REPORTING
The Revolutionary War

BEFORE *it was*
HISTORY, *it was* NEWS

BY TODD ANDRLIK

Published by Sourcebooks, Inc.
P.O. Box 4410, Naperville, Illinois 60567-4410
(630) 961-3900
Fax: (630) 961-2168
www.sourcebooks.com

Library of Congress Cataloging-in-Publication Data

Reporting the Revolutionary War : before it was history, it was news / [compiled by] Todd Andrlik.
    p. cm.
 (hardcover : alk. paper) 1. United States—History—Revolution, 1775-1783—Sources. 2. United States—History—Revolution, 1775-1783—Press coverage. 3. American newspapers—History—18th century. I. Andrlik, Todd.
 E203.R44 2012
 973.3—dc23
                    2012022258

Printed and bound in the United States of America.
BG 10 9 8 7 6 5 4 3 2 1

CONTENTS

NORTH AMERICA
Barry Lawrence Ruderman Antique Maps,
raremaps.com

An early map of the British Colonies and the whole
of North America, shortly after the conclusion of the
French and Indian War and on the eve of revolution.

INTRODUCTION

By Todd Andrlik

THERE ARE NO PHOTOGRAPHS OF THE AMERICAN REVOLUTION. NO SNAPSHOTS EXIST TO SHOW ordinary life or depict the struggles and suffering of the late eighteenth century. Engravings and oil paintings, made long after the war ended, portray epic battles and heroism but often fail to realistically capture the moment.

Newspapers are the closest thing we have to photos of the Revolution. They transport readers back in time, providing unmatched insight about common life and life-altering events. Despite their small size and lack of headlines, eighteenth-century newspapers pack an intense, concentrated punch and demonstrate the incredible power of the printed word. Through newspapers, we realize that history is much more than a chronological list of battles as we eavesdrop on everyday life and witness everyday realities of the American Revolution through the eyes of the British and the American colonists. The eighteenth-century newspapers presented in this book help us see that history is real life, messy, and exciting. We learn firsthand what many historians claim: without newspapers, there would have been no American Revolution.

Through vivid eyewitness accounts, battlefield letters, and breaking news compiled from hundreds of newspapers—primarily printed from 1763 to 1783 on both sides of the Atlantic Ocean—this story of the American Revolution is unlike any version that has been told. It is raw and uncut, full of intense action, drama, and suspense. From start to finish, these frontline newspapers deliver incomparable insight about America's founding. As a collection, they provide one of the most reliable and comprehensive narratives of the Revolutionary Era, loaded with amazing characters, better-than-fiction plot twists, and the perfect climax. Before these famous and infamous events became the history and foundation of America, they were littered among the news of the day for colonial Americans. Mark Twain wrote "of the wide difference in interest between 'news' and 'history'; that news is history in its first and best form, its vivid and fascinating form; and that history is the pale and tranquil reflection of it."

Reporting the Revolutionary War brings to life precious first drafts of history and lets readers experience the charming rusticity of eighteenth-century newsprint, complete with stains, tears, imperfect ink and paper, typesetting mistakes, misspellings, and grammatical errors that were all typical of the era. Reading Revolution Era newspapers in their original form helps reproduce the same immediacy and uncertainty felt by those who first held them.

With each newspaper, readers gain valuable insight into the social, economic, political, and military histories of the American Revolution. Reading newspapers in their entirety—including advertisements, obituaries, and essays—provides more than a glimpse of all the obstacles and ideas of the period. It creates a 360-degree view of the American Revolution and the formation of the United States.

Another important history lesson to be gained from this book relates to journalism. We live in a time of instant and on-demand news. Journalists and bloggers work frantically around the clock, competing to break news stories before anyone else. Cable news channels and websites stream updated headlines nonstop across their screens. Using Twitter and Facebook, millions of citizen reporters scramble to share the latest news affecting their lives, practically in real time. Despite the debated endangerment of printed newspapers, it is difficult to imagine a time when media were more important. However, 250 years ago, newspapers were the fundamental form of mass media and were more important than in any other time in America's history.

Just as social media helped ignite and organize the Arab Spring revolutions of the Middle East and Northern Africa, colonial newspapers fanned the flames of rebellion, provided critical intercolonial communication during the war, sustained loyalty to the Patriot cause, and aided in the outcome of the war—all of which becomes evident after reading straight from the pages of newspapers. In *Reporting the Revolutionary War*, readers will see that Americans maintained "Liberty or Death! Join or Die!" attitudes with blood, as well as ink, on their hands. David Ramsay, who twice served as a delegate in the Continental Congress, wrote that "in establishing American independence, the pen and the press had merit equal to that of the sword."

Not only do eighteenth-century newspapers contain the exclusive essays, reports, and advertisements of the day, but they also include reprinted extracts from other primary sources such as private letters, journal entries, official government documents, and war-zone intelligence direct from merchants, travelers, soldiers, officers, and common colonists. They are a proverbial gold mine of information. Since the day the Revolutionary War ended, historians and authors have relied heavily on newspapers as the basis for their own analysis and interpretations of the course of the war. The endnotes of practically every history book about the Revolution are loaded with references to the up-close-and-personal perspectives found in newspapers.

Reporting the Revolutionary War brings to life eighteenth-century newspapers in a firsthand account of America's founding, distinct from the history we receive in high school and university texts. Never before has such a significant collection of American Revolution newspapers been made available to the general public in such color and detail. Never before has access to such an archive been made so easy. And never before has *this* version of the American Revolution been told.

THE EIGHTEENTH-CENTURY NEWSPAPER BUSINESS

By Carol Sue Humphrey

NEWSPAPERS PLAYED AN IMPORTANT ROLE DURING THE AMERICAN REVOLUTION BECAUSE THEY had already become an essential part of life for many Americans, more so than all other media (books, pamphlets, magazines, or broadsides) combined. Ever since John Campbell founded the first successful newspaper in Boston in 1704, Americans either sought out copies of the newspapers themselves or went someplace where they could hear them being read aloud. People wanted to know what was happening elsewhere, particularly in the colonies and Europe, and newspapers were the major source of such information.

Over the course of the 1700s, more newspapers appeared in the American colonies, but printing was always a difficult business. The French and Indian War had provided a major encouragement for the further growth of newspapers in the colonies because of the desire for information about the conflict. By the end of the war in 1763, each of the thirteen mainland colonies had at least one printer, and the number of newspapers had grown from eleven to twenty-three. By the time the Revolutionary War broke out in 1775, there were thirty-eight newspapers being printed on fifty presses in America. All printers looked for ways to increase business, and newspapers were a possibility. Postmasters founded the earliest newspapers in the colonies because they had easy access to information for the paper. However, they had to hire a printer if they could not produce the newssheets themselves. Many printers saw the financial possibilities and began to produce their own weekly newspapers as a way to bolster their income.

Along with an increase in the number of newspapers came an increase in the circulation of these papers. In 1750, the average newspaper circulation was about 600 copies per week. By 1770, some printers produced 1,500 copies a week, and these numbers continued to rise throughout the conflict with Great Britain. Throughout the colonies, the population of the cities did not grow as rapidly as the percentage of newspapers during the same period, indicating that more people were reading these publications. Some larger cities had several newspapers, another indication that newspaper readership was sizeable enough to sustain a growth in circulation. For example, in 1760, Philadelphia had approximately 25,000 people, and it had only grown to just over 28,000 when the first official U.S. census was taken in 1790. During the same period, the number of newspapers published in Philadelphia grew more rapidly, going from two in 1760 to seven in 1775. The total remained at seven in 1783, but there had been a number of starts and stops during the Revolution as people sought news and information and printers struggled to continue in business because of the problems created by the war.

A steady increase in literacy helped fuel the growth of publications. Newspapers were sold through subscription, but local taverns and coffeehouses often subscribed, and customers either read them directly or listened while someone else read them aloud, thus making the information available to many more people.

Delivering the newspapers to subscribers proved somewhat complicated as well. Within town, they were delivered by carrier, often a hired boy or an apprentice from the print shop. Along the coast, newspapers could be sent from one seaport to another by ship, but that would not work for inland delivery. Newspapers to outlying areas and other colonies were delivered by post riders, which could be haphazard, since the colonies did not have an organized postal system until the 1750s. There were official post roads between the colonies, but they often were not well maintained—many were more like dirt trails through the woods that were difficult to travel. It could take weeks for the post to go from one end of the colonies to the other, and that would continue to be true into the nineteenth century. Historian Frank Luther Mott determined in a 1944 study that it took six weeks for the news of the Battle of Lexington and Concord to be published throughout the colonies. The last printed account appeared in the *Georgia Gazette* in Savannah on May 31, 1775.

Printing as a trade changed very little since Johannes Gutenberg developed the press with movable type. Acquiring the necessary materials often proved difficult as well. Each item—presses, types, paper, and ink—all came from different producers, so making sure all necessary supplies were readily available could be very complicated. Most of these supplies were imported from Great Britain during the colonial era, since local production was difficult and costly and because Americans lacked the mastery of trade skills found in England.

The printing trade also could be discouraging, since it was a very slow and involved process. Most newspapers had four pages, each about ten by fifteen or eleven by seventeen inches in size. Two pages were printed on one side of a piece of paper. When both sides were printed, the newspaper would be folded in half prior to being sold. Thus, pages one and four would be on one side of the original paper while pages two and three would be on the other side. In order to produce one side of this production, thirteen separate processes had to be performed by two men operating a press. Type had to be set by hand in the page form and then locked into place in the press. It took about twenty-four to twenty-eight hours to typeset an entire four-page issue by hand. On average, this constituted about 2,400 words (13,500 type characters) on page two or three and 2,000 words (11,500 type characters) on page one (which contained fewer words because of the masthead at the top of the page). Page four was often reserved for advertisements.

After the type form was locked on the press bed, one man (the "beater") would ink the type using two large animal-skin balls. Next, he would place a piece of damp paper on the tympan (cloth padding) of the press, close the frisket (rectangular frame), and then clamp the tympan over the types. Wetting the paper ahead of time helped the ink better absorb into the paper and reduced wear on the lead types. This being done, the second man (the "puller") would turn the handle and roll the press bed under the platen (flat plate). In a quick motion, the puller would pull the bar to print the first page, turn the handle a second time, pull the bar again to print the second page, then again turn the handle in the opposite direction to roll the bed out from under the press. The beater would open the tympan and remove the printed sheet. They would repeat this two thousand times a day, each time placing freshly printed sheets on top of each other. At the end of the day, all of the sheets would be hung up to dry overnight.

The Revolution also increased many problems for printers. The war cut off access to imported supplies from Great Britain. Americans attempted to produce the needed materials but could not keep up with demand. It would not be until the 1790s that enough printing presses were produced in America to make importing them totally unnecessary. A number of people also established type foundries in the decade prior to the Revolution, but with little success. Maintaining enough type to run the print shop became increasingly difficult as the Revolution continued.

The necessary paper and ink supplies also became increasingly difficult to obtain. Printers had begun to make their own ink long before the nonimportation agreements began in the 1760s, but it seldom became more than a cottage industry for producing what an individual shop needed. Paper mills had existed since the late 1600s and more had been built in the intervening years, but the quality of the paper was not as good as imported paper, and the mills could not produce enough paper to meet the needs of American printers. In addition, importations of paper from Great Britain had been greatly reduced for a brief time following the adoption of the Stamp Act in 1765 and were totally cut off in 1775. Local production of paper became essential if print shops were to remain in operation. Consequently, many printers began to take an active interest in paper-making ventures. As the Revolution got underway, printers urged their readers to save rags for making paper to contribute to the fight for independence. However, printers often had to reduce the size of their newspaper or not publish at all because of the lack of paper and other supplies.

Printers who attempted to publish newspapers in the eighteenth century had difficulty getting content to include in their publications. Because of how time-consuming the actual printing was, newspaper printers often placed essays and advertisements on one side of the paper, since this could be printed ahead of time and allowed to dry. The inner two pages would be printed last and filled with news gleaned from other newspapers or letters. Thus, the most current and local news would typically be found on pages two and three rather than page one. The increase in the number of newspapers being published throughout the 1700s provided more information sources because printers exchanged newspapers with each other and copied materials from these traded productions on a regular basis.

Readers were most interested in international news, which generally came from London newspapers. News from other colonies proved somewhat important, while local news appeared in very small amounts. The local news in one town would be reprinted elsewhere through the exchange system, and news and information thus spread throughout the colonies. These exchanges were not always easy due to weather issues and travel problems, but the process slowly improved over the years. By the end of the French and Indian War in 1763, newspaper printers had managed to improve their business to such an extent that they had an effective system for gathering and sharing news. When the fighting in the Revolution created new problems, printers sought to replace their usual supply of information through other sources. They did this primarily by urging their readers to supply any information they received so the news could easily be shared with others through the newspapers. All printers, both Patriots and Loyalists, hoped that such information would fill the news void created by the war.

As the conflict with Great Britain escalated, Americans wanted information about what was happening. This desire encouraged some printers to try to produce more issues of their newspapers. John Mein and Thomas Fleming had founded the *Boston Chronicle* as a weekly in December

1767 and began publishing the paper semi-weekly after a year because of their readers' desire for more news. In August 1770, Zechariah Fowle and Isaiah Thomas founded the *Massachusetts Spy* in Boston as a tri-weekly publication, but the problems of acquiring needed supplies made it difficult to continue such frequent publication schedules. The *Spy* slowed to semi-weekly in November 1770 and weekly in 1771. Weekly newspapers were most common during the Revolution, but routine schedules at any frequency proved difficult to sustain.

The Revolution only exacerbated problems printers faced in acquiring supplies and information to publish their newspapers, but the Revolutionary-era printers, like their predecessors, clearly believed their news productions were important to Americans, and they worked hard to keep printing them, no matter the obstacles that stood in the way. By the time the Revolution began, newspapers were a relatively common aspect of American culture and society. They had never been easy to produce, and the Revolution did not change that reality.

EIGHTEENTH-CENTURY
PRINTING PRESS
North Wind Picture Archives

REVOLUTIONARY NEWSPAPER
READING TIPS

By Todd Andrlik

EIGHTEENTH-CENTURY NEWSPAPERS ARE A FAVORITE SOURCE OF EARLY AMERICAN SCHOLARS BECAUSE they chronicle practically every event of the American Revolution, from the Stamp Act crisis through George Washington's resignation as commander in chief of the Continental Army. Even as we approach the 250-year anniversaries of the Revolution's first events, these contemporary news accounts are well preserved, thanks in large part to the rag linen paper on which they were printed. Prior to 1870, before the transition to wood pulp, newspapers were printed on durable paper handmade with acid-free linen rags, often from clothes or ship sails. Not long after printing, some newspapers were saved and preserved by individuals for future reference, and others were bound into large volumes by libraries and museums for long-term storage.

Despite the best preservation intentions, eighteenth-century newspapers had to survive countless natural and man-made disasters, including wars, floods, fires, and deaccession (removal from an institution's collection). As a result, many still show scars such as tears, holes, stains, and tape mends. Even in the best condition, these newspapers reflect centuries-old communication obstacles and writing styles, making them an entirely different reading experience compared to today's news. Primary sources are by far the best source of information on the American Revolution, but even when original documents are well preserved, they can still sometimes be difficult to read and comprehend.

To help twenty-first-century learners better read and digest eighteenth-century newspapers, here are some important tips to consider:

1. **Put Yourself in the Period**: Toss out all preconceived notions about how we became a country. Read these papers as if it is all happening now. It will help you get inside the heads of the writers and force you to think of both sides of the issues rather than our sanitized and propagandized version of American history.

2. **Perspective**: To fully appreciate and understand differing perspectives of the Revolution, be sure to read the British newspapers as well. You may be surprised to find that British papers often presented points of view agreeable with the Americans, despite Parliament's insistence otherwise.

3. **News Time Lag**: Breaking news traveled slowly in the eighteenth century, often taking weeks to reach other colonies and countries by treacherous postal roads or ship routes, so the

first report about a major event or battle was often published after a few days or even several weeks. As such, expect to get "breaking news" in bits and pieces, even within the same newspaper. Because private correspondence from distant towns and colonies was the number one source of colonial news, new information was printed as quickly as it came to town. Sometimes conflicting information appears in the same paper or in subsequent issues. One letter with some information and a certain point of view might appear on page two, but another letter with a different perspective on the same subject may appear on page three.

4. **Old English S**: Lowercase *s* letters in eighteenth-century newspapers are still the Old English, or long *s*, version and resemble a modern-day *f*. The Old English *s* better matches the handwritten *s* letters of the period. For example, the words "last," "house," and "congress" will often appear as "laft," "houfe," and "congrefs." Under a microscope, the lowercase *f* and long *s* are different as the crossbar does not continue through, stopping at the vertical stroke. Some long *s* characters have no crossbar at all.

5. **Bias and Propaganda**: Realize that most newspapers of the time were biased, published and written by partisan Loyalists or Patriots. Regardless of the newspaper's insistence on being impartial, the paper's point of view is often apparent in the selection of material printed. This is especially noticeable prior to war breaking out. However, similar to left- or right-leaning twenty-first-century media, contemporary readers of Revolutionary newspapers were completely aware of this bias. In the battle over mind control, Revolution Era newspapers—American and British—used a variety of propaganda tactics to boost morale and increase support. Common eighteenth-century propaganda tactics included name-calling, fear mongering, selective news printing and source gathering, incompleteness, and demonizing the enemy. Sound familiar? Most of these tactics, perfected during the Revolutionary War, are still being used by some media today.

6. **Emphasis on Extracts and Excerpts:** Rather than lengthy feature stories with bold headlines, printers filled most of their newspaper pages with several excerpts (sometimes only a paragraph long) most commonly from private letters. Almost every instance of published correspondence begins with "Extract of a letter from…" Aside from letters, official dispatches, and government communications, another popular eighteenth-century news source was oral reports—sometimes rumor or hearsay—by sea captains, merchants, travelers, and soldiers. This sometimes led to conflicting stories appearing on the same page but allowed the reader to make up his or her own mind.

7. **Datelines, Not Headlines**: Eighteenth-century newspapers didn't use headlines, and most reports were separated only by a dateline or the popular "Extract of a letter from…"

8. **Struggle for Credibility**: Despite exaggeration, distortion, and the obstacles of transatlantic communication, eighteenth-century printers still needed to maintain a strong newspaper subscriber and advertiser base, so they printed news from credible sources and

often added disclaimers to unknown or unreliable sources. Frequently, newspaper printers pieced together oral, manuscript, and printed intelligence—official and unofficial—to help corroborate accounts for their own readers.

9. **News Exchange System:** Before news wire services and before professional journalists or correspondents, eighteenth-century newspaper printers relied heavily on an intercolonial newspaper exchange system to fill their pages. Printers often copied entire paragraphs or columns directly from other newspapers and frequently without attribution other than a dateline. As a result, identical reports often appeared in multiple papers throughout America. While this seems like plagiarism today, the news-swapping technique was standard operating procedure then, helping to spread the ideas of liberty and uphold the colonists' resistance to British Parliament.

10. **Evolution of Language**: Pay attention to the change in language. After all, it took a good many years to get to the point where the Americans were in real combat with the British. For example: when exactly did we become "the enemy" instead of "the Americans?"

11. **Pace of Dissent**: Pay attention to the pace by which dissent grows among the Americans. Also note that the new government quickly comes under fire, even from its supporters. This was the birth of free speech as well as a nation.

12. **Inconsistent Grammar**: Be prepared for run-on sentences with considerable comma usage and alternative word spellings—and not just the British-English difference between "color" and "colour." Prewar papers especially seemed to lack a consistency in spelling, even of common words. Also, rules regarding capitalization and punctuation were equally fluid. For example, some papers capitalized every noun, not just the proper ones.

13. **Humor and Sarcasm**: Have a sense of humor. Since much of the content is publicly printed letters addressed between anonymous authors on both sides of various issues, the tone is often snarky and sarcastic. No sword needed here. These words are often sharp, satirical, and witty.

14. **Irony**: Enjoy the ironies. It's not unusual to find the same paper discussing preparations for war and celebrating the birthday of the king. As you become absorbed by the news of the time, you will find that newspapers have the ability to make you forget the outcome. Remember, colonists were not all committed to the idea of independence, and even until early 1776, there was hope among many that things could be resolved.

15. **Read for Context**: Don't skip the ads or obits. Many of these provide insight into daily life, personal values, indentured servitude, slavery, and commerce of the time.

vage and destructive manner broke and abused his Furniture, Chairs, Tables, Desk, Glasses, China, and in short every Thing they could lay their Hands on; at the same Time purloining his Money, and dispersing his private Books and Papers, until by the Effect of Wine and the other Stores of his Cellar, they ripened in Ebriety and Madness, and became fit for the next, more desolating and barbarous Operation.

Towards Ten o'Clock they were traced by the Noise and Tumult of a numerous and confused Rabble to the Mansion-House of His Honor the Lieut. Gov. This seemed to be reserved for the utmost Violence of their diabolical Phrenzy; for immediately on the Word given, that large and stately Edifice became a Prey to the Iron Hand of Outrage and Robbery; a few Hours and the House was a meer Skeleton, and deprived of Furniture, even Wainscot and Partition, broke, hacked and mangled: and the whole by Break of Day, at once a sad Spectacle of Indignation and Wonder!

In this violent and extraordinary Desolation, besides the House and it's Furniture of very considerable Value, his Honor and his Family sustained, the loss of between _____ nineHundred Pounds Sterling in Cash, _____ Wearing Apparel, a valuable and cu_____ Number of p_____ as well as curio_____ rs and Manu_____ and besides the _____ rds, occasio_____ in his Honor's P_____ e Clain_____ Title of this Provi_____ len, a_____ faced, so that the _____ Conseque_____ may be esteen_____ blickly _____ privately, _____ ious.

"To bear _____ own Misfortune _____ ith Firmness, and to feel _____ s," (th_____ Words o_____ the Occasion of an hono_____ wort_____ G_____ leman, _____ has lately taken_____ _____ ds) _____ t_____ t of true Philoso_____ _____ be_____ med

concern for this unhappy people: On his right hand stood the restless father of mischief with the stamp act in his hand, giving credentials to his all attentive pupil; the malignity of his heart was lively portray'd by the expressive cardinal knave at cards on his breast, accompanied with a cautious memento to all placemen, that *   *   *   *   *   *
"When vice prevails and impious men bear sway,
"The post of honour is a private station."
Their appearance was becoming, and procession glorious, attended by such invectives, huzza's and disdainful music as are the pure emanations of injured freedom: after passing thro' town, our hero with his companion, was conducted ————— ——————
"in all the Majesty of Greece" to the height of a lofty hill, perhaps the highest summit he will e'er ascend; and there in complaisance to his fellow, committed to the flames; and a few loyal and very constitutional healths crown'd the night.

NEW-LONDON, *August* 23.
We hear that a gentleman in one of the southern provinces being advised that his son, then in London, was appointed a *STAMP-OFFICER,* for said pro_____ _____ ately _____ e him, that if he _____ ught _____ that _____ detestable _____ fice, he w_____ ld _____ _____ that _____ ion of Stamps, _____ the Dev_____ repr_____ They w_____ re suspe_____ tw_____ and_____ ca_____ embo_____

❧ CHAPTER I ❧

THE CURSED STAMP ACT

Introduction

Stamp duty. When these two words touched American soil in April 1764 as a teaser of the internal tax following the Sugar Act, they set in motion a chain of events that soon united thirteen colonies, bolstered confidence, and forever altered the course of American history. First irritated by the Sugar Act, then seriously angered by the Stamp Act, colonies developed extensive intercolonial networks of resistance, chained together by independent organizations, such as the Sons of Liberty, and independent newspapers, which were widely read locally as well as raced by horseback and ship up and down the continent. The primary source of colonial communication, newspapers spread the word of mobs, violence, and boycott, which effectively prevented enforcement of the Stamp Act and led to its repeal. To avoid total humiliation, the same day Parliament passed the Stamp Act repeal, it also declared full power and authority over the colonies—a declaration it didn't hesitate to impose.

Supplement to the
Boston News-Letter
September 5, 1765

Stamp Act Riot, Boston
North Wind Picture Archives

ble
lofs
ling in Cafh. all his Plate, Wearing Apparell, a valuable and coftly Library, a great Number of private
as well as curious and fcarce Papers and Manufcript-
and b

provinces being advifed that his fon, then in London,
was appointed a STAMP OFFICER, for faid province, immediately wrote him, that if he thought
proper to accept that

JOIN, OR DIE.
Library of Congress

(*above*) Benjamin Franklin's cartoon in the *Pennsylvania Gazette*, May 9, 1754, urged the British North American colonists to join together against the French and the Indians. The symbol and phrase, along with other popular slogans like "Liberty or Death," "Die or Be Free," or "Don't Tread on Me" returned with new meaning—against a new enemy—during the Revolution.

KING GEORGE III, C. 1762–1764
BY ALLAN RAMSAY
The Bridgeman Art Library

(*left*) In 1760, at the age of 22, George III ascended the throne, where he served as King of Great Britain through the entire American Revolution until his death in 1820.

SUGAR ACT

By Todd Andrlik

IN 1763, THREE YEARS AFTER GEORGE III ASCENDED THE throne, Great Britain faced several serious economic challenges, including a massive national debt that skyrocketed during the Seven Years' War (1756–1763), known as the French and Indian War in North America. On the other side of the Atlantic Ocean, American colonists rejoiced after fighting alongside the mother country to defeat France. But by spring of 1764, details about new revenue-raising policies affecting colonial trade started arriving from England on packet boats, which carried the latest newspapers, private letters, and official correspondence. Immediately upon receiving word of the taxes, known as the Sugar Act because of its three-penny duty on molasses, Americans began the argument that echoed for centuries: no taxation without representation.

Printed five weeks after Parliament passed the Sugar Act, just long enough for the news' transatlantic journey, the May 10, 1764, edition of the *Pennsylvania Gazette* warned colonists that "a Scheme of Taxation of the American Colonies has for some time been in Agitation: That it had been previously debated in Parliament, whether they had Power to lay such a Tax on Colonies which had no Representatives in Parliament, and determined in the Affirmative."

From the Jamestown settlement in 1607 through 1763, Great Britain maintained an unwritten policy of salutary neglect toward its thirteen American colonies, leaving them to establish their own systems of government and taxation with the expectation that this apathetic attitude would help them flourish. A handful of regulations on colonial trade were introduced during that time, including the Navigation Act (1660) and the Molasses Act (1733), but they were not enforced or were easily evaded by bribery or smuggling.

What Americans found most upsetting about the Sugar Act of 1764 was (1) its plans for strict enforcement, essentially voiding the tranquil era of salutary neglect colonists had enjoyed since the first settlements; (2) the believed illegality of being taxed without having representatives in Parliament; and (3) the strong hint of a forthcoming stamp duty, the first internal tax on activities and transactions within the colony. At the conclusion of the same *Pennsylvania Gazette* article that delivered news of the Sugar Act was the first warning of a stamp tax:

"Besides this, an internal Tax was proposed, a Stamp Duty, &c. but many Members warmly opposing it, this was deferred till next Session; but it was feared that the Tax upon foreign Goods would pass into a Law this Session. That these Colonies are under great Disadvantages, in not having sufficient Interest in Parliament… Only, that Mr. Allen, of this Place, was indefatigable, in remonstrating to many of the Members, with whom he was acquainted, on the Illegality of an internal Tax, and had considerable Influence in preventing it."

By spring of 1764, details about new revenue-raising policies affecting colonial trade started arriving from England. Immediately upon receiving word of the taxes, Americans began the argument that echoed for centuries: no taxation without representation.

It wasn't long after news of the Sugar Act arrived in America that local newspapers began printing public concerns. According to a letter extract in the July 20, 1764, *New Hampshire Gazette*:

…the Destruction will be dreadful till their Eyes are open'd.——In Virginia they already feel it, Tobacco at Home, fetches little or nothing, most of their Bills are come back protested, and the Planters have no Money to pay with.——Though every one is convinced of the Unanimity amongst the Colonies, to ward off any Burden that may be intended for us; yet no Steps are taken, and all complain that they see with great Perspicnity, the Destruction that must befal us. I still flatter my self some fortunate Event will change the Face of Things, and relieve us from our Anxiety.

The PENNSYLVANIA GAZETTE

PHILADELPHIA, May 10.

On Monday next the GENERAL ASSEMBLY of this Province meets here.

Our other Advices by the Packet are, that a Scheme of Taxation of the American Colonies has for some Time been in Agitation: That it had been previously debated in Parliament, whether they had Power to lay such a Tax on Colonies which had no Representatives in Parliament, and determined in the Affirmative: That on the Ninth of March Mr. ———— made a long Harrangue on the melancholy State of the Nation, overloaded with heavy Taxes, and a Debt of 146 Millions, 52 Millions of which had arisen in the four last Years: That by a Computation, which he laid before the House, 360,000 l. Sterling per Annum was expended on North-America, and therefore it was but reasonable they should support the Troops sent out for their Defence, and all the other particular Expence of the Nation on their Account. To raise this Sum, he proposed that the Drawbacks on Re-exportation of particular Goods should be discontinued: That a Duty should be laid on East-India Goods; a Duty of 7 l. Sterling per Ton on all Wines from Madeira, the Western and Canary Isles; a Duty of 3 d. per Gallon on foreign Melasses, of 10 s. Per Hundred on Sugars; a high Duty on Coffee, Cocoa, &c. and that Rum should be wholly prohibited: That Wines from Spain, Portugal, &c. first landed in England, before sent to America, should have the Duty drawn back. Besides this, an internal Tax was proposed, a Stamp Duty, &c. but many Members warmly opposing it, this was deferred till next Session; but it was feared that the Tax upon foreign Goods would pass into a Law this Session. That these Colonies are under great Disadvantages, in not having sufficient Interest in Parliament; from the Want of which, the West-Indians have been able to carry any Point against them. —— Only, that Mr. Allen, of this Place, was indefatigable, in remonstrating to many of the Members, with whom he was acquainted, on the Illegality of an internal Tax, and had considerable Influence in preventing it.

PENNSYLVANIA GAZETTE (PHILADELPHIA)
May 10, 1764
—

On page two, a small news report that just arrived in port was published about a "Scheme of Taxation," which included the Sugar Act and a forthcoming stamp duty. Read closely and note the origins of the "no taxation without representation" debate. Newspapers spread dramatic details of mobs, violence, and boycotts in subsequent years, but historians can point to the May 10, 1764, *Pennsylvania Gazette* as one of the printed cornerstones of revolution.

... be very pleaſing to our Readers.

Two Days ago, Capt. Montour arrived with ſome of his Party at Johnſon-Hall, brought the Scalp, &c. taken ſome Time ſince. The Indian ſcalped, was a Head Warrior, Nephew to the Squaſh-Cutter, a Chief of the Delawares. Capt. Montour brought with him likewiſe, a lad named Emanuel Stover, of Rariton, New-Jerſey, taken laſt Year at Wioming, with 6 others, by the Delawares; and a Delaware who went to Johnſon-Hall, on the 20th Inſtant, under ſome ſpecious Pretences, was, on Diſcovery of his Villanies, apprehended. The 5 Nations (except thoſe in Purſuit of the Enemy) are returned Home, to be in Readineſs for accompanying the Troops.

The Public may confide in the following Report now in Town, viz. That by the Articles of Peace agreed on by the Five Nations, and Sir William Johnſon, they are to cede to his Majeſty, all the Country from Niagara to above the Great Falls, on both Sides of the River; being a Tract of 15 or 16 Miles in Length, and ſeveral in Breadth; very advantageous Conceſſions, equally intereſting to the Public.

PHILADELPHIA, May 10.

On Monday next the GENERAL ASSEMBLY of this Province meets here.

Our other Advices by the Packet are, that a Scheme of Taxation of the American Colonies has for ſome Time been in Agitation: That it had been previouſly debated in the Parliament, whether they had Power to lay ſuch a Tax on Colonies which had no Repreſentatives in Parliament, and determined in the Affirmative: That on the Ninth of March Mr. ————— made a long Harrangue on the melancholy State of the Nation, overloaded with heavy Taxes, and a Debt of 146 Millions, 52 Millions of which had ariſen in the four laſt Years: That by a Computation, which he laid before the Houſe, 360,000 l. Sterling per Annum was expended on North-America, and therefore it was but reaſonable they ſhould ſupport the Troops ſent out for their Defence, and all the other Expence of the Nation on their Account. To raiſe this Sum, he propoſed that the Drawbacks on Re-exportation of particular Goods ſhould be diſcontinued: That a Duty ſhould be laid on Eaſt-India Goods; a Duty of 7 l. Sterling per Ton on all Wines from Madeira, the Weſtern and Canary Iſles; a Duty of 3 d. per Gallon on foreign Melaſſes, of 10 s. per Hundred on Sugars; a high Duty on Coffee, Cocoa, &c. and that Rum ſhould be wholly prohibited: That Wines from Spain, Portugal, &c. firſt landed in England, before ſent to America, ſhould have the Duty drawn back. Beſides this, an internal Tax was propoſed, a Stamp Duty, &c. but many Members warmly oppoſing it, this was deferred till next Seſſion; but it was feared that the Tax upon foreign Goods would paſs into a Law this Seſſion. That theſe Colonies are under great Diſadvantages, in not having ſufficient Intereſt in Parliament; from the Want of which, the Weſt-Indians have been able to carry any Point againſt them.———— Only, that Mr. Allen, of this Place, was indefatigable, in remonſtrating to many of the Members, with whom he was acquainted, on the Illegality of an internal Tax, and had conſiderable Influence in preventing it.

FORT PITT, April 26, 1764.

Extracts from the Examination of GERSHOM HICKS, (a White Man) lately with the Indians, who came in here the 14th Inſtant as a Spy, taken at ſeveral different times.

THAT an Engliſh Army was expected by the Indians down the Ohio this Spring. That he left Hockhocking about 30 Days ago, in Company with 7 Delaware Indians, to go to War on the Frontiers. That they came in upon Shearman's Valley, murdered and ſcalped one James and his Wife, and took two little Boys, their Children, Priſoners. That they came with the Children within a few Miles of this Poſt, when he was deſired to come in here, under Pretence he had made his Eſcape from the Indians, and to enquire into the Strength of the Fort, Ammunition, Proviſions, &c. what Guards were out each Day, and to return to them in two Nights; and that if he met with any Indians, not to let them know any thing till he got to King Beaver. That the Night they came here a Party of 8 Shawaneſe came to their Sleeping Place, and had two Scalps, which they got between Ligonier and ...

---

that, with all poſſible Diſpatch, I ſhould proceed on my Voyage, which I could not do ſo ſoon as I deſired, for various Diſappointments which happened. I arrived at Campechy the 7th Inſtant, and having taken Poſſeſſion the 24th, I was informed of your Arrival at Balis in the Month of April, alſo five Veſſels, and that immediately the People were diſperſed as far as Rio Hondo, practiſing from that Time the cutting of Logwood, by Virtue of the Treaty of Peace. You did not preſent the Royal Schedule that my Sovereign expedited for this End, nor the Licence of the King of England for the aforeſaid Effect.

This being granted, I am obliged by the King my Lord, in his Royal Confidence of the Government of this Province, and to comply entirely with the ſaid 17th Article of the Definitive Treaty of Peace, as I ſaid before, to diſpatch the Commandant of the Fort of Bacalar, Don Joſeph Roſado, with this, requiring you, that in Conſideration of the Want of Inſtruments for your Introduction, and having extended yourſelves, gathering Fruits as in your own Country, without waiting to ſettle the Limits with the neceſſary Solemnity that ſhould have ſecured your Eſtabliſhment, you will be pleaſed, with all ſpeed, to give the neceſſary Advice to all your Community that are in Rio Hondo, to retire to Balis, and I expect you will preſent me with the Royal Schedule, that the King my Maſter diſpatched to this End, or with Orders from the King of Great-Britain for this Effect; and there is no Doubt but I ſhall then attend to it with that Care and Equity I am commanded, iſſuing for that Purpoſe the neceſſary Orders to all the Commandants, Cabos, Military and Juſticiary of all the Diſtricts in their Juriſdiction, by which Means the Suſpicion of the fatal Conſequences will ceaſe, which will be inevitable if ſuch Conduct is continued, ſufficient to deſtroy the good Harmony between the two Nations, and happy Tranquility that we enjoy; if the Remedy is not occurred to in time, and our Sovereigns will manifeſtly ſee how we intereſt ourſelves, that their juſt and laudable Intentions take Effect, for which I am ſo ready on my Part, as is manifeſt by my Toleration, that you and all your Nation remain at Balis, and I promiſe myſelf the ſame on your Parts, proteſting always, that for the Reſult of what may happen by ſuch irregular Introduction and Exceſs of cutting Logwood, thoſe who commit, or do not remedy, them, will be reſponſible after all. I hope you will favour me with an Anſwer by hand of the ſaid Commandant of Bacalar, and other Commands moſt to your Satiſfaction, to manifeſt to you the Deſire I have to ſerve you. God guard you many Years, as he can, and I deſire.

Your moſt humble Servant kiſſes your Hands,
PHILIPE REMIRES DE ESTINOS.

Merida in Jucatan, 29th December, 1763.
Sir DON JOSEPH MAUD.

DON JOSEPH ROSADO, Lieutenant of Infantry in the Battalion of Caſtilia, and Commandant of this Garriſon and royal Fort of St. Philip, of Bacalar, and its Juriſdiction.

NOtwithſtanding that the Serjeant Dioniſius Chavaria, who is detached to the Look-Out of St. Anthony, has the neceſſary Orders, that the Engliſh Logwood-Cutters of Rio Hondo, do retreat to Balis, without permitting them to make any Demur, becauſe that ſince the 4th Inſtant, when the Order of the Governor and Captain General, was by me intimated to them, they have had competent Time to evacuate the River, carrying away the Utenſils of their Houſes: I order and command the ſaid Serjeant, that he receive 11 Soldiers of this Garriſon, well armed, which, with 4 there before, compleats the Number of 15, to remain at the ſaid Look-Out; that with them he is not to permit any Engliſh Veſſel, under any Pretext, to enter the Mouth of this River; on the Contrary, if any Flats remain in the River, they are to go out, with the Utenſils of their Houſes, with ſo much Brevity, as not to permit them to ſtop any where, but retire totally; as likewiſe thoſe from the New-River, becauſe in the Order intimated to them, it is expreſſed, that the Retreat ſhall be to Balis, and no other Part; and to act on the Contrary, they expoſe themſelves to evident Danger, as by their Diſobedience they loſe their Negroes, and find themſelves under a violent Arreſt. This Order he ſhall manifeſt to ...

NEW YORK, July 9.

One of the Sloops that was carried into Cape Francois, in Company with Capt. Claxton, by a French Man of War, as mentioned under the Philadelphia Head, arrived here last Monday, and confirms the Account he brought; but we are since credibly informed, That an English Frigate, having Occasion to call at Turks Island, and observing the French erecting some Works there, ordered them to defist; but they not chusing to comply, the English Commander landed Part of his Crew, killed 28 Frenchmen, and took several Prisoners.

Tuesday last the Rev'd Mr. WHITEFIELD set out for the Southward, but the Day following his Servant, having drank some CYDER, and the Weather being very warm, he went into the Water at Mr. Watson's Ferry, to cool himself, and was soon after found drowned in not more than two feet of Water. This Misfortune, and the Heat of the Weather, obliged Mr. Whitefield to return to Long Island.

NEWPORT, July 2.

We hear from Providence, that Doctor Philip Bourne, of that Place, put an End to his Life, a few Days since, by a Dose of Poison.

July 9. The Sloop Elizabeth, Capt. Gardner, arrived here last Tuesday from the Coast of Africa, in 55 Days, with a Cargo of Slaves. Before he sailed, a Boat belonging to Capt. Remmington, of this Port, with a Mate and three Men on board, was overset in going into a River to the Windward of Cape Mount, by which Accident the 3 Men were drowned; but the Mate happily saved himself by swiming.

Capt. Elliot, of this Port, sailed before Captain Gardner with 160 Slaves, for the West Indies.

PROVIDENCE, July 7.

A Gentleman in a neighbouring Province, writing his Correspondent in this Town on the Scourges we are to suffer (by the late Act of Parliament) from our Mother Country, in Recompence for that Loyalty and Obedience for which this Country is so eminently distinguished, says, "Jealousy, that Bane of Society, has been the Cause of passing these Laws at Home; which will so embarrass Trade, that they will be under a Necessity to repeal what they have done in few Years, but the Destruction will be dreadful till their Eyes are open'd. —— In Virginia they already feel it, Tobacco at Home, fetches little or nothing, most of their Bills are come back protested, and the Planters have no Money to pay with. —— Though every one is convinced of the Unanimity amongst the Colonies, to ward off any Burden that may be intended for us; yet no Steps are taken, and all complain, that they see with great Perspicuity, the Destruction that must befal us. I still flatter myself some fortunate Event will change the Face of Things, and relieve us from our Anxiety."

came out in Company with Capt. Maitara, in a Mast Ship, bound to this Place; who sprung a Leak a few Days after they came away, and was obliged to put back. There was several Passengers on Board, who we hear are come in Capt. Jarvis.

Last Friday arrived here Capt. Benjamin Torry, from Fyall, having had 76 Days Passage. He spoke with Capt. White of Boston, off the Western Islands; who had been out five Weeks from Jamaica, bound for London; all well.

WANTED (for finishing

the STATE HOUSE) a Quantity of clear Boards Laths and Lime. Likewise Joyners, Painters and Masons will be wanted immediately to compleat the Same: Any Persons inclining to furnish any or all said Materials, as well those who incline to undertake the Joyner's, Painter's, or Mason's Work; are desired to send in their Names, and lowest they will do it for, next Wednesday to the Committee appointed to get the same done, who will attend on said Day at the Sign of the King's Arms; all are desired to take Notice in making their Calculations, that nothing but the Money, will be paid them, on the Completion of any of their Agreements. *Portsmouth July 19th By Order of the Committee.*

MARK HUNKING WENTWORTH, *Chairman.*

Richard Champney,

NOTIFIES his Customers and others, That he has Remov'd to his Shop near Mr. Beck's Hatter's Shop; where he continues to Sell at the lowest Cash Price, (for Cash only) Choice Green Coffee, by the Hundred, or Quarter, Bohea Tea, Best French Indigo, and Genuine Kippen's Snuff, per Dozen or Retail, Pepper, Allspice, Nutmegs, Raisons, Loaf and Brown Sugar, Table Oyl, per Jarr or Bottle, Chesheire Cheese and Cotton Wool —— His Customers may be supply'd with all sorts of Tin Ware as usual at said Shop.

Said Champney wants a good

smart LAD that inclines to learn the Tin Plate Workers Business.

TO BE SOLD

By HENRY NAGLEE,

Near Spring Hill, at Mr. JOSEPH ALCOCK's Store, Cheap for CASH,

POrk, Rice, Tar, Pitch, and Turpentine.

---

an half, in the house of Mr. Blackmore one said Messengers; when after a trial of seven his Lordship summed up the evidence in a g charge, and then the Jury went out, who, staying about three quarters of an hour, brow their verdict against the defendants for one th *pounds damages.* Upon the determination o Jury, there was an universal shout from a co rable number of spectators. The council fo defendants were, the Attorney and Sollicitor G ral, Mr. Serjeants Davey and Naires, and Wallis; and for the plantiff, Mr. Serjeant Gly Recorder of London, Mr. Stow, Mr. Denning Mr. Gardner.

At a late meeting at Newmarket, a gent of great fortune, in one day lost ten thousand neas; in two days more, this sum was treb'ed on the fourth he judiciously set out for town, ving to tempt his stars no further for that tim they wore so unfavourable an aspect.

We hear that a noble Personage won last at Newmarket, no less than 40,000 l.

The spirit of gaming is now so prevalent am the lower class of people, that a butcher in market lost 1000l. last week at Newmark

Last week a horse was sold in Smithfie weight at four pence per pound; the buyer seller differing on the price, they agreed o method of selling. It is said the buyer got a good bargain, as of all animals a horse is reck the lightest as to his size.

It is said above 12,000l. were depend bets last Saturday, at Newmarket, betwee Duke of Ancasters colt, and Lord Bolingb colt, which was won by the former, and knowing Gentlemen of the Turf were deep ken in.

A giant, 14 feet high (who was the same at nine years old) arrived the 14th ult. at Dr from Trent, to make a shew of himself.

It has been reported, that on Thursday l —— Ambassador presented a memo our court concerning the fisheries, on whic count the stocks fell 2 per cent.

The Order of the Bath, lately given to Clive, was promised to Col. Draper who his claim to accommodate his Lordship, as add to his respect and influence with the Na Bengal.

On a gentleman's applying to Lord Cliv commission for his son, he made answer, tha had been able to give commissions to all th applied to him, he should have had a suffici my of officers, without needing one private

Gen. Leighton's regiment has a fine set of scoth girls along with them; which, cons their polific nature, will, it is hoped, be an tage in peopling our West-India colonies.

NEW-HAMPSHIRE GAZETTE (PORTSMOUTH)
July 20, 1764
—

Private letters were one of the top sources of colonial news and were not always very private. It was normal for a letter to be opened and read along the delivery route or to find its way to the local print shop. In this case, the extract of a gentleman's letter about the economic stresses made worse by the Sugar Act first appeared in the July 7 *Providence Gazette* (Rhode Island). As that issue circulated among the colonies, other printers published the paragraph in their newspapers like Daniel Fowle did on page three of his *New-Hampshire Gazette*.

LONDON CHRONICLE
December 6, 1764
—

By late 1764, Great Britain received news of America's "uneasiness" about the Sugar Act and fears of the forthcoming Stamp Act. Here, it is being communicated that the idea of being taxed internally without representation in Parliament is alarming. Less than a year later, after the Stamp Act is passed in Parliament, alarm turns to rage.

HE Members of the House of

Guernsey; Polly, and John and Francis, from

to the Chancery in the palace.

The English factors who reside
their correspondents here
in their letters relati
ecause they were all

ch ship, Peter Klasen,
nd to Hamburg, is los
crew were saved.
ports of the sailing of
oned merely by order
fresh supply of ships
on, which is done ever
articles propagated of
seem calculated to serve

y the two Chief Justic
s, &c. will be elegantl
nsion-house, by the Ri
yor, as they could not
ast Friday, it being the
yal Highness the Princes
Wales.

The elegant cartoons, which
down some time ago in the saloon in
palace, to hang that room with a
mask of English manufacture, are
be replaced in the same apartment

Dr. Spry, who is appointed j
Court of Admiralty for the Nor
district, arrived with his family a
Nova Scotia, on the 23d of Septem

On Monday last the Marquis of
in town from Scotland.

His Majesty has appointed Rich
den, Gent. to be Adjutant to the
ment of Dragoons, in the room
Knigge, who has resigned.

Thomas Sandby, Esq; is appoin
to his Royal Highness the Duke
land, in the room of Mr. Ford, de

Last Saturday was married a
Shropshire, the Hon. Capt. George
Miss Clive, sister to Lord Clive; a
young lady with a handsome fortu

Yesterday died at her house in
Piccadilly, Mrs Cleveland, widow
Secretary Cleveland, belonging
miralty.

On Tuesday evening died, Mr
wholesale linen-draper in Cheapsid

On Monday last came on befo
Mansfield and a special jury, in th
King's Bench, Guildhall, a cause
foreign sailor was plaintiff, and the
East-India ship defendant. The
brought for the non-payment or
about twenty thousand rupees, of
upwards of 2000l. which the plain
had been delivered, while the shi
voyage from the East Indies, to the
and which he denied to have rece

mult be supposed to determine always with wisdom and integrity, thought fit further to prorogue the Assembly to the 10th of this month.

The late act of parliament (possibly for want of a thorough understanding of it) gives some uneasiness to the people of this province, and it is said of the northern colonies in general; and the fears of being taxed, internally, by the parliament, while we have no representation on the spot, are alarming to men of the greatest penetration and judgment among us: If the jealousies and fears of the people are groundless, who can so effectually remove them, as the General Assembly, in whom, while in solemn session, the wisdom of the whole is presumed to be collected: On the other hand, if those at home, whose intentions are always upright, yet whose wisdom, being human, is not infallible, have in any respect mistaken the rights of the American subjects, and the true interest both of the colonies and the mother country, what is to be done? By no means to resist the authority of the supreme power of the nation, but humbly to remonstrate our rights and privileges: And who can do this with so much propriety, as the General Assembly? As the colonies, with regard to these matters at least, are alike affected, it is prudent for them to acquaint each other with the measures they may take: The parliament, it is said, will meet in November next, or December at farthest: Considering then, the distance of the colonies from Great Britain, the great importance of the business we have to do; and the shortness of the time prudently to effect it, even from the 5th of September, we cannot but regret, that there should be any necessity for a farther prorogation.

Boston, Oct. 7. The Surveyor-General has

Island of Cape-Breton.
Capt. Hedge, who sailed from this port
yesterday se'nnight in a sloop laden with corn

Lloyd, Carbery, from Newfoundland, at Malaga.
Ann Gally, Smith, from Newfoundland, at Leghorn.
Cork Packet, Evans, from Bristol, at Cork,
Sarah Ann, Clark, from Bristol, at Waterford.
Polly, Evans, from Malaga; and Forbes, Burton, from Petersburgh, at Bristol.
Prince William, Graystock, from Rotterdam, in the River.
Lovely, Scheverick; and Polly, Fagg, from New-York; and Susannah, Lockhart, from Philadelphia, at Quebec.
Banker, Kerley, from Newfoundland, at Poole.
London Packet, Califf; Hawke, Coffin; Deep Bay, Dashwood, from London; John and Sukey, Bruce, in 26 days from Land's End; and St. George, Mallard, from London and Lisbon, at Boston.

LONDON.

We are informed that no money will be borrowed for the service of the ensuing year.

The Account of the Capitals at the Bank, South Sea, and India Houses, November 24, 1764.

Bank Stock, ——	£. 10,780,000
4 per Cent. Consol. Ann.	20,240,000
4 per Cent. 1763, ——	3,500,000
4 per Cent. Navy, ——	3,500,000
3 one half per Cent. 1756,	1,500,000
3 one half per Cent. 1758,	4,500,000
3 per Cent. Consol, ——	33,627,841
3 per Cent. Reduced, ——	17,701,323
3 per Cent. 1726, ——	1,000,100
South Sea Stock, ——	3,662,784
3 per Cent. Old Annuities,	12,404,270
3 per Cent. New, ——	8,958,255
3 per Cent. 1751, ——	2,100,000

Total, £. 129,674,553

some time, brought in a verdict for
for the value of the above amount

STAMP ACT

O N MARCH 22, 1765, THE STAMP ACT RECEIVED ROYAL assent with its fifty-five resolutions to go into effect on November 1. For the first time in 150 years of existence, Americans were going to be taxed on internal business, not external trade. Printers were to be among the hardest hit by the Stamp Act, but the effects would be felt by all colonists as it required government-issued stamps "upon every skin or piece of vellum or parchment, or sheet or piece of paper," including deeds, wills, newspapers, pamphlets, court judgments, liquor retail licenses, playing cards, etc. Among the first American newspapers to publish the Stamp Act in full was the April 18,1765, *Pennsylvania Gazette*, the same newspaper that Benjamin Franklin printed until 1748 and that continued to bear his name as printer until a partnership deal expired in 1766.

By the fall of 1765, uneasiness over the Stamp Act's internal taxes had escalated to outrage.

News of the Stamp Act spread quickly and was carried to Williamsburg, Virginia, while the House of Burgesses was still in session. The shock quickly changed the assembly's agenda as they soon found themselves debating several resolutions against the Stamp Act. Newly elected Patrick Henry delivered a passionate speech to inspire passage of more radical resolves. Despite Henry's best efforts, conservative representatives were able to successfully strike two radical resolutions from official record; however, the controversial resolves leaked to the press and were printed throughout the colonies and Great Britain, as seen in the October 17, 1765, *London Chronicle*, still making the statement Henry wanted.

By the fall of 1765, uneasiness over the Stamp Act's internal taxes escalated to outrage, as demonstrated in Boston on the morning of August 14, 1765, when two effigies were hung from a great elm tree, later called Liberty Tree, at the southern neck of town connecting Boston's 15,000 residents to the farms of Suffolk County and beyond. One effigy represented the commissioned stamp distributor Andrew Oliver and the other a green-soled "jackboot with a head and horns peeping out of the top" (*London Chronicle*, October 10, 1765) to mock George Grenville and Earl of Bute, John Stuart, whom the colonists labeled as the primary architects of the hated act.

At dusk, the effigies were lowered from the tree and paraded through town by a "great concourse of people, some of the highest reputation, and in the greatest order" until they stopped at stamp distributor Andrew Oliver's newly built stamp office on Kilby Street, not far from Long Wharf in Boston Harbor, and demolished the building. Afterward, the crowd continued to Oliver's home, where they burned his effigy and proceeded to destroy his barn, fence, garden, and, ultimately, his home. The goal was to intimidate Oliver and pressure his resignation, which it did. Oliver, who had fled his home, resigned the next day and avoided what was reported in the *London Chronicle* (October 10) as a planned second night of mob attacks against his property.

Less than two weeks later, on August 26, 1765, mobs attacked the homes of more crown-appointed officials, including Admiralty Court Deputy Register William Story, Customs Comptroller Benjamin Hallowell, and Lieutenant Governor Thomas Hutchinson. According to Massachusetts Royal Governor Francis Bernard's proclamation of August 28, reprinted in the October 19 *London Chronicle*, Hutchinson's home was left "a mere shell from top to bottom," with massive destruction to the wainscot, furniture, apparel, jewels, book, and papers, and £900 stolen from the home. Bernard's proclamation also served as a wanted poster, offering £300 for mob leaders and £100 for participants.

The intimidation of crown-appointed officials produced the result Bostonians craved. The resignation of the local stamp officer meant no one could distribute stamped paper, thereby avoiding enforcement of the Stamp Act, so businesses could proceed as usual without taxation. News of the effective revolt spread like wildfire throughout the thirteen colonies and became the tactic of choice up and down the continent with similar forced resignations taking place in Annapolis, Newport, Providence, New York, Albany, New Haven, Philadelphia, Portsmouth, Charleston, and Savannah. The Newport riot and resignation of August 27–29 is reported in detail on the back page of the *Supplement to the Boston News-Letter* on September 5, 1765, and presumably provided Bostonians with encouragement that the terror campaign they launched to help fight the Stamp Act was indeed catching on (coincidentally, a lengthy account of the August 26 attack on Story's, Hallowell's, and Hutchinson's homes in Boston was published on the front page). The episodes of Jared Ingersoll and Henry Van Schaick, appointed stamp distributors for New Haven and Albany, respectively, are well documented in the January 23, 1766, *Pennsylvania Journal*.

In October 1765, a congress of delegates from nine colonies convened in New York to author and adopt a Declaration of Resolves and Grievances; among them it was stated that Parliament could not tax the American colonies without representation.

Throughout the winter months of 1765–66, the Sons of Liberty, a term applied to both organized opposition groups as well as a generic label for any stamp tax opponent, were successful in opening correspondence channels and aligning colonial interests (see Savannah dateline in January 27, 1766, *Supplement to the Boston Gazette* containing reports originally from the *Georgia Gazette*). Using news-swapping techniques they perfected during the French and Indian War, colonial printers, among the hardest hit by the stamp duty, repurposed patriotic reports from other colonies and used their newspapers as the vehicle to lead and uphold the resistance (see Annapolis dateline in March 20, 1766, *Pennsylvania Gazette*, which was originally printed in the *Maryland Gazette* on March 6).

Beyond effigies and acts of intimidation, colonial leaders also collaborated on a joint boycott of British imports, which added financial stress to English merchants and effectively recruited them to lobby Parliament in favor of the act's repeal (see January 27 and February 17, 1766, *Boston Gazette*).

BURNING OF STAMP ACT, BOSTON
Library of Congress

News of the Boston riots spread like wildfire throughout the colonies and became the tactic of choice up and down the continent.

The PENNSYLVANIA GAZETTE.

Containing the Freshest Ad-   *vices, Foreign and Domestic.*

By Captain CALEF, arrived at Boston, in a short Passage from London, we have the following Advices, viz.
EXTRACT from the VOTES of the HOUSE OF COMMONS of GREAT-BRITAIN, in Parliament assembled.
Jovis, 7 Die Februarii, 1765.

MR. HUNTER (according to order) reported from the committee of the whole house, to whom it was referred to consider further of ways and means for raising the supply granted to his Majesty, the resolutions which the committee had directed him to report to the house; which he read in his place, and afterwards delivered in at the table, where the same were read, and agreed to by the house, and are as followeth, viz.

Resolved, That a stamp duty of 3 d. sterling money, be charged upon every skin or piece of vellum or parchment, or sheet or piece of paper, on which shall be ingrossed, written or printed, any declaration, plea, replication, rejoinder, demurrer, or other pleading, or any copy thereof in any court of law, within the British colonies and plantations in America.

Resolved, That a stamp duty of 2 s. sterling money, be charged upon every skin or piece of vellum or parchment, or sheet or piece of paper, on which shall be ingrossed, written or printed, any special bail, and appearance upon such bail, in any such court.

Resolved, That a stamp duty of 1 s. 6 d. sterling money, be charged upon every skin or piece of vellum or parchment, or sheet or piece of paper, on which shall be ingrossed, written or printed, any petition, bill, answer, claim, plea, replication, rejoinder, demurrer, or other pleading, in any court of chancery, or equity, within the said colonies and plantations.

Resolved, That a stamp duty of 3 d. sterling money, be charged upon every skin, or piece of vellum or parchment, or sheet or piece of paper, on which shall be ingrossed, written or printed, any copy of any petition, bill, answer, claim, plea, replication, rejoinder, demurrer, or other pleading, in any such court.

Resolved, That a stamp duty of 1 s. sterling money, be charged upon every skin or piece of vellum or parchment, or sheet or piece of paper, on which shall be ingrossed, written or printed, any monition, libel, answer, allegation, inventory, or renunciation in ecclesiastical matters, in any court of probate, court of ordinary, or other court, exercising ecclesiastical jurisdiction within the said colonies and plantations.

Resolved, That a stamp duty of 6 d. sterling money, be charged upon every skin or piece of vellum or parchment, or sheet or piece of paper, on which shall be ingrossed, written or printed, any copy of any will, other than the probate thereof, monition, libel, answer, allegation, inventory, or renunciation in ecclesiastical matters, in any such court.

Resolved, That a stamp duty of 2 l. sterling money, be charged upon every skin or piece of vellum or parchment, or sheet or piece of paper, on which shall be ingrossed, written or printed, any donation, presentation, collation, or institution, of or to any benefice, or any writ or instrument for the like purpose, or any register, entry, testimonial, or certificate, of any degree taken in any university, academy, college, or seminary of learning, within the said colonies and plantations.

Resolved, That a stamp duty of 1 s. sterling money, be charged upon every skin or piece of vellum or parchment, or sheet or piece of paper, on which shall be ingrossed, written or printed, any monition, libel, claim, answer, allegation, information, letter of request, execution, renunciation, inventory, or other pleading, in any admiralty court, within the said colonies and plantations.

Resolved, That a stamp duty of 6 d. sterling money, be charged upon every skin or piece of vellum or parchment, or sheet or piece of paper, on which any copy of any such monition, libel, claim, answer, allegation, information, letter of request, execution, renunciation, inventory, or other pleading, shall be ingrossed, written or printed.

Resolved, That a stamp duty of 10 s. sterling money, be charged upon every skin or piece of vellum or parchment, or sheet or piece of paper, on which shall be ingrossed, written or printed, any appeal, writ of error, writ of dower, ad quod damnum, cer-

Resolved, That a stamp duty of 20 s. sterling money, be charged upon every skin or piece of vellum or parchment, or sheet or piece of paper, on which shall be ingrossed, written or printed, letters of mart, or commission for private ships of war, within the said colonies and plantations.

Resolved, That a stamp duty of 10 s. sterling money, be charged upon every skin or piece of vellum or parchment, or sheet or piece of paper, on which shall be ingrossed, written or printed, any grant, appointment, or admission, of or to any public beneficial office or employment, for the space of one year, or any lesser time, of or above the value of 20 l. per annum, sterling money, in salary, fees, and perquisites, within the said colonies and plantations, except commissions of officers of the army, navy, ordnance, or militia, and of justices of the peace.

Resolved, That a stamp duty of 6 l. sterling money, be charged upon every skin or piece of vellum or parchment, or sheet or piece of paper, on which any grant of any liberty, privilege, or franchise, under the seal of any of the said colonies or plantations, or under the seal or sign manual of any governor, proprietor, or public officer, alone, or in conjunction with any other person or persons, or with any council, or any council and assembly, or any exemplification of the same, shall be ingrossed, written or printed, within the said colonies and plantations.

Resolved, That a stamp duty of 20 s. sterling money, be charged upon every skin or piece of vellum or parchment, or sheet or piece of paper, on which shall be ingrossed, written or printed, any licence for retailing of spirituous liquors, to be granted to any person who shall take out the same, within the said colonies and plantations.

Resolved, That a stamp duty of 4 l. sterling money, be charged upon every skin or piece of vellum or parchment, or sheet or piece of paper, on which shall be ingrossed, written or printed, any licence for retailing of wine, to be granted to any person who shall not take out a licence for retailing of spirituous liquors, within the said colonies and plantations.

Resolved, That a stamp duty of 3 l. sterling money, be charged upon every skin or piece of vellum or parchment, or sheet or piece of paper, on which shall be ingrossed, written or printed, any licence for retailing of wine, to be granted to any person who shall take out a licence for retailing of spirituous liquors, within the said colonies and plantations.

Resolved, That a stamp duty of 5 s. sterling money, be charged upon every skin or piece of vellum or parchment, or sheet or piece of paper, on which shall be ingrossed, written or printed, any probate of a will, letters of administration, or of guardianship for any estate, above the value of 20 l. of the same money within the British colonies and plantations upon the continent of America, the islands belonging thereto, and the Bermuda and Bahama islands, except probates of wills, and letters of administration to the effects of common seamen or soldiers, who shall die in the public service.

Resolved, That a stamp duty of 10 s. sterling money, be charged upon every skin or piece of vellum or parchment, or sheet or piece of paper, on which shall be ingrossed, written or printed, any such probate, letters of administration, or of guardianship, within all other parts of the British dominions in America.

Resolved, That a stamp duty of 6 d. sterling money, be charged upon every skin or piece of vellum or parchment, or sheet or piece of paper, on which shall be ingrossed, written or printed, any bond, for securing the payment of any sum of money, not exceeding the sum of 10 l. of the same money, within the British colonies and plantations upon the continent of America, the islands belonging thereto, and the Bermuda and Bahama islands.

Resolved, That a stamp duty of 1 s. sterling money, be charged upon every skin or piece of vellum or parchment, or sheet or piece of paper, on which shall be ingrossed, written or printed, any bond for securing the payment of any sum of money above 10 l. and not exceeding the sum of 20 l. of the same money, within such colonies, plantations, and islands.

Resolved, That a stamp duty of 1 s. 6 d. sterling money, be charged upon every skin or piece of vellum or parchment, or sheet or piece of paper, on which shall be ingrossed, written or printed,

charged upon every skin or piece of vellum or parchment, or sheet or piece of paper, on which shall be ingrossed, written or printed, any such original grant, or any such deed, mesne conveyance, or other instrument whatsoever, by which any quantity of land above 200, and not exceeding 320 acres, shall be granted, conveyed or assigned, and in proportion for every such grant, deed, mesne conveyance, or other instrument, granting, conveying or assigning every other 320 acres, within such colonies, plantations, and islands.

Resolved, That a stamp duty of 3 s. sterling money, be charged upon every skin or piece of vellum or parchment, or sheet or piece of paper, on which shall be ingrossed, written or printed, any such original grant, or any such deed, mesne conveyance, or other instrument whatsoever, by which any quantity of land not exceeding 100 acres, shall be granted, conveyed or assigned, within all other parts of the British dominions in America.

Resolved, That a stamp duty of 4 s. sterling money, be charged upon every skin or piece of vellum or parchment, or sheet or piece of paper, on which shall be ingrossed, written or printed, any such original grant, or any such deed, mesne conveyance, or other instrument whatsoever, by which any quantity of land above 100, and not exceeding 200 acres, shall be granted, conveyed or assigned, within the same parts of the said dominions.

Resolved, That a stamp duty of 5 s. sterling money, be charged upon every skin or piece of vellum or parchment, or sheet or piece of paper, on which shall be ingrossed, written or printed, any such original grant, or any such deed, mesne conveyance, or other instrument whatsoever, whereby any quantity of land above 200, and not exceeding 320 acres, shall be granted, conveyed or assigned, and in proportion for every such grant, deed, mesne conveyance, or other instrument, granting, conveying or assigning every other 320 acres, within the same parts of the said dominions.

Resolved, That a stamp duty of 4 l. sterling money, be charged upon every skin or piece of vellum or parchment, or sheet or piece of paper, on which shall be ingrossed, written or printed, any grant, appointment or admission, of or to any public beneficial office or employment, not before mentioned to be charged, above the value of 20 l. per annum sterling money, in salary, fees and perquisites, or any exemplification of the same, within the British colonies and plantations upon the continent of America, the islands belonging thereto, and the Bermuda and Bahama islands, except commissions of officers of the army, navy, ordnance, or militia, and of justices of the peace.

Resolved, That a stamp duty of 6 l. sterling money, be charged upon every skin or piece of vellum or parchment, or sheet or piece of paper, on which shall be ingrossed, written or printed, any such grant, appointment, or admission, of or to any such public beneficial office or employment, or any exemplification of the same, within all other parts of the British dominions in America.

Resolved, That a stamp duty of 2 s. 6 d. sterling money, be charged upon every skin or piece of vellum or parchment, or sheet or piece of paper, on which shall be ingrossed, written or printed, any indenture, lease, conveyance, contract, stipulation, bill of sale, charter party, protest, articles of apprenticeship, or covenant (except for the hire of servants not apprentices; and also except such other matters as are before mentioned to be charged) within the British colonies and plantations in America.

Resolved, That a stamp duty of 5 s. sterling money, be charged upon every skin or piece of vellum or parchment, or sheet or piece of paper, on which any warrant or order for auditing any public accounts, beneficial warrant, order, grant or certificate, under any public seal, or under the seal or sign manual of any governor, proprietor, or public officer, alone, or in conjunction with any other person or persons, or with any council, or any council and assembly, not before mentioned to be charged, or any pass-port, or let-pass, surrender of office, or policy of assurance, shall be ingrossed, written or printed, within the said colonies and plantations, except warrants or orders for the service of the navy, army, ordnance, or militia, and grants of offices under 20 l. per annum, in salary, fees and perquisites.

Resolved, That a stamp duty of 2 s. 3 d. sterling money, be charged upon every skin or piece of vellum or parchment, or sheet or piece of paper, on which shall be ingrossed, written or printed, any notarial act, bond, deed, letter of attorney, procuration,

PENNSYLVANIA GAZETTE (PHILADELPHIA)
April 18, 1765

This issue features one of the first full printings of the infamous Stamp Act, still more than six months from taking effect. During the summer of 1764, Benjamin Franklin, who printed the *Pennsylvania Gazette* until 1748 and remained a partner with the paper until 1766, sailed to London to protest the taxation. Franklin wrote back to a friend in Philadelphia that "we might well have hindered the sun's setting. That we could not do. But since it is down, my friend, and it may be long before it rises again, let us make as good a night of it as we can. We may still light candles." With these sentiments of moderation and compliance, Franklin's political reputation was tarnished, so he responded with a letter-writing publicity campaign to restore his image and convince colonists that he was working diligently to repeal the act.

The London Chronicle.

Vol. XVIII.   Nº 1377.

From TUESDAY, October 15, to THURSDAY, October 17, 1765.

To the PRINTER of the LONDON CHRONICLE.

Ecce! iterum CRISPINUS.   HOR.

Ah! what! my friend THE COBLER! come again!—

YOURS, good Sir, as witness O RARE BEN!—

SIR,

T has been obferv'd with no lefs humour than truth by the ingenious Author of the firft number in the *Spectator*, That the Reader of a Paper is fometimes curious and inquifitive to know *who*, and what *fort* of a man the *Writer* is: not only to his talents or abilities (if he has *any*) but alfo as to his *make* or *figure*, whether a fhort, tall, long or round-fac'd man; —in fhort his whole *perfon*—whether he wears a peruke, or bis own *hair* frizz'd out by *Signior* TOWZERARO (a famous Italian hair-dreffer juft arrived from *Italy* with a frefh cargo of *Naples dew*, and other Italian cofmetics and effences for the *folly* of the ENGLISH Ladies) or whether he wears a *buckle* in his breeches, or tied behind with one of his Landlady's old *top-knots*, with various other *particulars* of the like *importance*: I fay, till the *Reader* is fomewhat fatisfy'd in *all* fuch particulars, or at leaft *fome* of them, his judgment is at a full ftop: and if afk'd his opinion of him, he proceeds with great deliberation—begs leave to fufpend his judgment—fhrugs his fhoulders, and fhakes his head, with many looks and airs of confequence—gives many fignificant nods, and at laft fends in the formal grimace of " Why really, " Sir, as to my opinion of this Writer—I—I " — I could fay—ay — that I could — now " mark what I am going to fay—I don't know " what to think of him—and fo, Sir, your " fervant."—As to *myfelf*, Mr. Printer, I look upon a COBLER to be of that *vaft* confequence as a *Writer*, that nobody cares a fingle farthing about him what *fort* of fellow he is — whether he *has* a *head* or none at all, or walks up and down the city with a large roundy *turnip* fet between his fhoulders by way of an head—whether he wears a *wig*, his own *hair*, or a tatter'd *cap* of cotton or flannel—whether a fharp *eye*, or *fquints* with one — or, laftly, whether he has a good pair of *legs*, or a *wooden* one: I fay, *all*, or any *one* of thefe things, are points of the utmoft indifference to a fmart, fenfible Reader — the things which *he* has in view, are—can he write any thing *tolerably* clever, funny, or humourous to divert the *town*, which, like the *Athenians* of old, is daily fond of feeing and hearing *novelties?* Is he a *good* hand at bearing a part in a REVIEW, in cenfuring feverely what he does *not* underftand, and *worrying* (like fo many H—ds) the characters of Writers, who either can't afford, or difdain to fend a *broad piece* or two, in order to court their favour? or has he any *fmart* talents (like my friend ——) at affifting at a Com—n C——l in drawing up a CITY ADDRESS with a " *nocet empta dolore voluptas*," i. e. in plain modern English, " A LICK at the COURT," or " a SUGAR-ROLL for *Statefmen* dipp'd in MOLASSES and VINEGAR." I fay, if he has but a *Scull* for any of thefe things, he'll foon find it will do — it's no matter whether the GENIUS is a COBLER or a STATESMAN, fince he will want neither *Money* nor *Fame* — and with this advantage, that fometimes the STATESMAN is the greater

Cobler or *Bungler* of the two, as the families of the WRONG-HEADS and COBLERS have a very clofe relation and connection with each other, and have been famous for their exploits time immemorial. —— Hence, it feems, it is a common thing with us to call a Blockhead a *Wrong-headed* Whelp, or a *Cobbling* Cur, which are terms exactly of the fame meaning; for when a man is fit for nothing elfe, he will do for a COBLER; it being obferved that all *Fools* are *Coblers*; tho' it don't follow that all *Coblers* are *Fools*, as (with modefty be it fpoken, and humbly hoping) witnefs your very humble fervant,

The COBLER *of Chancery-lane*.

P. S. I fhall take an opportunity to endeavour to entertain your Readers with fome account of our COBBLING family, and the great Hero of it SIR FRANCIS. And in fome *future* Papers,

Quicquid agunt homines, votum, timor, ira, voluptas,
Gaudia, difcurfus, noftri eft farrago libelli.

Which for the benefit of the Ladies, runs thus, according to Ben *Johnfon*,

The *folly, vice,* and *nonfenfe* of the Town,
Shall in *your* CHRONICLE be fully fhewn.
O RARE BEN!

WEDNESDAY, OCTOBER 16.
The London Gazette. No. 10565.

St. James's, October 15.

THE King has been pleafed to grant unto the Right Rev. Dr. Frederick Keppel, Bifhop of Exeter, the Deanry of the Chapel Royal in the Caftle of Windfor, with the Deanry of Wolverhampton, and Regiftry of the Knights of the moft Noble Order of the Garter, thereunto annexed, the fame being void by the death of Dr. Peniftone Booth.

The King has been pleafed to prefent Richard Penneck, Clerk, M. A. to the rectory of St. John of Herflydown, Southwark, void by the refignation of Dr. James Trail.

The King has been pleafed to prefent John Warner, Clerk, M. A. to the vicarage of Weft-Ham in Effex, void by the refignation of Dr. James Trail.

Lord Chamberlain's Office, Oct. 15. Orders for the Court's going out of mourning on Sunday next, the 20th inftant, for the late Emperor of Germany, and the late Duke of Parma.

BANKRUPT.
Thomas Afhhurft Maclane, of Lime-ftreet, London, Merchant. To appear Oct. 22, 31, Nov. 30, at Guildhall.

Dividends to be made.

Nov. 6. William Farnworth of Cullum-ftreet, London, Merchant and Warehoufeman, at Guildhall.

Nov. 7. William Hutchefon, of Briftol, Merchant, at the Fountain Tavern in the High-ftreet, Briftol.

Nov. 8. William Penkett, late of Chefter, Grocer, at the Golden Fleece in Liverpool.

AMERICA.

Wilmington, in Virginia, Auguft 22.

THE following are the refolutions the Houfe of Burgeffes are come to very lately with refpect to the Stamp-duty, immediately on the receipt of a copy of the act of parliament from England, on which the Governor diffolved the affembly

WHEREAS the Hon. ***** of ******* in England have of late drawn into queftion, how far the General Affembly of this colony hath power to enact laws for laying taxes and impofing duties, payable by the people of This his

Majefty's moft ancient colony: For fettling and afcertaining the fame to all future times, the Houfe of Burgeffes of this prefent General Affembly have come to the feveral following refolutions:

Refolved, That the firft adventurers and fettlers of This his Majefty's colony and dominion of Virginia, brought with them, and tranfmitted to their pofterity, and all other his Majefty's fubjects fince inhabiting in this his Majefty's colony, all the privileges and immunities that have at any time been held, enjoyed and poffeffed by the people of Great Britain.

Refolved, That by the two royal charters granted by King James the Firft, the colonifts aforefaid are declared entituled to all privileges and immunities of faithful Liege and natural born fubjects, to all intents and purpofes, as if they had been abiding and born within the realm of England.

Refolved, That his Majefty's liege people of This his moft ancient colony have enjoyed the right of being thus governed by their own Affembly in the article of taxes and internal police, and that the fame have never been forfeited, or any other way yielded up, but have been conftantly recognized by the King and people of Great Britain.

Refolved, therefore, That the General Affembly of this colony, together with his Majefty or his Subftitute, have in their reprefentative capacity the only exclufive right and power to lay taxes and impofitions upon the inhabitants of this colony; and that every attempt to veft fuch a power in any perfon or perfons whatfoever other than the General Affembly aforefaid, is illegal, unconftitutional, and unjuft, and has a manifeft tendency to deftroy Britifh as well as American freedom.

The following RESOLVES *were not paffed, only drawn up by the Committee.*

Refolved, That his Majefty's liege people, the inhabitants of this colony, are not bound to yield obedience to any law or ordinance whatfoever, defigned to impofe any taxation whatfoever upon them, other than the laws and ordinances of the General Affembly aforefaid.

Refolved, That any perfon who fhall, by fpeaking or writing, maintain that any perfon or perfons, other than the General Affembly of this colony, have any right or power to impofe or lay any taxation whatfoever on the people here, fhall be deemed an enemy to This his Majefty's colony.

Bofton, New-England, Auguft 22. The General Affembly of Virginia is, by Governor Faquier's Proclamation, prorogued to the 17th of October next.

Governor Wentworth has prorogued the affembly of New-Hampfhire to the 19th of November next.

Accounts received from feveral of our Whaling-Veffels on the Labrador Coaft are, that they meet with fome delays in regard to their fifhing, in confequence of orders from the Commending Officers on that ftation, a copy of which is as follows.

Memorandum,

" In purfuance of the Governor's directions, all mafters of whaling-veffels, and others whom it may concern, are hereby moft ftrictly required to obferve the following particulars, viz.

" 1. To carry the ufelefs parts of fuch whales as they may catch, to at leaft three leagues from the fhore, to prevent the damage that the neighbouring fifhers for cod and feal fuftain, by their being left on the fhore.

[Price Two-pence Halfpenny.]

The LONDON CHRONICLE

AMERICA.

Wilmington, Virginia, August 22.

THE following are the resolutions the House of Burgesses are come to very lately with respect to the Stamp-duty, immediately on the receipt of a copy of the act of parliament from England, on which the Governor dissolved the assembly

WHEREAS the Hon. ***** of ******* in England have of late drawn into question, how far the General Assembly of this colony hath power to enact laws for laying taxes and imposing duties, payable by the people of This his Majesty's most ancient colony: For settling and ascertaining the same to all future times, the House of Burgesses of this present General Assembly have come to the several following resolutions:

Resolved, That the first adventurers and settlers of This his Majesty's colony and dominion of Virginia, brought with them, and transmitted to their posterity, and all other his Majesty's subjects since inhabiting in this his Majesty's colony, all the privileges and immunities that have at any time been held, enjoyed and possessed by the people of Great Britain.

Resolved, That by the two royal charters granted by King James the First, the colonists aforesaid are declared entitled to all privileges and immunities of faithful Liege and natural born subjects, to all intents and purposes, as if they had been abiding and born within the realm of England.

Resolved, That his Majesty's liege people of This his most ancient colony have enjoyed the right of being thus governed by their own Assembly in the article of taxes and internal police, and that the same have never been forfeited, or any other way yielded up, but have been constantly recognized by the King and people of Great Britain.

Resolved, therefore, That the General Assembly of this colony, together with his Majesty or his Substitute, have in their representative capacity the only exclusive right and power to lay taxes and impositions upon the inhabitants of this colony; and that every attempt to vest such a power in any person or persons whatsoever other than the General Assembly aforesaid, is illegal, unconstitutional, and unjust, and has a manifest tendency to destroy British as well as American freedom.

The following RESOLVES *were not passed, only drawn up by the Committee.*

Resolved, That his Majesty's liege people, the inhabitants of this colony, are not bound to yield obedience to any law or ordinance whatsoever, designed to impose any taxation whatsoever upon them, other than the laws and ordinances of the General Assembly aforesaid.

Resolved, That any person who shall, by speaking or writing, maintain that any person or persons, other than the General Assembly of this colony, have any right or power to impose or lay any taxation whatsoever on the people here, shall be deemed an enemy to This his Majesty's colony.

LONDON CHRONICLE
October 17, 1765

—

On May 29, 1765, at Virginia's House of Burgesses, Patrick Henry gave a passionate speech to inspire the passage of resolutions against the Stamp Act. The two most radical resolves—including one that was intended to give Virginians the right to disobey any tax not enacted by the Virginia assembly—were struck from official record but still leaked to the public and eventually reached London newspapers.

Thursday, October 10.

SCOTLAND.

Edinburgh, October 5.

R. William Ogilvy is elected Professor of Humanity in the King's College at Aberdeen, in place of Mr. Thomas Gordon, admitted Professor of Philosophy.

On Tuesday Night last, about five score of sheep belonging to two fleshers in Musselburgh, which were grazing a little eastward of the town, had betaken themselves for shelter from the storm, to a hollow, when they were surrounded by a high tide, carried off to the sea, and all perished. The whole number were cast ashore on Aberlady Sands.

On the 28th ult. died at Lamington, Lanerkshire, the Rev. Mr. David Blinshall, in the 47th year of his ministry there. Though in the 97th of his age, he performed all the duties of his office until about twelve months ago, retaining his memory and judgment to the last hour of his life.

Last night came down a further reprieve of fourteen days, from Wednesday next, for Lieutenant Patrick Ogilvie, now prisoner in the Tolbooth here.

COUNTRY NEWS.

Gloucester, Octob. 7. On Tuesday last died at Beckford, in this county, Benedict Wakeman, Esq; of that place.

Lately died at Rochelle in France, whither he had been for his health, George Pritchard, Esq; of Hopen, in Herefordshire.

Salisbury, Octob. 7. A few days ago, at Southampton, a girl of sixteen, being long troubled with an ague, was advised by a lad of her acquaintance to try white hellebore, of which having obtained a pennyworth, she took one half immediately, which not having the least effect, she took the remainder on the approach of the next fit, and in less than half an hour after she was seized with convulsions, and expired in a few minutes.

LONDON.

Yesterday his Majesty came from Richmond to St. James's, where there was a numerous levee, at which were present the Archbishop of Canterbury, the Duke of Newcastle, with many others of the Nobility, foreign Ministers, &c. to pay their respects to his Majesty, as being the birth-day of the Prince of Brunswick.

Neither his Royal Highness the Duke of Cumberland, nor his serene Highness the Prince of Brunswick, are yet returned from Newmarket. They are at present making several visits at the Duke of Grafton's, Duke of Rutland's, and other noble personages in Cambridge and Lincolnshires.

Extract of a Letter from Boston in New England, Aug. 26.

"Very early on Wednesday morning, the 14th instant, were discovered hanging on a limb of the great trees, so called, at the south part of this town, two effigies, one of which by the labels appeared to be designed to represent a Stamp-Officer; the other a Jackboot with a head and horns peeping out of the top: The report of the images soon spread thro' the town, brought a vast number of spectators, and had such an effect on them that scarce any could attend to the talk of day-labour; but all seemed on the wing for Freedom. About dusk the images were taken down, placed on a bier, supported in procession by six men, followed by a great concourse of people, some of the highest reputation, and in the greatest order, ecchoing forth Liberty and Property! No Stamp, &c.— Having passed thro' the town-house they proceeded down King-street, and thro' Kilby-street, where an edifice had been lately erected, which was supposed to be designed for a Stamp-Office.

Here they halted, and went to work to demolish that building. This being finished, many of them loaded themselves with the wooden trophies, and proceeded (bearing the two effigies) to the top of Fort-hill, where a fire was soon kindled, in which one of them was burnt. The populace after this went to work on the barn, fence, garden, &c. And here it would have ended, had not some indiscretions, to say the least, been committed by his friends within, which so enraged the people they were not to be restrained, though hitherto no violence had been offered to any one. But it is very remarkable, though they entered the lower part of the house in multitudes, yet the damage done to it was not so great as might have been expected.

The next day the honourable gentleman who had been appointed to the duty of Distributor of the Stamps when they should arrive, supposing himself to be the object of their derision, informed the principal gentlemen of the town, that as it appeared so disagreeable to the people, he should request the liberty of being excused from that office; and in the evening the populace re-assembled, erected a pyramid, intending a second bonfire; but upon hearing of the resignation, they desisted, and repaired to the gentleman's gate, gave three cheers, and took their departure without damage; but having heard it propagated that an honourable gentleman at the north part of the town, had been accessary in laying on the Stamp Duties, &c. they repaired to his house, where, upon being informed by some gentlemen of integrity and reputation, that he had not only spoke but wrote to the contrary, they retired, and having patroled the streets, returned to their respective habitations, as quietly as they had done the night before."

They write from Warsaw of the 21st ult. that the Sieur Kozlobrocki, having been guilty of murder, and had fled to the church for refuge, was taken from thence by a detachment of troops, by express orders of the supreme Court of Justice at Peterkau, where he was tried and condemned. To the breach of this privilege, the Clergy of Poland would never before submit.

Letters from Amsterdam of the 4th instant bring advice, that a further account had been received there, touching the violent hurricane which happened at St. Eustatia the 31st of last July; that the small vessels got out to sea in time, but the storm reaching to Martinico, thirty-three French, English, and Spanish ships were lost; at Guadaloupe, six ships and ten small vessels: and at Dominica, nine vessels, with a large quantity of Coffee on board, were drove on shore and lost: And on the 7th ult. another great storm happened at St. Eustatia, by which three barks and a snow were lost in the road.

Yesterday the purser of the Earl of Lincoln, Hardwick, came to the India, with the news of the above ship being safe arriv'd at Plymouth, from Fort St. George and China.

The Earl of Lincoln East-Indiaman, just arrived from China, brought home 427,500 lb. of bohea, 36,600 lb. congou, and 172,800 lb. of single Tea; five whole chests, 45 half ditto, and one box of china-ware; besides several other goods.

Yesterday Sir Jarvis Clifton, Bart. was introduced to his Majesty at St. James's by Lord Berkeley of Stratton, and was graciously received.

The Hon. Mr. Wallop, brother to the Earl of Portsmouth, is appointed Ensign in the 3d regiment of foot-guards, in the room of Lord Offaley, deceased.

William Newton, Gent. is appointed, by his Majesty, a Lieutenant in the 10th regiment of dragoons, in the room of Lieut. Floyer preferred. George Poyntz Ricketts, Gent. succeeds Mr. Newton, as Cornet in the said regiment.

Yesterday Col. Keene, Gentleman of horse to his Excellency the Earl of Hertford, set out for Ireland. As did likewise the Hon Col Hotham, and Lieut. Col. Paterson, to join their regiment in that kingdom.

As the alteration of the rates of postage of letters takes place this day, it may not be unacceptable to our readers to inform them, that, by an act passed the last sessions of parliament, it is enacted, that from and after the 10th day of October, 1765, the rates now payable for the postage of letters sent by the General Post not exceeding two post-stages shall cease and determine, and in place thereof the following rates shall be taken, viz. " For the conveyance of every single letter, not exceeding one whole post-stage from the office where such letter may be put in, the sum of one penny; for every double letter, two-pence; for every treble letter, three-pence; and for every ounce, four-pence; and so in proportion for every packet of deeds, writs, or other things. And for the conveyance of every single letter above one post-stage, and not exceeding two post-stages, the sum of two-pence; for every double letter, four-pence; and for every treble letter, six-pence; and for every ounce, eight-pence; and so in proportion for every pacquette of deeds, writs, or other things."

Yesterday David Durell, D. D. Principal of Hertford College, was chosen Vice-Chancellor of the university of Oxford; and Dr. Barton, Warden of Merton; Dr. Leigh, Master of Baliol; Dr. Brown, Provost of Queen's; and Dr. Randolph, President of Corpus Christi, were chosen Pro-Vice Chancellors.

Yesterday the Rev. Mr. Pearce was collated by the Dean and Chapter of St. Paul's, to the Rectory of the United Parishes of St. Mary Magdalen and St. Gregory's, Old Fish-street.

A few days ago died at Wickham, near Gosport, in Hampshire, in a very advanced age, Samuel Atkins, Esq; the second on the list of superannuated flag-officers on half-pay.

On Monday died, at his house on the Gunwharf, at Portsmouth, John Eddowes, Esq; many years storekeeper of the ordnance, &c. there.

On Tuesday last died, at Pendley hall, near Webley in Surry, Dame Margaret Estcombe, relict of Sir William Estcombe.

On Tuesday died in Lombard-street, Capt. Michael Butler, in the West-India trade.

The same day died Mr. Green, master of the Oval tavern in Grosvenor-street.

On Sunday last the Collector of the toll at Kensington Gravel-pits, was suddenly taken ill, fell down, and expired immediately.

On Tuesday the body of Mr. Parkinson, an overseer to persons employed in unloading ships, was taken up near Stone-stairs; he fell over the side of a West Indiaman last Friday-night, and was drowned.

On Monday night Mary Davers (who accused herself some years ago of the murder of her bastard child, for which she was tried and acquitted, and also charged herself with being concerned, with others, in the murder of the Turnpike man at Mary-le-bon) hanged herself in Bucket-Court, in Tottenham-Court road.

Tuesday se'nnight, at the clearing the prisoners at Guildhall, it was again argued by several eminent Counsellors, Whether a spunging-house was to be deemed a prison or not? when it was finally determined by the Court in the negative. —At the last sessions at Guildford, a Captain, who was arrested in December last, and did not surrender to the gaol before March, was cleared, the Court at that place being of opinion, that a spunging-house was a prison.

Yesterday John M'Kenzie for stealing two silver pint mugs from Mr. Abedward, a Publican in Nightingale-lane; and James Haines, for robbing Joseph Dupree, Esq; on the highway, were executed at Tyburn.

Yesterday a young fellow was carried before the Lord Mayor, being charged with forging a certificate, signed by a Captain of a Man of war, in order to receive some wages, and was committed to the Poultry-Compter.

D. L.   Jealous Wife, with Fortunatus.

C. G.   The Wonder, with Perseus and Andromeda.

that it would be full seven years before the payments could be completed.

Letters from Stockholm advise, that the subsidy treaty between Sweden and France meets with great opposition.

A proclamation was publish'd at Boston in New-England by his excellency the Governor Bernard on the 28th of August last, purporting, that "Whereas on the 26th of August, towards the evening, a great number of people unlawfully assembled together in the town of Boston, arm'd with clubs, staves, &c. and did first of all attack the dwelling house of William Story, Esq; deputy register of the Court of Admiralty within that province, break his windows, and enter his said house, and the office wherein the books and files belonging to the said court were lodged, and did scatter, burn or destroy the same, and most of his own papers, &c. and did destroy a great part of his furniture. After which the rioters did proceed to the dwelling house of Benjamin Hallowell, Esq; comptroller of his Majesty's Customs, for the port of Boston, break down the fence before it, and enter the house, destroy the wainscot and furniture, take away his apparel, break open his desk and trunks, and take out all his papers, and about thirty pounds sterling in money.

"And whereas these or other rioters did, on the same night, attack the dwelling-house of the Hon. Thomas Hutchinson, Esq; Lieutenant-Governor of the said province, and destroy the wainscot, leaving the house a mere shell from top to bottom, destroy all the furniture, destroy or carry off all the apparel, jewels, books, and papers of his honour and his family, drink, take away, or destroy eight pipes and three quarter casks of wine, and all provisions and stores of what kind soever in his cellars, and carry off about 900 l. sterling in money, together with all his honour's plate, pillaging and destroying every thing in the said house of what kind soever.

"His Excellency promises a reward of 300 l. for the discovery of the leader or leaders, of any of the parties aforesaid, so that he or they may be convicted, and a reward of 100 l. for the discovery of any other person of such parties. And any person (such principal leaders only excepted) shall, over and above the reward aforesaid, upon discovery of any of his accomplices, receive his Majesty's gracious pardon."

Extract of a Letter from Boston in New-England, dated Sept. 2.

"At a meeting of the freeholders and other inhabitants of the town of Boston, on Tuesday

appear, that he was led into an error by symptoms which have hitherto been always thought certain.

The French Comedians had fixed up bills at Paris for the tragedy of Phædra and Hypolitus, to be performed on the 30th ult. but when the curtain was drawn up that evening, one of the Actors appeared on the stage, and requested permission to play a new comedy, which was granted by a clapping of hands; and the piece, which is called *The Guardian duped*, met with great applause. It is wrote by M. Caillevac de l'Etendoux, who made use of this stratagem to avoid the cabals generally attendant on a new play.

A letter from Dunkirk, dated Oct. 7, says, "While all are in despair here on account of the English ministry insisting so peremptorily on the destruction of our port, we acknowledge some obligations to them for being instrumental in having the Chevalier de Mezieres removed from being our Governor. He left this town yesterday, to the universal satisfaction of the first inhabitants of the place, as well as of the meanest peasants in the adjacent villages, who have equally been exposed to his tyrannical and capricious humour. It is reported here, that the British Ministry made a point with our Court to recall the man who had distinguished himself here in his command with so much violence against their nation. It is well known, that he extended his oppression equally to the natives of the place, and acted, in every respect, as if tyranny was his sole delight."

From Rome they write, that a great quantity of gold coin has been lately discovered in the land of Poggio-Mirleto; and that the grand treasurer's lieutenant was gone to examine them.

It is said the Prince and Princess of Brunswick, with several other Royal Personages, will honour the City with their presence at Guildhall next Lord Mayor's Day.

Yesterday the Right Hon. Lady Holland was at Court at St. James's, for the first time since her arrival from France.

On Wednesday evening the Tripoline Ambassador arrived in town from Portsmouth; and yesterday he notified his arrival to the Secretaries of State.

Yesterday set out for Ireland the Right Hon. —— Fortescue, Esq; Postmaster General of that kingdom.

His Majesty has been pleased to appoint Henry Bassett, Esq; to be a Major in the 10th regiment of foot, in the room of Major Percival. And Robert Nettle, Esq; succeeds Major Bassett

for the benefit of the owner. To perpetuate this circumstance this fair is annually kept, where horn, and all toys made of horn, are publickly purchased.

On Tuesday last Capt. Hayter, of St. Martin's, was married to Miss Millis, of Thames Ditton, in Surry.

M. Filengeri, Governor of Viterbo, died lately, and has left an immense fortune to the different abbeys of Sicily. Having, as he says in his will, got all his riches by the church, he thought himself therefore obliged to let them return thither.

Letters from Barbadoes of the 28th of August, bring advice of the death of Col. Edward Carleton.

On Wednesday died, in Crutched Friars, Bartholomew Ibbot, Esq; formerly one of the Inspectors of the customs in the port of London.

Last week died at Bath, Lady Chapple, widow of the late Sir William Chapple, one of the Judges of the Court of King's Bench.

Mr. John Steers, an eminent English merchant at Lisbon, died there lately.

Yesterday died at his house in Marybone-street, Piccadilly, —— Leslie, Esq; who supplied the army in Germany with wine during the late war. He died worth 20,000.

On Monday Langley and Everett, two Bargemen, who had for some time bore animosity to each other, went on board a barge below Chertsey to navigate it to London, where they fought, and in the fray Everett was knocked overboard, and drowned. Langley escaped.

On Wednesday John Willis, and his son, carpenters, pulling down some old houses at Duke's Place, near Aldgate, found as much Spanish silver coin as they sold for seventeen pounds and upwards.

Yesterday the sessions ended at the Old-Bailey, when 20 prisoners were tried, two of whom were capitally convicted, viz. Andrew Fitzgerald and William Richardson, for forging seamens wills, seven were cast for transportation, and eleven acquitted. At this sessions two received sentence of death, 19 to be transported for seven years, one branded, and one to be fined and imprisoned. It is remarkable there were five prisoners tried this sessions who were tried the September sessions.

The next Sessions will begin on Monday the 9th of December at Guildhall, and on Wednesday the 11th at the Old-Baily.

Wednesday last a young woman was tried at the Old Bailey, for stealing, in an amour with a sailor, seven guineas, his property; the proof not being sufficient, and the evidence of the sailor very favourable, she was acquitted. The —— caught her in his arms, —— —— rapture, swearing —— keep all, but that she —— smacks were so hard —— Court was much surprise —— ling at the oddity. —— plan is under considerat —— of milk, and obliging —— to sell by statute measur

—— RACES.
—— for five year-olds, —— grey horse, Trimm —— 50 l. weight for age, —— bay horse, Young Bar —— with Daphne and Amint —— ith Perseus and Andromed

---

LONDON CHRONICLE
October 10, 1765

—

Three weeks before the Stamp Act took effect, news of the August 14 riots in Boston arrived in London. English readers were likely glued to the following issues as more details of colonial anger and protest arrived by ship.

LONDON CHRONICLE
October 19, 1765

—

Soon after reading about the Virginia Resolves and the Boston riot of August 14, the *London Chronicle* continues to barrage its readers with terrifying American news. This time, it prints the dreadful details of the destruction of homes of Crown officials, including Lieutenant Governor Thomas Hutchinson. Here, Londoners read the proclamation by Royal Governor Francis Bernard, who offered a £300 reward for the capture of the riot leaders.

The following is from one of the Monday's Papers.

BOSTON, *September 2.*

ABOUT Twilight last Monday, a small Bonfire appeared to be kindled in King-Street, and surrounded only by a few Boys and Children ; but one of the Fire-Wards perceiving it to rise to a dangerous Height, interposed and used his Endeavours to extinguish or at least to diminish it ; in which salutary attempt, after several Whispers from a Person unknown, warning him of danger, he received a Blow, and such Tokens of Insult and Outrage, as obliged him to desist and take his Departure.

Soon after this, Day-light being scarce in, the Fire gradually decaying, a peculiar Hoop and Whistle was observed to be sounded from various Quarters, which instantaneously drew together a great Number of disguised Ruffians, (for this Appellation we hope not improperly applied,) armed with Clubs, Staves, &c. No sooner were they assembled, than Attack was made on the Dwelling-House of *William Story*, Esq: opposite the North side of Court-House ; the lower Part of which, being his Office as Deputy-Register of the Court of Vice-Admiralty, was in a few Minutes laid open : The public Files and Records of that Court, Mr. *Story*'s private Papers, Books of Account &c. exposed to Ravage and Destruction, and improved as Fuel to revive the expiring Flames : Little more than half an Hour sufficed them here, for it seems much greater Exploits, were reserved for the Heroism of the Night.

Boisterous and intrepid, from this first Object of their Rage, they rushed onward, encreasing still in Number and Fury, to the new and elegantly finished Building of *Benjamin Hallowell*, jun. Esq; where after tearing down the Fences, breaking the Windows, &c. they at length entered the House, and in the most savage and destructive manner broke and abused his Furniture, Chairs, Tables, Desk, Glasses, China, and in short every Thing they could lay their Hands on ; at the same Time purloining his Money, and dispersing his private Books and Papers, until by the Effect of Wine and the other Stores of his Cellar, they ripened in Ebriety and Madness, and became fit for the next, more desolating and barbarous Operation.

Towards Ten o'Clock they were traced by the Noise and Tumult of a numerous and confused Rabble to the Mansion-House of His Honor the Lieut. Gov. This seemed to be reserved for the utmost Violence of their diabolical Phrenzy ; for immediately on the Word given, that large and stately Edifice became a Prey to the Iron Hand of Outrage and Robbery ; a few Hours and the House was a meer Skeleton, and deprived of Furniture, even Wainscot and Partition, broke, hacked and mangled : and the whole by Break of Day, at once a sad Spectacle of Indignation [...]er !

[...]t and extraordinary Desolation, be[...] [...]d it's Furniture of very considera[...] [...]onor and his Family sustained, the [...]ght and nine Hundred Pounds Ster[...] [...]his Plate, Wearing Apparel, a valu[...] [...]brary, a great Number of private [...] and scarce Papers and Manuscripts, [...] large Files and Records, occasionally [...]ssession, relating to the Claims and [...]ince ; all dispersed, stolen, and de[...] [...]e Damage in it's Consequences [...] publickly as well as privately, In[...]

[...]'s own Misfortune with Firmness, [...]thers," (the Words on the Occasion [...] and worthy Gentleman, who has [...]Residence among us) is the Part of [...] who then can blush, or be ashamed [...] those who have so severely felt the [...] a misguided and merciless Rabble.

The Sufferings of the other Gentlemen, tho' truly grievous, seems to be absorbed in the greater Misfortune of his Honor and his Family, their loss being computed at near twenty five Hundred Pounds Sterling exclusive of the Building.

The Peace and good Order of the Town has been [...]er since preserved by a Military Watch, which we hope in Time will have a Tendency to allay the present strange and tumultuous Spirit ; tho' we would not be understood, not to distinguish this, from the truly noble Opposition to the imposition of internal Taxes, without the intervention of the respective Legislatures of the Colonies, or an equal Representation, which seems to be not only of this Province, but the united Voice of the whole British Continent.

The morning after the late Tumult and Devastation, being the Time for opening the Superiour Court of Judicature, Court of Assize, &c. His Honor the Chief Justice was obliged to attend, notwithstanding his great Distress, there not being a Quorum of the Court without him. His Brethren of the Bench, and the Gentlemen of the Bar habited in their respective Robes, and he in his only Suit ! A Scene truly affecting to every humane and feeling Breast.

Several Persons were taken up and committed to Goal in this Town, last Week, on a voilent Suspicion of their being concerned in the Riot of the 26th Instant.

Since our last we have received a Number of Accounts that in the neighbouring Colonies they have gone great Lengths in their Resentment to the Stamp-Officers, some of them we here insert.

NORWICH, *August 22.*

The noble patriotic fire which has lighted up in one place and another, and of late shone so conspicuous at Boston, blazed here with all the vehemence and splendor of a comet, guided by the dictates of prudence and decorum. 'Twas last night our reputable STAMP-MASTER, in effigy, made his public appearance in this town, clad in a suit of white, trim'd with black, the gift of his native country, both as an emblem of his purity and innocence, and his sorrow and tender concern for this unhappy people : On his right hand stood the restless father of mischief with the stamp act in his hand, giving credentials to his all attentive pupil ; the malignity of his heart was lively portray'd by the expressive cardinal knave at cards on his breast, accompanied with a cautious memento to all placemen, that * * * * * *

" When vice prevails and impious men bear sway,
" The post of honour is a private station."

Their appearance was becoming, and procession glorious, attended by such invectives, huzza's and disdainful music as are the pure emanations of injured freedom : after passing thro' town, our hero with his companion, was conducted——

" in all the Majesty of Greece" to the height of a lofty hill, perhaps the highest summit he will e'er ascend ; and there in complaisance to his fellow, committed to the flames ; and a few loyal and very constitutional healths crown'd the night.

NEW-LONDON, *August 23.*

We hear that a gentleman in one of the southern provinces being advised that his son, then in London, was appointed a *STAMP-OFFICER*, for said province, immediately wrote him, that if he thought proper to accept that most detestable Office, he would not expect any thing from him, and that he might never see his face more

Newport, August 26.

We hear from New-London, that about 4 o'Clock last Thursday Afternoon, was exhibited, in the most public Part of the Town, the Effigies of a Distributor of Stamps, with a Boot on one of the Shoulders, and the Devil represented as looking out of the same.—— They were suspended in the Air, on a Gibbet, between 20 and 30 Feet from the Ground ; and after being exposed about an Hour, were taken down, and carried through the Town, attended by the principal Part of the Inhabitants. The Cannon of the Fort were repeatedly discharged during the Time of Exhibition. Between Ten and Eleven the Effigies were consumed amidst the Acclamations of the People. 'Tis said the most perfect Decorum was observed in all their Behaviour ; and no Person suffered the least Injury.

From several Letters wrote at Newport, Rhode-Island, and from the Newport Mercury of Monday last, we have collected the following Particulars of the Populace there :

Newport, September 2.

The latter End of the Week before last, the Effigies of three Gentlemen were prepared, in order for an Exhibition, on the Tuesday following, the Day for the Choice of Deputies to represent the Town in the General Assembly ; one of the Effigies represented the Distributor of the Stamps ; the other two those who were suspected of countenancing the Stamp-Act.—On Monday one of the Gentlemen published the following Advertisement in the Mercury ; by many thought to be a very imprudent Action at that Juncture, viz

THE Author of the Halifax Letter gives out to the Public, That he is a Native of the Colonies, and has a Heart as warmly attached to their true Interest as any Man whatever : That the Sentiments he has adopted, in Print, have since appeared to be the Judgment of the Parliament of Great Britain ; and the Opinion of Nine-Tenths of the British Nation : and he has published them with that Freedom, which is the Privilege, and ought to be the Boast of every English-man. He therefore cannot repress his Astonishment at the mistaken Notions of those, who, under a Pretence of serving the Cause of Liberty, would take away the Right of private Judgment, and stop the Avenues to Truth, by instigating the Populace, and endeavouring to point their Fury against the Person and Interest of a Man, meerly because he happens to differ in Opinion from his Countrymen : And in that Instance, only exercises the same Privilege which they claim and enjoy.

The Writer does not retract any Position contained in the Halifax Letter ; and therefore does not meanly sollicit any Favour or Exemption from the Abuse intended him, because if his Person and Interest become the Objects of popular Revenge for these Sentiments, he thinks he shall never lament the Cause, whatever may be the Consequences.

On Tuesday Morning the 27th, between 5 and 6 o'Clock a Mob assembled, erected a Gallows near the Town House and dispers'd, and about 10 o'Clock reassembled, when the Effigies were carted up Thames Street, and then up King-street to the said Gallows where they were hung by the Neck, suspended near 15 Feet in the Air, and about 5 o'Clock in the Afternoon they made a Fire under the Gallows which consumed the Effigies and Gallows to Ashes. After the Effigies were burnt the Mob dispers'd, and no Violence was offered to the Persons or Property of any Man.

On the Effigies were the following Labels.

On the Stampman, an *S* painted on his Forehead, and *Stampman* in Capitals on his Breast.

At his Left Hand, *M--t-n H-w--d*, with an *S* on his Forehead, and on his Breast, *That fawning, insidious, infamous Parricide, Martinus Scriblerus.*—His Neck, with that of his Accomplice, connected with a Rope, to which was appended a Paper with this Inscription, *We have an hereditary, indefeasible Right to an Halter ;---besides, we encouraged the Growth of Hemp you know.*—In his Right Hand he held his Halifax Letter, and on his Right Arm inscribed, *The only filial Pen.*—From his Mouth issued this Label, directed towards his Left Arm, *What avails my boasted independence---Posterity will curse my Memory.*—And on his Left Arm this Sentence, *Curs'd Ambition, accursed Clan, ye have ruined me.*

On the Right Hand of the Stampman hung, with the Letter *S* painted on his Forehead, *Dr. Murphy,* and on his Breast, *That formule, miscreated, tearing Jacobite, Dr. Murphy.* Out of his mouth issued this Label, *We cannot complain Martinus, we deserve this, and more.*—In his Right Hand he held a Letter, directed, *To that Mawgawgeene of Knowledge, Dr. —— Murphy, Newport, Rhode Island.* And on his Right arm, *If I had received this Letter from the Earl of —— but a Week sooner.* And on his Left arm, *It is too late now, Martinus, to tack about, we are all aground.*

On one of the Posts out of Reach, *Whoever attempts, in any Way whatsoever, to render ineffectual this Mark of public Contempt, will be deem'd an Enemy to Liberty, and incur the Resentment of the Town.*

The same Day, at a Meeting of the Inhabitants of the Town, Metcalfe Bowler, Esq ; Esq ; Mr. John G. Wanton, George Hazard, Esq ; Mr. Benjamin Green, Capt. Samuel Carr, and Capt. William Read, were chosen Deputies of the Town, to represent them in the General Assembly to be held in October next.—The Town also chose a Committee to prepare Instructions for their Deputies relative to the Stamp Act.

Early on Wednesday Evening, as four Gentlemen, among whom was Martin Howard, jun. Esq ; were walking down Queen-Street, a Person, in consequence of a private Pique, assaulted one of them, the Collector of his Majesty's Customs for that Port, the Collector soon disengaged himself, and retreated. The other Gentlemen manifested some Resentment in his Behalf ; but the Return they met with, induced them to withdraw, and go towards Mr. Howard's House.—An account of this Affair immediately spread among the People, a Mob collected, and marched directly to Mr. Howard's ; and not finding the Gentlemen there, they shattered some of the Windows, and went off. But not satisfied with the Mischief they had done, they soon returned to the Charge with redoubled Fury, broke the Windows and Doors all to pieces, damaged the Partitions of the House, and ruined such Furniture as was left in it, the best part being happily removed out between the attacks.—This being done, the Mob drew off, and proceeded to the hired House that Doctor Moffat lived in, where they committed Outrages equally terrible, in tearing the House to pieces, and demolishing the Furniture. The Cellars of both Houses were ravaged, and the Provisions, Wines, &c. destroyed and lost—From the Doctor's they went in quest of the Gentleman first aimed at, who had luckily, by that Time, got on board the Cygnet Man of War, which lay at the back of the Fort. After this they surrounded the House of the then Stamp-Master ; but upon promises of his resigning that Office, they offered no Violence to his Habitation.—It was eleven o'clock when they were about to perform this last act of devastation ; but desisting from this they contented themselves with rendering more compleat the Ruin of the two Houses beforementioned.—Next Morning the Stamp-Master's Resignation being publickly read, the People anounced their Joy by repeated Huzza's, &c. and the Storm ceased. Things, however, did not continue long in this easy State ; an Irish young Fellow, who had been but a few Days in Town, stood forth, like Massaniello, openly, declared that he was at the Head of the Mob the preceding Night, and triumphed in the Mischief that was done. Some Gentlemen, to prevent any further Evil, thought it best to seize immediately upon this Desperadoe, and put him on board the Man of War, which they accordingly did : But this, instead of answering the designed Purpose, kindled a new Fire. The Mob began again to collect ; and a Number of Persons, who it seemed, were so irritated at his being carried on board the Man of War, that it became necessary to bring him on shore again. This was done ; and upon his promising immediately to quit the Government, he was released, and the Night passed without Tumult. The Morning following, Massaniello appeared again in the publick Streets, boldly declaring himself to have been the Ring-leader of the Mob, and threatning Destruction to the Town, more particularly to the Persons and Houses of those who seized him the preceding Day, unless they made him Presents agreeable to his Demands. The Attorney-General, who was the late Stamp-Master, being met and insulted by him, heroically seized upon him ; and some Gentlemen running to his assistance, they carried him off to Goal. This proved effectual ;—nobody appeared to rescue him, nor to say a Word in his Favour. He is now under Confinement ; — the Town is again in Peace, and we sincerely wish it may continue so.

The Ship Friendship, Capt. Lindsey, sailed for England Yesterday. Dr. Thomas Moffat, and Martin Howard, jun. Esq ; of this Town, went Passengers.

The Lot of Land and the late Dwelling-House of Mr. Howard is advertised for Sale. His Loss sustained is computed to be about 1000£. sterl.

The Town of Little-Compton have given Instructions to their Deputies, but we have not Room to insert them. — In general they are like those lately given to the Members for Providence, which have been published.

PENNSYLVANIA JOURNAL (PHILADELPHIA)

January 23, 1766

The Stamp Act was technically effective from November 1, 1765, until its repeal on March 17, 1766. Despite being published within that time frame, this *Pennsylvania Journal* showed no signs of stamps as there were no stamp distributors to enforce it. This issue reports on events surrounding the intimidation of New Haven, Connecticut, and Albany, New York, stamp distributors.

The following Resolves were unanimously agreed to, and ordered to be printed in the New-London Gazette, viz.

1. THAT allegiance and the strictest loyalty is ever due from the people of the English American colonies, to our [...]

[...] rights. And that every person who endeavours the execution of the same, is an inveterate enemy to our public weal and tranquility.

5. That whereas our Stamp-man was appointed agent for this colony at the Court of Great-Britain, in confidence that he would exert his utmost abilities to prevent said Act; nevertheless he return'd, the executioner of those evils he was sent to defend us from. And notwithstanding his solemn engagements to the contrary, has, and still obstinately persists, by every way and means his malice and craft suggests, or his unbridled audacity can attempt, to plot the ruin and total overthrow of his native country, to which he is allied by the tenderest ties, and strongest bonds of gratitude; and thereby has set his own interest in competition with the interest of his country, and forfeited all privilege of protection from the same,—is no longer to be believed, his friendship no more to be trusted,—nor his malignant designs any longer to be endured; and that assuredly unless he instantly desists from plotting our ruin, writing, or sending any thing prejudicial to the government, or even relative to the same, he shall forthwith feel the weight of his injured country's righteous indignation, and know by sad experience, all the horrors of falling a defenceless prey to the justice of a free, injured and enraged people, whose bosoms glow with the free spirit of British liberty, and who count not their lives dear in defence of it.

6. That as to the matters of charge in the aforesaid articles against Mr. Ingersol, we challenge him to deny, or vindicate himself from them, at any of our public meetings: And we do hereby give him full assurance, that if he will come, he shall have as fair a hearing as he can desire; and safe protection from any insult or injury to his person or property, while with us at our meeting.

7. That Mr. Ingersol's letters be read publickly in all the counties in this colony, at their public meetings, if desired.

8. That copies of Mr. Ingersol's letters be given out to some one person in every county, to be kept for the benefit of the Freemen.

9. That we most critically inspect every avenue and way by which the Stamp Papers may be introduced into the colony; and on appearance of danger give the most speedy notice to the Freemen.

10. That we most earnestly recommend to the civil authority in this colony, to proceed in business as usual; as our cessation and delay of business will be construed an implicit acknowledgement of the validity of the Stamp Act. To this purpose we recommend a piece wrote by a master of reason, and a true friend to liberty in Pennsylvania, and inserted in the New-London Gazette of the 20th instant. Also we do fully concur with and adopt the Resolves of the county of New-London, of the 10th instant.

11. That another meeting is appointed to be held on the first Thursday in March next, at the Meeting House, in the first society in Canterbury, at 10 o'clock on said day.

NEW-HAVEN. January 19.

WHEREAS I have lately received two anonymous letters, calling on me (among other things) to give the public some farther assurance with regard to my intentions about executing the office of distributor of stamps for this colony, as some others have done since the receiving our commissions or deputations for that purpose; and that I confirm the same by oath. And altho' I don't think it best ordinarily to take notice of such letters, nor yet to take oaths upon such kind of occasions; yet (as I have good reason to think that those [...]

of them (especially of any particular detached sentences) but by me, or by mutual consent; —that those paragraphs which have lately been published in the New-London Gazette, I conceive to be, in some parts, by some mistake, differently worded from the originals, and com[...] what I imagine would [...] whole of my said [...]er. This I intend [...] the papers again; [...] public will not un[...] the matter. And [...]se particular letters [...] are recalled; and if, [...] was said in them that [...]urable to the colony [...] be always ready to [...] they shall call upon [...] at all trouble of [...] to write no letters [...] than they now are) [...]ntlemen as, at this

J. I.

[...]ecember 30.

[...] in New-London was [...]els are cleared out there as usual, without STAMPS: —And that the justices and Lawyers, in that county, go on with business in the old way......

Last Friday Se'nnight, was found in her house, in New-Haven, lying on a fire dead, the Widow Smith:—On examining her body, several wounds were found; by which it was determined that she had been murdered.——Her only son is taken up, on suspicion of having been the perpetrator of the horrid fact, and is confined in goal for tryal.

NEW-YORK, January 20.

Extract of a letter from a gentleman in London, to his friend in this city, dated Nov. 9, 1765.

"I am fully sensible of the malignity of the late measures, and your————has well delineated the authors. Your zeal is commendable; but you should not impute your grievances to the whole, which were imposed by the influence of a ministry universally detested, and now removed, and the new ministry entirely in your favour. An entire new system in your favour is adopted, and the truly noble Lord Dartmouth at the head of the Board of Trade, your friend out of judgment, being fully convinced of the mutual interest of the colonies and their Mother Country; so that a few months will give a new face to your affairs.

"I contributed my mite to his information, and he was so condescending as to call on me and thank me, and opened his sentiments without reserve.——He is a charming man."

On Saturday the 4th instant, many of the inhabitants of Albany, having heard that Mr. Van Schaick, of that place, merchant, had applied for the office of distributor of the Stamps there, a number of them went to him and demanded a resignation of the office if he had it, and a solemn engagement that he nor any for him, should ever act in it.——That he would not enter into such an engagement without some reserve, in case the act should hereafter take place; which by no means satisfying the people, several hundreds of them assembled the next Monday evening, and again insisted on his absolute renunciation of the office, which he not complying with, they put a haltar about his neck, dragged him through the town, and it was thought would absolutely have hanged him, if he had not found means to make his escape, and take sanctuary in the fort. This so enraged the multitude, that they returned to his house, and demolished all his furniture that they could find, to the value of 4 or 500l.

——Two other persons there, we hear, had also applied for employments in the Stamp office, one of which was very roughly used, and the other had fled.

The following letter from Mr. James M'Evers, of this city, to Mr. Henry Van Schaick, of Albany, is inserted by particular desire, to satisfy the sons of Liberty in this place.

SIR,   NEW-YORK, January 13, 1766.

I HAVE received yours of the 7th instant, acquainting me, that through a report being propagated of your having made application to me for the distribution of Stamps at Albany, you had incured the displeasure of your fellow citizens, and the resentment of the populace. I am very sorry that through such a supposition, you should meet with any insult, as it is groundless. I therefore (in consequence) think myself in duty bound, to declare that you never made any application to me

[...]navigation stop'd.

* There is now at the store kept by WILLIAM SMITH, on the north side of Market-street, one door below Water-street, between thirty and forty pieces of CLOTHS, of different colours and qualities, all our own Produce and Manufactory; some of which little, if any ways, inferior to the super cloths imported from England; also home made Linens, Shalloons, Blankets, Swanskins, Flannels, Ink Powder, &c. &c

* Was found, on the Lower Ferry Road, a SILVER WATCH. The Owner, by applying to John Lort, and proving his Property, may have it again.

SUPPLEMENT TO THE BOSTON GAZETTE

January 27, 1766

Throughout the winter of 1765–66, the Sons of Liberty, a term applied to both organized opposition groups as well as a generic label for any stamp tax opponent, were successful in opening correspondence channels and aligning colonial interests. Using news-swapping techniques perfected during the French and Indian War, printers—many being Sons of Liberty and among the hardest hit by the stamp duty on paper—repurposed patriotic reports from other colonies, thereby using newspapers as the vehicle to lead and uphold the resistance. The article shown here from the January 27, 1766, *Supplement to the Boston Gazette* contains an article originally from the *Georgia Gazette*, which includes details about the Sons of Liberty meeting at Machenry's tavern in Savannah.

---

annulled. If the colonists are prevented from endeavouring to have their grievances redressed in this manner, can we blame them if they attempt it in another? Or is it not naturally to be expected they should, though perhaps that other may be left...

This month Deputies [from Ame]rica were to assemble... they will again attempt... your business, Sir, to... not treated as some we... are reasonable, justice... if they are otherwise, p... nity of pointing out to... requests; and I am we... nothing that is unreaso... parliament will be w... member will advise an... is the interest of Britain... to alienate the affection... done only by kind usa... them, as they most certain... same footing with ourselves... very privilege we in Britain enjoy.

The colonies are so many distant provinces of the British Empire, founded upon which it will rise firm and strong, and defy the shock of ages. But if, instead of improving this accession of dominion for the purpose of strengthening the State, we make enemies of our friends, and convert this blessing of Heaven into a curse, then indeed may we have cause to weep over our late conquests, and Britain may in the end be conquered in America. But I hope better things, tho' I thus write. I trust the favourable opportunity will be eagerly embraced of uniting and incorporating the colonies with Great Britain, and that they shall be henceforth considered as one state. Never was there an ampler field for acquiring honour; never a fairer occasion of securing immortality. The man, who shall do this piece of real service to the State, will infallibly insure to himself everlasting renown, and his memory will be endeared to latest ages—Whoever he may be, who nobly undertakes it, may success accompany him in this great and good work!—My warmest wishes are for the prosperity of Britain.

WILL. ALFRED.

SAVANNAH, in Georgia, Oct. 24.

LAST week advice was received from Augusta, that three white men, two of them named Payne, and the other Hoggs, were killed by the Creeks, on whose lands it is said they were hunting. We also hear, that an Officer was lately killed near Pensacola, by two of these Indians, who were put to death by their father immediately on their arrival in their own country.

Oct. 31. About seven o'clock last Friday night the effigy of a Stamp-officer was carried thro' the streets and afterwards hanged and burnt, amidst the acclamations of a great concourse of people of all ranks and denominations assembled together on the occasion.

Novem. 7. One Mr. Angus we hear is appointed for this province; the stamp paper we are also told, is brought over to Charlestown, and is to be sent to this place in his Majesty's ship Speedwell.

At a meeting of the *Sons of Liberty*, on Monday night last, at Machenry's tavern, in order to consult upon the properest measures to be taken at this very alarming and critical juncture, it was unanimously agreed upon, that the Stamp-master appointed for this province, immediately on his arrival, be waited upon, and, that as that gentleman is a stranger to this place, and consequently unacquainted with the sentiments of the people, be desired to resign an office so universally disagreeable to his Majesty's American subjects, and the execution of which may be attended with very bad consequences.

Tuesday last being the anniversary of the Gun Powder Plot, the same was observed here by firing of the great guns, &c. A number of sailors having assembled together in order to parade thro' the streets, as

---

able satisfaction to see one of the finest countries in the world; from this fort, which is built near the banks of the river Mississippi, for about 40 miles back, is absolutely delightful, the soil the richest I ever saw...

James Hogg, William Payne, and his brother a boy, went off to Togoolo in the Lower Cherokee, but did not own the murder. Fourteen white men, among whom are Payne's brothers, set out from Augusta after them, who has sworn not to return without having revenge.

The miscreants who murdered the Cherokees in Virginia some time since, are fled from that province, and are said to be amongst the Paxton-boys in Pennsylvania.

They write from Pensacola, that a Dutch subject, a Native of Surrinam, having engaged to introduce the Manufacture of Cochineal in West-Florida, on promise from the Merchants of a valuable Consideration, had received his Death by Poison; and it was strongly suspected, that the Spanish Emissaries had a hand in the affair.

The Black Vomit and sweating Sickness, continued to carry off great Numbers of the French Settlers in Cayenne colony, when the last letters were received from thence.

We have the Georgia papers to the 21st of Nov. by which we find that they had no stamp paper there and that business went on as usual.

PHILADELPHIA, *January 2.*

On Thursday last an Express passed through this City, from Fort Pitt to the General, with the agreeable and important News that Capt. Stirling, and his Party, had arrived safe at Fort Chartres, in the Illinois Country, and were there received with open Arms by the Natives.------A full Confirmation this, of Colonel Croghan's Influence, and judicious Negociations, with Pondiac, and other Chiefs of many numerous Western Nations.

By Letters from Detroit of a late Date, we hear, that every Thing was in the most perfect State of Peace with the Natives.

Extract of a letter from Charlestown, South-Carolina, Dec. 2, 1765.

"The Petitions which were drawn up at the Congress were agreed to, without any Alteration, and signed afterwards by our Assembly. The Members who attended at New York, have received the Thanks of the House, and are re-elected again. At present every thing is very quiet here; our Liberty Boys being content to keep out the Stamps, do not injure, but protect, the Town; for some Time ago a Parcel of Sailors, having a Mind to make the most of this Suspension of Law, formed a Mob, to collect Money of the People in the Streets; but these Sons of Liberty suppressed them instantly, and committed the Ringleaders to Goal. While they act thus cooly and determinately, we have little Reason to fear they will give up the Point, especially as the Country People are all unanimous in it; besides we have had an Offer of the whole Force of North-Carolina, should it be wanted-----At Bermuda they had taken the stamps,

---

RY 27, 1766.

...ve the colonists ...of the most valu- ...lament of Great ...of the subjects, ...by birth-right, ...abundantly able ...power of par- ...: They may of ...habitants of any ...of being tried ...and must not ...colonists I am ...to parliament ...the manner of ...would present ...forms of the ...in the way of ...their most va- ...that the H--- ...ms? If a chap- ...it should be ...from endea- ...in this manner, ...another? Or is ...though per- ...us? ...blies of Ame- ...it is probable ...ment. It is ...petitions be ...their demands ...be granted; ...an opportu- ...priety of their ...will insist on ...wisdom of ...asion; and no ...of power. It ...tain, and not ...and this can be ...considering ...as on the ...entitled to e-

is usual on that day, one of them representing a stamp master, was placed upon a scaffold supported by six others, having a paper in his hand, and a rope fastened under his arms and round his neck: at certain stages they made a stand, where this pretended Stamp master was obliged by several severe blows with a cudgel to call out in a pitiful tone, *No Stamps, No riot act, Gentlemen, &c.* After having thus sufficiently exposed him to the view of the inhabitants, and used him with every indignity they could think of, they conducted him to Machenry's tavern, before which they concluded the whole by hanging him up for a little while, and afterwards cut him down, in the presence of a croud of spectators, who were highly diverted with the humour of the tars. In all the exhibitions here of this kind, private as well as public property has remained unmolested, and no outrages been committed.

Extract of a letter from a gentleman at Natchez fort to his friend in Savannah, dated 12th of Aug. last.

"I arrived here the 12th ult. and had the agreeable satisfaction to see one of the finest countries in the world; from this fort, which is built near the banks of the river Mississippi, for about 40 miles back, is absolutely delightful, the soil the richest I ever saw, though born in Old England, the oak, hickory, cedar, poplar, and beech remarkably large: It would be the greatest crime in the world to suffer this part of the river to remain unsettled, as the inhabitants would reap every advantage that could be expected from the richest lands. Every kind of grain that Europe produces would grow here in the greatest perfection."

Seven families, consisting of about 76 people, arrived here on Saturday last, from Maryland, in order to settle in this province; amongst them are a good many who have been used to farming, and tradesmen.

CHARLES-TOWN, *South-Carolina, Oct. 23.*

Five several Parties of Cherokees, are gone out to war against the Northern tribes; one of them is headed by Oucconnostora or the Great Warrior, and another by Attakullakulla.

The seven Creeks who about three weeks ago killed James Hogg, William Payne, and his brother a boy, went off to Togoolo in the Lower Cherokee, but did not own the murder. Fourteen white men, among whom are Payne's brothers, set out from Augusta after them, who has sworn not to return without having revenge.

...America. But ...braced of uni- ...sylvania.

They write from Pensacola, that a Dutch subject,

...formed that indulgence into a Right; and a general pretence parliament being only judicially supposed, is thus rendered ...thing more than a legal fiction; hence the maxim prevail-... "that every one was a party to all acts of parliament."

PENNSYLVANIA GAZETTE (PHILADELPHIA)

March 20, 1766

Under the Annapolis, March 6, dateline in the *Pennsylvania Gazette* printed March 20, 1766, is another important report of the inaugural Sons of Liberty meeting in the Maryland capital.

statute-law, or a mere act of parliament, independantly of any ...iliary jurisdiction derived from the blended exertion of pre-...ative in cases of that legal Repugnancy, which in terminis are ...epted by their said charters; and wherein Prerogative singly, ...conjunctively with both Houses, has and may acknowledgedly ...erpose, pursuantly to the same. This obedience would cer-...ly be, with respect to him, a naked duty; an ex-parte obli-...ion obtruded upon him, which is repugnant to the nature of ...legal ties, and destructive of that principle wherein English ...erty essentially consists. But farther, were the English Ame-...ans not only to be bound there by the acts of the British par-...ent in all cases, but also by those of their own Assemblies:---...re would be a subjection within a subjection, which might ...ordinate their actions to alternate contrarieties and cross penal-...s! a duplicity of jurisdiction over the same objects, and equal-...in the first instance, unknown to the law! a superfetation in ...legislative system, which seems monstrous and unnatural! ...e delegation therefore of a legislative power to the colonies ...st, one would think, from its necessary efficacy, be considered ...only as unconcurrent with, but as exclusive of all parliamen-...y participation in the proper Subjects of their legislation; that ...o say, in cases not repugnant to the laws of Great-Britain. ...d in all such cases may not the maxim be fitly applied;---...Designatio unius est exclusio alterius, et expressum facit cessare ...tum?"

That such a question should be occasioned at this time of day, ...ms altogether surprizing; after our very parliaments having ...en occasional notices of, and impliedly confirmed the acts of ...American Assemblies in local levies and assessments: And ...Administration itself having had frequent recourses to them ...supplies in such pressing seasons, when, if the Mother-coun-...had a right of imposing taxes, the importance of the occasion ...uld have worthily becomed her to have done so, and, on the ...position of that right, should have done it,---for the sake of ...tainty and dispatch.

But it has been asserted with more justice and consistency, that ...King's Scepter is the instrument of power over the colonies, ...d Prerogative the rule by which their obedience must be re-...lated. In this case, however, have not royal charters been ...nted, establishing a constitution, and delegating to them the be-...e mentioned qualified power of legislation? To which the be-...wn, even for the necessary provision and maintenance of their ...ernment, has frequently referred itself, as to an essential prin-...al concurring party; thereby recognizing that vested right in ...colonies, the establishment whereof itself had originally pre-...bed and chartered. Moreover, is not the King a perpetual ...stituent branch of their legislatures; representedly present in ...ry assembly, and an actual party to all their laws? And this ...ng the case, prerogative must indeed be owned to have herein ...pered its operations agreeably to the spirit of the English con-...ution, and to have thus generously bound and limited itself. ...r could it well have happened otherwise: For if, as has been ..., the common-law followed the subject to America, it is pre-...ned that prerogative could have only acted there consistently ...h, and in conformity to it. Further, with particular respect ...he point in question, numerous are the instances of money-...ies and assessments enacted by the American assemblies, that ...we travelled through occasional examinations of the several ...ards and cognizances here, and nevertheless been confirmed, ...received the royal approbation: And no instance that I can ...d has occurred, where any such act has been disallowed merely ...account of its particular tendency, or of those legislatures hav-...exercised a power which did not appertain to them. And ...royal confirmation of the actual exercise of this power pro-...ded, no doubt, from a due respect to, and consideration of the

...nduary ties which the Crown and Parliament have upon them: ---the Navigation Act, by which they are directly excluded from all foreign markets;---the power of laying duties on their ex-ports---transmitted to Britain;---the right of Port-entry and ...ir castles, fortifications, and mi-...several officers, civil as well as ...government;---the right of ...ing their assemblies;---the ...e determination of appeals ...nd, as a clincher, the abso-...acts, when their before-...o have been exceeded. This ...at supremacy, which, with ...-country has retained over ...ow little has been left ...ow taken away, how soon, ...e deserted. To conclude; ...condition of our Americans ...er English subject: A con-...intemperate folly and perverse-ness to reduce them to! A folly and perverseness, which must not be imputed to the policy of the English Nation!

I am, Sir, yours, &c. &c.

London, Nov. 27.   ÆQUUS.

A N N A P O L I S, March 6.

On Monday, the 24th of February, a considerable Number of the principal Gentlemen of Baltimore County, met at the Mar-ket-House in Baltimore-Town, formed themselves into a Society for the Maintainance of Order and Protection of American LI-BERTY, by the Name of the SONS OF LIBERTY, and resolved to meet at Annapolis, on Friday last, to oblige the several Officers there, to open their respective Offices, and proceed in Business, as usual, without stamped Paper: And that the Society and Application might be still the more respectable, the SONS OF LIBERTY in Baltimore, gave the most speedy Notice to Gentlemen of the neighbouring Counties, to form themselves into the like Societies, and co-operate with them in this so laudable Work. Saturday last, a much greater Number of the SONS OF LIBERTY than could be expected from the Shortness of the Notice, met, by Adjournment, at the Court-House in Annapolis; those of Baltimore and Anne-Arundel Counties were present personally, and those of Kent were repre-sented by their Deputy; and after hearing different Proposals, and debating thereon with great Decency, Coolness and Order, Re-solved, To make a written Application to the Chief Justice of the Provincial Court, the Secretary and Commissary-General, and Judges of his Lordship's Land Office, to open their respective Offices, and proceed as usual in the Execution of their Duties, on the 31st Day of March instant, or sooner, if a Majority of the Supreme Courts of the Northern Governments should pro-ceed in Business before that Time. And therein to propose, "That if the above Officers would proceed agreeable to the Re-"quest, that then an Indemnification be signed by the SONS "OF LIBERTY, and as many others as could be induced "thereto, and that the respective Officers be requested to give "an Answer in Writing under their Hands to that Proposition." A Committee having been ordered to deliver the Requisition of the SONS OF LIBERTY to the above mentioned Gentle-men, afterwards returned and reported the verbal Answer of the Chief Justice of the Provincial Court, and Doctor Steuart, one of the Judges of the Loan-Office, and communicated the written Answer of the Secretary, to this Effect; That if he should con-tinue in Office, the Clerk of the Provincial Court would receive his Directions to act as the Judges should in their judicial Capa-city, at the next Court, order him as their Minister; but before the Meeting of the Provincial Court, he could not undertake to give Directions to the Clerk, to issue Process, whatever the De-termination of the Majority of the Northern Colonies might be, whose Courts might sit before ours. The Commissary General not being in Town, the Committee could not deliver the Requi-sition to him: The verbal Answer of the Chief Justice, and that of one of the Judges of the Land-Office, were taken under Con-sideration, and in Consequence of the Order of the SONS OF LIBERTY, the Committee again waited on those Gentlemen, and having informed them, "That their Refusal to give their "Answers in Writing, to the Proposition aforesaid, was deemed "a great Indignity offered to the SONS OF LIBERTY, "and that their Answers in Writing were instantly expected;" they received and reported their following Answers.

GENTLEMEN,

IN Answer to your Application of this Day, my Connections and Circumstances speak my Attachment to the Liberty of the Subject here. The carrying on Business at the adjourned Provincial Court will, as to myself, depend on the Opinion I

lately happened in the Bay, on the Eastern Shore. Last Month Mr. Jacob Bromwell, a Man of good Character, and well esteem-ed, left Oxford, in his Boat (the Oxford Packet) in order to Pilot one or two Ships down the Bay: Saturday the 15th, in the Afternoon, the Packet left Captain Peacock's Ship off Sharp's Island, in order to work up to Captain Laing's, off the Mouth of Wye River, the Wind then being easterly, and very tempestuous, and in the Evening suddenly came about to West, blowed extreme hard, and became very cold. The Boat being missing for some Time, and Captain Laing waiting for his Pilot, occasioned a Sus-picion of an Accident; and after a diligent Search, they found the Boat, with a little of her Masts to be seen, at the Westward of Poplar-Island, in three Fathom Water. We are told that three Persons were in her, beside Mr. Bromwell, viz. John Row-landson, and Edward Brining, both young Men, and a Dutch-man, who, undoubtedly, all perished together.

We hear that Captain Robert Bryce, in the Brig Nancy, be-longing to this Place, outward bound with a Load of Wheat, sprung a Leak, and was obliged to put into Norfolk to stop it.

March 20, 1766.   NUMB. 1943.

The PENNSYLVANIA GAZETTE.

Containing the Freſheſt Ad- *vices, Foreign and Domeſtic.*

To the PRINTER of the LONDON CHRONICLE.

SIR,

AN ex poſt facto queſtion, ſoon expected to be adviſedly diſcuſſed is, " Whether the Mother country has a right of impoſing local taxes on all her American colonies?" The precedent fact is ſuppoſed to have been miniſterially prereſolved, and influentially eſtabliſhed. This neceſſary previous queſtion, as to the Right, remains ſtill to be put: And it is hoped the wiſdom and equity of both Houſes will not ſuffer it to be craftily ſlurred over, and much leſs precipitately carried;---as it were by a Coup de Main.

The proper arguments, ſtript of all political refinements and expediences, muſt turn on the conſideration of two principal points, viz. the conſtitutional Power of the Britiſh Parliament, reſpecting the aforementioned fact; and the actual Exertions of royal prerogative, in the point of Right; under which it is admitted that the colonies lay claim to, and avow their reſpective legiſlative privileges.

Engliſh Liberty is a propriety attached to the individuals of the community, founded on the original frame or conſtitution of our government, and might be defined, " the primitive right that every freeholder had of conſenting to thoſe laws by which the Community was to be obliged." Time and change of circumſtances extended this circle of comprehenſion, and made every ſubject in ſome reſpect or other a member of the legiſlature; his conſent at firſt perſonally denoted, was afterwards allowed to be given by a proxy or repreſentative. Uſage and conveniency transformed that indulgence into a Right; and a general pretence in parliament being only judicially ſuppoſed, is thus rendered ſomething more than a legal fiction; hence the maxim prevailed,---" that every one was a party to all acts of parliament." This privilege of becoming a Party to the laws, or of being in effect his own governor, was as it were the conſideration or price of individual ſubjection: And from the expreſs or implied exerciſe of it, the duty of our legal Obedience is inferred. But an Engliſhman in America has no means of being preſent or repreſented in the Britiſh Legiſlature, quaſi a Coloniſt: Where then is to be found his conſent to parliamentary acts operative there; and by what conſtruction can he be ſaid to give his voice? being thus in neither ſenſe a party, as wanting the fundamental privilege above-mentioned; and not having been ſubjected to any obligation of this kind by original patent or charter; but, on the contrary, an expreſs power being thereby granted to the colonies of enacting their own Laws, provided the ſame be not repugnant to thoſe of Great-Britain. It is hard to conceive from what conſtitutional principle, applicable to a colony, not a conquered country, his obedience to our ſtatute-law can be deduced. I ſay, to ſtatute-law, or a mere act of parliament, independantly of any auxiliary juriſdiction derived from the blended exertion of prerogative in caſes of that legal Repugnancy, which in terminis are excepted by their ſaid charters; and wherein Prerogative ſingly, or conjunctively with both Houſes, has and may acknowledgedly interpoſe, purſuantly to the ſame. This obedience would certainly be, with reſpect to him, a naked duty; an ex-parte obligation obtruded upon him, which is repugnant to the nature of all legal ties, and deſtructive of that principle wherein Engliſh Liberty eſſentially conſiſts. But farther, were the Engliſh Americans not only to be bound there by the acts of the Britiſh parliament in all caſes, but alſo by thoſe of their own Aſſemblies:--- Here would be a ſubjection within a ſubjection, which might ſubordinate their actions to alternate contrarieties and croſs penalties! a duplicity of juriſdiction over the ſame objects, and equally, in the firſt inſtance, unknown to the law! a ſuperfetation in the legiſlative ſyſtem, which ſeems monſtrous and unnatural!

ſtatute, De tallagio non concedendo; or, " The prohibition of impoſing any taxes or aids without the univerſal conſent of the freemen," &c. An exemption, founded on common law, and antient Engliſh Liberty! which it ſeems the coloniſts do conceive themſelves intitled to, as their birthright; that birthright, by which they are themſelves tied in intereſt to the Mother-country, and bound to a correlative loyalty, which thus requires not any military force to be ſecured or vindicated. So that whether this queſtion, of a ſubſiſting right to impoſe œconomical taxes on the colonies, be applied to the Britiſh parliament, independantly as before noticed; or to the royal prerogative, excluſive of the American aſſemblies; in both caſes it would ſeem, as matters are circumſtanced, to be a loſt point. On the other hand, ſhould this right, ſo delegated to the colonies, be now conſidered by any after-thought as a reverſible error: Be it remembered, that it was at firſt ſo delegated by ſolemn acts of government, that it proved the means of their vaſt increaſe and cultivation, and by conſequence of thoſe immenſe profits and advantages which have thence accrued to us; that it is ſanctified by ſucceſſive uſage, grounded upon a generous reliance on Engliſh Faith and Compact, and that uſage---ratified by repeated authoritative acquieſcence: And laſtly, that any violation of their conſtitutions, by what means ſoever executed, might unhinge the principles of their natural and civil attachment to the Mother-country; thereby opening to our foreign enemies a direct paſſage into our palladium itſelf.

Nor, this privilege being left them, let it be thought that the colonies will of courſe be independent. No! numerous are the reſiduary ties which the Crown and Parliament have upon them: ---the Navigation Act, by which they are directly excluded from all foreign markets;---the power of laying duties on their exports---transmitted to Britain;---the right of Port-entry and clearance;---the command of their caſtles, fortifications, and militia;---the appointment of their ſeveral officers, civil as well as military;---the executive power of government;---the right of convening, proroguing, and diſſolving their aſſemblies;---the Governor's negative to any bill;---the determination of appeals from their Courts of Judicature;---and, as a clincher, the abſolute juriſdiction of annulling their acts, when their beforementioned legiſlative power appears to have been exceeded. This is a general ſketch of the nature of that ſupremacy, which, with ſome partial exceptions, the Mother-country has retained over her colonies.----By it, it will appear how little has been left them; and, were that little to be now taken away, how ſoon, at the beſt, they might probably be deſerted. To conclude; were it not for this privilege, the condition of our Americans would be worſe than that of any other Engliſh ſubject: A condition, that would argue the moſt intemperate folly and perverſeneſs to reduce them to! A folly and perverſeneſs, which muſt not be imputed to the policy of the Engliſh Nation!

I am, Sir, yours, &c. &c.

London, Nov. 27.   ÆQUUS.

ANNAPOLIS, March 6.

On Monday, the 24th of February, a conſiderable Number of the principal Gentlemen of Baltimore County, met at the Market-Houſe in Baltimore-Town, formed themſelves into a Society for the Maintainance of Order and Protection of American LIBERTY, by the Name of the SONS of LIBERTY, and reſolved to meet at Annapolis, on Friday laſt, to oblige the ſeveral Officers there, to open their reſpective Offices, and proceed in Buſineſs, as uſual, without ſtamped Paper: And that the Society and Application might be ſtill the more reſpectable, the SONS OF LIBERTY in Baltimore, gave the moſt ſpeedy Notice to Gentlemen of the neighbouring Counties, to form themſelves

have as yet to form. I ſhall meet my Brethren on the Day to which the Court is adjourned, and be governed by thoſe Reaſons and Principles which ought to actuate every Man who ſits in Stations ſimilar to that which is filled by

March 1,   Your humble Servant,
1766.   JOHN BRICE.

A PROPOSITION being this Day given in to me, requeſting that Buſineſs ſhould be done in the Land Office of this Province as uſual; to which I anſwered, That the Land Office was open, and the Records thereof ſubject to the Peruſal of all Perſons who have Occaſion to make Searches; and that Copies of the Records, authenticated by the Regiſter, ſhould be made out to any Perſon ſo applying, paying the uſual Fees; and, as I apprehend the Sale of the Lord Proprietary's Lands, are Matters of private Concern, reſpecting his own Intereſt, he may grant Warrants, or refuſe to grant them, as he ſhall think proper. Given under my Hand, at Annapolis, this Firſt Day of March, 1766.   GEORGE STEUART.
To the SONS of LIBERTY, of Baltimore, Anne Arundel, and Kent Counties.

After reading of which Anſwers, it was ordered, that Copies of the Proceedings be tranſmitted to the ſeveral Counties, and their SONS OF LIBERTY invited to enter into the like Aſſociations, and a Number, not leſs than Twelve, from each County, be requeſted to attend at Annapolis, on the 31ſt Inſtant, to ſee the Event of, or repeat, if neceſſary, the Applications already made.

We have an Account of a very melancholy Cataſtrophe which lately happened in the Bay, on the Eaſtern Shore. Laſt Month Mr. Jacob Bromwell, a Man of good Character, and well eſteemed, left Oxford, in his Boat (the Oxford Packet) in order to Pilot one or two Ships down the Bay: Saturday the 15th, in the Afternoon, the Packet left Captain Peacock's Ship off Sharp's Iſland, in order to work up to Captain Laing's, off the Mouth of Wye River, the Wind then being eaſterly, and very tempeſtuous, and in the Evening ſuddenly came about to Weſt, blowed extreme hard, and became very cold. The Boat being miſſing for ſome Time, and Captain Laing waiting for his Pilot, occaſioned a Suſpicion of an Accident; and after a diligent Search, they found the Boat, with a little of her Maſts to be ſeen, at the Weſtward of Poplar-Iſland, in three Fathom Water. We are told that three Perſons were in her, beſide Mr. Bromwell, viz. John Rowlandſon, and Edward Brining, both young Men, and a Dutchman, who, undoubtedly, all periſhed together.

We hear that Captain Robert Bryce, in the Brig Nancy, belonging to this Place, outward bound with a Load of Wheat, ſprung a Leak, and was obliged to put into Norfolk to ſtop it.

Imported from England, and to be ſold by
JAMES HARDING,
At his Store, in Water-ſtreet (three Doors above Arch-ſtreet)
A GOOD Aſſortment of European and Eaſt-India Goods, ſuitable to the Seaſon.   6 W.

TO be SOLD or Lett, by the Subſcribers, a fine Griſt Mill, with two Pair of Stones, fit for Country or Merchant Work; together with 60 Acres of exceeding good rich Land (the greateſt Part of which may be mowed) a Dwelling-houſe, Kitchen, Barn and Stable, Orchard, &c. with the Advantage of having an Opportunity of purchaſing a fine improved Tract of Land adjoining the ſame, and may be entered upon immediately; ſituate in Hunterdon County, New-Jerſey, on Stony Brook, a Branch of Millſtone, which empties into Rariton River, being about 12 Miles from Trenton, 3 Miles from Penington, 7 or 8 M es from Princetown, and 20 Mi es from Brunſwick; lying in a good and

tary participation in the proper Subjects of their legiſlation; that is to ſay, in caſes not repugnant to the laws of Great-Britain. And in all ſuch caſes may not the maxim be fitly applied:---

Shortneſs of the Notice, met, by Adjournment, at the Court-Houſe in Annap is; thoſe of Baltimore and Anne-Arundel Counties were preſent perſonally, and thoſe of Kent were repre-

TO BE SOLD,
SUNDRY Lots of Ground, of about 10 Acres each, ſome of them very well wooded, and are pleaſantly ſituated, about 4

in some dispatches just received from a gentleman in high office in America, we are credibly informed he has mentioned, that should the late act of parliament be carried into execution for enforcing the stamp duty

... called.

A number of merchants in Boston have wrote to England for goods to be sent, upon condition only that the stamp act is repealed.

'Tis now pretty confidently asserted, that a great nobleman is making over all his estates in trust, and intends to make a speedy retreat to another country.

It is said Lord Grosvenor has offered 35,000l. for the late Duke of Cumberland's running horses at Newmarket.

His Majesty has conferred the honour of Knighthood on Sir William Johnson's son, who lately arrived from America.

It is said, that his late Royal Highness the Duke of Cumberland gave away near 6000l annually in private charities.

Lord Campden, we hear, will deliver his opinion concerning the legality of warrants issued by Secretaries of state on Wednesday next.

A letter from Madrid say, " The public are greatly pleased with the liberty which the King has granted to all his subjects indiscriminately, of trading to our American colonies."

NEW-YORK, January 6.

Tuesday last Capt. Haviland arrived here from London, and had ten Boxes of the detestable Stamp Papers on board—But about 12 a Clock last Night a Company of armed Men went on board his Brig, and after obliging the People to deliver up the Keys, and get Lights, they opened the Hatches, and seized the stamped Papers for this Province and Connecticut, amounting to 10 Boxes, with which they loaded a large Boat, and proceeded with them up the River to the Shipyards where they broke the Packages to Pieces, and with some Tar-Barrels and other Combustibles, made a Bonfire of them and their Contents.—When the whole was entirely consumed, they all quietly dispersed, without doing any MISCHIEF, or even alarming the City.

destroying their Houses, &c. no thinking sober Man can justify, and if encouraged, will tend to prevent ... and trample upon all Order and good Government, and ... in Murders, Anarchy, Confusion and every ... that is dreadful to Society. The House of Re... ... will be (with you I dare say they are ... Guardians and Defenders of the People they ... and of themselves : the People should meet ... them their Instructions, and they I dare say ... Care to guard their Liberties, and to defend ... (when obliged) from Rapine, and ministe... ... well as gubernatorial Avidity. I have ever ... by the Principles of this most free Govern... ... People could not be taxed without their Con... ... nothing I have lately read has altered my ... if I am mistaken, I am open to Conviction, ... to receive Instruction, but not by an ipse ... of a King.—Trials by Jury is establish'd ... Magna Charta ; and an Act of Parliament ... Contradiction to that glorious Charter, Lord Coke tells us void.—Perhaps you may find, or I may see a Scot's Lawyer give his Opinion the other Way."—

Friday last the Halifax Packet in 17 Days, and Yesterday Capt. Pepper, in 10 Days, arrived here from Halifax ; neither of which confirm the (pretended) Orders the Captains of the Cruizers at New York have assum'd to take ; but on the contrary say, that Vessels are enter'd there (without Stamps) as usual, which may more fully appear by the following

Extract of a Letter from Halifax, dated Jan. 1. 1766.

—"IT gives us great Pleasure to find the Port again open, so that an Intercourse is not likely to be further interrupted.—The Vessels are admitted to an Entry here as usual, without exacting the Penalty of Ten Pounds as prescribed in the —— Stamp Act. —The Distributor of the Stamps with us has received Instructions from the Commissioners of the Stamp Duties, not to prosecute any Person upon the Penalties of the Act, but only to represent to them who the Persons are that refuse Obedience, &c.——This has the Appearance of Conviction among the Learned on the other Side the Water, that the Act is unconstitutional ; wherefore they seem to decline a legal and judicial Determination upon it. Surely this forbodes good Tidings—— I pray God that the next Parliament may by some wise and prudent Measures remove every Obstacle of Jealousy between the Old and New England Men, and the Benefits of Britons under the British Constitution for ever hereafter be mutually enjoyed"—

The public Prints brought by the Lord Hyde Packet are of no later Date than we have already published.

It was strongly reported in England we shall very soon be relieved from the late grievous Impositions, and that Measures the most salutary and beneficial to the Colonies had been resolved upon, in some important Councils at the West end of the Town ; as a London Paper mentions.

The Inferiour Court of Common Pleas at Portsmouth, carry on Business as usual, without Stamps.

for Relief ; but it is not suitable or Dignity of the British Emp... under the Pretence of redress... presume to violate the publick ...

Extract of a Letter from a ... Credit in London to a Frien... November 9 1765.

"WE have now the Plea... our new Ministry ... retrieving you from the Oppressi... laid you under, which has rende... the People here; and a few Mont... the Face of Affairs, for they are ... take off the Stamp Duty and Dut... to give you several positive Adva...

An Account from England abo... says, That They at Home have ac... with respect to America, they wil... to Trade, the Stamp Act they wil... relax, but will not repeal.

LONDON, ...

It is now again confidently as... American Governor is actually supe...

The reconciliation that has lat... tween two certain great personages ... ed this evening with a supper and a...

We hear that the Sun Fire Office ... by the late fire, to the amount ... pounds.

We are informed that there is ... apprehend, what the anti ministerial... trumpet forth, that a change of ad... precede, or at least soon follow the ... liament.

The right hon. the Lord Chance... much better.

IMPORTED in the last ...
LONDON and BRISTOL, and ...
Samuel Allyne
At his Store No. 5, South Side of ...

Ticklinburgs	*	ALS...
Oznabrigs	*	sa...
Russia Duck No. 1 to 4	*	Best...
Cod & Mackrel Hooks and Lines	*	Cordage...
	*	Quart &...
Twine	Starch	* Cotton
Allum	Copperas	* West In...
3d 4d 6d 8d 10d & 20d Nails	*	Engla...
	*	Melasses...
Pipes	Glass	* Flour
Powder	Steel	* Iron Pot...
Pepper	Mustard	* Mackrel...
Spices of all kinds.	*	A few Q...
	*	cha...

AND sundry other Articles at the ...

Monday Night last arrived here Capt. Dixcey from London, in 35 Days; by whom we have the public Prints to the 27th of December, from which we have extracted the following Articles: viz.

From the LONDON GAZETTE.

WESTMINSTER, THIS day his Majesty came December 17. to the House of Peers, and being in his royal robes seated on the throne with the usual solemnity, Sir Francis Molineux, Knt. Gentleman Usher of the Black Rod, was sent with a message from his Majesty to the House of Commons, commanding their attendance in the House of Peers. The Commons being come thither accordingly, His Majesty was pleased to make the following most gracious SPEECH

My Lords and Gentlemen,

"THE present general state of tranquility "in Europe, gave me hopes, that it "would not have been necessary to as- "semble my Parliament sooner than is "usual in times of Peace.

"BUT, as matters of importance have lately oc- "curred in some of my Colonies in America, which "will demand the most serious attention of Parliament "and as further informations are daily expected from "different parts of that country, of which I shall "order the fullest accounts to be prepared for your "consideration; I have thought fit to call you to- "gether, in order that opportunity may thereby be "given, to issue the necessary writs on the many "Vacancies that have happened in the House of Com- "mons since the last Session; so that the Parliament "may be full, to proceed, immediately after the "usual recess, on the consideration of such weighty "matters as will come before you."

The Humble ADDRESS of the Right Honorable the Lords Spiritual and Temporal in Parliament assembled.

Most Gracious Sovereign,

WE, Your Majesty's most dutiful and loyal Subjects, the Lords Spiritual and Temporal in Parliament assembled, beg Leave to return your Majesty our humble Thanks for your most Gracious speech from the Throne.

We should be wanting in our Duty, not to assure your Majesty, that when your Majesty shall have been pleased to communicate to your Parliament those Informations and Advices which have been, or shall be, received from America, we will proceed to the Consideration of those weighty Matters, with an Attention equal to the Importance of the Subject, and with a Resolution to do every Thing which the Exigency of the Case may require.

ATTENTIVE to every Event which affects your Majesty, permit us to congratulate your Majesty on the Birth of a Prince. Whatever adds to your domestic Happiness, and the Stability and Encrease of that illustrious House from which these Kingdoms have received the most important Benefits, must always afford the highest Satisfaction to your faithful Subjects.

ANIMATED by the same Sentiments of Zeal and Duty to your Majesty and your Royal Family, and under the deepest Impressions of Concern, we beg Leave to approach your Throne with our sincere Condolence on the Loss of His late Royal Highness the Duke of Cumberland.

THE many eminent publick and private Virtues, the Extent of Capacity, and the Magnanimity of Mind, the Affection for your Majesty's Person, and the eminent Services performed for this Country, which distinguished that great and excellent Prince, as they have left a lasting Memorial in your Royal Breast, so have they

The Humble ADDRESS

Most Gracious

WE your Maje the Comm assembled, beg Le Thanks of this Hou from the Throne: we will not fail, with its Members Diligence and Atte cies in America, w our Consideration, devours for the H ment, and the tru Parts of your exter

Permit us, at the sa Majesty on the late Increase of your Royal Family, by the Birth of a Prince. Your Majesty's Happiness and that of your People are one; and every Increase of your Majesty's Illustrious Family is considered by your faithful Commons, as a further Security to that Religion, and those Liberties we enjoy under your Majesty's most auspicious Government.

We also beg Leave to offer to your Majesty our sincere Condolence on the great Loss, which your Majesty and this Kingdom have sustained by the Death of his late Royal Highness the Duke of Cumberland; whose private and public Virtues, whose Duty and Affection to your Majesty, and whose distinguished Merits and Services to this Country, as they made his Person dear to this Nation while he lived, so they cannot fail to render his Memory sacred to the latest Posterity.

The following is His Majesty's answer to the address of the Honourable House of Commons, presented to him on Thursday last for his most gracious speech from the Throne, viz.

"*Gentlemen,*

"I return you thanks for this loyal and dutiful address.

"The satisfaction you express in the increase of my family, and the affectionate share you take in the great loss I have sustained by the death of the Duke of Cumberland, are fresh proofs of your zeal and loyalty

"Your resolution at the same time to support the honour of my government, and to provide for the true interest of all my people, cannot but be acceptable to me. My conduct shall always shew, that I consider their interest as inseparable from my own."

The following is her Majesty's answer to a congratulatory message, sent by the House of Commons to her Majesty, on her happy delivery of another Prince during the vacation of Parliament.

"*Gentlemen,*

"This fresh instance of your duty to the King, and attention to Me, cannot but meet with my most hearty acknowledgements, and insure a continuance of that affection I bear to this nation, whose welfare and prosperity will be for ever the first object of my wishes.

Last Sunday died at Bath, his Grace Dr. William Carmichael, Archbishop of Dublin.

St. James's, Dec. 21. The King has been pleased to constitue and appoint the Right Hon. John Earl of Egmont of the Kingdom of Ireland, and Lord Lovel and Holland of Enmore in the County of Somerset in the Kingdom of Great Britain, Sir Charles Saunders, Knt. of the Bath, Augustus Keppel, and Charles Townsend, Esqrs. Sir William Meredith, Bart. John Buller, and John Yorke, Esqrs. to be Commissioners for executing the Office of High Ad-

that Memorials have been actually sent up from the Manufacturers and Merchants; by which such Measures are pointed out, as, it is hoped, will restore our Commerce to its former flourishing State."

Extract from another Letter.

"The Disturbances in North America about the Stamps are very alarming, and causes great Uneasiness to those Gentlemen who have large Sums due to them there: the Stagnation of Remittances for a few Months may be attended with bad Consequences.----You are very right with regard to the Method of that Trade from the Body of Merchants trading to the several Provinces, who in Conjunction with those concerned in the Trade thither, intend to apply to Parliament for some Redress with respect to the American Trade; and 'tis hoped the Government will repeal the Stamp Act, from a Conviction that the late Ministry have done wrong."

Extract of a private Letter from London, dated 24th Dec. 1765.

"On Tuesday 18th December there was a warm Debate in the H——se of C——ns, what should be done with the rebellious Americans (for 'tis the general Opinion that your Opposition has led you into Measures rather too licentious, tho' God knows I am no Friend to the Stamp Act) Mr. G——nv——lle was excessively warm on the Occasion, and urged that a large Force be sent out to destroy you, to my Amazement 29 of the present Members concurred with him; but there were 80 Members who as warmly opposed those Measures, and you may rest satisfied that every thing will be settled to your Satisfaction very soon."

Extract of a Letter from a Gentleman in London, dated Dec. 22, 1765.

"The Parliament met last Tuesday; two Days they were debating the American Riots, which many called Rebellion: The present Ministry are calm and dispassionate, willing to redress all Grievances; and thank God, have a Majority in both Houses. Much Heat and Altercation will arise to make it a long and warm Sessions. In my next I hope to give you some more favourable Accounts."

Extract of another Letter of the same Date.

"I am now at the Court End of the Town, and have the Pleasure to inform you, that the City and Country are all in your Favour: I make no doubt the Stamp Act will be repealed."

On the 13th of December a Deputation from the Merchants of London, trading to North-America, waited on the Ministry, to request their Countenance and Support, in the intended Application to Parliament, for the Relief of the Colonies, and of the Trade to these Parts —— A List of the Deputation is as follows. For *Canada* Mr. John Strettel; Mr. Anthony Vialars

STAMP ACT REPEAL

By Todd Andrlik

BY FEBRUARY 1766, THE STAMP TAX CRISIS HAD BECOME such a nuisance that Parliament passed its repeal and George III gave his royal approval on March 17. News of the repeal was instantly met with great joy and relief by London merchants, who would soon benefit from the end of boycotts on their goods. In fact, before the King and Parliament went into session to repeal the Stamp Act, measures were taken by local merchants to quickly communicate the great news with their colonial clients.

According to the March 20, 1766, *London Chronicle*, "The instant his Majesty came out of the Parliament house yesterday, an express with letters to different persons in America, set off for Falmouth; at which place, a light ship, hired and prepared by the Merchants, lay ready to set sail, the very moment the express arrives."

> *America's social revolution, incubated by newspapers, successfully pressured Great Britain, the world's greatest superpower, to retreat from its unprecedented legislation. Printers demonstrated the power of the press to incite political debate and influence a favorable government response, which would not soon be forgotten.*

Reaching American ports in May, news of the Stamp Act repeal set off another wave of celebrations. The repeal festivities in New York quickly circulated around the colonies, such as the report from the May 29, 1766, *Pennsylvania Journal* that printed:

> *On Tuesday last we were favoured with the authenticated glorious and interesting news of the repeal from different quarters, which was instantly spread throughout the city, diffusing joy and gladness in every face : whereupon, all the bells of the different churches were rung, and the next day there was a manifestation of the greatest gratitude shewn by the True Sons of Liberty.*

One of the express letters from London, "signed by 55 of the principal Merchants trading to North America," was published in the June 16, 1766, *Boston Gazette*, addressed to "John Hancock, Esq; and the Rest of the Merchants in Boston." The letter encourages Boston merchants to support public order and gratitude toward the mother country, "which by the Repeal of this Act has given such incontestable Proof of her Moderation." It also suggests that had Americans obeyed the law and simply communicated their hardships, "[r]elief would have been more speedy."

No matter how long it took, America's social revolution, incubated by newspapers, successfully pressured Great Britain, the world's greatest superpower, to retreat from its unprecedented legislation. Printers demonstrated the power of the press to incite political debate and influence a favorable government response, which would not soon be forgotten. As Benjamin Franklin pointed out near the end of the Revolutionary War, "the same truths may be repeatedly enforced by placing them daily in different lights in newspapers, which are everywhere read... And we now find, that it is not only right to strike while the iron is hot, but that it may be very practicable to heat it by continually striking."

To save face, the Declaratory Act was passed the same day of the Stamp Act repeal and asserted Parliament's authority over the colonies as having "full power and authority, to make laws and statutes of sufficient force and validity to bind the colonies, and people of America, subjects of the Crown of Great-Britain, in all cases whatsoever."

It would not be long before Parliament picked the scab and again demonstrated its authority to tax the American colonies, stirring renewed ferment and continuing a back-and-forth struggle for power.

THE REPEAL, OR THE FUNERAL PROCESSION, OF MISS AME-STAMP, 1766
The Bridgeman Art Library

(*left*) This popular satire shows supporters of the Stamp Act gathering at a dock to carry a small coffin containing the remains of the bill toward an open vault.

ADVERTISEMENT
February 17, 1766, Boston Gazette

(*below*) In addition to the *Boston Gazette*, printers Benjamin Edes and John Gill also printed other works, including the American reprint of this anti–Stamp Act pamphlet from London.

Now in the PRESS, And in a few Days will be Re Printed, (From the London Edition,) THE NECESSITY of *Repealing* the *American* STAMP-ACT demonstrated : Or, A PROOF that GREAT-BRITAIN must be injured by that ACT. In a LETTER to a MEMBER of the BRITISH HOUSE of COMMONS.

condemned to be hanged; John Yemm, and George Lypiatt, were also condemned for sheep-stealing, but have since been reprieved. Thomas Dee, condemned last assizes and reprieved, to be transported for 14 years.

LONDON.

His Majesty was attended in the state coach yesterday to the House of Peers by the Earl of Buckinghamshire and Lord Cadogan; when the following acts, besides those mentioned in our last, received the royal assent.

An act to remove a doubt concerning such part of an act made in the last session of parliament, as relates to the ascertaining of the duties upon the importation of certain linnen cloth of the manufacture of Russia; and to obviate all doubts with respect to the importation of tea, under certain licences authorized to be granted by an act made in the 18th year of the reign of his late Majesty.

An act to indemnify such persons as have omitted to qualify themselves for offices and employments; and to indemnify Justices of the Peace, Deputy Lieutenants, and officers of the militia, or others, who have omitted to register or deliver in their qualifications within the time limited by law, and for giving further time for those purposes, &c.

An act for the better regulation of pilots for the conducting of ships and vessels into and out of the port of Liverpool.

The act for repealing the American stamp duties, is thus intituled: — "An act to repeal an act made in the last session of Parliament, intituled, An act for granting and applying certain stamp duties and other duties in the British Colonies and Plantations in America, towards further defraying the expences of defending, protecting, and securing the same, and for amending such parts of the several acts of Parliament relating to the trade and revenues of the said Colonies and Plantations, as direct the manner of determining and recovering the penalties and forfeitures therein mentioned."

A great number of Merchants met yesterday at the King's Arms Tavern, in Cornhill; from whence they went in their coaches to West-

King Stanislaus of Poland has left to each his executors, the Intendant and Farmer General of Lorrain, a ring worth 20,000 crowns.

We hear the Right Hon. Lord Cant now Earl of Delawar, will be appointed the honours his late father enjoyed.

The Court of Aldermen having lately an order, than whenever there should not sufficient number of Aldermen to make a by one o'clock, the Lord Mayor might ad the said Court, without sending to the Al men's houses, as has been lately the cu and yesterday there not being a sufficient ber of Aldermen, who attended by one o' his Lordship soon after went away, pursua the above order of Court.

Yesterday a dispensation passed the sea enable the Rev. Dr. William Digby, one Majesty's chaplains, to hold the rector Sheldon, and also the vicarage of Colesh Warwickshire, worth 240l. per annum.

The Rev. James Fletcher, B. A. was a days since presented to the vicarage of M Minster in Norfolk, void by the cession o late minister.

The Rev. Mr. Henry Pepperell is pres by William Crofts, Esq; to the rectory of Harling, with Middle Harling, in Norfolk.

A letter from Plympton in Devonshire, "We have had nothing but rejoycings and all round the country, in every parish village, bells ringing, and bonfires at ni ever since Tuesday's post, which brought port that the repeal of the late Cyder-tax passed the House of Commons. Three bouring Justices of the Peace gave a t cyder each to the inhabitants of their se parishes."

On Monday died at his chambers in Co Court, Gray's-Inn, Samuel Chalmers, Esq; merly Governor of Gibraltar.

On the 7th instant died, at his seat, Stradb Hall, Pole Cosby, Esq; by whose death an of 4000l. per annum devolves to Dudley ander Sidney Cosby, late British minister a court of Denmark.

On Friday died in Stanhope-Street, May-James Jessup Essup, Esq.

and at Morpeth, it was called and a reward offered: After man went to Mr. Turnbull delivered it, telling him she before on the road near Al bull immediately sent it to t turned her three guineas.

Tuesday died at Kirkhar land, Mr. John Brown, Stev the Duke of Portland.

Wednesday died at Matfi land, Mr. John Armstrong, ward Blackett, Bart.

Thursday se'nnight died the county of Durham, Wm.

On the 7th inst. died at thumberland, Rebecca Hug memory she retained to the and could read without spect posterity survive her, viz. 6 children, and 26 great grand

Gloucester, March 17. W of a very extraordinary inst vengeance that happened ab Chalford in this county; On a young man of that place, wa and he most profanely wished and his eyes never shut, if h next game. When he was g served a black spot upon his l mortification began immedia over his body, so that he die his flesh being quite rotten; be shut, notwithstanding all friends to close them. The attested by many of the nei with him. [Gloucester Jour

At our assizes, which were turday, Thomas Evans and condemned to be hanged; George Lypiatt, were also con stealing, but have since been r Dee, condemned last assizes an transported for 14 years.

LONDO

His Majesty was attended yesterday to the House of Pe Buckinghamshire and Lord C acts, besides those the royal assent. to remove a doub act made in the la lates to the ascertai importation of cer facture of Russia; respect to the in licences author made in the 18th ye his late Majesty.

An act to indemnify such omitted to qualify themselve employments; and to indemn Peace, Deputy Lieutenants, militia, or others, who have o

LONDON CHRONICLE
March 20, 1766
—

By February 1766, the stamp tax crisis had become such a nuisance that Parliament passed its repeal and King George III gave his royal approval on March 17. News of the repeal was instantly met with great joy and relief by London merchants, who would soon benefit from the end of boycotts on their goods. In fact, before the King and Parliament went into session to repeal the Stamp Act, measures were taken by local merchants to quickly communicate the great news with their colonial clients.

bellman, an old wo-wick, and the night Mr. Turn-, who re-

minfter, to exprefs their fatisfaction on the royal affent being given to the bill for the repeal of the Stamp Act. The bells rang in every part of the city on the fame occafion; and in the afternoon the Merchants had a grand entertainment at the above Tavern, at which were prefent many perfons of diftinction. At night many coffee-houfes and other houfes in the city were finely illuminated, and other demonftrations of joy were fhewn on this event.

The inftant his Majefty came out of the Parliament houfe yefterday, an exprefs with letters to different perfons in America, fet off for Falmouth; at which place, a light fhip, hired and prepared by the Merchants, lay ready to fet fail, the very moment the exprefs arrives.

We are informed, that 1,800,000 l. will be granted for paying off and difcharging the Exchequer Bills made out in 1764 and 1765.

It is faid, the fum of thoufand, three hundred fhillings and fixpence granted, towards defra expences of his Majefty fervices incurred to the

Letters from Lower the 10th of January Georgians, under the Heraclius, again attack fent to reduce them to of whom were cut to fued to the mountain C

We are told, that ordered 10,000 troops be on account of an from the Province of the proceedings of th ftrict.

King Staniflaus of P his executors, the Inte ral of Lorrain, a ring

We hear the Righ now Earl of Delawar the honours his late

The Court of Alde an order, than whene fufficient number of by one o'clock, the the faid Court, with men's houfes, as ha and yefterday there ber of Aldermen, wh his Lordfhip foon aft the above order of C

Yefterday a difpe enable the Rev. Dr. Majefty's chaplains Sheldon, and alfo Warwickfhire, wor

The Rev. James days fince prefented Minifter in Norfolk late minifter.

The Rev. Mr. by William

Yefterday died at her houfe in Dover-ftreet Mrs. Dafhwood, mother of Mrs. Dafhwood, of the won jefty.

On S Woolpac

Yefter berland,

On M in good pay a vi in Cold-rand, th in the been feiz

Six of breaking Maidftone gaol, and prefent at the murder of the keeper, were executed on Satur-

iron. There may be fome others; but thefe are the principal regulations; I hope they will all pafs, but the fpirit of oppofition muft certainly overfet fome of them."

Extract of a Letter from Briftol, March 25.

" We have the trade bill now much at heart, and are battling it out with the London Weft-India merchants, and hope in the conclufion we fhall be able to procure you in America fuch advantages as you could wifh yourfelves to and from the Spanifh and French fettlements in America.

NEW-YORK, May 26.

On Tuefday laft we were favoured with the authenticated glorious and interefting news of the *repeal* from different quarters, which was inftantly fpread throughout the city, diffufing joy and gladnefs in every face; whereupon, all the bells of the different churches were rung, and the next day there was a manifeftation of the greateft gratitude fhewn by the *True Sons of Liberty*, who could not withold any longer their open and liberal rejoicings, on a matter which fo nearly concerned them; and in order to give public notice of a rejoicing was printed and diftributed.

Accordingly, preparations being made without a moment's lofs of time, and meafures adopted for carrying on the feftival, a number of the Sons of Liberty repaired to Trinity Church, having been very politely acquainted by the Rector, of his intentions to preach on another fubject, a congratulatory difcourfe on the joyful occafion. After which repairing to the Field of Liberty, a royal falute of 21 cannon was fired, and that fucceeded by a confiderable body of the Sons of Liberty, collecting at their ufual houfe of public refort, where an elegant entertainment was prepared, attended with a band of mufick, and when they had dined in the moft focial manner, twenty-eight loyal and conftitutional toafts were cheerfully drank.

The evening concluded with bonfires and other illuminations; and notwithftanding the tranfports of our joy, and the vaft concourfe of people which were affembled, the whole tranfactions of the day was conducted and finifhed with the greateft loyalty, harmony and good order.

The Sons of Liberty of New-York, take this early opportunity, of moft cordially faluting and congratulating all their American brethren on this glorious and happy event.

A letter from London, dated March 29, fays, The relief for the colonies, faid to be intended, is, reducing the duty on fugar to one fhilling per cent molaffes to one penny per gallon; with liberty to import wine, fruit, and oil, from Cadiz; and perhaps the price of tea reduced.

His Majefty's fnow of war the Hind, arrived at Sandy-Hook from Plymouth, yefterday afternoon, with difpatches from the miniftry for the different Governors on the continent, acquainting them of the total repeal of the Stamp Act; which intelligence his Excellency our Governor immediately made public at the Coffee-Houfe, and added, That the acts of trade were taken into confideration, and 'twas hoped would terminate in favour of the colonies. The Hind left Plymouth the 7th of April, in which veffel came paffenger, Major

6 The Doctor then delivered his effay, which was received with the higheft approbation by the audience After which the Provoft proceeded as follows---

" Sir, as the reward of your great merit in this elegant performance, I am, in the name of the Truftees and Faculty of this college, as well as in behalf of the worthy donor, to beg your acceptance of this *Gold Medal*---Its intrinfic value may not be an object of much confideration to you; but the truly honourable circumftances by which it now becomes yours, muft render it one of the moft valuable jewels in your poffeffion.

" That the firft literary prize in this inftitution fhould fail to the fhare of one of its eldeft fons, who to much genius and application, has joined much knowlege of the world, will not feem ftrange. Yet ftill for the honour of this feminary, and what will not derogate from your honor, it will appear that you have obtained this preheminence over no mean competitors.

" Some of our younger fons (among whom we ought not to omit the name of the modeft and candid *WATTS*, with fome others even of inferior ftanding) have exhibited fuch vigorous efforts of genius, and tread fo ardently on the heels of you their feniors, that it will require the utmoft exertion of all your faculties, the continual ftraining of every nerve, if you would long wifh to lead the way to them, in the great career of fame.---

" Truly delicate and difficult, we confefs, gentlemen, was the fubject prefcribed to you---to treat of the reciprocal advantages of a perpetual *union* between Great-Britain and her colonies, at a time when a fatal mifunderftanding had untwifted all the cords of that *union*, and the minds of many were too much inflamed! This difficulty was likewife encreafed to us by other confiderations.

" Great-Britain, who by her liberality has raifed this college from a helplefs to a flourishing ftate, had an undoubted demand on us for all the returns of gratitude. Yet we could not, we durft not, divert the ftreams of learning from their facred courfe----Our country, nay all America, had a right to expect that they fhould be directed pure along to water the goodly *Tree of LIBERTY*, nor ever be fuffered to cherifh any rank weed that would choak its growth.

" In this moft difficult conjuncture, we rejoice to behold you, in your early years, exercifing all the temper and prudence of the moft experienced patriots. We rejoice that ever we had the leaft fhare in forming fentiments, which have led you fo powerfully to fhow that on the everlafting bafis of reciprocal intereft, and a participation of conftitutional privileges, our union fhall be perpetuated and our bleeding wounds healed up without fo much as a fcar by way of remembrance------Here you have fhewn yourfelves entituled to the name of *true* SONS OF LIBERTY----SONS OF LIBERTY indeed! neither betraying her facred caufe on the one hand, nor degenerating into licentioufnefs on the other, &c."

This eulogium entered

never lessen the Repu-
oth it need a Veil on
be found in the best
nd whatever Excesses
a, under our late dif-
lief kindly granted us
racious Sovereign and
how to distinguish the
strances of loyal Sub-
s aggrieved, from the
le. Notwithstanding
pped from your Excel-
per generally prevails
ead the Parliament to
othing that can afford
se who were for main-
Sorrow and Concern
al.
further to say, " When
d in Form, when there
prive it of it's best and
nlyCrime is their Fide-
t be indifferent, but find
every legal and consti-
n the King's Authority
ill-timed Oppugnation
have been your Excel-
ording to the more ob-
lions, an heavy Charge,
or any Order of Men
Speech to both Houses
World is left to place

says, there has been an
orm, and an ill judged
f the King's Authority.
ter, to Truth and Jus-
the Province in which
HisMajesty,oblige us to
reedom in which we are
isrespect to your Excel-
Occasion would merit
may be ready from your
y upon us, and would
of the Choice that has
xcellency's Approbation.
his Province been guilty
ent in Form, or of any
Authority—We declare
of no such Thing—the
of Sovereigns, and sen-
ection with and subordi-
ry, have given new and
hese happy Dispositions
upon the lateIndulgence
rejoiced with the high-
ratitude to the King, to

upon Government, or an Oppugnation of the King's
Authority : and should any Thing like this be ever
attempted, your Excellency would find this Board
zealous to defend our Sovereign's Honour, and the
constitutional Power of His Representative.

We beg Leave to assure your Excellency, that
we shall heartily join with you in healing Divisions
and burying Animosities, should they arise ; and that
we shall chearfully contribute all in our Power to
the Peace and Honour of your Administration.

May it please your Excellency,

The Letter from the Right Honorable Mr. Secretary CONWAY to your Excellency, accompanying
your second Speech from the Chair, affords us a
most agreeable Occasion of repeatedly declaring the
strong Sentiments of Respect and Gratitude, with
which we regard the Lenity and Tenderness already
so remarkably manifested on the Part of His Majesty
and the Parliament, to the American Colonies,
and the Prospect given us of some additional Indul-
gences ; for all which it will be our Pleasure as it
must be our Glory, to make the most dutiful and affectionate Returns.—These are the Dispositions which
have uniformly influenced this Board before we saw
this Letter so happily adapted to confirm us in
them.—And we beg Leave to assure your Excellency
that from these Dispositions we shall continue to act.

There are several Paragraphs in your Excellency's
Speeches that have been construed to bear hard on
the Gentlemen who now constitute the Board : But
your Explanation of them in Council, and your repeated Declaration, that you had no such Intention,
have given Satisfaction to the Board.

We again beg Leave to assure your Excellency,
that our best Abilities shall faithfully be employed,
in promoting His Majesty's Honor and Interest, and
in making every Part of your Administration easy and
happy : And such Testimonials of your Conduct as
are contained in Mr. Secretary CONWAY's Letter,
will not suffer us to conclude without recognizing
your Excellency in the united Character of a true
Friend to the Province and a faithful Servant to the
Crown.

———————

*To which ADDRESS His Excellency was pleased
to return the following ANSWER.*

Gentlemen,

I Thank you for your Congratulations on the Repeal of the Stamp-Act, and for your Assurances
that nothing shall be wanting on your Part that may
contribute towards a proper Improvement of this
happy Event.

However, I doubt not but that with your Assistance,
I shall soon see this Government restored to its Peace
and Honour, and the Character of every Person concerned in it brought to its true Estimation.

Fra. Bernard.

*THE following is the Copy of a Letter from the
principal Merchants in London trading to the
Colonies, sent by Express when the Act for repealing the Stamp-Act receiv'd the Royal Assent,
which Express has not yet arrived that we have
heard of.*

To JOHN HANCOCK, Esq; *and the
Rest of the Merchants in* BOSTON.

LONDON, *March* 18. 1766.

GENTLEMEN,

WE have now the Satisfaction of informing
you by Capt Wray, sent by us Express in the Ship Dispatch, that the Bill
for repealing theStamp-Act received the
Royal Assent this Day.

To enumerate the Difficulties which we have had
in this Affair, would be a disagreeable Task to us ;
as it may seem calculated to enhance our own Merit,
at the Expence of Characters whom we respect for
their Situation, however they may have been induced
to act a Part we could not approve, or thoroughly
reconcile to the true Interests of the British Empire.

Nevertheless, we think ourselves entituled, from
the Pains we have taken to serve you, to the Privilege of imparting our Sentiments on your past and
future Conduct, with that Freedom and Impartiality
which Observation and Experience dictate.

You must know better, than to imagine that any
well regulated Government will suffer Laws, enacted
with a View to public Good, to be disputed by lawless Rioters, with Impunity.

There is no Government so perfect, but that thro'
Misinformation, and the Frailties even of the most
elevated human Understandings, Mistakes, or at least
the Appearance of such, may arise in the Conduct of
Affairs, even in the wisest Legislature—but, is it just,
is it tolerable, that without Proof of Inconvenience,
tumultuous Force shall be encouraged by a Part, to
fly in the Face of Power established for the Good of
the Whole ? We are persuaded, Gentlemen, that you
cannot be of that Opinion, and that you will exert
your utmost Endeavours to cancel the Remembrance
of such flagrant Breaches of public Order, and to manifest your Gratitude and Affection to your Mother
Country, which by the Repeal of this Act has given
such incontestible Proof of her Moderation

What Sentiments you ought to entertain on this
Occasion, and whatConduct we would wish you to observe, will sufficiently appear from our former Letter

BOSTON GAZETTE
June 16, 1766

A letter from fifty-five merchants in London to John Hancock and the merchants of Boston encourages public order and gratitude toward the mother country and suggests that had Americans obeyed the law and simply communicated their hardships, "your Relief would have been more speedy."

dated 28th February last, and sent by the first Conveyance, the Moment we could inform you, with any Degree of Certainty what was likely to be the Fate of the Stamp-Act.

We shall only observe, that under Providence, you are indebted for this Event to the Clemency and paternal Regard of His Majesty for the Happiness of his Subjects, to the publick Spirit, Abilities and Firmness of the present Administration; and to the Humanity, Prudence, and Patriotism of the Generality of those who compose the Legislature, and the most considerable Persons of every Rank in this Kingdom.

We hope Gentlemen, that this Conduct in the British Legislature; provoked by the most irritating Measures on your Side, will forever be a Lesson to your Posterity; as it is the most convincing Proof, that if by any Means, Laws are, or should be, enacted, detrimental or seemingly oppressive to any Part of the British Subjects; the British Legislature, will at all Times, with the utmost Tenderness consider every Grievance, & redress them the Moment they are known.

We cannot but acquaint you, that had the Americans endeavoured to acquiesce with the Law, and dutifully represented the Hardships as they arose, your Relief would have been more speedy, and we should have avoided many Difficulties as well as not a few unanswerable mortifying Reproaches on your Account.

Such however is the Patriotism and Magnanimity of those in Power, that, unaffected, by the Conduct of many on your Side the Water, and the strenuous Efforts of an Opposition here to every Measure of Lenity and Indulgence towards America; they are endeavouring to establish its Commerce in particular, as well as that of the British Empire in general, upon the most solid Foundation, & the most extensive Plan of Utility.

On your Parts we hope that nothing will be wanting to obliterate the Remembrance of what is passed, by setting the Example yourselves, and promoting the like Sentiments in others; of a dutiful Attachment to your Sovereign and the Interests of your Mother Country, a just Submission to the Laws, and respect for the Legislature; for in this you are most effectually promoting your own Happiness and Security.

By a Conduct like this, Gentlemen, you will both encourage and enable us to serve you with Zeal on future Emergencies, should any such arise; and to support our mutual Interests; the Interest of the Colonies, which are inseparable from the common Interests of Great-Britain, with Efficacy and Success.

We are, Gentlemen,
Your assured Friends,
and very humble Servants
[Signed by 55 of the principal Merchants trading to North America.]

Hartford, in Connecticut, June 9.

Last Tuesday died at Weathersfield, in the 47th Year of his Age, Dr. Jonathan Marsh, of Norwich. He was sent for to this Town, at the Time the late unhappy Accident happened here, on Account of his great Skill in Surgery, and was very useful for a few Days; but one of his Arms, in which he had received a great Strain, grew so painful that he was obliged to leave his Practice, and retire to his Brother-in-Law, (Dr. Porter of Weathersfield) where his ... grew worse and worse, till it put an End to his

21, 27, 29, 35, 30, ...
57, 63, 66, 68. 6...
97, 100. Of the ...
raised December ...
quent, viz. No. 5...
47, 54, 68, 70, 78...
7s. Tax lawful M...
and to be apportion...
and was laid equal...
third Division 25...
second Division 3d...
delinquent in the f...
31, 41, 42, 44, 4...
In the second Divi...
46, 47, 48, 55, 5...
99, 100: In the th...
17, 18, 20, 29, 32, 42, 43, 59, 70, 74, 78, 79, 80, 81, 85, 88, 89, 92, 93, 94, 95, 118, 121, 124, 137, 162, 192. Of the 2d. 1q. Tax lawful Money Voted to be raised May 1760, on each Acre laid out, the following Lots are delinquent, viz. In the first Division, No. 6, 22, 27, 39, 41, 45, 58, 62, 68, 78, 79, 85, 88, 89, 91, 98: In the second Division, No. 1, 4, 6, 7, 8, 9, 10, 20, 22, 25, 26, 59, 69, 94, 95, 98, 99: In the third Division, No. 4, 6, 9, 11, 12, 13, 18, 20, 26, 27, 34, 35, 37, 40, 43, 51, 55, 58, 59, 60, 62, 69, 70, 73, 74, 77, 79, 80, 81, 85, 88, 91, 93, 94, 98, 108, 118, 121, 132, 138, 139, 143, 148, 158, 164, 182, 192; and also Fayerweather's Farm containing 500 Acres. Of the 4 d. Tax lawful Money Voted to be raised March 1761, on each Acre laid out, the following Lots are delinquent, viz. In the first Division, No. 3, 6, 27, 35, 41, 44, 45, 66, 68, 69, 80, 88, 89, 100: In the second Division, No. 10, 14, 21, 24, 25, 27, 59, 89, 94, 95, 98, 99: In the third Division, No. 1, 4, 6, 9, 11, 13, 18, 20, 26, 27, 29, 40, 43, 51, 55, 58, 59, 60, 62, 69, 74, 77, 79, 83, 88, 90, 94, 95, 106, 111, 118, 121, 132, 138, 139, 143, 148, 158, 164, 182, 185, 192, and also Fairweather's Farm, containing 500 Acres, and Newberry's Farm in the Gore, containing 264 Acres. Of the 1d. 2q. Tax lawful Money Voted to be raised March 1765, on each Acre of Land laid out and voted to be laid out, the following Lots are delinquent, viz. In the first Division, No. 2, 3, 5, 6, 8, 11, 14, 15, 17, 19, 20, 22, 23, 24, 25, 27, 29, 30, 31, 32, 33, 35, 39, 42, 43, 45, 49, 54, 55, 62, 63, 66, 68, 69, 73, 74, 79, 81, 85, 86, 88, 89, 91, 94, 95, 96, 97, 98, 100: In the second Division, No. 1, 2, 3, 4, 5, 6, 7, 8, 10, 11, 12, 13, 14, 15, 20, 21, 22, 23, 24, 25, 26, 27, 49, 55, 56, 57, 59, 60, 61, 62, 63, 64, 65, 69, 72, 73, 89, 91, 96, 98, 100: In the third Division, No. 1, 3, 4, 6, 7, 11, 12, 14, 16, 17, 18, 23, 26, 27, 29, 32, 34, 35, 36, 37, 43, 51, 52, 54, 55, 56, 59, 60, 62, 64, 68, 69, 70, 74, 76, 77, 78, 79, 80, 81, 83, 89, 90, 93, 94, 95, 96, 97, 98, 103, 104, 105, 106, 108, 111, 112, 117, 118, 120, 121, 122, 125, 128, 129, 131, 132, 133, 134, 136, 137, 138, 139, 141, 142, 144, 145, 147, 148, 153, 158, 160, 162, 163, 164, 166, 167, 169, 170, 171, 176, 178, 180, 182, 183, 184, 185, 187, 189, 192, 194, 195, 197, 198, 199, 200, also Fayerweather's Farm containing 500 Acres, and Colbey's and Newberry's Farm in the Gore, containing 264 Acres each.

And that every Proprietor may know the Sum he has to pay on the several Taxes, we would inform them, that in the first and second Divisions the following Lots contain

Irish linnens, garlix, dowlais, Ruina linnens, Irish sheeting, Russia diaper and clouting ditto, bedticks, striped holland, cotton gowns, silk damascus, cotton velves, thicksetts, pillow fustians, duroys, silk sagathies, worsted ditto, fine double allapeens, grezetts, brunetts; a fine assortment of calicoes and chints, fine broad black russell, brolioes, worsted grograms, calimancoes, russells, tammies and durants, shalloons, plain and sprigg'd half-yard and yard-wide venetian poplins, worsted and silk sprigg'd camblets, stripped ditto, yard-wide stuffs, mecklenburghs, fine coloured crapes, cloth coloured English taffities, white & brown buckrams, yellow holland, stay cord and braids, cambricks, 7-8 and yard wide lawns, long lawns, book russia, plain & flower'd white and black gauze, white cat-gutt, bengalls, black, cloth, buff and crimson worsted breeches patterns, mens, womens and childrens cotton and thread hose, worsted caps, green and crimson mock velvet ditto, black worsted mitts, black, pink, crimson, blue & white pelon sattin, black, pink, crimson and blue figur'd capuchin silks, narrow black alamode, black lutestring, yard-wide white farsnet for handkerchiefs, 3, 4 black ditto, kid and lamb gloves and mittens of all sorts, womens and childrens black and colour'd silk mitts, womens black and white silk gloves; a variety of womens and childrens fans, plain and drawn'd sattin hatts and bonnets, plain black ditto, chip hatts and bonnetts, half-ell and ell-wide persians, a fine assortment of new-fashion ribbons, tippets and turbans, linnen and silk handkerchiefs, large black gauze ditto, wax threads, Scotch and nuns threads, gimps, English and French wax necklaces and earings, silk ferrets, white & black trolly lace, black bone ditto, white cap lace, tapes and pins of all sorts, white chapple, common, darning & Glover's needles, Lynn-made shoes, black sattin ditto, children's morrocco shoes, silk & hair, best scarf twist, silk twist, and basket-work'd buttons, knee garters, silk purses, shirt buttons, cotton and silk laces, garters, fine shoe bindings, London qualities, bellindine silks, ivory combs, Raven's duck, &c. &c. &c.

THESE are to give Notice to the Candidates for their Second Degree this Year, That They attend at the College in this Place, on or before the 9th Day of July next, and if any neglect to give their Attendance accordingly, without sufficient Reason therefor, They may not expect their Degrees this Year.

EDWARD HOLYOKE, President.
Cambridge, June 5. 1766.

Life, in the 25th Year of his Age, greatly lamented, Mr. William Gardiner of this Town, Merchant; he ... of those that were wounded, at the late un-

| No. 19 | 55 | No. 1 | 7 | No. 24 | 6 | No 71 | 6 |
| 20 | 60 | | 6 6 | 25 | 6 | 72 | 7 |

the Proprietors of New Framingham, alias Lanesborough, in the County of Berkshire (legally warn'd)

A LIST of the Names of *those* who AUDACIOUSLY continue to counteract the UNITED SENTIMENTS of the Body of Merchants thro'out NORTH-AMERICA; by importing British Goods contrary to the Agreement.

John Bernard,

James McMasters & Comp'y.

John Mein,

The following is a Copy of the AGREEMENT the Merchants of this Town entered into Oct. 17. 1769.

WHEREAS the Merchants and Traders in the Town of Boston, taking into Consideration the Deplorable Situation of the Trade, and the many Difficulties that it laboured under, did on the First Day of August 1768, by a Subscription under their Hands, agree, that they would not send for, or Import from Great-Britain, any Kind of Goods or Merchandize, either on their own Accounts or on Commissions, or otherwise, from the First Day of January 1769, to the First Day of January 1770, excepting, Coals, Salt, Fish-Hooks & Lines, Hemp, Duck, Bar-Lead, Shott, Wool-Cards, Card-Wire. And Whereas it appears to us the Subscribers that, as the said Agreement has been very Generally adheared to, so it has already had a good Effect, and affords a promising Prospect of answering the important Ends designed thereby, provided it should be continued, Therefore in order effectually to promote the Design of relieving the Trade, from the many Difficulties and Oppressions under which it labours, and to preserve to ourselves and Posterity, the Liberties and Privileges which we were wont to enjoy, WE now _____ and Engage with each other as follows,

1. THAT we will not import _____ of Goods or Merchandize _____ Britain, either on our own Accounts _____ mmons, or otherwise, until the Acts imp _____ America for raising a Reve _____ Seeing the A _____ cles of Coa _____ Hemp _____

Aug. 23. *A farmer at Granchester in Cambridgshire, was bound over to the quarter sessions by the humanity of the Rev. Dr. Plumtree, for forcing a poor woman of Caldecot into the water to prove her a witch, and otherwise maltreating her.*

Aug. 31. *The French ambassador has lately presented a memorial to the States General, in which he acquaints them that the Island of Corsica is united to the dominions of France, and hopes that in case any ships for the future shall appear under Corsican colours, their H. M. will look upon them as pirates, and treat them accordingly.*

Sept. 1. *A Correspondent says, the prodigious Increase of the French Navy is truly alarming, and should instigate the Great to lay aside Contentions and Party Squabbles, and unite in taking Care of the most essential Interests and Security of the Nation, which demand a powerful Navy well kept up and ready to defeat the Attempts of our artful and naturable Enemy.*

The French, from a Calculation lately made, reckoned in the Island of Corsica, 57 Pieves, or Ecclesiastical Districts, 10 Jurisdictions, 26,336 Houses with Chimneys, 32,322 Men able to bear Arms, and 130,680 Souls in all.

Aug. 31. Last Thursday died in Cavendish square, aged 97, Edmund Hoyle, Esq; well known in the polite world for writing the celebrated treatise on the games of Whist, Quadrille, Piquet, Chess and Backgammon, which he lived to see pass thro' no less than thirteen editions.

Yesterday several colony agents waited upon the Earls of Rochfort and Weymouth, on the subject of recent instructions from their respective colonies.

Sept. ___. Saturday the Right Hon. the Earl of Bute ___ ntinues in a declining state ___ set o ___ eat at Luton Hoo, in Bedfo ___

A ___ of artillery and ordnance ___ ping ___ ower and Woolwich for ___ N ___

___ day evening his Royal Highn ___ ___ ved at his house in Gr ___ ___ from hi ___ through ___ day ___ l on ___ ___ g ___ ales,

The Westminster Petition to different Parishes throughout been signed by a great numb ___ there is no time yet fixed f ___ his Majesty.

On Wednesday evening t ___ rived in Town from his Reg ___ and was yesterday at Court.

Wednesday several Ger ___ American Colonies, waited ___ cers of State, on affairs ___ North America.

Sept. 9. A great man has ___ duct of the Bostonians, tha ___ now begun to prove true, ___ ricans would only grow mo ___ were indulged." — He adde ___ the Revenue-Act entirely, ___ of the Admiralty Courts, ___ plain of, their Agents in ___ the boldness to assert, that ___ fied, without Concessions" ___ be, is surely a matter well ___ the Mother-Country.

The affairs relating to t ___ Bay, and also the Petition ___ vernor, are postponed till ___ Hilsborough from Ireland ___ course of next week.

A Letter from Cante ___ Gentleman, just come f ___ that Gen. Paoli was to ___ Dutch Ship, for Dover, ___

It is said that a meetin ___ ding to North America ___ consider on a proper ___ relative to the present stag ___ on produce the most de ___ ely remedi ___

___ HARLE ___ that the ___ in the A ___

___ from H ___ ___ n England a ___ ___ o the farther ___ ___ e in North-America.

___ tember 12. It is ___ ___ on in the Russian ___ ___ Sea, is to b ___ ___ the Port ___ ___ selves ___ ___ was a ___ ___ s were ___ ___ eir rigg ___ ___ ails her ___ ___ l here ___ ___ they ___

FRUGALITY
AND INDUSTRY

Introduction

THE DECLARATORY ACT OF 1766—REITERATING GREAT BRITAIN'S "FULL POWER and authority" over the American colonies "in all cases whatsoever"—was a hard pill for colonists to swallow following the repeal of the Stamp Act, but Americans had little to fear until Parliament enforced it, which came one year later in the form of a new tax proposal by Charles Townshend. With both sides learning valuable lessons from the Stamp Act crisis, the Townshend Acts focused on external taxes and included laws for proper enforcement. Colonists leveraged the newfound power of the newspaper press and coupled domestic manufacturing with continent-wide boycotts—tactics that helped distinguish Patriot rebels from Crown-supporting Loyalists.

BOSTON GAZETTE
November 20, 1769

COLONIAL AMERICAN FAMILY
North Wind Picture Archives

CHARLES TOWNSHEND
North Wind Picture Archives

His namesake acts included revenue-raising taxes on goods
imported from England, an act establishing a new system
of customs commissioners, and an act for suspending the
New York assembly.

JOHN DICKINSON, A PORTRAIT
BY C. W. PEALE, 1741–1827
The Bridgeman Art Library

Philadelphia lawyer, politician, and author of twelve letters
"from a farmer" that clearly stated objections to British
authority.

TOWNSHEND ACTS

RESPONSIBLE FOR BRITAIN'S FISCAL POLICIES, CHARLES Townshend needed to defray the expense of colonial American defense and operations, which was magnified after a reduction in British property taxes left a gaping hole in the national budget. Plus, with the embarrassment of the Stamp Act repeal still fresh on the mind, new taxes would reassert imperial authority and shift the balance of power back to Great Britain.

To avoid the passionate internal tax debate from two years earlier, Townshend opted for external tariffs only. On June 29, 1767, Parliament passed the Townshend Acts, a series of laws that imposed strict revenue-raising taxes on goods imported from England, including paint, glass, lead, paper, and tea (see list of the duties in the October 12, 1767, *Pennsylvania Chronicle*). Tea had become a symbol of aristocracy in England and therefore the drink of choice among wealthy American women. The hope that external duties would be more easily stomached was quickly rejected as Americans argued that taxes on the use of paper were no different than those on the importation of it.

To ensure enforcement and payment of the new taxes, the Townshend Acts included laws for sending customs collectors to America and establishing new admiralty courts in Boston, Philadelphia, and Charleston. Yet another law dissolved New York's assembly after it had recently refused to provide housing, food, and drink for British troops.

After reading about the riots and mobs of 1765–66, Londoners, fearing further violence, cautioned friends in America about going to extremes and, thus, making more enemies. This was made evident in a letter from London, dated August 6, 1767, that was published in the *Pennsylvania Chronicle*'s October 12 issue:

The Opposition to America seems to increase. Every Step is taking to render the Taxation of the Colonies a popular Measure, and it is contended that they should be obliged explicitly to acknowledge that Right. I know not what to advise on this Occasion, but that the Friends of America, on both Sides the Water, should exert their utmost Endeavours to lessen the present Unpopularity of the American Cause; conciliate the Affections of the People here towards you, increase by all possible Means the Number of your Friends, and be careful not to weaken their Hands, and strengthen those of your Enemies, by rash Proceedings, the Mischiefs of which are inconceivable.

The Townshend Acts took effect November 20, 1767, and caused a resurgence of anti-taxation prose and protests. Among the colonial chorus of dissenting voices, John Dickinson's stood out. Dickinson, a well-known Philadelphia lawyer and politician, wrote a series of twelve

> *With the embarrassment of the Stamp Act repeal still fresh on the mind, new taxes would reassert imperial authority and shift the balance of power back to Great Britain.*

letters "from a farmer" that were printed and reprinted in newspapers from New Hampshire to Georgia (see the first letter in the December 21, 1767, *Boston Chronicle*). His articulate and reasonable public objections to British authority helped unite the colonies and urged nonviolent resistance. Privately, Dickinson shared copies of his letters with Boston statesman James Otis, Jr., suggesting that Massachusetts lead the charge against the Townshend Acts as it did against the Stamp Act.

WHEREAS it is expedient that a revenue should be raised, in your Majesty's dominions in America, for making a more certain and adequate provision for defraying the charge of the administration of justice, and the support of civil government, in such provinces where it shall be found necessary; and towards further defraying the expences of defending, protecting, and securing the said dominions; We, your Majesty's most dutiful and loyal subjects, the commons of Great-Britain, in parliament assembled, have therefore resolved to give and grant unto your Majesty the several rates and duties herein aftermentioned; and do most humbly beseech your Majesty that it may be enacted, and be it enacted by the King's most excellent Majesty, by and with the advice and consent of the lords spiritual and temporal, and commons, in this present parliament assembled, and by the authority of the same, that from and after the twentieth day of November, one thousand seven hundred and sixty seven, there shall be raised, levied, collected, and paid unto his Majesty, his heirs, and successors, for and upon the respective goods herein after mentioned, which shall be imported from Great-Britain into any colony or plantation in America, which now is, or hereafter may be under the dominion of his Majesty, his heirs or successors, the several rates or duties following; that is to say,

For every hundred weight aveirdupois of crown plate, flint, and white glass, Four shillings and eight-pence.

For every hundred weight aveirdupois of green glass, One shilling and two-pence.

For every hundred weight aveirdupois of red lead, Two shillings.

For every hundred weight aveirdupois of white lead, Two shillings.

For every hundred weight avoirdupois of painters colours, Two shillings.

For every pound weight avoirdupois of tea, Three-pence.

For every ream of paper, usually called or known by the name of Atlas Fine, Twelve shillings.

For every ream of paper, called Atlas Ordinary, Six shillings.

For every ream of paper, called Bastard, or double Copy, One shilling and six-pence.

For every single ream of blue paper, for sugar bakers, Ten-pence halfpenny.

For every ream of paper, called German Crown, nine-pence.

For every ream of paper, called Fine Printing Crown, Nine-pence.

For every ream of paper, called Second Ordinary Printing Crown, Six-pence three farthings.

For every ream of paper, called Crown Fine,

For every ream of any other paper, called Fools Cap Fine, not made in Great-Britain, One shilling and ten-pence halfpenny.

For every ream of any other paper, called Fools Cap Fine Second, not made in Great-Britain, One shilling and six-pence.

For every ream of paper called Fools Cap Fine, made in Great-Britain, Nine-pence.

For every ream of paper, called Fools Cap Second, made in Great-Britain, Six-pence three farthings.

For every ream of paper, called Imperial Fine, Twelve shillings.

For every ream of paper, called Second Writing Imperial, Eight shillings and three-pence.

For every ream of paper, called German Lombard, Nine-pence.

For every ream of paper, called Medium Fine, Four shillings and six-pence.

For every ream of paper, called Genoa Medium, One shilling and ten-pence halfpenny.

For every ream of paper, called Second Writing Medium, Three shillings.

For every ream of painted paper, not made in Great-Britain, Six shillings.

For every ream of paper, called Fine large Post, One shilling and ten-pence halfpenny.

For every ream of paper, called Small Post, One shilling and one penny halfpenny.

For every ream of paper, called fine Genoa Pot, Six-pence three farthings.

For every ream of paper, called Second Genoa Pot, Six-pence three farthings.

For every ream of other paper, called Superfine Pot, not made in Great Britain, One shilling and six-pence.

For every ream of other paper, called Second Fine Pot, not made in Great-Britain, One shilling and one penny halfpenny.

For every ream of paper, called Ordinary Pot, not made in Great-Britain, Six-pence three farthings.

For every ream of paper, called Fine Pot, made in Great-Britain, Nine-pence.

For every ream of paper, called Second Pot, made in Great-Britain, Four-pence halfpenny.

For every ream of paper, called Super Royal Fine, Nine shillings.

For every ream of paper, called Royal Fine, Six shillings.

For every ream of paper, called Fine Holland Royal, Two shillings and five-pence farthing.

For every ream of paper, called Fine Holland Second, One shilling and six-pence.

For every ream of paper, called Second Fine

... Royal,

... Genoa Royal,

... Writing ... fpenny ... Writ-

... of paste ... made in ... ence.

... of paste ... made in ... ence.

... shall be ... tain, to ... farthings ... the duties ...

For every ream of paper, called German Crown, nine-pence.

For every ream of paper, called Fine Printing Crown, Nine-pence.

For every ream of paper, called Second Ordinary Printing Crown, Six-pence three farthings.

For every ream of paper, called Crown Fine,

... not been printed, painted, or stained, and after those rates respectively, for any greater or less quantity.

And it is hereby further enacted by the authority aforesaid, That all other paper (not being particularly rated and charged in this act) shall pay the several and respective duties that are charged, by this act, upon ...

... day last at a Meeting of the Common ... ISAAC JONES, Esq; was elected ... of this City for the ensuing Year; Mr. ... GIBSON was made an Alderman; Messieurs ANDREW and JAMES AL- ... WILLIAM FISHER, JOSHUA ... ELL, WILLIAM PARR, JOSEPH ... T, GEORGE CLYMER, and JOHN ... COCKS, Common Council Men.

Extract of a Letter from a Merchant in London, August 7, 1767.

It is truly melancholy, to reflect on the present ... of public Affairs here:—The Confusion ... our great men still continues—who, instead ... exerting their Abilities, in this Time of Peace, ... foreign Powers, to extend the Commerce of ... Kingdom, pay off the National Debt, and in- ... the Strength and Power of the Nation to ... a future War, are wasting their whole, ... in Party Contentions, Intrigues, and Cabals ... establish their own Power, and the Profit at- ... it; and in abusing one another.

Extract of another Letter from London, dated August 7, 1767.

" A late Attempt to coalesce the different Parties ... a new Ministry, has proved ineffectual—and ... seems probable, that the present Set will conti- ... some Time longer—This seems not unfortu- ... for America, as some of them who were pro- ... to come in, were professed Adversaries of A- ... erica—The prevailing Distinction of Parties here, ... those who in the two last Sessions of Parl—t, ... have been disposed to favour America, are cal- ... by their Opponents, (by Way of Reproach) ... AMERICANS! while the Adherents to G——le ... d B——d, boast of their being true to the Inte- ... est of Britain, and zealous for maintaining its ... Sovereignty over the Colonies—This Declaration ... seems every Day to be more and more fixt; and ... it is much to be feared will be carried higher, in ... the next Session of Parliament, for the political ... Purposes of influencing the ensuing Election—It is ... already said, that the Act for Quartering the Sol- ... diers at New-York, without taking Notice of its ... being done in Obedience to the Act of Parliament, ... is *evasive* and *unsatisfactory*; that it is high Time ... to put the Right of taxing America out of Dis- ... pute, by an Act of Taxation, effectually carried ... into Execution, &c. &c.

Extract of another Letter from London, dated August 6, 1767.

" The general Affairs of America here, bear a ... very disagreeable Aspect; the present Ministry are ... like to continue some Time longer—some *particu- ... cular Changes* will happen, and I fear the princi- ... pal Structure will not be of long Duration, but ... probably there will be another Session of Parlia- ... ment before a considerable Alteration is made.— ... The Opposition to America seems to increase. ... Every Step is taking to render the Taxation of the ... Colonies a popular Measure, and it is contended ... that they should be obliged explicitly to acknow- ... ledge that Right. I know not what to advise on ... this Occasion, but that the Friends of America, on ... both Sides the Water, should exert their utmost ... Endeavours to lessen the present Unpopularity of ... the American Cause; conciliate the Affections of ... the People here towards you, increase by all possi- ... ble Means the Number of your Friends, and be ... careful not to weaken their Hands, and strengthen ... those of your Enemies, by rash Proceedings, the ... Mischiefs of which are inconceivable."

About a Month ago the young Wife of an old ... Gentleman, of this City, about 84 Years of Age, ... was safely delivered of a fine Daughter. They ... are the same Couple whose Marriage was men- ... tioned in this Paper of the 9th of February last.

The Captains Adam, and Ford, from Virginia, ... Captain Briggs, from Rhode-Island, Captain So- ... merville, from Piscataqua, and the Captains Che-

---

PENNSYLVANIA CHRONICLE (PHILADELPHIA)
October 12, 1767

A series of laws, known as the Townshend Acts, were printed in this issue with the front page filled with a long list of the new taxes on paint, glass, lead, paper, tea, and more. Fresh off the Stamp Act, a general fear of politically incited violence and retaliation was common. Inside, a letter from London, dated August 6, 1767, cautions about growing opposition to America and encourages colonists to make more friends than enemies.

The PENNSYLVANIA CHRONICLE

WHEREAS it is expedient that a revenue should be raised, in your Majesty's dominions in America, for making a more certain and adequate provision for defraying the charge of the administration of justice, and the support of civil government, in such provinces where it shall be found necessary ; and towards further defraying the expenses of defending, protecting, and securing the said dominions ; We, your Majesty's most dutiful and loyal subjects, the commons of Great-Britain, in parliament assembled, have therefore resolved to give and grant unto your Majesty the several rates and duties herein after-mentioned ; and do most humbly beseech your Majesty that it may be enacted, and be it enacted by the King's most excellent Majesty, by and with the advice and consent of the lords spiritual and temporal, and commons, in this present parliament assembled, and by the authority of the same, that from and after the twentieth day of November, one thousand seven hundred and sixty seven, there shall be raised, levied, collected and paid unto his majesty, his heirs, and successors, for and upon the respective goods herein after mentioned, which shall be imported from Great-Britain into any colony or plantation in America, which now is, or hereafter may be under the dominion of his Majesty, his heirs or successors, the several rates or duties following ; that is to say [...]

Extract of another Letter from London, dated August 7, 1767.

"A late Attempt to coalesce the different Parties in a new Ministry, has proved ineffectual—and it seems probably, that the present Set will continue some Time longer—This seems not unfortunate for America, as some of them who were proposed to come in, were professed Adversaries of America—The prevailing Distinction of Parties here, is, those who in the two last Sessions of Parl—t, have been disposed to favour America, are called, by their Opponents, (by Way of Reproach) AMERICANS ! while the Adherents to G----le and Is-------d, boast of their being true to the Interest of Britain, and zealous for maintaining its Sovereignty over the Colonies—This Declaration seems every Day to be more and more fixt ; and it is much to be feared will be carried higher, in the next Session of Parliament, for the political Purposes of influencing the ensuing Election—It is already said, that the Act for Quartering the Soldiers at New-York, without taking Notice of its being done in Obedience to the Act of Parliament, is evasive and unsatisfactory ; that it is high Time to put the Right of taxing America out of Dispute, by an Act of Taxation, effectually carried into Execution, &c. &c.

Extract of another Letter from London, dated August 6, 1767.

"The general Affairs of America here, bear a very disagreeable Aspect ; the present Ministry are like to continue some Time longer—some particular Changes will happen, and I fear the principal Structure will not be of long Duration, but probably there will be another Session of Parliament before a considerable Alteration is made.---The opposition to America seems to increase. Every Step is taking to render the Taxation of the colonies a popular Measure, and it is contended that they should be obliged explicitly to acknowledge that Right. I know not what to advise on that Occasion, but that the Friends of America, on both Sides the Water, should exert their utmost Endeavours to lessen the present Unpopularity of the American Cause ; conciliate the Affections of the People here towards you, increase by all possible Means the Number of your Friends, and be careful not to weaken their Hands, and strengthen those of your Enemies, by rash Proceedings, the Mischiefs of which are inconceivable."

To the PUBLIC.

ON the first appearance of the Boston Chronicle, we should think ourselves worthy of the great encouragement we have received, if we neglected to return thanks to our Subscribers in general whose number has far exceeded our most sanguine expectations; this, tho' an agreeable circumstance to us, is, not unattended with its cares; for as the list increased, we felt ourselves more and more sensible of the importance of our task, that, of endeavouring to entertain and engage the attention of such a number of gentlemen, as appeared to encourage our undertaking.——Gratitude for this encouragement calls for our utmost industry.

We have already mentioned, that, we considered the plan pointed out to us by our friends with diffidence: We therefore hope that our readers will be candid, and not expect to see it fully executed either in one or a few papers: As the winter already set in, will deprive us, for some time, of the benefit of our British and foreign intelligence.

In this situation, we will endeavour, by a variety of entertaining and instructive pieces to please our Subscribers: and we will be glad if we succeed sometimes in making them laugh, when we have little to interest them.

It is with pleasure we inform the public, that several gentlemen of distinguished abilities have promised us their assistance.

We should esteem it a very great favour, if gentlemen of experience and knowledge (of whom we know there are many in this country) would lay before the public, their experiments and discoveries, as well in Husbandry, as in the other arts and Sciences, by the channel of our paper: such a correspondence would be a benefit to the whole——The societies at home, to which are owing the late great improvements in the Arts, have been mostly established by a few public spirited men:—Great improvements generally arise from small beginnings and repeated efforts.—Here probably a few pieces in a news-paper, might be the foundation of a lasting advantage to the country.

As some of our Subscribers have intimated their hopes that the Chronicle will not be filled up with advertisements, we shall explain ourselves upon that head: we do not intend to exclude advertisements; yet we promise our customers, that no one paper shall contain more of them than can be included into two pages.

We beg to be excused for having taken up so much of the paper about our own affairs, as we consider every thing of the kind an encroachment on the property of our Subscribers; we however hope to be pardoned from our motive. Gratitude impelled us to speak, as Silence might have been construed into Negligence.

LETTERS

From a Farmer in Pennsylvania, to the inhabitants of the British colonies.

By JOHN DICKINSON, Esq;

LETTER I.

Beloved Countrymen,

I am a farmer, settled after a variety of fortunes, near the banks, of the river Delaware, in the province of Pennsylvania. I received a liberal education, and have been engaged in the busy scenes of life: But am now convinced, that a man may be as happy without bustle, as with it. My farm is small, my servants are few, and good; I have a little money at interest; I wish for no more; my employment in my own affairs is easy; and and with a contented grateful mind, I am compleating the number of days allotted to me by divine goodness.

Being master of my time, I spend a good deal of it in a library, which I think the most valuable part of my small estate, being acquainted with two or three gentlemen of abilities and learning, who honour me with their friendship, I believe I have acquired a greater share of knowledge in history, and the laws and constitution of my country, than is generally attained by men of my class, many of them not being so fortunate as I have been in the opportunities of getting information.

From infancy I was taught to love humanity and liberty. Inquiry and experience have since confirmed my reverence for the lessons then given me, by convincing me more fully of their truth and excellence. Benevolence towards mankind excites wishes for their welfare, and such wishes endear the means of fulfiling them. Those can be found in liberty alone, and therefore her sacred cause ought to be espoused by every man, on every occasion, to the utmost of his power: as a charitable but poor person does not withold his mite, because he cannot relieve all the distresses of the miserable, so let not any honest man suppress his sentiments concerning freedom, however small their influence is likely to be. Perhaps he may " † touch some wheel" that will have an effect greater than he expects.

These being my sentiments, I am encouraged to offer to you, my countrymen, my thoughts on some late transactions, that in my opinion are of the utmost importance to you. Conscious of my defects, I have waited some time, in expectation of seeing the subject treated

† Pope.

by persons much better qualified for the task; but being therein disappointed, and apprehensive that longer delays will be injurious, I venture at length to request the attention of the public, praying only for one thing,—that is, that these lines may be read with the same zeal for the happiness of British America, with which they were wrote.

With a good deal of surprise I have observed, that little notice has been taken of any act of Parliament as injurious in its principle to the liberties of these colonies, as the stamp-act was: I mean the act for suspending the legislation of New-York.

The assembly of that government complied with a former act of parliament, requiring certain provisions to be made for the troops in America, in every particular, I think, except the articles of salt, pepper, and vinegar. In my opinion they acted imprudently, considering all circumstances, in not complying so far, as would have given satisfaction, as several colonies did: but my dislike of their conduct in that instance, has not blinded me so much, that I cannot plainly perceive, that they have been punished in a manner pernicious to American freedom, and justly alarming to all the colonies.

If the British parliament has a legal authority to order, that we shall furnish a single article for the troops here, and to compel obedience to that order; they have the same right to order us to supply those troops with arms, cloaths, and every necessary, and to compel obedience to that order also; in short, to lay any burdens they please upon us. What is this but taxing us at a certain sum, and leaving to us only the manner of raising it? How is this mode more tolerable than the stamp-act? Would that act have appeared more pleasing to Americans, if being ordered thereby to raise the sum total of the taxes, the mighty privilege had been left to them, of saying how much should be paid for an instrument of writing on paper, and how much for another on parchment.

An act of parliament commanding us to do a certain thing, if it has any validity, is a tax upon us for the expence that accrues in complying with it, and for this reason, I believe, every colony on the continent, that chose to give a mark of respect for Great-Britain, in complying with the act relating to the troops, cautiously avoid the mention of that act, least their conduct should be attributed to its supposed obligation.

ed of the privileges of making laws, only for insisting on that exclusive privilege of taxation. If they may be legally deprived in such a case of the privilege of making laws, why may they not, with equal reason, be deprived of every other privilege? Or why may not every colony be treated in the same manner, when any of them shall dare to deny their assent to any impositions that shall be directed? Or what signifies the repeal of the stamp-act, if these colonies are to lose their other privileges, by not tamely surrendering that of taxation?

There is one consideration arising from this suspicion, which is not generally attended to, but shews it's importance very clearly. It was not necessary that this suspension should be caused by an act of parliament. The crown might have restrained the Governor of New-York, even from calling the assembly together, by its prerogative in the royal governments.—This step, I suppose, would have been taken, if the conduct of the assembly of New-York, had been regarded as an act of disobedience to the crown alone: but it is regarded as an act of "disobedience "to the authority of the British legisla-"ture." This gives the suspension a consequence vastly more affecting. It is a parliamentary assertion of the supreme authority of the British legislature over these colonies in the part of taxation: and is intended to compel New-York unto a submission to that authority. It seems therefore to me as much a violation of the liberty of the people of that province, and consequently of all these colonies, as if the parliament had sent a number of regiments to be quartered upon them till they should comply. For it is evident, that the suspension is meant as compulsion; and the method of compelling is totally indifferent. Is is indeed probable, that the sight of red coats, and the beating of drums would have been most alarming, because people are generally more influenced by their eyes and ears than by their reason: But whoever seriously considers the matter, must perceive, that a dreadful stroke is aimed at

three shillings and four pence, was tried all the people of England, with anxious expectation, interested themselves in the important decision; and when the slightest point touching the freedom of a single colony is agitated, I earnestly wish, that all the rest may with equal ardour support their sister. Very much may be said on this subject, but I hope, more at present is unnecessary

With concern I have observed that two assemblies of this province have sat and adjourned without taking any notice of this act. It may perhaps be asked, what would have been proper for them to do? I am by no means fond of inflammatory measures. I detest them.——I should be sorry that any thing should be done which might justly displease our sovereign or our mother-country. But a firm, modest exertion of a free spirit, should never be wanting on public occasions. It appears to me, that it would have been sufficient for the assembly, to have ordered our agents to represent to the King's ministers, their sense of the suspending act, and and to pray for its repeal. Thus we should have borne our testimony against it; and might therefore reasonably expect that on a like occasion, we might receive the same assistance from the other colonies.

"*Concordia res parvæ crescunt.*
Small things grow great by concord.
A FARMER.

Lord BALTIMORE's *remarks on the city of* CONSTANTINOPLE *late as*

" I

ous as we
more cor
mic feve

" Con
one of th
is said to
thousand
ler of i
would adn
equal ground; and the streets are consequently the same; they are paved

ty, very cheap, and proceeds from its being Grand Vizir himself, th the Empire after the gr who certainly is the first in eminence and power, different parts of the c and shops, which he doe month or oftner; at followed, at a distance whom he precedes, dre man, enquires into the and examines their value bad, over-rated, or defic measure, then he assume calls to his attendants, mediately the offenders seldom with death.

" There are few Phy pothecaries, and no Sur inhabitants therefore, little of the horrid misc by a certain disease we great cities.

" The religion, laws, the Turks are, as much them, in direct oppositio eat, write, sleep, and sit their dead they carry ou foremost, their cloaths short; they have many wi es allowed by law, we have few wh—s, we a r believe in One God, we they believe in predestina our potentates send amb other, the grand Signio they say on this head, t

parliament may lawfully deprive New-

The houses are built of wood and plaister

in opposition to our fash

* An order of the Turkish infantr Signior's guard, and the main strength

NONIMPORTATION AND NONCONSUMPTION

By Todd Andrlik

IN FEBRUARY 1768, AFTER PETITIONING KING GEORGE III for a repeal of the Townshend Acts, the Massachusetts House of Representatives delivered to the other colonial legislatures a circular letter, drafted by Boston politicians Samuel Adams and James Otis, Jr. The letter, as published in the March 21, 1768, *Boston Chronicle*, encouraged harmony among the colonies and provided plenty of fodder for the other assemblies to draft their own petitions.

Boycotts of British goods were a double-edged sword. They unified all walks of life—men, women, young, old, wealthy, poor—but began driving a wedge between Patriots and Loyalists.

Furious from Massachusetts's attempt to ignite a multi-colony response, Lord Hillsborough, British secretary of state for the American colonies, demanded that the body rescind the letter. In June, the House voted 92 to 17 not to rescind (see July 14, 1768, *Pennsylvania Gazette*). As a result

of their disobedience to the Crown, Massachusetts's Royal Governor Francis Bernard dissolved the colonial assembly. Now with the New York and Massachusetts assemblies dissolved, the struggle for power intensified as royal executive orders were extinguishing the colonies' long-standing government by the people. Invoking the Magna Carta and Petition of Right, early English freedom documents, Americans focused their Townshend arguments on constitutional rights, liberties, and privileges.

Boycotts of British goods helped overturn the Stamp Act a couple years earlier, so mercantile abstinence was seen as a proven counterpunch to the Townshend Acts. After the unsuccessful petitions for relief, nonimportation and nonconsumption agreements were formed across the colonies and were supported, sometimes reluctantly, by various public, merchant, or mechanic organizations (see July 10, 1769, *Boston Gazette*).

American manufacturing was encouraged to help starve English merchants and simultaneously free colonists of their financial chains to the mother country by allowing them to pay off their debts to London shopkeepers and agents. New paper mills were built to supply the colonial printing industry, which was growing and gaining importance as tensions worsened. Lamb was eaten less for the purpose of increasing reserves of sheep's wool, which Daughters of Liberty used during meetings to spin hundreds of skeins of yarn at a time (see May 21, 1770, *Boston Gazette*).

The boycotts, however, were a double-edged sword. They unified all walks of life—men, women, young, old, wealthy, poor—but began driving a wedge between Patriots and Loyalists (see letter by "The Sons of Liberty" to Nathaniel Rogers, followed by "A LIST of the Names of those who AUDACIOUSLY continue to counteract the UNITED SENTIMENTS of the Body of Merchants thro'out NORTH-AMERICA; by importing British Goods contrary to the Agreement" in the May 21, 1770, *Boston Gazette*). While the strict nonimportation and nonconsumption agreements were violated by those loyal to the crown, they were also sometimes difficult to obey for wealthy Patriots, who were accustomed to the luxuries of London and made their riches by smuggling.

Loyalist printer John Mein published in his *Boston Chronicle* the names of patriotic gentlemen who broke the agreements, alleging Patriot merchant John Hancock, one of the richest men in Boston, was among the greatest offenders. Mein soon found himself in a dangerous confrontation, as described in the November 6, 1769, *New-York Gazette; or, Weekly Post-Boy*:

Last Saturday afternoon, as Mr. John Mein, publisher of the Boston Chronicle, was returning from his shop in King-street, some gentlemen then upon Change, who thought themselves ill-treated in a late publication of his, took occasion to 'catechise' him; upon which, after a few words had passed between them, he drew a pistol out of his pocket, and threatened to fire if they did not stand off; but that was so far from intimidating them, that they followed up in order to seize him…

Tensions escalated between Loyalists and Patriots, and with British troops occupying Boston since October 1768, incidents soon became more tragic.

JOHN HANCOCK, BY JOHN SINGLETON COPLEY, 1765
Museum of Fine Arts, Boston (current location)

(*left*) Patriot John Hancock was a prominent merchant and one of the wealthiest men in Boston. Loyalist printer John Mein accused Hancock of violating the boycott of British goods.

DAUGHTER OF LIBERTY
North Wind Picture Archives

(*opposite page*) Patriotic American woman spinning to avoid importing British cloth.

BOSTON CHRONICLE
March 21, 1768

Circulated to the other colonies, this letter by the Massachusetts House of Representatives served as the template for the other colonial assemblies to draft their own petitions for repeal of the Townshend Acts.

oe they found in the vessel—
Antigua, distant 7 leagues.
apt. David Young of the ship

ry material transaction that
e, I connot help acquainting
affair that passed here a few
s it may be a means of pre-
ny who trade here, from be-
ey to the villany and cowar-
of our public officers. The
an English vessel now in this
ing a file of soldiers carrying
to the fort, begged he might
erty of seeing who they were
ht know whether any of his
mong them. The corporal,
ery insolently, took him to
here the Com—d—nt treated
extreme ill language, and
him with corporal punish-
captain, not used to such
told him he was an officer as
self, and dared him or his
him with any violence. The
immediately ordered him out
telling him, at the same time,
ld see him in the morning.
ish captain, not doubting but,
—d—nt bore a commission, he
ive him a gentleman's satis
being altogether ignorant
ous character his antagonist
s being recorded a liar, went
d next morning coming on
is sword on, met the Com—
im aside, and, told him he
wait upon him wherever he
per: that he was a gentle-
ad been ill treated by him.
Com—d—nt replied, that he
im satisfaction, and turning
ed up to some gentlemen
anding at Mr. Dickson's ta-
bauled out, "Sir you have
d me, and I will complain to
nor." In this he was as good
, and aggravated his com-

prove the contrary, by which means he
has recorded himself a coward. I hope
this will be a caution to all gentlemen
... so great a
the first of-
himself a
,) *Dec.* 22.
hath been
e Commons
rd to Mr.
ville parish,
for making public his invention of a machine for beating rice, which with six ordinary horses, will, in one season, beat out
six hundred barrels of rice.

New York, March 4. Wednesday March
second, arrived here Capt. Finglass from
South-Carolina, in eight days passage,
who informs us that Capt. Farrell arrived there the 13th. of February, after a
disagreable passage of 27 days; who on
29th. of January off Cape Hatteras, was
struck by a violent flash of lightening,
which carried away his main topmast,
and the head of his main-mast: But on
the 12th. of Febuary being the day before he arrived, being at anchor off Carolina, in weighing his anchor at seven
o'clock in the morning, he had the most
melancoly sight and accident that ever
he saw, which was his mate John Stud-
don, killed dead on the spot, without e-
ver making the least motion of life; It
happened by the stop of the windless giving way, and the hand-spike took him
under his right ear.

Providence, February 17. By Captain
Joseph Tilling, from the West-Indies we
are advised that Captain Pray, of this port,
who sailed from hence just before the
storm which happened on the 15th of
December last, is arrived at St Eustatia:
he had been but 14 hours from this Harbour, when, about noon, the wind met
him at S. E. which increased to a violent
storm, and lasted till midnight, without
the least intermission: then suddenly shift-
ing to W. S. W. blew a more terrible
Hurricane than perhaps has been known
in these parts for many years, which obliged him to throw over a number of
horses, cattle and sheep, with a quantity
of hay, stove the water on deck, and broke
his boom. The extreme severity of the
weather added greatly to his distress, most

a wet season, and no rational account
given how it could happen by any accident.—In the large barn, (which was 100
feet in length, and of proportionable
breadth, well finish'd) there were con-
sum'd nineteen head of neat cattle, and
some swine, the flames having prevail'd
so far, before the fire was discover'd that
there was no possibility of saving the cattle, so much as their hides after they were
dead, in the other barn some young cattle
and sheep were saved—the loss is great
to the public, as many milch cows and
calfs were destroy'd, besides other useful
stock. How much the loss is to the owner we are not able at present to say—
we wou'd only observe, that such flagrant
wickedness is most amazing and alarming,
as it threatens the destruction of the place
where is exists: for in such cases no man's
person nor property is safe; and every
one would chuse to fly from such a place
as fast as from one infected with the most
malignant contagion, 15 load of hay
was also burnt.

BOSTON.

*Copy of a letter written by the Hon. the House
of Representatives, in the last Session of
the General Assembly, and sent to the respective Assemblies on the continent.*

Province of the Massachusetts-Bay, *Feb 11.*
*To the Honourable the Speaker of the Honour-
able House of Representatives of the province of*

S I R,

THE House of Representatives of this
Province, have taken into their serious consideration, the great difficulties
that must accrue to themselves and their
constituents, by the operation of the several acts of parliament imposing duties
and taxes on the American colonies.

As it is a subject in which every colony
is deeply interested, they have no reason
to doubt but your assembly is duly impress'd with its importance; and that such
constitutional measures will be come into,
as are proper. It seems to be necessary,
that all possible care should be taken that
the representations of the several assemblies, upon so delicate a point, should
harmonize with each other: The House
therefore hope that this letter will be
candidly considered in no other light
than as expressing a disposition freely to
communicate their mind to a sister colony, upon a common concern, in the same

cannot over-leap the bounds of it, without destroying its own foundation : That the constitution ascertains and limits both sovereignty and allegiance ; and therefore his Majesty's American subjects who acknowledge themselves bound by the ties of allegiance, have an equitable claim to the full enjoyment of the fundamental rules of the British constitution : That it is an essential unalterable right in nature, ingrafted into the British constitution, as a fundamental law, and ever held sacred and irrevocable by the subjects within the realm, that what a man hath honestly acquired, is absolutely his own, which he may freely give, but cannot be taken from him without his consent : That the American subjects may therefore, exclusive of any consideration of charter rights, with a decent firmness adapted to the character of free men and subjects assert this natural constitutional right.

It is moreover their humble opinion, which they express with the greatest deference to the wisdom of the parliament ; that the acts made there, imposing duties on the people of this province, with the sole and express purpose of raising a revenue, are infringements of their natural and constitutional rights ; because, as they are not represented in the British parliament, his Majesty's commons in Britain, by those acts, grant their property without their consent.

This House further are of opinion, that their constituents, considering their local circumstances, cannot by any possibility, be represented in the parliament ; and that it will for ever be impracticable that they should equally be represented there, and consequently not at all ; being seperated by an ocean of a thousand leagues : that his Majesty's royal predecessors, for this reason, were graciously pleased to from a subordinate legislative here, that their subjects might enjoy the unalienable right of a representation. And that considering the utter impracticability of their being fully and equally represented in parliament, and the great expence that must unavoidably attend even a partial representation there, this house think that a taxation of their constituents, even without their consent, grievous as it is, would be preferable to any representation that could be admitted for them there.

Upon these principles, and also consi-

They have also submitted it to consideration, whether any people can be said to enjoy any degree of freedom, if the crown, in addition to its undoubted authority, of constituting a governor, should also appoint him such a stipend as it shall judge proper, without the consent of the people, and at their expence : and whether, while the judges of the land, and other civil officers, hold not their commissions during good behaviour, their having salaries appointed for them by the crown, independent of the people, hath not a tendency to subvert the principles of equity, and endanger the happiness and security of the subjects.

In addition to these measures, the house have wrote a letter to their agent Mr. DeBerdt, the sentiments of which he is directed to lay before the ministry ; wherein they take notice of the hardship of the act for preventing mutiny and desertion, which requires the governor and council to provide enumerated articles for the King's marching troops, and the people to pay the expence : and also of the commission of the gentlemen appointed commissioners of the customs to reside in America, which authorises them to make as many appointments as they think fit, and to pay the appointees what sums they please, for whose malconduct they are not accountable—From whence it may happen that officers of the crown may be multiplied to such a degree, as to become dangerous to the liberty of the people, by virtue of a commission which doth not appear to this house to derive any such advantages to trade, as many have been led to expect.

These are the sentiments and proceedings of this house ; and as they have too much reason to believe that the enemies of the colonies have represented them to his Majesty's ministers and parliament, as factious, disloyal, and having a disposition to make themselves independant of the mother country, they have taken occasion, in the most humble terms, to assure his Majesty, and his ministers, that with regard to the people of this province, and as they doubt not of all the colonies, the charge is unjust.

The house is fully satisfied that your assembly is too generous and enlarged in sentiment, to believe, that this letter proceeds from an ambition of taking the

The PENNSYLVANIA GAZET

Containing the Freſheſt Ad-   vices, Foreign

MERCY   JUSTICE

To the PRINTERS of the PENNSYLVANIA GAZETTE.
Lancaſter, June 28, 1768.

As the following Remarks on a Propoſition of one Woods, publiſhed in the Chronicle of the 20th of June, for diſcovering the Longitude of a Ship at Sea, may be ſerviceable to the Public, ſo your giving them a Place in your Paper, may be acceptable to your Readers.

I APPREHEND the Gentleman is greatly miſtaken, in his Notion of others attempting to meaſure the exact Space of a ſolar Day, a Thing never propoſed by any that I ever underſtood: But what Harriſon and all others mean by a Time Piece, is ſuch an one as will meaſure true Time, which is the Quantity of Time any one Point, on the terraqueous Globe, takes up in revolving round from any one Point in the celeſtial Globe, until it interſect the ſame again, which is equal to the Sun's mean Motion; and as the Sun's Equation is known, conſequently a Machine to meaſure the mean Motion, will be far preferable to any other Method yet propoſed; and were not Harriſon's Machines upon that erroneous Principle of Springs, they would undoubtedly anſwer the Intention, which he ſays were finiſhed about Chriſtmas 1765; in which he is likewiſe miſtaken, for his Father made three, and I ſaw them in Motion about 18 Years ſince; but as to finiſhing, neither the Father, or his Son, will be ever able to perform that Part, though they are a curious Performance.------And as to the Gentleman's Method of meaſuring Time, it may anſwer for one Revolution of the Earth; but as the Glaſs muſt contain a large Quantity of Sand, at leaſt three or four Pounds, let the Obſerver be ever ſo careful, the Glaſs cannot be turned without a conſiderable Loſs of Time, for the Sand muſt all run out before it is turned, and veral Minutes in Time.------He concludes, and ſays, " Thus the main Point of Navigation may be determined, without any Regard to ſolar Time." And above he ſays, " and a good Watch, or Spring Clock, will ſhew the Time between, &c."------So it is obvious, his Works are full of Errors, and his Writing Contradiction, and the Sea-faring Gentlemen left to their Log Line and Lead as before.   C. S.

unhappy Diviſions and Diſtractions which have operated ſo prejudicially to Great-Britain and the Colonies.-----After what paſſed in the former Part of the Seſſions, and after the declared Senſe of ſo large a Majority when the Houſe was full-----His Majeſty cannot but conſider this as a very unfair Proceeding, and the Reſolutions taken thereupon to be contrary to the real Senſe of the Aſſembly, and procured by Surpriſe; and therefore it is the King's Pleaſure, that ſo ſoon as the General Court is again aſſembled at the Time preſcribed by the Charter, you ſhould require of the Houſe of Repreſentatives, in His Majeſty's Name, to to Reſcind the Reſolution that gave Birth to the Circular Letter from the Speaker, and to declare their Diſapprobation of, and Diſſent to that raſh and haſty Proceeding.

" His Majeſty has the fulleſt Reliance on the Affections of His good Subjects in the Maſſachuſetts-Bay, and has obſerved with Satisfaction that Spirit of Decency, and Love of Order, which has diſcovered itſelf in the Conduct of the moſt conſiderable of its Inhabitants, and therefore His Majeſty has the better Ground to hope, that the Attempt made by a deſperate Faction to diſturb the public Tranquility, will be diſcountenanced, and that the Execution of the Meaſure recommended to you, will not meet with any Difficulty."-----

The Houſe by Meſſage deſired the Governor to ſend them the Remainder of the above Letter, alſo another Letter from his Lordſhip, which had been communicated to his Majeſty's Council, and Copies of ſuch Letters as his Excellency had wrote on the Subject contained in his Meſſage, with the King's Inſtruction to him on this Matter.

In Conſequence of which Meſſage his Excellency the Governor ſent the following Anſwer, viz.

Gentlemen of the Houſe of Repreſentatives,

I ſhould have communicated to you the whole of the [Hil]lſborough's Letter relating to the Buſineſs which [you] on the 21ſt Inſtant, if I had not been deſirous [com]pliance with his Majeſty's Requiſition might have [...] by its appearing to be entirely dictated by a Senſe [...] but ſince you deſire to know what my further [...] herewith ſend you a Copy of the Part of the Let[ter] this Buſineſs, which contains all my Inſtructions [...] as I know you will not expect that I ſhould diſ[...]'s poſitive Commands, I muſt deſire, that if you [...] oblige me to execute them, you will, previouſly [...] your final Anſwer, prevent the Inconvenience that [...] the People for want of the annual Tax-Bill, [...] derſtand is not yet ſent up to the Board.----If I am obliged to Diſſolve the General Court, I ſhall not think myſelf at Liberty to call another, till I ſhall receive his Majeſty's Commands for that Purpoſe, which will be too late to prevent the Treaſurer iſſuing his Warrant for the whole Tax granted by the Act of the laſt Year.

As to the Letter of the Earl of Hillſborough which I communicated to the Council, I may beg Leave to be the proper

B Y virtue of a writ, [...] 3d day of Auguſt ne[xt] will be ſold by vendue, a c[...] or parcel of land thereun[...] acres, more or leſs, ſituate of Cheſter, bounded by la[...] Wilſon, John M'Konkey, Cunningham, deceaſed, ſei[...]
July 9, 1768.

B Y virtue of two writs [...] Saturday, the 6th da[...] Matthias Kerlin's tavern, i[...] vendue, the following piec[...] ſhip, to wit, a meſſuage, an[...] to the ſouth by the river De[...] and extending back 565 fee[...] of the ſtreet, as laid out b[...] with land of Thomas How[...] lands of the widow Howell, [...] from the river to the King's [...] piece or parcel of land, in [...] bounded by lands of Johann[...] mas Howell, deceaſed, and [...] containing 20 acres and 60 [...] liam Clayton, junior, Jere[...] laid out to Marcus Hook [...] Howell, deceaſed, ſeized in [...]
July 9, 1768.

B Y virtue of a writ, t[o...] day of Auguſt next, [...] be ſold by vendue, a certain [...] the name of the Blue-ball [...] 20 years paſt, where Thom[...] with a good orchard, barn, a[...] land thereunto belonging, b[...] ther road leading to Marcus [...] land, lying near the aforeſai[...] ſquare perches; late the eſta[...] in execution, and to be ſold [...]
July 9, 1768.

W HEREAS Iſaac [...] Roxborough, and [...] having abſconded from his [...] perſonal Eſtate of him in [...] to ſatisfy his Creditors, [...] Court of Common Pleas [...] ſaid Court did appoint us [...] make Diſtribution of th[...] Creditors: We do herel[...]

A MESSAGE from the GOVERNOR to the ASSEMBLY.

Gentlemen of the House of Representatives,

I CANNOT consistently with my Sense of my Duty, prorogue or adjourn the General Court, until I have received your Answer to his Majesty's Requisition. I must therefore repeat my Request to you to bring this Matter to a Conclusion.

Council-Chamber, June 29, 1768.

F. BERNARD.

On Thursday, the 30th of June, the Committee reported a Letter to the Right Honourable the Earl of Hillsborough, setting forth to his Lordship, the several Votes and Resolutions which passed in the last House of Representatives, relating to the Circular Letter; and showing that the whole of these Matters were transacted in the Height of the Session, in a full House, and by a large Majority. This Letter was distinctly read several Times; and afterwards accepted by a Majority of Ninety-three out of One Hundred and five Members present, and a fair Copy was ordered to be taken for the Speaker to sign and transmit to his Lordship as soon as might be. Then it was moved that the Question be put, whether the House will rescind the Resolution of the last House, which gave Birth to their circular Letter to the several Houses of Representatives and Burgesses of the other Colonies on the Continent? and passed in the Negative, by a Division of Ninety-two to Seventeen.

Hereupon the Committee reported an Answer to the Governor's Messages of the 21st and 24th of June, which was accepted by a large Majority, and is as follows.

A MESSAGE from the ASSEMBLY to the GOVERNOR, June 30, 1768.

May it please your Excellency,

THE House of Representatives of this His Majesty's antient and loyal Province of the Massachusetts-Bay, have, with the greatest deliberation, considered your Messages of the 21st and 24th instant, with the several extracts from the letter of the Right Hon. the Earl of Hillsborough, His Majesty's principal Secretary of State for North-American affairs, dated the 22d of April last, which your Excellency has thought fit to communicate. We have also received the written answer which your Excellency was pleased to give the Committee of this House directed to wait on you the 29th inst. with a message, humbly requesting a recess, that the Members might be favoured with an opportunity to consult their constituents at this important crisis, when a direct and peremptory requisition is made of a new and strange construction, and so strenuously urged, viz. That we should immediately rescind the Resolution of the last House, to transmit circular letters to the other British Colonies on the continent of North-America, barely intimating a desire that they would join in similar dutiful and loyal petitions to our most gracious Sovereign, for the redress of the grievances occasioned by sundry late Acts of Parliament, calculated for the sole purpose of raising a revenue in America. We have most diligently revised, not only the said resolution, but also the circular letter, written and sent in consequence thereof; and after all, they both appear to us, to be conceived in terms not only prudent and moderate in themselves, but respectful to the authority of that truly august body the Parliament of Great-Britain, and very dutiful and loyal in regard to His Majesty's sacred person, crown and dignity; of all which we entertain sentiments of the highest reverence and most ardent affection; and should we ever depart from these sentiments, we must stand self-condemned, as unworthy the name of British subjects, descended from British ancestors, intimately allied and connected in interests and inclination with our fellow subjects the commons of Great-Britain. We cannot but express our deep concern that a measure of the late House, in all respects so *innocent*, in most so virtuous and laudable, and as we conceive so truly patriotic, should have been represented to *Administration*, in the odious light of a party, and factious measure, and that pushed through by reverting in a thin House to, and reconsidering, what in a full Assembly had been rejected. It was, and is a matter of notoriety, that more than eighty Members were present at the re-consideration of the vote against the application to the other Colonies. The vote of reconsideration was obtained by a large majority. It is laudable, and as well known, that the prefer——

of the one, or the censure of the other.

On the whole, Sir, we will consider His most sacred Majesty under God, as our King, our best protector and common Father; and shall ever bear him true and faithful allegiance. We also regard your Excellency as the Representative of the greatest Potentate on earth, and at all times have, so far as could consist with the important purposes of preserving Life, Liberty and Property, been most ready and willing to treat you with all that respect justly due to your high rank and station. But we are constrained to say, that we are disagreeably convinced that your Excellency entertains not that parental regard for the welfare of the good people of this province, which you have sometimes been pleased to profess, and which they have at all times an irrefragible right to expect from their Governor. Your Excellency has thought fit not only to deny us a recess to consult our constituents, in regard to the present requisition, but hath assured us, in effect, that you shall take silence, at least a delay, not, as usual, for a consent, but a denial. You have also thought fit to inform us, that you cannot think yourself at liberty, in case of the Dissolution of this, to call another Assembly, without the express orders of His Majesty for that purpose: At the same time, your Excellency has been pleased to assure us, that you have communicated the whole of Lord Hillsborough's Letter, and your Instructions, so far as relate to the Requisition. In all this, however, we cannot find that your Excellency is more than directed to dissolve the present Assembly, in case of a non-compliance on the part of the House. If the Votes of the House are to be controuled by the direction of a Minister, we have left us but a vain semblance of Liberty. We know it to be the just prerogative of the Crown, at pleasure, to dissolve a Parliament: We are also sensible that, consistently with the great Charter of this Province, your Excellency, when you shall think fit, with or without the Intervention of a Minister, can dissolve the Great and General Court of this Colony, and that without the least Obligation to convene another within the Year. But should it ever grow into use, for any ill-disposed Governor of the Province, by means of a mistaken, or wilfully wrong state of facts, to procure orders for a Dissolution, that same Charter will be of no value.

We take this opportunity faithfully and firmly to represent to your Excellency, that the new Revenue Acts and Measures are not only disagreeable to, but in every view are deemed an insupportable burthen and grievance, with a very few exceptions, by all the Freeholders and other Inhabitants of this Jurisdiction: And we beg leave, once for all, to assure your Excellency, that those of this opinion are of no " *party or expiring faction.*" They have at all times been ready to devote their lives and fortunes to his Majesty's service. Of Loyalty, this Majority could as reasonably boast as any who may happen to enjoy your Excellency's smiles. Their Reputation, Rank, and Fortune, are at least equal to those, who may have been sometimes considered as the only friends to good Government; while some of the best blood of the colony, even in two Houses of Assembly, lawfully convened, and duly acting, have been openly charged with the unpardonable crime of " Oppugnation against the Royal Authority." We have now only to inform your Excellency, that this House have voted not to Rescind, as required, the Resolution of the last House; and that, on a Division on the Question, there were 92 Nays, and 17 Yeas. In all this we have been actuated by a conscientious, and finally, a clear and determined Sense of Duty to God, to our King, our Country, and to our latest Posterity: And we most ardently wish, and humbly pray, that in your future conduct your Excellency may be influenced by the same Principles.

[The Governor, after having received the last foregoing Message from the House, directed their Attendance in the Council, and then and there *adjourned* the Great and General Court to Wednesday, the Third Day of August next.]

Charles-Town, South-Carolina, June 6.

A calculation having been made of the value of the produce of this province, exported since the 1st of November last, and of what remains to be shipped by the same day in the present year, at the price the planter and manufac——

it at the Charles-T——

William Brow——
Peter Frye, E——
Dr. John Cale——
Jacob Fowle——
Richard Salton——
Israel Williams——
Mr. Jonathan ——
Mr. Jonathan A——
Capt. Joseph Ro——
John Ashley, E——
John Chadwick,——
Timothy Ruggle——
Chillingt. Foster,——
Jonathan Sayware——
Mr. William Jen——
Matt. Mayhew,——
Josiah Edson, Esq——

pealed to him
ose his friend-
manner said,
in Chester, a
cel of damn'd
nperious info-
truck at this
it is said he
e in Philadel-
linate a gen-
sooner out of
f the schooner
redoubled his
ithout offering
fti... my
ich, with an
strike me on
did not, that
edly. " You
ow dare you
Vith that they
for the mate,
e commander
ner. When
at they might
e put in irons,
e they thruft
ore he would
light, nor to
me to Halifax.
reats and me-
the protection
ce and info-
, he order-
on board my
his pardon.—
e ordered his
rd my boat,
ring this in-
ome nigh the
BEVAN.

he followed
to make up
scorn'd, and
each of the

Lisbon to his

delatory and
rious to the
that a small
vill take near
terally true.)
erchant that
his Influence
Effects of so

3.
er of Gentle-
d voluntarily
e Non-impor-
that Govern-
ed into by

Numbers of
ed at the Af-
e were warm

---

that Place, since the Troops were withdrawn, is really difficult to be described ; several poor Families are in a starving Condition, and many of the Inhabitants daily deserting the Town.

SALEM, July 4.

WHEREAS Information has been made to the Merchants and Traders of this Town, that sundry Persons belonging to Boston, have sent Quantities of English Goods in this Town for Sale, which were imported since the General Agreement of the Merchants (not to import such Goods) took Place :—— We therefore, the Merchants and Traders of the Town of Salem, at a Meeting at the King's Arms this 30th Day of June, Anno Domini 1769, do publickly DECLARE our Disapprobation thereof, and resolve, that we will do all in our Power to discourage the Sale of such Goods, by not purchasing any of them ourselves, or suffering any Person for or under us to purchase them. We think (in Justice to those Merchants and Traders who have strictly adhered to their Agreement) we ought to inform all Persons, that the Shop lately kept by Mr. John Gool, now 'tended by John Norris in this Town, is now owned and supplied by Merchants in Boston, who have taken the Advantage of others not sending for Goods, to import double the Quantity of Goods which they did at other Seasons, expecting to make their Fortunes, while others were sinking theirs for the Benefit of their Country. We hereby caution all Persons, who have the Interest of their Country at Heart, against purchasing Goods of any Persons who come from Boston and offer Goods to sale, such as Tea, Loaf-Sugar, Crates of Earthen Ware, &c. as we have great Reason to suspect, that those Goods are sent out of that Town, because of the Discouragements the Owners meet with in the Sale of them by the Friends of Liberty there. We also request the Town of Marblehead to join with their Neighbours (for the general Good) not to send for any more Goods, contrary to the Intent and Meaning of the Agreements entered into by the Inhabitants of the Town of Boston and other neighbouring Towns, which Request, if still refused, we must desire all who are real Friends to their Country, properly to take Notice of. We also request those Traders in this Town, who (it is well known) have deviated from their Contract, that they would (for the future) strictly adhere thereto ; for it is determined at this Meeting, that we will make publick the Names of all those who shall hereafter break through their Engagements by purchasing Goods of those who have not subscribed the Agreements, or by any other Way.

All GENTLEMEN of NOTE, in their respective Towns, are desired to caution their Families and Neighbours from purchasing at the abovementioned Shop, or of any traveling Traders who are sent out to sell Goods imported since the Agreements aforementioned.

BOSTON, July 10.

Thursday last Major Robert Rogers came to Town from New-York ; and set out the same Day for Portsmouth.

Early last Saturday Morning 4 Companies of the 64th Regiment embarked on board the Launceston, in Order to proceed to Halifax.

Same Afternoon the Body of a Man was taken up in Charles's River, suppos'd to be one Thomas Nolen, who was drowned last Tuesday Se'nnight.

CUSTOM-HOUSE, BOSTON.

ENTERED In

Brooks from New-Haven ; Davis from New-London ; Bates fr. Canso ; Childs, Murphy & Southerland fr. Virginia Arnold from Newfoundland ; Wier, Clift and Helpman from Quebec ; Smith from New-York ; Harman from Porto Rico ; Taylor from Figuira ; Somes from Turks-Island ; Waters from Hispaniola ; Andrews from St. Croix ; Hathom from St. Lucia ; White from Dominica and St. Eustatia.

Buried in the Town of Boston since our last,
Ten Whites. No Blacks.
Baptiz'd in the several Churches, Six.

The BOSTON GAZETTE

SALEM, *July 4.*

WHEREAS Information has been made to the Merchants and Traders of this Town, that sundry Persons belonging to Boston, have sent Quantities of English Goods in this Town for Sale, which were imported since the General Agreement of the Merchants (not to import such Goods) took Place :—We therefore, the Merchants and Traders of the Town of Salem, at a Meeting at the King's Arms this 30th Day of June, Anno Domini 1769, do publickly declare our Disapprobation thereof, and resolve, that we will do all in our power to discourage the Sale of such Goods, by not purchasing any of them ourselves, or suffering any Person for or under us to purchase them. We think (in Justice to those Merchants and Traders who have strictly adhered to their Agreement) we ought to inform all Persons, that the Shop lately kept by Mr. John Gool, now 'tended by John Norris in this Town, is now owned and supplied by Merchants in Boston, who have taken the Advantage of others not sending for Goods, to import double the Quantity of Goods which they did at other Seasons, expecting to make their Fortunes, while others were sinking theirs for the Benefit of their Country. We hereby caution all Persons, who have the Interest of their Country at Heart, against purchasing Goods of any Persons who come from Boston and offer Goods to sale, such as Tea, Loaf-Sugar, Crates of Earhten Ware, &c. as we have great Reason to suspect, that those Goods are sent out of that Town, because of the Discouragements the Owners meet with in the Sale of them by the Friends of Liberty there. We also request the Town of Marblehead to join with their Neighbours (for the general Good) not to send for any more Goods, contrary to the Intent and Meaning of the Agreements entered into by the inhabitants of the Town of Boston and other neighbouring Towns, which Request, if still refused, we must desire all who are real Friends to their Country, properly to take Notice of. We also request those Traders in this Town, who (it is well known) have deviated from their Contract, that they would (for the future) strictly adhere thereto ; for it is determined at this Meeting, that we will make publick the Names of all those who shall hereafter break through their Engagements by purchasing Goods of those who have not subscribed the Agreements, or by any other Way.

ALL GENTLEMEN of NOTE, in their respective Towns, are desired to caution their Families and Neighbours from purchasing at the abovementioned Shop, or of any traveling Traders who are sent out to sell Goods imported since the Agreements aforementioned.

BOSTON GAZETTE
July 10, 1769
—

BOSTON, May 21.

Laft Wednesday Forty five Daughters of Liberty, met in the Morning at the Houfe of the Rev. Mr. MOORHEAD in this Town; in the Afternoon they exceeded Fifty. By the Evening of faid Day they fpun 232 Skeins of Yarn, fome very fine, their Labour and Materials were all generoufly given the worthy Paftor.

Nothing appeared in their whole Conduct, but Love, Feftivity and Application. They were, by a great Majority, of his own Congregation; the reft of the Ladies belong'd to other Societies in the Town, who generoufly offer'd their Service. For all which, the Recipient is under great Obligations to the whole.

Their Entertainment, was wholly American Production, excepting a little Wine, &c. Many Ladies and Gentlemen were pleafed to vifit this agreeable Collection, and appear'd highly gratified. There are above 100 Spinners in Mr. Moorhead's Society; and confidering they are comparatively fmall, 'tis fuppos'd that no Congregation in the Province can produce fo great a Number, of the fame Number of Families.

The whole was concluded with many agreeable Tunes, Anthems and Liberty Songs, with great Judgment; fine Voices perform'd and animated on this Occafion, in all their feveral Parts, by a Number of the Sons of Liberty.

Let this ferve as a Specimen, to excite the numerous Fair in this Metropolis, and Country Towns, to exert their Parts in rendering this happy Climate oppulent and flourifhing.——*Quid Enim tentare nocebit?*

Thursday Morning the 29th Regiment quitted the Barracks at Caftle-Ifland, and landed at Dorchefter-Neck, from thence they began their March for Providence, where they arrived laft Saturday Noon, and immediately embarked on board the Tranfports then ready to proceed to the Jerfeys.

Capt. Jenkins and Capt. Hall, in Brigs, Capt. Jacobfon and Capt. Daverfon, in Ships, were to leave London foon after Capt. Symmes. Mr. Samuel Eliot, of this Town, Merchant, had taken his Paffage in Capt. Jacobfon.

A Letter from London, by Capt. Burnell, mentions, that it was tho't the Eaft-IndiaCompany would fettle the

[...] or three Hours.

Laft Saturday fail'd with a fair Wind for London, to the fad Mortification of all the Tories Male and Female, who have been ufing all the Tricks which the grand Cabal were capable of inventing to embarrafs and hinder her Voyage, the good Ship Lydia, Capt. Scott, laden in Part

JUST PUBLISHE[D]
And to be fold by RICHARD DR[...]
Second EDITION: With Addit[ions]

A Plan of Exercife for the [MILI]TIA of the Province of the *Maffachufetts*-B[ay] ed from the Plan of Difcipline, for the NORF[OLK]

Country Traders, Shopkeepers and others, are invited to the Auction[...] Queen-Street,

On *Wednefday* and *Thurfd[ay]* 23d and 24th Inftant,

At TEN o'Clock in the Morning, and [in] the Afternoon of each Day.

At which Times and Place will be Sold by P[...] a large and valuable Affortment of GO[ODS] *Among which are,*

Rich blue, white, green, crim[fon] mazarene, ftraw, cloth color'd, fcarlet and [...]ties—cloth color'd Grograms,—yellow, buf[f] green, drab, blue and cloth color'd Sattins [...] ftrings, black Padufoy, pink and cloth-co[lor'd] —Perfian Sarfnets,——Broad Cloths, Bea[ver] Ratteens, Frize, Shalloons and Tammies [...] Poplins, Dorfetteens, Fuftians, Jeans, Dim[ity] fets, Camblets, Mens and Womens cotto[n] worfted Hofe, Nankeens, Buckram, green [...] crimfon and fcarlet knit Waiftcoat and Bre[eches] Cotton Gowns, 3 4, 7 8 & yard wide Chec[k] Allopeen, a few Lawns, yellow Hollands [...] Gauze Handkerchiefs, Mens and Wome[ns] Mitts, kid and lamb ditto. A variety of [Rib]bons, filk Ferrets, Qualities, Capuchin S[...] nets, Blond Lace, white Wax Necklaces, [...] Hair, Womens & Childrens Stays, Cotton [...] white and yellow metal Coat and Breaft B[...] Head ditto, &c. &c. &c.

N. B. The Sale to begin on *Wednefday* at TEN o'Clock in the Morning, [and conti]nued till *Thurfday* Evening.

J. Ruffell,

TO BE SOLD, B[Y]

Joseph Peirce,

At his Shop the North Side of the T[own] [N]ew *Philadelphia* FLO[UR] [...]mens, fuperfine Broad Cloths, a Vari[ety] ALSO,

The Remains of Meffrs. COX and B[...] [wh]o are embarked for England, confifti[ng] [...]ver Lace, and Bindings, Gold & Silver B[...] *N. B.* The higheft Price given for old [...] Lace.

On WEDNESDAY next Forenoon, will be Sold by PUBLI[C] the Houfe of MILES GREENWOO[D] Part of BOSTON.

an exprefs avowal of it [...] We would not *willingly* [...] other fecretary of ftate eve[r] *commend* the alteration of [...] the province in one of its [...] dicates himfelf by faying, [...] of which was dictated to [...] "fignified by his——[...] alfo when the houfe charge [...] fitions to the miniftry *priv[ately]* denying it; but *alertly* anf[wer] ferred to muft be thofe whic[h] tranfmitted to his Majefty'[s] *Majefty's* commands fignif[ied] he fays "he is forry that h[e] fo much as *may have been e[...]* he receiv'd fuch command[...] people to give their teftimon[y] have been glad to have had [...] ed pains and penalties for a [...] cult to procure *voluntary* e[vidence] not execute the King's comm[ands] Certain it is however that *evidence of fome perfons*; an[d] poffibly believe that Gov. B[ernard] part he did, as he declares, i[f he] would be condemn'd, much *advis'd to fuch orders,* h[...] have been to the people [...] himfelf properly enough [...] cafe, the charges muft be [...] againft his——'s adminiftr[ation] *wrong*—This is a maxim al[l mi]nifters may, for which in for[...] to feel the vengeance of an in[...] to overthrow the conftitution [...] of another, is the higheft crim[e] bro't an haughty *Safford* to [...] Traitors will always plead *th[at]* *Great* therefore are accounta[ble] have given them orders to *opp[refs]* are made to atone for their cr[...] crept from the dunghill and [...] *their funfhine,* will retreat & r[...]

In confequence of this com[...] prefentatives, Bernard, it feem[s] *vernment,* tho' the Petition li[...] great city of London, is deer[...] fcandalous.

TO BE [SOLD] On THURSD[AY] By Benjamin [...]

At his ufual Pl[ace]

BROAD Cloths, Forreft [...] Stuffs, Irifh and Scotch H[...] Checks, Handkerchiefs, Mens [...] Sundry Articles of Houfhol[d] Chairs, Looking-Glaffes, Bed[s] Apparel, Watches, &c.

[...] Half Pipes of choice [...] [...] the Day of [...]

... presence.——

Lord H—— or any
Gov. Bernard to re-
lished constitution of
parts; tho' he vin-
of the acts, the doing
special commands
of state":——Thus
sending over depo-
, &c. he is far from
the depositions re-
y be *suppos'd to have*
in *obedience to his*
for that purpose";
done in that respect
m him", for " when
no power *to oblige*
no doubt he would
ower to have inflict-
" He found it diffi-
and therefore could
that punctuality &c."
rocure the voluntary
he whole one could
as ordered to act the
tional to suppose he
ish'd by those *who*
grievous they may
Province; for he
that in such a
od to be directed
he *King can do no*
lege; but his Mi-
s some were made
ople—An attempt
ow the expression
the State——This
nely death—Little
f the great—The
unishable, if they
eople; when *they*
vermin who have
themselves under
native obscurity.
the House of Re-
led from the go-
monstrance of the
me people, to be

D

ext.

urch,

Sale;

Camblets, figured
awns, Cambricks,
ats, Caps, &c. &c.
ure, as Tables,
dsteads, Wearing

WINE—Samples

---

bances had happened there; and that further distur-
chief has ordered, once more, ALL the king's ships in A-
merica before that town, as the likeliest means to awe
those SONS OF LIBERTY.

PHILADELPHIA, May 10.
Extract of a Letter from London, dated March 6.

" I have had many to visit me this Morning, asking
this Question, What will now be done? I answered, the
Ships in the North-America Trade must go there empty;
I pray the People may stand firm in the Agreement they
have entered into for another Year; and it is much wished by all, who are Friends to the Liberties of free born
Englishmen here, of whom there are a great Number in this
Kingdom.—— Lord North, I was informed, before I got
into the House of Commons, said to this Effect, That the
People of Boston, who began the Association, were going
on with their Importations from hence, nearly as before,
having broke their Faith with New-York and Philadelphia, who had been true to their Agreement; which, tho'
unwarrantable and illegal, yet their being true to their
Agreements did them Honour. How it will prove, I
do not pretend to say, but certain it is, that great Quantities of Goods are gone, and going to that Place.—— I hope
they have not been ordered by any that entered into the
Non-Importation Agreement, but by Governor Bernard's
Son, and those who joined in the Opposition; tho' his Father, Mein the Printer, and many others, say, that it is in
a great Degree general; but be it as it may, it has much
hurt the Cause of America, if not lost it, for the present
Year.

" I can assure you, from all I have observed, or can
learn, the most serious and sensible People in England, are
much and deeply impressed with a Sense of their and our
Situation; inasmuch as the Ministry, and such a one as
they think it is, can carry every Point they please in Parliament, without any Regard to the constitutional Rights
of the Subject. In short, unless this Nation gets engaged
in a War, or something turns up which we cannot foresee,
I have no Idea (nor have I heard one good Reason given
by any Body, to make me think) that the present Ministry,
or the Majority, which is the same Thing, will not hold
their Ground, and continue their Schemes of ministerial
Oppression, until their Measure is full.

On Sunday last the Rev. Mr. WHITEFIELD arrived
here from Georgia, in the Georgia Packet, Capt. Souder.
Monday Evening he preached at the New Presbyterian
Church, and again last Night at St. Paul's Church, to
very crowded Auditories.

NEW-YORK, May 14.

IT being publickly known here, that NATHANIEL
ROGERS, (one of the Boston Merchants, who has
all along refused to come into the Non-Importation
Agreement) was in Town, and it being suspected that his
Design in visiting this City, was to use his Endeavours to
prevail on the Merchants here, to break thro' and put an
End to their Agreement; his Effigy was exhibited (last
Thursday Evening) hanging on a Gallows, with Labels
on the Back and Breast of it, expressing his Crime. It
was attended by some Thousand Spectators, who after
parading through Part of the City, went from the Coffee-
House to his Lodgings, about 9 o'Clock, in order to pay
their Respects to himself, in which they were disappointed,
as he din'd out of Town and had not yet returned.——
They then proceeded through several of the principal

... Vessels from Bristol are coming out in Ballast.

TO BE SOLD,

A Quantity of good Indian Corn.
Inquire of the Printers.

A LIST of the Names of those
who AUDACIOUSLY continue to counteract the UNIT-
ED SENTIMENTS of the BODY of Merchants thro'out
NORTH-AMERICA; by importing British Goods
contrary to the Agreement.

JOHN GILLESPIE,
In Queen-Street, has imported a Quantity of Glass
contrary to the Agreement of the Merchants, and
refuses to reship them.

John Bernard,
(In King-Street, almost opposite Vernon's Head.

James McMasters,
(On Treat's Wharf.

Patrick McMasters,
(Opposite the Sign of the Lamb.

Nathaniel Rogers,
(Opposite Mr. Henderson Inches Store lower End
King-Street.

William Jackson,
At the Brazen Head, Cornhill, near the Town-House.

Theophilus Lillie,
(Near Mr. Pemberton's Meeting-House, North-End.

John Taylor,
(Nearly opposite the Heart and Crown in Cornhill.

Ame & Elizabeth Cummings,
(Opposite the Old Brick Meeting House, all of Boston.

Israel Williams, Esq; & Son,
(Traders in the Town of Hatfield.

And, Henry Barnes,
(Trader in the Town of Marlboro'.

IT must evidently appear either by Importing British
Goods contrary to the Agreement, or by breaking their
Contract with the Merchants, that they have prefered their
own little private Advantage to the Welfare of America: It is therefore highly proper that the Public should
know who they are, that have at this critical Time, sor-
didly detached themselves from the public Interest; and
as they will be deemed Enemies to their Country, by all
who are well-wishers to it; so those who afford them their
Countenance or give them their Custom, must expect to
be considered in the same disagreeable Light.

We are desired to insert the following.

IF Mr. *Lemuel Spear* of Braintree, and Mrs. *Mary*
Belcher living near the Fortification in Boston, will
desist from purchasing Goods of the *McMasters*, IM-
PORTERS, nothing *further* will be said of the Matter!
And Mrs. *Wingfield* and Mrs. *Curtis* are requested to desist from *visiting* the said *McMaster's* Shop, least it should
be taken for granted that their Visits are *for no other End*
but to purchase *unallowed Goods.* *A Hint to the Wise.*

NEW-YORK GAZETTE; OR, THE WEEKLY POST-BOY

November 6, 1769

—

Not long after alleging that John Hancock and other local Patriots were violating the nonimportation agreement, Boston Loyalist printer John Mein found himself in a dangerous confrontation. Shortly after the incident described here, in 1770, Hancock put Mein out of business. Just by coincidence, publishers in London asked Hancock to be their attorney in collecting debts from Mein. The Scottish printer had evidently bought books on credit to sell in Boston and hadn't paid the bill. Hancock thus got legal authority to seize Mein's property, which he did with undoubtable happiness. That took out the pro-Crown *Boston Chronicle*. Other Boston papers, including the *Post-Boy* and *News-Letter*, started receiving the Customs Office business again and became Crown mouthpieces.

Last Evening the following melancholy accident happened to Mr. Jonathan Lowder, Post Rider, between Boston and Hartford—an honest worthy man, extensively known and as generally respected. As he was riding through the town, his horse being touch'd by a Cart, took fright and threw his head against the wheel, which went over his shoulder and down his side. He was immediately carried into a house and surgeons sent for. He had his senses till they came, but died in about an hour. It was his birth day, being then 55 years of age.

Oct. 30. Tuesday last Mr. Robert Pierpoint, and several other inhabitants at the south part of the town, made complaint to a Magistrate, that they had been greatly abused, the preceding night, and that morning, by some of the guard at the Fortification; likewise that when the guards were relieved, on their march one of the soldiers took his firelock off his shoulder, and fired it; and had not another soldier with his bayonet knock'd up the muzzle, the bullet which was discharged would have gone among a number of Persons, that were very near standing at a blacksmith's shop, but providentially the bullet entered the upper part of the shop, and hurt no person.----These matters have since been examined by the magistrates, and some of the parties concerned, bound to appear at the next Court of Assize, to answer for their misdemeanors.

Last Saturday afternoon, as Mr. John Mein, publisher of the Boston Chronicle, was returning from his shop in King-street, some gentlemen then upon Change, who thought themselves ill-treated in a late publication of his, took occasion to " catechise" him; upon which, after a few words had passed between them, he drew a pistol out of his pocket, and threatened to fire if they did not stand off; but that was so far from intimidating them, that they followed up in order to seize him, and he apprehending some danger to himself from the resentment of the people, who began to collect together pretty fast, precipitately retreated to the main guard, which was near, with the pistol in his hand, where, as soon as he entered the door, he discharged it at random among those who closely followed him (tho' without doing any other damage than wounding the sleeve of the coat of a grenadier who was upon guard) and then immediately took shelter in the house under the protection of the military conservators of the peace :----Application was soon after made to Mr. Justice Dana, and a warrant issued for apprehending him, in order to answer for this atrocious offence; but tho' search was made in the Guard-house and other places, by the proper civil officers, to whom the warrant was committed, they have not yet been able to serve it upon him.

The large French ship, which put in here some time ago in distress, having been refitted, is sailed for France.

Saturday afternoon a person who lately belonged to the

Tuesday the 21st of November Instant, Circular Letters having been wrote to the respective Members, requiring their Attendance on that Day.

In order to amend the Breed of Sheep, if possible, we are assured, one Mr. Deshon, has imported into New-London, from Barbary, two RAMS, which are much larger, and finer Wool, than any of our American Sheep: One of those Rams is said to be of the true Turkey-Breed, the Tail of which alone generally weigh from 6 to 12 Pound weight, and are most delicious Mutton.----Any Person bringing a Ewe to propagate from the Broad Tail Ram, pay 1 s. 6 d. Lawful Money.

Last Friday Night about 9 o'Clock, a Fire broke out in the Sugar-House belonging to John Van Cortland, Esq; at the North-West Corner of Trinity Church-Yard; which having got to a Head when it was discovered, burnt with great Violence near an Hour, before it could be conquered :----But the Out Side being all of Stone, and the Night wet, the Fire was prevented from spreading, or doing any other Damage. Mr. Cortland's Loss is said to be very considerable.

Last Monday Night one Nicholas Lockerman, a Shoemaker by Trade, and a single Man, having been drinking at a Tavern near the Upper Barracks, kept by James Shaw, ---he left it about 10 o'Clock with an Intent to go home; but the next Morning was found lying at Shaw's Door speechless :---He was thereupon taken up and put into a Bed, but not recovering, he was carried next Day to the Poor-House, where he died, without being able to give any Account of himself.--The Coroner's Inquest brought in his Death occasioned by excessive Drinking.------Whilst he was lying on Shaw's Stoop, it appeared he was robbed of his Hat, Shoes and Buckles; and it has been since found, that the Woman who was last Monday carted round the Town, in Company with two others, had sold them to a Soldier for 1 s. 6 d. and a Pint of Rum ;--and the three Thieves are all since committed to Bridewell.

CUSTOM-HOUSE, NEW-YORK, INWARD ENTRIES.
Sloop Nancy, J. Waddell from Roscoft. Sloop John, C. Anderson, and Sloop Polly, P. Dennis from St. Thomas. Sloop Little Betsy, B. Smith from St. Croix. Sloop Sally and Polly, W. Rhodes, and Sloop Lydia, J. Frebody jun. from Rhode-Island. Sloop Herring, C. Bowne from Philadelphia. Sloop Lydia, S. Clark, Sloop Newburgh, I. Belknap, and Sloop Olive, Ed. Cottle, from Nantuckett. Sloop Conway, R. Elder from Madeira.

OUTWARD.
Ship New-Hope, P. De Peyster, for Hull. Ship Buchannan, T. Cockran for Lisbon. Brig Boon, G. Brass for Gibraltar. Sloop Nancy, J. Rogers for Pensacola. Sloop Endeavour, G. Ellis for Philadelphia. Schooner George, T. Dent for Maryland.

CLEARED.
Ship Beaver, C. Miller, Ship Charming Polly, A. Shoemaker, and Snow General Gage, Peter Berrien to London. Brig Jeany, W. Hunter to Madeira. Brig Charlotte, H. Coupar to Antigua. Brig Polly, I. M'Con-

ors of John
of February, at
County of Mon-
their Accompts
h Creditor receive
lvent Act.-------
son, } Affignees

D,
containing
at Fifh-Kill, in
t is well watered
, lying but feven
rm 20 Acres of
cleared. In faid
or the Plow, of
is on it a new
House ; a large
: There is two
Fruit of the beft
rels of Cyder a
On it is a good
the dryeft Time.
ith other fmall
ublick Bufinefs,
y handy to Mill,
chafe faid Farm,
utable Title for
BARGAR.

on Tuefday the
o'Clock in the

ts, Peices
in the County
mber Two and
and fifteen, are
River, called in
Number Thirty-
t, and the Main
Southweft and
Tracts, Peices
ws, to wit : Lot
on the Main.
is a large Heap
umber 8, and a
ow Land on the
nd of an Ifland,
) thence down
h 76 Degrees
xteen, Chains ;
North 54 Deg.
irteen Chains ;
North 20 Deg.
Weft thirty-two
nd fifty Links ;
South 15 Deg.
urteen Chains ;
76 Deg. Weft
; then North
20 Deg. Weft
Chains ; then
; then North
36 Deg. Weft
Chains ; then
35 Deg. Weft
Chains ; then
g. and an half,
ifteen Chains ;
South 55 Deg.
South 36 Deg.
wo Chains and

NOVEMBER 6, 1769

The
NEW–YORK GAZETTE;
OR, THE WEEKLY POST-BOY

BOSTON, October 28.

[…]

Last Saturday afternoon, as Mr. John Mein, publisher of the Boston Chronicle, was returning from his shop in King-street, some gentlemen then upon Change, who thought themselves ill-treated in a late publication of his, took occasion to "*catechise*" him; upon which, after a few words had passed between them, he drew a pistol out of his pocket, and threatened to fire if they did not stand off; but that was so far from intimidating them, that they followed up in order to seize him, and he apprehending some danger to himself from the resentment of the people, who began to collect together pretty fast, precipitately retreated to the main guard, which was near, with the pistol in his hand, where, as soon as he entered the door, he discharged it at random among those who closely followed him (tho' without doing any other damage than wounding the sleeve of the coat of a grenadier who was upon guard) and then immediately took shelter in the house under the protection of the military conservators of the peace: --- Application was soon after made to Mr. Justice Dana, and a warrant issued for apprehending him, in order to answer for this atrocious offence; but tho' search was made in the Guardhouse and other places, by the proper civil officers, to whom the warrant was committed, they have not yet been able to serve it upon him.

❧ CHAPTER III ❧

THE LATE HORRID MASSACRE

Introduction

In October 1768, following multiple infractions between Patriots and Loyalists, Boston soon found itself with a ratio of one British soldier to every five inhabitants. The shock and awe of encamped redcoats and bayonets was temporarily counterattacked by calm and civility as the colonists collectively bit their lips. Frustration mounted and colonists again turned to newspapers to journal their tyrannical experiences. Bickering over boycotts and partisan loyalties escalated and incidents soon became deadly. In March 1770, as news of the Boston Massacre raced across the Atlantic to London, news from England about the repeal of the Townshend Acts headed to American ports. Americans soon read that all of the import duties were lifted with one exception—the tax on tea—and, in the wake of another tragic event in Rhode Island, colonists developed an alternative method of intercolonial communication.

BOSTON CHRONICLE
October 31, 1768

BRITISH OFFICER HARASSED
BY BOYS IN BOSTON
North Wind Picture Archives

A VIEW OF PART OF THE TOWN OF BOSTON IN NEW ENGLAND AND BRITTISH SHIPS OF WAR LANDING THEIR TROOPS! 1768

BRITISH SHIPS OF WAR LANDING THEIR TROOPS
Randall J. Stephens, Eastern Nazarene College

This engraving by Paul Revere states: "At noon on Saturday, October the 1st, the fourteenth & twenty-ninth Regiments, a detachment from the 59th Regiment, and Train of Artillery, with two pieces of Cannon, landed on the Long Wharf; there Formed and Marched with insolent Parade, Drums beating, Fifes playing, and Colours flying, up King Street. Each Soldier having received 16 rounds of Powder and Ball."

ARRIVAL OF THE
TROOPS IN BOSTON

By Robert J. Allison

PARLIAMENT CREATED A FIVE-MEMBER BOARD OF Customs Commissioners in 1767 to oversee the ineffective customs apparatus, which had never raised as much in revenue as it cost to maintain. The 1767 Townshend duties on lead, paint, glass, and tea would pay the salaries of the commissioners, as well as the agents the commissioners hired to inspect cargoes. The commissioners would ensure that colonial trade, which benefitted from Britain's control of the seas, would help to pay for the fleet that controlled those seas.

Basing the board in Boston, the center of opposition to the Sugar Act and scene of riots over the Stamp Act, made less sense. The commissioners feared for their lives from the moment they arrived in Boston in late 1767.

On March 18, 1768, the anniversary of the Stamp Act repeal, mobs paraded to the houses of Governor Francis Bernard and the customs commissioners. The fifty-gun warship *Romney* arrived in June. A few days later, John Hancock's sloop *Liberty* docked, laden with Madeira wine. [He] locked the customs inspector in the hold while [quickly] and illegally unloaded the cargo. When the [seized] the *Liberty*, Bostonians rioted, forcing the [commis]sioners to take refuge on the warship.

[Thoma]s Gage, the New York–based com[mander of Briti]sh forces in North America, ordered the [Fourteenth a]nd Twenty-Ninth Regiments from Halifax to [Boston. A]fter a stormy passage, the troops reached Boston [on O]ctober 1, 1768. Lord Hillsborough, British secretary of state for the colonies, sent two regiments from Ireland, which reached Boston in mid-November.

The Twenty-Ninth Regiment pitched its camp on Boston Common; Bernard knew their tents would not be adequate for the winter. The Fourteenth Regiment had no tents, but the town refused Bernard's request to quarter them. They allowed some soldiers temporarily at Faneuil Hall (where town meetings took place), and with the assembly suspended, Bernard placed others in the Old State House.

To highlight the town's seizures and sufferings, an anonymous diarist logged a day-by-day account of Boston's military occupation, which was circulated and published as the "Journal of the Times" by several colonial newspapers. "The troops still keep possession of Faneuil Hall, the court house, the representatives' chambers, &c.," the Journal of the Times reported in its October 14 entry (*Pennsylvania Chronicle*, October 31, 1768). But this was a temporary expedient. In the first two weeks, between forty and seventy soldiers deserted, encouraged by Bostonians. Officers placed guards at Boston Neck and patrolled the ferries to stop desertions, and the few deserters captured were executed to discourage others.

General Gage arrived to inspect in October. "The arrival of this gentleman from N. York at this time," the October 15 entry of Journal of the Times reported (*Pennsylvania Chronicle*, October 31, 1768), "is a very agreeable circumstance, to the friends of their country," as Gage was better able than the customs commissioners to "see and judge for himself." The Governor's Council hoped Gage would report that the troops were unnecessary. They explained to him (*Boston Chronicle*, October 31, 1768) that the June riot "appeared to have originated with those who ordered the seizure" of Hancock's ship, provoked to "furnish a plausible pretense for requesting troops." Gage did report that Boston was not in a state of rebellion, but the taxes would remain in place, and so would the customs commissioners and soldiers. Bernard rented barracks for them in empty warehouses. An uneasy peace settled on Boston, with soldiers garrisoning a town that insisted it neither needed nor wanted them. Using armed troops to keep peace in Boston, Benjamin Franklin warned, was like setting up a blacksmith forge in a gunpowder magazine.

Mr. GODDARD,

Your correspondents furnish you with intelligence so expeditiously, that I observe you have already published many of the particulars mentioned in the Journal of the Times; nevertheless, as numbers of your customers would be glad to see the extraordinary transactions, &c. of the present day, in one comprehensive view, &c. of the invaluable paper, on their behalf I beg the favour of you to give the following continuation a place, without any alteration.

AMICUS.

B O S T O N.
JOURNAL of the TIMES.
[Continued.]

Oct. 3. TWO circular letters of Lord Hillsborough's this day seen in print, whereby it appears that the commissioners of the board of customs had repeatedly complained of being obstructed in the execution of their office. The proceedings of council on the 27th and 29th of July last, which G——r B——d hitherto prevented being made public, declares to the world, that no insult had been offered the commissioners;—That, " what happened on the 10th of June, seems to have sprung wholly from those who complain of it, and that it seems probable, an uproar was hoped for and intended to be seconded by the manner of proceeding, in making the seizure of the sloop Liberty; that their quitting the town was a voluntary act, without any sufficient ground for the same, and that when at the castle, there was no occasion for men of war to protect them." " That it is their unanimous opinion, the civil power does not need the support of troops; that it is not for his Majesty's service, nor the peace of this province, that any troops be required, or that any came into the province; and that they deem any persons who may have made application for troops to be sent hither, in the highest degree unfriendly to the peace and good order of this government, as well as to his Majesty's service and the British interest in America." *How detested and abhorred by the people must that G——r and those men then be, who, not content with having by their misrepresentations introduced troops into this province, are now leaving no stone unturned in order*

to procure quarters for them in this metropolis, to the great vexation and distress of the inhabitants, as also in violation of law and justice, which must be the case, while they are quartered in the town, to disturb and annoy the inhabitants, and while the barracks provided by the province, at a very considerable expence, remain empty!——The prints of this day contain a very extraordinary advertisement, published by order of the commissioners of customs, whereby it appears that the inhabitants of Nantucket, who are mostly of the persuasion called Quakers, have not accommodated Mr. Samuel Procter, an officer of the customs lately sent among them, with an office, and that therefore orders are issued to their several officers in America, to make seizure of all vessels, and their cargoes, that shall arrive from that island, without proper documents, signed by the Collector and D. Comptroller of the port of Boston.——*If quarters are to be provided by the people for custom-house officers, who are daily increasing upon us, as well as for his Majesty's troops, we shall quickly perceive that we are without quarters ourselves.*

Oct. 11. We have certain information, that at a full meeting of the inhabitants of Lebanon, (a large town in Connecticut) convened the 26th of September last, in consequence of intelligence that troops were soon expected in Boston, to be quartered upon the town; said inhabitants unanimously expressed their sentiments and resolutions as follows, " That an union of measures is absolutely necessary, at this important crisis, in order to maintain our liberties and immunities; and that they fully agreed with their brethren of Boston, in the resolves they passed in a late town meeting; and that considering themselves connected by the strongest ties to their fellow subjects, in this and the neighbouring colonies, they should look upon an attack upon them, as though they themselves were the immediate sufferers, and that with a determinate, unalterable resolution and firmness, they would assert and support their American brethren, at the expence of their lives and fortunes; should their welfare, which is so intimately blended with their own, demand the sacrifice." *As it is thought the above shews the disposition, not only of the other towns in that colony, but of the rest of the provinces; how must the friends of Britain applaud the prudence and wisdom of the late committee of convention in Boston, who in tenderness to the mother country, and loyalty to their Sovereign, under all their grievances, while they adhered strictly to their rights, yet strongly recommended peace and quietness to the people, until the effect of their last representations and petitions could be known.*

Oct. 12. Advice received that the merchants in Connecticut, have agreed as those in Massachusetts, and New-York, &c. had done before them, not to import any goods from Great-Britain, till the late revenue acts, &c. are repealed.—*A measure that must have the greatest tendency to awaken the attention of the mercantile and manufactoral part of Britain to their own immediate interest, which they lately seem to have quite lost sight of.* The rumour of Castle William being delivered up by the G——r to the King's troops, arose from his having permitted a number of mariners from the ships of war, to land at Castle Island, six of whom it is said went off in a boat last night.

Reports of great desertions and a general disposition to desert from the regiments here, which it is said left Halifax under great dejection of spirits; about 21 of the soldiers absconded the last night, and parties from the troops with other clothing, instead of their regimentals are sent after them.—*Some of the consequences of bringing the troops into this town, in direct violation of the act of parliament, and disregard to the advice of his Majesty's Council, instead of quartering them in the barracks at Castle island, are like to be the scattering proper tutors through the country, to instruct the inhabitants in the modern way of handling the firelock, and exercising the men, and also in the various manufactures which the ingenuity and industry of the people of Great-Britain have hitherto furnished us with.*—This night a surgeon of one of the ships of war, being guilty of very disorderly behaviour, was committed to gaol by Mr. Justice Quincy, as was also a person, not belonging to this province, by Mr. Justice Hutchinson, on complaint of a soldier, that he had been enticing him to desert; said stranger was first taken and confined by Captain Willson, in the town house for some time, without warrant or authority from any Magistrate.——*If the oaths of soldiers who are promised 10 Guineas for such discoveries, are to be taken as sufficient proof, we know not what proscriptions may take place.*

Oct. 13. A private letter from Halifax contains some particulars relative to the Boston expedition, not known before, viz. " That in consequence of orders received Sept. 11th, from this place, all the workmen in the King's yard, necessary to equip the ships, were set to work on Sunday; a strict embargo laid, and guard vessels sent to the mouth of the harbour to prevent intelligence being sent, and more caution used than when fitting out for the Louisbourg

has or may commit to them, as a secret, unless the B——d shall judge it for his Majesty's interest so to do.

Oct. 14. The troops still keep possession of Faneuil-Hall, the court-house, representatives' chambers, &c. Guards placed at the passage way into the town, near the neck. Patrolling companies near the ferry ways, and parties sent into the country to prevent desertions: In the forenoon one Rogers, a New-England man, sentenced to receive one thousand stripes, and a number of other soldiers, were scourged in the common by the black drummers, in a manner, which however necessary, was shocking to humanity; some gentlemen who had held commissions in the army, observing, that only 40 of the 170 lashes received by Rogers, at this time, was equal in punishment to 500, they had seen given in other regiments.

Oct. 15. A deserter from the 14th regiment was brought in last evening by one of the decoy parties, sent into the country, also a labouring man from Roxbury, with a soldier's regimentals on his back, he was confined for some time in a tent, without lawful warrant, and afterwards committed to prison by Mr. Just Hutchinson.—This afternoon the troops were drawn up, on the common, on the appearance of General Gage; at sunset there were 17 discharges from the field cannon; he passed the front of the battalion in his chariot, preceded by a number of aid de camps on horseback. *The arrival of this gentleman from N. York, at this time, is a very agreeable circumstance, to the friends of their country; as his mild and judicious behaviour, in that province, has been justly applauded; and he comes here determined to see and judge for himself.*

Oct. 16. This day Capt. Jenkins arrived from London, who brought a print of August 13th, in which there is the following article, " There are 4000 troops ordered for Boston, which it is thought will sufficiently intimidate those people to comply with the laws enacted in England; especially as the other Colonies seem to have deserted them." The design of sending troops among us was before fully comprehended; all the Colonies that have been permitted to meet, have united with us in humble petitions and remonstrances, and it is hoped that the merchants of Philadelphia have, or will soon co-operate in a measure our friends at home represent as the most likely to procure a redress of grievances.

BOSTON, October 20.

It has been reported that the Head Quarters for the army is to be in this town.

Tuesday last sailed from hence, his Majesty's ship Launceston of 40 guns, the Martin sloop of 14 guns, and the St. Lawrence armed schooner, for Halifax.

to town; and that the troops embarked in as great hurry as was ever known in time of war—And a

gal, and Hope schooner,

Among the many writers in the London papers, one who signs *Anglo Americanus* says, that in the pro-

m from Quebec,
hed through the
e; and this morn-
them was difem-
k the fame rout.
ad eleven years.
look hearty and

The following is
eceived here from
ft 2.

2d inftant, about
a very uncommon
in this neighbour-
or large body of
on Dungavel-hill,
out fix miles fouth
its way into the
the rock, making
ards broad, and a-
; it then rufhed
the hill, with the
urling the largeft
tities of earth be-
ening of the fame
y down the hill.
g appearance, and
with a fevere fe-
grounds on that
d deep under wa-
ers have loft their
ounds covered with
At the fame time
s of water rufhed
f the hill, as put
grounds in the
d a houfe fo in-
ater, that had not
efcape by the win-
been drowned, as
ning through the
after. It carried
fwept every thing
a paffage into a
rtoun-Burn, which
year is commonly
fuch an enormous
f a houfe; and had
ftructions which it
oufe, which made
ferent courfe, the
ould have been in

O N.

n London, Aug. 30.
t of foot command-

gentlemen of the Council, in behalf of themfelves and the other members who fubfcribed it, being all that were prefent.

To his Excellency General GAGE, Commander in Chief of his Majefty's forces in America.

The Addrefs of the fubfcribers, members of his Majefty's Council of the province of Maffachufets-Bay.

SIR,

A General Council being held yefter-day gives the diftant members of it, together with the members in the town and the neighbourhood the pleafure of addreffing you ——We take this firft opportunity of doing it, and at the fame time to pay our compliments to your Excellency.

In this time of public diftrefs, when the General Court of the province is in a ftate of diffolution; when the metropolis is poffeffed by troops, and furrounded by fhips of war; and when more troops are daily expected, it affords a general fatisfaction that your Excellency has vifited the province, and has now an opportunity of knowing the ftate of it by your obfervation and enquiry.

Your own obfervation will give you the fulleft evidence that the town and province, are in a peaceful ftate.——Your own enquiry will fatisfy you, that tho' there have been diforders in the town of Bofton, fome of them did not merit notice; and that fuch as did, have been magnified beyond the truth.

Thofe of the 18th of March, and 10th of June are faid to have occafioned the above-mentioned armament to be ordered hither.——The firft was trivial, and could not have been noticed to the difadvantage of the town, but by perfons inimical to it; efpecially as it happened in the evening of a day of recreation. The other was criminal, and the actors in it were guilty of a riot: but we are obliged to fay it had its rife from thofe perfons who were loudeft in their complaints about it, and who by their overcharged reprefentations of it have been the occafion of fo great an armament being ordered hither. We cannot perfuade ourfelves to believe they have fufficient evidence to fupport fuch reprefentations; which have moft unjuftly brought into queftion the loyalty of as

proceedings that have taken place in the town of Bofton. We deteft them, and have repeatedly and publickly expreffed that deteftation; and in council have advifed Governor Bernard to order the Attorney General to profecute the perpetrators of them: but at the fame time we are obliged to declare in juftice to the town, that the diforders of the 10th of June laft, occafioned by a feizure made by the officers of the cuftoms, appeared to have originated with thofe who ordered the feizure to be made. The hour of making the feizure (at or near fun fet) the threats and armed force ufed in it, the forcibly carrying the veffel away, and all in a manner unprecedented, and calculated to irritate, juftify the apprehenfion that the feizure was accompanied with thefe extraordinary circumftances in order to excite a riot, and furnifh a plaufible pretence for requefting troops. A day or two after the riot, and as if in profecution of the laft mentioned purpofe, notwithftanding there was not the leaft infult offered to the commiffioners of the cuftoms, either in their perfons or property, they thought fit to retire, on the pretence of fecurity to themfelves, on board the Romney man of war, and afterwards to Caftle William; and when there, to keep up the idea of their being ftill in great hazard, procured the Romney and feveral other veffels of war to be fo ftationed as to prevent an attack upon them which they affected to be afraid of.

Thefe proceedings have doubtlefs taken place, to induce a belief among the officers of the navy and army, as they occafionally came thither, that the commiffioners were in danger of being attacked, and to procure from thofe officers reprefentations co-incident with their own, that they really were fo. But their frequent landing on the main, and making excurfions to the country, where it would have been eafy to have feized, if any injury had been intended them, demonftrates the infincerity of their declarations; that they immured themfelves at the caftle for fafety. This is rather to be accounted for as being an effential part of the concerted plan for procuring troops to be quartered here, in which they and their coadjutors have fucceeded to their wifh; but unhappily to the mutual detriment and uneafi-

if
true
fure
his
regi
a g
bita
to
barr
or t
of i
can

A
fro
roug
inte
men

I
inco
they
firft
eafe
vinc

A
his
for
ing
mak
Exc
difo
fes
hav
whi
ver
tive
pea
of w
ther
you

can

then

GENTLEMEN,

I Return you thanks for the honour you do me in this Address, and am greatly obliged to you, for the good opinion you are pleased to conceive of me.

Whatever may have been the particular causes of the disturbances, and riots, which have happened in the town of Boston, these riots, and the resolves which were published, have induced his Majesty to order four regiments to this town to protect his loyal subjects, in their persons and properties, and to assist the civil magistrates in the execution of the laws. The discipline and order which will be preserved amongst the troops, I trust, will render their stay, in no shape, distressful to his Majesty's dutiful subjects in this town; and that the future behaviour of the people, will justify the best construction of their past actions, which I flatter myself will be such, as to afford me a sufficient foundation to represent to his Majesty the propriety of withdrawing the most part of the troops *Thomas Gage.*

Boston, Oct. 28th, 1768.

Tuesday last George Erving, Esq; of this Town, merchant, was married to Miss Lucy Winslow, daughter to Isaac Winslow, Esq; of Roxbury.

Last Sunday se'night as Mr Turner the Coxswain of the Pinnace belonging to his Majesty's ship the Romney, was coming from the ship to the Long-Wharf, with three other men in a small skiff, they accidentally overset, when the Coxswain

BOSTON CHRONICLE

October 31, 1768

—

The British fifty-gun warship *Romney* arrived in June. A few days later, John Hancock's sloop *Liberty*, laden with Madeira wine, docked. The crew locked the customs inspector in the hold while they quickly and illegally unloaded the cargo. When the *Romney* seized the *Liberty*, Bostonians rioted, forcing the customs commissioners to take refuge on the warship. The Governor's Council hoped Gage would report that the troops were unnecessary and explained to him that the June riot "appeared to have originated with those who ordered the seizure" of Hancock's ship, provoked to "furnish a plausible pretense for requesting troops." Gage did report that Boston was not in a state of rebellion. But the taxes would remain in place, and so would the customs commissioners and soldiers.

BOSTON MASSACRE

By Robert J. Allison

"FACTS ARE STUBBORN THINGS," JOHN ADAMS SAID IN HIS defense of the soldiers on trial for their role in the Boston Massacre. The facts of March 5, 1770, were not in dispute—eight soldiers, under command of Captain Thomas Preston, fired into a crowd of several hundred people, killing five and wounding half a dozen. But were the soldiers guilty of murder?

John's cousin Samuel Adams certainly thought so. He orchestrated the town of Boston's public response. *A Short Narrative of the Horrid Massacre*, published two weeks after the event, traces the crisis to the Stamp Act (1765) and the arrival of customs commissioners (1767). Preceding the narrative in the pamphlet was a "Report of the Committee of the Town of Boston" taken from a March 12 town meeting. The exact report was reprinted in the March 20, 1770, *Essex Gazette*.

Samuel Adams demanded removal of all soldiers from town, warning of grave danger if they stayed.

Two British regiments arriving in 1768 made the tragic conflict inevitable. Boston artist Henry Pelham sketched the scene in a print, "The Fruits of Arbitrary Power." Paul Revere copied the print, creating one of American history's most important images, showing the soldiers in line firing at unarmed townsfolk while the spires of the Town House and the First Church, symbolizing civil and spiritual power, stand impotent in the background.

John Robinson took a set of depositions to London, where a different version appeared: *A Fair Account of the Late Unhappy Disturbance at Boston*. This tells of the "Unhappy Disturbance" that began on Friday, March 2, when a group of rope workers beat an off-duty soldier; he came back with more soldiers to get revenge, but again the rope workers beat them, and all weekend Boston toughs and soldiers fought. The March 20 *Essex Gazette* (dateline Monday, March 19) said this was "stopping far short of the real source of the matter," and the May 8, 1770, *London Chronicle* talks of "repeated acts of provocation" on both sides, with the soldiers spoiling for a fight.

The evening of March 5, two hundred people tried to attack the British barracks in Brattle Square; as they were driven off, they saw sentry Hugh White defending himself in front of the Custom House from a group of harassing apprentices. The mob surrounded White. Someone alerted Captain Thomas Preston, who led seven soldiers through the crowd to White's rescue. The crowd—now three hundred or more, brandishing clubs and swords and throwing rocks—pressed them against the Custom House. Private Hugh Montgomery fired, killing Crispus Attucks, and Private Matthew Kilroy fired without aiming, blowing a hole through Samuel Gray's head. Two other soldiers fired; Benjamin Caldwell fell dead, and Samuel Maverick and Patrick Carr were mortally wounded as musket balls tore through others. Lieutenant Governor Thomas Hutchinson arrived, ordered Preston and his men to their barracks, urged the crowd to go home, and spent the rest of the night hearing witnesses. Before dawn, he ordered Preston and the soldiers arrested for murder.

Samuel Adams demanded removal of all soldiers from town, warning of grave danger if they stayed. He arranged the largest funeral North America had seen: ten thousand people followed the caskets through the streets to their common grave.

Preston and the soldiers went on trial that fall. Patriot Josiah Quincy joined John Adams in defending the soldiers, eager to prove that Bostonians would give them a fair trial. All were acquitted but Montgomery and Kilroy. Guilty of manslaughter, they pled benefit of clergy, were branded on the thumbs, and were sent to join their regiment in New Jersey.

Five witnesses testified that someone had fired from the Custom House. A servant, according to the March 12 report printed in the *Essex Gazette* (March 20), testified that his master, Manwaring, forced him to fire from the Custom House; Revere's engraving shows a musket firing from the window. After Preston's and the soldiers' trials, a jury acquitted Manwaring, then convicted the servant of perjury and had him whipped. But Samuel Adams ensured that his version of events on March 5—soldiers firing on unarmed civilians—would remain a vivid memory, with annual commemorations of the Massacre on King Street.

The unhappy Sufferers were Messrs Saml Gray, Saml Maverick, Jam^s Caldwell, Crispus Attucks & Pat^k Carr
Killed. Six wounded; two of them (Christr Monk & John Clark) Mortally

Published in 1770 by Paul Revere

THE BLOODY MASSACRE
Library of Congress

This sensationalized portrayal of the Boston Massacre is titled "The bloody massacre perpetrated in King Street Boston on March 5th 1770 by a party of the 29th Regiment." It was engraved, printed, and sold by Paul Revere, but copied from a Henry Pelham print.

ESSEX GAZETTE (SALEM, MA)

March 20, 1770

—

The Boston Massacre was a major PR crisis with each side scrambling to control the news. Two weeks later, additional details and eyewitness accounts about the March 5 riot were published in the *Essex Gazette*, printed 15 miles north of Boston in Salem, Massachusetts. According to one report, a servant was forced to fire a gun upon the people from the Custom House, which was depicted in Paul Revere's engraving of the event.

... Efq; Andrew Oliver, ... which, in Confequence ... wicked and defigning Men, to bring us into a State of Bondage and Ruin, in direct ... *Boston, 12 ...*

... &c. Peter Frye, Efq; ... Joſeph Flint, Thomas ...

From a South-Carolina Paper, we have

His Majeſty's moſt graci-

SPEECH, to both Houſes of ... ment on Tuesday the 9th Day ... anuary, 1770.

y Lords and Gentlemen,

... with much concern, that I find ... felf obliged to open this Parlia- ... with acquainting you, that the ... per among the horned Cattle, has ... broke out in this kingdom, not- ... anding every precaution that could ... d for preventing the infection from ... n parts. Upon the firft notice of ... ual appearance, my next atten- ... on was to ſtop, if poſſible, its fur- ... progreſs, and as the ſucceſs of thoſe ... endeavours muſt, in all probability, ... have been entirely defeated, by any the ... leaſt degree of delay in the application ... of them, I thought it abſolutely ne- ... ceſſary, with the advice of my Privy ... Council, to give immediate directions ... for every ſtep to be taken, that appeared ... moſt capable of checking the inſtant ... danger of the ſpreading the infection, ... until I could have an opportunity of ... conſulting my Parliament upon ſome ... more permanent meaſures, for ſecuring ... us againſt ſo great a calamity ... your immediate and moſt ſeri- ... deration, I earneſtly recom- ... very important object.

I have given my parliame ... aſſurances, that it has alway ... fixed purpoſe, to preſerve ... tranquility, maintaining ... time, the dignity and ho ... Crown, together with the ... intereſt of my people. ... mon burthens which my ... borne ſo chearfully, in ... the late War to a happ ... muſt be an additional m ... me vigilant to prevent ... turbances in Europe fro ... any part, where the ſec ... intereſt, of this nation, ... ceſſary for my Crown ... ty. The aſſurances I ... other great Powers, a ... believe, that my ende ... nue to be ſucceſsful ; ... the general intereſt ... ject of my attention ... dily ſupport my ow ... equally careful, not ... claims of any other

NEW-YORK, March ... On Thurſday Night laſt, bet ... the Hours of 11 and 12 o'Clock, ... broke out in Scotch Street, and it ... nerally agreed that it began in a ... belonging to Mr. Hampton, and k ... by the Name of the Lodge, and it ... muſt have conſumed a conſiderab ... of the Inſide before it was diſcove ... the Building was reduced in le ... Twenty Minutes after the Di ... was made.—The Rapidity with ... it burnt, baffled the moſt active Vi ... of People of all Ranks and Cond ... Hours ...

... have out ... view, and which may be moſt likely ... give authority & efficacy to the re ... of your deliberations : Such a condu ... on your parts, will, above all thin ... contribute to maintain, in their pro ... luſtre, the ſtrength, the reputation, ... the proſperity of this country ; ... ſtrengthen the attachment of my ... jects to that excellent conſtitution ... government from which they de ... ſuch diſtinguiſhed advantages ; an ... cauſe the firm reliance and confide ... which I have in the wiſdom of my ... liament, as well as in their zeal fo ... true intereſt of my people, to be ... proved both at home and abroad.

... d received Inſtructions ... ſembly at Cambridge," ... indiſpenſible Duty to ... your Honor againſt any ... proroguing this Court ; ... fraction of our eſſential ... and Citizens, as well ... d to us by the Britiſh ... nd the Charter of this ...

... further beg Leave to ... to your Honor, that the ... eral Aſſembly in Harvard ... erly repugnant to the In- ... Seminary of Learning, ... ntly to the Deſigns of the ... es of this People, in ſo ... ting the Monies of their ... for its Emolument and ...

Reaſons, the Houſe of ... ves are indiſpenſably obli- ... your Honor, to exert the ... erived to you from his Ma- ... Commiſſion, agreeable to ... of this Colony, and veſted ... in adjourning this Great ... al Aſſembly to its ancient ... Court-Houſe in Boſton. ... ear particularly to mention ... nor, the great Inconvenien- ... attend the Sitting of the Aſ- ... Cambridge, where the Mem- ... ot be accommodated ; but ... ially as they are at a Diſ- ... the Place where the Records ... embly are kept. ... which his Honor was pleaſed ... the following ANSWER. ... of the Houſe of Repreſentatives, ... E being reſerved by the Royal ... rter to this Province certain

... Priſoners out of the Hand of Juſtice, and even firing upon the Inhabitants in the Street, when in the Peace of God and the King, and when we have applied for Re- dreſs in the Courſe of the Law of the Land, our Magiſtrates and Courts of Juſtice have appeared to be overawed by them, and ſuch a Degree of mean Submiſſion has been ſhewn to them, as has given the greateſt Diſguſt even to the coolest and moſt judi- cious Perſons in the Community. Such has been the general State of the Town.

On Friday the ſecond Inſt. a Quarrel aroſe between ſome of the Soldiers of the XXIXth, and the Ropemakers Journeymen and Apprentices, which was carried to that Length as to become dangerous to the Lives of each Party : This contentious Diſpoſi- tion continued until the Monday Evening following, when a Party of ſeven or eight Soldiers, detached from the Main Guard under the Command of Capt. Preſton, and by his Orders fired upon the Inhabitants promiſcuouſly in King ſtreet without the leaſt warning of their Intention, and killed three on the ſpot, another has ſince died of his wounds, and others are dangerouſly not to ſay mortally wounded ; Capt. Preſton and his Party are now in Goal. An En- quiry is now making into this bloody Af- fair ; and by ſome of the Evidence there is Reaſon to apprehend that the Soldiers have been made uſe of by others as Inſtru- ments in executing a ſettled Plot to Maſ- ſacre the Inhabitants. There had been but a little Time before a Murder committed in the Street by two Perſons of infamous Character, who had been employed by the Commiſſioners and Cuſtom-Houſe Officers. In the preſent Inſtance there are Witneſſes who ſwear, that, when the Soldiers fired, ſeveral Muſquets were diſcharged from

134

THE

SALEM, March 20.

A LIST of Officers choſen at an an- nual Meeting of the Town of SALEM, held the 12th, and continued by Ad- journment to the 19th of March, 1770.

Town-Clerk ; John Higginſon, Eſq;
Town-Treaſurer ; Joſeph Bowditch, Eſq;
Selectmen and Aſſeſſors ; Meſſrs. Samuel Barton, jun. George Dodge, George Williams, Elias Haſket Derby, John Felt.
Overſeers of the Poor and of the Work-Houſe ; Meſſrs. Joſeph Hodges, Jonathan Gardner, jun. Jo- nathan Ropes, jun. Richard Derby, jun. Benjamin Goodhue.
Conſtables ; Meſſrs. David Smith, Robert Foſter, Benjamin Hooper, jun. William Clough.
Clerks of the Market ; Meſſrs. Benjamin Oſgood, Edmund Whittemore, Joſeph Flint.
Sealers of Leather ; Meſſrs. John Bray, Stephen Webb, Peter Cheever, jun.
Surveyors of Highways ; Meſſrs. Joſeph Hodges, Thorndike Proctor, jun.
Hayward of the Neck and Winter Iſland ; Mr. Stephen Webb.
Tything-Men ; Meſſrs. Benjamin Sawyer, Jere- miah Newhall, Samuel Silſbee.
Viewers and Cullers of Staves and Hoops ; Meſſrs. Joſeph Hodges, Samuel Murry, Edmund Hendfield, Arthur Jeffry, Thomas Maſon, Joſhua Phippen, Benjamin Ropes.
Surveyors and Meaſurers of Boards, and Surveyors of Shingles & Clapboards ; Meſſrs. Abraham Watſon, Atwater Phippen, James Gould, David Phippen.
Meaſurers of Salt ; Meſſrs. Nathaniel Archer, Edmund Hendfield, Samuel Murry.
Keeper of the Town Pound by the Alms-Houſe ; Mr. Joſeph Elſon.

his Majeſty ... whilſt I am ... what Man ... exerciſed I t ... form to it.

I wish tha ... tration, whe ... ions or other ... to the Memb ... muſt not de ... King. If I ... Deſire of the ... Proroguing I ... prehend I ſh ... Diſpleaſure ; ... will not be e ... I ſhall never t ... ciſe of any P ... tionally in th ... Powers ſhou ... quence of In ... Members of ... ſtituents.

Cambridge, March 1 ... (We hear t ... tives have ſent a ... Board upon th

The ESSEX GAZETTE

The following is the Substance of Letters addressed by the Committee of the Town to divers Gentlemen of the first Distinction in London.

SIR,

THE Town of Boston, now legally convened at Faneuil Hall, have directed us their Committee to acquaint you of their present miserable Situation, occasioned by the Exorbitancy of the Military Power, which, in Consequence of the Intrigues of wicked and designing Men, to bring us into a State of Bondage and Ruin, in direct Repugnance to those Rights which belong to us as Men, and as British Subjects, have long since been stationed among us.

The Soldiers ever since the fatal Day of their Arrival, have treated us with an Insolence which discovered in them an early Prejudice against us, as being that rebellious People which our implacable Enemies had maliciously represented us to be.—They landed in the Town with all the Appearance of Hostility!—They marched thro' the Town with all the Ensigns of Triumph! and evidently designed to subject the Inhabitants to the severe discipline of a Garrison. They have been continuing their Enormities by abusing the People, rescuing Prisoners out of the Hand of Justice, and even firing upon the Inhabitants in the Street, when in the Peace of God and the King, and when we have applied for Redress in the Course of the Law of the Land, our Magistrates and Courts of Justice have appeared to be overawed by them and such a Degree of mean Submission has been shewn to them, as has given the greatest Disgust even to the coolest and most judicious Persons in the Community. Such has been the general State of the Town.

On Friday the second Inst. A Quarrel arose between some of the Soldiers of the XXIXth, and the Ropemakers Journeymen and Apprentices, which was carried to that Length as to become dangerous to the Lives of each Party: this contentious Disposition continued until the Monday Evening following, when a Party of seven or eight Soldiers, detached from the Main Guard under the Command of Capt. Preston, and by his Orders fired upon the Inhabitants promiscuously in King street without the least warning of their Intention, and killed three on the spot, another has since died of his wounds, and others are dangerously not to say mortally wounded; Capt. Preston and his Party are now in Goal. An Enquiry is now making into this bloody Affair; and by some of the Evidence there is Reason to apprehend that the Soldiers have been made use of by others as Instruments in executing a settled Plot to Massacre the Inhabitants. There had been but a little Time before a Murder committed in the Street by two Persons of infamous Character, who had been employed by the Commissioners and Custom-House Officers. In the present Instance there are Witnesses who swear, that, when the Soldiers fired, several Musquets were discharged from the House where the Commissioners Board is kept, before which the shocking Tragedy was acted; and a Boy, Servant of one Manwaring, a petty Officer in the Customs, upon Oath accused his Master of firing a Gun upon the People out of a Window of the same House, a number of Persons being at the same Time in the Room; and he confesses that himself being threatened with Death if he refused, discharged a Gun twice by the Orders of that Company; but as it has been impossible for any Persons to collect a State of Facts hitherto, we are directed by the Town to give you this short intimation of the Matter for the present, and to intreat your Friendship to prevent any ill Impressions from being made upon the Minds of his Majesty's Ministers and others against the Town by the Accounts which the Commissioners of the Customs and others our Enemies may send, until the Town shall be able to make a full Representation of it; which will be addressed to you by the next Conveyance.

This horrible Transaction has occasioned the greatest Anxiety and Distress in the Minds of the Inhabitants, who have ever since need necessitated to keep up their own Military Watch. And his Majesty's Council were so soon convinced of the imminent Danger of the Troops being any longer in the Town, that upon Application being made by the inhabitants, they immediately and unanimously advised the Lieut. Governor to effect their Removal; And Lt. Col. Dalrymple, the present commanding Officer, is now removing all the Troops to Castle William. We are With strict Truth, Sir, Your most

Faithful, and obedient Servants.

Boston, 12 March, 1770.

[…]

Extract of a Letter from a Gentleman in Boston, to his Friend in the Country, in Answer to one, desiring to be impartially informed how the late Disturbances arose.

" To trace the massacre of the 5th instant no further back than the preceding week, (a very candid account of its prelude in Mr. Gray's rope-walks, was published on that day in Fleet's paper, and since in the Essex Gazette)

wou'd be stopping far short of the real source of the matter. Abundant evidence appears to warrant a very opposite conclusion! The projectors and promoters of the favorite scheme of drawing people's substance from them without their consent, have ever been the patrons of standing armies.----These must be taught to believe the people a licentious and rebellious rabble; which their lordships the common soldiery must awe into peace and good order; and if they will not be held in proper subjection by sound drubbings with lusty cudgels, heavy cutlasses, and pushes with fixed bayonets; a few discharges of powder and double quantity of lead may be occasionally necessary to disperse the people raised by the fore-mentioned gentle discipline, and learn them better manners than to huzza and whistle at their masters!

"To be serious in the enquiry, whether the outrages perpetrated by an ignorant and misinstructed soldiery originated from the provocation of a vulgar expression or stroke of a snow ball, would be solemn trifling indeed! No man, in the least acquainted with the workings of the human mind, could ever have expected, that such mortal foes as enslaving dragoons (*for the express purpose of guarding public plunderers*) and free, brave and sensible, pillaged, affronted and butchered citizens, could long live in amity together. ------I deplore the fall of my countrymen; but shall be very agreeably disappointed if these be the last victims to a bound'ess rage for lawless dominion! The inhabitants are blameless, to the amazement of their enemies! Their moderation has been mistaken for most abject timidity; & well am I assured, that a firm conviction of the fallacy of this conception will have more weight in procuring a restoration of our civil constitution than all the proofs of innocency, loyalty and affection, that could be collected from Canada to Pensacola. Your abhorrence of standing armies can be no greater than mine is of revenue officers, tho' their exportions from the people were but a bare maintenance for three tide waiters on the whole continent, and that to be independent on the people. By this entering wedge of taxing without our consent, in other terms, levying tribute at discretion, has been introduced the slavery of every state we read of in modern history. To prefer a speedy and glorious death to a lingering and shameful torture, becomes a Briton, becomes a sagacious, uncorrupted and hardly American!---------- Our friends on the Isle of Britain tell us we have no further protection to expect from them, we must therefore be madmen if we neglect to inform ourselves in every article of necessary knowledge for our own defence.---The native goodness of our Prince is as strongly presumed, and fully acknowledged in this capital as any part of his wide dominions; and none more sensibly feel the pertinency of your modest conclusion, that all those offenders may be imputed to his bad servants."

From the continuance of these, and such a force as would embolden them to hazard the fatal experiment, nothing short of carnage, devastation, and utter destruction, could be expected. Nor is there any method to escape, but the single one of convincing them that the universal voice of the colonies, at least is F r e e d o m o r D e a t h !

The accounts in this Paper and the Boston Gazette are as authentic as could then be collected; the inquiry is still continuing, and new patter turns up every day, of which,

when completed, a digest will be published, which will lay open such a plot as will render the Fifth of November below the notice of even of boys and children.

The honourable John Robinson, Esq; sailed the 16th for London (it is said) with a number of depositions, to manifest that the cause of the massacre was the defence of the treasure in the custom-house, from the inhabitants, whose design the deponents verily believe was to break in and plunder it. One would think it very strange the intended robbers should take it in their heads to begin the action at Murray's barracks, at least in Boylston's alley!

The dependency of the colonies is confessedly an object long in view---Two powers independent on an inimical to their civil constitutions will soon make work enough for appeals---The expence and discouragement in which these will be involved, bids fair to dishearten the most hardy from contending, and when that becomes the case let any one determine for himself how far the British American Colonies will differ from Roman provinces, in the most corrupt era of that despotic state!

hereof.
en to take
ngthen the
ative to the
t ; and for
ncouraging

19.
ceeding in a le-
great Numbers
at is relative to
Evidence will
the Aggreffors,
reated by them
Number of Evi-
m the Cuftom-
and a Track is
te the intended
of the perjured
d from thence
ng Snider was
hen clearly ap-
and abandoned
mploy'd by our

Work to form
oners and their
ainft us---The
ir Property and
ed ; and what
n the ftrongeft
infamous & de-

there only the whole difficulty lies."
Extract of a Letter from a Gentleman in Boston, to his Friend in the Country, in Answer to one, defiring to be impartially informed how the late Difturbances arofe.
" To trace the maffacre of the 5th inftant no further back than the preceeding week, (a very candid account of its prelude in Mr. Gray's rope-walks, was publifhed that day in Fleet's paper, and fince in the Effex Gazette) wou'd be ftopping far fhort of the real fource of the matter. Abundant evidence appears to warrant a very oppofite conclufion ! The projectors and promoters of the favorite fcheme of drawing people's fubftance from them without their confent, have ever been the patrons of ftanding armies.----These muft be taught to believe the people a licentious and rebellious rabble ; which their lordfhips the common foldiery muft awe into peace and good order : and if they will not be held in proper fubjection by found drubbings with lufty cudgels, heavy cutlaffes, and pufhes with fixed bayonets ; a few difcharges of powder and double quantity of lead may be occafionally neceffary to difperfe the people raifed by the fore-mentioned gentle difcipline, and learn them better manners than to huzza and whiftle at their mafters !
" To be ferious in the enquiry, whether the outrages perpetrated by an ignorant and mifinftructed foldiery originated from the provocation of a vulgar expreffion or ftroke of a fnow ball, would be folemn trifling indeed ! No man, in the leaft acquainted with the workings of the human mind, could ever have expected, that fuch mortal foes as enflaving dragoons *(for the exprefs purpofe of guarding publick plunderers)* and free, brave and fenfible, pillaged, affronted and butchered citizens, could long live in

ment her with warm Affection ; and fhe is mentioned with Regret, Efteem and Honor, by all her large Acquaintance.

SALEM, March 20.

By a Veffel in a fhort Paffage from Lifbon, which arrived at Cape-Ann laft Week, we are informed, that a War between the Englifh and French was much expected and talked of at that Place.

We hear from Hampton, that a large Barn was confumed there by Fire laft Friday Night, and it is faid 15 Tons of Hay, and about 15 Head of Cattle, were deftroyed in the Flames. The Barn and its Contents were the Property of one Mr. ----- Smith.

By Capt. George Cabot, who arrived here laft Saturday in 39 Days from Bilboa, we have Advice, that the Weather, as he heard, was very tempeftuous, in the Bay of Bifcay, in December and January laft ; in which 13 Sail of Veffels were loft, and 5 of them fuppofed to be Fifh Veffels ------- which ------ N ------- foundland. It was faid ------- ------ ------ Quintals of Fifh on board, ------ ------ ------ to her all loft.

At an annual Meeting of ------ ------ Inhabitants of the Town ------ ------ qualified to vote in Town Affairs, began and held at the Court-Houfe (fo called) in faid Salem, on Monday the 12th of March, A. D. 1770.
VOTED, That Joseph Bowditch, Efq; be appointed Moderator of this Meeting.
VOTED, That the Inhabitants of this Town will ufe their Endeavours, that none they are con-

Whereas a Load of Ha belonging to Uriah Gibbs of Sudbury, fta the Town-Houfe, laft Night, in this Tow fome evil minded Perfon or Perfons, difpe the Town, and feveral Bundles loft : Thi fore to give Notice, that a Reward of Fi will be given to any Perfon who will di Offender or Offenders, fo that he or the brought to Juftice.
N. B. As fuch Proceedings are a fca Town, and ought to be difcountenanced by ber Perfon, it is hoped that every one w utmoft Endeavours to bring the Offender or to condign Punifhment. Salem, Ma

GASPEE AFFAIR

By Steven H. Park

MANY HISTORIANS HAVE REFERRED TO THE PERIOD between the Boston Massacre (or, depending upon one's perspective, the King Street Riot) and the Boston Tea Party as "the lull," a period of relative quiet in the North American colonies. One notable exception to that fleeting peace was the burning of the armed schooner *Gaspee* by a colonial mob in the Providence River in 1772. Boston attorney and later President John Adams admitted in his diary that what became known as "the *Gaspee* Affair" brought back all of his old hostile feelings against British rule. Initially, the colonial raiders seemed motivated by the desire for compensation for some illegal rum that had been seized and was being held by the *Gaspee* crew, but Patriot printers and ministers soon exploited the event for their own political purposes.

Initially, the colonial raiders seemed motivated by the desire for compensation for some illegal rum that had been seized and was being held by the Gaspee *crew, but Patriot printers and ministers soon exploited the event for their own political purposes.*

Lieutenant William Dudingston took command of the *Gaspee* in 1768. It was one of several vessels commissioned after the French and Indian War (or the Seven Years' War in Europe) to patrol the fishing waters off Canada and northern New England. When Dudingston patrolled as far south as Philadelphia in 1769 and 1771, doing basic customs enforcement with his rough manner, he made some enemies who pressed civil charges. It was not unusual for sea officers to have arrest warrants issued against them by colonials, making it difficult for them to go ashore. For this reason, and to diffuse public dislike for particular officers, the admiralty moved unpopular commanders like Dudingston around frequently. (See Davis Bevan's account from the *Pennsylvania Journal* on June 29,

1769, reprinted in the *Boston Gazette* on July 10, 1769). Sea officers and customs officials did not believe they could get a fair hearing in the courts in the thirteen colonies and would try to take colonial smugglers to a vice-admiralty "super court" in Halifax.

Rhode Island had a reputation in London for its smuggling and trading with the enemy during times of war (*London Chronicle*, July 18, 1772). All of British America could not produce enough molasses for even a small colony like Rhode Island to maintain its production of rum. Consequently, Rhode Island merchants and shipmasters went looking elsewhere to meet the demand. Lieutenant Dudingston was sent to Rhode Island by Admiral John Montagu in Boston because he was so effective at suppressing smuggling and enforcing customs regulations. When the *Gaspee* ran aground in Narragansett Bay in June 1772, a group of colonial raiders rowed out to the schooner at night, shot the commander, put the crew ashore, and burned the vessel. The *London Chronicle* report was incorrect in stating that the Lieutenant was killed, although he was so badly hurt that he did make an official statement suspecting that he would not live through the night. Dudingston did recover and was court-martialed in Great Britain for the loss of the *Gaspee*, but he continued his naval career and retired as a rear admiral.

There were several instances in the 1760s when His Majesty's Government took no administrative action following colonial attacks on customs vessels, but they could not overlook such an attack on a naval vessel like the armed schooner *Gaspee* while in active service. They could not impose a royal court on a colonial government that already had a court system in place, but they could send over a "royal commission of inquiry" to investigate. By putting Rhode Island Governor Joseph Wanton in charge of the commission, the London government virtually doomed it to failure. Wanton scheduled witnesses in such a way that no raider or *Gaspee* mariner was in Colonial House at the same time. Other commissioners thought that some of the *Gaspee* mariners could identify colonial raiders if given the opportunity. The report in the *London Chronicle* from March 25, 1773, noted that "several persons were examined." They merely asked witnesses for a physical description of the raiders and their leaders but did not bring the two parties face-to-face.

Frustrated by what seemed like colonial efforts to obstruct justice and weak excuses by witnesses for failure to appear after being summoned, the commissioners agreed to take a recess until summer. Their efforts were merely stirring up more Patriot and rebel sentiment against His Majesty's program of colonial reforms. On August 14, 1773, the *London Chronicle* reported accurately that no one was "discovered." A black slave named Aaron

Biggs was the only colonial who did come forward and name the names of some powerful Rhode Island merchants. Governor Wanton worked diligently to discredit his testimony, and to this day, we do not know how much Biggs might have been "coached" by mariners aboard another British vessel, the *Beaver*.

The *Gaspee* Affair left two important Patriot developments in its wake. The Committees of Correspondence grew directly out of the frustration over the slow and inaccurate communication that followed the *Gaspee* events. It spurred direct communication between Richard Henry Lee in Virginia and Samuel Adams in Boston. Additionally, a little-known itinerant preacher named John Allen gave a highly political Thanksgiving Day sermon about the *Gaspee* Affair in Boston that became one of the most popular pre-independence pamphlets in the colonies.

BURNING OF THE *GASPEE*
North Wind Picture Archives

Angry Rhode Island colonists burn the *Gaspee* in Providence River in 1772, before the American Revolutionary War.

tius,) on *Green's Wharf*, opposite to *John Rowe*, Esq; where he has to sell very cheap for Cash, a good Assortment of English and India Goods, Cutlery Ware, Paper, French Indigo, &c. &c. &c.

PHILADELPHIA, June 29.

From the Pennsylvania Journal, June 29, 1769.

As the late outrageous insult and cruel treatment I have received from William Didingston, commander of the armed schooner Gaspey, and David Hay, captain of the Train, is become the common topic of conversation, I think I am bound in justice to myself and the public, to give a full and true narrative of the whole matter.—— What was my case yesterday, may be the case of every freeman, who may unfortunately fall within the power of such cowardly insolent officers, who disgrace the commissions they hold, and who seem to think that their office intitles them to treat their fellow subjects with outrage, insolence, and abuse.

On the 26th inst. going a fishing with Mr. Thomas Pedrix, of Chester, I saw a top-sail schooner coming up. As I wanted to speak with a Pilot, who I was informed was in such a schooner, I went near and hailed her, and asked what pilot was on board? The Capt. of the schooner replied, that the pilot did not chuse to tell his name. Such an uncivil, ungentleman-like answer provoked me to tell him, that a civil question deserved a civil answer, and that I thought both the Captain and Pilot blackguards. Upon which the Captain ordered out his boat and five men, to bring me on board, at the same time presenting his firelock, and swearing most violently, that he would fire upon me, if I did not come along side directly. All this time I had no apprehension of its being a King's armed Schooner. When the boat came up the Cockson immediately seized me, and in a piratical manner dragged me into the boat and put me on board the schooner, when the Captain accosted me with the most abusive language.——Finding in what hands I had fallen, I endeavoured to mollify him, by making all the concessions which gentlemen ought to demand. I assured him I did not know he was a King's officer; that if I had offended him I asked his pardon. Just at this time happening to see Capt. Hay, to whom I was known, I appealed to him for my character, expecting he would interpose his friendly offices. But Capt. Hay in a rude insulting manner said, " I know him very well, a tavern-keeper in Chester, a " damned horse-jockey. They are all a parcel of damn'd " rascals." Tho' I heard much of the imperious insolence of the man, yet I was quite thunder struck at this instance of it. He did not seem drunk, as it is said he was when he committed the violent outrage in Philadelphia some years ago, and attempted to assassinate a gentleman of that city. The words were no sooner out of Capt. Hay's mouth, than the commander of the schooner struck me in the face with his fist, and redoubled his strokes, which I endeavoured to ward off, without offering to return a blow. But in sending off his boat, my hand happened to touch his face; on which, with an oath, he cried out, " you rascal, will you strike me on " board my own vessel." I told him, I did not, that if my hand touched him, it was not designedly. " You " lie, you rascal," said Capt. Hay, " how dare you " strike a Captain of a man of war?" With that they both fell upon me; at the same time calling for the mate, who seized and held my hands, while the commander and Hay both beat mn in a most cruel manner. When they had tired themselves with beating me, that they might add insult to cruelty, they ordered me to be put in irons, and as if nothing could glut their revenge they thrust me into the hold, where the commander swore he would keep me and would not suffer me to see the light, nor to have pen, ink, or paper, till he had carried me to Halifax. When the commander found that all his threats and menaces did not break my spirit, trusting to the protection of the laws of my country, I defied his malice and insolence: His rage being somewhat abated, he ordered the boat with five men to put me on board my boat, if I would fall on my knees and ask his pardon.—— Finding he could not bring me to this, he ordered his men to carry me, bloody as I was, on board my boat, which was about half a mile distant, and during this inhuman scene he would not suffer to come nigh the schooner.   DAVIS BEVAN.

As soon as Mr. Bevan got to Chester, he followed them to this place, where they endeavoured to make up

---

here from Boston.

And next Day Brigadier General Pomeroy arrived here from Boston also, in his Majesty's armed Schooner Sultana.

New-York, June 25, 1769.

To the PUBLIC.

AS I have justly incurred the Resentment of my Fellow Citizens, from my Behaviour, as set forth in an Advertisement *Of great Importance to the Public*; I beg Leave to implore the Pardon of the Public, assuring them that I am truly sorry for the Part I have acted; declare and promise that I never will again attempt an Act contrary to the true Interest and Resolutions of a People zealous in the Cause of *Virtue* and *Liberty*; and by my future Conduct, not only convince them of my Contrition, but make it my whole Study to maintain inviolate the Resolutions they have entered into,——beseeching the Public in general to believe me,

Their ready devoted, and most
Obedient Humble Servant,
Alexander Robertson.

I Also declare, That the Goods were returned back to Philadelphia by the Stage last Monday, and that a Certificate of the same shall be produced to the Public.

The last three Lines } ELIAS DESBROSSES.
sworn to before me, }

PROVIDENCE, June 24.

Saturday last the Honourable General Assembly of this Colony adjourned to the second Monday in September next, then to be convened at East-Greenwich.

During the Session a Letter was received by the Speaker from Virginia, inclosing a Copy of the Resolutions entered into by the late House of Burgesses of that Colony; to which we are told the Assembly have agreed, and a Committee is accordingly appointed for preparing an Address to be presented to his Majesty.

From Louisbourg we have Advice, that the Distress of that Place, since the Troops were withdrawn, is really difficult to be described; several poor Families are in a starving Condition, and many of the Inhabitants daily deserting the Town.

SALEM, July 4.

WHEREAS Information has been made to the Merchants and Traders of this Town, that sundry Persons belonging to Boston, have sent Quantities of English Goods in this Town for Sale, which were imported since the General Agreement of the Merchants (not to import such Goods) took Place:—— We therefore, the Merchants and Traders of the Town of Salem, at a Meeting at the King's Arms this 30th Day of June, Anno Domini 1769, do publickly DECLARE our Disapprobation thereof, and resolve, that we will do all in our Power to discourage the Sale of such Goods, by not purchasing any of them ourselves, or suffering any Person for or under us to purchase them. We think (in Justice to those Merchants and Traders who have strictly adhered to their Agreement) we ought to inform all Persons, that the Shop lately kept by Mr. John Gool, now 'tended by John Norris in this Town, is now owned and supplied by Merchants in Boston, who have taken the Advantage of others not sending for Goods, to import double the Quantity of Goods which they did at other Seasons, expecting to make their Fortunes, while others were sinking theirs for the Benefit of their Country. We hereby caution all Persons, who have the Interest of their Country at Heart, against purchasing Goods of any Persons who come from Boston and offer Goods to sale, such as Tea, Loaf-Sugar, Crates of Earthen Ware, &c. as we have great Reason to suspect, that those Goods are sent out of that Town, because of the Discouragements the Owners meet with in the Sale of them by the Friends of Liberty there. We also request the Town of Marblehead to join with their Neighbours (for the general Good) not to send for any more Goods, contrary to the Intent and Meaning of the Agreements entered into by the Inhabitants of the Town of Boston and other neighbouring Towns, which

---

should be taken down notice shall be given them;—the Physicians of the Town have also declared, that they know not of any one Person, who has the Distemper or the Symptoms of it, excepting Mrs. Tyler at the Orange Tree, Mrs. Crafts at a House near Liberty Tree, and a Soldier, Sailor and two Women at the Province Hospital at New-Boston; at which Places a Red Flag is hung out as a signal of the Small Pox, Guards Placed; and the Passages stopt, to prevent a spread of the Infection:—A strict Enquiry will be continued and immediate Notice given in all the Papers if any other Person should be visited with the Distemper.—It is hoped that no one will conceal the Small-Pox from the Selectmen, if it should break out in their Family, as in such case they would be prosecuted to the rigor of the Law.

By Order of the Selectmen,
WILLIAM COOPER, Town-Clerk.

Messieurs EDES & GILL,

I Lately had occasion to search into the meaning of the word BARONET, and I find it to be a *diminutive* Term, as the Grammarians speak, and that it denotes little, tiny Baron. And the word Baron is derived from the Latin Baro, which in its *primary* Signification and as used by Cicero, means a *Blockhead*, a *Sot*, a *Dolt*, a *Fool.*   Vid. Ainsworth in voc.

At a Meeting of the FREE-AMERICAN *Fire-Society*, the Bunch of Grapes Tavern, *July 6, 1769.* Present 23 Members out of 25.

VOTED unanimously,

THAT Mr. ———————— be expelled the Society; as unworthy of being a Member of same, for having imported, and still persisting to import Goods from G. B. contrary to the general Agreement of the worthy and patriotic Merchants in this Town; for having been concern'd in publishing a partial, evil, and scandalous Advertisement, tending to cast an Odium on the respectable Merchants of this Town, and frustrate their good Intentions for the public Advantage.

Messieurs EDES & GILL,

The following Method of grafting the Mulberry Tree is mitted to your Inspection; if you shall think it a publishing, please to give it a Place in your valuable Gazette, and you will oblige a Friend to American produce and Manufactures.

TAKE from the Mulberry-Tree a Root ½ of an Diameter, and 7 or 8 Feet in Length, splice the and let it be fixed into the great End of the Root after usual Manner of grafting, wind a Woolen Thread the Root to keep the Cion in its Place, bury the Root the same Depth you found it, raising the great End 3 Inches of the Surface of the Ground, which bring Cion near perpendicular. The above Experiment tried in April 1768. The Cion grew two Feet that Year, and now appears very thrifty. The same in April 1769, grafted seven, some into shorter & Roots, even to two Feet in Length; they all appear to do well.

On FRIDAY next,

At Ten o'Clock in the Morning, Will be sold by PUBLIC VENDUE at the Auction Room in Queen-Street.

A Variety of Goods, among which Irish Linens, Sheetings, Callicoes, India Patch Lutestring, white Jeans, Ivory-stick Fans, Pieces, Mens and Boys Worsted Hose, Womens Cotton ditto, spotted Bandannoes, Indigo, Snuff of Pipes, &c. &c.

J. RUSSELL, Auction
Next Friday TEN o'Clock.

TO BE SOLD
On THURSDAY next.

By Benjamin Church

At his usual Place of Sale;

A great Variety of valuable Artic

Captains.

Extract of a Letter from a Gentleman in Lisbon to his Correspondent in this City.

THE sale of Grain here is rendered so delatory and

---

is well known) have deviated from their Contract, that they would (for the future) strictly adhere thereto; for it is determined at this Meeting, that we will make publick the Names of all those who shall hereafter break

---

Hollands—Bed Ticken—Irish Holland—She nens—Handkerchiefs—Mens, Womens and Hose, &c. &c. Likewise some House Furniture

BOSTON GAZETTE

July 10, 1769

Some sea officers had a lack of respect for colonials well before 1775, believing that colonials had traded with the enemy during the Seven Years' War (French and Indian War). Rhode Islanders had a very low reputation among English officers, on a par with pirates. After pieces like this one appeared in the local press, admirals would move their officers and vessels to a different city where their reputation for harsh treatment of colonials was not yet known. Since this Philadelphia story appeared in a Boston newspaper, their strategy did not work as well as they hoped.

LONDON CHRONICLE

July 18, 1772

In his haste to get information to London, Admiral Montagu mistakenly reported that Lieutenant Dudingston was dead. In fact, the commander returned to naval service in North America.

Thursday, March 25.

AMERICA.

Boston, (New-England) January 18.

WE hear from Newport the Commissioners for enquiring into the circumstances of attacking, plundering and burning his Majesty's schooner Gaspee, sat in the Court-house last week, when several persons were examined before them.

Boston, Jan. 21. It is said, that 45 towns and districts (out of 150 towns and districts that are in this Province) have had meetings, and sent their resolves, instructions to their Representatives, and other proceedings, in consequence of circular letters from this Town, to the Committee of Correspondence, appointed by the Town, and received.

COUNTRY NEWS.

Birmingham, March 22. At the assizes at Shrewsbury on Monday last, Thomas Brinford, for stealing six horned cattle; Richard Williams, for stealing one weather sheep; Francis Tipton, for stealing 18l. and Thomas Davies, for stealing a mare, received sentence of death.

SHIP NEWS.

Deal, March 23. Wind at S. S. W. Arrived and sailed for the River his Majesty's ship the Carcase. Remain in the Downs the ships as before, and the Great Marlow, Kitchen, for Jamaica; the William and Hopewell, Fenwick, for Maryland; the Rachael, Henry, for the Granades; and the Arabella, Bryan, for Neath.

LONDON.

The latter part of the decision of the House of Lords on Monday last on the appeal in which Alexander M'Clatchie was Appellant, and Mrs. Burnet, widow, Respondent, when their Lordships affirmed the interlocutors of March and

lity, it could not be pleaded in bar of his competency. Lord Mansfield was therefore fully of opinion, that Malcolm's testimony in the present case could not be refused; and that on the whole, it was an incontrovertibly just exception to the general rule of Law, that an Agent, Attorney, or Solicitor, was always competent to give testimony in any cause in which they might be employed, when it was impossible to resort to that species of evidence in any other manner whatever.

On Tuesday the House of Commons passed a bill for lighting, paving, and cleansing, the streets in the town of Brighthelmstone; and a bill for making new piers, regulating ships, and cleansing the harbour of Aberdeen.

Also the bill for making a new harbour, and for supplying the Inhabitants with fresh water in the town of Greenock in Scotland.

A new writ is issued for the election of a Member for Dover, in the room of Sir Thomas Pym Hales, deceased.

The election of a Member for Dover is expected to be strongly contested.

On Tuesday, at a meeting of a number of Freeholders of the county of Huntingdon now in town, a Gentleman moved that a similar engagement to that proposed by the late Common Hall, for shortening the duration of Parliaments, should be subscribed by the Candidates at the next Election, which was unanimously approved of.

Orders are sent to Woolwich for a Company of the Royal Regiment of Artillery to be in readiness to embark for Scotland, to relieve the Company now on that station.

Yesterday arrived a Mail from Flanders, but brought nothing material.

Yesterday Lord Stormont took leave of his Majesty, and to-morrow will set out on his embassy to the Court of France.

The same day the Earl of Suffolk arrived in town from his seat at Charlton in Wilts, and went to Court.

The same day Lord Viscount Townshend was

themselves against Re have other entrench quarter of Grand Sabl wish they would ma could trust themselves numbers of the Carib Lucia and the other daily going, to wait treat of the troops fr return to their own co

Basseterre in St. K which arrived here or formed that all the me train of artillery and coast, in order effectu that in a few days we my's surrendering, or

Letters are said to b St. Vincent's, which Infantry, under the c had come up with an Caribbs, headed by a regiment, when after a lasted near an hour, oth and their ringleader irons, and sent to the h

Extract of a Letter " The packet boat fr yesterday, and this brought in it were carri one directed to the C other to the Chancellor without any consideratio opened them both, and several books not permit Magistrates of the town to be made of them all the Court of Justice.

Extract of a Letter fro " This day sevennig goons arrived here, wi quelling the mutiny an nock and Port Glasgo marched on Friday, bu their assist and Lig cured a of 40 o were dif of actor istrate Inhabita ut to su n the latt disagre isperse turned to the ships they

under the command of Capt. Crafton, who had been left behind when the bill in party, however, put them to flight, and found five of their carcases in the woods, also several fuzees, habersacks, &c. thrown away in their

This deed was drawn up, and witnessed by Mr. Archibald Malcolm, his ordinary Attorney;

colm's evidence, as being the adviser of the settlement, and by reputation interested in the issue,

mentioned to have bee dead, and the life of ano On Monday sevenni

uld try at a speech of my own;
re prologue, the fancy is new,
eaves, you shall judge what Tom
on can do.

time, it was in Shakespeare's days,
common sense embellish'd plays,
nglish humour turn'd buffoon,
er Operas put wit out of tune,
time, folks did not think by rules,
felt, they spoke;—our fathers were
ols.
was, mirth admit me of your crew,
's old; 'tis not the thing—'twont do.
now—We must have something

we've had, new grand illuminations,
ees, and Trips, and Installations.
Trip to-night to shew some shipping,
ight the Author a'nt caught tripping,
e Play-jobbers, tho' it is surprising,
rs send me on apologizing,
come o'er me. Weston, you're a soul,
my prologue, you're so dry, so droll.
go then, I'm serv'd so to-night,
on bail for what bad poets write.
hope not—if we're brought to shame.
Author, or the Actors blame;
n one request, good sirs, be friended,
t give sentence till the piece is ended.

rday, August 14.

y arrived the Mail from FRANCE.

Constantinople, June 18.

HE last advices from Egypt
confirm the accounts of Ali
Bey's defeat and death, and
mention that Mehemet Abou-
daab has renewed the protestations of his zeal and fidelity to
the Porte; and it is hoped that
cha, the new Caimacan, who is to re-
Cairo, will now find but little trouble
ute the commission he is sent upon.
was wanting to complete the triumph
Porte in Egypt, after defeating Ali Bey,
conquering the Rebels who sided with
hich their avarice has happily spared
e trouble of doing; for no sooner was
ws arrived of Ali's defeat, than the
who were of his party, began to quar-
t dividing his treasures; and the Druses,
abs, and the Mutualis, took up arms.
Daher, that old and renowned warrior,
age of upwards of 80, full of courage
our, had the grief to see some of his
ildren in arms against him; upon which
unted his horse, and at the head of his
gave battle to his children and former
, with their forces; when he had the
tune not only to be defeated, but killed,
was fighting with amazing courage. The
accounts add, that all is in confusion in
and it seems as if the Pacha of

---

vate the earth for the use of others, which they
are not permitted the enjoyment of themselves;
and after having felt the intemperance of the
seasons, the scorchings of the sun, cold, snow,
and frost, they have no other retreats than the
abovementioned, from whence they are to issue
forth on the return of the day to renew their
labour. Touched with this sad picture, her
Imperial Majesty has given orders that this class
of her subjects shall be better accommodated,
by building for them more commodious habitations, wherein they may enjoy themselves with
tranquillity, and no longer look on themselves
as the most unfortunate class of her Majesty's
subjects.

AMERICA.

Boston, New England, June 21. Last Thursday twelve persons, belonging to Salem, went
from thence in a boat on a party of pleasure;
but in the evening a squall of wind came up,
attended with thunder and lightning, by which
the boat was sunk off Marblehead, and the following persons were drowned; viz. Mr. William Ward and wife, Mr. Diggadon and wife,
Mr. John Kimball and wife, the widow of Mr.
Eleazar Giles, a daughter of Dr. Fairfield's, one
other woman, and the wife of Mr. John Becket,
Boat-builder.

Newport, (Rhode Island) June 28. The
Court of Enquiry is broke up, without having
been able to discover any of the parties concerned in destroying the Gaspee schooner.

New-York, July 5. On Wednesday last Sir
John Johnson, son of the truly worthy, gallant,
and Hon. Sir William Johnson, Bart. was married to Miss Polly Watts, daughter of the Hon.
John Watts, Esq; of his Majesty's Council.

SHIP NEWS.

Deal, August 12. Wind at South. Arrived
and sailed for the River, the Active, Henzell,
from Oporto. Came down and sailed, with the
ships as per last, the Magna Charta, Maitland,
for Carolina; and the Molly and Betsey, Nicholson, for Maryland. Remains in the Downs
the Swift, Lante.

LONDON.

Yesterday a Mail from New York, brought by
the Lord Hyde packet boat, Capt. Goddard, in
29 days to Falmouth.

The following particulars are extracted from
the minutes of the Council Board of Boston in
New England, which met the 21st of June last,
containing the substance of their proceedings
that day.

The Council sent a message to his Excellency
Thomas Hutchinson, Governor, informing him,
that the House of Representatives have communicated to the Board a number of letters written
from Boston to Gentlemen in England, which
have occasioned great uneasiness; six of them
they said appeared to be written by his Excellency. The Board referred the consideration of

---

furnish the Lieutenant Governor, the Hon.
Andrew Oliver, with copies of four letters,
which appear to them to be written by him;
and to desire that he will inform the Board whether he has written letters to England of the
tenor of the copies aforesaid. The Lieutenant
Governor returned the following answer to the
Secretary:

" I have received from you a copy of a resolve
of the Hon. Board, setting forth, That among
the letters communicated by the House of Representatives, which have occasioned great uneasiness, and which are to come under consideration to-morrow, there are four from me,
bearing date from 7th May 1767, to 12th Aug.
1769, which appear to the Board to be written
and signed with my own hand, copies of which
they have been pleased to cause to be sent to
me, desiring that I would inform them whether
I had written letters to England of the tenor of
the said copies.

" I am obliged to the Board for their candour in furnishing me with those copies before
they take the matter under consideration. It
does not appear by the copies that either of the
letters were directed to any person in England,
or elsewhere. It is very material to know to
whom they were wrote, for there is an essential
difference between a free correspondence among
friends, and letters wrote to persons in public
office. I cannot therefore think it incumbent
on me to authenticate imperfect copies, even if
it were in my power.

" If I should be favoured with a sight of the
originals, which it is to be supposed are entire
and compleat, I will not deny my hand writing,
if they are really such: Nor will I contest any
kind of evidence which ought to be admitted in
proof before the Board of their having ever
been in England; although I own I should be
much surprised to see any letters of mine returned from thence; for I never corresponded
with any Gentleman there, whom I can suspect
to be capable of so much baseness, as to betray
a confidential correspondence: And it is very
evident these letters are of that kind.

" I have not heard that there has been any
attempt as yet to evidence so material a fact as
that of the letters coming from England: I cannot therefore think that the Hon. Board will
expect me to explain myself further on the subject, or that they will act upon it themselves
until this has been done.

Hon. Mr. Sec. Flucker,
  to be communicated   AND. OLIVER."
  to the Hon. Board.

Some letters from Berlin mention, that the
Jews of all ranks are preparing to leave the
Prussian dominions by order, on account of
some of them being suspected to be concerned in
the circulation of base ducats.

We hear from Dublin, that Mr. Gardiner,
Mr. Leslie, Mr. Bagnelle, Mr. Dawson, and
other Gentlemen of Distinction, have offered to
advance, upon Government security, a sum sufficient to satisfy, for the present, the numerous

COMMITTEES OF CORRESPONDENCE

By Carol Sue Humphrey

RELATIONS WITH GREAT BRITAIN REMAINED TENSE BUT relatively calm for most Americans in the years after the Boston Massacre of 1770. However, some people believed the fight was not over and sought ways to be prepared for future conflicts. In November 1772, Patriot leaders in Boston established a committee of correspondence to provide an organized mechanism for communication and protest when needed. Such committees had been used on a random and ad-hoc basis since 1764 to deal with specific issues, but people like Samuel Adams and Joseph Warren wanted to develop a more standardized system by tying the committees directly to the existing town meeting structure in order to provide official standing for the committee in the community and regular meetings to deal with ongoing concerns.

Other towns in Massachusetts organized similar groups. Word of the creation of Committees of Correspondence in Massachusetts soon spread to other colonies as communities in those areas organized their own groups. By March 1773, the colony of Virginia had formed a permanent colony-wide committee. They communicated this action to the other colonies and urged them to do the same. In late May, the House of Representatives of Massachusetts voted to establish its own colony-wide committee, charged with three primary duties:

> *to obtain the most early and authentic Intelligence of all such Acts and resolutions of the British Parliament, or Proceedings of Administration, as may relate to, or affect the British Colonies in America; and to keep up and maintain a Correspondence and Communication with our Sister Colonies respecting these important Considerations; and the result of such their Proceedings, from Time to Time, to lay before the House.*

On June 3, the *Massachusetts Gazette; and the Boston Weekly News-Letter* published this report and the resolutions related to the creation of the Massachusetts committee, as well as reports of the creation of similar groups in New Hampshire and Connecticut. Such detailed coverage reflected the growing awareness among many Americans that these committees were going to be increasingly important in the conflict with Great Britain. This assumption proved correct because the Committees of Correspondence became the de facto governments of the colonies when the royal institutions ceased to function properly as the arguments with Great Britain grew worse.

In each colony, these committees provided a means of communication separate from the official government that enabled the Patriots to organize to protest various British actions. In Massachusetts, for example, the committee played an important role in the events that led up to the Battle of Lexington and Concord. The Boston Committee of Correspondence worked hard to get the citizens of Boston organized to protest the shipment of East India Tea that led to the Boston Tea Party, and after the Tea Party occurred, their communication network spread the word to the rest of Massachusetts and the other colonies about what had happened in Boston.

When word of the Coercive Acts reached the colonies in the spring of 1774, the Committees of Correspondence in Massachusetts organized protests and demonstrations throughout the colony. In the wake of these events, prisoners were freed, courts were closed, and British-appointed officials were forced to resign. As a result of these revolutionary actions, the British colonial government ceased to function throughout Massachusetts, and the Committees of Correspondence stepped up to fill the gap. They eventually would provide the impetus for forming a new

THE Maſſachuſetts Gazette:
AND
Boſton Weekly
THE News-Letter.

Number 3635.

Draper's.]   THURSDAY, June 3, 1773.

The Treaſurer for the

County of SUFFOLK Notifies the Conſtables and Collectors of Taxes who are in Arrears for the Years preceding 1772, that he has received Order from the Court of General Seſſions of the Peace, to iſſue his Warrants againſt them, unleſs they immediately pay him their reſpective Ballances.   May 19th. 1773.

BOSTON, June 3.

Laſt Thurſday, upon Complaint to the Honourable Houſe of Repreſentatives, from ſome of the Inhabitants of the Town of Weſton, of Corruption in the Election of the Repreſentative for that Place; the Houſe took the Matter under Conſideration, when, after examining a Number of Witneſſes relative thereto, the Member was diſmiſſed the Houſe, and a new Precept ordered to be iſſued for another Choice.

The ſame Day after the Houſe of Repreſentatives had determined a conteſted Election, and agreed upon rules and Orders for their own Government, the Speaker communicated a Letter from the Speaker of the Houſe of Burgeſſes in the Colony of Virginia, incloſing a Reſolution of that Aſſembly, to keep up and maintain a Correſpondence and free Communication with the Siſter Colonies, and requeſting the Houſe to appoint a Committee to join with their Committee for that Purpoſe: The Speaker communicated alſo a Letter from the Speaker of the Houſe of Repreſentatives of the Colony of Rhode-Iſland, acquainting him that they had agreed to the ſalutary Meaſure propoſed by Virginia; and the ſame being read, the Houſe aſſigned the next Morning Nine o'Clock, to take them under Conſideration, and then adjourned.

The ſaid Letter and the Incloſures were accordingly read again on Friday Morning, and after due Conſideration thereon, the Houſe came into the following Reſolutions, there being 113 Members preſent, and only four Diſſentients.

WHEREAS the Speaker hath communicated ...

this Continent, incloſing the aforeſaid Reſolves; and requeſting them to lay the ſame before their reſpective Aſſemblies rately and chearfully the Reſolves of the ſince,

YEAS.
Mr. Samuel Adam
Hon. John Hancock
William Phillips,
Capt. William Hea
Mr. Samuel Howe
Mr. Joſiah Howe
Ebenezer Thayer, ju
Mr. Nathaniel Bai
Benjamin Lincoln,
Mr. Abner Ellis
Mr. Moſes Bullen
Mr. Jabez Fiſher
Capt. Benjamin W.
Richard Derby, jun
Mr. John Pickering
Dr. Samuel Holten
Capt. Michael Far
Hon. Joſeph Gerriſh
Capt. Jonathan Gr.
Mr. Elbridge Gerry
Azor Orne, Eſq;
Ebenezer Burrell, E
Mr. Moody Bridge
Capt. Henry Herri
Mr. Samuel Smith
Nathaniel Allen, E
Mr. John Gould
Aaron Wood, Eſq;
Iſaac Merrill, Eſq;
Capt. Daniel Thur
Capt. Thomas Gar
Mr. Nathaniel Go
Capt. Jonathan B
Mr. Samuel Wyma
Capt. James Barre

Hon. John Whitcomb, Eſq;
Capt. Ephraim Doolittle
Mr. Paul Mandell
Mr. Samuel March
Mr. John Lewis
Mr. Wentworth Stewart

James McCobb, Eſq;
David Ingerſol, Eſq;
Mr. Samuel Brown jun.
Mr. Peter Curtis
Mr. David Noble

NAYS.
Abijah White, Eſq;
Thomas Gilbert. Eſq;

Capt. Jeremiah Learned
John Murray, Eſq;

Then the Houſe immediately made Choice of the following Gentlemen to be the Committee of Correſpondence and Communication with the other Colonies.

Mr. Speaker, Mr. Samuel Adams, Hon. John Hancock, Eſq; Mr. William Phillips, Capt. William Heath, Hon. Joſeph Hawley, Eſq; Hon. James Warren, Eſq; Richard Derby, jun. Eſq; Mr. Elbridge Gerry, Jerathmeel Bowers, Eſq; Jedediah Foſter, Eſq; Daniel Leonard, Eſq; Capt. Thomas Gardner. Capt. Jonathan Greenleaf, and, James Preſcott, Eſq;

We hear that the Honorable Houſe of Repreſentatives of the Province of New-Hampſhire, have taken into their wiſe Conſideration the Plan of Union between the Colonies, as propoſed by the Honourable Houſe of Burgeſſes in Virginia, and have choſen a Committee of Correſpondence to communicate with the other Colonies;—have wrote Letters to the Houſes of Aſſembly in Virginia and Rhode-Iſland, and aſſured them that the Houſe of Repreſentatives of the Province of New-Hampſhire are ready to co-operate with all their Siſter Colonies to recover and perpetuate the Liberties of America.

We hear that the Houſe of Aſſembly of the Colony of Connecticut, have alſo adopted the ſame Meaſures.

Proceedings of the Town of Barnſtable.

the Water's Edge.——The Fire, caſioned by ſome Coals falling fr the Cabouſe on to the Deck, wh pay'd over with Turpentine, and Rapidity that Nothing could be —The Captain, with his Wife and uſually kept on board, likewiſe a ple belonging to her being aſhore be taken out of the Cabin Windo able to ſave the leaſt Thing but —A report prevailing at the Tim a large Quantity of Powder was Inhabitants in general into great fear of the Conſequences that mi Exploſion thereof; but being after none was in her, they became per Hills and Wharfs were covered view ſo uncommon a Sight. Som the Hold, ſuch as Cordage, Cab which were under Water befor reach them, will be ſaved.

About the ſame Time a Fire Goal at Cambridge, but by the dance of the Students, with the it was extinguiſhed.

Yeſterday Afternoon arrived Sloop of War from North Caroli

The ſame Day a Schooner arriv Mole, being one of thoſe lately whom we learn, that moſt or all th detained are likewiſe releaſed.

We hear from Boxford, that on had a terrible Storm of Hail, a ſevere Thunder and Lightning: that fell, we are informed, meaſ and a Half round.

---

government structure in Massachusetts that was totally independent of the British system.

As relations with Great Britain worsened in all the colonies, the colony-wide Committees of Correspondence played a major role in the planning of the First Continental Congress and thus helped in the initial stages of establishing an intercolonial government that could successfully fight the British during the American Revolution.

MASSACHUSETTS GAZETTE;
AND THE BOSTON WEEKLY NEWS-LETTER
June 3, 1773
—

are to be grounded any Instructions, that shall tend to lessen the Rights of either House, or any other Way affect the Interests of the Province?

On this Occasion it is obvious to observe that within these few Years the Ministry seem to have considered the Governors of this Province, not as CrownOfficers with Commissions under the Great Seal, but as Officers within their Department and under their Direction. This remarkably appeared in the Administration of Governor Bernard, who very probably was the means of it: For there is Reason to suppose, and his Letters shew it, that he laid a Plan for depriving Americans in general, and this Province in particular, of their Liberties: And being a Volunteer in the executing it, in order to secure himself seems to have procured from the Minister Letters of Instruction from time to time, as he had occasion for them: Whereby without giving the Province an opportunity of being heard, its Rights, Interests and Character have been greatly injured. And as the same mode of proceeding has been continued, there is the same reason to complain of it. But it is humbly hoped from the Goodness and Justice of his Majesty, and the distinguished Virtues of the Earl of Dartmouth, (his Majesty's Minister for the American Department) that this Province will be made happy by the Removal of all its Grievances.

In the mean time the Board are affected with the deepest concern, that any part of their Conduct should be disapproved by his Majesty: but they humbly trust, that when his Majesty shall be informed of the Reasons on which it is grounded, it will notwithstanding be the Object of his Gracious Approbation.

Extract of the proceedings of the town of Marshfield. on the 31st of January, 1774.

THIS town taking into consideration the late tumultuous and as we think illegal proceedings in the town of Boston, in the detention and destruction of the teas belonging to the East-India company, which we apprehend will affect our properties if not our liberties, think it our indispensible duty to show our disapprobation of such measures and proceedings:——Therefore Voted and Resolved, as the opinion of this town, That the late measures and proceedings in the town of Boston, in the detention and destruction of the teas belonging to the East-India company, were illegal and unjust & of a dangerous tendency.——That Abijah White, Esq; the present Representative of this town, be and hereby is instructed and directed to use his utmost endeavours that the perpetrators of those mischiefs may be detected and brought to justice. And as the country has been heretofore drawn in to pay their proportionable part of the expence which accrued from the riotous and unruly proceedings and conduct of certain individuals in the town of Boston,——if application should be made to the general court by the East-India company or any other persons for a consideration for the loss of said teas, you are by no means to acquiesce, but bear your testimony against any measures by which expence may accrue to the province in general, or to the town of Marshfield

Uxbridge, purchased a male infant of one of his tenants, who had lain in a few days, and was left a widow: he gave one hundred guineas for the child, on consideration the mother was never to own it, and intends adopting it as his own son.

Nov. 15. *One Mr. Fabrigas, a resident in Minorca, on account of some very heavy oppressions from General Mostyn, his Majesty's Governor of that island, last summer, brought an action against that officer.—— The cause was tried before Lord Chief Justice Mansfield, and a verdict of three thousand pounds damages was found for the plaintiff; afterwards the defendant's counsel moved the Court for a new trial, which occasioned the Governor to be summoned before a very awful tribunal, where the following particulars occurred:*

One day last week a command was sent to the culprit to attend immediately at Kew, his Majesty having business with him of the utmost importance. This command was immediately obeyed, and on the ministerial officer's arrival, he was introduced into the royal closet, where he found Lord North and Lord Mansfield, who had likewise received particular messages to attend, but were entirely ignorant of the business on which they were summoned, until the Viceroy gave immediate[...]*tion that it was on his ac*[...]*the gre*[...] appeared, and c*[...]*opinio*[...] himself to L*[...]

"*It is f*[...] account of [...] gentleme*[...] already [...] so indis[...] implicit t*[...] vestigatin*[...] nearly aff*[...] in foreig*[...] ing hims*[...] not alone [...] you that [...] any man, w*[...] shall use [...] his [...] Vi*[...] an*[...] th*[...] ap*[...] hav*[...] which [...] Marsh*[...] cumstan*[...] he recite*[...] stile that se*[...] injuries to [...] louring [...]

Wheeler, of [...] from Worcester goal, in the Massachusetts-Bay) was apprehended on the night of the 21st January last, for passing counterfeit dollars; also, one Peter Hobart, an accomplice, who has turned King's evidence, & given such a clue to Wheeler's plans, as cannot fail of the most salutary effect.

BOSTON, Thursday, February 3.

We hear that on Monday last the Corporation of Harvard-College, made Choice of the Honorable JOHN WINTHROP, Esq: LL.D. and F.R.S. to be PRESIDENT; but that he decl[...] accepting that Office.

We have authentic intelligence from [...] bridge, that the three Persons in Capt. [...] Family, who have been supposed to ha[...] Small-Po[...] all perfectly [...]over[...] House [...] cleansed t[...] Dist[...] now in any [...] [...]rehended [...] to th[...] [...]ation [...] B[...]

❦ CHAPTER IV ❦

THE DETESTABLE TEA

Introduction

WITH THE TEA ACT OF 1773, BRITISH PARLIAMENT PROVIDED A GOVERNMENT bailout to the East India Company, the monopoly importer of tea and one of Britain's biggest and most important businesses, which faced serious financial doom. Instead of imposing new or additional taxes, the Tea Act provided tax breaks, lowering the price of the East India Company's products and underselling American smugglers and legitimate middlemen alike. In the closing months of 1773, as tea ships sailed for America, colonists mobilized to determine exactly how the soon-arriving tea chests should be handled. With an important customs deadline looming and the threat of the tea cargo being forced into the American marketplace, a party of rebels took matters into their own hands, destroying hundreds of tea chests in Boston Harbor—a decision with revolutionary consequences.

ESSEX GAZETTE (SALEM, MA)
February 8, 1774

DISGUISED COLONISTS WIELDING
AXES AND DUMPING BOXES OF TEA
INTO BOSTON HARBOR
North Wind Picture Archives

TEA ACT IN AMERICA

By Benjamin L. Carp

POLITICS IN BOSTON, AND MUCH OF THE REST OF COLO-nial America, had been relatively quiet since the Boston Massacre of 1770. True, the people of Massachusetts were becoming increasingly angry with Governor Thomas Hutchinson, but the town of Boston was largely free of violent crowd action.

Then in October 1773, Boston began to learn about the provisions of the Tea Act. Parliament had passed this law on behalf of the East India Company, which had a monopoly on British tea imports from China but was deeply in debt and needed better access to the American market (see the letter in the *Boston Gazette* of March 22, 1773). The law imposed no taxes; in fact, it gave significant tax breaks to the East India Company, which would now be able to sell tea directly to designated agents, or consignees, in the American colonies. The result would be cheaper tea for colonial consumers.

The Tea Act gave privileges to a monopoly company and its consignees, which would drive other merchants out of the tea trade. Many Americans feared Parliament would extend such monopoly privileges to other commodities.

Many of the colonists were outraged, for three reasons: first, they were afraid cheap tea would seduce Americans into paying the duty (or tax) on tea that had been imposed in 1767; second, the revenue from the tea tax paid the salary of Hutchinson and other civil officials in Massachusetts—the people of Massachusetts would have preferred these salaries be paid from the coffers of the House of Representatives, so as to keep these officials accountable; and finally, the Tea Act gave privileges to a monopoly company and its consignees, which would drive other merchants out of the tea trade. Many Americans feared Parliament would extend such monopoly privileges to other commodities.

Egged on by New York City and Philadelphia (both centers for smuggling tea from foreign countries), the Bostonians protested the Tea Act in several ways. The Boston Committee of Correspondence, the local political caucus, and the newspapers coordinated protests. Crowds confronted the consignees at their homes and shops, trying to force the consignees to resign their commissions. Bostonians gathered at official town meetings on November 5, 6, and 18 to deliberate about the tea, challenge the consignees, and pass resolutions against the Tea Act.

Then the first of the tea ships hired by the East India Company, the *Dartmouth*, arrived on November 28. The next day, the people of Boston and its surrounding towns began gathering at more expansive meetings of the "body of the people." Such meetings took place November 29 and 30 and December 14 and 16. As was reported in the *Boston Evening-Post* of December 6, 1773, Faneuil Hall (the site of town meetings) was too small to contain the thousands of interested spectators, so the meetings were moved to the Old South Meeting House, the largest building in town. The meetings overtly defied Governor Hutchinson, and they continued to challenge the consignees, owners, and captains of the tea ships to send the tea back to London. The gathered subjects appointed guards to watch over the ships at night to make sure no one tried to unload the tea. Finally, the assembly announced that anyone who tried to import tea from Great Britain would be deemed "an Enemy to his Country," and everyone present agreed to prevent the tea from landing "at the Risque of their Lives and Property."

OLD SOUTH MEETING HOUSE
North Wind Picture Archives

(*at right*) The largest building in Boston, where thousands met in November and December 1773 to discuss the tea crisis.

The House of P——— and B———, at Stockholm, has stopped payment for the sum of *one million four hundred thousand Dollars*, (about 313.000l. sterl.) There is, no doubt but this failure will in its consequences involve many other capital houses in all the great commercial cities of Europe.

NEW-YORK, March 15.

Extract of a Letter of the 29th of January, from a Gentleman in the West-Indies.

" The Caribs are resolute, and seem determined that the Loss of Liberty and Property shall be accompanied with that of Life ;—a Determination worthy of a Briton; and as such, should be rever'd by one, tho' found in the Breast of a poor oppress'd Carib.—Our Troops are sickly and appear to want that Animation, which has, hitherto always appeared on more glorious Occasions ; they seem sensible that Justice has not drawn the Sword.—The Expedition was ill-judged, and is condemned by every rational Being in the West-Indies.—One Third of the Sum expended, given to the Caribs, would have purchased the Lands, and they would have retired from the Island.—They are by no Means Savages ; many of them own 20 and 30 Negroes, and have Plantations under good Cultivation."

BOSTON, March 22.

Extract of a Letter from a Gentleman in London to his Friend in this Town, dated January 5. 1773.

" Some Circumstances are working in Favor of America with Regard to the Duties ; it is found by the last Year's Accounts transmitted by the Commissioners that the Balance in Favor of Britain is but about Eighty-Five Pounds, after Payment of Salaries, &c. exclusive of the Charge of a Fleet to enforce the Collection.— It is further observed, that the India Company is so out of Cash that it cannot pay the Bills drawn upon it, and at the same Time so out of Credit that the Bank does not care to assist them ; whence they find themselves obliged to lower their Dividend, the Apprehension of which has sunk their Stock from 280 to 160, whereby several Millions of Property are annihilated, occasioning private Bankruptcies and other Distress, besides a Loss to the public Treasury of £.400 000 per Ann. which the Company by Agreement are not to pay into it as heretofore, if they are not able to keep up their Dividend at 12½ ; and as they have at the same Time Tea and other India Goods in their Warehouses, to the Amount of Four Millions as some say, for which they want a Market, and which if it had been sold, would have kept up their Credit. This shews the great Importance of losing the American Market, by keeping up the Duties on Tea, which has thrown the Trade into the Hands of Foreigners. This gives some Alarm, and begins to convince People more and more of the Impropriety of Quarrelling with the Americans."

Extract of a Letter from New-York, dated March 10, 1773.

" THE present political Transactions of your Province, especially of your General Court, excites the Attention of all Ranks here :—Your Assembly's *Reply* to your Governor's late *extraordinary* Speech, meets with general Approbation ; & well

... any of the American Colonies. I think, however, that we ought not to be inattentive to the Subject. The Episcopal Clergy we know will not, and sure we ought not. The Comic Satiric Lecture, call'd The Times, which was to have been deliver'd this Evening at Concert-Hall, is postpon'd on Account of the Weather to Monday Evening next.

Folks may strip us stark naked, and turn us out of Doors in Mid-winter, we hold the Blessings of Heaven on very precarious Tenure. Planners and Abettors of such a Conspiracy as this, and for them only the modern *Juvenal* boasts his Desire to maintain the Freedom of his Press.

Quere, Should not Emboweling and Quartering have been added to the well deserved Punishments this P——— drawn up for himself ?

On Tuesday the 30th will be Sold at Public Auction at a Store opposite to the Sign of Admiral Vernon, King — Fourteen Hogsheads of Choice — vado SUGAR.

Lost last Thursday, a — ther Pocket Book, containing sundry P— Ticket No. 928, in Faneuil-Hall Lottery Ruddock. Whoever has found the same bring it to the Printers hereof, shall be — their Trouble.

A Brigantine.

Now on the Stocks at North River ; a B— about 130 Tons, built of good Stuff and by — (can be Launch'd in April.) To be Sold Cash or part West India Goods.—A so a fi— Brig of three Years old, about 97 ons, a p— and well found. Inquire of Edes & Gill.

To be Sold on Reasonable Term

A Likely Well-built B— about 115 Tuns, single Deck, 5 Years old, w— and a tall Sailer. Inquire of the Printers. N. B. A Vessel of 70 Tuns would suit —

TO BE SOLD.

The Estate of Capt. Edward S— late of Boston, Mariner, deceased, consisting of — ling House with two Rooms on a Floor, a g— and Garden, and fine Well of Water, pleasa— ed on Cambridge-Street, N w-Boston. For Particulars, inquire of Hannah Stone, Admini said Estate. AND all Persons that have any Demands Estate, are desired to bring in their Accounts, the Estate being rendered Insolvent.

TO-MORROW at 11 o'Clock, Will be Sold by PUBLIC VENDUE, at the Auction-Room Foot of Royal Exchange Lane.

A Variety of ENGLISH GOODS, Among which are, 30 Pieces of Irish Linnens, Bedticks,

Daniel Parks.

LOST at the late Fire at Mr. Ivis's, a Leather Bucket, mark'd *Wm. Homes.* If any Person will return it to him opposite the Golden Key, they shall be satisfied for their Trouble.

... of the — best E— — the — — eas'd — — OT, — made — ell'd — on—

— the — — — nt — on — the — — d — — his — — may — that good Order will be observ'd. The Days propos'd for public School are Mondays and Thursdays. N. B Said CURTIS was Educated in *Paris,* and has taught Dancing in several Towns in this Province.—Any Persons that are disposed to employ him, are desired to leave a Line with Capt. GORE, at the Painters Arms.

At Bowman's Dying Auction Room, North Side of the Market, On FRIDAY Morning next, Sold by Public Vendue, — —— Consisting of, erseys, Duffils, Coating, Threads, Serge Denim, figured and plain Lawns 7 8 and yard-wide Irish Callicoes, Checks, check and Thread Hose, a Writing Paper, Table s of Hard Ware, &c.— amongst which are, an Book Case, one Meho-eather Beds, &c. &c. Ten o'Clock.

TON, since our last, No Blacks. — Churches, Fourteen.

High Water at BOSTON for this present Week.

Monday,	0 min. after 11	Friday,	40 m aft. 1
Tuesday,	40 min. af. 11	Saturday,	12 m. af. 2
Wednesday,	10 m. aft. 12	Lord's Day 0 m. af. 3
Thursday	48 min. after 12	New Moon this Night

BOSTON GAZETTE
March 22, 1773

—

Parliament passed the Tea Act on behalf of the East India Company, which had a monopoly on British tea imports from China but was deeply in debt and needed better access to the American market. A letter from a gentleman in London to his friend in Boston tells "that the India Company is so out of Cash that it cannot pay the Bills drawn upon it" and that the Company has a surplus inventory of tea "to the Amount of Four Millions as some say, for which they want a Market." As the writer summarizes, this shows "the great Importance of losing the American Market, by keeping up the Duties on Tea" and suggests it will convince Great Britain to quarrel less with America.

trator be chosen, and

ONATHAN WILLIAMS, Esq;
Was then chosen Moderator of the Meeting.

A MOTION was made that as the Town of Boston had determined at a late Meeting legally assembled, that they would to the utmost of their Power prevent the landing of the Tea, the Question be put, Whether his Body are absolutely determined that the Tea now arrived in Capt. Hall shall be returned to the lace from whence it came at all Events. And the question being accordingly put, it passed in the affirmative. Nem. Con.

It appearing that the Hall could not contain the People assembled, it was Voted, that the Meeting be immediately Adjourned to the Old South Meeting-House, Leave having been obtained for is Purpose.

The People met at the Old South according to djournment.

A Motion was made, and the Question put, viz. Whether it is the firm Resolution of this Body that the Tea shall not only be sent back, but at no Duty shall be paid thereon; & pass'd in the affirmative. Nem. Con.

It was moved, that in order to give Time to the consignees to consider and deliberate, before they sent in their Proposals to this Body, as they had given Reason to expect would have been done at the opening of the Meeting there might be an Adjournment to Three o'Clock, P. M and the Meeting was accordingly for that Purpose adjourned.

THREE o'Clock, P. M. met according to Adjournment.

A Motion was made, Whether the Tea now arrived in Captain Hall's Ship shall be sent back in the same Bottom—Pass'd in the Affirmative, Nem. Con.

Mr. Rotch the Owner of the Vessel being present, informed the Body that he should enter his Protest against their Proceedings.

It was then moved and voted, nem. con. That Mr. Rotch be directed not to enter this Tea; and that the Doing of it would be at his Peril.

Also Voted, That Captain Hall the Master of
[...] Ship [...] that at his Peril he is not

they had hitherto expended upon them to no Purpose, were prevailed upon to adjourn to the next Morning Nine o'clock.

Nine o'Clock,
[...] journment.

[...]ds were at length [...] directed to the Mo[...], Esq; one of the [...]ted that the same [...] follow, viz.

[...]ov. 29th, 1773.

[...]ld not return to the [...]ers to their two late [...]eas; we beg Leave [...]ectmen that we have [...] the Honorable East-

[...] do all in our Power [...], but as we under-
[...] Gentlemen Selectmen at Men. Clarkes Interview with you last Saturday, that this can be effected by nothing less than our sending back the Teas, we beg Leave to say, that this is utterly out of our Power to do, but we do now declare to you our Readiness to Store the Teas until we shall have Opportunity of writing to our Constituents and shall receive their further Orders respecting them; and we do most sincerely wish that the Town considering the unexpected Difficulties devolved upon us will be satisfied with what we now offer.

We are, SIR,
Your most humble Servants,
Tho. & Elisha Hutchinson,
Benja. Faneuil, jun. for Self and
Joshua Winslow, Esq;
Rich'd Clarke & Sons.

John Scollay, Esq;

Mr. Sheriff Greenleaf came into the Meeting, and begg'd Leave of the Moderator that a Letter he had received from the Governor, requiring him to read a Proclamation to the People here assembled might be read; and it was accordingly read.

Whereupon it was moved, and the Question put, Whether the Sheriff should be permitted to read the Proclamation—which passed in the Affirmative, nem. con.

The Proclamation is as follows, viz.

Massachusets-Bay. } By the Governor.

To JONATHAN WILLIAMS, Esq; acting as Moderator of an Assembly of People in the Town of Boston, and to the People so assembled:

WHEREAS printed Notifications were on Monday the 29th Instant posted in divers Places in the Town of Boston and published in the News-Papers of that Day calling upon the People to assemble together for certain unlawful Purposes in such Notifications mentioned: And whereas great Numbers of People belonging to the Town of Boston, and divers others belonging to several other Towns in the Province, did assemble

And the same being read by the Sheriff, there was immediately aft[...] a loud and very general Hiss.

A Motion was th[...] made, and the Question put, Whether the Assembly would disperse and surcease all further Proceedings, according to the Governor's Requirement——It pass'd in the Negative, nem. con.

A Proposal of Mr. Copley was made, that in Case he could prevail with the Mess. Clarkes to come into this Meeting, the Question might now be put, Whether they should be treated with Civility while in the Meeting, though they might be of different Sentiments with this Body; and their Persons be safe until their Return to the Place from whence they should come——And the Question being accordingly put, passed in the Affirmative, Nem. Con.

Another Motion of Mr. Copley's was put, Whether two Hours shall be given him, which also passed in the Affirmative.

Adjourn'd to Two o'Clock, P. M.

TWO o'Clock P. M. met according to Adjournment.

A Motion was made and passed, that Mr. Rotch and Capt. Hall be desired to give their Attendance.

Mr. Rotch appeared, and upon a Motion made the Question was put, Whether it is the firm Resolution of this Body, that the Tea brought by Capt. Hall shall be returned by Mr. Rotch to England in the Bottom in which it came; and whether they accordingly now require the same, which passed in the Affirmative, Nem. Con.

Mr. Rotch then informed the Meeting that he should protest against the whole Proceedings as he had done against the Proceedings on Yesterday, but that tho' the returning the Tea is an involuntary Act in him, he yet considers himself as under a Necessity to do it, and shall therefore comply with the Requirement of this Body.

Capt. Hall being present was forbid to aid or assist in unloading the Tea at his Peril, and ordered that if he continues Master of the Vessel, he carry the same back to London; who reply'd he should comply with these Requirements.

Upon a Motion, Resolved, That John Rowe, Esq; Owner of Part of Capt. Bruce's Ship expected with Tea, as also Mr. Timmins, Factor for Capt. Coffin's Brig, be desired to attend.

Mr. Ezekiel Cheever was appointed Captain of the Watch for this Night, and a sufficient Number of Volunteers gave in their Names for that Service.

VOTED, That the Captain of this Watch be desired to make out a List of the Watch for the next Night, and so each Captain of the Watch for the following Nights until the Vessels leave the Harbour.

Upon a Motion made, Voted, that in Case it should happen that the Watch should be any Ways molested in the Night, while on Duty, they give the Alarm to the Inhabitants by the tolling of the Bells—and that if any Thing happens in the Day Time, the Alarm be by ringing of the Bells.

VOTED, That six Persons be appointed to be in Readiness to give due Notice to the Country Towns when they shall be required so to do, upon any important Occasion. And six Persons were accordingly chosen for that Purpose.

A Motion was made, That in Order for the security of Captain Hall's Ship and Cargo, a Watch may be appointed—and it was Voted

Moderator, and to consult, deba[...] and resolve upon Ways and Means for carrying such un[...]

carry back the Tea [...] brou't in the same Bottom, or that it was the Expectation of this Body that he does the same by the Tea expected in Capt. Bruce; where[...] reply'd that he was under the Care

Confignees, be in the leaft Degree fatisfactory to this Body, & paffed in the Negative. Nem. Con.

Whereas a Number of Merchants in this Province have inadvertently imported Tea from Great-Britain, while it is fubject to the Payment of a Duty impofed upon it by an Act of the British Parliament for the Purpofe of raifing a Revenue in America, and appropriating the fame without the Confent of thofe who are required to pay it :

RESOLVED, That in thus importing faid Tea, they have juftly incurr'd the Difpleafure of our Brethren in the other Colonies.

And Refolved further, That if any Perfon or Perfons fhall hereafter import Tea from Great-Britain, or if any Mafter or Mafters of any Veffel or Veffels in Great-Britain fhall take the fame on Board to be imported to this Place, until the faid unrighteous Act fhall be repeal'd, he or they fhall be deem'd by this Body, an Enemy to his Country ; and we will prevent the Landing and Sale of the fame, and the Payment of any Duty thereon. And we will effect the Return thereof to the Place from whence it fhall come.

RESOLVED, That the foregoing Vote be printed and fent to England, and all the Sea-Ports in this Province.

Upon a Motion made, Voted, That fair Copies be taken of the whole Proceedings of this Meeting, and tranfmitted to New-York & Philadelphia, And that   Mr. SAMUEL ADAMS,
Hon. JOHN HANCOCK, Efq;
WILLIAM PHILLIPS, Efq;
JOHN ROWE, Efq;
JONATHAN WILLIAMS, Efq
Be a Committee to tranfmit the fame.

Voted, That it is the Determination of this Body, to carry their Votes and Refolutions into Execution, at the Rifque of their Lives and Property.

Voted, That the Committee of Correfpondence for this Town, be defired to take Care that every other Veffel with Tea that arrives in this Harbour, proper Watch appointed for her —— Alfo Voted, That thofe Perfons who are defirous of making a Part of thefe Nightly Watches, be defired to give in their Names at Meffieurs Edes and Gill's Printing-Office.

Voted, That our Brethren in the Country be defired to afford their Affiftance upon the firft Notice given ; efpecially if fuch Notice be given upon the Arrival of Captain Loring, in Meffieurs Clarkes' Brigantine.

Voted, That thofe of this Body who belong to the Town of Bofton do return their Thanks to their Brethren who have come from the neighbouring Towns, for their Countenance and Union with this Body in this Exigence of our Affairs.

VOTED, That the Thanks of this Meeting be given to JONATHAN WILLIAMS, Efq; for his good fervices as Moderator.

VOTED, That this Meeting be Diffolved —— And it was accordingly Diffolved.

Frazier & Geyer

HEREBY inform the PUBLIC,

That their Co-partnerfhip is this Day mutually DISSOLVED ; wherefore, all Perfons having any Demands on, and who are indebted to faid Company, are defired to call on *Frederick Wm. Geyer,* at the Store lately improved by them, for an immediate Settlement.   *November* 16, 1773.

N. B. The Bufinefs is ftill continued at faid Store by faid *Geyer* as ufual.——

---

of the Town of Roxbury, legally affembled on Friday, December 3, 1773.

After mature Deliberation, the Town came into the following Refolutions, which paffed unanimoufly, *viz.*

WHEREAS it appears by an Act of the Britifh Parliament paffed at their laft Seffion, That the Eaft India Company in London, are by faid Act allowed to export their Teas to America " *difchaaged from the Payment of any Cuftoms or Duties whatfoever*" in London, but " *liable to the fame Rules, Regulations, Penalties and Forfeitures,*" in America, as if faid Act had not been paffed ; from which there is too much Reafon to apprehend the faid Act was defigned to take in the Unwary, and to continue and eftablifh the Tribute extorted from, and fo much, and fo juftly complained of by the Americans. Upon due Confideration thereof, *Refolved,* That the Senfe of this Town cannot be better exprefs'd upon this Occafion, than in the Words of certain judicious, and truly patriotic Refolves lately entered into by the worthy Citizens of Philadelphia, & fince adopted by our much refpected Brethren, the Inhabitants of the Town of Bofton.

And Whereas it appears that notwithftanding the repeated Application which hath been made by the Inhabitants of the Town of Bofton to the Perfons appointed by the Eaft India Company, to receive and fell faid Tea, to refign faid Truft, they ftill, regardlefs of their own Characters, or of the Peace, Quiet and Profperity of the People, not only of the Town of Bofton, or of this Town and Province, but from the moft undoubted Intelligence, America in general.

Therefore *Refolved,* That fo long as faid Perfons appointed by the Eaft India Company as aforefaid, fhall perfift in refufing to refign their Appointment to that Truft, or otherwife eafe and fatisfy the prefent Uneafinefs of this People, fo greatly enhanced by their repeated Refufals, they difcover a want of Fellow-feeling of the Grievances under which this People are Groaning, that they prefer their own private Emolument, to the public Happinefs—a Difpofition to facilitate and eftablifh the detefted Tribute. ——A Temper enemical to the Rights, Liberties and Profperity of America, and that in fuch light they will be viewed by this Town, from whom they may not expect the leaft Protection.

Refolved alfo, That if any other of the Inhabitants of this Province fhall hereafter, directly or indirectly, import any Tea into this Province, fubject to a Duty in America, fuch Perfon or Perfons fhall be viewed by this Town as Enemies to their Country, and may not expect either Countenance or Protection.

And Whereas the Inhabitants of the Town of Bofton, have repeatedly heretofore, and on the prefent occafion in particular, given frefh proof of their vigilance and unwearied Endeavors, to recover and preferve the Rights and Liberties of America.

Refolved, That this Town look upon themfelves, as in Duty bound to themfelves and Pofterity, to ftand faft in that Liberty wherewith the Supreme Being hath made them free, & that they will readily join with the Town of Bofton & other Sifter Towns, in fuch Conftitutional Meafures, as fhall be judged proper to preferve and hand down to Pofterity inviolate, thofe ineftimable Rights & Liberties, handed down to us (under Providence) by our worthy Anceftors.   The foregoing is a true Copy,

Atteft,   SAMUEL GRIDLEY, Town Clerk.

AT a legal Meeting of the Freeholders and other Inhabitants of the Town of Charleftown, Nov. 27, 1773, *and continued by Adjournment to the* 4th *of December, the following* RESOLVES *were unanimoufly Voted, viz.*

WHEN we his Majefty's dutiful and loyal fubjects the Inhabitants of this Town, reflect on the glorious Attachment of our Anceftors to Liberty ; an Attachment fo ftrong as to induce them (during the Tyranny of the Stuarts) to quit their native Homes, and feek for Freedom in the howling Wildernefs of America : When we confider that this once inhofpitable Defart has by their Labor and at the Expence of their Blood and Treafure, been brought to its prefent flourifhing Situation : When we contemplate our ftrong Attachment to the Perfon and Family of our moft gracious Sovereign, & recollect that Harmony and mutual Affection that lately fubfifted between our Parent State and her Colonies, the Reftoration of which we moft ardently wifh, we cannot but have our Minds moft deeply affected, and our Fears greatly alarmed at the Encroachments on our Rights and Privileges ; by Adminiftration's raifing

---

in the Colonies, that the retaining the Duty on Tea, for the exprefs Purpofe of raifing a Revenue in America, and impowering the Eaft India Company to fend their Tea here for Sale, while fubject to faid Duty, is a ftriking Inftance of their Determination to perfevere in their Attacks, and thereby reduce us to the moft abject State of Wretchednefs and Slavery.

IV. Refolved, That whoever fhall be directly or indirectly concerned in landing, receiving, buying or felling faid Tea, or in importing any Tea from Great Britain, whilft fubject to Duty, is an Enemy to America, and ought to be treated accordingly.

V. Refolved, That we highly approve the Vigilant, Wife and Steady Conduct of our Brethren the Inhabitants of the Town of Bofton at this alarming Crifis, and beg their Acceptance of our moft cordial Thanks for the fame.

VI. Refolved, That we are and will be on all proper Occafions ready in Conjunction with our oppreffed American Brethren to rifque our Lives and Fortunes in the fupport of thofe Rights, Liberties and Privileges with which GOD, Nature and our happy Conftitution has made us free.

The foregoing is a true Copy,
Atteft.   SETH SWEETSER, Town-Clerk.

At a Meeting of the Freeholders and other Inhabitants of the Town of Dorchefter, on the 30th of November 1773.

THE Committee of Correfpondence laid before the Town a Letter which had been agreed upon by the Committees of feveral Towns, to be fent to all the Towns in the Province, in order to know their Minds at this critical Juncture, and alfo the Votes and Proceedings of the Town of Bofton thereon :

VOTED, That we highly approve of the public Conduct of the Towns of Bofton and Cambridge, in their late Town-Meetings, and the Refolves that came into, in order to prevent the Act of Parliament refpecting the Eaft-India Company being allowed to fend their Teas to America, to take effect.

2. But being at prefent engaged in private matters within the Town, and having not long fince made our Minds known to the Public in fundry Refolves, which were voted unanimoufly, we muft now cut fhort ; but we can affure the Public, that fhould this Country be fo unhappy as to fee a day of trial, for the recovery of its Rights, by a laft and folemn appeal to him who gave them, we fhould not be behind the braveft of our patriotic brethren, and that we will at all times be ready to affift our neighbours and friends, when they fhall need us, though the greateft dangers fhould attend it.

3. And whereas feveral Perfons, who are deemed Enemies to their Country, have of late by their guilty confciences been drove into this and the neighbouring Towns, to fhelter themfelves from the juft Vengeance of their Fellow-Citizens, that we will ufe our endeavours, that the juft indignation they there feared, fhall here overtake them, and that we, though we are not all of one Town, yet are all embarked in one common Caufe.

Voted, That the Town-Clerk be directed to forward a Copy hereof to the Committee of Correfpondence in the Town of Bofton.

A true Copy from Dorchefter Records.
Atteft.   NOAH CLAP, Town-Clerk.

NEW-YORK, Nov. 25.

George Clarke, Efq; having furrendered the office of Secretary of this Province, it has been conferred, for life, upon William Knox, Efq; Under Secretary to the Earl of Dartmouth.

The Ship Grace, Capt. William Chambers, will fail for Briftol on Sunday next. This is the commander's 72d paffage over the Atlantick.

Lieut. John Nordberg, of the firft Battalion of the Royal Americans, now in Jamaica, is appointed Commandant of Fort George, near Lake George, with the Rank of Captain in America.

We have Advice by Capt. Couper from London, that ten Days before him failed,

A Ship for Bofton, with Tea, Chefts	600
A Ship for Philadelphia, with	600
A Ship for Charleftown, ready to fail, with	200
A Ship for Rhode Ifland, ditto,	200
And another for New York, taking in	600
Total,	2200

NEWPORT (*Rhode-Ifland*) Nov. 29.

We are affured from the beft authority, that Bohea TEA in New-York is no more than Half a Dollar a pound, by wholefale, and but 3/4½ lawful, by the fingle Pound.

The French nation having found Bohea Tea very pernicious, have almoft entirely eradicated the ufe of it, through the whole kingdom ; and even in England, there is but very little ufed, there being fcarcely a drop drank in any public-houfe in London.

Laft Tuefday arrived here, from New-York, the Lady who has paffed thro' feveral of the fouthern colonies under the name and character of CAROLINA MATILDA, Marchionefs de WALDEGRAVE, &c.

BOSTON, December 6, 1773.

Laft Saturday Capt. Shephard, in a Ship, arrived here from London : He failed from the Downs in Company with Capt. Bruce, but has none of the obnoxious Tea on board.

We have advice by the laft Veffels from England, that on the end of September the fame Ships

Americans throwing the Cargoes of the Tea Ships into the River, at Boston

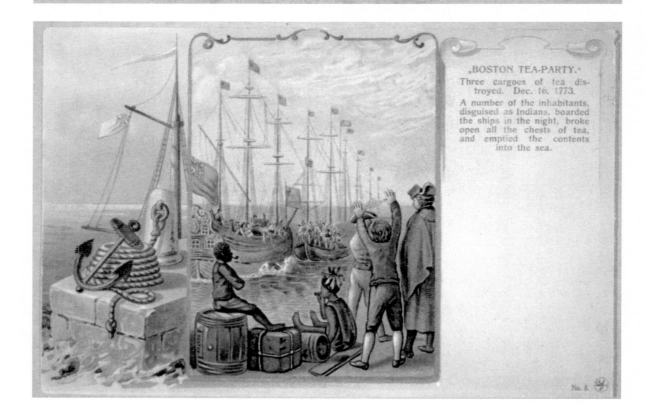

DESTRUCTION OF THE TEA
Library of Congress

(*top*) "Americans Throwing the Cargoes of the Tea Ships into the River, at Boston" from *The History of North America* (London, 1789) and (*bottom*) "Boston tea-party." Three cargoes of tea destroyed, December 16, 1773. This print, created in 1903, is a reproduction of the 1789 engraving.

"BOSTON TEA-PARTY."
Three cargoes of tea destroyed. Dec. 16, 1773.

A number of the inhabitants, disguised as Indians, boarded the ships in the night, broke open all the chests of tea, and emptied the contents into the sea.

REPORTING THE
BOSTON TEA PARTY

By Benjamin L. Carp

B Y DECEMBER 16, 1773, THERE WERE THREE SHIPS loaded with tea at Griffin's Wharf: the *Dartmouth*, the *Eleanor*, and the *Beaver*. The *Dartmouth* had been in Boston Harbor for almost twenty days, and when this deadline elapsed, any ship with taxable goods aboard was liable to seizure by customs officials. It was illegal for the *Dartmouth* and the other ships to return to London without unloading their cargo, but the Bostonians refused to allow the tea to land. If customs officials or the governor were willing to look the other way, then the ships might travel back across the Atlantic with the accursed tea aboard.

By December 16, customs officials had already refused to go along with the Boston crowd. So the people of Boston and the surrounding towns gathered at the Old South Meeting House and ordered Francis Rotch, owner of the *Dartmouth*, to travel to Milton and ask Governor Thomas Hutchinson to permit his ship to leave Boston Harbor. Hours later, Rotch returned to the Meeting House with the governor's refusal.

Soon afterward, the gathered Bostonians heard a war whoop, and a group of men disguised as Indians led the crowd down to Griffin's Wharf. About a hundred men boarded the three ships, lifted 340 tea chests above decks, smashed them open, and emptied their contents—over forty-six tons of tea—into the harbor. (Although the newspapers reported a figure of 342 chests, the East India Company claimed that 340 chests were destroyed.) The task took two or three hours, and the destroyers made sure not to damage anything other than the tea. The East India Company would later claim £9,659 in damages.

The *Pennsylvania Packet* jokingly reported: "Letters from Boston complain much of the taste of their fish being altered."

The "Impartial Observer" whose letter was printed in the *Essex Gazette* of December 21, 1773, was anything but impartial: "I cannot but express my admiration at the conduct of this People!" he exclaimed. He insisted that the "wise and considerate body" at the Old South Meeting House "evidently tended to preserve the property of the East-India Company." Furthermore, the writer observes that it was not the gathered people from Boston and the surrounding towns who destroyed the tea, but "a number of Persons, supposed to be the Aboriginal Natives from their complections." Yet everyone knew that in reality, disguised white men, not American Indians, had destroyed the tea. In other words, the writer supported the protestors at the meetinghouse by making them blameless for the property destruction. Even the actual tea destroyers were careful to leave the rest of the ships' cargo untouched and replaced a broken lock. Meanwhile, other Boston newspapers joined the "Observer" in blaming the stubbornness of the consignees and the governor for the "fatal necessity" that "rendered this catastrophe inevitable."

The gathered Bostonians heard a war whoop, and a group of men disguised as Indians led the crowd down to Griffin's Wharf.

The *Essex Gazette* also illustrates that the people of Massachusetts were deeply interested in other American tea protests: they exulted at Philadelphia's approval, and they noted that several neighboring Massachusetts towns were publicly burning tea and pledging support for Boston.

BOSTON, December 20.

Messrs. PRINTERS,

HAVING accidentally arrived at Boston upon a visit to a Friend, the Evening before the Meeting of the Body of the People on the 29th of November, curiosity and the pressing invitation of my most kind host induced me to attend the Meeting; I must confess I was most agreeably, and I hope I shall be forgiven by this People if I say so unexpectedly entertained and instructed by the regular, reasonable and sensible conduct and expression of the People there collected, that I should rather have entertained an idea of being transported to the British senate than to an adventitious and promiscuous assembly of People of a remote Colony; were I not convinced by the genuine uncorrupted integrity and manly hardihood of the Rhetoricians of that assembly, that they were not yet corrupted by venality, or debauched by luxury. The conduct of that wise and confederate body in their several transactions, evidently tended to preserve the property of the East-India Company: I must confess I was very disagreeably affected with the conduct of Mr. Hutchinson, their pensioned Governor, on the succeeding day, who very unseasonably, and as I am informed, very arbitrarily (not having the sanction of law) framed and executed a mandate to disperse the People, which in my opinion, with a people less prudent and temperate, would have cost him his head: The force of that body was directed to effect the return of the Teas to Great-Britain; much argument was expended, much entreaty was made use of to effect this desirable purpose—Mr. Rotch behaved in my estimation very unexceptionable; his disposition was seemingly to comport with the desires of the People to convey the Teas to the original proprietors. The Consignees have behaved like Scoundrels in refusing to take the consignment, or indemnify the owner of the ship which conveyed this detestable commodity to this port; every possible step was taken to preserve this property; the people being exasperated with the conduct of administration in this affair, great pains were taken, and much policy exerted to procure a stated watch * for this purpose. The body of the people determined the Tea should not be landed; the determination was deliberate, was judicious; the sacrifice of their Rights, of the Union of all the Colonies, would have been the effect, had they conducted with less resolution: On the Committee of Correspondence they devolved the care of seeing their resolutions seasonably executed; that body, as I have been informed by one of their members, had taken every step prudence and patriotism could suggest, to effect the desirable purpose, but were defeated. The Body once more assembled, I was again present; such a collection of the people as to me a novelty; near seven thousand persons from several towns, Gentlemen, Merchants, Yeomen and others, respectable for their rank and abilities, and venerable for their age and character, constituted the assembly; they decently, unanimously and firmly adhered to their former resolution, that the baleful commodity, which was to rivet and establish the duty, should never be landed; to prevent the mischief, they repeated the desires of the committee of the Towns, that the owner of the ship should apply for a clearance; it appeared that Mr. Rotch had been managed, and

assembly, gave the War-Whoop, which was answered by a few in the galleries of the house where the assembly was convened; silence was commanded, and a prudent and peaceable deportment again enjoined. The Savages repaired to the ships which entertained the pestilential Teas, and had began their ravage previous to the dissolution of the meeting--they applied themselves to the destruction of this commodity in earnest, and in the space of about two hours broke up 342 chests and discharged their contents into the sea. A watch as I am informed was stationed to prevent embezzlement, and not a single ounce of Tea was suffered to be purloined by the populace: One or two persons being detected in endeavouring to pocket a small quantity were stripped of their acquisitions and very roughly handled—It is worthy remark that although a considerable quantity of goods of different kinds were still remaining on board the vessels, no injury was sustained; such attention to private property was observed that a small padlock belonging to the Captain of one of the Ships being broke, another was procured and sent to him.—I cannot but express my admiration at the conduct of this People! Uninfluenced by party or any other attachment, I presume I shall not be suspected of misrepresentation.—The East-India Company must console themselves with this reflection, that if they have suffered, the prejudice they sustain does not arise from enmity to them: a fatal necessity has rendered this catastrophe inevitable—the landing the tea would have been fatal, as it would have saddled the col... imposed without their conse... power on earth can effect. T... numbers, spirit and illuminati... periment dangerous, the det... Consignees must attribute to... of the property of the East-In... they seasonably quieted the ... by a resignation, all had been ... house, and the man who disgr... presenting him, acting in co... inveterate enemies of America... every measure concerted to re... That American virtue may d... to enslave them, is the warme... I shall return home doubly forti... tion to prevent that deprecated calamity, the landing the teas in Rhode-Island, and console myself with the happiest assurances that my brethren have not less virtue, less resolution than their neighbours.   An IMPARTIAL OBSERVER.

Another Account concludes thus: "The Masters and Owners are well pleased that their Ships are thus cleared; and the People are almost universally congratulating each other on this happy Event."

Capt. Loring in a Brig from London for this Place, having 58 Chests of the detested Tea on board, was cast ashore on the Back of Cape-Cod last Friday se'nnight: 'Tis expected the Cape Indians will give us a good Account of the Tea against our next.

Extract of a letter from Philadelphia, dated December 11, 1773.
—"Your Resolutions of the 29th ult. were publickly read at our Coffee-House last Thursday, to a large Company of our Merchants, who gave three Cheers by Way of *Approbation*."

We hear from Philadelphia, that Capt. Ayres, in a Ship chartered by the East-India Company, Company's importing Tea into America, subject to a duty here; and have entered into a number of spirited Resolves relative to the same; fully agreeing with those of the Town of Boston, and their determination to assist in carrying them into Execution, at the hazard of their Lives and Fortunes.

Immediately on the Proceedings of the People here, on the 29th ult. being received in Philadelphia, all the Bells in the City were set a ringing.

A CARD.

DETECTOR presents his due respects to Messieurs A. B. C. and D. and informs those dark and villainous *Assassins* that their *Conspiracies* against the Lives and Liberties of a Number of the most worthy *Patriots* in this *Metropolis*, and the *Vicinity*, are well known; their execrable Measures to secure and transport them abroad, are seasonably discovered, their Persons are marked, and if they are disposed for a concealed Plot, they may probably fall into the Pit they are digging for others.   *Boston Gaz.*

SALEM, December 21.

We are informed, that 130 Patients, who were inoculated at Salem Hospital last Thursday sevennight, are now broke out with the Small-Pox, and are all in a fair Way of coming out well in a few Days. Two Children, inoculated several Days after the other Patients, are not yet broke out.

Divine Service was performed at the Hospital last Sunday, when the Rev. Mr. Payson again officiated.

The ESSEX GAZETTE

BOSTON, December 20.

Messrs. Printers,

HAVING accidentally arrived at Boston upon a visit to a Friend, the Evening before the Meeting of the Body of the People on the 29th of November, curiosity and the pressing invitation of my most kind host induced me to attend the Meeting ; I must confess I was most agreeably, and I hope I shall be forgiven by this People if I say so unexpectedly entertained and instructed by the regular, reasonable and sensible conduct and expression of the People there collected, that I should rather have entertained an idea of being transported to the British senate than to an adventitious and promiscuous assembly of People of a remote Colony ; were I not convinced by the genuine uncorrupted integrity and manly hardihood of the Rhetoricians of that assembly, that they were not yet corrupted by venality, or debauched by luxury. The conduct of that wise and considerate body in their several transactions, evidently tended to preserve the property of the East-India Company [...]

Previous to the dissolution, a number of Persons, supposed to be the Aboriginal Natives from their complection, approaching near the door of the assembly, gave the War-Whoop, which was answered by a few in the galleries of the house where the assembly was convened ; silence was commanded, and a prudent and peacable deportment again enjoined. The Savages repaired to the ships which entertained the pestilential Teas, and had began their ravage previous to the dissolution of the meeting—they applied themselves to the destruction of this commodity in earnest, and in the space of about two hours broke up 342 chests and discharged their contents into the sea. A watch as I am informed was stationed to prevent embezzlement, and not a single ounce of tea suffered to be purloined by the populace : One or two persons being detected in endeavouring to pocket a small quantity were stripped of their acquisitions and very roughly handled—It is worthy remark that although a considerable quantity of goods of different kinds were still remaining on board the vessels, no injury was sustained ; such attention to private property was observed that a small padlock belonging to the Captain of one of the Ships being broke, another was procured and sent to him.—I cannot but express my admiration at the conduct of this People ! Uninfluenced by party or any other attachment, I presume I shall not be suspected of misrepresentation.—The East-India Company must console themselves with this reflection, that if they have suffered, the prejudice they sustain does not arise from enmity to them : a fatal necessity has rendered this catastrophe inevitable—the landing the tea would have been fatal, as it would have saddled the colonies with a duty imposed without their consent, and which no power on earth can effect. Their strength and numbers, spirit and illumination render the experiment dangerous, the defeat certain: The Consignees must attribute to themselves the loss of the property of the East-India Company : had they seasonably quieted the minds of the people by a resignation, all had been well ; the custom-house, and the man who disgraces Majesty by representing him, acting in confederacy with the inveterate enemies of America, stupidly opposed every measure concerted to return the Teas.----That American virtue may defeat every attempt to enslave them, is the warmest wish of my heart. I shall return home doubly fortified in my resolution to prevent that deprecated calamity, the landing the teas in Rhode-Island, and console myself with the happiest assurances that my brethren have not less virtue, less resolution than their neighbours.

An IMPARTIAL OBSERVER

APRIL 18, 1774

The
PENNSYLVANIA PACKET

Jan. 28. Letters from Boston complain much of the taste of their fish being altered: Four or five hundred chests of tea may have so contaminated the water in the harbor, that the fish may have contracted a disorder not unlike the nervous complaints of the human body. Should this complaint extend itself as far as the banks of Newfoundland, our Spanish and Portugal fish trade may be much affected by it.

[…]

It is said that the tea thrown into the Sea at Boston is valued at 18,000 l. at 1s. 6d. per pound. The whole sent to America is said to be worth about 300,000 l. which is returning home, not being suffered to be landed.

---

the lift of those gentlemen who were recommended by the House of Commons to his Majesty for some adequate employment, when the act was repealed, yet he is the only one of them who has not been provided for. All these circumstances, so highly recommendatory of him, with a character perfectly unexceptionable, seem only to have operated as a bar to his preferment, till Lord Dartmouth, who has always been distinguished for his upright and equitable conduct, rewarded his long-neglected merit. The propriety of his choice redounds much to his Lordship's wisdom, as well as to his honour; for Colonel Mercer's perfect knowledge of that country, his thorough acquaintance with the American laws, and the well-known candour, integrity, and firmness of his mind (exclusive of his other fair pretensions) render him better qualified for that appointment than almost any other man.

Jan. 26. Advice is received from Tunis, that three Barbarian vessels have been equipped against the vessels of any christian powers that shall approach near that port.

Letters from Petersburgh advise that Admiral Spiritoff is recalled from the Mediterranean, and that Admiral Basbaille will succeed him.

It is now said to be settled by a great Personage for the Queen of Denmark to come to England the ensuing summer.

When the Duke of Gloucester was at Paris, Morgan, the highwayman, presented a petition to him, praying that his highness would procure him a pardon: The Duke gave him two guineas but told him his offences were of that nature that he could do nothing else for him.

It is again in agitation to appoint a commander in chief on the British establishment; and it is generally supposed that his royal highness the Duke of Gloucester will succeed to it.

The following shocking affair happened at Munich the beginning of this month:—Baron Waldeck was stabbed by his Valet de Chambre in his bed; the murderer was instantly detected, but he begged leave of the guard to go with him into his room, as he wished to take along with him some papers of consequence. This was granted, and the guards posted themselves at the doors and windows: but not minding farther what the prisoner was about, he took a well charged pistol and shot himself. It since appears by some notes found upon him, that he was promised 3000 florins for that heinous action; and the hand writing appears to be that of his young master, the only son of the Baron, about seventeen years of age, who was immediately secured upon suspicion.

Jan. 28. Letters from Boston complain much of the taste of their fish being altered: Four or five hundred chests of tea may have so contaminated the water in the harbour, that the fish may have contracted a disorder not unlike the nervous complaints of the human body. Should this complaint extend itself as far as the banks of Newfoundland, our Spanish and Portugal fish trade may be much affected by it.

An act, it is said, will pass this session, disqualifying all persons from voting for members of Parliament that do not possess a freehold of ten pounds a year.

Council, last week, only voted two regiments to America. His Majesty has ordered five more from Ireland. The Bostonians are to be chastised, and are to drink tea, though ever so great an emetic.

The Polly, Captain Ayres, is just arrived at Dover, returned from North-America with

---

Tea. On her arrival at Philadelphia, the inhabitants informed the Captain that they would not suffer him either to land or enter his cargo at the Custom-House.

It is said that the tea thrown into the Sea at Boston is valued at 18,000 l. at 1s. 6d. per pound. The whole sent to America is said to be worth about 300,000 l. which is returning home, not being suffered to be landed.

Extract of a letter from an English gentleman at Copenhagen, Dec. 14.

" By some of the English new-papers which have lately fallen into my hands, I find that you, in England, think that the King of Denmark is in a state of imbecility; be that as it will, however if he is so, his subjects are happy, and his actions every day prove that his mind is less tainted than the minds of any neighbouring Princes. He has lately struck out a number of pensions which were burthensome to his people, and has found a scheme himself to lessen several heavy taxes very much. Are these actions that denote a weak mind? If they are I should not be sorry to hear that —— —— was in a state of imbecility; you would perhaps then be happier than you are.—The first opportunity that offers, I intend writing again."

Extract of a letter from the Hague, Jan. 21.

" One of the two commissaries who went over

---

no notice would be taken of dering the matter, it was th refer it to the privy cou were thus obliged to take i trial was resolved upon, tha legations might be affectedl upon which some judgmen and reported to the King. last Saturday, before the Franklin attended accordi Attorney and Solicitor-Gen of Administration, council foa, Dr. Franklin was allo He had Mr. Serjeant Glynn The matter turned chiefly u letters (which have been publ and Lieutenant-Governor to It was sometime doubted wh could be admitted as eviden possible to obtain the origina the House of Assembly, the admitted. The event of t made public.—The fate of of Great-Britain, depends rather report, which the pr to the King upon this occasi affairs in America is become than ever. The union thro to reject the tea, while it is and this Province in particular, of their Liberties: And being a Volunteer in the executing it, in order to secure himself seems to have procured from ... to ... wi... bei... hav... mo... the... bly... Ma... of ... Ame...

made happy by the Removal of all its Grievances.

In the mean time the Board are affected with the deepest concern, that any part of their Conduct should be disapproved by his Majesty: but they humbly trust, that when his Majesty shall be informed of the Reasons on which it is grounded, it will notwithstanding be the Object of his Gracious Approbation.

Extract of the proceedings of the town of Marshfield. on the 31st of January, 1774.

THIS town taking into consideration the late tumultuous and as we think illegal proceedings in the town of Boston, in the detention and destruction of the teas belonging to the East-India company, which we apprehend will affect our properties if not our liberties, think it our indispensible duty to show our disapprobation of such measures and proceedings:——Therefore Voted and Resolved, as the opinion of this town,—— That the late measures and proceedings in the town of Boston, in the detention and destruction of the teas belonging to the East-India company, were illegal and unjust & of a dangerous tendency. ——That Abijah White, Esq; the present Representative of this town, be and hereby is instructed and directed to use his utmost endeavours that the perpetrators of those mischiefs may be detected and brought to justice. And as the country has been heretofore drawn in to pay their proportionable part of the expence which accrued from the riotous and unruly proceedings and conduct of certain individuals in the town of Boston,—if application should be made to the general court by the East-India company or any other persons for a consideration for the loss of said teas, you are by no means to acquiesce, but bear your testimony against any measures by which expence may accrue to the province in general, or to the town of Marshfield

counsel moved the Court for a new trial, which occasioned the Governor to be summoned before a very awful tribunal, where the following particulars ...

... this account. The great personage soon appeared, and confirmed this opinion, by addressing himself to Lord Mansfield in the following manner: "It is from you, my Lord, that we expect a clear account of the heavy charge brought lately against this gentleman, in one of our courts of justice; the relations already given us have been so partially coloured, and so indistinctively confused, that we must rely on the implicit truth of your recital, as the only means of investigating to our own satisfaction, a matter that so nearly affects ourselves, and the safety of our subjects in foreign governments. We have, my Lord (addressing himself to Lord North) desired your attendance, not alone to have the benefit of your advice, but to shew you that we will not in the least encourage or support any man, who, trusted with our delegated authority, shall use it to the worst of purposes, that of oppressing his fellow subjects. And you, Sir (speaking to the Viceroy) we thought proper to command your attendance, to bear our sincere opinion of your conduct, and to convince you, that all reliance upon our protection, assistance, or future favour is in vain, if we find you have merited by oppression and injustice, the stigma which has been thrown on your character." Lord Mansfield then entered into a minute detail of the circumstances, but eloquently palliated the most flagrant; he recited the provocations given to the Viceroy, in a stile that set them on a level with the most provoking injuries to his person and government; in which colourings he was more than once interrupted by Lord North, which set them in their true light. When his Lordship had finished, the King demanded his positive and real opinion, whether the verdict given was just and adequate? To this plain demand, enforced by a determinate voice and accent, the equivocating P—— was obliged to give an affirmative reply. Lord North was then asked his opinion, who replied, that he had not the least doubt of the justness of the verdict; that the tyranny and cruelty of the Viceroy were but too palpable; though it must be confessed, some provoca-

REBELLION

Introduction

SOON AFTER NEWS OF THE BOSTON TEA PARTY ARRIVED IN LONDON, PARLIAMENT struck back with an iron fist that included closing the Port of Boston and stripping Massachusetts of its right to self-govern. In April 1774, King George III appointed General Thomas Gage, a veteran of the French and Indian War, as commander in chief of the British forces in America and royal governor of Massachusetts, replacing the much-hated Governor Thomas Hutchinson. Tensions escalated and an arms race unfolded as New England militia and Gage's army scrambled to secure and hide powder and shot from one another. Meanwhile, Massachusetts colonists assembled their own de facto government to effectively rule the colony from the countryside. On the brink of war, a twelve-colony congress is called to discuss and debate a united resistance.

BOSTON GAZETTE
March 7, 1774

"THE BOSTONIANS
PAYING THE EXCISE-MAN
OR TARRING & FEATHERING"
Library of Congress

COERCIVE ACTS

By Ray Raphael

COLONISTS DID NOT UNITE BEHIND THE ACT OF POLITI-cal vandalism we now celebrate as the Boston Tea Party. John Adams called it "the grandest event, which has ever yet happened since the controversy with Britain opened," but George Washington chided Bostonians for "their conduct in destroying tea," and Benjamin Franklin thought the East India Company should be compensated for the ruined merchandise.

People did unite, however, around the harsh repression that followed. To punish the vandals and those who supported them, Parliament passed four acts it thought would bring rebels to their knees. People in Britain called them the Coercive Acts, but in America, they were labeled the Intolerable Acts.

The first is the best known: the Boston Port Act, which closed Boston Harbor until somebody paid for the destroyed tea. Related acts, to facilitate enforcement, permitted British soldiers to be housed in unoccupied buildings and allowed for the removal of Massachusetts residents to Britain to stand trial.

To punish the vandals and those who supported them, Parliament passed four acts it thought would bring rebels to their knees. People in Britain called them the Coercive Acts, but in America, they were labeled the Intolerable Acts.

Instead of isolating Bostonians, these measures triggered a sympathetic response from other colonies. Political groups passed supportive resolutions (posts from Connecticut House of Representatives, Newark, New York, and Philadelphia in June 20, 1774, *Pennsylvania Packet*), organized relief efforts (*Boston Evening-Post*, October 31, 1774), and selected delegates for an intercolonial assembly—the future Continental Congress—to coordinate their efforts.

The most consequential act of repression, though, was the "act for the better regulating the Government of the province of the Massachusetts Bay" (known today as the Massachusetts Government Act), which disenfranchised the province's citizens and spurred them to shed British rule. No longer could residents gather in town meetings, unless the royal governor gave his assent and approved all agenda items. The powerful council, formerly chosen by the people's representatives, would henceforth be selected by the Crown, while sheriffs and judges would be chosen by the Crown-appointed governor, not the people. Even the selection of jurors was now out of the people's hands. The very heart of the Massachusetts Charter of 1691, the provincial constitution, had been unilaterally set aside.

Resistance was immediate, widespread, and multifaceted:

* Town meetings continued despite the ban. In Salem, one block from the temporary headquarters of Governor Thomas Gage, citizens held a meeting. When Gage ordered the arrest of seven alleged ringleaders, three thousand local residents marched on the jail to force their release. In neighboring Danvers, citizens held a town meeting "and continued it two or three howers longer than was necessary, to see if he would interrupt 'em," one man reported. "He was acquainted with it, but reply'd—'Damn 'em! I won't do any thing about it unless his Majesty sends me more troops.'"

* All thirty-six Crown-appointed councilors (called "mandamus counsellors" at the time) were intimidated by groups of angry citizens and forced either to resign or to flee to Boston, where they would be protected by British troops. Timothy Ruggles, for instance, had his horse mutilated, while Abijah

Willard chose to sign a humiliating recantation to secure his safety, asking "forgiveness of all the honest, worthy gentlemen, that I have offended" by taking the oath to serve under the new act, which undermined "the Charter Rights and Liberties of this province" (August 25 Sturbridge dateline in September 5, 1774, *Massachusetts Gazette; and the Boston Post-Boy and Advertiser*).

❈ Finally, and most significantly, crowds numbering in the thousands closed the county courts (Barnstable dateline in October 31, 1774, *Boston Evening-Post*), the farthest reach of British imperial authority under the hated Massachusetts Government Act. More on these dramatic events in the next three sections.

The BOSTONIANS in DISTRESS.

The able Doctor, or America Swallowing the Bitter Draught.

THE BOSTONIANS IN DISTRESS
Library of Congress

(*above*) Depicting Boston's sufferings as a result of the Coercive Acts, this print shows three sailors feeding starving Bostonians suspended in a cage from the Liberty Tree.

THE ABLE DOCTOR, OR AMERICA SWALLOWING THE BITTER DRAUGHT
Library of Congress

(*left*) Lord North forces tea down the throat of America, represented by a Native American, and she spits it back in his face. In North's pocket is a copy of the Boston Port Bill.

In the House of Representatives of the English Colony of Connecticut.

THIS House taking into their serious consideration sundry acts of the British Parliament, in which their power and right to impose duties and taxes upon his Majesty's subjects in the British colonies and plantations in America, for the purpose of raising a revenue, are declared, attempted to be exercised, and in various ways enforced and carried into execution, and especially a very late act, in which pains and penalties are inflicted on the capital of a neighbouring province, a precedent justly alarming to every British colony in America, and which being admitted, and established, their lives, liberties, and properties are at the mercy of a tribunal where innocence may be punished upon the accusation and evidence of wicked men, without defence, and even without knowing the accuser. A precedent calculated to terrify them into silence and submission whilst they are stripped of their invaluable rights and liberties—do think it their duty, and expedient at this time to renew their claim to the rights, liberties and immunities of freeborn Englishmen, to which they are justly intitled by the laws of nature, by the royal grant and charter of his late Majesty King Charles the second, and by long, and uninterrupted possession, and thereupon do declare and ———— as follows, viz.

III. That the only lawful representatives of the freemen of this colony are the persons they elect to serve as members of the General Assembly thereof.

IV. That it is the just right and privilege of his Majesty's liege subjects of this colony to be governed by the General Assembly in the article of taxing, and internal police, agreeable to the powers and privileges recognized and confirmed in the royal charter aforesaid, which they have enjoyed for more than a century past, and have neither forfeited nor surrendered, but the same have been constantly recognized by the King and Parliament of Great-Britain.

V. That the erecting new and unusual Courts of Admiralty, and vesting them with extraordinary powers, above, and not subject to the common law courts in this colony, to judge and determine in suits relating to the duties and forfeitures contained in said acts, foreign to the accustomed and established jurisdiction of the former Courts of Admiralty in America, is, in the opinion of this House, highly dangerous to the liberties of his Majesty's American subjects, contrary to the great charter of English liberty, and destructive of one of their most darling rights, that of trial by juries, which is justly esteemed one chief excellence of the British constitution, and a principle branch of English liberty.

but has been verified in fact, and by long experience, found to produce, according to our extent, and other circumstances, as many loyal, virtuous, industrious, and well governed subjects, as any part of his Majesty's dominions; and as truly zealous of and warmly engaged, to promote the best, good and real glory of the grand whole, which constitutes the British empire.

XI. That it is an indispensible duty, which we owe to our King, our country, ourselves and our posterity, by all lawful ways and means in our power, to maintain, defend and preserve these our rights and liberties, and to transmit them entire and inviolate to the latest generations. And that it is our fixed, determined, and unalterable resolution, faithfully to discharge this our duty.

At their sessions at Hartford, on the second Thursday of May, 1774, in the 14th year of his Majesty's reign, the foregoing resolutions, reported to the House by their committee, were unanimously voted and ordered to be entered on their journal or record.

June 9. Monday afternoon two young Gentlemen came into Boston from the county of Worcester, relating that they had been alarmed with the report that a regiment of soldiers had been posted at the entrance of this city, to cut off its communication with the country.—Many respectable persons, they said, had assembled upon the occasion, ——————— Sabbath evening, to ——————— intelligence as ——— case they ——— report, they ——— and strong,

Their ex——— be the minds ——— r of their li——— ry at all dif——— in their act. ——— that by the ———ed, and the ——— is utterly va——— province and ——— solved, they ——— in what man——— tual security. ——— sail of wood ———ward, bound ——— unload and load again, before they are permitted to take their departure.

At a meeting of the Freeholders and Inhabitants of the county of Essex, in the province of New-Jersey, at Newark in the said county, on Saturday the 11th June, 1774.

THIS meeting taking into serious consideration some late alarming measures, adopted by the British parliament, for depriving his Majesty's American subjects of their undoubted and constitutional rights and privileges; and particularly, the act for blockading the port of Boston, which, appears to them, pregnant with the most dangerous consequences, to all his Majesty's dominions in America: do unanimously resolve and agree,

I. That under the enjoyment of our constitutional privileges and immunities, we will ever cheerfully render all due obedience to the crown of Great-Britain, as well as full faith and allegiance to his most gracious Majesty, King George the Third; and do esteem a firm dependance on the mother-country, essential to our political security and happiness.

II. That the late act of Parliament relative to Boston, which so absolutely destroys every idea of safety and confidence, appears to us, big with the most dangerous and alarming consequences; especially, as subversive of that very dependance, which we would earnestly wish to continue, as our best safeguard and protection; and that we conceive, every well-wisher to Great-Britain and her colonies, is now loudly called upon to exert his utmost abilities, in promoting every loyal and pru-

The port of Boston was on Tuesday last cleared of every vessel intended for sea, it being the day on which the late act of Parliament prescribes, that no vessel, except in his Majesty's service, shall be allowed to depart from that port until the King in Council may be pleased to suspend its operation.

PHILADELPHIA, *June 20.*

At a meeting of the Freeholders and other inhabitants of the county of Frederick, and Gentlemen practising at the bar, held at the town of Winchester, the 8th of June, 1774, to consider of the best mode to be fallen upon to secure their liberties and properties, and also to prevent the dangerous tendency of an act of Parliament passed in the fourteenth year of his present Majesty's reign, entitled, An act to discontinue in such manner and for such time as are therein mentioned, the landing and discharging, lading and shipping of goods, wares and merchandize at the town, and within the harbour of Boston, in the province of Massachusetts-Bay, in North-America, evidently has to invade and deprive us of the same.

The Rev. Mr. Charles M. Thruston being voted Moderator, a Committee of the following gentlemen, viz. the Rev. Charles M. Thruston, Isaac Zane, George Rootes, Angus M'Donald, Alexander White, George Johnson, and Samuel Beall 3d, were appointed to draw up Resolves suitable to the same occasion, who withdrawing for a short time, returned with the following Votes, viz.

VOTED,

I. THAT we will always chearfully pay due submission to such acts of government as his Majesty has a right by law to exercise over his subjects, as sovereign of the British dominions, and to such only.

II. That it is the inherent right of British subjects to be governed and taxed by Representatives chosen by themselves only; and that every act of the British Parliament respecting the internal policy of North America, is a daring and unconstitutional invasion of our said rights and privileges.

III. That the act of Parliament above mentioned is not only in itself repugnant to the fundamental laws of natural justice, in condemning persons for a supposed crime unheard, but also a despotic exertion of unconstitutional power, calculated to enslave a free and loyal people.

IV. That the enforcing the execution of the said act of Parliament by a military power, will have a necessary tendency to raise a civil war, thereby dissolving that union which has so long happily subsisted between the Mother Country and her Colonies; and that we will most heartily and unanimously concur with our suffering brethren of Boston, and every other part of North-America that may be the immediate victims of tyranny, in promoting all proper measures to avert such dreadful calamities, to procure a redress of our grievances, and to secure our common liberties.

V. It is the unanimous opinion of this meeting, that a joint resolution of all the Colonies to stop all importations from Great-Britain, and exportations to it, till the said act be repealed, will prove the salvation of North-America and her liberties: On the other hand, if they continue their imports and exports, there is the greatest reason to fear that fraud, power, and the most odious oppression, will rise triumphant over right, justice, social happiness and freedom.

VI. That the East-India Company, those servile tools of arbitrary power, have justly forfeited the esteem and regard of all honest men; and that the better to manifest our abhorrence of such abject compliance with the will of a venal Ministry in ministering all in their power, an increase of the fund of peculation; we will not purchase Tea, or any other kind of East-India commodities, either imported now, or hereafter to be imported, except salt-petre, spices and medicinal drugs.

VII. That it is the opinion of this meeting that Committees ought to be appointed for the purpose of affecting a general association, that the same measures may be pursued through the whole continent: That the Committees ought to correspond with each other, and to meet at such places and times as shall be agreed on, in order to form such general association, and that when the same shall be formed and agreed on by the several Committees, we will strictly adhere thereto; and till the general sense of the continent shall be known, we do pledge ourselves to each other and to our country, that we will inviolably adhere to the votes of this day.

VIII. That Charles M. Thruston, Isaac Zane, Angus M'Donald, Samuel Beall 3d, Alexander White, and George Rootes, be appointed a Committee for

of Massachusetts Bay into a military ——— and the other impowering the Gover——— tenant Governor to send any person ——— England to be tried for actions comm——— colony, are subversive of every idea ——— serves as a prelude to the fate of ea——— British colony on this continent.

4. That a congress of deputies from ———lonies is the most probable and prop——— curing relief for our suffering Breth——— redress and preserving our natural rig——— ties, and the establishing peace and mor——— between the mother-country and her ——— constitutional foundation.

5. That we will concur and join w——— thren of the city and county of Phila——— siring the Speaker of the Honourable ———presentatives of this province, to wr——— ral Members of Assembly, requesting ——— in the city of Philadelphia on any ——— than the first of August next, to take——— rious consideration our very alarmin——— appoint deputies to attend at a gener——— the colonies, at such time and pla——— agreed on.

As the notice of this meeting was ——— agreed that a general meeting be fix——— the 25th instant, at the dwelling h——— James, at the sign of the Turk's He——— at one o'clock, P. M. in order to cho———tee of Correspondence, and to resolv——— modes or propositions as may be nece——— tain redress from those grievances, th——— now groan under; at which time ——— those who are entitled to vote for M———sembly, and wish well to their poste——— can liberty, are requested to attend ——— advice in this alarming crisis.

Last Saturday afternoon many th——— spectable inhabitants of this city ——— near the State-house, agreeable to a ——— take into their consideration certain ——— positions prepared to be laid befor——— as it is impossible to insert the pre——— meeting in this paper, we must defer t——— CUSTOM-HOUSE, PHILA———

INWARD ENTR———
Ship King of Prussia, W. Adam——
Ship Molly, G. Johnston, Genoa.
Brig Fancy, T. Murdoch, St. Vin——
Sloop Rebecca, A. Culnan, Antig——
Ship Nancy and Suky, J. Robinso——
Brig Mount-Holly, G. Bayley, Ja——
Sloop Little Welcome, J. Lambert——
Sch. Felicity, A. Keeble, Virginia
Sch. Betsy, F. Savage, Virginia.
Sch. Two Brothers, B. Clark, Ne——
Sloop Lively, A. Lowell, Piscataq——
Sloop Discovery, A. Gall, North——
Sch. Happy Return, G. Simpson,
Sloop Susanna, T. Chadwick, No——
Sch. Sally, J. Buck, North Caroli——
Sloop Robert, C. Metcalf, Virgi——
Sloop Polly, J. Attwood, Nova-S——
Sch. North-Island, J. Hannah, Se——

OUTWARD
Brig Samuel and Charles, T. W——
Ship Molly, G. Johnston, Lisbo——
Sloop Betsy, V. Wightman, Rho——
Sloop Hope, T. Atheton, Seni-G——
Snow John & William, W. Britto——
Sloop Adventure, J. Hutchings,
Brig Chance, J. Craig, Grenado——
Sloop Lively, A. Lowell, Piscat——
Ship Nancy, C. Donavan, Lisbo——
Ship Clementina, P. Brown, Ca———

CLEARED
Sch. Experiment, D. Livingst———
Sloop Industry, C. Gale, North——
Brig Cornelia, J. Fortter, Jamai——
Sch. Betsy, F. Savage, Virginia.
Sch. Polly, J. Vicary, Dominca.
Brig Industry, P. Hodgkinson, J——
Brig Mercury, J. Trimingham,
Brig Charlotte, P. Parker, Jam——
Sch. Ambrose, J. Wooren, New——
Sloop Robert, C. Metcalf, Virg——
Sloop Friendship, R. Parini, Vi——
Sloop Ranger, W. Picett, Virg——
Brig Adrian, J. Duncan, St. C——
Brig Ranger, C. Biddle, Jamai——
Sloop Betsy and Ann, P. Light——
Brig Lucy, J. Pyner, Jam tes——
Sch. Felicity, A. Moore, Jamai——
Schooner Mary, J. Perott, St.——
Sch. Betsy, R. Alcock, Domin——
Ship James and Mary Ann, W.——
Sch. Peggy, J. Keogh, Domini——

or by their representatives, and are not to be disseised of their liberties and free customs, sentenced and condemned but by lawful judgement of their peers, and that the said rights and immunities are recognized and confirmed to the inhabitants of the colony by the royal grant and charter aforesaid, and are their undoubted right to all intents, constructions and purposes whatsoever.

VI. That the apprehending and carrying persons beyond the sea, to be tried for any crime alledged to be committed within this colony; or subjecting them to be tried by commissioners, or any court constituted by act of Parliament; or otherwise within this colony, in a summary way, without a jury, is unconstitutional, and subversive of the liberties and rights of the free subjects of this colony.

VII. That any harbour or port duly opened and constituted, cannot be shut up and discharged, but by an act of the legislature of the province or colony, in which such harbour or port is situated, without subverting the rights and liberties, and destroying the property of his Majesty's subjects.

VIII. That the late act of Parliament inflicting pains and penalties on the town of Boston, by blocking up their harbour, is a precedent justly alarming to the British Colonies in America, and wholly inconsistent with, and subversive of their constitutional rights and liberties.

IX. That whenever his Majesty's service shall require the aid of the inhabitants of this colony, the same fixed principles of loyalty, as well as self preservation which have hitherto induced us fully to comply with his Majesty's requisitions, together with the deep sense we have of its being our indispensible duty (in the opinion of this House) will ever hold us under the strongest obligations, which can be given, or desired, most chearfully to grant his Majesty, from time to time, our further proportion of men and money, for the defence, protection, security and other services, of the British American dominions.

X. That we look on the well-being, and greatest security of this colony, to depend, under God, on our connections with Great-Britain, which is ardently wished, may continue to the latest posterity, and that it is the humble opinion of this House that the constitution of this colony being understood and practised upon, as it has ever since it existed (till very lately) is the surest bond of union, confidence, and mutual prosperity, of our mother-country and us, and the last foundation on which to build, the good of the whole, whether considered in a civil, military or mercantile light; and of the truth of this opinion, we are the more confident, as it is not founded on speculation only, but has been verified in fact, and by long experience, found to produce, according to our extent, and other circumstances, as many loyal, virtuous, industrious, and well governed subjects, as any part of his Majesty's dominions; and as truly zealous of and warmly engaged, to promote the best, good and real glory of the grand whole, which constitutes the British empire.

XI. That it is an indispensible duty, which we owe to our King, our country, ourselves and our posterity, by all lawful ways and means in our power, to maintain, defend and preserve these our rights and liberties, and to transmit them entire and inviolate to the latest generations. And that it is our fixed, determined, and unalterable resolution, faithfully to discharge this our duty.

At their sessions at Hartford, on the second Thursday of May, 1774, in the 14th year of his Majesty's reign, the foregoing resolutions, reported to the House by their committee, were unanimously voted and ordered to be entered on their

dential measure towards obtaining, a repeal of the said act of Parliament, and all others subversive of the undoubted rights and liberties of his Majesty's American subjects.

III. That it is our unanimous opinion, that it would conduce to the restoration of the liberties of America, should the colonies enter into a joint agreement not to purchase or use any articles of British manufactory; and especially any commodities imported from the East-Indies, under such restrictions as may be agreed upon by a general congress of the said colonies hereafter to be appointed.

IV. That this county will most readily and chearfully join their brethren of the other counties in this province, in promoting such congress of deputies, to be sent from each of the colonies, in order to form a general plan of union, so that the measures to be pursued for the important ends in view, may be uniform and firm: to which plan when concluded upon, we do agree faithfully to adhere. And do now declare ourselves ready to send a committee to meet with those from the other counties, at such time and place, as by them may be agreed upon, in order to elect proper persons to represent this province in the said general congress.

V. That the freeholders and inhabitants of the other counties in this province, be requested speedily to convene themselves together, to consider the present distressing state of our public affairs; and to correspond, and consult with such other committees, as may be appointed as well as with our committee, who are hereby directed to correspond and consult with such other committees, as also with those of any other province: and particularly, to meet with the said county committees, in order to nominate and appoint deputies to represent this province in general congress.

VI. We do hereby unanimously request the following Gentlemen, to accept of that trust; and accordingly do appoint them our committee for the purposes aforesaid, viz. Stephen Crane, Henry Garritse, Joseph Riggs, William Livingston, William P. Smith, John De Hart, John Chetwood, Isaac Ogden and Elias Boudinot, Esqrs;

NEW-YORK, June 16.

The port of Boston was on Tuesday last cleared of every vessel intended for sea, it being the day on which the late act of Parliament prescribes, that no vessel, except in his Majesty's service, shall be allowed to depart from that port until the King in Council may be pleased to suspend its operation.

PHILADELPHIA, June 20.

At a meeting of the Freeholders and other inhabitants of the county of Frederick, and Gentlemen practising at the bar, held at the town of Winchester, the 8th of June, 1774, to consider of the best mode to be fallen upon to secure their liberties and properties, and also to prevent the dangerous tendency of an act of Parliament passed in the fourteenth year of his present Majesty's reign, entitled, An act to discontinue in such manner and for such time as are therein mentioned, the landing and discharging, lading and shipping of goods, wares and merchandize at the town, and within the harbour of Boston, in the province of Massachusetts-Bay, in North-America, evidently has to invade and deprive us of the same.

The Rev. Mr. Charles M. Thruston being voted

the purposes aforesaid; and that they, or any three of them, are hereby fully impowered to act.

Which being read, were unanimously assented to and subscribed.

On Monday the 6th instant tickets were posted up in different parts of Frederick county, Virginia, signed by the friends of liberty, requesting the Gentlemen Merchants, Freeholders, and other inhabitants of the county to meet at the Court-house, on the ensuing Wednesday, at three o'clock in the afternoon, to consider of the most proper measures to prevent the fatal consequences apprehended from the act of Parliament mentioned in the votes, and to defend and secure the rights and liberties of America. In consequence of which (though the notice did not exceed 48 hours) a great concourse assembled at the time and place appointed. The Court-house being too small to contain the company, they adjourned to the Church, where the above votes were unanimously agreed to. The general opinion of the people there seems to be, that the Boston scheme of non-importation from Great-Britain, and exportation to it, is the only probable means to obtain redress of our grievances, and shew great eagerness that it may be universally adopted.

We hear from Fort-Pitt, that the Shawanese have lately murdered eighteen White People, within nine miles of that place; and that several parties of Indians have gone forth to war against the defenceless inhabitants of the frontiers of Virginia and Pennsylvania: That it is supposed all the English traders in the Shawanese towns are killed by the Savages, and about fifteen hundred families, settled to the westward of the Allegany mountains, have deserted their habitations, and fled for sanctuary to the more interior parts of the country; and that the traders at Fort Pitt are about leaving that place as soon as they can form a party strong enough to venture forth. An Indian war seems inevitable.

At a meeting of a respectable body of the Freeholders, Inhabitants of the county of Chester, on Saturday the 18th of June, 1774. The following resolutions were deliberately and unanimously agreed on, viz.

1. THAT it is an absolute right, inherent in every English subject, to have the free use, enjoyment and disposal of all his property either by himself or representative, and that no other power on earth can legally divest him of it.

2. That we apprehend the act of Parliament for shutting up the port of Boston (until his Majesty's duties be duly collected, &c.) is highly arbitrary and oppressive to the inhabitants of that town, and, in its consequences may endanger the liberties of all the British colonies in America.

3. That the two bills mentioned in the last advices from London to be passing in Parliament, one changing the charter'd constitution of the province of Massachusetts Bay into a military government, and the other impowering the Governor, or Lieutenant Governor to send any person or persons to England to be tried for actions committed in that colony, are subversive of every idea of liberty and serves as a prelude to the fate of each charter'd British colony on this continent.

4. That a congress of deputies from the said colonies is the most probable and proper mode of procuring relief for our suffering Brethren, obtaining redress and preserving our natural rights and liberties, and the establishing peace and mutual confidence between the mother-country and her colonies on a constitutional foundation.

5. That we will concur and join with our Brethren of the city and county of Philadelphia in desiring the Speaker of the Honourable House of Representatives of this province, to write to the several Members of Assembly, requesting them to meet in the city of Philadelphia on any day, not later than the first of August next, to take into their serious consideration our very alarming situation, to appoint deputies to attend at a general congress for

cester, relating that they had been alarmed with the report that a regiment of soldiers had been posted

der White, George Johnson, and Samuel Beall 3d, were appointed to draw up Resolves suitable to the same occasion, who withdrawing for a short time,

agreed that a general meeting be fixed on Saturday the 25th instant, at the dwelling house of Jacob James, at the sign of the Turk's Head, in Goshen,

BARNSTABLE, October 10, 1774.

ON Tuesday the 27th ult. the Time for the Court of General Sessions of the Peace, and Inferior Court of Common Pleas for this County to sit, a great number of People from this, and the neighbouring Counties of Plymouth and Bristol, being assembled before the Court-House door in this Town; after choosing a Moderator, Voted and Resolved, That it was inexpedient for said Courts to sit, under the present situation of our public affairs, until the opinion of the Continental or of a Provincial Congress could be known; and therefore chose a Committee, viz. Dr. *Nathaniel Freeman* and Mr. *Stephen Nye*, of Sandwich, Capt. *Daniel Crocker* of Barnstable, Capt. *Noah Fearing*, of Wareham, and Dr. *John Pitcher* of Rochester, to present the following Address to the Justices of said Court, then convened at the House of Mr. Crocker, Innholder in this Town.

To the Honorable Justices of his Majesty's Inferior Court of Common Pleas, and Court of General Sessions of the Peace, for the County of Barnstable.

May it please your Honors,

THE Inhabitants of this Province, being greatly alarmed at the late unconstitutional Acts of the British Parliament, considering them as calculated to establish tyranny and oppression instead of the once happy constitution of this Province; in consequence of which many respectable Counties in the same have prevented the sitting of the Inferior Courts, as well as Superior; we judge, not from an apprehension, merely, that they were not constitutional; but, from a supposition, that there might be appeals from them to the *Superior Court*, the Chief Justice of which receiving his support from the Crown, independent of the grants of the People, cannot fail to have an unhappy bias in favor of said unconstitutional Acts; and two others, of the superior Judges, having sworn to carry the same Acts into execution; and judging, that by proceeding upon appeals from a Court friendly to the Constitution, and zealous for their Country's cause, to the said *Superior Court*, we might in this way, if no other, open a door for the said Chief Justice and his assistants to execute their Commissions on the plan of the said oppressive Acts.

Wherefore a great number of the Inhabitants of the County of Barnstable, being now convened, with several others from the several Counties in Old Plymouth Colony, taking into serious consideration the necessity of using every precaution to prevent the operation of said Acts, & believing the following one necessary, do humbly request your Honors to desist from all business in said Courts, and from holding any Sessions thereof, till the minds of the Continental, or of a Provincial Congress, be obtained:----And that your Honors would assure this body, that you will not, in any manner, assist in carrying said unconstitutional Acts into execution, nor hold any commission in consequence of said Acts, and upon the new establishment, or in any manner conform thereto; but that you will use your utmost endeavors to prevent the same from taking place.

N. Freeman, | A Committee chosen
S. Nye, | by the Body of the
D. Crocker, | People to present this
N. Fearing, | Address to your Ho-
T. Pitcher, | nors in their Name.

Barnstable,
Sept. 27, 1774.

The Address being presented accordingly, the Justices after taking the same into consideration, returned the following Answer, viz.

TO *Nathaniel Freeman, John Pitcher, Stephen Nye, Daniel Crocker,* and *Noah Fearing, a Committee, as they say, chosen by the Body of the People, to present an Address, this 27th of September, 1774, to the Honorable Justices of his Majesty's Inferior Court of Common Pleas, and Court of General Sessions of the Peace.* ---Said Address being presented to the Justices of said County, or at least as many as are present: The said Justices in answer thereto, say, That they are as much concerned at the late uncon-

provincial congress can be fully known, as we can by no means apprehend that any ill consequences can attend the setting of said Courts, until this month expires. James Otis,

David Thatcher,   Kenelm Winslow,   Thomas Smith,
Daniel Davis,   Joseph Otis,   Edward Bacon,
Meletiah Bourn,   Isaac Hinkley,   David Gorham,
Shearjashub Bourn, Nymphas Marston,   Solomon Otis,

The answer being communicated to the people, after taking

---

and just indignation of the people towards them for addressing the late infamous governor Hutchinson, upon his departure from this province, whereby they used their endeavours to support, encourage and applaud, a *known Traitor*, and *inveterate Enemy*, to the country. ---That said address was, in the apprehension of the people, no less false and designing, than flattering and fulsome, and discovered the unparalleled vanity, insolence and audacity of the addressors, in daring, openly, to contradict the the united express'd sentiments of both houses of the General Court, as well as of all America; by which conduct, they have forfeited the esteem of the public, and enlisted under the banners of said Hutchinson, as enemies to the cause of liberty; for which they ought immediately to make satisfaction to the offended public.

The Justices and Sheriff signed the respective *declarations*, and the Addressors the respective *confessions* enclosed herewith, which were voted satisfactory. [*But the Publication of them, for want of Room, must be defer'd till next Week.*]

The body of people then voted and resolved, That the Military officers, holding commissions under a Captain-General, at the head of forces raised against the Rights and Properties, and consequently the Lives of the inhabitants of this country and who is constantly making hostile preparations against it, must themselves be considered as enemies to the country likewise, unless they immediately resign their commissions: And therefore a committee was chosen to apply to, and acquaint them herewith, and to desire them to resign accordingly; and also to apply to the deputy-sheriffs for them to sign a declaration, respecting said oppressive acts, suitable to their office.

The body of the people also voted to address the honorable James Otis, Esq; of this Town, as one of the constitutional Councellors of the Province, and pray his Honor's Attendance at the General Court, to be holden at Salem on the 5th Day of October next---The whole body accordingly marched in procession to him, and presented to him the following Address, viz.

To the Honorable JAMES OTIS, Esq;

May it please your Honour,

THE body of people assembled from the several counties of Barnstable, Plymouth and Bristol, on the 28th day of Sept. 1774, at or near the court house in Barnstable, beg leave to address your Honour, as one of his Majesty's constitutional council of this province; and to assure you that we entertain a very high and grateful sense of that *integrity*, and of those *abilities*, which have long distinguished you, as in every important trust reposed in you by the public, so especially in the capacity we now consider you.

And whereas his Excellency the Governor of this Province, hath issued writs for electing a new house of representatives, to meet at Salem, on the 5th day of October next, and notwithstanding a number of councellors have been appointed by mandamus from his Majesty, in consequence of a late act of the British parliament; but presuming the representatives of this people, yet determined to be free, never will, or ought, to consent to do any business with them, and we look upon the council chose last May by the great and general court, according to charter, to be the only constitutional council of this Province; we do therefore pray your Honour, that you would attend the great and general court at Salem the next sessions, in said capacity; and that you would continue those endeavours to obtain a redress of the grievances so justly complained of by the People, which have long distinguished you as an able defender of our constitution and liberties: And now wishing your Honour the support of Heaven in your advanced age, that you may much longer remain a blessing to this Province, and enjoy the happiness of seeing those Rights restored, which have been most injuriously wrested from us, we beg leave to subscribe ourselves, your Honour's most obedient

Nath'l Freeman, | A Committee
Stephen Nye, | in Behalf of
Jos. Haskel, 3d. | the People.
Noah Fearing, |
John Pitcher, |

----d Otis was pleased to return the ----Answer, viz.

----ress to me as a constitutional Coun-
----aring me to attend my Duty at Salem
----when the General Court is to set,
----r putting me in Mind of my Duty;
----at Salem at that Time, in case my
----Your very humble Servant,

74.   JAMES OTIS.

----high esteem of that honourable
---- of his past Services, their sanguine
----ions, and hearty approbation of his
----s, by giving him three cheers, and
----ession to the court-house.

The People voted and resolved, that as the town of Boston was now suffering in a common cause, they would use their endeavours to relieve them, by encouraging and procuring donations for their support---that they would immediately provide themselves with arms and ammunition, and hold themselves in readiness to assist, in defending the town of Boston, and the rights and liberties of this country, which they never would give up, but with their lives and fortunes---that they would not import any more goods from Great-Britain, or purchase any imported by others, after

---

NEW-HAVEN, October 21.

Colony of Connecticut, October 20, 1774.
In the House of Representatives,

RESOLVED unanimously,

THAT Contributions from all the Towns in this Colony for supplying the Necessities, and alleviating the distresses of our Brethren at Boston, ought to be continued in such Manner, and so long as their Occasions may require. RICHARD LAW, Clerk.

From Baltimore, in Maryland, we learn that a Vessel arrived there the 6th instant, sent by General Gage to purchase a load of Flour, a quantity of Blankets, &c. for the Troops under his Command at Boston; but that the Committee of Correspondence for that Place refused to furnish any of the Articles until they heard from the General Congress, where they had sent an express to receive directions how they should act upon the Occasion.

** *The Notification from the Treasurer of the Province, relative to the Sheriffs bringing into the Treasury such Public Monies as they now have in their Hands, &c. we received too late to be inserted this Day; but will be in our next.*----
All Advertisements, intended for Monday's Paper, must be sent on Saturday Afternoon preceeding, if it is expected they have a Place therein.

---

with the declarations and refignations abovefaid, and paffed in the affirmative, nem. con.

It was then moved to know whether that body would fignify their abhorrence of mobs, riots, and the deftruction of private property, and paffed in the affirmative, nem. con.

Col. Phips, the high fheriff of the county, then came before the committee of the body and complained that he had been hardly fpoken of for the part he had acted in delivering the powder in Charleftown magazine to the foldiery; which, the committee candidly confidered and reported to the body, that it was their opinion the high fheriff was excufeable, as he had acted in conformity to his order from the commander in chief. Col. Phips alfo delivered the following declaration by him fubfcribed viz.

Colonel Phips's Anfwer to the Honorable body now in meeting upon the Common, viz.

THAT I will not execute any Precept that fhall be fent me under the new Acts of Parliament for altering the Conftitution of the Province of the Maffachufetts Bay, and that I will call in the Venires that I have fent out under the new Eftablifhment.

Cambridge, Sept. 2, 1774. DAVID PHIPS.

Which was accepted as fatisfactory.

About 8 o'clock his honor Lieut. Governor Oliver fet off from Cambridge to Bofton, and informed Governor Gage of the true ftate of matters, and the bufinefs of the people; which, as his honor told the Admiral, were not a mad mob, but the freeholders of the county, promifing to return in two hours and confer further with them on his own circumftance, as prefident of the council. On Mr. Oliver's return he came to the committee and fignified what he had delivered to the body in the morning, viz. that as the commiffions of Lieut. Governor, and prefident of the council, feemed tacked together, he fhould undoubtedly incur his Majefty's difpleafure if he refigned the former, and pretended to hold the latter; and no body appeared to have any objection to his enjoying the place he held conftitutionally, he begged he might not be preffed to incur the difpleafure at the inftance of a fingle county, while any other councellor held on the new eftablifhment. Affuring them however, that in cafe the mind of the whole province collected in congrefs or otherwife appeared for his refignation, he would by no means act in oppofition to it. This feemed fatisfactory to the committee, and they preparing to deliver it to the body, when Mr. commiffioner Hallowell came through the town on his way to Bofton. The fight of this perfon fo inflamed the people that in a few minutes above an hundred horfemen were drawn up and proceeding in purfuit of him on the full gallop. Capt. Gardner of Cambridge firft began a parley with one of the foremoft, which caufed them to halt till he delivered his mind very fully in diffuafion of the purfuit, and was feconded by Mr. Deavens, of Charleftown, and Dr. Young, of Bofton. They generally obferved that the object of the body's attention that day feemed to be the refignation of unconftitutional councellors, and that it might introduce confufion into the proceedings of the day if any thing elfe was brought upon the carpet till that important bufinefs was finifhed: And in a little time the gentlemen difmounted their horfes and returned to the body.

But Mr. Hollowell did not entirely efcape, as one gentleman, of a fmall ftature, pufhed on before the general body, and followed Mr. Hollowell, who made the beft of his way till he got into Roxbury, where Mr. Bradfhaw overtook and ftopped him in his chaife; Mr. Hollowell fnapped his piftols at him, but could not difengage himfelf from him till he quitted the chaife, and mounted his fervant's horfe, on which he drove into Bofton with all the fpeed he could make; till the horfe falling within the gate, he ran on foot to the camp, through which he fpread confternation, telling them he was purfued by fome thoufands, who would be in town at his heels, and deftroy all friends of government before them.

A gentleman in Bofton, obferving the motion in the Camp, and concluding they were on the point of marching to Cambridge, from both ends of the town, communicated the alarm to Dr. Roberts, then at Charleftown ferry, who having a very fleet Horfe, brought the news in a few minutes to the committee, then at Dinner. The intelligence was inftantly diffufed, and the people whofe arms were neareft fent Perfons to bring them; light horfemen were difpatched both ways to gain more certain advice of the true ftate of the foldiery. A greater fervor and refolution probably never appeared among any troops. The difpatches foon returning and affuring the body that the foldiers ftill remained, and were likely to remain, in their camp, they refumed their bufinefs with fpirit, and refolved to leave no unconftitutional officer, within their reach, in poffeffion of his place. On this the committee affembled again, and drew up the paper, of which the following is a copy, and at the head of the body delivered it to Lieut. Governor Oliver to fign, with which he complied, after obtaining their confent to add the latter claufe implying the fource by which he was compelled, to do it. Mr. Mafon, clerk of the county of Middlefex, alfo engaged in his office to do no one thing in obediance to the new Acts of Parliament impairing our Charter. *Cambridge, Sept. 2, 1774.*

---

mittee, who went to the houfe, and being admitted, enquired for the Colonel; his fons informed them he was not at home, but had fet off for Bofton the preceding evening; the committee made report to the company, which did not give fatisfaction, they infifted upon fearching the houfe, which was done, as alfo the barns, out houfes and ftables, after which the committee wrote a letter to Col. Murray, informing ... office by the tenth of this mo... the Bofton news-papers, he ... turn home; and then difperf...

The fpirit of the people, w... the firft fettlement of the co... in the country for hundreds ... to "DIE or be FREE"...

MARRIED.] M... chant, to Mifs Pricilla ... Scollay, Efq; of this ...

Mr. William Evans, ... Shilcock.

Mr. Thomas Moore, ... nah Dinmore, only I... Archibald Dinmore, d...

DIED.] Mrs. Sara... Tyler.---At Charleftow... ed 82.---At Dunftable, ... Town, Merchant.---A... Crocker, aged 55.

Want of Room obliges us to om... Meeting, feveral Articles of Intelligence, ...

To my worthy Town and Countrymen.

Gentlemen,

AS I have given you great Offence by figning an Addrefs to Governor Hutchinfon (upon his leaving the Province) and as it always gives me Pain to affront or difoblige even a fingle Neighbour; this has been much increafed as the Public are fo much concerned in it: And had I conceived that the Generality of the People fo much diflikced an Addrefs to Mr. Hutchinfon, it fhould not have had my Name to it, as I always place the Friendfhip and Good-will of my Fellow-Men, in the firft Clafs of the World's Enjoyments. I am very forry I ever figned it, and hope the Public will freely forgive, Gentlemen,

Your humble Servant,
Charleftown, Sept. 3, 1774. JOHN WHITE.

Sturbridge, Aug. 25, 1774.

WHEREAS I ABIJAH WILLARD, of Lancafter, have been appointed, by mandamus, a Counfellor for this province, and having without due confideration taken the oath, do now freely and folemnly declare that I am heartily forry that I have taken the faid oath, and do hereby folemnly and in good faith promife and engage that I will not fit nor act in the faid Council, nor in any other that fhall be appointed in fuch manner and form; but that I will, as much as in me lies, maintain the Charter Rights and Liberties of this province, and do hereby afk forgivenefs of all the honeft, worthy gentlemen, that I have offended by taking the abovefaid oath, and defire this may be inferted in the public prints. Witnefs my hand,

ABIJAH WILLARD.

Meffieurs PRINTERS,

Pleafe to infert the following in your next paper, and you will oblige your moft humble fervant, E. G.

IN the Supplement to the laft Monday's Gazette, a writer under the fignature of Maffachufetenfis, after calling me by name, plainly intimates *that I have wounded the conftitution of my country in my department of clerk of the feffions.* This cruel infinuation not only tends to render me odious to the world of mankind, but exhibiting me to my countrymen as their enemy, at this time of public calamity, muft render me fingularly hateful. To one confcious of deferving a very different character, fuch treatment muft be a very fevere trial, as it muft affect every man of fentiment and feeling.---Soon after the arrival of an act of Parliament, entitled an act for better regulating the government of the province of the Maffachufetts-Bay, in North-America, two or three clerks of the court of feffions, of different counties, happening to meet; naturally fell into converfation upon the fubject of their duty in confequence of the requirements of that act. On this fudden meeting, and fhort confultation, finding ourfelves directed by that law, we fuppofed ourfelves bound in duty to iffue warrants for the return of jurors, in the manner thereby required. Upon this fudden opinion it was, that twenty warrants were iffued to the conftables of the feveral towns in the county of Suffolk, agreeable to the direction of the fame act; ten of which were figned by me, and the remaining ten by Mr. Ezekiel Price, joint clerk with me. At the time I figned, I did not fuppofe any one town in the county would take the leaft notice of fuch warrant, and with pleafure I find upon enquiry, that my expectations have been anfwered.

The fcience of the law hath never been my profeffed ftudy, tho' the mere mechanical bufinefs of a clerk's office hath been my employ for many years. As therefore it has not been my ftudy *to know any more than to determine what is the law of the land,* my erroneous fentiments (which I am now fully convinced they were)...

To to held at PHILADELPHIA, on the firft of September, 1774.

---

of Maffachufetts-Bay, which being a manifeft infringement of the charter rights and privileges of this people; I do hereby, in conformity to the commands of the body of this county now convened, moft ...

give. And I now publickly declare that it was not for the leaft inclination I had to comply with this, or any other of the acts of Parliament lately paffed, relative to North-America, that I figned ...

POWDER ALARM

LATE IN AUGUST 1774, WILLIAM BRATTLE OF Cambridge, a Massachusetts militia general, wrote to Royal Governor Thomas Gage that it might be wise to secure the province's gunpowder supply. On September 1, General Gage's troops emptied a powder house outside Boston and took two small cannons from Brattle's militia unit. The people of Cambridge saw those actions as curtailing their power to defend themselves. Hearing of his neighbors' anger, Brattle fled to the protection of the Royal Army. The next day, he wrote an open letter explaining himself, published alongside his original note in the September 5, 1774, *Massachusetts Gazette; and the Boston Post-Boy and Advertiser*. But it was too late.

An exaggerated rumor that the army was attacking Boston spread west September 1. Across Massachusetts, farmers mustered in their militia companies and marched to defend the capital. By the time they reached the outskirts of Cambridge early the next morning, they knew the rumor was false—but still the men came on, leaving their guns stacked at taverns, determined to make a show of numbers.

As a rumor that the army was attacking Boston spread west, farmers mustered in their militia companies and marched to defend the capital.

Lieutenant Governor Thomas Oliver hurried from his Cambridge mansion into Boston to warn Gage not to overreact. On his way, he passed Whigs summoned by Dr. Joseph Warren heading out to Cambridge to keep people calm. Neither side's leaders wanted violence.

On Cambridge Common, the militiamen—at least three thousand strong—had called on two locals appointed to Gage's council under the Massachusetts Government Act to publicly resign. Samuel Danforth and Joseph Lee did so. Sheriff David Phips apologized for helping the army remove the militia cannon. The crowd then voted unanimously to condemn riots. Newspapers like the September 9, 1774, *New-Hampshire Gazette* printed those transactions much like the record of an official public meeting.

Colonial newspaper publishers rarely left their print shops to gather news, but Isaiah Thomas of the *Massachusetts Spy* was on Cambridge Common that day. In fact, Thomas alerted the crowd that, by coincidence, the customs commissioners were passing by. Several men on horseback began to chase Benjamin Hallowell, the least popular of those officials. A few pursued Hallowell all the way to the Boston Neck.

Now riled up, the Cambridge crowd decided to visit Lieutenant Governor Oliver, who had returned home, and demand that he resign from the council, as well. Oliver refused. The crowd's emissaries pleaded, warning they could not control four thousand angry men. Around dusk, Oliver finally signed a resignation. Rain began to fall, and the farmers dispersed to their homes. Though the rumor about Boston continued to spread through New England for days, there were no further confrontations.

No one was hurt during this event, later dubbed the "Powder Alarm," but it demonstrated three things.

First, General Gage's authority stopped at the gates of Boston. The rest of Massachusetts was beyond royal control. Prominent Loyalists like Oliver soon moved into Boston for their safety.

Second, the Massachusetts countryside was now as committed to resistance as Boston. For weeks, Whig newspapers reported, and probably overstated, how many militiamen had mustered: "FORTY THOUSAND MEN in MOTION, and under ARMS," said an item in the September 16, 1774, *New-Hampshire Gazette*. The point was not that colonists wanted war, but that they could oppose any Crown aggression with overwhelming force and unity.

Third, people saw the next stage of the conflict as a race to control artillery and gunpowder. For example, the September 23, 1774, *New-Hampshire Gazette* told its readers how General Gage and the Royal Navy had disabled batteries in Boston Harbor. Newspapers did not report that New Englanders were spiriting other cannon into the countryside, beyond the governor's reach.

MASSACHUSETTS GAZETTE; AND THE BOSTON POST-BOY AND ADVERTISER
September 5, 1774

Massachusetts militia general William Brattle's open letter explaining his treasonous note to Royal Governor Thomas Gage was printed in newspapers along with the original "much-talked of" note to Gage.

The following is a Copy of the much-talked of Letter, wrote by Major-General Brattle, to the Commander in Chief, viz.

Cambridge, August 29, 1774.

MR. Brattle presents his Duty to his Excellency Governor Gage, he apprehends it his Duty to acquaint his Excellency from Time to Time with every Thing he hears and knows to be true, and is of Importance in these troublesome Times, which is the Apology Mr. Brattle makes for troubling the General with this Letter. Captain Minot, of Concord, a very worthy Man, this Minute informed Mr. Brattle that there had been repeatedly made pressing Applications to him to warn his Company to meet at one Minute's Warning, equipt with Arms and Ammunition, according to Law, he had constantly denied them, adding, if he did not gratify them he should be constrained to quit his Farms and Town; Mr. Brattle told him he had better do that than lose his Life, and be hanged for a Rebel; he observed that many Captains had done it, though not in the Regiment to which he belonged, which was and is under Colonel Elisha Jones, but in a neighbouring Regiment.

Mr. Brattle begs Leave humbly to quere, Whether it would not be best that there should not be one Commission Officer of the Militia in the Province.

This Morning the Select-Men of Medford, came and received their Town-Stock of Powder, which was in the Arsenal on Quarry-Hill, so that there is now therein, the King's Powder only, which shall remain there as a sacred Depositum till ordered out by the Captain General.

To his Excellency General Gage, &c. &c. &c.

TO THE PUBLIC.

Boston, September 2, 1774.

I Think it but Justice to myself to give an Account of my Conduct, for which I am blamed; and to obviate some Mistakes which are believed. His Excellency Governor Gage wrote me in the Words following: "Sir, as I am informed there are several Military Stores in your Charge, at Cambridge, I beg the Favour of you to send me a Return of them, as soon as convenient, specifying the different Sorts of each, T. Gage.---To Major General Brattle." Which Order I obeyed; the like I did to Governors Pownal, Bernard and Hutchinson: In doing of which, every Soldier will say, I did but my Duty. But it is affirmed, I advised the Governor to remove the Powder; this I positively deny, because it is absolutely false. It never so much as entered into my Mind or Thought. After I had made my Return, I never heard one Word about the Affair till the Night before last, when Sheriff Phips came to my House, with the Governor's Order to deliver him the Powder and Guns; the Keys of the Powder-House I then delivered him, and wrote to Mr. Mason, who had the Care of the Guns under me, to deliver them, which I suppose he did; both I imagine were taken, but where transported I know not. I wrote to the Governor what is contained in the above Letter; I did not write the Governor the Grounds and Reasons of the Query therein contained; but I will now mention them: They proceeded from a real Regard both to the Commission Officers and to the Province: First, to the Commission Officers; I thought, and still think, it was best for them; many of whom I thought would be unwilling to issue their Warrants, and if they did not, I apprehended they might meet with some Difficulty; and those that did, I was not convinced so great Good would result therefrom, as if another method was taken: Secondly, I thought, and still think, it would be much better for the Province; for supposing there was not one Commission Officer for the present in it, what Damage could the Province sustain? It may be answered, Commission Officers are supposed to be the most understanding in military Affairs; I grant it: But supposing their Commissions were vacated, supposing the respective Companies in the Province were disposed and determined to do any one Matter or Thing, which they imagined to be for its Safety; and proper Persons were to be employed to lead them, ... their not having Commissions in the least unfit them from being employed in the particular Services they may be chosen to execute; and in this Way cannot any One conceive that some bad Consequences might be possibly prevented. Is it not easy to conceive, that the Commission Officers, leading their respective Companies, might, in the Eyes of the Judicious, be looked upon more blameable in doing such and such Things, than they would be if they were not Military Officers, and did not act under Commission? Might not the Difference with respect to the Province be looked upon very great both at home and here. It was suggested that General Gage demanded the Towns Stocks of Powder; this certainly he did not; the above Order speaks for itself. As I would not have delivered the Provincial Powder to any One but to his Excellency, or Order, so the Towns Stocks I would have delivered to none but the Selectmen, or their Order. Upon the whole the Treatment I have met with, my Banishment from my own Home, the Place of my Nativity, my House being searched, though I am informed it was without Damage, and the Sense of the People, touching my Conduct, &c. for the present cannot but be grievous, yet this Grief is much lessened by the Pleasure arising in my Mind, from a Consciousness that I am a Friend to my Country; and, in the above Instances, that I really acted according to my best Judgment for its true Interest. I am extremely sorry for what has taken Place; I hope I may be forgiven, and desire it of all that are offended, since I acted from an honest, friendly Principle, though it might be a mistaken one.

W. BRATTLE.

Messieurs MILLS and HICKS,

Taking it for granted, that a Transaction so interesting to the Community as Major General B-----'s Letter to his Excellency the Governor, and his Address to the Public in defence of the same, will be quoted in your very useful and impartial Gazette, I must insist on your accompanying the Recital of these with the subsequent QUERIES. I am, Gentlemen, your's, &c. K. D.

1. WHETHER advising the Governor to dismiss the Militia Officers of every Order through the Province, with the confessed Intention of rendering them less criminal in any Oppugnation to the present Form of Government, in which they might engage, can entitle the Advisor to Confidence on Account of his extraordinary Loyalty, in the present Acceptation of the Word with Men in Power, and agreeable to his high Expectations, both in Consequence of his previous Exertions for Promotion under the present Establishment, and Protestations of Duty, ...

minute Detail of ...

a slight might not have induced him to himself, unless it had been of the last ...

5. Whether the uncouth Composition considered as the Production of a Man of Le... on any other Principle than the conscious and some secret Fear of a Discovery, ha... Writer?

6. Whether any Part of G----l B---... REVIEW on Cambridge Common ... to him, from a serious Concern for him) ...

Messieurs PRINTERS,

THE freemen who were returned at the Superior Court for this term in the Court-House yesterday; and ... bly, (Peter Oliver, Edmund Trowbrid... William Cushing and William Brown Esq as judges,) they all to the number of twe... as Jurors for reasons which they had previ... and signed, and appointed to be read there the above said Judges refusing to hear the ... to have the reading of it to themselves, wh... the Jurymen withdrew from the Court-... tavern, where they unanimously voted that refusal to the world, their aforementioned re... in the public papers.------I send you a ... and am your humble servant.

"Boston, ...

"COUNTY OF SUFFOLK.

"WE who are returned by the several to serve as Grand Jurors at the Superior C... term, being actuated by a zealous regard fo... and a sincere desire to promote justice, righte... vernment, as being essential to the happines... would now most gladly proceed to the discha... duty required in that department, could we p... by doing thus, it would tend to our own repu... welfare of our country: But when we consid... roads that have been made upon our civil co... attempts now making to alter and annul the r... our Charter, granted by the most solemn faith... peatedly recognized by British Kings and par... see the open and avowed design of establishing system of despotism in this province, and there... born inhabitants thereof to the most abject ... bondage; we feel ourselves necessarily constra... impannelled, for reasons that we are ready to ... permitted, which are as follows.

"First. Because Peter Oliver, Esq; who f... this Court, has been charged with high crimes a... the late Hon. House of Representatives, the g... province; of which crimes he has never been ... has been declared by that House to be unqualifie... this Court.

"Secondly. Because by a late act of the Brit... altering the constitution of this province, the ... present Judges of this Court, as well as the appo... from the first day of July last, is made to depe... King's pleasure, vastly different from the tenu... Judges; and as we apprehend they now hold the... consequence of that act, all the judicial proceedi... will be taken as concessions to the validity of the... we dare not consent.

"Thirdly. Because three of the Judges, being ... the Court, namely the said Peter Oliver, Esq; F... Esq; and William Brown, Esq; by taking the oat... under authority of the aforesaid act, are (as w... sworn to carry into execution, all the late griev... British parliament, among the last of which is one... for the impartial administration of justice in this... we fear, really for the impunity of such persons... pretext of executing those acts murder any of the i... of, which acts appear to us to be utterly repugna... of justice and common humanity, and are justly... throughout America, as highly injurious and oppre... people of this province, and manifestly destructive o... as well as constitutional rights.

"Fourthly. Because we believe in our conscienc... ing in concert with a Court so constituted, and und... stances, would be so far betraying the just and sacre... native land, which were not the gift of Kings, but... solely with the toil, the blood and treasure of our wor... ancestors, and which we look upon ourselves under ... and inviolable obligations to maintain, and to trans... entire to our posterity.

"Therefore we the subscribers unanimously decl... Grand Jurors at this Court.

"Ebenezer Hancock,	Boston,
Peter Boyer,	ditto,
Joseph Hall,	ditto,
Thomas Crafts, jun.	ditto,
James Ivers,	ditto,
Paul Revere,	ditto,
Robert Williams,	Roxbury,
William Thompson,	Brookline,
Abraham Wheeler,	Dorchester,
Joseph Jones,	Milton,
Nathaniel Belcher,	Braintree,
Samuel Hobart,	Hingham,
Joseph Poole,	Weymouth

logy, that Character of UNEXAMPLED DUPLICITY, which bars all Confidence in the Person who sustains it?

3. Whether the ...

Henry Plymton,	Medway,
Lemuel Kalloc,	Medfield,
Joseph Willet,	Wrentham,
Thomas Pratt,	Walpole,

Docks were blown up, but the Commander found Means to get her into port.

The Amount of the National DEBT, when it was stated in January last, is One Hundred Twenty-Eight Millions, Five Hundred Twenty-Four Thousand, and Three Hundred ...

Number of Frigates and small armed Vessels cruizing in the Mediterranean.

From the Massachusetts-Spy.

BOSTON, Sept. 1.

THE Freemen who were returned to serve as Grand Jurors at the Superior Court for this Term, made their Appearance in the Court House Yesterday; and before a numerous Assembly, (Peter Oliver, Edmund Trowbridge, Foster Hutchinson, William Cushing, and William Brown, Esquires sitting on the Bench as Judges) they all to the Number of Twenty-Two declined acting as Jurors for Reasons which they had previously drawn up in Writing and signed, and appointed to be read there by their Chairman, but the above said Judges refusing to hear the same openly read, desired to have the Reading of it to themselves, which being complied with, the Jurymen withdrew from the Court House to the Exchange Tavern, where they unanimously voted that in Order to justify their Refusal to the World, their aforementioned Reasons should be printed in the public Papers.——I send you a Copy for that Purpose, and am your humble Servant. A JURYMAN.

" BOSTON, August 30th, 1774.

" COUNTY OF SUFFOLK.

" WE who are returned by the several Towns in this County, to serve as Grand Jurors at the Superior Court for this present Term, being actuated by a zealous Regard for Peace and good Order, and a sincere Desire to promote Justice, Righteousness and good Government, as being essential to the Happiness of the Community; would now most gladly proceed to the Discharge of the important Duty required in that Department, could we persuade ourselves that by doing thus, it would tend to our own Reputation or promote the Welfare of our own Country: But when we consider the dangerous Inroads that have been made upon our civil Constitution, the violent Attempts now making to alter and annul the most essential Parts of our Charter, granted by the most solemn Faith of Kings, and repeatedly recognized by British Kings and Parliaments; while we see the open and avowed Design of establishing the most compleat System of Despotism in this Province, and thereby reducing the freeborn Inhabitants thereof to the most abject State of Slavery and Bondage; we feel ourselves necessarily constrained to decline being impanelled, for Reasons that we are ready to offer to the Court if permitted, which are as follows.

" 1st. Because Peter Oliver, Esq; who sits as Chief Judge of this Court, has been charged with High Crimes and Misdemeanors, by the late Hon. House of Representatives, the grand Inquest of this Province; of which Crimes he has never been legally acquitted, but has been declared by that House to be unqualified to act as Judge of this Court.

" 2d. Because by a late Act of the British Parliament, for altering the Constitution of this Province, the Continuance of the present Judges of this Court, as well as the Appointment of others, from the first Day of July last, is made to depend solely on the King's Pleasure, vastly different from the Tenor of the British Judges; and as we apprehend they now hold their Places, only in Consequence of that Act, all the judicial Proceedings of the Court, will be taken as Concessions to the Validity of the same, to which we dare not consent.

" 3d. Because three of the Judges, being the major Part of the Court, namely the said Peter Oliver, Esq; Foster Hutchinson, Esq; and William Brown, Esq; by taking the Oath of Counsellors, under Authority of the aforesaid Act, are (as we are informed) sworn to carry into Execution, all the late grievous Acts of the British Parliament, among the last of which is one, made ostensibly for the impartial Administration of Justice in this Province, but as we fear, really for the Impunity of such Persons, as shall under Pretext of executing those Acts, murder any of the Inhabitants thereof; which Acts appear to us to be utterly repugnant to every Idea of Justice and common Humanity, and are justly complained of throughout America, as highly injurious and oppressive to the good People of this Province, & manifestly destructive of their natural, as well as constitutional Rights.

" 4th. Because we believe in our Consciences that our acting in concert with a Court so constituted and under such Circumstances, would be so far betraying the just and sacred Rights of our native Land, which were not the Gift of Kings, but were purchased solely with the Toil, the Blood and Treasure of our worthy and revered Ancestors, and which we look upon ourselves under the most sacred and inviolable Obligations to maintain, and to transmit whole and entire to our Posterity.

" Therefore we the Subscribers unanimously decline serving as Grand Jurors at this Court.

" Ebenezer Hancock, Peter Boyer, Joseph Hall, Thomas Crafts, jun. James Ivers, Paul Revere, Robert Williams, Wm. ...

---

led to read it in Court, or after Reading the Court would promise to return it to them again.

The Petit Jurors were then called for, and a List of their Names being handed to the Court they appointed Mr. Bartholomew Kneeland, Foreman, of the first Jury, and Mr. Nathan ... posed to ... Rea- ... with ... ourt. ... pro- ... man. ... the ... beg- ... told ... with- ... one ... that ... inta- ... ne of ... for ... Rea- ... Jurors ... Worm, but he refused, and referred to the Paper for his Reasons, as aforesaid. The Chief Justice then desired the Court might peruse the Paper, which should be returned to the Jurors again; which was agreed to, read and returned. The Court then proposed the same Condition to the Grand Jury, which was complied with, and the Contents delivered, which are inserted in this Day's Paper, see the Piece signed ' A JURYMAN.'

The Reasons of the Petit Jurors were as follows.

" BOSTON, August 30, 1774.

" SUFFOLK, ss.

" To the Honourable the Justices of the Superior Court of Judicature, Court of Assize. &c.

" MAY IT PLEASE YOUR HONOURS,

" WE the Subscribers, returned by this County to serve as Petit Jurors this Term, beg Leave to acquaint your Honours, that as the Hon. Peter Oliver, Esq; stands impeached by the late Hon. House of Commons of this Province, in their own Name, and in the Name of the People of this Province, of high Crimes and Misdemeanors; which Impeachment, with the Reasons therefor, as they are public, would be needless for us to repeat.

" We would also beg Leave to acquaint your Honours, that as by a late Act of the British Parliament, the Continuance of the Judges of the Superior Court, is since the first of July last, made to depend upon said Act, which it is apprehended places their Dependance entirely upon the Crown, and which is esteemed a great Infringement of the Charter Rights of this Province.

" Taking the above Premises into our most serious Consideration, we beg Leave to acquaint your Honours, that we cannot in our Consciences, from a Sense of that Duty we owe to our Country, to ourselves, and to Posterity, act against the united Voice of this People:——Therefore beg your Honours will excuse us, when we say, we decline serving as Petit Jurors for this Court. (Signed)

" Josiah Waters, Samuel Ridgeway, Nathan Frazier, Robert Wire, Bartholomew Kneeland, Thomas Chase, John Cunningham, Joseph Brewer, Jacob Sharp, Timothy Tilestone, Samuel Sprague, Ebenezer Swift, Eliphalet Sawer, Thomas White, Thomas Nash, Nathaniel Holbrook, jun, Elijah Jenning, Elisha Cushing, Ignatius Orcutt, Elijah Monk, Henry Stone, William Draper, Jonathan Parker, Ebenezer Kingsbury, Samuel Payson, Joseph Morse, Ralph Day, Nathaniel Lewis, Eliakim Cook, Joseph Lovell, Elias Thayer, Theodore Mann, James Blake."

After the Court had read the Papers, the Clerk of the Court, by Order of the Chief Justice, asked them Seriatim, if they would be Sworn, and every ONE refused. The Court said they would consider of their Reasons, and the Juries withdrew.—— The Court then adjourned to Ten o'Clock next Day, when they met exclusive of Mr. Oliver, and to the inexpressible Grief of their Fellow Citizens, went on to such Business as is usually transacted without Juries.

BOSTON, Monday September 5.

ON Wednesday last the new Council took their Seats at the Board in Boston. Their Deliberations have not hitherto transpired; and with Secrecy, on Thursday Morning at half after Four, about 260 Troops embarked on Board 13 Boats at the Long Wharfe and proceeded up Medford River, to Temple's Farm, where they landed, and went to the Powder-House on Quarry Hill, in Charlestown Bounds, whence they have taken 250 Half Barrels of Powder, the whole Store, and carried it to the Castle.

A Detachment from the Corps went to Cambridge, and brought off two Field-pieces, which had lately been sent there for Colonel Brattle's Regiment. The Preparation for this Expedition caused much Speculation, as some who were near the Governor gave out that he had sworn the Committee of Salem should recognize or be imprisoned; nay, some said they would be put on Board the Scarborough and sent to England forthwith. The Committee of Boston sent off an Express after ten on Wednesday Evening to advise their Brethren of Salem of what they apprehended was coming against them, who received their Message with great Politeness, and returned an Answer purporting their Readiness to receive any Attack they might be exposed to for acting in Pursuance to the Laws and Interest of their Country as became Men and Christians.

From these several hostile Appearances the County of Middlesex took the Alarm, and on Thursday Evening began to collect in large Bodies, with their Arms, Provision and Ammunition, determining by some Means to give a Check to a Power which so openly threatened their Destruction, and in such a clandestine Manner robb'd them of the Means of their Defence. And on Friday Morning some Thousands of them had advanced to Cambridge, armed only with Sticks, as they had left their Fire-Arms, &c. at some Distance behind them. Some indeed had collected on Thursday Evening and surrounded the Attorney-General's House, who is also Judge of Admiralty on the new ...

---

of late Declaration, he delivered the following certificate drawn up by himself and sign'd with his own Hand, viz.

ALTHO' I have this Day made an open Declaration to a great Concourse of People who assembled at Cambridge, that I had resigned my Seat at the Council Board, yet for the further Satisfaction of all, I do hereby declare under my Hand, that such Resignation has actually been made, and that it is my full Purpose not to be any way concern'd as a Member of the Council, at any Time hereafter. Sept. 2, 1774. S. DANFORTH.
A true Copy, Attest. N. Cudworth, Cl.

Judge Lee was also on the court-house steps, and delivered his mind to the body in terms similar to those used by Judge Danforth, and sign'd by him.

Upon this a Vote was called for to see if the Body was satisfied with the Declarations and Resignations aforesaid, & passed in the Affirmative, nem. con.

It was then moved to know whether that Body would signify their Abhorrence of Mobs, Riots and the Destruction of private Property, and passed in the Affirmative, nem. con.

Col. Phips, the High Sheriff of the County, then came before the Committee of the Body and complained that he had been hardly spoken of for the Part he had acted in delivering the Powder in Charlestown Magazine to the Soldiery; which the Committee candidly considered and reported to the Body that it was their Opinion the High Sheriff was excusable as he had acted in Conformity to his Order from the Commander in Chief, Colonel Phips also delivered the following Declaration by him subscribed, viz.

Colonel PHIPS's Answer to the Hon. Body now in Meeting upon the Common, viz.

THAT I will not execute any Precept that shall be sent me under the new Acts of Parliament for altering the Constitution of the Province of the Massachusetts-Bay, and that I will recall all the Venires that I have sent out under the new Establishment.

Cambridge, Sept. 2d, 1774. DAVID PHIPS.
A true Copy, Test. NATH. CUDWORTH, Cl.
Which was accepted as satisfactory.

About Eight o'Clock his Honor Lieut. Governor Oliver set off from Cambridge to Boston, and informed Gov. Gage of the true State of Matters, and the Business of the People; which as his Honor told the Admiral, were not a mad Mob, but the Freeholders of the County, promising to return in two Hours and confer further with them on his own Circumstance as President of the Council. On Mr. Oliver's Return he came to the Committee and signified what he had delivered to the Body in the Morning viz. that as the Commissions of Lieut. Governor and President of the Council, seem'd tack'd together, he should undoubtedly incur his Majesty's Displeasure if he resign'd the latter, and pretended to hold the former; and no Body appeared to have any Objection to his enjoying the Place he held constitutionally he begged he might not be pressed to incur that Displeasure at the Instance of a single County, while any other Councellor held on the new Establishment. Assuring them however, that in Case the Mind of the whole Province collected in Congress or otherwise appeared for his Resignation, he would by no Means act in Opposition to it. This seemed satisfactory to the Committee, and they were preparing to deliver it to the Body, when Commissioner Hallowell came through the Town on his Way to Boston. The Sight of that obnoxious Person so inflamed the People that in a few Minutes above 160 Horsemen were drawn up and proceeded in pursuit of him on the full Gallop. Capt. Gardner of Cambridge first began a Parley with one of the Foremost, which caused them to halt till he delivered his Mind very fully in Dissuasion of the Pursuit, & was seconded by Mr. Deavens of Charlestown, and Dr. Young of Boston. They generally observed that the Object of the Body's Attention that Day seemed to be the Resignation of unconstitutional Councellors, and that it might introduce Confusion into the Proceedings of the Day if any Thing else was brought upon the carpet till that important Business was finished; and in a little Time the Gentlemen dismounted their Horses, and returned to the Body.

But Mr. Hallowell did not entirely escape, as one Gentleman of a small Stature pushed on before the general Body and followed Hallowell, who made the best of his Way till he got into Roxbury, where Mr. Bradshaw overtook and stopped him in his chaise. Hallowell snapped his Pistols at him, but could not disengage himself from him till he quitted the chaise and mounted his Servant's Horse on which he drove into Boston with all the Speed he could make; till the Horse falling within the Gate he ran on Foot to the Camp, thro' which he spread Consternation, telling them he was pursued by some Thousands, who would be in Town at his Heels and destroy all Friends of Government before him.

A Gentleman in Boston observing the Motion in the Camp, and concluding, they were on the point of Marching to Cambridge, from both Ends of the Town, communicated the Alarm to Dr. Roberts then at Charlestown Ferry, who having a very fleet Horse brought the News in a few Minutes to the Committee, then at Dinner. The Intelligence was instantly diffused, and the People whose Arms were nearest sent Persons to bring them, while Horsemen were dispatched both Ways to gain more certain Advice of the true State of the Soldiery. A greater Fervor and Resolution probably never appeared in any Troops. The Dispatches soon returning, and assuring the Body that the Soldiers still remained, and were likely to remain in their camp, they resumed their Business with Spirit, and resolved to leave no unconstitutional Officer within their Reach in Possession of his Place. On this the Committee assembled again, and drew up the Paper of which the following is a Copy, and at the Head of the Body delivered it to Lieut. Governor Oliver to sign, with which he complied, after obtaining their consent to add the latter Clause implying the Force by which he was compelled to do it. Mr. Mason, Clerk of the County of Middlesex, also engaged in his Office to do no one Thing in Obedience to the new Acts of Parliament impairing our Charter.

Cambridge, Sept. 2. 1774.

I THOMAS OLIVER being appointed by his Majesty to a Seat at the Council Board, none but in Conformity to the ...

The NEW-HAMPSHIRE GAZETTE

BOSTON, *Monday September 5.*

ON Wednesday last the new Council took their Seats at the Board in Boston. Their Deliberations have not hitherto transpired ; and with Secrecy, on Thursday Morning at half after Four, about 260 Troops embarked on Board 13 Boats at the Long Wharf and proceeded up Medford River, to Temple's Farm, where they landed, and went to the Powder-House on Quarry Hill, in Charlestown Bounds, whence they have taken 250 Half Barrels of Powder, the whole Store, and carried it to the Castle.

A Detachment from the Corps went to Cambridge, and brought off two Field-pieces, which had lately been sent there for Colonel Brattle's Regiment. The Preparation for this Expedition caused much Speculation, as some who were near the Governor gave out that he had sworn the Committee of Salem should recognize or be imprisoned ; nay, some said they would be put on Board the Scarborough and sent to England forthwith. The Committee of Boston sent off an Express after ten on Wednesday Evening to advise their Brethren of Salem of what they apprehended was coming against them, who received their Message with great Politeness, and returned an Answer purporting their Readiness to receive any Attack they might be exposed to for acting in Pursuance to the Laws and Interest of their Country as became Men and Christians.

From these several hostile Appearances the County of Middlesex took the Alarm, and on Thursday Evening began to collect in large Bodies, with their Arms, Provision and Ammunition, determining by some Means to give a Check to a Power which so openly threatened their Destruction, and in such a clandestine Manner robb'd them of the Means of their Defence. And on Friday Morning some Thousands of them had advanced to Cambridge, armed only with Sticks, as they had left their Fire-Arms, &c. at some Distance behind them. Some indeed had collected on Thursday Evening and surrounded the Attonery[sic]-General's House, who is also Judge of Admiralty on the new Plan for Nova-Scotia ; and being provoked by the Firing of a Pistol from a Window, they broke some Glass, but did little more Mischief. The Company however, concerned in this, were mostly Boys and Negroes, who soon dispersed.

On perceiving the Concourse on Friday Morning, the Committee of Cambridge sent Express to Charlestown, who communicated the Intelligence to Boston, and their respective committees proceeded to Cambridge without Delay. When the first of the Boston committee came up, they found some Thousands of People assembled round the Court-House Steps, and Judge Danforth standing upon them, speaking to the Body, declaring in Substance, that having now arrived at a very advanced Age, and spent the greater part in the Service of the public, it was a great Mortification to him to find a Step lately taken by him so disagreeable to his Country, in which he consciously meaned to serve them, but finding their general Sense against his holding a Seat at the Council Board on the new Establishment, he assured them that he had resigned said Office, and would never henceforth accept or act in any Office inconsistent with the Charter Rights of his Country ; and in confirmation of said Declaration, he delivered the following certificate drawn up by himself and sign'd with his own Hand, viz.

ALTHO' *I have this Day made an open Declaration to a great Concourse of People who assembled at Cambridge, that I had resigned my Seat at the Council Board, yet for the further Satisfaction of all, I do hereby declare under my Hand, that such Resignation has actually been made, and that it is my full Purpose not to be any way concern'd as a Member of the Council, at any Time hereafter. Sept. 2, 1774.* S. DANFORTH.

A true Copy, Attest. N. Cudworth, Cl.

Springfield, a great Concourse of People, judg'd to be about 3000, assembled at the Court-House in that Place, and appointed a Committee to wait on the Court, and request their Appearance among the People, which they immediately complied with, when they very willingly signed the following Engagement, viz.

WE the Subscribers, do severally Promise, and solemnly engage to all People now assembled at Springfield, in the County of Hampshire on the 30th Day of Aug. 1774, that WE never will take, hold, execute, or exercise any Commission, Office, or Employment whatsoever, under, or by Virtue of, or in any Manner derived from any Authority pretended or attempted to be given by a late Act of Parliament, entitled, "An Act for the better regulating the Government of the Province of the Massachusetts Bay in New England."

Israel Williams, Oliver Partridge, Timothy Dwight, Thomas Williams, John Worthington, Joseph Hawley, William Williams, Simeon Strong, Moses Bliss, Jonathan Ashley, Elisha Porter, William Billings, John Phelps, Solomon Stoddard, Justus Ely, Caleb Strong, Samuel Fowler, Jonathan Bliss.

BOSTON, Sept. 8.

Treasurer Gray, we are credibly informed has not resigned his Office as Councellor.

Yesterday General Gage, accompanied by Lord Percy, the Admiral, and other Officers, critically surveyed the Mill Creek, which divides the Town.

By Letters from Connecticut, and by several credible Gentlemen arrived from thence, we are informed, that there were not less than FORTY THOUSAND MEN in MOTION, and under ARMS, on their Way to Boston, on Saturday, Sunday, and Monday last, having heard a false Report that the Troops had fired upon Boston, and killed several of the Inhabitants: Twelve Hundred arrived at Hartford from Farmington, & other Places Forty Miles beyond Hartford, on Sunday last, on their Way to this Place, so rapidly did the News fly. But being informed by Expresses that it was a false Report, they returned

but small Quantities of CORN sent in, now our Ports are open: And further we have a very unpleasing Prospect of the next Year's Crop of WHEAT. The POOR are greatly oppressed, and many others much straitned.---That BOSTON is the Seat of MINISTERIAL REVENGE we too well know: The Issue we dread---How far the Colonies will yield, we know not; and if they do, how far they must they know not. The Ministry will endeavour, without Doubt, by all Means to caress one Part, while they oppress another; and if they can disunite you, they gain their End; and in Time oppress all by every TAX imposed upon us, for the Support of their Creatures; of this you need no Hints. We shall soon hear how Things will go down with you. May you have divine Direction. Your LIBERTY or SLAVERY are soon to be determined. Our Ministerial Tools are dogged hungry, and want to pick your Bones. The Ease with which Things passed through our Houses affords Matter for some Speculation. Whether the anti ministerial Part did not interest themselves in the Affair, or had rather the Ministry should by this Step entangle themselves, Time will probably discover,--- You will be careful how you express yourself, that neither of us be brought into Trouble, as it is very likely our Letters may be inspected."---

PORTSMOUTH.

THURSDAY last arrived here Captain NORMAN in the Fox Mastship, with 30 Chests of TEA, consigned to Edward Parry, Esq; who refused the Consignment; upon the People's being acquainted with this repeated Insult (of the East-India Company) to the Colonies, they were greatly alarmed, and had almost absolutely determined to oblige the Ship to return to London, with the Tea only, but through the polite

Schooner Polly, James Tilestone, Newfoundland.
Sloop Polly, William Furnell, Halifax.
Sloop Britannia, John Gray, Nantucket.
Sloop Revenge, Benjamin Dannell, West Indies.
Brig Abigail, John Wheelwright, Ditto.
Brig Success, Edmund Freeman, Ditto.
Ship Polly, John Gregory, Ditto.

TO BE SOLD

One Half of a Right of Land, In Rochester, originally belonging to Nicholas Harford, excepting the first Division.

Enquire of the Printer.

Whereas Mary, the Wife of me the Subscriber, has of late run me greatly in Debt, this is therefore to forbid all Persons trusting her on my Account, as I will not pay One Penny she may contract from the date hereof. Kittery, Sept. 14th 1774.
JOHN LILLEY.

TO BE SOLD,

For the Term of seven Years, pursuant to a Decree of Court,

George Madden,

An Excellent Weaver--- Whoever inclines to purchase the said George, may hear of the Terms by enquiring at the Printing Office.

---

hope, and expect this House will immediately adopt, I will be among the foremost of this illustrious Assembly, to move for such Measures as will effectually prevent a future Relapse, and make them feel what it is to provoke a fond and forgiving Parent; a Parent, my Lords, whose Welfare has ever been my greatest and most pleasing Consolation. This Declaration may seem unnecessary, but I will venture to declare, the Period is not far distant, when she will want the Assistance of her most distant Friends; but should the all disposing Hand of Providence prevent me from affording her my poor Assistance, my Prayers shall be ever for her Welfare. Length of Days be in her Right Hand, and in her left, Riches and Honor; may her Ways be Ways of Pleasantness, and all her Paths be Peace.

SALEM, Sept. 13, 1774.

Last Tuesday arrived here the Ship Julius Cæsar, Charles Fea, Master, from London, having on board thirty Chests and three half Chests of Tea, the Property of one Montgomery of London, consigned to Messrs. Smith and Atkinson, Merchants in Boston, who were equally surprized and offended at the Consignment, it being intirely unknown to them before the Ship's Arrival; and they solemnly declare, that Mr. Montgomery, previous to this Consignment, never had any Intercourse or commercial Correspondence with either of them. As soon as the Committee of Correspondence here had made Discovery of the Tea, the Master sent an Express to Smith and Atkinson; and the next Morning Mr. Smith came to Town, and frankly declared that the Tea should not be landed, nor any Duty paid on it here, if he

Home, declaring themselves ready at a Minute's Warning to arm again, and fight for their Country, and distressed Brethren of Boston.

A Number of the Poor of this Town are now employed about making Bricks at the new Yard, belonging to the Town on the Neck.

Lieutenant Governor Oliver has removed his Family and Goods from Cambridge to this Town.

In several Towns towards Connecticut, the Meeting-Houses were shut up on Sunday last, and the People all under ARMS.

We hear the Hon. Peyton Randolph, Esq; Speaker of the House of Burgesses of Virginia, is appointed President of the Congress.

Last Friday Morning one Valentine Ducket, a Deserter from the 65th Regt. now at Halifax, was shot in the Rear of the Camp in the Common, pursuant to the Sentence of a Court-Martial.

Since our last 4 24 pounders and 8 nine pounders have been transported from castle william to this town, and are now placed at the fortification on the neck.

The Hon. Mrs. GAGE, Lady of his Excellency the Governor, arrived in Town last Evening from New-York.

EXTRACT of a LETTER from GOVERNOR HUTCHINSON, LONDON, July 8, 1774.

"Let the TEA be paid for by or in behalf of the Town, as soon as may be; and I hope you will do as much to promote this as possible.------I find my APPLICATIONS every where to have more WEIGHT than I could EXPECT, and the PROSPECT of your speedy RELIEF to be fairer every DAY :----If finally obtained, I shall think it one of the most happy CIRCUMSTANCES of my LIFE."

LAST Monday the Select-Men of this Town waited on his Excellency General GAGE, to acquaint him that the People were surprized to find that he had ordered the Fortification on the Neck; that he would explain to them every Movement, that they might to quiet the Minds of the People; for the following Purpose: That up the Avenue to the Town, or any of the Country People, the Town as usual; that he had he was to protect his Majesty's troops in this Town; and that he hostile against the Inhabitants.

Sept. 12.

men of this Town again waited upon with the following ADDRESS, viz

EXCELLENCY,

Boston, at the earnest Desire of a Number of Gentlemen of the Town and Country, again wait on your Excellency to acquaint you, that since our late Application the Apprehensions of the People not only of this but of the neighbouring Towns are greatly increased, by observing the Design of erecting a Fortress at the Entrance of the Town; & of reducing this Metropolis in other Respects to the State of a Garrison.--- This with Complaints lately made, of Abuse from some of the Guards posted in the Quarter in assaulting and forceably detaining several Persons who were peaceably passing in and out of the Town, the Market People from coming in with

Behaviour of the Captain, who was ready to submit to any Thing the People thought proper upon the Occasion, he was permitted to send the Tea to Halifax, and it was put on Board Capt. Fernald, who sailed for Halifax with it last Sunday. In future no such Indulgence will be allowed to the Enemies of America.

Mr. PRINTER, Please to insert the following, and you will oblige your's, MEDICUS.

ON Saturday last was delivered of a perfect CHILD, the famous Personage Mrs. FOX, who arrived here from LONDON the 8th Instant: It was expected by many, she would have been provided with a MIDWIFE from Boston; as it was feared, if she was intrusted to the Unskilfulness of the obstetric Professors in Portsmouth, her tender Offspring might be stifled in the Birth. But as a more than ordinary Caution was observed on both Sides, the Event so much feared, has been happily prevented. The CHILD was immediately sent to Halifax, to be put under the Care of a faithful NURSE, where it will remain, until it be fit to appear in Public. The MOTHER will return to LONDON, when sufficiently recovered to venture abroad.

By a private LETTER from Boston since the Post, the following is said to be Governor GAGE's Answer to the COMMITTEE of the County of Suffolk, who waited on his EXCELLENCY, on Account of the uneasiness of said County, occasioned by his erecting a Fortress at the Entrance of the Town, &c.

I Hoped the Assurance I gave the Selectmen of Boston on the Subject you now address me, had been satisfactory to every Body.---- I cannot possibly intercept the Intercourse between the Town and the Country; it is my Duty and Interest to encourage it, and it is as much inconsistent with my Duty and Interest to form this strange Scheme you are pleased to suggest of reducing the Inhabitants to a State of Humiliation and Vassalage, by stopping their Supplies, nor have I made it easier to effect this, than what Nature has made it. You mention the Soldiers insulting, beating and abusing Passengers as a common Thing; an Instance perhaps may be given of the bad Behaviour of some disorderly Soldiers, but I must appeal to the Inhabitants of both Town and Country for their general good Behaviour, from their first Arrival to this Time.

I would ask what Occasion there is, for such Numbers going armed in and out of the Town, and thro' the Country in an hostile Manner? Or why were the Guns removed privately in the Night from the Battery at Charlestown? The refusing Subjection to the late Acts of Parliament I find general throughout the Province, and I shall lay the same before his Majesty.

A Town-Meeting is to be held in this Town on Monday next at 3 o'Clock Afternoon, when Matters of Importance are to be transacted, therefore it is desired there may be a general Attendance.

---

rations are now carrying

NEW-PORT, Sept. 5.

Yesterday an Express arrived at Providence from Plainfield, to inquire into the Account of the Powder's being stolen by Gage's Orders, informing that there were near Ten Thousand Men in Arms, in that Part of the Country, ready to march to Boston, if needed.

About 10 o'Clock last Night an Express arrived in this Town, for a Number of Military Officers in the wes-

---

NEW-HAMPSHIRE GAZETTE (PORTSMOUTH)
September 16, 1774
—

"FORTY THOUSAND MEN in MOTION and under ARMS," reported the *New-Hampshire Gazette* to show the Massachusetts countryside was committed to resistance and could oppose any Crown aggression with overwhelming force and unity.

NEW-HAMPSHIRE GAZETTE (PORTSMOUTH)
September 23, 1774

The next stage of the American Revolution was a race to arm, to control artillery and gunpowder. For example, we read here how General Gage and the Royal Navy had disabled batteries in Boston Harbor, but we do not read anything about how New Englanders were sneaking cannon into the countryside.

Union between Great-Britain and the Colonies, so ardently wished for by all good Men.

18. Whereas the universal Uneasiness which prevails among all Orders of Men, arising from the wicked and oppressive Measures of the present Administration, may influence some unthinking Persons to commit Outrage upon private Property :——We would heartily recommend to all Persons of this Community, not to engage in any Routs, Riots or licentious Attacks upon the Properties of any Person whatsoever, as being subversive of all Order and Government ; but by a steady, manly, uniform and persevering Opposition, to convince our Enemies that in a Contest so important, in a Cause so solemn, our Conduct shall be such as to merit the Approbation of the Wise, and the Admiration of the brave and free of every Age and of every Country.

19. That should our Enemies, by any sudden Manoeuvres, render it necessary for us to ask the Aid and Assistance of our Brethren in the Country, some one of the Committee of Correspondence, or a Selectman of such Town, or the Town adjoining, where such Hostilities shall commence, shall dispatch Couriers with written Messages to the Selectmen or Committees of Correspondence of the several Towns in the Vicinity, with a written Account of such Matter, who shall dispatch others to Committees more remote, 'till proper and sufficient Assistance be obtained ; and that the Expence of said Couriers be defrayed by the County, until it shall be otherwise ordered by the Provincial Congress. *Attest,*
WILLIAM THOMPSON, *Clerk.*

BOSTON, Sept. 19.

A melancholy Accident happened at Roxbury on Monday last, as two young Men were diverting themselves with military Exercise one exchanged his Gun with the other, who gave the Words of Command ; at the Word FIRE ! his Companion discharged his Piece, not knowing it was loaded, and a Ball entered the Head of Mr. Henry, and killed him on the Spot.

We have received from Worcester the Recantation of John Chandler, Esq; and 42 others, of the Protestors, against the Proceedings of that Town, which gave such Cause of Offence to the Public; as also the Acknowledgement of six Justices of that County, for having aspersed the People in an Address to General GAGE.

Last Wednesday Night all the Cannon in the North Battery were spiked up, said to be done by about 100 Men, who came in Boats from the Men of WAR.---They were, however, cleared again the next Day without much Difficulty.

The Newport Mercury of last Monday says, that "the Alarm which went thro' the Country last Saturday and Yesterday se'nnight, reach'd New York on Monday, & had not the Accounts been soon contradicted, it is very certain there would have been Sixty or Eighty Thousand Men in Arms, near Boston, in 2 Days, not as some Tories infamously insinuate, for the Purpose of REBELLION ; but in Defence of ALL that's valuable, dear, holy and sacred."

Last Week the Cannon at the Batteries back of Governor's Island were removed by Order of the General.

The TEA lately arrived in the Mary and Jane, Capt. Chapman, at Norfolk in Virginia, is to be returned in the same Ship by Orders of the Owners, in Consequence of their having been waited on by the Committee of that Town.

Patients for the Small Pox, during the sitting of the Congress, as several of the Northern and Southern Delegates have not had that Disorder."

We hear that Collections are making in the several Towns in the Colony of Rhode-Is... here : It is said 1500 Doll... Newport ; and that the... had generously subscribe...

A Correspondent obs... advise that the East-In... troyed at Boston ; they... Markets in the World ;... Teas to such Provinces,... pay the Duty, and they... vanced Price.

A great Number of... Barracks on the Common...

Advices from Lo...

" That notwithstanding... tion Association being... the Continent of Ameri... Custom House in the Co... is not among the List, th... about a Dozen more are... is said to be resolved, at all... Bill, as Lord North says, " It will keep good for Years in America, tho' not used."

S A L E M, Sept. 20.

Letters from a Gentleman in Philadelphia, to his Friends in this Place, dated the 2d Inst. say,---"The whole Attention and Conversation is wrapped up in the Congress, & every Mouth wishing them Success-----they are greatly respected, as Men of Wisdom, from whom the People ardently expect the Salvation of America. Every one prays for their Success. The Canada Bill serves greatly to cement our Welfare, and the Unanimity expected in their Councils almost assures them of it.------What Measures will be adopted is as yet very uncertain ; some think Non-Exportation and Non-Importation to the West-Indies and Great-Britain, others only to Great-Britain : But by what I can gather, it will be only with Great-Britain for the present, and the West-Indies conditionally, at some future Meeting of the CONGRESS, if they find the first ineffectual. General Gage is most severely handled in the Papers here and at Virginia, for his taking his Appointment. Government has not in this Place one who dares appear its Advocate. The Members from Virginia were just now received with Ringing of Bells, and other Marks of a most hearty Welcome. Upon the whole, every Thing bears the most promising Appearance for the future Welfare of America."

P H I L A D E L P H I A, Sept. 5.

Extract of a Letter from London, July 8.

" The Fox Indiaman, bound to New-England, has on board 30 Chests of Tea, shipped on the 6th Day of July, by Anthony Bacon, Esq; of London. This Tea is generally supposed to be a Speculation of the Minister."

Extract of a Letter from Boston, August 20.

" Letters by Capt. Scott have this Moment arrived :----He brings Intelligence that the People in England are rubbing up their Eyes, and begin to awake. Governor Tr---n is said not a little to contribute to this : He told the Lords of Council, that it would not do to treat the Yorkers as he did the Regulators ; they were a very different kind of Men. He said all the Force he had could not have saved the TEA, and therefore he sent it back. He was asked what he tho't of the present Measures adopted towards the Americans ? He answered, they would undoubtedly produce a Congress : And what would be the result of that ? He replied, he could not take upon him to say ; perhaps the Loss of all North-America."

WILLIAMSBURG (Virginia,) Aug. 18.

By an Express from the Frontiers, we learn that Col. M'Donald had just arrived from Wahatomakie, a Shawanese Town on the Muskingham, which he has destroyed, with all the Plantations round it, taken 3 Scalps, killed several of the Indians, and made one Prisoner, with the Loss of only two of his People, and 6 wounded ; and that an Expedition is planned against some of their other Towns, which, if successful, will probably put an End to the War. Several Parties of Indians are daily seen on this Side of the Allegheny Mountains, but they have done but little Mischief of late, except scalping one Family on the Head of Cedar Creek.

Country ? Have they not by a partial and ignominious inclosure of Commons, destroyed the Cottages who were the Supports of our Market, and (by Propagation) the Recruits of our Navy and Army ? Have they not, by a lawless and exorbitant Rise of the Price of Lands, driven the Husbandmen from...

...Country can be saved by you, and yet you suffer your Rights to be trampled on, nor turn again with the humble Spirit of a Worm. The Spirit of a Worm would save ye, but ye have it not ; and who must pursue the Man, who can stand with his Fingers in his Mouth, and suffer the Slaves of Power to pick his Pockets. The next Election may, in some Measure, snatch you from the Brink of Destruction, if ye can withstand the Potations offered you by the venal Candidates of Government. Retain yourselves sober, pride yourselves in a blunt and manly Refusal of Bribes, and give your Votes to such honest Men only, who can and will stand by you in the Hour of Need and in the Day of Destruction.

Let no intoxication warp your Resolutions ; drink with your own Money, nor swallow a Draught of Corruptions, that will most inevitably ruin ye all. There is scarce a Borough but will have Candidates of both Complexions ---You cannot be so blind as not to discern the white from the Black. Call up that antient Spunk and Virtue that so long distinguished your Forefathers ; and let the World see that though Kings and Nobles study to ruin a People,---that Englishmen alone can save their Country, in spite of all the Evils of evil Men. Rouse, Britons, rouse from your Lethargy ; nor forget your antient Spirit, that hath so often reclaimed this Land in the Hours of Sorrow and Despair. The Virtue is alone with you---if you tamely fold your Arms and talk of Maladies, without administring a Cure, this Island in fifty Years will be a Colony of France, and your Children the miserable Slaves of Arbitrary Power. Remember with Tears I give you the Caution,---remember the Prophecy ; or save the Land, by adopting the Advice of your steady and unshaken Friend
MARVELL.

L O N D O N, July 28.

According to an Estimate, it is said, the Navy of France at Midsummer last, consisted of 100 Ships of the Line and Frigates, said to be esteemed, upon an Average, superior in Strength to 100 English 64 Gun Ships.

It is said that a French Nobleman of great Quality is in London incog. settling some Business relative to Poland. He is so cautious of being seen that he never goes out of his Lodging till late at Night, when he goes in a Chair to Down-Street, from whence he is conveyed in a Coach, attended by a certain Lord, to such Places as their Business may require. 'Tis thought this will make the King of Prussia Sweat and Fret, when he is acquainted with it.

Orders are given for a general Survey of all the Fortifications in Great Britain, Ireland, and the Isles of Mann, Jersey, Guernsey and Scilly. Engineers are gone off for that Purpose. Every place of Strength is in future to be kept in thorough Repair.--- Some of the old Castles on the Sea Coasts are to be pulled down, and the old Materials applied towards the Building new Fortifications and Barracks for Soldiers at every Place where the former are erected.

July 30. There are now fitting out, in different Yards, three Men of War destin'd for the Coast of Affrica, where they are to be stationed for same Time, for the better Protection of the Trade, and are afterwards to sail down the Coast, to join the Fleet on the North-American Station.

We are assured that some further Orders and Instructions of an important Nature were last Week sent off to General Gage, Governor of Massachuset's Bay in New-England.

SUFFOLK RESOLVES

By Ray Raphael

WHILE THE RESPONSE TO THE POWDER ALARM WAS sudden and spontaneous, the lasting overthrow of British rule in all of Massachusetts outside of Boston was carefully considered. The local Committees of Correspondence, which enjoyed quasi-official status by their connection with town meetings, determined in advance to shut down the county courts after August 1, 1774, the date the Massachusetts Government Act was to take effect. (These courts, meeting quarterly, not only administered justice, but also served as the administrative arms of local government.)

The first court date was set for August 16 in Great Barrington, the "shiretown" of Berkshire County. On July 25, a local committee of correspondence told the Boston Committee it would not allow that court to sit, and on the appointed day, 1,500 people converged on the courthouse to make certain it did not. The Berkshire court would never again meet under British rule.

Springfield, in Hampshire County, was scheduled next. On August 30, before a crowd of some three thousand local citizens "in a sandy, sultry place, exposed to the sun," the Crown-appointed judges read their recantations, promising never to serve under the dreaded act (September 6 Hartford dateline in September 16, 1774, *New-Hampshire Gazette*.)

Other counties followed in turn. In the shiretown of Worcester, 4,622 militiamen from thirty-seven towns—half the adult male population of the county—assembled along both sides of Main Street as two dozen court officials slowly walked the gauntlet, hats in hand, reciting their recantations over thirty times apiece so all could hear.

In Plymouth, after some four thousand people had forced court officials to bow to their will, the victors were so enthused that they:

"attempted to remove a Rock (the one on which their fore-fathers first landed, when they came to this country) which lay buried in a wharfe five feet deep, up into the center of the town, near the court house. The way being up hill, they found it impracticable, as after they had dug it up, they found it to weigh ten tons at least."

And so it went. As each county closed its courts, that county's convention of the Committees of Correspondence issued a set of resolutions explaining why the people had subverted the law. Typical of these resolutions is that of Middlesex County, which detailed item-by-item the injustices of the Massachusetts Government Act while giving only one fleeting mention to the Boston Port Act (September 8 Boston dateline in September 16, 1774, *New-Hampshire Gazette*.)

Only one of the mainland contiguous counties in Massachusetts did *not* close the courts: Suffolk, whose shiretown was Boston. There, buttressed by the presence of three thousand British soldiers, Crown-appointed officials still exerted military and political power. But Suffolk County's Committees of Correspondence still met and voiced their discontent, even if they lacked the power to overturn British authority. Hence the famous Suffolk Resolves, which resembled the resolves of other county conventions in substance but exceeded them in literary flare. Simultaneous with issuing its resolves, the Suffolk Convention sent a committee to Governor Gage to protest the cannon he positioned at the gates of Boston after the militia mobilization on September 2 (September 15 Boston dateline in September 23, 1774, *New-Hampshire Gazette*.)

Joseph Warren, on behalf of the Suffolk Convention, dispatched Paul Revere to Philadelphia with a copy of the

Suffolk Resolves, and when Revere returned September 23, he bore news that the intercolonial congress meeting there had unanimously endorsed the resolutions and would stand by the people of Massachusetts in their firm resistance to the abuses of British authority (September 26 Boston dateline in September 30, 1774, *New-Hampshire Gazette*.)

"This was one of the happiest days of my life," John Adams, one of the delegates, noted in his diary. "In Congress we had generous, noble sentiments, and manly eloquence. This day convinced me that America will support the Massachusetts or perish with her."

Historians have long noted the historic importance of the Suffolk Resolves and their endorsement by leaders from other colonies, but they have generally overlooked one key element: by sanctioning the Resolves, Congress supported deeds as well as words. It vowed to stand behind a revolution that was in full swing throughout Massachusetts.

A Map of 100 Miles
Around Boston
Gentleman's Magazine,
London, 1775

This map illustrates the counties of Massachusetts.

It may be depended upon, that some copious instructions respecting the Effectuation of a Peace between the Russians and the Turks, were last Week sent off to our Ambassadors at Petersburgh and Constantinople.

BOSTON, Sept. 8.
Middlesex RESOLVES.

At a Meeting of 150 Gentlemen, being Committees from every Town and District in the County of Middlesex, and Province if Massachusetts-Bay, held at Concord in said County, on the 30th and 31st Days of Aug. 1774. to consult upon Measures proper to be taken at the present very important Day, viz.

The Hon. JAMES PRESCOT, Esq; chosen Chairman.

After having read the late Act of the British Parliament entitled, An Act for the better regulating the Government of the Province of Massachusetts Bay in New-England," and debated thereon;

Voted, That a Committee be appointed to take into Consideration the said Act, and report to this Meeting.

Voted, That Mr. *Jonathan Williams Austin,* of Chelmsford, Capt. *Thomas Gardner,* of Cambridge, Doctor *Isaac Foster,* of *Charlestown,* Capt. *Josiah Stone,* of Framingham, Mr. *Richard Deavens,* of *Charlestown,* Doctor *Oliver Prescott,* of *Groton,* Henry Gardner, Esq; of *Stow,* Mr. *William Brown* of *Framingham,* and Mr. *Ebenezer Bridge,* jun. of Billerica, be the Committee.

Who reported as follows,

IT is evident to every attentive Mind, that this Province is in a very dangerous and alarming Situation. We are obliged to say, however painful it may be to us, that the Question now is, whether by a Submission to some late Acts of the Parliament of Great-Britain, we are contented to be the most abject Slaves, and entail that Slavery on Posterity after us, or by a manly, joint and virtuous Opposition assert and support our Freedom.

There is a Mode of Conduct, which in our very critical Circumstances, we would wish to adopt, a Conduct, on the one Hand never tamely submissive to Tyranny and Oppression, on the other, never degenerating into Rage, Passion and Confusion. This is a Spirit which we revere, as we find it exhibited in former Ages, and will command Applause to latest Posterity.

The late Acts of Parliament pervade the whole System of Jurisprudence, by which Means, we think, the Fountains of Justice are fatally corrupted. Our Defence must therefore be immediate in Proportion to the suddenness of the Attack and vigorous in Proportion to the Danger.

We must NOW exert ourselves, or all those EFFORTS, which for Ten Years past, have brightened the Annals of this Country, will be totally frustrated. LIFE and DEATH, or what is more, FREEDOM and SLAVERY are in a peculiar Sense now before US, and the Choice and Success, under God, depend greatly upon ourselves. WE are therefore bound, as Struggling not only for ourselves, but future Generations, to express our Sentiments in the following RESOLVES; Sentiments, which we think, are founded in Truth and Justice, and therefore Sentiments we are determined to abide by.

RESOLVED, That as true and loyal SUBJECTS of our gracious SOVEREIGN GEORGE the THIRD, KING of Great Britain, &c. we by no MEANS intend to withdraw our ALLEGIANCE from him; but, while permitted the free Exercise of our natural and Charter RIGHTS, are resolved to expend LIFE and TREASURE in his SERVICE.

RESOLVED, That when our Ancestors emigrated from Great Britain, Charters and solemn Stipulations expressed the Conditions, and what particular Rights they yielded; what each party had to do and perform, and which each of the contradicting Parties were equally bound by.

RESOLVED, That we know of no Instance, in which this Province has transgressed the Rules on their Part, or any Ways forfeited their natural and chartered RIGHTS to any Power on Earth.

RESOLVED, That the Parliament of Great-Britain have exercised a Power contrary to the above-mentioned Charter, by passing Acts, which hold up their absolute Supremacy over the Colonists; by another Act blocking up the Port of Boston; and by two late Acts, the one entitled, An Act for better regulating the Government of the Province of Massachusetts-Bay, the other entitled, An Act for the more impartial Administration of Justice in said Province; and by enforcing all these iniquitous Acts with a large armed Force to dragoon and enslave us.

RESOLVED, That the late Act of Parliament, entitled an Act for the better regulating the Government of the Province of the Massachusetts-Bay in New England, expressly acknowledges the Authority of the Charter, granted by their Majesties King William and Queen Mary to said Province; and that the only Rea-

RESOLVED, That every People have an absolute Right of meeting together to consult upon common Grievances, and to Petition, Remonstrate and use every legal Method for their Removal.

RESOLVED, That the Act which prohibits these constitutional Meetings cuts away the Scaffolding of English Freedom, and reduces us to a most abject State of Vassallage and Slavery.

RESOLVED, That it is our Opinion, these late Acts if quietly submitted to, will annihilate the last Vestiges of Liberty in this Province, and therefore we must be justified by God and the World, in never submitting to them.

RESOLVED, That it is the Opinion of this Body, that the present Act, respecting the Government of the Province of Massachusetts-Bay, is an artful, deep laid Plan of Oppression & Despotism, that it requires great Skill & Wisdom to counteract it. This Wisdom we have endeavoured to collect from the united Sentiments of the County; And although we are grieved that we are obliged to mention any Thing that may be attended with such very important Consequences, as may now ensue, yet a Sense of our Duty as Men, as Freemen, as christian Freemen, united in the firmest Bonds, obliges us to resolve, that every civil Officer now in Commission in this Province, and acting in conformity to the late Act of Parliament, is not an Officer agreeable to our Charter, therefore unconstitutional, and ought to be opposed, in the Manner hereafter recommended.

RESOLVED, That we will obey all such civil Officers, now in Commission, whose Commissions were issued before the first Day of July 1774, and support them in the Execution of their Offices according to the Manner usual before the late Attempt to alter the Constitution of this Province; nay, even although the Governor should attempt to revoke their Commissions.—— But that if any of said Officers shall accept a Commission under the present Plan of arbitrary Government, or in any Way or Manner whatever, assist the Governor or Administration in the Assault now making on our Rights and Liberties, we will consider them as having forfeited their Commissions, and yield them no Obedience.

RESOLVED, That whereas the Hon. SAMUEL DANFORTH, and JOSEPH LEE, Esquires; two of the Judges of the Inferior Court of common Pleas, for the County have accepted Commissions under the new Act by being sworn Members of his Majesty's Council appointed by said Act: We therefore look upon them utterly incapable of holding any Office whatever.—— And whereas a Venire, on the late Act of Parliament, has issued from the Court of Sessions, signed by the Clerk, We think they come under a preceeding Resolve of acting in Conformity to the new Act of Parliament, We therefore Resolve that, a Submission to Courts thus acting and under these Disqualifications, is a Submission to the Act itself, and of Consequence, as we are resolved never to submit to Courts thus constituted and thus acting in conformity to said Act.

RESOLVED, That as, in consequence of the former Resolve all Business at the Inferior Court of common Pleas and Court of General Sessions of the Peace next to be holden at Concord, must cease; to prevent the many Inconveniences that may arise therefrom, we resolve that all Actions, Writs, Suits, &c. bro't to said Court, ought to remain in the same Condition, as at present, (unless settled by Consent of Parties) 'till we know the Result of a Provincial and Continental Congress. And we resolve, that no Plaintiff, in any Cause, Action or Writ aforesaid, ought to enter said Action in said Court thus declared to be unconstitutional. And we resolve, if the Court shall set in Defiance to the Voice of the County, and default Actions and issue Executions accordingly, no Officer ought to serve such Process. And we are also determined to support all Constables, Jurors and other Officers, who from these constitutional Principles shall refuse Obedience to Courts which we have resolved are founded on the Destruction of our Charter.

RESOLVED, That it is the Opinion of this Body of Delegates, that a provincial Congress is absolutely necessary, in our present unhappy Situation.

These are Sentiments which we are obliged to express, as these acts are intended *immediately* to take place. We must *now* either oppose them, or tamely give up all we have been struggling for. It is this that has forced us so soon on these very important Resolves. However we do it with humble deference to the Provincial and Continental Congress, by whose Resolutions we are determined to abide; to whom and the World we chearfully Appeal for the uprightness of our Conduct.

On the whole, these are "great and profound Questions," We are grieved to find ourselves reduced to the Necessity of entering into the discussion of them. But we deprecate a State of Slavery. Our Fathers left a fair Inheritance to us, purchased by a waste of Blood and Treasure. This we are resolved to transmit equally fair to our Children after us. No Danger shall affright, no Difficulties intimidate us. And if in Support of our Rights we are called to encounter even Death, we are yet undaunted, sensible that HE can never die too soon, who lays down

carried with him the esteem of every one; but as they are, they ought to be remembered as great Instances to instruct the World, to what a Stretch of Liberty Mankind will naturally attain when they are left to the free Exercise of themselves. And, my Lords, notwithstanding my Intention to give my hearty Negative to the Question now before you, I cannot help condemning in the severest Manner, the late turbulent and unwarrantable Conduct of the Americans in general, and the Riots in Boston in particular. But, my Lords, the Mode which has been pursued to bring them back to a Sense of their Duty to the parent State, has been so diametrically opposed to the fundamental Principles of sound Policy, that Individuals possessed of common Understanding, must be astonished at such Proceedings. By blocking up the Harbour of Boston, you have involved the innocent Trader in the same Punishment with the guilty Profligates who destroyed your Merchandize; and instead of making a well concerted Effort to secure the real Offenders, you clap a naval and military Extinguisher over their Harbour; and punish the Sin of a few lawless Raparees & their Abettors upon the whole Body of the Inhabitants.

My Lords, This Country is little obliged to the Framers and Promoters of this Tea-Tax; the Americans had almost forgot, in their Excess of Gratitude for the Repeal of the Stamp-Act, any Interest but that of the Mother Country; there seemed an Emulation among the different Provinces, who should be most dutiful and forward in their Expressions of Loyalty to their Royal Benefactor; as you will readily perceive by the following Extract of a Letter to from Governor Bernard to a noble Lord then in Office.

"The House of Representatives, (says he) from the Time of "opening the Session to this Day, has shewn a Disposition to "avoid all Dispute with me; every Thing having passed with "as much good Humour as I could desire. They have acted, "in all Things, with Temper and Moderation; they have a"voided some Subjects of Dispute, and have laid a Foundation "for removing some Causes of former Altercation."

This, my Lords, was the Temper of the Americans; and would have continued so, had it not been interrupted by your fruitless endeavours to tax them without their Consent : but the Moment they perceived your Intention was renewed to tax them, through the Sides of the East-India Company, their Resentment got the Ascendant of their Duty, and hurried them into Actions contrary to all Laws of Policy, Civilization and Humanity, which in their cooler Hours they would have thought on with Horror; for I seriously believe, the destroying the Tea was much more the Effect of Despair than that of Design.

But, my Lords, from the Complexion of the whole of the Proceedings, I am apt to think, that Administration has purposely irritated them into those late violent Acts for which they now so severely smart; purposely to be revenged on them for the Victory they gained by the Repeal of the Stamp-Act, a Measure to which they seemingly acquiesced, but at the Bottom they were its real Enemies. For what other Motive could induce them to dress Taxation, that Father of American Sedition, in the Robes of an East-India Director, but to break in upon that mutual Peace and Harmony which then so happily subsisted between them and the Mother Country ? My Lords, I am an old Man, and will advise the noble Lords now in Office, to adopt a more gentle Mode of governing America; for the Day is not far distant, when America may vie with these Kingdoms, not only in *Arms*, but in *Arts* also. It is an established Fact, that the principal Towns in America are *learned* and *polite*, and understand the Constitution of the Empire, as well as the noble Lords who *guide the Springs* of Government ----; and consequently, they will have a watchful Eye over their Liberties, to prevent the least encroachment of an arbitrary Administration on their hereditary Rights and Privileges.

This Observation so recently exemplified in an excellent Pamphlet which comes from the Pen of an American Gentleman,* that I shall take the Liberty of reading to your Lordships his Thoughts on the Competency of the British Parliament to tax America, which in my Opinion, sets that interesting Matter in the clearest Point of View.

"The high Court of Parliament (says he) is the supreme Legislative Power over the whole Empire; in all free States the Constitution is fixed; and as the supreme Legislative derives its Power and Authority from the Constitution, it cannot overleap the Bounds of it, without destroying it's own Foundation; for the Constitution ascertains and limits both Sovereignty and Allegiance; and therefore his Majesty's American Subjects, who acknowledge themselves bound by the Ties of Allegiance, have an *equitable* Claim to the full Enjoyment of the fundamental Rules of the English Constitution; and that it is an essential unalterable Right in Nature, ingrafted into the British Constitution as a fundamental Law, and ever held sacred and irrevocable by the Subjects within the Realm; and that what a Man has honestly acquired, is absolutely his own; which he may freely give, but which cannot be taken from him without his Consent."

of their having been forfeited, to which Charge the Province has had no Opportunity of answering.

RESOLVED, That a Debtor may as justly refuse to pay his

same, be collected by Yeas and Nays; which being done, there were 146 Yeas and 4 Nays.

Voted, That it be recommended to the several Towns and

licy, which neither the Exigencies of the State, or even the Acquiescence in the Taxes, could justify upon any Occasion whatever. Such Proceedings will never meet with their wished for

holiday Nights the Committee of Guards was fet.
Thursday Meffrs. Smith and Atkinson procured a Veffel to take
the Tea on board and carry it to Halifax. That Night alfo a
Guard was fet. And the next Morning, at Day-Light, the Tea
was taken out, and put on board the Veffel procured to receive
it, in Prefence of the Guard; who having the Marks & Numbers of the Chefts, found them to agree with the Bill of Lading
and the Cocket. By 7 o'Clock the Veffel, with the TEA on
board, got under Sail, and before 10 was out of the Harbour,
with a fair Wind.

Meffrs. Smith & Atkinfon in the whole Affair conducted like
Men of Honour, & entirely to the Satisfaction of the Committee, having ufed their utmoft Endeavours to difpofe of the Tea
in a Manner the leaft exceptionable.

The 59th Regiment from this Town, and two Companies of
the 64th from Danvers, marched to Bofton laft Saturday. The
former is ftationed on the Neck, at the Entrance of that Town,
where they are Entrenching, and where the moft hoftile Preparations are now carrying on.

NEW-PORT, Sept. 5.

Yefterday an Exprefs arrived at Providence from Plainfield,
to inquire into the Account of the Powder's being ftolen by Gage's
Orders, informing that there were near Ten Thoufand Men in
Arms, in that Part of the Country, ready to march to Bofton,
if needed.

About 10 o'Clock laft Night an Exprefs arrived in this Town,
for Commiffions for a Number of Military Officers in the weftern Parts of this Colony, and informs, that Col. Putnam had
marched from Connecticut, for Cambridge, with 1500 Men,
and that Col. Saltonftall was to march this Day with another
Body, and that all the Country were prodigioufly enraged, they
having been informed that a Party of Soldiers had marched to
Framingham, to feize the Powder in that Town, and had killed 6 of the Inhabitants outright.

NEW-LONDON, Sept. 2.

Laft Tuefday fe'nnight, Col. Willard, one of the *new Council*,
came to Union to do fome Bufinefs; when two Gentlemen
belonging to Windham, who had been his Attornies, in a
Cafe, met him and publickly refufed to affift him any more, as
they looked upon him a Traitor to his Country. The People
rofe, took & confined him one Night, then carried him to Brimfield, where the Province People, about 400 in Number, met
them: They called a Council of themfelves, and condemned
Col. Willard to Newgate Prifon in Symfbury, and a Number fet
off with and carried him 6 Miles on the Way thither. Colonel
Willard then fubmitted to take the Oath they required, on
which they difmiffed him.------One Capt. Davis, of Brimfield,
was prefent who fhewing Refentment and treating the People
with bad Language, they ftrip'd him, and give him the New-
Fafhion Drefs of Tar and Feathers.

PHILADELPHIA, Auguft 31.

Laft Week Col. Nathaniel Folfom, and Major John Sullivan,
Delegates from New-Hampfhire, arrived here.

On Monday Evening the Honorable Thomas Cufhing, Efq;
Samuel Adams, John Adams, and Robert Treat-Paine, Efq'rs
Delegates from Bofton, arrived in this City.

The Gentlemen Delegates from Connecticut are expected in
Town this Evening.

As are thofe from Virginia and Maryland on Friday.

HARTFORD, Sept. 6.

On Tuefday laft, being the Day the County Court was to fet at
Springfield, a great Concourfe of People, judg'd to be about
3000, affembled at the Court-Houfe in that Place, and appointed a Committee to wait on the Court, and requeft their
Appearance among the People, which they immediately complied with, when they very willingly figned the following
Engagement, viz.

WE the Subfcribers, do feverally Promife, and folemnly
engage to all People now affembled at Springfield, in
the County of Hampfhire on the 30th Day of Aug.
1774, that WE never will take, hold, execute, or exercife any
Commiffion, Office, or Employment whatfoever, under, or by
Virtue of, or in any Manner derived from any Authority pretended or attempted to be given by a late Act of Parliament, en-
tiled, "An Act for the better regulating the Government of
the Province of the Maffachufetts Bay in New England."
Ifrael Williams, Oliver Partridge, Timothy Dwight, Thomas
Williams, John Worthington, Jofeph Hawley, William Wil-
liams, Simeon Strong, Mofes Blifs, Jonathan Afhley, Elifha
Porter, William Billings, John Phelps, Solomon Stoddard, Juftus
Ely, Caleb Strong, Samuel Fowler, Jonathan Blifs.

BOSTON, Sept. 8.

Treafurer Gray, we are credibly informed has not refigned
his Office as Councellor.

Yefterday General Gage, accompanied by Lord Percy, the Admiral, and other Officers, critically furveyed the Mill Creek,
which divides the Town.

By Letters from Connecticut, and by feveral credible Gentlemen arrived from thence, we are informed, that there were
not lefs than FORTY THOUSAND MEN in MOTION, and
under ARMS, on their Way to Bofton, on Saturday, Sunday,
and Monday laft, having heard a falfe Report that the Troops
had fired upon Bofton, and killed feveral of the Inhabitants;

Excellency Governor GAGE, to acquaint him that the
Inhabitants were much alarmed to find that he had ordered the
breaking up the Ground near the Fortification on the Neck;
and requefted of his Excellency that he would explain to them
his Defign in that extraordinary Movement, that they might
thereby have it in their Power to quiet the Minds of the People;
when his Excellency replied to the following Purpofe: That
he had no Intention of ftopping up the Avenue to the Town, or
of obftructing the Inhabitants or any of the Country People,
coming in or going out of the Town as ufual; that he had
taken his Meafures, and that he was to protect his Majefty's
Subjects and his Majefty's Troops in this Town; and that he
had no Intention of any Thing hoftile againft the Inhabitants.

Monday, Sept. 12.

On Friday laft the Select-Men of this Town again waited upon
his Excellency the GOVERNOR with the following ADDRESS, viz.

MAY IT PLEASE YOUR EXCELLENCY

THE Select-Men of Bofton, at the earneft Defire of a Number of Gentlemen of the Town and Country, again wait on
your Excellency to acquaint you, that fince our late Application
the Apprehenfions of the People not only of this but of the neighbouring Towns are greatly increafed, by obferving the Defign of
erecting a Fortrefs at the Entrance of the Town; & of reducing
this Metropolis in other Refpects to the State of a Garrifon.----
This with Complaints lately made, of Abufe from fome of the
Guards pofted in the Quarter in affaulting and forceably detaining feveral Perfons who were peaceably paffing in and out of the
Town, may difcourage the Market People from coming in with
Provifions as ufual, and oblige the Inhabitants to abandon the
Town.--This Event we greatly deprecate, as it will produce Mi-
feries which may hurry the Province into Acts of Defperation.
We fhould therefore think ourfelves happy if we could fatisfy
the People that your Excellency would fufpend your Defign, and
not add to the Diftreffes of the Inhabitants occafioned by the
PORT-BILL, that of GARRISONING the TOWN.
JOHN SCOLLAY, Chairman of the Selectmen.

§§§§§

THE GOVERNOR's ANSWER.

GENTLEMEN,

WHEN you lately applied to me respecting my ordering
some Cannon to be placed at the Entrance of the Town,
which you term the erecting a Fortress; I so fully expressed my
Sentiments, that I tho't you was satisfied the People had nothing
to fear from that Measure, as no Use would be made thereof,
unless their hostile Proceedings should make it necessary; but as
you have this Day acquainted me, that your Fears are rather
increased, I have thought proper to assure you, that I have no
Intention to prevent the free Egress and Regress of any Person
to and from the Town, or of reducing it to the State of a GAR-
RISON, neither shall I suffer any under my Command to injure
the Person or Property of any of his Majesty's Subjects. But
as it is my Duty, so it shall be my Endeavour to preserve the
Peace, and promote the Happiness of every Individual; and I
earnestly recommend to you, and every Inhabitant, to cultivate
the same Spirit.----And heartily wish they may live quietly and
happily in the Town.
THO's GAGE.

Bofton, Sept. 9. 1774.
To the Gentlemen Selectmen of the Town of Bofton.

Extract of a Letter by the laft Ship from London.

PROVISIONS are very dear here,
but fmall Quantities
open: And further we
next Year's Crop of WH
and many others much ft
MINISTERIAL REVE
dread---How far the C
they do, how far they m
endeavour, without Dou
they oppress another; an
End; and in Time opp
for the Support of their
We shall soon hear how
you have divine Directi
soon to be determined.
and want to pick your
passed through our Ho
Whether the anti-minif
the Affair, or had rat
tangle themselves, Tim
careful how you expre
into Trouble, as it is ver

POR

THURSDAY
NORMAN in the Fox Mailfhip, with
30 Chefts of TEA, configned to Edward
Parry, Efq; who refufed the Confignment;
upon the People's being acquainted with
this repeated Infult (of the Eaft-India Company) to the Colonies, they were greatly a-
larmed, and had almoft abfolutely determi-

---

occafioned by his erecting a Fortress at the
Town, &c.

I Hoped the Affurance I gave the Selectmen of Bofton on the
Subject you now addrefs me, had been fatisfactory to every Body.---- I cannot poffibly intercept the Intercourfe between the
Town and the Country; it is my Duty and Intereft to encourage
it, and it is as much inconfiftent with my Duty and Intereft to
form this ftrange Scheme you are pleafed to fuggeft of reducing
the Inhabitants to a State of Humiliation and Vaffalage, by ftopping their Supplies, nor have I made it eafier to effect this, than
what Nature has made it. You mention the Soldiers infulting,
beating and abufing Paffengers as a common Thing; an Inftance
perhaps may be given of the bad Behaviour of fome diforderly
Soldiers, but I muft appeal to the Inhabitants of both Town and
Country for their general good Behaviour, from their firft Arrival
to this Time.

I would afk what Occafion there is, for fuch Numbers going
armed in and out of the Town, and thro' the Country in an
hoftile Manner? Or why were the Guns removed privately in the
Night from the Battery at Charleftown? The refufing Subjection to the late Acts of Parliament I find general throughout the
Province, and I fhall lay the fame before his Majefty.

A Town-Meeting is to be held in this
Town on Monday next at 3 o'Clock
Afternoon, when Matters of Importance are
to be tranfacted, therefore it is defired there
may be a general Attendance.

The Cuftomers of this Paper

are earneftly defired to pay off what they may be in Arrears
immediately, as the Publifher is under a Neceffity of raifing Money to carry on his Bufinefs, and purchafe Paper, which lie does
now with great Difficulty and extraordinary Charge, as it is
all brought 70 Miles on Land carriage-----------He hopes every
Cuftomer will fend at leaft one Dollar, that the Paper may not
be wholly ftopped, as there are now the moft interefting Matters depending that ever were in this Country.

The Merrimack Poft-Rider, whofe Year is now up, will not
carry News-Papers after this Month, unlefs the Cuftomers punctually pay off; Likewife the Eaftern Poft, and the other who
Rides up Connecticut River to the College.

THE annual Convention of Minifters is
to be held at the Houfe of the Rev'd
Dr. HAVEN in Portfmouth, on Wednefday
the 21ft of September current.

THE GAZETTE, CHRONICLE, FOREIGN AND DOMESTIC.

Vol. XVIII.

NO. 935 { Weeks since this Paper was first Publish'd. }

ountry, Ourselves and l Ways and Means in , defend and preserve s Rights & Liberties r Fathers fought——— d to hand them down ations.

cts of the British Par- p the Harbour of Bof- he established Form of olony ; and for screen- s Violaters of the Laws a legal Trial, are grofs ights to which we are Laws of Nature, the nd the Charter of the

ence is due from this any Part of the Acts a- that they be rejected wicked Administration

the Justices of our Su- cature, Court of Affize, very, & Inferior Courts this County, are ap- ir Places by any other hich the Charter & the e direct ; they must be undue Influence, & are ionalOfficers, & as such e paid them by the Peo-

Justices of the Superior Court of Affize, &c. t of Common Pleas, or ons of the Peace, fhall eir present disqualified will support and bear & their Deputies, Con- ther Officers, who fhall Execution the Orders of s far as is possible to pre- ences that must attend e Courts of Justice, we mend it to all Creditors nable and generous For- ebtors, and to all Debtors t Debts with all possible

offended by accepting said Department, and have not already, publickly resigned their Seats at the Council-Board, to make public Resignations of their Places at said Board, on or before the TWENTIETH Day of this Instant September ; and that all Persons neg- lecting so to do shall from and after said Day be considered by this County, as obstinate and incorrigible Enemies to this Colony.

9. That the Fortifications begun and now carrying on upon Boston Neck are justly a- larming to this County, and give us Reason to apprehend some hostile Intention against that Town, more especially as the Comman- der in Chief has in a very extraordinary Man- ner removed the Powder from the Magazine at Charlestown, and has also forbidden the Keeper of the Magazine at Boston to deliver out to the Owners the Powder which they had lodged in said Magazine.

10. That the late Act of Parliament for establishing the Roman Catholic Religion, and the French Laws in that extensive Coun- try now called Canada, is dangerous in an extreme Degree to the Protestant Religion, and to the civil Rights and Liberties of all America ; and therefore, as Men and Pro- testant Christians we are indispensibly obli- ged to take all proper Means for our Security.

11. That whereas our Enemies have flat- tered themselves that they shall make an easy Prey of this numerous, brave and hardy Peo- ple, from an Apprehension that they are un- acquainted with military Discipline, We therefore for the Honor Defence and Secu- rity of this County and Province advise, as it has been recommended to take away all Commissions from the Officers of the Mili- tia, that those who now hold Commissions or such other Persons be elected in each Town as Officers in the Militia as shall be judged of sufficient Capacity for that Purpose, and who have evidenced themselves the inflexi- ble Friends to the Rights of the People, and that the Inhabitants of those Towns and Districts who are qualified do use their ut- most Diligence to acquaint themselves with the Art of War as soon as possible, and do for that Purpose appear under Arms at least once

---

SEPTEMBER 23, 1774

The NEW-HAMPSHIRE GAZETTE

BOSTON, September 15, 1774.

At a Meeting of the Delegates of every Town and District in the County of *Suffolk*, on Tuesday the sixth of *September*, at the House of Mr. *Richard Woodward* of *Dedham*, and by Adjournment at the House of Mr. *Daniel Vose* of *Milton*, on Friday the Ninth Instant, JOSEPH PALMER, Esq; being chosen Moderator, and WILLIAM THOMPSON, Esq; Clerk, a Committee was chosen to bring in a Report to the Convention, and the following being several Times read and put Paragraph by Paragraph, was UNANIMOUSLY voted, *viz.*

Whereas *the Power, but not the Justice ; the Vengeance, but not the Wisdom of Great-Britain, which of old persecuted, scourged and exiled our fugitive Parents from their native Shores, now pursue us their guiltless Children with unrelenting Severity— And whereas this then savage and uncultivated Desart was pur- chased by the Toil and Treasure or acquired by the Valor & Blood of those our venerable Progenitors, who bequethed to us the dear bought inheritance, who consigned it to our Car & Protection ; the most sacred Obligations are upon us to transmit the glori- ous Purchase, unfettered by Power, unclogg'd with Shackles, to our innocent and beloved Offspring. On the Fortitude—on the Wisdom & on the Exertions of this important Day, is suspended the Fate of this New World, and of unborn Millions. If a bound- less Extent of Continent, |warming with Millions, will tamely submit to live, move and have their Being at the arbitrary Will of a licentious Minister, they basely yield to voluntary Slavery, and future Generations shall load their Memories with incessant Execrations.—On the other Hand, if we arrest the Hand which would ransack our Pockets, if we disarm the Parricide who points the Dagger to our Bosoms, if we nobly defeat that fatal Edict which proclaims a* Power to frame Laws for us in all

NEW-HAMPSHIRE GAZETTE (PORTSMOUTH)
September 23, 1774

Suffolk County, whose shiretown was Boston, was the only county in Massachusetts not to close the courts because it was occupied by three thousand British soldiers. Still, the county's Committees of Correspondence met and documented their discontent, which resulted in the famous Suffolk Resolves, "which resembled the resolves of other county conventions in substance but exceeded them in literary flare."

BOSTON, September 15. 1774.

At a Meeting of the Delegates

of every Town and Diſtrict in the County of *Suffolk*, on Tueſ-day the ſixth of *September*, at the Houſe of Mr. *Richard Wood-ward* of *Dedham*, and by Adjournment at the Houſe of Mr. *Daniel Voſe* of *Milton*, on Friday the Ninth Inſtant, JOSEPH PALMER, Eſq; being choſen Moderator, and WILLIAM THOMPSON, Eſq; Clerk, a Committee was choſen to bring in a Report to the Convention, and the following being ſe-veral Times read and put Paragraph by Paragraph, was UNANIMOUSLY voted, *Viz.*

WHEREAS the Power, but not the Juſ-tice ; the Vengeance, but not the Wiſ-dom of Great-Britain, which of old perſecuted, ſcourged and exiled our fugitive Pa-rents from their native Shores, now purſue us their guiltleſs Children with unrelenting Seve-rity—And whereas this then ſavage and uncul-tivated Deſart was purchaſed by the Toil and Treaſure or acquired by the Valor & Blood of thoſe our venerable Progenitors, who bequeathed to us the dear bought Inheritance, who conſigned it to our Care & Protection ; the moſt ſacred Obliga-tions are upon us to tranſmit the glorious Pur-chaſe, unfettered by Power, unclogg'd with Shackles, to our innocent and beloved Offspring. On the Fortitude—on the Wiſdom & on the Exer-tions of this important Day, is ſuſpended the Fate of this New World, and of unborn Millions. If a boundleſs Extent of Continent, ſwarming with Millions, will tamely ſubmit to live, move and have their Being at the arbitrary Will of a licentious Miniſter, they baſely yield to voluntary Slavery, and future Generations ſhall load their Memories with inceſſant Execrations.—On the the other Hand, if we arreſt the Hand which would ranſack our Pockets, if we diſarm the Par-ricide who points the Dagger to our Boſoms, if we nobly defeat that fatal Edict which proclaims a Power to frame Laws for us in all Caſes whatſoever, thereby entailing the endleſs and numberleſs Curſes of Slavery upon Us, our Heirs and their Heirs forever ; if we ſucceſsfully re-ſiſt that unparrallelled Uſurpation of unconſti-tutional Power, whereby our Capital is robbed of the Means of Life, whereby the Streets of Boſ-ton are thronged with Military Executioners, whereby our Coaſts are lined, & Harbours crow-ded with Ships of War, whereby the Charter of the Colony, that ſacred Barrier againſt the En-

we owe to G[...]
Poſterity, by [...]
our Power, t[...]
thoſe civil a[...]
for which n[...]
bled——and [...]
entire to fu[...]

3. That [...]
liament for [...]
ton, and ſo [...]
Governme[...]
ing the m[...]
of the Pro[...]
Infraction [...]
juſtly enti[...]
Britiſh Co[...]
Province.[...]

4. Th[...]
Province [...]
bovemen[...]
as the Att[...]
to enſlave [...]

5. That [...]
perior Cou[...]
& Gener[...]
of Comm[...]
pointed, [...]
Tenure [...]
Laws of[...]
conſider [...]
therefore[...]
no Regar[...]
ple of th[...]

6. T[...]
Court of [...]
Juſtices of the Court of [...]
of the General Seſſions of the Peace, ſhall ſit and act during their preſent diſqualified State, this County will ſupport and bear harmleſs all Sheriffs & their Deputies, Con-ſtables, Jurors and other Officers, who ſhall refuſe to carry into Execution the Orders of ſaid Courts : And as far as is poſſible to pre-vent the Inconveniences that muſt attend the Suſpenſion of the Courts of Juſtice, we do earneſtly recommend it to all Creditors to exerciſe all reaſonable and generous For-bearance to their Debtors, and to all Debtors to diſcharge their juſt Debts with all poſſible

croachments of *Tyranny, is mutilated, and in Effect annihilated ; whereby a murderous Law is framed to ſhelter Villains from the Hand of Juſtice ; whereby that unalienable and ineſti-mable Inheritance, which we derived from Na-ture, the Conſtitution of Britain, which was co-venanted to us in the Charter of the Province, is totally wrecked, annulled and vacated ;——Poſterity will acknowledge that Virtue which preſerved them free and happy ; and while we enjoy the Rewards and Bleſſings of the Faithful, the Torrent of Panegyrick will roll down our Reputations to that lateſt Period, when the Streams of Time ſhall be abſorbed in the Abyſs of Eternity.*

Therefore, WE HAVE RESOLVED, AND DO RESOLVE,

1ſt. THAT whereas his Majeſty GEORGE the Third is the rightful Succeſſor to the Throne of Great-Britain, & juſtly en-titled to the Allegiance of the Britiſh Realm and agreeable to *Compact*, of the Engliſh Co-lonies in America.—Therefore we the Heirs and Succeſſors of the firſt Planters of this Colony, do chearfully acknowledge the ſaid GEORGE the Third to be our rightful So-vereign, and that ſaid Covenant is the Te-nure and Claim on which are founded our Allegiance and Submiſſion.

2. That it is an indiſpenſable Duty which

to diſcharge their juſt Deb[...]
Speed, and if any Diſputes[...]
or Treſpaſſes ſhou'd ariſe, [...]
ſettled by the Parties, we [...]
them to ſubmit all ſuch C[...]
tion ; and if the Parties c[...]
ſhall refuſe ſo to do, they [...]
dered as co-operating with[...]
this Country.

7. That it be recomme[...]
lectors of Taxes, Conſtabl[...]
Officers who have publick[...]
Hands, to retain the ſame,[...]
any Payment thereof to [...]
County Treaſurers, until t[...]
ment of the Province is pl[...]
ſtitutional Foundation, or [...]
therwiſe be ordered by th[...]
vincial Congreſs.

8. That the Perſons w[...]
Seats at the Council-Boar[...]
Mandamus from the King, [...]
the late Act of the Britiſh Pa[...]
"An Act for regulating the [...]
Maſſachuſetts-Bay have ac[...]
olation of the Duty they ov[...]
try, and have thereby giv[...]
Offence to this People. T[...]
Reſolved, That this Co[...]
mend it to all Perſons who

it has been recommended [...]
Commiſſions from the Officers of the Mili-tia, that thoſe who now hold Commiſſions or ſuch other Perſons be elected in each Town as Officers in the Militia as ſhall be judged of ſufficient Capacity for that Purpoſe, and who have evidenced themſelves the inflexi-ble Friends to the Rights of the People, and that the Inhabitants of thoſe Towns and Diſtricts who are qualified do uſe their ut-moſt Dilligence to acquaint themſelves with the Art of War as ſoon as poſſible, and do for that Purpoſe appear under Arms at leaſt once

Juſtice ; whereby that unalienable and ineſti-mable Inheritance, which we derived from Na-

ſettled by the Parties, we recommend it to them to ſubmit all ſuch Cauſes to Arbitra-tion ; and if the Parties or either of them

pearances on the[...]
withſtanding the many Inſults and Oppreſ-ſions which we moſt ſenſibly reſent ; yet ne-

Cases whatsoever, *thereby entailing the endless and numberless Curses of Slavery upon Us, our Heir and their Heirs forever ; if we successfully resist that unparrallelled Usurpation of unconstitutional Power, whereby our Capital is robbed of the Means of Life, whereby the Streets of Boston are thronged with Military Executioners, whereby our Coasts are lined, & Harbours crowded with Ships of War, whereby the Charter of the Colony, that sacred Barrier against the Encroachments of Tyranny, is mutilated, and in effect annihilated ; whereby a murderous Law is framed to shelter Villains from the Hand of Justice ; whereby that unalienable and inestimable Inheritance, which we derived from Nature, the Constitution of Britain, which was covenanted to us in the Charter of the Province, is totally wrecked, annulled and vacated;----Posterity will acknowledge that Virtue which preserved them free and happy ; and while we enjoy the Rewards and Blessings of the Faithful, the Torrent of Panegyrick will roll down our Reputations to that latest Period, when the Streams of Time shall be absorbed in the Abyss of Eternity.*

Therefore, WE HAVE RESOLVED, and DO RESOLVE,

1st. That whereas his Majesty George the Third is the rightful Successor to the Throne of Great-Britain, & Justly entitled to the Allegiance of the British Realm and agreeable to *Compact*, of the English Colonies in America.—Therefore we the Heirs and Successors of the first Planters of this Colony, do chearfully acknowledge the said GEORGE the Third to be our rightful Sovereign, and that said Covenant is the Tenure and Claim on which are founded our Allegiance and Submission.

2. That it is an indispensable Duty which we owe GOD, our Country, Ourselves and Posterity, by all lawful Ways and Means in our Power, to maintain, defend and preserve those civil and religious Rights & Liberties for which many of our Fathers fought----bled----and died : and to hand them down entire to future Generations.

3. That the late Acts of the British Parliament for blocking up the Harbour of Boston, and for altering the established Form of Government in this Colony ; and for screening the most flagitious Violaters of the Laws of the Province from a legal Trial, are gross Infractions of these Rights to which we are justly entitled by the Laws of Nature, the British Constitution, and the Charter of the Province.

4. That no Obedience is due from this Province to either or any Part of the Acts abovementioned ; but that they be rejected as the Attempts of a wicked Administration to enslave America.

5. That so long as the Justices of our Superior Courts of Judicature, Court of Assize, & General Goal Delivery, & Inferior Courts of Common Please in this County, are appointed, or hold their Places by any other Tenure than that which the Charter & the Laws of the Province direct; they must be considered as under undue Influence, & are therefore unconstitutional Officers, & as such no Regard ought to be paid them by the People of this County.

6. That if the Justices of the Superior Court of Judicature, Court of Assize, &c. Justices of the Court of Common Please, or of the General Sessions of the Peace, shall sit and act during their present disqualified State, this County will support and bear harmless all Sheriffs & their Deputies, Constables, Jurors and other Officers, who shall refuse to carry into Execution the Orders of the said Courts : And as far as is possible to prevent the Inconveniences that must attend the Suspension of the Courts of Justice, we do earnestly recommend it to all Creditors to exercise all reasonable and generous Forbearance to their Debtors, and to all Debtors to discharge their just Debts with all possible Speed, and if any Disputes concerning Debts or Trespasses shou'd arise, which cannot be settled by the Parties or either of them shall refuse so to do, they ought to be considered as co-operating with the Enemies of this Country.

NEW-HAMPSHIRE GAZETTE (PORTSMOUTH)
September 30, 1774
—

Between 1773 and 1775, Paul Revere had two dozen revolutionary rides. One such ride was to share the Suffolk Resolves with the Continental Congress and return with their response, which was documented here.

BOSTON Sept. 22.

Upon receiving the last Answer of his Excellency, the Committee met together, and having carefully perused the same, were unanimously of Opinion, That his Excellency's Answer could not be deemed satisfactory to the County.——And further, that his Excellency in his Reply had been pleased to propose several Questions, which if unanswered by the Committee would leave on the Minds of People not fully acquainted with the State of Facts some very disagreeable Impressions concerning the Conduct and Behaviour of the People in the County and Province. And the following Address was unanimously voted to be presented to his Excellency.

May it please your Excellency,

THE Answer we have been pleased to favour us with to the Address this Day presented to you, gives us Satisfaction so far as it relates to your own Intentions; and we thank your Excellency for the Declaration which you have made, that it is your Duty & Interest to encourage an Intercourse between Town and Country; and we intreat your Indulgence while we modestly reply to the Questions proposed in your Answer. Your Excellency is too well acquainted with the Human Heart not to be sensible that it is natural for the People to be soured by Oppression, and jealous for their personal Security, when their Exertions for the Preservation of their Rights are construed into Treason and Rebellion. Our Liberties are invaded by Acts of the British Parliament, troops are sent to inforce those Acts. They are now erecting Fortifications at the Entrance of the Town of Boston, upon the compleating those, the Inhabitants of the Town of Boston will be in the Power of a Soldiery who must implicitly obey the Orders of an Administration who have hitherto evidenced no singular Regard to the Liberties of America. The Town is already greatly impoverished and distressed by the Operations of the barbarous Port-Bill. Your Excellency, we are persuaded from Principles of Humanity, would refuse to be an Actor in the tragical Scene that must ensue upon shutting up the Avenues to the Town, and reducing the Inhabitants by Distress and Famine, to a disgraceful and slavish Submission; but that cruel Work may possibly be reserved for a Successor, disposed and instructed thereto. Daily Supplies of Provisions are necessary for the Subsistence of the Inhabitants of the Town. The Country disgusted and jealous at the formidable Operations now carrying on, survey with Horror, a Plan concerted——whereby the Inhabitants of the Town of Boston may be imprisoned and starved at the Will of a Military Command. They kindly invite them to abandon the Town, and earnestly solicit them to share the homely Banquet of Peace in the Country. Should their Refusal involve them in Miseries hitherto unheard of, and hardly conceiv'd of, the Country must stand acquitted, and will not hold their Liberties so loosely as to sacrifice them to the Obstinacy of their Brethren in Boston.

Your Excellency has been pleased to order the Powder from the Magazine in Charlestown, to forbid the Delivery of the Powder in the Magazine of Boston to the legal Proprietors, to seize the Cannon at Cambridge, and bring a formidable Number from Castle William, which are now placed at the Entrance of the Town of Boston. And have likewise in Addition to the Troops now here, been pleased to send for Reinforcements to Quebec and other Parts of the Continent. These Things, Sir, together with the Disposition of the Ships of War, we humbly think sufficiently justify the Proceedings for which your Excellency seems to be at a Loss to account.

Your Excellency has suggested that Nature has made it easy to cut off the Communication between Town and Country.——Our only Request is, that the Entrance into the Town may remain as Nature has formed it.

If the Security to his Majesty's Troops is the only Design in the late Manœuvres, we beg leave to assure your Excellency that the most certain, and by far the most honourable Method of making them secure and safe, will be to give the People of the Province the strongest Proof that no Design is forming against their Liberties. And we again solicit your Excellency with that Earnestness which becomes us on this important Occasion to desist from every Thing which has a Tendency to alarm them, and particularly from fortifying the Entrance into the Town of Boston. We rely on your Excellency's Wisdom and Candor that, in your proposed Representation to our common Sovereign, you will Endeavour to redeem us from the Distresses which we apprehend were occasioned by the grossest Misinformation, and that you will assure his Majesty that no Wish of Independency, no adverse Sentiments or Designs towards his Majesty or his Troops now here, actuate his good Subjects in this Colony; but that their sole Intention is to preserve pure and inviolate those Rights to which, as Men, and English Americans, they are justly entitled, and which have been guaranteed to them by his Majesty's Royal Predecessors. By Order of the Committee,

JOSEPH WARREN, Chairman.

A COPY of the above was delivered to Mr. Sec'ty Flucker, by the Chairman, with a Desire that he would as soon as convenient, present it to the Governor, & request his Excellency

BOSTON, Sept. 26.

By Mr. PAUL REVERE, who returned Express from Philadelphia last Friday Evening, we have the following Important Intelligence.

PHILADELPHIA, Sept. 17, 1774.

SIR,

WE received your Favour of the 11th Inst. together with the Resolutions of the County of Suffolk, and communicated the same to the Congress: In Consequence of which they passed the several Resolutions which will be delivered to you by Mr. Revere, together with a Letter from the President. They highly applaud the wise, temperate and spirited Conduct of our People, in their Opposition to the late Act for altering our Constitution. These Resolves will, we trust, support and comfort our Friends, and confound our Enemies. In Behalf of myself and Brethren, I am with Respect,

Your most humble Servant,

JOSEPH WARREN, Esq; THOMAS CUSHING.

PHILADELPHIA, 17th Sept. 1774.

SIR,

YOUR Letter of the 11th Inst. directed "To the Hon'ble Thomas Cushing, Esq; and the other Gentlemen of the Congress, Members for Massachusetts Bay," together with the Resolutions entered into by the Delegates of the several Towns in the County of Suffolk, and their Address to his Excellency Governor GAGE, were communicated to the Congress, whereupon the Congress came into the following unanimous RESOLVES, which by their Order I transmit to you to be communicated to the Committee of Correspondence for the Town of Boston.

I am, SIR,

your most obedient Servant,

JOSEPH WARREN, Esq; PEYTON RANDOLPH.

IN CONGRESS, Saturday, Sept. 17, 1774.

A LETTER from Dr. JOSEPH WARREN, and sundry Resolutions entered into by the County of SUFFOLK, on Tuesday the 6th of this Instant, and an Address from the Delegates of the said County to his Excellency Governor GAGE, dated the 9th Instant, were read. Whereupon,

RESOLVED unanimously, That this Assembly deeply feels the suffering of their Countrymen in the Massachusetts-Bay, under the Operation of the late unjust, cruel and oppressive Acts of the British Parliament——that they most thoroughly approve the Wisdom and Fortitude with which Opposition to these wicked ministerial Measures has hitherto been conducted; & they earnestly recommend to their Brethren a Perseverance in the same firm and temperate Conduct, as expressed in the Resolutions determined upon at a Meeting of the Delegates for the County of Suffolk, on Tuesday the 6th Inst. trusting that the Effect of the united Efforts of North-America in their Behalf, will carry such Conviction to the British Nation, of the unwise, unjust, and ruinous Policy of the present Administration, as quickly to introduce better Men and wiser Measures.

RESOLVED unanimously, That Contributions from all the Colonies for supplying the Necessities and alleviating the Distresses of our Brethren at Boston, ought to be continued, in such Manner and so long as their Occasions may require.

A true Extract from the Minutes,

CHARLES THOMPSON, Secr.

DELEGATES who attend the CONGRESS.

From New Hampshire.

Major John Sullivan, and Col. Nathaniel Folsom.

From Massachusetts-Bay.

Hon'ble Thomas Cushing, Esq; Mr. Samuel Adams, John Adams, and Robert Treat Paine, Esq;

From Rhode-Island.

Hon. Stephen Hopkins, Esq; Hon. Samuel Ward, Esq;

From Connecticut.

Hon. Eliphalet Dyer, Silas Deane, and Roger Sherman, Esq'rs.

From New York.

James Duane, John Jay, Philip Livingston, Isaac Low, Col. William Floyd, and Henry Wisner, Esq'rs.

From New-Jersey.

James Kinsey, William Livingston, John D'Hart, Stephen Crane, and Richard Smith, Esq'rs.

From Pennsylvania.

Hon. Joseph Galloway, Samuel Rhoads, Thomas Mifflin, Charles Humphreys, John Morton, Edward Biddle, and George Ross, Esq'rs.

From Newcastle, Kent, and Sussex Governments.

Cæsar Rodney, Thomas M'Kean, and George Read, Esq'rs.

From Maryland.

Mathew Tilgham, Thomas Johnson, jr. Robert Gouldsborough, William Paca, and Samuel Chase, Esq'rs.

From Virginia.

Hon. Peyton Randolph, Richard Henry Lee, George Washington, Patrick Henry, Richard Bland, Benjamin Harrison, and Edmund Pendleton, Esq'rs.

From North Carolina.

19. The virtuous Few in both Houses of Parliament.
20. The CITY of London. 21. Lord Chatham. 22. Lord Cambden. 23. Bishop of St. Asaph. 24. Duke of Richmond. 25. Sir George Saville. 26. Mr. Burke. 27. General Conway. 28. Mr. Dunning. 29. Mr. Sawbridge. 30. Dr. Franklin. 31. Mr. Dulany. 32. Mr. Hancock.

The Acclamations with which several of them were received, not only testified the Sense of the Honor conferred by such worthy Guests, but the fullest Confidence in their Wisdom and Integrity, and a firm Resolution to adopt and support such Measures as they shall direct for the public Good at this alarming Crisis.

BOSTON Sept. 26.

Thursday last, being the Anniversary of his Majesty's Coronation, the Guns at Castle William, and of the Batteries in this Town, also on board the Men of War in the Harbour were fired at Noon.——His Excellency the Governor received the Compliments of the Gentlemen of the Army and Navy, &c. at the Council Chamber.

We hear the Town of Hartford in Connecticut, have contributed 1400 Bushels of Grain, Middletown about the same Quantity——Kensington 600——Middle Haddam 600, and other Towns in that Colony are doing the same for the Relief of the Poor in this Town.

Wednesday last the Freeholders and other Inhabitants of Boston met at Faneuil-Hall, for the Choice of Representatives to serve in the Great and General Court to be convened at Salem the 5th of next Month, when the following Gentlemen were chosen, viz. The Hon. Thomas Cushing, Esq; Mr. Samuel Adams, Hon. John Hancock, Esq; and William Philips, Esq;

Last Friday the Town made Choice of Dr. Joseph Warren, Dr. Benjamin Church, and Mr. Nathaniel Appleton, to serve as Delegates in the Provincial Congress, to be held at Concord on the second Tuesday of October next, in Addition to the four Representatives of this Town——and the following Instructions for our Representatives were voted, viz.

GENTLEMEN,

AS we have now chosen you to represent us in the Great and general Court to be holden at Salem on Wednesday the 5th Day of October next ensuing: we do hereby instruct you that in all your Doings as Members of the House of Representatives you adhere firmly to the Charter of this Province granted by their Majesty's King William and Queen Mary, and that you do no Act which can possibly be construed into an Acknowlegment of the Act of the British Parliament for altering the Government of the Massachusetts-Bay, more especially that you acknowledge the Hon. Board of Councellors elected by the General Court at their Session in May last, as the only rightful and constitutional Council of this Province. And as we have Reason to believe that a conscientious Discharge of your Duty will produce your Dissolution as an House of Representatives, We do hereby impower and instruct you to join with the Members who may be sent from this and the Neighbouring Towns in the Province, and to meet with them at a Time to be agreed on in a general Provincial Congress, to act upon such Matters as may come before you in such a Manner as shall appear to be most conducive to the true Interest of this Town and Province, and most likely to preserve the Liberties of all America.

At a Meeting of the Select-Men and Committee of Correspondence, Sept. 24, 1774.

OUR Friends in the Neighbouring Towns and the Country in general, having expressed their Uneasiness lest the Workmen in this Town, by assisting the Army in building Barracks should give Occasion of Umbrage to their Friends who dwell more remote, whether in this or the neighbouring Colonies, particularly to our Brethren of New-York, who have nobly rejected the Application of the Barrack-Master for Mechanicks and other Assistants from that place;——Therefore having debated this Matter in Compliance with the Application of our Friends in the Country,——It is the Opinion of this joint Committee that should the Mechanicks or other Inhabitants of this Town, assist the Troops by furnishing them with Artificers, Labourers, or Materials of any Kind to build Barracks or other Places of Accomodation for the Troops they will probably incur the Displeasure of their Brethren, who may withhold their Contributions for the Relief of the Town, and deem them as Enemies to the Rights and Liberties of America, by furnishing the Troops with Conveniences for their Residence and accomodation in this Town.

By the public Papers and Letters from London, to the 30th of July we are informed, that Governor Hutchinson's Representation of the State of our Affairs were very pleasing to the Ministry, who were led to expect a Payment of the Tea, and a Submission to, and acquiescence in, the late Acts of the British Parliament, by the Friendship and Zeal of the Addressers to Governor Hutchinson, who have been represented as a Majority of the Men of Property, and Consequence in this Town——that the Operation of the Boston Port would greatly contribute to

MASSACHUSETTS PROVINCIAL CONGRESS

By Ray Raphael

WORCESTER, SPRINGFIELD, PLYMOUTH—THE REVOlution that swept through Massachusetts in 1774 was a decentralized grassroots movement without any command post. Initially, this made it difficult to stop. "The flames of sedition," Governor Gage complained, had "spread universally throughout the Country beyond Conception." But how could the revolution be sustained without any central coordinating body?

On August 26 and 27, at the request of activists from Worcester, delegates from four counties convened in Boston for the first multicounty meeting of the Committees of Correspondence. Hoping to provide a more enduring structure to the movement, that meeting suggested that a Provincial Congress convene in Concord on the second Tuesday of October, and all the county committees, as they closed the courts, echoed this call.

For protocol, the towns also elected representatives to the official General Court, which had been scheduled to meet on October 5. This body convened in Salem, then the provincial capital, to demonstrate a willingness to work within the 1691 Provincial Charter—but not the Massachusetts Government Act. Governor Gage, though, had discontinued the General Court in advance. After waiting a full day for the governor to show up, knowing of course he would not, representatives transformed themselves into a new Provincial Congress, not beholden to any British authority. They then adjourned until October 11, the date set by the county conventions for a Provincial Congress to meet in Concord (October 10 Boston dateline in October 13, 1774, *Massachusetts Gazette; and the Boston Weekly News-Letter*).

The response to the call for the Provincial Congress was overwhelming: 209 of the province's 260 towns and districts sent representatives, a far greater showing than the General Court had ever mustered. The meeting was too large for Concord to host, so it moved to Cambridge instead.

Delegates differed on how to proceed from there. The town of Worcester had instructed its representative to "raise from the dissolution of the old constitution, as from the ashes of the Phenix, a new form, where all officers shall be dependent on the suffrages of the people." A new government? Were people ready to make such a dramatic break with Britain in October 1774? Many were, particularly from the western towns, but others were not. While western radicals might have comprised the majority, leadership positions went primarily to the better educated and more experienced political figures from Boston and other eastern towns. The push to declare "independency," form a new government, and raise an army to attack the British stronghold in Boston stalled in the Provincial Congress.

Even if it did not move as quickly as radicals would have liked, the Provincial Congress did take definitive steps to prepare Massachusetts for the counterrevolution British officials were expected to stage. The Congress proceeded on several fronts, as witnessed by entries from its journal reprinted in the October 31, 1774, issue of the *Boston Evening-Post*. On October 26, it recommended that militia companies choose officers and that these men reorganize their regiments, form battalions, and select field officers; this was to be a democratic army, top to bottom. Further, they encouraged the companies to arm and train. Then, since an army costs money, the Provincial Congress chose its own receiver general and recommended that all sheriffs pay the taxes they had collected to him rather than to the official tax collector.

The Provincial Congress did not claim to be a government, however, for that would amount to a declaration of independence. This meant it could not *require* towns to send it money, but it "earnestly recommended" and "strongly recommended" they do so. The army it raised, too, remained unofficial for months. Not until April 1775, as the British army prepared for its inevitable offensive, did the Provincial Congress formally sponsor an army.

After Lexington and Concord, the illusion of a government-that-is-not-a-government became more difficult to sustain. On May 16, the Provincial Congress asked the Continental Congress for "your most explicit advice, respecting the taking up and exercising the power of civil government," and the Continental Congress, which itself had no official standing, instructed the Provincial Congress to set elections for a new government and then disband. On July 19, 1775, the Massachusetts Provincial Congress dissolved itself, but the following day, the new government declared that all the "resolves, doings, and transactions" of the Provincial Congress be "confirmed and established, as lawful and valid."

MASSACHUSETTS GAZETTE; AND THE BOSTON WEEKLY NEWS-LETTER
October 13, 1774
—

Despite Royal Governor Gage's cancellation of the Massachusetts General Court meeting, it still met in Salem and voted to "resolve themselves into a Provincial Congress" with John Hancock as its chairman.

THE
Massachusett
AND
Boston Weekly

Draper's.]   TH

BOSTON, October 10, 1774.

WEDNESDAY laſt the Members choſen in Conſequence of Governor GAGE's Writ for calling a General Aſſembly, met at the Court-Houſe in Salem purſuant to the Precepts; and after waiting a Day without being admitted to the uſual Oaths, which ſhould have been adminiſtred by the Governor or other conſtitutional Officers; and having choſen the Honorable JOHN HANCOCK, Eſq; to be their Chairman, and BENJAMIN LINCOLN, Eſq; Clerk, they proceeded to Buſineſs, and paſſed the following Reſolves.

Province of the MASSACHUSETTS-BAY.

In the Court-Houſe at Salem, October 7, 1774.

WHEREAS Writs bearing Date the Firſt of September laſt, for the Election of Members to ſerve as Repreſentatives in a Great and General Court, which he did "think fit and appoint" to be convened and holden the 5th Day of October Inſtant, at the Court-Houſe in this Place: And whereas a Majority of Members duly elected in conſequence of ſaid Writs, did attend at ſaid Court-Houſe the Time appointed, there to be qualified according to Charter, for taking Seats and acting as Repreſentatives in ſaid Great and General Court; but were not met by the Governor, or other conſtitutional Officer or Officers by him appointed for adminiſtring the uſual Oaths, and qualifying them thereto. And whereas a Proclamation bearing date the 28th of September laſt, and publiſhed in ſundry News Papers, with the Signature of his Excellency, contains many Reflections on this Province, as being in a tumultuous and diſorderly State; and appears to have been conſidered by his Excellency as a conſtitutional Diſcharge of all ſuch Perſons as have been elected in Conſequence of his Excellency's ſaid Writ.——The Members aforeſaid ſo attending, having conſidered the Meaſures which his Excellency has been pleaſed to take by his ſaid Proclamation, and finding them to be unconſtitutional, unjuſt, and diſreſpectful to the Province, think it their Duty to paſs the following Reſolves. Therefore,

RESOLVED, as the Opinion of ſaid Members,

I. THAT by the Royal Charter of the Province, the Governor for the Time being, is expreſly obliged to convene "upon every laſt Wedneſday in the Month of May, every Year for ever, and at ſuch other Times as he ſhall think fit and appoint, a Great and General Court." And therefore that, as his Excellency had thought fit, and by his Writ appointed a Great and General Court to be convened on the 5th Day of October Inſtant, his Conduct in preventing the ſame is againſt the expreſs Words, as well as

adjourn, prorogue and diſſolve all Great and General Courts.
. . . have his Place after conſequence ſhall be appointed, until
II. That the Conſtitutional Government of the Inhabitants of

ed than Hoftilities with Great Britain—notwithstanding the Province has not the most diftant Design of attacking, annoying, or moleſting his Majeſty's Troops aforefaid, but on the other hand will confider and treat every Attempt of the Kind, as well as all Meaſures tending to prevent a Reconciliation between Britain and the Colonies as the higheſt degree of Enmity to the Province.——Nevertheleſs there is great Reaſon from the Conſiderations aforefaid to be apprehenfive of the moſt fatal Conſequences ; and that the Province may be in ſome Degree provided against the ſame, and under full Perſuaſion that the Meaſures expreſſed in the following Reſolves are perfectly conſiſtent with ſuch Reſolves of the Continental Congreſs as have been communicated to us,

It is *Resolved* and hereby recommended to the ſeveral Companies of Militia in this Province, who have not already choſen and appointed Officers, that they meet forthwith and elect Officers to command their reſpective Companies ; and that the Officers ſo choſen aſſemble as ſoon as may be ; and where the ſaid Officers ſhall judge the Limits of the preſent Regiments too extenſive, that they divide them and ſettle and determine their Limits, and proceed to elect Field Officers to command the reſpective Regiments ſo formed ; and that the Field Officers ſo elected, forthwith endeavour to enliſt one Quarter at the leaſt of the Number of the reſpective Companies, and form them into Companies of fifty Privates at the leaſt, who ſhall equip & hold themſelves in Readineſs to march at the ſhorteſt Notice ; and that each and every Company ſo formed, chooſe a Captain and two Lieutenants to command them on any neceſſary and emergent Service : And that the ſaid Captain and Subalterns ſo elected, form the ſaid Companies into Battalions to conſiſt of nine Companies each ; and that the Captains and Subalterns of each Battalion ſo formed, proceed to elect Field Officers to command the ſame. And this Congreſs doth moſt earneſtly recommend that all the aforefaid Elections be proceeded in and made with due Deliberation and general Regard to the public Service.

Also *Resolved*, That as the Security of the Lives, Liberties and Properties of the Inhabitants of this Province depends under Providence on their Knowledge and Skill in the Art Military, and in their being properly and effectual armed and equipt ; if any of ſaid Inhabitants are not provided with Arms and Ammunition according to Law, they immediately provide themſelves forthwith ; and that they uſe their utmoſt Diligence to perfect themſelves in Military Skill ; and that if any Town or Diſtrict within the Province is not provided with the full Town Stock of Arms and Ammunition according to Law, the Selectmen of ſuch Town or Diſtrict take effectual Care without Delay to provide the ſame. *A true Extract from the Minutes,*
BENJAMIN LINCOLN, Sec'ry.

In Provincial Congreſs, Octo. 28. 1774.

WHEREAS this Province has not as yet received from the Continental Congreſs ſuch explicit directions, reſpecting Non-Importation and Non-Conſumption Agreements as are expected ; And whereas the greateſt Part of the Inhabitants of this Colony have entered into Non-Importation & Conſumption Agreements, the good Effects of which are very conſpicuous.——Therefore,

RESOLVED, That this Congreſs approve of the ſaid Agreements, and earneſtly recommend to all the Inhabitants of this Colony, ſtrictly to conform to the ſame, until the further Senſe of the Continental or of this Provincial Congreſs is made public. And further, this Congreſs highly applaud the Conduct of thoſe Patriotic Merchants who have generouſly refrained from Importing British Goods ſince the Commencement of the cruel Boſton Port-Bill ; at the ſame Time with Pain on the Conduct of thoſe, who have ſordidly preferred their private Intereſt to the Salvation of their ſuffering Country, by continuing to Import as uſual ; and recommend it to the Inhabitants of the Province that they diſcourage the Conduct of ſaid Importers by refuſing to purchaſe any Article whatever of them.
A true Extract from the Minutes,
BENJAMIN LINCOLN, Sec'y.

In Provincial Congreſs, October 28. 1774.

IT has been recommended by the Congreſs, That whereas the Monies heretofore granted and ordered to be aſſeſſed by the General Court of this Province, and not paid into the Province Treaſury, the ſame ſhould not be paid to the Hon. Harriſon Gray, Eſq ; for Reaſons moſt obvious :

Therefore, *Resolved*, That Henry Gardner, Eſq ; of Stow, be and hereby is appointed Receiver-General, until the further Order of this or ſome other Congreſs, or Houſe of Repreſentatives of this Province ; whoſe Buſineſs it ſhall be to receive all ſuch Monies as ſhall be offered to be paid into his Hands, to the Uſe of the Province, by the ſeveral Conſtables, Collectors or other Perſons, by Order of the ſeveral Towns or Diſtricts, and to give his Receipt for the ſame.——And it is hereby recommended to the ſeveral Towns and Diſtricts within this Province, that they immediately call Town and Diſtrict Meetings, and give Directions to all Conſtables, Collectors and other Perſons, who may have any Part of the Province Tax of ſuch Town or Diſtrict in

for the Purpoſe aforefaid. And it is alſo recommended, that the ſeveral Towns and Diſtricts in ſaid Directions ſignify and expreſsly engage to ſuch Conſtable, Collector or other Perſon, as ſhall have

---

in that manner to levy the Contents of ſuch Aſſeſſments ; and that they do oblige and compel the ſaid Conſtables and Collectors to comply with and execute the Directions of this Reſolve, in as much as the preſent alarming Situation and Circumſtance of this Province do make it neceſſary for the Safety thereof.
A true Extract from the Minutes.
BENJAMIN LINCOLN, Sec'y.

In Provincial Congreſs, Octo. 29. 1774.

RESOLVED, That it be recommended to the Inhabitants of this Province, that in Order to their perfecting themſelves in the Military Art, they proceed in the Method ordered by his Majeſty in the Year 1764 ; it being in the Opinion of this Congreſs, the beſt calculated for Appearance and Defence.
A true Extract from the Minutes,
BENJAMIN LINCOLN, Sec'ry.

*** The Manual Exerciſe, recommended to be practiſed by the above Reſolve of the Congreſs, is to be had only of T. and J. FLEET, at the Heart and Crown in Cornhill, Boſton.

Extract of a Letter from a Gentleman in the Country, to his Friend in Boſton, dated Oct. 26, 1774.

"I Thank you for your laſt favor, of the 13th inſt. and I think I can ſubſcribe to your creed in every thing except where you ſay you believe that General B——tt—e is ſorry for what has happen'd, that is, he is ſorry he is found out, and am apt to think that is your meaning ; he is *ſemper idem*. All theſe diſturbances and altercations are in conſequence of his officious impertinent Letter to G. G. but as he is an original, the beſt way is to diſpiſe him, and let him alone ; if he aſks pardon, and replaces a ſimilar quantity of Gun-powder at Quarry-hill, in the room of what he moſt ſurreptitiouſly took therefrom, *but nothing leſs*. I could decypher him, but it is loſs of time, pen, ink, paper and breath.——I join with you, I think the troops ought to be ſupplied with ſtraw, &c. As to our Courts being ſhut up, I entirely acquieſce with you, it is WRONG, VERY WRONG.——Pray Sir, have not our Clerks of the Pleas, and Seſſions of the Peace witneſſed a good confeſſion under their hands publickly ? That man who holds up his hand for obedience to theſe late, moſt cruel and inhuman Acts of P——t, ought to have it cut off : Well, Sir, if our Courts can go on in the old channel, pray what hinders ? I think, Sir, with you, that the ſhutting up our Courts is rather a compliance with thoſe Acts, and will by our enemies be ſo conſtrued, as it has brought us to a pauſe ; for let us think but one minute, have not our Sheriffs, Deputies, Grand and Petit Jurors, openly and repeatedly abjured theſe infamous acts ? Where is the Attorney (ſhow me the man) who dare, being left of Heaven, to countenance theſe, I had almoſt ſaid, accurſed Acts ? but if that epithet is too harſh I recall it——Mark the end of that man, for I propheſy it will not be peace ; nay, there are only ſome ſeeking tools who do appear on that ſide of the queſtion.—If any of our Judges (and ſome there are) remain ſo abandoned, from the neceſſity of the thing, *they muſt be paddled aſide and good men put in their place*. When juſtice departs from, injuſtice enters a land, the precedent is alarming, it is hard, very hard, to come to rights after we have been accuſtomed to do wrong, and to live without law and juſtice, I foreſee a thouſand unconquerable difficulties ariſing ! All nature will be inverted ! The man who has the leaſt, or no property, will direct and controul the man of property : What proſtitution and inverſion is this ? I alſo deprecate with you the ignorance and blindneſs of the more common people in the Mother Country. If the truth of facts was not wickedly hid from them by wicked men, Bute, Manſfield and North would have been on the other ſide of the ferry long ago ; and I am alſo very ſenſible that truth is induſtriouſly hid by the ſame ſet of men from the eyes of our King, or the prejudices of his education are great. The people of England are honeſt, but they are wretchedly impoſed on, they will ſee it anon, and will riſe like Thunder and make publick examples of wicked men. Which God grant."——

THE Printers hereof have received the Declarations and Acknowledgments of ſeveral Deputy Sheriffs, and other Perſons, who by ſigning an Addreſs to Governor Hutchinſon had rendered themſelves obnoxious to the People ; but have not Room to publiſh them this Week :——Tho' bad the Recantations of the few who have lately taken Refuge in this Town, and obſtinately perſiſt in their new and unconſtitutional Appointments, been offered us, we ſhould have taken Pleaſure in poſtponing other Matters in order to inſert them, that ſo thoſe Exiles might return in Peace to their reſpective Families, and again enjoy that ſocial Domeſtic Happineſs and Friendſhip of their Fellow-Citizens, which by moſt People is eſteemed one of the greateſt Bleſſings that can be enjoyed in this Life, and which we wiſh to contribute what is in our Power to put all Mankind in the Poſſeſſion of.——The two following Acknowledgments, however, are ſo conciſe we can't omit obliging our Readers with them, as they may ſerve for a Specimen to other Addreſſers whoſe Principles are ſuch as not to incline them to make long Confeſſion, even when they know they were to blame.

---

tica on board the ſhips of war that have been fitted out there ; and that 8000 Men went on board the Eſſential Angelo, &c. which ſailed the firſt of Auguſt for America.——The reaſons of all theſe preparations, they ſay, may be eaſily gueſſed at, France and Spain certainly intend to attack the British Colonies in America, and to take advantage of the preſent diſputes between them and the mother-country, while they are ſo irritated againſt the British Government."

A Letter from Liſbon, as late as Sept. 6th, makes no mention of a War between them & the Spaniards. *Extract of a Letter from a Gentleman in* London, *to his Friend at New-York.*

"In reply to your Paragraph reſpecting the conduct of Philadelphia and your City, in regard to the Tea-Ships : I have not heard that Adminiſtration has caſt the leaſt reflection on either of thoſe Provinces or their conduct therein. Boſton is the preſent object of their reſentment, and ſhould they ſucceed therein, every other Province will have their reſentment in courſe, as opportunity offers."

Tueſday laſt being the anniverſary of his Majeſty's Acceſſion to the Throne, the ſame was obſerved here by the firing of the Guns at the Caſtle, at the Batteries in this Town, and of thoſe on board the Men of War in the Harbour.——At Noon the Piquet Guards of the ſeveral Regiments here marched into King-Street, where they fired three Vollies on the Occaſion.

The Provincial Congreſs is adjourned to the 23d Day of November next.

The two Whaling Veſſels, outward bound, lately mentioned to have been loſt on Nantucket Shoals and 21 Perſons left on board ſuppoſed to have periſhed, we have ſince the ſatisfaction to hear were all ſaved : One of whom gives the following account of their remarkable Preſervation, viz. That they lay on the Shoal two Nights and one Day, in which time one of the Veſſels went to pieces, the other beat over the Shoal and overſet ; they then made a Raft of the Veſſel's Spars, and 13 of the People got on the ſame, and there being a light Breeze of Wind, they happily drifted on Nantucket Iſland, after being 24 hours on the Raft in the moſt perilous Situation, as it was ſcarcely able to ſupport them above Water : The other 8 of the Crew got on the Quarter-deck of the Veſſel which beat to Pieces, and alſo drove on Nantucket Iſland. For three Days they had no other Proviſion than three Cod-Fiſh to ſubſiſt on.

The General Aſſembly of Pennſylvania has met, and after chooſing Edward Biddle, Eſq ; Speaker, they added John Dickinſon, Eſq ; to the general Congreſs.

Laſt Friday arrived a Tranſport Ship from Quebec, and Yeſterday two more with Troops on board from the ſame Place.

Laſt Saturday ſe'nnight the Dwelling Houſe of Aaron Wood, Eſq ; of Boxford, was conſumed by Fire, together with part of the Furniture.

ON Wedneſday laſt died at Charleſtown, after a tedious Illneſs, Mrs. *Mary Foſter*, relict of the late *Richard Foſter*, Eſq;——She was a Perſon of a truly Chriſtian diſpoſition, and peculiarly ſolicitous to diſcharge the ſeveral duties of life, *without partiality and without hypocriſy* :—very diſcrete, humane and charitable ; calm and unmoved at the various and inevitable events of Providence, and grieved only at the ſufferings of the meek and innocent, the wickedneſs of the wicked, and the evils of ſin ; the loſs of ſuch a Chriſtian, ſuch a Mother, ſuch a Relative, Neighbour and Friend, will always deeply affect the virtuous and good. She deſcended from anceſtors of the firſt characters in the Province, whom ſhe hath honour'd in the conduct of her life : and the voice of all remind us that
"The ſweet remembrance of the juſt,
Shall flouriſh when they ſleep in duſt."

MARRIED.] Capt. *Callahan* to Miſs *Lucretia Greene*, Daughter of Mr. *Benja. Greene*, Merchant.
DIED] Mr. *Watts*, Malſter, aged 79.——Miſs *Abigail Dennie* aged 16, Mrs. *Hannah Billings*

In the Alms-Houſe, Miſs *Mary Cook*, aged 81.
At Leiceſter, Colonel *Thomas Denny*, aged 50 :

WHereas I the Subſcriber ſigned an Addreſs to the late Governor Hutchinſon——I wiſh the Devil had had ſaid Addreſs before I had ſeen it.

Every impartial person will admit, that the Minister, by making the Parliament take such contradictory Resolutions within a few days, and without any intervening events that might occasion them, hath let down the dignity of Parliament to the lowest degree, and rendered the legal authority of the nation ridiculous. The minister has hereby shewn that he is absolute master of the Parliament, and can make the members of it jump backwards and forwards, like a parcel of Spaniels over a stick, just as he pleases?——What a contemptible idea must the people of England, from such inconsistent proceedings, entertain of their legislators?

When the three General Officers kissed his Majesty's hand, previous to their departure for America, he enjoined them in expressions the most affecting, to let humanity influence them more than courage, and to avoid an engagement with those deluded people, if it can be done with safety to his person and crown. From this we may rest satisfied, that neither their lives nor fortunes will be endangered, if their behaviour does not amount to that pitch of villainy that appeared in the Scotch Rebels in 1745.

The loss of Lord Coventry and the Duke of Northumberland to Government, has made a great turn in the scale of politics.

Several patriotic Gentlemen have actually entered into an agreement to embark for America, as soon as the present session is concluded.

House of Commons, March 1.

At three o'clock the House went into a Committee on the Bill for restraining the Commerce, and prohibiting the New-England Provinces from fishing on the Banks of Newfoundland. A strong opposition was expected on the part of the minority; but the field was left to Administration entirely clear; not a syllable being offered by way of either amendment or reprobation. The Victors however designed to make a few alterations, or what they pleased to call amendments, and to be reported on Monday.

The new Plan respecting America, proposed by the ostensible Agent, is one of the most insidious that ever entered the depraved heart of a corrupt Minister: being at once calculated to set the people here against their brethren in the Colonies, by a *seeming* proposals of conciliatory measures, and at the same time to sow divisions among the Americans, by holding out a deceitful lure to them to come in, if any one among them shall be found weak enough to swallow the bait.

In Provincial Congress, Concord, April 14. 1775.

WHEREAS Numbers of Persons from their unhappy situation in the Town of Boston, are removing with their Effects.——It is recommended to the good People of this Province, that they would rent their Houses, and assist such Persons with Teams for their removal, Provisions for their Support, and all other Necessaries upon as easy and cheap Terms as they can possibly afford; and that all Goods and Merchandize be sold in like Manner, agreeable to the Spirit of the Continental Association.

By Order of the Provincial Congress,
JOHN HANCOCK, President.

In Provincial Congress, Concord, April 15, 1775.

WHEREAS it has pleased the righteous Sovereign of the Universe, in just Indignation against the Sins of a People long blessed with inestimable Privileges, civil and religious, to suffer the Plots of wicked Men on both Sides of the Atlantic, who for many Years have incessantly laboured to sap the Foundation of our public Liberties, so far to succeed, that we see the New-England Colonies reduced to the ungrateful Alternative of a tame Submission to a state of absolute Vassalage to the Will of a despotic Minister——or of preparing themselves speedily to defend, at the hazard of Life, the unalienable Rights of themselves and Posterity, against the avowed Hostilities of their parent State, who openly threatens to wrest them from their Hands by Fire and Sword.

In Circumstances dark as these, it becomes us, as Men and Christians, to reflect that, whilst every prudent Measure should be taken to ward off the impending Judgments, or prepare to act a proper Part under them when they come; at the same Time, all Confidence must be with-held from the Means we use; and reposed only on that God who rules in the Armies of Heaven, and without whose Blessing the best human Counsels are but Foolishness—and all created Power Vanity.

It is the Happiness of his Church that, when the Powers of Earth and Hell combine against it, and those who should be nursing Fathers become its Persecutors—then the Throne of Grace is of the easiest Access—and its Appeal thither is graciously invited by the Father of Mercies, who has assured it, that when his Children ask Bread he will not give them a Stone:

THEREFORE, in Compliance with the laudable Practice of the People of God in all Ages, with humble Regard to the Steps of divine Providence towards this oppressed, threatned and endangered People, and especially in Obedience to the Command of Heaven, that binds us to call on him in the Day of Trouble,—

Resolved, That it be, and hereby is recommended to the good People of this Colony, of all Denominations, that THURSDAY the Eleventh Day of May next be set apart as a Day of Public Humiliation, Fasting and Prayer; that a total Abstinence from servile Labor and Recreation be observed; and all their religious Assemblies solemnly convened, to humble themselves before God under the heavy Judgments felt and feared, to confess the Sins that have deserved them, to implore the forgiveness of all

DONATION
MASS
From unknown Ha
Menson, 2 C. oqr.
8 1 i
Meal, 2 l
Hanover, From a
SOU
From Mess'rs *Cha*
Bill on Mr. *Na*
Part of nett Pr
at New-York,
N. B. *The Donatio
the 27th of Mar*

Elizab

At her Shop two
House, North-Side
An Assortment of
Ware, among wh
Sizes, and l
A few Crates o
Also Groce
Capers by the B
Keg, or Pound,
Anchovies, do. do
Choice Durham Mu
in Bottles of various
Flask Oil,
Double & single r
Loaf Sugar,
Coffee, Chocola
Spermaceti Candles
Hard Soap, Crown
Castile ditto,
Poland Starch,
Patent Sago, Ci
Most of the above
Retail, with m

For L
The Brig

rious Firings, &c. with a Precision seldom exceeded by any regular troops.

BOSTON, *April 17. 1775.*

In Capt. Collins came one of the Hands who sailed with Capt. Calef, to London: He informs, that the latter had a tedious P

We learn from Concord, that on Saturday last the Provincial Congress, which had been sitting there, adjourned to the 10th of May next; tho' if necessary, to be summoned to meet earlier:——We also have it from undoubted authority, that a perfect Unanimity

At TEN o'Cl
Will be Sold by
At RUSSELL's A
—A Variety

REPORTING THE
FIRST CONTINENTAL
CONGRESS

By Benjamin H. Irvin

ON MARCH 31, 1774, PARLIAMENT ENACTED THE PORT Bill, a severe piece of legislation intended to punish Bostonians for flagrantly destroying East India Company tea. The first of four detested Coercive Acts, the Port Bill closed Boston Harbor to maritime trade, depriving the town's fifteen thousand inhabitants of their subsistence. When news of the Port Bill reached the colonies in early May, it provoked an immediate outcry. In town meetings and provincial conventions, dismayed Americans pled for unified resistance. Many proposed that the colonists elect delegates to a general congress, as several colonial assemblies had done during the Stamp Act crisis nearly ten years before.

Delegates to the "Grand Continental Congress" journeyed to Philadelphia early that autumn. Representing twelve colonies—Georgia did not send delegates—their ranks included many of the most prominent statesmen in British North America. Among them were Peyton Randolph, speaker of the Virginia House of Burgesses; Joseph Galloway, speaker of the Pennsylvania Assembly; Stephen Hopkins and Samuel Ward, both former governors of Rhode Island; merchant Philip Livingston, the scion of a manorial New York family; the brothers John and Edward Rutledge, distinguished planter-lawyers from South Carolina; the cousins Samuel and John Adams, the former a firebrand assemblyman, the latter a prominent attorney of the Boston Massacre trials; and numerous other individuals of comparable stature and wealth.

On September 5, the delegates gathered at the City Tavern to address preliminary matters. For their meeting place, they chose Carpenters' Hall, a two-story brick building owned by a Philadelphia trade guild. To serve as secretary, they selected Charles Thomson, a local Patriot who had helped organize tea boycotts. The delegates then agreed to conduct their deliberations in secrecy. What historians know of the First Continental Congress comes chiefly from the delegates' private papers and from Congress's official resolutions, which were published as complete journals and also as piecemeal entries in colonial newspapers, as in the February 17, 1775, edition of the *New-Hampshire Gazette*.

Most congressmen resented Parliament's repeated efforts to tax the colonists and to subordinate their legislative assemblies, but delegates disagreed over the wisest course of resistance. More radical delegates, like Samuel Adams and Richard Henry Lee, favored the establishment of trade boycotts to exert economic pressure on Great Britain, as some American communities had intermittently done during the taxation controversies of the 1760s and early 1770s. Champions of economic resistance carried a forceful popular mandate. Throughout that summer, indignant colonists had urged their representatives to implement a strategy of commercial opposition. Virginia's provincial convention, for example, resolved to cease importation from Great Britain, as reported in the August 26, 1774, edition of the *New-Hampshire Gazette*. Nevertheless, several congressmen doubted that economic resistance would sway British policymakers. Joseph Galloway, Isaac Low, and others feared that boycotts would instead devastate American trade.

Before Congress could deliberate such matters, a dire report from Massachusetts disrupted its proceedings. On September 6, an express rider brought an urgent message: British soldiers had marched on Charlestown, a bloody skirmish had ensued, and naval vessels had cannonaded the town of Boston all through the night. This desperate account, dispatched at the height of the Powder Alarm, proved mostly untrue, but it distressed the inhabitants of Philadelphia and cast a somber tone over the delegates' affairs.

In the weeks that followed, Congress progressed steadily toward a platform of aggressive resistance. On September 17, it endorsed the incendiary Suffolk Resolves, delivered by the courier Paul Revere, which declared that no obedience was due to the Coercive Acts and that the people of Massachusetts ought diligently "to acquaint themselves with the art of war." In mid-October, Congress issued a statement of grievances that predicated American rights on "the immutable laws of nature." The following week, it composed addresses to the people of Great Britain and to the inhabitants of the British colonies, including Quebec, St. John's, and Nova Scotia. In those addresses, one of which appeared in the November 29, 1774, edition of the *Essex Gazette*, Congress recited a history of tyrannical British government. Exercising a right preserved by the Magna Carta, Congress also composed a petition to King George III. Published in the February 3, 1775, edition of the *New-Hampshire Gazette*, this petition implored the king to disavow "designing and dangerous" ministers.

Most significantly, before adjourning, Congress framed the Articles of Association, a comprehensive scheme of nonimportation, nonexportation, and nonconsumption boycotts. Circulated throughout the colonies and enforced by local committees of observation and inspection, the Association called upon Americans to withdraw from the transatlantic trade and to forgo expensive leisure activities. By pinching British pocketbooks, the Association might have compelled the Royal Ministry to pursue a peaceful resolution to the imperial conflict. But in April 1775, months before nonexportation went into effect, war broke out in Massachusetts, dashing hopes of reconciliation.

DELEGATES who attend the CONGRESS.

From New Hampshire.
Major John Sullivan, and Col. Nathaniel Folsom.

From Massachusetts Bay.
Hon'ble Thomas Cushing, Esq; Mr. Samuel Adams, John Adams, and Robert Treat Paine, Esqs;

From Rhode-Island.
Hon. Stephen Hopkins, Esq; Hon. Samuel Ward, Esq;

From Connecticut.
Hon. Eliphalet Dyer, Silas Deane, and Roger Sherman, Esq'rs.

From New York.
James Duane, John Jay, Philip Livingston, Isaac Low, Col. William Floyd, and Henry Wesner, Esq'rs.

From New-Jersey.
James Kinsey, William Livingston, John D'Hart, Stephen Crane, and Richard Smith, Esq'rs.

From Pennsylvania.
Hon. Joseph Galloway, Samuel Rhoads, Thomas Mifflin, Charles Humporys, John Morton, Edward Biddle, and George Ross, Esq'rs.

From Newcastle, Kent, and Sussex Governments.
Cæsar Rodney, Thomas M'Kean, and George Read, Esq'rs.

From Maryland.
Mathew Tilgham, Thomas Johnson, jr. Robert Gouldsborough, William Paca, and Samuel Chase, Esq'rs.

From Virginia.
Hon. Peyton Randolph, Richard Henry Lee, George Washington, Patrick Henry, Richard Bland, Benjamin Harrison, and Edmund Pendleton, Esq'rs.

From North Carolina.
William Hooper, and Joseph Hewes, Esq'rs.

From South-Carolina.
Hon. Henry Middleton, John Rutledge, Thomas Lynch, Christopher Gadsden, and Edward Rutledge, Esq'rs.

NEW-HAMPSHIRE GAZETTE
(PORTSMOUTH)
September 30, 1774

Shortly after the First Continental Congress convened in Philadelphia, this list of delegates was published.

Continental Congress continu'd

Tuesday, October 18th, 1774:

The congress resumed the consideration of the plan of association, &c. and after sundry amendments the same was agreed to and ordered to be transcribed that it may be signed by the several Members.

The committee appointed to prepare an address to the people of Great-Britain, bro't in a draught which was read and ordered to lie on the table for the perusal of the members and to be taken into consideration to-morrow.

Wednesday, October 19th, 1774.

The congress resumed the consideration of the address to the people of Great-Britain, and the same being debated by paragraphs, and sundry amendments made, the same was recommitted in order that the amendments may be taken in.

The committee appointed to prepare a memorial to these colonies reported a draught which was read and order'd to lie on the table. Ordered that this memorial be taken into consideration to-morrow.

Thursday, October 20th, 1774,

The association being copied, was read and signed at the table and is as follows,
See the Association in this Paper, Novem. 11.

The congress then resumed the consideration of the memorial to the inhabitants of these colonies, and after debates thereon, adjourned till to-morrow.

See the Memorial in this Paper, Novem. 18.

Resolved, That an address be prepared to the people of Quebec and letters to the colonies of St. Johns, Nova-Scotia, East and

---

The committee appointed to prepare a letter to the colonies of St. John's, &c. reported a draught which was read, and being amended was approved and is as follows,

PHILADELPHIA, October 22, 1774.

Gentlemen,

THE present critical and truly alarming state of American affairs, having been considered in a general congress of deputies from the colonies of New-Hampshire, Massachusetts-Bay, Rhode-Island, Connecticutt, New-York, New-Jersey, Pennsylvania, the lower counties on Delaware, Maryland, Virginia, North-Carolina, and South-Carolina, with that attention and mature deliberation which the important nature of the case demand, they have determined for themselves and the colonies they represent, on the measures contained in the inclosed papers, which measures, they recommend to your colony, to be adopted with the earnestness, that a well directed zeal for American liberty can prompt, so rapidly violent & unjust has been the late conduct of the British administration against the colonies, that either a base and slavish submission, under the loss of this ancient, just and constitutional liberty must quickly take place, or an adequate opposition be formed.

We pray to God to take you under his protection, and to preserve the freedom and happiness of the whole British empire.

We are, &c.

Monday, October 24, 1774,

The committee appointed to prepare an to the people of Quebec, which was d after debate recommitted.

committee to whom the address was itted, brought in a draught which and ordered to be taken into consi to-morrow.

Tuesday, October 25,

congress resumed the consideration of paragraphs was approved and ordered to be engrossed.

Ordered, That the address to the King, be enclosed to the several colony agents in

---

NEW-HAMPSHIRE GAZETTE (PORTSMOUTH)

February 17, 1775

—

Most of what historians know about the First Continental Congress comes from the delegates' private papers and Congress's official resolutions, which were published as complete journals and also as piecemeal entries in colonial newspapers.

---

that served like ad to be added to the ing your Favour from the purest diffembled Patrio acknowledged. tion, when it was of Mustard. I ha if has become a g that crawl upon the Root, the fou on its Branches. work immediate and cut it down cause it is a Pest led suddenly by a Thousands in the

An Apprehension of Great-Britain told you was the Week I endeavou Necessity of her re hing some Gover now to point out upon which the b was the violent A the East-India Co of their Tea. In ment of that Tra back & view the As the Government Spirit or Genius o narchical, aristocra and commercial. which is the most it is worthy of Re British Nation upo like injuring a Fr Honor. Commer tional Wealth, for by all Orders of M Cottage. In some held in Contempt they respect him. in the State, often the first Families i Blood flows in the Trade is founded mutually supplying dundances. Thus enriched, the Arpe away, and Mankin Husband Manu are its treple Supp these, it would cea

NEW-HAMPSHIRE GAZETTE (PORTSMOUTH)

August 26, 1774

In the summer of 1774, the Virginia provincial convention protested Parliament's Coercive Acts by boycotting British goods. That autumn, the Continental Congress adopted an even more comprehensive scheme of economic resistance known as the Articles of Association.

At a very full Meeting of DELEGATES from the different Counties in the Colony and Dominion of VIRGINIA, begun in Williamsburg the first Day of August 1774, and continued by several Adjournments to Saturday the 6th of the same Month, when a Number of RESOLVES were passed and signed by 108 Persons, being an ASSOCIATION unanimously resolved upon and agreed to. At the same Time the following INSTRUCTIONS were given for the DEPUTIES appointed to meet in GENERAL CONGRESS on the Part of the Colony.

THE unhappy Disputes between Great Britain and her American Colonies, which began about the third Year of his Majesty's Reign, and since, continually increasing, have proceeded to Lengths so dangerous and alarming as to excite just Apprehensions in the Minds of his Majesty's faithful Subjects of this Colony that they are in Danger of being deprived of their natural, ancient, constitutional, and chartered Rights, have compelled them to take the same into their most serious Consideration; and, being deprived of their usual and accustomed Mode of making known their Grievances, have appointed us their Representatives to consider what is proper to be done in this dangerous Crisis of American Affairs. It being our Opinion that the united Wisdom of North America should be collected in a General Congress of all the Colonies, we have appointed the Hon. PEYTON RANDOLPH, Esq; RICHARD HENRY LEE, GEORGE WASHINGTON, PATRICK HENRY, RICHARD BLAND, BENJAMIN HARRISON, and EDMUND PENDLETOE, Esquires, Deputies to represent this Colony in the said Congress to be held at Philadelphia on the first Monday in September next.

And that they may be the better informed of our Sentiments touching the Conduct we wish them to observe on this important Occasion, we desire that they will express, in the first Place our Faith and true Allegiance to his Majesty King George the Third, our lawful and rightful Sovereign; and that we are determined, with our Lives and Fortunes, to support Him in the legal Exercise of all his just Rights and Prerogatives. And however misrepresented, we sincerely approve of a constitutional Connexion with Great-Britain, and wish most ardently a Return of that Intercourse of Affection and commercial Connexion that formerly united both Countries, which can only be effected by a Removal of those Causes of Discontent which have of late unhappily divided us.

It cannot admit of a Doubt but that British Subjects in America are entitled to the same Rights and Privileges as their Fellow Subjects possess in Britain; and therefore, that the Power assumed by the British Parliament to bind America by their Statutes, in all Cases whatsoever, is unconstitutional, and the Source of these unhappy Differences.

The End of Government would be defeated by the British ... their local Circumstances, cannot be there represented. Of this Nature we consider the several Acts of Parliament for raising a Revenue in America, for extending the Jurisdiction of the ...

jesty's Forces in America. If he considers ... the Character of his Majesty's Representative ... him that the Statute 25th Edward III. has ... all treasonable Offences, and that the Legis... tain hath declared that no Offence shall be c... son but such that is pointed out by that Sta... was done to take out of the Hands of tyran... weak and wicked Ministers, that deadly ... structive Treason had furnished them wit... drawn the Blood of the best and honestest Me... and that the King of Great-Britain hath no ... clamation to subject his People to Imprison... Penalties.

That if the said General CAGE conceiv... to act in this Manner, as the Commander i... jesty's Forces in America, this odious and i... must be considered as a plain and full Decla... spotick Viceroy will be bound by no Law, ... stitutional Rights of his Majesty's Subjects... terfere with the Plan he has formed for ... People of the Massachusetts-Bay; and ther... cuting, or attempting to execute, such Proc... sy Resistance and Reprisal.

MARBLEHEAD

On Saturday last Capt. Calley, of this Place, ... Days from Falmouth in England, has bro... the 6th of July, from which we have take... Advices, viz.

LONDON, Ju...

THE following is a Sketch of a popular ... on American Affairs:

"My Lords, Want of Health has hit ... from giving my Sentiments on the several Bi... under your Consideration with respect to ... may therefore be indulged in the Opportun... of the Line of the present Matter of the Da... to speak with Tenderness and Caution; I k... can't bear much; I will be, if possible, voi... Was I in Boston I would say they were v... Property of the East-India Company; I say ... the original Aggressors; a-Law is past whic... but were I to speak what I think, and wha... stitutional, I would tell you----you have i... a dead Letter-----you have set up an Image ... own, and which the People of America la... tell you, you had no Right to touch the P... Life, of a fellow Subject in America; he f... Necessity of your Laws relative to Trade, ... of a national Commerce, because he sees ... grees to buy the Wool, employ the Weave...

his Coat, because he is no longer sure of ni... ches.

"My Lords, you have lived upon the ...

ESSEX GAZETTE (SALEM, MA)

November 29, 1774

Congress composed addresses to the people of Great Britain and to the inhabitants of British colonies, including Quebec. In the address printed in this edition of the *Essex Gazette*, Congress recited a history of tyrannical British government.

ESSEX GAZETTE

both foreig

NUM

From TUESDAY, *November* 22, to

TUESDAY,

SALEM: Printed by *Samuel* and *Ebenezer Hall*, at their Printing-Office near

American Continental CONGRESS, *Oct.* 1774.

To the INHABITANTS of the COLONIES Of *New-Hampshire, Massachusetts-Bay, Rhode-Island and Providence* Plantations ; *Connecticut, New-York, New-Jersey, Pennsylvania*, the Counties of *New-Castle, Kent* and *Suffex* on Delaware ; *Maryland, Virginia, North-Carolina* and *South-Carolina.*

Friends and Fellow Countrymen,

WE, the Delegates appointed by the good people of the above Colonies to meet at Philadelphia in September laft, for the purposes mentioned by our refpective Conftituents, have in pursuance of the truft repofed in us, affembled and taken into our moft ferious confideration the important matters recommended to the Congrefs. Our refolutions thereupon will be herewith communicated to you. But as the fituation of public affairs grows daily more and more alarming ; and as it may be more fatisfactory to you to be informed by us in a collective body, than in any other manner, of thofe fentiments that have been approved, upon a full and free difcuffion by the Reprefentatives of fo great a part of America, we efteem ourfelves obliged to add this Addrefs to thefe Refolutions.

In every cafe of oppofition by a people to their rulers, or of one ftate to another, duty to Almighty God, the Creator of all, requires that a true and impartial judgment be formed of the meafures leading to fuch oppofition ; and of the caufes by which it has been provoked, or can in

The inhabitants of thefe colonies, confiding in the juftice of Great-Britain, were fcarcely allowed fufficient time to receive and confider this act, before another, well known by the name of the ftamp-act, and paffed in the fifth year of this reign, engroffed the whole of their attention. By this ftatute the Britifh Parliament exercifed in the moft explicit manner a power of *taxing* us, and extending the jurifdiction of Courts of *Admiralty* and *Vice-Admiralty* in the Colonies, to matters arifing within the body of a county, directed the numerous penalties and forfeitures, thereby inflicted, to be recovered in the faid Courts.

In the fame year a tax was impofed upon us, by an act, eftablifhing feveral new fees in the cuftoms. In the next year the ftamp-act was repealed ; not becaufe it was founded on an erroneous principle, but, as the repealing act recites, becaufe " the continuance thereof would be attended with many inconveniencies, and might be productive of confequences greatly detrimental to the commercial intereft of Great-Britain."

In the fame year, and by a fubfequent act, it was declared, " that his Majefty in Parliament, " of right, had a power to bind the people of thefe " Colonies by ftatutes *in all cafes whatfoever.*"

In the fame year, another act was paffed, for impofing rates and duties payable in thefe colonies. In this ftatute the Commons avoiding the terms of *giving* and *granting*, " humbly befought his Majefty that it might be enacted, &c." But from a declaration in the preamble, that the rates and duties were " in lieu of" feveral others grant-

liament made in t Houfe of Reprefen hibited by a ftatute tioned, from maki or vote, except for ac until provifion fhou bly for furnifhing t not only with all the ftatute which t but alfo with thofe ftatutes, which we the twenty-fourth

Thefe ftatutes of prehenfions and dif fided on the repeal the juft fears and j ftatute wa lifh Courts of *Adm* new model, exprefl recovering the per by acts of Parliam raifing a revenue in

The immediate fubvert the right o by rendering Affen perty, by taking th out their confent ; fubftituting in thei Vice-Admiralty C fide, holding their and unduly to influ Law, by rendering pendant on the Cr

permitted to give a wrong bias to reafon, it may be enabled to take a difpaffionate view of all the

pears, that thefe duties were intended *for that* purpofe.

other, will be foun fyftem, in which

pare an address to the people of Great-Britain, and a memorial to the inhabitants of British America, and 3d, to prepare a loyal address to his Majesty agreeable to resolutions already entered into.

¶ To be continu'd.

🔹🔹🔹🔹🔹🔹🔹🔹🔹🔹🔹🔹🔹🔹🔹🔹🔹

The following is the PETITION of the CONTINENTAL CONGRESS, To the KING's most excellent MAJESTY.

TO a sovereign, who "*glories in the name of Briton*," the bare recital of these acts must we presume, justify the loyal subjects who fly to the foot of his throne and implore his clemency for protection against them.

From this destructive system of colony administration, adopted since the conclusion of the late war, have flowed those distresses, dangers, fears, & jealousies, that overwhelm your Majesty's dutiful colonists with affliction ; and we defy our most subtle & inveterate enemies to trace the unhappy differences between Great Britain and these colonies, from an earlier period, or from other causes than we have assigned ; had they proceeded on our part from a restless levity of temper, unjust impulses of ambition, or artful suggestions of seditious persons, we should merit the opprobrious terms frequently bestowed on us by those we revere. But, so far from promoting innovations, we have only opposed them, and can be charged with no offence, unless it be one to receive injuries and be sensible of them.

Had our Creator been pleased to give us existence in a land of slavery, the sense of our condition might have been mitigated by ignorance and habit ; but, thanks be to his adorable goodness, we were born the heirs of freedom, and ever enjoyed our rights under the auspices of your royal ancestors, whose family was seated on the British throne to rescue and secure a pious & gallant nation from the popery and despotism of a superstitious & inexorable tyrant. Your Majesty, we are confident, justly rejoices, that your title to the crown is thus founded on the title of your people to liberty ; and therefore we doubt not but your royal wisdom must approve the sensibility that teaches your subjects anxiously to guard the blessings they received from divine providence, & thereby to prove the performance of that compact which elevated the illustrious house of Brunswick to the imperial

was seated on the British throne to rescue and secure a pious & gallant nation from the popery and despotism of a superstitious & inexorable tyrant. Your Majesty, we are confident, justly rejoices, that your title to the crown is thus founded on the title of your people to liberty ; and therefore we doubt not but your royal wisdom must approve the sensibility that teaches your subjects anxiously to guard the blessings they received from divine providence, & thereby to prove the performance of that compact which elevated the illustrious house of Brunswick to the imperial dignity it now possesses.

The apprehension of being degraded into a state of servitude from the pre-eminent rank of English freemen, while our minds retain the strongest love of liberty, and clearly foresee the miseries preparing for us and our posterity, excites emotions in our hearts which, though we cannot describe, we should not wish to conceal. Feeling as men, and thinking as subjects, in the manner we do, silence would be disloyalty. By giving this faithful information we do all in our power to promote the great objects of your royal care, the tranquility of your government, and the welfare of your people!

Duty to your Majesty, and regard for the preservation of ourselves and our posterity, the primary obligations of nature and of society, command us to entreat your royal attention, and, as your Majesty enjoys the signal distinction of reigning over freemen, we apprehend the language of freemen cannot be displeasing. Your royal indignation, we hope, will rather fall on those designing and dangerous men who daringly interposing themselves between your royal person and your faithful subjects, and for several years past incessantly employed to dissolve the bonds of society, by

bunal before which all mankind

NEW-HAMPSHIRE GAZETTE (PORTSMOUTH)
February 3, 1774

In its 1774 petition to George III, the Continental Congress professed loyalty and dutifulness to the king, but it also proclaimed "the strongest love of liberty."

Filled with sentiments of duty to your Majesty, & of affection to our parent state, deeply impressed by our education, and strongly confirmed by our reason ; & anxious to evince the sincerity of these dispositions, we present

RAID ON
FORT WILLIAM AND MARY

ACCORDING TO NEW HAMPSHIRE HISTORY, THE American Revolution began four months before the famous Battle of Lexington and Concord. Royal Governor John Wentworth was well liked in his hometown of Portsmouth, New Hampshire, and saw his subjects as "more moderate" than those to the south in Boston. But by early December 1774, his effort to mollify the growing unrest was failing, and his friendly relations with the royal governors of Massachusetts angered locals. On December 13, Paul Revere rode his horse through frigid weather from Boston to alert citizens of Portsmouth that the Royal Navy was coming. Revere said British command was sending reinforcements to secure Fort William and Mary in nearby New Castle. Strategically located on an island at the mouth of New Hampshire's only seaport, the fort's armory held a major supply of gunpowder and weapons. The British and local authorities had recently taken or disabled guns from shore batteries and forts in Massachusetts and Rhode Island. Worse yet, as Revere told the Committee of Safety, the mother country now planned to ban the export of weapons to all her rowdy American children. The fuse was lit.

Roused by fife and drum the following morning, December 14, 1774, a crowd of about four hundred citizens from Portsmouth and nearby towns made its way to Fort William and Mary. Captain John Cochran commanded only five soldiers at the fort, which was in poor condition. Shots were fired. In his report to Governor Wentworth, Cochran wrote:

Had anyone been killed, American history texts would tell a different version of the start of the Revolution.

I immediately ordered three four-pounders to be fired on them, and then the small arms; and, before we could be ready to fire again, we were stormed on all quarters, and they immediately secured both me and my men.

Local rebels lowered the British colors and stole the king's munitions. Cochran and one of his men were injured in the battle. Had anyone been killed, American history texts would tell a different version of the start of the Revolution.

Governor Wentworth certainly recognized the significance of the raid as seen by his stern proclamation read at the Portsmouth State House on December 26 and reprinted in the January 9, 1775, *Boston Evening-Post*. As Wentworth reported, the crowd overpowered the guards, made treasonous insults, and stole over one hundred barrels of gunpowder and other munitions in a "most daring and rebellious manner." Despite his demands, none of the "high-handed offenders" were captured. Two of the supposed insurgent leaders, John Langdon and John Sullivan, became key figures in the Revolution and were both early governors of the state of New Hampshire. The gunpowder was hidden in several towns to make sure the royal authorities would not recover it, and according to local legend, it was later used at the Battle of Bunker Hill.

The details, including the presence of Paul Revere, were reported by Wentworth in a letter to General Gage the same day as the raid. In the letter, the governor blamed "the imbecility of this government" for not sending ships of war to Portsmouth to protect the fort. Contrary to his proclamation, it is clear from his private correspondence that he knew the names of the "popular leaders" who organized the raid. On December 15, Wentworth attempted to find thirty local men to protect the fort but without luck, as it was again invaded by a much larger force that carried away many light cannons and sixty muskets.

Delayed by a slow start, tides, and bad weather, British

warships HMS *Canceaux* and HMS *Scarborough* arrived well after the raids. On December 28, two days after his official proclamation, the governor sent a brief letter to his friend Lord Dartmouth in England to warn that the citizens of Portsmouth "are arming and exercising men as if for immediate war." Wentworth's family had been among the most powerful leaders of the colony since 1717. Despite his empathy for the protestors, he was unable to cool their outrage. John Wentworth and his family were forced from their home by an armed mob on June 13, 1775. After a brief stay at the fort and aboard HMS *Scarborough*, they fled to England, never to return under penalty of death. John Wentworth became governor of Nova Scotia, where he died in 1808. His ruined fort, renamed Fort Constitution, still stands as mute evidence of the revolutionary New Hampshire shots not heard around the world.

BOSTON, in New-England.

On Monday the 26th of December his Excellency Governor WENTWORTH, of New-Hampshire issued the following Proclamation, viz.

By the GOVERNOR,
A PROCLAMATION.

WHereas several Bodies of Men did, in the Day time of the 14th and Night of the 15th of this instant December, in the most daring and rebellious Manner invest, attack and forcibly enter into his Majesty Castle William and Mary in this Province, and overpowering and confining the Captain and Garrison, did, besides committing many treasonable Insults and Outrages, break open the Magazine of said Castle and plunder it of above 100 Barrels of Gunpowder, with upwards of 60 Stand of Small Arms, and did also force from the Ramparts of said Castle and carry off 16 Pieces of Cannon, and other Military Stores, in open Hostility and direct Oppugnation of his Majesty's Government, and in the most atrocious Contempt of his Crown and Dignity:

I DO, by Advice and Consent of his Majesty's Council, issue this Proclamation, ordering and requiring in his Majesty's Name, all Magistrates and other Officers, whether Civil or Military, as they regard their Duty to the KING and the Tenor of the Oaths they have solemnly taken and subscribed, to exert themselves in detecting and securing in some of his Majesty's Goals in this Province the said Offenders, in Order to their being brought to condign Punishment: And from Motives of Duty to the KING and Regard to the Welfare of the good People of this Province: I do in the most earnest and solemn Manner, exhort and enjoin you, his Majesty's liege Subjects of this Government, to beware of suffering yourselves to be seduced by the false Arts or Menaces of abandoned Men, to abet, protect, or screen from Justice any of the said high-handed Offenders, or to withhold or secrete his Majesty's Munition forcibly taken from his Castle; but that each and every of you will use your utmost Endeavours to detect and discover the Perpetrators of these Crimes to the civil Magistrate, and assist in securing and bringing them to Justice, and in recovering the King's Munition: This Injunction it is my bounden Duty to lay strictly upon you, and to require your Obedience thereto, as you value individually your Faith and Allegiance to his Majesty, as you wish to preserve that Reputation to the Province in general; and as you would avert the dreadful but most certain Consequences of a contrary Conduct to yourselves and Posterity.

Given at the Council Chamber in Portsmouth the 26th Day of December, in the 15th Year of the Reign of our Sovereign Lord GEORGE the Third, by the Grace of GOD, of Great Britain, France, and Ireland, KING, Defender of the Faith, &c. and in the Year of our Lord CHRIST, 1774.

By His Excellency's Command,
with Advice of Council,
               J. WENTWORTH.
THEODORE ATKINSON, Sec'ry.
GOD save the KING.

By Capt. Sinclair, *who is arrived at Marblehead in 40 Days from Falmouth, we have the following Advices from* London.

LONDON, October 22.
To LORD NORTH.

GOvernment hath a long time formed the plan for establishing episcopacy in America, and a considerable sum been left by private gentlemen for its support. The establishment is necessary, on ac-

Oct. 29. The letters received on Friday from Boston, dated the 21st of September, are of the most alarming nature. They assert that the inhabitants of Boston, and of the province of Massachusetts-Bay, are now in arms. They have put themselves into constant exercise, and observe the most regular discipline. The Governor (General Gage) alarmed to the last degree at this state of things, sent to New-York for more troops, but the people of New-York refused to furnish transports to convey the troops.—These steps have been taken without waiting for the deliberations of the congress.——It is very strange, and must very soon excite more than astonishment, that those men are continued in office, who have brought the public affairs to this horrid situation.

The state or importance of the American colonies is so little understood or regarded by the *cunning people* at the west end of the town, that we are told they have universally agreed that if all our settlements there were at the bottom of the sea, it would be much better for England. These to be sure are very pretty conclusions about those dominions which have brought in so ma[ny] [mil]lions to England; about those dominions w[hich] constantly employed an infinite number of shipping about those dominions, which rendered this natio[n] the last war. Fro[m] [impor]tance of our colonies capable they are of ma[king] and we may also guess of the exercise or such hopes every Englishm[an] welfare of the Americ[a] such a great dependance

Extract of a Letter f[rom] on board the True September 30, to

"On Wednesday the Glorious Memory form Bristol bound fo[r] inst. met with a viole[nt] lost her mizen mast, people washed overbo[ard] the cargoe shifted, above the cargoe in the just keep her up with the pumps constantly at work as the people was very much jaded, what with pumping and getting her as upright as they could (which indeed was but very indifferent at best) however the Captain desired I would keep him company till we either saw land or near a port, which I readily complied with and kept him company till six o'clock the next morning, w[hen] finding by sounding we

Nov. 3. The proclamation against sending guns and gunpowder out of this kingdom will be of very little use, or effect, because the Americans will certainly procure whatever quantity of them they want from Holland, France, and Spain; and if orders were given to stop and seize such ships as were laden with the above commodities by those nations, it would bring on an immediate war with them: An event which the present ministry dare not hazard with any foreign power, though they assume courage sufficient to send fleets and armies to cut the throats of our American brethren.

No less than ten acts of parliament have been made to teaze and persecute the Americans, since the accession of George III.

This morning the Lord Mayor elect went up in his new private coach, with a pair of cream coloured horses, attended by Alderman Crosby, Thomas, and Hayley, and the two sheriffs, and was presented to the Lord Chancellor, who expressed the usual approbation.

An Evening Paper says, the People were so enraged at Hereford with Alderman Harley that they burnt his Coach.

Nov. 5. When the Lord Mayor elect was presented

By the last letters from America we have the melancholy account of the burning of the town of Boston; and that this fire had been occasioned by a general skirmish between the army and the inhabitants, in consequence of the General's issuing press warrants to man the ships which are short of complement, through epidemical distemper. The General

BOSTON EVENING-POST
January 9, 1775
—

Four months before the Battle of Lexington and Concord, and the "shot heard round the world," the first armed exchange between American and British military units took place in Portsmouth, New Hampshire, about 50 miles north of Boston. To some historians, this confrontation signaled the start of the Revolutionary War because it was the first deliberate confrontation of the war and first use of deadly force to seize territory and ordnance.

e bravery of our troops; what men
a country furnished with fastnesses
ntimately known to the enemy you
is unavailing or embarrassing, and
than human power to succeed to
en forbid that the bravery of such
e so vainly, so fatally employed;
verthrow of BRADDOCK by a
rthrow incurred by the very disci-
trust, will be apt to doubt the fa-
by military force; they who re-
fforts of all the colonies were
arms in the late war against the
ubtful of this expedient.

ng been already said on the sub-
your valuable moments, which I
employed; indulge me, how-
most serious attention to the true
try, and to the welfare of our bre-
revered and esteemed by all good
ferred with honour to posterity,
ection, and esteem, be echoed
nd extensive empire.

        MEMENTO.

WN, July 31.

y Connonade at Roxbury since
We have not yet heard the par-
urnt.

granted to the inhabitants of
number of persons have since
ermitted to bring their effects.
rning two prisoners were taken
rlestown, and
hey were taken
e sentry ma
it i

---

it. The breastwork about two hundred. The rail fence stuffed
with straw four or five hundred. The reason why the square was
so thinly manned on the side toward Boston, was because the fire
from Cop's hill poured in so thick that there was no living in it.
The regulars when they found the fire slacked for want of ammunition, pushed over the walls with their guns in their left hand,
and their swords in the right, for it was such an unfinished piece
of work that they ran over it. Part of them had come round on
the side next Charlestown, so as to fire on the back of our people,
when they began to leave the entrenchment, and it was then we
lost our men. The ships and floating batteries prevented any
assistance, or support of consequence, being given to our men;
the fire from Cop's hill ceased when that with small arms began,
but that from a ship off New Boston killed and raked our men
quite up to the Sun tavern. —— thinks there was more than three
thousand of the regulars landed. They advanced in open order,
the men often twelve feet apart in the front, but very close after
one another in extraordinary deep or long files. As fast as the
front man was shot down, the next stepped forward into his place;
but our men dropt them so fast, they were a long time coming up.
It was surprising how they would step over their dead bodies, as
though they had been logs of wood. Their officers, it is said,
were obliged to push them on behind, notwithstanding which they
once ran and filled some of the boats, the fire was so hot. One
of ———'s Captains told me he fired about thirty five times,
and after that threw stones. ———says when they pushed over
the breastwork, what with the smoke and dust, it was so dark in
the square that he was obliged to feel about for the outlet, the
earth, which they threw up for a breastwork, being very dry and
loose, for they had only one of these short nights to execute it in.

Extract of a letter from LONDON, *June 1.*

"IT is my indispensable duty to inform my countrymen on
your side the water, of whatever resolutions are form
this side injurious to your sacred rights, that ye
on your guard to defeat the pernicious
and tyrannical

---

consist of 8000 men, in order to co-operate
in forcing a relinquishment of the present i
in supporting constitutional liberty through
nions."

SPEECH *of the Hon.* TEMPLE LUTTRELL,
*mons, on the conduct of Administration wit
affairs.*

IT is but too visible, from the rash meas
Ministers of your government here in En
temper and situation of your American colon
will be inevitable.

Gentlemen on the other side of the House h
favourite proposition, that protection and obe
duties; and, of course, that the withdrawing
the other. Now, Sir, by these bills you ar
protection to some purpose; I therefore presum
no longer to be treated as rebels, but, whatso
zard of battle, will be entitled to the same n
the same acts of clemency and of grace that a
according to the modern system of war, by ev
in the world. You have a striking exampl
conduct from ancient time, in the most flagrant
all the wars the Romans ever waged: I mea
their own countrymen, commonly called the
that, in many of it's circumstances, bears so
to the present unhappy æra in our history, t
asking leave of the House to say a fe
sions of mankind,
nearly ali
look

BLOODY NEWS

Introduction

On the morning of April 19, 1775, war erupted along a country road west of Boston as colonial forces stood their ground and exchanged deadly fire with the world's largest and most feared army, the British regulars (soldiers). Bloody news about Lexington and Concord ignites the colonies as a swarm of militia and minutemen from all over New England race to surround Boston, trapping the British. The Continental Congress urgently reconvenes in Philadelphia to manage the hostilities while militia units capture heavy artillery from Fort Ticonderoga and prove their strength and steadfast determination at Bunker Hill. George Washington is appointed commander in chief of the Continental Army, helping to lay siege to Boston while an invasion of Canada is soon approved.

Virginia Gazette
(Williamsburg)
(Dixon and Hunter)
August 26, 1775

Battle of Bunker Hill
North Wind Picture Archives

NEWS OF THE FIRST FULL BATTLE OF THE REVOLUTIONARY War spread gradually. For Massachusetts militia officers in towns along the roads from Boston to Concord, it came on April 18, 1775, as neighbors reported seeing British army officers on horseback, cloaks over their uniforms and pistols. That night, provincial riders, alarm bells, and signal guns transmitted the warning that eight hundred infantrymen had crossed the Charles River and were marching west. Militia companies began to muster.

On the morning of April 19, the news grew grim: royal troops had fired on a militia company on Lexington common, killing eight. At midday, people learned that those British regulars were searching Concord, destroying the Provincial Congress's supplies and cannons. Another exchange of fire at Concord's North Bridge left dead on both sides. Meanwhile, a reinforcement column had marched out of Boston.

As soon as the royal troops left the center of Concord, the Middlesex County militia began a concerted counterattack. The regulars met their reinforcements in Lexington, and the combined force struggled east to Charlestown through growing hostile fire. By the end of the day, about 3,800 militiamen had seen action against about 1,500 regulars. More than 270 British were left dead, wounded, or missing; for the Americans, only ninety-four.

On April 21, the New-Hampshire Gazette *published a front-page article on the "BLOODY NEWS" from Massachusetts, reflecting the regional importance of the battle.*

On April 21, the *New-Hampshire Gazette* published a front-page article on the "BLOODY NEWS" from Massachusetts. A collection of rumors, this early printed report on the battle was wrong in several major details, but it reflected the regional importance of the event.

Normally, colonial newspapers started with foreign news set in type over the preceding week; in this one paper, the battle in Massachusetts pushed those columns aside.

The Massachusetts Provincial Congress worked to shape the news of the battle, issuing a detailed report that portrayed the militiamen as victims of aggression. Magistrates gathered eyewitness accounts favorable to the provincials; some even came from captured British soldiers, as John Dixon and William Hunter reprinted in the June 3, 1775, *Virginia Gazette*.

The legislature also commissioned John Derby of Salem to sail his family's schooner *Quero* to Britain with no cargo except a few copies of the April 21 and 28, 1775, *Salem Gazette,* containing Congress's report on the battle. Derby arrived in London on the evening of May 28. His news was soon discussed all over the capital. The Secretary of State's office had to issue a reminder, published in the June 1, 1775, *London Chronicle*, that there was still no official word from Massachusetts.

General Thomas Gage's report finally arrived in London on June 9. As quoted in the June 13, 1775, *London Chronicle*, Gage stated that the fight at Lexington began when "guns were fired upon the King's troops from behind a stone wall." He suggested the rebels had suffered "very considerable" losses and did not mention how his army was now besieged in Boston. Reflecting British army priorities, the general named casualties among the officers but merely numbered the enlisted men. The *Chronicle* continued to print news from America culled from newspapers, official dispatches, and private letters.

Back in Massachusetts, the printers of the *Essex Gazette* moved their press to Cambridge, headquarters of the new New England army, and began issuing the *New-England Chronicle*. They published letters between

General Gage and Governor Jonathan Trumbull of Connecticut (who sided with the resistance), soldiers' letters intercepted on their way to England, and Gage's widely derided proclamation of amnesty for rebels who surrendered.

American newspapers formed a consensus that one goal of the British army's march had been to arrest Massachusetts's political leaders, particularly John Hancock and Samuel Adams. General Gage described his aim as destroying rebel supplies in Concord; his orders and private files, made available in the twentieth century, confirm this. But the early American assumptions still shape how historians retell the event.

One part of the Battle of Lexington and Concord that did not appear in newspapers of the day was the story of Paul Revere. As dramatic as his experiences were, they had a limited effect on the fight, and Massachusetts officials did not wish to publicize how they had prepared for war. It took almost a century before Henry W. Longfellow's poem "Paul Revere's Ride" made the silversmith into an American icon. On April 19, 1775, he was just one of thousands of men caught up in the start of the war.

THE FIGHT ON LEXINGTON COMMON
North Wind Picture Archives

(*right*) British regulars fire on a militia company, killing eight and starting the first full battle of the Revolutionary War.

BRITISH RETREAT FROM CONCORD, MA
North Wind Picture Archives

(*left*) By the end of the royal troops' retreat from Concord to Boston, more than 270 British were left dead, wounded, or missing; for the Americans, only ninety-four.

BLOODY NEWS.

PORTSMOUTH, April 20, 1775.
Early this Morning, we were alarmed, with an Express from Newbury-Port, with the following Letter, to the Chairman of the Committee of Correspondence in this Town.

SIR,   Newbury-Port, April 19, 1775.

THIS Town has been in a continual Alarm since Mid-day, with Reports of the TROOPS having marched out of Boston to make some Attack in the Country—— The Reports in general concur, in part, in having been at Lexington.—And it is very generally said they have been at Concord.—— We sent off an Express this Afternoon, who went as far as Simons's at Danvers, before he could get Information that he thought might be depended upon—— he there met two or three Gentlemen who affirmed, the Regular *Troops* and our Men had been engaged chief of the Morning, and that it is supposed we had Twenty-five Thousand Men engaged against Four Thousand Regulars; that the Regulars had begun a Retreat—— Our Men here are setting off immediately——And as the *Sword is now drawn*, and *first drawn on the Side of the Troops*, we scruple not, you will give the *readiest and fullest Assistance in your Power*—— And send this Information further on—— In Behalf of the Committee for this Town,
            Your humble Servant,
                JAMES HUDSON, Chairman.

By the Express who brought the above Letter, we hear the Attack began at Lexington,

bers had been slain on both Sides. A Rein-

leaving one Thousand only to guard the Town. Thursday One o'Clock. Another Express

By the Nautilus and Falcon Ships of War, arrived at Boston from London, we have the following important Advices, viz.

LONDON, February 16.

ORDERS are sent to Commanders of his Majesty's Guard Ships at Portsmouth & Plymouth, to take on board an extra Number of Hands to be ready to man the Ships fitting out for Sea.

The Ministry complain very loudly of the Alteration in the Temper of a certain American Governor, since his being made Commander in Chief of the Forces in that Quarter. An Addition of Power it was expected would have produced additional Zeal; But they say, like all others, he is dwindled into the same Magistrate.

Orders are given from the War Office, for the Lord Lieutenants of every County in England to give in Accounts of the State and Condition of the Militia, as well Officers as private Men.

Not a Commission has been lately bestowed either at the War-Office or the Admiralty for the American Service, but to Persons whose Opinions with Respect to the Opposition of the Colonies have been first very scrupulously canvassed.

Orders are sent to the commanding Officers of Marines, at Chatham and Portsmouth, to raise a Number of Recruits to compleat the several Companies to their full Compliment of Men, to supply the Draughts that have been made for Boston.

We learn that in Virginia they have now 15000 Troops under Arms, 1000 Horse, and 5000 free Negroes.

Feb. 21. All the Deserters from the Troops on the other Side the Atlantic, we are assured, are English and Irish; not a Scotchman having yet flinched from his Duty, or betrayed the least Desire to depart from the very Letter of his Commission.

Is is not somewhat remarkable, says a Correspondent, that our Quarrels with Spain and France should be settled by drawing our Purse Strings; but those with America, by Fire and Sword.

A Morning Paper observes, that a Spanish Fleet is absolutely cruizing off Boston, and it is added, that the Americans have refused to supply the Troops under General Gage with any kind of Provisions, for which Purpose several Regiments of Provincials were encamped near that City, who have cut off all Communication between the Soldiers and the Country People.

Upwards of 3000l. have been raised privately in London since the Meeting of Parliament, for the Relief of the distressed Americans, and transmitted there.

Among the many Reasons assigned to account for Monday's American Motion, are the certain Loss of the Revenue of Trade and Commerce, the Uncertainty whether the Troops would act against their Fellow-Subjects, the utter impracticability of enslaving Americans, and lastly, an almost certainty of the Militia being soon wanted nearer Home, to oppose European Invaders.

Lord Adam Gordon, in the late Debate in Parliament, was for urging the American Acts with Vigour. His Reasons he begged to read from a Diary he himself had written when in America, which Diary, as he confessed, the Ministry did him the to consult, as a Guide in their Proceedings against the Americans.——The Substance of this Diary was, "That the People of Boston were naturally sensible and extremely polite, but very much inclined to Faction; that Governor Hutchinson was the best of Men, but rendered very uneasy in his Office by the turbulent Spirit of the People; that the Colony Governments inclined too much to the popular Scale, and therefore Lord Adam urges in this Diary the absolute Necessity of altering the Charters, in order to constitute a Government of a more Royal Nature.

gland, she meditates a more serious Blow, by securing America against her natural Friend.

The spirited Behaviour of the People of Jamaica, has thrown a

are to be bro't to some any Merchandize, wi to the said Province said Provinces or C Great-Britain, or so and that no other M the said Provinces o been imported into t shipped from any of cept Great Britain o dies, on Forfeiture o

"Also, that after of Wines, Salt, or a Horses, Victual, and of Ireland, and Goo for his Majesty's Fo tish Islands in the W tence whatsoever, u and carried directly Vessel.

"Likewise, tha or Ireland, or the Is after the limited Tim North America, or b less the Master do p jesty's Ships of War American Fisheries, vernor of the Color Nova-Scotia, New Virginia, N. Carolin Florida, setting forth one of the said Colon jesty's Subjects, Inh ful for any of the Co stationed for the Prot America to seize, an That nothing herein longing to the Frenc not carrying on any

"These restraints Laws shall be restore declared incapable of pains and Penalties."

From the St. JA

AN Opinion havi Lord has made with the Address of t made last Monday in the following authent

See the Motion i This Motion, Sir, heres in every Thing Offer of Lives and Fo cies, by Parliament, a nies return to their D Legislature, their real Application, be remov nise, the noble Lord a define the utmost Con the Mother Country g above Motion. Thes son to complain, that

this Country over Am ned Firmness by his M

opposition to our engagements, may ......

those ships, on hearing how things are at your Capes, do not land their dry goods in some part of the Bay. All goods on board should be taken possession of by the committee, and ship and all should be sent back, the salt at least thrown into the sea, and the goods returned by the ship."

WILLIAMSBURG, June 3.

LAST Monday morning a detachment of cavalry from the WILLIAMSBURG VOLUNTEERS, in their uniforms, mounted and equipped, with a waggon containing their baggage and provisions, set out in a regular military procession, to meet the Hon. PEYTON RANDOLPH, Esq; late President of the Grand Continental Congress, on the way hither from Philadelphia, his presence being requisite at our General Assembly now sitting here. On Tuesday, about noon, the troop of horse met that Gentleman at Ruffin's ferry, accompanied by Col. CARTER BRAXTON, and escorted them to Williamsburg, after having been joined by a company of infantry, who marched out the distance of two miles for the same purpose. They arrived here at sunset, and were attended to the honourable Gentleman's house by the whole body of cavalry and infantry, whose very martial appearance gave great satisfaction to the spectators. The bells began to ring as our worthy Delegate entered the city, and the unfeigned joy of the inhabitants, on this occasion, was visible in every countenance; there were illuminations in the evening, and the volunteers, with many other respectable Gentlemen, assembled at the Raleigh, spent an hour or two in harmony and cheerfulness, and drank several patriotic toasts.

Yesterday the Honourable House of Burgesses appointed committees to proceed on the ordinary business of the country.

We hear from King and Queen, that on Monday the 22d ult. a most dreadful whirlwind happened in that county. It seemed to rise from two thunder clouds meeting in the west; about one o'clock its course was easterly, and tore up every thing in its way near a quarter of a mile wide. Many poor people have felt its direful effects; no less than eight plantations are swept in as many miles, some not having a house left; 4 persons, viz. a young man, a woman, a boy, and a child in its mother's arms, were crushed to death, and several so much bruised and wounded that their recovery is doubtful. In short, such a scene of horrour and devastation was never seen before by winds in this country.

Extract of a letter from PHILADELPHIA, *May 23.*

" A Gentleman from Rhode Island brings an account that a Captain of a man of war at Boston had sent out a cutter to take a sloop arrived in a river there, with provisions for the provincial army, which was done; but the people collected in armed boats, regained their own, and took the other vessel, sending the crew prisoners into the country. Accounts from England and Ireland are, that the troops at the former are said to be countermanded, and at the latter an unwillingness to embark had produced a skirmish, in which many were killed, and the embarkation stopped."

In a late Philadelphia paper have been published, by order of the Congress, affidavits and depositions of sundry persons of Lexington, Concord, &c. by which it appears that the provincials were first attacked at both places by the King's troops. The following are depositions of three of the wounded regulars, which were published with those of the provincials.

LINCOLN, *April 23, 1775.*

" I JOHN BATEMAN, belonging to the 52d regiment, commanded by Col. Jones, on Wednesday morning the 19th day of April instant, was in the party marching to Concord; being at Lexington, in the county of Middlesex, and being nigh the meeting-house in said Lexington, there was a small party of men gathered together in that place when our said troops marched by; and I testify and declare, that I heard the word of command given to the troops to fire, and some of said troops did fire, and I saw one of said small party lay dead on the ground, nigh said meeting-house; and I testify that I never heard any of the inhabitants so much as fire one gun on said troops. JOHN BATEMAN."

CONCORD, *April 23, 1775.*

" I JAMES MARR, of lawful age, testify and say, that in the evening of the 18th instant I received orders from George

---

to their full scope, and that your gift, if you should be inclined to offer any, may be, in the completest manner, free. The civil government of this country being already provided for, you will only have to declare what proportion, and by what means, you are willing to contribute towards the public burthens of the state, burthens to which the mother country hath cheerfully submitted to secure the colonies from the encroachments of a dangerous and vigilant enemy: And I am warranted to say, that as it is never intended to require you to tax yourselves, without Parliament's taxing the subjects of Great Britain on the same occasion, in a far greater proportion, no prudence which you shall think necessary to observe for your security in that particular can be disapproved of.

And I can likewise assure you, that if you should judge fit to adopt the principle, and imitate the example of justice, equity, and moderation, in your proposals, which actuated the House of Commons in their resolution, declaring at once what was ultimately expected of you; such a compliance on your part will be considered by his Majesty not only as a testimony of your reverence for Parliament, but also as a mark of your duty and attachment to your Sovereign, who has no object nearer his heart than the peace and prosperity of his subjects in every part of his dominions.

I must recommend to you to fall upon means of paying the officers and private men employed in repelling the late invasion and incursions of the Indians, as I make no doubt you will think their services on that occasion deserving of your attention.

Gentlemen of the COUNCIL, Mr. SPEAKER, *and Gentlemen of the* HOUSE *of* BURGESSES,

You may be assured of my cheerful concurrence in all measures, and ready assent to all laws, which it may be found expedient to adopt for the present peace, tranquillity, and advantage of the country; and I hope you will think it necessary to these ends, that the courts of justice should forthwith be opened, in order that the laws may again have their due course.

I cannot conclude without exhorting you in the most earnest manner, to enter upon the subject matter, now recommended to you, with that patience, calmness, and impartiality, which its great importance requires, and to reflect upon the benefits this country hath received from the support given to it by the parent state, which I hope will animate your zeal, now you have it in your power, to restore that harmony and mutual confidence which rendered both countries so flourishing, and, in short, to pursue your true interest, which will convert our present gloomy apprehensions into prospects of peace, happiness, and lasting security.

AT a general meeting of the freeholders of Mecklenburg county, convened on Monday the 8th day of May 1775, at the courthouse of said county, in order to elect a committee, pursuant to a resolution of the American Continental Congress, the better to secure a due observation of the association entered into by the said Congress, the freeholders then proceeded to the choice of

For the London Chronicle.

To the P U B L I C. [...]

AS a doubt of the authenticity of the account from Salem, touching an engagement between the King's Troops and the Provincials in the Massachusetts Bay, may arise from a paragraph in the Gazette of this evening, I desire to inform all those who wish to see the original affidavits which confirm that account, that they are deposited at the Mansion House with the Right Hon. the Lord Mayor for their inspection.

ARTHUR LEE [...]

ADVICES from AMERICA.

The following Affidavits and other Particulars, relative to the late Skirmish between his Majesty's Troops and the Provincials in Massachusett's Bay, were received on Monday last. Lexington, April 23, 1775.

WE John Hoar, John Whithed, Abraham Gearfield, Benjamin Munroe, Isaac Park, William Hosmer, John Adams, Gregory Stone, all of Lincoln, in the county of Middlesex, Massachusett's Bay, all of lawful age, do testify and say, that on Wednesday last we were assembled at Concord in the morning of said day, in consequence of information received, that a brigade of regular troops were on their march to the said town of Concord, who had killed six men at the town of Lexington ; about an hour afterward we saw them approaching, to the number of 1200 ; on which we retreated to a hill about 80 rods back ; and the said troops then took possession of the hill where we were first posted. Presently after this, we saw the troops moving towards the North Bridge, about one mile from the said Concord Meetinghouse. We then immediately went before them, and passed the bridge, just before a party of them, to the number of about 200, arrived. They there left about one half of their 200 at the Bridge, and proceeded with the rest towards Col. Barrett's, about two miles from the said Bridge. We then seeing several fires in the town, thought the houses in Concord were in danger, and marched towards the said Bridge ; and the troops who were stationed there, observed our approach, marched back over the Bridge, and then took up some of the planks. We then hastened our march towards the Bridge ; and when we had got near the Bridge they fired on our men first, three guns one after the other ; they also fired a considerable number more ; and then, and not before (having orders from our commanding officer not to fire till we were fired upon) we fired upon the regulars, and they retreated. On their retreat through this town, Lexington, to CharlesTown, they ravaged and distressed private property, and burnt three houses, one barn, and one shop.

The above affidavit was signed by the persons whose names are mentioned at the beginning of it, and sworn before William Reed, John Cuming, Jonathan Hastings, and Duncan Ingraham, Esqrs. four of his Majesty's Justices of the Peace. And Nathaniel Gorham, Notary Public, certifies that full faith is to be given to the transactions of the said Justices.

Lexington, April 23. I James Barrett, of Concord, Colonel of a regiment of militia in the county of Middlesex, do testify and say, that on Wednesday morning last, about day-break, I was informed of the approach of a number of the regular troops to the town of Concord, where were some magazines belonging to this province, and where there were assembled some of the militia of this and the neighbouring towns, when I ordered them to march to the North Bridge (so called) which they had passed, and were taking up. I ordered said militia to march to said Bridge, and pass the same, but not to fire on the King's troops unless they were first fired upon. We advanced near said bridge, when the said troops fired upon our militia, and killed two men dead on the spot, and wounded several others, which was the first firing of guns in the town of Concord. My detachment then returned the fire, which killed and wounded several of the said King's troops.

JAMES BARRET.

VOL. XXXVII. The London Chronicle. N° 2883.

From TUESDAY, May 30, to T...

For the London Chronicle.

To the PUBLIC.

Tuesday, May the 30th, 1775.

AS a doubt of the authenticity of the account from Salem, touching an engagement between the King's Troops and the Provincials in the Massachusetts Bay, may arise from a paragraph in the Gazette of this evening, I desire to inform all those who wish to see the original affidavits which confirm that account, that they are deposited at the Mansion House with the Right Hon. the Lord Mayor for their inspection.

ARTHUR LEE,
Agent for the House of Representatives of the Massachusetts Bay.

ADVICES FROM AMERICA.

The following Affidavits and other Particulars, relative to the late Skirmish between his Majesty's Troops and the Provincials in Massachusett's Bay, were received on Monday last.

Lexington, April 23, 1775.

WE John Hoar, John Whithed, Abraham Gearfield, Benjamin Munroe, Isaac Park, William Hosmer, John Adams, Gregory Stone, all of Lincoln, in the county of Middlesex, Massachusett's Bay, all of lawful age, do testify and say, that on Wednesday last we were assembled at Concord in the morning of said day, in consequence of information received, that a brigade of regular troops were on their march to the said town of Concord, who had killed six men at the town of Lexington; about an hour afterward we saw them approaching, to the number of 1200; on which we retreated to a hill about 80 rods back; and the said troops then took possession of the hill where we were first posted. Presently after this, we saw the troops moving towards the North Bridge, about one mile from the said Concord Meeting-house. We then immediately went before them, and passed the bridge, just before a party of them, to the number of about 200, arrived. They there left about one half of their 200 at the Bridge, and proceeded with the rest towards Col. Barrett's, about two miles from the said Bridge. We then seeing several fires in the town, thought the houses in Concord were in danger, and marched towards the said Bridge; and the troops who were stationed there, observing our approach, marched back over the Bridge, and then took up some of the planks. We then hastened our march towards the Bridge; and when we had got near the Bridge they fired on our men first, three guns one after the other; they also fired a considerable number more; and then, and not before, (having orders from our commanding officer not to fire till we were fired upon) we fired upon the regulars, and they retreated. On their retreat through this town, Lexington, to Charles-Town, they ravaged and distressed private property, and burnt three houses, one barn, and one shop.

The above affidavit was signed by the persons whose names are mentioned at the beginning of it, and sworn before William Reed, John Cuming, Jonathan Hastings, and Duncan Ingraham, Esqrs. four of his Majesty's Justices of the Peace. And Nathaniel Gorham, Notary Public, certifies that full faith is to be given to the transactions of the said Justices.

Lexington, April 23. I James Barrett, of

the county of Middlesex, de... on Wednesday morning la... I was informed of the appr... the regular troops to the... where were some magazine... province, and where there,... of the militia of this and... towns, when I ordered them... North Bridge (so called) which... and were taking up. I ordered said militia to march to said Bridge, and pass the same, but not to fire on the King's troops unless they were first fired upon. We advanced near said bridge, when the said troops fired upon our militia, and killed two men dead on the spot, and wounded several others, which was the first firing of guns in the town of Concord. My detachment then returned the fire, which killed and wounded several of the said King's troops.

JAMES BARRET.

Sworn before Wm. Reed, Jonathan Hastings, and Duncan Ingraham, Justices of the Peace.

Lexington, April 23. We Bradbury Robinson, Samuel Spring, Thaddeos Bancroft, all of Concord, and James Adams, of Lincoln, all in the county of Middlesex, all of lawful age, do testify and say, that on Wednesday morning last, near ten of the clock, we saw near one hundred of regular troops, being in the town of Concord, at the North Bridge in the said town (so called) and having passed the same, they were taking up the said bridge, when about three hundred of our militia were advancing towards the said bridge, in order to pass the said bridge, when without saying any thing to us, they discharged a number of guns on us, which killed two men dead on the spot, and wounded several others, when we returned the fire on them, which killed two of them, and wounded several, which was the beginning of hostilities in the town of Concord.

Sworn before W. Reed, W. Stickney, and Jon. Hastings, his Majesty's Justices of the Peace.

Lincoln, April 23. I John Bateman, belonging to the fifty-second regiment, commanded by Colonel Jones, on Wednesday morning, on the 19th of April instant, was in the party marching for Concord, being at Lexington in the county of Middlesex; being nigh the meeting house in said Lexington, there was a small party of men gathered together in that place, when our said troops marched by; and I testify and declare, that I heard the word of command given to the troops to fire, and some of the said troops did fire, and I saw one of the said small party lie dead on the ground, nigh the said meeting house; and I testify, that I never heard any of the inhabitants so much as fire one gun on the said troops.

Sworn before John Cuming and Duncan Ingraham, Justices of the Peace.

Concord, April 23. I James Marr, of lawful age, testify and say, that in the evening of the 18th instant, I received orders from George Hutchinson, Adjutant of the fourth regiment of regular troops stationed at Boston, to prepare and march, to which orders I attended, and marched to Concord, where I was ordered by an officer, with about one hundred men, to guard a certain bridge there; while attending that service, a number of people came along, in order, as I suppose, to cross the said bridge, at which time a number of the regular troops first fired upon them.

Sworn before Duncan Ingraham and Jonas

place, we saw a body of provincial troops armed, to the number of about sixty or seventy men. On our approach they dispersed, and soon after firing began; but which party fired first I cannot exactly say, as our troops rushed on shouting and huzzaing, previous to the firing, which was continued by our troops so long as any of the provincials were to be seen. From thence we marched to Concord. On a hill near the entrance of the town, we saw another body of provincials assembled. The light infantry companies were ordered up the hill to disperse them. On our approach they retreated towards Concord. The grenadiers continued the road under the hill towards the town. Six companies of light infantry were ordered down to take possession of the bridge, which the provincials retreated over. The company I commanded was one. Three companies of the above detachment went forward about two miles. In the mean time, the provincial troops returned, to the number of about three or four hundred. We drew up on the Concord side of the bridge. The Provincials came down upon us, upon which we engaged and gave the first fire. This was the first engagement after the one at Lexington: A continued firing from both parties lasted through the whole day. I myself was wounded at the attack of the bridge, and am now treated with the greatest humanity, and taken all possible care of by the committee of Newhaven, and attested by the correspondence from town to town. Test. Jon. Sturges, And. Rowland, Silleck Silliman, Thad. Burr, Job Bartram.

WEDNESDAY, MAY 31.

The London Gazette. No. 11565.

Secretary of State's Office, Whitehall,
May 30, 1775.

A Report having been spread, and an account having been printed and published, of a skirmish between some of the people in the Province of Massachuset's Bay and a detachment of his Majesty's troops; it is proper to inform the Public, that no advices have as yet been received in the American department of any such event.

There is reason to believe, that there are dispatches from General Gage on board the Sukey, Capt. Brown, which, though she sailed four days before the vessel that brought the printed account, is not yet arrived.

Warsaw, May 13.

The very uncommonly dry and cold weather, which we have had for some time past, has occasioned a great mortality in and about this town.

Copenhagen, May 16. On the 13th a placart was published here, by Government, contradicting the report lately propagated of an intention to suppress or reduce the Bank Notes of one rixdollar, and promising a reward of 1000 rixdollars for discovering the author of the...

Chelmsford, June 9. M. Lingard, at Writtle, fowed three wheat kernels in his garden early this spring, which have produced what is hardly credible, not less than 151 stalks of wheat, which are all in a thriving state.

LONDON.

From the LONDON GAZETTE.

Whitehall, June 10. Lieutenant Nunn, of the Navy, arrived this morning at Lord Dartmouth's office, and has brought letters from General Gage, Lord Percy, and Lieutenant Colonel Smith, containing the following particulars of what passed on the 19th of April last, between a detachment of the King's troops in the province of Massachusett's Bay, and several parties of Rebel Provincials, viz.

General Gage having received intelligence of a large quantity of military stores being collected at Concord, for the avowed purpose of supplying a body of troops to act in oppsition to his Majesty's government, detached, on the 18th of April, at night, the Grenadiers of his army, and the Light Infantry, under the command of Lieutenant Colonel Smith of the 10th regiment, and Major Pitcairne of the Marines, with orders to destroy the said stores; and the next morning eight companies of the 4th, the fame number of the 23d and 49th, and fone Marines, marched under the command of Lord Percy, to support the other detachment.

Lieutenant Colonel Smith finding, after he had advanced some miles on his march, that the country had been alarmed by the firing of guns, and ringing of bells, dispatched six companies of Light Infantry, in order to secure two bridges on different roads beyond Concord, who, upon their arrival at Lexington, found a body of the country people drawn up under arms on a green, close to the road; and, upon the King's troops marching up to them, in order to inquire the reason of their being so assembled, they went off in great confusion, and several guns were fired upon the King's troops from behind a stone wall, and also from the Meeting-house and other houses, by which one man was wounded, and Major Pitcairne's horse shot in two places. In consequence of this attack by the rebels, the troops returned the fire, and killed several of them; after which the detachment marched on to Concord, without any thing further happening, where they effected the purpose for which they were sent, having knocked off the trunnions of three pieces of iron ordnance, burnt some new gun carriages, and a great number of carriage wheels, and thrown into the river a considerable quantity

Colonel Smith and Major Pitcairne did every ing that men could ... general; and th... ual intrepidity.

...turn of the ...fficers, Drum... and wounded, ...9th of April, 4th, or King's Knight, killed. and prisoner. wounded. 7 rank 8 missing.

5th regiment. ... Lieutenant William Cox, Lieutenant Thomas Hawkshaw, wounded. 5 rank and file killed, 1 wounded, 1 missing.

10th regiment. Lieutenant Colonel Francis Smith, Captain Lawrence Parsons, Lieutenant Wald. Kelly, Ensign Jeremiah Lester, wounded. 1 rank and file killed, 13 wounded, 1 missing.

18th regiment. 1 rank and file killed, 4 wounded, 1 missing.

23d regiment. Lieut. Colonel Bery Bernard, wounded. 4 rank and file killed, 26 wounded, 6 missing.

38th regiment. Lieut. William Sutherland wounded, 1 Serjeant wounded. 4 rank and file killed, 11 wounded.

43d regiment. Lieut. Hull wounded and prisoner. 4 rank and file killed, 5 wounded, 2 missing.

47th regiment. Lieut. Donald M'Cloud, Ensign Henry Baldwin, wounded. 1 Serjeant wounded. 5 rank and file killed, 21 wounded.

52d regiment. 1 Serjeant missing. 3 rank and file killed. 2 wounded.

59th regiment. 3 rank and file killed, 3 wounded.

Marines. Captain Souter, Second Lieutenant M'Donald, wounded. Second Lieutenant Isaac Potter missing. 1 Serjeant killed, wounded, 1 missing. 1 Drummer killed. 5 rank and file killed, 36 wounded, 5 missing.

TOTAL.

1 Lieutenant killed.
2 Lieutenant-Colonels wounded.
2 Captains wounded.
9 Lieutenants wounded.
1 Lieutenant missing.
2 Ensigns wounded.
1 Serjeant killed, 7 wounded, 2 missing. 1 Drummer killed, 1 wounded. 62 rank and file killed, 157 wounded, 24 missing.

N. B. Lieutenant Isaac Potter reported to be wounded and taken prisoner.

Signed   THO. GAGE.

Extract of a Letter from Edinbur...

...where the lives of so many men de... as the security of the nation.

" The smugglers upon this co... seized from them within this mo... wards of 1200 ankers of brandy, r... besides teas, by the custom-house ...

" The crops of grass, barley, ... like to turn out very bad, owing ... dry spring; the wheat is thin and ...

" We have had great plenty of ... this coast this season, which have ... to 1s. 6d. per dozen.

" His Majesty's ship Kent, Cap... is ordered to join the grand fleet ... Portsmouth; the Romney of 50 g... Duff, is at anchor in the Sound ... Dublin, Albion, Raisonable, and T... ships, are at their moorings in the H... Hunter sloop of war hath been ... sheathed for the American station... sloop of war is going into dock; ... and Fame are in the docks repair... Prudent, late from the East Indies ... being very leaky."

Extract of a Letter from Chatha...

" Sunday arrived here the Au... with Lord Sandwich, &c. on board... ship was saluted with 15 guns fr... jesty's ship Ramillies, Commodore ... Vernon, which compliment was r... the Augusta yacht, with seven ... Sandwich did not come on shore th...

" Monday morning his Lordsh... shore at the dock-yard, accompan... Seaford, Sir Hugh Pallifer, Dr. ... Omiah, the native of Otaheite; th... ceived in the yard by Col. M'K... Marines, Maurice Suckling, Esq; ... Sir John Williams, Surveyor, Will... Esq; Comptroller of the victualling ... his Majesty's navy, Commissioner ... the principal officers of the doc... Grenadier company of Marines we...

great numbers of the rebels assembled in many parts, and a considerable body of them attacked

de Guines arrived at his house in Great George-street, from France. His Excellency, immedi-

Their Lordships, &c. walked roun... and took a view of the ships build...

We are constantly stating the great obligation we have conferred on the Colonies by our former behaviour towards them; if it was ever so good, we can claim no merit from hence in private or public concerns, to do injury in future; they do not complain of your former behaviour, but they say, you have altered this very system from whence you would now derive their submission.

There are two arguments of the noble Lord which I must remark upon before I sit down; the first is, "the comparative view of "Taxation between this country and the Colonies, according to "the number of inhabitants." His Lordship says, "we pay about "twenty-five shillings a head, and they pay about six-pence." Who is there so unacquainted with political arithmetic as not to know that the small sum people pay in Taxation is often a proof of their poverty, and the large sum a proof of their prosperity, by demonstrating the riches from the greatness of the consumption? Let this kind of reasoning be applied to Ireland or Scotland, where we know the multitude to be poor in comparison to the inhabitants of London, whom we know to be rich; besides, if the Colonist does not pay in *palpable Cash* from his own hand, does not he pay all the *Taxes* on the four millions of *Manufactures* he receives, and part of those Taxes on the raw materials he sends hither.

The other argument is still more extraordinary. The noble Lord says, "if we fail in our attempt of forcing America, we shall "still be in the same situation we are in at present." What! after our armies have been disgraced, our fellow-subjects destroyed, all the irritation of a civil war, public confidence, and fair opinion lost!---Does the noble Lord think he will be in the same situation *himself?*---I really speak it with regret, for *personally* I have much regard for the noble Lord, and particularly because I perceive, from his *faint* manner of stating his propositions, that they are not the dictates of his own mind, and that they are forced on him.

I cannot see my other memorandums, and therefore I shall conclude by *heartily concurring* with the noble Lord who moved for the recommitment of this Address.

CAMBRIDGE, May 12.
Copy of a Letter to his Excellency General GAGE, from the Hon. JONATHAN TRUMBULL, Esq; Governor of his Majesty's Colony of Connecticut, in behalf of the General Assembly of said Colony.
SIR, Dated HARTFORD, April 28th, 1775.
THE alarming situation of public affairs in this country, and the late unfortunate transactions in the province of the Massachusetts Bay, have induced the General Assembly of this colony, now sitting in this place, to appoint a committee of their body to wait upon your Excellency, and to desire me, in their name, to write to you relative to these very interesting matters.

The inhabitants of this colony are intimately connected with the people of your province, and esteem themselves bound by the strongest ties of friendship, as well as of common interest, to regard with attention whatever concerns them. You will not therefore be surprised that your first arrival at Boston, with a body of his Majesty's troops, for the declared purpose of carrying into execution certain acts of parliament, which, in their apprehension, were unconstitutional and oppressive, should have given the good people of this colony a very just and general alarm; your subsequent proceedings in fortifying the town of Boston, and other military preparations, greatly increased their apprehensions for the safety of their friends and brethren; they could not be unconcerned spectators of their sufferings in that which they esteemed the common cause of this country; but the late hostile and secret inroads of some of the troops under your command into the heart of the country, and the violences they have committed, have driven them almost into a state of desperation. They feel now not only for their friends, but for themselves, and their dearest interests & connections. We wish not to exaggerate, we are not sure of every part of our information; but, by the best intelligence that we have yet been able to obtain, the late transaction was a most unprovoked attack upon the lives and property of his Majesty's subjects; and it is represented to us, that such outrages have been committed as would disgrace even barbarians, and much more Britons, so highly famed for humanity as well as bravery: It is feared therefore that we are devoted to destruction, and that you have it in command and intention, to ravage and desolate the country. If this is not the case, permit us to ask, why have these outrages been committed? Why is the town of Boston now shut up? And to what end are all the hostile preparations that are daily making, and why do we continually hear of fresh destinations of troops for this country? The people of this colony, you may rely upon it, abhor the idea of taking arms against the troops of their Sovereign, and dread nothing so much as the horrors of civil war; but at the same time we beg leave to assure your Excellency, that as they apprehend themselves justified by the principle of self-defence, so they are most firmly resolved to defend their rights and privileges to the last extremity; nor will they be restrained from giving aid to their brethren, if any unjustifiable attack is made upon them. Be so good, therefore, as to explain yourself upon this most important subject, so far as is consistent with your duty to our common Sovereign.--- Is there no way to prevent this unhappy dispute from coming to extremities? Is there no alternative but absolute submission, or the

happy for them if they had sought relief, only in the way which the constitution, their reason, and their interest pointed out.

You cannot wonder at my fortifying the town of Boston, or making any other military preparations, when you are assured, that previous to my taking these steps, such was the open threats, ar, such the warlike preparations throughout this province as rendered it my indispensable duty to take every precaution in my power, for the protection of his Majesty's troops under my command, against all hostile attempts. The intelligence you seem to have received, relative to the late excursion of a body of troops into the country, is altogether injurious and contrary to the true state of facts; the troops disclaim, with indignation, the barbarous outrages of which they are accused, so contrary to their known humanity. I have taken the greatest pains to discover if any were committed, and have found examples of their tenderness both to the young and the old, but no vestige of cruelty or barbarity: It is very possible that in firing into houses, from whence they were fired upon, that old people, women or children, may have suffered, but if any such thing has happened it was in their defence, and undesigned. I have no command to ravage and desolate the country, and were it my intention I have had pretence to begin it, upon the sea ports, who are at the mercy of the fleet. For your better information, I inclose you a narrative of that affair, taken from gentlemen of indisputable honor and veracity, who were eye-witnesses of all the transactions of that day. The leaders here have taken pains to prevent any account of this affair getting abroad, but such as they have thought proper to publish themselves; and to that end the post has been stopped, the mails broke open, and letters taken out; and by these means the most injurious and inflammatory accounts have been spread throughout the continent, which has served to deceive and inflame the minds of the people.

When the resolves of the Provincial Congress breathed nothing but war, when those two great and essential prerogatives of the King, the levying of troops, and disposing of the public monies, were wrested from him; and when magazines were forming by an assembly of men, unknown to the constitution, for the declared purpose of levying war against the King, you must acknowledge it was my duty, as it was the dictate of humanity to prevent, if possible, the calamities of civil war, by destroying such magazines.--- This, and this alone, I attempted. You ask why is the town of Boston now shut up? I can only refer you, for an answer, to those bodies of armed men, who now surround the town, and prevent all access to it. The hostile preparations you mention, are such as the conduct of the people of this province has rendered it prudent to make, for the defence of those under my command.

You assure me the people of your colony abhor the idea of taking arms against the troops of their Sovereign, I wish the people of this province, for their own sakes, could make the same declaration. You enquire, is there no way to prevent this unhappy dispute from coming to extremities? Is there no alternative, but absolute submission, or the desolations of war? I answer, I hope there is; the King and Parliament seem to hold our terms of reconciliation, consistent with the honor and interest of Great-Britain, and the rights and privileges of the colonies; they have mutually declared their readiness to attend to any real grievances of the colonies, and to afford them every just and reasonable indulgence, which shall, in a dutiful and constitutional manner, be laid before them; and his Majesty adds, it is his ardent wish that this disposition may have a happy effect, on the temper and conduct of his subjects in America: I must add likewise the resolution of the 27th February, on the grand dispute of taxation and revenue, leaving it to the colonies to tax themselves, under certain conditions; here is surely a found... people who wish a reconciliation... tween countries so nearly conne... terest; but I fear that the leade... still are, intent only on shedding...

I am much obliged by your fa... character, and assure you, as it ... deavour hitherto, so I shall con... protect all his Majesty's liege su... sons and property. You ask, w... my duty to suspend the operatio... menced no operations of war bu... me to suspend, while I am surr... have already begun, and threat... war, and are now violently dep... many others of the King's sub... tion, of all the conveniences ... the country abounds; but it mu... able people, when I assure you, th... jure or molest quiet and peaceable subjects; but on the contrary, shall esteem it my greatest happiness to defend and protect them, against every species of violence and oppression.
I am, Sir, &c. THO. GAGE.
Hon. Governor Trumbull.

The following is an exact Copy of a Letter which was intercepted at Roxbury last Week.
Boston, 4th May, 1775.

tants, till on the Night of the 18th of April, twenty-one Companies of Granadiers and Light Infantry were ordered into the Country about 18 Miles; where, between 4 and 5 o'Clock in the Morning, we met an incredible Number of People of the Country in Arms against us. *Col. Smyth of the 10th Regiment ordered us to rush on them with our Bayonets fix'd;* at which Time some of the Peasants fired on us, and our Men returning the Fire, the Engagement begun; they did not fight us like a regular Army, only like Savages, behind Trees and Stone Walls, and out of the Woods and Houses, where in the latter we killed Numbers of them, as well as in the Woods and Fields. The Engagement began between 4 and 5 in the Morning, and lasted till 8 at Night. I can't be sure when you'll get another Letter from me, as this extensive Continent is all in Arms against us: These People are very numerous, and full as bad as the Indians for *scalping and cutting the dead Men's Ears and Noses off, and those they get alive, that are wounded and can't get off the Ground.*"

April 28, 1775.
"The Granadiers and Light Infantry marched for Concord, where were Powder and Ball, Arms, and Cannon mounted on Carriages; but before we could destroy them all, we were fired on by the Country People, who are not brought up in our military Way as ourselves, were surrounded always in the Woods; the Firing was very hot on both Sides; about 2 in the Afternoon the 2d Brigade came up, which was 4 Regiments and Part of the Artillery, which were of no Use to us, as the Enemy were in the Woods, and when we found they fired from Houses, we set them on Fire, and they ran to the Woods like Devils. We were obliged to retreat to Boston again, over Charles-River, our Ammunition being all fired away. We had 150 wounded and killed, and some taken Prisoners; we were forced to leave some behind, who were wounded. We got back to Boston about 2 o'Clock next Morning, and them that were able to walk were forced to mount Guard and lie in the Field. I never broke any Fast for 48 Hours, for we carried no Provisions, and thought to be back next Morning. I had my Hat shot off my Head 3 Times, 2 Balls through my Coat, and carried away my Bayonet by my Side, and near being killed. The People of Boston are in great Trouble, for G. Gage will not let the Town's People go out. Direct for me to Chatham's Division of Marines."

"Dear Parents, April 30, 1775.
"Before this reaches you, you may hear that our Regiment has been engaged with the Provincials. The Granadiers and Light Infantry marched about 9 at night. At 6 next Morning 423 Soldiers and 47 Marines, in all 1500, marched to reinforce the Granadiers and Light Infantry; joined about 1 o'Clock, and found them not engaged, which they had been 8 Hours before; for we had 2 Pieces Cannon, which made us march very slow.--- As soon as we came up we fired the Cannon, which brought them from behind the Trees, for we did not fight as you did in Germany; for we could not see above 10 in a Body, for they were behind Trees and Walls, and fired at us, and then loaded on their Bellies. We had but 36 Rounds, which obliged us to go Home that Night, and as we came along they got before us and fired at us out of the Houses and killed and wounded a great many of us, but we *levelled their Houses* as we came along. It was thought there were about 6000 at first, and at Night double that Number. The King's Troops lost in killed and wounded 150, and the Americans 500 Men, Women and Children, for there was *a Number of Women and Children burnt in their Houses.* Our Regiment has 5 killed and 31 wounded, particularly Col. Bernard, in the Thigh, which all the Regiment is sorry for. The Shot flew thick. I got a wounded Man's Gun, and killed two of them, as I am sure of..."

NEW-ENGLAND CHRONICLE (CAMBRIDGE, MA)
May 12, 1775

The printers of the *Essex Gazette* moved their press from Salem to Cambridge, the headquarters of the new New England army, and began publishing the *New-England Chronicle*. This is the first issue after the move and title change.

much, by cutting down their Liberty Poles and Alarm Posts. We have had a great many died in our Regiment last Winter, so that what with wounded Men and what has deserted, we have not 300 Men, and Duty is so hard that we come off Guard in the Morning and mount Pickets at Night."

"Honour'd Mother, April 25, 1775.
"The Rebels, when we came to Concord, burnt their Stores, fired upon the King's Troops, and a smart Engagement ensued. About th...

WILLIAMSBURG GUNPOWDER INCIDENT

WILLIAMSBURG WAS THE CAPITAL OF VIRGINIA AT the outbreak of the American Revolution. The city was home to many prominent Virginians who supported the cause of American liberty, including Peyton Randolph, later the president of the first Continental Congress, and George Wythe, signer of the Declaration of Independence.

After the Port of Boston's closing, the House of Burgesses called for a day of fasting, humiliation, and prayer in support of the people of Massachusetts. John Murray, the Fourth Earl of Dunmore and governor of Virginia, quickly denounced this act and dissolved Virginia's representative body. The Burgesses moved their session to the Raleigh Tavern and commenced the First Virginia Convention on August 1, 1774. Taking matters into their own hands, the Burgesses, along with merchants in the city, decided to stop importing goods from England. By the fall of 1774, independent companies formed across the colony. These men kept watch over the colony as tensions ran high and helped to enforce the nonimportation agreement. Only a month after the Second Virginia Convention and Patrick Henry's infamous "Liberty or Death" speech, Lord Dunmore made a decision that forever changed the course of the colonies' history.

On the morning of Friday, April 21, 1775, Lord Dunmore gave orders to Captain Henry Collins of the armed schooner *Magdalen* to remove fifteen barrels of gunpowder from the magazine at Williamsburg. Under the cover of darkness, plans were executed successfully between 3:00 and 4:00 a.m., losing only a bayonet scabbard when the sailors

Only a month after the Second Virginia Convention and Patrick Henry's infamous "Liberty or Death" speech, Lord Dunmore made a decision that forever changed the course of the colonies' history.

returned. Later that morning, the citizens of Williamsburg were outraged and immediately armed and mobilized the Independent Company.

The news of the powder being taken spread across Virginia rapidly. Editors William Hunter and John Dixon printed in their newspaper, the *Virginia Gazette*, an address from the mayor of Williamsburg on April 22, 1775. They wrote "that the inhabitants of this city were this morning exceedingly alarmed by a report that a large quantity of gunpowder was in the preceding night, while they were sleeping in their beds, removed from the public magazine in this city." The citizens requested:

> *...as guardians of this city, we therefore humbly desire to be informed by your Excellency, upon what motives, and for what particular purpose, the powder has been carried off [...]*

Militia and independent companies across Virginia mustered and prepared to march on Williamsburg to forcibly, if necessary, take the powder back. The *Pennsylvania Evening Post* reported on May 9, 1775, that Mann Page Jr., Esq., rode from Fredericksburg to Williamsburg to find out if the powder was returned. The newspaper reported that the taking of the powder "had spread a general alarm, and greatly exasperated all ranks of people." Patrick Henry publicly demanded that Dunmore either return the gunpowder or pay £330 for it. Thousands of armed men marched on Williamsburg under the command of Henry. Lord Dunmore, enraged over Henry's request, demanded his arrest. While camped at Doncastle's Ordinary, nearly fifteen miles from the capital, word was received that the governor paid the treasury for the powder. This stalled armed conflict in Virginia.

Many of the organized militia companies continued and camped in Williamsburg, setting the tone for the next several months. A continuous guard was placed on the capital and magazine. The homes of Robert Carter Nicholas, treasurer of the colony of Virginia, and Peyton Randolph were also placed under guard. News of the first shots at Lexington arrived in Williamsburg by express rider on the evening of April 28. The Revolution had already begun. The Williamsburg gunpowder incident prompted the Third Virginia Convention, which established an interim government and allowed the raising of regiments within the colony. This posture of defense allowed Virginia to prepare and organize for their first major battle against the British at Great Bridge.

PATRICK HENRY
North Wind Picture Archives

Patrick Henry publicly demanded that Lord Dunmore, royal governor of Virginia, return the gunpowder he had removed from the Williamsburg magazine or pay £330.

M of New York, gives us the following in that place:—On the 13th
unhappy difturbance which happened in that place:—On the 13th
inftant a number of people, to the amount of about 50, collected

went armed to the courthoufe, with an intent to kill the fheriff and clerk of the Court, but finding the Court reinforced by a number of men from New Hampfhire, they defifted from their purpofe. The Court then adjourned to the next feffions. No Courts have been eftablifhed in the county till within thefe three years paft; and the people were very uneafy, and exclaimed highly againft the eftablifhment; in fo much that in March 1774 a militia was raifed in the county to fupprefs riots and difturbances among them. It muft be obferved that the Court party were enemies to diforder, and zealous affertors of the rights and liberties of the people, and were fenfible how neceffary to the peace and happinefs of fociety is the regular adminiftration of juftice; and have fhewn the fame readinefs in oppofing any forms of government not known by the conftitution, as in erecting and defending legal Courts of juftice.

NEWPORT, *March 27.*

WE are well informed that General Gage has four hundred of Rivington's papers regularly fent him every week by the poft, which are diftributed among the army, navy, and fuch others as are thought moft proper to promote the infamous plan of enflaving this country. Thefe papers are doubtlefs paid for out of the American revenue: Thus, Americans, you already begin to fee your own money employed for enflaving yourfelves and your children.

It is confidently afferted that 60,000 pounds fterling, has been remitted from the treafury in England, to be diftributed among fome hungry d—gs at New York.

We are well affured that his Honour our Governor has received a circular letter from Lord Dartmouth, of January 4th, in which

upon his word and honour, whenever it was wanted on any infurrection, it fhould be delivered in half an hour; that he had removed it in the night time to prevent any alarm, and that Captain Collins had his exprefs commands for the part he had acted; he was furprifed to hear the people were under arms on this occafion, and that he fhould not think it prudent to put powder into their hands in fuch a fituation.

The John, Capt. Taylor, from Liverpool, is arrived in James river, by whom we have received London advices to the 21ft of February. Captain Taylor failed on the 27th, and fays that a

---

My Lord,

WE his Majefty's dutiful and loyal fubjects, the Mayor, Recorder, Aldermen, and Common Council, of the city of Williamfburg, in Common Hall affembled, humbly beg leave to reprefent to your Excellency, that the inhabitants of this city were this morning exceedingly alarmed by a report that a large quantity of gunpowder was in the preceding night, while they were fleeping in their beds, removed from the public magazine in this city, and conveyed, under an efcort of marines, on board one of his Majefty's armed veffels lying at a ferry on James river.

We beg leave to reprefent to your Excellency, that as this magazine was erected at the public expence of this colony, and appropriated to the fafe keeping of fuch munition as fhould be there lodged from time to time, for the protection and fecurity of the country, by arming thereout fuch of the militia as might be neceffary in cafes of invafions and infurrections, they humbly conceive it to be the only proper repofitory to be reforted to in times of imminent danger.

We further beg leave to inform your Excellency, that, from various reports at prefent prevailing in different parts of the country, we have too much reafon to believe that fome wicked and defigning perfons have inftilled the moft diabolical notions into the minds of our flaves, and that therefore the utmoft attention to our internal fecurity is become the more neceffary.

The circumftances of this city, my Lord, we confider as peculiar and critical. The inhabitants, from the fituation of the magazine, in the midft of their city, have, for a long tract of time, been expofed to all thofe dangers which have happened in many countries from explofions, and other accidents. They have, from time to time, thought it incumbent on them to guard the magazine. For their fecurity they have, for fome time paft, judged it neceffary to keep ftrong patrols on foot; in their prefent circumftance, then, to have the chief and neceffary means of their defence removed, cannot but be extremely alarming. Confidering ourfelves as guardians of the city, we therefore humbly defire to be informed by your Excellency, upon what motives, and for what particular purpofe, the powder has been carried off in fuch a manner; and we earneftly entreat your Excellency to order it to be immediately returned to the magazine.

To which his EXCELLENCY *returned this verbal anfwer:*

THAT, hearing of an infurrection in a neighbouring county he had removed the powder from the magazine, where he did not think it fecure, to a place of perfect fecurity; and that

---

actually taken place, which, it was generally thought, would occafion a turn of meafures in favour of the Americans.

GOODS

That their remittances are almost intirely made by means of the fisheries, and consequently the ruin brought on those colonies will deeply injure the commercial interest of Great-Britain, and ultimately fall on the landed property of these kingdoms.

That among other grievances, of which our fellow subjects in America so generally complain, is their being deprived of trial by jury in particular cases, and the extension of the jurisdiction of the Admiralty Courts; which grievances, your Petitioners with much concern find, are not only continued, but extended by the present bill; and they think it their duty to represent it as their firm opinion to this Right Honourable House, and the disquietudes which universally prevail in the minds of their fellow subjects in America, will be increased and confirmed by this bill; which is, unjust as they conceive, because it involves the punishment of those who are allowed to be innocent, with those who are supposed to be guilty; and that these disquietudes will never be removed, unless lenient measures are pursued, and their grievances redressed.

Your Petitioners, therefore, most humbly pray, that the said bill may not pass into a law.

Published by order of the Committee.

THOMAS LANE, *Chairman.*

CHARLESTOWN (*South-Carolina*) April 17.

By a vessel which was 22 days ago at Havannah, we learn, that harbour was then full of men of war; and that the Spaniards were very inquisitive concerning the present dispute between Great-Britain and her colonies; also, that a fleet with troops, from old Spain, had arrived there about Christmas.

The General Assembly of this Province met here last week and is now sitting.

WILLIAMSBURG, *April 28.*

Yesterday, about ten o'clock, Mann Page, jun. Esq; one of the Representatives for Spotsylvania, arrived here in twenty-four hours from Fredericksburg; being charged by a number of people of the different counties, now assembling there, to inquire whether the gunpowder had been replaced in the public magazine, the removal of which had spread a general alarm, and greatly exasperated all ranks of people. Expresses had been sent into several counties, and it was expected that upwards of 2000 men would be assembled in Fredericksburg by this evening; and the militia of Caroline were ordered to meet to-morrow, at ten o'clock, to be in readiness to join those of the upper counties. Mr. Page returned again in the evening, and carried a letter from the Hon. the Speaker, to endeavor to pacify the people; and as that gentleman sets out to-morrow, by land, to attend the General Congress, we hear he proposes meeting them, and it is hoped, from his great influence, that he will be able to prevail on them to return home, and rest satisfied with the Governor's promise that the powder shall be given up when there is occasion for it.—The independent companies of Caroline and

---

NEWPORT, May 1.

Last Wednesday, as Mr. John Brown, of Providence, merchant, was going from this town to Providence, in one of the packets, the packet was stopped, by order of Captain Wallace, of the ship Rose, and Mr. Brown taken on board the ship Swan; soon after which another packet was stopped as she was going up. These packets had on board a quantity of flour, which Mr. Brown had purchased for a number of vessels he was fitting out. Part, or all, of the flour was taken on board the ship; and the next day Mr. Brown was sent off in one of the packets, to be carried to Admiral Graves, at Boston, without having a single reason given for his being thus violently seized and carried out of this colony, contrary to all law, equity and justice.

Extract of a letter from Roxbury, dated April 28.

"Notwithstanding your many neglects, notwithstanding my many avocations, I once more salute you—*jacta est alea.* What folly could induce Gen. Gage to act a part so fatal to Britain.—It is all over with them—their withering laurels will soon be plucked from their brows by the rapacious Bourbon.—I pity the madness which effected their destruction. —You have, no doubt, been informed of the affair of last Wednesday.—Is it not truly amazing, that such a body of regulars, so thoroughly appointed, with artillery, &c. should be defeated, and put to flight, by a handful of raw, undisciplined peasants?—We have lost but forty one, and but few, not exceeding ten, wounded—they have near three hundred killed, wounded and missing.—Our countrymen swarm to our defence from all quarters—we are busily organizing our troops, and shall soon have a well constructed army in the field, of 30,000 men.—Gage and his troops are immured within the walls of Boston; and what is a delay to our satisfaction, our friends are entrapped by them:—We have some hopes they will be liberated this day; Gen. Gage has proposed, upon their surrendering their arms, that they may march out; they surrendered their arms yesterday.

"Poor Quincy, alas, he is no more! He returned to his native country, pressed the beloved soil, and died—We did not see him; he breathed his last, the night before last, at Cape Ann.

"We have had an express, by the way of Connecticut, inclosing transcripts from letters sent lately to New-York,—such a vile system of slavery is preparing for us, as might make a Domitian blush.—Thank God, our enemies will assuredly be defeated."

NEW-YORK,

with six ships and a brig, from Plymouth, bound to Boston with troops.

Thursday last the Harriot Packet, Captain Lee, sailed with the mail for Falmouth, in whom went passengers, the Hon. John Watts, and Roger Morris, Esqrs. Members of his M-

T HE CONTINENTAL CONGRESS RECONVENED ON MAY 10, 1775, scarcely three weeks after British regulars and Massachusetts militiamen clashed at Lexington and Concord. News of the battle spread quickly across the Atlantic seaboard, provoking thousands of men and boys to turn out in defense of their liberties. As they journeyed back to Philadelphia, through every town they passed, members of Congress observed scores of volunteers performing military exercises to the music of fife and drum. At the outskirts of New York City, a corps of nearly one thousand soldiers waited to escort the New England delegates—including John Hancock and the cousins Samuel and John Adams—into town. "[T]he roads were lined with greater numbers of people than were ever known on any occasion before," reported the *Pennsylvania Evening Post* on May 9: "Their arrival was announced by the ringing of bells."

The Second Continental Congress met in the Pennsylvania State House and immediately began sifting through eyewitness accounts of the skirmishes in Massachusetts. Turning its attention to New York City, where shiploads of British reinforcements were daily expected, Congress admonished inhabitants to "act on the defensive, so long as may be consistent with their safety." But, in an alarming resolution reprinted in the *Pennsylvania Gazette* of May 24, 1775, it further advised them to "repel force by force" and to prepare "places of retreat" for women and children. Two weeks later, Congress dispatched an inflammatory address to "the oppressed Inhabitants of Canada," urging them to join the fight against a "licentious" British ministry.

Momentously, in anticipation of the war's escalation, Congress voted in mid-June to provision the New England militias that had gathered outside of Boston with flour and gunpowder. It determined to augment those troops by raising ten companies of riflemen. It commissioned George Washington, a war-seasoned colonel in the Virginia militia, to command American troops. And it appointed a committee to draft rules to govern the military. By these measures, Congress established the Continental Army, or, as the *Virginia Gazette* boasted on July 29, 1775, "the forces of *the united colonies of North America.*"

No sooner had Congress voted to build this army than British and American forces again clashed. The desperately hard-fought Battle of Bunker Hill left little doubt that a deadly war had begun. Nevertheless, Congress wished to justify Americans' military preparations, so on July 6, it issued the Declaration on Taking Arms. Drafted in its final form by the Pennsylvania congressman John Dickinson, this declaration rebuked Parliament's "cruel and impolitic" efforts to subjugate the colonists. The American people had been driven to arms not by a desire for independence, but rather, as the declaration proclaimed, by Parliament's "intemperate rage."

Though vigilant of his liberty, Dickinson fervently hoped the American colonies and the British Empire would soon be reconciled. Even as he revised the Declaration on Taking Arms, Dickinson prevailed upon Congress to assure King George III of Americans' allegiance. The so-called Olive Branch Petition—adopted by Congress on July 8 and widely reprinted, as in *Lloyd's Evening Post* of September 6, 1775—once again beseeched the king to protect the colonists from his ministers' "delusive pretences, fruitless terrors, and unavailing severities." To the dismay of the Crown's loyal subjects, the king not only rejected the Olive Branch Petition, but also, by a proclamation issued August 23, commanded that the American rebellion be suppressed.

In the months that followed, Anglo-American relations

deteriorated rapidly. On November 7, Lord Dunmore, the royal governor of Virginia, offered freedom to all slaves and indentured servants who took arms against their rebel masters. In December, Parliament passed the Prohibitory Act, casting American ships out of the Royal Navy's protection. On January 1, 1776, Dunmore ordered a British man-of-war to bombard Norfolk, Virginia's largest port. Soon after, King George secured treaties with numerous German sovereigns to provide auxiliary soldiers for the war. And on March 23, as reported in the May 2, 1776, edition of the *New-England Chronicle*, the Continental Congress authorized American privateers to raid British vessels. Thus, long before Congress declared independence in July 1776, Great Britain and the United Colonies began treating each other as enemies.

As the Revolution unfolded, Congress struggled to provision the Continental Army. Because it possessed no power to tax, Congress financed much of the war by printing unbacked paper dollars. It also aggressively pursued diplomatic relations with King Louis XVI of France, who provided essential military and financial assistance. To strengthen the United States, Congress drafted the Articles of Confederation, formally ratified in 1781. By the time Franco-American forces compelled Cornwallis's surrender at Yorktown, the power of Congress had greatly declined. The failure of its military procurement policies and the collapse of the continental currency weakened Congress, as did the stringent, supermajority voting requirements adopted under the Articles of Confederation. After the war, aside from the notable land ordinances of the mid-1780s, the states left the federal union in precarious drift. Not until the Constitutional Convention of 1787 did Americans take up federal governance in earnest again.

SECOND CONTINENTAL CONGRESS
North Wind Picture Archives

Congress leaves the Pennsylvania State House in Philadelphia to hear the first public reading of the Declaration of Independence.

PENNSYLVANIA EVENING POST (PHILADELPHIA)

May 9, 1775

In Philadelphia, the journey and arrival of the delegates of the Second Continental Congress was big news as the who's who from around the colonies gathered for the first time since bloodshed in Massachusetts.

their way for Philadelphia, to attend the Continental Congress, the Hon. John Hancock, and Thomas Cushing, Esqrs. Samuel Adams, John Adams, and Robert Treat Paine, Esqrs. Delegates for the province of Massachusetts-Bay ; and the Hon. Eliphalet Dyer, and Roger Sherman, Esqrs. and Silas Dean, Esq; Delegates for the colony of Connecticut. They were met a few miles out of town by a great number of the principal gentlemen of the place, in carriages and on horseback, and escorted into the city by near a thousand men under arms; the roads were lined with greater numbers of people than were ever known on any occasion before. Their arrival was announced by the ringing of bells, and other demonstrations of joy. They have double centries placed at the doors of their lodging.

We hear the above gentlemen, accompanied by the Delegates for this city, set out this day for Philadelphia.

PHILADELPHIA, May 9.

We hear from Charlestown, South-Carolina, that on the 21st of March, at night, about eight hundred stand of small arms, two hundred cutlasses, and all the cartouch boxes, fit for service, with several bundles of match and some flints, were taken out of the public armoury in the state-house ; and on the same night the public powder magazine, built about four miles from the town, was broke open, and all the powder carried off, being about five hundred weight. The Governor has offered a reward of one hundred pounds sterling for apprehending the offenders.

Saturday last Gen. Lee arrived in town from the Southren Colonies.

Last night the brig Charlestown Packet, Capt. Barton, arrived from Charlestown. In this vessel came passengers the Hon. Henry Middleton, Christopher Garden, John Rutledge, and Edward Rutledge, Esqs. Delegates for South-Carolina.

Thomas Lynch, Esq; the other Delegate, sailed the day before in a schooner. It is said she is in the river.

And this day arrived the Hon. Peyton Randolph, Esq; George Washington, Patrick Henry, Richard Henry Lee, Edmund Pendleton, Benjamin Harrison, and Richard Bland, Esquires, Delegates for Virginia.——Richard Caswell, and Joseph Hewes, Esquires, Del. for North-Carolina. Also Samuel Chace, Thomas Johnson, and John Hall, Esquires, Del. for Maryland.

This afternoon the brig Chance, Craig, arrived from Grenada.

The Delegates for Massachusetts-Bay, Connecticut, and New-York, are expected here to-morrow about noon.

Capt. Wright, of the brig Charlestown Packet, died the 21st of April, off Cape Fear, on his passage to Charlestown.

In an alarming resolution reprinted in this *Pennsylvania Gazette*, the Second Continental Congress advised inhabitants of New York, where shiploads of British reinforcements were expected soon, to "repel force by force" and to prepare "places of retreat" for women and children.

---

attack is made upon them. Be fo good, therefore, as to explain yourfelf upon this moft important fubject, as far as is confiftent with your duty to our common Sovereign. Is there no way to prevent this unhappy difpute from coming to extremities? Is there no alternative but abfolute fubmiffion, or the defolations of war? By that humanity which conftitutes fo amiable a part of your character, for the honour of our Sovereign, and by the glory of the Britifh empire, we intreat you to prevent it, if it be poffible; furely it is to be hoped that the temperate wifdom of the empire might, even yet, find expedients to reftore peace, that fo all parts of the empire may enjoy their particular rights, honours and immunities: Certainly this is an event moft devoutly to be wifhed for; and will it not be confiftent with your duty, to fufpend the operations of war on your part, and enable us on ours to quiet the minds of the people, at leaft, till the refult of fome further deliberations may be known. The importance of the occafion will, we doubt not, fufficiently apologize for the earneftnefs with which we addrefs you, and any feeming impropriety which may attend it, as well as induce you to give us the moft explicit and favourable anfwer in your power. *I am, with great efteem and refpect,*

In behalf of the General Affembly, Sir, &c.

(Signed) JON. TRUMBULL.

His Excellency THOMAS GAGE, *Efq;*

His Excellency General GAGE's *Anfwer, to the foregoing Letter.*

SIR, Dated Bofton, May 3, 1775.

I Am to acknowledge the receipt of your letter of the 28th of April laft, in behalf of the General Affembly of your colony, relative to the alarming fituation of public affairs in this country, and the late tranfactions in this province: That this fituation is greatly alarming, and that thefe tranfactions are truly unfortunate, are truths to be regretted by every friend to America, and by every well-wifher for the peace, profperity and happinefs of this province. The intimate connections and ftrong ties of friendfhip, between the inhabitants of your colony and the deluded people of this province, cannot fail of inducing the former to interpofe their good offices, to convince the latter of the impropriety of their paft conduct, and to perfuade them to return to their allegiance, and to feek redrefs of any fuppofed grievances in thofe decent and conftitutional methods, in which alone they can hope to be fuccefsful.

That troops fhould be employed for the purpofe of protecting the Magiftrates in the execution of their duty, when oppofed with violence, is not a new thing in the English or any other government: That any acts of the Britifh Parliament are unconftitutional or oppreffive, I am not to fuppofe; if any fuch there are, in the apprehenfion of the people of this province, it had been happy for them if they had fought relief, only in the way which the conftitution, their reafon, and their intereft pointed out.

You cannot wonder at my fortifying the town of Bofton, or making any other military preparations, when you are affured, that previous to my taking thefe fteps, fuch was the open threats, and fuch the warlike preparations throughout this province, as rendered it my indifpenfable duty to take every precaution in my power, for the protection of his Majefty's troops under my command, againft all hoftile attempts. The intelligence you feem to have received, relative to the late excurfion of a body of troops into the country, is altogether injurious and contrary to the true ftate of facts; the troops difclaim, with

NEW-PORT, May 15.

A gentleman, who left Roxbury, near Bofton, on Wednefday laft, fays, that juft before he came away letters were received there from England, by a veffel in a fhort paffage to Salem, one was dated the 3d, and the other the 9th of April; both of which gave an account, that moft of the troops, which had been feveral times ordered to embark and countermanded, were, on account of the great difturbances among the people, finally ftopped.

The whole regiment of light dragoons, to a man, has refufed to come over to fight againft this country; this we have from a Gentleman who left Liverpool the 30th of March.

NEW-YORK, May 18.

In CONGRESS, *at* Philadelphia, *May* 15, 1775.

THE City and County of New-York having through Delegates applied to the Congrefs for their advice how to conduct themfelves with regard to the troops expected there, the Congrefs took the matter into their moft ferious deliberation, and came to the following refolution:

" *That it be recommended for the prefent to the inhabitants of New-York, that if the troops which are expected fhould arrive, the faid colony act on the defenfive, fo long as may be confiftent with their fafety and fecurity: That the troops may be permitted to remain in the barracks, fo long as they behave peaceably and quietly, but that they be not fuffered to erect fortifications, or take any fteps for cutting off the communication between the town and country; and that if they commit hoftilities, or invade private property, the inhabitants fhould defend themfelves, and their property, and repel force by force:——That the warlike ftores be removed from the town:——That places of retreat, in cafe of neceffity, be provided for the women and children of New-York; and a fufficient number of men be embodied, and kept in conftant readinefs for protecting the inhabitants from infult and injury.*"

A true copy from the Minutes,

CHARLES THOMPSON, Secretary.

Gentlemen,

Inclofed, we fend you the advice of the Congrefs, on the fubject on which you requefted it, and left the advice to remove the military ftores might be conftrued to extend to thofe belonging to the Crown, we think it prudent to fuggeft to you, that the contrary conftruction is the true one.

You would have received this advice before, had not fundry circumftances not material, or perhaps not proper to explain, concurred in deferring it till now.

We are, Gentlemen, Your humble fervants,

James Duane, Francis Lewis, John Jay, Lewis Morris

We hear that orders ere fent down to Scotland for the officer to fill up their regiments to the full complement of men, as foon as poffible.

A report prevails, that the King of Denmark is dangeroufly ill, fome fay dead.

Extract of a letter from PORTSMOUMH, *May 17.*

"Every floop of war and fmall veffel at this port and Plymouth is now put into commiffion, and various fervices; but we have not yet received any particular orders for large fhips, though war is talked of as ftrong here as in London."

A morning paper fays: A letter juft received from Copenhagen fays, every thing in that city is in the greateft confufion; the Queen Dowager durft not appear in public, and the King, on account of the death of the Queen, is almoft diftracted. The populace, many of whom were the Queen's enemies when living, now fay fhe was innocent, and that her death was occafioned by the falfe accufations brought againft her by the Queen Dowager's party.

There are now living in the parifh of St. Bees, Cumberland, two brothers, and three fifters, whofe ages are 71, 81, 83, 85, and 87.

CAMBRIDGE, *June 26.*

NONE of the men who have been raifed by this, and feveral other colonies, are, in future, to be diftinguifhed as the troops of any particular colony, but as the forces of *the united colonies of North America*, into whofe joint fervice they have been taken by the Continental Congrefs, and are to be paid and fupported accordingly.

We hear from Exeter, New-Hampfhire, that a committee from the Congrefs fitting there waited on the province treafurer for what money he had by him belonging to the province, and received from him 1590l. which was fafely conveyed to Exeter.

Laft monday night died of the wounds he received in the battle of the 17th ult. the amiable, the gallant Colonel Thomas Gardner, of this place.

The following is thought to contain a true account of the lofs of the enemy, including thofe who died of their wounds; taken June 29th, 1775.

Return of the killed at Charelftown the 17th of June, taken from an orderly ferjeant in Bofton.

Commiffion officers 92, ferjeants 102, corporals 100, rank and file 753, total of killed 1047; wounded, 445. Total of killed and wounded, 1492.

HARTFORD, *July 10.*

Extract of a letter from FORT GEORGE (near TICONDEROGA) *dated June 29, 1775.*

THE reports from the northward are various. It is thought, from the beft accounts, that the Canadians will be very reluctant to enter into the fervice againft the colonies, and it is

---

An intermiffion of three weeks between our two laft publications, is the reafon why the following important Refolves did not appear fooner.

AMERICAN UNITED COLONIES.

IN CONGRESS, March 23, 1776.

WHEREAS the Petitions of thefe United Colonies to the King, for the Redrefs of great and manifeft Grievances, have not only been rejected, but treated with Scorn and Contempt; and the Oppofition to Defigns evidently formed to reduce them to a State of fervile Subjection, and their neceffary Defence againft hoftile Forces actually employed to fubdue them, declared Rebellion: And Whereas an unjuft War hath been commenced againft them, which the Commanders of the Britifh Fleets and Armies have profecuted and ftill continue to profecute with their utmoft Vigour and in a cruel Manner; wafting, fpoiling and deftroying the Country, burning Houfes and defencelefs Towns, and expofing the helplefs Inhabitants to every Mifery from the Inclemency of the Winter, and not only urging Savages to invade the Country, but inftigating Negroes to murder their Mafters: And Whereas the Parliament of Great-Britain hath lately paffed an Act, affirming thefe Colonies to be in open Rebellion; forbidding all Trade and Commerce with the Inhabitants thereof, until they fhall accept Pardons and fubmit to defpotic Rule; declaring their Property, wherever found upon the Water, liable to Seizure and Confifcation; and enacting that what had been done there, by Virtue of the Royal Authority, were juft and lawful Acts, and fhall be fo deemed: From all which it is manifeft, that the iniquitous Scheme, concerted to deprive them of the Liberty they have a right to by the Laws of Nature and the English Conftitution, will be pertinacioufly purfued. It being, therefore, neceffary to provide for their Defence and Security, and otherwife to annoy to make Reprifals upon their Enemies, and according to the Laws and Ufages of Nations; the CONGRESS, trufting that fuch of their Friends in Great-Britain (of whom it is confeffed there are many intitled to Applaufe and Gratitude for their Patriotifm and Benevolence, and in whofe Favour a Difcrimination of Property cannot be made) as fhall fuffer by Captures, will impute it to the Authors of our common Calamities, DO DECLARE AND RESOLVE as followeth, *to wit* :

RESOLVED, That the Inhabitants of thefe Colonies be permitted to fit out Armed Veffels to cruife on the Enemies of thefe United Colonies.

RESOLVED, That all Ships and other Veffels, their Tackle, Apparel, and Furniture, and all Goods, Wares and Merchandizes belonging to any Inhabitant or Inhabitants of Great-Britain, taken on the high Seas, or between high and low water Mark, by any Armed Veffel fitted out by any private Perfon or Perfons to whom Commiffions fhall be granted, and being libelled and profecuted in ...

VIRGINIA GAZETTE (WILLIAMSBURG) (DIXON AND HUNTER)

July 29, 1775

In anticipation of the war's escalation, Congress established the Continental Army, or, as printed here, "the forces of *the united colonies of North America.*"

NEW-ENGLAND CHRONICLE (BOSTON)

May 2, 1776

The Second Continental Congress authorized American privateers to raid British vessels.

Lloyd's EVENING POST

Vol. XXXVII.] From MONDAY, September 4, to WEDNESDAY, September 6, 1775. [Numb. 28

Copy of the PETITION from the GENERAL CONGRESS in AMERICA to his MAJESTY, which was delivered to Lord DARTMOUTH the first of this Month, and to which, his Lordship said, no Answer would be given.

RICHARD PENN.
ARTHUR LEE.

Sept. 4, 1775.

To the KING's Most Excellent MAJESTY.

Most Gracious SOVEREIGN,

E your Majesty's faithful Subjects of the Colonies of New Hampshire, Massachusetts Bay, Rhode Island and Providence Plantations, Connecticut, New York, New Jersey, Pennsylvania, the Counties of New Castle, Kent and Sussex in Delaware, Maryland, Virginia, North and South Carolina, in Behalf of ourselves and the Inhabitants of these Colonies, who have deputed us to represent them in General Congress, entreat your Majesty's gracious Attention to this our humble Petition.

The Union between our Mother Country and these Colonies, and the Energy of mild and just Government, produced Benefits so remarkably important, and afforded such Assurance of their Permanency and Increase, that the Wonder and Envy of other Nations were excited, while they beheld Great Britain rising to a Power the most extraordinary the World had ever known. Her Rivals observing that there was no Probability of this happy Connection being broken by Civil Dissentions, and apprehending its future Effects, if left any longer undisturbed, resolved to prevent her receiving so continual and formidable an Accession of Wealth and Strength, by checking the Growth of these Settlements, from which they were to be derived.

In the Prosecution of this Attempt, Events so unfavourable to the Design took place, that every Friend to the Interest of Great Britain and these Colonies, entertained pleasing and reasonable Expectations of seeing an additional Force and Extension immediately given to the Operations of the Union hitherto experienced, by an Enlarge-

by domestic Dangers in their Judgement of a more dreadful Kind.

Nor were their Anxieties alleviated by any Tendency in this System to promote the Welfare of the Mother Country : For though its Effects were more immediately felt by them, yet its Influence appeared to be injurious to the Commerce and Prosperity of Great Britain.

We shall decline the ungrateful Task of describing the irksome Variety of Artifices practised by many of your Majesty's Ministers; the delusive Pretences, fruitless Terrors, and unavailing Severities, which have from Time to Time been dealt out by them in their Attempts to execute this impolitic Plan, or of tracing through a Series of Years past the Progress of the unhappy Differences between Great Britain and these Colonies, which have flowed from this fatal Source. Your Majesty's Ministers persevering in their Measures, and proceeding to open Hostilities for enforcing them, have compelled us to arm in our own Defence, and have engaged us in a Controversy so peculiarly abhorrent from the Affections of your still faithful Colonists, that when we consider whom we must oppose in this Contest, and if it continues, what may be the Consequence; our own particular Misfortunes are accounted by us only as Parts of our Distress.

Knowing to what violent Resentments and incurable Animosities civil Discords are apt to exasperate and in[flame]
Parties, we think ou[r in]-
dispensable Obligat[ion]
to your Majesty, t[o]
and ourselves, imm[ediate]
Means in our Power [to]
our Safety, for stop[ping the effu]-
sion of Blood, and [avert]-
ing Calamities that [threaten the Em]-
pire. Thus called [upon to address your]
Majesty on Affairs o[f Ame]-
rica, and probably [to]
we are earnestly desi[rous]
Office with the utm[ost]
Majesty; and we th[ink]
Royal Magnanimity a[nd]
make the most favou[rable construction]
of our Expressions on so uncommon an
Oc[casion]

Generations in both Countries; and to transmit your Majesty's Name to Posterity, adorned with that signal and lasting Glory that has attended the Memory of those illustrious Personages, whose Virtues and Abilities have extricated States from dangerous Convulsions, and by securing Happiness to others, have erected the most noble and durable Monuments to their own Fame.

We beg Leave further to assure your Majesty, that notwithstanding the Sufferings your loyal Colonists, during the Course the present Controversy, our Breasts retain too tender a Regard for the Kingdom from which we derive our Origin, to request such a Reconciliation, as might in any Manner be inconsistent with her dignity or her Welfare. These, related as we are to her, Honour and Duty, as well as Inclination, induce us support and advance; and the Apprehension that now oppress our Hearts, with unspeakable Grief, being once removed, your Majesty will find your faithful Subjects, on the Continent, ready and willing, at all Times as they have ever been, with their Lives and Fortunes, to assert and maintain the Rights Interests of your Majesty and of our Mother Country.

We therefore beseech your Majesty, that your Royal Authority and Influence may graciously interposed, to procure us Relief from our afflicting Fears and Jealousies occasioned by the System before mentioned

LLOYD'S EVENING POST (LONDON)

September 6, 1775

—

The Olive Branch Petition, adopted by the Second Continental Congress on July 8, took almost two months to reach London. Letters to the editor and advertisements for *Lloyd's Evening Post* were received at Lloyd's Coffee Shop, located above the Royal Exchange, which was a prominent interchange of port news, and its reports often fed other London newspapers.

to a greater Distance.
At the Conclusion, therefore, of the late

the Sentiments which agitate the Minds of us, your dutiful Subjects, we are persuaded your Majesty would ascribe any seeming

your American People, we are convinced your Majesty would receive such satisfactory that the wished-for Opportunity would be restored to them, of evincing the Sincerity of their Professions by every Testimony

CAPTURE OF
FORT TICONDEROGA

By William P. Tatum III

O N MAY 10, 1775, AMERICAN FORCES STRUCK THE first of a series of blows that nearly unraveled British control of Canada by seizing Fort Ticonderoga. Built by the French in 1756, Ticonderoga had been the focus of two major battles in 1758 and 1759. After the conclusion of the French and Indian War, the fort acted as a secure storage facility for cannons and other military stores. By 1775, it was a sleepy backwater located well within the defensive perimeter of Britain's North American holdings.

In the spring of 1775, Fort Ticonderoga became the focus of several competing American expeditions. Connecticut, Massachusetts, and the contested Hampshire Grants (modern Vermont) sought to seize the fort for themselves. Massachusetts retained the services of Benedict Arnold, a native of Connecticut, who proceeded west from the siege of Boston in early May to raise militia volunteers for an attack on the fort. Ethan Allen, leader of the frontier force known as "The Green Mountain Boys," was making preparations for his own assault on Ticonderoga to secure territorial claims for Vermont. The two officers met at a council of war in Castleton, where Arnold was appointed the titular head of the force, though the majority of the soldiers owed their allegiance to Allen.

By the evening of May 9, 1775 (a day earlier than what was noted in the *Pennsylvania Gazette* article of May 24, 1775), the Arnold-Allen expedition was assembled across Lake Champlain from the fort. A scarcity of boats delayed the crossing until the early hours of May 10 and forced the Americans to send several detachments over instead of advancing en masse. As the *Pennsylvania Gazette* reported, Allen and Arnold rushed the fort with only a handful of soldiers, which nevertheless outnumbered the oblivious British garrison. Ignorant of the events at Lexington and

Concord, as well as of the larger American rebellion, the British forces were quickly overwhelmed, with many of the soldiers and their officers captured while still asleep in their barracks. While no one was killed in the engagement, Allen's undisciplined troops immediately set to looting the garrison, an act that led to their eventual dismissal. Allen eventually sent the British troops to Connecticut as a gift to Governor John Trumbull.

The capture of Fort Ticonderoga had a number of short- and long-term effects on the course of the American Revolution. As noted in the article, the fort contained large amounts of military stores, particularly cannons, which played a crucial role in supplying American forces. Henry Knox transported several of the larger cannons to Boston, where they were employed in the final stages of the siege. Its capture by American forces also returned Fort Ticonderoga to its former glory as a vital frontier post. In August 1775, Continental General Richard Montgomery launched his invasion of Quebec from the fort. His expedition quickly rolled up a string of British border posts, captured Montreal, and laid siege to Quebec City, where the campaign stalled and ultimately collapsed in early 1776. In the summer and autumn of the same year, the fort became the front line of American defenses against a British invasion from Canada, as well as the base of Benedict Arnold's American fleet on Lake Champlain. Ticonderoga's formidable appearance played a vital role in British General Guy Carleton's decision not to continue his attacks after the Battle of Valcour Island in October. While captured by British troops under General John Burgoyne the following year, the fort quickly fell back into American hands following the British surrender at Saratoga, serving out the remainder of the war as a relatively quiet American base.

John Lawrence, arrived here from Falmouth, in 6 weeks; by him we learn, that all the acts depending in Parliament, relative to American affairs, had received the Royal assent; and that the packet for this port was to sail the day after him.

PHILADELPHIA, May 24.

On Wednesday evening last arrived here, John Brown, Esq; from Ticonderoga, express to the General Congress, from whom we learn, that on the beginning of this instant, a company of about fifty men, from Connecticut, and the western part of Massachusetts, and joined by upwards of one hundred from Bennington, *in New-York government*, and the adjacent towns, proceeded to the eastern side of Lake Champlain, and on the night before the 11th current, crossed the Lake with 85 men (not being able to obtain craft to transport the rest) and about day-break invested the fort, whose gate, contrary to expectation, they found shut, but the wicker open, through which, with the Indian war whoop, all that could, entered one by one, others scaling the wall on both sides of the gate, and instantly secured and disarmed the centries, and pressed into the parade, where they formed the hollow square; but immediately quitting that order, they rushed into the several barracks on three sides of the fort, and seized on the garrison, consisting of two officers, and upwards of forty privates,* whom they brought out, disarmed, put under guard, and have since sent prisoners to Hartford, in Connecticut. All this was performed in about ten minutes, without the loss of a life, or a drop of blood on our side, or but very little on that of the King's troops.

In the fort were found about thirty barrels of flour, a few barrels of pork, seventy odd chests of leaden ball, computed at three hundred tons, about ten barrels of powder in bad condition, near two hundred pieces of ordnance of all sizes, from eighteen pounders downwards, at Ticonderoga and Crown-point, which last place, being held only by a corporal and eight men, falls of course into our hands.

By this sudden expedition, planned by some principal persons in the four neighbouring colonies, that important pass is now in the hands of the Americans, where we trust the *wisdom* of the Grand Continental Congress, will take effectual measures to secure it, as it may be depended on that administration means to form an army in Canada, composed of British regulars, French and Indians, to attack the colonies on that side.

Mr. Brown brought intercepted letters from Lieut. Malcom Fraser, to his friends in New-England, from which appear, that Gen. Carleton has almost unlimited powers, civil and military, and has issued orders for raising a Canadian regiment, in which Mr. Fraser observes, the officers find difficulty, as the common people are by no means fond of the service. He likewise remarks, that all the King's European subjects are disaffected at the partial preference given to the late converts to loyalty, as he phrases it, to their utter exclusion from all confidence, or even common civility. Matters are indeed in such a situation, that many, if not most of the merchants talk of leaving the province.

Mr. Brown also relates, that two regular officers of the 26th regiment, now in Canada, applied to two Indians, one a head warrior of the Caughanawaga tribe,

College of [Phila]delphia, May 17, 1775.

THIS day the public Commencement for Graduates in the Arts was held here, in the presence of the most illustrious assembly this Seminary ever beheld.

About half an hour after nine o'clock, agreeable to an invitation previously given to them, the Honorable Members of the CONTINENTAL CONGRESS were pleased to proceed in a body from the State-House to the College, where they were received at the gate by the Provost, and conducted to the places prepared for their reception in the Hall. As soon as they were seated, the *Trustees*, with the Governor as President at their head, followed by the Provost, Vice-provost, Professors, Graduates and other Students, in their proper habits, entered the Hall, and took their places, the Galleries and other parts of the house being filled with as many of the respectable inhabitants of the city as could find room. The business then proceeded in the following ORDER, viz.

1. Part of the Church Service, and an occasional Prayer, by the Provost.
2. An Anthem, accompanied with the organ and other instrumental music.
3. Latin Salutatory Oration, de Amicitia, by Henry Ridgely.
4. On the *Education of young Ladies*, by Francis Brown Sappington.
5. Latin Syllogistic Dispute, Utrum detur Sensus Moralis? Respondent, William Moore Smith; Opponents, Benjamin Chew and John Mifflin.
6. On *Ancient Eloquence*, by Thomas Ennals.
7. On *Politeness*, by John Mifflin.
8. On the *Fall of Empires*, by William Moore Smith.
9. The degrees were then conferred as follows, viz.

BACHELORS OF ARTS.
Benjamin Chew, *Townsend Eden, *Thomas Ennals, John Farrel, John Mifflin, *Henry Ridgely, *Francis Brown Sappington, and William Moore Smith.

MASTERS OF ARTS.
Samuel Armor, John Park and John Thomas. Honorary Master of Arts, James Ross.

10. A Dialogue and two Odes set to music. The speakers in the Dialogue were John Farrel, F. B. Sappington, and W. M. Smith.
11. Valedictory Oration, by B. Chew.
12. CHARGE to the Graduates, by the Provost.
13. *Concluding Prayer* [...]

[...] nature, are herewith communicated.
* The young Gentlemen who [...]

A Hea[...]
She [...]
hereof.

WA[...]
a [...]
he now li[...]
reading, the[...]
and several [...]
geometry, [...]
practice in [...]
war; which [...]
any of his [...]
him. He w[...]
the first of [...]
will be forw[...]

WHE[...]
my [...]
Presbyterians[...]
went to relea[...]
public manner[...]
the propagator[...]
malicious a sla[...]
to my hurt. [...]
approved the [...]
just rights and [...]
the capacities [...]
the risque of r[...]
assert the cause [...]
gress and Comm[...]
or inadvertently [...]
report.

N. B. I am [...]
further satisfac[...]
report, and my [...]
should not prove[...]

THIS is [...]
HEES, p[...]
ton, that they [...]
Esq; and the H[...]
Supreme Court [...]
Perth-Amboy, [...]
shew cause (if a[...]
discharged [...]

[...] and farther on said course [...] the Indians at Cohass, where they at length arrived [...] the Indians say they were [...]

[*To be concluded in our next.*]

one named Eben[...]
sandy complexion[...]
round the edges [...]
breeches, &c. St[...]
which it is in [...]

BY THE END OF MAY 1775, THE AMERICAN ARMY SURrounding Boston was feeling pretty good about itself—and they had reason. On April 19, they had battered the redcoats at Lexington and Concord, chased them into Boston, and cut off all interaction with the countryside. Confidence was not so high, however, that anyone wanted to launch a frontal assault on Boston, so the Americans contented themselves with depriving the British of food, hay, straw, and firewood. The two articles shown here, one from the *New-York Journal* and the other from the *New-England Chronicle*, describe the Battle of Noddle's Island, the sharpest fight between American and British forces to take place between Lexington and Concord and the Battle of Bunker Hill. It was a fight for sheep and hay.

Noddle's and Hog Islands, a chief source for hay and grazing land, sat just across the mouth of the Charles and Mystic rivers from Boston. Today, they are a great jumble of urban sprawl, but in 1775, they were just humps of pasture, home to hundreds of sheep, hayfields, and a few houses.

The two newspaper articles describe, with varying degrees of accuracy, two different parts of the same battle. In the predawn hours of May 27, 1775, about six hundred American troops splashed across the narrow river that separated Hog Island from the shore. For most of the morning, they drove livestock from the islands unseen by the British. It was only in the afternoon, when they set fire to the hayfields, that the redcoats took notice.

The British landed marines and some field artillery on the island and tried to flank the American troops by boat. Oddly, neither article mentions the fighting that took place on shore, perhaps because the most dramatic fighting took place on the water. The sloop mentioned in the *New-England Chronicle*'s article is no doubt the *Britannia*, which was mauled by American small arms and artillery. Worse off was the schooner *Diana*, featured prominently in both articles. *Diana* found herself caught between Noddle's Island and the mainland with no wind and a falling tide. Once aground, she was pounded into a near wreck by men under the command of Israel Putnam, abandoned by the British, and burned the next morning by the Yankees.

The *New-York Journal* article is quite accurate in its description of events, insofar as it closely matches other accounts and official reports of the action. In both cases, the American victory is greatly exaggerated. It is unlikely the British were as frightened as the *New-England Chronicle* suggests, and the claim that the British "killed and wounded exceed 300" is way off the mark. The British had two men who died; the Americans, none. It was only a few weeks after this that the British and the Americans would get a taste of how formidable their enemies really were on the slopes of nearby Bunker Hill.

virtuous Attendants assembled above) in Consequence of which, Application was made (by him) for the Keys, belonging to the same ; but not being able through Impatience to obtain them, a Bayonet, together with his ferocious Countenance, and a Centry penetrated these otherwise impregnable Vaults, and gave to a most thorough Examination of their Contents ; overturning and re-overturning all that could conceal Combustibles, without discovering any Thing capable of taking on Fire, except a few empty Powdering-Tubs, or Fawks's except an half famished Rat or two, the mighty nation began to subside, and the Gentry aloft to enter full the important business of the day. Whether the same tremor took possession of the troops (posted in Kingstreet on the occasion) as of their Masters, we cannot precisely inform our Readers ; but this is certain, no sooner was the word Present given, than a most hideous and irregular popping was heard thro' their whole Ranks, which sounded neither like Gun, Drum, Trumpet, Blunderbuss or Thunder. This frightful Noise, was once or twice heard to the no small Astonishment of many Eye and Ear Witnesses to the whole.

CAMBRIDGE, June 15.

Extract of a Letter from Falmouth, Casco-Bay, dated June 4, 1775.

"Capt. ——, (who on his Passage to New-York from this Place with a Load of Spars, was lately seized by Admiral Greaves and carried into Boston) returned here last Thursday Evening.—— He says he was at the Wharf at Noddle's-Island when the Battle began, and has given us a particular Account of the same. He says the Sloop near Winnisimmit, that had the first Brush, cut or slipped her Cables, and came and fastened to his Stern : He was shocked to see the Blood running out of the Scuppers ; there was a Number of Dead and Wounded lying on the Deck, but the Survivors did not care to tell how many. The Diana Schooner next engaged, and the Master of her told Capt. ——, that Guns never were better served than ours were, that not a Shot missed him.—— I have not Time to write you all he says : One Man was carried on board for dead, but next Morning came too, and had not the least Wound about him ; others were frighted almost to Death, &c. and that there was an amazing Difference in the Looks and Behaviour of the Enemy after the Battle, from what there was before ; before there was nothing but Noise and Confusion, afterwards all were still and quiet, insomuch that you could hardly perceive that there was any Fleet or Army there. From the General down to the common Soldier, they seemed to be in a great Panic, were afraid to go to Bed, for fear the Yankees should kill them before Morning."

In one of our late Papers, a Captain of the Militia was said to be killed, in the Battle at Concord, by our own People, owing to their firing at too great a Distance. We are since well assured, by a Person who was very near him at the Time, that the said Captain was killed by the Regulars, before a Gun was discharged on our Side. However, as Accidents of that Kind may happen, it is hoped the Caution against firing at too great Distance, in any future Engagement, will be duly observed.

Last Tuesday a Soldier belonging to the New-Hampshire Troops, bathing in Mistick River, was unfortunately drowned.

The patriotic Ladies of the Town of Concord are desired to accept the unfeigned Thanks of the Publick for their Care and Kindness in collecting and sending to the Hospital a Chest of old linen Rags, &c. This Instance of their Humanity and publick Spirit does Honour to the Town, and will we hope induce others to imitate so good an Example.

THE Printers of this Paper request their Customers at Salem and Marblehead to pay the Amount of their respective Accounts to Mr. JOSEPH HILLER, of Salem, Watchmaker.

[...] thority, Post-Rider from CAMBRIDGE to EXETER ; and that he is under Oath for the faithful Performance of his Trust. He sets out from the Post-Office here every Thursday, and returns the Saturday following. All Persons who may please to [...] Month, unless for those Persons who shall signify, either to himself or the Printers, their Willingness to pay the Postage, agreeable to the above Prices.

In Provincial Congress, at the City of New-York,
May 25, 1775.

WHEREAS the Enemies of American Liberty are indefatigable in their Endeavours to disunite these Colonies ; and in prosecuting of this Measure, evil minded Persons may insinuate that the northern Colonies have hostile intentions against our Fellow-Subjects in Canada.

Resolved, That this Congress do most earnestly recommend it to all Persons, whatsoever, not to commit any Hostilities against the People of that Country, and do hereby declare to the World, that we do consider every such Step as infamous and highly inimical to all the Colonies.

Ordered, That the above Resolution be published.
A true Copy from the Minutes,
ROBERT BENSON, Secretary.

---

**(left margin column)**

om St. Kitts, ad-
e news of the en-
ected in much the
s of St. Eustatia.
iladelphia, at their
d the last Thursday
ongregations under
Prayer on account
e Affairs. Should
ast, the Synod have
ference to the Day
it is not more than
ursday of June ;—
ordered both Days

e Congregations in
n of the last Thurs-
er, during the Con-

June 5.
phia, of a late date.
talians, consisting of
ade such rapid pro-
e able to go through
reat ease and quick-
ndered at, when we
they have been un-
day not always ex
large company well
mpany of about 100
ear, have one extra-
mission of every man
fers to enroll himself
her he can hit a cir-
imes out of 6, at the
ot, he is put by until.
What will not a
ed? Every county
ir forces."
don, 1756, entitled
et in the Mediterra-
a letter to a member
hor, speaking of the
ss of the lives an
d army, has this re
r Peter Warren re
Breton he happened
of land and Sea offi-

NEW-YORK JOURNAL

June 15, 1775

—

The two articles printed in the *New-England Chronicle* and *New-York Journal* describe the Battle of Noddle's Island, the sharpest fight between American and British forces to take place between Lexington and Concord and the Battle of Bunker Hill. It was a fight for sheep and hay.

who have since marched the important fortresses d Crown-Point.

4th regiment of troops, ay of Connecticut, under ol. Hinman, marched for conderoga.

returned from the east-n Goddard, who has been oliciting the establishment constitutional principles, last succeeded, the mat-aken up by the Commit-Congresses, or Assemblies, New Hampshire, Massa-de Island, and Connecti-hich, offices, post masters, f postage are established, fore the Continental Con-approved, or altered as pedient—It is hoped this, ernments, will come into the rates of postage have before. In our next, it is particular account of this

May last, the new Provin-e Massachusetts Bay, met fore whom the Rev. Dr. nt of the College, preach-adapted to the occasion, in Isaiah i. 26. "And I udges as at the first, and at the beginning: after-called, the city of righte-al city.

Association, until two vessels shall arrive from London with goods into this Colony, after a general importation from Great Britain to

obert y are rcial o'the

ry d 5th

and Cus-

worth of goods, to be shipped on board his Majesty's April Packet as baggage.—I now give you a hint that seven persons from America are in Scotland, ordering goods in the ship Lilly, Capt. Thomas Cochran, from Greenock; as he does not sail before the tenth of April, you will receive this first. Capt. Cochran sails for New-York, and not for Philadelphia."

In consequence of the above letter having been published in one of the Philadelphia papers, a sub-committee was appointed to wait on Captain Cochran, who declared that Messrs. George and John Buchanan, owners of the ship Lilly, had been so par-ticularly careful to prevent any goods being ship'd on board said ship; that they gave strict orders to Capt. Cochran, that no trunks, chests, or packages should be shipp'd without strict examination: And Captain Cochran further declared, he was ready to make oath, that no goods, wares, or mer-chandize was shipp'd on board said ship to his knowledge.

ON the 13th day of June, 1775, perso-nally appeared before me David Mat-thews, Esq; Alderman, of the East Ward, in the city of New York, Thomas Cockran, commander of the ship Lilly, who being duly sworn on the holy evangelists of al-mighty God; deposeth and faith, that ha-ving seen the above extract of a letter rela-tive to goods being ordered to be shipped in the ship Lilly, whereof he is master, published in one of the Philadelphia news papers; the same is false and groundless: That not

which were from officers of the army at Boston. That those letters in general are full of complaints and expressions of uneasi ness. Some of the officers desire and entreat to sell out, others say they are fighting in a bad cause, and apprehensive of a mutiny, others mention a difference between the Ge-neral and the Admiral, and that the army in general are disheartened and uneasy; other letters are full of invectives against the poor *Yankees*, as they call us ——— We hear the Provincial Congress will keep Temple as an hostage, but I hope they will let the vessel go, with the above letters."

We hear a man of war is stationed off Portsmouth, has taken two vessels laden with provisions, and has orders to take all such, and all that have West India goods on board, &c.

We hear that on Sunday last, the house of William Bayard, Esq; at Greenwich was struck with lightning, when several looking glasses were shattered, other furniture da-maged, and a Negro woman hurt, but not dangerously. It is supposed the lightning was conducted into every room in the house by the means of a bell wire.

The following Extract of a letter, dated the first of June instant, in the Provincial Camp, at Cambridge from a gentleman of undoubted veracity and intelligence, gives a more authentic, and in many respects, a more particular account of the late action at Noddle's and Hog-Islands, than any that has appeared in the public papers, and therefore will doubtless be acceptable to the reader.

"When our people were engaged in ta-king the stock, &c. from Noddle's and Hog-Islands, the king's troops made an attack upon them. On Hog Island, the combat began about 5 o'clock in the afternoon, and continued almost incessantly till midnight. The attack was made with cannon, swivels and small arms, from an armed schooner, sloop, and eight or ten barges, upon our people, who had small arms only, but were very advantageously posted by Colonel Putnam who got to them just in season to station and command them properly. He placed them in a ditch, up to their waists in water, and covered by the bank, to their

town, ceeding ha not a sing some of the cause, dec them in th

"An in but as we cers, we fe

Last Mo litary store the King's ried clear

Yesterda had been under Gen was taken a party of Provincial was examin We hear t made.

On Tu an exchang tween the was manag part, and t [*Want of many in*

perated the people, that
...eft in the province, and
...gotted, have quitted the
...r the people, and join
...spirited measures, &c."
...expedition was on foot,
...ived no news of its suc-
...miscarried."

...ning a quantity of mi-
...ken from what are called
...t Turtle Bay, and car-

...Donald, who it is said
...inlisting men to serve
...against their country,
...ody, and conducted by
...Grenadiers, before the
...the fitting, where he
...returned in custody.—
...rtant discoveries were

...6th instant there was
...ners at Cambridge, be-
...and Regulars, which
...en, Putnam on the one
...oncrief on the other.
...revents the publication of
...articles.]

E LET,
...f a genteel house, neatly
...the Coffee-House.—
...er.   93—

...who is in every
..., offers his service to any
...entlemen in the country, to
...youth; and instruct them,
...methods, in every essential
...nglish education.
...e most satisfactory testimo-
...moral character, a genteel

...otherwise, to G. D. at the
...   93 6

...h Castle, May the 25, 1775.
...ing now in actual confine-
...ouse, do hereby notify my
...ion to present a petition to
...of this colony, at their next
...t of an insolvent act; and
...y debts, agreeable to what
...ed to make in my favour.
...ICHABOD OGDEN:

ship Lilly, on her last arrival here,
...deponent's knowledge, or belief:
...e owners of said ship gave strict or-
...hat no trunks, bales, or packages
...put on board the said ship, with-
...examination; and that if any came
...containing merchandize, they
...e relanded, which orders were
...omplied with, and further saith not.
      Thomas Cochran.
...his 13th day of June, 1775,
...me David Matthews.

...lford, Litchfield County, Connecti-
...cut, May 29th, 1775.
...OLT.
...insert the following in your next
...and you will serve the public in
..., and oblige many of your constant
...ers in particular.
...Committee of observation, for said
...w Milford, having duly notified
...Ferriss, Joseph Ferriss, jun.
...borne, Daniel Taylor, Nathaniel
...Hezekiah Stevens jun. all of said
...ord, to appear before said Com-
...day, to give reason, if any they
...hey, and each of them, should
...rtified, as FOES to the rights of
...erica, and said Zechariah Ferriss,
...ss, jun James Osborne, Daniel
...Hezekiah Stevens, jun. having
...appear, and to give any satis-
...said Committee; and said Na-
...lor having appeared, and decla-
...osition to the doings of the Con-
...ongress, and said Committee
...deliberated upon, and finding
...aforenamed persons obstinately
...eir opposition to the doings of
...fs, and the (now bleeding) cause
...thinks itself in duty bound, to
...blication, that each of said per-
...universally neglected, and treat-
...igible enemies to the rights of
...rica, according to the eleventh
...he association, entered into by
...ls.
...of the Committee,
...UEL CANFIELD, Com. Cle.

...above, have made
...tion, and signed a compliance in

necks: The schooner, sloop and boats fu
...of men, came within 12 or 15 rods of them,
...and gave our people a fine opportunity to
...place their shot well. About midnight the
...fire ceased a little, and our people retreated
...to the main land, where they were soon after
...joined by Capt Foster with two field pieces,
...which were planted on the way of Winne-
...simit ferry. At day light the combat was re-
...newed,—as the schooner passed the ferry way,
...she was briskly attacked by our people, with
...the field pieces and small arms; which soon
...clearing her deck, she drifted on shore,
...where our people set fire to her, and she
...blew up, notwithstanding the utmost endea-
...vours of the people in the boats, &c. to tow
...her off, and save her from destruction.—In
...this they exposed themselves much to our fire,
...and suffered greatly. When they found the
...schooner was lost, they with difficulty tow-
...ed off the sloop, much disabled, and retired
...to their den; and thus ended the combat,
...at about 7 o'clock in the morning. In the
...afternoon, (Sunday) our people got out of
...the wreck, 12 four pounders, 6 swivels, and
...every thing else that was valuable, without
...molestation; they afterwards removed or
...destroyed from both the Islands, all the
...stock, &c. viz. about 5 or 600 sheep, 30
...horses, about as many cattle, a large quan-
...tity of hay, and burned all the barns and
...houses."

"All this was done in fight, and as we
...may say, under the noses of the whole fleet
...and army at Boston, without molestation.—
...The killed of the enemy (viz. Gen. Gage's
...crew of enemies to the English constitution)
...they themselves allow to be more than 100,
...besides wounded; others who have good
...opportunity to know, say, their killed and
...wounded, exceed 300, and I believe they
...have suffered as much as in their precipitate
...flight from Lexington, on the memorable
...19th of April." Our killed, none! wound-
...ed, three! "Heaven apparently, and most
...evidently fights for us; covers our heads in
...the day of battle, and shields our people
...from the assaults of our common enemies.—
...What thanks can speak our gratitude."

"These interpositions, and our determi-
...ned resolutions, may perhaps

...treat, in some distant quarter of the globe;
...and leave us peaceably

SURROUNDED BY AN INCREASING NUMBER OF COLONISTS coalescing into an army, the British in Boston welcomed the mid-June arrival of two thousand reinforcements that would allow them to conduct offensive operations. Situated on a peninsula that projected into the harbor like a leaf from a tree, Boston was flanked by two other peninsular hills that would threaten the town if not secured. General Thomas Gage intended to occupy Bunker Hill to the north, then Dorchester Heights to the south, starting June 18. But British plans had a way of instantly reaching American ears, and the nascent colonial army made the bold stroke of seizing Bunker Hill during the night of June 16, 1775, building a redoubt on the summit, fortifying a rail fence that led down the slope on one side, and securing the town of Charlestown on the other side. Separated from Boston by a quarter-mile of water, these hastily built fieldworks were an affront that the British army could not allow to stand.

News of the first major battle in a new and unintended war spread quickly throughout America and to England.

The ensuing battle is well known: the early morning discovery by British warships, rapidly assembled British boats landing troops at the hill's base, a failed attempt by British light infantry to outflank the rail fence, the British grenadiers' frontal assault bogged down by terrain obstacles and murderous musketry, harassing American shots from Charlestown silenced by incendiary mortar shells that burned the town to ashes, and a final columnar assault on the redoubt's weak right corner that carried it at bayonet point, resulting in carnage among the defenders. All of this is well chronicled in numerous histories and continued modern scholarship.

News of the first major battle in a new and unintended war spread quickly throughout America and to England, but none of the news bearers had the clear and detailed understanding of events that we have today. The battle dominated colonial newspapers in late June and early July; by August, accounts began to appear in the British press. As such, it provides an excellent case study of how news traveled and the challenges readers faced in understanding events based on accounts that were partial in terms of completeness and perspective. Newspapers published what information they could obtain from letters and travelers, with no means of verification.

Supporters of both sides viewed the epic fight as a victory. The June 29, 1775, *Pennsylvania Evening Post* carried news from a person who arrived outside of Boston while the battle was in progress. The spirited writer overstates by a factor of two the number of regulars engaged while indicating only a quarter of the actual colonial force; considering that he was in the American camp, it is interesting that his estimate of British casualties is quite accurate while he understates American losses. Two famous fatalities are singled out: Major Pitcairn of the British Marines, known for his role on April 19, and Joseph Warren, the doctor-cum-soldier-statesman whose death in the redoubt made him a battlefield hero. The same day's *New-England Chronicle* was informed by an escapee from Boston and included a eulogy to America's new hero. Surely the British army would hesitate to face such staunch opponents again.

The Edinburgh Advertiser of August 1, 1775, broke the news with General Gage's official report on the front page and four further pages of extracts from letters by witnesses and participants. Their military terminology gives credibility to the accounts, with talk of fascines and gabions (bundles of saplings and brush used to reinforce fortifications), light infantry and grenadiers (specialized troops detached from their regiments and formed together to lead the assault), battalions (the main portion of a regiment), carcasses (incendiary shells thrown by mortars), and three-, six-, and twelve-pounders (cannons defined by the weight of iron ball they fired). They emphasize the courage of outnumbered troops who stormed a fortified position in spite of fearsome casualties. Surely the rebellious colonists would hesitate to face such determined professionals again.

A remarkable piece of journalism appeared in Dixon and Hunter's *Virginia Gazette* on August 26, 1775. The illustrations that dotted newspapers of the era were mostly generic images complementing advertisements or decorative nameplates similar to the one atop the front page of the *Gazette*. Skilled hands could typeset text quickly, but it was not feasible to illustrate a current event because of the time required to prepare a printing block. However, based on an eyewitness description, the Virginia publishers ingeniously and quite accurately rendered a schematic diagram of the battlefield of Breed's Hill using only standard typesetting components. This is the only known newspaper illustration of a current event during the entire American Revolution and the only illustration in any period source—newspaper, book, magazine, or other—to use this diagrammatic technique.

BATTLE OF BUNKER HILL
George E. Ellis,
U.S. Army Images

An illustrated map of the battleground on Charlestown peninsula, encompassing Bunker and Breed's Hills.

Lord Dunmore's *answer to the address of the* House of Burgesses *of* Virginia. (*See page* 259.)

IT is with real concern I can discover nothing in your address that I think manifests the smallest inclination to, or will be productive of, a reconciliation with the mother country.

PHILADELPHIA, June 29.

Extract of a letter from Watertown, dated June 21.

"I arrived at this spot on Saturday last in good health, though much exhausted with a rapid and lengthy journey in so warm a season. The thunder of cannon reached my ears some miles before I got here; the army of Britain had sallied out, and were then engaging our people, who had attempted a lodgment on Bunker's Hill; the line of battle ships, one frigate, the batteries from Boston, a number of floating batteries, and the musquetry of 5000 British troops were discharging incessant torrents of shot, for the space of six hours on about 1200 Americans, without any artillery except three three-pounders. And what renders the matter more remarkable, the regulars were twice repulsed with excessive slaughter, and finally gained the lines with the loss of seventy officers killed and wounded, and 1000 men. Our men have entrenched on an eminence in Charlestown, about three quarters of a mile from the enemies encampment. We have lost sixty men, and upwards of an hundred wounded. Our troops are in high spirits, and eagerly wish for another trial. We have met with one capital loss; our worthy friend Doctor Warren was slain in the trenches, bravely struggling for the liberties of his country. We have lost a few brave officers. On the part of the British troops Major Pitcairn, and a number of capital officers are among the dead."

Extract of a letter from a Gentleman at Stockbridge (Massachusetts-Bay) to a Gentleman of the Congress, dated June 22.

"A firm foundation now turns up to view, for the influence of the Stockbridge Indians amongst the SIX NATIONS, and matters stand well with the Canadian Indians. If I had time, I would relate to you every particular of what befel the messengers of our Indians to the Six Nations and the Canadian Indians. To be short, they were taken and bound by the regulars, and carried into Montreal, where, by a court

have taken Mr. Gibbs's brig, with a load of flour from [Phi]ladelphia, and have taken her cargo on board for fear [it] should be retaken."

COMMITTEE CHAMBER, *June* 26, 17[ ]

A quantity of salt and a box of wine glasses having [been] imported in the ship Albion, Thomas Crippen, master, [from] Liverpool, it was resolved, that the said ship and cargo o[ught] to be returned forthwith, and that the Captain have n[otice] thereof immediately.

Ordered, That the District Committee see the above [reso]lution complied with.

On Motion, Resolved, That Mr. Joseph Whittall, [one] of the owners of the ship Albion, does not appear to h[ave] had any knowledge of or concern in the shipping the salt, [&c.] in said vessel.

Resolved, That Mr. Henry Cour, merchant, of Liver[pool] in Great-Britain, half owner of the ship Albion, has kn[ow]ingly violated the Association of the American Congress, [by] shipping the salt to America; and that it is the duty of [this] Committee to advertise him accordingly.

Resolved, That Nicholas Ashton, Esq; of or near Live[r]pool, in the county of Lancaster, in Great-Britain, owner [of] the abovementioned salt, has wilfully violated the Associat[ion] of the American Congress by shipping the said salt to A[me]rica, and that it is the duty of this Committee to adver[tise] his conduct herein.

Resolved unanimously, That, agreeable to the resolutions [of] the Grand American Congress, it is the duty of us and of [all] our constituents the inhabitants of the City and Liberties [of] Philadelphia, *from henceforth not to have any commercial int[er]course whatsoever* with the said Henry Cour and Nicholas A[sh]ton: And it is recommended that an inviolable regard [be] paid to this resolution.

Extract from the minutes.

J. B. SMITH, Secretary.

☞ Genteel BOARDING and LODGINGS to be had [in] a public Part of the City, on reasonable Terms. Inquire [of] the Printer.

Just PUBLISHED (Price 1s. 6d.)

By Robert Bell and Benjamin Towne,

THE CHRONICLE OF THE KINGS OF ENG[-]LAND, from the Reign of William the Conquer[or,] first King of England, down to his present Majesty Georg[e] III. containing a true History of their Lives, and the Chara[c]ter which they severally sustained, whether in Church a[nd] State, in the Field, or in private Life.

This Book, though published under the fictitious Title [of] Nathan Ben-Saddi, was wrote by the ingenious Author of th[e] ECONOMY of HUMAN LIFE, and has gone through a[l]most every Press in Europe.

offered us money to fight for you, but we would not take it, as

hang these our brothers, that came a great way to see us, do it, but remember we shall not forget it. Upon these threatenings

TO BE SOLD BY HENRY DROUGHERTY, at [his] GROCERY STORE at Cuthbert's Wharf, next [to] Willing and Morris's

the magazine, who have placed a guard...
concerted for its better security.

NEW-YORK, June 22.

Extract of a letter from London, dated April 25, 1775.

"A steady friend to America called upon me this afternoon, to acquaint me with the following intelligence, communicated to him by ------ this day, which you may rely upon as a fact. The ------ said that Administration on Friday received advices from General Gage, to the 18th of March, where he acknowledges the receipt of the King's order to apprehend Messrs. Cushing, Adams, Hancock, &c. and send them over to England to be tried; but that the second orders, which were to hang them in Boston, he said the General had not then received. The General expressed his fears on the occasion, and in hopes of their being reversed he should delay the execution a while longer; because he must, if the orders were fulfilled, come to an engagement,---the event of which, he had every reason to apprehend would be fatal to himself, and the King's troops; as the Massachusetts Government had at least 15,000 men, ready trained for the onset,---and besides, had every public and private road occupied by the militia, so as to prevent his marching into the country, and which were at the same time ready to facilitate any attempt against the army: On which unwelcome situation he earnestly wished for a reinforcement, if that disagreeable order must be effected. The General also wrote that the standard was hoisted by the people at Salem, and multitudes flocked to it, which would not be the case should the royal standard be erected---added, that he now believed America would carry their point---That many of the Administration were of the same mind, and sincerely wished they had pursued more gentle measures with the Colonies.------ He said Lord North was evidently uneasy, and that Government dreaded the news by the April packet---that they suppressed this intelligence from General Gage, because of the instant effect it would have on the stocks. He acknowledged the nation was ready for a revolution, if any enterprising genius would step forth, and which would certainly be the case, if blood was ever drawn in America. He blames Hutchinson much, and says Administration charges him with duplicity, in telling them they ought to have been more active, and that they would have made the Massachusetts submit. To others, that Administration had gone much further than he advised: Be this as it may, he added that the King consults him, places a confidence in what he says, and has actually fixed his salary at 2000l. per annum *for life*, which had much chagrined some of the Administration, who ardently wished him given up, as a sacrifice to both countries. My intelligencer wishes, if this letter should be published, that ------ name might be omitted as the information was confidential. I shall only add, that my country may be free if she will; and that she may have the virtue to play the man, is the aspiration of Sir, your most obedient servant."

Extract of a letter from St. John's, Newfoundland, May 30th, 1775, to his friend in this city.

"Here we are starving for bread and flour, and no hopes of redress,---and the ports in America being shut up, we are at a loss what to do."

A Gentleman that come in the Coach from Philadelphia, last Saturday Evening, informs us, That a Letter had been just received there from Virginia, acquainting them, That his Excellency Lord Dunmore, with all his Family had retired on board a Man of War in Consequence of some Guns that were fixed in such a Position in the Provincial Magazine there, that as soon as the Door was opened several went off, and wounded three Men.

Yesterday, we hear General Haldiman, who, it is reported, is recalled to England,

---

our Men were killed, and we wounded...
Mr. Robert Avery, of Norwich, in Connecticut, who was on board the Tender, a Prisoner, was unhappily killed...

CA...
Generals W... from the Sou...
Writs are i... tinental Cong... Watertown u...
The Gene... met at Portsm... Day to the 1...
A Man of... the Time of... from Admira... took the Opp... rived there t... Day of the Battl... brought over in Boats, to the Amount of at least 500; that 36 of them died before they arrived at the Hospital; that 84 Officers were killed and wounded, 3 of which were Field Officers; and that the whole of the Killed and Wounded amounted to 13 or 1400.

Various other Accounts confirm Mr. King's Intelligence, and give us great Reason to conclude that the Havoc among the ministerial Troops was very considerable. The Loss on our Side is not yet ascertained; but at the most is supposed to be from 150 to 200 killed and wounded. Major-General WARREN, late President of the Provincial Congress, is among the Slain. Col. Parker of Chelmsford, and 27 Privates from different Towns, are Prisoners in Boston Gaol.

The Hon. JAMES WARREN, Esq; is chosen President of the Provincial Congress, in the Room of the late Major-General Warren, slain in Battle.

On Saturday the 17th June, 1775,
fell in Battle,
in the American Army,
Major-General JOSEPH WARREN,
A Gentleman worthy that Office, to which, the Day before,
by the free Votes of his Countrymen,
he was honourably elected.
As a Friend to Britain, he wished the mutual Happiness
of her and America:
And conscious their Interests were inseparable,
He strenuously opposed the unjust Claims
of a venal Parliament,
Who attempted to ruin the latter, by depriving them of their Rights
sacred by Charter.
Twice, to crowded Audiences,
He wail'd the Fate of those massacred March 5, 1770;
and twice,
receiv'd the Thanks of his Fellow Citizens therefor.
To enumerate his Virtues
would be a Subject worthy of an abler Pen.
Sufficient for us, we add,
He by them has laid the Foundation of a Fame
that shall not be impaired
by the Tooth of Time.
Over his Grave his mourning Countrymen may justly say,
Here lies the Body of a worthy Man;
Whose Name shall live and fill the World with wonder,
Although his Ashes scarcely fill an Urn.
His Virtues shall remain when we have left the Stage:
His Praises shall be spoke for many an Age to come.

Since the Battle of the 17th Instant, a considerable Body of the Army have been employed in fortifying Prospect-Hill, Winter-Hill, and other Eminences near Charlestown. The former, which is a very fine Situation, and in full View of the Enemy on Bunker Hill, is said to be now rendered almost impregnable.----

---

place. She left that place the 21st of June; and by a letter come in the above ship we hear, that not more than 300 of the provincials were killed in the late skirmish of the 17th of June, and that they behaved with the greatest courage.

Yesterday it was currently reported, and it is imagined not without some foundation, that an eminent American house in this city had a letter from Boston, dated the 26th of last month, which gives an account, the provincials had actually began bombarding Boston; and that General Gage had sent over an express to government, that he was under some apprehension that the rebels would certainly make themselves masters of Boston, or burn it down.

The day after the late battle in America, some of the regulars searched the pockets of Dr. Warren, who was killed, and found three letters sent to him from some spies at Boston, which were immediately sent there, and the writers being soon discovered were sent to prison, and it is said they were to be hanged next day.

During the late engagement, thirty of the provincials who were taken prisoners, and brought to Boston, desired to be shot, but were confined in a prison, and attended by a clergyman, to whom they declared they were led on entirely by their ministers enforcing the doctrine of resistance.

The news of a battle between General Carleton and the provincials is hourly expected.

Extract of a private letter from an officer in the engagement of the 17th of last month, near Boston, to his friend an eminent merchant in London.

" The engagement, whilst it lasted, was the hottest, I ever saw, and in all the actual service I ever was in, I never saw troops keep up a more constant fire than the provincials.

" The left wing of our troops gave way, a little and it is not to be wondered at considering what numbers they had firing at them; at this time our regiment came up very fortunately to support them, and our men behaved with great intrepidity; they had seen, that nothing was to be done but by continuing a brisk fire, which they did with great spirit, and at length drove the provincials off the field in the utmost confusion. Their loss must be very considerable; and as they seemed afraid of us in the field, and kept in their entrenchments in this engagement, in which they have sustained great loss, I am of opinion, they will not be desirous of meeting the King's troops again; but we are preparing for another re-encounter, though it is uncertain where is to be the scene."

Part of a genuine letter from Boston, dated July 23, 1775, brought by the Cerberus.

" There is no instance in history of the mother country knowing so little of her colonies, as Great Britain does of America At least, this is the best excuse that can be made for your conduct. Our troops are as well disciplined as yours; and they are better marksmen, as your officers know very well. An account of the late action you will have in

---

a minute he was quite alone. His Aid de Camp was killed at his side. The officers brought up the men, and suffered for their temerity. General Clinton, with another corps, presently followed. General Putnam, who had not quite four thousand Connecticut men, thought the whole army was coming, and without the least disorder, or even being pursued a single step, left Bunker's hill, and went to another hill about half a mile further; where he has remained ever since, without the least disturbance. If the mercenaries had offered to march a yard after him General Ward, with his New-England men, was ready to give a good account of them. General Howe is come back to Boston, having had better than two thirds of his men killed and wounded.

" General Howe will do justice to the bravery of our troops. He makes no secret of saying he never saw troops behave better during the whole war. It has been proposed to attack Roxbury-hill; but the design is laid aside. The officers all declare, it will cost more men than the post is worth. So the army must remain cooped-up in Boston, or go on board the ships."

Extract of a letter from Plymouth, July 24.

" This morning a snow arrived in the Sound from Boston; what news she has brought we cannot tell, no person belonging to her being suffered to come on shore; the Captain is gone for London in a post chaise and four; it is said here that Boston has been burnt down, but by whom we do not know."

During the engagement near Charlestown, Gen. Ward, with the grand provincial army, remained quiet within his lines on Roxbury hill.

Major Pitcairn, of the marines, who was killed in the late action in America, has left eight children ——Four balls were lodged in his body, and he was taken off the field upon his son's shoulders.

A very promising youth, cousin to General Gage's lady, who was an officer under General Putnam, was killed in the late battle between the regulars and the provincials.

Our letter from Portsmouth, of this day, says, we hear by the Cerberus, that about 700 provincials were killed and wounded, in the engagement near Charlestown.

Yesterday, at two o'clock, an express arrived at Lord Dartmouth's office, from General Gage, which was laid before the cabinet at St. James's; afterwards Lord Dartmouth held a conference with the King.

The watch word of the provincial detachment, in the morning of the 17th, we are told was *Wilkes*; the next hour it was *Bull.*

From the NEW-YORK GAZETTE *of June* 19.

Providence, June 10. Sunday last the schooner Pelican, Capt. Tucker, arrived at Marblehead from London, in ballast, and brought dispatches for Gen. Gage and Admiral Graves, which were immediately secured by the committee of that place, and sent to the Provincial Congress at Watertown. The contents of them have not yet transpired.

Cambridge, June 8. Whereas the Provincial Congress, on the 3d day of May ult. empowered and directed the receiver general of this colony to borrow the sum of one hundred

---

Yesterday both Houses of Parliament met, and were further prorogued until Thursday the 14th day of September next.

Advice is received in town of a dreadful engagement between the Spanish fleet and the Emperor of Morocco's, reinforced by other Barbary states, wherein several of the Spanish men of war were sunk, amongst which was the Spanish Admiral's ship. It is said the Moors obtained a complete victory, and that with a savage brutality peculiar to those infidels, they massacred numbers of the Spaniards in cool blood.

Yesterday, after the usual business was over, the Lady who has been suspected of contributing to the death of the late —— Scawen, Esq; was examined before Sir John Fielding in the parlour, at the public office in Bowstreet, where Mr. Scawen, the member for Surrey, an eminent counsel for the prisoner, and a great number of gentlemen attended. She denied any knowledge of the circumstance of Mr. Scawen's being poisoned; and behaved with great propriety and composure. After a short hearing she was committed on suspicion to Tothill fields Bridewell, for further examination. She was elegantly dressed in mourning for the deceased Mr. Scawen, is remarkably handsome, and appears to be about five or six and twenty years of age.

Bank stock, 141 7-8 India ditto, ——
Lottery tickets, 12l. 18s.

EDINBURGH.
Extract of a letter from London, July 28.

" Many letters are received from Boston, but there is no particular account yet come of the loss on the side of the rebels, neither has the colony agents here received any accounts of the late action at Charlestown; but it is generally believed that the provincials must have suffered more than the King's troops.——The general proposed that the ships' boats, well manned and armed, should attack the rebels on both sides of Boston neck, which at last the admiral ordered to be done, but they came rather too late, to do effectual service: had the boats arrived sooner, it is supposed that all the rebels who were first engaged must have been cut off. Charlestown, which contained near a thousand houses, is entirely destroyed: as all the American ports were to be shut up the 1st of July, no accounts can come but by ships of war, or government packets.——It is confidently reported that more troops will be sent over soon to Boston, the army there being found by much too small for the service: this reinforcement cannot be great, till after the meeting of parliament, there being no funds for raising more men, which makes the situation of the army at Boston very critical, as it is probable the rebels will take advantage of the smallness of their number.

" Letters received this day from Carolina mention, that that province has agreed to raise two regiments of foot and one of horse, to join the rebels; Georgia has also acceded to the alliance, so that all America, Canada excepted, is leagued together.

" Last week Lieutenant General Houston was appointed to the command of one of the

THE DEATH OF GENERAL WARREN
AT THE BATTLE OF BUNKER'S HILL,
JUNE 17, 1775, BY JOHN TRUMBULL
Museum of Fine Arts, Boston (current location)

EDINBURGH ADVERTISER
August 1, 1775

This eight-page newspaper issue is loaded with page after page of details about the biggest and bloodiest confrontation yet experienced in the American Revolutionary War.

The VIRGINIA GAZETTE

PHILADELPHIA, August 2.

Another Account of the late Action at BUNKER'S hill.

As to camp news, I was there for the first time last Saturday. Our people appear hearty and very happy. The great numbers who crowd to view it, and see their friends, and the parading of the regiments upon the commons, make a grand appearance. The famous Prospect hill is just by the stone house, on the left hand as you go to Charlestown. I believe the regulars will hardly venture out, for they must lose a vast many men if they should, and they cannot afford to purchase every inch of ground as they did at Charlestown. The number the regulars lost, and had wounded, you have seen in the account taken from the orderly serjeant, which agrees pretty nearly with a variety of accounts we have received from people, who have come here from Boston, in fishing boats. They must have suffered greatly, for the first continued with small arms sixty one minutes, and the great part of the time very close fighting. My classmate, Col. ——, was in the entrenchment, and was wounded in the head and leg. He says there was no need of waiting for a chance to fire, for as soon as you had loaded, there was always a mark at hand, and as near as you pleased. His description of the entrenchment, &c. was this:

[see map]

The square, or fort, had about one hundred and fifty men in it. The breastwork about two hundred. The rail fence stuffed with straw four or five hundred. The reason why the square was so thinly manned on the side toward Boston, was because the fire from Cop's hill poured in so thick that there was no living in it. The regulars when they found the fire slacked for want of ammunition, pushed over the walls with their guns in their left hand, and their swords in the right, for it was such an unfinished piece of work that they ran over it. Part of them had come round on the side next Charlestown, so as to fire on the back of our people, when they began to leave the entrenchment, and it was then we lost our men. The ships and floating batteries prevented any assistance, or support of consequence, being given to our men; the fire from Cop's hill ceased when that with small arms began, but that from a ship off New Boston killed and raked our men quite up to the Sun tavern.—— thinks there was more than three thousand of the regulars landed. They advanced in open order, the men often twelve feet apart in the front, but very close after one another in extraordinary deep or long files. As fast as the front man was shot down, the next stepped forward into his place; but our men dropt them so fast, they were a long time coming up. It was surprising how they would step over their dead bodies, as though they had been logs of wood. Their officers, it is said, were obliged to push them on behind, notwithstanding which they once ran and filled some of the boats, the fire was so hot. One of ——'s Captains told me he fired about thirty five times, and after that threw stones. —— says when they pushed over the breastwork, what with the smoke and dust, it was so dark in the square, that he was obliged to feel about for the outlet, the earth, which they threw up for a breastwork, being very dry and loose, for they had only one of these short nights to execute it in.

VIRGINIA GAZETTE (WILLIAMSBURG) (DIXON AND HUNTER)
August 26, 1775
—

Truly one of a kind, this issue of the *Virginia Gazette* contains the only known newspaper illustration of a current event published during the entire American Revolution. It depicts the battlefield at Breed's Hill, based on an eyewitness account, and is made entirely of standard typesetting components found in a print shop.

suffer me to entreat you to STAY the SWORD, and suspend any further operations against the colonies, until some happy conciliating means may be devised, some fortunate expedient may be hit upon to heel the bleeding wounds, and re-unite us again with that unfortunate and distracted country. It is, my Lord, the sincere wish of every true friend of freedom, who are too sensibly afflicted, adequately to express their feelings on the above most melancholy event.

As a well-wisher to your Lordship and all mankind, I entreat you, from every motive of humanity, to listen to the dictates of sound reason and policy, and you cannot fail of being convinced of the justice and expediency of a measure so essentially requisite to stop the further effusion of the BLOOD of our COUNTRYMEN, and prevent us from being engaged in all the horrors of a civil and intestine war; the bare apprehension of which, my Lord, fills me with the most poignant anxiety, and makes me dread the impending consequences, with a torture of mind utterly impossible to be described.

If by those extraordinary exertions, which have often proceeded from people contending for their liberties, or by any of those accidents which have frequently decided the fate of battles and of empires, taking the victory from the strong, and the race from the swift, we should be REPULSED, to what a state of humiliation should we be reduced? Such is the insuperable absurdity of the measure, that whether victors, or vanquished, we are sure of being sufferers.

With ties so strong to bind us to each other, is it not strange, is it not deplorable, that we should differ? Do they who talk of chastising our colonies, and reducing them to obedience, consider how much we hazard when we dissolve those ties? What are we to substitue in their place, FORCE and FEAR, which Tacitus wisely tells us are insecure restraints, and always succeeded by inveterate hatred? When these consequences follow from the coercive measures we are now pursuing, will the counsellors who have compelled us to them by representations, not, I am sure, very fair, defend us from their fatal effects?

It is from experience only, my Lord, that men learn wisdom, but unhappily, sometimes the injury of the experiment is irretrievable; we have too much reason, I think, to apprehend that this will be the event of our present contest with America.

I acknowledge, I admire the bravery of our troops; what men can do, they will do; but in a country furnished with fastnesses and defiles without number, intimately known to the enemy you are to combat, where discipline is unavailing or embarrassing, and valour useless, it requires more than human power to succeed to any permanent purpose. Heaven forbid that the bravery of such troops as the English should be so vainly, so fatally employed; they who remember the fatal overthrow of BRADDOCK by a few Indians in ambush, an overthrow incurred by the very discipline in which he vainly put his trust, will be apt to doubt the facility of reducing the colonies by military force; they who reflect that the united aid and efforts of all the colonies were necessary to give success to our arms in the late war against the Canadians, will be still more doubtful of this expedient.

But, my Lord, so much having been already said on the subject, I will not take up more of your valuable moments, which I am persuaded must now be fully employed; indulge me, however, once more to entreat your most serious attention to the true interest and happiness of this country, and to the welfare of our brethren in America, so shall you be revered and esteemed by all good men, your name deservedly transferred with honour to posterity, and the tribute of gratitude, affection, and esteem, be echoed from every quarter of this great and extensive empire.

MEMENTO.

---

on the left hand as you go to Charlestown. I believe the regulars will hardly venture out, for they must lose a vast many men if they should, and they cannot afford to purchase every inch of ground as they did at Charlestown. The number the regulars lost, and had wounded, you have seen in the account taken from the orderly serjeant, which agrees pretty nearly with a variety of accounts we have received from people, who have come here from Boston, in fishing boats. They must have suffered greatly, for the fire continued with small arms sixty one minutes, and great part of the time very close fighting. My classmate, Col.————, was in the entrenchment, and was wounded in the head and leg. He says there was no need of waiting for a chance to fire, for as soon as you had loaded, there was always a mark at hand, and as near as you pleased. His description of the entrenchment, &c. was this:

The square, or fort, had about one hundred and fifty men in it. The breastwork about two hundred. The rail fence stuffed with straw four or five hundred. The reason why the square was so thinly manned on the side toward Boston, was because the fire from Cop's hill poured in so thick that there was no living in it. The regulars when they found the fire slacked for want of ammunition, pushed over the walls with their guns in their left hand, and their swords in the right, for it was such an unfinished piece of work that they ran over it. Part of them had come round on the side next Charlestown, so as to fire on the back of our people, when they began to leave the entrenchment, and it was then we lost our men. The ships and floating batteries prevented any assistance, or support of consequence, being given to our men; the fire from Cop's hill ceased when that with small arms began, but that from a ship off New Boston killed and raked our men quite up to the Sun tavern. ———— thinks there was more than three thousand of the regulars landed. They advanced in open order, the men often twelve feet apart in the front, but very close after one another in extraordinary deep or long files. As fast as the front man was shot down, the next stepped forward into his place; but our men dropt them so fast, they were a long time coming up. It was surprising how they would step over their dead bodies, as though they had been logs of wood. Their officers, it is said, were obliged to push them on behind, notwithstanding which they once ran and filled some of the boats, the fire was so hot. One of————'s Captains told me he fired about thirty five times, and after that threw stones. ———— says when they pushed over the breastwork, what with the smoke and dust, it was so dark in

---

the navy and a tion of the en the General, fact, it could tions were im lars from Quel to obtain the n can vessels at cursed plan, determination acts of butcher 50,000l. was

" The Gen spike up the ca up the King's this nation ! and the consoli threats, and forming this i Canada, they they would du lacious contra believing that cut off, or igne board the men

" Such also patched some contradict the men, cajole th effection of the expedients; fe supine landed given to the fur America, by blish her righ most flagitious wisdom and cl

" This eve meet, revive a consist of 8000 in forcing a r in supporting nions."

❋❋❋❋❋❋

SPEECH of th mons, on the affairs.

IT is but to Ministers o temper and fit will be inevita

Gentlemen favourite prop duties; and, the other. N protection to no longer to b zard of battle the same acts according to in the world conduct from all the wars th their own cou that, in man to the presen

GEORGE WASHINGTON TAKES COMMAND

By Robert J. Allison

BEFORE LEAVING VIRGINIA ON MAY 4, 1775, TO ATTEND the Congress in Philadelphia, Washington heard that British marines raided the Williamsburg gunpowder depot; the next day, he heard about the battle at Lexington and Concord. The political crisis had turned violent. Still, he expected to be home by July to attend to his own business. Instead, by early July, he was in Massachusetts taking command of an army.

Congress had him chair the committees to plan New York's defenses, to supply the army, and to devise rules for governing the army. Drawn from four different New England colonies, the army had no regular order. Men came and went at will, and men from one colony would not listen to orders issued by officers from another.

In the midst of this discussion, John Adams said he had a candidate to lead the army—"a gentleman of private fortune, a skilled, experienced officer, whose talents and character merited the praise of all America." Washington discretely left the room. The next day, June 15, Congress unanimously appointed him commanding general. It also appointed Charles Lee, a retired British officer who had served in Poland's army; Artemas Ward, the Massachusetts officer already in command in Cambridge; Philip Schuyler of New York; and Israel Putnam of Connecticut as major generals.

Washington wanted "it remembered by every Gentleman in the room" that he had not sought the position and did not "think myself equal to the command I am honoured with" (*New-England Chronicle and Essex Gazette*, January 11, 1776). He declined the $500 monthly salary and rode from Philadelphia on June 23 to take command. Three days later, he reached New York, whose provincial congress welcomed him, deploring "the calamities of this divided Empire," which forced them "to defend their dearest rights and privileges" and looked forward to an accommodation with England that would allow Washington to retire to private life (*New-England Chronicle*, July 6, 1775).

When "we assumed the Soldier," Washington told the Congress, "we did not lay aside the Citizen," agreeing on the goal of restored harmony between the colonies and England but pledging to fight for "the establishment of American Liberty, on the most firm and solid foundation" (*New-England Chronicle*, July 6, 1775). While in New York, he learned of Bunker Hill, which seemed to prove that the army would fight. He believed another such battle would convince the British public to give up the war.

He reached Cambridge on July 2, 1775, after briefly stopping in Watertown, where the Massachusetts Provincial Congress welcomed him. They told him his "naturally brave" soldiers had no real military experience and the "Youth in the Army are not possessed of the absolute necessity of Cleanliness in their Dress, and Lodging, continual Exercise, and strict Temperance" (*New-England Chronicle*, July 6, 1775).

Washington assured the Congress that in putting aside his private affairs to take on these duties, he emulated "the Virtue and publick Spirit of the whole Province of Massachusetts Bay," that his only ambition was to vindicate their rights and restore all to "Peace, Liberty, and Safety." Whatever his troops' deficiency, he was confident their "native Bravery and Spirit" would quickly end the "Distresses which now overwhelm this once happy Country" (*New-England Chronicle*, July 6, 1775).

But it would be Washington's task to organize this army; keep it fed, clothed, and armed; and turn it from an enthusiastic summertime encampment into a disciplined, effective fighting force.

The earliest portrait of George Washington wearing his colonel's uniform of the Virginia Regiment from the French and Indian War, likely the uniform he wore while accepting command of the Continental forces.

NEW-ENGLAND CHRONICLE (CAMBRIDGE, MA)
January 11, 1776
—

As shown in the Congressional journal for June 16, 1775, printed a half-year later, Washington understood this was a "momentous duty." Demonstrating his character, Washington made sure everyone knew he did not "think myself equal to the command I am honoured with" and turned down the $500 monthly salary.

EXTRACTS from the JOURNAL of the CONGRESS.

In CONGRESS, JUNE 15, 1775.

Resolved,

THAT a General be appointed to command all the Continental Forces raised or to be raised for the defence of American Liberty.

That five hundred dollars per month be allowed for the pay and expences of the General.

The Congress then proceeded to the choice of a General by ballot, and *George Washington*, Esq; was unanimously elected.

JUNE 16, 1775.

The President informed Col. Washington that the Congress had yesterday unanimously made choice of him to be General and Commander in Chief of the American Forces, and requested he would accept of that employment; to which Col. Washington, standing in his place, answered:

" *Mr. President,*

" Though I am truly sensible of the high honour done me in this appointment, yet, I feel great distress from the consciousness, that my abilities and military experience may not be equal to the extensive and important trust: However, as the Congress desire it, I will enter upon the momentous duty, and exert every power I possess in the service and for support of the glorious cause. I beg they will accept my most cordial thanks for this distinguishing testimony of their approbation.

" But left some unlucky event should happen unfavourable to my reputation, I beg it may be

stores and provisions.

That his pay be *Eighty Dollars* per month.

That there be one Quarter-Master-General for the Grand Army, and one Deputy under him for the separate Army.

That the pay of the Quarter-Master-General *Eighty Dollars* per month, and that of the Deputy *Forty Dollars* per month.

That there be one Pay-Master-General, and Deputy under him for the army in a separate department; that the pay for the Pay-Master-General himself be *One Hundred Dollars* per month, and for the Deputy Pay-Master under him *Fifty Dollars* per month.

That there be one Chief Engineer at the Grand Army, and that his pay be *Sixty Dollars* per month.

That two Affistants be employed under him, and that the pay of each of them be *Twenty Dollars* per month.

That there be one Chief Engineer for the Army in a separate department, and two Affistants under him; that the pay of the Chief Engineer be *Sixty Dollars* per month, and the pay of the Affistants each *Twenty Dollars* per month.

That there be three Aids-de-Camp; and that their pay be *Thirty-three Dollars* per month each.

That there be a Secretary to the Major-General acting in a separate department; and that his pay be *Thirty-three Dollars* per month.

That there be a Commissary of the Musters.

JUNE 17, 1775.

The Committee appointed to draught a Commission to the General, reported the same, which being read by paragraphs and debated, was agreed to as follows:

In CONGRESS.

The DELEGATES of the UNITED COLONIES of *New-Hampshire, Massachusetts-Bay, Rhode-Island, Connecticut, New-York, New-Jersey, Pennsylvania,* the Counties of *New-Castle, Kent* and *Sussex* on *Delaware, Maryland, Virginia, North-Carolina, and South-Carolina.*

To GEORGE WASHINGTON, ESQUIRE.

WE reposing especial trust and confidence in your patriotism, valour, conduct and fidelity, do by these presents constitute and appoint you, to be General and Commander in Chief, of the army

NEW-ENGLAND CHRONICLE OR, ESSEX GAZETTE.

VOL. VIII.

NUMB. 389.

THURSDAY, *January* 4, to

THURSDAY, *January* 11, 1776.

CAMBRIDGE: Printed by SAMUEL and EBENEZER HALL, at their Office in Stoughton-Hall, HARVARD-COLLEGE.

Officers, non-commiffioned Officers and Soldiers, belonging to any of the Corps of the Army of the United Colonies, under the immediate Command of his Excellency General WASHINGTON, who are abfent on Furlough, Recruiting, or by Permiffion of the Commanding Officers, are to join their refpective Regiments by the firft Day of February next. Any Officer neglects to pay due Obedience to this Order, he will be immediately cafhiered, and any non-commiffioned Officers, and Soldiers, offending therein, will be tried and punifhed as Deferters.

By his EXCELLENCY's Command,
HORATIO GATES, Adjutant-General.

Head-Quarters at Cambridge, *Jan.* 11, 1776.

A TRUNK OF LINNEN LOST.

About the End of May laft, a TRUNK, containing Table Cloths, Napkins, Towels, Pillow Cafes, and fundry other Articles, brought from Bofton, in a Veffel to Marblehead, were taken away by fome Perfon unknown.

No Enquiry has been made till now, becaufe it was thought they might have been put (by Miftake) on board a Veffel bound for London, but it is now certain they were not.

Several Goods brought for feveral People in the fame Veffel, fome of which went to the Water, and 'tis probable this Trunk went the fame Way.

Whoever is poffeft of it, will fend Word to the Printer, it will be kindly received, but if it is through any Defign to defraud him, and any Perfon will give Information, that the Trunk and Articles may be recovered and the Thief brought to Juftice, they fhall receive a Reward of TWO DOLLARS, with Thanks.

JOSEPH BARRELL.

N. B. Moft of the Linnen was mark'd I A,

---

remembered by every Gentleman in the room, that I this day declare with the utmoft fincerity, I do not think myfelf equal to the command I am honoured with.

"As to pay, Sir, I beg leave to affure the Congrefs, that as no pecuniary confideration could have tempted me to accept this arduous employment, at the expence of my domeftic eafe and happinefs, I do not wifh to make any profit from it. I will keep an exact account of my expences.—Thofe I doubt not they will difcharge, and that is all I defire."

Refolved, That a Committee be appointed to draught a Commiffion and Inftructions for the General.

The perfons chofen to compofe the Committee were Mr. *Lee,* Mr. *E. Rutledge* and Mr. *J. Adams.*

The Congrefs refumed the confideration of the report from the Committee of the whole, and came to the following refolution:

Refolved, That two Major-Generals be appointed for the American Army.

That the pay of each of the Major-Generals be *One Hundred* and *Sixty-fix Dollars* per month.

That when any of thefe act in a feparate department, he be allowed for his pay and expences *Three Hundred* and *Thirty two Dollars* per month.

That there be eight Brigadiers-General.

That the pay of each of the Brigadiers-General be *One Hundred* and *Twenty five Dollars* per month.

That there be one Adjutant-General.

That his pay be *One Hundred* and *Twenty five Dollars* per month.

That there be one Commiffary-General of ftores and provifions.

That his pay be *Eighty Dollars* per month.

That there be one Quarter-Mafter-General for the Grand Army, and one Deputy under him for the feparate Army.

That the pay of the Quarter-Mafter-General be *Eighty Dollars* per month, and that of the Deputy *Forty Dollars* per month.

---

of the United Colonies, and of all the forces now raifed or to be raifed by them, and of all other who fhall voluntarily offer their fervice, and join the faid army for the defence of American liberty, and for repelling every hoftile invafion thereof. And you are hereby vefted with full power and authority to act as you fhall think for the good and welfare of the fervice.

And we do hereby ftrictly charge and require all officers and foldiers under your command, to be obedient to your orders, and diligent in the exercife of their feveral duties.

And we do alfo enjoin and require you, to be careful in executing the great truft repofed in you, by caufing ftrict difcipline and order to be obferved in the army, and that the foldiers be duly exercifed and provided with all convenient neceffaries.

And you are to regulate your conduct in every refpect by the rules and difcipline of war (as herewith given you) and punctually to obferve and follow fuch orders and directions from time to time, as you fhall receive from this or a future Congrefs of thefe United Colonies or Committee of Congrefs.

This Commiffion to continue in force, until revoked by this or a future Congrefs.

By order of the Congrefs.

Ordered, That the fame be fairely tranfcribed, figned by the Prefident, attefted by the Secretary, and delivered to the General.

Refolved unanimoufly, Whereas the Delegates of all the Colonies from Nova Scotia to Georgia, in Congrefs affembled, have unanimoufly chofen GEORGE WASHINGTON, Efquire, to be General and Commander in Chief of fuch forces as are or fhall be raifed for the maintenance and prefervation of American Liberty; this Congrefs doth now declare, that they will maintain and affift him, and adhere to him the faid George Washington with their lives and fortunes in the fame,

...rn, for the pay he gives them: ...loy'd that old mungy Jacobite ...ary Johnson, alias the Rambler, ...s in a Pamphlet entitled, Tax-... A piece full of sophistical quib-bedantick bombast language. I ...answer to it; and am pleased to ...e authors of the Monthly Review, ...(March) have cut him down in ...u ever see that periodical work ..., it will give you pleasure to read ...on the subject. If we may be-...hings with you threaten war; in ...d the standard of liberty had been ...m, and that it was repaired to by ...etermined to fight or die; should ...worsted in any general action, of ...is the greatest probability, what ...ake in England? And then let the ... If the troops beat you, you can ...ey gain five battles and lose but ...them, so great is the disadvantage ...ngage, besides what arises from the ...ate, and fighting against those who ... persuaded they fight pro Aris et ...n their own ground

...Ambassador at the Hague applied ...id their subjects supplying the Ame-...and ammunition. The states pub-...under the penalty of a 1000 Guil-...£ 90 Sterling: I leave you to com-...ur leisure, and judge if where the ...are so great as a voyage of that ...not worth the merchants while to

---

TON, Generalissimo of all the Forces raised, and to be raised in the Confederated Colonies of America.

May it please your Excellency,

AT a time when the most loyal of his Majes-ty's subjects, from a regard to the laws and constitution, by which he sits on the throne, feel themselves reduced to the unhappy necessity of tak-ing up arms, to defend their dearest rights and pri-vileges; while we deplore the calamities of this divided Empire, we rejoice in the appointment of a Gentleman, from whose abilities and virtue, we are taught to expect both security and peace.

Confiding in you, Sir, and in the worthy Ge-nerals, immediately under your command, we have the most flattering hopes of success, in the glorious struggle for American Liberty, and the fullest as-surances that whenever this important contest shall be decided, by that fondest wish of each Ameri-can soul, an accommodation with our Mother Country, you will cheerfully resign the important Deposit, committed into your hands, and re-as-sume the Character of our worthiest Citizen.

By Order,

P. V. B. LIVINGSTON, President.

June 26th, 1775.

His EXCELLENCY's Answer.

Gentlemen,

AT the same time that with you, I deplore the unhappy necessity of such an appointment, as that with which I am now honoured, I cannot but feel sentiments of the highest gratitude, for this affecting instance of distinction and regard.

...on that point, it is own'd by our Ambassador at this place that a Dutch ship is lately got into Virginia where it has landed 400 Barrels Powder, and 1400 Stands of arms. France was apply'd to, to forbid its subjects furnishing you with any military stores —— France it is well known could easily have crushed all such assistance by an express prohibition; but France knows better than to do it and therefore only tells its subjects, if they do it, it is entirely at their own risque, which is plainly saying, If you will venture you may. Spain when applied to, roundly refused to give any hindrance to her subjects supplying you; and I dare say from present appearances will soon act openly against England. An article lately appeared in the English papers, that a Prussian ship sailed from Stetten to some part of America with 30 field pieces, a good store of Powder, Ball and small arms, and 6 or 7 Prussian Generals...

...on that point ...ocent in one ..., and for the ..., distress and ...se not your ... and fellow ...he power of ...tholic neigh-...oint of tax-...ect humilia-...rize would ...ur national ...ur liberties, ...men. We ...l somewhat ...you should ...ll you then

---

May your warmest wishes be realized in the success of America, at this important and interest-ing period; and be assured, that every exertion of my worthy colleagues and myself, will be equally extended to the re-establishment of peace and har-mony, between the Mother Country and these Colonies:—As to the fatal but necessary operations of War———————— when we assumed the Soldier, we did not lay aside the Citizen, and we shall most sincerely rejoice with you, in that happy hour, when the establishment of American Liberty, on the most firm and solid foundations, shall enable us to return to our private stations, in the bosom of a free, peaceful, and happy Country.

G. WASHINGTON.

June 29th, 1775.

NEW-YORK, June 29.
"On Tuesday General Wooster, with the advanced body of the Connecticut forces, arrived in the...

We would not presume to prescribe to your Excellency, but supposing you would choose to be informed of the general Character of the Soldiers who compose this Army, beg Leave to represent, that the greatest Part of them have not before seen Service. And although naturally brave, and of good Understanding, yet for Want of Experience in military Life, have but little Knowledge of divers Things most essential to the Preservation of Health, and even of Life. The Youth in the Army are not possessed of the absolute Necessity of Cleanliness in their Dress, and Lodging, continual Exercise, and strict Temperance, to preserve them from Diseases frequently prevailing in Camps; especially among those, who, from their Childhood, have been used to a laborious Life.

We beg Leave to assure you, that this

---

by private and public Distress.
GEO. WASHINGTON.

To the Honourable CHARLES LEE, Esq;
Major-General of the Continental Army
SIR,

THE Congress of the Massachusetts Colony, possessed of the fullest Evidence of your Attachment to the Rights of Mankind, and Regard to the Distresses which America in general, and this Colony in particular, are involved in, by the impolitic, wicked and tyrannic System, adopted by Administration, and pursued with relentless and savage Fury, do, with Pleasure, embrace this Opportunity to express the great Satisfaction and Gratitude they feel on your Appointment as a Major-General in the American Army.

We sincerely congratulate you on your safe Arrival here, and wish you all possible Happiness and Success in the Execution of so important a Trust. We admire and re-

---

of the Enemy, including
June 29. 1775.

Return of the Killed at C
an order
Commission Officers
Serjeants
Corporals
Rank and File

Total of killed
Wounded

Total of killed and wo
On Thursday, June 15th
plexy, in the 68th Year of
tuous Consort of AARON W
were happily united the affe
gent Mistress, sincere Frie
Christian.——Her Friends a
they rejoice in the Reason th
a World of Misery and Trou
——Her Remains were inter
Mark of Respect, and in a fle
commended by the Honorabl

STOLEN or lost,
of June, a Pocket-Book,
Bills, and some Notes of Han
said Bills and Notes, and deliv
Printers of this Paper, shall
necessary Charges paid by
Cambridge, July 5, 17

TO B
A handsome new fal
ness. Inquire of Mr. P

---

presented to his Excellency
or-General Lee.

ency
...INGTON, Esq;
Chief of the Con-

...ellency,
...e Massachusetts
...ith every Senti-
...ect, beg Leave
...r safe Arrival:
...ble Happiness
...n of the impor-
...Station. While
that Attention to the public
...ested in your Appointment, we
...ire that disinterested Virtue,
...ished Patriotism, which alone
...from those Enjoyments of do-
...which a sublime and manly
...with a most affluent Fortune,
...hazard your Life, and to en-
...igues of War, in the Defence
...s of Mankind, and the Good
...ntry.

...ble Zeal for the common Cause
...and Compassion for the Dis-
...Colony, exhibited by the great
...de in your Journey hither, fully
...niversal Satisfaction we have,
...e, observed on this Occasion;
...nising Presages that the great
...formed from your personal
...nd military Abilities, are well

A ppointment,
warmest Acknowledgments, and will ever be retained in grateful Remembrance.

In exchanging the Enjoyments of domestic Life for the Duties of my present honourable, but arduous Station, I only emulate the Virtue and publick Spirit of the whole Province of Massachusetts-Bay, which with a Firmness, and Patriotism without Example in modern History, has sacrificed all the Comforts of social and political Life, in Support of the Rights of Mankind, and the Welfare of our common Country. My highest Ambition is to be the happy Instrument of vindicating those Rights, and to see this devoted Province again restored to Peace, Liberty and Safety.

The short Space of Time which has elapsed since my Arrival does not permit me to decide upon the State of the Army. The Course of human Affairs forbids an Expectation, that Troops formed under such Circumstances, should at once possess the Order, Regularity and Discipline of Veterans—Whatever Deficiencies there may be, will I doubt not, soon be made up by the Activity and Zeal of the Officers, and the Docility and Obedience of the Men. These Qualities united with their native Bravery and Spirit will afford a happy Presage of Success, and put a final Period to those Distresses which now overwhelm this once happy Country.

I most sincerely thank you, Gentlemen,

---

bation of your own Conscience, and eternal Happiness hereafter.

His Honour's Answer.
To the Gentlemen of the Provincial Congress of Massachusetts.

Gentlemen,

NOTHING can be so flattering to me as the good Opinion and Approbation of the Delegates of a free and uncorrupt People. I was educated in the highest Reverence for the Rights of Mankind, and have acquired by a long Acquaintance a most particular Regard for the People of America. You may depend therefore, Gentlemen, on my Zeal and Integrity. I can promise you nothing from my Abilities. God Almighty grant us Success equal to the R

NEW-ENGLAND CHRONICLE (CAMBRIDGE, MA)
July 6, 1775

Washington's travel from Philadelphia to Cambridge to assume command of the Continental Army is documented in this issue. On July 2, he reached the army's headquarters at Cambridge, where this newspaper was printed.

---

from
Treasurer, for what Money he had by him, belonging to the Province, and received from him 1500 £. which was lately conveyed to Exeter

---

Discipline already established
as may be agreeable to your

Duties of my Station; they are so complicated, and extended, that I shall need the

heavy Fire upon the Town of Roxbury, both from their Cannon and Mortars. They set one House on Fire, which was consumed; but did little other Damage.

IN 1775, FEW CITIES COULD CLAIM THE STRATEGIC SIGNIFIcance of Norfolk. Virginia's largest and wealthiest city, it commanded one of the finest anchorages on the eastern seaboard and riverine access to the interior of the colony. It was also a Loyalist stronghold to which Tories from across the colony fled in the autumn of 1775. Among these was the Royal Governor John Murray, better know as Lord Dunmore and reviled throughout the region for offering freedom to slaves who would take up arms against their masters. This "cruel policy" horrified Virginians, who disingenuously accused Dunmore of exploiting African Americans. Those who answered Dunmore's call saw things in a different light, as they formed the Royal Ethiopian Regiment and embroidered "Liberty to Slaves" on their uniforms. Nevertheless, not enough Tories—black or white—responded to Dunmore's call to arms, leaving Norfolk ripe for Patriot picking.

Surrounded by water or low ground on nearly every side, Norfolk was most vulnerable from the south, where a single highway ran through the Great Dismal Swamp and on to Suffolk. Approximately nine miles south of Norfolk, the road crossed the Elizabeth River at the village of Great Bridge, incongruously named for the simple wooden structure that spanned this waterway. Realizing its importance, both the British and the Americans sent forces to defend the crossing. In mid-November, the British constructed a paltry stockade (Fort Murray) on the eastern bank; by month's end, Lieutenant Colonel Charles Scott and 215 men of the 2nd Virginia Regiment occupied the town on the opposite shore. On December 2, Colonel William Woodford arrived with the remainder of the regiment. Although he commanded seven hundred "shirtmen" (so-called because of their hunting shirts), Woodford did not realize that he faced fewer than one hundred British defenders and hesitated to await the arrival of artillery.

Lord Dunmore better appreciated the vulnerability of his little post, however, and sent reinforcements to mount a preemptive attack on the morning of December 9. Unfortunately for the British, little went according to plan. Two companies of the Ethiopian Regiment that were to conduct a feint downstream never received their orders. Meanwhile, the British tactical commander, Captain Samuel Leslie, assumed he outnumbered the Americans about 350 to three hundred when reinforcements had swollen Woodford's ranks to nearly nine hundred men. Mitigating this disparity was the geography of Great Bridge, which lay astride a narrow causeway scarcely wider than the road itself. While this prevented the Americans from bringing their superior numbers to bear, it confined attackers to a predictable, exposed approach.

The ensuing battle was one of few that conformed to subsequent American mythology about the superiority of the American rifleman over his red-coated antagonist. Although Leslie's light infantry replanked the bridge and secured its far side without being detected, the grenadiers commenced their attack just after Patriot drummers beat reveille. Unable to either surprise the Americans or envelop them, the grenadier commander, Captain Charles Fordyce, committed his men to a frontal assault across 150 yards of a narrow causeway against prepared defensive works. After withstanding a withering fire and losing perhaps thirty men (including Captain Fordyce), the British fell back to their bridgehead. There, they traded long-range shots with the Americans, eventually losing this contest to Virginia's Culpepper Minutemen, who wielded their Pennsylvania long rifles with deadly accuracy. With half of his 120 regulars dead, wounded, or captured, Captain Leslie abandoned not merely the attack, but also Fort Murray; he spiked his guns and retired to Norfolk. In his after-action report (reproduced in the *New-England Chronicle* of January 11, 1776), Woodford gloated that he had won "a second Bunker's-hill affair" in which American amateurs fighting from prepared positions had once again bested His Majesty's regulars.

But whereas the British continued to occupy Boston for nine months following the Battle of Bunker Hill, the much smaller fight at Great Bridge had more immediate consequences. Realizing that Norfolk was indefensible, Dunmore immediately withdrew his forces and Norfolk's Loyalist population to ships in Hampton Roads. When the Americans denied Dunmore access to provisions, he threatened to bombard the city—and did so New Year's Day. Landing parties also set fire to port facilities that sheltered snipers, which the Patriots used

as a pretext to burn much of the hated city to the ground. American commanders omitted this fact in their reports (see the *New-England Chronicle*, February 1, 1776), creating the impression that the British had burned the city in a fit of vengeance. When Patriot forces withdrew in February, they razed whatever remained of the town.

The loss of Norfolk—a direct consequence of the Patriot victory at Great Bridge—was a serious blow to the British. Dunmore not only lost a precious port and bastion of Loyalist support, but also handed the Patriots one of the most significant propaganda victories of the war. Writing under the pseudonym "An American" in the *Virginia Gazette* (reprinted in the *New-England Chronicle*, February 1, 1776), Patrick Henry used the destruction of Norfolk to argue for independence. Outraged by these latest "specimens of British cruelty" and simultaneously moved by Thomas Paine's *Common Sense*, most Americans agreed.

EASTERN VIRGINIA
Library of Congress

Detail of a 1770s map of eastern Virginia, oriented with north to the bottom and south to the top.

NEW-ENGLAND CHRONICLE (CAMBRIDGE, MA)

January 11, 1776

In his after-action report, Col. William Woodford gloated that he had won "a second Bunker's-hill affair" in which American amateurs fighting from prepared positions had once again bested His Majesty's regulars. But whereas the British continued to occupy Boston for nine months following the Battle of Bunker Hill, the much smaller fight at Great Bridge had more immediate consequences.

"A servant belonging to Major Mushall, who deserted the other night from Col. Scott's

and Capt. Fordyce, of the grenadiers, led the van with his company, who, for his coolness and bravery, deserved a better fate, as well as the brave fellows who fell with him, who behaved like heroes. They marched up to our breast-work with fixed bayonets, and perhaps a hotter fire never happened, or a greater carnage, for the number of troops. None of the blacks, &c. in the rear with Capt. Leslie, advanced farther than the bridge. I have the pleasure to inform you, that the victory was complete, and that most of the dead and wounded, with two pieces of cannon, were carried off under cover of their guns from the fort. We buried 12, besides the Captain (him with all military honours due to his rank) and have prisoners Lieut. Batut and 16 privates, all wounded; 35 stands of arms and accoutrements, 3 officers fusees, powder, ball and cartridges, with sundry other things, have likewise fallen into our hands. This was a second Bunker's-hill affair, in miniature, with this difference, that we kept our post, and had only one man wounded in the hand."

On Tuesday last, a large schooner from the West-Indies bound for Norfolk, was taken and bro't into Hampton by our men stationed there. She was laden with rum and sugar, and had 2,700 dollars on board, for the use of our enemies.

Lord Dunmore, we hear, swears most furiously, that he will bombard Norfolk, should the shirt men come into it. They most certainly will, so that we need not be amazed to hear soon, of that place's being laid in ashes.

NEW-YORK, January 4.

that place but 14 days ago, that 7000 French troops, and nine sail of the line were arrived there; that two vessels belonging to North-America were at that place, but not having any credentials from the Congress, the inhabitants refused to trade with them; and that the Congress was in high esteem there.

We hear, that yesterday came to town, a gentleman from Canada, who has brought letters from thence to several gentlemen in town, signifying, that on the 5th ult. Gen. Montgomery with his army, were on the heights of Abraham, that he had taken into pay 2500 Canadians, that his army consisted of near 5000 men, and that he had invested the city of Quebec on every side.

By the latest Accounts from Williamsburgh, in Virginia, we learn, That Lord Dunmore intends shortly for the West-Indies, with his Cargo of Slaves, to make the most of them before his Departure for England; and by Letters lately received, it is affirmed, that he would be speedily recalled, his Conduct in Virginia being much censured by the Ministry.—That 6 Men had deserted from the Otter Man of War; who, when they were asked, what induced them to leave Dunmore? Answered, *Hungry Bellies, naked Backs, and no Fuel*; besides, in other Respects, the most cruel and inhuman Treatment—That Lord Dunmore had requested an Exchange of Prisoners; and that the King's Soldiers killed and wounded in the Battle amounted to 102.

CAMBRIDGE, January 11.

Last Monday evening Major Knowlton was dispatched with 100 men, to make an incursion into Charlestown. He crossed the Mill Dam, which lays between Cobble Hill and Bunker's Hill, about nine o'clock, and immediately proceeded down the street on the westerly side of Bunker's-Hill; a part of the men, under the command of Capt. Keyes, at the same time were ordered to take post on the East side of the street, just under the hill, in order to intercept any persons who might escape from the houses in the street, some of which were occupied by the enemy. These houses, which were a little without the compact part of the town, the enemy suffered to remain unburnt in June last, for their own conveniences.—They were now surrounded and set fire to by our men. In one of them they found six soldiers and one woman, all of whom, except one refractory fellow, who was killed, were brought off. In another of the houses, according to the information of the prisoners,

WILLIAMSBURG, January 5.

A letter from Cols. Howe and Woodford, to the Hon. the President of the Convention, dated Norfolk, 10 o'clock at night, January 1, 1776.

BETWEEN 3 and 4 o'clock a severe cannonade began from all the shipping, under cover of which they landed small parties, and set fire to the houses on the wharves. The wind favoured their design, and we believe the flames will become general. In the confusion which they supposed would ensue, they frequently attempted to land; but this, by the bravery of our officers and men, we have hitherto prevented, with only a few men wounded on our side, and we persuade ourselves with a good deal of loss on theirs. Their efforts, and our opposition, still continue. We have stationed ourselves in such a manner as will, we believe, render every thing but burning the houses ineffectual. We wait with impatience your farther orders, and are respectfully, &c.

Extract of a letter from Col. Howe, to the President of the Convention, January 2.

"The burning of the town has made several avenues, which yesterday they had not, so that they may now fire with greater effect. The tide is now rising, and we expect at high water another cannonade. I have only to wish it may be as ineffectual as the last; for we have not one man killed, and but a few wounded. I cannot enter into the melancholy consideration of the women and children running through a crowd of those got out of the town, some of them with children at their breast. A few have, I hear, been killed. Does it not call for vengeance, both from God and man! It is but justice to inform you, that I had the pleasure to find every officer ready to execute orders at a moment's warning, and that the men behaved with steadiness and spirit. Col. Stevens went down at my command, and headed some men near the water, where he engaged a party who had landed, with the spirit and conduct of a good officer. Of my friend Colonel Woodford, it is almost needless to speak; but I cannot avoid expressing, that I received from him every assistance which conduct and spirit could give me."

Extract of a letter from Col. Elliott, to Col. Patrick Henry, dated Hampton, January 5. 1776.

"Inclosed you have the copy of a letter from Col. Woodford to me, dated 3 o'clock yesterday, since which a snow and two small vessels have gone up to Norfolk. She appeared to have a

Great-Bridge, with 17 Tories, and 11 negroes, arrived in town, under guard, from Norfolk. The wounded soldiers are sent to the hospital, most of the tories and negroes lodged in the publick jail, and Lieut. B--t, with a few others, admitted on their parole.

Yesterday afternoon an express arrived from

From the Virginia Gazette, January 5.

I HOPE our countrymen will not be at all dispirited at the destruction of Norfolk, but rather rejoice that half the mischief our enemies can do us is done already. They have destroyed one of the first towns in America, and the only one (except 2 or 3) in Virginia, which carried on any thing like a trade. We are only sharing part of the sufferings of our American brethren, and can now glory in having received one of the keenest strokes of the enemy, without flinching. They have done their worst, and to no other purpose than to harden our soldiers, and learn them to bear, without dismay, all the most formidable operations of a war carried on by a powerful and cruel enemy; to no other purpose than to give the world specimens of British cruelty, and American fortitude, unless it be to force us to lay aside that childish fondness for Britain, and that foolish tame dependence on her. We had borne so long with the oppression of an ungenerous restriction of our trade, of a restriction, in some instances, which seemed calculated merely as badges of our subjection, and had been contented so long with

without the assistance of Roman Catholicks and Indians, and endeavouring to raise amongst us a domestick enemy? Was this like a brave and generous nation! If they were lost to all the feelings of Britons, for men contending for the

Mr. Fox deceived by believe that America, th there would selves, secu peace; tha

NEW-ENGLAND CHRONICLE (CAMBRIDGE, MA)
February 1, 1776

Landing parties also set fire to port facilities that sheltered snipers, which the Patriots used as a pretext to burn much of the hated city to the ground. American commanders omitted this fact in their reports, creating the impression that the British had burned the city in a fit of vengeance. When Patriot forces withdrew in February, they razed whatever remained of the town.

IN EARLY SEPTEMBER 1775, BENEDICT ARNOLD AND ABOUT 1,100 American soldiers marched out of Cambridge, Massachusetts. Sent by General Washington, their objective was to capture Quebec City as part of a two-pronged attack aimed at wresting control of the colony of Quebec (or "Canada") from the British. The other "arm"—about two thousand men led by Richard Montgomery—had left Ticonderoga in late August, bound for Montreal. After taking the forts of Chambly and St. John's, Montgomery and his men reached Montreal; the British fled before their advance, and the Americans entered the town on November 12. After fortifying Montreal, Montgomery and three hundred of his men proceeded to Quebec to join Arnold and his troops. However, the campaign against Quebec would not meet with the same success.

The failure of the Battle of Quebec and the march on Canada was a serious setback for the American cause, ensuring that Canada would remain a British stronghold throughout the war.

In the first place, Benedict Arnold had lost many of his men en route to Quebec, an arduous journey that took them through the forests and swamps of northern New England. Clothes torn and boots worn out from the hard march, the men suffered from exposure, sickness, and dwindling provisions; some were even forced to eat their dogs. By the time Arnold arrived at Quebec, he had only about six hundred men left; many had died from starvation, exposure, or disease, and about three hundred deserted. Given their reduced strength, Arnold decided to withdraw to Pointe-aux-Trembles to await the arrival of Montgomery in early December. The Americans had no heavy artillery, nor were they able to construct any siege lines, owing to the ground being frozen solid.

The British defenders were only slightly better off.

There were only seventy British regular troops in Quebec and about 1,200 defenders in total. There was also some doubt concerning the loyalty of the local French-speaking inhabitants, some of whom resented their new British governors. Indeed, revolutionary leaders were counting on support from the local population (see letter from Arnold, November 1775, published in the *New-England Chronicle*, December 28, 1775). However, while some of the Canadiens aided the revolutionary army, others supported the British defenders, and many more remained neutral. This was partly because the British commander, General Carleton, had supported the passage of the Quebec Act of 1774, which guaranteed the right of the inhabitants to practice Catholicism.

In contrast to the optimistic tone of the letter written December 6 (published January 11, 1776, in the *New-England Chronicle*), the revolutionaries under Arnold and Montgomery were not in a strong position. However, they decided to launch an attack in late December, due in part to concern that many of their men would leave—a significant number had only enlisted until the end of the year. Thus, Arnold and Montgomery launched their attack during a snowstorm on December 31, 1775, hoping the weather conditions would provide some cover for their men. The attack was a failure: British fire repulsed the Americans, killing about fifty men, including Montgomery, and wounding Arnold and more than thirty others, while more than four hundred were taken prisoner. Despite this setback, the Americans remained encamped outside of Quebec for months, suffering from serious food shortages and outbreaks of smallpox and other diseases.

As the months passed, the chances of victory decreased. When spring arrived, the ice that had blocked the St. Lawrence River started to melt; this opened the way for reinforcements from Britain. On May 6, 1776, British ships arrived at Quebec, and the Americans were forced to withdraw. With the British in pursuit, they retreated along the St. Lawrence and Richelieu rivers until they reached Crown Point at the southern tip of Lake Champlain, where they began to build a fleet. The British began similar construction at the northern end of the lake. On October 11, 1776, the two fleets met in action in the Battle of Valcour Island. The American fleet suffered significant damage, and Arnold decided to retreat to Fort Ticonderoga farther south. The British did not

follow but withdrew to Canada due to the approach of winter. Had Carleton and the British forces continued their pursuit, the outcome of the war may have been very different. As it was, the failure of the Battle of Quebec and the march on Canada was a serious setback for the American cause; not only was it their first significant military defeat, but it also ensured that Canada would remain a British stronghold throughout the war. Indeed, no significant attempts were made to invade Canada again until the War of 1812. The fate of the Revolution would be decided farther south.

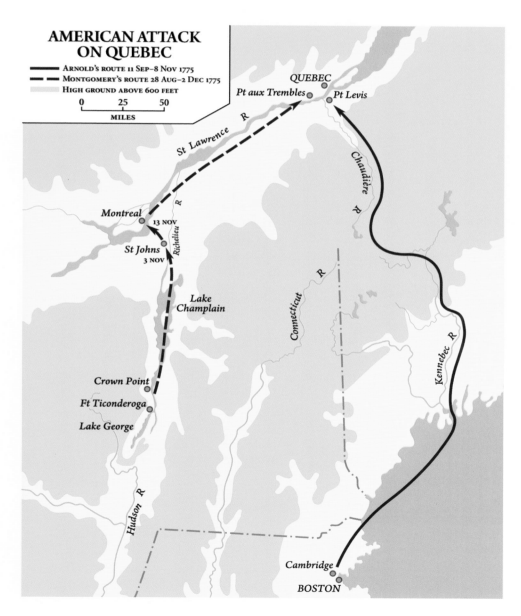

AMERICAN ATTACK ON QUEBEC
United States Army Center of Military History

Map showing the routes taken by the Benedict Arnold and Richard Montgomery expeditions into Quebec.

NEW-ENGLAND CHRONICLE (CAMBRIDGE, MA)
December 28, 1775
—

In late 1775 and early 1776, despite frequent reports about the Continental Army's attack on Quebec, newspapers rarely featured details of Benedict Arnold's arduous expedition. A few particulars emerged in December 1775 when the Continental Congress ordered a series of letters by Montgomery, Schuyler, and Arnold to be published. At least a half-dozen newspapers from Philadelphia to Newburyport published the letters, including the December 28, 1775, *New-England Chronicle*. In the front page printing of the letters, Arnold hints at the exhausting terrain while adding some spin about the army's happy and healthy condition.

Newbury-Port, on Friday, the week before last, a pair of SADDLE BAGS, almost new, very large, with a linen lining.—Whoever has found the same, and will send them to Col. Joseph Gerrish's of Byfield, or to the Printers hereof, shall be entitled to one dollar, paid by NATH. PEIRCE.

Jamaica Rum, Sugar, and English Goods, to be sold cheap. Apply to the red shop next to the Blue Anchor Tavern in Cambridge.

STOLEN from me the subscriber, on Saturday evening, the 16th inst. a brownish grey Horse, about 14 hands high, paces and trots, a small white spot in his forehead, one hind foot white, his right hind foot something broke. Whoever will take up said horse, and convey him to the subscriber in Attleborough, shall be handsomely rewarded, and all necessary charges paid by LEVI MAXCY. Dec. 16, 1775.

STOLEN, on Monday evening last, from the door of Mr. Vose, innholder in Milton, a redish Mare, whitish mane and tail, about 8 years old, natural pacer, a white strip in her forehead, carries a high dock, with her head something low, about 13 hands and half high, had on a redish saddle and housing, and a poor bridle. Whoever takes up said mare shall have two dollars reward upon conveying her to my dwelling-house in Taunton, and all necessary charges paid by GEORGE REED.

N. B. Two old shirts and an old grey coat were fastened on the saddle with 2 garters. Cambridge, 18th Dec. 1775.

PHILADELPHIA, December 15.

The following LETTERS are published by order of the Hon. Continental Congress.

"My dear General, Montreal, Nov. 17.

"With great pleasure I transmit you a letter from Col. Arnold for Gen. Washington, together with the copy of his letter to me. Col. Easton has six guns mounted on shore, three twelve pounders, one nine ditto, and two sixes, at the Sorrel, and the two row gallies. Mr. Carlton, with his 11 sail, has not yet been able to pass him by. Indeed Easton has obliged him twice to weigh anchor, and remove higher up the river. I am making all dispatch to attack him on my side, with field artillery mounted in batteaus. I have had great difficulty about the troops. I am afraid many of them will go home; however, depending on my good fortune, I hope to keep enough to give the final blow to ministerial politics in this province, as I hope effectual measures will be taken to prevent their leaving

much apprehensive of one half of the difficulties we had to encounter, of which I cannot at present give a particular detail. Can only say we have hauled our batteaus up over falls, up rapid streams, over carrying places, and marched through morasses, thick woods, and over mountains, about three hundred and twenty miles, many of which we had to pass several times to bring over our baggage. These difficulties the soldiers have with the greatest fortitude surmounted, and about two thirds of the detachment are happily arrived here, and within two days march, most of them in good health and high spirits.

"The other part, with Col. Enos, returned from the Dead river contrary to my expectation, he having orders to send back only the sick, and those that could not be furnished with provisions. I wrote General Schuyler the thirteenth of October, by an Indian I thought trusty, inclosed to my friend in Quebec, and as I have had no answer from either, and he pretends being taken at Quebec, I make no doubt he has betrayed his trust, which I am confirmed in as I find they have been some time apprised of our coming to Quebec, and have destroyed all the canoes at Point Levy, to prevent our passing. This difficulty will be obviated by birch canoes, as we have about twenty of them, with forty Savages who have joined us, and profess great friendship, as well as the Canadians, by whom we have been very friendly received, and who will be able to furnish us with a number of canoes.

I am informed by the French there are two frigates and several small armed vessels lying before Quebec, and a large ship or two lately arrived from Boston; however I propose crossing the St. Lawrence as soon as possible; and if any opportunity offers of attacking Quebec with success shall embrace it, otherwise shall endeavour to join your army at Montreal. I shall as often as in my power advise you of my proceedings, and beg the favour of hearing from you by every opportunity.

The inclosed letter to his Excellency Gen. Washington beg the favour of your forwarding by express.

I am very respectfully, dear Sir,

wives and children, under pain of being treated as Rebels and Spies. In consequence of which, a great number of the principal inhabitants came out with their families, but were obliged to leave all their property behind, except some wearing apparel, and a little houshold furniture, &c ——— Our men are in high spirits, being now well clothed with the regimentals destined for the 7th and 26th regiments, who were taken prisoners at St. John's.—This is a circumstance, which, I believe the like never before happened to the British troops, as two regiments of them to be made prisoners at one time. Providence smiles on us in a most remarkable manner. The Canadians say, 'Surely God is with this people, or they could never have done what they have done.'— They are all astonished at our march through the wilderness, which they say was impossible, and would not believe our coming, until they had ocular demonstration of it. I hope the next time I write you, it will be from Quebec, for if the in-

when the Lord Lieutenant made a speech to both houses, in which he tries to persuade the poor Irish (notwithstanding the many oppressions continually heaping upon them by the "best of Sovereigns" and his blessed ministry) that they were the happiest people under heaven. Respecting America, his Lordship said,---

"I am persuaded that you entertain a grateful sense of the blessings you enjoy under the mild and firm government of the best of Sovereigns; and his Majesty relies on the known zeal and loyalty of his subjects of Ireland, that, whilst his government is disturbed by a rebellion existing in a part of his American dominions, you will be ready to shew your unavoidable attachment to his person and government, in the assertion of his just rights, and in the support of his legal authority."

We hear from Groton, that Mr. Amos Farnsworth, 70 years of age, and his son, aged 18, in attempting to cross a river in that town, in a canoe, on the 5th ult. were both unhappily drowned. The former has left a wife and five children.

Mr. Joseph Loring jun. of Lexington, lately had a child baptized by the name of JOHN HANCOCK.

Last Sabbath se'nnight died at Wenham, Mrs. MARY HALL, aged 21, Wife of Ebenezer Hall, one of the Printers of this Paper, and Daughter of the late Capt. Josiah Orne of Salem. Her remains were interred at Salem the Thursday following.

As several persons of the name of Brimmer, friends to the country, have lately come out of Boston, we are desired to insert, that the cargo of a vessel, sometime since taken by Capt. Manly, was not consigned to one Brimer in Boston, (as mentioned in a late paper) but to Alexander Brymer, a Scotchman, agent to the victuallers of the navy.

MSBURG, (Virginia) Dec. 13.

...letter from Col. William Woodford to ...dward Pendleton, Esq; President of the ...nvention.

...nt belonging to Major Marshall, ...the other night from Col. Scott's ...ompletely taken his Lordship in.— ...who is wounded, and at present my ...rms, that this fellow told them that ...an three hundred shirtmen were ...at imprudent man catched at the ...ing Capt. Leslie with all his regu-...o) who arrived at the bridge about ...he morning, joined by about 300 ...hite slaves, laid planks upon the ...ssed just after our reveille had beat; ...o ur, and you'll say rather an im-...for them to made...

...sulting for does not surrender shortly, I believe it is the General's intention to carry the town by storm."

A gentleman from Hispaniola informs, he left that place but 14 days ago, that 7000 French troops, and nine sail of the line were arrived there; that two vessels belonging to North-America were at that place, but not having any credentials from the Congress, the inhabitants refused to trade with them; and that the Congress was in high esteem there.

We hear, that yesterday came to town, a gentleman from Canada, who has brought letters from thence to several gentlemen in town, signifying, that on the 5th ult. Gen. Montgomery with his army, were on the heights of Abraham, that he had taken into pay 2500 Canadians...

Last Lord's Day se'nnight, Lieut. Jonathan W... baptized, by the Rev. Mr. M'Gregore of Londo... JOHN SULLIVAN.

THIS DAY IS PUBLISHED, and to be sold, who by S. and E. HALL, in Cambridge; B. EDES, and I. THOMAS, in Worcester,----The

North-American's Alm...

For 1776.

By SAMUEL STEARNS, Student in Physic an...

LEFT on the seat of a necessary ...longing to the Free-Mason's arms tavern in Camb... 4th instant, a silver WATCH, china face, almost n... name Moses Peck. Whoever has taken up the f... leave it at Messrs. Halls' printing-office, shall receiv... two dollars.——N. B. The watch was left at ab... in the afternoon.

FOUND...

NEW-ENGLAND CHRONICLE (CAMBRIDGE, MA)
January 11, 1776
—

In contrast to the optimistic tone of the letter written December 6, published January 11, 1776, in the *New-England Chronicle*, the revolutionaries under Arnold and Montgomery were not in a strong position. However, they decided to launch an attack in late December, due in part to concern that many of their men would leave – a significant number had only enlisted until the end of the year. The failure of the Battle of Quebec and the march on Canada was a serious setback for the American cause. It was their first significant military defeat.

...nt commanded ...dyce, of the gre... ...pany, who, for ...ed a better fate, ...ll with him, wh... ...arched up to eu... ...and perhaps ... ...greater carnage, ...ne of the blacks, &c. in the rear ...fle, advanced farther than the ...the pleasure to inform you, that ...complete, and that most of the ...ded, with two pieces of cannon...

...Otter Man of War; who, when they were asked, what induced them to leave Dunmore? Answered, Hungry Bellies, naked Backs, and no Fuel; besides, in other Respects, the most cruel and inhuman Treatment —That Lord Dunmore had...

...particularize.

To be SOLD on reasonable terms.

A neat house, with a shop, almost ne... about an acre and an half of good land, just 3 mile... vard college, on the great road, in a good place for bu... pleasantly situated, with a small...

NATIVE AMERICANS CHOOSING SIDES

By Daniel J. Tortora

WHEN THE AMERICAN REVOLUTION BEGAN, Native Americans had to choose sides. The British, Patriots, and Tories coveted the services of Native American guides, interpreters, and spies, and they valued their bravery and intimidation in battle. Native American warriors played vital roles in the struggle for independence, but the Revolution devastated Native American lives and communities.

In the spring of 1775, when councils of safety pressed them to join the Patriot cause, Native Americans began to pick sides. The Continental Congress sent presents, letters, and wampum to the tribes in the east during the summer of 1775, reports the *Connecticut Journal* of August 23, 1775. The tribes of the Iroquois Confederacy initially declared neutrality as the same *Connecticut Journal* indicates, but most Native Americans sided with the British. Since 1763, they had seen white settlers overrun their lands. Natives believed that if Britain won, the Crown would limit white settlement in the west. Some fought with the Americans. They did so to escape poverty, pushed by family tradition and Christian missionaries, and the hopes, as one Mashpee Wampanoag put it, that the colonists' sufferings "would naturally lead them to respect and relieve ours."

Dozens of Native American Patriots fought in the siege of Boston, as the *Pennsylvania Evening Post* of June 29, 1775, reveals. Fifteen Native Americans saw action at Bunker Hill. Maine Native Americans escorted Benedict Arnold to Quebec in 1775. "Stockbridges" from western Massachusetts and eastern New York fought with the Continental Army from 1775 to 1778. On August 31, 1778, the Queen's Rangers decimated the Stockbridge unit in a battle in the Bronx.

Along the New York and Pennsylvania frontier, the Revolution devastated Native American communities. By 1777, a civil war broke out between, and even within, the six tribes of the Iroquois Confederacy. Mohawks, Senecas, Onondagas, and Cayugas joined the British. They raided and fought Patriot militias and Continental troops and provided food for British armies in New York, New Jersey, and Pennsylvania. Oneidas and Tuscaroras fought with Patriot militias.

Four hundred natives served with British General John Burgoyne. They pillaged, scalped, and killed without restraint. After suffering massive casualties, most of them deserted before the Battle of Saratoga. From late 1777 through summer 1779, hundreds of Native Americans and Tories, led by Mohawk Joseph Brant, Colonel John Butler, and Captain William Butler, raided the frontier along the Cherry Valley, Mohawk Valley, and the Wyoming Valley in New York and Pennsylvania. They seized supplies for the British Army and intimidated Patriot-leaning settlers and Native Americans.

In the south, Catawbas aided the American defense of Sullivan's Island, South Carolina, in 1776. At the same time, British agents incited Cherokees led by Dragging Canoe to attack the southern frontier. But southern militias and Catawbas destroyed most of the Cherokee settlements in response. Cherokee survivors ceded large tracts of land. Cherokee resistance was limited to sporadic raiding. Creek Native Americans helped the British defend the Gulf Coast region in 1780 and 1781. Catawbas defended Charleston in May 1780. They fought with General Thomas Sumter at King's Mountain and at Eutaw Springs. Lumbees, Pamunkeys, and other Native Americans fought in militia, state, and continental units.

In the west, George Rogers Clark and his Virginia militia took white settlements in Indiana and Illinois and quelled Shawnee resistance.

At war's end, it did not matter which side Native Americans had chosen. Tradition and grief led them to plunder, scalp, and mutilate. This reinforced land-hungry Americans' perceptions of Native Americans as "savage" and inhuman. With few exceptions, Patriot Native American veterans faced discrimination and marginalization. Massachusetts sold Maine Native American lands to pay white soldiers. Frontiersmen rapidly overtook Native American lands. Driven from their homelands, most Iroquois moved to Canada. Native communities reeled from the loss of their hunting grounds, men, and dignity. Survivors slipped into poverty, alcoholism, and despair, but they continued to fight to preserve their cultures.

PENNSYLVANIA EVENING POST (PHILADELPHIA)
June 29, 1775

Dozens of Native American Patriots fought in the siege of Boston, as this newspaper reveals. Fifteen saw action at Bunker Hill, and some from Maine escorted Benedict Arnold to Quebec in 1775.

CONNECTICUT JOURNAL (NEW HAVEN)
August 23, 1775

When the American Revolution began, Native Americans had to choose sides. The British, Patriots, and Tories coveted the services of Native American guides, interpreters, and spies and valued their bravery and intimidation in battle. The Continental Congress sent presents, letters, and wampum to the tribes in the east during the summer of 1775. The tribes of the Iroquois Confederacy initially declared neutrality as the same *Connecticut Journal* indicates, but most Indians sided with the British.

Extract of a letter from a Gentleman at Cambridge (Massachusetts-Bay) to a Gentleman of the Congress, dated June 22.

"A firm foundation now turns up to view, for the influence of the Stockbridge Indians amongst the SIX NATIONS, and matters stand well with the Canadian Indians. If I had time, I would relate to you every particular of what befel the messengers of our Indians to the Six Nations and the Canadian Indians. To be short, they were taken and bound by the regulars, and carried into Montreal, where, by a court martial they were condemned to be hanged, for a slight suspicion that they were sent to engage the Indians to fall upon the regulars. This event turned much to our advantage, and has fully fixed the minds of the Indians there against the regulars. High threatening words passed between the General and the Indian Sachems, who were raised far and near on the occasion, and a wonderful spirit of benevolence appeared towards the young men that were taken by the Indians there. They told them, in the strongest terms, *That they would take their place, they would die for them.* The whole story is very affecting. The Indian Sachems told the General, *You have offered us money to fight for you, but we would not take it, as we would have nothing to do with your quarrel, but now we shall know who are our enemies. If you think it best for you to hang these our brothers, that came a great way to see us, do it, but remember we shall not forget it.* Upon these threatenings they thought it best to let the prisoners go, who got away with some difficulty. The Canadian Indians farther told our Indians, *That if they did fight at all, they would FIGHT AGAINST the REGULARS, for they did not like them.*"

Extract of a letter from Providence, June 20.

"Our government have ordered two cruizers to be equipped and sent out to protect the trade. They have retaken Lindsay's packet in sight of the men of war. The men of war

Commission superseded.

John Carr, of Scotland-yard, Coal-merchant, (Partner in Trade with James Farrer and Edward Arrowsmith, of the same Place, Coal-merchants.)

Bankruptcy enlarged.

James Farrer, Edward Arrowsmith, and John Carr, of Scotland-yard, Coal-merchants and Partners, to surrender Aug. 29, at Guildhall.

Dividends to be made.

Sept. 3. John Gardner, late of Romsey, in Hants, Clothier, at the Angel in Romsey.

11. Richard Ford, of Coalbrookdale, in the County of Salop, Ironmaster, at Mary Corbett's, in High-street, Bridgnorth, Salop.

20. Benjamin Cooper, late of Walsall, in Staffordshire, and Joseph Hodgkin, late of Aldridge, in the said County, Merchants and Traders, at the King's-head in New-street, Birmingham.

Certificate to be granted.

Aug. 31. William Richardson, of Fenchurch street, London, Linen-draper.

LONDON.

Advice is received that the Congress resolved upon independence the 4th of July; and, it is said, have declared war against Great Britain in form.

When General Thompson was conducted in the guard-room at Montreal with the rest of the prisoners of that day, he reque   lier of his brother General,   bart tern waited on him wi   hich Carleton refused compl   ur for answer, "that he n   tion with rebels."

A letter from   says, "that the   refused to give an

On Tuesday last was married at Ash, in Kent, the Rev. Mr. Hutchinson of Norbourn, to Miss Elizabeth Beale Pery, of Ash.

On Saturday last was married at Crayford, in Kent, Mr. Essex, of Southampton-street, Covent-Garden, to Miss Nancy Wright, of Crayford.

Yesterday was married Mr. Samuel Fenn, of this City, to Miss Tate of the Old Change.

On Friday last died at Greenwich, Captain Francis Minshull

On Saturday last died, at his house in St. James's-street, Mr. Matthew Crane, Apothecary to the Houshold.

At Shrewsbury assizes John Herbert for sheep-stealing, was capitally convicted, but afterwards reprieved.

H. M. The Nabob, with Taste.

This Day was published, Price 1s 6d.
A New Edition, corrected to the present time, on a broad sheet of elephant paper, proper for framing, with an elegant engraved border,

A COMPLETE TITHE-TABLE: Wherein the nature of tithes, and all things tithable, are shewn at one view. With an account of compositions, custom, prescription, and privilege, distin   hed under their proper heads; with reference to   ged cases, and statutes relating to tithes.

      oper for   ll Vestries, Halls of Clergymen and   ntleme   ell as Attorneys.

      rinted   and C. Rivington, No. 62, in St.   e Ch   d.

          hom may be had,
          anner above-menti
          Wherein all the
       w. Price

SOCIETY for the Discharge and Relief imprisoned for Small Debts.
Craven-street, Strand, July

Benefactions since the last report, viz.

W. W. a Lady
Lord Chief Baron Smythe, annual
Lady Smythe, ditto
Mr. Hull, ditto
W. J. 3d benefaction
A. B.
D. B.
D. C. July 10
J. H. by J. R.

Discharged from the several prisons in polis, and other parts of the kingdom, 2 who could not be relieved by the Insolven 39 l. 6 s. 2 d.

Approved the recommendations of 24 Referred for Enquiry 19 Petitions.

The books may be seen by any person promote this undertaking, between the Eleven and Three, at No. 7, Craven-str benefactions are received, and where the S meet on Wednesday the 22d of Augu in the Afternoon.

      actions are also received by Mr.   atch'd house   the London   Compan   Nield,   St. Ja   Messrs   Finch   Messr

THE SPIRIT OF LIBERTY

Introduction

As the snow began melting in the early months of 1776, colonists warmed to the idea of independence thanks to a forty-eight-page pamphlet titled *Common Sense* that colonial presses printed in unprecedented quantities. Early military engagements in North Carolina, Georgia, and South Carolina reinforced the Patriot spirit while Washington's troops fortified the heights around Boston and successfully forced the British to withdraw from town. In June 1776, a committee of five legislators drafted and presented the Declaration of Independence to the Continental Congress. On July 2, Congress voted for independence, and two days later it approved the text of its official Declaration. Celebrations were short-lived as General Washington's focus quickly turned to New York and the middle colonies for what was certain to be a large-scale retaliation attack by the British.

LONDON CHRONICLE
August 13, 1776

DECLARATION OF INDEPENDENCE
BY JOHN TRUMBULL
Architect of the Capitol

COMMON SENSE AND THE AMERICAN CRISIS

By Jim Piecuch

A
T THE START OF 1776, MANY AMERICAN COLONISTS had begun to believe that independence might be the only solution to their decade-long dispute with the British government. However, the prospect appeared daunting. Independence not only meant challenging the military might of the world's most powerful empire, but also rejecting the authority of a king who many believed ruled by divine right and replacing monarchy with a new system of government. That January, Thomas Paine published *Common Sense* in Philadelphia. More than one hundred thousand copies of the pamphlet were sold, and it was also serialized or excerpted in many American newspapers. Using a variety of clearly stated arguments based on history, biblical scripture, and Enlightenment rationalism to appeal to the widest possible audience, Paine convinced a large number of Americans that independence was necessary and attainable (noted in the *New-England Chronicle* of March 27, 1776). He denounced the institution of monarchy, offered an alternative form of government, and asserted that the colonists had the means to defeat the British armed forces. Although the ringing words of Thomas Jefferson's Declaration of Independence are better remembered, it is possible that without *Common Sense*, the Declaration would never have been written. Later, when military reverses raised questions about the ability of the colonists to triumph, Paine wrote a series of essays, *The American Crisis*, to boost morale and urge Americans to persist in their struggle.

When King George III advocated tougher policies toward the colonies following the publication of *Common Sense*, Paine's arguments appeared to have been validated. The colonial press took up the cause of independence, using Paine's arguments (as stated in the *New-England Chronicle*, March 27, 1776).

Some Americans disagreed with Paine and published their own essays challenging *Common Sense*. One religious group, the Quakers (Society of Friends), argued against independence based on their pacifist tenets. Paine responded by appending an address to the Quakers to later editions of *Common Sense* that countered the points they had raised (this address was reprinted in the *New-England Chronicle* of April 4, 1776). Paine asserted that those Quakers who opposed independence misunderstood both the principles of their own religion and the serious political situation.

British writers also disputed Paine's contention that the colonies could defeat the British armed forces. Challenging Paine's statement that New England shipyards had the capability to build a fleet that could challenge the Royal Navy, Admiral Clark Gayton declared that New England had thus far produced only two large warships and that these had been of such poor quality that British naval authorities quickly condemned both (Gayton's letter appeared in the *London Chronicle*, August 29, 1776).

After the Continental Congress declared independence and the war dragged on, Paine wrote his *American Crisis* essays exhorting Americans to continue the struggle. The first appeared in December 1776, when the Continental Army was in full retreat across New Jersey following a series of disastrous defeats around New York City. Like *Common Sense*, the *Crisis* essays were widely reprinted in American newspapers. In the third essay, published in the

Although the ringing words of Thomas Jefferson's Declaration of Independence are better remembered, it is possible that without Common Sense, *the Declaration would never have been written.*

spring of 1777, Paine reminded Americans of the reasons why they had declared independence, accused the opponents of independence of acting from fear, laziness, and greed, and urged Americans to risk everything for their cause (see the *Independent Chronicle*, May 22, 1777). Three years later, in *The American Crisis No. VIII*, Paine reminded Americans of how, despite the "wanton cruelty" of the British army in its efforts to subdue the rebellion, five years had elapsed since the fighting had begun and the Americans remained unconquered.

Having played a crucial role in convincing the colonists to declare independence, Paine remained a steadfast advocate of the American cause throughout the Revolution. His writings not only helped give birth to the United States, but also nurtured the infant nation during the difficult wartime years until independence was finally attained.

THOMAS PAINE
*National Portrait Gallery, London
(current location)*

Thomas Paine wrote *Common Sense*, which sold more than one hundred thousand copies and used clearly stated arguments to convince the widest possible audience that independence was necessary and attainable.

The NEW-ENGLAND CHRONICLE

The public in general having read, and (excepting a few timid Whigs or disguised Tories) loudly applauded that *truly excellent pamphlet, intitled,* COMMON SENSE; *our readers will doubtless be pleased with the perusal of the following* APPENDIX *written by the same ingenious author, and printed in Philadelphia since the publication of the second edition of* Common Sense.

SINCE the publication of the first edition of this pamphlet, or rather, on the same day on which it came out, the King's Speech made its appearance in this city.---- Had the spirit of prophecy directed the birth of this production, it could not have brought it forth at a more seasonable juncture, or a more necessary time. The bloody-mindedness of the one, shows the necessity of pursuing the doctrine of the other. Men read by way of revenge. And the Speech, instead of terrifying, prepared a way for the manly principles of Independence.

Ceremony, and even silence, from whatever motive they may arise, have a hurtful tendency, when they give the least degree of countenance to base and wicked performances; wherefore, if this maxim be admitted, it naturally follows, that the King's Speech, as being a piece of finished villany, deserved, and still deserves, a general execration both by the Congress and the people.— Yet, as the domestic tranquility of a nation depends greatly on the *chastity* of what may properly be called NATIONAL MANNERS, it is often better to pass some things over in silent disdain, than to make use of such new methods of dislike, as might introduce the least innovation, on than guardian of our peace and safety. And, perhaps, it is chiefly owing to this prudent delicacy, that the King's Speech hath not, before now, suffered a public execution. The Speech, if it may be called one, is nothing better than a willful audacious libel against the truth, the common good, and the existence of mankind; and is a formal and pompous method of offering up human sacrifices to the pride of tyrants. But this general massacre of mankind, is one of the privileges, and the certain consequence of Kings; for as nature knows them *not*, they know *not her;* and although they are beings of our *own* creating, they know not *us,* and are become the gods of their creators. The Speech hath one good quality, which is, that it is not calculated to deceive, neither can we, even if we would, be deceived by it. Brutality and tyranny appear on the face of it. It leaves us at no less: And every line convinces, even in the moment of reading, that He, who hunts the woods for prey, the naked and untutored Indian, is less a Savage than the King of Britain.

Sir John Dalrymple, the putative father of a whining jesuitical piece, fallaciously called, *"The address of the people of* ENGLAND *to the inhabitants of* AMERICA," hath, perhaps, from a vain supposition, that the people *here* were to be frightened at the pomp and description of a king, given, (though very unwisely on his part) the real character of the present one: "But," says this writer, "if you are inclined to pay compliments to an administration, which we do not complain of," (meaning the Marquis of Rockingham's at the repeal of the Stamp-Act) "it is very unfair in you to withhold them from that prince, *by whose* NOD ALONE *they were permitted to do any thing."* This is toryism with a witness! Here is idolatry even without a mask: And he who can calmly hear, and digest such doctrine, hath forfeited his claim to rationality—an apostate from the order of manhood; and ought to be considered—as one, who hath not only given up the proper dignity of man, but sunk himself beneath the rank of animals, and contemptibly crawl through the world like a worm. [...]

NEW-ENGLAND CHRONICLE (CAMBRIDGE, MA)
March 27, 1776

Even at the start of 1776, the prospect of independence appeared daunting, but Thomas Paine's pamphlet, *Common Sense,* which was excerpted in many American newspapers, helped convince a large number of Americans that independence was necessary and attainable.

NEW-ENGLAND CHRONICLE: OR, ESSEX GAZETTE.

VOL. VIII. NUMB. 399.

From THURSDAY, March 21, to THURSDAY, March 27, 1776.

CAMBRIDGE: Printed by SAMUEL HALL, at his Printing-Office in Stoughton-Hall, HARVARD-COLLEGE.

The public in general having read, and (excepting a few timid Whigs or disguised Tories) loudly applauded that truly excellent pamphlet, intitled, COMMON SENSE; our readers will doubtless be pleased with the perusal of the following APPENDIX, written by the same ingenious author, and printed in Philadelphia since the publication of the second edition of Common Sense.

SINCE the publication of the first edition of this pamphlet, or rather, on the same day on which it came out, the King's Speech made its appearance in this city.— Had the spirit of prophecy directed the birth of this production, it could not have brought it forth at a more seasonable juncture, or a more necessary time. The bloody-mindedness of the one, shews the necessity of pursuing the doctrine of the other. Men read by way of revenge. And the Speech, instead of terrifying, prepared a way for the manly principles of Independance.

Ceremony, and even silence, from whatever motive they may arise, have a hurtful tendency, when they give the least degree of countenance to base and wicked performances; wherefore, if this maxim be admitted, it naturally follows, that the King's Speech, as being a piece of finished villany, deserved, and still deserves, a general execration both by the Congress and the people.— Yet, as the domestic tranquility of a nation depends greatly on the chastity of what may properly be called NATIONAL MANNERS, it is often better to pass some things over in silent disdain, than to make use of such new methods of dislike, as might introduce the least innovation, on that guardian of our peace and safety. And, perhaps, it is chiefly owing to this prudent delicacy, that the King's Speech hath not, before now, suffered a public execution. The Speech, if it may be called one, is nothing better than a wilful audacious libel against the truth, the common good, and the existence of mankind; and is a formal and pompous method of offering up human sacrifices to the pride of tyrants. But this general massacre of mankind, is one of the privileges, and the business of the reign of a king more than all other men; for they are beings of our own creating, they know not us, and are become the gods of their creators.

wickedly broken through every moral and human obligation, trampled nature and conscience beneath his feet; and by a steady and constitutional spirit of insolence and cruelty, procured for himself an universal hatred. It is now the interest of America to provide for herself. She hath already a large and young family, whom it is more her duty to take care of, than to be granting away her property, to support a power who is become a reproach to the names of men and christians:— Ye, whose office it is to watch over the morals of a nation, of whatsoever sect or denomination ye are of, as well as ye, who are more immediately the guardians of the public liberty, if ye wish to preserve your native country uncontaminated by European corruption, ye must in secret wish a separation.— But leaving the moral part to private reflection, I shall chiefly confine my farther remarks to the following heads.

First. That it is the interest of America to be separated from Britain.

Secondly. Which is the easiest and most practicable plan, RECONCILIATION or INDEPENDANCE? with some occasional remarks.

In support of the first, I could, if I judged it proper, produce the opinion of some of the ablest and most experienced men on this continent; and whose sentiments, on that head, are not yet publickly known. It is in reality a self-evident position: For no nation in a state of foreign dependance, limited in its commerce, and cramped and fettered in its legislative powers, can arrive at any material eminence. America doth not yet know what opulence is; and although the progress which she hath made stands unparalleled in the history of other nations, it is but childhood, compared with what she would be capable of arriving at, had she, as she ought to have, the legislative powers in her own hands. England is, at this time, proudly coveting what would do her no good, were she to accomplish it; and the Continent hesitating on a matter, which will be her final ruin if neglected. It is the commerce and not the conquest of America, by which England

trames, in which a sufficiency of the former remains, and a proper increase of the latter is obtained; And that point of time is the present time.

The reader will pardon this digression, as it does not properly come under the head I first set out with, and to which I again return by the following position, viz.

Should affairs be patched up with Britain, and she to remain the governing and sovereign power of America, (which, as matters are now circumstanced, is giving up the point intirely) we shall deprive ourselves of the very means of sinking the debt we have, or may contract. The value of the back lands which some of the provinces are clandestinely deprived of, by the unjust extention of the limits of Canada, valued only at five pounds sterling per hundred acres, amount to upwards of twenty-five millions, Pennsylvania currency; and the quit-rents at one penny sterling per acre, to two millions yearly.

It is by the sale of those lands that the debt may be sunk, without burthen to any, and the quit-rent reserved thereon, will always lessen, and in time, will wholly support the yearly expence of government. It matters not how long the debt is in paying, so that the lands when sold be applied to the discharge of it, and for the execution of which, the Congress for the time being, will be the continental trustees.

I proceed now to the second head, viz. Which is the easiest and most practicable plan, RECONCILIATION or INDEPENDANCE; with some occasional remarks.

He who takes nature for his guide is not easily beaten out of his argument, and on that ground, I answer generally---That INDEPENDANCE being a SINGLE SIMPLE LINE, contained within ourselves; and reconciliation, a matter exceedingly perplexed and complicated, & in which a treacherous capricious court is to interfere, gives the answer without a doubt.

The present state of America is truly alarming to every man who is capable of reflection. Without law, without government, without any other mode of power than what is founded on

they are beings of our own creating, they know not us, and are become the gods of their creators.

of each other as France and Spain; because in many articles, neither can go to a better market. But it is the independance of this country on

nevertheless subject to change, and which, every secret enemy is endeavouring to dissolve. Our this production, it could not have brought it forth at a more seasonable juncture, or a more necessary time. The bloody-mindedness of the one, shews the necessity of pursuing the doctrine of the other. Men read by way of revenge. And the Speech, instead of terrifying, prepared a way for the manly principles of Independance.

Ceremony, and even silence, from whatever motive they may arise, have a hurtful tendency, when they give the least degree of countenance to base and wicked performances; wherefore, if this maxim be admitted, it naturally follows, that the King's Speech, as being a piece of finished villany, deserved, and still deserves, a general execration both by the Congress and the people.—Yet, as the domestic tranquility of a nation depends greatly on the *chastity* of what may properly be called NATIONAL MANNERS, it is often better to pass some things over in silent disdain, than to make use of such new methods of dislike, as might introduce the least innovation, on than guardian of our peace and safety. And, perhaps, it is chiefly owing to this prudent delicacy, that the King's Speech hath not, before now, suffered a public execution. The Speech, if it may be called one, is nothing better than a willful audacious libel against the truth, the common good, and the existence of mankind; and is a formal and pompous method of offering up human sacrifices to the pride of tyrants. But this general massacre of mankind, is one of the privileges, and the certain consequence of Kings; for as nature knows them *not*, they know *not her*; and although they are beings of our *own* creating, they know not *us*, and are become the gods of their creators. The Speech hath one good quality, which is, that it is not calculated to deceive, neither can we, even if we would, be deceived by it. Brutality and tyranny appear on the face of it. It leaves us at no loss: And every line convinces, even in the moment of reading, that He, who hunts the woods for prey, the naked and untutored Indian, is less a Savage than the King of Britain.

Sir John Dalrymple, the putative father of a whining jesuitical piece, fallaciously called, "*The address of the people of ENGLAND to the inhabitants of AMERICA*," hath, perhaps, from a vain supposition, that the people *here* were to be frightened at the pomp and description of a king, given, (though very unwisely on his part) the real character of the present one: "But," says this writer, "if you are inclined to pay compliments to an administration, which we do not complain of," (meaning the Marquis of Rockingham's at the repeal of the Stamp-Act) "it is very unfair in you to withhold them from that prince, *by whose* NOD ALONE *they were permitted to do any thing.*" This is toryism with a witness! Here is idolatry

However, it matters very little now, what the king of England either says or does; he hath

to preserve your native country uncontaminated by European corruption, ye must in secret wish a separation.—But leaving the moral part to private reflection, I shall chiefly confine my farther remarks to the following heads.

First. That it is the interest of America to be separated from Britain.

Secondly. Which is the easiest and most practicable plan, RECONCILIATION or INDEPENDANCE? with some occasional remarks.

In support of the first, I could, if I judged it proper, produce the opinion of some of the ablest and most experienced men on this continent; and whose sentiments, on that head, are not yet publickly known. It is in reality a self-evident position: For no nation in a state of foreign dependance, limited in its commerce, and cramped and fettered in its legislative powers, can arrive at any material eminence. America doth not yet know what opulence is; and although the progress which she hath made stands unparalleled in the history of other nations, it is but childhood, compared with what she would be capable of arriving at, had she, as she ought to have, the legislative powers in her own hands. England is, at this time, proudly coveting what would do her no good, were she to accomplish it; and the Continent hesitating on a matter, which will be her final ruin if neglected. It is the commerce and not the conquest of America, by which England is to be benefited, and that would in a great measure continue, were the countries as independant of each other as France and Spain; because in many articles, neither can go to a better market. But it is the independance of this country on Britain or any other, which is now the main and only object worthy of contention, and which, like all other truths discovered by necessity, will appear clearer and stronger every day.

First. Because it will come to that one time or other.

Secondly. Because, the longer it is delayed the harder it will be to accomplish.

I have frequently amused myself both in public and private companies, with silently remarking, the specious errors of those who speak without reflecting. And among the many which I have heard, the following seems the most general, viz. that had this rupture happened forty or fifty years hence, instead of *now*, the Continent would have been more able to have shaken off the dependance. To which I reply, that our military ability, *at this time*, arises from the experience gained in the last war, and which in forty or fifty years time, would have been totally extinct. The Continent would not, by that time, have had a General, or even a military officer left; and we, or those who may ... been as ignorant of mar ... ent Indians: And this ... ended to, will unanswer ... ent time is preferable to ... ent turns thus—at the ... ar, we had experience, ... and forty or fifty years hence, we should have numbers, without experience; wherefore the proper point of time must be some particular point between the two extremes.

of the back lands which some of the provinces are clandestinely deprived of, by the unjust extension of the limits of Canada, valued only at five pounds sterling per hundred acres, amount to upwards of twenty-five millions, Pennsylvania currency; and the quit-rents at one penny sterling per acre, to two millions yearly.

It is by the sale of those lands that the debt may be sunk, without burthen to any, and the quit-rent reserved thereon, will always lessen, and in time, will wholly support the yearly expence of government. It matters not how long the debt is in paying, so that the lands when sold be applied to the discharge of it, and for the execution of which, the Congress for the time being, will be the continental trustees.

I proceed now to the second head, viz. Which is the easiest and most practicable plan, RECONCILIATION or INDEPENDANCE; with some occasional remarks.

He who takes nature for his guide is not easily beaten out of his argument, and on that ground, I answer *generally---That* INDEPENDANCE *being a* SINGLE SIMPLE LINE, *contained within ourselves; and reconciliation, a matter exceedingly perplexed and complicated, & in which a treacherous capricious court is to interfere, gives the answer without a doubt.*

The present state of America is truly alarming to every man who is capable of reflection. Without law, without government, without any other mode of power than what is founded on, and granted by courtesy. Held together by an unexampled concurrence of sentiment, which is nevertheless subject to change, and which, every secret enemy is endeavouring to dissolve. Our present condition, is, legislation without law; wisdom without a plan; a constitution without a name; and, what is strangely astonishing, perfect independance contending for dependance.—The instance is without a precedent; the case never existed before; and who can tell what may be the event? The property of no man is secure in the present unbraced system of things. The mind of the multitude is left at random, and seeing no fixed object before them, they pursue such as fancy or opinion starts. Nothing is criminal; there is no such thing as treason; wherefore, every one thinks himself at liberty to act as he pleases. The Tories dared not have assembled offensively, had they known that their lives, by that act, were forfeited to the laws of the state. A line of distinction should be drawn, between English soldiers taken in battle, and inhabitants of America taken in arms. The first are prisoners, but the latter traitors. The one forfeits his liberty, the other his head.

Notwithstanding our wisdom, there is a visible feebleness in some of our proceedings which gives encouragement to dissentions. The Continental Belt is too loosely buckled. And if something is not done in time, it will be too late to do any thing, and we shall fall into a state, in which, neither *Reconciliation* nor *Independance* will be practicable. The king and his worthless adherents are got at their old game of dividing the Continent, and there are not wanting among us, Printers, who will be busy in spreading specious falsehoods. The artful and hypocritical letter which

THE
NEW-ENGLAND
OR,
ESSEX
VOL. VIII.

CHRON
GAZE

From THURSDAY, *March* 28, to

THURSDAY, *Apr*

NUMB.

CAMBRIDGE: Printed by SAMUE

The following Address was lately published in Philadelphia, as an Addition to "COMMON SENSE."

Representatives of the religious Society of the people called Quakers, *or to so many of them as were concerned in publishing a late piece, entitled,* "The ANTIENT TESTIMONY and PRIN-"CIPLES of the people called QUAKERS re-"newed, with respect to the KING and Go-"VERNMENT, and touching the COMMOTI-"ONS now prevailing in these and other parts "of AMERICA, addressed to the PEOPLE in "GENERAL."

THE writer of this, is one of those few, who never dishonours religion either by ridiculing or cavelling at any deno-mination whatsoever. To God and not to man, are all men accountable on the score of re-ligion. Wherefore, this epistle is not so proper-ly addressed to you as a religious, but as a politi-cal body, dabbling in matters, which the pro-fessed quietude of your principles instruct you not to meddle with.

As you have, without a proper authority for so doing, put yourselves in the place of the whole Body of the Quakers, so, the writer of this, in order to be on an equal rank with yourselves, is under the necessity of putting himself in the place of all those who approve the very writings and principles against which, your testimony is direct-ed: And he hath chosen this singular situation, in order, that you might discover in him that presumption of character which you cannot see in yourselves. For neither he nor you can have any claim or title to *political representation.*

When men have departed from the right way, it is no wonder they stumble and fall. And it is evident from the manner in which ye have ma-naged your testimony, that politics (as a religious body of men,) is not your proper walk; for how-ever well adapted it might appear to you, it is, nevertheless, a jumble of good and bad put un-

O y ledged the fir differe able d from tical h world our ene us proof James's to the A ravaging creants whom y of *Ba* King and w spend y and insu would are peu authors upon y that we are *Qua* NOT Q

Alas some pa your co compre that by mistake neral te And it i to many see them instant mon of ter it wi tite as keen as death.

hope, end, and aim. *Our plan is peace for ever.* We are tired of contention with Britain, and can see no real end to it but in a final separation. We act consistently, because for the sake of in-troducing an endless and uninterrupted peace, do we bear the evils and burdens of the present day. We are endeavouring, and will steadily continue to endeavour, to separate and dissolve a connection which hath already filled our land with blood, and which, while the name of it remains, will be the fatal cause of future mischiefs to both countries.

We fight neither for revenge nor conquest; neither from pride nor passion; we are not in-sulting the world with our fleets and armies, nor ravaging the globe for plunder. Beneath the shade of our own vines are we attacked; in our own houses, and on our own lands, is the violence committed against us. We view our enemies in the character of highwaymen and housebreakers, and having no defence for ourselves in the civil law, are obliged to punish them by the military one, and apply the sword in the very case where you have, before now, applied the halter.---Per-haps we feel for the ruined and insulted sufferers in all and every part of the continent, with a de-gree of tenderness which hath not yet made its way into some of your bosoms. But be ye sure that ye mistake not the cause and ground of your testimony. Call not coldness of soul, religion; nor put the *Bigot* in the place of the *Christian.*

only an
"It
"ple, fi
"Chris
"to thi
"kings
"regat
"And
"hand
"bodie
"contr
"but t
"tion,
"live
"and
"is ple
your pr
Why d

a "Thou
"est w
"ruled
"ing o
"oppre
"ings,
"Lord
"thee
"vanit
"whic
"or do
"and p
"of Ch
"ther
"case i

the exciting and stirring u

THE CHRONICLE: THE GAZETTE.

NUMB. 400.

THURSDAY, *April* 4, 1776.

at his Printing-Office in Stoughton-Hall, HARVARD-COLLEGE.

of your own acknow-
...bearing arms be sinful,
...be more so, by all the
...al attack and unavoid-
...fore, if ye really preach
...can not to make a poli
...religion, convince the
...iming your doctrine to
...wise bear ARMS. Give
...by publishing it at St.
...ers in chief at Boston,
...ains who are piratically
...all the murdering mis-
...authority under HIM.
Had ye the honest soul
...ach repentance to *your*
...royal wretch his sins,
...ruin. Ye would not
...es against the injured
...ke faithful ministers,
...none. Say not that ye
...eavour to make us the

work, to be managed by himself? These very
principles instruct you to wait with patience and
humility, for the event of all public measures,
and to receive that event as the divine will towards
you. Wherefore, what occasion is there for your
political testimony if you fully believe what it contains? And the very publishing proves, that either
ye do not believe what ye profess, or have not
virtue enough to practise what ye believe.

The principles of Quakerism have a direct
tendency to make a man the quiet and inoffensive
subject of any, and every government *which is set*
over him. And if the setting up and putting down
of kings and governments is God's peculiar prerogative, he most certainly will be robbed thereof by us; wherefore, the principle itself leads you
to approve of every thing which ever happened,
or may happen to Kings as being his work.
OLIVER CROMWELL thanks you. CHARLES,
then, died not by the hands of man; and should
the present proud imitator of him, come to the

tains, to applaud the fact. Kings are not taken
away by miracles, neither are changes in governments brought about by any other means than
such as are common and human; and such as we
are now using. Even the dispersion of the Jews,
though foretold by our Saviour, was effected by
arms. Wherefore as ye refuse to be the means
on one side, ye ought not to be meddlers on the
other; but to wait the issue in silence; and unless ye can produce divine authority, to prove,
that the Almighty, who hath created and placed
this *new* world, at the greatest distance it could
possibly stand, east and west, from every part of
the old, doth, nevertheless, disapprove of its being
independent of the corrupt and abandoned court
of Britain; unless I say, ye can shew this, how
can ye on the ground of your principles, justify
the exciting and stirring up of the people, " firm-
" ly to unite in the *abhorrence* of all such *writings*
" and *measures,* as evidence a desire and design to
" break off the *happy* connection we have hither-
" to enjoyed, with the kingdom of Great-Bri-
" tain, and our just and necessary subordination
" to the King, and those who are lawfully placed
" in authority under him," What a slap of the face
is here! the men, who in the very paragraph
before, have quietly and passively resigned up the
ordering, altering, and disposal of kings and governments, into the hands of God, are now, recalling their principles, and putting in for a
share of the business. Is it possible, that the conclusion, which is here justly quoted, can any
ways follow from the doctrine laid down? The
inconsistency is too glaring not to be seen; the
absurdity, too great not to be laughed at; and
such as could only have been made by those,
whose understandings were darkned by the narrow and crabby spirit of a disparing political party; for ye are not to be considered as the whole
body of the Quakers, but only as a fractional and
fractional part thereof.

Here ends the examination of your testimony;
(which I call upon no man to abhor, as ye have
done, but only to read and judge of fairly;) to
which I subjoin the following remark; " That
the setting up and putting down of kings," most
certainly mean, the making him a King, who is
yet not so, and the making him no King who is
already one. And pray what hath this to do in
the present case? We neither mean to *set up* nor
to *put down,* neither to *make* nor to *unmake,* but
to have nothing to do with them. Wherefore,
your testimony, in whatever light it is viewed,
serves only to dishonour your judgment, and for
many other reasons had better have been let alone
than published.

First, Because it tends to the decrease and reproach of all religion whatsoever, and is of the ut-

NEW-ENGLAND CHRONICLE (CAMBRIDGE, MA)

April 4, 1776 (continued)

Samuel Hall moved his press out of Cambridge,
headquarters of Washington's army, after printing this
issue of the *New-England Chronicle: Or, the Essex Gazette*
(full title). On April 25, he resumed publication in Boston,
which the British had evacuated in March, now calling his
paper simply the *New-England Chronicle.*

morning through the Downs, for the River, the Ankerwyke East Indiaman; and the Anne, Kennedy, for Jamaica; the Golden Fleece, Dixon, for Corke; the Succefs Increase, Tifdale, for Halifax; and the Grange, Parker, for Liverpool. Remain in the Downs, the Prince Frederick, Sawyer; and the Amity's Experiment, Moore, for orders.

LONDON.

Extract of a Letter from Jamaica, dated June 29, 1776.

"A pamphlet has been circulated here under the title of "Common Senfe," which was fent hither from America. It is written with great virulence against the Englifh adminiftration; and its defign is to ftir up the colonifts to affert their independency on the mother country. There are many falfe affertions in it, one of which Admiral Gayton has thought proper to contradict in the Jamaica Gazette, in the following words:

"I have feen a pamphlet publifhed in Philadelphia, under the title of *Common Senfe*, wherein the Author fays, that 40 years ago there were 70 and 80 gun fhips built in New England: In anfwer to which I do declare, that, at that very period of time I was in New England, a midfhipman on board his Majefty's fhip Squirrel, with the late Sir Peter Warren, and then there never had been a man of war built of any kind. In 1747 (after the reduction of Louifburgh) there was a fhip of 44 guns ordered to be built at Pifcataqua by one Mr. Meffervey, fhe was called the America, and failed for England the following year; when fhe came home, fhe was found fo bad, that fhe never was commiffioned again. There was afterwards another fhip of 20 guns built at Bofton, by Mr. Benjamin Hollwell, which was called the Bofton, fhe run but a fhort time before fhe was condemned, and thofe were the only two fhips of war ever built in America; therefore I thought it my duty to publifh this, to undeceive the Public in general, to fhew that what the Author has fet forth is an abfolute falfity. CLARK GAYTON."

On Monday their Majefties vifited Lady Sufanna Clayton, at her feat near Great Marlow in Bucks; and Tuefday they paid a vifit to Lady Effingham Howard, at her feat at Stowe-Green, near Windfor.

Yefterday (and not before) the Earl of March kiffed his Majefty's hand, on being appointed Lord High Commiffioner to the General Affembly of the Church of Scotland, and Firft Commiffioner of the Police in that kingdom, in the room of Lord Cathcart, deceafed.

The fame day Baron D'Airing, lately arrived here from the Electorate of Hanover, was introduced by Baron Alvenfleben, the Hanoverian Minifter, to his Majefty.

Yefterday John Hely Hutchinfon, Provoft of

Charleftown Bar to attack the town, and cover the landing of the army. In confequence thereof the fquadron weighed, confifting of the Briftol, Experiment, A_____ A__ire, and S____ There were 10_____ Briftol was lig_____ The cannonad_____ hours; but th_____ board the Act_____ At low water _____ heeled into th_____ kept up by th_____ with fuch acti_____ the whole fqu_____ fort. The fp_____ fhot away, fho_____ the fort; and _____ the transports _____ able to get acr_____ conftructed o_____ the batteries l_____ fhips went over_____ 16 men, and 13_____ tified in the fame way, and is capable of making an equal refiftance. Gen. Lee with his army attacked the flying rear of Gen. Clinton's army, and defeated them. If they had not made a precipitate retreat and embarkation, they had been all cut off. Gen. Lee was feen to command on Sullivan's Ifland; and till he came into the province they were in no ftate of defence. The Ranger, which came home with this exprefs, was attacked by a one maft floop privateer an hour and 40 minutes, and got off. The pilots were quite unacquainted with the navigation of Charleftown River."

Another account fays, that when the Ranger failed, General Lee was then engaged with Clinton's army; and thofe troops who were embarked were ordered to land again; the fire obferved by the Ranger's people appeared to be very hot, and confifted of mufquetry and field pieces.

The rebel army at prefent at Bofton, it is faid, does not exceed 7000 men, the others have been fent in detached parties, from Cambridge to New York, and other places.

All the officers allow, that if it had not been for the intrepid conduct of Capt. Scot, of the Active, and Lieutenant Reddall, that the fquadron had been quite deftroyed.

By a letter from an Officer in Canada, it appears, that the article in the London Papers, which fays that the Indians had murdered all the rebels that were taken at the Cedars, is not true. The following is an extract from a genuine letter. "Capt. Fofter, of the 8th regiment, on his way down the river St. Lawrence from Ofwegatchey, with his company of light infantry, 200 Indians, and a few Canadians, attacked a rebel poft at the Cedars that confifted of 500 men, which he carried, after killing fome and making the reft prifoners. The In-

of war.

Extract of a Letter from Portfmouth, Aug.

"Yefterday feveral of the fhips from Downs paffed by St. Helen's, and this mor_____

der convoy from St. Kitts, is fafe arrived Dover, after being chafed by an American vateer, but outfailed her.

The Holland, Capt. Taylor, from Jama which is one of the miffing fhips, on which per cent. was given, was fpoke with by Taunton, Capt. Fowler, the 10th of July, the Colleradoes, all well.

Capt. Young, of the Matthew, who arri at Dover on the 26th of July, in Lat. 34. fa fhip taken by a Provincial privateer.

The Seahorfe, Collinfon, from Greenland, three fifh, and the Ankerwyke, Barwell, f Bengal, are arrived in the River.

A gentleman juft arrived from Derbyfh fays, that they have had fourteen days co nual rain there, which has damaged imme quantities of hay. He adds, that the crop wheat and oats are greater than ever reme bered, but that hands are fo fcarce, they k not how they fhall get in the harveft.

The Court of Directors of the Eaft I Company will nominate writers this feafon the prefidencies of Bengal, Madrafs, and B bay. It is aftonifhing the intereft that is m ing at the Weft end of the town for the no nations of the Bengal writers; and fo diffi has it been to fucceed, that, it is faid, 40 was actually offered laft week by a gentle near St. James's for an appointment to a Be writerfhip for his fon, owing, it is fuppo to a determination not to fend out any m for thefe three years to come; and alfo to fons of the firft gentry in the kingdom g thither fince the eftablifhment of the fupr council.

A difpenfation has paffed the great feal, bling the Rev. James Topham, M. A. Ch lain to Sir John Shelley, Treafurer of his jefty's houfhold, to hold the united rectorie

INDEPENDENT CHRONICLE (BOSTON)
May 22, 1777

After the Continental Congress declared independence and the war dragged on, Paine wrote his *American Crisis* essays exhorting Americans to continue the struggle. In the third essay, published in the spring of 1777, Paine reminded Americans of the reasons why they had declared independence, accused the opponents of independence of acting from fear, laziness, and greed, and urged Americans to risk everything for their cause.

the latter end of March. This it. Had Independence rendered the dose still more dangerous by continuing ... king of England, who seduced and several governors, then in being, before ... tain has advanced) she ought to have *doubled* her importation, and ... took into keeping a sister of their society, is reverenced and supeach province; and the first Assembly before prohibited in some degree her exportation. ... ported with repeated testimonies, while the friendly nodle from whom as the Assembly of Pennsylvania, in May folstance is sufficient. And this single circum ... she was taken (and who if now in this city) continues a drudge in a just state of the case ... any jury of nations of ... the service of his rival, as if proud of being cuckolded by a creature called a king.

Our support and success depend on such a variety of men and circumstances, that every one, who does but wish well, is of some use: There are men who have a strange awkwardness to arms, yet have hearts to risk every shilling in the cause, or in support of those who have better talents for defending it. Nature, in the arrangement of mankind, has fitted some for every service in life: Were all soldiers, all would starve and go naked, and were none soldiers, all would be slaves. As disaffection to Independence, is the badge of a Tory, so affection to it is the mark of a Whig; and the different services of the Whigs down from those who nobly contribute every thing, to those who have nothing to render but their wishes, tend all to the same centre, though with different degrees of merit and ability. The larger we make the circle, the more we shall harmonize, and the stronger we shall be. All we want to shut out, is disaffection, and that excluded, we must accept from each other such duties as we are best fitted to bestow. A narrow system of politics, like a narrow system of religion, is calculated only to sour the temper, and live at variance with mankind.

All we want to know in America is simply this, Who is for Independence, and who is not? Those who are for it, will support it, and the remainder will undoubtedly see the reasonableness of their paying the charges; while those who oppose, or seek to betray it, must expect the more rigid fate of the jail and the gibbet. There is a kind of bastard generosity, which, by being extended to all men, is as fatal to society, on one hand, as the want of true generosity is on the other. A lax manner of administring justice, falsely termed moderation, has a tendency both to dispirit public virtue and promote his patronage. I happened, when a school boy, to pick up a pleasing natural history of Virginia, and my inclination from that day of seeing the western side of the atlantic never left me. In October, Seventy-five, Dr. Franklin proposed giving me such materials as were in his hands, towards completing a history of the present transactions, and seemed desirous of having the first volume out by the next spring. I had then formed the outlines of *Common Sense*, and finished nearly the first part; and as I supposed the Doctor's design in getting out a history, was to open the new year with a new system, I expected to surprize him with a production on that subject much earlier than he thought of; and without informing him of what I was doing, got it ready for the press as fast as I conveniently could, and sent him the first pamphlet that was printed off.

...

THE AMERICAN CRISIS.
NUMBER III.
By the Author of COMMON SENSE.
(Continued from our last.)

HAVING thus gone over some of the principal points in support of Independence, I must now request the reader to return back with me to the period when it first began to be a public doctrine, and examine the progress it has made among the various classes of men. The era I mean to begin at, is the breaking out of hostilities, April 19th, 1775. Until this event happened, the Continent seemed to view the dispute as a kind of lawsuit for a matter of right, litigating between the old country and the new; and she felt the same kind and degree of horror, as if she had seen an oppressive plaintiff, at the head of a band of ruffians, enter the court, while the cause was before it, and put the judge, the jury, the defendant and his council to the sword. Perhaps a more heart-felt convulsion never reached a country with the same degree of power and rapidity before, and never may again. Pity for the sufferers, mixt with indignation at the violence, and heightened with apprehensions of undergoing the ...

in England. But the principal scheme, and that which has marked their character in every part of their conduct, was a design of precipitating the Colonies into a state which they might afterwards deem rebellion, and under that pretence put an end to all future complaints, petitions and remonstrances, by seizing the whole at once. They had ravaged one part of the globe, till it could glut them no longer; their prodigality required new plunder, and through the East-India article TEA, they hoped to transfer their rapine from that quarter of the world to this. Every designed quarrel has its pretence and the same barbarian avarice accompanied the *Plant* to America, which ruined the country that produced it.

That men never turn rogues without turning fools, is a maxim, sooner or later, universally true. The commencement of hostilities, being in the beginning of April, was, of all times, the worst chosen: The Congress were to meet the tenth of May following, and the distress the Continent felt at this unparalleled outrage gave a stability to *That Body*, which no other circumstance could have done. It suppressed too all inferior debates, and bound them together by a necessitous affection, without giving them time to differ upon trifles. The suffering likewise, softened the whole body of the people into a degree of pliability, which laid the principal foundation stone of union, order and government; and which, at any other time, might only have fretted and then faded away unnoticed and unimproved: But Providence, who best knows how to time her misfortunes as well as her immediate favours, chose this to be the time: And who dares dispute it?

It did not seem the disposition of the people at this crisis to heap ...

BATTLE OF MOORE'S CREEK BRIDGE

By William P. Tatum III

OUGHT ON FEBRUARY 27, 1776, THE BATTLE OF Moore's Creek Bridge effectively ended major organized resistance to the American Revolution in North Carolina. The engagement played on imperial and local divisions, pitting resettled Scots Highlanders and backcountry Regulators against Tidewater Whig militia. The former hailed from the north of Scotland and had resettled in America following their defeat during the Jacobite Uprising of 1745–46. Before immigrating, the Scots swore oaths of loyalty to the Crown, which they now honored. The Regulators had rebelled against the colonial assembly between 1769 and 1771 over taxation issues but were crushed by the Tidewater elites in a pitched battle at Alamance (near modern Burlington, North Carolina).

In early 1775, Royal Governor Josiah Martin of North Carolina laid the groundwork for the battle to come by organizing the Loyalists. After escaping from a Whig mob in April, Martin continued to coordinate resistance from his headquarters on HMS *Cruiser*. In the latter half of 1775, the Scottish settlements in the interior began mobilizing and were soon joined by British army officers. Among these officers was Donald MacDonald, who would lead the Loyalist forces during the ensuing campaign. In early 1776, Martin received word of a major British relief expedition bound for the Carolinas, which he ordered MacDonald to rendezvous with in February.

Events began to move quickly, as seen in the March 23, 1776, issue of the *Providence Gazette*. Following a meeting at Cross Creek on February 5, the Loyalist forces began their march to the coast. This news reached the Whig authorities by February 13, though the initial strength of the Loyalist force was closer to 3,500 men than the

seven hundred reported. A steady stream of desertions weakened MacDonald's ranks throughout the march. By February 19, the opposing forces faced off at Rockfish Creek, where MacDonald began an exchange of letters with Whig General James Moore, which were later published in the April 25, 1776, issue of the *New-England Chronicle*. MacDonald's force slipped away the next day, crossing the Cape Fear River and continuing toward the coast. The Loyalists found their path unavoidably blocked at Moore's Creek Bridge by entrenched militia under Colonels Alexander Lillington and Richard Caswell. After sending an envoy to spy on the Whig camp, MacDonald elected to storm the position early on February 27, directing Lieutenant Colonel Donald MacLeod to lead the assault.

Shortly after dawn that morning, the Loyalist force of about seven hundred men advanced toward the bridge. Finding a redoubt on the west bank unoccupied, the mostly Scottish force quickly moved toward the bridge and exchanged fire with Whig sentries. Unbeknownst to MacLeod, Caswell's force had changed their position from the preceding day, redeploying in earthworks on the far side of the creek, supported by two small cannon. The militia had also removed the planks from the bridge and greased the rails that remained. As the April 4, 1776, issue of the *New-England Chronicle* reported, the Loyalist army attempted to storm across the bridge, led by a company of hand-picked swordsmen with MacLeod at their head. A withering volley of Whig musketry and cannon fire stopped the attack, killing MacLeod and upward of fifty soldiers. The surviving Loyalists fled, with the Whig militia in hot pursuit. Moore's Creek Bridge quickly became an irrecoverable strategic defeat: Whig forces arrested hundreds of Loyalists in its aftermath and confiscated

PROVIDENCE GAZETTE (RHODE ISLAND)

March 23, 1776

Fought on February 27, 1776, the Battle of Moore's Creek Bridge effectively ended major organized resistance to the American Revolution in North Carolina.

... and I will venture to speak ... he will not bestow great commenda-.—The Athenians, a wise and polished ... banished their best citizens, from ... of their power—a glorious reward ... citizen, who, as was the case in more ... one, had preserved his country from ... In the latter times of the Carthagenian republics, what constant scenes of blood ... does history present to us.—The ... perpetual ferment, like the ocean in a storm; did I say—like the waters of the ... a dreadful whirlwind, nothing but ... party encountering the rage of another. ... of humanity being thus lost, men ... creatures, and become as fierce and savage ... tygers.

... descend nearer to modern times—let us ... peace and security in the republic of ... often mentioned, and so little known; ... the fate of the two brothers, Corne-... de Wit, Dutch ministers, who were ... the people in the year 1672. Holland ... a republic, is become a downright ... liberty did not continue long in that ... the blood and treasure that ...

but did say who they were.

"His Lordship is not recalled, but has leave to go if he chooses. His conduct is approved of, and he has unlimited power to draw on the treasury. Col. Corbin says, that he, General Clinton, and Capt. Hammond, all appeared in good humour, the latter declaring he had forbid his tenders to offer injury to individuals or their property, his sole design being to watch the water, and enforce the acts of trade. General Clinton had four companies, who had not landed, but, on the contrary, the transports, with the Mercury, had fallen down into the road (Hampton) under sailing orders; he did not mention his destination, but it was gathered from the young officers, that they were to pay a visit to Governor Martin, at Cape Fear, and then proceed to South-Carolina. On hearing that part of our letter to Col. Corbin read, "that we were not authorized or inclined to intermeddle in the mode of negociation, which must be left to Congress," the General said, there was nothing America could ask in a constitutional way but would be granted; but if we relied on the Congress, we had nothing to expect from Parliament. Lord Dunmore wanted to borrow his troops to drive ours from Kemp's; he asked if ours would not return; the other said, he supposed they would; then says the General, I don't think it worth while to meddle with them.

up, took him and his company on board, and on the first of January arrived at Falmouth. Capt. Johnson says, that in Martinico the inhabitants universally, warmly espoused the cause of the brave injured Americans, and wished them to continue firm and united; which in a little time would certainly crown them with success to the utmost of their wishes, and that they might be assured of powerful assistance in a short time.

Extract of a letter from Montreal, Feb. 26.
"We have nothing material new, from camp before Quebec, except a few deserters now and then, who report, that there is a scarcity of provisions, and that General Carleton has promised the sailors in town one hundred pounds each, and 200 acres of land, wherever they chose it, if they will defend the town till a reinforcement comes in the spring.—Captain Lamb and the rest of the prisoners we hear are well."

Extract of a letter from Newbern (North-Carolina) February 13.
"An express arrived yesterday from the back country, informing us that the regulators and tories were making head there, and intended marching to Cross Creek, and from thence to Cape Fear; but am of opinion they will get well flogged before they get there, if they will fight. Our minute men and part of the militia march to-morrow, and will join Col. Caswell, in Dobb's county, from which place he will march in two or three days, with near 1000 men. I am just informed that Col. Ashe was on his march from New-Hanover two days ago, against the regulators, with near 2000 men. If three or four more of our Colonels raise as many men, which I expect will be the case, we shall be able to attack 10 000 tories, and beat them too."

By Captain Hayman, from Newbern, North-Carolina, we learn, that Governor Martin had found means to raise 700 tories, whom he had joined at Cross Creek; that one or two of the parties who marched in quest of Martin's party, had fell in with

thousands of weapons, crippling any potential further attempts at resistance.

The Loyalist defeat at Moore's Creek Bridge revealed that southern Loyalists could not operate effectively against their Whig counterparts without support from British regular troops. The Scottish contingent had suggested as much at the Cross Creek meeting, where they argued for delaying the march until British troops were in a position to provide immediate aid. Unsupported Loyalist uprisings throughout South Carolina and Georgia repeatedly failed throughout the rest of the war. Thus, in the greater scheme of the American Revolution, the Battle of Moore's Creek Bridge stands out as the archetype for the majority of subsequent significant confrontations between Whig and Loyalist militias in the South.

The following letters passed between General Moore, and the Tory General M'Donald, before the late battle in North-Carolina.

A letter from Donald M'Donald, Esq; lately erected Brigadier General in the Tory army by Governor Martin, to Brigadier General Moore.

SIR,

I herewith send the bearer, Donald Morrison, by advice of the Commissioners appointed by his Excellency Josiah Martin, and in behalf of the army now under my command, to propose terms to you as friends and countrymen. I must suppose you unacquainted with the Governor's proclamation, commanding all his Majesty's loyal subjects to repair to the King's royal standard, else I should have imagined you would ere this have joined the King's army now engaged in his Majesty's service. I have therefore thought it proper to intimate to you, that in case you do not, by 12 o'clock to morrow, join the royal standard, I must consider you as enemies, and take the necessary steps for the support of legal authority.

I beg leave to remind you of his Majesty's speech to his Parliament, wherein he offers to receive the misled with tenderness and mercy, from motives of humanity. I again beg of you to accept the proffered clemency. I make no doubt, but you will shew the gentleman sent on this message every possible civility; and you may depend in return, that all your officers and men, which may fall into our hands, shall be treated with an equal degree of respect. I have the honor to be, in behalf of the army, Sir, Your most obedient humble servant,

DON. M'DONALD.

Head Quarters, Feb. 19, 1776.

His Excellency's proclamation is herewith inclosed.

Brigadier General Moore's answer.

SIR,

Your's of this day I have received, in answer to which, I must inform you that the terms which you were pleased to say, in behalf of the army under your command, are offered to us as friends and countrymen, are such as neither my duty or inclination will permit me to accept, and which I must presume you too much of an officer to expect of me. You were very right when you supposed me unacquainted with the Governor's proclamation, but as the terms therein proposed are such as I hold incompatible with the freedom of Americans, it can be no rule of conduct for me. However, should I not bear farther from you before twelve o'clock to morrow, by which time I shall have an opportunity of consulting my officers here, and perhaps Col. Martin, who is in the neighbourhood of Cross-creek, you may expect a more particular answer: mean time you may be assured that the feelings of humanity will induce me to shew that civility to such of your people as may fall into our hands, as I am desirous should be observed towards those of our's, who may be unfortunate enough to fall into your's. I am, Sir, your most obedient, and very humble servant,

JAMES MOORE.

Camp at Rockfish, Feb. 19, 1776.

From Brigadier General Moore, to Brigadier General M'Donald.

SIR,

Agreeable to my promise of yesterday, I have consulted the officers under my command, respecting your letter, and am happy in finding them unanimous in opinion with me. We consider ourselves engaged in a cause the most glorious and honourable in the world, the defence of the liberties of mankind, in support of which we are determined to hazard every thing dear and valuable, and in tenderness to the deluded people under your command, permit me, Sir, through you to inform them, before it is too late, of the dangerous and destructive precipice on which they stand, and to remind them of the ungrateful return they are about to make for their favourable reception in this country. It is not sufficient to recall them to the duty which they owe themselves and their posterity, inform them that they are engaged in a cause in which they cannot succeed, as not only the whole force of this country, but that of our neighbouring provinces, is exerting and now actually in motion to suppress them, and which must end in their utter destruction. Desirous, however, of avoiding the effusion of human blood, I have thought proper to send you a test recommended by the Continental Congress, which if they will yet subscribe we are willing to receive them as friends and countrymen. Should this offer be rejected, I shall consider them as enemies to the constitutional liberties of America, and treat them accordingly.

I cannot conclude without reminding you, Sir, of the oath which

you and some of your officers took at Newbern, on your arrival to this country, which I imagine you will find it difficult to reconcile to your present conduct. I have no doubt that the bearer, Capt. James Walker, will be treated with proper civility and respect in your camp. I am, Sir, your most obedient, and very humble servant,

Camp at Rockfish, Feb. 20, 1776. JAMES MOORE.

From Brigadier General M'Donald to Brigadier General Moore.

SIR,

I received your favour by Capt. James Walker, and observed your declared sentiments of revolt, hostility, and rebellion to the King, and to what I understand to be the constitution of the country. If I am mistaken, future consequences must determine; but while I continue in my present sentiments, I shall consider myself embarked in a cause which must, in its consequences, extricate this country from anarchy and licentiousness. I cannot conceive that the Scotch emigrants, to whom I imagine you allude, can be under greater obligations to this country than to the King, under whose gracious and merciful government they alone could have been enabled to visit this western region: And I trust, Sir, it is in the womb of time to say, that they are not that deluded and ungrateful people which you would represent them to be. As a soldier, in his Majesty's service, I must inform you, if you are to learn, that it is my duty to conquer, if I cannot reclaim, all those who may be hardy enough to take up arms against the best of masters, as of kings. I have the honour to be, in behalf of the army under my command, Sir,

Your most obedient servant,

DON. M'DONALD.

To the commanding officer at Rockfish.

To be sold by Doc. ZECHARIAH HARVEY,

of Westminster, in the county of Worcester, the FARM he now lives on, which is situated in the middle of the town, near the Meeting-House, lies on the great road that leads from Boston to Deerfield, and is well situated for public business of any sort. Said farm has a large new House on it, almost finished, with five fire places. On the farm is a good young orchard of about 180 acres, two barns, and a shop suitable for a trader. The land is all under good improvement, well fenced, and excellent land for mowing, and pasturage, well watered in every part; a good place for a corn-mill or fulling-mill. Said Harvey has also 400 acres of other lands in town to sell, very good and suitable for settlements, and will be sold in such parcels as will suit the purchaser. All which will be sold very cheap for cash or short credit. Any person inclining to purchase, by applying to said Harvey, will be well used in the affair.

DESERTED from the Continental Hospital,

ONE JOEL PIRKINS, belonging to Captain Sayer's company, in Col. Patterson's regiment; he is about five feet two inches high,

NEW-ENGLAND CHRONICLE (CAMBRIDGE, MA)

April 4, 1776

The Loyalist defeat at Moore's Creek Bridge revealed that southern Loyalists could not operate effectively against their Whig counterparts without support from British regular troops. Unsupported Loyalist uprisings throughout South Carolina and Georgia repeatedly failed throughout the rest of the war.

Extract of a letter from Brigadier General James Moore, in the Continental service, to the Honourable Cornelius Harnet, Esq; President of the Provincial Council, North-Carolina, dated Wilmington, March 2d, 1776.

THE 25th of February, by four o'clock, we arrived at Dollison's landing, but as we could not possibly march that night, for want of horses for the artillery, I despatched an express to Moore's creek bridge, to learn the situation of affairs there, and was informed that Col. Lillington, who had the day before taken his stand at the bridge, was that afternoon reinforced by Col. Caswell, and that they had raised a small breastwork, and destroyed a part of the bridge. The next morning, the twenty-seventh, at break of day, an alarm gun was fired, immediately after which, scarce allowing our people a moment to prepare, the Tory army with Capt. M'Cloud at their head, made their attack on Col. Caswell and Col. Lillington, & finding a small intrenchment next to the bridge on our side empty, concluded that our people had abandoned their post, and in the most furious manner advanced within thirty paces of our breast work and artillery, where they met a very proper reception. Capt. McCloud and Captain Campell fell within a few paces of the breast-work, the former of whom received upwards of twenty balls through his body; and in a very few minutes their whole army was put to the flight, and most shamefully abandoned their General, who was next day taken prisoner. The loss of the enemy in this action, from the best accounts we have been able to learn, is about 30 killed and wounded; but as numbers of them must have fallen into the creek, besides many more that were carried off, I sup-

by the men of war, who now lie just below the town, gave the inhabitants reason to apprehend every thing that could be suffered from their disappointed vengeance; however the committee have most spiritedly determined rather to suffer the

---

His Excellency's ANSWER.

To the Select-men and Citizens of Boston.

GENTLEMEN,

YOUR congratulations on the success of the American arms, gives me the greatest pleasure.

I most sincerely rejoice with you, on your being once more in the quiet possession of your former habitations; and, what greatly adds to my happiness, that this desirable event has been effected with so little effusion of human blood.

I am exceedingly obliged by the good opinion you are pleased to entertain of my conduct. Your virtuous efforts in the cause of freedom, and the unparralleled fortitude with which you have sustained the greatest of all human calamities, justly entitle you to the grateful remembrance of your American brethren; and I heartily pray that the hand of tyranny may never more disturb your repose; and that every blessing of a kind Providence may give happiness and prosperity to the town of Boston.

GEO. WASHINGTON.

Thursday last the Lecture, which was established, and has been observed from the first settlement of Boston, without interruption, until within these few months past, was opened by the Rev. Dr. Elliot. His Excellency General Washington, the other General Officers and their suites, having been previously invited, met in the Council Chamber, from whence, preceded by the Sheriff with his Wand, attended by the Members of the Council who had had the Small Pox, the Committee of the House of Representatives, the Selectmen, the Clergy, and many other Gentlemen, they repair'd to the Old Brick Meeting-House, where an excellent and well adapted Discourse was delivered from the 33 chap. Isaiah, 20 verse.

After Divine Service was ended, his Excellency, attended and accompanied as before, returned to the Council Chamber, from whence they proceeded to the Bunch of Grapes Tavern, where an elegant Dinner was provided at the Public Expence; after which many very proper and pertinent Toasts were drank.

Joy and gratitude sat on every countenance, & smiled in every eye. The whole was conducted and concluded to the satisfaction of all.

The Sukey, a large Transport Ship, with 4 Tories at least on board, is ashore on George's Island, and 'tis said cannot be got off.

We hear the Baron De WOEDLKE, formerly a General Officer in the Prussian Service, and lately arrived in Philadelphia, is appointed a Brigadier-General in the Continental Service, and is to do duty in Canada.

A favourite toast, in the best companies, is, "May the INDEPENDENT principles of COMMON SENSE be confirmed throughout the United Colonies."

We hear that about 10 or 12 transport vessels, supposed to be from England, arrived, last Tuesday, in Nantasket road, where 4 or 5 of the enemy's ships of war remain.

The Honourable Continental Congress have declared and resolved, That all ships and other vessels, and all goods, wares and merchandizes, belonging to any inhabitants of Great-Britain, taken on the high seas, or between high and low water mark, shall be deemed and adjudged to be lawful prize.

The Resolves of Congress, respecting the above, will be inserted in our next. Some further accounts from N. Carolina, new advertisements, &c. must also be deferred.

Last Tuesday died at Littleton, aged 38 years, Capt. EBENEZER SYMMES, of Boston. He has left a tender wife, and one daughter, an aged father and a great number of other near relatives to lament the loss of a kind husband, a tender father, a dutiful child and a very affectionate brother and sincere friend. He was a warm friend to his oppressed country, and consequently a determined opposer of the measures pursuing by its present unnatural and cruel enemies, by whom he was drove from his habitation in the capital, (where he lived in affluent circumstances) to seek an asylum in the country.

IT is presen of this Gazette of paper, the sumption of the versal, that almost price from his rise of many of reasonable to value of what w delphia Evening num, owing to Printer hereof that the price per Annum, e 6s. 8d. will be which each sub desirous of rem requested to sig

The Printer next Tuesday building in Sch Boston; where paper, and to se Printing, as we

N. B. The of removing the

AS all the Hills, have mar notice that I wa or any thing els

P. S. Whoe Hay, &c. are de between Prospe

Next week wil

J. FLE

A New E addressed to the in the body of an address to th

N. B. This any former one.

THIS is c cerned in the p of about 15 ton of the date here salvage, may ha plying to the su

Cohasset,

TO be sol part of Methue barn, and chief head of cattle; o ed, with a good ent to keep the

TO be so part of Methu orchard, and a goo ther stock acco and well watere advertised above

JOHN C begs leave to in gagement und hopes for punc papers. He fil

---

PUBLIC NOTICE is hereby given to such

REPORTING THE
BATTLE OF
THE RICE BOATS

By Hugh T. Harrington

FTER THE BATTLE OF LEXINGTON AND CONCORD AND its long wretched retreat, the British were confined to Boston, under siege. It was immediately apparent that food would soon become scarce.

In December 1775, General William Howe ordered a small fleet to Savannah in search of rice and other provisions. The intent was to purchase the supplies rather than antagonize and alienate the population by confiscation. However, use of force was authorized if necessary.

The May 2, 1776, edition of the *New-England Chronicle*, in splendid detail, describes the events. The appearance of the British fleet caused the government, controlled by the Whigs whose Provincial Congress and Council of Safety had replaced the Royal Assembly, to put Royal Governor James Wright under house arrest. Wright believed that the fleet would help restore him and Royal government to power over the Whigs. The Whigs called up the militia and asked for military assistance from South Carolina because it was feared that the British intended to seize Savannah.

Wright, fearing for his safety, fled along with several members of his Royal Council to one of the British ships. When the British Commander, Captain Andrew Barclay, communicated to the Whigs that he wished to negotiate for the sale of food, the Whigs refused and moved twenty rice-filled merchant vessels, referred to as the "rice boats," upriver in hopes of preventing their capture. Barclay went on the offensive, sending ships upriver to Savannah to capture the rice boats.

Musket and light artillery fire erupted as the Whigs tried to protect Savannah while retaining control of the boats. Men were captured on both sides. The British were successful, however, in securing most of the rice boats.

The Whigs, without the artillery power needed to halt the British, intentionally set other ships on fire and drifted them down the river in attempts to burn the captured rice boats. Their efforts were only marginally successful.

In the end, the British made off with most of the rice boats. Savannah had never been their objective, nor was restoring Governor Wright and Royal government to Georgia. Captain Barclay did not have the resources and the time required to subdue the Whigs and reestablish the Royal government. Governor Wright sailed away with the British fleet, ending the Royal presence in Georgia. Temporarily, Georgia was in the hands of the Whigs.

The hastily assembled militia could boast that they had saved Savannah from the marauding British. While they had lost the rice boats, they had given up nothing of value to the Revolution. In fact, it was a time for celebration. The president of the Council of Safety wrote that the burning vessels, "passed and re-passed [Savannah] with the tide, which in any other but the present times would be truly horrible, but is now a subject only of gratulation [sic] and applause."

The *New-England Chronicle* accurately reported and concentrated on the dishonorable accounts of the British firing on unarmed Whig representatives and taking other envoys prisoner. Such spotlighting of these events would enflame readers and discredit the British.

The British had suffered a significant defeat as news of the Battle of the Rice Boats emerged as both a military and political victory for the Whig forces. The British had been repulsed from the vicinity of Savannah and had taken the remnants of the Royal government with them. The attack at Savannah transformed Georgia from being on the sidelines in the war to a colony in opposition to British authority.

your province, in a particular manner, renders it necessary, to acquaint you with the occurrences in the former, since the date of our last; to which, and the dispatches proceeding, we refer you.

"Our dispositions in the evening of the 2d, were such as appeared to our officers the most likely to prevent the landing of our enemy; and so as, if they should make their landing good, either above or below the town, to prevent their getting in; however, notwithstanding our vigilance, they, by collusion with the masters and others on board the merchant shipping, which hawled near the shore of Hutchinson's Island in the night time, got on board these ships, about four o'clock yesterday morning; to the number, as far as we are competent to judge, from observations we made, and the intelligence we received, of between two and three hundred, where they affected to conceal themselves.

"We had our fears respecting these shipping, and therefore kept a good watch upon them; but it was impossible for centinels, on this shore, to descry them in boarding from the other, the vessels being betwixt.

"Captain Rice, who commanded a boat of observation, was sent on board the shipping about nine o'clock, to order the rigging on shore, and was, without any noise, or the smallest knowledge of us, kidnapped. This we did not know, till about half an hour afterwards: Two sailors, under pretence of coming on shore for cloaths, gave information of the troops being on board the shipping, and of Rice's being taken: about three hundred were then immediately marched to Ya-

ker, by a discharge down directly upon them of near two hundred shot, both from swivels and small arms; which was kept up while they were in reach; the Captains and men in the boat, not in the smallest degree confused, or even, perhaps, disappointed by the attack, fired their rifles, most of them three several times, and as they say, not without execution: And, wonderful to tell! not a man of them killed; one man only received a slug in the fleshy part of his shoulder, which was immediately cut out, without the smallest inconvenience or danger. The spectators all declare, as we now do, that such a providential deliverance has not yet been known. This unmanly attack, upon a few men in an open boat, produced a general fire from our field pieces and intrenchments; and a smart return from two four pounders and several swivels from the shipping; which lasted from about twelve o'clock to four; and, although they often fired langridge, which continually whistled about our men, not a single man was even touched; but we have no doubt a number of the enemy met with a worse fate, as they were seen frequently to fall.

"About four o'clock, we called a Council, and determined to have the vessels immediately burnt; and issued orders to Col. M'Intosh accordingly, whereupon the Inverness, late Capt. M'Gillivray, loaded with rice and deer-skins, was set on fire, and cut loose, to the amount of 15,000l sterl. Upon this the soldiers, in the most laughable confusion, got ashore in the marsh; while our rifle-men, and field-pieces, with grape shot, were incessantly galling them. The shipping were now also in confusion, some got up the river, under cover of

NEW-ENGLAND CHRONICLE (BOSTON)
May 2, 1776

The British had suffered a significant defeat as news of the Battle of the Rice Boats emerged as both a military and political victory for the Whig forces. This edition of the *New-England Chronicle* describes the events of the battle in splendid detail. It accurately reports and concentrates on the dishonorable accounts of the British firing on unarmed Whig representatives and taking other envoys prisoner. Such spotlighting would enflame readers and discredit the British.

NEW-ENGLAND CHRONICLE.

(Vol. VIII.)   THURSDAY, *May* 2, 1776.   (Numb. 402.)

BOSTON: Printed by SAMUEL HALL, at his Office next to the OLIVER CROMWELL Tavern, in SCHOOL-STREET.

SAVANNAH, [*Georgia*,] February 7.

THE petition from the Congress of this province to the King, was presented to his Majesty by Governor Johnstone, on the 3d of November last.

February 14. Last Friday arrived a large transport with soldiers from Boston.

February 21. The ship which arrived at Cockspur, on Monday the 12th instant, proves to be a transport from Boston with more soldiers.

On the 12th instant, our Governor and his family took themselves on board the Scarborough, from which he has wrote a letter, to endeavour to persuade us to let the officers, lately arrived in our river, land in this town, and declaring the fleet only want water and fresh provisions, which they will pay for, with a great deal of stuff, to lull the people asleep.

February 28. The Cherokee, the two transports from Boston, a sloop and three small vessels, are now laying at anchor within three miles of this town.

Besides the militia of the town and district of Savannah, there are a number of companies from the country now in this place.

CHARLESTOWN, (S. Carolina) Feb. 16.

We hear from Georgia, that the Scarborough man of war, of 20 guns, lately arrived in Savannah river, with a prize schooner, having 4000lb. of gunpowder on board.

March 8. On Sunday a detachment of 120 men of the Charlestown volunteer companies, set out for Savannah.

We hear from Savannah, that two armed schooners and a sloop had got above the town, through Back River, and had taken a brig and a schooner lying there; that the Syren was arrived in the river; and that some more large vessels were in the offing; that the troops, said to be about 5 or 600, were in transports near the town; That it was expected they would attempt to land, to prevent which, upwards of 1000 Georgia and Carolina militia-men were in Savannah; and that there is too great reason to fear there will be much blood shed.

The troops are said to be the 40th regiment, and a detachment of marines; Majors Grant and Maitland are among them, also Capt. Pitcairn.

Copy of a letter just received, by express, from Georgia. In the Council of Safety, Savannah, March 4, 1776.

"THE intimate connection between this and your province, in a particular manner, renders it necessary, to acquaint you with the occur-

macraw, opposite the shipping, with three four-pounders, and threw up a breast-work. The armed schooner, Hinchinbrook, of — guns, with a number of men on board, which with others, went up the Back river in the afternoon of the day preceding, about this time set sail down the South River, with intent, no doubt, of covering the landing of the troops, from on board the merchant shipping: But being continually fired at, by two companies of rifle-men who were placed in ambuscade, she was obliged to come very slowly, and when came to, and returned a very smart fire at every place where the rifle-men fired from, until the tide was spent, and she could not get down. During the course of their firing, only one of our men got wounded, and that slightly in the thigh; but on board, several were seen to fall.

"In town we had exhibited a still more interesting scene; we found the officers and men clamorous, about the capture and detention of Rice; and two gentlemen, Lieut. Daniel Roberts, of the St. John's rangers, and Mr. Raymond Demere, of St. Andrew's parish, solicited and were permitted to go on board, to demand a surrender of Rice and his people. They accordingly divested themselves of arms, and were rowed by a negro on board a vessel, in which were Captain Barclay, the Commodore, and Major Grant; and these officers, contrary to all the principles which cement society, and govern mankind, immediately arrested our deputies, and yet detain them as prisoners. We waited with anxious expectation for near half an hour, when we demanded our deputies, by the help of a trumpet, without getting any other but insulting answers; whereupon we fired two fourpounders directly into them; and then they informed us, that they would send an answer in writing; which they presently after did, signed by Lieutenant Roberts and Mr. Demere, purporting, that if we would send two of the persons in whom the people most confided, they would treat with them.

"Capt. Screven, of the St. John's rangers, and Capt. Baker, of the St. John's rifle-men, chagrined, no doubt (the former particularly, on account of his Lieutenant) by the detention of our deputies, took about a dozen of rifle men in a boat, and rowed directly under the stern of Capt. Inglis, in whose vessel were a great part of the soldiery, and, in peremptory terms, demanded the deputies; and were answered, after one shot from Capt. Baker, by a discharge down directly upon them of near two hundred shot, both from swivels and

the armed schooner, while others caught the flame, and as night approached exhibited a scene, as they passed and repassed with the tide, which in any other but the present times would be truly horrible, but is now a subject only of gratulation and applause.

"The ships of Captains Inglis and Wardell neither got up the river, or on fire, they were ordered on shore, and are now prisoners of Captain Screven in the country, and their vessels brought down close into a wharff. They were permitted to write to Capt. Barclay in the evening, to inform of their situation, and to request an exchange of prisoners, which the latter peremptorily refused.

"We have thus given you a particular detail of things, as they really happened, to prevent the belief of any erroneous intelligence; and, from which, you will be competent to judge of our situation.

"Col. M'Intosh laid before the board a resolution of your Congress to aid us, accompanied by a letter from Mr. Lowndes; and we are very glad that you have determined to afford us farther assistance. We wish it may arrive in time.

By order of the Council of Safety,
WILLIAM EWEN, President."
To the Hon. the Congress, or Council of Safety, for South-Carolina.

BOSTON VIEWED FROM DORCHESTER HEIGHTS
North Wind Picture Archives

(*left*) Using the artillery that Henry Knox helped procure from Fort Ticonderoga, General Washington fortified the hill just south of Boston known as Dorchester Heights, which gave the Continental Army a military advantage by placing key British positions within range of bombardment.

WASHINGTON WATCHING EVACUATION OF BRITISH TROOPS FROM BOSTON
North Wind Picture Archives

(*right*) Threatened with destruction, the British army hastily evacuated the city by sea, taking along numerous loyal Bostonians. By March 17, 1776, the last British troops boarded ships, and Boston was again in colonial hands.

FORTIFICATION OF DORCHESTER HEIGHTS

By Don N. Hagist

THE STALEMATE HAD TO BE BROKEN. FOR NEARLY A YEAR the British army had been holed up in Boston, surrounded by a determined pro tem military of American inhabitants. The Boston garrison was too strong to dislodge, too weak to take the offensive; the besieging colonists were numerous but had neither a navy to blockade the city nor sufficient artillery to bombard it. Each side could only harass the other. British reinforcements would surely arrive in the spring. The Americans needed a decisive blow before then.

A substantial quantity of artillery had fallen into American hands when Fort Ticonderoga was seized in May 1775. It was, however, three hundred miles away; conventional transport by sea was impossible due to British naval dominance. Instead, General Washington's staff formulated a bold plan to move the ordnance over land during the coldest part of winter, when snow would allow transportation on sleds over the rugged New England terrain. Young Henry Knox was sent in November to carry out this scheme and masterfully assembled the necessary men, oxen, and equipment to haul some sixty tons of heavy guns and stores.

After ten weeks of toil over ice and snow, the guns arrived outside of Boston in late January. Preparations and planning proceeded apace; by March Washington's army was ready to commence a bombardment. Their existing positions were in range of British defenses, but the outcome of the siege hinged on a hill called Dorchester Heights. This prominence allowed artillery to bombard troops in the city and ships in the harbor. The British had moved to take the Heights immediately after storming Bunker Hill; after failing to seize it immediately, American troops occupied it. British officers, including Lieutenant-General John Burgoyne, repeatedly recommended taking the Heights, but their army lacked the strength to risk incurring heavy casualties.

The March 6, 1776, edition of the *New-England Chronicle* recounted the American stratagem: Beginning on March 2, guns in existing fortifications began an incessant bombardment of British positions, creating a distraction and drawing return fire. On the night of March 4, Washington's army fortified Dorchester Heights. When the works were discovered at dawn, they quickly organized an assault, but inclement weather made it impossible to ferry troops across the channel between the city and the Heights. By the time favorable conditions were present, so too were American guns; an assault was impossible. Threatened with destruction, the British army hastily evacuated the city by sea, taking along numerous loyal Bostonians. By March 17, the last British troops boarded ships. Boston was in colonial hands. The fleet stood for a week by Castle William, a British-held fortified island in the harbor, awaiting fair weather. They stocked their transports with water and destroyed the Castle's fortifications, all the while under threat of American guns. On March 27, they departed Boston harbor, never to return.

Americans were jubilant. It was common for newspapers to enumerate the spoils of a great victory; readers of the March 23, 1776, *Providence Gazette* saw for the first time a tally of weapons and supplies captured by a wholly American army. There were no ministerial troops remaining in the thirteen colonies. Rhode Island would soon declare independence, followed by a similar declaration from Congress itself. But the exhilaration would be short-lived; British reinforcements were on the way, and few foresaw the long war that was just beginning.

was one of memorable minority of five, in the house of Lords, on the question some time ago, that the British parliament had no right to tax

is, to treat with each province separately about an accommodation, and to dispatch this business: ——they are not now to treat with the Congress, as was first reported.

A plan is now under consideration, for all criminals in Great-Britain, sentenced for transportation, to be sent to the British settlements on the coast of Africa.

Mr. Glover has formed a calculation upon undoubted authority of the national loss for the present year owing to the American quarrel, and he makes it twenty-seven millions sterling.

Gov. Cornwallis is making the necessary preparations for the spring campaign, to go to Virginia with 5000 men.

Dec. 8. In pursuance of an advertisement for a meeting of the West-India merchants at the London tavern, a very numerous and opulent assembly met yesterday. Administration, through their emissaries, hoped for a petition in conformity to what the minister had thrown out in the House lately, that he expected an application for bounties from *Nova-Scotia*, Canada, and both Floridas, and the regions of Nova-Zembla; yet no sooner was this business opened by Mr. Edwards and Mr. Walker, than the attention of all present was engaged by the alarming danger of the Colonies from the purport of the bill now pending in Parliament, which denounces famine, and utter destruction to 500,000 of his Majesty's quiet subjects, concerned in the West-Indies.——A bill which inflicts the same punishment alike on the innocent subjects of the islands, as was in mockery of human woes held forth to the interested, yet infatuated landed interests of Britain, as a measure that would reduce America into subjugation; but which failing hitherto of that effect in America,

ative justice in all the colonies.

Should the consequence of the present ruinous

vided; ayes for admitting the troops 68, noes 106. Majority against admitting the foreign troops 38.

We are informed that 600 Georgian troops had marched for St. Augustine, to reduce that important place to the obedience of COLONIES.

___ it. a Schooner from Hingham, bound to Wil___ ad of Corn, was taken by a Tender, and car___ k.

JACOB RUSH, Esq; is appointed Secretary to the CONGRESS.

___ ince, the YANKEY-HERO sent into *Newbury-* ___ , a fine Brig, of about 200 tons burthen, laden ___ , &c. bound from *White-Haven*, for the use of ___ chers, under the command of General Howe, ___ n. This is the fifth prize out of eight which ___ bove Port, and we are in hopes of giving a good ___ ree remaining.

___ which arrived at Cape-Cod last week from London, ___ passengers, Capt. Samuel Carlton, Capt. John Battin, and Mr. Samuel Bacon, of Salem, Capt. Holmes of Ipswich, Capt. Wyer of Cape-Ann, Capt. Nutter and Capt. Shores of Portsmouth, Capt. Smallcorn of Kittery, Capt. Hutch of Old-York, and John Greenough, Esq; of Wellfleet.

The Continental Army, assisted by a large body of Militia, are now carrying on the siege of Boston with great vigor. Last Saturday night our artillery at the fortresses of Cobble-Hill and Lechmere's-Point, below this town, and at Lamb's-Dam in Roxbury, bombarded and cannonaded the town; the following night the same was continued with great briskness; and the whole of Monday night the artillery from all the above fortresses played incessantly. Our shot and shells were heard to make a great crashing in the town, but we have not learnt any particulars of the execution done thereby. The enemy returned the fire, from their batteries at West-Boston, and from their lines on the Neck, very vigorously. They threw many shells into the battery at Lechmere's-Point, one into the fort on Prospect-Hill, and one or two as far up as fort No. 2, within a quarter of a mile of the College. On Monday night we had two killed, Lieut. Mayo at Roxbury, by a cannon ball; and a man at Lechmere's Point by a shell, which, with one or two wounded, is all the loss, of any consequence, that we have sustained. We have had but little firing since Tuesday morning.

On Monday night a body of the Continental troops took possession of two large hills at Dorchester, about a mile from the south part of Boston, where they are now strongly fortified.—These are two of the heights which General Burgoyne said, in a letter to a noble Lord, commanded the town of Boston, and which, he also said, it was absolutely necessary the British troops should be possessed of.

Yesterday was the anniversary of Preston's massacre, in King-Street, Boston, 1770, when Gray, Maverick, Caldwell, Carr and Attucks, were cruelly murdered by a band of ruffians, sent hither by George, the brutal tyrant of Britain, in order to execute his infernal plans for enslaving a free people. An Oration, to commemorate this event, and to impress upon our minds the fatal tendency of standing armies being posted in populous cities, in time of peace, was pronounced, at the meeting-house in Watertown, by the Rev. Mr. Thatcher of Malden, preceded by a prayer by the Rev. Doctor Cooper.

DIED.] At Danvers, last Sabbath, Mr. WILLIAM POOL, of that place. His death is a great loss to the Town in which he lived, and much lamented by his numerous friends and acquaintance;——to his bereaved family, consisting of a widow and 7 or 8 children, it is inexpressibly distressing. He was son to Mr. Zechariah Pool of Medford, whose death was mentioned in our last.

——At Stoneham, Mrs. Osgood, the virtuous consort of Mr. John Fisk Osgood, of Boston.

——At Rowley, the 26th ult. Mrs. Mighill, widow of Captain Nathaniel Mighill, in her 93d year.——And, not long since, Mrs.

Adams, of said Rowley, in her 91st year.——There is yet living, in the said town of Rowley, twenty persons who are 80 years old

A Farm in the ___ about half a mile from the Ra ___ miles from Cambridge, on the ___ Hartford, containing about one ___ proportioned for mowing, pastu ___ land, and is fenced in fifteen ___ good stone wall, with two dwel ___ house, 5 rooms on a floor (alm ___ warehouse, chaise-house, grana ___ with works for the manufactur ___ commodious for a private gent ___ been kept at said place for alme ___ clining to purchase or hire the ___ applying to WILLIAM JENN ___ premises. Mendon Fe ___

To be sold by THOM ___

At their shop opposite the S ___
Silk handkerchiefs, li ___ baize, half thick, velvet, mens ___ calamanco, thread per pound, w ___ white drilling serge, red plush, ___ buckle brushes per dozen; che ___ files; chest, desk and table hing ___ knobs, brass cocks, brass ink- ___ pound, plated shoe and knee buc ___ of most sorts by the card, shoe ___ tongues by the dozen, fiddle-str ___ raizors per dozen, shoemakers ___ stamped awl blades and shoe-ta ___ spike gimblets, smaller do. pins, ___ by the hundred, barbers hair-p ___ snuff-boxes, tobacco do. women ___ sattin, black alamode, black bl ___ garters, nankeens, damascus, car ___ ——Cinnamon, nutmegs, mace ___ hogshead, loaf sugar and coffee

LOST, yesterday, a ___
ing twenty-one dollars in pape ___ of ten pounds, two of four pou ___ shillings, with several other pap ___ found said pocket pocket, and th ___ and papers, to the Printer here ___ shall be intitled to a reward of ___

To be sold, a Farm i ___
ing about one hundred acres, w ___ portion of tillage, pasturage and ___ and barn, half a mile from Mr. ___ be sold together or in parts, as ___ further particulars, inquire of M ___ of said Wrentham.

Whereas we the subs ___
tofore appointed commissioners ___ of the creditors of the estate of ___ deceased; and not being able to ___ pointed for that purpose, the ___ Judge of the probate of wills for ___ a further time of five months, fo ___ the creditors of said estate to brin ___ cordingly this is to give notice ___ scribers will attend that busines ___ and the four following months, ___ the afternoon, at the house of F ___

To be sold, the riggi ___

burning the Barracks and other Buildings on the Island, they fell down to Nantasket Road, where they remained when the last Accounts came away.— So very precipitate was their Flight, that they left behind them a great Quantity of Ordnance, Stores, Provisions, &c. among which are the following.

100 Pieces of Cannon in the Town, from 9 to 32 Pounders.
100 Ditto at the Castle.
.. Mortars, ...
   Beds, weighing 5 Tons each.
2500 Chaldrons of Sea-Coal.
25000 Bushels of Wheat.
1300 Bushels of Barley.
600 Bushels of Oats in one Store.
100 Jars of Oil, containing one Barrel each.
150 Horses, marked G. R.

A Number of Cannon and Mortars have been since discovered in the Water.

Extract of a Letter from an Officer in the Continental Army, dated Boston, March 18.

"We are now in firm Possession of Boston and Charlestown.—On Sunday the 17th Instant (being just 9 Months since Bunker's Hill was taken) we observed a large Body of Troops move from thence to Boston. Many were the Conjectures concerning its being evacuated. Two Soldiers of our Company offered to ascend the Hill and examine, which they resolutely did, and discharged their Muskets as Signals for us to enter, when we found the Works extremely advantageous and strong. During this the Shipping in Boston sailed down to the Castle, and anchored.— General Putnam, with a large Party, entered Boston in Boats, by the Way of Cambridge River; a Party from Generals Green and Sullivan's Brigades entered by the Ferry-Way, and others by the Neck.—It would be difficult to describe the Joy of the Inhabitants on this Occasion. "My dear Countrymen and Friends, you are welcome—God bless you—now we are happy, notwithstanding our late unparalleled Distresses"— was the Cry of Fathers, Mothers, Children, &c.— Were I to attempt giving an Account of their truly deplorable Situation, the Cruelties they have experienced, together with the Destruction of Houses and other Property in many Parts of the Town, the Task would be arduous.—Let it suffice to say, they were not suffered by the ministerial Butchers to look out of their own Windows, or speak unless commanded— their Houses ravaged before their Eyes; their Property thrown into the Streets, and destroyed; Vessels scuttled; Masts, Yards and Rigging, wantonly demolished; Houses torn down, and the Furniture, of whatsoever excellent Kind, broke to Pieces, and strewed about the Streets.—The ministerial Army left a Number of Cannon, of various Sizes, which were spiked, and the Trunnions of many broke off. Those who were supposed to have been forward in the Cause of Liberty experienced their utmost Malice.

Congress; but said Bird soon after applied to the Committee, desiring their Pardon for the Crime, and promising Reformation: They therefore have stopped all Proceedings against him, and recommend him to the future good Opinion of the Continent, on his signing the following Paper. By Order of the Committee, JAMES WILLIAMS, jun. Clerk.

Whereas I the Subscriber, a Shopkeeper in this Town, have been repeatedly guilty of passing Paper Currency in Pay for my Goods, ... that ... ... the Resolutions of the Continent, and for the General Court of this Province. I therefore in this humble and public Manner ask the Forgiveness of my Country, and promise for the future to abide by and personally support the Resolutions of the Congress, and General Court of this Province, as far as lies in my Power.
                                        N. BIRD.

Taunton, March 18, 1776.
   A true Copy.
   Attest. SAMUEL WILLIAMS, jun. Clerk.

LOST, on Monday the 18th Instant, a large black Hogskin Pocket-Book, containing sundry Accounts, Notes, &c. together with about Four or Five Pounds in Cash. As the Papers can be of no Use to any but the Owner, he would give a handsome Reward to any Person who will produce him the Book, and its Contents. DAVID LAWRENCE.

N. B. Among the Cash was a Maryland Bill of small Value, and one of the Currency of Pennsylvania.

To be SOLD or LETT,
A FARM, lying in the Northerly Part of Gloucester, containing 250 Acres, adjoining on Herring Pond; 150 Acres are within good Fence, 7 or 8 Acres of Rye in the ...

Doctor James Howard, late of Cumberland, deceased, are hereby requested to make immediate Payment; and all Persons having any Demands against said Estate, are desired to come and ...

BATTLE OF SULLIVAN'S ISLAND

By David Lee Russell

Abandoning the Cape Fear region of North Carolina after the Loyalist defeat at Moore's Creek Bridge and "having received intelligence that the fortress erected by the rebels on Sullivan's Island…was in an imperfect and unfinished state" (*London Chronicle*, August 27, 1776), on June 1, 1776, Major General Henry Clinton and Commodore Sir Peter Parker, with a British Royal Navy fleet of forty ships and seven regiments under Major General Lord Earl Charles Cornwallis, weighed anchor and sailed away to Sullivan's Island.

Major General Charles Lee, commander of the Southern Department of the Continental Army, firmly held that Fort Sullivan, built at the entrance to Charleston Harbor, could not be defended, but Colonel William Moultrie, commanding the militia, disagreed. Clinton planned to wade across from Long Island to Sullivan's Island and attack the rear of the fort while Parker's naval forces simultaneously bombarded the fort from the channel side. On June 8, Clinton, with Lord Cornwallis's 2,200 redcoats, disembarked on Long Island from the British transports. On June 18, Clinton learned that that the low tide depth at Breach Inlet across to Sullivan's Island was not eighteen inches as expected but seven feet, which would force him to use his fifteen available flat boats to cross over only four hundred troops at a time.

The night before the battle there were 435 men at Fort Sullivan, but the fort was not completed in the rear, and on the front the logs were only seven feet high. On the northeastern point of Sullivan's Island were 780 Patriot Rangers commanded by Colonel William Thomson. Not counting his transports, Commodore Parker's attack fleet consisted of two fifty-gun ships, five frigates, and four other vessels, with a total of 270 naval guns.

At 9:00 a.m. on June 28, Commodore Parker ordered his men-of-war to begin moving to anchor off Fort Sullivan. By 11:30 a.m., Parker's First Division with four British warships—*Solebay, Experiment, Bristol*, and *Active*—moved into position at four hundred yards off the beach in seven fathoms of water. The bombship *Thunder* with the twenty-two-gun *Friendship* anchored to the southeast and began firing. Meanwhile, the Second Division, with the twenty-gun *Sphinx*, the twenty-eight-gun *Acteon*, and the twenty-eight-gun *Syren*, moved past the fort, raking it with fire as it tried to reach a position behind the fort. Two of these frigates soon ran aground.

As soon as the fleet began the bombardment of Fort Sullivan, Clinton began his attempt to cross Breach Inlet. Clinton's small boat flotilla rowed toward Thomson's men as they opened fire on the flotilla, raking their decks with grapeshot from the cannon and accompanying expert rifle fire. The flotilla dispersed in response to the deadly fire. Clinton and his men looked on in quiet disbelief. Discouraged, Clinton made the decision to abandon the crossing.

At 10:20 a.m., the rebels began to fire on the *Bristol* and then at all the British warships. The cannon battle was intense as the shells of the fleet landed in and around the fort, but it did no damage as the shells buried themselves in the loose sand of the fort, lodged in the soft Palmetto logs, or flew over the fort. At noon, the British fleet was fully engaged off the fort. By 2:00 p.m., Captain Morris reported: "we silenc'd the Fort until ½ past 3… during which time the Rebels fired one Gun" (*Journal of HMS Bristol, Captain John Morris, PRO, Admiralty 51/137*). Moultrie had decided to slow down his cannon firing to conserve his ammunition, but it restarted an hour later. The battle raged on the entire day as the fort and its men took their punishment. At 9:00 p.m., Parker's warships withdrew and moved to their former moorings. The twelve-hour battle was over.

It was a clear Patriot victory. As reported in the *London Chronicle* of August 27, 1776, the British suffered forty dead and seventy-one wounded aboard the *Bristol*, while there were twenty-three dead and fifty-six wounded on the *Experiment*. The *Solebay* lost eight wounded, and the *Active* saw one killed with six wounded. Colonel Moultrie had lost only twelve men and twenty-five wounded. On July 4, President Rutledge visited the garrison for a victory celebration, where he promoted William Moultrie to Brigadier General, and the fort was renamed Fort Moultrie.

With their defeat at the Battle of Sullivan's Island, the British expedition to establish a foothold in the south had failed, and the southern colonies would remain invasion-free for another thirty months.

AMERICAN DEFENSE OF FORT SULLIVAN
North Wind Picture Archives

The cannon battle was intense as the shells
of the fleet landed in and around the fort,
but there was no damage.

Abandoning the Cape Fear region of North Carolina after the Loyalist defeat at Moore's Creek Bridge and "having received intelligence that the fortress erected by the rebels on Sullivan's Island…was in an imperfect and unfinished state," on June 1, 1776, Major General Henry Clinton and Commodore Sir Peter Parker, with a British Royal Navy fleet of forty ships and seven regiments under Major General Lord Earl Charles Cornwallis, sailed to Sullivan's Island. The Battle of Sullivan's Island was a clear Patriot victory and helped keep the southern colonies invasion-free for another two and a half years.

MONDAY, AUGUST 26.

The London Gazette. No. 11671.

Whitehall, August 24.

CAPTAIN Hope arrived on Wednesday evening last from South Carolina with dispatches from Commodore Sir Peter Parker and Lieutenant General Clinton.

Extract of a Letter from Sir Peter Parker to Mr. Stephens, Secretary of the Admiralty, dated within Charlestown-bar, July 9, 1776.

"It having been judged adviseable to make an attempt upon Charlestown in South Carolina, the fleet sailed from Cape Fear on the 1st of June, and on the 4th anchored off Charlestown-bar. The 5th founded on the bar, and laid down buoys preparatory to the intended entrance of the harbour. The 7th all the frigates and most of the transports got over the bar into five fathom Hole. The 9th General Clinton landed on Long Island with about four or five hundred men. The 10th the Bristol got over the bar with some difficulty. The 15th gave the Captains of the squadron my arrangement for the attack of the batteries on Sulivan's Island, and the next day acquainted General Clinton that the ships were ready. The General fixed on the 23d for our joint attack, but the wind proving unfavourable, prevented its taking effect. The 25th the Experiment arrived, and next day came over the bar, when a new arrangement was made for the attack. The 28th, at half an hour after nine in the morning, informed General Clinton by signal that I should go on the attack. At half an hour after ten I made the signal to weigh; and about a quarter after eleven the Bristol, Experiment, Active, and Solebay, brought up against the fort. Thunder Bomb, covered by the Friendship armed vessel, brought the saliant angle of the east bastion to bear N. W. by N.

for near an hour and a half; but the rebels finding that our army could not take possession, about six o'clock a considerable body of people re-entered the fort, and renewed the firing from two or three guns, the rest being, I suppose, dismounted. About nine o'clock, it being very dark, great part of our ammunition expended, the people fatigued, the tide of ebb almost done, no prospect from the eastward, and no possibility of our being of any farther service, I ordered the ships to withdraw to their former moorings. Their lordships will see plainly by this account, that if the troops could have co-operated on this attack, his Majesty would have been in possession of Sulivan's Island. But I must beg leave here to be fully understood, left it should be imagined that I mean to throw the most distant reflection on our army: I should not discharge my conscience, were I not to acknowledge, that such was my opinion of his Majesty's troops, from the general down to the private soldier, that after I had been engaged some hours, and perceived that the troops had not got a footing on the north end of Sulivan's Island, I was perfectly satisfied that the landing was impracticable, and that the attempt would have been the destruction of many brave men without the least probability of success; and this, I am certain, will appear to be the case, when General Clinton represents his situation.—The Bristol had 40 men killed, and 71 wounded; the Experiment 23 killed and 56 wounded, and both of them suffered much in their hulls, masts, and rigging; the Active had Lieutenant Pike killed, and 6 men wounded; and the Solebay 8 men wounded. Not one man who was quartered at the beginning of the action on the Bristol's quarter-deck escaped being killed or wounded. Capt. Morris lost his right arm, and received other wounds, and is since dead; the master is wounded in his right arm, but will recover the use of it: I received seve-

[Price Three-pence.]

ral contusions at different times, but as none of them are on any part where the least danger can be apprehended, they are not worth mentioning. Lieutenants Caulfield, Molloy, and Nugent, were the Lieutenants of the Bristol in the action; they behaved so remarkably well that it is impossible to say to whom the preference is due; and so indeed I may say of all the petty officers, ship's company, and volunteers. At the head of the latter I must place Lord Wm. Campbell, who was so condescending as to accept of the direction of some guns on the lower gun deck. His Lordship received a contusion on his left side, but I have the happiness to inform their Lordships that it has not proved of much consequence. Capt. Scott, of the Experiment, lost his left arm, and is otherwise so much wounded, that I fear he will not recover. I cannot conclude this letter without remarking, that when it was known we had many men too weak to come to quarters, almost all the seamen belonging to the transports offered their service with a truly British spirit, and a just sense of the cause we are engaged in. I accepted of upwards of fifty to supply the place of our sick. The Masters of many of the transports attended with their boats, but particular thanks are due to Mr. Chambers, the Master of the Mercury.

All the regiments will be embarked in a few days. The first brigade, consisting of four regiments, will sail in a day or two, under convoy, for New York; and the Bristol and Experiment will, I hope, follow with the remainder.

Sir Peter Parker's squadron consisted of the following ships and vessels:

Ships, &c.	Guns.	Commanders.
Bristol	50	Ad. Sir Peter Parker, Capt. John Morris.
Experiment	50	Alexander Scot.
Active	28	William Williams.
Solebay	21	Thomas Symonds.
Actæon	28	Christopher Atkins.
Syren	28	Tobias Furneaux.
Sphynx	20	Anthony Hunt.
Friendship	22	Charles Hope.
Ranger sloop	8	Roger Wills.
Thunder bomb	8	James Reid.
St. Laurence schooner	—	Lieut. John Graves.

Whitehall, August 24.

IT appears by Lieutenant General Clinton's letter to Lord George Germaine, dated July 8, 1776, from the camp on Long Island, province of South Carolina, that Sir Peter Parker and the General having received intelligence that the fortress erected by the Rebels on Sulivan's Island (the key to Charlestown harbour) was in an imperfect and unfinished state, resolved to attempt the reduction thereof by a coup de main; and that, in order that the army might co-operate with the fleet, the General landed his troops on Long Island, which had been represented to him, by a ford passable at low water; but that he, to his very great mortification, found that the channel, which was reported to have been eighteen inches deep at low water, to be seven feet deep; which circumstance rendered it impossible for the army to give that assistance to the fleet in the attack made upon the fortress, that the General intended, and which he, and the troops under his command, ardently wished to do.

St. James's, August 24. The King has been pleased to grant the dignity of a Baronet of the Kingdom of Great Britain, to them and their

George Baker, Doctor in [Physic] sician in ordinary to her Majesty.

St. James's, August 24. Mr. Robert Halifax and Mr. Edward Holdich are appointed joint Apothecaries to his Majesty's household.

The King has been pleased to grant unto Benjamin Wheeler, D. D. the office and place of Regius Professor of Divinity in the University of Oxford, together with the place and dignity of a Canon of the cathedral church of Christ in the said University, properly belonging to the Regius Professor of the said University; being both void by the death of Dr. Edward Bentham.

BANKRUPTS.

Richard Bishop, late of Holborn, Baker, to surrender Aug. 31, Sept. 14, Oct. 5, at Guildhall. Attorney, Mr. Jennings, of Shoe-lane.

David Riz, of Sweedland-court, in the Parish of St. Botolph Bishopsgate Without, London, Soapmaker, to surrender Sept. 3, 6, Oct. 5, at Guildhall. Attorney, Mr. Collet, Lamb's-conduit-street.

Samuel Cole, of Dartmouth, in Devonshire, Dealer, to surrender Sept. 9, 10, Oct. 5, at the Bear Inn in Southgate-street, Exeter. Attorney, Mr. Walter Prideaux, Dartmouth.

John Law, late of Stratton grounds, Westminster, Scrivener, to surrender Aug. 30, Sept. 11, Oct. 5, at Guildhall. Attorney, Mr. Wright, of Holborn-court, Gray's-inn.

William Holyland, of West Smithfield, London, Linen-draper, to surrender Aug. 31, Sept. 16, Oct. 5, at Guildhall. Attorney, Mr. Lowten, Middle Temple.

William Clarke and Robert Collins, of Paternoster-row, in the City of London, Booksellers, Dealers, and Chapmen, (surviving Copartners of Lacey Hawes, late of the same Place, Bookseller, deceased) to surrender Sept. 3, 6, Oct. 5, at Guildhall. Attorney, Mr. Edmunds, Cursitors-street, Chancery-lane.

Bankruptcy enlarged.

John Radenhurst, late of Dolgun Forge, in the Parish of Dolgelley, in Merionethshire, North Wales, Ironmaster, but now of the Parish of Heswall, in Cheshire, Merchant, to surrender Sept. 14, at Guildhall, London.

Dividends to be made.

Sept. 13. John Coster, jun. of Romsey, in the County of Southampton, and Matthew Jenkins, of the same Place, Common Brewers, at the Dolphin Inn in Romsey.

16. John Davy and Henry Hounsom, of Church-lane, near Whitechapel, Sugar-refiners, at Guildhall.

Certificate to be granted.

Sept. 14. David Goodsman, of the Strand, Bookbinder.

LONDON.

Last Saturday's Gazette contains his Majesty's Order in Council, that a former Order for prohibiting the exporting out of this kingdom, or carrying coastwise, gunpowder, saltpetre, or any sort of arms or ammunition, be continued for three months longer, to commence from the 23d of this inst. August.

A letter from Maryland mentions, "That the body of people which rose in arms against the congress grow every day stronger and stronger, as also that the latter has sent a considerable force to oppose them, and that the two parties lay intrenched at a few miles distance from each other; but unhappily the greater part of the British forces from the south, had little prospect of success, unless Lord Dunmore should leave his [coast] and attempt something for their assistance.

The troops on the expedition at [Charlestown] under General Clinton, consist of the 15th, 33d, 37th, 54th, and 57th regiments, and two companies of artillery, making in the whole 3395, to which the marines of the shipping may be added, who are about 300 in number.

General Lee is said to have commanded the Provincial forces at the attack of fort Sulivan.

A considerable number of the English troops were encamped on Long Island during the attack of fort Sulivan. Long Island is about a quarter of a mile distant from Sulivan's Island.

According to the plan of action, the English forces were to have forded from Long Island to Sulivan's Island, and to have attacked the Provincials by land, whilst the ships of war endeavoured to annoy them by a maritime attack. The Commodore was misinformed as to the depth of water between the two islands. The water was found to be seven feet deep.

Extract of a Letter from Amsterdam, Aug. 19.

"Several letters from Madrid, by yesterday's mail, have the following paragraph:—" It is universally reported here, that two members of the Continental Congress of North America have been at our court a few days ago; that they had several private audiences with our King, and actually concluded a treaty of alliance with Spain; and that orders were sent Don Michael de Caston in consequence thereof to sail for North America with his fleet, and act in conjunction with the Americans." But how far this is grounded in truth, a very short time must discover."

On Friday a packet with letters was received at Gloucester-house from his Royal Highness the Duke of Gloucester, which bring advice that the health of his Royal Highness was so good as it was some months ago, and a relapse of his former disorder was greatly feared.

An insurrection of the Negroes at Barbadoes is said to have happened, on account of a scarcity of provisions.

Extract of a Letter from Penzance, Aug.

"Last Friday morning, about eight o'clock, came in here the William and Mary, W. Phillips, Master, from Madeira, with [wine]. She was chased all the morning, and the day before, by two American privateers, one mounting 12, the other 24 guns. When the alarm was given, all the inhabitants of Penzance, Mousehole, &c. and all the adjacent parts belonging to the Land's-end, went to see them landing on the glasses. They were so near, that we could plainly see the men and guns; they steered towards the Scilly Islands."

Extract of a Letter from Gosport, Aug.

"A letter from Capt. Dickson, Commander of the Greyhond, says, he had taken five American prizes, but has lost four of them, being retaken by the rebels, with his men he had put on board to take care of them, they are made prisoners. He has but one left, which he kept by him. He is going to New York to join Lord Howe."

"Thursday a company of the 4th or King's own, arrived here from Havre, are to embark this day for America."

The Hero, Strivens, from Granada to London, was taken in lat. 21, by the Privateer, Capt. Sumner, of the Sunbury, who arrived in the river, met with a French [ship] had on board Capt. Strivens, and two English Captains; all three have [been] ships.

The Favourite man of war at Dep[tford]

DECLARATION OF INDEPENDENCE

By Matthew P. Dziennik

AFTER THE EVACUATION OF BOSTON IN MARCH 1776, William Howe, commanding the British army in America, turned his attention toward the capture of New York. The battle of New York was to be the first military campaign undertaken by the independent United States of America.

In the months after April 1775, when tensions between the colonists and Great Britain had exploded into open hostilities, a series of events had pushed the United Colonies toward a formal declaration of independence. Until the autumn of 1775, many colonists still hoped that their grievances might still be addressed by a sympathetic king and that their troubles were primarily the result of corrupt ministers and the machinations of Parliament. As the November 16, 1775, *New-England Chronicle* had reported of a congressional investigation into British hostilities which would later make up part of the Declaration of Independence, atrocities had been committed by "ministerial troops," implicitly distinguishing between the king and his ministers. The King's Proclamation of August 23, 1775, which declared that the colonies were in "open and avowed Rebellion" and no longer subject to his protection, revealed the naivety of this line of thinking and pushed increasing numbers of colonists toward republicanism.

A new sense that the king was part of the problem was fully demonstrated by the phenomenal success of Thomas Paine's *Common Sense*, published in January 1776. In its bitter denunciation of the king, *Common Sense* both reflected and encouraged an increasing belief that independence was the only viable means of effecting change. Indeed, by the time Richard Henry Lee presented his resolution on independence to Congress on June 7 (following an earlier preamble by John Adams on May 15), the majority of colonists were probably already supportive of independence. At least

ninety local "declarations" preceded the Declaration of Independence between April and July 1776. Congress formally declared independence on July 2 and on July 4 finalized the text of the Declaration, which was drafted by John Adams, Benjamin Franklin, Thomas Jefferson, Robert Livingston, and Roger Sherman. On the night of July 4, a handwritten copy of the document was rushed from Congress to a local printer, John Dunlap, who published the first broadsides the following day (the July 6, 1776, issue of the *Pennsylvania Evening Post*, printed by Benjamin Towne, was the first newspaper to publish the Declaration). John Hancock forwarded a copy of the Dunlap broadside to George Washington with instructions that it was to be read to the army defending New York.

While future generations have come to emphasize the stirring evocation of natural rights enshrined in the Declaration—"that all Men are created equal"—revolutionary leaders were intently aware of the Declaration's more immediate value. Washington hoped that it would improve enlistment and inspire his troops to face the regulars of the British army. As the report that appeared in the *London Chronicle* of September 26, 1776, makes clear, when the Declaration was officially read out on July 9, it had the desired effect. The reading was "everywhere received with loud huzzas, and the utmost demonstrations of joy." That same evening, a crowd gathered on the Bowling Green in lower Manhattan, where they proceeded to pull down and decapitate the equestrian statue of George III erected there in 1770. The statue was then delivered to Litchfield, Connecticut, where local women melted it down to make musket balls, something also referenced in the same report.

Most colonists, however, did not elevate the Declaration of Independence to the heights it has since attained. As the articles in the *New-England Chronicle* of August 29, 1776, and the *Pennsylvania Evening Post* of September 28, 1776, demonstrate, the revolutionaries did not idly congratulate themselves on a job well done but immediately turned to the question of the form of the new state and national governments. Much of the work done by Congress over the summer of 1776 was also directed toward international recognition of the United States. As the depth of analysis in the *Scots Magazine* of that August reveals, the audience for the Declaration was foreign as well as domestic. The Declaration was as much about declaring the United States to be a free and sovereign state within the international community as it was about appealing to the loyalties of the colonists. The

appearance of the Declaration in the London newspapers is, therefore, significant. The small note contained in the *London Chronicle* from August 13, 1776, was likely a reprint of a government communique that had first appeared in numerous newspapers the previous day. More than half of the world's countries now have their own declarations of independence.

In a series of engagements in the autumn of 1776, Howe savaged the Continental Army and ejected it from New York. The riotous behavior reported on the evening of July 9, however, serves to demonstrate the significance of the Declaration of Independence, a work that would help sustain the revolutionary movement until Britain finally recognized that independence in 1783.

AMERICANS TEARING DOWN
STATUE OF GEORGE III
North Wind Picture Archives

The same evening the Declaration of Independence was read in New York, a crowd gathered in lower Manhattan to pull down and decapitate the equestrian statue of George III. The statue was later melted to make musket balls.

dispatched to the aid of Hampton, and the Col. of the 2d regiment sent to take the command of ... swimming away with Mr. King's Negro man, who are on shore, and a pursuit, it is hoped, may overtake them. There were in the vessel two men mortally wounded, one is since dead, and the other near his end ; besides which, we are informed nine men were seen to be thrown overboard from one of the vessels. We have not a man even wounded. The vessels went over to Norfolk, and we are informed the whole force from thence is intended to visit Hampton to-day. If they come, we hope our brave troops are prepared for them, as we can with pleasure assure the public that every part of them behaved with spirit and bravery, and are wishing for another skirmish.

PHILADELPHIA, November 4.

In CONGRESS, Wednesday, Oct. 18, 1775.

RESOLVED, That a just and well authenticated account of the hostilities committed by the ministerial troops and navy in America since March last, be collected, with proper evidence of the truth of the facts related, the number and value of the buildings destroyed by them. Also the number and value of the vessels, inward and outward bound, which have been seized by them since that period, as near as the number and value can be ascertained. Also the stock taken by them from different parts of the continent.

That Mr. Deane, Mr. John Adams, and Mr. Wythe, be a Committee for this purpose.

A true copy from the minutes,

CHARLES THOMSON, Secretary.

Capt. Stiles arrived here yesterday from Bermuda. Coming out he spoke with a vessel that left London the 10th of September, the Captain of whom informed him that he sailed with three men of war and twenty five transports, with 5000 Hanoverians, bound for Charlestown South Carolina,

---

the Martiers ; and out of five Galloons, that sailed from Campeachy, four were dismasted, two of which put into Georgia, two more into South Carolina, and the fifth supposed to be lost.

The Captain of the Tamar Frigate took the Powder and Cash out of the Galloons, on their Arrival at Carolina ; but the Spanish Capts in a few Days after took Charge of the Money themselves.

CAMBRIDGE, November 16.

Yesterday se'nnight Captain Robbins, bound from Ireland to Boston, in a schooner, laden with Beef, Tongues, Butter, Potatoes, and Eggs, (all much wanted for the butchering assassins there) was taken by a two-mast boat from Beverly, and carried in there. Capt. Robbins, who has been brought to town, informs us, that he left Ireland the 24th of September, at which time five regiments were embarking on board seven ships and one brig, for Boston, and 'twas said that those were all the troops destin'd hence this fall, though a large reinforcement was to be sent in the spring, to make up an army of 22,500 men. Capt. Robbins brought papers to the 16th of September, which are not come to hand ; also the King's proclamation (inserted in the last page) declaring the Colonists rebels. Capt. Robbins says, The common people of Ireland were almost unanimous in favour of the Americans, and that only those in favour of government, appeared against us.

Thursday last, at one o'clock P. M. about 300 of the enemy landed at Lechmere's point, covered by the guns of 2 or 3 men of war, which lay off the westerly part of Boston. The tide was very full, and our men were retarded in getting on to the point by being obliged to pass a ford near breast high. The enemy (urged on by the prospect of getting a little lean beef) took the advantage of stealing away 5 or 6 cows, and 2 or 3 horses ; and then, on discovering our men advancing towards them, run down to their boats with the greatest precipitation. Our troops fired upon them as they went off, and killed and wounded several ; but how many they lost we have not been able to learn. Two of our soldiers were wounded by cannon balls from the ships, which kept up an incessant fire upon our men while in pursuit of the regulars.

A gentleman who lately came out of Boston, assures. That the ministerial rebels in Boston, by order of their General, How, have taken down the pulpit and all the pews in the old south meeting-house, and are using it for a riding school ;---this he saw. Thus we see the house once set apart for the true worship and service of GOD, turned into a den for thieves !

Tuesday last week, a privateer from Beverly, took and carried in there a vessel, Richie master, bound from Boston to Annapolis-Royal, laden with dry goods, &c. on a trading voyage.

Last week the privateers from Plymouth, took and carried in there several vessels employed in the service of the ministerial butchers in Boston ; among others, Capt. Jabez Hatch of Boston.

Governor Martin's proclamation of the 8th of August, was burnt at Hillsborough, in North-Carolina, by the hands of the common hangman, in pursuance of an order from the congress for that purpose.

Saturday last the general assembly of this colony adjourned to Wednesday the 29th of November instant.

MARRIED.] At East-Greenwich, John Singer Dexter, Esq; to Miss Polly Pearce, of that Town.

STRAYED or stolen from the Subscriber, in Salem, last Thursday morning, a small red HORSE, with a roan swaggle tail, and a white star in his face. Whoever will return the said horse to the Subscriber, or leave him with the Printers hereof, shall receive TWO DOLLARS reward, and be paid all necessary charges. JOSEPH HILLER.

---

laid deceased's ...

RAN awa...
Sellon, formerl...
Isaiah Foxon, ...
little round-sho...
on the right ha...
turn him to his ...
dollar reward.
Leicester, ...

WHERE...
of the townshi...
unto the first W...
morning, at the ...
the county of W...
(or such part th...
of taxes heretof...
dered to be paid...
or to Capt. Eli...
Woodstock.

JOSEPH ...
A Quantity ...
Cheese, ...
Cash given for ...
Saie Hovey ...
in Cambridge, ...
articles cheap f...

BENJ ...
INFORMS ...
six months ...
the 23d instant...
payment to the ...
that his custom...
before or at the ...
as he is at prese...
post road, are de...
that their paper...

DESERT...
regiment. and C...
Nash, of Granb...
5 feet 8 or 9 in...
had with him a ...
dark short hair, ...
to the tavern-k...
make, a cartrid...
the province.
bring him to t...
necessary charge...
Camp n...
P. S. Said ...
the Selectmen ...
any town where...
send him forthw...

STRAYE...
ber last, from th...
as a middling tw...
trots all, with t...
from it ; her m...
said colt and bri...
for his trouble b...
the county of F...

WANTE...
Any such one, ...
by applying im...

Commission superseded.

John Carr, of Scotland-yard, Coal-merchant, (Partner in Trade with James Farrer and Edward Arrowsmith, of the same Place, Coal-merchants.)

Bankruptcy enlarged.

James Farrer, Edward Arrowsmith, and John Carr, of Scotland-yard, Coal-merchants and Partners, to surrender Aug. 29, at Guildhall.

Dividends to be made.

Sept. 3. John Gardner, late of Romsey, in Hants, Clothier, at the Angel in Romsey.

11. Richard Ford, of Coalbrookdale, in the County of Salop, Ironmaster, at Mary Corbett's, in High-street, Bridgnorth, Salop.

20. Benjamin Cooper, late of Walsall, in Stafford-shire, and Joseph Hodgkin, late of Aldridge, in the said County, Merchants and Traders, at the King's-head in New-street, Birmingham.

Certificate to be granted.

Aug. 31. William Richardson, of Fenchurch street, London, Linen-draper.

LONDON.

Advice is received that the Congress resolved upon independence the 4th of July; and, it is said, have declared war against Great Britain in form.

When General Thompson was conducted in the guard-room at Montreal with the rest of the prisoners of that day, he requested an audience of his brother General, Carleton, and a subaltern waited on him with the message, which Carleton refused complying with, and returned for answer, " that he never held any conversation with rebels."

A letter from Paris received on Saturday, says, " that the French Court have absolutely refused to give any answer to the demand made by the English Ambassador, ' What they were arming for?' "

A number of men, employed by the Board of Works, are now repairing and taking down the battlements at St. James's, to make the building more uniform, according to the present taste.

Since the brigade of foot guards have embarked for America, upwards of 500 recruits have been raised and incorporated in the said regiments; the remaining number to compleat the same to the full complement of men, are now raising.

The Jameson and Peggy, the Kingston, Benham, from London, and the Britannia, Sommers, from Waterford, are all arrived at Halifax.

Letters from Jamaica mention, that advice has been received there of the loss of the Septentrion, a Spanish man of war of 74 guns, about 20 leagues from the Havannah (supposed by lightning) and all the crew perished.

The Ulysses, Littleton, from London, is lost at Gambia.

The Thomas, Sides, from Newfoundland, foundered at sea; the crew were saved.

The four 60 gun ships now fitting out for

On Tuesday last was married at Ash, in Kent, the Rev. Mr. Hutchinson of Norbourn, to Miss Elizabeth Beale Pery, of Ash.

On Saturday last was married at Crayford, in Kent, Mr. Essex, of Southampton-street, Covent-Garden, to Miss Nancy Wright, of Crayford.

Yesterday was married Mr. Samuel Fenn, of this City, to Miss Tate of the Old Change.

On Friday last died at Greenwich, Captain Francis Minshull.

On Saturday last died, at his house in St. James's-street, Mr. Matthew Crane, Apothecary to the Houshold.

At Shrewsbury assizes John Herbert for sheep-stealing, was capitally convicted, but afterwards reprieved.

H. M. The Nabob, with Taste.

This Day was published, Price 1s 6d.

A New Edition, corrected to the present time, on a broad sheet of elephant paper, proper for framing, with an elegant engraved border,

A COMPLETE TITHE-TABLE: Wherein the nature of tithes, and all things tithable, are shewn at one view. With an account of compositions, custom, prescription, and privilege, distinguished under their proper heads; with reference to adjudged cases, and statutes relating to tithes.

Proper for all Vestries, Halls of Clergymen and Gentlemen, as well as Attornies.

Printed for J. F. and C. Rivington, No. 62, in St. Paul's Church-yard.

Or whom may be had,
Printed in the manner above-mentioned,
A Sporting Table: Wherein all the laws touching game are shewn at one view. Price 1s. 6d.

For the TEETH and GUMS.

JACOB HEMET, Dentist to her MAJESTY, and the PRINCESS AMELIA, begs leave to recommend to the Public his ESSENCE of PEARL, and PEARL DENTIFRICE, which he has found to be greatly superior, not only in elegance, but also in efficacy,
plaint ...
will p...
to ol...
out i...
as are...
becom...
cure t...
firm a...
breath...
disord...
Sol...
and r...
street, ...
retail by...
and no where else in London. Sold also by Mr. Purdie, Perfumer, at Bath, price 2s. 6d. each.

For the COMPLEXION, and DISORDERS of the SKIN,

FAU DE FLEURS DE VENICE: or, Venetian Bloom Water. This curious

SOCIETY for the Discharge imprisoned for Sma Craven-street, St

Benefactions since the last viz.

W. W. a Lady
Lord Chief Baron Smythe, ann
Lady Smythe, ditto
Mr. Hull, ditto
W. J. 3d benefaction
A. B.
D. B.
D. C. July 10
J. H. by J. R.

Discharged from the several polis, and other parts of the ki who could not be relieved by th 39 l. 6 s. 2 d.

Approved the recommendatio
Referred for Enquiry 19 Peti

The books may be seen by a promote this undertaking, b Eleven and Three, at No. 7, benefactions are received, and v meet on Wednesday the 22d o'Clock in the Afternoon.

Benefactions are also receive the Thatch'd-house Tavern; t Banking Company; and M surer, in St. James's-street; and Co. in Finch-lane, Cornh in Fleet-street; Mess. Biddu Charing Cross; Mess. Fullers; Co. in Lombard-street; and seller, at Charing-Cross.

DR. JAMES's ANAL GEORGE the Thir ROBERT JAMES, of county of Middlesex, Doctor i represented unto us, that he ha

year of our reign. By writ o

These are the Pills which th so many years in his private pra been always in such high estim tients. They are particularly u gestions, flatulencies, and hab

For the NEW-ENGLAND CHRONICLE.

LETTER III.

To the PEOPLE of the MASSACHUSETTS-BAY.

Friends and Countrymen,

YOU are upon the eve of an event, that will prove of the utmost consequence to the State. We congratulate ourselves upon the Declaration of Independency: but the liberties of the present and future generations remain to be secured by a proper Form of Government. What we had taken up pro tempore by the advice of the Continental Congress is now necessarily expiring; for we no longer mean to receive a Governor from the King of Great-Britain, though he should appoint one that would conform to the Charter. It might be questioned, whether the General Court can with consistency pass any new acts, till the Form of Government has been settled by the voice of the publick.— However, it may be proper enough, by reason of the times, to connive at their proceedings, till you can have digested matters, and prepared duly for the important service before you: they being careful to act up to the *spirit* of liberty, and not to abuse the confidence of the people. Suffer me to exhort you, upon every consideration, not to be hurried or drawn in to any one particular Form of Government, without examining the nature and tendency of it with the greatest accuracy. The weak and designing may tell you, that as you have the power of altering it when you find it defective, it does not so much signify what it is. The same set of persons will argue against altering it, when once adopted, upon the plea of your not having given it a fair trial, and the inconvenience that arises from fre... ...anges, till they have got it established

having received the instructions of their constituents upon the head. Whoever are appointed to form a Plan of Government would do well in consulting the several Plans that have been already, or may be adopted by the other Colonies, ere they have finished it. It would be well indeed were all these Plans published in each of our news-papers, that so you might have an opportunity of canvassing the subject in your own thoughts, and of culling out the excellencies, and marking the defects to be found in them.

I would now observe to you, my Friends and Countrymen, that I have reason to believe that there are some Gentlemen in the House, who wish to have the legislature rest in that body only, and to have no Council or any check upon them. Such Gentlemen may design well, but appear to me to be egregiously mistaken. I do not say that the *House* mean to engross the legislature: but they may possibly be led insensibly into the measure by those that see further than the majority. They have been thought by some to have trespassed already upon the right of the Council, to have lessened their power, and to have encroached upon their authority as one Branch of the Constitution. This is certain, that they have neglected calling in the assistance of the Council in forming the Plan of Government, and taken the whole to themselves. One reason assigned for this omission, by a popular Member, (as I have been told) was very extraordinary, viz. that they were more the Representatives of the people than the Council. Truly not in this case; for they were never elected by the people for that purpose, and therefore could be no more the Representatives of the people in that, than the Council. Besides, if the Council consist of the ablest persons, whom we must suppose the House would be careful to elect annu-

a day of fasting, hu... Almighty GOD, sho... *imploring of his divin... zation and establishme... ment* for the security civil and religious ri... kind; no less than protection in the America.

STATE of ...
In COUNCI...

ORDERED, Th... ble Congress of th... ing Persons app... Letters of Marque and R... several News-Papers in... fitting out such Vessels... plication for their Comm...

By Order...
JOHN...

In CONGR...

RESOLVED, Tha... set forth and fit out... War, and applying for... Marque and Reprisal fo... a Writing, subscribed b... and Tonnage or Burther... Number of her Guns,... the Name and Place of... Owners, the Names of t... cers, the Number of the... Provisions and Warlike... be delivered to the Secr... Clerk of the House or... or Council, or Commit... which the Ship or Vesse... the said Secretary, an... And that the Command... the Commission or Le...

Price THREE Coppers.   Published every *Tuesday, Thursday,* and *Saturday* Evenings.

Vol. II.]   SATURDAY, SEPTEMBER 28, 1776.   [Num. 264.

For the PENNSYLVANIA EVENING POST.

HOWEVER censurable a man may become, by differing in opinion with some part of the community, it ought not to lessen his right and his duty to communicate his sentiments, whenever he apprehends the happiness and safety of the people to be in danger.

The right of publishing my sentiments, I claim on the general principles of liberty and self preservation—The Convention for the state of Pennsylvania have preserved this right *defensible,* by inserting of it in the Declaration of Rights, and intending to admit it in their proposed frame of government, to wit, " that the printing presses shall be free to every person who undertakes to examine the proceedings of the legislature, or *any part* of the government," &c. therefore I am induced to examine into *some* part of the proceedings of the Convention, and hope no evil tendency to the public will arise from the examination.

Public affairs being brought, by the American contest with Great-Britain, to a crisis, it was thought conducive to the people's security, that a change in the powers of government should be made, without the interference of any other authority than the voice of the people.—A number of people were accordingly chosen, out of the several counties, to meet in Provincial Conference, in order to consider, what measures might be judged best to be taken on the alarming occasion—On consultation, among other things, the Provincial Conference resolved, N. C. D. " that it is necessary a Provincial Convention be called by this Conference, for the *express purpose of forming a new government* in the province"—A Convention was therefore chosen and met, and although above one hundred days (at above 3000 pounds expence in wages) have expired since their first meeting, a frame of government hath not yet been concluded upon; but in the mean time, several ordinances have been passed by them, touching the liberty, property, and happiness of the people in their most essential points—from the spirit and tenor of the powers given by the Provincial Conference, as well as by the resolves of the several county Committees, it appears the Convention were only chosen to form a plan of government, *not to legislate,* or *execute* any laws or ordinances whatsoever.

This being premised, I shall beg leave to point out the ordinance passed Sept. 12th, wherein it is enacted, " that any person speaking, &c. against the measures carrying on by the United States of America, on complaint and proof made on oath before any Justice or Justices, such person so offending shall be committed to the common jail, for such term as they shall deem proper, not exceeding the duration of the present war with Great-Britain," &c.

By virtue whereof, it is in the power of any two justices nominated by the Convention, on the evidence of a *single* witness, without the least *semblance* of trial by a jury, to abridge a freeman of his liberty, by committing of him to the common jail, perhaps forever. An appeal is indeed permitted to be made to the Council of Safety, who may *annul* or *confirm* the sentence of the Justices aforesaid. But who are the Council of Safety? They are nominated by the Convention, without order or authority, no code of laws to govern their proceeding, but left, like the Justices, to do as to them seem meet. " The supposed offender being in close confinement, the writ of *Habeas Corpus,* the most *celebrated* writ in the law, is hereby rendered void, so that he has no other satisfaction under the Ordinance before recited, than to rest *there* in durance," till chance of war, or any other adventitious circumstance, may deliver him; that great oracle of the law, Judge *Blackstone,* asserts, that " the personal liberty of the subject is a natural inherent right, which cannot be surrendered, or ought to be *abridged* in any case, without the special permission of law." The Honorable Congress of the United States considered the form of trial by jury, and the benefits of a Habeas Corpus writ, to be of such importance, to the preservation of the liberty of the subject, that in their Declaration of Independence, they advance the breach of them as solemn testimonials of the tyranny and usurpation of George III. Our wise ancestors *fought, bled* and *conquered,* in support of these grand bulwarks of liberty, and handed them down, notwithstanding the violence of conquest, or the ferocity of the times; but why their posterity should esteem them of less moment in this day, can only be accounted for by those whose views and interests may be obtained by destroying of them.

Another Ordinance, passed in Convention in the same month, I shall next consider—By authority of this Ordinance a tax and fines are imposed on the estates and personal service of the freemen of the province, who are above the age of fifty years, or do not either from conscientious principles, or other solemn obligations, enter into a military state of defence—the effects of which must, if carried into execution, be destructive to common justice, common honesty, and the rights of mankind in general—the Convention have, in their Declaration, declared, that " no part of a man's property can be justly taken from him without his own consent, or that of his *legal* representatives"—and their intended frame of government expressly declares, " that no tax or contribution shall be *raised* or *paid* by *any* of the people of this state, except by a *law* made for that purpose," and farther, " that it shall appear clearly to the legislature to be of more service to the community than the money would be, if not collected."—The wildest enthusiast for popular government will not be bold enough to prove, that the Convention is a *legislative body,* or that the money, when raised by virtue of the above intended Ordinance, will be better in coffers than circulating among its *proper owners*—there is not, and I hope will not be, any occasion for the *use* of the money as *specified* in the Ordinance, as from *experience* it has been found better to raise men into a well disciplined state of defence, to remain so during the present unhappy war, than by leading the inhabitants out of the province in a *militia* situation; though I admit that a militia, acting within its respective province, to be a good security.—I shall not at this time enter into the propriety, or otherways, of what may be most advantageous on this head; but, from the tenor of the above recited Ordinance, I shall beg leave to ob-

---

LE.

UMB. 419.)

Queen-Street.

n and prayer to
observed for the
ce in the *organi-*
Form of Govern-
epetuation of the
liberties of man-
licate his further
t now rages in

setts-Bay.

ust 22, 1776.
solve of the honora-
April last, respect-
Commissions, or
e published in the
e, that all Persons
how to make ap-

cil.

Y, Dep. Sec'ry.

ril 3, 1776.
erson intending to
Ship or Vessel of
ission or Letters of
pose, shall produce
ntaining the Name,
Ship or Vessel, the
Weight of Metal,
e of the Owner or
ander and other Offi-
nd the Quantity of
which Writing shall
Congress, or to the
tatives, Convention
ety of the Colony in
to be transmitted to
registered by him.
Ship or Vessel, before
Marque and Reprisal

A Declaration by the Repre-sentatives of the UNITED

SCOTS MAGAZINE (EDINBURGH)
August 1776

This Scottish periodical was among the first of books, pamphlets, and periodicals to publish the Declaration of Independence in full. Unlike most other printings of the Declaration, *Scots Magazine* included extensive analysis, beginning with the question "In what are they created equal?"

dent: That all men are created equal *; That they are endowed by their Creator with certain unalienable rights: That a-mong these are life, liberty, and the pur-suit of happiness †: That to secure these rights,

* [In what are they created equal? Is it in size, strength, understanding, figure, mo-ral or civil accomplishments, or situation of life? Every ploughman knows that they are not created equal in any of these. All men, it is true, are equally created: but what is this to the purpose? It certainly is no reason why the Americans should turn rebels, be-cause the people of G. Britain are their fel-low-creatures, i. e. are created as well as themselves. It may be a reason why they should not rebel, but most indisputably is none why they should. They therefore have introduced their self-evident truth, either through ignorance, or by design, with a self-evident falsehood; since I will defy any A-merican rebel, or any of their patriotic re-tainers here in England, to point out to me any two men throughout the whole world of whom it may with truth be said, that they are created equal.]

† [The meaning of these words the Con-gress appear not at all to understand; among which are life, liberty, and the pursuit of happiness. Let us put some of these words together.—All men are endowed by their Creator with the unalienable right of life. How far they may be endowed with this un-alienable right I do not yet say, but, sure I am, these gentry assume to themselves an unalien-able right of talking nonsense. Was it ever heard since the introduction of blunders into the world, that life was a man's right? Life or a-nimation is of the essence of human nature, and is that without which one is not a man; and therefore to call life a right, is to betray a total ignorance of the meaning of words. A li-

rights, governments are instituted among men, deriving their just powers from the [consent] of the governed; and whenever [...], i. e. a man with life, hath a right [to] many things; but to say that a man [...]e hath a right to be a man with life, [...]urely American, that I believe the [...] of no other brain upon the face of [...]h will admit the idea. Whatever it [...], I have tried to make an idea out of [...]own I am unable. Prior to my ha-[...]y right at all as a man, it is certain I [...] a man, and such a man I certainly [...]e if I have no life; and therefore if [...]d that I have a right to life, then [...]d I must signify something without [...] and, consequently, something without life must be supposed to have a property, which without life it is not possible it can have.

Well, but they say, all men have not only a right to life, but an unalienable right. The word *unalienable* signifies that which is not alienable, and that which is not alien-able is what cannot be transferred so as to become another's; so that their unalienable right is a right which they cannot transfer to a broomstick or a cabbage-stalk; and be-cause they cannot transfer their own lives from themselves to a cabbage-stalk, there-fore they think it absolutely necessary that they should rebel; and, out of a decent re-spect to the opinions of mankind, alledge this as one of the causes which impels them to separate themselves from those to whom they owe obedience.

The next assigned cause and ground of their rebellion is, that every man hath an unalienable right to liberty: and here the words, as it happens, are not nonsense; but then they are not true: slaves there is in America; and where there are slaves, their liberty is alienated.

If the Creator hath endowed man with an unalienable right to liberty, no reason in the world will justify the abridgement of that liberty, and a man hath a right to do every thing that he thinks proper without controul or restraint; and upon the same principle, there can be no such things as ser-vants, subjects, or government of any kind whatsoever. In a word, every law that hath been in the world since the formation of A-dam, gives the lie to this self-evident truth, (as they are pleased to term it); because e-very law, divine or human, that is or hath been in the world, is an abridgement of man's liberty.

Their next self-evident truth and ground of rebellion is, that they have an unalien-able right to the pursuit of happiness. The pursuit of happiness an unalienable right! This surely is outdoing every thing that went before. Put it into English: The pur-

any form of gove[...] structive of these e[...] the people to alter [...] to institute new g[...] foundation on suc[...] ganizing its powers [...] them shall seem mo[...] safety and happine[...] will dictate, that g[...] blished should not [...] and transient cause[...] experience hath she[...] more disposed to [...] sufferable, than to [...] bolishing the forms [...] customed: but wh[...] buses and usurpati[...] ably the same obje[...] reduce them under [...] is their right, it is [...] off such governmen[...] guards for their f[...] has been the pati[...] colonies, and such [...] which constrains t[...] mer systems of gov[...] of the present Kin[...] a history of repeate[...] tions; all having i[...] blishment of an a[...] these states. To p[...] submitted to a can[...]

He has refused h[...] most wholesome an[...] blic good.

He has forbidde[...] laws of immediate [...] ance, unless suspen[...] till his assent shou[...] when so suspended[...] glected to attend t[...]

He has refused t[...] accommodation of [...] unless those peopl[...] rights of representa[...] a right inestimable [...] dable to tyrants on[...]

suit of happiness i[...] Creator hath endow[...] neither be taken fro[...] it to another. Di[...] hear of taking a pu[...] man? What they[...] these words, I own,[...] hension. A man m[...] or a cow, or I may[...] from myself, as I [...] that I have; but ho[...] me, or alienated, w[...] left for the solution of[...]

LONDON CHRONICLE

September 26, 1776

When the Declaration was officially read out in New York on July 9, it was "everywhere received with loud huzzas, and the utmost demonstrations of joy." That same evening, a crowd gathered on the Bowling Green in lower Manhattan, where they proceeded to pull down and decapitate the equestrian statue of King George III erected there in 1770.

for the government and immolony, adjourned themselves
lay in October next.

June 13, 1776. Resolved, that
e immediately established, and
ten thousand men, to make up
resolved, that the colony of
requested to furnish of their
aryland, of their militia, 3400;
ment, of theirs, 600.
tia be engaged to the first day
xt, unless sooner discharged by
of the militia commence from
marching from home, and that
one penny a mile, lawful mo-
rations for travelling expences,
y for every 20 miles, between
general rendezvous, going and
provincial brigadier generals
r the flying camp, two from
d one from Maryland.
CHARLES THOMPSON, Sec.

June 26, 1776. Resolved, that
dollars be given to every non-
cer and soldier who will enlist
rm of three years.
CHARLES THOMPSON, Sec.

---

rom Lieut. Colonel Campbell
General Howe.

Boston, June 19th. 1776.
nform you, that it has been
t to have fallen into the hands
in the middle of Boston har-
he circumstances which have
safter are understood, I flatter
on will arise to myself or my
t of it.

June, the George and Anna-
with two companies of the
ighlanders, made the land of
passage of seven weeks from
he course of which we had
of speaking to a single vessel
the smallest information of
having evacuated Boston. On
ht we found ourselves oppo-
s mouth at Boston, but from
was necessary to make several

Four schooners, which we
armed vessels in the service
which were afterwards found
n privateers, of eight carriage
nd 40 men each) were bear-
at four o'clock in the morn-
our thereafter two of them
out eleven o'clock the other
ng-side. The George trans-
which major Menzies and I,
e 2d battalion, the adjutant,
two lieutenants, five volun-
rs, had only six pieces of

---

receive protection either from a fort or from
some ship of force stationed there for the security of our fleet.

"Toward the close of the evening w
ceived the four schooners that were
with us in the morning, joined by
Defence, of 16 carriage guns, 20 swi
117 men, and a schooner of 8 carria
12 swivels, and 40 men, got under w
made towards us. As we stood up for l
road, an American battery opened u
which was the first serious proof we
there could scarcely be many of our l
Boston; and we were too far embaye
treat, especially as the wind had die
and the tide of flood not half expended
each of the vessels had twice run a-gro
anchored at George's island, and prep
action; but the Annabella, by some misf
or other, got a-ground so far a-stern of the
George, we could expect but a feeble support
from her musketry. About eleven o'clock four
of the schooners anchored right upon our bow,
and one right astern of us; the armed brig took
her station on our starboard-side, at the distance
of 200 yards, and hailed us to strike the British
flag. Although the mate of our ship, and every
sailor on board, (the captain only excepted) refused positively to fight any longer, I have the
pleasure to inform you, that there was not an
officer, non-commissioned officer, or private
man, of the 71st, but what stood to their quarters with a ready and cheerful obedience. On
our refusing to strike the British flag, the action
was renewed with a good deal of warmth on
both sides, and it was our misfortune, after a
sharp combat of an hour and an half, to have
expended every shot that we had for our artillery. Under such circumstances, hemmed in as
we were with six privateers, in the middle of
an enemy's harbour, beset with a dead calm,
without the power of escaping, or even the
most distant hope of relief, I thought it became
my duty not to sacrifice the lives of gallant men
wantonly in the arduous attempt of an evident
impossibility; in this unfortunate affair major
Menzie and 7 private soldiers were killed; the
quarter-master and 12 private soldiers wounded.
The major was buried with the honours of war
at Boston.

"Since our captivity I have the honour to
acquaint you, that we have experienced the utmost civility and good treatment from the people of power at Boston, insomuch, Sir, that I
should do injustice to the feelings of generosity,
did I not give this particular information with
pleasure and satisfaction.—I have now to request
of you, that so soon as the distracted state of
this unfortunate controversy will admit, you
will be pleased to take an early opportunity of
settling a cartel for myself and officers.—I have
the honour to be with great respect, Sir, your
most obedient and most humble servant,
ARCHIBALD CAMPBELL,
Lieut. Col. of the 2d bat. 71st reg.

"P. S. On my arrival at Boston I found that

Flint, volunteer; Dougald Campbell, ditto;
Donald M'Bane, John Wilson, 3 serjeants, 4
corporals, 2 drummers, 00 private men.
ARCHIBALD CAMPBELL,
Lieut. col. of the 2d battal. 71st regiment."

NEW YORK, July 8.

A sloop of 12 six-pounders, belonging to the
fleet from Halifax, lying in the Kills, near Mr.
Decker's ferry, was almost torn to pieces last
Wednesday morning, by a party under the command of general Herd, from the opposite shore,
with two eighteen-pounders. The crew soon
abandoned the sloop, and we suppose she is rendered entirely unfit for further service.

July 11. On Wednesday last, the declaration
of independence was read at the head of each
brigade of the continental army, posted at and
near New York, and every where received with
loud huzzas, and the utmost demonstrations
of joy.

The same evening the equestrian statue of
George III. which tory pride and folly raised
in the year 1770, was by the sons of freedom
laid prostrate in the dirt. The lead wherewith
this monument was made is to be run into
bullets, to assimilate with the brains of our infatuated adversaries, who to gain a pepper-
corn have lost an empire. "*Quos Deus vult
perdere prius dementat.*"

Trenton, (New Jersey) July 8. The declaration of independence was proclaimed here,
together with the constitution of the colony, of
late established, and the resolve of the provincial
congress, for continuing the administration of
justice during the interim.

Princetown, New Jersey, July 10.

"Last night Nassau-hall was grandly illuminated, and independency proclaimed under a
triple volley of musketry, and universal acclamations for the prosperity of the united colonies. The ceremony was conducted with the
greatest decorum."

Williamsburgh, Aug. 3. Wednesday an express arrived here, with the following account
of a battle fought by a party of the Fincastle militia, with a number of Cherokee and Creek
Indians, near the Great-island of Holdein, the
20th of July ult.

"Our scouts returned and informed that
they had discovered a large number of Indians

New York Campaign

A T Boston and Charlestown in 1775–76, the narrow necks of the peninsulas had enabled the Americans to bottle up the king's powerful army, while the Charles and Mystic Rivers were too small for the navy's ships to penetrate the countryside. So the British shifted their focus to New York for a decisive blow against the American rebellion. By sending one army up from New York City and another down from Canada, they hoped to control the Hudson River, splitting New England from the rest of the colonies.

This misguided strategy, which focused on seizing territory instead of destroying the rebel army, was agreeable to General William Howe and Admiral Richard Howe, the co-commanders in chief. The two brothers were opposed to shedding American blood and had agreed to serve only if they were also named as peace commissioners, empowered to grant pardons and negotiate an end to the rebellion. Their older brother, George, was a popular officer who had been killed in the previous war while leading Massachusetts troops at Ticonderoga in 1758. The Massachusetts government funded a monument to him in Westminster Abbey, and his brothers remained grateful. In 1776, the Howes hoped to cow the Americans into submission, not crush them, with the largest expeditionary force Britain had ever assembled: more than thirty-four thousand troops and sailors—roughly the population of Philadelphia, America's largest city—aboard some 430 vessels, including thirty warships.

William Howe arrived in New York's Lower Bay with much of the fleet at the end of June, and on July 2, the day Congress voted for independence, he landed his troops on Staten Island. Richard was delayed in London by final discussions about the peace commission with the king and the secretary of state for the colonies, Lord George Germain,

and did not arrive until July 12. The *London Chronicle* (September 26, 1776) describes the Americans' rejection of the admiral's peace initiative. For the next several weeks, the British probed the American defenses. A report in the *New-England Chronicle* (August 29, 1776) dated August 21 and a letter dated August 22 noted that the British were embarking their troops on flatboats, clearly preparing for an attack, and that a terrible storm on the night of August 21 seemed a portent of disaster for the Americans.

On the clear, bright morning of August 22, the British began landing troops on Long Island and soon had a total of twenty thousand ashore. On the night of August 26, the British flanked the American positions on Gowanus Heights and nearly surrounded them in the battle the following day—the largest of the war, with almost thirty thousand troops engaged. Describing the British victory in the Battle of Brooklyn in his report to Germain, printed in the *Continental Journal* (January 23, 1777), General Howe greatly exaggerates the number of Americans killed (see also the *London Chronicle*, October 10, 1776). Howe defends his puzzling decision—infuriating to his subordinates—not to press his advantage and overrun the American lines on Brooklyn Heights when half the rebel army was cornered, its back to the water. Then he explains, without comment, how the rebels escaped across the East River to Manhattan on the night of August 29. The British had lost their best chance to win the war at a stroke.

The Howes repeatedly launched amphibious assaults, beat the Americans on the battlefield, and then let them slip away: at Brooklyn in August, on Manhattan after the Kips Bay landing in September, and at White Plains in October. General Howe gave military explanations for pausing each offensive, but the American general Israel Putnam said it best: "He's either our friend, or he's no general." Despite the loss of 2,800 men taken prisoner at Fort Washington in November, enough of Washington's army escaped to carry on the war. With news often taking more than six weeks to cross the Atlantic, General Howe learned he had been knighted for the Battle of Brooklyn in December—just before Washington struck back at Trenton and Princeton. And the seven-year British occupation of New York would sap their efforts: while defending their principal base, the British failed to send timely support to Burgoyne at Saratoga and Cornwallis at Yorktown—the key turning points of the war.

BATTLE OF BROOKLYN
U.S. National Guard

The Battle of Brooklyn was the largest of the war, with almost thirty thousand troops engaged. The British were victorious but lost their best chance to win the war at a stroke.

LONDON CHRONICLE
September 26, 1776
—

British General William Howe arrived in New York's Lower Bay with much of the fleet at the end of June, and on July 2, the day Congress voted for independence, he landed his troops on Staten Island. William's brother Admiral Richard Howe was delayed in London by final discussions about the peace commission with the king and the secretary of state for the colonies, Lord George Germain, and did not arrive until July 12. The *London Chronicle* describes the Americans' rejection of the admiral's peace initiative.

New York, July 15.

Esterday Lord Howe sent up a flag, with the captain and lieutenant of the Eagle man of war. The adjutant general met them, after some little ceremony, but as the letter was directed to Geo. Washington, Esq; he could not receive it; the officers insisted much on his receiving it, saying it was of a civil nature, his lordship being invested with unlimited powers, and was sorry he had not arrived a few days sooner. This morning we have accounts that the ships, &c. which passed the town are 50 miles up, opposite to Tary-town, where the river is four miles wide, and they may be safe.

On Tuesday another flag from the fleet appeared, and was met as before, when a letter was again offered, but for the same reason as the former rejected.

Philadelphia: In Congress, July 19. Resolved, that general Washington, in refusing to receive a letter said to be sent from lord Howe, addressed to George Washington, Esq; acted with a dignity becoming his station, and therefore this congress do highly approve the same, and do direct that no letter or message be received, on any occasion whatever, from the enemy, by the commander in chief or other the commanders of the American army, but such as shall be directed to them in the characters they respectively sustain.——By order of the congress.   JOHN HANCOCK, President.

Congress, July 19. Resolved, that a copy of the circular letters, and of the declarations they inclosed from Lord Howe to Mr. W. Franklin, Mr. Penn. Mr. Eden, Lord Dunmore, Mr. Martin, and Sir James Wright, late governors, sent to Amboy by a flag, and forwarded to congress by general Washington, be published in the several gazettes, that the good people of these united states may be informed of what nature are the commissioners, and what the terms

province of New Jersey, as will render the same of the most public notoriety.

"Assured of being favoured with your assistance in every measure for the speedy and effectual restoration of public tranquility, I am to request you will communicate, from time to time, such information as you may think will facilitate the attainment of that important object in the province over which you preside. I have the honour to be, with great respect and consideration, Sir, your most obedient humble servant,   HOWE."

By *Richard Viscount Howe,* one of the King's commissioners for restoring peace to his Majesty's colonies and plantations in *America,* &c.

DECLARATION.

Whereas, by an act passed in the last session of parliament, to prohibit all trade and intercourse with the colonies of New Hampshire, Massachusetts Bay, Rhode Island, Connecticut, New York, New Jersey, Pennsylvania, the three lower counties on Delaware, Maryland, Virginia, North Carolina, South Carolina, and Georgia, and for other purposes therein mentioned, it is enacted, that "it shall and may be lawful to and for any persons or person appointed and authorised by his majesty, to grant a pardon or pardons to any number or description of persons by proclamation in his Majesty's name, to declare any colony or province to be at the peace of his majesty;" and that, "from and after the issuing of any such proclamation, in any of the aforesaid colonies or provinces, or if his Majesty shall be graciously pleased to signify the same by his royal proclamation," the said "act, with respect to such colony or province, colonies or provinces, county, town, port, district, or place, shall cease, determine, and be utterly void:"

And whereas the king, desirous to deliver all his subjects from the calamities of war, and other oppressions which they now undergo, and to restore the said colonies to his protection and peace, as soon as the constitutional authority of

r. 26, 1776.

conducive to the ——ment and peace, most gracious p——

——rd his majesty's fl—— ——ast of the province —— ——ett's-bay, the 20th day of Ju——

By order of the congress,
JOHN HANCOCK

From the Virginia Gazette, W—— *July* 5.

The following are the appointmen—— new plan of governmen——

Patrick Henry, junior, Esq; gove——Page, Dudley Digges, John Taylo——Benjamin Harrison of Berkeley, —— Dandridge, Charles Carter of Shirl——jamin Harrison of Brandon, counse——Thomas Whiting, John Hutchin——Travis, Thomas Newton, jun. —— Webb, Esqrs. commissioners of —— James Husband, Joseph Prentis, a——ler, Esqrs. judges of admiralty —— Randolph, Esq; attorney general —— Everard and James Cocke, Esqrs. c—— for settling accounts.

God save the Com——

Upon Colonel Henry's being ch—— vernor by the honourable convent—— mittee of the house was directed —— his excellency, to notify to him —— ment, to whom he delivered th—— letter:

To the honourable the president —— convention.

"Gentlemen, The vote of th—— pointing me governor of this con—— has been notified to me, in the m—— obliging manner, by Geo. Mason, —— Dudley Digges, John Blair, and —— Dandridge, Esqrs.

A sense of the high and unmer—— conferred upon me by the conventi—— heart with gratitude, which I tru—— life will manifest. I take this earli—— nity to express my thanks, whic—— convey to you, gentlemen, in t—— terms of acknowledgment.

All smuggled arts wou'd be expell'd the land !
Unsully'd Nature shou'd revive again,
And rosy Virtue bloom, without a stain !

Postscript.

FRESH ADVICES *from* AMERICA.

An express is arrived from Lord Howe, giving an account that on Aug. 22, he had obtained possession of Long Island ; with the loss only of fifty men killed, and 200 slightly wounded. Of the Provincials 3500 were killed upon the spot, and above 1000 taken prisoners, among whom are Lord Sterling, and Generals Sullivan and Udal. The Rebels on this defeat were retreating from New York with the utmost precipitation ; but two men of war were sent up East River to prevent their escape. On our side only Colonel Grant and two or three other Officers were killed, and Col. Monckton wounded, but not mortally.—It is not expected that the Provincials will set fire to New York, as they have no less than 4000 sick in that place, which it is expected soon after this action fell into our hands.—All the artillery of the Provincials were taken ; and as there was an epidemical distemper in their camp, all their baggage was instantly burnt.

Several Merchants of this City have received letters of the above-mentioned defeat, which differ only in some trifling particulars. The Coffee-houses about the 'Change this morning were crowded with Merchants who expressed great joy on the occasion.

Private letters from a Gentleman of veracity in New York affirm, that the most horrid cruelties are inflicted on the American Loyalists. They are driven from their homes, on refusing to take the oaths of allegiance to the Congress, and are obliged to take shelter in the woods to escape loathsome gaols and the most horrid tortures; tortures peculiar to that country, of which tarring and feathering is the least. They oblige a man to ride on the ridge of a sharp rail, full of splinters, carried by two men, who take care to shake him so as to bruise him in a most shocking manner. That of carting is another species of torture; it consists in exposing the unfortunate sufferer to ride on a wooden horse, fixed in a cart, and to be pelted by the populace, while he is in this distressed attitude.

Dr. Auchmuty, the rector of New York, together with several other clergymen of that city, have been obliged to shut up their churches, as the leaving out the prayers for the King in the church service, and substituting the Congress, was required of them; and if they refused to comply, they were given to understand they must expect the consequences. So that the church of England is as much persecuted by American republican fanatics at this time, as it was in the days of Oliver in Britain.

Many of the zealous friends of liberty, such as have stood forth against American taxation by a British Parliament, are imprisoned and otherways persecuted, for refusing to renounce their allegiance to his Majesty.

LONDON CHRONICLE
October 10, 1776

The October 10, 1776, *London Chronicle* summarizes General Howe's exaggerated report of his lopsided victory in the Battle of Brooklyn on August 27, 1776 (see also the January 23, 1777, *Continental Journal*). The paper also emphasizes that New York's loyal merchants were celebrating the British victory. The next few paragraphs contain sharp descriptions of the cruelties inflicted on American Loyalists by the Whigs and assert that some of these persecuted Loyalists were outspoken friends of liberty, too: they opposed taxation by Parliament, without renouncing their loyalty to the king. The Revolution forced Americans to choose between king and country, creating divisions at every level of society and turning the struggle, in some areas, into a civil war.

cargo to ſome Yorkers, who for fear of another female attack, forwarded the nefarious ſtuff to the North-River, precipitately; where it is now afloat, but the women have planted their guards on each ſide.

We can aſſure the public, that the foreign-ers in Burgoyne's army, are beginning to de-

... came to Anchor near Fiſher's Iſland.

Laſt Saturday a number of gentlemen were brought to this town from New-York, where they were lately taken up on ſuspicion of enter-... friendly to the American

ted to "the laſt Enemy, which will be deſtroyed —Death."

Extract of a letter from New-York, Aug. 22.

"I have but a moment in which to tell you what I have to ſay. It is ſaid the enemy are now at-tempting to land on Long-Iſland. There is a ſmoke there, from whence a General Officer told me he concluded that our people were burning dwelling-houſes, barns, grain and hay, for which orders have been ſome time iſſued in caſe the enemy ſhould attempt to land there. He told me they had cer-tain intelligence that the enemy could not remain on Staten-Iſland, and they could not return to England; they were therefore under a neceſſity of attacking. They are expected here to-day if the wind ſhould favour; it is now a head. Laſt night was the moſt diſmal I ever ſaw. The Almighty appeared among us in terrible majeſty. The ſharp-eſt and almoſt inceſſant lightning, from darkneſs thick as Egyptian, and accompanied with dread-ful thunder, formed a moſt awful ſcene. A New-York Captain and two Lieutenants were killed in one tent; the Sentinel was ſtruck deaf and dumb, and ſtill continues ſo. A Private in town was killed."

NEW-ENGLAND CHRONICLE (BOSTON)

August 29, 1776

A report in the *New-England Chronicle*, under the New-York August 21 dateline, and an "Extract of a letter from New-York, Aug. 22" noted that the British were embarking their troops on flatboats, clearly preparing for an attack, and that a terrible storm on the night of August 21 seemed a portent of disaster for the Americans.

PHILADELPHIA, Auguſt 20.

We are informed by a Captain of a veſſel be-longing to this City, who eſcaped a few days ago from Staten-Iſland, that the German troops lately arrived from Halifax are landed on the iſland, where it is ſaid they are to wait the arri-val of another reinforcement (which is hourly expected) before the attack will be made on New-York. He adds, that the Britiſh troops ſpeak with great contempt of General Waſhing-ton's army, and are aſſured that they will have the pleaſure of ſoon meeting and ſpending the winter with General Burgoyne and his troops in New-York.

We hear that Lord Dunmore, with the re-mains of his Æthiopian regiment, joined his Britannic Majeſty's troops on Staten-Iſland, on the 13th of this month.

NEW-YORK, Auguſt 21.

For ſome days paſt, the Britiſh army, on Staten-Iſland, have been embarking on board the tranſports; ſo that we expect their whole force before this city every tide. We hope to give them a reception, worthy the free born ſons of America, and may every freeman of A-merica make this his Toaſt, "That New York is now an aſſylum for American Liberty."

Yeſterday a number of the miniſterial fleet left their ſtation at Staten-Iſland, and went through the Narrows; it is ſuppoſed they mean to land part of their troops on Long-Iſland.

Extract of a letter from Ticonderoga, July 20.

"We have lately ... high ſpirits. Our marine force conſiſts of eight gondolas and four ſchooners. We ...

On the 26th Inſt. Capt. Nott, of the Privateer Sloop Broome, of New-Haven, arrived at Dartmouth with 4 valuable Prizes, viz.—the Ship Charming Sally, John Stell, Captain, bound to Europe from Dominico; had on board 465 Hogſheads, 31 Teirces, 35 Barrels of Sugar and 25 Tons of Fuſtic:--- The Snow Ann, John Bowes, Captain, from Tobago to Lancaſter; had on board 169 Hogſheads, 20 Teirces, 26 Barrels of Sugar, 40 Bags of Ginger and 118 Bales of Cotton:---The Brig Carolina Packet, Mark Towel, Captain, bound from Antigua to London; had on board 151 Hogſheads, 12 Teirces, 10 Barrels of Sugar, 2 Hogſheads of Rum, and 14 Tons of Lignum Vitæ and Fuſtic:---And the Brig John, Daniel McKay, Captain, from Grenada to Dublin; had on board 90 Hogſheads and 2 Teirces of Rum.

Yeſterdy the General Aſſembly of this State convened at Watertown, agreeable to Ad-journment.

The Convention of the State of New-York, on the 17th Inſtant (Auguſt) Reſolved, "That the Women, Children and infirm Perſons, in that City, be immediately removed from the ſame, agreeable to a Requeſt of his Excellency General WASHINGTON."

One Day laſt Week, the Viper Sloop of War, belonging to the Royal Pirate, and which has been cruiſing off Cape-Ann ſome Days, took two Sloops, from the Eaſtward.

Laſt Sunday Morning ſafely arrived at Mar-blehead, a Prize Ship from Jamaica, with a Car-go of Sugars, Cotton, &c. She was chaſed in by the Milford Frigate, who being ...

State of the Maſſachuſetts Bay, Middle Diſtrict, ſſ.

NOTICE is hereby ...

Libels are filed before me, ...ing Veſſels, their Cargoes and ... wit—in Behalf of Captain Joſe... Company, and the Owners of th... Revenge, againſt the Ship ANNA... tiam Pringle late Maſter; and ... POLLY, of about 170 Tons Burthen Maſter:—In Behalf of the Capt... Skimmer and their Companies, of ... armed Schooners Hancock and Fra... Brigantine PERKINS, burthened ... William Jenkins late Maſter:—In ... Wingate Newman and his Company ... of the Privateer Brigantine Hancock ... NANCY, burthened about 220 Ton... late Maſter; and againſt the Sloop ... burthened about 95 Tons:---In Beh... John Phillips and his Company, and ... the Privateer Sloop Warren, againſt t... burthened about 400 Tons, George Aſl... ter: And in Behalf of Caleb Hog an... againſt the Schooner DEBORAH, b... 45 Tons, Samuel Nickerſon late Maſt... Veſſels, their Cargoes and Appurtenanc... are ſaid to have been taken and bro... County of Eſſex. And another Libel ... me by Bartholomew Putnam and A... againſt the Ship LORD DARTMOUTH... Tons Burthen, her Boats, Sails, Cab... Rigging and Appurtenances ...

Whitehall, September 10, 1776.

THIS morning Major Cuyler, First Aid de Camp to the honorable General Howe, arrived with the following letter from General Howe, to Lord George Germaine:

Camp at Newtown, Long-Island, Sep. 3, 1776.

My Lord,

ON the 22d of last month, in the morning, the British, with Colonel Donop's corps of Chasseurs and Hessian grenadiers, disembarked near Utrecht on Long-Island without opposition, the whole being landed, with forty pieces of cannon, in two hours and an half, under the direction of Commodore Hotham; Lieutenant General Clinton commanding the first division of the troops.

The enemy had only small parties on the coast, who, upon the approach of the boats, retired to the woody heights, commanding a principal pass on the road from Flat-Bush to their works at Brooklyn. Lord Cornwallis was immediately detached to Flat-Bush with the reserve, two battalions of light infantry, and Colonel Donop's corps, with six field pieces, having orders not to risk an attack upon the pass, if he should find it occupied; which proving to be the case, his Lordship took post in the Village, and the army extended from the Ferry to the Narrows, through Utrecht and Gravesend to the Village of Flatland.

On the 25th Lieutenant General de Heister, with two brigades of Hessians from Staten Island, joined the army, having one brigade of his troops, a detachment of the 14th regiment from Virginia, some Convalescents and recruits, under the command of Lieutenant Colonel Dalrymple, for the security of that island.

On the 26th Lieutenant General de Heister took post at Flat-Bush, and in the evening Lord Cornwallis with the British drew off to Flatland; about nine o'clock the same night the van of the army, commanded by Lieut. General Clinton, consisting of the light dragoons and brigade of light infantry, the reserve, under the command of Lord Cornwallis, excepting the 42d regiment, which was posted to the left of the Hessians, the first brigade, and the 71st regiment, with fourteen field pieces, began to move from Flatland, across the country through the new lotts, to seize a pass in the heights, extending from east to west along the middle of the Island, and about three miles from Bedford, on the road to Jamaica, in order to turn the enemy's left, posted at Flat-Bush.

General Clinton being arrived within half a mile of the pass about two hours before day-break, halted, and settled his disposition for the attack. One of his patrols, falling in with a patrol of the enemy's officers, took them; and the General learning from their information that the rebels had not occupied the pass, detached a battalion of light infantry to secure it, and advancing with his corps upon the first appearance of day, possessed himself of the heights, with such a disposition as must have insured success, had he found the enemy in force to oppose him.

The main body of the army, consisting of the guards, 2d, 3d, and 5th brigades, with 10 field pieces, led by Lord Percy, marched soon after General Clinton, and halted an hour before day in his rear. This column (the country not admitting of two columns of march) was followed by the 49th regiment, with four medium twelve pounders, and the baggage closed the rear with a separate guard.

As soon as these corps had passed the heights, they halted for the soldiers to take a little refreshment, after which the march was continued, and about half an hour past 8 o'clock, having got to Bedford, in the rear of the enemy's left, the attack was commenced by the light infantry and light dragoons upon large bodies of the rebels, having cannon, who were quitting the woody heights beforementioned to return to their lines upon descovering the march of the army, instead of which they were drove back, and the army still moving on to gain the enemy's rear, the grenadiers and 33d regiment being in front of the column, soon opposed them within musquet shot of the enemy's lines at Brooklyn, from whence these battalions, without regarding the fire of cannon and small arms upon them, pursued numbers of the rebels that were retiring from the heights so close to their principal redoubt, and with such eagerness to attack it by storm, that it required repeated orders to prevail upon them to desist from the attempt. Had they been permitted to go on, it is my opinion they would have carried the redoubt; but it was apparent the lines must have been ours, at a very cheap rate by regular approaches. I would not risk the loss that might have been sustained in the assault and ordered them back to a hollow way, in front of the works, out of the reach of musquetry.

Lieut. Gen. de Heister began soon after day-break to cannonade the enemy in his front, and, upon the ap-

ferred considerably: Numbers of them however did get into the Morass, where many were suffocated or drown'd.

The force of the enemy detached from the lines where General Putnam commanded, was not less, from the accounts I have had, than 10,000 men, who were under the orders of Major Gen. Sullivan, Brigadier Generals Lord Stirling and Udell. Their loss is computed to be about 3,300 killed, wounded, prisoners, and drowned; with five field pieces, and one howitzer taken.——A return of the prisoners is inclosed.

On the part of the king's troops, five officers, and sixty six non-commissioned officers and rank and file killed; twelve officers and 245 non-commissioned officers, and rank and file wounded: One officer and 20 Grenadiers of the Marines taken by mistaking the enemy for the Hessians.

The Hessians had two privates killed, three officers, and twenty-three rank and file wounded. The wounds are in general very slight. Lieut. Col. Monckton is shot through the body, but there are the greatest hopes of his recovery.

The behaviour of both officers and soldiers, British and Hessians, were highly to their honour. More determined courage and steadiness in troops have never been experienced, or a greater ardour to distinguish themselves, as all those who had an opportunity have amply evinced by their actions.

In the evening of the 27th the army encamped in front of the enemy's works. On the 28th, at night, broke ground 600 yards distant from a redoubt upon their left, and on the 29th at night, the rebels evacuated their entrenchments, and Red-hook, with the utmost silence, and quitted Governor's Island the following evening, leaving their cannon and a quantity of stores in all their works. At day break on the 30th, their flight was discovered, the pickets of the line took possession; and those first advanced reached the shore opposite to New-York, as their rear guard was going over, and fired some shot among them.

The enemy is still in possession of the town and island of New-York, in force, and making demonstrations of opposing us in their works on both sides of King's-Bridge.

The inhabitants of this Island, many of whom had been forced into rebellion, have all submitted, and are ready to take the oaths of allegiance.

This dispatch will be delivered to your Lordship by Major Cuyler, my first Aid de Camp, who I trust will be able to give your Lordship such further information as may be required. I have the honour to be, &c.

W. HOWE.

P. S. I have omitted to take notice, in its proper place, of a movement made by the King's ships, towards the town on the 27th, at day-break, with a view of drawing off the attention of the enemy from our real design, which I believe, effectually answered the intended purpose.

Return of Prisoners

Three Generals
Colonels; three
Lieutenants; e
one hundred an
ninety-seven.
Privates, of thr

Return of brass
in the engage
found in the
Governor's-Is
Cam
Brass ordnan
1776. 1 five-a
1 three-pounder

Iron ordnanc
Island and Gov
1 twenty-four p
ers; 3 three pou

A quantity o
tools, small arm
on carts, and m
(Signed)
Commander

Return of killed

1 Lieutenant
Serjeants, 53 rank
3 Captains, 8 Lieutenant, 11 Serjeants, 3 Drummers, 231 rank and file wounded; 1 Lieutenant, 1 Serjeant 350 rank and file missing.

List of Officers killed, wounded and missing.
KILLED,
Captain Sir Alexander Murray, 17th regiment.
Lieutenant Colonel Grant, 40th ditto.
Captain Nelson 52d ditto.
Captain Logan, 2d regiment marines.

NEW-YORK, *December 23.*

The brave Col. Harcourt of Burgoyne's light horse, took LEE the deserter from the king's service and late rebel general, with a party of less than 50 Men, in the face of all his vagabond retinue, without the loss of a single man. The Col. by several circumstances, found out his quarters, rode up to the house, and surrounded it. Lee, fearful of being put to the sword, begged his life in a manner, which shews that, where just and loyal principles are not, true courage is never to be found. His life was granted by the brave commander, for further confideration. Lee was brought to Brunswick, and is now confined under a strong guard at that place.

Gen. Clinton, Lord Percy, and the troops under their command, have taken possession of Rhode-Island without firing a single gun. Sir Peter Parker, Commodore Hotham, and his majesty's ships under their command are safely moored in Newport harbour.

The rebels are every where mouldering away like a rope of sand. With the most impudent bravadoes, they have not yet had the spirit to make any thing like a stand in a single encounter. The New-England people have neither money nor recruits; and the rest of the colonies are nearly drained of their resources. Ruin, therefore, and destruction must be the consequence to them of continuing the War any longer.

Mr. Washington, with about two thousand poor wretches, who can get no subsistance but by following him, has fled to Lancaster in Pennsylvania. Many people of Philadelphia have retired with their goods and effects into the back country, with but little provision for the winter.

The chain of posts, formed by the British troops, reach within 17 miles of Philadelphia upon the banks of the Deleware; and the first strong frost will afford them a natural bridge over it.

The *Allens* and some other principal people of Philadelphia, are come in, and have claimed the protection of his majesty's army.

Great numbers in the Jersies have likewise come in, and taken the oaths; and two whole counties have laid down their arms together, and subscribed the tests required in the commissioner's proclamation. Most of them express the deepest sorrow for their late delusion, and freely acknowledge that when they left British protection, they fell into real slavery, and into slavery of the worst kind—the slavery of weak and wicked men.

It is reported, that some of the coal ships from Louisburg are taken by rebel privateers, fitted out from the coasts of New-England. Those unhappy people will soon see, that such ill gotten and pirated goods will only lay the foundation of their own ruin.

Several captures have been sent in by the men of war in the course of last week.

We hear that the colony of Connecticut have scarce

Newport. These were the only buildings that remained on the island after Wallace's expedition up the bay last winter.

Capt. Ayres, who lately went with a flag of truce to Newport, returned on Wednesday, and brought with him about 50 Americans, in exchange for a number of prisoners he delivered

---

CONTINENTAL JOURNAL (BOSTON)
January 23, 1777

—

Describing the British victory in the Battle of Brooklyn in his report to Germain, printed in the *Continental Journal* (January 23, 1777), General Howe greatly exaggerates the number of Americans killed (see also the *London Chronicle*, October 10, 1776). Howe defends his puzzling decision—infuriating to his subordinates—not to press his advantage and overrun the American lines on Brooklyn Heights when half the rebel army was cornered, its back to the water. Then he explains, without comment, how the rebels escaped across the East River to Manhattan on the night of August 29. The British had lost their best chance to win the war at a stroke.

acquainted with the course
ur the smallest doubt of our

glorious struggle of the Uni-
he power of Spain, to which
ed. Their extent was small,
people far from numerous,
and in the neighbourhood
t that time, the most power-
er fleet formidable ; her ar-
and led by the best Generals
sury overflowing with the
ru, endeavoured to enslave
nonstrated against the design,
t with contempt, and fire and
eir country to compel sub-
ved to be free, they declared
ates, and after an obstinate
cked intentions of Spain.
s with another instance of
ntry was oppressed by cruel
ased to continue in bondage ;
they expelled those tyrants,
ts the portion of freedom.
nius now blushes for the de-
afforded examples of opposi-
worthy to be imitated by all
ty Charles I. lost his head and
to enslave his subjects ; and
. was for the same reason ex-
his whole family, and the
ing in his stead. The En-
eve, that the person of any
nd never suffered any man to
mpted to exercise the power
on of the people from whom
. This practice is not only
son, but perfectly consonant
f God himself : You know
his peculiar direction, and
d of the many instances in
from such of their kings, as
g to the laws of the Jews.
freedom, are we not respon-
ll as other talents ? If it
ell it for a mess of p
us by the hand of
are in our power.
What excuse sha
eator ? These
s all. Th
happinss

Judge. If success crown your efforts, all the blessings
of freedom will be your reward. If you fall in the con-
test, you will be happy with God and liberty in Heaven.
By the unanimous order of the Convention,
ABRAHAM TEN BROECK, *President.*
Fish-Kill, December 23, 1776.

BALTIMORE, *December 31, 1776.*
This Morning CONGRESS received the following
Letter from General WASHINGTON.
Head-Quarters, Newtown, 27th Dec. 1776.
SIR,

I HAVE the pleasure of congratulating you upon
the success of an enterprize, which I had formed a-
gainst a detachment of the enemy lying in Trenton,
and which was executed yesterday morning.

The evening of the 25th, I ordered the troops intended for this service, to parade back of M'Kenky's Ferry, that they might begin to pass as soon as it grew
dark, imagining we should be able to throw them all
over, with the necessary artillery, by 12 o'clock, and
that we might easily arrive at Trenton, by five in the
morning, the distance being about nine miles. But
the quantity of ice made that night, impeded the passage of the boats so much, that it was three o'clock
before the artillery could all be got over, and near four
before the troops took up their line of march.

I formed my detachment into two divisions, one to
march up the lower or river road, the other by the upper or Pennington road. As the divisions had nearly
the same distance to march, I ordered each of them immediately upon forcing the out guards, to push directly into the town, that they might charge the enemy before they had time to form. The upper division
arrived at the enemy's advanced post exactly at 8 o'-
clock, and in three minutes after, I found, from
fire on the lower road, that that division had also
up. The out guards made but a small opp
though, for their , they behaved v
keeping up a const treating fire from h
ses.

We presently main
from their moti med
to act. Being
ready got poi
tempted to f ng to
Princeton ; ew a
dy of troo eck-
the they
y d

should do great injustice to the others.
Col. Baylor, my first aid-de-camp, will have the h
nor of delivering this to you, and from him you may
made acquainted with many other particulars : H
spirited behaviour upon every occasion, requires me
recommend him to your particular notice.
I have the honor to be, with great respect,
Sir, your most humble servant,
G. WASHINGTON.

Inclosed I have sent you a particular list of the pri
soners, artillery, and other Stores.
RETURN of Prisoners taken at Trenton, the 26th
December, 1776, by the army under the comman
of his Excellency General WASHINGTON.
Regiment of LANDSPATCH.
1 Lieutenant Colonel, 1 Major, 1 Captain, 3 Lieut
4 Ensigns, 38 Serjeants, 6 Drummers, 5 Musicians,
Officers Servants, 206 Rank and File.
Regiment of KNIPHAUSEN.
1 Major, 2 Captains, 2 Lieutenants, 3 Ensigns, 2
Serjeants, 6 Drummers, 6 Officers Servants, 258 Ran
and File.
Regiment of ROHL.
1 Colonel, 1 Lieut. Col. 1 Major, 1 Capt. 2 Lieut.
5 Ensigns, 2 Surgeons Mates, 25 Serjeants, 8 Drummer
4 Musicians, 9 Officers Servants, 244 Rank and File.
Regiment of ARTILLERY.
1 Lieut. 4 Serjeants, 1 Officer's Servant, 32 Ran
and File.
TOTAL——1 Colonel, 2 Lieut. Colonels, 3 Major
4 Captains, 8 Lieutenants, 12 Ensigns, 2 Surgeons, 9
Serjeants, 20 Drummers, 9 Musicians, 25 Officers Se
ants, 740 Rank and File. 918 Prisoners.
6 double-fortified Brass 3-pounders, with Carriage
complete.
3 Ammunition Waggons.
As many Muskets, Bayonets, Cartouch-Boxes, an
Swords, as there are Prisoners.
12 Drums. 4 Colours.
Published by Order of Congress,
CHARLES THOMSON, Sec'y.

STATE OF MASSACHUSETTS-BAY.
Council-Chamber, January 17, 1776.
ORDERED, That each Recruiting Officer withi
this State, belonging to the sam are Re
cruisi the Continental Army, be, here
Return to the of thi
St suc
wha

❧ CHAPTER VIII ❧

CUT TO PIECES

Introduction

After crushing, lopsided defeats in New York, General Washington's war-torn army retreated to New Jersey, where the pivotal day-after-Christmas victory against German mercenaries inspired the American troops to persevere. Confidence in Washington and the Continental Army is restored, but enlistment goals are increasingly difficult to achieve and an alliance with France is needed more than ever. While the French remain noncommittal, British General John Burgoyne returns to America in hopes of delivering a quick and decisive blow by taking the Hudson River, the strategic artery separating the north and south colonies. Fort Ticonderoga and Philadelphia, America's political capital, fall into British hands. Without aid, General Burgoyne surrenders at Saratoga to American Generals Horatio Gates and Benedict Arnold, changing the face of the war.

CONTINENTAL JOURNAL
January 23, 1777

WASHINGTON CROSSING
THE DELAWARE
BY EMANUEL LEUTZE
*Metropolitan Museum of Art
(current location)*

THE FABLED NIGHTTIME CROSSING OF THE DELAWARE River by George Washington's army on Christmas Day 1776 in a blizzard and freezing cold has long been a part of American legend. In truth, it was not a flag-waving, drums-beating crossing at all but a quiet, difficult sail across turbulent, freezing waters filled with large, heavy, flat chunks of ice and riverbanks covered with glistening snow.

After the treacherous crossing, the Continental Army, with men hauling just eight cannon, trudged some nine miles south on the New Jersey side of the river and surprised the Hessians at Trenton, attacking them through the snowstorm shortly before 8 a.m. The Hessians, reportedly England's toughest soldiers, were startled. Their colonel, Johann Rall, was shot dead during the assault and his troops had no one to lead them. They were defeated in a battle that lasted less than an hour. Near the end of the war, British General Charles Lord Cornwallis told his American captors that the crossing of the Delaware turned the tide of the war in favor of the Americans.

The story was well told—with sizable gaps—by George Washington in his letter to Congress, which was reprinted in many American newspapers and badly told by British sympathizers writing in their newspapers.

Near the end of the war, British General Charles Lord Cornwallis told his American captors that the crossing of the Delaware turned the tide of the war in favor of the Americans.

Washington, who saw most of the battle as he raced back and forth through Trenton on his horse with musket balls flying through the air around him, wrote a colorful and explosive letter that was published in the January 23, 1777, *Continental Journal*. It was written not only to state the facts, but also to drum up Congressional, press, and public support for his army. Washington offered a straightforward account of the battle. He wrote near the end of it that the Hessians surrendered because they knew they were about to be "cut to pieces," a dramatic phrase. He did not know the extent of the Hessians killed or wounded and did not exaggerate, as the British always did. He praised his men, writing that their behavior reflected "the highest honor" upon them and that they had passed over an entire river, faced a violent snow and ice storm, and marched a great distance.

The British press dismissed the battle and the Continental Army. The editor of one pro-British paper called the American army a "vagabond retinue." He also wrote that the army was comprised of "Mr. Washington (they often disdainfully called him "mister" and not General) and his two thousand poor wretches."

In its story, the *London Chronicle* (February 25, 1777) acknowledged that Washington had defeated the Hessians, but in the next line reminded readers that the British army, strong as ever, was marching throughout New Jersey and had nothing more to fear. It also wrote that many of Washington's ten thousand men were deserting. (He actually had about five thousand men but had spies feeding the British the much higher figure.)

A remarkable story from the January 13, 1777, *New-York Gazette*, reprinted in the March 4, 1777, *London Chronicle*, wrote of the British defeat ten days later at Princeton in such a way that any reader would have thought they had won the battle. The writer invented quotes from the dying American General Hugh Mercer that the British were even braver than he had heard and from British troops hailing their redcoat toughness and ability to conduct a very orderly retreat. Conversely, an American soldier sent a letter to an American paper in which he correctly described the Princeton engagement as a huge victory for the Americans, adding, as General Washington often told people, that if they only had more men they might have moved on to New Brunswick, defeated another British army there, and possibly won the war (see extract of letter from "Morris Town," January 8, in the January 23, 1777, *Continental Journal*).

Following his surprising two victories in ten days, George Washington realized that his army might win the war and that the public would now flock to its cause. Over the next few weeks, as word of the victories spread throughout the country, dozens of other newspapers agreed.

And James Rivington, the editor of the strong pro-British newspaper the *New-York Gazette* and who was close friends with all the British generals and insulted the Americans in all of his stories? One year later, he agreed, too, and became Washington's top spy.

TRENTON, 1776
U.S. Army Center of Military History

George Washington witnessed most of the battle as he raced back and forth through Trenton on his horse with musket balls flying through the air around him.

The CONTINENTAL JOURNAL

BALTIMORE, *December 31, 1776.*

This Morning CONGRESS received the following Letter from General WASHINGTON.

Head-Quarters, Newtown, 27th Dec. 1776.

SIR,

I HAVE the pleasure of congratulating you upon the success of an enterprize, which I had formed against a detachment of the enemy lying in Trenton, and which was executed yesterday morning.

The evening of the 25th, I ordered the troops intended for this service, to parade back of M'Kenky's Ferry, that they might begin to pass as soon as it grew dark, imagining we should be able to throw them all over, with the necessary artillery, by 12 o'clock, and that we might easily arrive at Trenton, by five in the morning, the distance being about nine miles. But the quantity of ice made that night, impeded the passage of the boats so much, that it was three o'clock before the artillery could all be got over, and near four before the troops took up their line of march.

I formed my detachment into two divisions, one to march up the lower or river road, the other by the upper or Pennington road. As the divisions had nearly the same distance to march, I ordered each of them immediately upon forcing the out-guards, to push directly into the town, that they might charge the enemy before they had time to form. The upper division arrived at the enemy's advanced post exactly at 8 o'clock, and in three minutes after, I found, from the fire on the lower road, that the division had also got up. The out guards made but a small opposition, though, for their numbers, they behaved very well, keeping up a constant retreating fire from behind houses.

We presently saw their main body formed, but, from their motions, they seemed undetermined how to act. Being hard pressed by our troops, who had already got possession of part of their artillery, they attempted to file off by a road, on their right leading to Princeton ; but perceiving their intention, I threw a body of troops in their way, which immediately checked them. Finding, from our disposition, that they were surrounded, and they must inevitably be cut to pieces, if they made any further resistance, they agreed to lay down their arms. The number submitted, in this manner, was 23 officers, and 886 men. Col. Rohl, the commanding officer, and seven others, were found wounded in the town. I do not exactly know how many they had killed ; but I fancy not above twenty or thirty, as they never made any regular stand. Our loss is very trifling indeed ; only two officers and one or two privates wounded.

I find that the detachment of the enemy consisted of the three Hessian regiments of Landspatch, Kniphausen, and Rohl, amounting to about 1500 men, and a troop of British light-horse, but immediately upon the beginning of the attack, all those who were not killed or taken, pushed directly down the road towards Borden-town. These would likewise have fallen into our hands, could my plan have been completely carried into execution. Gen. Ewing was to have crossed before day at Trenton ferry, and taken possession of the bridge leading out of town ; but the quantity of ice was so great, that though he did every thing in his power to effect it, he could not get over. This difficulty also hindered Gen. Cadwallader from crossing, with the Pennsylvania militia, from Bristol ; he got part of his foot over, but finding it impossible to embark his artillery, he was obliged to desist. I am fully confident, that could the troops under Generals Ewing and Cadwallader have passed the river, I should have been able, with their assistance, to have driven the enemy from all their posts below Trenton ; but the numbers I had with me being inferior to theirs below me, and a strong battalion of light infantry being at Princeton, above me, I thought it most prudent to return the same evening with the prisoners, and the artillery we had taken. We found no stores of any consequences in the town. [...]

I have the honor to be, with great respect,

Sir, your must humble servant,

G. WASHINGTON.

THE
CONTINENTAL JOURNAL,
AND
WEEKLY ADVERTISER.

THURSDAY, JANUARY 23, 1777.   [NUMB. XXXV.

BOSTON: PRINTED BY JOHN GILL, IN QUEEN-STREET.

☞ THE ENTIRE PROSPERITY OF EVERY STATE, DEPENDS UPON THE DICIPLINE OF ITS ARMIES.   *The KING of PRUSSIA.*

The remainder of the Address of the Convention of th Representatives of the State of New-York to their Conftituents, began in our laft.

WHOEVER therefore confiders the natural ftrength and advantages of this country, the diftance it is moved from Britain, the obvious policy of many European powers, the great fupplies of arms and ammunition chearfully afforded us by the French and Spaniards, and the feeble and deftitute condition of Britain : That fhe is mined of men and of money, obliged to hire foreign mercenaries for the execution of her wicked purpofes ; arrears to her troops for a twelve month's pay, which cannot or will not difcharge ; her credit funk ; her made ruined ; her inhabitants divided ; her king unpopular, and her minifters execrated : That fhe is overwhelmed with a monftrous debt ; cut off from the vaft revenue heretofore obtained by taxes on American produce ; her Weft-India iflands in a ftarving condition ; her fhips taken ; her merchants involved in bankruptcy ; her defigns againft us wicked, unjuft, cruel, contrary to the laws of God and man, purfued with implacable, unrelenting vengeance, and in a manner barbarous, and oppofed to the ufage of civilized or barbarous nations : Whoever confiders that we have humbly fought peace, and been refufed ; that we have been denied even a hearing ; all our petitions rejected ; all our remonftrances difregarded ; that we fight not for conqueft, put only for fecurity ; that our caufe is the caufe of God, of human nature and pofterity : Whoever, we fay, ferioufly confiders thefe things, muft entertain very proper ideas of the divine juftice, to which we have appealed, and be very little acquainted with the courfe of human affairs, to harbour the fmalleft doubt of our being fuccefsful.

Remember the long and glorious ftruggle of the United Netherlands, againft the power of Spain, to which they had once been fubjected. Their extent was fmall, their country poor, their people far from numerous, and unaccuftomed to arms, and in the neighbourhood of their enemies. Spain, at that time, the moft powerful kingdom in Europe ; her fleet formidable ; her armies great, inured to war, and led by the beft Generals of the age ; and her treafury overflowing with the wealth of Mexico and Peru, endeavoured to enflave them. They dutifully remonftrated againft the defign, their petitions were treated with contempt, and fire and word were carried into their country to compel fubmiffion. They nobly refolved to be free, they declared themfelves Independent States, and after an obftinate ftruggle, fruftrated the wicked intentions of Spain.

Switzerland prefents us with another inftance of magnanimity. That country was oppreffed by cruel tyrants, but the people refufed to continue in bondage ; with arms in their hands they expelled thofe tyrants, and left to their defcendants the portion of freedom.

Even England, whofe genius now blufhes for the degeneracy of her fons, hath afforded examples of oppofition to tyranny which are worthy to be imitated by all nations. His facred majefty Charles I. loft his head and his crown, by attempting to enflave his fubjects ; and his facred majefty James II. was for the fame reafon expelled the kingdom with his whole family, and the Prince of Orange chofen king in his ftead. The Englifh were too wife to believe, that the perfon of any tyrant could be facred ; and never fuffered any man to wear the crown, who attempted to exercife the power of royalty to the deftruction of the people from whom thofe powers were derived. This practice is not only confiftent with human reafon, but perfectly confonant to the will and practice of God himfelf : You know that the Jews were under his peculiar direction, and you need not be informed of the many inftances in which he took the crown from fuch of their kings, as refufed to govern according to the laws of the Jews.

If then God has given us freedom, are we not refponfible to him for that, as well as other talents ? If it be our birth-right, let us not fell it for a mefs of pottage, nor fuffer it to be torn from us by the hand of violence ! —If the means of defence are in our power, and we do not make ufe of them ; What excufe fhall we make to our children and our Creator ? Thefe are queftions of the deepeft concern to us all. Thefe are queftions which materially affect our happinefs, not only in this world, but in the world to come. And furely, "if ever a teft for the trial of fpirits can be neceffary, it is now. If ever thofe of liberty and faction ought to be diftinguifhed from each other, it is now. If ever it is incumbent on the people to know truth and to follow it, it is now."

Roufe, therefore, brave citizens ! Do your duty like men ! And be perfuaded, that divine Providence will not permit this weftern world to be involved in the horrors of flavery. Confider ! That from the earlieft ages of the world, religion, liberty and empire have been bending their courfe toward the fetting fun. The holy gofpels are yet to be preached to thofe weftern regions, and we have the higheft reafon to believe, that the Almighty will not fuffer flavery and the gofpel to go hand in hand. It cannot ! It will not be !

But if there be any among us, dead to all fenfe of honor and love of their country ; if deaf to all the calls of liberty, virtue and religion ; if forgetful of the magnanimity of their anceftors, and the happinefs of their children : If neither the examples and fuccefs of other nations, the dictates of reafon and nature, or the great duties they owe to their God, themfelves and their pofterity have any effect upon them : If neither the injuries they have received, the prize they are contending for, the future bleffings or curfes of their children, the applaufe or reproach of all mankind, the approbation or difpleafure of their great Judge, or the happinefs or mifery confequent upon their conduct, in this and a future ftate can move them : Then let them be affured that they deferve to be flaves, and are entitled to nothing but anguifh and tribulation. Let them banifh from their remembrance, the reputation, the freedom and happinefs which they have inherited from their forefathers : Let them forget every duty human and divine, remember not that they have children, and beware how they call to mind the juftice of the Supreme Being : Let them go into captivity like the idolatrous and difobedient Jews, and be a reproach and a bye-word among the nations.

But we think better things of you. We believe, and are perfuaded, that you will do your duty like men, and cheerfully refer your caufe to the great and righteous Judge. If fuccefs crown your efforts, all the bleffings of freedom will be your reward. If you fall in the conteft, you will be happy with God and liberty in Heaven.

By the unanimous order of the Convention,

ABRAHAM TEN BROECK, *Prefident.*

Fifh-Kill, December 23, 1776.

BALTIMORE, *December* 31, 1776.

This Morning CONGRESS received the following Letter from General WASHINGTON.

Head-Quarters, Newtown, 27th Dec. 1776.

SIR,

I HAVE the pleafure of congratulating you upon the fuccefs of an enterprize, which I had formed againft a detachment of the enemy lying in Trenton, and which was executed yefterday morning.

The evening of the 25th, I ordered the troops intended for this fervice, to parade back of M'Kenky's Ferry, that they might begin to pafs as foon as it grew dark, imagining we fhould be able to throw them all over, with the neceffary artillery, by 12 o'clock, and that we might eafily arrive at Trenton, by five in the morning, the diftance being about nine miles. But the quantity of ice made that night, impeded the paffage of the boats fo much, that it was three o'clock before the artillery could all be got over, and near four before the troops took up their line of march.

I formed my detachment into two divifions, one to march up the lower or river road, the other by the upper or Pennington road. As the divifions had nearly the fame diftance to march ; I ordered each of them immediately upon forcing the out-guards, to pufh directly into the town, that they might charge the enemy before they had time to form. The upper divifion arrived at the enemy's advanced poft exactly at 8 o'clock, and in three minutes after, I found, from the fire on the lower road, that that divifion had alfo got up. The out guards made but a fmall oppofition, though, for their numbers, they behaved very well, keeping up a conftant retreating fire from behind houfes.

We prefently faw their main body formed, but, from their motions, they feemed undetermined how to act. Being hard preffed by our troops, who had already got poffeffion of part of their artillery, they attempted to file off by a road, on their right, leading to Princeton ; but perceiving their intention, I threw a body of troops in their way, which immediately checked them. Finding, from our difpofition, that they were furrounded, and they muft inevitably be cut to pieces, if they made any further refiftance, they agreed to lay down their arms. The number that fubmitted, in this manner, was 23 officers, and 886 men. Col. Rohl, the commanding officer, and feven others, were found wounded in the town. I do not exactly know how many they had killed ; but I fancy not above twenty or thirty, as they never made any regular ftand. Our lofs is very trifling indeed ; only two officers and one or two privates wounded.

I find that the detachment of the enemy confifted of the three Heffian regiments of Landfpatch, Kniphaufen, and Rohl, amounting to about 1500 men, and a troop of Britifh light-horfe ; but immediately upon the beginning of the attack, all thofe who were not killed or taken, pufhed directly down the road towards Borden-town. Thefe would likewife have fallen into our hands, could my plan have been completely carried into execution. Gen. Ewing was to have croffed before day at Trenton ferry, and taken poffeffion of the bridge leading out of town ; but the quantity of ice was fo great, that though he did every thing in his power to effect it, he could not get over. This difficulty alfo hindered Gen. Cadwallader from croffing, with the Pennfylvania militia, from Briftol ; he got part of his foot over, but finding it impoffible to embark his artillery, he was obliged to defift. I am fully confident, that could the troops under Generals Ewing and Cadwallador have paffed the river, I fhould have been able, with their affiftance, to have driven the enemy from all their pofts below Trenton ; but the numbers I had with me being inferior to theirs below me, and a ftrong battalion of light infantry being at Princeton, above me, I thought it moft prudent to return the fame evening with the prifoners, and the artillery we had taken. We found no ftores of any confequence in the town.

In juftice to the officers and men I muft add, that their behaviour upon this occafion reflects the higheft honor upon them. The difficulty of paffing the river, in a very fevere night, and their march through a violent ftorm of fnow and hail, did not in the leaft abate their ardour ; but when they came to the charge, each feemed to vie with the other in preffing forward, and were I to give a preference to any particular corps, I fhould do great injuftice to the others.

Col. Baylor, my firft aid-de-camp, will have the honor of delivering this to you, and from him you may be made acquainted with many other particulars : His fpirited behaviour upon every occafion, requires me to recommend him to your particular notice.

I have the honor to be, with great refpect, Sir, your moft humble fervant,

G. WASHINGTON.

Inclofed I have fent you a particular lift of the prifoners, artillery, and other ftores.

RETURN of Prifoners taken at Trenton, the 26th of December, 1776, by the army under the command of his Excellency General WASHINGTON.

Regiment of LANDSPATCH.

1 Lieutenant Colonel, 1 Major, 1 Captain, 3 Lieutenants, 4 Enfigns, 38 Serjeants, 6 Drummers, 5 Muficians, 2 Officers Servants, 206 Rank and File.

Regiment of KNIPHAUSEN.

1 Major, 2 Captains, 2 Lieutenants, 3 Enfigns, 19 Serjeants, 6 Drummers, 6 Officers Servants, 258 Rank and File.

Regiment of ROHL.

1 Colonel, 1 Lieut. Col. 1 Major, 1 Capt. 2 Lieutenants, 5 Enfigns, 2 Surgeons Mates, 25 Serjeants, 3 Drummers, 4 Muticians, 9 Officers Servants, 276 Rank and File.

TOTAL.
4 Captains, 8 ...
2 Enfigns, 10 ...
... vants, 740 Rank and File.
6 double-fo...
complete.
3 Ammunition ...
As many M...
Swords, as th...
12 Drums.

STATE ...

ORDERED, ... this Stat... cruiting for th... by are directe... State, for p... Men as they h... Company and ...

A tr... Atteft.

Every Finger a Fifh-Hook.

TAKEN by accident from SPEAR's wharf a few days fince, a fingle fortified four pounder. The perfons who took it are defired to return it on faid wharf ; if they do not they will foon repent it.

Bofton, December 23, 1776.

---

y 4.
Trenton, ... ting in the ... this city, ... moft of ... ilities by a ... every gar... ry power. ... e 26th of ... ngagement ...

... we are ... n, a party ... n with a... ... ated them, ... horfes ;—— ... Philadelphia ...

... parties met ... in New-

17.
in a floop ... of Novem... hg put into ... hip arrived ... which in... taken place ... e was daily ... The cargo ... ng of blan... n into New... ped being ... the harbour

... gentleman ... York, dated ...

... communi... lie in heaps ... have died by ... ommon mo... ... e boafted ... erifhed under ... e no idea of ... fuch treatment ... nd neceffary, ... intryman, and ... ke fituation, ... and infults, ... I am, &c. ... o. 20. ... ding our arm ... been received

... rs and foldiers ... 160 more are ... f the 500 who ... as mentioned ...

... hibited of the ... ly boaft being ... lian and Wal... Jerfey, it gives ... y outraged tha ... were fo unhap... rly the fair fex, ... power of lan... the curious ... ublic library at ... y the celebrated ... age at Princeton, ... tutored favage, ... ve beheld with ... are our cruel ... nd the arts and ...

ry 23. ... Sloop Union's ... n'd with 600 ...

Extract of a another Letter from Morris Town, Jan. 8.

The 17th Regiment ufed their Bayonets with too much feverity upon a Party they put to Flight, but they now paid for it in proportion, very few efcaping, near 60 were killed on the Spot, befides the wounded ; we have taken between 3 and 400 Prifoners, all Britifh Troops, they muft have loft very confiderable in this Affair.——We loft feveral gallant Officers. Brigadier General Mercer was wounded, he had three Stabs with a Bayonet, but will get better. The Enemy tock his Parole after we left Princeton ; a Lieutenant Colonel Flemming was killed, and a Captain Neil of the Artillery. We took their Cannon, which confifted of two Brafs 6 pounders, a confiderable Number of Military Stores, Blankets, Guns, &c. They loft among a Number of other Officers, a Captain Leflie, Son to the Earl of Leven, and Nephew to General Leflie ; him we buried with the Honors of War. After we had been about two Hours at Princeton, Word was bro't that the Enemy was advancing from Trenton. As we had other Objects in View, viz. of beating up their Quarters, we purfued our March to Somerfet Court-Houfe, where we had been informed there were 1300 Men Quartered, they however had marched off, and joined the Army at Trenton. We at firft intended to have made a forced March to Brunfwick, at which Place was the Baggage of their whole Army and General Lee ; but our Men having been without either Reft, Rum or Provifions for two Days, and Nights, were unequal to the Tafk of marching 17 Miles further. If we could have procured 1000 frefh Men at Princeton, to have pufhed for Brunfwick, we fhould have ftruck one of the moft brilliant Strokes in all Hiftory. However our Advantages are very great already ; we have collected their whole Force, and drawn themfelves to one Point, viz. Brunfwick. A Party of ours two Days ago attacked 60 Waldeckers, who were all killed or taken in Monmouth County, in the lower Part of the Jerfeys. Another Party have routed a Party of Tories, killed and taken 200 Prifoners. They have fent their Baggage to Staten Ifland from the Jerfeys, and we are very well informed they are doing the fame from New-York.

Extract of a letter from Morris Town, Jan. 9.

"The enemy have abandoned Elizabeth-Town. Our people have entered it and taken 30 Waldeckers and 50 Highlanders, and about 30 Baggage Waggons fully loaded—The enemy who had all the Jerfies, are now only in poffeffion of Amboy and Brunfwick—this is a great reverfe in the courfe of a fortnight, to the Britifh power—Whether they mean to collect their whole force at Brunfwick and give us battle, or whether they mean to pufh for Staten-ifland, and abandon the Jerfies entirely is matter of doubt— We fhall make a move towards them to day, with a view to avail ourfelves of circumftances— The enemy appear to be panic ftruck in the extreme—God profpers our arms in an extraordinary manner—there is to be an eclipfe of the Sun to day—We mean if poffible to attack the Germans as foon as it begins, and take the advantage of their ignorant fuperftition—Endeavour to animate and awaken all ranks of people.—Let them view the diftreffed and lately fubjugated people of the Jerfies, complaining of their property being wrefted from them by the lawlefs banditti that have infefted thefe places.—Hufbands and Fathers being oblig'd to be witneffes of the luftful Brute ravifhing the dear object of their affections before their eyes—Thefe enormities have been committed and will be again committed, where tyranny reigns uncheck'd, and uncontroul'd—May God give my countrymen to fee thofe things neceffary for their political falvation, and may he avert from their country the horrid calamities of war."

We learn by the Hartford poft, that the Britifh

... they were to be ... t Capt. Johnfon ... rance ; that he ... November ; and ... ance of a French ... was 2000 Seamen

---

Which hangs out DEATH in one eternal night, A night which glooms us in the Morning Ray And wraps our tho'ts at banquets in a fhroud.

THE fale of the remaining part of the cargo of the brig Countefs of Eglinton, as advertifed in our laft will certainly begin at Taunton on Tuefday next, at ten o'clock in the morning.

Christian Majesty's flag, and the Bey caused the accustomed presents to be carried on board. Some days after, Mr. de Saizieu, Consul and Chargé des Affaires of his most Christian Majesty at this place, presented the Chevalier de Coriolis d'Espinouse, and the officers of the frigate to the Bey, who gave them a most distinguished reception. At the close of the audience, the Bey notified to his Court that he had resolved to send an Envoy to his most Christian Majesty, and had conferred this very important commission on Suleiman Aga, general of the cavalry, his relation, who was then standing at the side of the Bey's throne, and who, after returning thanks to that Prince, received the compliments of the Grandees of the country. He is now preparing for his departure.

"The Bey hath already ordered a vessel to sail for France, which he hath freighted with slaves, horses, lions, and divers effects, intended to be presented to his Most Christian Majesty by his Envoy."

Extract of a Letter from Portsmouth, Feb. 24.

"The Bristol man of war arrived here, brings a confirmation of General Lee being a prisoner at Brunswick in the Jerseys, where it is said he will remain till orders are sent how he is to be disposed of."

The North Star, Sanders; Henry, Stuart, King George, Redmond, Concord, Randal, Unity, Moore, Stag, French, Favourite, Cousins, William and Ann, Seal, Bridget, Gilbody, Betsey, Wolfe, and Nancy, Sellers, transports, from Corke, are all safe arrived at New York, with provisions, &c. for the use of his Majesty's forces.

The Thomas and William, Smith, from New York to Corke, and Friendship, Shotten, from Quebec to Barcelona, are retaken by our men of war, and carried into Halifax.

Extract of a Letter from Newcastle, Feb. 22.

"Wednesday morning there was a very nu-

British were ordered to advance, to bring off Dunhoff's corps, which they effected, but with great loss. The left of our army is now at Princess-town, in the mid-way between New York and Philadelphia, and about twenty miles from Trentown. He further adds, that Gen. Lee was made prisoner by Col. Harcourt, who had marched near forty miles from the army with his party of forty light dragoons, who surrounded the head quarters of the rebel Gen. about three miles from the provincial army, which was guarded by near fifty men; that on hearing the firing, Gen. Lee ran to the door, with two French officers, one of whom was shot dead by his side: that being thus taken by surprise, he was put upon a horse, and galloped off with, in despite of all his overtures for a parley; that Lee, when he was brought in, demanded to be received under the proclamation; but on being refused the benefit thereof, and told that he would be tried as a deserter, he flew into the most unbounded rage, and exclaimed against the repeated acts of false faith, and treachery, which had reduced him to his present situation. —He is now a close prisoner at Brunswick.

Col. White further says, that the Congress had removed from Philadelphia on the approach of Gen. Howe to Lancaster, about forty-five miles distant from their late place; that it was now rendered very contemptible by the divisions that had long agitated it, and the revolt of several of its principal members, particularly the family of the Alleynes, who had all quitted their seats in this congressional senate, come into government, and taken the benefit of the proclamation;—that Gen. Washington continues to occupy the heights with a reduced and mutinous force of about 10,000 men; for that the time being up of the principal part of the rebel army, they were quitting the service, and returning home in a state the most wretched and discontented, &c.

Extract of a Letter from Deal, Feb. 24.

LONDON.

From the New York Gazette, Jan. 13.

Several skirmishes between the King's troops and the rebels have lately happened in the Jerseys. But the most distinguished rencounter occurred on the 3d instant near Prince-town. The 17th regiment, consisting of less than 300 men fell in with the rebel army of very superior force, whom they attacked with all the ardour and intrepidity of Britons. They received the fire from behind a fence, over which they immediately leaped upon their enemies, who presently turned to the right about with such precipitation as to leave their very cannon behind them. The soldiers instantly turned their cannon, and fired at least twenty rounds upon their rear; and had they been assisted with another regiment or two, the rebels would have found it rather difficult to make good their retreat. This has been one of the most splendid actions in the whole campaign, and has given a convincing proof that British valour has not declined from its antient glory. Of Col. Mayhood, their gallant commander, and of his conduct in the affair, too many encomiums cannot be said. The loss was about 20 killed and 80 wounded, of the troops. Of the rebels above 400 were killed and wounded. Among their slain were eleven officers. Mr. Mercer (one of the wounded rebel officers, since dead) when he was taken up by our people, asked how many the numbers were who had thus attacked him, and upon being told, he cried out with astonishment, "My God; is it possible? I have often heard of British courage; but never could have imagined to find such an instance as this!"

Another account says, that the 17th regiment just before they charged the rebels, deliberately pulled off their knapsacks, and gave three cheers, then broke through the rebels, faced about, attacked, and broke through them a second time. Col. Mawhood then said, it would be prudent, as they were so few, to re-

the rest: and it is tho inspect all the parts of incendiaries, and to stif to a dangerous height, n proper means to prevent

Many of the principa plied to me to form such offered to watch in perse

I do therefore require sons may take a part in out to watch when calle and interest will lead all zens cheerfully to give th

Any who refuse to ta the city, will be judged w

JAMES ROBERT
Commander

Copy of GENE

January

THE owners of public or soldiers in their hou will be committed to the niture of their houses a and lights are to be put at nine at night.

WILLIAM BA

Yesterday morning, p going to the Chapel F waited on him, and h rence.

Yesterday their Maj Queen's Palace to St. and heard a sermon prea Oxford: The sword of r from Chapel by the Duke Majesties return from di drawing-room, and aft Townshend had a con jesty.

Yesterday morning a held at Lord Townshend square: There were pre Sir Charles Frederick, an of the Board; at the br Messenger was dispatche orders for an augmentati train of artillery of one dition, previous to a dr the train to go to Americ

Saturday last the Glou obliged to adjourn, on one of the committee, ill.

The following were the Howe's army on the 6th o an authentic account.

At New York.—The f consisting of the 4th, 15t giments; a squadron of 17th; and three Hessian ditary Prince, Cassel and

At Harlem.—The sixth sisting of the 23d, 44th, a a brigade of Hessians.

At Amboy.—33d and 7 mains of 7th and 6th reg of dragoons, and the Wal

At Brunswick.—The gu light infantry. Second sisting of the 5th, 28th, ments. Fourth brigade, B 17th, 40th, 46th, and 55 42d regiment, which is Donop's corps, Hessian seurs.

At Bergen.—The 57th Amboy, and preparing to

At Rhode-Island.—Thir British, consisting of the 52d; of the 22d, 43d, 54 a battalion of grenadiers, fantry; a troop of light ment of artillery, and two

This account shews clea Howe is in possession of that in Jersey he has

---

LONDON CHRONICLE

February 25, 1777

—

In its story, the *London Chronicle* acknowledged that Washington had defeated the Hessians but in the next line reminded readers that the British Army, strong as ever, was marching throughout New Jersey and had nothing more to fear. It also wrote that many of Washington's ten thousand men were deserting (he actually had about five thousand men but had spies feed the British the much higher figure).

LONDON CHRONICLE

March 4, 1777

—

A remarkable story from the January 13, 1777, *New-York Gazette*, reprinted in the March 4, 1777, *London Chronicle*, wrote of the British defeat ten days later at Princeton in such a way that any reader would have thought they had won the battle.

Sir Gilbert Elliott, Bart. who vacated his seat for that borough to stand for the shire of Roxburgh."

Yesterday Lieut. Col. White, aid de camp to Gen. Howe, arrived at Lord George Germain's office from America, with the following intelligence:—That about Christmas last Gen. Washington, at the head of a large body of Provincials, attacked the left wing of the King's forces near Trentown in New Jersey, consisting of several brigades of Hessians. The night preceding the grand affair, they drove in our advanced posts, and the next morning began their attack very briskly about six o'clock, when, after a smart engagement, the Hessians, who were unfortunately detached, were routed, 700 of whom were taken prisoners, and their Col. Reyne killed. The 49th, and 17th regiments of

was an uncommon quantity of corn brought in; which shews there is great plenty in the country.

Winchester, Feb. 22. At our fair on Monday last, we had a great quantity of cheese pitched, which sold from 29s. to 36s. per cwt.

A farmer coming to the said fair with cheese, fell from his horse, and died on the spot.

STOCKS.

Bank Stock, 138	Dit. Ind. An. —
India Ditto, 169 ½	3 ½ per Ct. 1758, —
South-Sea Ditto, —	4 per Ct. con. 1762, —
Do. Old An. 79 ¾	Ind. Bonds, 16s. a 17s.
Ditto New Ann. —	Prem.
3 per Ct. Bank red. 81	Navy and Vict. Bills, a
3 per Ct. cons. 80 ¾	¾ per cent. dis.
3 per Cent. 1726, —	Long Annuities, —
Ditto 1751, —	

men, lying at Raway. They were bravely repulsed, with the loss of one man killed and three slightly-wounded. The rebels left nine killed behind them. They fled with the more precipitation upon seeing Lieut. Col. Dongan with about 20 Jersey volunteers, belonging to Col. Lucee's battalion, coming up to Lieutenant Cameron's assistance.

A party of highlanders, about fifty in number, escorting some waggons and baggage, fell in with 3 or 400 rebels, who commanded them to surrender by a flag of truce. But the soldiers instead of surrender, gave them a salute of cannon which they had with them, drove them off with some precipitation, and brought their convoy safe to the next post.

PROCLAMATION.

By Major-general James Robertson.

WHEREAS there is ground to believe, that the rebels, not satisfied with the destruction of part of the city, entertain designs of burning

SIEGE OF FORT TICONDEROGA

By Eric H. Schnitzer

N O ONE READING THE *LONDON GAZETTE Extraordinary*'s headline report for August 25, 1777, could have interpreted the news as being anything less than a complete victory for British arms in the northern New York theater of military operations. Lieutenant-General John Burgoyne's glowing—and generally accurate—descriptions of events for the opening phase of his campaign in June and July no doubt left readers with an assurance that everything was going perfectly as planned for the British general.

Burgoyne's army from Canada was a multinational force of nearly ten thousand officers and men from Great Britain and Ireland, the German states of Braunschweig and Hessen-Hanau, warriors from dozens of First Nations, Royalist Americans, and French-Canadians, with an extensive mechanism of army support personnel, and women, children, refugee, and sutler followers. His plan was to invade New York from Canada, moving south on Lake Champlain, after which he would put his army onto Lake George and Wood Creek, eventually recombining his forces at Fort Edward on the Hudson River. Then, marching his army south alongside the river, he planned to capture the city of Albany and there receive further instructions from the British commander in chief of America, General Sir William Howe. The distance of nearly two hundred miles across lakes and rivers, over mountains and hills, through old-growth forests, deep ravines, and valleys dotted with small industry and farming communities was not going to be an easy task. Further, in order to achieve complete victory, a number of forts needed to be captured and the Northern Department of the Army of the United States defeated. With initial British tactical dominance in those late June and early July days—the conquering of Forts Crown Point, Ticonderoga,

Independence, and Anne, the routing of Revolutionary forces at Hubbardton and Skenesborough, and the capture of hundreds of tons of ordnance, armed vessels, provisions, and all manner of war matériel—seemed to make Burgoyne's plans for domination a certainty.

But these substantial victories were misleading. At the time Burgoyne's report to Lord George Germain was written on July 11, the army from Canada's rapid progress slowed to a crawl, in great part due to American troops destroying bridges, flooding streams, and blocking roads. This gave time for the army of the United States, commanded by Major General Philip Schuyler, to withdraw further south, receive reinforcements, and plan new defensive strategy. As the campaign wore on into August, Burgoyne's army effectively stalled when it reached the Hudson River as attempts were made to bring its disparate and far-flung parts—infantry, artillery, provisions, naval department, baggage, heavy baggage, and more—together. This considerable delay of nearly one and a half months bought Schuyler, and afterward his congressionally appointed replacement Major General Horatio Gates, even more time. When the report of Burgoyne's decisive successes was being read in the *London Gazette Extraordinary* on August 25, 1777, detachments of his army had already suffered major defeats near Bennington, Vermont (August 16), and in western New York a small supporting army intending to cooperate with Burgoyne retreated back to Canada after its unsuccessful siege of Fort Stanwix (August 23). Although Burgoyne still held the initiative and the dismal situation of his army as described in the November 8, 1777, issue of the *London Chronicle* was exaggerated, transportation delays, battle defeats, and isolation of communication were setting the stage for a complete reversal of fortune for the British general.

The London Gazette Extraordinary.

Published by Authority.

MONDAY, AUGUST 25, 1777.

Whitehall, August 25, 1777.

THE following Letter from Lieutenant-General Burgoyne to Lord George Germain was received the 23d Instant, by Captain Gardner, First Aid de Camp to Lieutenant-General Burgoyne, who arrived in the Royal George Armed Transport from Quebec.

Head Quarters, Skenesborough House,
July 11, 1777.

MY LORD,

I HAVE the Honour to acquaint your Lordship, that the Enemy dislodged from Ticonderoga and Mount Independance on the 6th Instant, and were driven on the same Day beyond Skenesborough on the Right, and to Huberton on the Left, with the Loss of 128 Pieces of Cannon, all their Armed Vessels and Batteaux, the greatest Part of their Baggage and Ammunition, Provision and Military Stores to a very large Amount.

This Success has been followed by Events equally fortunate and rapid. I subjoin such a Detail of Circumstances as the Time will permit; and, for His Majesty's further Information, I beg Leave to refer your Lordship to Captain Gardiner, my Aid de Camp, whom I have thought it necessary to dispatch with News so important to the King's Service, and so honourable to the Troops under my Command.

Journal of the late principal Proceedings of the Army.

HAVING remained at Crown Point Three Days, to bring up the Rear of the Army, to establish the Magazines and the Hospital, and to obtain Intelligence of the Enemy, on

June 30, I ordered the advanced Corps, consisting of the British Light Infantry and Grenadiers, the 24th Regiment, some Canadians and Savages, and Ten Pieces of Light Artillery, under the Command of Brigadier-General Frazer, to move from Putnam Creek, where they had been encamped some Days, up the West Shore of the Lake to Four

Artillery, and a large Square of Barracks within it.

The Foot of the Mount, which projects into the Lake, was intrenched and covered with a strong Abattis close to the Water. This Intrenchment was lined with heavy Artillery pointing down the Lake, flanking the Water-battery above described, and sustained by another Battery about half-way up the Mount. On the West Side the Mount runs the main River, and in its Passage round is joined by the Water which comes down from Lake George. On the East Side of the Mount the Water forms a small Bay, into which falls a Rivulet, after having encircled in its Course Part of the Mount to the South East. The Side to the South could not be seen, but was described as inaccessible. There was a Bridge between the Mount and Ticonderoga, which also was unseen.

July 2. About Nine in the Morning a Smoke was observed towards Lake George, and the Indians brought in a Report that the Enemy had set Fire to their further Blockhouse and had abandoned the Saw Mills; and that a considerable Body were advancing from the Lines towards a Bridge upon the Road which led to the Right of the British Camp. A Detachment of the advanced Corps was immediately put in March under Brigadier Frazer, supported by a Brigade of the Line and some Artillery, under the Command of Major-General Phillips, with Orders to proceed towards Mount Hope, which is to the North of the Lines, to reconnoitre the Enemy's Position, and to take Advantage of any Post they might abandon or be driven from.

The Indians under Captain Frazer, supported by his Company of Marksmen, were directed to make a Circuit to the Left of Brig. Frazer's Line of March, and endeavour to cut off the Retreat of the Enemy to their Lines; but this Design miscarried through the Impetuosity of the Indians, who attacked too soon, and in Front, and the Enemy were thereby able to retire with the Loss of one Officer and a few Men killed, and one Officer wounded. Major-

tance of the Fort of Ticonderoga. ...

Reserve, consisting of the Brunswick Chasseurs, ... Grenadiers under Lieutenant-

tageous Post of Mount Hope and the ... Enemy were thereby entirely cut off from a Com- ... with Lake George

LONDON GAZETTE EXTRAORDINARY
August 25, 1777

—

No one reading the *London Gazette Extraordinary*'s headline report for August 25, 1777, could have interpreted the news as being anything less than a complete victory for British arms in the northern New York theater of military operations. But the news was misleading, as Burgoyne's army slowed to a crawl and the American troops were posturing for a new defensive strategy.

ported this Hill to have the entire Command of the Works and Buildings both of Ticonderoga and Mount Independence; that the Ground might be levelled so as to receive Cannon; and that a Road to convey them, though difficult, might be made practicable in Twenty-four Hours. This Hill also entirely commanded in Reverse the Bridge of Communication, saw the exact Situation of the Vessels, nor could the Enemy during the Day make any material Movement or Preparation without being discovered, and even having their Numbers counted.

It was immediately determined that a Battery should be raised upon Sugar Hill for light Twenty-four Pounders, medium Twelves, and Eight-Inch Howitzers. This very arduous Work was carried on so rapidly that the Battery would have been ready the next Day.

It is a Duty in this Place to do some Justice to the Zeal and Activity of Major-General Phillips, who had the Direction of the Operation; and having mentioned that most valuable Officer, I trust it cannot be thought a Digression to add, that it is to his judicious Arrangements and indefatigable Pains, during the general Superintendency of Preparations which Sir Guy Carleton entrusted to him in the Winter and Spring, that the Service is indebted for its present Forwardness; the Prevalence of contrary Winds and other Accidents having rendered it impossible for any Necessaries prepared in England for the Opening of the Campaign yet to reach the Army.

July 6. Soon after Day-light an Officer arrived express on board the Royal George, where in the Night I took my Quarters as the most centrical Situation, with Information from Brigadier Frazer that the Enemy were retiring, and that he was advancing with his Piquets, leaving Orders for the Brigade to follow as soon as they could accoutre, with Intention to pursue by Land. This Movement was very soon discernable, as were the British Colours which the Brigadier had fixed upon the Fort of Ticonderoga. Knowing how safely I could trust to that Officer's Conduct, I turned my chief Attention to the Pursuit by Water, by which Route I had Intelligence One Column were retiring in Two Hundred and Twenty Batteaux, covered by Five Armed Gallies.

The great Bridge of Communication, through which a Way was to be opened, was supported by Twenty-two sunken Piers of large Timber at nearly equal Distances: The Spaces between were filled by separate Floats, each about Fifty Feet long and Twelve Feet wide, strongly fastened together by Chains and Rivets, and also fastened to the sunken Piers. Before this Bridge was a Boom made of very large Pieces of round Timber, fastened together by rivetted Bolts and double Chains made of Iron an Inch and Half Square.

The Gun Boats were immediately moved forward, and the Boom and one of the intermediate Floats

Colonel Hill, commanding the Enemy had been reinforced in the consider a Body of fresh Troops; that he could not retire before them with his Regiment, but would maintain his Ground. The two remaining Regiments of the First Brigade under Brigadier Powell were ordered to quicken their March; and, upon second Intelligence of the Force of the Enemy, and Firing being heard, the 20th Regiment was ordered forward, and Major General Phillips, with some Pieces of Artillery, was sent to take the Command. A violent Storm of Rain, which lasted the whole Day, prevented these Troops from getting to Fort Anne so soon as was intended; but the Delay gave the 9th Regiment an Opportunity of distinguishing themselves by standing and repulsing an Attack of six Times their Numbers. The Enemy finding the Position not to be forced in Front, endeavoured to surround it; and, from the Superiority of their Numbers, that Inconvenience was to be apprehended, and Lieutenant-Colonel Hill therefore found it necessary to change his Ground in the Heat of Action. So critical an Order was executed by the Regiment with the greatest Steadiness and Bravery. The Enemy, after an Attack of Three Hours were totally repulsed with great Loss. The fled towards Fort Edward, setting Fire to Fort Anne, but leaving a Saw Mill and Block House in good Repair, which latter was afterwards possessed by the King's Troops. The 9th Regiment acquired, during their Expedition, about Thirty Prisoners, Stores and Baggage, and the Colours of the Second Hampshire Regiment. The Accidents to counterballance these several Successes are few. The service has lost an Officer of great Gallantry and experience in Major Grant. The other Officers are also to be much regretted. Captain Montmery of the 9th Regiment, an Officer of Merit, was wounded in the Leg early in the Action, and was in the Act of being dressed by the Surgeon, when the Regiment changed Ground; being to help himself, he and the Surgeon were taken soners. I hear he has been well treated, and recovering at Albany. The

"In that trunk (said I) Amelia, I have, with-out any ceremony put up every thing with which

LONDON CHRONICLE
November 8, 1777

Although Burgoyne still held the initiative and the dismal situation of his army as described in the November 8, 1777, issue of the *London Chronicle* was exaggerated, transportation delays, battle defeats, and isolation of communication were setting the stage for a complete reversal of fortune for the British general.

scruples had there been any feathers of objection remaining. I could easily see, that side of the heart was touched which contains those vessels that feed the passions of pleasure—I saw consent bloomingly written on every feature—I took my little cabinet under my arm, handed Amelia into the chaise, and heard, with pleasure, the wheels rattle over the pavement."

FRIDAY, NOVEMBER 7.
COUNTRY NEWS.
Leeds, Nov. 4.

ON Thursday last, as an Auctioneer was selling some houshold goods at Blackhouse-lane, near Colne, the chamber-floor gave way, bruised a number of persons in the fall, and among the rest the Auctioneer; happily no lives were lost.

The same kind of caterpillars which have been found in the haystacks and mows in the neighbourhood of Otley, Bradford, &c. are also found in the stacks in this neighbourhood.

LONDON.
NEWS from AMERICA.
State of MASSACHUSETTS-BAY.
Council-Chamber, Sept. 1, 1777.

WHEREAS it is represented to this board, that some men who were drafted in consequence of the resolution of the general court, of the 8th of August last have not marched, although they have received orders,

Therefore ordered, That the militia officers in each town, where any person dwells that has been drafted, and agrreeable to the resolves of the general court, of the 8th of August last, be and they hereby are directed to apprehend all such persons in their respective towns, as have been drafted, ordered to march, and have neglected as aforesaid, and forward them, under guard, to the regiment to which they belong, without delay, and take a receipt of the commanding officer of the regiment to which said delinquents belong, and return the same, with the account of the expences, into the secretary's office.

A true copy.
Attest,   JOHN AVERY, Dep. Sec.

From the MARYLAND JOURNAL, Aug. 26.

---

counties, where they shall receive orders.—To ... requires our exertions; our ... our country, implore ... mply sufficient to arm ... led a man.

... his 22d day of August, ... rd, one thousand seven ... -seven.

T. JOHNSON.
August 26.

... part of the continental ... ut 10,000 men, with ... hington at their head, ... ity, and immediately ... Scuyikill, on their way ... Maryland, where the ... ely been seen, and it is thought will make a descent upon that state. And yesterday morning Gen. Nash's brigade of North Carolina forces, and Col. Procter's regiment of artillery, passed through this city. They are to pursue the same route, in order to join our most illustrious General.

On the enemy's fleet appearing off Baltimore, the disaffected inhabitants were all seized and sent under a strong guard to Fredericktown.

August 28. Congress proceeded to the election of a committee to collect evidence and facts respecting the evacuation of Ticonderoga, and the ballot being taken, Mr. Laurens, Mr. R. Henry Loyde, and Mr. John Adams, were elected.

A letter received from a young gentleman who went to America with Gen. Burgoyne in a private capacity, transmitted to his father, Mr. C——, at Hackney, gives a most dismal picture of the state of that General's army: the troops are in so great distress for want of provisions, that the gentleman who wrote the letter, though he dines at the second table immediately after the General, has not been able, by reason of the scarcity of the fare, to make a hearty meal for several weeks. What then, may we suppose, must be the situation of the inferior officers and the common soldiers? The letter proceeds, that the troops lay for a month upon the bare earth, which has greatly emaciated them; that the foraging parties had proved so very unsuccessful, as to be almost cut off to a man; that a party of 800 were surrounded, and only three returned alive.

By the last returns made to the Adjutant-general's office from Sir William Howe, it appears, that there were above 900 of the rank and file incapable of duty, from a violent flux, which they got soon after landing in the southward.

A letter was yesterday received by a gentleman of consideration in office from Corke, written by a person that landed there from Chesapeak-bay, the 29th of Oct. which mentions, that the battle between Gen. Howe's army and Washington's happened on the 11th of Sept. that Washington's army was entirely routed, with the loss of near 5000 killed and taken prisoners; and that Gen. Howe took possession of Philadelphia on the 14th.

Yesterday there was a very numerous and splendid Court at St. James's, when his Majes-

---

consisted of English property, consigned to Spanish Merchants."

Extract of a Letter from Bilboa, Oct. 15.

"An American ship has brought in a prize loaded with 3000 quintals of fish, and as she brings none of her real crew, we do not know what vessel she is. Yesterday we received advice from Capt. Salmon, of the brig Peter, who was coming consigned to us with 2600 quintals of cod fish: In his letter he says, that in lat. 44, long. 9, he was taken the 5th inst. by an American privateer, bound from Bourdeaux to Philadelphia, who, after having plundered him of all his sails, rigging, ship's stores, and a large quantity of fish, returned him the vessel, not being capable of manning her, and she has since got safe into this port."

Extract of a Letter from Bourdeaux, Oct. 23.

"This city is as much the seat of American politics as ever, though the privateering is not so brisk as formerly. Trade, however, was never brisker, as a proof of which the Officers of the King's Customs here are augmented, there not being enough before to do the business."

Extract of a Letter from St. Eustatia, Aug. 12.

"An English armed vessel belonging to Barbadoes chased an American brig into this harbour two days ago. Two American vessels were taken just without this port, about a fortnight ago, and carried off, which has made the English cruisers frequent this island, in hopes of meeting some more of them. Martinico has been so well watched lately, that the Provincials have paid us more visits than they were used to do, and Surinam has had some trade with them."

Extract of a Letter from Beerhaven, Oct. 22.

"An American privateer, which had been cruising for some time off Cape Clear, put in here two days ago, in order to heel ship, on account of a leak. They gave out that they were a letter of marque belonging to London, and on a cruise; this took with the common people, and many others; they bought a great quantity of live stock, and some spirits, for which they paid in dollars, and after lying here almost 24 hours, put again to sea."

They write from Halifax in Nova Scotia, that a large French ship had lately been wrecked in the Gulph of St. Lawrence, and deserted by the crew, on board of which were found a large quantity of gunpowder, a great number of firearms, and divers other military stores, supposed to be intended for the Americans.

The Brothers, Kelly, from Dublin to Oporto, is taken by Capt. Cunningham, off the coast of Portugal.

Extract of a Letter from Chatham, Nov. 4.

"Yesterday sailed from hence for Blackstakes, the Sultan, Capt. Farker, a new ship of 74 guns; she is to take in her powder and guns at Blackstakes, after which she is to proceed to Spithead.

"Tuesday sailed from this port to the Nore, the Conquestadore of 74 guns, Capt. Thompson; she is to be stationed at the Nore, to receive imprest men.

"Mr. John Blackmore is appointed Inspector of the new work of his Majesty's dock-yard at this place, in the room of Mr. Foot ...

PROCLAMATION.
THIS state being now actually invaded by a formidable land and sea force, and the enemy,

of another Princess.
Yesterday a prodigious number of persons partook of cake and caudle at St. James's; the

of the Marines quartered in this town."
Extract of a Letter from Portsmouth, Nov. 5.
"We have just now heard the Monarque is

REPORTING THE
BATTLE OF ORISKANY

By Daniel J. Tortora

B Y JUNE 1777, GENERAL JOHN BURGOYNE HAD recruited four hundred Indian auxiliaries to join his campaign. He gave each warrior a silver medallion, explains the *Independent Chronicle* of September 11, 1777. Silver medallions symbolized the shine and luster of the idealized British-Iroquois alliance.

Burgoyne soon grew frustrated with the Indians. He could not stop them from plundering and killing. The warriors resented British officers' arrogance and hierarchy. Iroquois families were destitute, and the British paid for scalps. Further, by killing non-Indians, native warriors satisfied the evil spirits and honored their war dead. When the Indians murdered Jane McCrea, the fiancée of a Loyalist, Burgoyne feared alienating Loyalists and the uncommitted, so he stopped rewarding the Indians for taking colonists' scalps. However, he still threatened New Yorkers with Indian violence. The British used their native warriors in dangerous roles.

As Burgoyne advanced south, Lieutenant Colonel Barry St. Leger left Montreal. St. Leger aimed to take the forts in New York's Mohawk Valley and then to meet Burgoyne at Albany. The colonel led 1,500 men—half were Indian allies; half were Canadians, British and Hanau regulars, and Tory militiamen.

Colonel Peter Gansevoort commanded 750 militiamen at Fort Schuyler (formerly Fort Stanwix). In mid-June, Iroquois scouts killed five workers outside the fort and captured eight more. The prisoners exaggerated the fort's defenses and manpower. St. Leger delayed. The colonel finally arrived on August 3, 1777. Gansevoort refused to surrender. St. Leger commenced bombardment, and his Indian snipers picked off Gansevoort's men.

General Nicholas Herkimer left Fort Dayton on August 4 to reinforce Gansevoort. He led eight hundred Tryon County militiamen and some Oneida scouts. The *Independent Chronicle* of September 11, 1777, reveals that St. Leger's troops attacked a detachment sent from Fort Schuyler to meet Herkimer. Herkimer feared that his impatient men would mutiny, so he continued. Four hundred Iroquois and four hundred Tories under Mohawk Joseph Brant, Colonel John Butler, and Sir John Johnson lay in wait six miles from Fort Schuyler, near the Indian village of Oriskany. On August 6, 1777, they attacked after most of Herkimer's army had crossed a marshy ravine.

The Battle of Oriskany evolved into hand-to-hand combat. British officers had incited the Indians with liberal doses of rum. Many fought clumsily, but many American officers fell dead in the first few minutes of the chaos. Herkimer was shot in the leg. Many militiamen fled. A sudden thunderstorm enabled American forces to regroup on high ground. Herkimer organized his men into a defensive circle as he smoked a pipe, propped up on his saddle. Tory commander Colonel John Butler briefly breached the Patriot defenses, ordering his men to turn their green coats inside out so that they resembled American uniforms. Britain's Indians, fearing a rear attack and discouraged by their heavy losses, retreated. Tories Butler and Johnson then had to withdraw.

Both sides sustained heavy casualties in the six-hour-long battle. One Indian recalled that blood flowed in a stream down the battlefield. More than half of Herkimer's command were killed, wounded, or captured, so he retreated to Fort Dayton. He died there eleven days later. Of the Tory forces, at least sixty to eighty Indians—many of them Senecas—and a handful of Loyalists were killed or wounded. Neither side won, though both claimed victory.

St. Leger threatened that if Fort Schuyler refused to surrender, his Indians, "much exasperated and mortified from their losses," would destroy white settlements along the Mohawk River. Meanwhile, the article shows that Tories recruited for Burgoyne by threatening to unleash the natives against any who refused. St. Leger's subordinate, Colonel Daniel Claus, sought native allies in Canada.

Major General Benedict Arnold, already on his way from Saratoga to relieve the beleaguered fort, took prisoners and forced them to give misleading information to St. Leger. St. Leger's Indians fled. The colonel lifted the siege on August 22 and returned to Canada. The November 15, 1777, *London Chronicle* reflects his frustration. The British questioned the Indians' "bravery," without acknowledging the opportunistic nature of Indian warfare. Denied payment and discouraged by high casualties at Freeman's Farm, Burgoyne's Indians deserted. This contributed to the American victory at Saratoga.

Thereafter, brutal raids and ambushes pitted white and Indian brothers and neighbors against each other for months and even years. General Sullivan destroyed dozens of villages and fields in 1779.

KINGSTON, August 25.

By a gentleman from Albany, we are favoured with the following anecdote.—That at the late battle between General Harkman and the enemy, at Oneyda Creek, there was a friendly Indian, with his wife and son, who distinguished themselves remarkably on the occasion. The Indian killed nine of the enemy, when having received a ball through his wrist that disabled him from using his gun, he then fought with his tomahawk. His son killed two, and his wife on horseback, fought by his side, with pistols, during the whole action, which lasted six hours. That in this and Lieut. Col. Willet's action near the fort, three hundred and fifty Indians were killed, a greater number than they ever lost in any battle during the last war. That they having discovered some reluctance to engage our troops, were plied with liquor till they were half intoxicated, to heighten their courage, and prepare them for the slaughter they meditated against us, but suffered themselves, in much greater numbers. This circumstance occasioned their standing the battle with such unusual perseverance. That upon the arrival of a troop of our light horse, at Schenectady, our friends there (who lately had been menaced by the Indians, and worse Savages the Tories) joined the troop in great numbers, and soon put the infamous M'Donald and his base, ungrateful clan, to the rout. That General Arnold, with about a thousand men, above half of whom were Continental troops, having a few days since, marched from Albany for the relief of Fort Stanwix, he was daily joined on the way, by great numbers of volunteers, and by Wednesday it was expected he arrived in the neighbourhood of the more than Savage Butler, and his tawny companions. It is greatly to be feared that this motly banditti of Indians, Tories, Bastards and Britons will retreat to their boats, and escape before our forces can come up with them.

That a son of Butler, with eighteen other savages, came a few days ago to the German recruits, and threatened the inhabitants, if they did not turn out immediately to join the bloody tyrant of Britain, a party of Indians sent to their houses, who should not spare infants in the cradle. But the brave and [...] men there, disdaining their brutal threat [...] surrounded, and took them all prisoners. [...] soon after sent off for Albany, where p[...] are now confined.

[Has not Providence delivered these [...] our hands, as hostages for the security of [...] fenceless inhabitants, whose fears must be [...] leviated by this happy event ?]

That at Bennington, in the battle of S[...] 16th inst. when the enemy made their [...] they received a reinforcement, headed by [...] mock Governor, named Skeene, [*since dead*] on seeing our troops file off to the right and left, with a view to flank him, had so little penetration, as to imagine they were flying before him, when he insultingly bawled out, " Stand Yankies, stand, don't run away." They very soon got into the position they intended, bravely attacked the enemy, and gal-

dence, Fort Schuyler, and were all his, and as soon as his army appeared before them, would be delivered to his commanders, without firing a gun. And he, Col. Clause, only told them these things, because he had a good will to them, and wanted to keep them from hurting themselves by joining the Rebels, but that if they did join them, it would not make the least alteration in the King's affairs, nor stop him a moment from taking all that the Rebels had, whenever he had a mind to it.

That this speech was delivered with so much confident assurance, that many believed it on that account, while others doubted it. But that on the strange and shameful delivery of Ticonderoga, and all its Stores, Fort Independence, &c. all the rest that Clause had asserted was generally believed, both by Indians and Tories. But they have now reason to think they shall find all the rest of the speech to be false.

Col. Baum, who commanded the whole of the enemy's forces at the late battle near Bennington, is among the slain. We have taken 900 swords of the dragoons, upwards of 1000 stands of arms, four brass field-pieces, viz. one 12, two 9, and one 4 pounders. Our loss 20 or 30 killed, and not more than 50 wounded.

INDEPENDENT CHRONICLE (BOSTON)
September 11, 1777

By June 1777, General John Burgoyne had recruited four hundred Indian auxiliaries to join his campaign. He gave each warrior a silver medallion, which symbolized the shine and luster of the idealized British-Iroquois alliance. The *Independent Chronicle* reveals that Lieutenant Colonel Barry St. Leger's troops attacked a detachment sent from Fort Schuyler to meet General Nicholas Herkimer. Four hundred Iroquois and four hundred Tories lay in wait six miles from Fort Schuyler, near the Indian village of Oriskany.

SIR,

WHEN the scheme was first adopted of taking a body of Indian savages to assist the British army, it was very generally affirmed, and almost as generally believed, that this circumstance alone would decide the controversy against the Americans; for nothing, it was said, could exceed the terror which the Americans entertained of these same savages. At that time I wrote you a letter contradicting the report, and assuring you, from my own personal knowledge, that nothing could be worse founded.

As individuals indeed, and man opposed to man, the savages are dreadful to the peaceable inhabitants of the Colonies; but as an open enemy, and forming an army, they are justly held in the most supreme contempt. In a word, the savages have all the cunning of the fox, and all the cruelty of the tyger; but they have none of the open bravery of the lion. And this opinion of mine is now confirmed by authority; for Colonel St. Leger, in his last dispatches, says that the Indians in his army were so alarmed at the report of the approach of a body of Continental forces, that they could not be persuaded to continue the attack upon Fort Stanwix, but immediately abandoned his colours, and took to their heels.　R. M.

To be Sold by private Contract,

ALL that the Manor, or reputed Manor, or Lordship, of Stallington in the parish of Stone, in the county of Stafford.

Also all that capital and elegantly finished Mansion-house called Stallington-hall, now in the possession of Thomas Ashwood, Esq; situate in Stallington aforesaid, with a good kitchen garden, pleasure grounds, fish ponds, and all manner of convenient offices thereunto belonging, together with 78 acres, 3 roods, 24 perches of rich arable, meadow, and pasture land, tythe-free, lying round the said Mansion-house.

Also all that capital Messuage called Leacroft-hall, and convenient outbuildings thereunto belonging, situate in Fulford in the parish of Stone aforesaid.

And also several Chief Rents arising in the same Manor or Lordship, amounting in the whole to 18 l. per annum, together with such herriotts and rights of common as will be specified in the particular.

The Mansion-house is most agreeably situated, being very contiguous to several good turnpike roads

---

STATE LOTTERY, 1777.

RICHARDSON and GOODLUCK respectfully acquaint the Public, that the Tickets in the present State Lottery are sold and divided into Shares, Chances, and Shares of Chances; from a Half to a Sixteenth Part, at their Offices in the Bank-buildings, Cornhill, and No. 8, facing the King's Mews, Charing-cross, where every legal business of the Lottery is transacted with correctness and fidelity.

The Chances and Shares of Chances intitle the Purchasers to every Prize in the Lottery above 20 l. for more than One-third less than the price of a Ticket.

Chances at One Guinea each are also selling at the above Offices, by which the fortunate Purchasers will gain the following large sums, viz.

l.						l.
2,000	if the number of the Chance is a Prize of	-	}	20,000
1,000	-	-	if a Prize of	-		10,000
500	-	-	if a Prize of	-		5,000
200	-	-	if a Prize of	-		2,000
100	-	-	if a Prize of	-		1,000
50	-	-	if a Prize of	-		500
10	-	-	if a Prize of	-		100
5	-	-	if a Prize of	-		50

The above plan is by much the most advantageous to Adventurers of any ever offered, as they will have the Chance of 768 Prizes, and may gain the sum of Two Thousand Pounds for the trifling consideration of One Guinea.—The money for the above Chances will be paid to the fortunate Adventurers as soon as drawn, without any deduction, the Original Tickets being in the possession of Messrs. Richardson and Goodluck, pursuant to Act of Parliament.

The Lottery will begin drawing on Monday next.

LEGAL CHANCES for the STATE LOTTERY, 1777, at One Pound each; and at Four Shillings each, are now selling by HORNSBY and Co. Stock brokers, at the Original King's Arms State Lottery Office, No. 19, corner of Pope's-head-alley, Cornhill, and No. 16, near the Saracen's-head-inn, Aldgate; and No. 5, Bridges-street, opposite Drury-lane Theatre, where the following Capital Prizes were sold, shared, and registered, 10,000 l. in Cox's Museum, 20,000 l. in the State Lottery for 1774, 5,000 l. 2,000 l. and 1,000 l. in the last State Lottery.

... ONE POUND:

... Purchasers will gain the following sums, viz:

		l.
the Chance is }	Prize of -	20,000
	Prize of -	10,000
	Prize of -	5,000
	Prize of -	2,000
	Prize of -	1,000
	Prize of -	500
	Prize of -	100
	Prize of -	50

... UR SHILLINGS:

		l.
either of the	2	20,000
either of the	3	10,000
either of the	4	5,000
either of the	8	2,000
... either of the	11	1,000
... is either of the	40	500
2 2 if the number is either of the	200	100
1 1 if the number is either of the	500	50

Total 768

The advantages arising to the Purchasers of Chances on the above Plans are superior to any thing yet offered to the Public, as they will have the

---

A NEW SYSTEM OF HUSBANDRY.

This Day was published,

Printed on a new type, and fine paper, in Quarto, Price 10 s. 6 d. in Boards,

CLARKE's TRUE THEORY and PRACTICE of HUSBANDRY, deduced from Philosophical Researches, and Experience.—This Work consists of Three Parts or Sections.—Sect. I. Contains a philosophical and practical investigation of the most essential matters in the walk of husbandry; a fair and impartial method of estimating the value of land; the education of youth designed for Husbandmen, &c. &c. II. The elements of mechanics illustrated with plates, and so explained and applied, as to enable the Husbandman to direct the making and repairing his various utensils in a true mechanical manner. III. Consists of, 1st—An explanation of the figures contained in the five demy folio plates given in the Work, viz. Exact drawings of the best natural and artificial grasses for pasture, meadow, and pleasure grounds; two drain ploughs; a trenching plough; a paring plough; a turn-wrist plough, or plough for banky land; the common plough; a plough that requires the least force possible to draw it; an improved drill plough, &c. for the invention of which the Author has had the first premiums given by the Honourable Society, instituted in London, for the Encouragement of Arts. 2d—Full directions for making and managing a cheap and durable machine for threshing corn, which may be worked by wind, water, horses, or men, to great advantage.

Printed for the Author, and sold by G. Robinson, Pater-noster-row; and T. Slack, Newcastle.

For the TEETH, SCURVY in the GUMS, and TOOTH ACH,

Mr. GREENOUGH's TINCTURES.

THESE Tinctures have now been in general use for more than thirty years past, and as the standing the test of time and experience is the strongest proof of real excellence, it is hoped the universal esteem they have acquired during that period, is a sufficient evidence of their merit, efficacy, and safety: But as their success has occasioned many counterfeits, Mr. Greenough requests, that every purchaser will observe, that his genuine Tinctures are in oblong square bottles, on each of which is a label with the following words, PREPARED BY T. GREENOUGH,

---

LONDON CHRONICLE

November 15, 1777
—

Colonel Daniel Claus, St. Leger's subordinate, lifted the siege of Fort Schuyler on August 22 and returned to Canada. The November 15, 1777, *London Chronicle* reflects his frustration. The British questioned the Indians' "bravery," without acknowledging the opportunistic nature of Indian warfare. Denied payment and discouraged by high casualties at Freeman's Farm, Burgoyne's Indians deserted. This contributed to the American victory at Saratoga.

REPORTING THE
BATTLES OF BRANDYWINE AND GERMANTOWN

By Bruce E. Mowday

O N THE MORNING OF SEPTEMBER 11, 1777, AMERICAN General George Washington's troops were well entrenched behind the banks of the Brandywine River near Chadds Ford, Pennsylvania. Washington picked the Brandywine as the perfect place to defend the young nation's capitol of Philadelphia against the British and to defeat King George III's army.

Late in August 1777, General William Howe's British army landed at the Head of the Elk in Maryland and began a campaign to capture Philadelphia. Howe's planning for the operation began in the waning months of 1776 and was approved by his superior Lord George Germain in London. The campaign had three objectives. The first was to capture Philadelphia, the second was to deprive Washington's army of supplies furnished by the inhabitants of the region, and the third was to rally citizens loyal to King George III to fight the rebels.

Before daybreak on the day of the Battle of Brandywine, Howe split his army into two segments. Howe and General Charles Cornwallis led more than half of the British army on a seventeen-mile march to flank Washington. The remaining segment of the British army under General Wilhelm Knyphausen was ordered to march from Kennett Square, Pennsylvania, and force Washington's light infantry back to the Brandywine. Knyphausen was ordered to cross the river and attack the rebels when Howe attacked the rear portion of Washington's army.

The plan almost worked perfectly for the British. Several British officers wrote after the battle that if they had an hour's additional daylight, Washington's army would have been destroyed. The Continental Congress fled Philadelphia after the defeat at Brandywine, and on September 26, 1777, the British took control of one of America's most important cities.

The Philadelphia campaign was a disaster for Washington, including General Anthony Wayne's defeat at Paoli on the evening of September 21, 1777. Washington attempted to surprise the British army at Germantown on October 4, 1777, and had initial success. Fog, friendly fire, and a stubborn British defense at the Cliveden mansion contributed to Washington's withdrawing from Germantown.

The early reporting on the Battle of Brandywine in the October 28, 1777, edition of the *London Chronicle* had few details and overstated the number of casualties of both armies. The paper estimated Washington's losses at two thousand and the British at seven hundred to eight hundred. The Americans actually lost about 1,300 and the British almost six hundred. The same newspaper on November 15, 1777, again inflated losses for Washington's army and reported that the British took possession of a city in ruins after rebels set fire to Philadelphia. While some supplies were destroyed, no widespread destruction of the city was done before the British took control.

A report from an American officer that first appeared in the *New-York Gazette* on September 22, 1777, was reprinted in the *London Chronicle* on November 8, 1777. That report was written at 5:00 p.m. on the day of the Battle of Brandywine, and the author didn't have a complete view of what was taking place that day. He wrote about his limited experiences and was overly optimistic about the American fortunes.

The *London Chronicle* reprinted a letter from a British officer attached to Hessian troops at Germantown that contained a great amount of details on the fighting. The letter was penned a week after the battle and was printed on January 6, 1778.

The Philadelphia campaign was a triumph for the British army as Howe's forces forced the Americans to retreat to Valley Forge, where Washington's army suffered through a hard winter.

Tuesday, Oct. 28.

IRELAND.

Tralee, Oct. 6.

FEW days ago a Gentleman of Tubridbeg gave an order on one of his tenants to two brothers, Smiths, with power to distrain: accordingly they

---

LONDON CHRONICLE

October 28, 1777

—

The early reporting on the Battle of Brandywine in the October 28, 1777, edition of the *London Chronicle* had few details and overstated the number of casualties of both armies.

SCOTLAND.

Edinburgh, Oct. 22. Thursday last were interred in the church-yard of Aberdeen a man and a woman, whose ages amounted to 190.

At Haddington, on the 19th inst. died, Dr. James Lundie, Physician there, in the 92d year of his age.

COUNTRY NEWS.

Liverpool, Oct. 24. Yesterday the John and Sally arrived from the Smalls, with Mr. Whitesides and the workmen she took from hence, and those who went down before her, in perfect health. It is remarkable, that this is the fourth season the people have returned from this supposed hazardous enterprize, without hurt or blemish. We hear, the building was left in a condition to stand the winter, though not habitable.

Bristol, Oct. 25. Thursday evening the Birmingham diligence returning to the White Hart in this city, was stopped within 100 yards of Stokes Croft Turnpike by two footpads, who robbed the passengers of between 5l. and 6l. On the arrival of the carriage, Mr. White informed Mr. Weekes of the event, who, anxious for the safety of his own diligence expected in, ordered a whiskey, and, accompanied by a friend, with only a brace of pistols, proceeded that road himself. Just at the cross posts, between the turnpike and Redland, the same two footpads ordered them to stop, when Mr. Weekes's companion rather too precipitately discharged his pistol, on which the fellows instantly fired a brace of blunderbusses, but happily without effect. The horse on the discharge of the fire arms set out full speed, and the Gentlemen thought it most expedient to hasten home by another road, when they procured more assistance, and again sallied out in pursuit of the offenders, but they eluded a diligent search of several hours.

Salisbury, Oct. 27. Last week the unanimous thanks of the parish of Milton was sent to Philip Pulse, Esq; Patron of that church, for

Oxford, Oct. 25. Last Saturday morning a coach and a diligence were robbed between four

---

Reading, Oct. 25. On Wednesday last a gentleman of Savernacle Park, near Marlborough, aged 72, was married to Miss Molly Tuch, aged 27. The coming of this couple together was not a little singular, and is as follows: The old gentleman was paying his addresses to a widow in Marlborough, on whom he had offered to settle 50l. a year for her life, besides leaving her a considerable sum at his decease, which she rejected, when the above young lady falling into their company, and Mr. Tarrant submitting to ... the proposals he had made ... and honourable? she ... such an offer." The ... the young woman, ... s her candour, and in ... ervice to her, which

NEWS.

...d and sailed for the ...dshall, from Oporto; ...m Bristol; the Plenty, ... and the Dublin, Rider, from Chester. Remain in the Downs the ships as before; and the Nile, Goldsmith, for orders; the Duke of Cumberland, Passmore, for Ancona; the Princess Mary, Arthur, for Jamaica; the ———, Wilson, for St. Ube's; and the Fleece, Moore, for Plymouth. Wind South West, blows hard.

LONDON.

Accounts received yesterday by the way of France say, that there has been a general engagement between Washington and Gen. Howe, near Philadelphia. On the approach of the British army Gen. Washington called a counsel of war, whether they should defend their magazines, which was agreed to, the consequence of which was a total defeat, with the loss of 2000 men killed and wounded, and all their magazines. About seven or eight hundred of the British troops fell in the action. Policies were opened at Lloyd's to receive fifteen guineas to pay an hundred if the above is not true.

A report prevails that Lieut. Kniphausen insisted on the release of the Hessian officers taken at Trenton last December, according to the terms proposed by Mr. Washington; in consequence of which Gen. Lee was given in exchange for them, and for Col. Campbell an English officer taken in his passage to America two years since. Sir Wm. Howe is said to have been unwilling to part with Lee, but the Hessian General insisting on having his officers, he was under the necessity of complying.

Yesterday some dispatches were received at the Admiralty from Admiral Montague on the Newfoundland station, brought by the Active frigate, arrived at Portsmouth, which are to be laid before the Privy Council.

The army in America is to be reinforced next campaign with 17,000 troops, and early in the sessions the House of Commons is to be moved for supplies, to enable government to defray the expence. The minority Members are busy collecting all their strength.

Yesterday his Majesty took an airing on horseback to Windsor, and returned to the Queen's Palace at three o'clock.

... cester House.

It is said Lord North intends to raise the principal additional supplies next session, by

---

lings. By this a... collected without...

Yesterday the... Cofferer's and of... hold a quarter's...

It is said that... powers to trea... Princes, and to... service for next...

It is said that... for the America... cluded with the... body of troops... it be found nece...

A letter from... tenant of a ma... having boarded... Ireland, the cr... chest, and shot...

Advice is sai... town, South C... very great distu... cipal inhabitant... properties seize... prison, because... currency issued...

The Irish nat... veral establishm... ing Lady-day r... the two years e... to 2,561,065l. a... at the former ... the latter amou...

The first regi... by his Majesty... next week; as... soon after; wh... from each regi... America.

Extract of a ...

" Arrived th... from Plymouth... here this even... ships, viz. on... ship Squirrel,... with about 16... under his conv... the Hero, Cap... lona; on the ... Alarm, off Lif...

Extract of a ...

" Yesterday... several passeng... of the West I... was taken off... of 36 guns. ... tacked the D... sailer, and was... rica, in 63 v... prizes, among... from Jamaica... mouth, for... schooner, con... New York, w... Jamaica fleet.... on board a Fre... they obtained...

Extract of a ...

" Arrived t... jesty's ship th... Capt. William...

Warsaw, Oct. 25.

E have accounts her... Porte has declared w... the Tartars, because... chosen a new Chan,... in consequence of... Russians have sent 12... to their assistance, a... Romanzow is to command the Russia... It is added, that if war is declared the... will act upon a new plan, which will... Turks very much; but we do not hear... plan is.

Madrid, Oct. 30. By advices from... we hear, that the coasts of Biscay are... with American privateers, which ta... English vessels, and that Capt. John F... the Success privateer has taken sever... vessels in one month.

Naples, Oct. 21. We have the satisf... hear that all the royal children, who we... inoculated, are perfectly recovered, w... gained great honour to Dr. Gaskin... given the utmost satisfaction to the C... the Public.

Rome, Oct. 25. Our letters from... mention, that a violent shock of an ea... had been felt there, without mentio... consequences of it, only that it had... general alarm throughout that city... shocks have also been felt in the provi... patrimony of St. Peter, but happily di... mage.

Marseilles, Oct. 23. The following i... of the letter written by the Minister of... rine Department, and sent to all the... France.

" You could not, Gentlemen, be ig... the orders so often renewed by his M... the fittings of the different Admiraltie... ports, not to permit the sale of any priz... by foreign privateers, or to suffer the... and their prizes to remain any longe... ports than is absolutely necessary to... them the provisions and assistance th... might want. This prohibition, which... from a principle of faithfully observing... once made, ought not to be eluded on a... tence whatever; and it is not without g... pleasure, that his Majesty hears that ill... gal methods have been made use of to e... vigilance of his Officers, and to buy... the goods belonging to the above-me... prizes; and I am charged by the King... give notice to the Chambers of Trac... through them to the Merchants, that... not directly or indirectly buy any of th... chandizes which in any shape belong... prizes brought into any of his ports,... of answering for it personally, and being... to return the goods or their value.

" I desire you will make these intent... his Majesty known to the Merchants,... the same time that the King will not per... least evasion of his orders to go unpu... and, I am persuaded, that the Mercha... shew the utmost alacrity to prove the... mission to the King's pleasure. I am... order you, that those who counteract th... ders be rigorously proceeded against; an... further to add, that as the ports of the... dom are open for the trade of all natio... Merchant ships from North America may... mitted with their cargoes, which they m... pose of, and take in return any merch... which is permitted to be exported, exce... munition, &c. and his Majesty particularly... all Merchants to avoid the introducing... American prizes, under pretence of their... Merchantmen."

... cher cutter,... with eight fa... laden with li...

... Oxford, Oct. 25. Last Saturday morning a coach and a diligence were robbed between four and five o'clock: one of them near the Obser-

IRELAND

Dublin, Nov. 8. The Lord Mayor, Sheriffs, Aldermen, and Common Council of the county of the town of Drogheda, having unanimously voted the freedom of said town, in an elegant silver box, unto Lambert Brabazon, Esq; of his Majesty's navy, in consideration of his intrepid and attentive conduct, in protecting the trade and commerce of this kingdom, whilst the coast was infested with American privateers; at the request of their corporation, Wm. Mead Ogle, Esq; one of their representatives in parliament, on Tuesday last delivered Lieut. Brabazon this distinguishing mark of their approbation.

And the principal Merchants of the city of Dublin have also presented by their representative, Dr. Wm. Clement, a memorial to his Excellency the Lord Lieutenant, representing the spirited and active conduct of Lieut. Brabazon, and the essential service rendered by him to the commercial and trading interest of this kingdom, and in particular to the merchants of this city, praying that their representation be laid before his Majesty that this officer might receive a reward equal to his merit and services.

The Lord Lieutenant has appointed the Right Hon. Murrough Earl of Inchiquin, to be Governor of the County of Clare, in the room of the late Earl of Inchiquin.

Wednesday Walter Hussey Burgh, Esq; Prime Serjeant at Law in this kingdom, and John Scott, Esq; Attorney General, were sworn of his Majesty's most Hon. Privy Council.

Letters by Thursday's post from Kilkenny advise, that one Magher, a labouring man, was taken and lodged in the county gaol there, charged with the murder and robbery of one Collier, a lad, near Ballyragget, when he was about to pay a sum of money.

Kilkenny, Nov. 5. Miss Vize has been rescued from the persons who forcibly took her away from the house of Mr. Parsons, of Ballinatten, near Clonmell, and restored to her family, by the activity of Lord Doneraile, the Tipperary rangers, and many other gentlemen of the counties of Tipperary and Corke.

COUNTRY NEWS.

Penzance, Nov. 7. The beginning of this week a woman was committed to the county gaol of Launceston from Liskeard, by the name of Jones, for horse-stealing.

SHIP NEWS.

Deal, Nov. 13. Came down his Majesty's ship Boston, and remain in the Downs with the ships as before, and the Lapwing, Scott, for Gibraltar; the Hope, Warman, the Montserrat Packet, Clark, for Montserrat. Sailed for the river the Allen, Liddey, from Dublin. Wind south.

LONDON.

Yesterday morning his Majesty, attended by the officers of the train, went on horseback to Woolwich to see a proof of several pieces of cannon intended for New York; after which his Majesty returned to the Queen's palace.

The same day, after breaking up of the Levee at St. James's, a Privy-council was held, at which all the great Officers of State assisted.

In the House of Commons of Ireland on Thursday Nov. 6, Mr. Gorges Lowther moved to enquire into the state of the civil and military pensions.

The address of the house, thanking his majesty for his gracious answer to their former address, was presented by Mr. Charles Henry Coote, and agreed to by the house.

The petition of Mr. Thomas Johnson, praying relief for his losses incurred by his importation of cattle for improving the live stock of Ireland, was reported by Mr. Lodge Morris, as being fully proved, and the petitioner worthy of parliamentary aid.

Mr. Frederick Flood moved, that the proper officer do lay before the house a particular account of incidents on the civil establishment of this kingdom, from Lady-day 1775, to Lady-day, 1777, which was carried.

It appeared in the returns of the payments out of the concordatum, that Mr. Supple and Mr. Hackett had received money, and it had not been expressed in the warrant of the privy-council for what reason they had been paid the sums specified. To attain information on that head, Mr. Barry Barry moved that the report of the committee of the privy-council on which these warrants were grounded should be laid before the house. Mr. Prime Serjeant replied, though he would not wish any information should be withheld, yet the house was to judge what information was to be asked, and whether it was asked properly; which was not the present case, as the privy-council were all on oath.

Mr. Recorder, Mr. Daly, Mr. Grattan, and Mr. Barry, urged the right of members to call for any papers they pleased, and the latter made many remarks on the excesses on concordatum.

Mr. Leigh thought the motion improper; and Mr. Attorney General explained these two articles, by informing Mr. Barry that Mr. Supple had been very active in prosecuting to conviction some very atrocious criminals, and out of revenge their accomplices had set on him, and left him for dead, with 18 wounds. Still he survived, and successfully prosecuted the offenders; but had been long reduced to misery and distress, till the council had considered his case, and given him the above relief. As to Mr. Hackett, he was a messenger, and the money he had received was for travelling charges for his journey to London, and attendance there on Sir John Blaquiere. His information giving satisfaction, the motion was withdrawn.

General Cunningham informed the house, that for two journeys, one through all Ireland, and another to embark the troops at Corke, he had refused to receive any gratification, but it being insisted upon that his charges should be paid, he had received the expence of his post horses, which had been set down in the civil expences, without any explanation, and mixed with other accounts, that might induce the house to think he had charged for his trouble, which he scorned to do; and this matter had been thus set down by a person in office, in resentment for his not being so pliable as he could wish.

Mr. Gardiner also spoke concerning the money charged for works done in the Phœnix Park, and said he never had signed any paper for such works, and that the roads there were in very bad order.

On Friday, Nov. 7. The committee of accounts finished all its business previous to preparing their report.

Mr. Barry Barry began a revision of the case of Mr. Supple, as mentioned the day before, but being reminded it was time to go up with the address, he desisted, and the house adjourned, and went to present to his Excellency the address to his majesty, and request it may be transmitted to the king.

Some of the morning papers contain the following article: The Bienfaisant man of war, which arrived at Plymouth on Wednesday last, from Halifax, (from whence she sailed October 16.) at the mouth of Halifax harbour met the Grayhound frigate, the Capt. of which sent on board the Bienfaisant a Newport gazette extraordinary, of Sunday October 5, and another from New York of the same date, containing a letter from Gen. Howe, brought by a sloop of war from Chesapeak Bay to General Clinton, and also a letter from Lord Howe to Sir Peter Parker at Rhode Island, giving an account of what had happened since the disembarkation of the troops, viz. that General Howe came up with the rebels at Brandywine, on the

---

11th of September, about five o'clock in the afternoon, having had several skirmishes with the enemy's out-posts in the course of the day, and the rebels were at last brought to a general action, which lasted till dark, when Washington, taking the advantage of the night, made a precipitate retreat, leaving behind all his cannon, baggage, and 1800 of their dead on the field. That on the 17th another action had happened near the Schuylkill, where Washington was again defeated with great loss. That Gen. Howe took possession of Philadelphia the 24th, which the rebels instantly abandoned, setting it on fire in three places, but, from the vigilance of the troops, and the assistance afforded by the inhabitants, it was soon got under, with very little loss. The rebels likewise set fire to three frigates in the harbour, and several floating batteries. Gen. Howe left three regiments to garrison the town, and set off, full speed, with the grenadiers, light infantry. &c. into the Jerseys, after Washington. Provisions of all sorts have been sent into Philadelphia from the country around, and the inhabitants have promised to furnish the army with every necessary, in abundance. And the counties of Newcastle, Kent, and Sussex, had also sent delegates to the General, offering to supply him with provisions, if they could be protected, and that he had left a brigade there for that purpose. The Dispatch sloop of war had arrived at New York from Chesapeak-bay, and the Bristol and Experiment with their convoys from England.

When the Bienfaisant left Halifax, the reports were, that the provincials had set fire to Philadelphia in four places previous to their abandoning it. So that our troops are in possession only of the ruins of the city.

Philadelphia, Sept. 3.
In Congress, Sept. 1, 1777.
Resolved, That Gen. Washington be directed to appoint a court of enquiry relative to the late expedition by Gen. Sullivan, against the British forces on Staten-island.
Copy from the journals,
WM. CH. HOUSTON, Dep. Sec.

A letter from Port Antonio, in the island of Jamaica, dated Sept. 2, says, " The 6th inst. two American privateers, both of them ships of considerable force, stood into, and cut three vessels out of this harbour; and a few days before, the same privateers took a large ship within a few miles of this place. There is at present nine of those provincial vessels of war cruising round this island, in defiance of the small squadron the Admiral has at Port Royal, which are too few in number to check their progress."

From New York, intelligence has been received, that Capt. T. was killed in a duel there, by Capt. P. of the guards, immediately after

---

dropped down to St.
ship Ariel is put back to
remains with the outw
fleet."

Yesterday the Earl of
Levee at St. James's, an
with his Majesty.

On Thursday an extra
of the Governors was
hospital, St. George's
election (by ballot) of
preachers. The candida
Wm. Sellon, Minister
well; the Rev. Mr. Rich
Brompton-chapel; the
ler, Preacher at Charlott
Mr. T. Bowen, Reader a
ing up the ballot there a
180, Mr. Harrison 115,
Bowen 30, whereupon t
men were declared duly

Last week was married
Bath, to Miss Eliz. Sher

On Wednesday died,
Sir Lau. Dundas at Mo
wood, Esq; of Soho-squ

On Tuesday last died,
port, George Clarke, Es
Justices of the Peace for
and Lancaster.

On Thursday died, at
Theamon, formerly an of

Yesterday died, at his
Mr. Clarke, Builder.

Yesterday the body of a
found drowned in the
Tower. He was laid up
to be owned.

D. L. The School for Scand
a Stage.

C. G. The Duenna, with T

---

the Mary Cutter, Lieutenant Donavan, are arrived from Dublin, having safely convoyed from thence to Dungenness, the London, Herd, the Success, Dunn, and the Allen, Liddey, all bound to London, loaded with linen for that port.

" Arrived about 14 sail of outward-bound ships from the Downs, and two large ordnance

Chronology, small size, the
may be had, price 1s. 6d.
12mo, price 3 s. half-bound
Sold by R. Baldwin, Pat
News-carriers.

New editions of this
lished the first day of every
zines; any corrections there
Trusler, to the care of

LONDON CHRONICLE
November 15, 1777

The November 15, 1777, *London Chronicle* again had overinflated losses for Washington's army and reported that the British army took possession of a city in ruins after rebels set fire to Philadelphia. While some supplies were destroyed, no widespread destruction of the city was done before the British took control.

The LONDON CHRONICLE

From the NEW YORK GAZETTE, *Sept. 22.*

Yesterday the following account of the action of the 11th instant, between the King's troops under the command of his Excellency Sir Wm. Howe, and the rebel army under Mr. Washington, near Brandywine, came to hand, as the same was published by order of Congress. Chad Ford, Sept. 11, 1777, 5 o'clock.

SIR,

WHEN I had the honour of advising you this morning, I mentioned that the enemy were advancing: I had begun a cannonade. I would now beg leave to inform you, that they have kept up a brisk fire from their artillery ever since their advanced party were attacked by our light troops under Gen. Maxwell, who hemmed the Brandywine for that purpose, and had posted his men on some high ground on each side the road. The fire from our people was not of long duration (as the enemy pushed on fast), but was very severe. What loss the enemy sustained cannot be ascertained with precision; but from our situation, and briskness of the attack, it is the general opinion (particularly those that were engaged) that they had at the least 300 killed and wounded. Our damage is not exactly known, but from the best account we have been able to obtain, it does not exceed 50 in the whole. After this affair, the enemy halted upon the heights, where they have remained ever since, except a detachment of them which filed off about eleven o'clock from their left, and have since passed Brandywine at John's Ford, between five and six miles above Chad's; the amount of it is not known, accounts respecting it being various, some making it to be two or three thousand strong, and others more. Generals Sullivan, Stirling, and Stephens, with their divisions, are gone in pursuit of them, and to attack if they can with any prospect of success. There has been a scattering fire between our parties on each side the brook since the action in the morning, which just now becomes warm, when Gen. Maxwell pushed over with his corps, and drove them from their ground, with the loss of 30 men left dead on the spot, amongst them a Captain of the 49th, and a number of intrenching tools, with which they were turning up a battery. At half after four o'clock the enemy attacked Gen. Sullivan at the Ford, and above this, and the action has been violent ever since; it still continues a very severe cannonade, has begun here, and I suppose we shall have a very hot evening. I hope it will be a happy one. I have the honour to be, ROBT. H. HANNISON.

Hon. John Hancock, Esq;

Published by Order of Congress,

CHARLES THOMSON Sec

LONDON CHRONICLE

November 8, 1777

—

A report from an American officer that first appeared in the *New-York Gazette* on September 22, 1777, was reprinted in the *London Chronicle* on November 8, 1777. That report was written at 5:00 p.m. on the day of the Battle of Brandywine, and the author didn't have a complete view of what was taking place that day. He wrote about his limited experiences and was overly optimistic about the American fortunes that day.

Saturday, Nov. 8.

Yesterday arrived the Mails from FRANCE *and* HOLLAND.

Petersburgh, October 10.

ON the 6th of this month we had another tempest here, but happily no inundation; we are daily more sensible of the effects of the last, which has occasioned the price of corn to be very high, as all that was in the magazines is spoiled.

Cologne, Oct. 30. It is said that the Prince of Anhalt Zerbst is to send a corps of his troops into the British service, and that some of his Officers are already gone to London.

Madrid, Oct. 14. We have accounts from South America, that a great difference has arisen there between the two Commanders of our fleet, Don Cevallos and the Marquis of Cassa Tilly, insomuch that the former has complained to the Court, who it is said has given orders for the command of the fleet to be given to a Commodore, till the arrival of another Lieutenant-general, whom the King shall appoint to take the command of that fleet.

Lisbon, Oct. 7. It is said that peace is concluded between Spain and Portugal, on condition that the Spaniards shall return the Island St. Catherine to the Portuguese, but that the former are to keep the colony of St. Sacrament.

The departure of the Queen Dowager for Spain is fixed for the 21st of this month. Their Majesties and the royal family will accompany her Majesty to Villa Viciosa.

A shock of an earthquake was felt here on the 1st of this month, at six o'clock in the morning, and a subterraneous noise was heard at the same time.

Paris, Oct. 31. The Cardinal de la Roche Aymon, Archbishop and Duke of Rheims, first Peer and Grand Almoner of France, &c. died on the 27th of this month.

SHIP NEWS.

Deal, Nov. 6. Came down and sailed this morning, with several of the outward-bound ships, the Trecothick, Moore, the St. James Planter, Steward, for Jamaica. Came down, and remain in the Downs with the rest of the ships as before, his Majesty's ship Cornwall, the Thomas, Mann, for Montserrat; and the Resolution, Cox, for Grenada. Wind W S.W.

LONDON.

Yesterday the Lord Mayor, Aldermen, and Common Council, attended his Majesty according to his royal will and pleasure, and presented the following address.

To the KING's Most Excellent Majesty.

The humble Address of the Lord Mayor, Aldermen, and Commons of the City of London, in Common Council assembled:

Most Gracious Sovereign,

"We your Majesty's most dutiful and loyal subjects the Lord Mayor, Aldermen, and Commons of the city of London, in Common Council assembled, humbly beg leave to express our unfeigned joy upon the happy delivery of our Most Gracious Queen, and the birth of another Princess, an event which we consider as an ad-

To which the King returned the following answer:

"I thank you for this dutiful address, and your loyal congratulations on the happy delivery of the Queen, and the birth of another Princess.

"It is my invariable object to preserve, and transmit entire, the constitutional liberties of my people, which I shall ever consider as forming the basis of my government."

The Lord Mayor, the Lord Mayor Elect, and the following Aldermen, were present on the above occasion, viz. Alsop, Kennett, Thomas, Hayley, Pugh, and about 130 Common Councilmen, in 33 coaches and chariots; the Chamberlain, the City Remembrancer, the Town Clerk, and other officers.

They were all received very graciously, and had the honour of kissing the King's hand. After which they were regaled with cake, wine, &c.

Yesterday some dispatches were received at St. James's from the Hon. Robert Walpole, Esq; his Majesty's Ambassador at the Court of Lisbon, brought by the Squirrel man of war, arrived at Portsmouth.

It is said that General Faucett, who is gone to Germany, has received orders to contract with the different German States for 7000 men, who are to be in readiness to embark for America on the first notice.

On Thursday evening their Graces the Dukes of Leeds and Chandos arrived in town from their respective country seats, and were yesterday at Court.

The William, Norris, from New York, is arrived at Liverpool.

From the ROYAL AMERICAN GAZETTE, *received yesterday.*

New York, Sept. 11. On Monday last a vessel, with a flag of truce, arrived here from Martinico. Their business, we hear, is to solicit the release of the French officers taken in the vessels trading with the rebels.

New York, Sept. 15. Wednesday arrived here from Tobago, the ship Catharine, John Freeman, Master, laden with rum and sugar; she was on the 13th ult. taken by a rebel privateer sloop called the Baltimore Hero, commanded by one Hasey, who put on board the ship one Lieutenant, a prize-master, and three hands. They kept possession of her nine days; but in the night of the 22d past, Capt. Freeman, being assisted by the hands left on board belonging to the ship, resumed the command, and brought her safe into his destined port.

We hear that Commodore Hotham has very generously given up the salvage of the above ship to the master and mariners that rescued her from the hands of the Rebels, and brought her into this port.

Tuesday last the ship Peace and Plenty, Capt. M'Kenzie, the ship King George, Capt. Redmond, and the ship Nelly, Capt. North, arrived here from Corke, with provisions, &c. after a tedious passage of 10 weeks: They sailed from thence under convoy of the ship British King, and in company with the Jane, Diana, Unity, Walters, Mary and Anne, Stagg, Indian King, Union Island, Concord, and Lord Howe; and left them the 19th of August, in lat. 38. 30. long. 60. being ordered by the Commodore to give chace to a rebel privateer schooner of 12 guns, that appeared among the shipping; but after a pursuit of several hours, the wind falling away, the privateer took to her oars, and got

Yesterday the following account of the action of the 11th instant, between the King's troops under the command of his Excellency Sir Wm. Howe, and the rebel army under Mr. Washington, near Brandywine, came to hand, as the same was published by order of Congress.

Chad Ford, Sept. 11, 1777, 5 o'clock.

SIR,

WHEN I had the honour of advising you this morning, I mentioned that the enemy were advancing: I had begun a cannonade. I would now beg leave to inform you, that they have kept up a brisk fire from their artillery ever since their advanced party were attacked by our light troops under Gen. Maxwell, who hemmed the Brandywine for that purpose, and had posted his men on some high ground on each side the road. The fire from our people was not of long duration (as the enemy pushed on fast), but was very severe. What loss the enemy sustained cannot be ascertained with precision; but from our situation, and briskness of the attack, it is the general opinion (particularly those that were engaged) that they had at the least 300 killed and wounded. Our damage is not exactly known, but from the best account we have been able to obtain, it does not exceed 50 in the whole. After this affair, the enemy halted upon the heights, where they have remained ever since, except a detachment of them which filed off about eleven o'clock from their left, and have since passed Brandywine at John's Ford, between five and six miles above Chad's; the amount of it is not known, accounts respecting it being various, some making it to be two or three thousand strong, and others more. Generals Sullivan, Stirling, and Stephens, with their divisions, are gone in pursuit of them, and to attack it if they can with any prospect of success. There has been a scattering fire between our parties on each side the brook since the action in the morning, which just now becomes warm, when Gen. Maxwell pushed over with his corps, and drove them from their ground, with the loss of 30 men left dead on the spot, amongst them a Captain of the 49th, and a number of intrenching tools, with which they were turning up a battery. At half after four o'clock the enemy attacked Gen. Sullivan at the Ford, and above this, and the action has been violent ever since; it still continues a very severe cannonade, has begun here, and I suppose we shall have a very hot evening. I hope it will be a happy one. I have the honour to be,   ROBT. H. HARRISON.

Hon. John Hancock, Esq;

Published by Order of Congress,

CHARLES THOMSON, Sec.

The following extraordinary news, dated Bourdeaux, Oct. 15, appeared in the Avignon Gazette, and arrived by yesterday's mail.

"Letters received yesterday from l'Orient advise, that two vessels dispatched by the Congress, had arrived in that port; the Captains of the ships say, that Gen. Washington having sent a reinforcement of troops under the command of Arnold to join the army of Gen. St. Clair, these two Generals attacked Gen. Burgoyne under the cannon of Fort Edward; that they entirely defeated his army, and took him prisoner. This news, which prudence should forbid us to believe until well authenticated, has had strange effects in this city: and though there are wanting the most essential marks of authenticity, such as dates, &c. yet there are numbers of people here who believe it merely

STATE OF MASSACHUSETTS-BAY.
COUNCIL-CHAMBER, October 20, 1777.

STATE OF MASSACHUSETTS-BAY.
In the House of Representatives, October 13, 1777.

J. WARREN, Speaker.

In COUNCIL, October 13, 1777.
Read and concurred. JOHN AVERY, D. Sec'y.

STATE OF MASSACHUSETTS-BAY.
COUNCIL-CHAMBER, Boston, October 21, 1777.

JOHN AVERY, D. Sec'y.

An Express arrived here last Wednesday Evening from the Honorable Major-General GATES, to the honorable the President of the COUNCIL of this State, with the following important Advices, viz.

Albany, 19th October, 1777.

SIR,

Camp near Pawling's Mill, Oct. 5, 1777.

GEORGE WASHINGTON.

To the Hon. JOHN HANCOCK, Esq; President of CONGRESS.

BATTLES OF SARATOGA

By Eric H. Schnitzer

THE NORTHERN CAMPAIGN OF 1777 ENTERED A NEW phase in September, during which time both armies prepared to confront each other; no longer was Major General Horatio Gates's Northern Department of the Army of the United States retreating, and Lieutenant-General John Burgoyne's army from Canada was finally prepared to make its push to capture the city of Albany. Gates's force, at first deployed near Albany itself, moved about twenty miles north to Bemis Heights. The Heights, overlooking the valley and Hudson River below, were part of a continuity of stunning natural defenses, made stronger by man-made ones. Gates commanded an army of nearly eight thousand officers and men from Massachusetts, New York, New Hampshire, Connecticut, Virginia, and Pennsylvania, the great majority of whom were Continentals.

On September 19, Burgoyne's slightly larger army advanced to attack the American defenses. Gates's second-in-command, Major General Benedict Arnold, took the initiative and brought the battle to the British in the farm fields and woods one and a half miles north of Bemis Heights, with the primary fighting occurring on American Royalist John Freeman's Farm. The battle ended in a tactical British victory, albeit a pyrrhic one—British casualties numbered 590 to the Americans' 325. After a day of resting his army following the hard-fought battle, Burgoyne received a message from the commander of the City of New York, Sir Henry Clinton, who offered to assist Burgoyne by making a diversion in the Hudson Highlands with the hope that Gates would be forced to split his army in two. Relying wholly on this new plan, Burgoyne built a fortified camp on and around Freeman's Farm and waited. The wait lasted for two and a half weeks, during which time Gates's army was joined by militia regiments and grew to over twelve thousand, whereas attrition dwindled Burgoyne's to nearly seven thousand.

On October 7, having heard nothing further of Clinton's movements, Burgoyne took the initiative and, with a probing force of 1,500, moved south to observe the American lines in search of a weakness that could be exploited. But neither he nor anyone in his detachment got close enough to see the Revolutionary army's defenses. Gates ordered an immediate and decisive attack on the British probing force, which in little more than one hour was beaten back to its fortified camp. In close pursuit, the Americans attacked two fortifications and captured one of them, Breymann's Post, at which place Arnold was severely wounded. Having suffered over six hundred casualties to the Americans' 150, and having lost one of his key forts, Burgoyne ordered a retreat.

Thunderstorms, fatigue, and poor coordination slowed the British withdrawal to Saratoga, eight miles north of Freeman's Farm. Gates belatedly ordered a pursuit on October 10 but quickly caught up with Burgoyne at Saratoga later that day. The small village was surrounded by the army of the United States, now numbering nearly seventeen thousand, and the British were forced to surrender—by the generally favorable terms outlined in the *Articles of Convention*—on October 17.

The *Articles of Convention*, a transcript of which was published in the December 11, 1777, issue of the *London Chronicle*, stated that Burgoyne's surrendered troops would be allowed to return to Europe. However, Congress interposed a series of objections to the *Articles* (as reported in the April 4, 1778, issue of the *Pennsylvania Ledger*) by questioning Burgoyne's integrity on account of supposedly missing arms, accoutrements, and other war matériel. Burgoyne's and Gates's responses to Congress's inquiries on the matter proved unsatisfactory, and Congress doomed the Convention Army (as Burgoyne's surrendered army was called) to de facto prisoner of war status on January 8, 1778.

Gates's capture of an entire army commanded by a British Lieutenant-General—something which was never done before—was astonishing and inspired the new nation's first day of Thanksgiving on December 18, 1777. But the greatest effect of the victory at Saratoga was the resultant February 6, 1778, Treaty of Alliance between the United States and France, the decisiveness of which came to fruition at Yorktown, Virginia, in 1781. That is why the victory at Saratoga is known as the great "Turning Point of the Revolutionary War."

SURRENDER OF GENERAL BURGOYNE
Architect of the Capitol

On October 10, 1777, British Lieutenant-General John Burgoyne found his army surrounded at Saratoga, New York, by American forces totaling nearly seventeen thousand. One week later, he surrendered.

The LONDON CHRONICLE

Postscript.
LONDON.
ADVICES *from* AMERICA.
Albany, Oct. 19, 1777.

SIR,

I Have the pleasure to send your honourable council the inclosed copy of a convention, by which lieutenant general Burgoyne surrendered himself and his whole army on the 17th instant into my hands. They are now upon their march towards Boston. General Glover and general Whipple, with a proper guard of militia, escort them, and are to provide all such necessary articles as may be wanted upon the march. I am so extremely busy in pushing the army forward to stop the cruel career of general Vaughan up Hudson's-river, that I have only time to acquaint you, that my friend general Lincoln's leg is in a fair way of doing well, and to testify with what respect I am, your much obliged and most obedient humble servant,

HORATIO GATES.

To the honourable the President of the Council of the State of Massachusetts Bay.

ARTICLES *of* CONVENTION *made between*
Lieutenant-general BURGOYNE, *and Major-general* GATES.
ARTICLE. I.

The troops under lieutenant-general Burgoyne, are to march out of their camp with the honours of war, and the artillery of the intrenchments, to the verge of the river where the old fort stood, where the arms and artillery are to be left.—The arms are to be piled by word command from their own officers.

II. A free passage to be granted to the army under lieutenant-general Burgoyne to Great Britain, upon condition of not serving again in North America, during the present contest; and the port of Boston to be assigned for the entry of transports, to receive the troops, whenever general Howe shall so order.

III. Should any cartel take place, by which the army under lieutenant-general Burgoyne, or any part of it, may be exchanged, the foregoing article to be void, as far as such exchange shall be made.

IV. The army under lieutenant-general Burgoyne is to march to Massachusetts-bay, by the easiest, most expeditious, and convenient route; and to be quartered in, near, or as convenient as possible to Boston, that the march of the troops may not be delayed when transports arrive to receive them.

V. The troops to be supplied on the march, and during their being in quarters, with provisions, by general Gates's orders, at the same rate of rations as the troops of his own army; and, if possible, the officers horses and cattle are to be supplied with forage at the usual rates.

VI. All officers are to retain their carriages, but horses and other cattle and no baggage to be molested or searched; lieutenant general Burgoyne giving his honour there are no public stores secreted therein. Major general Gates will of course take the necessary measures for the due performance of this article: should any carriages be wanted during the march for the transportation of officers baggage, they are, if possible, to be supplied by the country at the usual rates.

VII. Upon the march, and during the time the army shall remain in quarters, in the Massachusets Bay, the officers are not, as far as circumstances will admit, to be separated from their men. The officers are to be quartered according to rank, and are not to be hindered from assembling their men for roll calling, and other purposes of regularity.

VIII. All corps whatever of general Burgoyne's army, whether composed of sailors, batteaumen, artificers, drivers, independant companies and followers of the army of whatever country, shall be included in the fullest sense, and utmost extent of the above articles, and comprehended in every respect as British subjects.

[…]

(Signed)　　　　J. BURGOYNE.
Camp at Saratoga, Oct. 16, 1777.

The Battles of Saratoga, fought eighteen days apart, resulted in the surrender of British Lieutenant-General John Burgoyne's entire army and helped convince France to ally with the United States. The favorable terms of Burgoyne's surrender were published in the December, 11, 1777, *London Chronicle*.

Congress interposed a series of objections to the articles, or terms, of surrender by questioning Burgoyne's integrity on account of supposedly missing arms, accoutrements, and other war matériel. The objections are reprinted from "Rebel Papers" in this Tory newspaper, published in Philadelphia while occupied by the British.

---

cleaning woollen cloth, it instantly removes every kind of spot (even paint, although it may have been dried in for several weeks) without leaving the smallest trace behind. It is so easily used, that cloaths which are only soiled (and not spotted) require very little trouble to clean them, and is brushed out as readily as the dust after a day's wear. It being used dry does not make the cloth appear rough, but on the contrary, if the cloaths are carefully brushed (with the grain) they will be as smooth as when new.

It will be found exceedingly useful to gentlemen of the army and navy, as it makes white and buff-coloured cloth and kersymier appear as beautiful as new.

It is also particularly recommended for the linings of carriages, &c.

By appointment of the Patentee this Powder is sold wholesale and retail only by W. Bayley, Perfumer, in Cockspur-street; and Mess. Smyths, Perfumers to his Majesty in New Bond-street. Sold also retail by J. Price, Perfumer, in Leadenhall-street, price 2s. a box.

†‡† Proper brushes may be had at the same places.

Postscript.

LONDON.
ADVICES from AMERICA.

SIR,   Albany, Oct. 19. 1777.

I Have the pleasure to send your honourable council the inclosed copy of a convention, by which lieutenant general Burgoyne surrendered himself and his whole army on the 17th instant into my hands. They are now upon their march towards Boston. General Glover and general Whipple, with a proper guard of militia, escort them, and are to provide all such necessary articles as may be wanted upon the march. I am so extremely busy in pushing the army forward to stop the cruel career of general Vaughan up Hudson's-river, that I have only time to acquaint you, that my friend general Lincoln's leg is in a fair way of doing well, and to testify with what respect I am, your much obliged and most obedient humble servant,
HORATIO GATES.

To the honourable the President of the Council of the State of Massachusetts Bay.

ARTICLES of CONVENTION *made between Lieutenant-general* BURGOYNE, *and Major-general* GATES.

ARTICLE I.

THE troops under lieutenant-general Burgoyne, are to march out of their camp with the honours of war, and the artillery of the intrenchments, to the verge of the river where the old fort stood, where the arms and artillery are to be left.—The arms are to be piled by word command from their own officers.

VI. All officers are to retain their carriages, but horses and other cattle and no baggage to be molested or searched; lieutenant general Burgoyne giving his honour there are no public stores secreted therein. Major general Gates will of course take the necessary measures for the due performance of this article: should any carriages be wanted during the march for the transportation of officers baggage, they are, if possible, to be supplied by the country at the usual rates.

VII. Upon the march, and during the time the army shall remain in quarters, in the Massachusets Bay, the officers are not, as far as circumstances will admit, to be separated from their men. The officers are to be quartered according to rank, and are not to be hindered from assembling their men for roll calling, and other purposes of regularity.

VIII. All corps whatever of general Burgoyne's army, whether composed of sailors, batteaumen, artificers, drivers, independant companies and followers of the army of whatever country, shall be included in the fullest sense, and utmost extent of the above articles, and comprehended in every respect as British subjects.

IX. All Canadians and persons belonging to the Canadian establishment, consisting of sailors, batteaumen, artificers, drivers, and independant companies, and many other followers of the army who come under no particular description, are to be permitted to return there. They are to be conducted immediately by the shortest route to the first British post on Lake George; are to be supplied with provisions in the same manner as the other troops, and are to be bound by the same condition of not serving during the present contest in North America.

X. Passports are to be immediately granted, for three officers, not exceeding the rank of captains, who shall be appointed by lieutenant-general Burgoyne, to carry dispatches to Sir William Howe, Sir Guy Carleton, and to Great Britain, by way of New York. And major-general Gates engages the public faith, that these dispatches shall not be opened. These officers are to set out immediately after receiving their dispatches, and are to travel by the shortest routes, and in the most expeditious manner.

XI. During the stay of the troops in Massachusets-bay, the officers are to be admitted on parole, and are to be allowed to wear their side-arms.

XII. Should the army under lieutenant general Burgoyne find it necessary to send for their clothing and other baggage to Canada, they are to be permitted to do it in the most convenient manner, and the necessary passports granted for that purpose.

---

528   THE LONDO

The Capitulation between Generals Gates *and* Burgoyne *concluded from the preceding Page.*

XIII. These articles are to be mutually signed and exchanged to-morrow morning at nine o'clock, and the troops under lieutenant-general Burgoyne are to march out of their intrenchments at three o'clock in the afternoon.
(Signed)   J. BURGOYNE.
Camp at Saratoga, Oct. 16, 1777.

In consequence of the foregoing convention at Saratoga the 17th Oct. 1777, the following numbers laid down their arms, and surrendered to Gen. Gates, viz. British troops 2442; Brunswick and other German troops 2198; Canadians, volunteers, &c. 1100; staff 12; total 5752.

Sick and wounded left in the British camp when general Burgoyne began his retreat 528. Besides the above, there were killed, wounded, taken, and deserted, of British, German, and Canadian troops under general Burgoyne, between the 6th July, and 16th Oct. 2933; in all 9213.

Account of Brass Ordnance, &c. delivered up to General Gates *on the 17th of Oct. viz.*

Two 24 pounders, four 12 ditto, eighteen 6 ditto, four 3 ditto, Royal Howitzers five 5½ inch, brass mortars, two inch; in all 35, all of brass, besides those taken at Bennington.

Stands of arms complete, 7000, besides the military chest, large quantities of ordnance stores, cloathing for 7000 Provincials, tents, &c. &c.

By the last accounts from America, received by a packet arrived in France, we learn, that General Gates had returned to Albany on the 19th of October, and was pushing forward his army (consisting of 12,000 men) with all possible speed to attack the British troops under General Vaughan, on the North-river: General Putnam was advancing up that river, in their rear, with 5000 men, so that it was scarce possible they could escape a disaster similar to that of general Burgoyne. Generals Gates and Putnam, after having overcome gen. Vaughan's troops, were immediately to join general Washington, whose army, by various reinforcements, had been increased to 25,000 men, and was laying siege to Philadelphia.

This day arrived the mails from Flanders, but brought nothing new.

MARKET-DAY ADVERTISER

SATURDAY,   DIEU ET MON DROIT   APRIL 4, 1778.

☞ *Philadelphia:* Printed by JAMES HUMPHREYS, Jun. in *Market-street*, between *Front* and *Second* streets, and nearly oppofite the *Guard-houfe:*—By whom Effays, Articles of News, Advertifements, &c. are gratefully received and impartially inferted: And where Subfcriptions are taken in for this Paper.

CITY VENDUE,

THIS DAY, precifely at eleven o'clock, at the London Coffee-houfe, by public auction, will begin the fale of

MUSCOVADO, } Single refined } fugar;
Rum,—*fubject to the regulations in the proclamation;*
Madeira, }
Port, } wines, by the quarter-cafk, hogfhead and
Sherry, } pipe;
Teneriff }
Rice;
Soap;
Fine falt;
And a few hogfheads of very good tobacco.

N. B. The City Vendue-ftore (between Chefnut and Walnut-ftreets, on the eaft fide of Front-ftreet) will continue to receive all forts of goods and merchandize for public and private fale; where they will be kept at a very moderate expence, and expofed to the greateft advantage, in an elegant room fitted up for that purpofe; and where purchafers will always have the advantage of chufing out of a general and large affortment, on low terms.

Commiffions for purchafing or difpofing of any article, for the gentlemen of the army or navy, will be particularly attended to.

April 4.   DAVID SPROAT, Vendue-Mafter.

By his Excellency Sir WILLIAM HOWE, K. B.
General and Commander in Chief, &c. &c.

PROCLAMATION.

WHEREAS, by my proclamation bearing date the fourth day of this inftant, " All mafters " of merchant fhips were ordered and commanded " immediately on their arrival, to make entry of " the veffels, and deliver in proper manifefts of their " cargoes, on oath, at the Superintendent's office," and it was further ordered, that " No goods or " merchandize whatever fhould be laden on board " any fhip or veffel, (fuch as are in his Majefty's " fervice excepted) until permiffion in writing fhould " firft be obtained from the faid Superintendent's " office, fpecifying the quantity and quality of the " goods fo intended to be laden, with the veffel " and mafter's name, and where bound:" And, " That no fhip or veffel (fuch as are in his Majefty's " fervice excepted) fhould leave this port, until " the mafter fhould deliver in, at the Superinten- " dent's office, a manifeft on oath, fpecifying the " quantity and quality of the goods, and by whom " fhipped, together with the permiffion granted for " the lading the veffels." And whereas, the maf- ters of tranfports, victuallers, and other veffels in his Majefty's fervice, may conceive themfelves jufti- fied under the exceptions aforefaid, in importing into, and exporting goods and merchandize from, this port, without complying with the regulations in my faid proclamation contained, whereby great frauds may be committed, and the true intent and meaning of the faid proclamation eluded: For pre- vention whereof, I do hereby declare and order, that the faid exceptions, relating to fhips or veffels in his Majefty's fervice, fhall be void, and that all fhips and veffels whatever, that are now in, or may hereafter come in, or go out of, this port, and the mafters thereof, fhall be liable to the fame regula- tions, pains and penalties, as merchant fhips are

---

The printer JAMES HUMPHREYS, jun.
Has for fale a few copies of
GAINE's UNIVERSAL REGISTER.
OR,
AMERICAN BRITISH KALENDER,
For the year 1778;
Containing befides a complete lift of the army, a variety of very ufeful matter

Juft publifhed, and to be fold by JAMES HUM- PHREY's, jun. printer hereof, at his Statio- nary Store in Market-ftreet,
(Price bound in leather Six Shillings and Six-pence, in vellum Five Shillings)

The GENTLEMAN and LADY's Pocket Memorandum Book for 1778.

Containing a page for memorandums for every week in the year; and for accounts of monies re- ceived, paid, or lent. Alfo a table reducing fter- ling money into Pennfylvania currency.—A table fhewing the amount of any number of dollars at 4s. 8d. fterling—Another fhewing the amount of any number of dollars at 7s. 6d. currency; a table fhewing the amount of any number of guineas at 35s. currency; and a table of the value and weight of coins

A Meeting of the Yorkfhire club will be held on Monday the 13ft inftant, at the bunch of grapes, Third ftreet,
JOHN VEVERS, Secretary.
N. B. Any gentlemen of the county defirous of being member's, are requefted to leave their names at the bar, on Friday the 10th inftant.

ANTI-VENERIAL ESSENCE,
Prepared and Sold by Dr. YELDALL, at his Medicinal Ware-houfe two doors from Walnut- ftreet in Second-ftreet.

THIS Effence not only cures the difeafe in all its degrees, and in fuch manner that the patient need not be hindered from his bufinefs, or his condition be made known to his moft intimate acquaintance, but will alfo effectually prevent catching the infection: Proper directions will be given in print, fo that no queftions need be afked, *(price two dollars.)*   April 4.

To be fold, wholefale and retail, by Henry Johns, four doors below the Friends meeting in Second- ftreet,

AN affortment of hard-ware:
Japanned & plated goods:
Jewellery, &c.
Table knives & forks in ivory, green wood and ftag hafts:
Splitbone, fham buck & various other forts of common ditto:
Carving knives and forks:
Fine convex, and Barlow's beft penknives:
Fine pocket knives:
Sciffors:
Lancets, and polifhed warrant- ed razors:
Scarificators for cupping:
Cork fcrews:
Plated and fteel fpurs:
Sewing needles:
Ivory and horn combs:

Japanned waiters and tea trays:
Tin and japaned tea pots and coffee-pots:
Tin difhes and plates for can- teens in parcels:
Pontypool japaned tea kettles:
Tea kitchens and table croffes:
Silver enamelled and japaned bottle labels:
Wine and beer glaffes:
Leather bottle ftands:
Brafs cocks:
Brafs and japanned table and tea candlekicks:
Chamber candleflicks, with fnuffers and extinguifhers:
Green and white wax tapers:
Pewter plates, bafons, & fpoons:
Plated table fpoons

In CONGRESS, *November 8, 1777.*
Refolved,

THAT Major General Heath be directed forth- with to caufe to be taken down the name and rank of every commiffioned officer, and the name, former place of abode, occupation, fize, age and defcription of every non-commiffioned officer and private foldier, and all other perfons comprehended in the Convention, made between Lieutenant-Gene- ral Burgoyne, and Major-General Gates, on the 16th of October, 1777, and tranfmit an authentic copy thereof to the Board of War, in order that if any officer, foldier, or any other perfon as above- mentioned of the faid army, fhall hereafter be found in arms againft thefe States in North-America, during the prefent conteft, he may be convicted of the offence, and fuffer the punifhment in fuch cafe inflicted by the law of nations.

That Major-General Heath be directed to take the parole in writing of the officers, according to the Convention, and tranfmit authenticated copies of fuch paroles to the Board of War.

NOVEMBER 22, 1777.
The Committee to whom were referred the return of ordnance and ftores, taken from the enemy fince the 19th day of September, and the letter from the Council of Safety of New-York, and to whom their former report was recommitted, having taken the fame into confideration, beg leave to obferve.

" That there is no mention in the faid return of ftandards, military cheft, medicines or tents.

" That the quantity of powder is very fmall, being only fifteen barrels grained, and two barrels mealed, and the quantity of fixed ammunition very inconfiderable. That the mufkets amount only to 4647, a number not equal to the prifoners who furrendered agreeable to the Convention of Sara- toga, and all thefe mufkets are returned " unfit for fervice." That there are only 638 cartouch boxes. That the number of bayonets is greatly inferior to the mufkets, and thefe as well as the cutlaffes, are returned " without fcabbards" or belts. In fhort, the whole return feems very inadequate to a well appointed army, and to what might be expected from the anfwers returned by Lieut. Gen. Bur- goyne to the firft propofitions made by Major Gen. Gates.

" Your Committee therefore are of opinion, that an enquiry ought to be made into the caufes of this deficiency." Whereupon,

Refolved, That the Prefident immediately fend an exprefs to Gen. Gates, and defire anfwers to the following queftions, viz.

What is become of the ftandards belonging to the refpective regiments in Gen. Burgoyne's army?

Where is the military cheft and medicines?

What is become of the cartouch boxes?

How comes the quantity of powder and cartridges to be fo fmall?

How comes it that the number of mufkets is lefs than that of the prifoners, and that all the muf- kets are unfit for fervice?

How comes the number of bayonets to be fo greatly inferior to that of mufkets?

Where are the fcabbards and belts of the bayonets and cutlaffes?

Was there any deftruction, wafte, removal or con- cealment, of the arms, tents, colours, treafure

WOMEN AND CHILDREN ON THE WAR FRONT

By Eric H. Schnitzer

REVOLUTIONARY WAR ARMIES GENERALLY INCLUDED "followers"—noncombatants who were sutlers, refugees, or (most commonly) soldiers' wives and children. Women and children endured the same living conditions and suffered the same privations as the soldiers in an army, which sometimes included a lack of food, clothing, and shelter. Like soldiers, women labored intensely, fulfilling the roles of laundresses, seamstresses, and nurses. Children were expected to work as well.

But there were exceptions. In rare cases, followers included women and children of the middle or upper classes whose husbands formed part of an army's officer corps. Such was the case in Lieutenant-General John Burgoyne's army, in which six such women and five children followed the British forces as they attempted to make their way from Canada to Albany, New York. Their class protected them from the labors that the hundreds of soldier wives and children toiled upon.

One upper-class woman, Lady Christian "Harriet" Acland, chose to brave the rigorous conditions of the Northern Campaign of 1777 in order to be with her husband, a major in the British army. Daughter of an Earl, Lady Acland suffered—she was almost burned to death when her tent caught fire from an overturned candle, and her husband was almost killed in the Battle of Bemis Heights (October 7, 1777). Both accounts of these events, and how Lady Acland dealt with them, were published in the February 29, 1780, edition of the *Edinburgh Advertiser*. However, other women suffered far worse; the husband of one of Lady Acland's traveling companions, Anne Reynell, was killed in the Battle of Freeman's Farm (September 19, 1777), leaving their four young children fatherless. Their stories are only two from the many followers whose husbands died in the service—in some cases, women and children lost their own lives while suffering an army life.

MOLLY PITCHER FIRING CANNON AT BATTLE OF MONMOUTH
Library of Congress

Although women were not allowed to fight, some took the initiative to do so anyway. One of the most famous was Mary Hayes ("Molly Pitcher") who helped load a cannon in the 1778 Battle of Monmouth, NJ.

The following true and affecting story, is taken from Lieutenant General Burgoyne's state of the expedition from Canada.

BESIDES the continuation of difficulties and general fatigue, this day was remarkable for a circumstance of private distress too peculiar and affecting to be omitted. The circumstance to which I allude is Lady Harriet Ackland's passage through the enemy's army, to attend her wounded husband then their prisoner.

" The progress of this lady with the army could hardly be thought abruptly or superfluously introduced, were it only for the purpose of authenticating a wonderful story. It would exhibit, if well delineated, an interesting picture of the spirit, the enterprize, and the distress of romance, realized and regulated upon the chaste and sober principles of rational love and connubial duty.

" Lady Harriet Ackland had accompanied her husband to Canada in the beginning of the year 1776. In the course of that campaign she had traversed a vast space of county, in different extremities of season, and with difficulties that an European traveller will not easily conceive, to attend her husband, in a poor hut at Chamblee, upon his sick bed.

" In the opening of the campaign of 1777, she was restrained from offering herself to a share of the fatigue and hazard expected before Ticonderago, by the positive injunctions of her husband. The day after the conquest of that place, he was badly wounded, and she crossed the Lake Champlain to join him.

" As soon as he recovered, Lady Harriet proceeded to follow his fortunes thro' the campaign; and at Fort Edward, or at the next camp, she acquired a two-wheel tumbril, which had been constructed by the artificers of the artillery, something similar to the carriage used for the mail upon the great roads of England. Major Ackland commanded the British grenadiers, which were attached to General Fraser's corps, and consequently were always the most advanced post of the army. Their situations were often so alert, that no person slept out of their clothes. In one of these situations a tent, in which the major and Lady Harriet were asleep, suddenly took fire. An orderly serjeant of grenadiers, with great hazard of suffocation, dragged out the first person he caught hold of. It proved to be the major. It happened, that in the same instant she had, unknowing what she did, and perhaps not perfectly awake, providentially made her escape, by creeping under the walls of the back part of the tent.

" The first object she saw, upon the recovery of her senses, was the Major on the other side, and in the same instant again in the fire, in search of her. The serjeant again saved him, but not without the major being severely burned in his face and different parts of the body. Every thing they had with them in the tent was consumed.

" This accident happened a little time before the army passed the Hudson's river. It neither altered the resolution nor the chearfulness of Lady Harriet; and she continued her progress, a partaker of the fatigues of the advanced corps. The next call upon her fortitude was of a different nature, and more distressful, as of longer suspense. On the march of the 19th, the grenadiers being liable to action at every step, she had been directed by the Major to follow the route of the artillery and baggage, which was not exposed. At the time the action began she found herself near a small uninhabited hut, where she alighted. When it was found the action was becoming general and bloody, the surgeons of the hospital took possession of the same place, as the most convenient for the first care of the wounded. Thus was this lady in hearing of one continued fire of cannon and musketry, for four hours together, with the presumption, from the post of her husband at the head of the grenadiers, that he was in the most exposed part of the action. She had three female companions, the Baroness of Reidesel, and the wives of two British officers, Major Harnage and Lieutenant Reynell; but in the event their presence served but little for comfort. Major Harnage was soon brought to the surgeons, very badly wounded; and a little time after came intelligence that Lieutenant Reynell was shot dead. Imagination will want no helps to figure the state of the whole groupe.

" From the date of that action to the 7th of October, Lady Harriet, with her usual serenity, stood prepared for new trials; and it was her lot that their severity increased with their numbers. She was again exposed to the hearing of the whole action, and at last received the shock of her individual misfortune mixed with the intelligence of the general calamity; the troops were defeated, and Major Ackland, desperately wounded, was a prisoner.

" The day of the 8th was passed by Lady Harriet and her companions in common anxiety; not a tent, nor a shed being standing, except what belonged to the hospital, their refuge was among the wounded and dying.

" When the army was upon the point of moving after the halt described, I received a message from Lady Harriet, submitting to my decision a proposal (and expressing an earnest solicitude to execute it, if not interfering with my designs) of passing to the camp of the enemy, and requesting General Gates's permission to attend her husband.

" Though I was ready to believe (for I had experienced) that patience and fortitude in a supreme degree, were to be found, as well as every other virtue, under the most tender forms, I was astonished at this proposal. After so long an agitation of the spirits, exhausted not only for want of rest, but absolutely for want of food, drenched in rains for twelve hours together, that a woman should be capable of such an undertaking as delivering herself to probably in the night, and unce ⸺ hands she might first fall into, ap ⸺ above human nature. The assista ⸺ bled to give was small indeed; I ⸺ cup of wine to offer her; but I w ⸺ found, from some kind and for ⸺ little rum and dirty water. All ⸺ to her was an open boat and a f ⸺ ten upon dirty and wet paper, to ⸺ recommending her to his protecti ⸺

HOUSE OF LORDS, *Feb.* 21.

THE *Marquis of Rockingham* when he brought up the petition from the planters and merchants trading to Jamaica, took notice of the shameful negligence of ministry, with respect to that valuable island, notwithstanding frequent representations from the Governor and Council which had been disregarded.—The dependence of that island on the crown of Great Britain could only be ascribed to the interposition of providence, as the expedition intended against it had proved abortive, by the troops being attacked with sickness. The petition stated three particulars. *First,* That no attention had been paid to frequent remonstrances by his Majesty's ministers. *Second,* That no force had been detached for defence of the island: and, *Third,* That its present situation was in the last degree precarious.

Lord Sandwich declared, that the three particulars stated in the petition were all false. He wished a day might be appointed to take it into consideration, when it would appear ministry had paid every attention to Jamaica, that at present it was in a state of security, and when the day of investigation did come, he and his colleagues in administration would, he trusted, be found to deserve honour in place of being found guilty of any neglect or criminality.

The *Marquis of Rockingham* replied, that Jamaica had been neglected, in proof of which he read part of a letter from Governor Dalling, to Sir Henry Clinton, which says, " D'Estaing is every day expected here. We rely upon you to send us the earliest assistance, as the military force at this time within the island is *extremely trifling, and entirely unequal to its defence.*"

Lord Sandwich said, that the Marquis should also have informed the house, that Sir H. Clinton had detached a proper naval and military force to the assistance of Jamaica, which was only stopt, on intelligence that D'Estaing had left those seas.

The *Marquis of Rockingham* maintained, that that detachment would have come too late had D'Estaing persisted in his attack.

Here a long altercation took place betwixt the Marquis and Lord Sandwich, upon stationing ships off the leeward and windward islands. Lord Sandwich said, he consulted Sir Hugh Palliser in most cases, and acted by his advice, as he always found it good. No man was better able to give good counsel. He did not care though all the world heard him say so, it was the truth. The petition was ordered to lie on the table.

HOUSE of COMMONS, *Feb.* 21.

Mr. Smith member for Nottingham informed ⸺ which the old ground of the nature of the petitions and protests was once more travelled over. The ministry condemned the petitions and associations as factious, libellous, and tending to harass government. They maintained, that the protestors ⸺

Another winter is over, and nothing has been either attempted, or done of consequence by his Excellency Gen. Howe. The British army, thank heaven, was in good health, and in good spirits, and the general continues to be preparing for something, if we are to credit report; but when any thing material is to be done, no common augur can tell. We were often told during the winter, that Mr. Washington's army was inferior in numbers to the British; sickly, dying, ill clothed, ill fed, dispirited, and by no means so well armed as our troops; all which I verily believe.

But what avails all this to us? although we might add, and with truth, that our troops are better officered, and better disciplined, without disrespect to Mr. Washington's officers; still it answers no good end to Britain, since the prudence of Gen. Howe does not think it fit to hazard a battle or disperse the rebels.

Neither ancient nor modern history can produce any thing equal to the campaigns spent in North America, since the sword has been unsheathed against the insurgents. Armies of regular, well disciplined troops, furnished amply with all necessaries for war, officered with a set of old experienced veterans, and troops that never turned their backs when led on! yet year after year goes on and no exertion is attempted to crush rebellion, and ... back to their revolted subjects, that ... judgment, or spirit, ... is to set the whole ...

Even t... graceful separa... nor the unfor... ate, seem...

... empire, in 1778 ... we are on the eve of losing an empire; unless some guardian spirit rises amongst us, like that which directed and conducted with honour and glory our last war with France and Spain.

PASTOR FIDO.

For the EDINBURGH ADVERTISER.
A REMEDY for the BITE of a MAD DOG.
Discovered by a GENTLEMAN of SILESIA, and published by order of the KING of PRUSSIA.
[Sent to Scotland by Earl MARSHAL, and approved of by some eminent physicians of this place.]

TWENTY-four of the insect called Meloë Majalis or May-bug, cut into small pieces:
Two drachms of ebony wood, finely scraped:
One drachm of Serpentaria or Virginia snakeroot, nicely pulverized.
One drachm of rasped lead.
Twenty grains of clunn cignn giglrium.
Two ounces of treacle; or, in place of it, the inspissated jui... the fruit of the ... tree.
All these ing... well kneaded ... and made into a ... aste with the hon... insects are kept in...

with scissars and thrown ... put into a glass with some ... be well covered, and ke... place. If, after some tim... to have dried up, some mo... and thus, with proper ... keep for two or three year... the black-coloured insects ... seventy-five of the gold... quart of honey, measure o...

DOS

Age.
From one to three years old
—— three to six
—— six to twelve
—— twelve to twenty
—— twenty to thirty
—— thirty upwards

N. B. This dose to be dim... the constitution of the patie... the breast, the nurse is to ta... When a person bit by a ... the medicine, as prescribed, ... for twenty-four hour... and for twelve hour ... t time he finds ... some tea ... can ...

GOOD AND FAITHFUL ALLIES

Introduction

DURING A HARSH WINTER AT THE VALLEY FORGE ENCAMPMENT, GENERAL Washington and Prussian military officer Baron von Steuben helped breathe new life into the American army with modernized drills, tactics, and disciplines. The poorly supplied soldiers began to see themselves as professionals. In spring 1778, British Commander William Howe returned to England with blame for the loss at Saratoga, an American victory that motivated a French alliance and further bolstered American confidence as demonstrated at the Battle of Monmouth, where the Patriots faced off against new British Commander Henry Clinton.

EDINBURGH ADVERTISER
May 29, 1778

WASHINGTON AND LAFAYETTE
AT VALLEY FORGE
BY JOHN WARD DUNSMORE
Library of Congress

VALLEY FORGE WINTER ENCAMPMENT

By Wayne Bodle

THE 1777–78 VALLEY FORGE WINTER CAMP WAS A harrowing experience for the Continental Army, but not one that brought it near the breaking point. It was neither the proverbial "darkest hour" nor the "turning point" of the Revolution. The operational effects of Friedrich Steuben's training of the troops at Valley Forge were real enough, but its decisive effect on the outcome of the Revolution has not been proven by historians. By July 1777, General Washington led a much different group of soldiers—newly recruited and inexperienced in combat—from the men who ended the 1776 campaign successfully at Trenton and Princeton. While losing battles at Brandywine and Germantown and surrendering the rebel capital at Philadelphia, they fought with spirit and some real effectiveness. Washington brought the army to Valley Forge in December as part of a political bargain to protect the fragile state government of Pennsylvania and persuade the Continental Congress to help professionalize the force.

At Valley Forge, the army experienced two brief periods of desperate material shortage for about ten days in late December and then for two weeks in February 1778. Fortunately for Washington, the second crisis hit during the two-month-long visit to camp by a committee from Congress. Sharing the crisis showed the politicians the weaknesses of America's first truly complex mass organization better than words ever could have. The May 12, 1778, *Edinburgh Advertiser* reprinted Washington's February 18 appeal to mid-Atlantic farmers to raise more cattle, reflecting hard realities. With the area

By July 1777, General Washington led a much different group of soldiers—newly recruited and inexperienced in combat—from the men who ended the 1776 campaign successfully at Trenton and Princeton.

near Valley Forge drained of provisions, flour and bread were imported from parts of the Chesapeake Region that had long since abandoned tobacco cultivation, while beef cattle were driven on the hoof from New England. Unless the middle states replenished their productive capacities, planning for a new campaign was futile. Washington's letter was written during the army's worst supply disruption of the year, however, which brought shared hardship to local civilians, and it is not clear what, if any, positive effects it had.

The March 7, 1778, letter from a "Gentleman in Philadelphia," printed in the *London Chronicle* nearly two months later, was insightful on a local scale but quite inaccurate in strategic terms. General William Howe exploited the Continental Army's midwinter paralysis by supporting local Loyalists in a "kidnapping campaign" to break the political backbone of the American rebellion. Exactly the kinds of individuals mentioned ("tax-gatherers," "committee-men," and "justices") were targeted, and important local revolutionaries did not sleep quietly that spring. British forces had no realistic hope, however, of "large reinforcements." France's entry into the war on the American side led British planners to shift forces from North America to focus on a West Indian and Atlantic defensive strategy. The continental war moved into the southern states, and the rebels were offered generous terms of peace essentially to repeal the Declaration of Independence. Congress ignored the proposal with a kind of studied contempt.

Congress's May 27, 1778, agreement on a new "Establishment" for the army, as printed in the August 26, 1778, *New-Jersey Gazette*, was a broad compromise between the continued resistance by many of its members, especially New Englanders, to an expensive, dangerous, unrepublican "standing army" and the growing realization by many Americans that independence could not be won by minutemen. Friedrich von Steuben's training of the army that winter paid important morale and other dividends, but how effectively it would intersect with the reorganization plan was unknowable before the American victory at Yorktown in 1781.

General John Burgoyne, the British general defeated at Saratoga in October of 1777, arrived in Britain on May 13, 1778, to defend his conduct in that battle. Far from bringing "good news," his arrival presaged a growing sense in British circles that the effort to crush the rebellion was doomed. Ironically, on May 18, as "Pastor Fido" wrote the *Edinburgh Advertiser* to articulate that pessimism, the resigned British commander William Howe was feted by his officers in Philadelphia in a "Meschianza" as he left them to contest Burgoyne's account. Fido's morose predictions may seem quite recognizable to members of a modern global generation for whom counterinsurgency operations have often proved more frustrating than gratifying. For most Britons, however, the decades after 1783 brought increasing "glory." The British state defeated Napoleonic France, consolidated in Asia and Africa a "Second Empire" more valuable than the first, and led the world into an industrial epoch. For Americans, the fruits of perseverance at Valley Forge were still five long and mostly exhausting years in the future.

The March to Valley Forge, December 16, 1777
by William B. T. Trego
American Revolution Center
(current location)

Valley Forge was not the proverbial "darkest hour," but the Continental Army did experience two brief periods of desperate material shortage.

defence, but it would appear in its pro-
, and then he would be ready to abide
gment of the house, which he doubted
ld be in favour of the king's servants.
Pulteney observed, that the minister had
d, that this country was in a state of de-
did he mean the island of Britain alone,
re all our dependencies to be left exposed?
, he could prove that government had
of the sailing of the Toulon fleet on
se'ennight; and though the wind had
r for some time, not a ship had been or-
to follow them, nor was even a council
pon so important a subject till Wednes-
This inactivity was the more inexcuseable,
had actually at Spithead eighteen sail of
e fit to put to sea. He mentioned this re-
cumstance, that it might be in the memo-
he house when it should come before them
ther shape hereafter.
motion went in the affirmative.

Wednesday, May 6.
order of the day being read for a vote of
to his Majesty of 1,000,000 l. Mr. T.
end rose to oppose it upon the ground of
tion, and incapacity in the servants of the
; drew an exaggerated picture of our na-
defence, having, as he said, a militia
t arms, who were going to be encamped
t tent equipage; and a navy, either not
l or not victualled, but lying embayed at
d for the mere parade of a naval review.
the Toulon fleet had sailed on its expedi-
which might prove fatal to the distant
ents of the British empire. As to Great
, its situation must be deplorable when
afts and towns are daily stripped, and the
thrown into consternation by the enemies
ers.

Fenton, one of the lords of the admi-
replied to that part which respected the
said he had the happiness of assuring the
that the fleet was both manned and vic-
d for any expedition. With regard to the
ations of the American privateer, it was
ptom of the national imbecility, as Thurot
very height of our glory last war, an-
our coasts in a similar manner; but he
ery reason to believe the American priva-
as by this time taken, four frigates having
spatched for that purpose.

C. Fox censured the conduct of the mi-

out time enough for the king to sign them, and
that they had gone through all the official forms.
and were despatched to Portsmouth before nine
o'clock that evening: therefore he wished, that
no *general* imputation might be thrown on the
ministry, but that a proper inquiry might take
place, and that the blame, if any there was,
might fall only where it was found due. As to
the sailing of any part of the fleet, it was judged
improper to detach any squadron of it, till the
internal safety of Great Britain could admit of
it.

Mr. *Fox* confessed the candour of the noble
lord, but urged, that the language of despondence now came from administration and not
from opposition; reprobated the narrow policy
that kept that vast fleet for the internal defence
of this island, which, he said, had force and
magnanimity enough still to repel any force
France could land in it; said he should rather
hear of a body of French troops having invaded
it, than that the distant territories of the empire
should be thus timorously sacrificed to her in-
glorious safety.

Lord *G. Germaine* said, he had spoken fairly
and openly, nor did he mean to hold a language
of despondency; so far from it, that should
Monf. D'Estaing have sailed to America, he
trusted our fleet would arrive in time to punish
him for any attempt to oppose the British arms.

Mr. *Burke* spoke next, for near two hours,
represented the premier as the man who had tri-
fled away the favourable winds of fortune; the
nodding Palinurus, who had lashed the rudder
fast, and left the state vessel in the midst of the
storm: he said Sir William Howe, with 36,000
men, was likely to be in a similar predicament
with that of Mr. Burgoyne; for as they received
their daily bread from the sea, who was their
present mother and guardian, as soon as the
French admiral domineered it over the American
seas, which must soon be the case, as Lord Howe
had no force to look him in the face, they
must surrender to him at discretion. He concluded, by lamenting that we had nothing but
prayers left for it, and that the only consolation
we could find was, that the noble Lord was
about to turn priest, when he found himself
incapable of being any longer a minister.

Sir *Edward Astley* said, he should not give his
assent to the vote of credit. He asked whether
government were sure of the allegiance of Canada? and whether they had not received ac-

The following letter was sent on the 18th
ult. from Gen. Washington to the inhabitants of
New Jersey, Pennsylvania, Delaware, Maryland,
and Virginia.

"Friends, Countrymen, and Fellow Citizens,

"After three campaigns, during which the
brave subjects of these States have contended,
not unsuccessfully, with one of the most powerful kingdoms upon earth, we now find ourselves
at least upon a level with our opponents; and
there is the best reason to believe, that efforts
adequate to the abilities of this country would
enable us speedily to conclude the war, and to
secure the invaluable blessings of peace, liberty,
and safety. With this view it is in contempla-
tion, at the opening of the next campaign, to
assemble a force sufficient, not barely to cover
the country from a repetition of those depredations which it hath already suffered, but also
to *operate offensively* and to *strike a decisive blow.*

"In the prosecution of this object, it is to
be feared that so large an army may suffer for
want of provisions. The distance between this
and the Eastern states, whence considerable supplies of flesh have been hitherto drawn, will
necessarily render those supplies extremely precarious. And unless the virtuous yeomanry of
New Jersey, Pennsylvania, Delaware, Maryland,
and Virginia, will exert themselves to prepare
cattle for the use of the army, during the
months of May, June, and July next, great difficulties may arise in the course of the campaign;
it is therefore recommended to the inhabitants
of those states, to put up and feed immediately
as many of their stock cattle as they can spare,
so that they may be driven to this army within
that period. A bountiful price will be given,
and the proprietors may assure themselves that
they will render a most essential service to the
illustrious cause of their country, and contribute
in a great degree to shorten this bloody contest.
But should there be any so insensible to the common interest, as not to exert themselves upon
these generous principles, the private interest of
those whose situation makes them liable to become immediate subjects to the enemy's incursions
should prompt them at least to a measure which
is calculated to save their property from plunder,
their families from insult, and their own persons
from abuse, hopeless confinement, or perhaps a
violent death.
GEORGE WASHINGTON.
Head quarters Valley Forge, Feb. 18.

In Congress Jan. 2. 1778. Congress having,
no further occasion for the service of Esek Hopkins, Esq; who on the 22d of December 1775,
was appointed commander in chief of the fleet
fitted out by the naval committee,

Resolved, that the said Esek Hopkins, Esq
be dismissed from the service of the United
States. CHARLES THOMPSON. Sec.

EDINBURGH ADVERTISER

May 12, 1778

The May 12, 1778, *Edinburgh Advertiser* reprinted
Washington's February 18 appeal to mid-Atlantic
farmers to raise more cattle, reflecting hard realities of
the Valley Forge winter camp.

But having scap'd so well last night,
To yield this time he thought was right.
   At Marlborough they stopt to dine,
Where Doctor Robert did not shine;
For tho' his fast he had not broke,
He cou'd not eat, she turn'd the joke:
And in the sequel you will find
The Lady's joke and how they din'd.

[To be continued in our next.]

Thursday, April 30.

SCOTLAND.

Edinburgh, April 25.

 THE beating orders for the new regiments of Fencible Men are now come down from the War-office.

We are informed that Government have resolved to give two guineas of levy-money in place of one, that being the price paid for Sutherland's Fensibles last war.

On the 24th of March last died abroad, Sir James Kinloch, Bart. He is succeeded in his titles by David Kinloch, of Gilmerton, Esq; his brother.

COUNTRY NEWS.

Northampton, April 27. Last Tuesday an inquisition was taken by William Jackson, Gent. at Mears-Ashby in this county, on view of the body of one Roger Grove, who in attempting to steal some fowls out of a cow-house belonging to one William Bayley, where there were some loose poles lay upon the beams on which the fowls roosted, fell to the ground, by which he received a mortal concussion of the brain, and instantly died. The jury brought in their verdict Accidental Death.

Reading, April 25. Wednesday last Mess. Ajax and Tomlinson, Officers of Excise, and Mr. Smallbone, Clerk to Mr. Pierce, collector, seized 4157lb. of black and green tea, and 431lb. of coffee, valued at upwards of 1000l. in a house, near Lambourne, in this county, which they lodged the same evening in this Borough (52 miles distant from the place of seizure.) The officers of our militia favoured Mr. Pierce with a proper guard for its security.

SHIP NEWS.

Deal, April 28. Came down and sailed immediately the Hercules, Russell, for Antigua; the Elliott, Squires, for Barcelona. Remain in the Downs his Majesty's ships Medway and Buffalo, the Ranger sloop of war, and Greyhound cutter. Wind E. N. E.

LONDON.

Yesterday there was a very numerous Levee at St. James's to pay their compliments to his Majesty on his arrival in town from surveying the dock-yard, &c. at Chatham.

---

clear of incumbrances.

Extract of a Letter from Dantzick, April 10.

" The regiments in Prussia are upon the march, and there are said to be great desertions from them. The Prussian ——— went a few days ago to Pu—— several recruits, and as ot—— at Schidlitz and other Pr—— of them took refuge in th—— zic, and concealed ther—— threw the inhabitants in—— that many of them fled w—— were pursued to the very ——— who seized those they can—— The officers at Dantzick —— the gates sent out some m—— fire upon those who com—— which obliged the Prussia—— sent however our inhabita—— out on account of the ins—— but we hope our tranqu—— when the detachment retu——

" The navigation of t—— interrupted by the like e—— be feared will also affect t—— Vistula, by which the produc—— brought hither."

They write from Cadiz that the departure of the flota, which was fixed for the 16th of April, was still further postponed by order from Court, and that it was not now to put to sea without a strong convoy, which would not be ready before the end of May.

Extract of a Letter from a Gentleman at Philadelphia, to his Father in Glasgow, dated March 7.

" We are all much encouraged by the assurances from Britain of a large reinforcement of troops the ensuing summer, which, I hope, providence will make the happy means of crushing this unprovoked rebellion. The rebel army (and indeed the whole country) are in a most miserable situation for want of almost every necessary. The King's troops in this city are uncommonly healthy. Sickness even to a contagion prevails in the rebel camp; and never a day passes but some deserters come in here, sometimes 40 or 50 together. Several thousands have come in here within these last three months, many of them with their arms. The poor people are so oppressed by Congress and their minions, that we have had several instances lately of tax-gatherers, committee-men, justices, and military officers being brought in, and delivered up here, by the poor people whom they have oppressed. These men have formed themselves into volunteer companies, and have been so active in kidnapping these gentry, that any kind of officer under Congress is not safe to sleep within 20 miles of this city. I think matters at present look very favourable, as the poor deluded people begin to see that they have made an unhappy choice, in renouncing British liberty in exchange for the most cruel slavery ever before exhibited in the large compass of the known world. They rob people indiscriminately of every thing they want for their miserable army;

The March 7, 1778, letter from a "Gentleman in Philadelphia," printed in the *London Chronicle* nearly two months later, was insightful on a local scale but quite inaccurate in strategic terms. General William Howe exploited the Continental Army's midwinter paralysis by supporting local Loyalists in a "kidnapping campaign" to break the political backbone of the American rebellion. Exactly the kinds of individuals mentioned ("tax-gatherers," "committee-men," and "justices") were targeted, and important local revolutionaries did not sleep quietly that spring.

ces this kingdom now labours under, is actually agitating in his Majesty's cabinet; and that the first object of reformation is to be the abolishing the places of governors to dismantled and nomi——

a mixture of rudeness and civility, who they were, and that all the plate must be delivered to them. Lady Selkirk behaved with great composure and presence of mind. She soon directed her plate to be delivered, with which, without doing any other damage, or asking for watches, jewels, or any thing else, (which is odd) the gentlemen made off. Something, however, had been said about their returning; and the Kirkcudbright people were in expectation of a visit last night. There is reason to think that there were some people among them acquainted with persons and places, and in particular, one fellow, supposed to have been once a waiter at an inn in Kirkcudbright. The leader of the party, who was not the Captain of the vessel, told, that their intention was to seize Lord Selkirk, who is now in London; that two other privateers were at hand; and that they had been at Whitehaven, where they had burnt some small vessels, but did not get done what they intended. When the affair was ended, Lady Selkirk, with her family and visitors, left the house. Her Ladyship remained last night at Carlingworth, in order to be near information.

" It appears, that the privateer which did the damage at Whitehaven, landed at one o'clock yesterday morning, and did not sail till ten, so that it could not be the same with the one which landed at the Isle. It is said there are some ships of force at Belfast."

Extract of a Letter from Glasgow, April 27.

" On Friday and Saturday last the 70th regiment of foot arrived here in two divisions from Edinburgh, and on the same days several additional companies belonging to different corps in America passed through here for Greenock in order to be embarked there.

" On Monday the new raised regiment of Argyleshire highlanders marched for Greenock,

[VOL. I.]

THE
NEW-JERSEY GAZETTE.

[NUMB. 38.]

WEDNESDAY, AUGUST 26, 1778.

To the PRINTER of the NEW-JERSEY GAZETTE.

SIR,

SOMETIME ago I had occasion to extract the cube-root to four or five places of figures, but could not recollect the common methods for doing it; and not having logarithms at hand, I sat down to make a rule to answer the present exigency: This led me to consider the subject much further than I at first intended, and produced the following theorems, which may be useful to the mathematician; therefore their publication in your paper will greatly oblige

EXPONENT.

The first and most simple that offered are,

$$\frac{d}{\frac{m}{r}+2rr} = e, \text{ or}$$

$$\frac{2m+r^3}{\frac{m}{r}+2rr} = R$$

$m=$ Resolvend given.
$r=$ Root assumed.
$e=$ Part sought.
$R=$ Root found, and
$d=$ Difference between the resolvend and r^3

These theorems converge fast, and may serve very well for common use, when no great exactness is required at one operation. The third theorem is,

$$2 : \frac{\overline{m}|\frac{1}{2}}{r} + r = R \text{ for the cube root.}$$

$$2 : \frac{\overline{m}|\frac{1}{2}^3}{rr} + 2r = R \text{ for the 4th power.}$$

$$2 : \frac{\overline{m}|\frac{1}{2}^4}{r^3} + 3r = R \text{ for the 5th power, &c. &c.}$$

These expressions always give the value of R too much, if not exactly true; but as the excess is in a

many of first figures in the quotient by 5 as there are correspondent figures to the left hand, between $\frac{m}{r} + rr$, and $2r : \overline{m}|\frac{1}{2}$

But universally, the value of e may be found to six, eight, or ten places of figures, by the first and third

---

In CONGRESS, May 27, 1778.

ESTABLISHMENT of the AMERICAN ARMY.

I. INFANTRY.

RESOLVED, That each battalion of infantry shall consist of nine companies, one of which shall be of light infantry; the light infantry to be kept complete by drafts from the battalion, and organized during the campaign into corps of light infantry:

That the battalion of infantry consist of

1 Colonel and Captain,	75 dollars per month.	
1 Lieut. Col. and Captain,	60	
1 Major and Captain,	50	
6 Captains, each - -	40	
1 Captain Lieutenant, -	26 2-3	
8 Lieutenants, each -	26 2-3	
9 Ensigns, each - -	20	

Paymaster, Adjutant, Quartermaster — To be taken from the line. — 20, 13, 13 — In addition to their pay as officers in the line.

1 Surgeon, - - -	60	
1 Surgeon's Mate, - -	40	
1 Serjeant Major, - -	10	
1 Quartermaster Serjeant,	10	
27 Serjeants, each - -	10	
1 Drum Major, - -	9	
1 Fife Major, - -	9	
18 Drums and Fifes, each	7 1-5	
27 Corporals, each - -	7 1-3	
477 Privates, each - -	6 2-3	

Each of the field officers to command a company. The Lieutenant of the Colonel's company to have the rank of Captain Lieutenant.

II. ARTILLERY.

That a battalion of artillery consist of

1 Colonel,	100 dollars per month.	
1 Lieutenant Colonel, -	75	
1 Major, - -	62 1-2	
12 Captains, each - -	50	
12 Capt. Lieutenants, each	33 1-3	

72 Gunners, each - -	8 2-3	
24 Drums and Fifes, each	8 2-5	
336 Matrosses, each - -	8 1-3	

III. CAVALRY.

That a battalion of cavalry consist of

1 Colonel,	93 3-4ths dollars per month.	
1 Lieutenant Colonel,	75	

---

1 Captain, - - -	50 dollars per month.	
3 Lieutenants, each -	33 1-3	
4 Serjeants, each -	10	
4 Corporals, each -	9	
60 Privates, each -	8 1-3	

These companies to be instructed in the fabrication of field works, as far as relates to the manual and mechanical part. Their business shall be to instruct the fatigue parties to do their duty with celerity and exactness; to repair injuries done to the works by the enemy's fire, and to prosecute works in the face of it. The commissioned officers to be skilled in the necessary branches of the mathematics; the non-commissioned officers to write a good hand.

Resolved, That the Adjutant and Quartermaster of a regiment be nominated by the field officers out of the Subalterns, and presented to the Commander in Chief or the commander in a separate department for approbation; and that, being approved of, they shall receive from him a warrant agreeable to such nomination:

That the Paymaster of a regiment be chosen by the officers of the regiment out of the Captains or Subalterns, and appointed by warrant as above; the officers are to risque their pay in his hands; the Paymasters to have the charge of the cloathing, and to distribute the same.

Resolved, That the Brigade Major be appointed as heretofore by the Commander in Chief, or commander in a separate department, out of the Captains in the brigade to which he shall be appointed:

That the Brigade Quartermaster be appointed by the Quartermaster General, out of the Captains or Subalterns in the brigade to which he shall be appointed.

Resolved, That two Aids-de-Camp be allowed to each Major General, who shall for the future appoint them out of the Captains or Subalterns.

Resolved, That in addition to their pay as officers in the line, there be allowed to

An Aid-de-Camp,	24 dollars per month.	
Brigade Major, -	24	
	15	

The Staff officers appointed above the ranks effectively appointed shall thereupon be vacated.

Brigade Majors to ...

Brigade Majors and ... appointed from ... ranks, and be admitted ... same rank they held ... provided that no Aid, Brigade Major or Quartermaster shall have the command of any officers who commanded him while in the line.

Resolved, That whenever the Adjutant General shall be appointed from the line, he may continue to hold his rank and commission in the line.

Resolved, That when supernumerary Lieutenants are continued under this arrangement of the battali...

VOL. XXIX.

THE
EDINBURGH ADVERTISER.

No. 15○

From TUESDAY May 26, to FRIDAY May 29, 1778.

To the PRINTER.

SIR, Hungerford Coffee-house, May 18.

THE arrival of Gen. Burgoyne gave hopes to many loyal subjects, that he had come home with some good news from America.—But alas! nothing has transpired of the kind. Another winter is over, and nothing has been either attempted, or done of consequence by his Excellency Gen. Howe. The British army, thank heaven, was in good health, and in good spirits, and the general continues to be preparing for something, if we are to credit report; but when any thing material is to be done, no common augur can tell. We were often told during the winter, that Mr. Washington's army was inferior in numbers to the British; sickly, dying, ill clothed, ill fed, dispirited, and by no means so well armed as our troops; all which I verily believe.

But what avails all this to us? although we might add, and with truth, that our troops are better officered, and better disciplined, without disrespect to Mr. Washington's officers; still it answers no good end to Britain, since the prudence of Gen. Howe does not think it fit to hazard a battle or disperse the rebels.

Neither ancient nor modern history can produce any thing equal to the campaigns spent in North America, since the sword has been unsheathed against the insurgents. Armies of regular, well disciplined troops, furnished amply with all necessaries for war, officered with a set of old experienced veterans, and troops that never turned their backs when led on! yet year after year goes on and no exertion is attempted to crush rebellion, and bring back to their duty revolted subjects, that either bespeaks wisdom, judgment, or spirit, in those whose province it is to set the whole in motion.

Even the disgraceful captivity of our whole separate army, nor their remaining in the same unfortunate state, seems to have the least effect on the British chief commander in America.—Nor does the declaration of France, of her avowing the American rebels to be an independent people, seem to have any more effect upon our ministers at home, than if such a declaration had never been made.

The business of this kind of war, seems to be nothing more than the sending, at an enormous expence to the nation, a great army and fleet to America, to spend millions of hard guineas amongst a people who have revolted from

him, will slip away where the prospect of less taxes and trade is apparent.

Good God, Mr. Printer, what times do we live in! Was the British spirit ever at such an ebb, or the British glory ever so sunk, for want of men of spirit, resolution and wisdom, to guide and conduct the national concerns? In 1764 we gained and secured an empire; in 1778 we are on the eve of losing an empire; unless some guardian spirit rises amongst us, like that which directed and conducted with honour and glory our last war with France and Spain.

PASTOR FIDO.

For the EDINBURGH ADVERTISER.
A REMEDY for the BITE of a MAD DOG.
Discovered by a GENTLEMAN of SILESIA, and published by order of the KING of PRUSSIA. [Sent to Scotland by Earl MARSHAL, and approved of by some eminent physicians of this place.]

TWENTY-four of the insect called Meloë Majalis or May-bug, cut into small pieces:
Two drachms of ebony wood, finely scraped:
One drachm of Serpentaria or Virginia snakeroot, nicely pulverized.
One drachm of raf
Twenty grains
Two ounces o
inspissated ju

All these ing
and made into
sects are kept i

As the princi
insect above me
particular descri
it is to be gather
the patient.

The common
Scarabæus Melo
use of is a Melo
indifferently.
bæus, also called
his Elem. Eutom.
this insect. It is almost as large as the finger, and an inch and a half long. The female is larger than the male. It has no wings, but small elytra, that is, a kind of strong hard wings, or rather sheaths, (jus coleopter), which serve as a cover for their softer wings, not for flying with, and reach to the half length only of the body. They are softer than in other kinds, black, mark'd with points, without lustre; for this reason the insect cannot fly, but moves slowly. His body is in general soft, tender, and black, surrounded with blue, green, and

are to be gathered in the month of May, in dry and warm day; but particular care must taken not to touch them with the fingers, b cause they will immediately drop their juice, ar therefore they must be taken up with small bi of wood, or pincers, without squeezing then and put into a vase. The heads are to be cut o with scissars and thrown away, and the bodie put into a glass with some fine honey, which mu be well covered, and kept in a dry temperat place. If, after some time, the honey is foun to have dried up, some more fresh may be added and thus, with proper care, the insects wil keep for two or three years. Two hundred o the black-coloured insects, or a hundred an seventy-five of the gold coloured, require quart of honey, measure of Berlin.

DOSE.

Age.	Men.		Women	
	dra.	gr.	dra.	gr
From one to three years old	0	24	0	20
—— three to six	0	30	0	26
—— six to twelve	0	40	0	30
—— twelve to twenty	1	0	0	50
—— twenty to thirty				

ell, or burnt.—In winter the chamber is to be kept warm. If the bite has caused a wound, it must be washed with some wine, beer, or vinegar, which last is to be mixed with fine salt, but salt-water alone will do as well. This to be repeated from time to time. The wounded part to be wrapped up in a linen cloth dipped in warm vinegar, and the wound dressed with a plaister of basilicon, or with fresh wet salt butter, and often touched with oil of scorpion, or with oil of olives wherein Meloës have been steeped. This is done in order to keep the wound open that it may be well cleaned; it will afterwards heal of itse

EDINBURGH ADVERTISER
May 29, 1778

General John Burgoyne, the British general defeated at Saratoga in October of 1777, arrived in Britain on May 13, 1778, to defend his conduct in that battle. Far from bringing "good news," his arrival presaged a growing sense in British circles that the effort to crush the rebellion was doomed. Ironically, on May 18, as "Pastor Fido" wrote the *Edinburgh Advertiser* to articulate that pessimism, the resigned British commander William Howe was feted by his officers in Philadelphia.

himself in removing his head quarters from Boston to New York; and from New York to Philadelphia. Where he is next to go

antenna are composed of twelve articulations; the fore and middle feet have five of them, but the binder feet have only four. Whenever it

overheat him; all strong liquors, and, in general, all kinds of excess.

As to animals, the following rules are to be

FRENCH-AMERICAN ALLIANCE

By Julia Osman

THE FRENCH-AMERICAN ALLIANCE CONSISTED OF MORE than the Treaties of Amity and Commerce and of Alliance, signed on February 6, 1778. While the treaties stipulated that France would send America aid in its war against Great Britain, France had already been unofficially supporting the colonists for two years. With the support of King Louis XVI, Caron de Beaumarchais, the famous French playwright, had created a special merchant company specifically to send substantial amounts of military supplies and money to the American colonies. French officers, such as the Marquis de Lafayette, frustrated at the lack of opportunity to prove their worth in combat in Europe, sailed to America to offer their military expertise to the American Congress. The rebelling American colonies had excited the French state and its people for two major reasons: on one hand, Great Britain, France's greatest rival for European and global power, would suffer greatly if it lost its thirteen American colonies. Eager to incapacitate Britain, the French were happy for any reason to make "unjust seizures…upon the ships and goods" of the English king (*London Gazette*, August 1, 1778). While King George III took care to justify his decision to "procure reparation," the "two crowns" had never been interested in maintaining peace for too long. On the other hand, the possibility of an independent America generated a great deal of genuine excitement, as American colonists seemed to be pursuing a way of life and government that closely mirrored French Enlightenment ideals of virtue and patriotism.

The possibility of an independent America generated a great deal of genuine excitement, as American colonists seemed to be pursuing a way of life and government that closely mirrored French Enlightenment ideals of virtue and patriotism.

Adding fuel to the pro-American fire, Ben Franklin arrived in Paris in December 1776 to facilitate an alliance with France that would include supplies and military aid. He wooed the French court and intellectual circles by presenting himself as the quintessential "American" that French readers had come to expect. With the victory of the Battles of Saratoga, Louis XVI finally expressed his happiness in "acknowledging the Independence of America" in 1778 (*Continental Journal*, May 14, 1778). While desiring an American victory over Britain for years, France now felt for certain that it could enter the war on the side of the victors. Louis XVI resolved to send military aid. Initial attempts to land French troops in America under the command of General d'Estaing were unsuccessful, but the Comte de Rochambeau arrived with several French regiments in 1780 in Newport, Rhode Island. Rochambeau, in turn, served "under the orders of General Washington." While European armies had reputations as plunderers and looters, French troops did prove to be "under the strictest discipline" while in America, and relationships between American citizens and the French army were generally cordial (*London Chronicle*, October 17, 1780)

The treaty of Amity and Commerce sealed the French-American alliance, but it also hints at more revolution to come. Made "for reciprocal advantage of their subjects and citizens," the treaty itself recognized that "subjects" of a monarchy were becoming "citizens" in an American Republic, a condition that would soon apply to the French, just six years after the Treaty of Paris ended the American Revolution (*Independent Chronicle*, December 10, 1778). By pledging money, supplies, and troops, and by celebrating the American Revolution, France had set the stage for its own.

Numb. 11896.

The London Gazette.

Published by Authority.

From **Tuesday** July 28, to **Saturday** August 1, 1778.

AT the Court at *St. James's*, the 29th of *July*, 1778,

PRESENT,

The KING's Most Excellent Majesty in Council.

WHEREAS many Injuries and Acts of Hostility have been committed, and many unjust Seizures made, by the French King and his Subjects, unto and upon the Ships and Goods of His Majesty's Subjects, contrary to the Faith of Treaties; and whereas His Majesty has lately received Advice, that such Acts of Hostility are now Publickly encouraged and authorized by the French King's Orders: His Majesty has taken into Consideration these injurious Proceedings of the French Court; and His Majesty, being determined to take such Measures as are necessary for vindicating the Honour of His Crown, and for procuring Reparation and Satisfaction for His injured Subjects, is pleased, by and with the Advice of His Privy Council, to order, and it is hereby ordered, That General Reprizals be granted against the Ships, Goods and Subjects of the French King, so that as well His Majesty's Fleet and Ships, as also all other Ships and Vessels that shall be commissionated by Letters of Marque or General Reprizals, or otherwise by His Majesty's Commissioners for executing the Office of Lord High Admiral of Great Britain, shall and may lawfully seize all Ships, Vessels and Goods belonging to the French King or his Subjects, or others inhabiting within any of the Territories of the French King, and bring the same to Judgment in any of the Courts of Admiralty within His Majesty's Dominions; and to that End His Majesty's Advocate-General, with the Advocate of the Admiralty, are forthwith to prepare the Draught of a Commission, and present the same to His Majesty at this Board, authorizing the Commissioners for executing the Office of Lord High Admiral, or any Person or Persons by them empowered and appointed, to issue forth and grant Letters of Marque and Reprizal to any of His Majesty's Subjects, or others whom the said Commissioners shall deem qualified in that Behalf, for the apprehending, seizing and taking the Ships, Vessels and Goods belonging to the French King, and the Vassals and Subjects of the French King, or any inhabiting within his Countries, Territories or Dominions; and that such Powers and Clauses be inserted in the said Commission as have been usual, and are according to former Precedents: And His Majesty's Advocate-General, with the Advocate of the Admiralty, are also forthwith to prepare the Draught of a Commission, and present the same to His Majesty at this Board, authorizing the said Commissioners for executing the Office of Lord High Admiral, to will and require the High Court of Admiralty of Great Britain, and the Lieutenant and

Judge of the said Court, his Surrogate or Surrogates, as also the several Courts of Admiralty within His Majesty's Dominions, to take Cognizance of, and judicially proceed upon, all and all Manner of Captures, Seizures, Prizes and Reprizals of all Ships and Goods that are or shall be taken, and to hear and determine the same; and according to the Course of Admiralty, and the Laws of Nations, to adjudge and condemn all such Ships, Vessels and Goods as shall belong to the French King, or the Vassals and Subjects of the French King, or to any others inhabiting within any of his Countries, Territories and Dominions; and that such Powers and Clause be inserted in the said Commission as have been usual, and are according to former Precedents: And they are likewise to prepare, and lay before His Majesty at this Board, a Draught of such Instructions as may be proper to be sent to the Courts of Admiralty in His Majesty's Foreign Governments and Plantations, for their Guidance herein; as also another Draught of Instructions for such Ships as shall be commissionated for the Purposes afore-mentioned.

AT the Court at St. *James's*, the 10th of *July*, 1778,

PRESENT,

The KING's Most Excellent Majesty in Council.

WHEREAS the Names of many of the Officers serving in the respective Regiments and Battalions of Militia, within the several Counties in England and Wales, have been frequently returned by the Judges in the List of Persons proper to be appointed Sheriffs, notwithstanding such Officers are by Law exempted from serving the Office of Sheriff, during the Time of their Service in the Militia: And whereas the Impropriety of such Returns has proceeded from the Want of Information being given to the Judges of the Names of the several Officers serving in the Militia, from whence many Inconveniencies have arisen: His Majesty, in order to

---

LONDON GAZETTE
August 1, 1778

The rebelling American colonies had excited the French state and French people. Eager to incapacitate Britain, the French were happy for any reason to make "unjust seizures . . . upon the ships and goods" of the English king.

MAY 14, 1778

The
CONTINENTAL
JOURNAL

Extract of a letter from a gentleman in Nantes, to another in this town, dated 25ᵗʰ March, 1778.

"It must undoubtedly give you great pleasure, my dear friend, to hear that our Independency is acknowledged in form by the Court of France. On the 20th instant, the Commissioners were received at Versailles as Ministers Plenipotentiary of the United States of America, and the next day the English Ambassador went off without taking leave. Orders are given to seize all English vessels that are found in any French port, and an open declaration of war is daily expected. At the reception of our ministers, the King (addressing himself to Dr. Franklin) said, he was happy in acknowledging the Independence of America, and that the conditions of the treaty on the part of France, should be faithfully observed: The Doctor answered to the same effect on the part of Congress. In England they are in the most humiliating confusion, they are driven to the last resource, and want to make peace with us at any rate; peace, peace is the cry of the nation; but as the weak ministers have still the foolish hope of persuading us to renounce our Independence, I imagine their plan will only be another public proof of their foolish obstinacy."

It is rumoured, That the late news from England, is very unpleasing to the Tories in New York--has fixed a surly gloom on their countenances---fear works so hard on some of them that they are privately packing up in order to decamp.

CONTINENTAL JOURNAL (BOSTON)
May 14, 1778
—
With the victory of the Battles of Saratoga, Louis XVI finally expressed his happiness in "acknowledging the Independence of America" in 1778.

NEW-HAVEN, May 6.

Monday last came to town, Major-General BENEDICT ARNOLD; he was met on the road by several Continental and Militia Officers, the Cadet Company, and a number of respectable inhabitants from this place, to testify their esteem for one who has, by his bravery, rendered his country many important services. On his arrival in town, he was saluted by a discharge of thirteen cannon.

PROVIDENCE, May 9.

Capt. Whipple, in the Providence frigate, who sailed from this port last week, in his passage down the Bay, was fired on by the Lark frigate, which lay near Warwick Neck, and had got under way; Capt. Whipple returned the compliment with a broadside, and we since learn killed three and wounded seventeen of the Lark's crew; her hull and rigging were likewise much damaged. The Juno frigate, the lowermost of the enemy's ships, fired a broadside at the Providence as she passed, and received another, but with what effect we have not yet learnt. Capt. Whipple likewise poured a broadside into a tender that got under sail, and shattered her so much that the enemy were obliged to haul her to a wharf at Newport, where she sunk. The enemy's ships did not follow Capt. Whipple to sea as was reported.

BOSTON, May 14.

Yesterday being the annual meeting for the choice of Representatives for this town the ensuing year, the following Gentlemen were chosen, viz.—Hon. JOHN HANCOCK, Esq; Hon. WILLIAM PHILLIPS, Esq; Hon. JOHN PITTS, Esq; OLIVER WENDELL and CALEB DAVIS, Esq'rs; Mr. ELLIS GRAY and JOHN LOWELL, Esq;

Extract of a letter from a gentleman in Nantes, to another in this town, dated 25th March, 1778.

"It must undoubtedly give you great pleasure, my dear friend, to hear that our Independency is acknowledged in form by the Court of France. On the 20th instant, the Commissioners were received at Versailles as Ministers Plenipotentiary of the United States of America, and the next day the English Ambassador went off without taking leave. Orders are given to seize all English vessels that are found in any French port, and an open declaration of war is daily expected. At the reception of our ministers, the King (addressing himself to Dr. Franklin) said, he was happy in acknowledging the Independence of America, and that the conditions of the treaty on the part of France, should be faithfully observed: The Doctor answered to the same effect on the part of Congress. In England they are in the most humiliating confusion, and are driven to the last resource, and want to make peace with us at any rate; peace, peace is the cry of the nation; but as the weak ministers have still the foolish hope of persuading us to renounce our Independence, I imagine their plan will only be another public proof of their foolish obstinacy."

It is rumoured, That the late news from England, is very unpleasing to the Tories in New-York—has fixed a surly gloom on their countenances---fear works so hard on some of them that they are privately packing up in order to decamp.

Tuesday last arrived a Ship from Nantz in five weeks.

A Letter from Head-Quarters, dated May 2d, mentions as a report, that General Amherst and Admiral Keppel were arrived at Philadelphia.

The lengthiness of the Valuation Act, obliges us to omit several articles of intelligence, particularly the late patriotic exertions of the ladies in the towns of Andover and Mendon, towards their pastors.

STATE of MASSACHUSETTS BAY.

A Proclamation for Dissolving the Great and General Court of said State.

WHEREAS the Great and General Court of

STATE OF MASSACHUSETTS BAY.

In COUNCIL, Roxbury, April 6 1778.

WHEREAS it is represented to this Court, that some of the Men inlisted into the public Service for the Defence of Rhode-Island, are not possessed of Fire Arms, but are willing to furnish themselves, if they knew where to purchase them:

Therefore, RESOLVED, That the Board of War, be, and they hereby are impowered and directed to sell Fire Arms to any such Persons as are, or may be engaged in the public Service of this State, and shall apply to them for the same, at such Price as they may judge reasonable. And the Secretary is directed to publish this Resolve in the next Thursday News Papers.

Sent down for Concurrence.

JNO. AVERY, Dep. Sec'y.

In the House of REPRESENTATIVES,
April 29, 1778. Read and concurr'd.
J. PITTS, Speak. pro Tem.

Consented to by the Council,

A true Copy. Attest J. AVERY, D. Sec'ry.

STATE OF MASSACHUSETTS-BAY.
IN THE HOUSE OF REPRESENTATIVES,
APRIL 28. 1778.

WHEREAS it appears by the Returns made into the Secretary's office, that in many instances the same have been returned for several towns as one seventh part of their male inhabitants for the Continental army, by which means the compleating this State's quota of said army has been greatly delayed. For remedy whereof, and in order that the deficiencies of each town may be exactly and speedily known:

RESOLVED, That Daniel Perry, Abner Ellis, and Thomas Crane, Esq'rs; be a committee for the county of Suffolk; Samuel Osgood, Esq; Col. Israel Hutchinson and Major Joseph Page, a committee for the county of Essex; Col. Eleazer Brooks, Capt. Joseph Hosmer and Col. Cyprian Howe, a committee for the county of Middlesex; Mr. Willis Hall, Israel Nichols, Esq; Col. Jacob Davis, Dr. William Dunsmore and Capt. Timothy Page, a committee for the county of Worcester; Justin Ely, Esq; Mr. Elijah Hunt and Col. Ruggles Woodbridge, a committee for the county of Hampshire; John Turner, Esq; Mr. Benjamin Thomas and Col. John Gray, a committee for the county of Plymouth; John Greenough, Solomon Freeman, Esq'rs; and Mr. Joseph Snow, a committee for the county of Barnstable; Thomas Durfee, Shubael Peck and Samuel Toby, Esq'rs; a committee for the county of Bristol; Joseph Simpson, John Frost and Thomas Cutts, Esq's; a committee for the county of York; John Waite, Esq; Mr. Paul Little, and John Lews, Esq; a committee for the county of Cumberland; Dummer Sawall, Esq; Col. Samuel McCobb, and Nathaniel Thwing, Esq; a committee for the county of Lincoln; and Capt. William Bacon, Joel Woodbridge, Esq; and Capt. William King, a committee for the county of Berkshire.

And it is further RESOLVED, That said committees be, and hereby are invested with full powers to hear and determine all disputes arising from returns made in manner aforesaid, between the several towns and companies within the county for which they are respectively appointed; and said committees are hereby directed as soon as may be to notify by writing the time and place at which they will meet the selectmen and military officers of the several towns within the county for which they are respectively appointed; and in case the officers or selectmen of any such town or company as shall have made returns in manner aforesaid, shall refuse or neglect to appear and defend their claims before said committees, they shall nevertheless proceed to hear and determine the cause upon such evidence as they shall be able to obtain; and said committees are hereby directed to transmit to the Secretary's office on or before the 20th of June next, a particular account of their proceedings, together with the number of men each town within their county is deficient, in order to compleat one seventh part of their male inhabitants, in consequence of having made such wrong returns as aforesaid. And it is further

Resolved, That there be allowed said committees for each man per day the sum of eighteen shillings for his time and expences (including horse-hire) whilst attending said service; which together with all other charges arising thereon, shall be paid as the General Court shall hereafter order.

And whereas it is represented to this Court that several towns or companies have returned men as part of their respective quotas of the Continental army, who were inlisted or drafted to do duty as guards, or otherwise for short terms in Continental pay:

Resolved, That the aforesaid committees be directed to make full enquiry into this matter, and make report to this Court of those towns or captains of companies who have returned such men, and order said captains immediately to detach other men, agreeable to the true

TO BE SOLD, BY
JOSEPH RUSSELL, and SON,
At their Store in BEDFORD,

ABOUT 3000 wt. of Spermaceti Candles, cheap for Cash.

TO BE SOLD,
By PUBLIC AUCTION,
On WEDNESDAY the 20th current,
At Nine in the morning,
At the shop of the late THOMAS LEVERETT, deceased, in Cornhill,

All the Stock in Trade belonging to the estate of the said deceased;—Consisting of a large and valuable collection of BOOKS, in divinity, law, history, and the classicks.—Among the collection are the following, viz.—Bibles; testaments, psalters, primers, spelling-books, Watts's psalms and hymns, Tate and Brady's psalms, singing-books, Dodridge's rise and progress, &c. &c.—A large assortment of account-books, and sundry other stationary, &c. &c.

RUSSELL & CLAP, Auctioneers.

TO BE SOLD, BY
J. HOOPER and F. BOARDMAN,
At Cruft's wharf, North end, Boston,
On WEDNESDAY the 20th May instant,
The following articles, viz.

Sundry Sails very good, suitable for a ship of 350 tons; a quantity of cordage, blocks, iron, &c. a ship's bell; an anchor about 1800 wt. some twine, duck, &c.

The sale to begin at eleven o'clock, A. M.

TO BE SOLD, by T. & J. FLEET,
Mr. FISKE's SERMON,
preached at Brookfield, on the day of the interment of Mr. Joshua Spooner, who was most barbarously murdered at his own gate by three ruffians, who were hired for the purpose by his wife.

STRAYED from the subscriber in Reading, the 22d of April last, TWO COLTS, one a brown Mare, three years old, has a small star in her forehead, shoes on her fore feet, has been but little used, trots and paces both; the other a red horse-colt, one year old.——Whoever will take up said colts and bring them to the subscriber at Reading, or inform him of them, so that he can find them, shall have TEN DOLLARS Reward and all necessary charges paid by JOSEPH HOLT.

RAN-AWAY from me the subscriber, a NEGRO MAN named FORTUNE, about 50 years of age, talks very broken English; had on when he went away, a grey coat and jacket, and leather breeches. Whoever will take up said run-away, and return him to his master at Reading, shall be handsomely rewarded, and all necessary charges paid by me,
NATHAN PARKER.

NOTICE is hereby given that the proprietors unimproved Land belonging to THOMAS FLUKER, Esq; and the heirs of Col. SAMUEL WALDO, deceased, lying in Warren, in the county of Lincoln, are taxed in the sum of thirty five pounds four shillings and three pence; the owners of said Lands are requested to pay the same speedily, to prevent further proceeding according to law. JOSEPH COPELAND, Constable.

PUBLIC NOTICE.

TAKEN into Custody by Jonas Dix and Leonard Williams, Esqrs; of Waltham, in the County of Middlesex, a Person, with two Pieces of 7 8 Linnen Cloth, not of the best Kind, loose roll'd, and which no doubt were stolen. The Owner by applying to the Justices, may serve both himself and the Public.

IN the County of Hampshire, in the Province of the Massachusetts Bay.

AGreeable to the Directions given in the present Tax-Bill,—Public Notice is hereby given, That the non-resident Land hereafter named, lying in the Town of Leverett, are indebted by a Tax in equal Proportion to the other Lands in said Town, (viz.) Mr. Thomas Dickenson for Lot No. 12, £1 0 3. Huppin's Heirs for Lot No. 15, £1 6 10, and Lot No. 16, £1 10 10. Owners not known, Lot No. 19, £0 16 8. Lot No. 50, £1 1 5. Captain Ayres's Land, £2 9 2. George Nye's Land, £3 10 10. Samuel Hinckley's Land, £1 0 0. James Convus's Land, £0 9 2. Mr. Chandler's Land, £0 12 0.—The above Sums are to be paid to Joseph Smith and Moses Keep. The Owners of which are requested

LONDON CHRONICLE

October 17, 1778

While European armies had reputations as plunderers and looters, French troops did prove to be "under the strictest discipline" while in America, and relationships between American citizens and the French army were generally cordial.

INDEPENDENT CHRONICLE (BOSTON)

December 10, 1778

On February 6, 1778, the French signed two treaties: the Treaty of Alliance and the Treaty of Amity and Commerce, which officially sealed the French-American alliance with political and commercial support. However, France had been unofficially supporting the colonists for two years already with military supplies, money, and French officers, such as the Marquis de Lafayette.

REPORTING THE
BATTLE OF MONMOUTH

By Michael S. Adelberg

THE AMERICAN REVOLUTION FUNDAMENTALLY changed for the British in 1778. France's entry into the war forced the British to shift military resources elsewhere in the Empire and shift from an offensive to a defensive posture in America. The first task of the new British commander, Henry Clinton, was quitting Philadelphia and consolidating forces in New York.

In June, the British army began its march across New Jersey. The march was slow and difficult from the start. In his July 5, 1778, report (printed in the *London Gazette Extraordinary* on August 24, 1778), Clinton complained "the obstructions we met with were frequent," as the New Jersey Militia felled bridges, fouled wells, and skirmished with their advance parties. Clinton also reported being "encumbered by an enormous provision train" that "extended near 12 miles." Another report suggested fourteen miles. On June 27, Clinton paused at Freehold (Monmouth Court House) to rest his weary troops.

After enduring the famous winter encampment at Valley Forge, the Continental Army was improved by newly arrived European drill masters—such as Baron von Steuben—and fresh recruits. Under command of the Marquis de Lafayette and then Charles Lee, the vanguard of the Continental Army marched into New Jersey with the main body of the army, commanded by George Washington, trailing behind.

On the morning of June 28, Clinton sent his provision train east toward Sandy Hook and turned to face the gathering Continentals. The British drove the Continentals back through the morning, but the Continental lines stiffened when Washington arrived with more men. Well-positioned artillery gave the Continentals the upper hand in the late afternoon. Lee was blamed for disorderly leadership that morning and court-martialed shortly after the battle (see December 22, 1778, *London Chronicle*). Clinton ignored all

of this in his report, claiming instead that his men halted because they "were so over-powered with fatigue" and heat. Indeed, officers from both armies claimed that the heat took as many lives that day as the enemy.

At sundown, the battlefield quieted. Clinton reported taking "advantage of the moonlight" to retreat and reunite with his provision train. The evacuation to New York was completed without serious opposition. Clinton's report downplayed the high cost of the Monmouth Campaign, omitting mention of the massive desertions (reportedly 1,800 men) and the humiliation of leaving behind forty-five wounded at Freehold. He also neglected to mention soldier misconduct during the march, including the arson of a dozen homes near Freehold.

After the battle, stories swirled about the wife of a Continental soldier who risked her life carrying water and munitions to the men during the battle and taking her husband's place at his cannon when he fell. Tales of heroic women at different Revolutionary War battles mixed together, resulting in the Molly Pitcher legend. Though much of the Molly Pitcher legend is unlikely, it is well understood that hundreds of women—wives, daughters, mistresses, and refugees—followed the armies and performed important support roles throughout the war.

Both commanders claimed victory after the Battle of Monmouth. Clinton reported that his strategic objective—reaching New York—was achieved. He claimed that he merely wished to protect his provision train, but the British maneuvers at the Battle of Monmouth suggest he was trying to rout the Continentals. Though the Battle of Monmouth is often discussed as a draw, it marked the first time that the main body of the Continental Army engaged the main body of the British army and held the battlefield. It was also reported as a Continental victory throughout America, persuading wavering Americans to support the war effort.

The London Gazette

EXTRAORDINARY.

Published by Authority.

MONDAY, AUGUST 24, 1778.

Whitehall, August 24, 1778.

THE following Letter from Lieutenant-General Sir Henry Clinton, Knight of the Bath, to Lord George Germain, One of His Majesty's Principal Secretaries of State, was received on Saturday Night by Colonel Patterson, who arrived in the Grantham Packet from New York.

New York, July 5, 1778.

MY LORD,

I Have the Honor to inform your Lordship, that, pursuant to His Majesty's Instructions, I evacuated Philadelphia on the 18th of June, at Three o'Clock in the Morning, and proceeded to Gloucester Point without being followed by the Enemy. Every Thing being from thence passed, in Safety across the Delaware, through the excellent Disposition made by the Admiral to secure our Passage, the Army marched at Ten o'Clock, and reached Haddonfield the same Day. A strong Corps of the Enemy having, upon our Approach, abandoned the difficult Pass of Mount Holly, the Army proceeded without any Interruption from them, excepting what was occasioned by their having destroyed every Bridge on our Road. As the Country is much intersected with marshy Rivulets, the Obstructions we met with were frequent, and the excessive Heat of the Season rendered the Labour of repairing the Bridges severely felt.

The advanced Parties of our Light Troops arriving unexpectedly at Crosswicks on the 23d, after a trifling Skirmish, prevented the Enemy from destroying the Bridge over a large Creek at that Village, and the Army passed it the next Morning. One Column, under the Command of his Excellency Lieutenant-General Knyphausen, halted near Amely's Town; and as the Provision Train and heavy Artillery were stationed in that Division, the other Column, under Lieutenant-General Earl Cornwallis, took a Position at Allen's Town, which

join them on the Rariton. As I could not hope that, after having always hitherto so studiously avoided a general Action, General Washington would now give into it against every Dictate of Policy; I could only suppose that his Views were directed against my Baggage, &c. in which Part I was indeed vulnerable. This Circumstance alone would have tempted me to avoid the difficult Passage of the Rariton; but when I reflected that from Sandy Hook I should be able, with more Expedition, to carry His Majesty's further Orders into Execution, I did not hesitate to order the Army into the Road which leads through Freehold to the Navesink. The Approach of the Enemy's Army being indicated by the frequent Appearance of their Light Troops on our Rear, I requested his Excellency Lieutenant-General Knyphausen to take the Baggage of the whole Army under the Charge of his Division, consisting of the Troops mentioned in the Margin * Under the Head of Baggage was comprized, not only all the Wheel Carriages of every Department, but also the Bât Horses; a Train which, as the Country admitted but of one Route for Carriages, extended near 12 Miles. The indispensible Necessity I was under of securing these is obvious; and the Difficulty of doing it, in a most woody Country, against an Army far superior in Numbers, will, I trust, be no less so.

I desired Lieutenant-General Knyphausen to move at Day-Break on the 28th; and, that I might not press upon him in the first Part of the March, in which we had but one Route, I did not follow with the other Division† till near Eight o'Clock. Soon after I had marched, reconnoitring Parties of the Enemy appeared on our Left Flank. The Queen's Rangers fell in with and dispersed some Detachments among the Woods in the same Quarter. Our Rear Guard having descended from the Heights above Freehold into a Plain near Three Miles in Length, and about One Mile in Breadth, several Columns of the Enemy appeared likewise descending into the Plain,

formed, of near 12,000 Men, from two strong Positions; but it will, I doubt not, be considered as doubly creditable, when I mention, that they did it under such Disadvantages of Heat and Fatigue, that a great Part of those we lost fell dead as they advanced, without a Wound.

Fearing that my first Order had miscarried, before I quitted this Ground I sent a second, for a Brigade of Infantry, the 17th Light Dragoons, and 2d Battalion of Light Infantry, to meet me on the March, with which additional Force, had General Washington shewn himself the next Day, I was determined to attack him; but there not being the least Appearance of an Enemy, I suspected he might have pushed a considerable Corps to a strong Position near Middletown; I therefore left the Rear Guard on its March, and detached Major General Grant to take Post there, which was effected on the 29th. The whole Army marched to this Position the next Day, and then fell back to another, near Navesink, where I waited two Days, in the Hope, that Mr. Washington might have been tempted to have advanced to the Position near Middletown, which we had quitted; in which Case I might have attacked him to Advantage.

During this Time the Sick and Wounded were embarked, and Preparations made for passing to Sandy Hook Island by a Bridge, which by the extraordinary Efforts of the Navy was soon compleated, and over which the whole Army passed in about two Hours Time; the Horses and Cattle having been previously transported.

Your Lordship will receive herewith a Return of the Killed, Wounded, Missing, &c. of His Majesty's Troops on the 28th of last Month. That of the Enemy is supposed to have been more considerable, especially in Killed.

The Loss of Lieutenant Colonel Monckton, who commanded the 2d Battalion of Grenadiers, is much to be lamented.

I am much indebted to Lord Cornwallis for his zealous Services on every Occasion; and I found great Support from the Activity of Major General Grey, Brigadier Generals Mathew, Leslie, and Sir William Erskine.

I beg Leave to refer your Lordship for any other Particulars, which you may wish to be informed of, to Colonel Patterson, who will have the Honor of delivering these Dispatches, and whose Services in this Country entitle him to every Mark of your Lordship's Favor.

I have the Honor to be, &c.
H. CLINTON.

Return of the Killed, Wounded, Missing, &c. of the Troops under the Command of General Sir Henry Clinton, in an Engagement with the Rebel Army, on the Heights of Freehold, County of Monmouth, New Jersey, the 28th of June, 1778.

TOTAL BRITISH.

1 Lieutenant-Colonel, 1 Captain, 2 Lieutenants, 4 Serjeants, 56 Rank and File, *killed*; 3 Serjeants, ... Rank and File, *died with* ... File, *wounded*; 3 Serjeants, 61 Rank and File, *missing*.

1st Battalion of Light Infantry. Hessian Grenadiers, Guards, 3d, 4th, 5th Brigades British.

[Price Three-pence Halfpenny.]

LONDON GAZETTE EXTRAORDINARY
August 24, 1778

France's entry into the war forced the British to shift military resources elsewhere in the Empire and shift from an offensive to a defensive posture in America. The British army's march from Philadelphia across New Jersey to New York was slow and difficult.

EXTRACT from the TRIAL of MAJOR-GENERAL LEE.

Major-general Lord STIRLING, *Prefident.—Brigadier-generals,* Smallwood, Poor, Woodford, *and* Huntington. *Colonels,* Irvine, Shepherd, Swift, Wiggelfworth, Angel, Clarke, Williams, Fehiger, *Members.*
JOHN LAWRENCE, *Judge Advocate.*

Brunfwick, July 4, 1778.

THE Judge Advocate produces the General's orders (Wafhington) for the court to fit. The Prefident, Members, and Judge Advocate, being fworn, the Judge Advocate profecuting in the name of the United States of America, the court proceed to the trial of Major-general Lee, who appears before the court, and the following charges are exhibited againft him: Firft, for difobedience of orders, in not attacking the enemy on the 28th of June, agreeable to repeated inftructions. Secondly, for mifbehaviour before the enemy on the fame day, by making an unneceffary, diforderly, and fhameful retreat. Thirdly, for difrefpect to the Commander in Chief in two letters, dated the 1ft of July and the 28th of June.

Major-general Lee pleads, Not Guilty.

[The letters on which the third charge is founded are as follow:]

Sir, *Camp, Englifh Town, July* 1.
FROM the knowledge I have of your Excellency's character, I muft conclude, that nothing but the mifinformation of fome very ftupid or mifreprefentation of fome very wicked perfon, could have occafioned your making ufe of fo very fingular expreffions as you did, on my coming up to the ground where you had taken poft: they implied, that I was guilty either of difobedience of orders, of want of conduct, or want of courage: your Excellency will therefore infinitely oblige me, by letting me know on which of thefe three articles you ground your charge, that I may prepare for my juftification, which I have the happinefs to be confident, I can do to the army, to the Congrefs, to America, and to the world in general. Your Excellency muft give me leave to obferve, that neither yourfelf nor thofe about your perfon could, from your fituation, be in the leaft judges of the merits or demerits of our manoeuvres, and, to fpeak with a becoming pride, can affert, that to thefe manoeuvres, the fuccefs of the day was entirely owing: I can boldly fay, that had we remained on the firft ground, or had we advanced, or had the retreat been conducted in a manner different from what it was, the whole army and the interefts of America would have rifked being facrificed. I ever had (and I hope ever fhall have) the greateft refpect and veneration for Gen. Wafhington; I think him endued with many great and good qualities, but in this inftance, I muft pronounce, that he has been guilty of an act of cruel injuftice towards a man, who certainly has fome pretenfions to the regard of every fervant of this country; and, I think, Sir, I have a right to demand fome reparation for the injury committed; and, unlefs I can obtain it, I muft in juftice to myfelf, when the campaign is clofed (which I believe will clofe the war), retire from a fervice, at the head of which is placed a man, capable of offering fuch injuries; but, at the fame time, in juftice to you, I muft repeat, that I from my foul believe, that it was not a motion of your own breaft, but inftigated by fome of thofe *dirty earwigs*, who will for ever infinuate themfelves near perfons in high office; for I am really convinced that, when Gen. Wafhington acts from himfelf, no man in his army will have reafon to complain of injuftice or indecorum.

His Excellency Gen. Wafhington.

Head Quarters, Englifh Town, June 28.

Sir,
I RECEIVED your letter (dated through miftake the 1ft of July) expreffed, as I conceive, in terms highly improper. I am not confcious of having made ufe of any very fingular expreffions at the time of my meeting you, as you intimate. What I recollect to have faid, was dictated by duty, and warranted by the occafion. As foon as circumftances will permit, you fhall have an opportunity, either of juftifying yourfelf to the army, to Congrefs, to America, and to the world in general; or of convincing them, that you were guilty of a breach of order; and of mifbehaviour before the enemy on the 28th inftant, in not attacking them as you had been directed, and in making an unneceffary, diforderly, and fhameful retreat. I am, Sir, your moft obedient fervant,
GEORGE WASHINGTON.

General Lee.

Sir, *Camp, June* 30.
SINCE I had the honour of writing my letter by Col. Fitzgerald, I have reflected on both your fituation and mine, and beg leave to tell you, that I think it would be for our mutual convenience and honour, that a Court fhould be immediately ordered—it might be a Court-martial—drawn into length, and all the neceffary evidence collected on a paper war betwixt the parties, which muft keep up feuds on the continent, nor all your admiffion from your love of juftice immediately exhibit your conduct in its true colours, till I may be brought, Sir, your moft obedient humble fervant,
CHARLES LEE.

His Excellency General Wafhington.

The Court met by feveral adjournments till the 12th of Auguft.

The Court having confidered the firft charge againft Major General Lee, the evidence, and his defence, are of opinion, that he is guilty of difobedience of orders, in not attacking the enemy on the 28th of June, agreeable to repeated inftructions; being a breach of the latter part of article 5, fec. 2, of the articles of war.

The Court having confidered the fecond charge againft Major General Lee, the evidence and his defence, are of opinion he is guilty of mifbehaviour before the enemy on the 28th of June, by making an unneceffary, and in fome few inftances a diforderly retreat, being a breach of the 13th article, of the 13th fec. of the articles of war.

The Court having confidered the 3d charge againft Major General Lee, are of opinion, that he is guilty of difrefpect to the Commander in Chief in two letters dated 1ft July and 28th of June, being a breach of the 2d art. 2d fec. of the articles of war.

The Court do fentence Major General Lee to be fufpended from any command in the armies of the United States of North America, for the term of 12 months.
STIRLING,
M. G. and Prefident.

The Court adjourn without day.

This Day was publifhed,
Neatly printed on a fine paper, in 2 vols. 12mo, price 6s. fewed, or 7s. bound, and embellifhed with a Half fheet Profpective View, engraved by Walker, of the Royal Review of the Encampment,

COXHEATH CAMP: A NOVEL.
In a SERIES of LETTERS.
By a LADY.
Printed for Fielding and Walker, Pa—

LONDON CHRONICLE
December 22, 1778
—
Despite a strong engagement and demonstration of America's more professional army, the Battle of Monmouth resulted in the court-martial of American Major General Charles Lee for disorderly leadership.

h ult. arrived here a Virginia
pilot boat, which was cut out
ur last Friday night, by 38 Bri-
ho had effected their escape from
here. The schooner had lately
e West Indies, and had part of her
d. These brave men, rendered
e by the hard usage they receiv-
els, had, some time before, pro-
, for their deliverance, and were
ave boarded and brought off the
, of 36 guns; but that vessel be-
e draught of water, and all of
inted with the channel, they
to desist from the enterprize:
owen, late prize-master of the
formerly of this port having
to get on shore last Thursday,
riday night a large boat along-side
hip, with which they boarded the
ere they found three rebels, (now
hip here) a very small quantity
ork, and only ten gallons of wa-
wever, on their passage, boarded
el schooners; and obliged them to
t of their provisions. Off the back
d, they were chased by two rebel
the southward of Barnegat, but
m."

MERICA
Aug. 18. It is reported tha
tely concerted a plan to cut a
woods from the Upper Caho
river, to Canada, in order to
arties into that province; a
gly sent out, under the comma
rk, but before they had m
s they were surrounded b
and totally routed: those
ing in almost famished, in
or fo

from LLOYD's LIST
Sir Charles Hardy ha
f...w all officers to b
...his...d...epare for...

New-York; she proceeds with a fleet of
victuallers.
"The Alexander, Monkhouse, from Granada to Halifax, was taken the 14th of July, by
three American privateers, and carried into Cal-
co Bay.
"The St. Carolo and Pedro, a Genoese ship,
from Sallo to Ferrol, with 340 pipes of wine,
designed for the use of the Spanish fleet, is taken
and sent into Falmouth by the Union and Phœnix cutters belonging to Folkstone.
"The brig Hazard from Scotland, and a brig
from Liverpool, the one of 18 and the other of
16 guns, are taken by Captain Manley, and sent
into Boston.
"The Nancy privateer of New London, of
16 six-pounders, is taken by the Greyhound man
of war, and sent into New York.
"The Snow Bristol Packet, loaded with
dry goods, and the Dashwood Packet, Captain
Roberts, who sailed from Falmouth with the
June mail, are retaken by the Perseus man of
war, Capt. Elphinston, and sent into New York;
the mail thrown overboard.
Bank stock, 111⅞. India ditto, 142¾.
3 per ct. b. red. —— Do. con. 61¼ a ⅜.
L.t Tick. 13l. 14s. 0d Dub. Ex. 7⅝.

EDINBURGH.
Extract of a letter from London, Oct.
everal letters from Amsterdam men
aul Jones was arrived in the Texel
erapis and his other prizes, in a f
on.
rliament, which is to meet on t
mber, will only sit for a few
supplies, and then adjourn for th
is still talked off, the terms o
d, will be, to make America in
ibraltar to Spain, and G
abo...t has agreed to
vo hundred thousan
of Pondich
ycastle

---

party of them had the assurance to come within a
mile of this city, at a place called Paulus Hook,
surprised and carried off with them a number of
British and Hessian soldiers. Within these few
days two rebel privateers have been sent in here
by the Greyhound, frigate."
The following particulars, relative to the
late engagement between Paul Jones and the Serapis man of war, may be depended on as authentic: when Jones first attacked the Serapis, he
was a-head of his little fleet several leagues; notwithstanding this, he engaged with all the fury
of a man determined to conquer or die. The
engagement soon grew desperate, and Jones,
besides having a great part of his crew shot round
him, had his rigging on fire for about seven minutes. In this interval, the Captain of the Serapis, who was so near him as to be audible, called out to him to strike, or he must infallibly
go to the bottom. Jones replied, with an oath,
"I may sink, but I'll be d—d if I strike." At
this instant, one of his men attempted to strike
the colours, when Jones, turning round, shot
him dead on the spot. Two more attempted
the same thing, and met with the same fate; a
mutiny then was expected to take place, as the
ship was appe...sinking, when, fortunately
for Jones, ...his squadron immediately
came up t...ce, which turned the ta-
s on t...and she was obliged to
e, af...degree of co...ch
ould, ...ty, have m...
sful...enemy.
A le...ton in I...
an in...
a...

❧ CHAPTER X ❧

CONQUER
OR DIE

Introduction

BEYOND THE ATLANTIC COAST OF NORTH AMERICA, IMPORTANT BATTLES OF THE
Revolutionary War were also fiercely fought in remote forts of the frontier, as far west as the Mississippi River, and even at the doorstep of Great
Britain. George Rogers Clark, older brother to William Clark of Lewis and Clark
fame, led the militia actions against British posts and their Indian allies in territories
of modern day Ohio, Kentucky, Michigan, Indiana, and Illinois. Also on the western front, General John Sullivan led a force of 4,000 on a scorched-earth campaign
through Iroquois country. Across the globe, American naval captain John Paul
Jones, commanding the forty-two-gun *Bonhomme Richard*, was leading an effective
maritime terror campaign against the British.

EDINBURGH ADVERTISER
October 12, 1779

JOHN PAUL JONES'S
BONHOMME RICHARD
VS THE BRITISH *SERAPIS*
Library of Congress

REVOLUTIONARY WAR IN THE WEST AND GEORGE ROGERS CLARK

By John Reda

I N THE AUTUMN OF 1777, SEVERAL AMERICAN SETTLEMENTS in the future state of Kentucky were under siege. Hostile Indians, supplied and encouraged by British officials in Detroit, posed an ongoing threat to the very lives of the Americans. In desperation, twenty-six-year-old George Rogers Clark started for Virginia—where he had been born and raised—to pitch a desperate plan by which the American settlements might be protected. On his way east, Clark joined a party of seventy-six men and women who had given up on the West and were returning to their old homes.

Once in Virginia, Clark huddled with a group including Virginia's governor, Patrick Henry, as well as Thomas Jefferson, George Mason, and George Wythe. Clark had met a year earlier with these same men to request five hundred pounds of powder desperately needed for the defense of the western settlements. Now his plan involved a daring attack on British holdings in the Illinois Country. Clark explained to Virginia's leaders that spies he had sent to Illinois had returned with the news that the British fort in Kaskaskia was undefended and that the mostly French inhabitants of the scattered Illinois villages were lukewarm in their support of the British. Clark's ultimate target was Detroit, where Lieutenant Governor Henry Hamilton was coordinating the Indian attacks that were ravaging the frontier. Known to settlers as the "Hair Buyer," Hamilton was rumored to be paying a bounty for scalps taken in the raids. Clark's plan was to occupy Illinois as a stepping-stone to an attack on Detroit that might stop the Indian raids at their source.

With no hope of receiving help from the near destitute Continental Congress, Clark's appeal to Virginia's leaders reflected that state's claim on much of the West—based on its original colonial charter. Armed with the authorization

for an expedition described to Virginia's Assembly as a defense of Kentucky, Clark headed west to recruit volunteers. His efforts met with meager results as most men already in the West were more concerned with protecting their families and farms than attacking British holdings.

When Clark set out on June 26, 1778, from the Falls of the Ohio (present-day Louisville), his forces numbered just 175 men, although all were buoyed by the recent news that France had formally agreed to join the American war against Great Britain. After traveling ten miles down the Ohio River, Clark and his men set off on foot on a 120-mile overland march to Kaskaskia, where they arrived on July 4, 1778, surprising the fort's commander, Rocheblave, and taking the town without losing a man. In fact, Clark's men did not even fire a shot. Gathering the inhabitants the next morning, Clark offered American citizenship to all willing to take an oath in support of the United States. The Kaskaskians, relieved to learn that the feared Americans meant them no harm, accepted Clark's offer and sent representatives ahead to the other Illinois villages where similar scenes ensued.

Two months later, Clark convened a council of Indians where he bluntly offered them a choice between war and peace. Although many would later again take up arms against the people they called the "Long Knives," the American Indians accepted Clark's offer and the winter of 1778–79 saw a marked decrease in Indian attacks against American settlements. In the meantime, however, Henry Hamilton led a British and Indian force down from Detroit to capture the American-held fort at Vincennes on the Wabash River.

In February 1779, Clark responded to Hamilton's move by collecting ninety American and eighty French volunteers for an excruciating 180-mile march across waterlogged lands to come to the relief of Vincennes. Wading for days through water often up to their chests, Clark's force surprised Hamilton and forced his surrender. The fort, now renamed Patrick Henry, was again in American hands.

Because of the distances involved, numerous inaccuracies about Clark's exploits made it into eastern newspapers. Contrary to an item in the *Connecticut Journal* (June 9, 1779), Clark did not put Hamilton to death, but rather placed him in custody and sent him east to be held as a prisoner of war at Virginia's capital of Williamsburg.

Nor did Clark and his men move on to capture Fort Detroit, as claimed by the *Boston Gazette* (January 18, 1779). In fact, Clark spent much of the next three years trying to organize an expedition against Detroit but failing at any point to gather the necessary men or supplies to do so. Instead, as printed in Clark's own words by the *Pennsylvania Gazette* (October 25, 1780), the Americans had to settle for a 1780 attack against Indian villages north of the Ohio River. Clark led another such attack in 1782 before the 1783 Treaty of Paris brought the Revolutionary War to an end.

GEORGE ROGERS CLARK
AND THE MARCH TO VINCENNES
North Wind Picture Archives

In February 1779, George Rogers Clark, with ninety American and eighty French volunteers, marched 180 miles across waterlogged lands to Vincennes.

WEDNESDAY, June 9, 1779.

THE CONNECTICUT JOURNAL.

[Numb. 606.

NEW-HAVEN: Printed by THOMAS and SAMUEL GREEN, near the College.

WILLIAMSBURG, (Virginia) May 15.

Extract of a letter from Col. Lawson, to his Excellency the Governor, dated Smithfield May 13.

"I Presume your Excellency by this time, is pretty well informed of the strength and movements of the enemy. From accounts which I have received, the cruel and horrid depredations and rapine committed on the unfortunate and defenceless inhabitants who have fallen within their reach, exceed almost every thing yet heard of within the circle of their tragic display of savage barbarity!—Houshold furniture, stock of all kinds, houses, and in short almost every species of perishable property, are effectually destroyed, with unrelenting fury, by those devils incarnate; murder, rape, rapine and violence, fill up the dark catalogue of their detestable transactions!—They surprised and took a small body of Frenchmen, at the Great-Bridge, whom they murdered immediately on the spot, to the amount of seven.—The feelings of humanity are deeply wounded with reflections, on the various and pointed cruelties exercised towards our suffering countrymen, and call aloud for the most strenuous exertions."

Extract of another letter from the same gentleman:

"On my way down from Smithfield, towards Suffolk, I met numbers of the unfortunate inhabitants flying from the rapid approach of the enemy, with such circumstances of distress, as language cannot paint.—I feel no pleasure (I believe your Excellency will think) in numerating and dwelling upon the distresses of our countrymen and fellow creatures; but on the present occasion, they exceed any thing in imagination. The enemy are now in possession of Suffolk, a part of

[...]ning, who is constantly watching his motions, and will not quit it till he sees the end of it."

On the 6th instant, the brig Monmouth, Captain Ingersol, took the brig Constance, Capt. Devereaux, from N York to Surinham; and the sloop Nancy, Capt. Bunyan, from

intercepted by the militia, fourteen killed & sixteen taken prisoners. The enemy have with them three thousand men only; and I have the pleasure to inform you that the militia of the lower counties are turning out with great alacrity."

Published by order of Congress,
CHARLES THOMSON, Sec'ry.

MAY 25.

Extract of a letter from Baltimore, dated May 23.

"The town is nearly clear of all kinds of goods, and many families have moved out; many more daily moving. The militia are getting under arms, and march in freely if required. Our last advices from below are from Hampton, dated on Tuesday night after burning Suffolk and some Whig's houses in its vicinity, the enemy divided their force there, and marched part for South-Quay, and part for Smithfield, a little town higher up James's river. At the latter place our militia were collecting, tolerably well armed, and to all appearance anxious to meet the barbarians, who were committing [...] and wanton outrages on [...] neighbours and countrymen. [...] unjustly to brand an enemy wi[...] inhumanity, but alas! stubborn [...]ly justify the charge.—A ge[...] near Suffolk, assures me, they d[...] tleman of consequence, in bot[...] private life, (one is an inhabit[...] mond county and an old ac[...] yours, therefore it would be pa[...] particularize him) together w[...] ters from their house, and car[...] board their shipping, and th[...] wretched father was loaded w[...] chains, on board the same vessel, the still more wretched [...] were pos[...] of those [...] was shot [...] family, [...] [...]—s, [...] was carried [...] not been [...] 't rouse [...]es. Ar[...] but is [...] he Vir[...] ter, and [...] enemy, [...]ken in [...]oregoing [...] Goodrich is with them, and as insolent as ever. Our town will be cleared of stores and goods in a day or two, and then, if they visit us, we will give them a warm reception. It is time the Whigs should rouse; we have been too long languid and supine."

post St. Vincent, was surprized in the garrison, by a party of Col. Clarke's men, and taken prisoner with all his people and stores; that the Governor and some others were certainly put to death, in consequence of their former cruelties; that a party of warriors, twenty in number, who had been sent to Kentuckey settlement, happened soon after to return, and not knowing of the Fort being re-taken, marched boldly within a few yards of it, expecting that their father (the Governor) was still there ready to receive them with open arms; but were prepared for their reception, killed eighteen the first fire, the other two made their escape with the news to Detroit. This is the third time we have received these accounts, and from different quarters."

In CONGRESS, May 28, 1779.

The Board of Treasury having reported, "That in their opinion it will be impracticable to carry on the war by paper emissions, at the present enormous expences of the [...]"

MAY 27.

Extract of a letter from Fort Pitt, dated May 14.

"The 11th inst. four Delaware Indians arrived here from Muskingum, and brought letters for Col. Broadhead; they say, that Henry Hamilton, Lieut. Governor of Detroit, having some time ago got possession of [...]"

[...] Committee of three, and [...] they be directed to report a plan for the purpose.

The Members chosen, Mr. Dickenson, Mr. Huntington, and Mr. Burke.

Extract from the Minutes,
CHARLES THOMSON, Sec'ry.

In CONGRESS, May 28, 1779.

WHEREAS, it is indispensibly necessary that the greatest œconomy should be introduced in public expenditures.

Resolved, That a Committee of three be appointed to make strict enquiry into the establishments and contingent expences of the respective Boards and Departments, and to consider and report the retrenchments and reformations which shall appear to be practicable and expedient, and that they have power to call for returns from the offices, and for information from the officers of any Department, and to confer thereupon with the Commander in Chief.

The Members chosen, Mr. Dickenson, Mr. Sherman, and Mr. Scudder.

Extract from the Minutes.
CHARLES THOMSON, Sec'ry.

four top-sail sloops, about number of sla[...]

Last Lord[...] eight miles b[...] consisting of [...] infantry, wi[...]

A gentleman from Staten Island, we are told that 30,000 tons of shiping has been taken New York for government service, and that total embargo is laid.

A letter from John Goodrich, sen. to Lord more, at New York, dated at St. George's, Bermuda, 26th July, 1778.

MY LORD,

Be free to trouble you with a few lines of the 8th and 18th of May, from Philadelphia; I g leave to inform your Lordship, after my from the rebels of the 18th of March, I proto New York, from thence to Philadelphia; places I obtained permission for two armed to come with me to this place, to remove ilies, and the small property we saved from their hoyers, to New York, which we are putting r a fine new brig we make free to call the re, and expect to sail in a few days. The of this island are very unfriendly to governd we don't think ourselves or property safe them; we took in our passage to this place ooners and one sloop, one of them a fine long f the pilot-boat construction, with one hundred two hogsheads of tobacco on board; her e armed with twenty carriage guns, and sent a cruise, commanded by Bridger Goodrich, eventy five men. I beg leave to inform your ip, we have now five sail of vessels, well ard compleated with warlike stores, but in the situation of affairs are much retarded in the tion of the business; we have commissions his island as letters of marque; after the exand detention of time in getting them manned, ver they arrive in port where the men of war ey press all our men, and two thirds of our ost in getting a new set of them, of course rs to the service, and we are often obliged to ur vessels out half manned.

g leave to inform your Lordship, that I have tender of our services to Sir Henry Clinton rd Howe, with the whole of our vessels and t, whenever they may choose to call on us, Majesty's service. I humbly implore your i's interposition in endeavouring to secure n we sail those vessels, from being taken on his Majesty's ships, when I assure your Lordt myself, my sons, and every of our vessels, a minute's warning ready for his Majesty's

We have now purchased my old sloop Edand are loading her for London, with tobacg part of the schooner's cargo: I have been

t trade is now carried on from Maryland h Carolina in swift sailing vessels from so

---

Major Rogers Clark, the conqueror of the Illinois, has sent in the late Governor of the British settlement there, a Frenchman by birth, who is now in this city upon his parole, where he will be able to form a judgment of the friendly intentions of his nation to the United States of America, and see clearly the declining state of his employer's power on this continent, now ready to expire.—Major Clark, after regulating the affairs of his late conquest, and having received the submission of sundry Indian nations (many of them hitherto unknown to us) had marched with a chosen body of men and a number of Indian warriors, against Fort D'Etroit, which, from the best accounts, being in a very defenceless condition, and in great want of provisions, there is good reason to conclude is now reduced to the obedience of these States, which will put a finishing stroke to the British interests in these parts, and secure to us the friendship of all the Indian nations who have been chiefly issued out on their scalping expeditions from that abominable magazine. And indeed it appears, that the savages themselves began to suspect the boasted strength of the British Worthies, and to slacken in their readiness to serve them; for some time ago, on being summoned against our settlements, which they were told they could easily plunder and destroy, for that the Big Knives, as the Indians call the Americans, were no more to be dreaded than flies, one of their chiefs, to keep up the allegory, told them, that he had lately seen those very harmless flies turn into wasps and hornets, and sting the Great King's men most severely, and he should not be surprised to behold them quickly turn into snakes and swallow them up, as those animals are accustomed to serve the miserable and helpless frogs.

On TUESDA o'Clock, will be Store on GRAY'S
THE following the Privateer double-fortified En Swivels, 1 Suit Sai cine Chest, a Barge,

To be sold by PUB on TUESDAY (if not previously ALL the Real E Binney situate New-South Meeting commodious and gen extensive Garden well stock'd with an elegant Variety of the very best English Fruit Trees

---

NOTICE is hereby given, before me, In Behalf of E others, against the armed Schoo burthen about 20 Tons, in the ser Great Britain, George Douglas late to be taken and brought into said the Trial of the Justice of the Maritime Court will be held for East Precinct of Pownalborough, 25th Day of February, 1779, at the Forenoon, when all Persons m Cause (if any they have) why the Guns, Tackle and Appurtenances, demned. T. LANGDON, Judg

State of Massachusetts-Bay, Middle District.

NOTICE is hereby given, before me, against the follo Cargoes and Appurtenances, viz. el Nicholson, Esq; Commander Ship of War Deane, and all concer the Snow LIVELY, of about 140 T Morgan late Master: In behalf of Commander of the armed Brigantin and all concerned therein, against FRIENDS, of about 100 Tons bur riot late Master: In behalf of Sam mander of the armed Brigantine concerned therein, against the Sno 100 Tons burthen, John Ness lat of Nicholas Ogilbe, Commander Bunker Hill, and all concerned Schooner DELAWARE, of about Thomas Butler late Master: In Burnell, and others, against the DEL CARMEN, of about 80 Tons late Master: In behalf of George der of the armed Ship Marlborou ed therein, against the Brigantin about 100 Tons burthen, James and against the Effects, Wares an

the SECOND CLASS of the

Dollars in the FIRST CLASS, who ed their Tickets, are requested to or send their Tickets, to be excha

---

BOSTON GAZETTE
January 18, 1779
—

While George Roger Clark's ultimate target was Detroit, Clark and his men did not move on to capture Fort Detroit, as claimed by the *Boston Gazette* (January 18, 1779). In fact, Clark spent much of the next three years trying to organize an expedition against Detroit but failing at any point to gather the necessary men or supplies to do so.

Carriages, and a good Pasture of several Hundred Feet in length and breadth, all adjoining. A fair and un-

is a man of nice ho-
the temptation was
ver his error.
ton and others were
, that Andre came
h a paffport from a
confequently could
deputation compof-
Mr. Elliot, and Mr.
id, the true ftate of
m t Robinfon, and
ch he reiterated the
afe as a perfonal fa-
any friend of ours
g could have been
was ufed. The fact
and object of the
circumftances, there
with flags; and the
t to Mr. Anderfon.
all the formalities,
y, the fanction of a
y his trull
pofe would
ggravation.
rgument b
ination b
s to urge it
Arnold o
out of our
had taken
interview
een in his
This furmi of
linton mire
, and a gs.
t to the la
n. He d at
fo much er
revious to in
fince B
affuring ig
m him, an
ng officer y
t he would
ry t write
with the y
ence thou
d the farce of fend-
in every fenfe defpi-

will not fuffer themfelves to be *perfuaded to give up*, what they have thus become poffeffed of by virtue of one of the *wifeft* laws of this State. A law effentially neceffary to the fafety of the lives and property of the people, who have a right to infift on the ftricteft adherence to it.

Oct. 12. Yesterday a ship of 20 guns, prize to the Mifflin privateer, arrived fafe in port. She was bound from New-York to Newfoundland.

NEW-HAVEN, *October* 12.

Monday and Tuesday laft, Admiral Arbuthnot's fleet left Gardner's-Bay, and ftood to the eaftward;—their deftination not known, but fuppofed to be for Newport.

FISH-KILL, *October* 19.

By the arrival of yefterday's poft from Albany, we have it reported, That Sir John Johnfton had, with a party, faid to be about 500 men, come down the Mohawk river, and advanced within fix miles of Johnftown; when, hearing that a party of our three month's men lay there, he contented himfelf with burning a few houfes, killing and carrying off fome inhabitants—Another party of about 800, commanded by Major Carleton, nephew to Gen. Carleton, came down the Lakes from St. John's and ad... the enemy, are to be included.

RICHMOND, (Virginia) *October* 4.

Extract of a letter from Colonel George Rogers Clarke, to his Excellency the Governor, dated Louifville, Auguft 22, 1780.

By every poffible exertion, and the aid of Colonel Slaughter's corps, we compleated the number of 1000, with which we croffed the river at the mouth of Licking on the 1ft day of Auguft, and began our march the 2d. Having a road to cut for the artillery to pafs for feventy miles, it was the 6th before we reached the firft town, which we found vacated, and the greateft part of their effects carried off. The general conduct of the Indians on our march, and many other corroborating circumftances, proved their defign of leading us on to their own ground and time of action. After deftroying the crops and buildings of Chelcauthy, we began our march for the Picawey fettlements, on the waters of the Big Miame, the Indians keeping runners continually before our advanced guards. At half paft two in the evening of the 8th, we arrived in fight of the town and forts, a plain of half a mile in width laying between us. I had an opportunity of viewing the fituation and motions of the enemy, near their works.

" I had fcarcely time to make the neceffary difpofitions, before the action commenced on our left wing, and in a few minutes became almoft general, with a favage

may if you can catch him."

The Governor of this State hath iffued a proclamation,

fierceness on both fides. The confidence the enemy had in their own ftrength and certain victory, or the want of generalfhip, occafioned feveral neglects, by which thofe advantages were taken that proved the ruin of their army, being flanked two or three different times, drove from hill to hill in a circuitous direction for upwards of a mile and a half; at laft took fhelter in their ftrong holds and woods adjacent, when the firing ceafed for about half an hour, until neceffary preparations were made for diflodging them. A heavy firing again commenced, and continued fevere until dark, by which time the enemy were totally routed. The cannon playing too brifkly on their works, they could afford them no fhelter. Our lofs was about 14 killed and 13 wounded, theirs at leaft triple that number. They carried off their dead during the night, except 12 or 14 that lay too near our lines for them to venture. This would have been a moft decifive ftroke to the Indians, if unfortunately the right wing of our army had not been rendered ufelefs for fome time by an uncommon chain of rocks, that they could not pafs, by which means part of the enemy efcaped through the ground they were ordered to occupy.

" By a French prifoner we got the next morning, we learn that the Indians had been preparing for our reception ten days; moving their families and effects; that the morning before our arrival, they were 300 Warriors, Shawanefe, Mingoes, Wiandatts, and Delawares. Several reinforcements coming that day, he did not know their numbers; that they were fure of deftroying the whole of us; that the greateft part of the prifoners taken by Byrd were carried to Detroit, where there were only 200 regulars, having no provifions except green corn and vegetables. Our whole ftore at firft fetting out being only 300 bufhels of corn, and 1500lb. of flour, having done the Shawanefe all the mifchief in our power, after deftroying Picawey fettlements, I returned to this poft, having marched, in the whole, 480 miles in 31 days. We deftroyed upwards of 800 acres of corn, befides great quantities of vegetables, a confiderable proportion of which appear to have been cultivated by white men, I fuppofe for the purpofe of fupporting war parties from Detroit. I could wifh to have had a fmall ftore of provifions, to have enabled us to have laid wafte part of the Delaware fettlements, and falling in at Pittfburgh, but the exceffive heat and weak diet fhewed the impropriety of fuch a ftep. Nothing could excel the few regulars and Kentuckyans that compofed this little army, in bravery and implicit obedience to orders. Each company vying with the other who fhould be the moft fubordinate."

PHILADELPHIA, *October* 25.

Extract of a letter from his Excellency Governor Jefferfon, of Virginia, to the Prefident of Congrefs, dated Richmond, October 15, 1780, fix o'clock, P. M.

S I R,

" I DO myfelf the pleafure of congratulating your Excellency on the fmall dawn of good fortune which at length appears in the fouth, as you will find by the difpatches I have the honour of inclofing to you, and which I this moment received from General Gates."

S I R, *Burk county, 2d October, 1780.*

" I am, at prefent, about 70 miles from Salifbury, in the fork of the Catabaw, with about 450 horfemen, in purfuit of Colonel Fergufon. On my croffing the Catabaw river I difpatched to different quarters for intelligence, and this evening I was favoured with this news, which you may depend on: That Colonel Clark, of the State of Georgia, with 100 riflemen, forced his way through South-Carolina to Georgia [...] being joined by 700 men, he proceeded to the town of Augufta, and has taken it with a large quantity of goods; but not finding it prudent to continue there, he has retreated to the upper parts of South-Carolina, in Ninety-fix diftrict, and made a ftand with 800 brave men.

" This moment another of my expreffes is arrived from

ded down with oxe-
ll repeat with r ve-
ULDING and WIL-

djutant General, to
c. &c.

ptember 29, 1780.
ady apprifed of the

... Van... Jared Sexton, John Law-
bert, Efquires.

Burlington county. Council, Peter Tallman, Efquire. Affembly, Thomas Fenimore, William Trent, William Hough, Efquires.

Gloucefter county. Council, John Cooper, Efquire. Affembly, John Sparks, Thomas Rennard, Ifaac Kay, Efquires.

The PENNSYLVANIA GAZETTE

RICHMOND *(Virginia) October 4.*
Extract of a letter from Colonel George Rogers Clarke, to his Excellency the Governor, dated Louisville, August 22, 1780.

By every possible exertion, and the aid of Colonel Slaughter & corps, we completed the number of 1000, with which we crossed the river at the mouth of Licking on the 1st day of August, and began our march the 2d. having a road to cut for the artillery to pass for seventy miles, it was the 6th before we reached the first town, which we found vacated, and the greatest part of their effects carried off. The general conduct of the Indians on our march, and many other corroborating circumstances, proved their design of leading us on to their own ground and time of action. After destroying the crops and buildings Chelcauthy, we began our march for the Picawey settlements, on the waters of the Big Miame, the Indians keeping runners continually before our advanced guards. At half past two in the evening of the 8th, we arrived in sight of the town and forts, a plain of half a mile in width laying between us. I had an opportunity of viewing the situation and motions of the enemy, near their works.

"I had scarcely time to make the necessary dispositions, before the action commenced on our left wing, and in a few minutes became almost general, with a savage fierceness on both sides. The confidence the enemy had in their own strength and certain victory, or the want of generalship, occasioned several neglects, by which those advantages were taken that proved the ruin of their army, being flanked two or three different times, drove from hill to hill in a circuitous direction for upwards of a mile and a half; at last took shelter in their strong holds and woods adjacent, when the firing ceased for about half and hour, until necessary preparations were made for dislodging them. A heavy firing again commenced, and continued severe until dark, by which time the enemy were totally routed. The cannon playing too briskly on their works, they could afford them no shelter. Our loss was about 14 killed and 13 wounded, theirs at least triple that number. They carried off their dead during the night, except 12 or 14 that lay too near our lines for them to venture. This would have been a most decisive stroke to the Indians, if unfortunately the right wing of our army had not been rendered useless for some time by an uncommon chain of rocks, that they could not pass, by which means part of the enemy escaped through the ground they were ordered to occupy.

"By a French prisoner we got the next morning, we learn that the Indians had been preparing for our reception ten days; moving their families and effects; that the morning before our arrival, they were 300 Warriors, Shawanese, Mingoes, Wiandatts, and Delawares. Several reinforcements coming that day, he did not know their numbers; that they were sure of destroying the whole of us; that the greatest part of the prisoners taken by Byrd were carried to Detroit, where there were only 200 regulars, having no provisions except green corn and vegetables. Our whole store at first setting out being only 300 bushels of corn, and 1500lb. of flour, having done the Shawanese all the mischief in our power, after destroying Picawey settlements, I returned to this post, having marched, in the whole, 480 miles in 31 days. We destroyed upwards of 800 acres of corn, besides great quantities of vegetables, a considerable proportion of which appear to have been cultivated by white men, I suppose for the purpose of supporting war parties from Detroit. I could wish to have had a small store of provisions, to have enabled us to have laid waste part of the Delaware settlements, and falling in at Pittsburgh, but the excessive heat and weak diet shewed the impropriety of such a step. Nothing could excel the few regulars and Kentuckyans that composed this little army, in bravery and implicit obedience to orders. Each company vying with the other who should be the most subordinate.

SULLIVAN EXPEDITION

By Daniel J. Tortora

BRITAIN RECRUITED INDIAN ALLIES WITH GENEROUS gifts and promised to halt the white settlers that overran native lands. Of the six members in the Iroquois Confederacy, Senecas, Mohawks, Onondagas, and Cayugas joined the British. Christian Tuscaroras and Oneidas sided with the Americans. Since the Battle of Oriskany, Colonel John Butler and Captain William Butler and their Tory militias, along with Mohawk Joseph Brant and his Iroquois, had decimated New York's Cherry Valley and Pennsylvania's Wyoming Valley. Frontiersmen refused to join the Continental Army because they feared for their families' safety, and Indian villages in the region fed and supplied the British army.

General George Washington wanted revenge. He wished to cut off the supplies of Indians and the British, to end the devastating frontier raids, and to free up land for American settlers. In 1779, he ordered an invasion of Indian towns in Northern Pennsylvania, the Finger Lakes, and the Genesee Valley in New York. The *London Chronicle* of October 19, 1779, details the pivotal events of the "Sullivan Expedition" of 1779.

With preparations for the campaign underway, on July 20, Mohawk Joseph Brant, with Indians and Tories, attacked Minisink (letter dated Philadelphia, August 19). A militia company overtook the attackers and a bloody engagement followed.

Major General John Sullivan marched from Easton, Pennsylvania. He traveled across the Poconos to Wyoming. He then followed the Susquehanna River north to Tioga. Brigadier General James Clinton marched west from Schenectady to Otsego Lake. The forces then combined. They had orders to "lay waste" to Indian villages and fields.

On August 11, Sullivan arrived at Tioga. The next day, Sullivan sent a detachment to burn the Indian town of Chemung. When the men completed their task, they chased some Iroquois. The Iroquois ambushed the soldiers, killing several and wounding fourteen.

On August 22, Clinton arrived at Tioga. The combined force of three thousand to four thousand left four days later. On August 29, near the Indian village of Newtown, 1,200 Tories and Indians hid in a breastworks concealed by saplings. Pennsylvania Continentals under Brigadier General Edward Hand, with some Virginia riflemen, detected the intended ambush. Sullivan ordered an attack. The *London Chronicle*'s coverage (October 19, 1779, dateline New York, September 1) exaggerates. In the battle that followed, Sullivan suffered three dead and thirty-nine wounded. The Tories and Iroquois narrowly escaped as the Americans took the high ground, but a dozen of the Tory-Indian force died, and two fell captive.

Sullivan's army then traversed dangerous terrain, burning Indian villages and destroying crops and orchards. Its only major setback involved an ambush set by Colonel John Butler and his Indians. They killed and mutilated most of the men in a small American detachment. Some reports claimed that the killers had even resorted to ritual cannibalism.

Meanwhile, Colonel Daniel Broadhead led Pennsylvanians up the Allegheny from Fort Pitt on August 11. The October 26, 1779, *Maryland Journal* details the expedition. Broadhead's men drove off Indian attackers fifteen miles north of Venango. They advanced "without the least interruption," destroying ten Indian villages before returning to Fort Pitt thirty-three days later.

Citing a shortage of supplies and fearing the dangerous paths, Sullivan ended his campaign in late September without linking up with Clinton and without attacking Fort Niagara. Sullivan, Clinton, and Broadhead destroyed fifty villages, 1,200 houses, vast cornfields, two hundred thousand bushels of grain, and ten thousand fruit trees.

Indians raided the frontier in 1780 and 1781, killing two hundred settlers, but Sullivan's expedition had permanently crippled the Iroquois. The expedition destroyed Britain's food supplies, and the British struggled to support five thousand Indian refugees. It prevented a British campaign in the region and also underscored the divisions that were not unique to New York: brother fought brother. Tribesman fought tribesman. And it secured land along the frontier for American settlers. Many Iroquois settled in Canada and never returned. The British ceded Iroquois lands to the Americans in the 1784 Treaty of Fort Stanwix. Patriot soldiers and speculators soon populated the Indian lands cleared by the Sullivan Expedition.

LONDON CHRONICLE

October 19, 1779

General George Washington wished to cut off the supplies of Indians and the British, to end the devastating frontier raids, and to free up land for American settlers. In 1779, he ordered an invasion of Indian towns in Northern Pennsylvania, the Finger Lakes, and the Genesee Valley in New York. Major General John Sullivan and Brigadier General James Clinton had orders to "lay waste" to Indian villages and fields.

rmed, that the fleet under the
es Hardy, had put into Torbay
to wait for a reinforcement of
, which are to join him from
uth. The sudden return of our
sioned by their having received
united squadrons of France and
ips of the line, besides frigates.
Majesty last Tuesday sent for the
Lord Howe, and having closet-
, jointly the command of the
e Admirals demanded an hour's
ich they returned, and thank-
jesty's offer, on condition that
oved from the board of Admi-
nder his auspices they must ever
eir King and Country.

th-Carolina *Gazette.*

S T O W N, *Sept. 22.*
ve had no direct advices from
ployed upon the Southern ex-
ly know, is, That Count d'Es-
troops as he thought necessary,
site to the Orphan-House, 12
in the night between the 11th
out the least opposition; and
ad been opened between him
hat General Lincoln had been
intosh; and that the Head-
a week ago, were at Cherokee-
annah: That General Count
ith the cavalry, and had not
picket of the enemy, but also
aptains and three privates at
Maitland had abandoned Port-
whole force he had there, on
king off the trunnions from the
ied upwards of 200 men, leav-
groes, for want of means of
s embarkation was made ra-
he Vigilante, the Gallies, and
with an intent to push through
General Prevost at Savannah:

perintendant of Indian affairs)
ped falling into the General's

possible be could have any objection to what concerned the
*Lady; but the plate, he had been informed, was ob-
tained in such a way, from the Allies of his King, that he
was confident the General could not mean to disgrace himself with keeping possession of it.*"

PHILADELPHIA, *October 16.*
Last Sunday arrived from Bordeaux (Old France)
the ship General Mercer, Captain Robinson, and bro't
in with her the ship Minerva, Capt. ———, from Halifax bound to Surinam, loaded with fish, &c.
Extract of a letter from Nantz, dated July 3, 1779.
"The French have 32,000 men at St. Malo, ready to
embark; it is said they only wait the arrival of Compte
D'Orvilliers in the Channel, accounts of which
may be daily expected, as the wind has been for 36
hours past from the westward, and likely to continue.
It is supposed that there is a descent intended on England or Ireland. It is reported that the ships the
Spaniards were to furnish by compact, which is ten sail
of the line, have joined D'Orvilliers, and that the Cadiz
fleet sailed about the fifth ult. The sailing of the English fleet you'll find by the papers. The French have
an army of 40,000 men on the frontiers of Holland,
which will keep the Dutchman quiet, if even his inclination was to be troublesome."

*Extract of a letter from a Gentleman in Bordeaux, dated
July 22, 1779.*
"We have no certain advices from the combined
fleets, expect some very interesting; if any arrives before
the present conveyances leave the river, shall embrace
the opportunity to forward them. Mr. Wedderburne
is nominated to succeed Lord Suffolk; other new nominations are daily expected in the different ministerial
departments of that Kingdom.
"Advices from Spain agree in the determination of
that Court on the blockade of Gibraltar.
"An army is marching into Flanders, under the command of Monsieur, said to pay a visit to Hanover, and
thereby oblige that Electorate to resal her troops in
the pay of Britain from Minorca and Gibraltar, or to
watch the Dutch, and hold them to a strict neutrality."
Extract of a letter from Bordeaux, dated July 20, 1779.
"The grand French fleet, consisting of 32 sail of the
li—— ——h ——lid from B—— ——th of June.
—— ———— ———— coast of
————— ———— e Dutch
———— ———— he coast
———— as a de-
——— l of the
——— the line,
———— adiz the
——— th Am-
——— ain have
——— the line,
——— nation not
known.
"On the ninth of July arrived at Brest, a fleet of

our route upon its banks. But here our march was
rendered still more difficult by the mountains which
jutted close upon the river, forming a continued narrow
defile, allowing us only the breadth of an Indian path
to march upon. In the midst of one of these defiles,
our advanced party, consisting of 15 white m—— ——
Delawares, discovered between 30 ——
landing from their canoes, who having also seen part
of our troops, immediately stripped themselves and prepared for action. Lieutenant Harding, who commanded our advance, disposed his men in a semicircular
form, and began the attack with such irresistible fury,
tomahawk in hand, that the Savages could not long
sustain the charge, but fled with the utmost horror and
precipitation, some plunging themselves into the river,
and others, favoured by the thickness of the bushes,
made their escape on the main, leaving five dead on
the field, without any loss on our side, except three men
slightly wounded. Upon the first alarm, supposing it
to be more serious, the army was arranged for fight,
both officers and men, enraged at their former cruelties, and animated by the calmness, resolution and intrepidity of the commandant, shewed the utmost ardor
to engage; and had the action been general, we had
every prospect of the most ample success from a brave
commander, at the head of brave men. Continuing
our march, we arrived the same day at Buchaloons,
where leaving our baggage, stores, &c. under a guard,
proceeded to their towns with the utmost despatch,
which we found at the distance of about twenty miles
farther, with extensive corn-fields on both sides of the
river, but deserted by the inhabitants on our approach.
Eight towns we set in flames, and committed their pagod and war posts to the river; the corn was our next
object, which, in three days, we cut down and piled into heaps, amounting in the whole to near 600 acres,
without the least interruption from the enemy.
"Upon our return we several times crossed a creek
about ten miles above Venango, remarkable for an oily
liquor, which ouzes from the sides and bottom of the
channel, and the adjacent springs, much resembling
British oil, and if applied to woolen cloth, burns it in
an instant.
"After burning the old towns of Conauwago and
Mahusquachiakoeken, we arrived at Pittsburgh the
14th inst. with the scalps we had taken, and 30,000
dollars worth of plunder, having in the course of 33
days compleated a march of near 400 miles, through a
country the Indians had hitherto thought impenetrable
by us, and considered as a sufficient barrier for the security of their towns, and indeed nothing but the absolute necessity of such a measure, and a noble spirit of
enterprize, could be a sufficient inducement to undertake so arduous a task, and encounter those difficulties
and obstacles which require the most consummate fortitude to surmount."

In C O N G R E S S, *October 14, 1779.*
Resolved, That the thanks of Congress be given to
His Excellency General Washington, for directing, and
to Major-General Sullivan, and the brave officers and
soldiers under his command, for effectually executing

MARYLAND JOURNAL (BALTIMORE)
October 26, 1779

Simultaneous to Sullivan's expedition, Colonel Daniel
Broadhead led Pennsylvanians up the Allegheny from
Fort Pitt on August 11. Broadhead's men drove off Indian
attackers fifteen miles north of Venango. They advanced
"without the least interruption," destroying ten Indian
villages before returning to Fort Pitt thirty-three days later.

The MARYLAND JOURNAL

Extract of a letter from Pittsburgh, September 16, 1779.

"The many savage barbarities and horrid depredations, committed by the Seneca and Muncy Nations upon the Western frontiers, had determined Col. Broadhead, as the most effectual way to prevent such hostilities in the future, and revenge the past, to carry the war into their own country, and strike a decisive blow at their towns.

"On the 11th of August, our little army, consisting only of six hundred and five, rank and file, marched from Pittsburgh with one month's provision; at Mahoning, 15 miles above the Old Kittanning, we were detained four days by the excessive rains, from whence (leaving the river which rolls in a thousand meanders) we proceeded by a blind path leading to Cuscushing, thro' a country almost impassable, by reason of the stupendous heights and frightful declivities, with a continued range of craggy hills, overspread with fallen timber, thorns and underwood, here and there an intervening valley, whose deep impenetrable gloom has always been impervious to the piercing rays of the warmest sun. At Cuscushing (which is 15 miles above Venango) we crossed the Alleghany, and continued our route upon its banks. But here our march was rendered still more difficult by the mountains which jutted close upon the river, forming a continued narrow defile, allowing us only the breadth of an Indian path to march upon. In the midst of one of these [...] our advanced party, consisting of 15 white men [...] Delawares, discovered between [...] landing from their canoes, who having also seen part of our troops, immediately stripped themselves and prepared for action. Lieutenant Harding, who commanded our advance, disposed his men in a semicircular form, and began the attack with such irresistible fury, tomahawk in hand, that the Savages could not long sustain the charge, but fled with the utmost horror and precipitation, some plunging themselves into the river, and others, savoured by the thickness of the bushes, made their escape on the main, leaving five dead on the field, without any loss on our side, except three men slightly wounded. Upon the first alarm, supposing it to be more serious, the army was arranged for fight, both officers and men, enraged at their former cruelties, and animated by the calmness, resolution and intrepidity of the commandant, shewed the utmost ardor to engage; and had the action been general, we had every prospect of the most ample success from a brave commander, at the head of brave men. Continuing our march, we arrived the same day at Buchaloons, where leaving our baggage, stores, &c. under a guard, proceeded to their towns with the utmost dispatch, which we found at the distance of about twenty miles farther, with extensive corn fields on both sides of the river, but deserted by the inhabitants on our approach. Eight towns we set in flames, and committed their pagod and war posts to the river; the corn was our next object, which, in three days, we cut down and piled into heaps, amounting in the whole to near 600 acres, without the least interruption from the enemy.

"Upon our return we several times crossed a creek about ten miles above Venango, remarkable for an oily liquor, which ouzes from the sides and bottom of the channel, and the adjacent springs, much resembling British oil, and if applied to woolen cloth, burns it in an instant.

"After burning the old towns of Conauwago and Mahusquachiakouken, we arrived at Pittsburgh the 14th inst. with the scalps we had taken, and 30,000 dollars worth of plunder, having in the course of 33 days completed a march of near 400 miles, through a country the Indians had hitherto thought impenetrable by us, and considered as sufficient barrier for the security of their towns, and indeed nothing but the absolute necessity of such a measure, and a noble spirit of enterprize, could be a sufficient inducement to undertake so arduous a task, and encounter those difficulties and obstacles which require the most consummate fortitude to surmount."

COURSES OF JOHN PAUL
JONES'S SHIPS
North Wind Picture Archives

John Paul Jones's two cruises
into British waters with
Continental ships *Ranger* (1778)
and *Bonhomme Richard* (1779).

BATTLE OF FLAMBOROUGH HEAD AND JOHN PAUL JONES

By Dennis M. Conrad

JOSEPH CALLO, A RECENT BIOGRAPHER OF JOHN PAUL Jones, has written of the battle between the Continental ship *Bonhomme Richard* and HMS *Serapis* that took place on September 23, 1779, off Flamborough Head, a promontory on England's Yorkshire coast:

"It was an isolated struggle, albeit a particularly bloody one, between two ships that weren't even large enough to be classified as capital ships in the age of sail.... [but it] was to the naval component of the American Revolution what the battle of Saratoga was to the land campaign—it changed everything. The battle's unlikely outcome broadcast to the world that the American Continental Navy not only could fight, it could fight and win."

John Paul Jones was "projecting power" and bringing the war to England. The October 4, 1779, *Birmingham Gazette* report is correct in suggesting that Jones had planned to capture a British city or port town and hold it hostage for ransom. Earlier in the cruise, Jones had tried to capture Leith, the port city for Edinburg, and when thwarted by bad weather had sailed to Newcastle-on-Tyne with the intention of seizing its waterfront and burning the British collier fleet loading there but was dissuaded by the captains of other vessels in his squadron who argued that the attempt was too risky. By the time of the battle, Jones had given up his plans and was preparing to sail to Texel, where a French fleet of merchantmen awaited escort, when his lookouts spied the Baltic fleet approaching Flamborough. This fleet was valuable as it carried naval stores—canvas, rope, and timber—essential to equip the Royal Navy, so Jones decided to attack it.

As the newspaper accounts indicate, the action was long, obstinate, and bloody, although whether the *Alliance* helped or hurt the American cause is still debated. Jones's answer when asked if he was prepared to surrender is probably what was reported in the *Edinburg Advertiser* of October 12, 1779. However, Richard Dale, an officer serving with Jones, in a book written long after the battle, quoted Jones as saying "I have not yet begun to fight," and those words are now immortalized. Contrary to the report in the *Birmingham Gazette* of October 4, 1779, Jones did not shoot members of his crew. When he found two petty officers trying to lower the flag, he ran at them shouting "stop them, shoot them," but when he discovered his pistols were unloaded he threw them at the sailors, knocking one senseless, but he did not shoot or kill them. Portraying Jones as a merciless brute and pirate was a staple of British press coverage of him.

Finally, the newspaper accounts are correct that the shaken Royal Navy leadership sent warships—at least eight—to capture Jones. Arriving at Flamborough Head after Jones had departed, some of the British warships sailed northeast toward Scandinavia, others southeast toward France, and still others cruised British waters, but none spotted Jones's squadron, which zigzagged in the North Sea for ten days and then sailed directly to Texel, the deep-water anchorage for Amsterdam, a neutral, and therefore safe, port.

LONDON, THURSDAY, Sept. 30.

Some Particulars of the Proceedings of PAUL JONES's *Squadron.*

A LETTER from Bridlington, dated Sept. 24, says, " I doubt not but you have heard of the alarming Situation we have been in since Tuesday Night; but thank God, as yet we have been only terrified by this Paul Jones. An Engagement took Place at seven last Night, and continued till two this Morning, between the Serapis Frigate of 44 Guns, assisted by the Countess of Scarborough armed Ship of 22 Guns, and Paul Jones's Ship, the Bonne Homme of 44 Guns, with some smaller Vessels, off Flamborough head, and I am sorry to say that Jones hath now our two Ships with their Commanders, who distinguished themselves in a most gallant Manner, though obliged at last to surrender to superior Force, after having made almost a Wreck of Jones's own Ship. The Serapis had her Masts shot away. Several Sailors made their Escape, and have been examined this Afternoon at the Key, but their Stories are different as to Jones's Loss; some of them say he had 140 Men killed, and his Ship quite a Wreck. They say his Design was to destroy Scarborough, Bridlington, and Hull, with some other Places; and that he intended landing at Flamborough Yesterday Morning, but the Sea ran too high."

A Letter from Hull, dated Sept. 26, which may be depended on, says, " A little past five this Afternoon an Express arrived from Mr. Foster, of Bridlington, to the Mayor of this Place, which relates, that between Eight and Nine this Morning, Paul Jones, with his Fleet, was seen off Flamborough Head, steering to the Northward; that he was scarcely out of Sight, when three Frigates, two large armed Ships, and two Sloops appeared there, (sent by the Admiralty) who immediately pursued the same Course after him, and we are in the most sanguine Expectation of hearing an Account of Jones and his

Service, made the Remainder drunk, sent them on Shore by their own Desire, brought the Ship into the Humber, and she is now in our Dock. We are this Day (Sunday) at Work in mounting 28 Pieces of Cannon, viz. 20 Eighteen pounders, the rest of a smaller Size. The Marquis

On Tuesday morning his of Wales, and the Bishop the Diversion of Stag-hunti rest.

Monf. le Comte D'Orvill signed the Command of the France and Spain, as some Tin in this Paper, it being confir Journal of the 15th Instant. Article. viz-

" Monf. le Comte d'Orvilli ed the Kings Permission to re of the Naval Armament, hir cepted of his Resignation; an Duchauffault is named his S Command: this Officer w vered of the Wound he rece ment off Ushant, arrived h

Lord S―― has assure within these few Days, t respecting the home Defer engage to have 64 Ships c proceed to Sea by the 15th

According to Letters fr have been given there for of the Troops of that Elec embark for America early i Prince Charles of Meckle Brother, goes along with t

A Letter from Portsmo says, " This Day arrived se The rest of the Convoy, cc 100 Sail, were left well 200 of Scilly, under the Care o and a Sloop of War. The Capt. Cornwallis, put into 40 Men killed in the Acti

Another Letter from Por Pearl Frigate, of 32 Guns, George Mountagu, from in here, a Spanish Frigate, ers, and two six Pounders, the St. Dominique. She tern Islands after a bloody Hours and a Half, in whic had 18 Men killed and 58 wounde

T S ― gh H s of F v. 9, a of Ne Wigar Herm Wm. r.―J rchant Andr ilson o Fryer o

DIVIDENDS *to be ma*
Oct. 15, Peter Nouaille of Silk-merchant.――8, Nathan Lancashire, Fustian-manufactu mas late of Bristol, but now o Dealer.――11, George Hudson

into the Humber, and she is now in our Dock. We are this Day (Sunday) at Work in mounting 28 Pieces of Cannon, viz. 20 Eighteen pounders, the rest of a smaller Size. The Marquis of Rockingham has been here some Days, and has had several Meetings with the Gentlemen of the Town respecting its defenceless State. A Man who escaped from Jones's Ship has made Oath before the Mayor, that Jones stood on the quarter-Deck with a Brace of Pistols, and shot by six of his own Men during the Action."

By an Affadavit made by Thomas Berry on 24th Instant, before Humphrey Osbaldiston, one of his Majesty's Justices of the Peace for the East-Riding of Yorkshire, it appears, that Paul Jones's Squadron had been six Days between Berwick and the Humber, and his declared Intentions were to make a Descent somewhere on the Coast; that on Tuesday he ordered all his Oars to be muffled, and the Boats ready to be hoisted out; that on Wednesday Morning the Alliance and Pallas rejoined Jones off Flamborough-Head: and on Thursday Evening about seven o'Clock, they met with the East-Country Fleet, convoyed by a 40 Gun Ship, and an armed Ship, the 40 Gun Ship engaged Jones alone about 4 Hours, till Jones's Fire ceased; having been several Times on Fire and very near sinking, he called to the Alliance for Assistance, which came up, and gave the 40 Gun Ship a Broadside, which being totally disabled struck. Jones's Officers called to the Alliance to hoist out their Boats, as their Ship was sinking, in one of which the Deponent and Six other Men made their Escape to Filey.

In the Engagement between the Serapis and Paul Jones, his Vessel was so disabled, that the Captain of the Serapis called out to Jones to strike, or else he would sink him. To which the latter replied, " that he might if he could; for whenever the Devil was ready to take him, he would rather obey his Summons, than strike to any one." And if another of Jones's Squadron had not come to his Assistance, he would soon have gone to the Bottom. The foregoing Account is from the Affidavits of seven Seamen who made their Escape after the Engagement, before the Mayor of Hull; and they add, that during the Engagement, Paul Jones (who was dressed in a short Jacket and long Trowsers, with about a Dozen of charged Pistols slung in a Belt round his Middle, and a Cutlass in his Hand) shot seven of his Men for deserting from their Quarters; and to his Nephew whom he thought a little dastardly, he said, that " D――n his Eyes, he would not blow his Brains out, but he would pepper his Shins," and had actually the Barbarity to shoot at the Legs of the Lad, who is a Lieutenant on board Jones's Ship.

It was this Morning asserted as a Fact in the City, that Paul Jones's Ship absolutely sunk before the Engagement with the Seraphis was over, and that he got on board another Ship, of equal Force, not above three Minutes before his Ship went to the Bottom.

No Accounts whatever were received of Paul Jones by the several Mails which came to the Post Office this Day, nor by any Express or other

Silk-merc Lancashire mas late of Dealer.―1 Ironmonger London, Gl square, Lond ter, Sussex, and Nathan 19, Wm. E 21, Thomas Wm. Hooke Cooper.―16 Master, Mar of Rippon, V Wood-street and Wright ler.――8, (church-street Mumford-co

Certificate minster, Gro cester; Woo

S T A T
The TI stamped at th liament, are r NICHOLSO Lottery Office where six C and shared; No. 31,591, each, besides

Also their Guinea, Half each, simila (on which t of upwards o liament-street Farmer, at I to Mr. Lane proved for th more from e gained in an as these Plan least Risk be presumed wi Adventurer, be had gratis to any Thin Whole Time others are.

THE
l. s.
Half, 7 1
Quarter, 3 12
Eighth, 1 16
Sixteenth 1
Besides the P

Schemes of ness relative t with that k that cannot Public.

The Lottery

H ORN moved Cornhill, to near the Sara sincere thank in the last a candid plans advantageous cure and ben gain a consid SHILLING the course of such yearly

OCTOBER 4, 1779

Aris's BIRMINGHAM GAZETTE

SATURDAY's POST.
LONDON, Thursday, Sept. 30.

Some Particulars of the Proceedings of PAUL JONES's *Squadron.*

A LETTER from Bridlington, dated Sept. 24, says, " I doubt not but you have heard of the alarming Situation we have been in since Tuesday Night ; but thank God, as yet we have been only terrified by this Paul Jones. An Engagement took Place at seven last Night, and continued till two this Morning, between the Serapis Frigate of 44 Guns, and Paul Jones's Ship, the Bonne Homme of 44 Guns, with some smaller Vessels, off Flamborough head, and I am sorry to say that Jones hath now our two Ships with their Commanders, who distinguished themselves in a most galant Manner, though obliged at last to surrender to superior Force, after having made almost a Wreck of Jones's own Ship. The Serapis had her Masts shot away. Several Sailors made their Escape, and have been examined this Afternoon at the Key, but their Stories are different as to Jones's Loss ; some of them say he had 140 Men killed, and his Ship quite a Wreck. They say his Design was to destroy Scarborough, Bridlington, and Hull, with some other Places ; and that he intended landing at Falmborough Yesterday Morning, but the Sea ran too high. "

A Letter from Hull, dated Sept. 26, which may be depended on says, "[…] A Man who escaped from Jones's Ship has made Oath before the Mayor, that Jones stood on the quarter-Deck with a Brace of Pistols, and shot some of his own Men during the Action."

By an Affadavit made by Thomas Berry on 24th Instant, before Humphrey Osbaldiston, one of his Majesty's Justices of the Peace for the East-Riding of Yorkshire, it appears, that Paul Jones's Squadron had been six Days between Berwick and the Humber, and his declared Intentions were to make a Descent somewhere on the Coast ; that on Tuesday he ordered all his Oars to be muffled, and the Boats ready to be hoisted out ; that on Wednesday morning the Alliance and Pallas rejoined Jones off Flamborough-Head : and on Thursday Evening about seven o'Clock, they met with the East-Country Fleet, convoyed by a 40 Gun Ship, and an armed Ship, the 40 Gun Ship engaged Jones alone about 4 Hours, till Jones's Fire ceased ; having been several Times on Fire and very near sinking, he called on the Alliance for Assistance, which came up, and gave the 40 Gun Ship a Broadside, which being totally disabled struck. Jones's Officers called to the Alliance to hoist out their Boats, as their Ship was sinking, in one of which the Deponent and Six other Men made their Escape to Filey.

In the Engagement between the Serapis and Paul Jones, his Vessel was so disabled, that the Captain of the Serapis called out to Jones to strike, or else he would sink him. To which the latter replied, " That he might if he could ; for whenever the Devil was ready to take him, he would rather obey his summons, than strike to any one." And if another of Jones's Squadron had not come to his Assistance, he would soon have gone to the Bottom. The foregoing Account is from the Affidavits of seven Seamen who made their escape after the Engagement, before the Mayor of Hull ; and they add, that during the Engagement, Paul Jones (who was dressed in a short Jacket and long Trowsers, with about a Dozen of charged Pistols slung in a Belt round his Middle, and a Cutlass in his Hand) shot seven of his Men for desrting from their Quarters ; and to his Nephew whom he thought a little dastardly, he said, that " D—n his Eyes, he would not blow his Brains out, but would pepper his Shins," and had actually the Barbarity to shoot at the Legs of the Lad, who is a Lieutenant on board Jones's Ship.

The EDINBURGH ADVERTISER

Extract of a letter from New-York, dated Aug. 12.

" I arrived here about a month ago, to very glutted market for provisions. The Yankies are perplexing us greatly ; a few nights ago, a party of them had the assurance to come within a mile of this city, at a place called Paulus Hook, surprised and carried off with them a number of British and Hessian soldiers. Within these few days two rebel privateers have been sent in here by the Greyhound, frigate."

The following particulars, relative to the late engagement between Paul Jones and the Serapis man of war, may be depended on as authentic : when Jones first attacked the Serapis, he was a-head of his little fleet several leagues; notwithstanding this, he engaged with all the fury of a man determined to conquer or die. The engagement soon grew desperate, and Jones, besides having a great part of his crew shot round him, had his rigging on fire for about seven minutes. In this interval, the Captain of the Serapis, who was so near him as to be audible, called out to him to strike, or he must infallibly go to the bottom. Jones replied, with an oath, " I may sink, but I'll be d—d if I strike. " At this instant, one of his men attempted to strike the colours, when Jones, turning round, shot him dead on the spot. Two more attempted the same thing, and met with the same fate ; a mutiny then was expected to take place, as the ship was apparently sinking, when, fortunately for Jones, another of his squadron immediately came up to his assistance, which turned the tables on the Serapis, and she was obliged to strike, after exerting a degree of courage which would, in all probability, have made her successful with any other enemy.

EDINBURGH ADVERTISER
October 12, 1779
—

As the newspaper accounts indicate, the action was long, obstinate, and bloody. Jones's answer when asked if he was prepared to surrender is probably what was reported in the *Edinburgh Advertiser* of October 12, 1779. However, Richard Dale, an officer serving with Jones, in a book written long after the battle, quoted Jones as saying "I have not yet begun to fight," and those words are now immortalized.

A LIST of SHIPS TAKEN or DESTROYED by our ENEMIES or by ACCIDENT, within the Space of the last five Years.

LONDON CHRONICLE
October 26, 1779

Guns.	Ships Names.	Year.	Where, and by whom, taken, or destroyed.
14	Ferret	1774	On the Jamaica station, lost with all the crew.
14	Pomona	1776	On the Antigua station, lost with all the crew.
32	Repulse		On her passage from New York to the West Indies, lost, all her crew.
28	Actæon		Burnt near Charlestown, having run ashore.
64	Augusta	1777	Burnt near Philadelphia, a few of the crew perished.
20	Vestal		Lost on the Newfoundland station, with their crews.
16	Pegasus		
16	Merlin		Burnt near Philadelphia, the crew saved.
8	Cruiser		Burnt on the coast of Carolina, the crew saved.
8	Savage		Lost near Louisburgh, the crew saved, except two.
70	Somerset	1778	Lost near Boston, with part of the crew.
32	Minerva		Taken on the Jamaica station, by a French ship of 50 guns.
32	Flora		
32	Juno		Burnt at Rhode Island, to prevent their falling into the hands of the French fleet, the crews saved.
32	Lark		
32	Orpheus		
28	Cerberus		Ditto.
28	Mermaid		Lost near Philadelphia, attempting to escape the French fleet, the crew saved.
28	Liverpool		Lost near New York, the crew saved.
28	Syren		Lost near Rhode Island, the crew saved.
28	Active		Taken on the Jamaica station by two French frigates.
28	Fox		Taken in the Channel by a French frigate of 36 guns.
20	Lively		Taken by several French frigates.
20	Mercury		Lost near New York, the crew saved.
16	King's Fisher		Burnt at Rhode Island, to prevent her falling into the hands of the French, the crew saved.
16	Otter		Lost near St. Augustine, the crew saved.
16	Senegal		Taken by the French fleet near Rhode Island.
16	Drake		Taken by Paul Jones near Belfast.
16	Thunder Bomb		Taken by the French fleet near Rhode Island.
8	Zephyr		Taken by the French in the Mediterranean.
64	Ardent	1779	Taken by the combined fleets near Plymouth.
44	Serapis		Taken by Paul Jones near Hull.
32	Quebec		Burnt near Ushant, in an engagement with a French frigate of 40 guns, and only 30 of the crew saved.
32	Montreal		Taken by two French 74 gun ships in the Mediterranean.
32	Arethusa		Lost near Brest, the crew saved.
26	Supply storeship		Burnt in the West Indies, the crew saved.
20	Glasgow		
20	Countess of Scarborough		Taken by Paul Jones near Hull, the crew saved.
16	Ceres		Taken on the Antigua station by a French frigate of 36 guns.
16	Weazle		Taken near St. Eustatia.
12	York		Taken at the Grenades by the French.

Total number, one of 70 guns, two of 64, one of 44, nine of 32, seven of 28, one of 26, five of 20, eight of 16, two of 14, one of 12, three of 8, and one bomb.

I believe the Zebra of 16 guns was lost with the Somerset, and the Swift of 16, since, near Virginia. There are also several armed vessels, such as brigs, schooners, cutters, &c.

A LIST of SHIPS TAKEN or DESTROYED from the FRENCH, SPANIARDS and AMERICANS.

AMERICANS.

Guns.	Ships Names.	Year.	Where, and by whom, taken, or destroyed.
32	Delaware	1777	Taken near Philadelphia, by the army.
32	Hancock		Taken near Halifax, by the Rainbow of 44 guns.
36	Randolph	1778	Blown up near Barbadoes, in an engagement with the Yarmouth of 64 guns, and only five of the crew saved.
32	Raleigh		Taken near Boston, by the Experiment of 50 guns, and Unicorn of 20, the crew saved.
26	Warren	1779	Burnt, with sixteen others of inferior force, at Penobscot, by Sir George Collier's fleet.
40	Bon Homme Richard		Sunk in an engagement with the Serapis of 44 guns, which she took before she went down.

FRENCH.

Guns.	Ships Names.	Year.	Where, and by whom, taken, or destroyed.
32	Licorne	1778	Taken by Admiral Keppel's fleet in the Channel.

They arrived in the house just before day & stay'd there until the next evening, when Major Andre became extremely sollicitous to return by the way he came, but that was impossible, for the two men who Arnold and Smith had seduced to bring on shore, refused to carry him back. It then was absolutely necessary he should return to New-York by land. He chang'd his dress and name, and thus disguised, pass'd our post of Stoney and Verplank's Points, on the evening of the 22d ult. in company with the said Joshua Smith, brother to William Smith, Esq; Chief Justice within the British lines; he lodged that night at Cron Pond, with Smith, and in the morning left Smith, and took the road to Tarry-Town, where he was taken by some militia lads about 15 miles from Kings Bridge. He offered them any sum of money, and goods, if they would permit him to escape, but they readily declared and inflexibly adhered to it, that 10 000 guineas, or any other sum, would be no temptation to them. It was this virtue as glorious to America as Arnold's apostacy is disgraceful, that his abominable crimes were discovered.

"The lads, in searching him, found concealed under his stockings, in his boots, papers of the highest importance, viz.

1 Returns of the ordnance and its distributions at West-Point and its dependencies.

2. Artillery orders, in case of an alarm.

3. Returns of the number of men necessary to man the works at West Point and its dependencies.

4 Remarks on ----- at West Point, with the strength ----- of each.

5. Returns ----- ----- and their distribution.

6. State of ----- ----- eral Washing ----- which state ha ----- officers i -----

" Besid ----- ----- carried ----- of West -----

Gen. Robertson, Andrew Elliot and William Smith, Esqrs; the two latter were not permitted to land. General Greene met Gen. Robertson; he had nothing material to urge—" but that Andre had come on shore under the sanction of a flag, and therefore could not be considered as a spy:" But this is not true, for he came at night, had no flag, and on business totally incompatible with the nature of a flag. He also said they should retaliate on some people at New-York and Charlestown; but he was told that such conversation could neither be heard nor understood. After which he urged the release of Andre on motives of humanity, and because Sir Harry Clinton was much attached to him; and other reasons equally absurd

" I have been particular in this narration, well knowing what strange stories you will have on the subject."

The following is a Copy of a Letter from Major Andre to his Excellency General Washington.

SIR,

" Buoyed above the fear of death, by the consciousness of a life spent in the pursuit of honor, and fully sensible that it has at no time been stained by any action, which at this serious moment could give me remorse—I have to sollicit your Excellency if there is any thing in my character which excites your esteem; if aught in my circumstances can impress you with compassion; that I may be permitted to die the death of a soldier: —It is my last request and I hope it will be granted." I have the honor to be, &c.

All Persons indebted to the

Estate of Mr. Benjamin Star, late of Boston, Cordwainer, deceas'd; and all to whom said Estate is indebted ----- desired to bring in their Accounts for Settlement ----- BENJAMIN EDES, Administrator.

A fe ----- arlestown and L ----- may be had of the Pr -----

MARKS OF HEROISM

Introduction

Hoping to stir Loyalist support and restore British authority in the South, the British army realigns its strategy and shifts more than ten thousand troops loyal to the Crown, under the command of Henry Clinton, southward. In scorching heat and humidity, the Patriot-Loyalist civil war is fierce. Many of the bloodiest scenes unfold, including some of the worst Patriot defeats as well as the most pivotal victories. Despite the heroism of Patriot forces, "treason of the blackest dye" is uncovered among America's highest ranks and sends a shock wave through the Continental Army.

Boston Gazette
October 16, 1780

Capture of John André
and discovery of Benedict
Arnold's treason
North Wind Picture Archives

SIEGE OF SAVANNAH

By Rita Folse Elliott

BUNKER HILL, SARATOGA, YORKTOWN. WHILE SOME think the American Revolution happened only in New England and the mid-Atlantic, southern landscapes were also deadly scenes of strategic battles, with Georgia serving as the springboard for British military operations in the second half of the war. Casualties were not limited to the military, as civilians suffered intensively in what amounted to civil war. A Georgian's eyewitness account in the *London Chronicle* on October 26, 1779, stated, "the whole country to within 25 miles of Savannah has been plundered in the most cruel manner." The British taking of Savannah in December 1778 set the stage for one of the most decisive American defeats. The epic 1779 saga involved eight thousand to twelve thousand multinational forces consisting of American, African, British, French, Haitian, Hessian, Irish, Scottish, and Native American troops.

The British taking of Savannah in December 1778 set the stage for one of the most decisive American defeats.

Southern colonial importance is reflected in British Lieutenant Colonel Archibald Campbell's proclamation printed March 18, 1779, in the *American Journal*, three months after British troops took Savannah in little more than a heavy skirmish. The proclamation mentioned "all his Majesty's faithful subjects of the southern provinces," and the British mistakenly believed that applied to most residents. Perhaps for that reason, Major General Augustin Prevost seemed in no hurry to reinforce the city's weak defenses, even when word arrived that French Admiral Count Charles Henri d'Estaing's fleet was in route to America from the nearby West Indies.

While Prevost remained composed, British political and military figures from Florida to Rhode Island were fearful of being d'Estaing's target. A *Maryland Journal* article printed October 26, 1779, is a typical compilation of fact, fiction, and biased optimism. It correctly reported Count d'Estaing landing troops downstream from Savannah but failed to mention why d'Estaing was so terrifying. He brought one of the world's largest military flotillas: twenty-two ships of the line. The article mentioned American Major General Benjamin Lincoln, commander of the war's southern theater. The 1779 battle represented the first time French and American forces allied in ground combat. Lincoln and d'Estaing proved a disastrous combination of character flaws, cultural incompatibility, and poor judgment.

Unbeknownst at the time of the article, British Lieutenant Colonel John Maitland mustered eight hundred troops in Beaufort, South Carolina. Contrary to the article, he did "effect a junction with General Prevost" by slogging through back swamps and inlets through enemy lines. Meanwhile, Prevost ordered engineers, five hundred African Americans, militia, and regulars to reinforce four redoubts and construct nine new ones surrounding the city. Inside, Royal Georgia Governor James Wright and petrified civilians, including Prevost's wife Anne and children, waited. Prevost bought time with a twenty-four-hour truce. The same newspaper article optimistically stated "officers gave their opinions publicly that [Savannah] must capitulate." This may have happened had the allies attacked immediately in lieu of laying a siege. The allies bombarded Savannah for two weeks with little effect, other than torching houses and killing women and children cowering in basements. The futile siege ended with an unsuccessful attack on October 9, 1779.

It would be weeks before George Washington learned

of the catastrophic loss at Savannah. French and American military casualties numbering eight hundred contrasted with fifty British. D'Estaing himself was among officers wounded. Count Casimir Pulaski, mentioned in the newspaper as victoriously taking the picket, suffered mortal wounds leading a cavalry charge. This loss was significant as the Polish Pulaski had created America's first cavalry.

The *London Chronicle* celebrated the British victory in its December 28, 1779, issue more than seventy days after the battle. It published an accurate battle account by Prevost. The 1779 battle of Savannah, Georgia, resulted in a rift in the fragile Franco-American alliance and a strategic victory for the British, enabling them to hold Georgia, take Charleston, South Carolina, and launch an attack from the southern front.

SIEGE OF SAVANNAH,
BY A. I. KELLER
North Wind Picture Archives

The epic 1779 Siege of Savannah, one of the most decisive American defeats, involved eight thousand to twelve thousand multinational forces consisting of American, African, British, French, Haitian, Hessian, Irish, Scottish, and Native American troops.

Extract of a Letter from a Gentleman of the first Distinction in Georgia, dated Savannah, July 27.

"During near three months that the royal army was in South Carolina, the whole province, excepting our three posts of Savannah, Ebenezer, and Sanbury, was entirely in the rebels power; and the consequence has been, that the whole country to within 25 miles of Savannah has been plundered in the most cruel manner, and almost every man who had submitted to, and received the protection of government, either killed or taken prisoners, and the few that have escaped that fate have been obliged to submit to such terms as the rebels pleased to prescribe.

"On the 26th ult. we were alarmed with accounts of a large body of horse having penetrated into the heart of our lower settlements; having a few days before received a small reinforcement from our army, a detachment of about 50 men was sent out from this garrison to watch their motions, but by very bad conduct they fell in with and were surprised by upwards of 100 of the enemy, within 17 miles of Savannah; in consequence of which the Commanding Officer, Capt. Muller, and several privates, were killed, and the remainder of the detachment made prisoners.

"Col. Maitland now commands at Beaufort, with about 1500 men; the rest of the army is here with Gen. Prevost. We have force enough to defend the part of the country that we are in possession of, until the season will admit of operations in the field, for at present the weather is so excessive hot that nothing material could be attempted. Our reinforcements, we doubt not, will be with us early enough to complete the work we have so happily begun in these southern provinces.

"Our worthy Governor, Sir James Wright, arrived here in the Experiment, Commodore Sir James Wallace, on the 13th inst. He was much disappointed on finding a descent had been made upon Carolina, which, it was hoped in England, would have been deferred till the arrival of the

Three battalions, making upwards of 2500 men, will go out to the Leeward islands, in the

taking soundings of the coast along shore under English colours."

Extract of a Letter from Milford Haven, dated Oct. 19.

"A coaster from the northward was chased in here on the 17th by a large cutter; she is said to be one of those fitted out at Dunkirk as smugglers, or privateers; they are commanded by an American, and have a commission from the Congress, and the crew are Irish, English, and French, and, in short, whatever they can get: she had 18 guns, and was full of men."

Extract of a Letter from Weymouth, Oct. 20.

"This morning was brought in here a French privateer belonging to Cherburg, mounting 12 guns, called the St. Amiand, taken by the Rover privateer, after an engagement of two hours, in which the French had 12 men killed and 20 wounded. The Rover had only two men killed and three wounded."

Extract of a Letter from Gosport, Oct. 22.

"His Majesty's ship Garland is appointed convoy to Newfoundland, and is this day sailed; she gave instructions to all ships that would go with her, bound to New York; accordingly the Hannah, Watson, and the ——, Moor, with a ship bound to Bermuda, and several others, are all this day sailed under her convoy, with a fine N. E. wind."

Extract of a Letter from Dunwich, in Suffolk, October 19.

"The violent blowing weather we have had for several days has done a great deal of damage amongst the shipping on our coast; every tide presents to our view a melancholy scene of dead bodies, and pieces of wrecks thrown on the sands. It likewise did great havoc on shore, blowing down rows of large trees, barns, outhouses, &c. and unroofing dwelling houses; in short, the damage done amounts to many thousands of pounds. A man, his wife, and several children, were buried under the ruins of a house, and all killed."

A Captain of a ship arrived from Yarmouth mentions, that the whole of the Society's busses are safely arrived at Southwold from the Shetland fishery, with full cargoes.

... ...rday last, at one o'clock, William ...; finding that most of his friends ...d to poll for Henry Kitchen, Esq; ...licited their favours, he therefore ...ng on with the poll, and desired that ...ight be finally closed, to prevent the ...r and the Gentlemen of the Ward ... further trouble; which request was ...th, and thereupon the Lord Mayor ...nry Kitchen, Esq; duly elected Alderman ...Farringdon Ward within, in the ...late Wm. Bridgen, Esq.

...nday last as some workmen were sinking a grave in the north ayle of the parish church of Danbury in Essex, they discovered a leaden coffin, which enclosed a stout elm coffin, about one inch and a quarter thick, in which was a shell of about half that thickness, containing the body of a Knight Templer, supposed to be of...

Shoe-lane, Fleet-street.

On Saturday last died, at Bal...ham, Surry, Mrs. Elizabeth Scri...

On Tuesday last died, at Camb... Thomas Hooper, A. M. a pre... and Rector of Barley, in Hertfor...

Saturday morning at 1 o'clock, ... of the Royal George West India... ped near the end of Virginia-... fellows, who beat him most cruel... him of near 30l. which he had ... afternoon received from his owne...

On Saturday nine prisoners we... Old Bailey, one of whom was ca... ed, viz. Wm. Russell, for brea... dwelling-house of Mr. James E... court, in the night-time, with i... five were convicted of grand lar... of petit larceny.

Lea Josepha Salomons was co... lawfully setting fire to a wooden ... ers, in her dwelling-house, in the ... inu-passage, in Warwick-lane, ... burn and destroy the said house ... sentence to be imprisoned two ... gate, and pay a fine of 100l. ... victed on his own confession for ... rupt perjury, and his sentence re...

The same day the session en... prisoners received sentence of dea...

The Recorder, in passing sen... last Saturday, addressed himself ... Mr. Taylor. He said, it was ... course of his trial that he had at ... function, the more easily to i... world; that a man capable of f... a character with any sort of suc... suppose, was possessed of some a... from a liberal education, and f... considered the unfortunate convi... was far from his wish to aggrava... of a man in so deplorable a si... crime of the prisoner was so de... comercial interests of this kingd... could be no expectation of mer... those feelings which a sensible m... would make a proper impression o... and dispose him to think serious... of the state of his soul, in order ... employ the short time he had t... manner as to entitle him to the ... ven.—This serious address, hov... to be thrown away upon the p... appeared very inattentive and i... spoke not a word. The other pri... with a becoming decency.

The Sessions of the Peace is a... the 3d of November at Guildhall ... sions of Gaol Delivery of Newga... of December at the Old Bailey.

D. L. Love in a Village with Fa...
C. G. Macbeth, with Plymouth...

For DISORDERS in the BO... THE sudden alteration of the ... produce a state of air very...

and when Capt. Delmley brought to, all his own topmasts fell over the side; the lower masts would likewise have gone, had not the weather proved fine."

AMERICAN JOURNAL (PROVIDENCE, RI)
March 18, 1779

—

Southern colonial importance is reflected in British Lieutenant Colonel Archibald Campbell's proclamation printed March 18, 1779, in the *American Journal*, three months after British troops took Savannah in little more than a heavy skirmish.

CHARLESTOWN, January 12.

The commanders of the British armament in Georgia, in humble imitation of their superiors to the northward, have entertained the good people of the southern states with a proclamation; which, notwithstanding it militates directly against the cause of America, in order to shew how little apprehension is entertained of its producing the effect the framers of it have in view, is here published: Indeed those who at this time can put any confidence in their promises would richly merit that share of misery and want, which has invariably attended all those Americans who have been apostates to the cause of freedom, and inlisted themselves under the banners of their country's foes.

By HYDE PARKER, jun. Esquire, Commodore of a Squadron of his Majesty's Ships of War; and Lieut. Col. ARCHIBALD CAMPBELL, commanding a Detachment of the Royal Army, sent for the Relief of his Majesty's faithful Subjects in North and South-Carolina and Georgia.

A PROCLAMATION.

WHereas the blessings of peace, freedom, and protection, most graciously tendered by his Majesty to his deluded subjects of America, have been treated by Congress with repeated marks of studied disrespect, and to the disgrace of human nature have had no effect in reclaiming them from the bloody persecutions of their fellow citizens: BE IT THEREFORE KNOWN to all his Majesty's faithful subjects of the southern provinces, that a fleet and army, under orders, are actually arrived in Georgia for their protection, to which they are desired to repair without loss of time, and, by uniting their force under the royal standard, rescue their friends from oppression, themselves from slavery, and obtain for both the most ample satisfaction for the manifold injuries sustained.

To all other well disposed inhabitants, who, from a just regard to the blessings of peace, reprobate the idea of supporting a French league, insidiously framed to prolong the calamities of war, and who, with his Majesty's faithful subjects wish to embrace the happy occasion of cementing a firm and perpetual coalition with the parent state, free from the imposition of taxes by the Parliament of Great-Britain, and secured in the irrevocable enjoyment of every privilege, consistent with that union of interests and force on which their mutual advantage, religion and liberties depend. WE offer the most ample protection to their families and effects, on condition they shall immediately return to the class of peaceful citizens, acknowledge their just allegiance to the crown, and with their arms support it.

To those who shall attempt to oppose the re-establishment of legal government, or who shall presume to injure such whom the dictates of reason, honor and conscience prompt to embrace it; WE lament the necessity of exhibiting the rigours of war, and call God and the world to witness, that they only shall be answerable for all the miseries which may ensue.

Deserters of every description, who, from a due sense of their error, wish to return to their colours, have also our pardon, provided they return within the space of three months from the date of this proclamation.

GIVEN at Head-Quarters at Savannah, this 4th day of January 1779, and in the nineteenth year of his Majesty's reign,

HYDE PARKER,

ARCHIBALD CAMPBELL.

PHILADELPHIA, Feb. 22.

have deferted into the city to their friends, perhaps half as many more.

(To be continued.)

LEGHORN, June 15.

ACCORDING to a private letter from an officer on board the Chatham, fix French ships of the line keep Gibraltar blocked up; that fortrefs is provided with ammunition and provifions for nine months, with a garrifon of 8000 men. That letter adds, that Admiral Roddam has been feen off Cape St. Vincent, making proper difpofitions to clear the Streights of Gibraltar.

DUBLIN, July 3.

The Amfterdam Gazette, which arrived here yefterday, in the Paris article contains a regulation of the ceremonial obferved at the junction of the French and Spanifh fleets, and the difpofition for embarking the army under M. de Vaux, which the French affectedly call L'Armee Irlandoife. This army, which confifts of 30,000 foot, and 1000 horfe, were on the 20th of June to go on board 300 tranfports, which had been fome time waiting for them. The fame Gazette gives an account of the arrival of a frigate at Breft, which had left the fquadron under the command of M. de la Mothe Piquet off the Azores, where they had captured fix Englifh privateers, which they fay were lying in wait for the French homeward-bound Weft-India fhips.

July 13. By Gentlemen who are arrived here in the laft packet we are informed, that the fleet under the command of Sir Charles Hardy, had put into Torbay the 5th inftant, there to wait for a reinforcement of eight fhips of the line, which are to join him from

---

CHARLESTOWN, Sept. 22.

Since our laft, we have had no direct advices from either of the armies employed upon the Southern expedition. All we certainly know, is, That Count d'Efting did land as many troops as he thought neceffary, at Beulah, nearly oppofite to the Orphan-Houfe, 12 miles from Savannah, in the night between the 11th and 12th inft. and without the leaft oppofition; and that a communication had been opened between him and General Lincoln; that General Lincoln had been joined by General Mackintofh; and that the Head-Quarters of our army, a week ago, were at Cherokee-hill, 9 miles from Savannah: That General Count Pulafki was advanced with the cavalry, and had not only taken an advanced picket of the enemy, but alfo furprized one of their captains and three privates at Ebenetzer. That Col. Maitland had abandoned Port-Royal Ifland, with the whole force he had there, on the 12th inft. after breaking off the trunnions from the cannon, and having buried upwards of 200 men, leaving behind alfo 300 negroes, for want of means of tranfportation: That his embarkation was made rather haftily, on board the Vigilante, the Gallies, and fome other fmall craft, with an intent to pufh through Skull Creek, and join General Prevoft at Savannah

---

tachments, one at Brewton's plantation, with 36 pieces of brafs cannon, the other at Girardeau's point: That the active and enterprizing General Count Pulafki, with the cavalry, had fo thoroughly cleared the way, and broke up all the enemy's advanced pofts, as to afford Major-General Lincoln the opportunity of an interview with the French General, at the Orphan-houfe, on the 16th, when and where the plan of operations was fettled: That fome of the French men of war had got into the harbour, and poffeffed themfelves of all the Britifh fhipping below Brewton's, amongft them the Fowey man of war, which, tho' grounded, had all been got off and into the fleet: That the fortifications at Savannah were but trifling, confifting only of 9 redoubts (no lines) and abbatis: That the force to defend thefe, confifted of about 1000 regulars, and 1200 militia, refugees, and protection gentry: That Sir James Wright, governor, &c. was in Savannah: That Col. Maitland had not been able to effect a junction with General Prevoft, and it was fuppofed had been repulfed in an attempt to get thro' Skull-creek, yefterday morning, when we heard a heavy cannonade: That the enemy's foldiery, in general, were much diffatisfied; and tho' it was pretended, that Savannah would be defended, even the officers gave their opinions publicly, that it muft capitulate. And that General Prevoft had applied to the Count d'Eftaing, for a fafe conduct and permiffion to remove his lady, plate and effects, to Florida; to which the gallant French General politely replied, *"That it was impoffible he could have any objection to what concerned the Lady; but the plate, he had been informed, was obtained in fuch a way from the Allies of his King, that he was confident the General could not mean to difgrace himfelf in poffeffion of it."*

PHILADELPHIA, October 16.

... rived from Bordeaux (Old France) ... ercer, Captain Robinfon, and bro't ... Minerva, Capt. ———, from Ha... am, loaded with fifh, &c.

... from Nantz, dated July 3, 1779.

... e 32,000 men at St. Malo, ready to ... ey only wait the arrival of Compte ... e Channel, accounts of which ... ected, as the wind has been for 36 ... weftward, and likely to continue. ... here is a defcent intended on Eng... It is reported that the fhips the Spaniards were to furnifh by compact, which is ten fail of the line, have joined D'Orvilliers, and that the Cadiz fleet failed about the fifth ult. The failing of the Englifh fleet you'll find by the papers. The French have an army of 40,000 men on the frontiers of Holland, which will keep the Dutchman quiet, if even his inclination was to be troublefome."

Extract of a letter from a Gentleman in Bordeaux, dated July 22, 1779.

" We have no certain advices from the combined fleets, expect fome very interefting; if any arrives before the prefent conveyances leave the river, fhall embrace the opportunity to forward them. Mr. Wedderburne is nominated to fucceed Lord Suffolk; other new nominations are daily expected in the different minifterial departments of that Kingdom.

" Advices from Spain agree in the determination of that Court on the blockade of Gibraltar.

" An army is marching into Flanders, under the command of Monfieur, faid to pay a vifit to Hanover, and thereby oblige that Electorate to refal her troops in the pay of Britain from Minorca and Gibraltar, or to watch the Dutch, and hold them to a ftrict neutrality."

Extract of a letter from Bordeaux, dated July 20, 1779.

---

fhortly be on that coaft. They are fortifying all poffible expedition, every advantageous place about the city, and have eleven veffels rea... fink in the channel at the Hook. Every poffible... tion is making on board their fhipping, in cafe of... tack. In fhort, the whole city is one fcene o... fufion and fear."

Extract of a letter from Pittfburgh, September 16,

" The many favage barbarities and horrid... dations, committed by the Seneca and Muncy N... upon the Weftern frontiers, had determined... Broadhead, as the moft effectual way to preven... hoftilities in future, and revenge the paft, to car... war into their own country, and ftrike a decifive... at their towns.

" On the 11th of Auguft, our little army, con... only of fix hundred and five, rank and file, ma... from Pittfburgh with one month's provifion; a... honing, 15 miles above the Old Kittanning, we... detained four days by the exceffive rains, from w... (leaving the river which rolls in a thoufand mean... we proceeded by a blind path leading to Cufcu... thro' a country almoft impaffible, by reafon of th... pendous heights and frightful declivities, with a... tinued range of craggy hills, overfpread with... timber, thorns and underwood, here and there an... vening valley, whofe deep impenetrable gloo... always been impervious to the piercing rays... warmeft fun. At Cufcufhing (which is 15 miles... Venango) we croffed the Alleghany, and cont... our route upon its banks. But here our marc... rendered ftill more difficult by the mountains... jutted clofe upon the river, forming a continued n... defile, allowing us only the breadth of an Indian... to march upon. In the midft of one of thefe t... our advanced party, confifting of 15 white m... Delawares, difcovered between ... landing from their canoes, who having alfo feen... of our troops, immediately ftripped themfelves an... pared for action. Lieutenant Harding, who... manded our advance, difpofed his men in a femici... form, and began the attack with fuch irrefiftible... tomahawk in hand, that the Savages could not... fuftain the charge, but fled with the utmoft horro... precipitation, fome plunging themfelves into the... and others, favoured by the thicknefs of the b... made their efcape on the main, leaving five de... the field, without any lofs on our fide, except three... flightly wounded. Upon the firft alarm, fuppof... to be more ferious, the army was arranged for... both officers and men, enraged at their former... ties, and animated by the calmnefs, refolution a... trepidity of the commandant, fhewed the utmoft... to engage; and had the action been general, w... every profpect of the moft ample fuccefs from a... commander, at the head of brave men. Contin... our march, we arrived the fame day at Buchal... where leaving our baggage, ftores, &c. under a g... proceeded to their towns with the utmoft defp... which we found at the diftance of about twenty... farther, with extenfive corn-fields on both fides o... river, but deferted by the inhabitants on our appr... Eight towns we fet in flames, and committed their... god and war pofts to the river; the corn was our... object, which, in three days, we cut down and pile... to heaps, amounting in the whole to near 600 a... without the leaft interruption from the enemy.

" Upon our return we feveral times croffed the... about ten miles above Venango, remarkable for an... liquor, which oozes from the fides and bottom o... channel, and the adjacent fprings, much refeml... Britifh oil, and if applied to woolen cloth, burns... an inftant.

" After burning the old towns of Con...

Province of Georgia, to the Right Honourable Lord George Germaine, one of his Majesty's Principal Secretaries of State, dated Savannah, November 1, 1779: Received by Captain Shaw, Aid de Camp to Major General Prevost.

AS I look upon it to be always of Importance, and my indispensable Duty, that your Lordship should directly be made acquainted with every material Occurrence in this Quarter affecting his Majesty's Service; and as it is probable the very unexpected Visit of the Count d'Estaing to this Coast, with so powerful a Squadron, and a considerable Body of Land Troops, when known, would have excited some Uneasiness for our Safety; it is with very sincere Pleasure I do myself the Honour to inform you, that we have seen the last of the French Fleet this Day depart,—we hope off the Coast,—got both them and their American Allies off our Hands, in a Manner which we humbly hope our gracious Sovereign will not think unhandsome.

September 4th. When Intelligence was received from Tybee, that five Sail of French Men of War, with some Sloops and Schooners, were off the Bar, as it was impossible to determine whether this was a Whole or only Part of a larger Force; whether they had landed Troops in Carolina, or this was their first Appearance on the Coast; Orders were sent to all the Out-Posts to hold themselves in Readiness to join: And as it was very possible that the Enemy might push their Frigates into Port Royal Bay, and cut off the Communication with Beaufort, an Order was sent to the Honourable Colonel Maitland, commanding there, forthwith to evacuate that Place, and cross to Hilton Head Island, from whence, if he was not stopped by a further Order, he was to proceed to this Place. The Officer who was charged with this Order was taken by the Rebels, going through Skull Creek; but this Accident was then judged of no other Consequence, as the French disappearing, and their coming on the Coast being hoped, for various Reasons, to be only accidental, Colonel Maitland was next Day directed to remain; but embarking all his heavy Baggage and other Incumbrances, to hold himself in constant Readiness to come away on the shortest Notice: Or if, through any other Channel, he received Intelligence which should induce that Measure, he was immediately to adopt it, without waiting the Ceremony of Orders, as best for his Majesty's Service; his great Care being always to run no Risque, possibly to be avoided, of being cut off from this Place, which was our principal Concern.

6th. The French Ships re-appeared with one of Addition, and from the Northward. Captain Moncrief, the Commanding Engineer, with one hundred Men and a Howitz, was sent to Tybee to reinforce the Post and Battery there; and an Order to be forwarded to Colonel Maitland to join without Loss of

an Attack.—Repair and strengthen the Abbatis.—A very superior Force approaching the Bar, our Ships, the Fowey and Rose, of twenty Guns each, the Keppel and Germain armed Vessels, obliged to retire towards Town. The Battery on Tybee destroyed, the Guns spiked, and the Howitz and Stores carried off. Four large Frigates came over the Bar.

10th. All the Out-posts in Georgia join. Lieutenant-Colonel Cruger from Sunbury came by Land with all his Men able to march; his Sick and Convalescents he embarked on board an armed Vessel to come inland.—By contrary Winds they were detained till the Passage was seized by the Enemy. They however put up Ogechy River, where, finding the Communication by Land also cut off, Captain French (commanding) landed and took Post, and for many Days continued to defend himself, until obliged, by Want of Provisions, to capitulate to a very superior Force. Began new Redoubts and Batteries, and strengthen the Abbatis. The Troops encamped.

11th. Busy in landing Cannon from the Shipping.—Making Fascines.—The Engineer hard at Work.

12th. Several French and Rebel Vessels come over Ossiban Bar.—At Ten o'Clock, Evening, the French landed at Beaulieu.

13th. Having confined our Views to the Defence of the Town, as our sole Object, which we determined, by the Blessing of God, to be vigorous, and worthy of British Troops, continued our Works with unremitting Ardour. Captains Henry, Brown, and Fisher came on Shore, their Assistance being required in the Defence of the Place, on which every Thing depended.—They chearfully agreed, and proceeded directly to land their whole Force, Men, Guns, &c. Some Masters of Transports, and a Privateer with their Men, made voluntary Offers of their Services. Capt. Watson of the Tweed, Tate, Nancy, Higgins, Betsey, Mr. Manley, Merchant of Jamaica, all had their Posts assigned; the Seamen on the Batteries, the Marines joined to the 60th Grenadiers.—Report, that the Rebels from Augusta were at Hudson's, and General Lincoln from Carolina approaching Zubly's Ferry.

14th. The Engineer hard at Work.—Certain Intelligence that Lincoln was crossing at Zubly's Ferry, from intelligent Spies, who crossed with him.—His Numbers about 1500. More on their Way from all Parts of Carolina. Polaski, already crossed and joined by the Horse from above, advanced to within eight Miles of the Town.

15th. Some French and Polaski's Lighthorse appear in Front. Force in a Subaltern's Piquet, of which six are taken: They are forced to retire in Turn with some killed, and an Officer taken. No further Loss on our Side, our Men not being suffered to pass beyond the Cover of our Cannon.

16th. Receive a Summons (No. I.) from the Count d'Estaing, *To surrender to the Arms of France.* No Stranger to the unanimous Opinion of the Army; but, for Form's Sake, assemble the Field Officers at the Governor's—

twenty-four Hours to deliberate, which is agreed to (No. IV. and No. V.).

17th. By Noon, and in the Night before, all the rest of the Army fit for Duty from Beaufort arrive, and take their Posts in the Line. The Enemy being in Possession of the Ship Channel, Colonel Maitland had been obliged to come round Dawfuskie, and land on the Marshes; and dragging his Boats empty through a Cut, got into Savannah River above the Enemy, and so to this Place.—Again assemble the Field Officers, Sea and Land, with the Governor and Lieutenant Governor in Camp.—Unanimously determined to defend ourselves to the last Man, which is communicated to Count d'Estaing, (No. VI.) Our Evening Gun fired an Hour before Sunset, to be the Signal for recommencing Hostilities. — Review the Troops under Arms at their Posts, all in high Spirits, and the most pleasing Confidence expressed in every Face—The Sailors not to be prevented from giving Three Cheers.

18th and 19th. We continue to work hard on Redoubts and Batteries—Further strengthen the Abbatis.

20th. A Frigate and Gallies at Four Mile Point. Captain Moncrief prepares Fire Rafts. The Rose and Savannah sunk in the Channel.

21st. A new Work for seven 6 and 9 pounders begun in Front of the Barracks—Hearing the Rebels were making Fire Rafts above the Town, we get the Boom across, and Vessels ready to be sunk, a small Galley, and the Germain to cover the Boom, and occasionally to scour Yamacraw Swamp on our Right.—Some Houses and Barns on our Flanks, judged too near, are burnt, unfortunately the Property of Friends.

22d. The Enemy appear in Force all along our Front—In Readiness to fight, but continue our Works—Boats and other Craft of the Enemy go up Augustine Creek, probably with Cannon and Stores.

23d. As the Day before.

24th. The Enemy had been hard at Work the whole Night; and when the Morning Fog cleared off, were discovered to have pushed a Sap to within Three Hundred Yards of our Abbatis, to the Left of the Center.—At Nine o'Clock Three Companies of Light Infantry (97 Rank and File) were sent out under Major Graham, of the 16th, to give an Opportunity of reconnoitring, and probably judging of the Enemy's Force, and to draw them exposed to our Cannon. It had been once intended to send the whole Light Infantry with Major Graham,

7[...]
T[...]
A[...]
o[...]
and the Vicinity of the French Camp, which was discovered to be very near, there was Reason to apprehend an Affair more general than we wished for, might be brought on; it was judged sufficient to draw the remaining Three Light Companies along the Abbatis, and the Highlanders concealed behind the Barracks, in

LONDON CHRONICLE
December 28, 1779

SIEGE OF CHARLESTON

By David Lee Russell

O N MARCH 8, 1778, LORD GERMAIN, THE SECRETARY of state for the American Department, signed final directives to General Henry Clinton specifying his future military operations against the colonies, revealing that "it is the King's intention that an attack should be made upon the southern colonies, with a view to the conquest and possession of Georgia and South Carolina." This "Southern Strategy" as it became known, led to the British capture of Savannah on December 29, 1778, and the defeat of a Franco-American siege against British-held Savannah in October of the following year led by General Benjamin Lincoln and French Admiral Charles Henri d'Estaing. Clinton's next target was Charleston, South Carolina.

At 10:00 the morning after Christmas in 1780, British Vice Admiral Arbuthnot's fleet of ninety-six ships (eighty transports), with General Clinton's 6,975 British and German Hessian troops, sailed from Sandy Hook, New York, for Charleston. The British landed below the city on Simmons Island (Seabrook Island) on February 11, and by the afternoon of March 31, they broke ground on their siege works 1,200 yards from the Patriot main defensive line opposite Charleston.

It was the greatest victory in the war for the British, and there was great celebration in England over the fall of the city.

When the British works reached only 250 yards off the city's works on April 21, General Lincoln sent a flag of truce with his terms consisting of articles of surrender. Clinton rejected Lincoln's terms and asked for the immediate surrender of the city. The Patriot Council refused, and the bombardments began again.

By May 8, the British held all escape routes from Charleston. That day, Clinton sent a summons to General Lincoln to surrender, as recorded in the *New-Jersey Gazette* of June 28, 1780:

Circumstanced as I now am with respect to the place invested, humanity only can induce me to lay within your reach the terms I had determined should not again be proffered [...] By this last summons therefore, I throw to your charge whatever vindictive severity exasperated soldiers may inflict on the unhappy people, whom you devote by preserving in a fruitless defence. I shall expect your answer until eight o'clock, when hostilities will commence again, unless the town be surrendered.

Again Clinton rejected Lincoln's revisions, and when that time arrived on May 9, Hessian Captain Hinrichs recorded in his diary, "The enemy rang all the bells in the city and after a threefold 'Hurray!' opened a cannonade more furious than any before." On May 11, the British crossed the lines within twenty-five yards of the Patriot works. Hinrichs noted, "At two o'clock in the afternoon the enemy hoisted a large white flag on the hornwork and dispatched a second flag, offering the capitulation of the city."

The *London Chronicle* dated June 17, 1780, printed Sir Henry Clinton's account of the May 12 surrender of Charleston:

On the 12th Major-General Leslie took possession of the town. There were taken seven general officers, a commodore, ten continental regiments, and three battalions of artillery, together with town and country militia, French and seamen, making about six thousand men in arms. The titular deputy governor, council, and civil officers, are also prisoners. Four frigates and several armed vessels, with a great number of boats, have likewise fallen into our possession, and about four hundred pieces of canon.

Clinton continued with his warm appreciations to Lieutenant-General Earl Cornwallis, his army corps, and to Admiral Arbuthnot's fleet for their service. The British and German Hessian losses were "2 ensigns, 1 sergeant, 73 rank and file, killed; 1 captain, 7 lieutenants, 2 sergeants, 179 rank and file, wounded."

This was a tragic end to the Siege of Charleston.

King George III was out riding when Clinton's aide, the Earl of Lincoln, told him of the good news. It was the greatest victory in the war for the British, and there was great celebration in England over the fall of the city. The returning British troops were paraded before their cheering citizens. Charleston remained under British control until they evacuated it in 1782. It was the largest surrender of an American armed force until the 1862 surrender of Union forces at Harper's Ferry during the Civil War.

SIEGE OF CHARLESTON
North Wind Picture Archives

By May 8, 1780, the British held all escape routes from Charleston, and British General Henry Clinton sent a summons to American General Benjamin Lincoln to surrender.

NEW-JERSEY GAZETTE.

WEDNESDAY, JUNE 28, 1780.

PHILADELPHIA, June 17.

Last Wednesday evening arrived Lieutenant Colonel Ternant, with the following Dispatches from Major-General Lincoln to Congress.

SIR, Charlestown, May 24, 1780.

THE enclosed papers will inform Congress of each important circumstance which has occurred in this department since I did myself the honor to write them on the 9th ult. by Mr. Cannon.

They will hereby observe, that after every effort and exertion made by a handful of brave troops, contending with numberless hardships and difficulties, (to all which they most chearfully submitted) we were reduced to the sad necessity of treating with Sir Henry Clinton, and acceding to the terms of capitulation, which accompany this letter.

I shall not at present go into a detail of the matter as I expect to reach Congress before this—but should I not, Lieutenant Colonel Ternant, who is the bearer of this letter, will be able to give a minute state of things: I must beg leave therefore to refer Congress to that gentleman, and to assure them, that his steady attention to duty, and zeal for the service, entitle him to every respect.

I have the honor to be, with the highest regard and esteem, your Excellency's most obedient servant, B. LINCOLN.

Lieutenant-Colonel Ternant will be able to inform Congress what has caused so much delay in getting off the dispatches.

His Excellency Samuel Huntington, Esq.
President of Congress.

No. I.

Camp, before Charlestown, April 10th, 1780.

SIR Henry Clinton, K. B. General and Commander in Chief of his Majesty's forces, in the colonies lying on the Atlantic, from Nova Scotia, &c. &c. &c. and Vice-Admiral Arbuthnot, Commander in Chief of his Majesty's ships in North-America, &c. &c. &c. regretting the effusion of blood, and the distresses which must now commence, deem it consonant to humanity to warn the town and garrison of Charlestown of the havock and desolation with which they are threatened from the formidable force surrounding them by land and sea.

An alternative is offered at this hour to the inhabitants of saving their lives and property (contained in the town) or of abiding by the fate of the

letter, and my request that the battery on James island may desist firing. I have the honor to be, &c.
(Signed) H. CLINTON.
Major-General Lincoln.

No. V.

Articles of Capitulation proposed by Major-Gen. Lincoln.

Art. 1. That all acts of hostility and works shall cease between the naval and land forces of Great-Britain and America, in this state, until the articles of capitulation shall be agreed on, signed and executed, or collectively rejected.

2. That the town, forts, and fortifications belonging to them, shall be surrendered to the Commander in Chief of the British forces such as they now stand.

3. That the several troops garrisoning the town and forts including the French and American sailors, the French invalids, the North-Carolina and South-Carolina militia, and such of the Charlestown militia as may choose to leave this place, shall have thirty-six hours to withdraw to Lampriere's after the capitulation has been accepted and signed on both sides—and that those troops shall retire with the usual honours of war, and carry off during that time their arms, field artillery, ammunition, baggage, and such of their stores as they may be able to transport.

4. That after the expiration of the thirty-six hours mentioned in the preceding article, the British troops before the town shall take possession of it, and those now at Wappetaw shall proceed to Fort Moultrie.

5. That the American army, thus collected at Lampriere's, shall have ten days, from the expiration of the thirty-six hours before-mentioned, to march where-ever General Lincoln may think proper to the eastward of Cooper River, without any movement being made by the British troops, or part of them out of the town, or Fort Moultrie.

6. That the sick and wounded of the American and French hospitals, with their medicines, stores, the Surgeons, and Director-General, shall remain in the town, and be supplied with the necessaries requisite, until provision can be made for their removal, which will be as speedily as possible.

7. That no soldier shall be encouraged to desert, or permitted to enlist on either side.

8. That the French Consul, his house, papers, and other moveable property, shall be protected and untouched, and a proper time granted him for retiring to any place that may afterwards be agreed upon between

[...] providence, [...] with the [...] have liberty [...] on board, [...] Philadelphia, [...] French in-

[...] their persons

[...] as do not [...] ment, to [...] in the state, [...] remove such families, and that during that time, they or any of them may have it at their option to reside occasionally in town or country.

12. That the same protection to their persons and properties, and the same time for the removal of their effects, be given to the subjects of France and Spain, residing amongst us, as are required for the citizens in the preceding articles.

No. VII.

SIR, Camp before Charlestown, May 8, 1780.

CIRCUMSTANCED as I now am with respect to the place invested, humanity only can induce me to lay within your reach the terms I had determined should not again be proffered.

The fall of Fort Sullivan, the destruction (on the 6th instant) of what remained of your cavalry, the critical period to which our approaches against the town have brought us, mark this as the term of your hopes of succour, (could you ever have formed any) and as an hour, beyond which resistance is temerity.

By this last summons therefore, I throw to your charge whatever vindictive severity exasperated soldiers may inflict on the unhappy people, whom you devote by persevering in a fruitless defence.

I shall expect your answer until eight o'clock, when hostilities will commence again, unless the town be surrendered, &c. &c.
(Signed) H. CLINTON.
Major-General Lincoln.

No. VIII.

SIR, Charlestown, May 8, 1780.

YOUR letter to me of this date is now under consideration—there are so many different interests to be consulted, that I have to propose that hostilities do not again commence till twelve.
(Signed) B. LINCOLN.
His Excellency Sir Henry Clinton.

No. IX.

SIR, May 8, 1780.

I CONSENT that hostilities shall not again commence before the hour of twelve, as you desire.
I have the honour to be, Sir, &c.
(Signed) H. CLINTON.
Major-General Lincoln.

No. X.

SIR, May 8, 1780.

AS more time has been expended in consulting the different interests than I supposed there would be, I have to request that the truce may be continued until four o'clock.
(Signed) B. LINCOLN.
His Excellency Sir Henry Clinton.

No. XI.

Articles of Capitulation proposed by Major-Gen. Lincoln.

Art. 1. That all acts of hostility and work shall cease between the besiegers and besieged, until the articles of capitulation shall be agreed on, signed, and executed, or collectively rejected.

2. The town and fortifications shall be surrendered to the Commander in Chief of the British forces, such as they now stand.

3. The continental troops and sailors, with their baggage, shall be conducted to a place to be agreed on, where they will remain prisoners of war, until exchanged—While prisoners, they shall be supplied with good and wholesome provisions, in such quantity as is served out to the troops of his Britannic Majesty.

4. The militia now in garrison shall be permitted to return to their respective homes, and be secured in their persons and property.

5. The sick and wounded shall be continued under the care of their own Surgeons, and be supplied with medicines, and such necessaries as are allowed to the British hospitals.

6. The officers of the army and navy shall keep their horses, swords, pistols and baggage, which shall not be searched, and retain their servants.

No. II.

Head-Quarters, (Charlestown) April 10, 1780.

Gentlemen,

I HAVE received your summons of this date. Sixty days have passed since it has been known that your intentions against this town were hostile, in which has been afforded to abandon it; but duty and inclination point to the propriety of supporting it to the

LONDON CHRONICLE

June 17, 1780

The *London Chronicle* dated June 17, 1780, printed Sir Henry Clinton's account of the May 12 surrender of Charleston. Charleston remained under British control until they evacuated it in 1782. It was the largest surrender of an American armed force until the 1862 surrender of Union forces at Harper's Ferry during the Civil War.

main.

, *Charles Town, May 13, 1780.*

trouble your Lordship with a repe- delays and difficulties which pro- us operation until the 29th of which day the landing on Charles was effected.

ne a depot was formed; the Admi- d the Bar, and I had the essential officers and seamen of the Royal operations. I was also strengthened s from Georgia, under Brigadier- rson, which, through a country in- rivers, and rendered more difficult as, had advanced, not unopposed, f twelve days, from Savannah to re of Ashley, under the conduct of ninstone, and by the good service s and sailors of the fleet, was ac- with order and expedition, and ance on the part of the enemy.

ucceeding it the army moved to- s Town, and on the night of the broke ground within 800 yards of ks.

our guns were mounted in bat- ad the satisfaction to see the Ad- o Charles Town Harbour, with s conduct deserved, though under fire from Sullivan's Island.

eriod we judged it adviseable to osed summons to the place, which answer I have the honour to trans-

ries were opened the next day. ffect we soon observed the fire of advanced works to abate conside- ttention of the engineers, and di- troops but encreasing as they pro- econd parallel was completed on April, and secure approaches open- e were now within 450 yards of

unications had hitherto required attention. They had been chosen au's landing in Stono River across and by small inlets, leaving only d carriage into the part of Ashley te our camp.

the protection of the stores and Stono, others on the communica- eyeral redoubts and batteries on the labours necessary to give se- mportant a point.

ice of the fleet in the harbour re- om apprehension on that part, and

effect, in presence of a very superior cavalry, which might harass him much. It was there- fore of the utmost importance to strike at this corps, and, as suddenly as poss[ible] principal passes of the country.

The surprize and defeat of [the] valry and militia of the rebels, a[t] Biggin's Bridge over Cooper by lonel Tarleton with the horse, t[he] Major Ferguson's detachment, mand of the country to Colonel into his hands great supplies of enabled him to take a post n[ear] Wandoo River, forbidding by access to the town from Coope[r] Navigation. An armed naval fo[rce] Admiral sent into Servee Bay, and another stationed in Spencer's Inlet, completed the in- vestiture to the sea.

A considerable reinforcement joining me from New York the 18th of April, I immediately strengthened the corps beyond Cooper river, which, thus augmented, I requested Lieutenant General Earl Cornwallis to take under his com- mand.

On the 6th of May the third parallel was compleated close to the edge of the rebel canal, and a ship carried to the dam, which contained its water on the right, by which means a great part was drained to the bottom.

We could now form juster opinions of the de- fences of the town towards the land, which ex- tended in a chain of redoubts, lines and batte- ries, from Ashley to Cooper. In front of either flank of the works, swamps, which the canal connects, ooze to each river; betwixt these im- pediments and the place are two rows of abba- tis, various other obstructions, and a double pic- ketted ditch; a horn work of masonry, which, during the siege, the enemy closed as a kind of citadel, strengthened the center of the line and the gate, where the same natural defences were not found as nearer the water: eighty pieces of cannon or mortars were mounted in the extent of these lines.

On the 6th of May our batteries were ready in the third parallel.

New and very forcible motives now prevailed to induce the place to capitulate. Admiral Arbuthnot had landed a force of seamen and mariners on Sullivan's Island under Captain Hudson, to whom, on the threat that ships should batter the fort, the garrison delivered themselves up on terms.

Lieutenant-General Earl Cornwallis had been no less successful in the country. The ca- valry under Lieutenant-Colonel Tarleton had

proposals for a surrender far too extensive pre- tensions, the Admiral and myself could not re- frain from...

quiescence in the terms he had two days before objected to. Whatever severe justice might dictate on such an occasion, we resolved not to press to unconditional submission a reduced ar- my, whom we hoped clemency might yet re- concile to us. The articles of capitulation were therefore signed, such as I have the honor to inclose them.

On the 12th Major-General Leslie took pos- session of the town.

There are taken seven general officers, a commodore, ten continental regiments, and three battalions of artillery, together with town and country militia, French and seamen, mak- ing about six thousand men in arms. The ti- tular deputy governor, council, and civil offi- cers, are also prisoners.

Four frigates and several armed vessels, with a great number of boats, have likewise fallen into our possession, and about four hundred pieces of canon.

Of the garrison, artillery, and stores, your Lordship will have as perfect returns as I shall be able to collect.

I have yet, my Lord, to add to this letter the expressions of gratitude I owe to the army, whose courage and toil have given me suc- cess.

I have most warmly to thank Lieutenant- General Earl Cornwallis, Major Generals Les- lie, Huyne, and Kosborth, and Brigadier-Ge- neral Paterson, for their animated assistance.

I trust I do no not flatter myself vainly, that the good services during the siege of the officers and soldiers of the royal artillery, of Captain Elphinstone, and the officers and seamen of the royal navy serving with us on shore, of the corps of engineers, of the officers and soldiers of every corps, British and Hessian, and particularly the Yager detachment, will receive his Majesty's gra- cious approbation.

CAROLINA BACKCOUNTRY
MILITIA ACTIONS
By Charles B. Baxley

THE BRITISH SOUTHERN STRATEGY WAS PAYING OFF IN the summer of 1780—Georgia and the South Carolina coast were again under the Crown's control. Lord Cornwallis established his inland posts at Camden and Ninety Six in the South Carolina backcountry and reestablished Royal governance and militias to subdue the rebellion in North Carolina. Ninety Six controlled the route into Cherokee country linking the British with her Native American allies. Camden controlled the roads to central North Carolina and Virginia.

A December 5, 1780, letter from Charlotte, North Carolina, printed in the February 15, 1781, Connecticut Journal *accurately summarized the summer's actions: "Such a train of important victories obtained by raw militia, has no parallel in history."*

The infamous British Legion, a Loyalist-American-comprised infantry and cavalry commanded by Banastre Tarleton, raced through Camden to catch the last remnant of Continentals commanded by Colonel Abraham Buford as he retreated from the South Carolina Lowcountry in late May 1780. Tarleton caught Buford at the Waxhaws near the North Carolina border. While it was a British victory, "massacre" echoed through the Carolina backcountry. British overall commander General Henry Clinton's political proclamations also polarized the backcountry militiamen: loyal British citizens to arm and put down this rebellion. It was civil war.

Backcountry Patriot militia leaders from both Carolinas and Georgia, alive with zeal for liberty and self-determination, cooperated. North Carolina acted as the safe base for organization and recruitment and as a source of money and supply for South Carolina militiamen like Cols. Thomas Sumter, John Thomas Jr., and James Williams. They cooperated with the North Carolina leaders Colonel Charles McDowell in the west, General Griffith Rutherford in the central area, and General Henry William Harrington in the east.

Sumter's troops countered the British raids into the New Acquisition District of South Carolina by annihilating Captain Christian Huck's British Legion detachment at Williamson's Plantation in July. Sumter, supported by North Carolina militia, next attacked the strongly fortified British outpost at Rocky Mount, South Carolina, on July 30, 1780. Volunteers of New York and South Carolina Loyalists commanded by Lieutenant Colonel George Turnbull garrisoned Rocky Mount. Sumter's troops withdrew after a five-hour fight, without artillery to force the fortifications, when a rainstorm soaked the fire set by two intrepid soldiers to burn the British-occupied buildings. Although the August 29, 1780, excerpt from "Robertson's *New-York Gazette*," printed in the *Providence Gazette* of September 16, 1780, reported a general bayonet charge by the British, this refers to the British sally out of the defensive works to drive back the two flame throwers.

Again on the offensive a week later, Sumter's troops with North Carolina militia attacked the main British outpost at Hanging Rock. The Americans dispersed Colonel Samuel Brian's North Carolina Loyalist militia regiment and so severely damaged the Prince of Wales's American (Loyalist) Regiment, it would never fight again. After almost five hours of combat, which pushed the surviving British into a defensive square, the combat ended upon the arrival of some British Legion cavalry and Sumter's troops exhausting all of their ammunition. Sumter withdrew with many prisoners and military supplies, militia having taken on British regulars and defeated them. Bias is again evident in the report of this battle in the September 16, 1780, *Providence Gazette* acknowledging that the partisans claimed victory but disputed Sumter's claim by relating that some Legion cavalry "dashed among the rebels, put them to flight, and pursued them some a considerable distance." Sumter's men controlled the battlefield for over four hours, marched through three regimental camps, took prisoners and supplies from all of the British camps, and captured the British artillery; his six hundred men did not decide to withdraw because thirty or forty cavalrymen arrived.

A December 5, 1780, letter from Charlotte, North Carolina, printed in the February 15, 1781, *Connecticut Journal*, accurately summarized the summer's actions: "Such a train of important victories obtained by raw militia, has no parallel in history."

Into this cauldron marched the new American Southern Army commander, General Horatio Gates, the hero of Saratoga, supported by militia from North Carolina and Virginia. He relied on the partisans who secured his flanks, but the Battle of Camden a week later was an unmitigated disaster.

THURSDAY, FEBRUARY 15, 1781. THE [Numb. 694.

CONNECTICUT JOURNAL.

NEW-HAVEN: Printed by THOMAS and SAMUEL GREEN, near the College.

St. John's, in Antigua, December 9.

ON the 4th instant arrived at, English Ha frigate, command ney, having lost he all her masts in a on her passage fror The same gale Rodney's fleet (wl fallen in with and thereto) and pro Sharke, a sloop of which over-set, an longing to her pe reas parted with board of which w. Triumph and the o'clock on Sunda bound for Barbad we hear they are gether with the T

Baltimore, (in Ma

A few days since of this port, carry a sharp engageme with the privateer nia, of 12 guns, The schooner, it i festly the advantag grounding, the schooner took the opportunity of sheering off, and im

"Although some pains has been taken to asperse the militia of this, as well as our sister States, on account of what happened on the memorable 16th and 18th of August; yet, I hope, that an impartial world will not loose sight of those striking marks of heroism displayed at Ramsour's, on the 20th of June, where Col. Locke commanded; at Packelet, in the night of the 15th of July, where Col. M'Dowel commanded; at Coleson's, the mouth of Rockey river, on the 21st of July, where Col. now General Davidson commanded, in which he was wounded; at Rocky-Mount, on the 23d of July, where the heroic Gen. Sumter commanded; at Hanging-Rock, on the 6th of August, where General Sumter commanded; at Enoree, the 19th of August, where the late intrepid Col. Williams commanded; at Augusta, in Georgia, on the 12th of September, where Col. Clarke commanded; at King's Mountain, on the 7th of October, where Col. Campbell com-

lege of every society of men that were under the dominion of any one or when they found ved, and had no ress, to withdraw nd either to throw the protection of h a government , on a basis of a ture, that of public rty, which might of the few, for the ole body. He was pretended embassy vered, he was no ador, itials for an

e que the se , &c. any baffad er, the him in

told, that he was the Tower, he violating the law of nations to detain an Ambassador;

manded; at Broad-River, on the 9th of November, where Gen. Sumpter commanded, & where Maj. Wemyss was made prisoner; at Blackstocks, on Tyger river, on the 20th of November, where Gen. Sumpter commanded, and was unfortunately wounded; besides several other rencounters. Such a train of important victories obtained by raw militia, has no parrallel in history.

"The firmness of the people in Mecklenburg, and Rowan counties, when the enemy advanced to Char-

ment, and conceived himself reinstated. The people generally abandoned their habitations, some fled with what of their property they could carry, others took the field,

CONNECTICUT JOURNAL (NEW HAVEN)

February 15, 1781

—

A December 5, 1780, letter from Charlotte, North Carolina, printed in the February 15, 1781, *Connecticut Journal*, accurately summarized the summer's actions: "Such a train of important victories obtained by raw militia, has no parallel in history."

The PROVIDENCE GAZETTE

CHARLES-TOWN (South-Carolina) July 19.

From different parts of the province we have the most agreeable accounts of there being every appearance of a very plentiful harvest. There has not been in the memory of the oldest planter a more favourable season.

July 26. On Thursday last arrived here his Majesty's ship Hydra, with five sail of transports under convoy, from Savannah, having on board the Hessian regiment of Trambach.

August 9. On Friday the 28th ult. the privateer schooner Highland Lass, Capt. Sloo, returned to Savannah. On the 12th of June, she was taken by the brigantine Wasp, formerly belonging to this port, but then in possession of Spaniard. Next day she fell in with and was retaken by his Majesty's ships Richmond and Camilla, who also took the Wasp the same day. On the day following, the men of war captured 4 vessels out of 25 that had come out from the Capes of Virginia.

The following are the particulars we have been able to procure of the action on the 30th of last month: Col. Turnbull receiving intimation of the approach of a large body of rebels, said to be led by Sumpter, formerly a Lieutenant-Colonel in one of the South-Carolina Continental battalions, retired with his men, consisting of the New-York volunteers, and some loyal militia, into a block-house of stockade, at Rocky Mount, where on the 30th he was summoned to surrender. Returning a defiance in answer, a considerable firing commenced, and continued for some hours; but the enemy hearing that a reinforcement was coming from a post 9 miles distant, made a precipitate retreat, in which their speed was encreased by Col. Turnbull's dashing his corps with fixed bayonets amongst them. A number of their killed and wounded were left on the field; among the former a Colonel Neil.

Some banditti from North-Carolina, and the northern parts of this province, have been lately skulking and plundering about the Cheraws, and towards Georgetown, and have kidnapped several gentlemen, who were friends to government. They are encouraged to make these inroads by the hopes of indiscriminate plunder, held out to them by the leaders of a desperate faction.

August 10. Yesterday intelligence was brought to town, that a body of rebels, consisting of about five thousand, attacked one of our posts near the Hanging Rock, thirty miles above Camden, on Sunday last, but were repulsed. The report is, that the rebels charged our brave troops, who consisted of about two hundred and fifty men, two different times, but were drove back with great loss; and on making the third, with their whole force, were so confident of victory, that the officer who was leading them on exclaimed with great vociferation, that the day was their own; at that instant, a detachment of the cavalry of the legion arrived, dashed in amongst the rebels, put them to flight, and pursued them a considerable distance.

PROVIDENCE GAZETTE (RHODE ISLAND)
September 16, 1780

Bias is evident in the Hanging Rock battle report in the *Providence Gazette*. It acknowledged that the partisans claimed victory but disputed Sumter's claim by relating that some Legion cavalry "dashed among the rebels, put them to flight, and pursued them some a considerable distance." Sumter's men controlled the battlefield for over four hours, marched through three regimental camps, took prisoners and supplies from all of the British camps, and captured the British artillery; his six hundred men did not decide to withdraw because thirty or forty cavalrymen arrived.

his manner of rejecting the bill.

At length it was read a first time, and on the motion of Lord Stormont the bill was rejected.

The second reading of the bill to amend an act of the 3d of the present King, intituled, " an act to prevent occasional freemen from voting at elections of members to serve in Parliament for cities and boroughs," was, upon motion, on Friday last, in the House of Commons, put off till to-morrow.

The House rose between ten and eleven o'clock.

June 6.

The idea of appointing Commissioners, who shall cross the Atlantic, and treat for peace with the Americans, is again revived. It is proper (from an authority that cannot be overthrown) to warn the public, that such a measure will only serve to aggravate the burthen of national expences. Mr. Adams (a Plenipotentiary now at Paris) is near at hand; and, although not permitted to make the first propositions, is *totally* and *absolutely* empowered to listen, in the name of the United States, to general (but not *particular*) overtures.

Extract of a letter from Chatham, May 18.

" We have had several riots this week, in this town and neighbourhood, between the naval, military, and dock-yard men. Scarce a night passes without hearing of three or four of them being dangerously wounded; and on Thursday night three of these desperate wretches received their death wounds in an affray on the fair ground, and are since dead."

From the ROYAL MAGAZINE.
A short Account of the Origin, ecclesiastical Government, and Religion, of the RUSSIAN EMPIRE.

THE Russians are originally from Sclavonia, a province in Hungary. Ancient history says, that in the fifth century, three Princes went with their followers to seek new habitations, their native country being too narrow for them. It is said they were brothers, and the eldest, named Chech, settled in Bohemia, and he and his successors reigned Kings there many ages; Lech, the second brother, proceeded yet further east, and settled in Poland, and there erected a kingdom; and Russ, the third brother, went still further east, and settled a principality at Muscow.

It is observed, that in the Sclavonic language, the Bohemians are called Chechy, the Poles Lechy, and the Russians Russy. The language of these three countries is the same, and only differ in dialect, as the High Dutch from the Low Dutch. The Bohemians and Poles about the year 800 embraced the Christian religion, at the persuasion of some Romish Priests, and consequently the rites and ceremonies of that church, which they observe to this day, and make use of Latin characters in writings. But the Russians, who embraced the Christian religion much about this time, were instructed by Greek monks from Constantinople, and adhered strictly to the doctrines of the Greek church. In printing and writing they make use of Greek characters. They never acknowledged the

able season.

July 26. On Thursday last arrived here his Majesty's ship Hydra, with five sail of transports under convoy, from Savannah, having on board the Hessian regiment of Trambach.

August 9. On Friday the 28th ult. the privateer schooner Highland Lass, Capt. Sloo, returned to Savannah. On the 12th of June, she was taken by the brigantine Wasp, formerly belonging to this port, but then in possession of a Spaniard. Next day she fell in with and was retaken by his Majesty's ships Richmond and Camilla, who also took the Wasp the same day. On the day following, the men of war captured 4 vessels out of 25 that had come out from the Capes of Virginia.

The following are the particulars we have been able to procure of the action on the 30th of last month: Col. Turnbull receiving intimation of the approach of a large body of rebels, said to be led by Sumpter, formerly a Lieutenant-Colonel in one of the South-Carolina Continental battalions, retired with his men, consisting of the New-York volunteers, and some loyal militia, into a block-house or stockade, at Rocky Mount, where on the 30th he was summoned to surrender. Returning a defiance in answer, a considerable firing commenced, and continued for some hours; but the enemy hearing that a reinforcement was coming from a post 9 miles distant, made a precipitate retreat, in which their speed was encreased by Col. Turnbull's dashing his corps with fixed bayonets amongst them. A number of their killed and wounded were left on the field; among the former a Colonel Neil.

Some banditti from North-Carolina, and the northern parts of this province, have been lately skulking and plundering about the Cheraws, and towards Georgetown, and have kidnapped several gentlemen, who were friends to government. They are encouraged to make these inroads by the hopes of indiscriminate plunder, held out to them by the leaders of a desperate faction.

August 10. Yesterday intelligence was brought to town, that a body of rebels, consisting of about five thousand, attacked one of our posts near the Hanging Rock, thirty miles above Camden, on Sunday last, but were repulsed. The report is, that the rebels charged our brave troops, who consisted of about two hundred and fifty men, two different times, but were drove back with great loss; and on making the third, with their whole force, were so confident of victory, that the officer who was leading them on exclaimed with great vociferation, that the day was their own; at that instant, a detachment of the cavalry of the legion arrived, dashed in amongst the rebels, put them to flight, and pursued them a considerable distance.

BALTIMORE, August 29.

An embarkation of troops lately took place at Charlestown, South-Carolina, it is said, for St. Augustine, which it is apprehended will be shortly in-

BATTLE OF CAMDEN

ON AUGUST 16, 1780, AMERICAN AND BRITISH FORCES engaged in one of the largest battles of the Revolution in an open pine forest eight miles north of Camden, South Carolina. The engagement, which lasted nearly an hour, resulted in a crushing American defeat.

The Continental Congress responded to the British capture of Charleston on May 12, 1780, by appointing Major General Horatio Gates, hero of Saratoga, to take command of a new southern army. Gates assembled eight Continental regiments and contingents of North Carolina and Virginia militia twenty miles north of the British post at Camden. He intended to occupy a strong position about six miles north of Camden while partisans cut the town's supply lines. The British would then be forced either to attack Gates or abandon Camden.

The British commander in the south, Lieutenant General Charles, Earl Cornwallis, recognized the danger and chose to fight (as he explained in his report published in the *London Chronicle* on October 10, 1780). At 10:00 p.m. on August 15, Cornwallis marched from Camden to attack the Americans in their camp. Coincidentally, Gates marched at the same hour to occupy the position he had selected.

The vanguards of both armies met at about 2:00 a.m., and after some inconclusive fighting both commanders deployed their troops to resume the battle at daylight (the *Providence Gazette* of September 16, 1780, correctly reported the time of the initial encounter, but the main battle did not begin at that time). The exact strength of the American army is unknown. The best estimate of American strength is about 4,100. American press accounts (such as that in the *Gazette*) tended to understate the numbers of their own army and exaggerate those of the British. A field return for Cornwallis's army listed 2,239 men present at the battle.

Gates deployed the militia on his left flank, a Continental brigade on his right, and held his second brigade of Continentals in reserve. Cornwallis positioned his regular British regiments on his right, his Loyalist (provincial) units on his left, and kept two regular battalions and his cavalry in reserve.

At first light Gates ordered the militia on his left to charge the British in their front. He also ordered the reserve Continental brigade to occupy the space vacated by the militia and instructed the commander of the other Continental brigade, Major General Johann de Kalb, to make a supporting attack. Cornwallis's orders mirrored those of Gates. He instructed his right under Lieutenant Colonel James Webster to attack the militia and his left under Lieutenant Colonel Francis, Lord Rawdon, to advance in support of Webster.

The attacking North Carolina and Virginia militiamen met the British regulars rushing toward them and panicked. Throwing away their muskets, the militia fled with the exception of one North Carolina regiment (the September 16, 1780, *Providence Gazette* accurately described the militia's flight but incorrectly credited the South Carolina militia as having fought well). Gates tried to rally the fugitives but was caught up in the mob and swept from the battlefield. Webster wheeled to meet the reserve Continental brigade, and the veterans of both armies exchanged volleys with neither side able to gain an advantage. Cornwallis reinforced Webster with a reserve battalion, yet the Continental line held (Cornwallis noted their strong resistance in the October 10, 1780, *London Chronicle*).

On the American right, the Continentals drove Rawdon's line back, captured a British cannon (as the

Gazette recounted), and nearly seized Rawdon himself. Cornwallis's other reserve battalion stabilized the line. Finally, Cornwallis ordered the cavalry to charge through a gap between the two wings of the American line. Threatened with encirclement, the Continentals fled. British cavalry pursued the Americans for twenty-two miles (as reported in the *Chronicle*).

British casualties totaled 324 killed, wounded, and missing. American losses can only be estimated.

Cornwallis reported capturing 695 Americans, and at least three hundred were killed, including de Kalb (heavier casualties than reported in the *Gazette*).

Congress responded by dismissing Gates and appointing Major General Nathanael Greene to replace him. Because Cornwallis lacked supplies, he could not pursue his beaten opponent. The Americans used the reprieve to regroup in preparation for the next British move.

BATTLE OF CAMDEN, 1780
The Bridgeman Art Library

The Battle of Camden was fought in an open pine forest eight miles north of Camden, South Carolina.

BATTLE OF CAMDEN,
DEATH OF DE KALB
North Wind Picture Archives

The Battle of Camden was one of the largest battles of the Revolution and resulted in a crushing American defeat that included the death of Major General Johann de Kalb.

MEMBERS *elected for the ensuing* PAR- *LIAMENT, continued.*

BREADENSHIRE. Alexander Gordon, Esq. *Anstruther, Pittenweem,* and *Kilrenny.* Sir John Anstruther, Bart.

St. Andrews, Forfar, Coupar, Perth, and Dundee. George Dempster, Esq.

Dunfermline, Culross, Stirling, and *Queensferry.* Major Campbell.

Dunbar, Lauder, North Berwick, Haddington, and *Jedburgh.* Francis Charteris of Beanston, Esq.

Rossshire. George Graham, Esq.

Rutherglen, Dumbarton, Glasgow, and *Renfrew.* James Crawford, of Auchinames, Esq.

Selkirk. John Pringle, Esq.

Wigtown, Whitehorn, New Galloway, and *Stranraver.* William Adams, Esq.

Postscript.

THE LONDON GAZETTE EXTRAORDINARY.

Whitehall, October 9, 1780.

THIS Morning Captain Ross, Aid de Camp to Lieutenant-General Earl Cornwallis, arrived in Town from South-Carolina with a letter from his Lordship

Sumpter, who, after having in vain attempted to force the Posts at Rocky Mount and Hanging Rock, was believed to be at that Time trying to get round the Left of our Position, to cut off our Communication with the Congarees and Charles-Town; that the disaffected Country between Pedee and Black River had actually revolted; and that Lord Rawdon was contracting his Posts, and preparing to assemble his Force at Camden.

In consequence of this Information, after finishing some important Points of Business at Charles-Town, I set out on the Evening of the 10th, and arrived at Camden on the Night between the 13th and 14th, and there found Lord Rawdon with our whole Force, except Lieutenant Colonel Turnbull's small Detachment, which fell back from Rocky Mount to Major Ferguson's Posts of the Militia of Ninety-six on Little River.

I had now my Option to make, either to retire or attempt the Enemy; for the Position at Camden was a bad one to be attacked in, and by General Sumpter's advancing down the Wateree, my Supplies must have failed me in a few Days.

I saw no Difficulty in making good my Retreat to Charles-Town with the Troops that were able to march; but in taking that Re-

solution, I must have not only left near 800 Sick and a great Quantity of Stores at this Place, but I clearly saw the Loss of the whole Province, except Charles-Town, and of all Georgia, except Savannah, as immediate Consequences, besides forfeiting all Pretensions to future Confidence from our Friends in this Part of America.

On the other Hand, there was no Doubt of the Rebel Army being well appointed, and of its Number being upwards of 5000 Men, exclusive of General Sumpter's Detachment, and of a Corps of Virginia Militia of 12 or 1500 Men, either actually joined, or expected to join the main Body every Hour; and my own Corps, which never was numerous, was now reduced, by Sickness and other Casualties, to about 1400 Fighting Men of Regulars and Provincials, with 4 or 500 Militia and North Carolina Refugees.

However, the greatest Part of the Troops that I had being perfectly good, and having left Charles-Town sufficiently garrisoned and provided for a Siege, and seeing little to lose by a Defeat, and much to gain by a Victory, I resolved to take the first good Opportunity to attack the Rebel Army.

Accordingly, I took great Pains to procure [...] and Po[...] [...]ncamp[...] ck, at [...]es from [...] People, [...] deter- [...] Night [...]break, [...]their [...]nce I [...]Colonel [...]g I re- [...] as had [...]g been [...]march- [...]e De- [...] Mili- [...]nt of [...]ounted [...]on the [...]e in the Course of the Night.

I had proceeded nine Miles when about Half an Hour past Two in the Morning my advanced Guard fell in with the Enemy. By the Weight of the Fire I was convinced, they were in considerable Force, and was soon assured by some Deserters and Prisoners that it was the whole Rebel Army on its March to attack us at Camden. I immediately halted, and formed, and the Enemy doing the same, the Firing soon ceased. Confiding in the disciplined Courage of his Majesty's Troops, and well apprized by several intelligent Inhabitants, that the Ground on which both Armies stood, being narrowed by Swamps on the Right and Left, was extremely favourable for my Numbers, I did not chuse to hazard the great Stake for which I was going to fight, to the Uncertainty and Confusion to which an Action in the Dark is so particularly liable: But having taken Measures that the Enemy should not have it in their Power to avoid an Engagement on that Ground, I resolved to defer the Attack till Day. At the Dawn I made my last Disposition, and formed the Troops in the following Order: The Division of the Right, consisting of a small Corps of Light Infantry, the 23d and 33d Regiments, under the Command of Lieutenant Colonel

Webster; the Division of the Left, consisting of the Volunteers of Ireland, Infantry of the Legion, and Part of Lieutenant Colonel Hamilton's North Carolina Regiment, under the Command of Lord Rawdon, with two Six and two Three Pounders, which were commanded by Lieutenant M'Leod. The 71st Regiment, with two Six Pounders, was formed as a Reserve, one Battalion in the Rear of the Division of the Right, the other of that of the Left, and the Cavalry of the Legion in the Rear, and the Country being woody, close to the 71st Regiment, with Orders to seize any Opportunity that might offer to break the Enemy's Line, and to be ready to protect our own, in case any Corps should meet with a Check.

This Disposition was just made when I perceived that the Enemy, having likewise persisted in their Resolution to fight, were formed in two Lines opposite and near to us; and observing a Movement on their Left, which I supposed to be with an Intention to make some Alteration in their Order, I directed Lieutenant Colonel Webster to begin the Attack, which was done with great Vigor, and in a few Minutes the Action was general along the whole Front. It was at this Time a dead Calm, with a little Haziness in the Air, which, preventing the Smoke from rising, occasioned so thick a Darkness, that it was difficult to see the Effect of a very heavy and well supported Fire on both Sides. Our Line continued to advance in good Order, and with the cool Intrepidity of experienced British Soldiers, keeping up a constant Fire, or making Use of Bayonets, as Opportunities offered; and, after an obstinate Resistance during Three Quarters of an Hour, threw the Enemy into total Confusion, and forced them to give Way on all Quarters.

At this Instant I ordered the Cavalry to complete the Route, which was performed with their usual Promptitude and Gallantry; and after doing great Execution on the Field of Battle, they continued the Pursuit to Hanging Rock, 22 Miles from the Place where the Action happened, during which many of the Enemy were slain, a Number of Prisoners, near 150 Waggons (in one of which was a Brass Cannon, the Carriage of which had been damaged in the Skirmish of the Night), a considerable Quantity of Military Stores, and all the Baggage and Camp Equipage of the Rebel Army, fell into our Hands.

The Loss of the Enemy was very considerable; a Number of Colours, and seven Pieces of Brass Cannon (being all their Artillery that were in the Action), with all their Ammunition Waggons, were taken; between Eight and Nine Hundred were killed, among that Number Brigadier-General Gregory, and about One Thousand Prisoners, many of whom wounded, of which Number were Major-General Baron de Kalb, since dead, and Brigadier General Rutherford.

I have the Honour to inclose a Return of Killed and Wounded on our Side. The Loss of so many brave Men is much to be lamented; but the Number is moderate in Proportion to so great an Advantage.

The Behaviour of his Majesty's Troops in general was beyond all Praise; it did Honour to themselves and to their Country.

I was particularly indebted to Colonel Lord Rawdon and to Lieutenant Colonel Webster for the distinguished Courage and Ability with which they conducted their respective Divisions; and the Capacity and Vi-

---

LONDON CHRONICLE
October 10, 1780

The Continental Congress responded to the British capture of Charleston on May 12, 1780, by appointing Major General Horatio Gates, hero of Saratoga, to take command of a new southern army. Gates assembled his forces twenty miles north of the British post at Camden and planned to occupy a strong position about six miles north of town. British commander in the South, Lieutenant General Charles, Earl Cornwallis, recognized the danger and chose to fight.

Parliament for cities and bo-
motion, on Friday last, in the
put off till to-morrow.
ween ten and eleven o'clock.

June 6.

ting Commissioners, who shall
treat for peace with the Ame-
d.' It is proper (from an au-
overthrown) to warn the pub-
e will only serve to aggravate
al expences. Mr. Adams (a
t Paris) is near at hand; and,
d to make the first propositions,
empowered to listen, in the
tates, to general (but not par-

from Chatham, May 18.

everal riots this week, in this
od, between the naval, mili-
en. Scarce a night passes with-
four of them being dangerous-
Thursday night three of these
eived their death wounds in an
und, and are since dead."

AL MAGAZINE.

Origin, ecclesiastical Govern-
f the RUSSIAN EMPIRE.

e originally from Sclavonia, a
gary. Ancient history says,
three Princes went with their
abitations; their native coun-
them. It is said they were
named Chech, settled in Bo
uccessors reigned Kings there
econd brother, proceeded yet
in Poland, and there erected
the third brother, went still
a principality at Muscow.

in the Sclavonic language,
d Chechy, the Poles Lechy,
The language of these three
d only differ in dialect, as the
ow Dutch. The Bohemians
r 800 embraced the Christian
n of some Romish Priests, and
d ceremonies of that church,
is day, and make use of La-
e. But the Russians, who
eligion much about this time,
k monks from Constantino-
o the doctrines of the Greek
d writing they make use of
y never acknowledged the
f the church, but the Patri-
ill the time Constantinople
and the Russ clergy elected
is residence at Muscow, and
ver in all ecclesiastical mat-
at thinking too great, depos
imself head of the church.
sent in secular and monastic
s are Archbishops, Bishops,
ecular order of priests may
die, they cannot officiate in
e to a monastery; which is
kind to their wives. The
St. Basil, whereof there are
ia; each monastery has a
andit. The monks are not
re are two or three nunne
are not very regular, for
eceive company.

August 9. On Friday the 28th ult. the privateer
schooner Highland Lass, Capt. Sloo, returned to Savannah. On the 12th of June, she was taken by the
brigantine Wasp, formerly belonging to this port, but
then in possession of a Spaniard. Next day she fell in
with and was retaken by his Majesty's ships Richmond and Camilla, who also took the Wasp the
same day. On the day following, the men of war
captured 4 vessels out of 25 that had come out from
the Capes of Virginia.

The following are the particulars we have been
able to procure of the action on the 30th of last
month: Col. Turnbull receiving intimation of the
approach of a large body of rebels, said to be led by
Sumpter, formerly a Lieutenant-Colonel in one of
the South-Carolina Continental battalions, retired
with his men, consisting of the New-York volunteers,
and some loyal militia, into a block-house or stockade, at Rocky Mount, where on the 30th he was
summoned to surrender. Returning a defiance in answer, a considerable firing commenced, and continued
for some hours; but the enemy hearing that a reinforcement was coming from a post 9 miles distant,
made a precipitate retreat, in which their speed was
encreased by Col. Turnbull's dashing his corps with
fixed bayonets amongst them. A number of their
killed and wounded were left on the field; among
the former a Colonel Neil.

Some banditti from North-Carolina, and the
northern parts of this province, have been lately
skulking and plundering about the Cheraws, and towards Georgetown, and have kidnapped several
gentlemen, who were friends to government. They
are encouraged to make these inroads by the hopes
of indiscriminate plunder, held out to them by the
leaders of a desperate faction.

August 10. Yesterday intelligence was brought to
town, that a body of rebels, consisting of about five
thousand, attacked one of our posts near the Hanging Rock, thirty miles above Camden, on Sunday
last, but were repulsed. The report is, that the rebels charged our brave troops, who consisted of about
two hundred and fifty men, two different times, but
were drove back with great loss; and on making the
third, with their whole force, were so confident of
victory, that the officer who was leading them on
exclaimed with great vociferation, that the day was
their own; at that instant, a detachment of the cavalry of the legion arrived, dashed in amongst the
rebels, put them to flight, and pursued them a considerable distance.

BALTIMORE, August 29.

An embarkation of troops lately took place at
Charlestown, South-Carolina, it is said, for St. Augustine, which it is apprehended will be shortly invested by the Spaniards.

Several valuable bay craft, some of them richly
laden, have, within a few days, been captured by the
enemy's small privateers, which are cruising between
the Capes and the mouth of Patuxent. One of the
captured vessels was commanded by Capt. Joseph
White, of this town, and had effects on board worth
upwards of 100,000 l.

We are assured, by good authority, that on the 16th
inst. at 2 o'clock, A. M. a bloody battle was fought
within 8 miles of Camden, South-Carolina, between
his Excellency General Gates, at the head of about
3000 men, 900 of whom were regulars, and the
British forces, under the command of Earl Cornwallis,
consisting of 1800 regulars, and 2400 refugees, &c.
The contending armies engaged each other with the
greatest fury, and the prospect, for some time, was
extremely favourable to the American troops, who
charged bayonets on the enemy, which obliged

them to give ground, and leave some of their artillery
in the possession of our advancing troops—But unfortunately, at this critical moment, the premature flight
of the militia terminated the conflict in favour of the
enemy—an event which hath proved fatal to many of
our brave countrymen of the regular troops, 4 or 500
of whom having been killed and taken—amongst
them are several valuable officers, whose names we
think it prudent to omit for the present. The enemy's loss hath been much more considerable. Lord
Cornwallis, or some other British General, it is con-
jectured, is amongst the slain.——Notwithstanding
this misfortune, General Gates, whose Head-Quarters
are at Hillsborough, is collecting a force much superior
to his late army, and appears resolved to try the fortune of another day.

The Virginians have completed their quota of
5000 men, who are marching, in detachments of 500
men each, to reinforce General Gates.

About 300 cavalry, under the Colonels White and
Washington, left Halifax, North-Carolina, a few days
ago, to join General Gates, at Hillsborough.

In justice to the South-Carolina militia, it must be
mentioned, that they greatly distinguished themselves
in the late action.

PHILADELPHIA, August 23.

A letter from Pittsburgh, of the 4th ult. says, that
a party of 600 Indians, with 150 English and French,
marched from Detroit, with four field-pieces, to take
possession of Kaintuck, in Virginia; when information being given, Major Lanckton, Superintendent of
Indian affairs, went and met them privately, and
soon persuaded the Indians to lay down their arms,
which they did; and two days after, the guide
came in, leaving the British to find their way back to
Detroit in the best manner they could—but 'tis generally believed they would all perish, unless they
came and surrendered themselves.

September 2. Captain Montgomery, who lately
arrived here from L'Orient, left the coast of France
about the 10th of July. He says, that the British
channel fleet had been seen near Ushant, about the
last of June. Some days after his departure, about
150 leagues from the land, just before day, he fell in
with 16 sail of large ships, and 2 frigates, lying too;
they chased him for some time. Perhaps they may
be a Spanish squadron, bound from Cadiz to Brest,
which had left the coast of Europe to avoid the northern winds, common in summer on the coast of

the brig Phoenix, be
her in.

At a Town-Mee
John Hancock, Esq
Governor of this Co

We hear from Po
night the tories burn
that place, whom th

PROVID

At the Superior C
than Carpenter an
been charged, as me
glary, in breaking a
Nathaniel Sprague,
quitted said Carpenter
a Nolle Prosequi un
for the same Offenc
also for Larceny, they
and on pleading gu
for that Crime, rece
That they should p
the Value of the Mon
of One Thousand One
and all Costs of Prosec
case the same should
stant, each to be whi
Stripes, at a Cart's
Providence, between t
of that Day; that if do
stolen, and all Costs of
were not paid by the f
be respectively sold by
the 1st Day of October
not to exceed three Y
and that each should re
Thousand Pounds, with
in the Sum of Five Tho
haviour for one Year, a
tence should be perform

A Letter from Philade
mentions, that in the
South-Carolina, General
land Line, was killed
wounded, and taken Pri

Sunday last arrived he
from Cape Francois, wh
Company with a French
a Number of Frigates,

which the inhabitants of the neighbourhood regularly attended; and the respect paid to private property
was such, that all the [dama]ge done in three weeks
did not amount to more than fifty pounds specie,
agreeable to an appraisement made by two freeholders of New-Jersey. They were well provided
with tents, and all other necessaries for actual field

tain Lot of Land, situate
about Four Acres, bounded
John Usher, and partly by h
East, West and South, by
otherwise the said Lot may
to be bounded.

Therefore Notice is here

PROVIDENCE GAZETTE (RHODE ISLAND)
September 16, 1780
—

The vanguards of both armies met at about two a.m.,
and after some inconclusive fighting both commanders
deployed their troops to resume the battle at daylight
(the *Providence Gazette* of September 16, 1780, correctly
reported the time of the initial encounter, but the main
battle did not begin at that time). Also, American
press accounts (such as that in the *Gazette*) tended
to understate the numbers of their own army and
exaggerate those of the British.

IN SEPTEMBER 1780, THE BRITISH ARMY UNDER Lieutenant General Charles, Earl Cornwallis, occupied Charlotte, North Carolina. Opposed by only a few partisans in South Carolina and the remnants of Major General Horatio Gates's Continental Army, defeated the previous month at the Battle of Camden, Cornwallis seemed on the verge of completing the conquest of the southern states. Then, at the Battle of Kings Mountain on October 7, 1780, the tide of war suddenly shifted in the Americans' favor.

Scottish Major Patrick Ferguson had been assigned the task of organizing South Carolina Loyalists into an effective militia. With a core of about one hundred veteran Loyalist troops from the north, Ferguson began training volunteers in the northwestern part of the state, where a large percentage of the populace remained loyal to Britain. While undertaking this task, Ferguson also conducted operations against American partisans.

Rebel partisans attacked the British-held town of Augusta, Georgia, in September 1780 (contrary to the report in the *Pennsylvania Gazette* of October 25, 1780, the Americans failed to capture the town). When the Americans abandoned the siege and withdrew northward, Ferguson received orders to intercept their retreat.

Ferguson took his one hundred provincials and seven hundred militia into western North Carolina. There they recruited about two hundred Loyalists but failed to catch the Americans. On several previous occasions, Ferguson had battled Americans who had come from west of the Appalachians to harass the British, and since he was close to their settlements, he sent them a

Cornwallis seemed on the verge of completing the conquest of the southern states, but the American victory at Kings Mountain marked a turning point in the campaign.

message threatening to raze their homes if they continued to fight.

The western settlers, called the "Overmountain Men," lived illegally on lands reserved to the Indians by the British government's Proclamation of 1763. Knowing that a British victory would result in their removal from the territory, the Overmountain Men opted to attack Ferguson. Colonels Isaac Shelby, John Sevier, William Campbell, and Benjamin Cleveland (as reported in the October 25, 1780, *Pennsylvania Gazette*) led the Overmountain Men, and Colonel James Williams joined them with a force of South Carolinians. Their strength was about three thousand men, although just over half were able to reach Kings Mountain in time to engage Ferguson (these figures were accurately reported in the *Gazette*).

Learning that this force was pursuing him, Ferguson retreated to Kings Mountain, about twenty-five miles from the main British army in Charlotte, on October 6. He occupied the hilltop and asked Cornwallis for reinforcements. Apparently Ferguson hoped to trap the Americans between his own force and British troops from Charlotte. Cornwallis, however, did not send Ferguson any aid, despite the pleas of his cavalry commander, Lieutenant Colonel Banastre Tarleton, that he be permitted to lead a detachment to assist Ferguson.

On the afternoon of October 7, the Americans surrounded Ferguson's Loyalists. Repeated assaults on the hill were repulsed by bayonet charges that dispersed the attackers (noted in the *London Chronicle* of January 13, 1781, although the report understated Ferguson's strength and exaggerated the Americans' numbers). After nearly an hour of fighting, the Americans gained a foothold on the southeastern end of Kings Mountain, and Ferguson ordered a desperate bayonet charge in an attempt to break out. He was killed in the effort (which was not a reconnaissance as stated in the *Chronicle*), and his troops surrendered.

About 135 Loyalists were killed and six hundred captured (fewer than claimed by the *Gazette*, but more than reported in the *Chronicle*). Americans losses were officially reported at twenty-eight killed, including Colonel Williams, and sixty-two wounded (the *Gazette* accurately noted Williams's death but understated American casualties); however, Loyalist prisoners estimated American casualties as equal to their own.

The American victory at Kings Mountain marked a turning point in the southern campaign. Cornwallis was forced to withdraw to South Carolina (as stated in the *Chronicle*), and the Americans soon seized the opportunity to mount their own offensive operations.

LONDON CHRONICLE
January 13, 1781
—

On the afternoon of October 7, 1780, the Americans surrounded Ferguson's Loyalists. Repeated assaults on the hill were repulsed by bayonet charges that dispersed the attackers (noted in the *London Chronicle* of January 13, 1781, although the report understated Ferguson's strength and exaggerated the Americans' numbers). After nearly an hour of fighting, the Americans gained a foothold on the southeastern end of Kings Mountain.

and land, have resolved, and do, by and with the advice of our Privy Council, hereby command, That a Public Fast and Humiliation be observed throughout that part of our kingdom of Great Britain called England, our dominion of Wales, and town of Berwick upon Tweed, upon Wednesday the 21st day of February next; that so both we and our people may humble ourselves before Almighty God, in order to obtain pardon of our sins; and may, in the most devout and solemn manner, send up our prayers and supplications to the Divine Majesty, for averting those heavy judgments which our manifold fins and provocations have most justly deserved, and imploring his blessing and assistance on our arms, and for restoring and perpetuating peace, safety, and prosperity, to us and our kingdoms: And we do strictly charge and command, that the said Public Fast be reverently and devoutly observed by all our loving subjects in England, our dominion of Wales, and town of Berwick upon Tweed, as they tender the favour of Almighty God, and would avoid his wrath and indignation; and upon pain of such punishment as we may justly inflict on all such as contemn and neglect the performance of so religious and necessary a duty. And for the better and more orderly solemnizing the fame, we have given directions to the most Reverend the Archbishops, and the Right Reverend the Bishops of England, to compose a form of

LONDON CHRONICLE

killed and took upwards of three hundred. This stroke obliged Lord Cornwallis to return into South Carolina, and by the last accounts from him, he was returning near Waxsaws towards Ninety Six.

" The rebels made an unsuccessful attempt upon Augusta. The garrison was relieved by a

Yesterday there was a levee at St. James's, when the Hon. Mr. North, son of Lord North, kissed his Majesty's hand on being appointed Secretary and Comptroller of her Majesty's household, in the room of James Harris, Esq; deceased.

Yesterday a deputation of the West India merchants waited on Lord Sandwich, at his house in the Admiralty, with whom they had an hour and an half's conference, when his Lordship assured them of every assistance in his power towards the relief of the West India Islands.

Extract of a Letter from New York, Nov. 30.

" After the battle of Camden, Lord Cornwallis advanced into North Carolina, and Col. Ferguson attempting to join him from Ninety Six, with about 400 militia, was attacked at King's Mountain by near 2000 rebels. He twice repulsed them, and went out with 30 men to reconnoitre, when he was unfortunately killed. This dispirited his party. The rebels made a third attack, and succeeded. They

The PENNSYLVANIA GAZETTE

PHILADELPHIA, *October 25.*

Extract of a letter from his Excellency Governor Jefferson, of Virginia, to the President of Congress, dated Richmond, October 15, 1780, six o'clock, P. M.

SIR,

" I DO myself the pleasure of congratulating your Excellency on the small dawn of good fortune which at length appears in the south, as you will find by the dispatches I have the honour of inclosing to you, and which I this moment received from General Gates."

SIR, *Burk county, 2d October, 1780.*

" I am, at present, about 70 miles from Salisbury, in the fork of the Catabaw, with about 450 horsemen, in pursuit of Colonel Ferguson. On my crossing the Catabaw river I dispatched to different quarters for intelligence, and this evening I was favoured with this news, which you may depend on: That Colonel Clark, of the State of Georgia, with 100 riflemen, forced his way through South Carolina to Georgia. On his route thither being joined by 700 men, he proceeded to the town of Augusta, and has taken it with a large quantity of goods; but not finding it prudent to continue there, he has retreated to the upper parts of South-Carolina, in Ninety-six district, and made a stand with 800 brave men.

" This moment another of my expresses is arrived from Colonels M'Dowell and Shelby: They were on their march, near Burk Court-house, with 1500 brave Mountain-men, and Colonel Cleveland was within 10 miles of them with 800 men, and was to form a junction with them this day. I expect to join them to morrow, in pursuit of Colonel Ferguson, and under the direction of

Heaven, I hope to be able to render your Honour a good account of him in a few days. I am, &c.

(Signed) JAMES WILLIAMS."

Major General GATES

SIR, *Hillsborough, 12th October, 1780.*

" This instant I received the great and glorious news contained in the inclosed letter from Brigadier General Davidson to General Sumner, who directly dispatched it to me by express. We are now more than even with the enemy. The moment the supplies for the troops here arrive from Taylor's Ferry, I shall proceed with the whole to Yadkin. General Smallwood and Colonel Morgan are on their way to that post; the latter, with the light-infantry, was yesterday advanced 18 miles beyond Guilford Court-house; the former, with the cavalry, lay, last night, 13 miles on this side that place. I desire your Excellency will forthwith dispatch copies of all the letters I now send you to the President of Congress. I am, &c.

HORATIO GATES."

Governor JEFFERSON.

[…]

SIR, *Camp, Rocky-river, October 10, 1780.*

" I have the pleasure of handing you very agreeable intelligence from the west Ferguson, the great partisan, has miscarried. This we are assured of by Mr. Tate, Brigade Major in General Sumpter's late command: The particulars from that gentleman's mouth stand thus: That Colonels Campbell, Cleaveland, Shelby, Seveer, Williams, Brandon, Lacey, &c. formed a conjunct body, near Gilbert-Town, consisting of 3000; from this body were selected 1600 good horse, who immediately went in pursuit of Colonel Ferguson, who was making his way to Charlotte. Our people overtook him well posted on King's Mountain, and on the evening of the 7th inst. at 4 o'clock, began the attack, which continued 47 minutes. Colonel Ferguson fell in the action, besides 150 of his men; 810 were made prisoners, including the British; 150 of the prisoners are wounded; 1500 stand of arms fell into our hands. Colonel Ferguson had about 1400 men. Our people surrounded them, and the enemy surrendered. We left about 20 men, among whom is Major Chronicle of Lincoln county. Colonel Williams is mortally wounded. The number of our wounded cannot be ascertained. This blow will certainly affect the British very considerable. The Brigade Major who gives us this was in the action. The above is true. The blow is great. I give you joy upon the occasion. I am, &c.

(Signed)   WILLIAM DAVISON."

Honourable General SUMNER.

PENNSYLVANIA GAZETTE (PHILADELPHIA)
October 25, 1780
—

Rebel partisans attacked the British-held town of Augusta, Georgia, in September 1780 (contrary to the report in the *Pennsylvania Gazette* of October 25, 1780, the Americans failed to capture the town). When the Americans abandoned the siege and withdrew northward, Ferguson received orders to intercept their retreat but failed to catch the Americans. Three thousand "Overmountain Men" then opted to attack Ferguson.

---

vain. This horse is
t De Lancey 200l.—
he brought him in—
nter of all his cattle
er went down with a
of taking his cattle,
s horse by way of re-
ingly replied, "You

ued a proclamation,
his State, to observe
er next, as a day of
ty God, for the re-
rought in behalf of
this State in particu-
e conspiracy for be-
lands into the hands
n for the evils preva-
re a continuance of

October 18.
election in this State,
the several counties
during the ensuing
were chosen.
-Stevens, Esquire.

Tallman, Esquire.
am Trent, William

ooper, Esquire. Af-
ard, Isaac Kay, Ef-

ripps, Esquire. Af-
eton, jun. William

min Manning, Esq.
uydam, Melancthon

Lawrence, Esquire.
aniel Scudder, Tho-

itherspoon, Esquire.
kpatrick, Christopher

are not yet come to

moved from Tapan
ergen county, previ-
e marched four bri-

tant says, that "On
Post at Bergen Point,
omas Ward, was at-
nd horse, consisting
a smart fire from the
ees, assisted by a can-
e forced to retreat."
he above, that the af-
Refugees.
oners has lately been
an troops, now with

nia) October 4.
ge Rogers Clarke, to
Louisville, August 22.

the aid of Colonel
the number of 1000,
he mouth of Licking
an our march the 2d.
y to pass for seventy
ached the first town,
greatest part of their
onduct of the Indians
oborating circumstan-
r us on to their own
destroying the crops
gan our march for the
f the Big Miame, the
before our advanced
vening of the 8th, we
orts, a plain of half a
I had an opportunity
s of the enemy, near

the necessary disposi-
on our left wing, and
neral, with a savage

I could wish to have had a small store of provisions, to have enabled us to have laid waste part of the Delaware settlements, and falling in at Pittsburgh, but the excessive heat and weak diet shewed the impropriety of such a step. Nothing could excel the few regulars and Kentuckyans that composed this little army, in bravery and implicit obedience to orders. Each company vying with the other who should be the most subordinate."

PHILADELPHIA, *October* 25.
Extract of a letter from his Excellency Governor Jefferson, of Virginia, to the President of Congress, dated Richmond, October 15, 1780, *six o'clock, P. M.*

S I R,
"I DO myself the pleasure of congratulating your Excellency on the small dawn of good fortune which at length appears in the south, as you will find by the dispatches I have the honour of inclosing to you, and which I this moment received from General Gates."

S I R,   *Burk county, 2d October,* 1780.
"I am, at present, about 70 miles from Salisbury, in the fork of the Catabaw, with about 450 horsemen, in pursuit of Colonel Ferguson. On my crossing the Catabaw river I dispatched to different quarters for intelligence, and this evening I was favoured with this news, which you may depend on: That Colonel Clark, of the State of Georgia, with 100 riflemen, forced his way through South Carolina to Georgia; being joined by 700 men, he proceeded to the town of Augusta, and has taken it with a large quantity of goods; but not finding it prudent to continue there, he has retreated to the upper parts of South-Carolina, in Ninety-six district, and made a stand with 800 brave men.

"This moment another of my expresses is arrived from Colonels M'Dowell and Shelby: They were on their march, near Burk Court-house, with 1500 brave Mountain-men, and Colonel Cleveland was within 10 miles of them with 800 men, and was to form a junction with them this day. I expect to join them to-morrow, in pursuit of Colonel Ferguson, and under the direction of Heaven, I hope to be able to render your Honour a good account of him in a few days. I am, &c.
(Signed)   JAMES WILLIAMS."
Major General GATES.

S I R,   *Hillsborough, 11th October,* 1780.
"This instant I received the great and glorious news contained in the inclosed letter from Brigadier General Davidson to General Sumner, who directly dispatched it to me by express. We are now more than even with the enemy. The moment the supplies for the troops here arrive from Taylor's Ferry, I shall proceed with the whole to the Yadkin. General Smallwood and Colonel Morgan are on their way to that post; the latter, with the light-infantry, was yesterday advanced 18 miles beyond Guilford Court-house; the former, with the cavalry, lay last night, 13 miles on this side that place. I desire your Excellency will forthwith dispatch copies of all the letters I now send you to the President of Congress. I am, &c.
HORATIO GATES."
Governor JEFFERSON.

D E A R S I R,
"I have the pleasure to enclose to you a large packet of dispatches taken yesterday, at M'Cappin's Creek, on the way to Camden, by a small party of my brigade. A detachment of 120 horse, under Rutledge and Dickson, almost surrounded Charlotte yesterday, attacked a picket at Col. Polk's mill, and at a certain Mr. Elliot's, brought off a centinel and eight tories, who are now on their way to you. A small party of riflemen brought off 50 horses from the tories at Col. Polk's plantation last night. I have the honour to be, &c. WILLIAM DAVISON.
Rocky-river, Sunday, 2 o'clock, 10th October, 1780.
"P. S. Dickson lost one man killed, and one officer wounded."
General SUMNER.

S I R,   *Camp, Rocky-river, October* 10, 1780.
"I have the pleasure of handing you very agreeable intelligence from the west. Ferguson, the great partizan, has miscarried. This we are assured of by Mr. Tate, Brigade Major in General Sumpter's late command: The particulars from that gentleman's mouth stand thus: That Colonels Campbell, Cleaveland, Shelby, Sevier, Williams, Brandon, Lacey, &c. formed a conjunct body, near Gilbert-Town, consisting of 3000; from this body were selected 1600 good horse, who immediately went in pursuit of Colonel Ferguson, who was making his way to Charlotte. Our people overtook him well posted on King's Mountain, and on the evening of the 7th inst. at 4 o'clock, began the attack, which continued 47 minutes. Colonel

---

Ferguson fell in the action, besides 150 of his men; 810 were made prisoners, including the British; 150 of the prisoners are wounded; 1500 stand of arms fell into our hands. Colonel Ferguson had about 1400 men. Our people surrounded them, and the enemy surrendered. We left about 20 men, among whom is Major Chronicle of Lincoln county. Colonel Williams is mortally wounded. The number of our wounded cannot be ascertained. This blow will certainly affect the British very considerably. The Brigade Major who gives us this was in the action. The above is true. The blow is great. I give you joy upon the occasion. I am, &c.
(Signed)   WILLIAM DAVISON."
Honourable General SUMNER.

      Camp, Yadkin-Ford, October 10, 1780.
S I R,   *Eight o'clock, evening.*
"With great satisfaction I inform you of the defeat of Major Ferguson, on King's Mountain, 4 o'clock, Saturday afternoon. The particulars I inclose you as I received them a few minutes ago: Also a letter from General Davison, of his securing 29 barrels of powder, which were secreted, some time since, near Charlotte. I am, Sir,
With great respect, your very humble servant,
JETHRO SUMNER."
Published by Order of Congress,
CHARLES THOMSON, *Secretary.*

On the above important intelligence being circulated in the city, the chearful countenances of the honest and virtuous part of the community fully evinced the heart-felt satisfaction they experienced on the joyful occasion; whilst the malignant aspects of the disaffected sufficiently betrayed their chagrin and disappointment.
Extract of a letter from Cadiz, dated August 16, 1780.
"The pleasure of communicating intelligence, that I suppose may prove interesting or acceptable, induces me

---

P R O C L A M
W H E R E A S it hath plea
Father of all mercies, an
calamities of war, to bestow ble
these states, which call for their d
knowledgments, more especially
interposition of his watchful pro
person of our commander in chi
imminent dangers, at the momen
ened for execution: in prospering
bandmen, and causing the earth
plentiful harvests; and above all,
enjoyment of the gospel of peace:

It is therefore recommended to
apart Thursday, the seventh day o
observed as a day of public thankf
all the people may assemble on t
praises of our Divine Benefactor
thiness of the least of his favours,
supplications to the God of all g
him to pardon our heinous transg
hearts for the future to keep all h
relieve our brethren who are anyw
to smile upon our husbandry and tr
lic councils and lead our forces by
to take our illustrious ally under
and favour our joint councils an
blishment of speedy and permane
fools and seminaries of educa
knowledge of Christianity to spre
*Done in Congress, this eighteen
and in the fifth year of the I
States of America.*
Attest.   SAMUEL HUNT
CHARLES THOMSON, *Secretary.*

EXECUTION OF
MAJOR JOHN ANDRÉ
The Bridgeman Art Library

Major John André, British army
officer, hanged October 2,
1780, by the Continental Army
for spying.

TREASON OF BENEDICT ARNOLD AND HANGING OF JOHN ANDRÉ

By Dennis M. Conrad

To this day, Benedict Arnold's attempt to treasonously surrender the American bastion at West Point to the British is considered an act of the vilest nature, and Arnold continues to be considered one of America's greatest villains. How Arnold's well-conceived plans were disrupted is laid out in the *Boston Gazette* article of October 16, 1780. Almost immediately, the British launched an attempt to save Adjutant-General of the British army, Major John André, who had served as Arnold's go-between and had been arrested out of uniform. The letters by Beverly Robinson, Sir Henry Clinton, and Arnold arguing that André was acting under a flag of truce and should not be considered a spy, which are printed in the *London Chronicle* of December 2, 1780, were part of that effort. They were presented to General Nathanael Greene, acting as Washington's representative, in a clandestine meeting with three important British officials on October 1. Greene countered with the letter from André of September 24, also printed in the *London Chronicle*. In that letter, conceded the Royal Governor of New York writing to Henry Clinton immediately after the meeting, André, admitted his actions were criminal. The British delegation then offered to release anyone in British possession in exchange for André, and Greene countered by saying that only by returning Arnold could the British secure André's release. Not surprisingly, the British found such an exchange to be unacceptable, and the Americans proceeded to hang André as a spy, releasing the documents printed in the *London Chronicle* of December 2 to justify their action.

As can be seen in the proclamations issued in Arnold's name printed in the *London Chronicle* of November 14 and December 2, the British hoped to capitalize on the defection of Arnold and appointed him a brigadier general in the British army and authorized him to raise an armed force comprised of American deserters and Loyalists. Arnold's efforts to spark wholesale defection were unsuccessful, and Arnold himself, though he became an active and successful leader for the British in America, was never embraced nor trusted by his new compatriots, who treated him with cold politeness. After the war, he was quickly shunted aside by British authorities and never again given a position of any importance. Legend has it that on his deathbed he said: "Let me die in this old uniform in which I fought my battles. May God forgive me for ever having put on another," though the story is probably apocryphal.

"It is an irony among ironies that Benedict Arnold managed to do what no one else had. He revitalized the Revolution."

According to historian Dave R. Palmer in his book *George Washington and Benedict Arnold: A Tale of Two Patriots*, reaction to Arnold's treason among Americans followed three distinct waves. First was "surprise, disbelief, and shock," followed quickly by "biting anger" and sheer hatred. "Arnold became almost at once a figure despised and reviled as none other has been in the entire history of the United States." The third wave concerned the nation itself. Seeing the "hand of Providence" in the foiling of the treasonous plot, Americans experienced something akin to a "religious revival." Palmer notes: "It is an irony among ironies that Benedict Arnold managed to do what no one else had. He revitalized the Revolution."

The
BOSTON
GAZETTE

BOSTON, October 16.

Extract of a letter from a gentleman, dated Tapan, October 2, 1780.

" You will have heard before you can receive this, of the *infernal* villainy of Arnold. It is not possible for human nature to receive a greater quantity of guilt than he possesses : Perhaps there is not a single obligation, moral or divine, but what he has broken thro'. It is deserved now, that in his most early infancy, hell mark'd him for her own, and infus'd into him a full proportion of her diabolical malice.

" His late apostacy is the summit of his character. He began his negotiations with the enemy, to deliver up West Point to them, long before he was invested with the command of it, and whilst he was still in Philadelphia ; after which he solicited the command of that post, for the ostensible reason, that the wound in his leg incapacitated him for active command in the field : It was granted him on the 6th of August last.—Since which he has been as assiduous as possible in ripening his plans, but the various positions the army assumed, prevented their being put into execution.

" On the night of the 21st ultimo, he had an interview with Major Andre, the Adjutant-General of the British army. This gentleman came on shore from the Vulture man of war, which lay not far from Taller's Point, to a place on the banks of the river, near to the Haverstraw mountain, where he met Arnold, who conducted him to the house of Joshua Smith (the white house) within our lines, and only two miles from Stony-Point. They arrived in the house just before day & stay'd there until next evening, when Major Andre became extremely sollicitous to return by the way he came, but that was impossible, for the two men who Arnold and Smith had seduced to bring on shore, refused to carry

him back. It then was absolutely necessary he should return to New-York by land. He chang'd his dress and name, and thus disguised, passed our post of Stoney and Verplank's Points, on the evening of the 22d ult. in company with the said Joshua Smith, brother to William Smith, Esq; Chief Justice within the British lines ; he lodged that night at Cron Pond, with Smith, and in the morning left Smith, and took the road to Tarry-Town, where he was taken by some militia lads about 15 miles from Kings Bridge. He offered them any sum of money, and goods, if they would permit him to escape, but they readily declared and inflexibly adhered to it, that 10,000 guineas, or any other sum, would be no temptation to them. It was this virtue as glorious to America as Arnold's apostacy is disgraceful, that his abominable crimes were discovered.

" The lads, in searching him, found concealed under his stockings, in his boots, papers of the highest importance, viz.

1. Return of the ordnance and its distributions at West-Point and its dependencies.

2. Artillery orders, in case of an alarm.

3. Returns of the number of men necessary to man the works at West-Point and its dependencies.

4 Remarks on the works at West Point with the strength and working of each.

5. Returns of the troops at West Point and their distribution.

6. State of our army &c transmitted by General Washington to Arnold for his opinion, which state had been submitted to all the general officers in the Camp, for their opinions.

" Besides which it appears, that Arnold had carried with him to the interview, a general plan of West Point and its vicinity, and all the works, and also particular plans of each work, on a large scale,—all elegantly drawn by the engineer at that post. But these were not delivered to Major Andre, and from their requiring much time to copy, it was supposed they were not to be delivered until some future period.

From some circumstances it appears, that it was not Arnold's intention to have deserted, but that he meant to be taken at his post, which, from his distributions of the troops, was very easy to have seized. [...]

trary notwithstanding.

[*This Act passed September 29, 1780*]

BOSTON, October 16.

Extract of a letter from a gentleman, dated Tappan, October 2, 1780.

"You will have heard before you can receive this, of the infernal villainy of Arnold. It is not possible for human nature to receive a greater quantity of guilt than he possesses: Perhaps there is not a single obligation, moral or divine, but what he has broken thro'. It is discovered now, that in his most early infancy, hell mark'd him for her own, and infus'd into him a full proportion of her diabolical malice.

"His late apostacy is the summit of his character. He began his negotiations with the enemy, to deliver up West Point to them, long before he was invested with the command of it, and whilst he was still in Philadelphia; after which he sollicited the command of that post, for the ostensible reason, that the wound in his leg incapacitated him for an active command in the field: It was granted him on the 6th of August last—Since which he has been as assiduous as possible in ripening his plans, but the various positions the army assumed, prevented their being put into execution.

"On the night of the 21st ultimo, he had an interview with Major Andre, the Adjutant-General of the British army. This gentleman came on shore from the Vulture man of war, which lay not far from Taller's Point, to a place on the banks of the river, near to the Haverstraw mountain, where he met Arnold, who conducted him to the house of Joshua Smith (the white house) within our lines, and only two miles from Stony-Point. They arrived in the house just before day & stay'd there until the next evening, when Major Andre became extremely sollicitous to return by the way he came, but that was impossible, for the two men who Arnold and Smith had seduced to bring on shore, refused to carry him back. It then was absolutely necessary he should return to New-York by land. He chang'd his dress and name, and thus disguised, pass'd our post of Stoney and Verplank's Points, on the evening of the 22d ult. in company with the said Joshua Smith, brother to William Smith, Esq; Chief Justice within the British lines; he lodged that night at Cron Pond, with Smith, and in the morning left Smith, and took the road to Tarry-Town, where he was taken by some militia lads about 15 miles from Kings Bridge. He offered them any sum of money, and goods, if they would permit him to escape, but they readily declared and inflexibly adhered to it, that 10 000 guineas, or any other sum, would be no temptation to them. It was this virtue as glorious to America as Arnold's apostacy is disgraceful, that his abominable crimes were discovered.

"The lads, in searching him found concealed under his stockings, in his boots, papers of the highest importance, viz.

1. Returns of the ordnance and its distributions at West-Point and its dependencies.

2. Artillery orders, in case of an alarm.

3. Returns of the number of men necessary to man the works at West Point and its dependencies.

4. Remarks on the works at West Point, with the strength and working of each.

5. Returns of the troops at West-Point and their distribution.

6. State of our army, &c transmitted by General Washington to Arnold for his opinion, which State had been submitted to all the general officers in the Camp, for their opinions.

"Besides which it appears, that Arnold had carried with him to the interview, a general plan of West Point and its vicinity, and all the works,

"The General proceeded to view the works, wondering where Arnold should be; but about 4 o'clock in the afternoon he was undeceived, by an express with the papers taken on Andre. The apostate at this time was on board the Vulture, which lay about 5 or 6 miles below Stoney and Verplank's Points.

"Major Andre was brought to the General at West Point, and from thence he was brought to this camp. A board of general officers have examined into his case, and upon his own most candid confession, were of opinion that he was a spy, and according to the custom & usages of nations, he ought to suffer death; and about two hours ago he was executed.

"This gentleman was in the highest degree of reputation in the British army, of the most polite and accomplished manners, extremely beloved by Sir Henry Clinton. His deportment while a prisoner was candid and dignified. He requested no favour, but to die the death of a soldier, and not on a gibbet. Rigorous policy forbid granting a favour which at first flush seems immaterial. Our army sympathizes in the misfortunes of this Chesterfield of the day: But if he possess'd a portion of the blood of all the Kings on earth justice and policy would have dictated his death.

The enemy from hints that some of the officers dropp'd, appeared to be inclined to deliver Arnold into our hands for Major Andre: But they have since declared it was impossible. If it could have been effected, our desire to get Arnold would have render'd the exchange easy on our part.

"The British army are in the utmost affliction on the account of Major Andre and have sent repeated flags on the subject. Yesterday they sent Gen. Robertson, Andrew Eliot and William Smith, Esqrs; the two latter were not permitted to land. General Greene met Gen. Robertson; he had nothing material to urge—' but that Andre had come on shore under the sanction of a flag, and therefore could not be considered as a spy:' But this is not true, for he came at night, had no flag, and on business totally incompatible with the nature of a flag. He also said they should retaliate on some people at New-York and Charlestown; but he was told that such conversation could neither be heard nor understood. After which he urged the release of Andre on motives of humanity, and because Sir Harry Clinton was much attached to him; and other reasons equally absurd.

"I have been particular in this narration, well knowing what strange stories you will have on the subject."

The following is a Copy of a Letter from Major Andre to his Excellency General Washington.

SIR,

"Buoyed above the fear of death, by the consciousness of a life spent in the pursuit of honor, and fully sensible that it has at no time been stained by any action, which at this serious moment could give me remorse—I have to sollicit your Excellency if there is any thing in my character which excites your esteem; if aught in my circumstances can impress you with compassion; that I may be permitted to die the death of a soldier:—It is my last request and I hope it will be granted." I have the honor to be, &c.

By their Honors Command,
JOHN AVERY, Dep. Sec.
GOD save the United States of America.

STATE OF MASSACHUSETTS BAY.
Council-Chamber, October 10th, 1780.

WHEREAS this Board have received intelligence from the Quarter Master General of the United States, that the Army have had a sufficient supply of Horses for the present Campaign:

Therefore Ordered, That the Agents appointed to procure Horses from the several Counties in this State, who were directed by the Resolve of the General Court of the twenty-third of June last, to procure Horses within the limits of their appointment for the use of the Army of the United States, be, and they are hereby directed to surcease all further proceedings on the aforesaid Resolve, and that no more Horses be procured or sent on to the Committee appointed to receive them at Springfield, in consequence of the Resolve aforesaid.

True Copy.   Attest.
JOHN AVERY, Dep. Sec'y.

COMMITTEE-OFFICE, Springfield, Oct. 11, 1780.

WHEREAS by the Resolutions of the General Court of the 25th of September last the several Towns in this State are ordered to furnish a Quantity of Beef for the Use of the Army, or to pay so much Money as in the Judgment of the Committee for superintending Purchases, may be sufficient to purchase the same:

THIS is therefore to GIVE NOTICE, That the Committee are of Opinion, that *Three Pounds* in New Money, or an *Hundred and Twenty Pounds* in the old Currency, may be received in Lieu of an Hundred Weight of Beef at present: And the Agents appointed by us in the several Counties, are hereby directed to receive the old or the new Money at the aforesaid Rate, and give Discharges agreeable to the Directions of the aforesaid Resolutions, for so much Beef as any Town or Plantation shall furnish Money to purchase, at the Rate aforesaid; provided the Money is paid before the Thirty first Day of this Instant October; after which Time, the Agents will wait the farther Directions of the Committee, as they cannot determine now, at what Price Beef may be at that Time,

And the Agents aforesaid are hereby directed to transmit all such Sums of Money as they may receive on the above Account, as soon as possible, to the Committee at Springfield, untill further Orders.   SAMUEL OSGOOD,   } Committee for
ELIJAH HUNT,   } superintend-
OLIVER PHELPS,   } ing Purchases

LONDON CHRONICLE

December 2, 1780

—

The letters by Beverly Robinson, Sir Henry Clinton, and Arnold arguing that Major John André was acting under a flag of truce and should not be considered a spy, which are printed in the *London Chronicle* of December 2, 1780, were part of an effort by the British to save André from being hanged.

the British Army, Sept. 29,

Major General GREEN, President.

Maj. Gen. Ld. Stirling	Brig. Gen. Knox
Major Gen. St. Clair	Brig. Gen. Glover
	Patterson
	Hand
	Hunting-

at Weft Point; whither I pro-
in order to vifit the poft. I
nold had not been there during
on my return to his quarters, he

In the mean time, a packet
m Lieutenant Colonel Jamiefon,
capture of a John Anderfon,
avouring to go to New York
erefting and important papers,
writing of Gen. Arnold. This
apanied with a letter from the
ing himfelf to be Major John
nt General to the Britifh army,
ner of his capture, and endea-
that he did not come under
of a fpy. From thefe feveral
and information that the Ge-
be thrown into fome degree of
ceiving a letter a little time be-
from his quarters, I was led to
ediately that he had heard of
captivity, and that he would, if
to the enemy, and accordingly
ures as appeared the moft pro-
end him; but he had embarked
d proceeded down the river,
the Vulture fhip of war, which
les below Stoney and Verplank's
ote me a letter after he got on
Andre is not arrived yet; but I
ure, and that he will be here
been, and am taking precau
truft will prove effectual, to pre-
tant confequences which this
e part of Gen. Arnold, was in-
uce. I do not know the party
or Andre; but it is faid that it
of a few militia, who acted in
upon the occafion, as does them
our, and proves them to be men
As foon as I know their names,
eafure in tranfmitting them to

Paramus, Oct. 7, 1780.
honour to inclofe Congrefs a
ceedings of a Board of General
caufe of Major Andre, Adjutant
Britifh army. This officer wa
fuance of the fentence of the

Gentlemen,

" Major Andre, Adjutant General to the Britifh army, will be brought before you for your examination. He came within our lines in the night, on an interview with Major General Arnold, and in an affumed character, and was taken within our lines, in a difguifed habit, with a pafs under a feigned name, and with the inclofed papers concealed upon him. After a careful examination, you will be pleafed, as fpeedily as poffible to report a precife ftate of his cafe, together with your opinion of the light in which he ought to be confidered, and the punifhment that ought to be inflicted. The Judge Advocate will attend to affift in the examination, who has fundry other papers relative to this matter, which he will lay before the Board.

" I have the honour to be, Gentlemen, your moft obedient humble fervant,
G. WASHINGTON."
The Board of General Officers,
convened at Tappan.

The names of the officers compofing the Board were read to Major Andre, and on his being afked whether he confeffed the matters contained in the letter from his Excellency General Wafhington to the Board, or denied them, *he faid, in addition to his letter to General Wafhington, dated Salem, the 24th of September 1780,* which was read to the Board, and acknowledged by Major Andre to have been written by him, which letter is as follows:

Sir, Salem, 24th Sept 1780.

" What I have as yet faid concerning myfelf, was in the juftifiable attempt to be extricated; I am too little accuftomed to duplicity to have fucceeded.

" I beg your Excellency will be perfuaded, that no alteration in the temper of my mind, or apprehenfion for my fafety, induces me to take the ftep of addreffing you, but that it is to fecure myfelf from an imputation of having affumed a mean character for treacherous purpofes or felf intereft. A conduct incompatible with the principles that actuated me, as well as with my condition in life.

" It is to vindicate my fame that I fpeak, and not to folicit fecurity.

" The perfon in your poffeffion is Major John

Thus become a prifoner, I had to concert my efcape; I *quitted my uniform*, and was paffed another way in the night without the American pofts to neutral ground; and informed I was beyond all armed parties, and left to prefs for New York. I was taken at Tarry Town by fome volunteers.

" Thus, as I have had the honour to relate, was I betrayed (being Adjutant General of the Britifh army) into the vile condition of an enemy in difguife within your pofts.

" Having avowed myfelf a Britifh officer, I have nothing to reveal but what relates to myfelf, which is true on the honour of an officer and a gentleman.

" The requeft I have to make to your Excellency, and I am confcious that I addrefs myfelf well, is, that in any rigour policy may dictate, a decency of conduct towards me may mark, that though unfortunate, I am branded with nothing difhonourable; as no motive could be mine, but the fervice of my King, and as I was involuntarily an impoftor.

" Another requeft is, that I may be permitted to write an open letter to Sir Henry Clinton, and another to a friend for clothes and linen.

" I take the liberty to mention the condition of fome gentlemen at Charleftown, who being either on parole or under protection; were engaged in a confpiracy againft us. Though their fituation is not fimilar, they are objects who may be fent in exchange for me, or are perfons whom the treatment I receive might affect.

" It is no lefs, Sir, in a confidence in the generofity of your mind, than on account of your fuperior ftation, that I have chofen to importune you with this letter. I have the honour to be, with great refpect, Sir, your Excellency's moft obedient, and moft humble fervant,
JOHN ANDRE, Adj. Gen."
His Excellency Gen. Wafhington, &c. &c.

That he came on fhore from the Vulture floop of war *in the* night of the 21ft of September inftant, fomewhere under the Haverftraw Mountain. That the boat he came on fhore in carried *no flag*, that he had on a furtout coat over his regimentals, and that he wore his furtout coat when he was taken. That he met General Arnold on the fhore, and had an interview with him there. He alfo faid, that when he left the Vulture floop of war, it was underftood he was to return that night; but it was then doubted, and if he could not return, he was promifed to be *concealed on* fhore in a place of fafety, until the next *night*, when he was to return in the fame manner he came on fhore; and when the next day came, he was folicitous to get back, and made enquiries in the courfe of the day how he fhould return, when he was informed he could not return that way, and he muft take the route he did afterwards. He alfo faid, that the firft notice he had of his being within any *of our pofts*, was, being challenged by the fentry, which was the firft night

"New York, Sept. 7, 1780.

"I am told *my name* is made known to you, and that I may hope your indulgence in permitting me to meet a friend near your out posts, I will endeavour to obtain permission to go out *with a flag* which will be sent to Dobb's Ferry on Monday next, the 11th, at 12 o'clock, when I shall be happy to meet Mr. G——†. Should I not be allowed to go, the officer who is to command the escort, between whom and myself no distinction need be made, can speak on the affair.

"Let me entreat you, Sir, to favour a matter so interesting to the parties concerned, and which is of so private a nature, that the public on neither side can be injured by it.

"I shall be happy on my part, of doing any act of kindness to you, in a family or property concern of a similar nature.

"I trust I shall not be detained; but should any old grudge be a cause for it, I should rather risk that, than neglect the business in question, or *assume a mysterious character*, to carry on an innocent affair; and, as friends have advised, get to your lines by stealth. I am, Sir, with all regard, your most obedient humble servant, JOHN ANDERSON."
Colonel Sheldon.

Major Andre observed, that this letter could be of no force in the case in question, as it was written in New York, when he was under the orders of General Clinton; but that it tended to prove that it was not his intention to come within our lines.

The Board having interrogated Major Andre about his conception of coming on shore under the sanction of a flag, he said, that it was impossible for him to suppose he came on shore under that sanction; and added, that if he came on shore under that sanction, he certainly might have returned under it.

Major Andre having acknowledged the preceding facts, and being asked whether he had any thing to say respecting them, answered, he left them to operate with the Board.

---

* Lest it should be supposed that Col. Sheldon, to whom the above letter is addressed, was privy to the plot carrying on by General Arnold, it is to be observed, that the letter was found among Arnold's papers, and had been transmitted by Col. Sheldon, who, it appears from a letter, on the 9th of September to Arnold, which inclosed it, had never heard of John Anderson before. Arnold, in his answer on the 10th, acknowledged he had not communicated it to him, though he had informed him that he expected a person would come from New York, for the purpose of bringing him intelligence.

† It appears, by the same letter, that Arnold had written to Mr. Anderson, under the signature of Gustavus. His words are, "I was obliged to write with great caution to him, my letter was signed Gustavus, to prevent any discovery; in case it fell into the hands of the enemy."

...too often experienced the ingratitude of my country to attempt it; but from the known humanity of your Excellency, I am induced to ask your protection for Mrs. Arnold, from every insult and injury, that a mistaken vengeance of my country may expose her to. It ought to fall only on me; she is as good and as innocent as an angel, and is incapable of doing wrong. I beg she may be permitted to return to her friends in Philadelphia, or to come to me, as she may choose. From your Excellency I have no fears on her account, but she may suffer from the mistaken fury of the country.

I have to request that the inclosed letter may be delivered to Mrs. Arnold, and she permitted to write to me.

I have also to ask that my clothes and baggage, which are of little consequence, may be sent to me; if required, their value shall be paid in money. I have the honour to be, with great regard and esteem, your Excellency's most obedient humble servant, B. ARNOLD."
His Excellency Gen. Washington.

N. B. In justice to the Gentlemen of my family, Col. Warrick and Major Franke, I think myself in honour bound to declare, that they, as well as Joshua Smith, Esq; (who I know is suspected) are totally ignorant of any transactions of mine, that they had reason to believe were injurious to the public.

Sir, *Vulture, off Sinsink, Sept. 25, 1780.*
"I am this moment informed that Major Andre, Adjutant General of his Majesty's army in America, is detained as a prisoner by the army under your command. It is therefore incumbent on me to inform you of the manner of his falling into your hands:—He went up with a flag at the request of General Arnold, on public business with him, and had his permit to return by land to New York. Under these circumstances Major Andre cannot be detained by you, without the greatest violation of flags, and contrary to the custom and usage of all nations; and, as I imagine you will see this matter in the same point of view as I do, I must desire you will order him to be set at liberty, and allowed to return immediately. Every step Major Andre took, was by the advice and direction of Gen. Arnold, even that of taking a feigned name, and of course not liable to censure for it. I am, Sir, not forgetting our former acquaintance, your very humble servant,
BEV. ROBINSON, Col. Loy. Americ."
His Excellency Gen. Washington.

Sir, *New York, Sept. 26, 1780.*
"Being informed that the King's Adjutant General in America has been stopped, under Major General Arnold's passports, and is detained a prisoner in your Excellency's army, I have the honour to inform you, Sir, that I permitted Major Andre to go to Major General Arnold, at the particular request of that General Officer. You will perceive, Sir, by the in-

...relating to myself, that officer, to your Excellency.

I commanded at the time at West Point, and had an undoubted right to send my flag of truce for Major Andre, who came to me under that protection; and having held my conversation with him, I delivered him confidential papers in my own hand writing, to deliver to your Excellency; thinking it much properer he should return by land, I directed him to make use of the feigned name of John Anderson, under which he had by my direction come on shore, and gave him my passports to go to the White Plains on his way to New York. This officer cannot therefore fail of being immediately sent to New York, as he was invited to a conversation with me, for which I sent him a flag of truce, and finally gave him passports for his safe return to your Excellency; all which I had then a right to do, being in the actual service of America, under the orders of General Washington, and Commanding General at West Point and its dependencies.

I have the honour to be your Excellency's most obedient and very humble servant,
B. ARNOLD."
His Excellency Sir Henry Clinton.

The Board having considered the letter from his Excellency General Washington respecting Major Andre, Adjutant General to the British army, the confession of Major Andre, and the papers produced to them,—*Report* to his Excellency the Commander in Chief the following facts which appear to them relative to Major Andre:

First, That he came on shore from the Vulture sloop of war, in the *night* of the 21st of September instant, on an interview with General Arnold, *in a private and secret manner.*

Secondly, That he changed *his dress within our lines, and under a feigned name, and in a disguised habit,* passed our works at Stoney and Verplanks Points, the evening of the twenty-second of September, instant, and was taken the morning of the twenty-third of September instant, *at Tarry-town, in a disguised habit,* being then on his way to New York, *and when taken* he had in his possession several papers, which contained intelligence *for the enemy.*

The Board having maturely considered these facts. *Do also report* to his Excellency General Washington, that Major Andre, Adjutant General to the British army, ought to be considered as a SPY from the enemy and that, agreeable to the law and usage of nations, it is their opinion, he ought to suffer death.

Nathaniel Green, M. General, President.
Stirling, M. G.
R. Howe, M. G.
Ar. St. Clair, M. G.
La Fayette, M. G.
Stuben, M. G.
H. Knox, B. G.
James Clinton, B. G.
John Paterson, B. G.

John Stark, B. G.
Edw. Hand, B. G.
Sam. H. Parsons, B. G.
John Glover, B. G.
Artillery;
J. Huntington, B. G.
J. Lawrens, J. A. G.

...hips as per last. Arrived the Shark
Nimble cutter from a cruize. Wind

LONDON.
...y a Chapter of the Order of the
...held at St. James's, and the fol-
...ights attended the ceremony, viz.
Irvin, Sir Charles Frederick, Sir
...ne, Sir Robert Gunning, and Lords
...and Amherst: when General Ri-
...son, who commanded the camp at
...aft Summer; Thomas Wroughton,
...ajesty's Ambassador at the Court of
...and Admiral Sir George Brydges
Bart. were the three new-elected
...he two last by proxy.
...dia Company have received advice
...al, by the way of Holland, that a
...dition is now fitting out in the Gan-
...supposed to be destined either against
...or the Manillas. They have the most
...opes of success from this expedition,
...great force, both naval and military,
...ollected, and they have even pressed
...from the India ships.
...of a Letter from Corke, Nov. 5.
...day arrived here his Majesty's ship
...of 48 guns, the Ranger sloop of war,
...ince George armed ship, with a fleet
...ers from Plymouth, bound to New
...
...ire from Nantz, bound to the West

To the INHABITANTS of AMERICA.

I SHOULD forfeit, even in my own opinion, the place I have so long held in yours, if I could be indifferent to your approbation, and silent on the motives which have induced me to join the King's arms.

A very few words, however, shall suffice upon a subject so personal; for to the thousands who suffer under the tyranny of the usurpers in the revolted provinces, as well as to the great multitude who have long wished for its subversion, this instance of my conduct can want no vindication; and as to the class of men who are criminally protracting the war from sinister views at the expence of the public interest, I prefer their enmity to their applause. I am, therefore, only concerned in this address, to explain myself to such of my countrymen, as want abilities, or opportunities, to detect the artifices by which they are duped.

Having fought by your side when the love of our country animated our arms, I shall expect, from your justice and candour, what your deceivers, with more art and less honesty, will find it inconsistent with their own views to admit.

When I quitted domestic happiness for the perils of the field, I conceived the rights of my country in danger, and that duty and honour called me to her defence. A redress of griev-... aim; however, I ... ought precipi- ... ence: to justify ... ons were urged, ... hen Great Bri- ... parent, offered ... ant the wished- ...

...ies are in her ... principles, if I ... ourselves being ... because fellow ... foe? You have ... ised our arms ... e the guilty pro-...rectors of these unnatural dissentions to resign their ambition, and cease from their delusions, in compassion to kindred blood!

I anticipate your question, Was not the war a defensive one, until the French joined in the combination? I answer, that I thought so. You will add, Was it not afterwards necessary, till the separation of the British empire was complete? By no means; in contending for the welfare of my country, I am free to declare my opinion, that this end attained, all strife should have ceased.

I lamented, therefore, the impolicy, tyran-...

to serve a nation wanting both the will and the power to protect us, and aiming at the destruction both of the mother country and the provinces. In the plainness of common sense, for I pretend to no casuistry, did the pretended treaty with the Court of Versailles, amount to more than an overture to America? Certainly not, because no authority had been given by the people to conclude it, nor to this very hour have they authorised its ratification. The articles of confederation remain still unsigned.

In the firm persuasion, therefore, that the private judgement of an individual citizen of this country is as free from all conventional restraints, since as before the insidious offers of France, I preferred those from Great Britain; thinking it infinitely wiser and safer to cast my confidence upon her justice and generosity, than to trust a monarchy too feeble to establish your independency, so perilous to her distant dominions; the enemy of the Protestant faith and fraudulently avowing an affection for the liberties of mankind, while she holds her native sons in vassilage and chains.

I affect no disguise, and therefore frankly declare, that in these principles I had determined to retain my arms and command for an opportunity to surrender them to Great Britain; and in concerting the measures for a purpose, in my opinion, as grateful as it would have been beneficial to my country, I was only solicitous to accomplish an event of decisive importance, and to prevent as much as possible, in the execution of it, the effusion of blood.

With the highest satisfaction I bear testimony to my old fellow soldiers and citizens, that I find solid ground to rely upon the clemency of our Sovereign, and abundant conviction that it is the generous intention of Great Britain not only to leave the rights and privileges of the colonies unimpaired, together with their perpetual exemption from taxation, but to superadd such further benefits as may consist with the common prosperity of the empire. In short, I fought for much less than the parent country is as willing to grant to her colonies as they can be to receive or enjoy.

Some may think I continued in the struggle of these unhappy days too long, and others that I quitted it too soon.—To the first I reply, that I did not see with their eyes, nor perhaps had so favourable a situation to look from, and that to our common master I am willing to stand or fall. In behalf of the candid among the latter, some of whom I believe serve blindly but honestly—in the bands I have left, I pray God to give them all the lights requisite to their own safety before it is too late; and with respect to that herd of censurers, whose enmity to me originates in their hatred to the principles by which I am now led to devote my life to the re-union of the British...

... dnesday last died, at his house on ... green, William Donaldson, Esq.
...r died, at Marlborough, James Houb-...yne, Esq.
...y died, at Tottenham, Charles Dower...
...day died, in Bloomsbury-Square, A-...ings, Esq.
...y died, in Wimpole-Street, Cavendish-...dward Clutterbuck, Esq.
...rday last died at Packington in War-...in the 21st year of his age, the Hon.
...ington Finch, youngest brother of the

...iel Hankerson, Knt.
...t last died, at Newton-House, near

...glected to take their collective sentiments of the British proposals of peace, and to negociate, un-...

...they may be assured, that, conscious of the rectitude of my intentions, I shall treat their malice...

From RIVINGTON'S NEW YORK ROYAL GAZETTE, Nov. 1.

By Brigadier General ARNOLD.

A PROCLAMATION.

To the Officers and Soldiers of the Continental Army, who have the real Interest of their Country at Heart, and who are determined to be no longer the Tools and Dupes of Congress, or of France.

HAVING reason to believe, that the principles I have avowed, in my address to the public of the 7th instant, animated the greatest part of this Continent, I rejoice in the opportunity I have, of inviting you to join his Majesty's arms.

His Excellency Sir Henry Clinton has authorized me to raise a corps of cavalry, and infantry, who are to be clothed, subsisted, and paid as the other troops are in the British service; and those who bring in horses, arms, or accoutrements, are to be paid their value, or have liberty to sell them: To every non-commissioned officer and private, a bounty of three guineas will be given; and as the Commander in Chief is pleased to allow me to nominate the officers, I shall with infinite satisfaction embrace the opportunity of advancing men, whose valour I have witnessed, and whose principles are favourable to an union with Britain, and true American Liberty.

The rank they obtain in the King's service, will bear a proportion to their former rank, and the number of men they bring with them.

It is expected that a Lieutenant Colonel of cavalry will bring with him, or recruit in a reasonable time, 75 men.

Major of horse	50 men.
Captain of ditto	30
Lieutenant of ditto	15
Cornet of ditto	12
Serjeant of ditto	6

Lieutenant-colonel of infantry 75 men.

Major of ditto	—	50
Captain of ditto	—	30
Lieutenant of ditto	—	15
Ensign of ditto	—	12
Serjeant of ditto	—	6

N. B. Each field officer will have a company.

Great as these encouragements must appear to such as have suffered every distress of want of pay, hunger, and nakedness, from the neglect, contempt, and corruption of Congress, they are nothing to the motives which I expect will influence the brave and generous minds I hope to have the honour to command.

I wish to lead a chosen band of Americans to the attainment of peace, liberty, and safety (the first objects in taking the field), and with them to share in the glory of rescuing our native country from the grasping hand of France, as well as from the ambitious and interested views of a desperate party among ourselves, who, in listening to French overtures, and rejecting those from Great Britain, have brought the Colonies to the very brink of destruction.

Friends, fellow soldiers, and citizens, arouse, and judge for yourselves—reflect on what you

threatens you.

Your country once was happy; and had the proffered peace been embraced, your last two

you to the field of battle, and is daily deluging your country with your blood?

You are flattered with independency as preferable to a redress of grievances, and for that shadow, instead of real felicity, are sunk into all the wretchedness of poverty by the rapacity of your own rulers. Already are you disqualified to support the pride of character they taught you to aim at, and must inevitably shortly belong to one or other of the great powers, their folly and wickedness have drawn into conflict. Happy for you that you may still become the fellow subjects of Great Britain, if you nobly disdain to be the vassals of France.

What is America now but a land of widows, orphans, and beggars?—and should the parent nation cease her exertions to deliver you, what security remains to you, even for the enjoyment of the consolations of that religion, for which your fathers braved the ocean, the heathen, and the wilderness? Do you know that the eye, which guides this pen, lately saw your mean and profligate Congress at mass, for the soul of a Roman Catholic in Purgatory, and participating in the rites of a church, against whose antichristian corruptions, your pious ancestors would have witnessed with their blood.

As to you, who have been soldiers in the Continental Army, can you at this day want evidence, that the funds of your country are exhausted, or that the managers have applied them to their own private uses? In either case, you surely can no longer continue in their service with honour or advantage; yet you have hitherto been their supporters in that cruelty, which, with an equal indifference to your's, as well as to the labour and blood of others, is devouring a country, that, from the moment you quit their colours, will be redeemed from their tyranny.

But what need of arguments to such as feel infinitely more misery than tongue can express? I therefore only add my promise of the most affectionate welcome and attention, to all who are disposed to join me in the measures necessary to close the scene of our afflictions, which, intolerable as they are, must continue to increase until we have the wisdom (shewn of late by Ireland) in being contented with the liberality of the Parent Country, who still offers her protection, with the immediate restoration of our ancient privileges, civil and sacred, and a perpetual exemption from all taxes, but such as we shall think fit to impose on ourselves.

B. ARNOLD.

New York, Oct. 20, 1780.

For Ink Spots, Iron Moulds, Stains, &c.
The true essential SALT of LEMONS.

THIS SALT is infinitely preferable to any other thing whatever for discharging of Iron Moulds, Ink Spots, Red Wine, and Stains of every kind out of Lace, Muslin, Lawn, Cambrick, and Linen immediately, and without any trouble, whitening them to admiration, if grown yellow, and rendering them as beautiful as when quite new. It is also excellent for all the purposes which the Lemon itself is used for, being nothing more than the pure acid part of that fruit, separated from the pulp and

and sauces, and has the advantage over the fruit itself, in being always ready, and never spoiling in keeping.

FOURTEENTH DAY's DRAWING.

Prize of 1000l.
No. 13,790.

Prizes of 100l. each.
No. 21,901, 38,214.

Prizes of 50l. each.

No. 357, 2,964, 5,537, 5,802, 6,147, 9,211, 11,453, 21,855, 21,910, 27,736, 40,159, 44,366.

Prizes of 20l. each.

102	184	418	525	583	940	1127
1311	1439	1620	1622	1652	1782	1956
1974	1983	2102	2146	2391	2483	2509
2521	2614	2623	2870	2939	2955	3105
3197	3328	3381	3575	3843	3887	4101
4198	4288	4440	4459	4465	4587	4652
4690	4722	4810	4832	4882	4892	4898
5084	5095	5120	5217	5618	5651	5706
6031	6083	6502	6525	6560	6581	6702
6819	6889	6995	7044	7177	7214	7215
7223	7351	7425	7523	7776	7785	8038
8237	8319	8355	8376	8387	8635	8994
9242	9312	9446	9488	9795	9816	9977
10050	10399	10476	10481	10850	10866	10928
11130	11143	11203	11279	11433	11492	11627
11766	11809	11874	11975	12029	12039	12319
12446	12706	12737	12800	12808	12883	12952
12968	13045	13080	13085	13225	13329	13344
13372	13467	13553	14099	14129	14131	14339
14414	14512	14529	14530	14556	14635	15005
15157	15187	15188	15272	15309	15528	15832
15837	15920	15975	16207	16288	16466	16665
16848	16861	16931	16959	17128	17157	17745
18141	18385	18544	18597	18677	18716	19129
19262	19486	19497	19619	19793	19917	20066
20162	20240	20244	20254	20351	20400	20666
20811	20861	20941	21035	21036	21117	21152
21242	21341	21516	21834	21994	22156	22234
22304	22333	22461	22469	22572	22608	22626
22839	22887	22977	23063	23306	23326	23404
23648	23747	23754	23874	23893	23937	23939
23998	24218	24311	24333	24526	24531	24603
24613	24687	25051	25185	25195	25302	25383
25441	25634	25655	25715	25731	25784	25856
25929	26065	26077	26094	26138	26150	26152
26154	26213	26224	26228	26241	26282	26311
26579	26653	26779	27001	27038	27074	27126
27203	27333	27377	27418	27672	27813	27890
27918	27987	28031	28175	28275	28475	28890
28995	29157	29353	29755	30031	30188	30268
30353	30403	30423	30492	30512	30552	30555
30604	30778	30811	31043	31077	31277	31318
31324	31617	31674	31764	31861	31911	32006
32132	32142	32354	32398	32427	32455	32503
32558	31968	33035	33078	33146	33513	33726
33738	34485	34498	34676	34750	34761	35001
35054	35263	35382	35417	35435	35513	35713
35720	35861	35887	36000	36070	36357	36490

42130	42239	42294	42441	42500	42659	42787
44668	44710	44938	45115	45388	45425	45552
45631	45800	45811	45819	45974	46103	46203
46286	46288	46361	46407	46508	46610	46690

enemy were under the command of the famous General Arnold, and by the best accounts consisted of from 1500 to 2000 men——They have burnt the greatest part of the towns of New-London, and Groton, near the water——The garrison at Fort-Trumbull evacuated the fort and went over to Fort Griswold, where Colonel Ledyard made a noble defence——repulsed the enemy two or three times, but at last was obliged to surrender the fort to superiour force. The enemy, after Col. Ledyard had surrendered, murdered him and a number of others; they left 73 of our men dead, and between 30 and 40 wounded in the fort; they also carried off about 40 prisoners, among which last number is Ebenezer Ledyard, Esquire. They evacuated the fort about 10 o'clock, in the evening. They blew up the magazines in both forts, did very little other damage to either of them. The enemy this morning were at the harbour's mouth on board their shipping, and came to about eight o'clock; they are still just out below the Light-House, as the wind is against them. Their shipping consists of about 30 sail, two of which appear to be about 20 guns each.

We cannot ascertain the loss the enemy suffered, but by the best accounts imagine it must be large as ours if not larger. We have taken on made a few prisoners, among which is an Ensign, mortally wounded.

The loss sustained in ___ goods, provisions, stores, shipping, &c. ___ at——A considerable number of vessels ___ escape up Norwich River."

___ letter, dated Fort Griswold, ___ton, 7th ___ o'clock, A. M. says, "That the enemy landed at New-London and Groton yesterday morning ___ took possession of the works on New ___ about one in the afternoon ___ Griswold, in Groton, ___ spirited resistance ___

A New-York city paper of the 30th ult. mentions the arrival of Rear Admiral Hood, at Sandy-Hook, from the West-Indies, with 14 sail of the line, four frigates, one sloop, and a number of troops, consisting of the first battalion of the royal, the 13th and 69th regiments. We are informed that these ships, together with the fleet which were before at New-York, amounting in the whole to 35 sail, under the command of Admiral Graves, have taken their departure from Sandy-Hook, bound to the Chesapeake, in order to give battle to the French squadron, which arrived there from Rhode-Island the latter end of last month, and are much inferiour in force to the British; the whole French squadron is said to consist of only 23 sail including frigates and inferiour vessels. The English fleet consist of one ship of 98 guns, one of 90, one of 70, eleven of 74, four of 64, two of 50, four of 44, three of 32, five of 28, one of 24, one Fire-ship of 8, and a sloop of war. All the British line of battle ships except one are said to be copper-bottomed.

It is not doubted but that his Excellency General Washington has marched, with 8000 choice troops including the French, to Virginia, where the troops in that quarter will join him; Lord Cornwallis is blocked up by the French fleet;—by the present appearance of things we are at the eve of some important event, which God grant may be propitious to the United States.

It is said that Sir George Rodney and General Vaughan have gone for England from the W. Indies.

We hear that Arnold when he landed at New-London, dined at a gentleman's house with whom he was formerly acquainted. After dinner he ordered the house to be plundered and set on fire. The traitor carried off all the plunder in the town that his short stay would permit him to take. Had he tarried in order to have taken breakfast the next morning, it is likely he would have been rewarded for all his villanies.

A large quantity ___ money, lately ___ from ___

❧ CHAPTER XII ❧

CONQUEST AND CAPTURE

Introduction

Propelled by success at Kings Mountain and a decisive American victory under Daniel Morgan at Cowpens, General Nathanael Greene begins a strategic retreat, leading Cornwallis's forces northward. As commander of the Southern Army, Greene safely establishes himself as one of America's greatest military minds, helping set the stage for a series of climactic battles, by land and sea, in Virginia. A remarkable American victory at Yorktown in October 1781 was a key step toward ending the American Revolution. With its military overextended around the globe, Britain began peace talks with America, France, and Spain a few months later.

MASSACHUSETTS SPY
September 13, 1781

SURRENDER OF
LORD CORNWALLIS
Architect of the Capitol

BATTLE OF COWPENS

JANUARY 1781. EARLY THE PREVIOUS YEAR, A BRITISH expeditionary force invaded South Carolina and won two big battles and some smaller actions. But throughout the Carolina Backcountry, mounted partisan militia rose and in a sweeping guerilla war of movement forced a stalemate. Then the new American commander in the south, Major General Nathanael Greene, sent the cream of his little army, six hundred light troops under the command of his brilliant deputy, Brigadier General Daniel Morgan, westward beyond the Catawba River, with orders "to give protection to that part of the country and spirit up the people, to annoy the enemy in that quarter." Lord Cornwallis, believing that Morgan endangered the key British strongpoint of Ninety Six, sent against him his own light troops commanded by a cavalry officer with a fearsome reputation: Lieutenant Colonel Banastre Tarleton. With about 1,100 infantry and cavalry, Tarleton, bold and confident, drove his men through the rain-soaked Carolina Backcountry in pursuit of Morgan's six hundred.

While the British won most of the battles during the Revolutionary War, the Americans won the key battles, including Cowpens.

Morgan met his pursuer on the ground called Cowpens. It was a location familiar to backcountry militia, and during the night before the battle hundreds rode in to join Morgan, until his force numbered 1,500 to 1,600, perhaps more. Yet in his report to Greene published in the *New-Jersey Gazette*, Morgan claimed he had only eight hundred men, thus drawing attention largely to his light troops, especially his regulars. But the militia, though untrained in formal warfare, was a vital element at Cowpens, and Morgan was the right man to instruct guerilla warriors on how to fight British regulars in an open field.

Before Cowpens, American generals often placed militia in the front line and expected them to behave as regulars. Morgan also placed them in the front line, but he did not ask them to stand fast in the face of advancing British regulars wielding fixed bayonets. He deployed militia skirmishers supported by a militia line behind them. "Boys, give me three fires," Morgan told the militia, then they could retire behind the Continentals on the third line and form as a reserve. The third line was commanded by the cool, unflappable Lieutenant Colonel John Eager Howard of Maryland, and in reserve behind Howard was Colonel William Washington with eighty-two Continental Light Dragoons and forty-five mounted militiamen.

Tarleton reached Cowpens at dawn on January 17, 1781, and immediately attacked. The militia behaved well and delivered a "heavy and galling fire" before retiring behind the Continentals. The British came on and exchanged volleys with the third line. Then a misunderstood order led to a rearward movement that Morgan in his report incorrectly described as planned. Howard's entire command about-faced and marched to the rear—but in good order. As the British, certain of victory, came on in disorder, the Americans marched to a spot chosen by Morgan. Suddenly, upon command, the American regiments faced about and at short range delivered destructive volleys in sequence into the stunned British. Howard ordered a bayonet charge. Washington's cavalry also charged, and Colonel Andrew Pickens's militia came storming back into the fight. The British regulars collapsed and, in the words of a teenager fighting with Washington's cavalry, "did the prettiest sort of running." Of Tarleton's 1,100, some eight hundred were casualties, while the Americans suffered about twenty-four killed and more than one hundred wounded, double what Morgan reported.

With the exception of the two-hundred-man British Legion Horse, which refused Tarleton's order to charge and fled the field, Cornwallis had lost his light troops, the eyes and ears of his army, and in his fury he would pursue first Morgan, then Greene, and in the process ruin his army. During the Revolutionary War, the British won most of the battles, but the Americans won the key battles. Cowpens was one of those key battles, the beginning of the road to Yorktown and the British loss of America—the real jewel in the crown.

BATTLE OF COWPENS
North Wind Picture Archives

Of Tarleton's 1,100 infantry and cavalry, some eight hundred were casualties, while the Americans suffered about twenty-four killed and more than one hundred wounded.

The NEW-JERSEY GAZETTE

PHILADELPHIA, February 8.

[...]

His Excellency
The President of Congress.
General MORGAN's letter to General GREENE.
Camp, near Cain-creek, January 19, 1781.

Dear Sir,

THE troops I have the honour to command have gained a complete victory over a detachment from the British army, commanded by Lieut. Col. Tarleton. The action happened on the 17th instant, about sunrise, at a place called the Cowpens, near Pacolet river.

On the 14th, having received intelligence that the British army were in motion, and that their movements clearly indicated their intention of dislodging me, I abandoned my encampment at Grendales Ford, and on the 16th, in the evening, took possession of a post about 7 miles from the Chrokee Ford, on Broad River. My former position subjected me at once to the operations of Lord Corwallis and Col. Tarleton, and in case of a defeat my retreat might easily have been cut off. My situation at the Cowpens enabled me to improve any advantages that I might gain, and to provide better for my security should I be unfortunate. These reasons induced me to take this post, notwithstanding it had the appearance of a retreat.

[...]

The enemy drew up in one line, 400 yards in front of our advanced corps. The first battalion of the 71st regiment was opposed to our right, the 7th to our left, the Legion Infantry to our centre, and two companies of light troops of 100 each on our flanks.

In their front they moved two pieces of artillery, and Lieut. Col. Tarleton, with 280 cavalry, was posted in the rear of his line. The disposition being thus made, small parties of riflemen were detached to skirmish with the enemy, on which their whole line advanced with the greatest impetuosity, shouting as they advanced. Majors M'Dowal and Cunningham gave them a heavy and galling fire, and retreated to the regiments intended for their support; the whole of Col. Picken's command then kept up a fire by regiments, retreating agreeably to orders. When the enemy advanced to our line, they received a well directed and incessant fire, but their numbers being superior to ours, they gained our flanks, which obliged us to change our position. We retired in good order about fifty paces, formed, advanced on the enemy, and gave them a brisk fire, which threw them into disorder. Lieutenant Colonel Howard observing this, gave orders for the line to charge bayonets, which was done with such address that the enemy fled with the utmost precipitation. Lieut. Col. Washington discovering that the cavalry were cutting down our riflemen on the left, charged them with such firmness as obliged them to retire in confusion. The enemy were entirely routed, and the pursuit continued upwards of 20 miles. Our loss was inconsiderable, not having more than 12 killed and 60 wounded. The enemy's loss was 10 commissioned officers, and upwards of 100 rank and file killed, 200 wounded, 29 commissioned officers, and above 500 privates, prisoners, which fell into our hands, with two pieces of artillery, two standards, eight hundred muskets, one travelling forge, thirty-five baggage-waggons, seventy Negroes, and upwards of one hundred dragoon horses, with all their musick. They destroyed most of their baggage, which was immense.

Although our success was complete, we fought only eight hundred men, and were opposed by upwards of one thousand of chosen British troops.

Such was the inferiority of our numbers, that our success must be attributed, under God, to the justice of our cause, and the bravery of our troops. My wishes would induce me to mention the name of every private centinel in the corps. In justice to the bravery and good conduct to the officers, I have taken the liberty to enclose you a list of their names, from a conviction that you will be pleased to introduce such characters to the world.

[...]

I am, Sir, your obedient servant,
DAN. MORGAN.

NEW-JERSEY GAZETTE (TRENTON)
February 14, 1781

—

Nathanael Greene's after-action report and Daniel Morgan's letter provided readers of the *New-Jersey Gazette* with vivid detail about the Battle of Cowpens. During the Revolutionary War, the British won most of the battles, but the Americans won the key battles. Cowpens was one of those key battles, the beginning of the road to Yorktown.

BALTIMORE, January 30.

On Monday, the 22d instant, the brig Hawk, Captain Bull; the brig Cato, Captain Weeks; and the schooner Nautilus, Capt. Kerstead, outward bound from this port, were chased on shore in Roman bay, a little below Cedar Point, by the Iris frigate and other vessels of war. The enemy immediately boarded the Cato, who, by some accident, took fire, and blew off her quarters. Fifteen of the enemy and 8 of her people perished. They set the Hawk on fire, and she burnt to the water's edge. The Captain of the Nautilus landed his guns, and prevented the enemy from boarding his vessel, and in all probability she and her cargo will be saved. The British left Cedar Point on Wednesday.

Extract of a letter from Richmond, dated the 19th of January, 1781.

"I am this moment informed that the enemy landed at Hardy's ferry, and marched from thence to Smithfield, and thence to Mackie's mills, where they staid some time, and then returned to Smithfield. Some of their vessels are up Nansemond river, as high as Sleepy-Hole ferry."

PHILADELPHIA, February 8.

This morning arrived here Major Giles, Aid de Camp to General Morgan, with dispatches to Congress, containing the following

Important Intelligence.

Camp, South-Carolina, on Pee-Dee,
January 24, 1781.

SIR,

I HAVE the honour to enclose, for the information of Congress, the copy of my letter to his Excellency General Washington, with the enclosures, announcing the defeat of a detachment of the British army, under Lt. Col. Tarleton. The action was important, and reflects the highest honour on General Morgan, and the troops under his command.

Major Edward Giles will deliver these dispatches, and have the honour to give Congress such further information as they may request.

The Deputy Commissary General of Prisoners will, as soon as possible, transmit a particular return of the prisoners taken on the 17th, by which conveyance I will forward the standards, to be laid at the feet of Congress.

I have the honour to be, with sentiments of the greatest esteem and respect,

Your Excellency's
Most obedient humble servant,
NATHANIEL GREENE.

His Excellency
The President of Congress.

General MORGAN's letter to General GREENE.

Camp, near Cain-creek, January 19, 1781.

Dear Sir,

THE troops I have the honour to command have gained a complete victory over a detachment from the British army, commanded by Lieut. Col. Tarleton. The action happened on the 17th instant, about sunrise, at a place called the Cowpens, near Pacolet river.

On the 14th, having received intelligence that the British army were in motion, and that their movements clearly indicated their intention of dislodging me, I abandoned my encampment at Grendales Ford, and on the 16th, in the evening, took possession of a post about 7 miles from the Chrokee Ford, on Broad River. My former position subjected me at once to the operations of Lord Cornwallis and Col. Tarleton, and in case of a defeat my retreat might easily have been cut off. My situation at the Cowpens enabled me to improve any advantages that I might gain, and to provide better for my security should I be unfortunate. These reasons induced me to take this post, notwithstanding it had the appearance of a retreat.

On the evening of the 16th the enemy occupied the ground we had removed from in the morning. An hour before daylight one of my scouts informed me that they had advanced within five miles of our camp. On this information the necessary dispositions were made, and, from the alacrity of the troops, we were soon prepared to receive them. The light-infantry, commanded by Lieut. Col. Howard, and the Virginia militia under Major Triplett, were formed on a

In their front they moved two pieces of artillery, and Lieut. Col. Tarleton, with 280 cavalry, was posted in the rear of his line. The disposition being thus made, small parties of riflemen were detached to skirmish with the enemy, on which their whole line advanced with the greatest impetuosity, shouting as they advanced. Majors M'Dowal and Cunningham gave them a heavy and galling fire, and retreated to the regiments intended for their support; the whole of Col. Picken's command then kept up a fire by regiments, retreating agreeably to orders. When the enemy advanced to our line, they received a well directed and incessant fire, but their numbers being superior to ours, they gained our flanks, which obliged us to change our position. We retired in good order about fifty paces, formed, advanced on the enemy, and gave them a brisk fire, which threw them into disorder. Lieutenant Colonel Howard observing this, gave orders for the line to charge bayonets, which was done with such address that the enemy fled with the utmost precipitation. Lieut. Col. Washington discovering that the cavalry were cutting down our riflemen on the left, charged them with such firmness as obliged them to retire in confusion. The enemy were entirely routed, and the pursuit continued upwards of 20 miles. Our loss was inconsiderable, not having more than 12 killed and 60 wounded. The enemy's loss was 10 commissioned officers, and upwards of 100 rank and file killed, 200 wounded, 29 commissioned officers, and above 500 privates, prisoners, which fell into our hands, with two pieces of artillery, two standards, eight hundred muskets, one travelling forge, thirty-five baggage-waggons, seventy Negroes, and upwards of one hundred dragoon horses, with all their musick. They destroyed most of their baggage, which was immense.

Although our success was complete, we fought only eight hundred men, and were opposed by upwards of one thousand of chosen British troops.

Such was the inferiority of our numbers, that our success must be attributed, under God, to the justice of our cause, and the bravery of our troops. My wishes would induce me to mention the name of every private centinel in the corps. In justice to the bravery and good conduct of the officers, I have taken the liberty to enclose you a list of their names, from a conviction that you will be pleased to introduce such characters to the world.

Major Giles, my Aid de Camp, and Capt. Brooks, acting as my Brigade-Major, deserve and have my thanks, for their assistance and behaviour on this occasion. The Baron de Glabuck, who accompanies Major Giles with these dispatches, served with me as a volunteer, and behaved in such a manner as to merit your attention.

I am, Sir, your obedient servant,
DAN. MORGAN.

tence of death for horsestealing. There others that escaped who were charged offences; one of whom, of the name of gether with a Negro man) is retaken.

On the 6th instant, about 11 o'clock noon, a certain Samuel Reed, of Philad on his way to Freehold in Monmouth robbed by three villains, disguised in froc sers, of sixty Guineas, twenty Half-Jo hundred Continental dollars, at the Sand half a mile this side Lawrence Taylor's t

To the Printer of the NEW-JERSEY G
SIR,

AS it is a matter of the utmost import value of the new money should be e culating medium to gold and silver, and citizen should endeavour to prevent its o it behoves us to enquire why the county are authorized to give higher prices for as they purchase for the public, than was value of them in gold or silver. They g the amount, and by this means the mon ciated before it comes into circulation. ably certain that grain can be purchased new money or the old continental at seve lars instead of one, at least thirty or fort less than is allowed by the public. The fore appears like a merchant whose circu desperate, and therefore offers a much than common, in order to obtain credit. proper that the money should be immedia into circulation, yet as we suppose it w paid in value equal to gold and silver, wh public be burthened with a debt of at lea part more than is necessary? This, Sir, of importance to all who have taxes to behoves our Representatives to inform public money is thus to be squandered.

February 1, 1781. A F

Mr. COLLINS,

VIRGINIA has at last communicated her resolution of ceding to the Unit the land on the west of the Ohio river, pro gress will pay her the expence of conquer conquered country, furnish land for the her troops, and guaranty to her all the east of the said river Ohio.

The sharper has her own consent for a She will give Congress the Indian country of the Ohio river, to which she has no rig gress will pay her the expence of sending those woods to hunt for and make enemi might have the better pretence to add to ed chartered claim, that of conquest, at deficient quota was wanted in the field to

RACE to the DAN

By Dennis M. Conrad

THE RACE TO THE DAN WAS A REMARKABLE STRATEGIC retreat that saved the American Continental Army in the south and shifted momentum to the Americans in the bitterly contested war in that region. This retreat began immediately after the Battle of Cowpens on January 17, 1781, and continued until Nathanael Greene's army crossed the Dan River into Virginia on February 14.

It was a rugged retreat for both armies, but especially for the Americans. Having divided his army in order to feed and reform it while still maintaining a presence in the western Carolinas, Greene had to reunite his ill-supplied army in the face of the British advance. One officer observed that you could track Greene's army "by the Blood from the feet of the men."

It was a reluctant retreat on Greene's part. Twice he engaged or tried to engage his British pursuers. The first time was at Cowan's Ford. With militia led by William Lee Davidson, Greene tried to defeat the British as they crossed the swollen Catawba River. That effort failed because Davidson, contrary to Greene's advice, posted most of his force away from the river. Thus, despite what Lord Cornwallis writes in his account of the crossing in his report published in the *Massachusetts Spy* of September 13, 1781, the British vanguard was able to cross the river against weak resistance. When Davidson arrived with reinforcements, he was killed, which demoralized his men, who broke and ran.

Again at Guilford Court House, Greene tried to stop and fight Cornwallis, but, as Cornwallis correctly noted in his after-action report, the militia of North Carolina and Virginia did not assemble, and after consulting a Council of War, the American general decided to abandon North Carolina and move his army across the Dan River into Virginia.

The newspaper report printed in the March 15, 1781, *Connecticut Journal* is taken from Greene's letter to George Washington of February 9, which was written during the race. Therefore, the successful conclusion is not given. As he reported here, Greene again split his army and created a light infantry unit, which marched off in a northwesterly direction toward Virginia. Cornwallis, unaware that Greene's quartermaster was collecting boats at Irwin's and Boyd's Ferries at South Boston, Virginia, and therefore convinced that Greene's army would be forced to use the shallower, upper fords of the Dan River, pursued Colonel Otho H. Williams's diversionary force, buying time for the slower-moving main force, which marched directly to Boyd's and Irwin's Ferries.

Although initially fooled, Cornwallis soon saw through the American deception and moved in direct pursuit of the American army with Williams's force between them. The race began in earnest. For three days, the van of Cornwallis's army and the rearmost unit of Williams's light infantry remained in almost constant sight of each other. At one point, Williams spied campfires ahead and, believing he had overtaken the main army, contemplated a suicidal attack in an attempt to save the main force. Before issuing those fateful orders, Williams discovered that the fires had been left burning for the use of his men. More telling is that the British pursuers were so near that Williams's troops were unable to halt and cook a meal.

On February 14, after averaging over thirty miles per day, the rear of Greene's army crossed the Dan just as the first troops of Cornwallis's army arrived on the opposite bank. Greene, not convinced that the race was over, prepared to retreat farther into Virginia, but as Cornwallis reported in his letter published in the September 13, 1781, *Massachusetts Spy*, his army being "ill suited to enter by that quarter so powerful as Virginia," he moved away from the Dan toward Hillsborough, North Carolina, where he "erected the King's standard," hoping to attract local Loyalists.

Greene was active as well. Recognizing the retreat as an opportunity to defeat Cornwallis, who was now far from reinforcements and his supply lines, Greene wrote local militia leaders begging them to reinforce him and promising that they would "injure" Cornwallis or "effect his ruin." The result was the Battle of Guilford Courthouse, covered in the next section of this chapter.

Along with the account of the Race to the Dan, the March 15, 1781, *Connecticut Journal* contains reports of the activities of Francis Marion, a partisan leader operating in northeastern South Carolina. The letters of January 31 and February 2 detail successful raids conducted against the British supply line up the Santee River by Marion's subordinates, Major James Postell and Captain John Postell. The letter from Colonel Henry "Light Horse Harry" Lee discusses a joint attack on Georgetown, South Carolina, by Marion and Lee. It was an ingenious and complicated effort that failed when the British garrison, instead of trying to move to the brick redoubt, barricaded themselves in their quarters outside of the fort. As mentioned, Captain Patrick Carnes captured Colonel George Campbell, whose quarters were also in the town. The British considered the operation inconsequential. Lee's failure to mention Marion's role in the Georgetown operation is inexplicable.

Finally, there are two reports of a British expedition, commanded by Major James Craig, which captured Wilmington, North Carolina. That capture was intended to support Cornwallis's planned invasion of North Carolina by providing a supply depot for Cornwallis on the North Carolina coast. The opposition of local militia, however, prevented Craig from moving up the Cape Fear River as planned to set up a line of communication and supply as far as Cross Creek (Fayetteville).

GENERAL NATHANAEL GREENE
North Wind Picture Archives

Despite having no decisive victories on his resumé, Nathanael Greene is widely regarded as America's most gifted military strategist.

Massachusetts Spy

Or, The WORCESTER GAZETTE.

The noble Efforts of a Virtuous, Free and United People, shall extirpate TYRANNY, and establish LIBERTY and PEACE.

VOL. XI.)   THURSDAY, SEPTEMBER 13, 1781.   (No. 540.

The following is taken from a Charlestown Paper of July 26, 1781.

from the LONDON GAZETTE.

WHITEHALL, June 4, 1781.

THIS morning Captain Brodrick, Aid-de-camp to Lieut. Gen. Cornwallis, arrived from Charlestown, South-Carolina, with dispatches from his Lordship, and Lieutenant Colonel Balfour, to the Right Honourable Lord George Germaine, one of his Majesty's principal Secretaries of State, of which the following are copies and extracts:

My LORD,   *Guilford, March 17, 1781.*

HAVING occasion to dispatch my Aid-de-camp Capt. Brodrick, with the particulars of the action of the 15th, in compliance with general directions from Sir Henry Clinton, I shall embrace the opportunity to give your Lordship an account of the operations of the troops under my command, previous to that event, and of those subsequent, until the departure of Capt. Brodrick.

My plan for the winter's campaign was to penetrate into North-Carolina, leaving South-Carolina in security against any probable attack in my absence.

Lord Rawdon, with a considerable body of troops, had charge of the defensive, and I proceeded about the middle of January upon the offensive operations. I decided to march up the upper, in preference to the lower roads, leading into North-Carolina, because fords being frequent above the forks of the rivers, my passage there could not easily be obstructed; and General Greene having taken post on the Pedee, and there being few fords in any of the great rivers of this country below their forks, especially in the winter, I apprehended being much delayed, if not entirely prevented from penetrating by the latter route. I was the more induced to prefer this route, as I hoped in my way to be able to destroy or drive out of South-Carolina the corps of the enemy, commanded by Gen. Morgan, which threatened our valuable district of Ninety-Six; and I likewise hoped by rapid marches, to be between Gen. Greene and Virginia, and by that means force him to fight without receiving any reinforcement from that province; or failing of that to oblige him to quit North-Carolina with precipitation, and thereby encourage our friends to make good their promises of a general rising to assist me in the re-establishing his Majesty's government.

The unfortunate affair of the 17th of January, was a very unexpected and severe blow; however, being thoroughly sensible that defensive measures would be certain ruin to the affairs of Britain in the southern colonies, this event did not deter me from prosecuting the original plan.

That General Greene might be uncertain of my intended route as long as possible, I had left Gen. Leslie at Camden, until I was ready to move from Winnsborough, and he was now within a march of me. I employed the 18th in forming a junction with him, and in collecting the remains of Lieutenant Colonel Tarleton's corps, after which great exertions were made by part of the army without baggage, to retake our prisoners, and to intercept General Morgan's corps, on its retreat to Catawba; but the celerity of their movements, and the swelling of the numberless creeks in our way, rendered all our efforts fruitless. I therefore assembled the army on the 25th, at Ramsoure's mill, on the south fork of the Catawba; and as the loss of my light troops could not be remedied by the activity of the whole corps, I employed a halt of two days in collecting some flour, and in destroying superfluous baggage, and all my waggons, except those loaded with hospital stores, salt and ammunition, and four reserved empty, in readiness for sick or wounded. In this measure, though at the expence of a great deal of officers baggage, and of all prospect in future of rum, and even a regular supply of provisions to the soldiers, I must, in justice to this army, say, that there was the most general and chearful acquiescence.

In the mean time the rains had rendered the North-Catawba impassible; and Gen. Morgan's corps, the militia of the rebellious counties of Rowan and Mecklenburg, under Gen. Davidson, or the gang of plunderers usually under the command of General Sumpter, not then recovered from his wounds, had occupied all the fords in a space of more than forty miles upwards from the fork. I approached the river, during its heighth, by short marches, so as to give the enemy equal apprehensions for several fords; and after having procured the best information in my power, I resolved to attempt the passage at a private ford (then slightly guarded) near M'Cowan's ford, on the morning of the first of February.

Lieutenant-Colonel Webster was detached with part of the army, and all the baggage to Battle's ford, six miles above M'Cowan's, where General Davidson was supposed to be posted with 500 militia, and was directed to make every possible demonstration, by cannonading and otherwise, of an intention to force a passage there; and I marched at one in the morning, with the brigade of guards, regiment of Bose, 23d regiment, 200 cavalry, and two 3-pounders, to the ford fixed upon for the real attempt. The morning being very dark and rainy, and part of our way through a wood, where there was no road, one of the three ponnders, in front of the 23d regiment and the cavalry, overset in a swamp, and occasioned those corps to lose the line of march; and some of the artillery men belonging to the other gun (one of whom had the match) having stopped to assist were likewise left behind. The head of the column, in the mean while, arrived at the bank of the river, and day began to break. I could make no use of the gun that was up, and it was evident, from the number of fires on the other side, that the opposition would be greater than I had expected. However, as I knew that the rain, then falling, would soon render the river again impassible, and I had received information the evening before, that General Greene had arrived in General Morgan's camp, and that his army was marching after him with the greatest expedition, I determined not to desist from the attempt; and therefore, full of confidence in the zeal and gallantry of Brigadier General O'Hara, and of the brigade of guards under his command, I ordered them to march on; but to prevent confusion, not to fire until they gained the opposite bank. Their behaviour justified my high opinion of them; for a constant fire from the enemy, in a ford upwards of 500 yards wide, in many places up to their middle, with a rocky bottom and strong current, made no impression on their cool and determined valour, nor checked their passage. The light infantry, landing first, immediately formed, and in a few minutes killed or dispersed every thing that appeared before them, the rest of the troops forming and advancing in succession. We now learned that we had been opposed by about 300 militia, that had taken post there only the evening before, under the command of General Davidson. Their General and two or three other officers were among the killed; the number of wounded was uncertain, and a few were taken. On our side, Lieutenant-Colonel Hall and three men were killed, and 36 wounded, and all of the light infantry and grenadiers of the guards. By this time the rear of the column had joined, and the whole having passed with the greatest dispatch, I detached Lieut. Col. Tarleton, with the cavalry and 23d regiment, to pursue the routed militia; a few were soon killed or taken, and Lieut. Col. Tarleton having learned that 3 or 400 of the neighbouring militia were to assemble that day at Tarrank's house, about ten miles from the ford, leaving his infantry, he went on with the cavalry, and finding the militia as expected, he with excellent conduct and great spirit, attacked them instantly, and totally routed them, with little loss on his side, and on theirs between forty and fifty killed, wounded or prisoners. This stroke, with our passage of the ford, so effectually dispirited the militia, that we met with no farther opposition on our march to the Yadkin, through one of the most rebellious tracts in America.

During this time, the rebels having quitted Beattie's ford, Lieut. Col. Webster was passing his detachment and the baggage of the army: This had become tedious and difficult by the continuance of the rain and the swelling of the river; but all joined us soon after dark, about six miles from Beattie's ford. The other fords were also abandoned by the enemy. The greatest part of the militia dispersed; and Gen. Morgan, with his corps, marched all that afternoon, and the following night, towards Salisbury. We pursued next morning, in hopes to intercept him between the rivers, and after struggling with many difficulties, arising from swelled creeks and bad roads, the guards came up with his rear, in the evening of the third, routed it, and took a few waggons at the trading ford of the Yadkin. He had passed the body of his infantry in flats, and his cavalry and waggons by the ford, during that day and the preceeding night; but at the time of our arrival the boats were secured on the other side, and the ford had become impassible. The river continuing to rise, and the ———

[column cut off]

the greatest part of the militia dispersed; ———— ing a small ———— and the h———— me two d———— the banks ———— friends, ———— army wa———— form a ju———— had time ———— having r———— concluded ———— er to avo———— and it b———— made gr———— the upper ———— fords are ———— could n———— was in g———— receiving ————

Noth———— of the o———— hardi———— him; ———— exceeding ———— bad ro———— and bri———— rendered ———— val at Boy———— guard had got over the night before, his baggage and main body having passed the preceeding day, at that and a neighbouring ferry, where more flats had been collected than had been represented to me as possible. My force being ill suited to enter by that quarter so powerful a province as Virginia, and North-Carolina being in the utmost confusion, after giving the troops a halt of one day, I proceeded by easy marches to Hillsborough, where I erected the King's standard, and invited by proclamation, all ————

BY authentic advices we learn, That General Morgan collected near one hundred prisoners, by parties sent out for the purpose, after the account given in his letter to General Greene, dated the 19th of January last. That upon receiving the news of Tarleton's defeat, Lord Cornwallis marched in pursuit of the light infantry and the prisoners. As soon as Gen. Greene was informed of the movements of Lord Cornwallis, he put the army in motion on Pedee, and, leaving it under the command of Gen. Huger, set out to join the light-infantry, in order to collect the militia & embarrass the enemy, until he could affect a junction of his forces. Gen. Morgan, after the defeat of Tarleton, had very judiciously made forced marches up into the country, and happily crossed the Catawba the evening before a great rain, which swelled the rivers to such a degree as prevented the enemy from crossing, for several days, during which time the prisoners were got over the Yadkin, and on their march for Dan river, which they likewise passed, on the 14th of this month had reached Bedford Court-house, in the State of Virginia.

Gen. Greene, on the latter end of January, arrived at the light infantry camp at Sherard's ford, on the Catawba. The enemy were a little lower down the river at M'Cowan's ford, and the river was still so high that they could not cross. They had ...s, and equip... as light ...consisted of ...roops, in-... & their ...first of ...an's ford, ...of militia ...order to op-...falling by ...emy made ...he militia ...rendezvous ...tia to col-...up and ...them halt-...rt of the ...were over-...dispersed. ...night at ...ading the ...the light infantry the next morning continued their march to Salisbury, and crossed the Yadkin. Before they got over all the baggage and stores, the ene-

enemy near the ford. The boats being secured, and the river continuing high from the late rains, the e...

junction as soon as was expected. Gen. Greene therefore, fearing that the river might fall so as to be fordable, ordered the army to file off to Guilford Court-House, where part of them arrived on the evening of the 8th, and the rest were expected to be in on the 9th. The enemy, finding they could not pass at the Trading ford, near Salisbury, marched up the south side of the Yadkin, and on the night of the 7th crossed at the Shallow-ford, and had on the 9th advanced towards Salem, one of the Moravian towns, within 25 or 30 miles of Guilford Court-House.

These rapid movements having prevented the junction of the militia, Gen. Greene ordered the stores and heavy baggage to be removed to Prince Edward Court-House, in the State of Virginia; and having formed a light army, composed of the cavalry of the 1st and 3d regiments, and Lieut. Col. Lee's legion, a detachment of light infantry under Col. Howard, and some few Virginia riflemen, making in the whole 700, ordered them with the militia to harrass the enemy in their advance, and check their progress, while he with the rest of the army crossed the Roanoke. In the mean while, Gen. Sumpter was ordered to collect the militia in the upper part of South-Carolina, and Gen. Pickens had orders to take the command of the men in arms in the rear of the enemy. Such was the situation of the two armies at the date of the last dispatches, which was the 10th of this month.

Extract of a letter from General Marion to General Greene, dated Santee, January 31.

"On the 29th inst. I sent over the Santee river two parties of horse, consisting of 30 each, one under the command of Major Postil, the other under Capt. Postil. The first to burn the enemy's stores at Thompson's; the other to burn those at Watboo-bridge. The Captain has executed his orders with great spirit and good conduct. At Watboo there were 15 hogsheads of rum, a quantity of pork, flour, rice, salt and turpentine. He marched from there to Keithfield, near Monk's Corner, attacked a British guard, killed two, wounded three, took and brought off two surgeons, one Quarter-Master, seven Waggons, one Waggon-Master, seven Waggons, one Steward, and twenty five non-commissioned officers and privates of the 7th, 23d, 33d, 63d, and 71st regiments. He had not one ... cloathing and baggage, 20 hogsheads of rum, and retired with his prisoners."

away some days before. But on his return he heard of a great quantity of rum, sugar, salt, flour, pork, soldiers cloathing and baggage, at Maringualt's Ferry. The guard had gone after Capt. Postil, and left only four men in a redoubt of wood, which the Major took, and entirely destroyed all the stores and redoubt, without receiving any loss or hurt."

Extract of a letter from Major General Greene, dated at Sherrad's Ford, on Catawba River, Jan. 31.

"I have received intelligence that 400 troops have sailed from Charlestown for Wilmington in North-Carolina."

Extract of a letter from Col. Drayton, to Major General Greene, dated Feb. 2.

"On Monday evening the 12th ult. the enemy's fleet appeared off. On Tuesday part got in, and the Thursday following the whole of them reached the first flatts. The inhabitants then held a consultation on the propriety of meeting their foes with a flag and concluded on it. In consequence they insisted on Col. Young, who commanded the militia, to withdraw the few he had (not more than fifty) and leave the town to make their own terms. This he did, and on Saturday a flag was sent, with an offer to surrender as prisoners of war, until exchanged. This the British answered, by taking possession of the town with two gallies and about 200 infantry on Monday the 19th, at 12 o'clock.

Extract of a letter from Major General Greene, to Congress, dated January 31, 1781.

"I HAVE the honor to enclose a copy of a letter from Lieut. Col. Lee, announcing the partial success of an enterprise against George-Town, which does honor to his corps. *Legion camp, on Sampit river, Jan. 25.*

"SIR,

"I have the honor to advise you of the compleat surprise of the post at George-Town, this morning, by the infantry of the legion; Captain Carnes, who conducted this enterprise, has claim to great merit, for the address exhibited on the occasion; the officers and soldiers under him distinguished themselves by their gallantry and firmness. My force was inadequate to the assault of the enemy's inclosed works, nor was the possession equivalent to the certain loss to be expected from such a measure; I therefore determined to pursue my principal object, by means more certain and less destructive to ... prevented a full correspondence in the movements of the cavalry and infantry, by which mistakes we were,

CONNECTICUT JOURNAL (NEW HAVEN)
March 15, 1781
—

The report printed in the March 15, 1781, *Connecticut Journal* is taken from Greene's letter to George Washington of February 9, which was written during the race. Therefore, the successful conclusion is not given. Along with the account of the Race to the Dan, the *Connecticut Journal* contains reports of the activities of Francis Marion, a partisan leader operating in northeastern South Carolina.

BATTLE of GUILFORD COURTHOUSE

By Dennis M. Conrad

THE BATTLE, FOUGHT AT CURRENT-DAY GREENSBORO, North Carolina, is the pivotal contest of the war in the south. While the British army commanded by Earl Cornwallis won a tactical victory, it was so crippled in the battle that it retreated to the coast, eliminating any British presence from the interior of North Carolina and giving the Americans an important strategic victory. In its aftermath, Cornwallis decided to abandon the contest in North Carolina and march instead into Virginia, where later in 1781 his army was captured at Yorktown. In discussing that capture, Greene wrote that although Washington's army had "bagged" the bird, it was the Southern Army that had "flushed" it at Guilford Courthouse.

While Greene provides a good overview of the battle, his report published in the *Independent Chronicle* of April 19, 1781, written in haste and with incomplete knowledge, contains omissions, errors, and inconsistencies. For example, Greene does not give the size of his force, which is now estimated as having numbered 4,000 to 4,400 men, with over half being militia. Cornwallis's army numbered about 2,000 men, all regulars. Cornwallis's after-action report, published in the *London Chronicle* of June 7, 1781, is equally flawed. For example, he reported that Greene's army "exceeded 7000 men."

Greene erred in describing his arrangement of the Southern Army in the battle. He states that there were 300 yards between the three American lines, but scholars have found that there were 400 yards between the first (North Carolina militia) and second line (Virginia militia) and 600 yards between the second and third (Continental troops). Some have argued that this distancing led the militia, particularly the North Carolinians, to feel unsupported and vulnerable.

Another point of controversy is the conduct of the North Carolina militia. Greene's assessment of their performance grew increasingly more critical from what he wrote in the after-action report that appeared in the *Independent Chronicle* on April 19, 1781. For example, on March 20, he wrote General Daniel Morgan that they "deserted the most advantageous post I ever saw & without scarsely firing a gun." Other battle participants, however, remember the North Carolinians discharging at least two volleys and inflicting a considerable number of casualties on the British. Moreover, while Greene praised the conduct of the North Carolina militia officers in the piece that appeared in the *Independent Chronicle*, Colonel William Davie, another participant in the battle, wrote that the militiamen were "wretchedly officered." Cornwallis's report is no more helpful as he summarizes the contest involving the two militia lines with the phrase, "[Major General Alexander Leslie] soon defeated every Thing before him."

Finally, the number of American casualties, compiled by Greene's adjutant general Otho H. Williams and published in the *Independent Chronicle*, was understated by as much as 20 percent in terms of killed and wounded. Though the official British casualty report, which is printed in the *London Chronicle* of June 7, 1781, listed 28 percent of Cornwallis's army as killed, wounded, or captured, historians believe that even that devastatingly high number is understated.

There is no argument, however, with Greene's contention that his army conducted an orderly retreat to a pre-arranged position and was willing and able to renew the contest. In fact, after the battle, it was the British who precipitously retreated—though Cornwallis maintained it was because his army needed to find provisions—and the Americans who pursued, at least until the time of service of the militiamen expired.

The battle's result may be best summed up in the words

of Cornwallis's second-in-command, General Charles O'Hara, who wrote his patron, the Duke of Grafton, that "nearly one half of our best Officers and Soldiers, were either Killed or Wounded, and what remains are so completely worn out…[that] *entre nous*, the Spirit of our little Army has evaporated a good deal."

LONDON CHRONICLE
June 7, 1781

—

Though the official British casualty report printed in the *London Chronicle* listed 28 percent of Cornwallis's army as killed, wounded, or captured, historians believe that even that devastatingly high number is understated.

June 5—7. THE LONDON CHR[ONICLE]

Attack was directed to be made in the following Order:

On the Right the Regiment of Bose, and the 71st Regiment, led by Major General Leslie, and supported by the 1st Battalion of Guards; on the Left the 23d and 33d Regiments, led by Lieutenant Colonel Webster, and supported by the Grenadiers and 2d Battalion of Guards, commanded by Brigadier General O'Hara; the Yagers and Light Infantry of the Guards remained in the Wood on the Left of the Guns; and the Cavalry in the Road, ready to act as Circumstances might require. Our Preparations being made, the Action began about Half an Hour past One in the Afternoon; Major General Leslie, after being obliged, by the great Extent of the Enemy's Line, to bring up the 1st Battalion of Guards to the Right of the Regiment of Bose, soon defeated every Thing before him; Lieutenant Colonel Webster having joined the Left of Major General Leslie's Division, was no less successful in his Front, when, on finding that the Left of the 33d was exposed to a heavy Fire from the Right Wing of the Enemy, he changed his Front to the Left, and being supported by the Yagers and Light Infantry of the Guards, attacked and routed it; the Grenadiers and 2d Battalion of Guards moving forward to occupy the Ground left vacant by the Movement of Lieut. Colonel Webster.

All the Infantry being now in the Line, Lieutenant-Colonel Tarleton had Directions to keep his Cavalry compact, and not to charge without positive Orders, except to protect any of the Corps from the most evident Danger of being defeated. The excessive Thickness of the Woods rendered our Bayonets of little Use, and enabled the broken Enemy to make frequent Stands, with an irregular Fire, which occasioned some Loss, and to several of the Corps great Delay, particularly on our Right, where the first Battalion of Guards and Regiment of Bose were warmly engaged in Front, Flank, and Rear, with some of the Enemy that had been routed on the first Attack, and with Part of the Extremity of their left Wing, which by the Closeness of the Wood had been passed unbroken. The 71st Regiment and Grenadiers, and second Battalion of Guards, not knowing what was passing on their Right, and hearing the Fire advance on their Left, continued to move forward, the Artillery keeping Pace with them on the Road, followed by the Cavalry. The second Battalion of the Guards first gained the clear Ground near Guildford Court-house, and found a Corps of Continental Infantry, much superior in Number, formed in the open Field on the Left of the Road. Glowing with Impatience to signalize themselves, they instantly attacked and defeated them, taking two Six-pounders, but, pursuing into the Wood with too much Ardour, were thrown into Confusion by a heavy Fire, and imme-

cond Battalion of Guar[ds] [rall]ied, and, supported by [...] returned to the Charge with [...]crity. The 23d Regiment [...] Instant from our Left, and [Colo]nel Tarleton having advan[ced...] the Cavalry, the Enemy [...] Flight, and the 2 Six-poun[ders] into our Hands; 2 Ammu[nition...] and 2 other Six-pounders, bei[ng...] tillery they had in the Field, were likewise taken. About this Time the 33d Regiment and Light Infantry of the Guards, after overcoming many Difficulties, completely routed the Corps which was opposed to them, and put an End to the Action in this Quarter. The 23d and 71st Regiments, with Part of the Cavalry, were ordered to pursue; the Remainder of the Cavalry was detached with Lieutenant Colonel Tarleton to our Right, where a heavy Fire continued, and where his Appearance and spirited Attack contributed much to a speedy Termination of the Action. The Militia, with which our Right had been engaged, dispersed in the Woods; the Continentals went off by Reedy Fork, beyond which it was not in my Power to follow them, as their Cavalry had suffered but little. Our Troops were excessively fatigued by an Action which lasted an Hour and a half; and our numerous Wounded, dispersed over an extensive Space of Country, required immediate Attention. The Care of our Wounded, and the total Want of Provisions in an exhausted Country, made it equally impossible for me to follow the Blow the next Day. The Enemy did not stop till they got to the Iron Works on Troublesome Creek, 18 Miles from the Field of Battle.

From our own Observation, and the best Accounts we could procure, we did not doubt but the Strength of the Enemy exceeded 7000 Men; their Militia composed their Line, with Parties advanced to the Rails of the Fields in their Front; the Continentals were posted obliquely in the Rear of their Right Wing. Their Cannon fired on us whilst we were forming from the Center of the Line of Militia, but were withdrawn to the Continentals before the Attack.

I have the Honour to inclose your Lordship the List of our Killed and Wounded. Captain Schutz's Wound is supposed to be mortal; but the Surgeons assure me, that none of the other Officers are in Danger, and that a great Number of the Men will soon recover. I cannot ascertain the Loss of the Enemy, but it must have been considerable; between 2 and 300 Dead were left upon the Field; many of their Wounded that were able to move, while we were employed in the Care of our own, escaped, and followed the routed Enemy; and our Cattle-Drivers and Foraging Parties have reported to me, that the Houses in a Circle of six or eight Miles round us are full of others; those that

and Spirit of Brigadier General O'Hara merit my highest Commendations; for, after receiving two dangerous Wounds, he continued in the Field whilst the Action lasted. By his earnest Attention on all other Occasions, seconded by the Officers and Soldiers of the Brigade, his Majesty's Guards are no less distinguished by their Order and Discipline, than by their Spirit and Valour.

The Hessian Regiment of Bose deserves my warmest Praise for its Discipline, Alacrity, and Courage, and does Honour to Major du Buy, who commands it, and who is an Officer of superior Merit.

I am much obliged to Brigadier-General Howard, who served as a Volunteer, for his spirited Example on all Occasions.

Lieutenant-Colonel Webster conducted his Brigade like an Officer of Experience and Gallantry. Lieutenant Colonel Tarleton's good Conduct and Spirit in the Management of his Cavalry was conspicuous during the whole Action; and Lieutenant Macleod, who commanded the Artillery, proved himself upon this as well as on all former Occasions, a most capable and deserving Officer. The Attention and Exertion of my Aids de Camp, and of all the other public Officers of the Army, contributed very much to the Success of the Day.

I have constantly received the most zealous Assistance from Governor Martin during my Command in the Southern District. Hoping that his Presence would tend to excite the loyal Subjects in this Province to take an active Part with us, he has chearfully submitted to the Fatigues and Dangers of our Campaign; but his delicate Constitution has suffered by his public Spirit, for, by the Advice of the Physicians, he is now obliged to return to England for the recovering his Health.

This Part of the Country is so totally destitute of Subsistence, that Forage is not nearer than nine Miles, and the Soldiers have been two Days without Bread; I shall therefore leave about 70 of the worst of the wounded Cases at the New Garden Quaker Meeting-house, with proper Assistance, and move the Remainder with the Army To-morrow Morning to Bell's Mill. I hope our Friends will heartily take an active Part with us, to which I shall continue to encourage them, still approaching our Shipping by easy Marches, that we may procure the necessary Supplies for further Operations, and lodge our Sick and Wounded where proper Attention can be

Head Quarters, Iron Works,
North-Carolina, March 10.

SIR,

SINCE I had the honour of addressing your Excellency last, there has been some changes in our circumstances. On the second, Lieut. Col. Lee with a detachment of riflemen, attacked the advance of the British army, under Col. Tarleton near Allamance and killed and wounded, by report, about thirty of them. On the 6th the British moved down towards High Rock, either with a view to intercept our stores, or cut off the light infantry from the main body of the army, then advanced near seven miles; but they were handsomely opposed, and suffered considerably without effecting any thing.

This manœuvre occasioned me to retire over the Haw river, and move down the north side of it, with a view to secure our stores, coming to the army, and to form a junction with several considerable reinforcements of Carolina and Virginia militia, and one regiment of Virginia eighteen months men, on the march from Hillsborough to High Rock. I effected this business, and retired towards Guilford Court-house.

Our militia had been on such a loose and uncertain foot...

North-Carolina. After this junction, finding that our force was much more respectable than it had been, and that there was a much greater probability of its declining than increasing, and that there would be the greatest difficulty of subsisting it long in the field in this exhausted country, I took the resolution of attacking the enemy without loss of time, and made the necessary disposition accordingly; being persuaded that if we were successful it would prove ruinous to the enemy, and if otherwise, would only prove a partial evil to us.

The enemy marched from the High Rock-Ford on the 12th, and on the 14th arrived at Guildford.—The enemy lay at the Quaker Meeting-House, on Deep-River, eight miles from our camp. On the morning of the 15th our reconnoitring parties reported the enemy advancing on the great Salisbury road. The army was drawn up in three lines. The front line was composed of the North-Carolina militia, under the command of Generals Butler and Eaton—the second line of Virginia militia, commanded by Generals Stevens and Lawson, forming two brigades—the third line consisting of two brigades, one of Virginia and one of Maryland Continental troops, commanded by General Hugar and Col. Williams. Lieut. Col. Washington, with the dragoons of the 1st and 3d regiments, a detachment of light infantry, composed of Continental troops, and a regiment of riflemen under Col. Lynch formed a corps of observation for the security of our right flank. Lieut. Col. Lee, with his legion, a detachment of light infantry and a corps of riflemen under Col. Campbell, formed a corps of obser-

...ed about twenty minutes, when the enemy advanced in three columns; the Hessians on the right, the guards in the center, and Lieut. Col. Webster's brigade on the left. The whole moved through the old fields to attack the North Carolina brigades, who waited the attack until the enemy got within about one hundred and forty yards, when part of them began a fire, but a considerable part left the ground without firing at all. The Generals and field officers did all they could to induce the men to stand their ground; but neither the advantages of the position nor any other consideration could induce them to stay. Gen. Stephens and Gen. Lawson, and the field officers of those brigades, were more successful in their exertions. The Virginia militia gave the enemy a warm reception, and kept up a heavy fire for a long time; but being beat back, the action became general almost every where. The corps of observation under Washington and Lee were warmly engaged, and did great execution. In a word, the conflict was long and severe, and [they gained] their point by superior dis[cipline]... broke the second Maryland [on] our left flank, and got into [the rear of the] brigade, and appearing [in] which would have encir[cled the con]tinental troops, I thought [proper to orde]r a retreat. About this [time Tarl]ton made charge with the [cavalry on the] brigade of guards; and [the Mar]ylanders, commanded by [... command]ed by Lieut. Col. Howard, [... with] their bayonets; near the [... a great] sacrifice. General Hu[ger was] engaged, and gave the [enemy... ret]reated in good order to the [... cro]ssed at the ford, about [... field] of action, and there halt[ed...] troops, until we collected most of our stragglers. We lost our artillery and two ammunition waggons, the greatest part of the horses being killed before the retreat began, and it being impossible to remove the pieces but along the great road. After collecting our stragglers, we retired to this camp, ten miles distant from Guilford.

From the best information I can get the enemy's loss is very great, not less in killed and wounded than 600 men besides some few prisoners that we brought off.

Inclosed I send your Excellency a return of killed, wounded and missing; most of the latter have gone home as is but too customary with militia after an action. I cannot learn that the enemy have got any considerable number of prisoners. Our men are in good spirits for another field day. I only lament the loss of several valuable officers who were killed and wounded in the action. Among the latter is General Stevens shot through the thigh, and General Huger in the hand, and among the former is Major Anderson of the Maryland line.

The firmness of the officers and soldiers during the whole campaign has been almost unparalleled. Amidst innumerable difficulties they have discovered a degree of magnanimity and fortitude that will forever add lustre to their military reputation.

I have the honour to be &c.
NAT. GREENE.

His Excellency SAMUEL HUNTINGTON, Esq;
President of Congress.

Continentals. Killed. 1 Major, 1 Captain, 3 subalterns, 5 sergeants 47 rank and file. Wounded. 8 Captains, 4 subalterns, 6 sergeants, 93 rank and file. Missing. 3 sergeants, 8 drummers, 150 rank and file. Total. 1 Major, 9 Captains, 7 subalterns, 14 sergeants, 8 drummers, 290 rank and file.

---

an end to the war—The enemy in this country, victories and defeats, have lost two thirds of their armies since the taking of Charlestown, and a little exercise of the States would totally destroy them. I fear you will not make these exertions before you are scourged to it by the enemy. It is a very foolish way to ruin an enemy by allowing him to obtain expensive victories when we might so easily do it by defeats, though I am certain his ruin is inevitable."

We hear that the Honorable Robert Morris, Esq; hath been appointed by Congress, Superintendant-General of the Finances of America; and that the abilities, integrity and patriotism of this gentleman, give room to hope, that ways and means will now be found to remove many of the embarrassments of this country, by furnishing her with the sinews of war, &c.

Capt. Cames in a privateer from Salem, has taken two prizes, one a brig with 200 pipes Madeira wine, which he ordered home; the other a schooner with fish, which was sent for Martinico.

By a vessel arrived at Beverly since our last, in 28 days from Port D'uphen, we learn it was reported there, that a French fleet, consisting of 17 sail of the line and a large number of transports, had arrived at St. Piero in Martinico.

By Capt. Thorndike, who also arrived at Beverly since our last, we learn, that the island of Curaçoa was in quiet possession of the Dutch the 1st March.

Arrived in a safe port, a ship from Cork, bound to New-York, laden with pork, flour, butter, peas and cordage; prize to the snow Rochambeau, Capt. Melaly.

Monday last arrived here the Continental frigate Deane, Capt. Nicholson, from the West-Indies.

☞ The Sale of several Absentees Estates, as advertised in our preceding Paper to have been at the Bunch of Grapes Tavern in State-Street, Boston on the 3d of May, is by order of the Committee adjourned to Friday the 4th, at 11 o'Clock, at the same Place—Thursday being appointed, by Authority, a Day of public Humiliation, Fasting and Prayer.

Commonwealth of Massachusetts.
Boston, April 18, 1781.

The absent Members of the honorable House of Representatives are required to give immediate Attendance on the House, as Matters of the greatest Importance are to be acted upon.
By Order of the House.
G. R. MINOT, Clerk pro tem.

INDEPENDENT CHRONICLE (BOSTON)
April 19, 1781

While Greene provides a good overview of the battle, his report published in the *Independent Chronicle* of April 19, 1781, written in haste and with incomplete knowledge, contains omissions, errors, and inconsistencies. For example, Greene does not give the size of his force, which is now estimated as having numbered 4,000 to 4,400 men, with over half being militia. Cornwallis's army numbered about 2,000 men, all regulars.

The INDEPENDENT CHRONICLE

PHILADELPHIA, April 4.

[…]

His Excellency Gen. Washington.

Camp at the Iron-Works, 10 miles from Guilford Court-House, March 16, 1781.

SIR,

ON the 10th I wrote to his Excellency General Washington, from the High-Rock Ford, on the Haw-River, a copy of which I enclosed your Excellency, that I had effected a junction with a Continental regiment of 8 months men, and two considerable bodies of militia belonging to Virginia and North-Carolina. After this junction, finding that our force was much more respectable than it had been, and that there was a much greater probability of its declining than increasing, and that there would be the greatest difficulty of subsisting it long in the field in this exhausted country, I took the resolution of attacking the enemy without loss of time, and made the necessary disposition accordingly; being persuaded that if we were successful it would prove ruinous to the enemy, and if otherwise, would only prove a partial evil to us.

The enemy marched from the High Rock-Ford on the 12th, and on the 14th arrived at Guildford.—The enemy lay at the Quaker Meeting-House, on Deep-River, eight miles from our camp. On the morning of the 15th our reconnoitering parties reported the enemy advancing on the great Salisbury road. The army was drawn up in three lines. The front line was composed of the North-Carolina militia, under the command of Generals Butler and Eaton—the second line of Virginia militia, commanded by Generals Stevens and Lawson, forming two brigades—the third line consisting of two brigades, one of Virginia and one of Maryland Continental troops, commanded by General Hugar and Col. Williams. Lieut. Col. Washington, with the dragoons of the 1st and 3d regiments, a detachment of light infantry, composed of Continental troops, and a regiment of riflemen under Col. Lynch formed a corps of observation for the security of our right flank. Lieut. Col. Lee, with his legion, a detachment of light infantry and a corps of riflemen under Col. Campbell, formed a corps of observation for the security of our left flank.

The greater part of this country is a wilderness, with a few cleared fields interspersed here and there. The army was drawn up upon a large hill of ground, surrounded by other hills, the greater part of which was covered with timber and thick under brush—The front line was posted with two field pieces just in the edge of the woods, and the back of a fence which run parallel with the line, with an open field directly in their front. The second line was in the woods about 300 yards in the rear of the first; and the Continental troops about 300 yards in the rear of the second, with a double front as the hill drew to a point where they were posted, and on the right and left were two old fields.

In this position we waited the approach of the enemy, having previously sent off the baggage to this place, appointed to rendezvous at in case of a defeat. Lieut. Col. Lee with his legion, his infantry, and part of his riflemen, met the enemy on their advance, and had a very severe skirmish with Lieut. Col. Tarleton, in which the enemy suffered greatly. Capt. Armstrong charged the British legion and cut down near 30 of their dragoons; but the enemy reinforced their advanced party, Lieut. Col. Lee was obliged to retire, and take his position in the line.

The action commenced by a cannonade which lasted about twenty minutes, when the enemy advanced in three columns; the Hessians on the right, the guards in the center, and Lieut. Col. Webster's brigade on the left. The whole moved through the old fields to attack the North Carolina brigades, who waited the attack until the enemy got within about one hundred and forty yards, when part of them began a fire, but a considerable part left the ground without firing at all. The Generals and field officers did all they could to induce the men to stand their ground; but neither the advantages of the position nor any other consideration could induce them to stay.

[…]

I have the honour to be &c.
NAT. GREENE.

I N MARCH 1781, FOLLOWING A LONG, DEBILITATING PURsuit, Lord Cornwallis defeated Major General Nathanael Greene at Guilford Courthouse, North Carolina. But though he was the tactical victor, Cornwallis's losses were so heavy that he was forced to withdraw to Wilmington on the coast to rest and refit his army. Greene, his army intact and ready to fight again, marched for South Carolina, his twin goals to drive the British from the state and restore civil government. Thus began the second phase of the Carolina campaign.

Greene bivouacked at Hobkirk's Hill, about a mile and a half north of a key British post, Camden, South Carolina, then occupied by some nine hundred British and Provincial regulars under a fine officer, Lieutenant Colonel Francis, Lord Rawdon, now commanding British troops in the Carolinas. Greene, with about 1,500 men, was not strong enough to assault Camden and waited for Rawdon to attack him. Rawdon bided his time until he learned that Greene's artillery had left. On April 25, 1781, Rawdon marched to the attack. He eluded observation until his advance bumped into Greene's pickets.

Rawdon had taken Greene by surprise, which Greene failed to mention in his report to Samuel Huntington, president of the Continental Congress, as printed in the *Connecticut Journal* (June 14, 1781). The troops had been eating breakfast and washing clothes when the firing at the picket line alerted them. But the Americans formed quickly "& received us bravely," Rawdon wrote. Greene decided to attack with his infantry while sending Colonel William Washington and his dragoons on a swing to get behind Rawdon and charge from the rear. It was Rawdon's turn to be surprised when American artillery that was supposed to have left appeared and shook his advance with grapeshot. Greene ordered his regiments to charge with the bayonet.

The Americans appeared to be on the verge of victory, then a company commander of First Maryland was killed by musket fire and some of his men were felled by a volley. This threw his troops and another company into confusion, whereupon Colonel John Gunby, commanding First Maryland, blundered. He ordered the entire regiment to retire and reform about fifty yards to the rear. This threw the entire American line out of kilter, the British again advanced, and Greene was forced to order a general retreat.

Colonel Washington had also committed a serious error of judgment. On his ride to Rawdon's rear, he encountered wounded British soldiers and surgeons and ignored his mission in order to take them captive. Yet in his report to Huntington, Greene said that the behavior of Washington and his regiment "did them the highest honour," which was not true, and his claim that Washington found the British "retiring with the greatest precipitation toward the town" was also untrue.

Rawdon suffered more than Greene, taking over 28 percent casualties. He awaited reinforcements before pursuing Greene, and when they arrived, he set out once more to bring the American general to battle but found his prey in too strong a defensive position. Meanwhile, the brilliant partisan commander General Francis Marion, in concert with Lieutenant Colonel "Light Horse Harry" Lee's Continental Legion of horse and foot, was operating in Rawdon's rear between Camden and Charleston. They had taken Fort Watson, one of a string of forts protecting the British supply line, and were now besieging Fort Motte. Rawdon, the tactical victor, was in strategic peril: a beaten but unbroken foe before him, hostile territory swarming with partisans behind him. It was an old story in this frustrating war. With the exception of the Saratoga campaign, British armies marched where they pleased and won most of their battles along the way. But after they passed, implacable enemies who had gotten out of the way reappeared from their sanctuaries and once again took control of the countryside.

On May 10 and 11, Rawdon evacuated Camden and marched for Charleston, and Nathanael Greene once again went on the offensive.

BATTLE OF HOBKIRK'S HILL
North Wind Picture Archives

The troops had been eating breakfast and washing clothes when the firing at the picket line alerted them. But the Americans formed quickly and Greene attacked with his infantry while sending Colonel William Washington and his dragoons on a swing to get behind Rawdon and charge from the rear.

THURSDAY, JUNE 14, 1781

CONNECTICUT JOURNAL

NEW-HAVEN, Printed by THOMAS and SAMUEL GREEN, near the College.

Philadelphia, May 26.

Camp, Sander's Creek, April 27, 1781.

SIR,

I Did myself the honor to address your Excellency on the 2d, and informed you that we lay before Camden, having found it impracticable to storm the town with a prospect of success, and nothing left but to make a position to induce the enemy to sally. We chose a hill about one mile from the town, on the main road leading to the Waxhaws. It was covered with timber, and flanked on the left by an impassible morass. The country between that and the town is covered by heavy wood and under brush. In this situation we lay constantly upon our arms, ready for action at a moment's warning.

About eleven o'clock on the morning of the 25th, our advanced pickets were fired upon, who gave the enemy a warm reception.

The line was formed in an instant, General Huger's brigade upon the right of the road, Colonel Williams's brigade of Marylanders on the left, and the artillery in the centre. Colonel Read, with a few militia, in the rear, as a second line. Captain Kirkwood and the light infantry lay in our front, and as the enemy advanced, he was soon engaged with them, and both he and his corps behaved with great gallantry.

The pickets, under the command of Captains Morgan and Benson, behaved with equal spirit, and good conduct.

As the enemy were found to be advancing only with a small front, Lieut. Col. Ford, with the Second Maryland regiment, had orders to advance and flank them upon the left. Lieut. Col. Campbell had orders to do the like upon the right. Col. Gunby, with the First Maryland regiment, and Lieut. Col. Haws, with the Second Virginia regiment, had orders to advance down the hill and charge them in the front. Lieut. Col. Washington had orders to turn the enemy's right flank, and charge them in the rear. The whole line was soon engaged in close firing, and the artillery under Col. Harrison playing on their front. The enemy were staggered in all quarters,

---

Lieut. Col. Washington had orders to turn the enemy's right flank, and charge them in the rear. The whole line was soon engaged in close firing, and the artillery under Col. Harrison playing on their front. The enemy were staggered in all quarters, and upon the left were retiring, while our troops continued to advance, when unfortunately two companies of the right, of the First Maryland regiment, got a little disordered, & unhappily Colonel Gunby gave an order for the rest of the regiment, then advancing to take a new position in the rear, where the two companies were rallying. This impres-

---

sed the whole regiment with an idea of a retreat, and communicated itself to the Second regiment, which immediately followed the first on their retiring. Both were rallied, but it was too late, the enemy had gained the hill, and obliged the artillery to retire. The Second Virginia regiment having advanced some distance down the hill, and the Maryland line being gone, the enemy immediately turned their flank, while they were engaged in the front. Lieut. Col. Campbell's regiment had got into some disorder and fallen back a little; this obliged me to order Lieut. Col. Haws to retire. The troops were frequently rallied but had got into too much disorder to recover the fortune of the day, which once promised us a complete victory, as Col. Washington found the enemy, both horse and foot, retiring with the greatest precipitation towards the town, and took upwards of 200 prisoners, and ten or fifteen officers, before he discovered our people had left the ground; more than 50 of which were brought off. The Colonel's behavior, and that of his regiment upon this occasion, did them the highest honour. We retired about two or three miles, without any loss of artillery or ammunition waggons, the baggage having been sent off at the beginning of the action. The enemy suffered very greatly. Our force was not materially different; but had we succeeded, from the disposition made, we must have had the whole prisoners, as well as full possession of Camden. Inclosed is the return of the killed and wounded. Among the former is Captain Beaty of the Maryland line, a most excellent officer, and an ornament to his profession. Our army is in good spirits, and this little repulse will make no alteration in our general plan of operations. Inclosed I send your Excellency the conditions of the capitulation and surrender of fort Watson, which, I hope, will be followed by others.

I have the honour to be,
With the greatest respect,
Your Excellency's most obedient,
And most humble servant,
NATH. GREENE.

P.S. The horse and part of the

---

rously wounded, elbow. Lt. Col. Campbell, Virginia, slight contusion, thigh. Capt. William Beaty, Maryland, killed. Capt. S. Smith, 3d Maryland, prisoner. Capt. Denholm, Virginia, slight contusion. Captain-Lieut. Bruen, Maryland, wounded in both ankles, prisoner on parole. Lieut. M. Galloway, slightly wounded. Lieut. B— Virginia, dangerously in the leg.

O. H. WILLIAMS, D. A.

RETURN of the killed and wounded in the action.

Killed: 1 sergeant, 17 rank & file.

Wounded: 7 sergeants, 101 rank and file.

Missing: 3 sergeants, 133 rank and file.

Most of the missing mistook the order to rally, at Saunders creek, and took a different route; some are killed, some wounded and in the British hospital; one third of the remainder have been heard of and expected to rejoin.

O. H. WILLIAMS, D. A.

Fort Watson, April 23, 17—

"SIR,

"Lieutenant Colonel Lee made a junction with me on Santee, the — instant, after a rapid march from —sey's Mill on Deep river, which I performed in eight days.

"The 15th we marched to this place and invested it; our hope was to cut off their water; some riflemen and continentals immediately took post between the fort and the lake.

"The fort was situated on a hill, forty feet high, stockaded, with rows of abbatis around it, and no trees near enough to cover our men from fire.

"The third day after we had invested it, we found the enemy had found well near the stockade, which we could not prevent them from, as we had no intrenching tools to make our approaches. We immediately determined to raise a work equal to the height of the fort. This arduous work was completed the — morning by Major Mabam, who first took it. We then made a lodgement on the side of the mount near the stockade; this was performed with great spirit and address, by Ensign Johnson and Mr. Lee, a volunteer in Colonel Lee's legion; who with difficulty ascended the hill and pulled away the abbatis, which induced the commandant to hoist the — Inclosed is the capitulation, which — hope may be approved of by you.

"The officers and men performed e-
very thing that could be expected, and
Major Mihan, of my brigade, had in a
particular manner a great share in this
success, by his unwearied diligence in
executing a tower, which was the principal occasion of the reduction of the fort.
In short, Sir, I have had the greatest
satisfaction from every one under my
command.

"Inclosed is a list of the prisoners &
stores taken, I shall, without loss of
time, demolish the fort; after which I
shall proceed to the high hills of Santee, and halt at Captain Richardson's
plantation till further orders.

I have the honor to be, with the
greatest respect, Sir, your most obedient
humble servant,
FRANCIS MARION, B. G."
TERMS of CAPITULATION proposed by Lieutenant M Kay, commandant of Fort Watson.

I. The officers to be permitted their
parole, to wear their side arms, and to
possess their private baggage. Agreed.

II. The British soldiers to be permitted
to march to Charlestown, where they are
to continue perfectly out of service till
exchanged, and liable to be ordered elsewhere by the commander in chief of the
American southern army. Agreed.

III. The irregulars to be treated as
prisoners of war. Agreed.

IV. All public stores to be delivered to
the legion Quarter-master, and the fort
to be delivered up to Captain Oldham,
who will take possession this evening with
a detachment of Marylanders.

The capitulation is acceded to, as it
now stands, in compliment to the gallantry
with which it has been defended.
(Signed)
PATRICK CARNS, JAMES M'KAY
Capt. Leg. Infantry.   Lieutenant
April 23, 1781.

A LIST of PRISONERS taken at
Scott's Lake, April 23, 1781.
Commanding Officers.
Lieutenant M'Kay, commandant of the
fort. Surgeon Campbell, King's American regiment. Ensign Robinson, Loyal American regiment. Lieutenant
Lewis, South Carolina rangers. Ensign and Quarter-master M'Kallam,
ditto. 73 British privates. 36 Tories. Total, 5 commissioned officers, and
109 privates.
Extract of a letter from Gen. Marion,
dated April 21, 1781.

"A small detachment which I sent
to watch the enemy's movements in Camden, took, at the mouth of Kershaw's
creek, a boat laden with corn, killed two,
wounded four, and took 6 British soldiers
and one Tory.

"Colonel Horry crossed the Pedee with
seventy men to intercept the Tories, who
I expected would join Colonel Watson
in his march up Pedee; he fell in with a
party of thirty foragers and as many
more to cover them, he charged them on
horseback, in Mr. M'Pherson's plantation, killed two and took 13 British soldiers, and two Tories, two negroes;
without the loss of a man.

"General Lillington reports that
the Bladen militia of North Carolina,

---

fell with great spirit on the rear of
Lord Cornwallis's army, as he was retreating to Wilmington, and killed
men, and took between fifteen an   13
ty prisoners.

"General Pickens rep
Col. Clarke, on the 23d of
an action with Major Du
Ninety-Six, killed thirty-fou
forty-two prisoners; among
the Major himself is number
Published by order of Con
CHARLES THOMSO
May 29.   Yesterday ar
the prize sloop Jane, from
town, bound to New-Yo
with rice, &c. sent in by th
Sun privateer, of this port.
been but a short time from
town, and brings advice
Rawdon's having burnt Ca
retreated towards Charlesto
that Lord Cornwallis had
from Wilmington to the same place.
Upwards of one hundred wounded
British officers and soldiers had been
shipped from Wilmington to Charlestown, supposed to have suffered at
the late action at Guilford Court-
House.

By a gentleman who left York-
Town on Friday evening, we learn,
that four of the soldiers of the Pennsylvania line were shot at that place
on Tuesday last for mutiny. Six had
been condemned and two were pardoned by Gen. Wayne.

These men, each of them, at different times, had behaved in a very
disorderly mutinous manner. discovering the most seditious temper, &
calling upon their fellow soldiers of
the several regiments to join them in
their revolt. They found however
no support from their comrades.
The whole line were drawn up under arms at the execution, and behaved in the most orderly manner.
A finer body of men never were collected. They were to have marched from that place on Wednesday,
but were obstructed solely by the
heavy rains. The men appear chearful and happy without the least appearance of tumult or discontent.
FISH-KILL, June 7.

We learn that the French & English fleets in the West-Indies have
had a severe engagement; that the
French have been victorious, and
have taken two ships of the line. A
New-York paper of the 2d instant
says also, that the British lost two
ships of the line; but reports from
thence add further, that two are taken and three sunk.

Last Friday the post from this office to Morristown was taken, with
the mail, by a party of the enemy,
near Col. Soward's. His horse, saddle and holsters, are found. As he
has not yet been heard of, it is supposed he is either murdered or carried to New-York.
NEWPORT, May 26.

Last Thursday night seven or
eight prisoners made their escape
from the prison ship in this harbour,

---

boarded a schooner of about fifty tons
lying in the road ready to sail the
next morning, and carried her off.

Six of the above ships of the line
were bound to the East-Indies, and
the remainder to the windward islands.—And it is reported, that the
French have the greatest prospect of
a most advantageous campaign.

The same day Capt. Young arrived here in 20 days from Martinico:
By him we have a confirmation that
the French fleet lately arrived at Martinico, had been in pursuit of and
drove the British from before St. Lucia, and landed 6000 troops there;
and that there is no doubt but the
island is now in possession of our allies.

Yesterday arrived here the Continental frigate Alliance, Capt. Barry,
from France; he sailed in company
with a French ship of 40 guns, which
he parted with six weeks ago in a
heavy gale of wind. Capt. Barry
has captured on his passage six prizes, viz. Two privateers, as formerly mentioned, two Jamaica men, and
two sloops of war, of 16 six-pounders, the two last he took about ten
days ago, on the banks of Newfoundland, after a severe conflict, in which
the Alliance had 8 men killed and
24 wounded. Capt. Barry is unfortunately among the latter. One of
the prizes was sent to Newfoundland, with 300 prisoners, taking a
receipt for them, and hostages for
the return of the vessel.

The Thorn, Capt. Tucker, has
sent into a safe port a prize, from
Eustatia bound to Halifax, and was
left in chase of four or five others.

A number of vessels were seen in
the offing yesterday, supposed to be
the French fleet which sailed from
France in March last for this place.
Extract of a letter from a gentleman
at Newbury-Port, to his friend in
Salem, dated the 4th instant.

"This day arrived the brig Weasel,
Capt. Combs, in 14 days from Port
Louis, in Guadaloupe, by whom we
learn that the French fleet and army
had laid siege to St. Lucia, and that
our informant on his passage, fell in
with (as he supposed) Rodney's fleet
beating up for it."

CONNECTICUT JOURNAL (NEW HAVEN)
June 14, 1781
—

Despite a tactical victory, Cornwallis's losses were so
heavy at Guilford Courthouse that he was forced to
withdraw to Wilmington on the North Carolina coast to
rest and refit his army. Greene, his army intact and ready
to fight again, began the second phase of the Carolina
campaign at Hobkirk's Hill. The *Connecticut Journal*
prints Greene's report to Samuel Huntington, president
of the Continental Congress.

Siege of Ninety Six

By Robert M. Dunkerly

THE SIEGE OF NINETY SIX, SOUTH CAROLINA, IN THE summer of 1781 was taxing for both sides. General Nathanael Greene led a small army into South Carolina to attack the various British-held posts across the state. With the main British army under General Lord Charles Cornwallis in Virginia (where other American forces were ready to receive him), Greene felt free to attack the many weakly defended forts and outposts here.

Ninety Six was a village on the Cherokee Trading Path in upper South Carolina. British forces occupied and fortified the site, with a large, earthen, star-shaped fort and a stockade around the town. They also converted its large brick jail into a fortress. Greene's army of Virginia, Maryland, and Delaware Continental troops, along with militia from both Carolinas, arrived and began to lay siege to the post. Defending Ninety Six was a garrison composed entirely of Loyalists led by Lieutenant Colonel John Cruger.

The July 19, 1781, *Independent Chronicle* reveals that at the same time as the Ninety Six operation, American forces were also attacking Augusta, Georgia, just seventy miles to the south. In fact, after capturing the important Georgia town, Lieutenant Colonel "Light Horse Harry" Lee brought his forces to Ninety Six to assist Greene. They arrived in time for the final assault on June 18. It was a tremendous effort, as the Americans charged through obstructions and up to the very walls of the star fort, but they could go no farther and suffered heavy losses.

The Siege of Ninety Six illustrates an important fact about the fighting in the Carolinas: it was a brutal civil war.

This article, written by an unidentified American officer, is optimistic as it was written in late May before many of the challenges of attacking Ninety Six surfaced. In fact, the article later proclaims that "the above post has surrendered." Inaccuracies have obviously crept into the reports coming out of South Carolina.

The August 16, 1781, *Continental Journal* reports the news using General Greene's letter—no better source could be found for a summary of the siege. As the writer notes, Greene knew that British reinforcements had landed in Charleston and were on the way to relieve the beleaguered garrison. General Thomas Sumter had been dispatched to delay their march but could not impede their progress. Unable to take the fort and with enemy reinforcements closing in, Greene had no choice but to pull back after investing much time, effort, and resources. It was extremely frustrating for the commander, his officers, and the common soldiers who struggled there. Greene later recorded, "Our poor fellows are worn out with fatigue."

The small American army tried everything to capture Ninety Six: artillery to batter it, infantry assaulting it, and even tunneling under it. Despite their efforts under grueling conditions, Cruger's stubborn Loyalist defenders held on.

The Siege of Ninety Six illustrates an important fact about the fighting in the Carolinas: it was a brutal civil war. The defending garrison contained not one British soldier: they were all Loyalist Americans fighting for the King. Many communities in the Carolinas were split, and rival militias sprang up across the region. The war here was much more bitter and personal than in other regions.

Greene's letter in the August 16, 1781, *Continental Journal* is dated June 20, but the news it conveys is obviously not printed until mid-August in Boston, illustrating how slowly news traveled and the uncertainty of reports. These newspaper accounts, fragmentary and sometimes inaccurate, illustrate how uncertain good news was in the eighteenth century. It took many months, and often from many sources, for contemporaries to piece together the facts of distant occurrences. Imagine the shock of readers who saw the July 19, 1781, *Independent Chronicle* article only to learn later that Greene not only failed to take the fort, but also was repulsed handily.

Of little help to historians is that there were no American newspapers active in the Carolinas in 1781. Newspapers came and went with frequency here during the colonial period, and to make matters worse, only fragments of issues survived.

It is a good reminder to us in the "information age," with infinite access to news and data, that it was not always so; that our ancestors struggled to understand their world and make good decisions based on what they obtained. Period newspapers are thus not only a wonderful primary source, but also a window into how we construct and understand the past.

BALTIMORE, June 19.

LETTERS from Fredericksburg, dated on Tuesday last, mention, that the British army had visited Goochland and Amelia counties, the former on the North, and the latter on the South side of James river, and that it was hoped they were on their retreat still more Southerly.---That their cavalry had made a rapid march, in two divisions, under command of Colonels Tarlton and Simcoe, one to Charlottesville, and the other to a place called "Point of Fork," where they had committed great excesses, the particulars of which had not been received.

A postcript to one of the above-mentioned letters, advises, that intelligence had just been received from the Southward, that the British forces were in march for Richmond.

JUNE 26.

Extract of a letter from an officer of distinction in General Greene's army, dated camp before Ninety-Six, South-Carolina, May 24, 1781.

"Lord Rawdon has retreated to Charlestown. Fort-Watson, on Santee, forts Mott and Granby, on Congary, Camden and Nelson's-ferry, are in our possession. General Pickens and Lieut. Col. Lee are before Augusta: General Marian is below, manoeuvering towards Charlestown, and General Greene has invested Ninety-Six. It is only possible we may not succeed. I expect soon to hear of the reduction of Augusta. What General Phillips is doing, or Lord Cornwallis intends to do, I cannot inform you; you will have it from better authority. We fear nothing before us."

Extract of a letter from Fredericksburg, dated on Tuesday last.

"It is said the enemy were, on Saturday last, at Richmond, destroying the tobacco and houses.---The Marquis, by the last accounts, lay 12 or 15 miles from them."

A letter from George-Town, dated on Sunday last, mentions, that the Baltimore and Frederick-Town troops of light-dragoons, were to cross Patowmack the next day, on their way to join the Marquis de la Fayette.

PHILADELPHIA, July 4.

On the 28th ult. His Excellency JOHN RUTLEDGE, Esq; set out from this city, in order to resume the reins of his government, where, we hear,

him, the paragraph in last Saturday's paper, wherein that gentleman is named, ought to be considered as a slander, circulated to injure his character.

Extract of a letter, (found on board the schooner Dolphin, taken by Capt. Angus) from Colonel Brathwaite to Mr. Mayne, of Lisbon, dated Madras, October 10 1781.

"IN July last, Hyder Ally entered the Carnatick with 60,000 horse, 20,000 foot, 20 battering guns and 40 field pieces. The country fell before him like ripe corn before the reaper's fickle. We had no where 3500 men. In the face of this army we were to make a junction to form any thing to oppose. I had with me about the number above mentioned, with 10 field pieces; I was ordered to join the General at the Presidency; I was at Pondicherry; on accout of rivers I was obliged to go inland, and the enemy was so situated that his second days march would have crossed my fourth, but by marching always suddenly in the night, and sending people to clear one road when I meant to take another, I made good my junction, with only the loss of a little baggage, which I could not protect from his numerous horse. I joined the General, and we marched to join Lieutenant-Colonel Bailie coming from the northward, and with such a force as I had, we got within ten miles of him, and even reinforced him by a detachment. The enemy, on this occasion, shewed a great piece of generalship, for he made as if he meant to attack us, slipt by us in the ... whole force, ... bravest condu... er of our arm... there was sca... tale; so com... happened to... suppose, had... about 4000 ... to believe th... horses. Th... the ammuni... answering fo... some of our... to see, for o... marched to f... about 4 miles... gitives met us, told us all ... moving off as fast as they could. As our's, ... the remains of an ...

means to send him to the West-Indies, as there is no Britain on the Continent who will serve with a man so infamous. O Arnold! dost thou think to find the British in the Islands, more hardened to dishonour than those at New-York? O wretched Arnold! the opprobium of thy country---the scorn of nations---dost thou think there is any corner of the universe, where thou canst find a shelter from devouring remorse, and from vengefull despair?"

In Rivington's New-York Gazette of June 30, the following is inserted in a letter from London, dated May 5. "Our Court, to please the Northern Powers, have issued Proclamations forbidding privateers and letters of marque from stopping or molesting any vessels, though belonging to our enemies, in the Baltic, so we keep them in good humor with us."

Yesterday was the anniversary commencement at Harvard-College, Cambridge, which being the first public one since the present war, a very great concourse of all ranks of people were collected on the occasion. The names of the young gentlemen who took their degrees, will be inserted in our next.

A small boat, one of the noted Shaving-Mills which continually infest our bay, was captured by two or three whale-boats, and sent in here last Saturday.

The privateer ship Rover, of 20 guns, from Salem---privateer sloop Kingbird, of 10 guns, from Providence---and the brig Good-Intent, Captain Trott, from this port, bound to St. Croix, wit... ... into New-York.

INDEPENDENT CHRONICLE (BOSTON)
July 19, 1781

The July 19, 1781, *Independent Chronicle* reveals that at the same time as the Ninety Six operation, American forces were also attacking Augusta, Georgia, just seventy miles to the south. In fact, after capturing the important Georgia town, Lieutenant Colonel "Light Horse Harry" Lee brought his forces to Ninety Six to assist Greene.

have the pleasure to announce ... good authority, that that State and Georgia are now entirely in the possession of the Americans ... and Savannah excepted) and as soon ...

gage, tents, &c. The enemy has began the siege of Arcot, in which he makes neither figure nor ... and as the periodical rains have now ...

GREENLEAF'S Office, ...
Broad-Cloths, German Serges, V... Callicoes, Chintzes, Muslins, Check... lands and Cottons, China Cups and Sauc... Starch, Hair-Powder, Nails of many Sizes, a...

George Thatcher

THE
CONTINENTAL JOURNAL,
AND
WEEKLY ADVERTISER.

THURSDAY, AUGUST 16, 1781.　　[NUMB. CCLXXXVI.]

BOSTON: Printed by JOHN GILL, in COURT-STREET.

☞ THE ENTIRE PROSPERITY OF EVERY STATE DEPENDS UPON THE DISCIPLINE OF IT'S ARMIES.　　*The King of Prussia.*

PHILADELPHIA, July 25.

The following are copies of some of the Letters found in a packet from England bound to N York, but taken on her passage and carried into France.

(Duplicate) Parliament-street, 17 Feb. 1781.

DEAR SIR,

WITH this letter I send a copy of account between you and Mr. Murray of Quebec, by which I find you had drawn yourself, from New-York in May for 1,104: 16: 3, the sum for which you left with me a set of bills, and which I had negociated through my friend Captain Matthews, General Haldimand's secretary, not knowing you had drawn again. I also send Messrs. Ross and Gray's account, in which I observe, what seems to me extraordinary, that you are credited only 185: 14: 6, for deficiences in appointments on receiving the battallion, and charged with 1.619: 14: 2, for deficiences on your getting the 16 regiment. I have wrote fully to General Arnold, that his money is invested in the stock he mentioned, which is a very desirable investment, and made at a good time; I did my best for him, and hope he will approve, I know it was as well laid out as possible.

I hope now all tumults are over. Lord G. Gordon was two days ago tried and acquitted for his share in the riots in July 1780. Nothing yet from Lord Cornwallis, his army is in good spirits and no doubt reinforced by this time. I have nothing material to trouble you with. Mrs. Meyrick desires me to offer her most respectful compliments, and joins me in sincere wishes for your health and happiness.

I am, dear Sir, with the highest respect, your obedient and most humble servant,
(signed) JAMES MEYRICK.
His Excellency General Robertson.

(Duplicate) Parliament street, 30 Jan. 1781.

SIR,

I AM honored with your several letters, inclosing bills on Harley and Drummond, to amount of 5000l. the receipt of which I have regularly, by packet, acknowledged. On the day they were paid, I invested the amount in the fund you mentioned, and as it was a very favourable time, I flatter myself it will meet your approbation, also the mode in which it was done.

As it is possible some directions might come from you for disposing of the money in some other mode, I thought it might not be so advantageous to lock it up totally, as it might be a long while before I could receive a power from you to transfer, had I put it in your name, and in the mean time the dividends could not be received for your use. The mode I have adopted has been used in like cases, and can be instantly altered to any you direct, on your favouring me with a letter. The account is as follows, viz.

Brought by Samuel and William Scholey, stock brokers, for Major General Arnold, 7000l. in new 4 per cents, at 71 1 4 new 1 4 as follows.

In the name of Major GeneralBene-
dict Arnold 100l. stock at 71 1 4 new 4 } paid
per cent consols 6900 stock at 71 1 4 do. } 4987 10

In the name of James Meyrick, Esq.
7000　commission paid the brokers 8 15
power of attorney to receive dividends 1 6
　　　　　　　　　　　　　　　　4996 6 6

There remains therefore 3l. 13s. 6 of the 5000l.

By this method in case I receive my instructions from you from a different application of your money, I can sell out the 6900 stock and follow them before you receive this letter, and if you wish to continue in this fund, it may, if you prefer, be all placed in your own name, by transferring the 6900l. to your 100l. and it was for the purpose of your having an account there, I bought the 100l. in your name. Also the power of attorney now inclosed will enable me to receive the dividends on the whole 7000l. stock, after I have made the transfer, should you choose I should do for. I hope I have made myself properly understood, and can assure you I have to the best of my abilities acted for you as for myself.

I have the honour to be, Sir,
Your obedient and humble servant,
(Signed)　JAMES MEYRICK.
Major Gen. Arnold.

[*Judas Iscariot betrayed his master for thirty pieces of silver, but repenting of his guilt, returned the money into the treasury, and went and hanged himself.*

Judas ARNOLD received five thousand pounds sterling for his treachery, and we find has lodged the money in the British funds, but he has not spirit enough to pursue the character in the only part worthy of imitation.]

(No. 82.)　Whitehall, March 7, 1781.
SIR,

YOUR letter, No. 103, inclosing a general state of his Majesty's provincial forces serving under your command, and the report of the deputy inspector general of provincial forces, of nine battalions, which you have thought worthy of being recommended to his Majesty for half pay and permanent rank in America, has been received and laid before the king.

The encouragement held out to the officers of the provincial troops, of having their ranks made permanent in America, and of being entitled to half pay upon the reduction of their regiments, as stated in my letter of the 23d January, 1779, was meant as a reward and compensation to those of his Majesty's faithful American subjects as had suffered the loss of their property on account of their loyalty, and had taken or should take arms in his Majesty's service, and should exert themselves in raising and compleating provincial regiments : but it never was the king's intentions that those indulgencies should be extended generally to all those who held or who should hold commissions in the provincial corps, nor even to all those who came within this description of loyal American sufferers ; but to such regiments only as should be compleated to the then establishment of the British regiments of foot, and should be recommended to his Majesty by his commander in chief, as being properly officered and fit for service.

It is true, this rule was in some measure departed from, in the instance of the establishment of the queen's rangers, and the New-York volunteers, neither of which regiments were compleat when they were recommended to the king ; and also in the case of the volunteers of Ireland, as many of the officers of that regt. were neither Americans, nor had property or connections in that country : but then it was done on account of the distinguished merit of those corps, and upon your particular recommendation ; but in cases in general, where there is no such extraordinary merit to claim particular and distinguished marks of favor, it is expected by his majesty that all the conditions specified in my letter of the 23d January, 1779, before-mentioned, should be complied with in order to the officers of the Provincial regiments availing themselves of the advantages there held out to them.

With respect to the British legion, which you in your separate letter recommended to his Majesty's favour in your separate

letter of the 1st June, 1780, and which you again mention in your letter of the 18th December, as it appears by a return of that corps, dated the 31st Dec. last, which I have lately received from South-Carolina, that their numbers at that time amounted to more than 600 rank and file ; and as they would long since have been greatly over complete, but for the losses they have sustained in the very active and important service in which they have been employed ; upon these considerations, and as a mark of his Majesty's royal approbation of the gallant behaviour of this corps, and of the services of that very deserving officer Lieut. Col. Tarleton, who commands it, the king has been graciously pleased to approve of your recommendation of the British legion for permanent rank in America ; and the officers will be recommended to Parliament for half-pay, whenever the corps shall be reduced ; and it is his Majesty's pleasure, that you do take the earliest opportunity of making known to them these his gracious intentions.

And as it appears by the deputy inspector general's report, that the king's American regt. (which stands first upon the list of those you have recommended) was raised at a very early period of the rebellion, and was nearly compleated in a short time, and has since been constantly employed in active service in the field, where it has more than once been distinguished for its gallant and spirited behaviour in action, particularly at the affair of Rhode-Island, on the 29th of August, 1778, under the command of Major General Pigot, his Majesty has been pleased to approve of your recommendation of that regiment to be put upon the American establishment, and you will please to notify it accordingly.

But in future it is his Majesty's pleasure, that no provincial regiment should be recommended to him for permanent rank and half pay, that is not actually compleat to ten companies, consisting of 70 men rank and file each, with a due proportion of officers ; and whenever any regiment shall be so recommended, I am to desire you will give directions to the inspector general of Provincial forces, or his deputy, to report specially upon the merit of each commissioned officer, stating the place of his birth ; the time of his residence in North-America, if not a native of that country ; his former occupation and place of residence ; and whether he has suffered in his property on account of his loyalty : in order that the king may see how far the establishing of such regiments will come up to the original intention of the encouragement held out to the Provincials by the new regulations.

I am Sir, your most obedient humble servant,
(Signed)　GEO. GERMAIN.
Sir Henry Clinton.

Extract of a letter from Maj. Gen. Greene, dated Camp, at Little river, near Ninety-Six, June 20.

IN my letter of the 9th I informed your Excellency that the enemy had received a considerable reinforcement at Charlestown, and that I was apprehensive they would march out and interrupt our operations. On the 11th I got intelligence that they were advancing : I immediately detached the cavalry, with orders to General Sumpter to collect all the force he could, and keep in their front, and by every means in his power retard their march. The enemy passed him at Congaree before he got his troops in motion ; afterwards he found it impracticable to gain their front. It was my intention to have fought them before they arrived at Ninety-Six, could I have collected a force sufficient for the purpose.

" We had pushed on our approaches very near to the enemy's works. Our third parellel was formed round their abbatis : A mine and two approaches were within a few feet of their ditch. These approaches were directed against the star fort, which stands upon the left of the town, as we approached it from the Saluda. On the right our approaches were very near the enemy's redoubt ; this was a

[*For remainder see last Page.*]

strong stockade fort, with two block-houses in it. These two works flanked the town, which is picketed in with strong pickets, a ditch round the whole, and a bank raised near the height of a common parapet. Besides these fortifications, were several little flushes in different parts of the town, and all the works communicated with each other by covered ways. We had raised several batteries for cannon, one upwards of twenty feet high, within one hundred and forty yards of the star fort, to command the works, and a rifle battery also within thirty yards, to prevent the enemy from annoying our workmen. For the last ten days not a man could shew his head but he was immediately shot down, and the firing was almost incessant day and night. In this stage of the approaches I found the enemy so near us that it would be impossible to reduce the place without hazarding a storm. This, from the peculiar strength of the place could not be warranted by the success of a partial attempt to make a lodgment on one of the curtains of the star redoubt, and a vigorous push to carry the aright-hand work. The disposition was accordingly formed, and the attack made. Lieutenant Colonel Lee, with his legion infantry, and Capt. Kirkwood's light infantry, made the attack on the right ; and Lieut. Colonel Campbell, with the first Maryland & first Virginia regiments, was to have stormed the star redoubt, which is their principal work, and stands upon the left. The parapet of this work is near 12 feet high, and raised with sand bags near 3 feet more. Lieut. Duval, of the Maryland line, and Lieut. Selden of the Virginia line, led on the forlorn hope, followed by a party with hooks to pull down the sand bags, the better to enable them to make the alodgment, A furious cannonade preluded the attack. On the right the enemy were driven out of their works, and our people took possession of it. On the left never was greater bravery exhibited than by the parties led on by Duval, and Selden, but they were not so successful. They entered the enemy's ditch, and made every exertion to get down the sand bags, which from the depth of the ditch, height of the parapet, and under a galling fire, was rendered difficult. Finding the enemy defended their works with great obstinacy, & seeing but little prospect of succeeding without heavy loss, I ordered the attack to be pushed no farther.

" The behaviour of the troops on this occasion deserves the highest commendation ; both the officers that entered the ditch were wounded, and the greater part of their men were killed or wounded. I have only to lament that such men fell in an unsuccessful attempt.

"Capt. Armstrong, of the first Maryland regiment, was killed, and Capt. Benson, who commanded the regiment, was wounded at the head of the trenches. In both attacks we had upwards of 40 men killed and wounded ; the loss was principally at the star fort, and in the enemy's ditch, the other parties being all under cover. The attack was continued three quarters of an hour, and as the enemy were greatly exposed to the fire of the rifle battery and artillery, they must have suffered greatly. Our artillery was well served, and I believe did great execution.

" The troops have undergone incredible hardships during the siege, and though the issue was not successful, I hope their exertions will merit the approbation of Congress.

" We continued the siege until the enemy got within a few miles of us, having previously sent off all our sick, wounded and spare stores.

" Inclosed is a list of our killed and wounded during the siege."

RETURN of the killed, wounded and missing, during the siege of Ninety-Six, in South Carolina

The 6th, I detached an advance corps under General Wayne, with a view of reconnoitring the enemy's situation. Their light parties being drawn in ; the picquets, which lay close to their encampment, were gallantly attacked by some riflemen, whose skill was employed to great effect.

Having ascertained that Lord Cornwallis has sent off his heavy baggage under a proper escort, and posted his army in an open field- fortified by the shipping, I returned to the detachment which I found more generally engaged. A piece of cannon had been attempted by the vanguard under Major Galvan, whose conduct deserves high applause. Upon this the whole British army come out and advanced to the thin wood occupied by General Wayne. His corps chiefly composed of Pennsylvanians and some light infantry, did not exceed 800 men, with three field pieces, but notwithstanding their number, at sight of the British army the troops ran to the rencounter ; a short skirmish ensued with a close warm and well directed fire ; but as the enemy's right and left of course greatly out flanked ours, I sent General Wayne orders to retire half a mile to where Colonels Vose and Barber's light infantry battalions had arrived by a most rapid move, and where I directed them to form. In this position they remained till some hours in the night. The militia under Gen. Lawson had been advanced and the continentals were at Norrell's mill, when the enemy retreated during the night, to James Island, which they also evacuated, crossing over to the south side of the river. Their ground at this place and the Island was successively occupied by General Muhlenberg. A number of valuable horses were left on their retreat. From every account the enemy's loss has been very great and much pains taken to conceal it. Their light infantry, the brigade of guards, and two British regiments, former the first line ; the remainder of their army the second.—The cavalry were drawn up but did not charge.

By the inclosed return you will see what part of General Wayne's detachment suffered most. The services rendered by the officers make me happy to think that although many were wounded we lost none. Most of the field officers had their horses killed ; the same accident to every horse of two field pieces, made it impossible to move them, unless men had been sacrificed. But it is enough for the glory of General Wayne and the officers and men he commanded, with a reconnoitering party only, to have attacked the whole British army close to their encampment, and by this severe skirmish hastened their retreat over the river.

Colonel Boyer of the riflemen is a prisoner.

I ha........

Major Genera.....

RETUR.....
detachment.....
mish with.....
in Virginia....

Total. 4....
tains, 1 Ca....
and file wo....

NA.....
Capt. Van....
Montgom.....
Lieutenants. ....
prisoner) Capt. Lieut. Crossly, of artillery.

STOP THIEF!

TWENTY GUINEAS REWARD.

STOLEN from the Store of

CONTINENTAL JOURNAL (BOSTON)
August 16, 1781
—
The August 16, 1781, Continental Journal reports the news of the Siege of Ninety Six using General Greene's letter. No better source could be found for a summary of the siege.

RAID on NEW LONDON

By Matthew Reardon

N O MAN WAS HATED MORE IN CONNECTICUT IN 1781 than its native son turned traitor, Benedict Arnold. In September, Arnold met with British General Sir Henry Clinton at his headquarters in New York City. Clinton had been meticulously planning a combined land-naval attack on Newport, Rhode Island, where a sizable French army and naval squadron were stationed. He had hoped to deal a decisive blow to the Franco-American alliance. However, before he could set his plan in motion, he learned that a British ship carrying messages related to the attack had been captured by an American privateer. With the element of surprise gone, the attack was cancelled.

In retaliation, Clinton attempted to deal a blow to the American privateer fleet. American privateers had been a constant nuisance to the British high command since the beginning of the war. Arnold was given 1,700 men and orders to attack New London, Connecticut. New London was, according to the Loyalist newspaper *Rivington's Gazette*, "a nest of pirates." Once there, they were to destroy the privateers and any military stores they could locate.

Arriving at the mouth of the Thames River in the early hours of September 6, the force divided into two divisions. The first landed on the west side of the river to march on New London, while the second landed on the east side with orders to secure Fort Griswold. The first division met little resistance and quickly occupied the town. Detachments of soldiers began setting fire to many of the warehouses and privateers along the riverfront. Others struck at the homes of rebel leaders and in the process discovered military stores hidden in several private barns, which were also burned. Despite attempts to prevent looting and extensive damage, chaos soon erupted. Some British soldiers disobeyed orders and, along with several unlawful citizens, began looting abandoned houses. The wind picked up off the river, which only helped spread the fires.

Arnold was supposedly witnessed to be in several locations throughout New London during the day. Many citizens would try to place the blame of the fire and looting on him personally, even though he had issued strict orders beforehand not to do so. In his report, he would credit one of his staff officers for "his endeavors to prevent plundering…and the destruction of publick buildings."

One example of this was included in the September 13, 1781, *Massachusetts Spy*. The newspaper wrote that he dined at a house of an acquaintance and then ordered the house to be plundered and burned. This claim cannot be substantially proven. Arnold was hated, and people were eager to put him in any situation that would make him appear worse. It is very difficult to find any contemporary American accounts that are unbiased and do not refer to him as "Traitor Arnold" or "the Traitor" or his troops as "Arnold's murdering corps."

However, there are a few accounts of British soldiers doing the exact opposite of what so many are accused of doing. When writing her *History of New London*, Frances Caulkins wrote about a story of a daughter of a militia captain who pleaded with a British officer not to burn their home. She told him that her father was very ill and could not leave the house. The officer stepped in and ordered the house to be spared. It is impossible to draw any conclusion as to what Arnold or any individual British soldier was doing that day and is unjustifiable to accuse every British soldier of committing heinous acts.

The September 13, 1781, *Massachusetts Spy* also reported that "after Colonel Ledyard had surrendered [Fort Griswold, he was] murdered." This was a rumor that came about after the battle and has remained around even until today. New research suggests that Ledyard was actually attempting to lead a counterattack and was killed in the melee that ensued. The *Spy* also reported that the powder magazine in the fort was destroyed and that a British ensign was captured. The British did make an attempt to destroy the powder magazine, but the fuse that was set was put out before it reached the magazine. In his official report written the day after the battle, Arnold does not list any missing or captured officers. Neither do the official rosters of the regiments engaged.

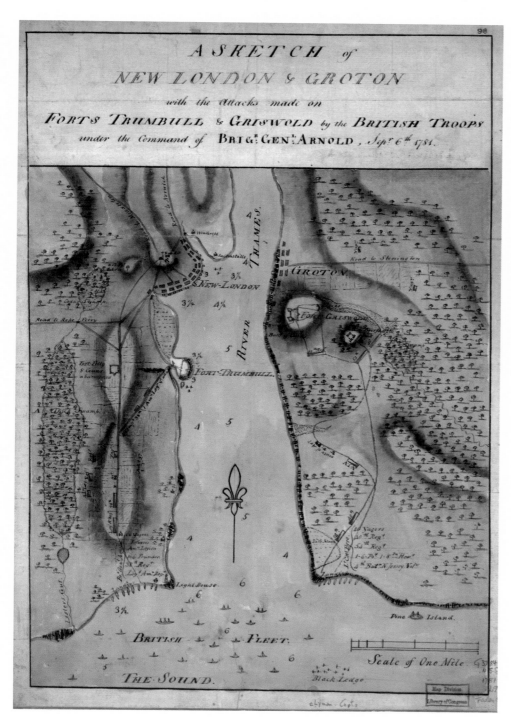

SKETCH OF NEW LONDON & GROTON
Library of Congress

The British targeted privateers and military stores in New London, Connecticut, which one Loyalist newspaper labeled "a nest of pirates."

said to have on board 19 head of cattle, which being to leeward, was the cause of her loss.

HARTFORD, September 11.

Extract of a letter from an officer commanding militia, dated New-London, Friday, 9 o'clock September 7, 1781.

" Yesterday morning at 10 o'clock, I received advice that the enemy were landing at New-London Harbour's mouth——I immediately ordered the regiment under my command to march to New-London for its defence. I arrived here, but it was too late to afford any great assistance in repelling the enemy, as they landed at 6 o'clock, and it was so late before I received advice of their arrival, that before the regiment could possibly get down, they were embarking.

" The enemy were under the command of the infamous General Arnold, and by the best accounts consisted of from 1500 to 2000 men——They have burnt the greatest part of the towns of New-London, and Groton, near the water——The garrison at Fort-Trumbull evacuated the fort and went over to Fort Griswold, where Colonel Ledyard made a noble defence——repulsed the enemy two or three times, but at last was obliged to surrender the fort to superiour force. The enemy, after Col. Ledyard had surrendered, murdered him and a number of others ; they left 73 of our men dead, and between 30 and 40 wounded in the fort ; they also carried off about 40 prisoners, among which last number is Ebenezer Ledyard, Esquire. They evacuated the fort about 10 o'clock, in the evening. They blew up the magazines in both forts, but did very little other damage to either of them.

" The enemy this morning were at the harbour's mouth on board their shipping, and came to sail about eight o'clock ; they are still just out beyond the Light-House, as the wind is against them. Their shipping consists of about 30 sail, two of which appear to be about 20 guns each.

" We cannot ascertain the loss the enemy sustained, but by the best accounts imagine it must be as large as ours if not larger. We have taken on this side a few prisoners, among which is an Ensign, mortally wounded.

" The loss sustained in this town, in goods, provisions, stores, shipping, &c. is very great——A considerable number of vessels made their escape up Norwich River."

Another letter, dated Fort-Griswold, Groton, 7th Sept. 10 o'clock, A. M. says, " That the enemy landed at New-London and Groton yesterday morning, and soon took possession of the works on New-London side the river ; and about one in the afternoon took possession of Fort-Griswold, in Groton, by storm, after a most severe and spirited resistance from our troops.——About seventy-five of our men found dead in the fort, officers included, among whom is the worthy and brave Lieut. Col. Ledyard, with several other officers of distinguished

---

tions we can to give them a warm reception."

Yesterday came up two victuallers, part of the fleet committed to the protection of his Majesty's frigate Pegasus, and dispatched by Rear Admiral Sir Samuel Hood to New-York ; the Pegasus and her convoy on the passage fell in with a French squadron of eight line of battle ships, supposed to be Monf. de Barras ; it was apprehended the whole consisting of six victuallers, and a vessel with the 40th regiment's cloathing, had fallen into the hands of the enemy, until happily those two effected a safe arrival in our harbour.

WORCESTER, September 13.

A New-York city paper of the 30th ult. mentions the arrival of Rear Admiral Hood, at Sandy-Hook, from the West-Indies, with 14 sail of the line, four frigates, one sloop, and a number of troops, consisting of the first battalion of the royal, the 13th and 69th regiments. We are informed that these ships, together with the fleet which were before at New-York, amounting in the whole to 35 sail, under the command of Admiral Graves, have taken their departure from Sandy-Hook, bound to the Chesapeake, in order dangerously wounded. French squadron, which ar Island the latter end of last feriour in force to the Bri squadron is said to consist o frigates and inferiour vess consist of one ship of 98 g 70, eleven of 74, four of 64 three of 32, five of 28, one of 24, one Fireship of 8, and a sloop of war. All the British line of battle ships except one are said to be copper-bottomed.

It is not doubted but that his Excellency General Washington has marched, with 8000 choice troops including the French, to Virginia, where the troops in that quarter will join him ; Lord Cornwallis is blocked up by the French fleet ;—by the present appearance of things we are at the eve of some important event, which God grant may be propitious to the United States.

It is said that Sir George Rodney and General Vaughan have gone for England from the W. Indies.

We hear that Arnold when he landed at New-London, dined at a gentleman's house with whom he was formerly acquainted. After dinner he ordered the house to be plundered and sat on fire. The traitor carried off all the plunder in the town that his short stay would permit him to take. Had he tarried in order to have taken breakfast the next morning, it is likely he would have been rewarded for all his villanies.

A large quantity of hard money, lately arrived from France, was a few days past carried through town, under a strong guard.

Last Friday Col. Armand, an active officer in the

" The enemy embarked on board their ships at about 11 o'clock last night, after burning most of the houses and other buildings on Groton bank, and many in New-London, among which are the Court-House, Church, &c."

From RIVINGTON's ROYAL GAZETTE.

---

old way, according to the number of colours, and the neatness of the flowers.

Any sort of produce or money will be received as pay for work done. Business in this way which individuals may order, will be cheerfully entered upon, and faithfully executed by their humble servant, SAMUEL JENNISON.

Oxford, September 5th, 1781.

N. B. A variety of patterns with different colours and figures may be seen at the house aforesaid.

BENJAMIN ANDREWS,
TAYLOR from BOSTON,

BEGS leave to inform the publick that he carries on his business near the Meeting-House in Worcester. Those gentlemen who will please to favour him with their commands, may be assured that his utmost endeavours shall be used to serve them with fidelity and dispatch.

S A D D L E S.

MEN's and Women's SADDLES, of all sorts, made and sold by
NATHANIEL COOLIDGE,
At his Shop in Worcester, near the Meeting-House.

...ublick that he carries its branches. Gen
...ease to favour him
...nd on being served
...ms.

...sses.

S, to be sold by
JOSEPH TRUMBULL,
At his Store near the Court-House in Worcester, Where may be had choice MADDER and OTTER, &c. &c.

STRAYED or stolen from the Subscriber, on or about the 26th day of last month, a very dark brown COW, low in flesh, the end of one of her horns a little broke, and about eight or nine years old. Whoever will give information to the Subscriber, of said Cow, so that he may have her again, shall have TWO DOLLARS reward ; and if stolen, will discover the thief, so that he may be convicted, shall be entitled to a further reward of one GUINEA. JOSEPH ALLEN.
Worcester, September 11, 1781.

DESERTED between Leicester and Springfield, one ASA KNOWLTON, of Bolton, aged 22 years, five feet 11 inches high, dark complexion, a farmer, engaged for six months for the town of Bolton. Whoever will take up said deserter and bring him to me, or to Col. Shepard at Springfield, shall have a handsome reward, and all necessary charges paid.
SETH WASHBURN, Superintendant.

MASSACHUSETTS SPY (BOSTON)
September 13, 1781

———

The *Massachusetts Spy* provides early accounts of the Raid on New London from letters, including one by "an officer commanding militia." Letters like these were among the top sources of colonial news. In a separate report under the Worcester dateline, Benedict Arnold is rumored to have dined with a former acquaintance in New London before ordering his house to be plundered and burned. Most Americans despised Arnold after his defection and were eager to make him appear worse in any situation.

The MASSACHUSETTS SPY

HARTFORD, September 11.

Extract of a letter from an officer commanding militia, dated New-London, Friday, 9 o'clock September 7, 1781.

"Yesterday morning at 10 o'clock, I received advice that the enemy were landing at New-London Harbour's mouth——I immediately ordered this regiment under my command to march on New-London for its defence. I arrived here, but it was too late to afford any great assistance in repelling the enemy, as they landed at 6 o'clock, and it was so late before I received advice of their arrival, that before the regiment could possibly get down, they were embarking.

"The enemy were under the command of the infamous General Arnold, and by the best accounts consisted of from 1500 to 2000 men——They have burnt the greatest part of the towns of New-London, and Groton, near the water——The garrison at Fort-Trumbull evacuated the fort and went over to Fort Griswold, where Colonel Ledyard made a noble defence——repulsed the enemy two or three times, but a last was obliged to surrender the fort to superiour force. The enemy, after Col. Ledyard had surrendered, murdered him and a number of others; they left 73 of our men dead, and between 30 and 40 wounded in the fort; they also carried off about 40 prisoners, among which last number is Ebenezer Ledyard, Esquire. They evacuated the fort about 10 o'clock, in the evening. They blew up the magazines in both forts but did very little other damage to either of them.

"The enemy this morning were at the harbour's mouth on board their shipping, and came to sail about eight o'clock; they are still just out beyond the Light-House, as the wind is against them. Their shipping consists of about 30 sail, two of which appear to be about 20 guns each.

"We cannot ascertain the loss the enemy sustained, but by the best accounts imagined it must be as large as ours if not larger. We have taken on this side a few prisoners, among which is an Ensign, mortally wounded.

"The loss sustained in this town, in goods, provisions, stores, shipping, &c. is very great—A considerable number of vessels made their escape up Norwich River."

Another letter, dated Fort-Griswold, in Groton, 7th Sept. 10 o'clock, A.M. says, "That the enemy landed at New-London and Groton yesterday morning, and soon took possession of the works on New-London side the river; and about one in the afternoon took possession of Fort-Griswold, in Groton, by storm, after most severe and spirited resistance from our troops.——About seventy-five of our men found dead in the fort, officers included, among whom is the worthy and brave Lieut. Col. Ledyard, with several other officers of distinguished merit. Captain Shapley of Fort Trumbull, is also dangerously wounded.

"The enemy embarked on board their ships at about 11 o'clock last night, after burning most of the houses and other buildings on Groton bank, and many in New-London, among which are the Court-House, Church, &c."

[...]

WORCESTER, September 13.
[...]

We hear that Arnold when he landed at New-London, dined at a gentleman's house with whom he was formerly acquainted. After dinner he ordered the house to be plundered and sat on fire. The traitor carried off all the plunder in the town that is short stay would permit him to take. Had he tarried in order to have taken breakfast the next morning, it is likely he would have been rewarded for all his villanies.

BATTLE OF EUTAW SPRINGS

By David Paul Reuwer

WE FIGHT, GET BEAT, RISE, AND FIGHT AGAIN," General Nathanael Greene said of his Southern Army's 1781 defeats at Guilford Courthouse and Hobkirk's Hill. Following partisan militia campaigns, Greene led the Southern Continental Army on a dynamic offensive attack.

Leading 2,100 troops for twenty-two days and 120 miles, Greene's intention was to crush Lieutenant Colonel Alexander Stewart's 1,690-man British force and eliminate the British threat in the Carolinas once and for all. The Patriots marched from the Santee High Hills to Camden, crossing the Wateree and Congaree rivers, then toward the Eutaws—within four miles of the British without their detection. The wooded topography of soft rises, swales, sinks, and steep-banked Eutaw Creek and its blackjack thickets influenced this battle.

Cavalry and infantry clashed on the morning of September 8 on the river road to the British encamped at Eutaw Springs, South Carolina. Hundreds of British foragers were then captured. Patriots arrayed in three lines, and the militia advanced two miles out, firing seventeen volleys, driving in the British skirmish line. The Maryland and Virginia Continentals "advanced in the face of the enemy's fire, a terrible cannonade and shower of bullets overturned all that presented, and the enemy were put to a rout" (*Glasgow Mercury*, December 13, 1781). Greene's army wielded four artillery pieces and the British five cannon plus two swivels; some were disabled and captured. Both armies employed extensive and repeated tactical use of cavalry, artillery, and infantry. Resilient British officers Coffin, Marjoribanks, and Sheridan bought time for Stewart to reform ranks, launch counterattacks, and check the American advance. Continentals utilized the bayonet with agility, such that Greene's report, reprinted in the December 13, 1781, *Glasgow Mercury*, stated, "I owe the victory which I have gained, to the brisk use the Virginians, Marylanders, and one party of the infantry made of the bayonet."

The intense, pitched fighting with infantry, artillery, and cavalry lasted four struggling hours until both sides wore out. Many leading Southern theater commanders fought together here. The drunken brawl portrayed by secondary sources is mostly myth; closed lines could not hold order fighting through the tented British camp. The Americans did not breach or dislodge the British from the three-storied brick house. This citadel anchored the British defense together with blackjack thickets along the creek. Both sides looked at each other from across the eight cleared acres as the afternoon sun broiled the wounded and bloated the dead. Greene's main force retired several miles to water, rest, and reorganize at Burdell's. Stewart broke one thousand arms, emptied rum barrels, abandoned supplies, and proceeded to withdraw the rest of his men who had not already fled toward Moncks Corner. In the end, Americans slaughtered Americans and 204 soldiers from both sides were buried at the battlefield.

Greene wrote to Governor John Rutledge the next day:

"We have had a most Obstinate and Bloody action. Victory was ours. We drove the Enemy, more than four Miles. We took between three and four hundred prisoners, and had it not been, for the large Brick Building, at the Eutaw Spring, and the peculiar kind of Brush that surrounds it, we should have taken the whole Army prisoners."

Marion, Lee, and Maham pursued and harassed Stewart's men retreating southeast toward Ferguson's Swamp even as British prisoners shuttled north to

Camden. Major Archibald McArthur's three hundred men up from Moncks Corner reinforced Stewart's retreat, but the whole army retired back there. Greene chased until September 13, short of Moncks Corner halfway to Charleston.

This fiercely fought engagement debilitated British field combat ability in the Carolinas. Unable to reinforce Cornwallis at Yorktown, the British ventured far from Charleston for more than another year, foraging and skirmishing at will. South Carolina Governor John Rutledge used this victory to declare qualified pardon to all those who had joined the British side. British officer Roderick Mackenzie journalized Greene in his diary: "the more he is beaten, the farther he advances in the end." Congress awarded Greene one of only six gold medals during the war for "a most signal victory" (*Pennsylvania Packet*, December 4, 1781) at Eutaw Springs.

PENNSYLVANIA PACKET (PHILADELPHIA)

December 4, 1781

—

Congress awarded Greene one of only six gold medals during the war for "a most signal victory" at Eutaw Springs.

THE VOICE OF THE PEOPLE, which supported thirteen columns, representing the states, supporting a frize, on which were wrote ILLUSTRIOUS SENATORS; and in a pediment, which covered the whole range of columns, were wrote, BRAVE SOLDIERY, with rays of light and support from the senate; the pediment ornamented with the following statues, Justice with her even scales, a flaming sword, and thirteen stars in the glory around the figure, emblematical of the justice of Congress; on the right, the statue of Hope, with her anchor; and on the left, the statue of Industry, with her bee hive. The second story of the Corinthian order, with statues in niches, with the words, HEROES FALLEN IN BATTLE; and an attic story, as the work compleated with the words AGRICULTURE, ARTS AND COMMERCE, and represented by the following statues: Agriculture, a figure holding a sheaf of wheat on her left arm, a sickle in her right hand, and a plow at her feet. The Arts represented by the statues of painting, sculpture, and architecture; Painting has a pallet and pencils in one hand, and the other supporting a picture; she has a golden chain hanging from her neck, with a medal, on which is IMITATION; the several links allude to the many parts necessary to be studied before a whole can be produced; or the combined qualifications of an able artist: and it being of gold, to shew that the art of painting cannot flourish without it is supported by the generosity of the opulent. Sculpture is represented by a statue, holding in one hand a mallet and chissel, and in the other a bust, ornamented with laurels. Architecture by a statue, having in one hand a plan of elevation, and in the other a square and a plummet. Commerce by a statue, holding a globe in one hand, and the other on the prow of a ship. A dome covers the building and finishes with the figure of Fame, blowing her trumpet to the east; which may easily be comprehended.

And at another window the genius of America, trampling on Discord, being a handsome female figure, the bigness of life, cloathed in white, a purple girdle with the word VIRTUE on it, and a blue mantle strewed with stars, a fillet on her head, with the word PERSEVERANCE: She holds in one hand her banner of thirteen stripes, with the words EQUAL RIGHTS, and in the other hand a globe with the word UNIVERSALITY on a circular index to the globe. The figure of Discord with his snakes instead of hair, and holding a torch, the flame of which turns down on himself.

By the UNITED STATES in CONGRESS assembled, October 29, 1781.

Resolved,

THAT the thanks of the united states in congress assembled, be presented to major general Greene, for his wise, decisive and magnanimous conduct in the action of the 8th of September last, near the Eutaw Springs in South-Carolina; in which, with a force inferior in number to that of the enemy, he obtained a most signal victory.

That the thanks of the united states in congress assembled, be presented to the officers and men of the Maryland and Virginia brigades, and Delaware battalion of continental troops, for the unparalleled bravery and heroism by them displayed, in advancing to the enemy through an incessant fire, and charging them with an impetuosity and ardour that could not be resisted.

That the thanks of the united states in congress assembled, be presented to the officers and men of the legionary corps and artillery, for their intrepid and gallant exertions during the action.

her, then pushed forward and closed the other which was engaged on our bow. In about thirty minutes she struck, sent a boat on board to take possession, and wore round after the other, who was making off, who also struck on our coming up. They proved to be the Hercules and Mars, two privateers belonging to Amsterdam, mounting 24 nine-pounders and 10 cohorns each, are perfectly new and alike, sail as fast as the Artois, and the compleatest privateers I ever saw, cost upwards of 20,000l. commanded by two Hogenboombes, father and son, inhabitants of Flushing. The father was well known last war, by the name of John Hardapple, had a schoote privateer, with a French commission, out of Flushing, and did much mischief to our trade; he was sent for on purpose to command these privateers. They sailed from the Texel the 30th of November, and had only taken one of our fishing smacks.

"The Hercules had 164 men on board; 13 were killed, and 20 wounded: the Mars 146 men, nine were killed, and 15 wounded. We had one man killed, and six wounded.

" I beg you to transmit to their Lordships, that I am much indebted to the attention of my officers and people in securing both these gentry. Our rigging and sails are cut, and fore-top mast unserviceable."

The capture of the two Dutch privateers by Capt. Macbride, most probably will prove of the happiest consequences to the trade. Their great force, and going in company, would have been very dangerous to the traders. The great object, we are informed, of these privateers, was to capture as many colliers as possible. The Hollanders are so very scarce of the article of coals, at present, that we are assured they sell at the amazing price of a penny the pound.

Yesterday the Lord Mayor held a common hall at Guildhall, in consequence of a requisition made for that purpose. Mr. Hurford came forward and moved that an address, petition, and remonstrance be presented to his Majesty on the present alarming state of affairs. The motion being seconded, the question was put and unanimously carried.

It concludes with beseeching his Majesty to abandon the attempt of reducing our fellow-subjects in America by force of arms, a fatal system, which he has been led to adopt from the misrepresentations and delusions of his ministers, and which, if persisted in, must terminate in the loss of all his possessions in the western world.—It declares to Europe, to America, the West-Indies, and the world in general, an abhorrence of the war against the Americans, with whom it re-

Petitions and remonstrances to the throne, of the same nature as the city of London's, are meditating in all the principal counties and towns in England. The minority are the promoters of them.

AMERICA.

Extract of a letter from General Green, to the President of Congress, from his head-quarters, at Martin's Tavern, near Ferguson's Swamps, in South Carolina, the 11th of September, 1781.

" We marched to attack the English army encamped at M'Leod's Ferry at four o'clock in the morning of the 8th. Our front line was composed of four small battalions of militia, two of North and two of South Carolina, our second line consisted of three small brigades of Continental troops, one of North Carolina, one of Virginia, and one of Maryland; Lieut Colonel Lee, with his legion, covered our right flank: and Lieut. Colonel Henderson, with the state troops, our left. Licut. Col. Washington with his cavalry, and the Delaware troops, formed the body of reserve. Two three-pounders were in the front of our line, and two six-pounders with the second line; the legion and the state troops formed our advanced guard, and were to retreat on our flanks when the enemy should form. We marched in this order to the attack. The legion and state troops met with a party of the enemy's horse and foot, about four miles from their camp, and put them to flight with fixed bayonets, having many killed and wounded. As we thought this was the van of the enemy, our first line was ordered to form, and the legion and state troops to take post on our flanks. From the place of action to Entow Springs, the whole country is covered with wood. The firing began at three miles from the English camp. The militia advanced firing, and the advanced posts of the enemy were routed; the fire redoubled, our officers behaved with the greatest bravery, and the militia gained much honour by their firmness; but the fire of the enemy, who continued to advance, being superior to ours, the militia were obliged to retreat.

The Carolina brigade, under General Sumner were ordered to support them, and though not above three months raised, behaved nobly. In this moment of action, the Virginans under Col. Campbell, and the Marylanders under Col. Williams advanced in the face of the enemy's fire, a terrible cannonade and shower of bullets overturned all that presented, and the enemy were put to the rout.

Lieutenant-Colonel Lee turned his left flank to the enemy, and charged them in the rear, while the troops of Maryland and Virginia charged them in the front. Col. Hampton, who commanded the troops of the State, charged one party, of whom he made 100 prisoners. Colonel Washington advanced with a corps-du-reserve upon the left, where the enemy appeared to prepare again to make resistance, and charged them so impetuously with his cavalry, and a body of infantry, that they had not time to rally.

We continued to pursue the enemy, after having broken them, until we attained their camp. A great number of prisoners fell into our hands, and some hundreds of fugitives escaped towards Charlestown: but a party having got into a brick house three stories high, and others took post in a pallisadoed garden, their rear being covered with springs and hollow ways, the enemy renewed the fight. Lieut. Col. Washington did his utmost to dislodge them from a thick wood, but found it impossible; his horse was killed under him, and himself wounded, and taken prisoner; four cannon were advanced against the house, but the fire from it was so brisk, that it was impossible to force it, or even to bring off the cannon, which

guard, and compleat our success. We lost two pieces of artillery to the enemy, and we have taken one of theirs.

The night of the 9th, the enemy retired, leaving more than 70 of their wounded behind them, and more than 1000 arms, which they had broken, and concealed in the springs of the Entows; they staved 20 or 30 barrels of rum; and destroyed a large quantity of provisions, which they could not carry with them.

We pursued them as soon as we had notice of their retreat, but they joined Major Arthur; General Marion, and Colonel Lee, not having troops enough to hinder them. At our approach they retired to Charlestown. We took 500 prisoners, including the wounded they had left behind, and I reckon they had no less than 600 killed and wounded. The fugitives spread such an alarm, that the enemy burnt their provisions at Dorchester, and quitted their post at Fair Lawn. A great number of negros and others have been employed to throw down trees across the roads, at some miles distance from Charlestown. Nothing but the brick house, and their strong post at Entows, hindered the remains of the English army from falling into our hands.

We have pursued them to the Entows, but could not overtake them. We shall rest here one or two days, and then retake our old position near the heights of Santee.

I think that I owe the victory which I have gained, to the brisk use the Virginians, Marylanders, and one party of the infantry, made of the bayonet. I cannot forbear praising the conduct and courage of all my troops.

Signed NATHANIEL GREEN.
State of the Continental troops.

Killed—1 Lieutetant Colonel, 6 Captains, 4 Subalterns, 4 Serjeants, 98 rank and file.

Wounded—2 Lieutenant-Colonels, 7 Captains, 20 Lieutenants, 24 Serjeants, 209 rank and file. Total 408 men.
State of the Continental troops of the state and militia.

Killed—1 Major, 4 Subalterns. 4 Serjeants, 16 soldiers.

Wounded—3 Lieutenant-Colonels, 6 Captains, Subalterns, 8 Serjeants, 91 soldiers.

Missing—8 soldiers Total 146 men.

Total of killed, wounded, and missing of the continental troops of the state and militia, 554 men. Published by order of Congress. CHARLES THOMSON, Sec.

STATE LOTTERY.

Monday, December 3. No. 25,653. a prize of 2000 l.— No. 11,485, a prize of 500l.—No. 46,985, 17,740, 47,884, prizes of 50l.

Tuesday, December 4. No. 31,217, a blank, but as first drawn 2,000l.—No. 36,376, a prize of 10,000l.— No. 3,810, a prize of 1,000l.—No. 42,752, and 2,698, prizes of 500l. each.—No. 39,605, and 34,613, prizes of 100l. each.—No. 6,838, 16,183, 26,019, 34,020, 41,732, 225, 2,049, 13,377, 21,640, and 45,102, prizes of 50l. each.

Wednesday, December 5. No. 37,991, as first drawn, 3000l.—No. 17,459, 616, prizes of 100l.—No. 15,997, 9153, 38,565, 16,913, 5707, 33,982, 26,008, 22,490, 8242, 131, 728. 43,229, prizes of 50l.

Thursday, December 6. No. 21,044. a prize of 1,000 l. No. 10,684, 30,514, and 10,684, prizes of 50l.

Intelligence from LLOYD'S LIST.
December 4.

The Magdalena, Hill, from Riga to Hull; the ———, Torres, from Riga to Oporto; and a ship from Bourdeaux to Stettin, are all lost in the Baltic.

The Henry Elisabeth, Shuttle, from London to Blackney, is taken and ransomed for 500 guineas; the Medway, Burches, from Arundel to Aberdeen, for 600 ditto; the William, Lamos, from Ostend to Overy, for 100 ditto;

GLASGOW MERCURY

December 13, 1781
—

"We fight, get beat, rise, and fight again," General Nathanael Greene said of his Southern Army's 1781 defeats at Guilford Courthouse and Hobkirk's Hill. Following partisan militia campaigns, Greene led the Southern Continental Army on a dynamic offensive attack at the Battle of Eutaw Springs. Greene's after-action report, reprinted in the December 13, 1781, *Glasgow Mercury*, stated, "I owe the victory which I have gained, to the brisk use the Virginians, Marylanders, and one party of the infantry made of the bayonet."

---

he would be graciously pleased to receive on his Throne, their humble petition, address, and remonstrance; to which his Majesty immediately replied in the following words.—

" *I shall take time to consider of the manner in*

forward under the fire of the house, and we returned to the bank, which we occupied in the morning, not finding water any where nearer, and our troops having great need for refreshment after a fight which had continued four hours. I left upon the field of battle a strong piquet. I shall send Colonel Lee, and General Marion, early to-morrow morning between Entow's and Charlestown, to pre-

flows over her every high water; they have scuttled her larboard side in two places, and work day and night to save as much of her cargo as possible.

The Ann and Francis, Thompson, of Whithaven for the Baltic, is totally lost in the Lewes, and two hands perished.

The Amazon privateer, of London, Capt. Hughes, ar-

The GLASGOW MERCURY

AMERICA.

Extract of a letter from General Green, to the President of Congress, from his head-quarters, at Martin's Tavern, near Ferguson's Swamps, in South Carolina, the 11th of September, 1781.

" We marched to attack the English army encamped at M'Leod's Ferry at four o'clock in the morning of the 8th. Our front line was composed of four small battalions of militia, two of North and two of South Carolina, our second line consisted of three small brigades of Continental troops, one of North Carolina, one of Virginia, and one of Maryland; Lieut. Colonel Lee, with his legion, covered our right flank: and Lieut. Colonel Henderson, with the state troops, our left. Lieut. Col. Washington with his cavalry, and the Delaware troops, formed the body of reserve. Two three-pounders were in the front of our line, and two six-pounders with the second line; the legion and the state troops formed our advanced guard, and were to retreat on our flanks when the enemy should form. We marched in this order to the attack. The legion and state troops met with a party of the enemy's horse and foot, about four miles from their camp, and put them to flight with fixed bayonets, having many killed and wounded. As we thought this was the van of the enemy, our first line was ordered to form, and the legion and state troops to take post on our flanks. From the place of action to Entow Springs, the whole country is covered with wood. The firing began at three miles from the English camp. The militia advanced firing, and the advanced posts of the enemy were routed; the fire redoubled, our officers behaved with the greatest bravery, and the militia gained much honour by their firmness; but the fire of the enemy, who continued to advance, being superior to ours, the militia were obliged to retreat.

The Carolina brigade, under General Sumner were ordered to support them, and though not above three months raised, behaved nobly. In this moment of action, the Virginans under Col. Campbell, and the Marylanders under Col. Williams advanced in the face of the enemy's fire, a terrible cannonade and shower of bullets overturned all that presented, and the enemy were put to the rout. […]

We collected all our wounded, except those who were too forward under the fire of the house, and we returned to the bank, which we occupied in the morning, not finding water any where nearer, and our troops having great need for refreshment after a fight which had continued four hours. I left upon the field of battle a strong piquet. I shall send Colonel Lee, and General Marion, early to morrow morning between Entow's and Charlestown, to prevent the reinforcements which may come to succour the enemy, or to retard their march, if they attempt to retreat; and to give room to the army to attack their rear guard, and compleat our success. We lost two pieces of artillery to the enemy, and we have taken one of theirs. […]

We pursued them as soon as we had notice of their retreat, but they joined Major Arthur; General Marion, and Colonel Lee, not having troops enough to hinder them. At our approach they retired to Charlestown. We took 500 prisoners, including the wounded they had left behind, and I reckon they had no less than 600 killed and wounded. The fugitives spread such an alarm, that the enemy burnt their provisions at Dorchester, and quitted their post at Fair Lawn. A great number of negroes and others have been employed to throw down trees across the roads, at some miles distance from Charlestown. Nothing but the brick house, and their strong post at Entows, hindered the remains of the English army from falling into our hands.

We have pursued them to the Entows, but could not overtake them. We shall rest here one or two days, and then retake our old position near the heights of Santee.

I think that I owe the victory which I have gained, to the brisk use the Virginians, Marylanders, and one party of the infantry, made of the bayonet. I cannot forbear praising the conduct and courage of all my troops.

Signed   NATHANIEL GREEN.

YORKTOWN CAMPAIGN

By Diane K. Depew

WE ARE AT THE EVE OF SOME IMPORTANT EVENT, WHICH God grant may be propitious to the United States" (*Massachusetts Spy*, September 13, 1781). Many Americans involved in the 1781 Siege of Yorktown anticipated the outcome could be crucial to the war, and when news of General Charles Lord Cornwallis's defeat at Yorktown reached Great Britain, the British government realized the war was over. But what is often lost in popular history of the war is the role France played. Without France, the siege and victory would not have happened.

In the summer of 1781, General George Washington, reinforced by a French army under General Jean-Baptiste Comte de Rochambeau, was planning an offensive against General Sir Henry Clinton's British garrison at New York City. Clinton, anticipating the attack, ordered Cornwallis, who was attempting to subdue Virginia, to establish a defensive naval base there and transfer some of his men to New York. Cornwallis moved his army to the port of Yorktown, on the York River, though his troops were never redeployed.

But for a chance at victory, Washington required a substantial navy. As he later wrote, "No land force can act decisively unless it is accompanied by a maritime superiority." On August 14, 1781, he learned a French battle fleet of twenty-eight ships of the line, commanded by Admiral François Joseph Paul Comte de Grasse, was sailing from the Caribbean to the Chesapeake Bay. Within less than five days, in an amazing accomplishment of logistics and organization, Washington changed his objective to Cornwallis and had most of his troops, including

When news of General Charles Lord Cornwallis's defeat at Yorktown reached Great Britain, the British government realized the war was over, but without France, the siege and victory would not have happened.

Rochambeau's army, headed south. It was a bold move. As Washington withdrew from New York, Clinton made no attempt to stop him, a decision at which, according to the December 13, 1781, *Glasgow Mercury*, "very sensible men express great surprise… [Clinton] did not offer him battle." Even some Americans were astonished, as the *Continental Journal* reported on October 18, 1781: "Sir Henry Clinton remains quiet in New York notwithstanding the imminent danger hanging over…Cornwallis."

Even without hindrance from Clinton, Washington lacked crucial information—would de Grasse gain control of the Chesapeake Bay and York River? But France's alliance with Spain and their joint effort against the British in the Caribbean benefited Washington. The British, discovering de Grasse was headed north, incorrectly deduced that he would leave part of his fleet to defend the French islands, but Spain's Admiral Bernardo de Galvez covered de Grasse's absence. With only nineteen ships of the line, Rear Admiral Sir Thomas Graves sailed from New York to stop de Grasse. On September 5, 1781, off the Virginia coast, the two fleets fought the largest naval battle of the Revolutionary War. Grave's fleet, outgunned and badly mangled, returned to New York for repairs. De Grasse, joined by another French fleet of eight battleships, now blockaded the mouth of the Chesapeake Bay and the York River. Washington had his naval advantage over Cornwallis. And on September 28, 1781, the allied army reached Yorktown.

Over the next week, Washington's soldiers prepared to besiege Cornwallis, who had encircled Yorktown with substantial earthen fortifications. On October 9, French artillery began pummeling Yorktown; a few hours later, Washington fired the first American cannon shot as his artillery joined the French in bombarding the British round the clock.

Throughout the siege, Clinton, still in New York, sent Cornwallis messages that he was coming with five thousand reinforcements. But Clinton had no control over the speed of repairs to Grave's ships; and as an article in the November 22, 1781, *Glasgow Mercury* notes, there was a celebrity in New York—King George III's son, Prince William Henry. The prince's presence was a distraction from important military matters, including the urgency to relieve Cornwallis.

On October 19, with defenses crumbling, most cannon damaged, many of his men sick, any chance of escape gone, and having lost expectation of help from Clinton, Cornwallis surrendered. The Articles of Capitulation, as accurately reported in the December 18, 1781, *London Gazette*, confirms it was an American and French victory. The first article of the terms stated: "The garrisons of York & Gloucester…to surrender themselves prisoners of war to the combined forces of America and France."

The November 22, 1781, *Glasgow Mercury* revealed irony to the British defeat. The same day Cornwallis surrendered, Clinton sailed from New York with Admiral Graves and "19 frigates and 8 fire ships." Noted on the listing of Graves's ships in the *Glasgow Mercury* was the seventy-four-gun vessel *Canada*, with a commander named Cornwallis. This was General Cornwallis's younger brother, Captain Sir William Cornwallis. The relief fleet, and Cornwallis's brother, reached Virginia five days later and too late to change history. However, less than six months later, Captain Cornwallis helped defeat Admiral de Grasse at the Battle of the Saints. This British victory improved Great Britain's strategic position during peace negotiations with the French—the same negotiations that resulted in the Treaty of Paris in 1783, in which Great Britain recognized the independence of the United States.

BATTLE OF THE VIRGINIA CAPES
*U.S. Naval History
and Heritage Command*

The French fleet successfully prevented the British fleet from entering the Chesapeake Bay and relieving Major General Lord Cornwallis's army at Yorktown.

ing immediately to their affistance. The brig is faid to have on board 19 head of cattle, which being to leeward, was the caufe of her lofs.

HARTFORD, September 11.

[...] officer [...] mili-
[...] arrival, that before the regiment could poffibly get down, they were embarking.

"The enemy were under the command of the infamous General Arnold, and by the beft accounts confifted of from 1500 to 2000 men———They have burnt the greateft part of the towns of New-London, and Groton, near the water———The garrifon at Fort-Trumbull evacuated the fort and went over to Fort Grifwold, where Colonel Ledyard made a noble defence———repulfed the enemy two or three times, but at laft was obliged to furrender the fort to fuperiour force. The enemy, after Col. Ledyard had furrendered, murdered him and a number of others; they left 73 of our men dead, and between 30 and 40 wounded in the fort; they alfo carried off about 40 prifoners, among which laft number is Ebenezer Ledyard, Efquire. They evacuated the fort about 10 o'clock, in the evening. They blew up the magazines in both forts but did very little other damage to either of them.

"The enemy this morning were at the harbour's mouth on board their fhipping, and came to fail about eight o'clock; they are ftill juft out beyond the Light-Houfe, as the wind is againft them. Their fhipping confifts of about 30 fail, two of which appear to be about 20 guns each.

"We cannot afcertain the lofs the enemy fuftained, but by the beft accounts imagine it muft be as large as ours if not larger. We have taken on this fide a few prifoners, among which is an Enfign, mortally wounded.

"The lofs fuftained in this town, in goods, provifions, ftores, fhipping, &c. is very great———A confiderable number of veffels made their efcape up Norwich River."

Another letter, dated Fort-Grifwold, Groton, 7th Sept. 10 o'clock, A. M. fays, "That the enemy landed at New-London and Groton yefterday morning, and foon took poffeffion of the works on New-London fide the river; and about one in the afternoon took poffeffion of Fort-Grifwold, in Groton, by ftorm, after a moft fevere and fpirited refiftance from our troops.———About feventy-five of our men found dead in the fort, officers included, among whom is the worthy and brave Lieut. Col. Ledyard, with feveral other officers of diftinguifhed

lie in fight of us. We are making all the preparations we can to give them a warm reception."

Yefterday came up two victuallers, part of the fleet committed to the protection of his Majefty's [...] difpatched by Rear Admiral [...] York; the Pegafus and [...] fell in with a French [...] cattle fhips, fuppofed to be [...] apprehended the whole [...] and a veffel with the [...] had fallen into the hands [...] thofe two effected a fafe

WORCESTER, September 13.

A New-York city paper of the 30th ult. mentions the arrival of Rear Admiral Hood, at Sandy-Hook, from the Weft-Indies, with 14 fail of the line, four frigates, one floop, and a number of troops, confifting of the firft battalion of the royal, the 13th and 69th regiments. We are informed that thefe fhips, together with the fleet which were before at New-York, amounting in the whole to 35 fail, under the command of Admiral Graves, have taken their departure from Sandy-Hook, bound to the Chefapeake, in order to give battle to the French fquadron, which arrived there from Rhode-Ifland the latter end of laft month, and are much inferiour in force to the Britifh; the whole French fquadron is faid to confift of only 23 fail including frigates and inferiour veffels. The Englifh fleet confift of one fhip of 98 guns, one of 90, one of 70, eleven of 74, four of 64, two of 50, four of 44, three of 32, five of 28, one of 24, one Fire-fhip of 8, and a floop of war. All the Britifh line of battle fhips except one are faid to be copper-bottomed.

It is not doubted but that his Excellency General Wafhington has marched, with 8000 choice troops including the French, to Virginia, where the troops in that quarter will join him; Lord Cornwallis is blocked up by the French fleet;—by the prefent appearance of things we are at the eve of fome important event, which God grant may be propitious to the United States.

It is faid that Sir George Rodney and General Vaughan have gone for England from the W. Indies.

We hear that Arnold when he landed at New-London, dined at a gentleman's houfe with whom he was formerly acquainted. After dinner he ordered the houfe to be plundered and fat on fire. The traitor carried off all the plunder in the town that his fhort ftay would permit him to take. Had he tarried in order to have taken breakfaft the next morning, it is likely he would have been rewarded for all his villanies.

A large quantity of hard money, lately arrived from France, was a few days paft carried through town, under a ftrong guard.

Laft Friday Col. Armand, an active officer in the

fhillings, and from that price to twelve fhillings the old way, according to the number of colours, and the neatnefs of the flowers.

Any fort of produce or money will be received as pay for work done. Bufinefs in this way which individuals may order, will be cheerfully entered upon, and faithfully executed by their humble fervant, SAMUEL JENNISON.

Oxford, September 5th, 1781.

N. B. A variety of patterns with different colours and figures may be feen at the houfe aforefaid.

BENJAMIN ANDREWS,
TAYLOR from BOSTON,

BEGS leave to inform the publick that he carries on his bufinefs near the Meeting-Houfe in Worcefter. Thofe gentlemen who will pleafe to favour him with their commands, may be affured that his utmoft endeavours fhall be ufed to ferve them with fidelity and difpatch.

SADDLES.

MEN's and Women's SADDLES, of all forts, made and fold by
NATHANIEL COOLIDGE,

At his Shop in Worcefter, near the Meeting-Houfe. He begs leave to inform the Publick that he carries on the Saddler's bufinefs in all its branches. Gentlemen and Ladies who will pleafe to favour him with their cuftom, may depend on being ferved with fidelity on reafonable terms.

Wine Glaffes.

Genteel WINE GLASSES, to be fold by
JOSEPH TRUMBULL,

At his Store near the Court-Houfe in Worcefter, Where may be had choice MADDER and OTTER, &c. &c.

STRAYED or ftolen from the Subfcriber, on or about the 26th day of laft month, a very dark brown COW, low in flefh, the end of one of her horns a little broke, and about eight or nine years old. Whoever will give information to the Subfcriber, of faid Cow, fo that he may have her again, fhall have TWO DOLLARS reward; and if ftolen, will difcover the thief, fo that he may be convicted, fhall be entitled to a further reward of one GUINEA. JOSEPH ALLEN.

Worcefter, September 11, 1781.

DESERTED between Leicefter and Springfield, one ASA KNOWLTON, of Bolton, aged 22 years, five feet 11 inches high, dark complexion, a farmer, engaged for fix months for the town of Bolton. Whoever will take up faid deferter and bring him to me, or to Col. Shepard at Springfield, fhall have a handfome reward, and all neceffary charges paid.

SETH WASHBURN, Superintendant.

feffions of his integrity.

General Vaughan fpoke to the fame points; and faid they had brought the ftores to fale on account of the private plunder, and for fear that they fhould be burnt by the wicked people in the ifland.

Lord Mahon recommended dividing the motion; as it ftood, he thought it too complex.

Lord George Germain could not vote for the motion, becaufe it bore relation to the claims agitating by the courts below.

Colonel Barré removed all difficulties, by perfuading Lord Mahon to withdraw his amendment, which his Lordfhip did; the Colonel then moved as an amendment, to add the words, " excepting fuch wares and merchandize as have been claimed in the Courts of Weftminfter Hall."

This amendment was received by the Houfe, and the queftion fo amended being put, the Houfe divided, Noes, — 163

Ayes, — 89

Wednefday, December 5.

The Houfe having gone into a committee of fupply,

Lord Lifburne ftated the neceffity of having a formidable navy in the prefent crifis. His Lordfhip moved, that 100,000 feamen, including 21,305 marines be voted for the year 1782, and that 4l. per man per month be granted for the fame.

An amendment was propofed to vote 110,000 men, which was oppofed by *Lord North* as unneceffary. The fact was, that the Admiralty employed as many men as they could get without regard to the vote of credit. His Lordfhip faid, fome gentlemen might be afraid that great augmentations were to take place in the army, and confequently that the American war was to be purfued with redoubled vigour. The largenefs of the fupply called for this day, might lull their apprehenfions on that head, for the motion without the amendment was ftill for 10,000 feamen more than were called for laft year, and confequently the fum of 520,000l. would be employed in the naval department more than laft year.

At half after nine o'clock the Houfe divided,

For the amendment — 73

For the original motion — 143

Advices have been received at the Admiralty, that the grand armament preparing at Breft had not failed from that harbour fo late as the 21ft of November laft, owing to an unexpected difficulty in obtaining the neceffary equipment of men. It was owing to this information, that Admiral Kempenfelt's departure was accelerated, his inftructions being to cruize, for the prefent, off the port of Breft; and, as he has a larger force with him than any the enemy poffefs in that quarter, it is expected he will be able to prevent the execution of their intended fcheme for this feafon, which is ftrongly believed, though not pofitively known by Adminiftration, to be directed againft our Weft India iflands.

Government have received, by the laft packet from the Leeward Iflands, the moft alarming accounts from the Governors refpecting the dangers that threaten them, and their incompetency for making any material refiftance. Information has been received from St. Lucia and Jamaica,

the ifland in the beft ftate of defence poffible; but the great misfortune, which it is feared will render all his efforts abortive, is, that a ftrong fpirit of party prevails amongft the people there, and many of the moft wealthy inhabitants in the ifland are the avowed patrons of the American defection. On this account the Governor finds great difficulty to ftimulate the natives and eftablifhed inhabitants, to take any fhare in the military preparations which are making on the part of this country; and Government at home have therefore determined to fend out 2000 men with the fleet that goes under the command of Admiral Rodney, for the further fecurity of this valuable ifland.

It has been ftrongly reported and believed, that the French fleet, immediately upon the capture of Lord Cornwallis, failed to the Weft Indies, as they had no further bufinefs in America. The probability of their purfuing this ftep greatly alarms the Weft India merchants, as at prefent we have no force there equal to cope with them, and therefore, although Jamaica is too ftrong for a detachment of the fleet, yet there is great reafon to be alarmed for its fafety, when invefted, as it probably may be, by the whole force of the enemy.

By a Gentleman lately arrived from Quebec, who made a very extenfive journey upon commercial bufinefs through the back fettlements of New England, New York, Jerfey, Pennfylvania, and Virginia, we learn, that almoft the whole Interior of the Colonies, out of the reach of the coaft and its immediate communication, are in affociation armed to refift the Congrefs, whofe meafures are execrated among them, for not making peace. No recruiting officer, nor one in any civil employment, much lefs a tax-gatherer, dares to appear there. In the country between Fort Pitt and the Ohio, there are not lefs than 300,000 inhabitants fettled, who fly to arms on any appearance of their own perfect independence being infringed. It is expected, that thefe and other territories, peopled with men of the fame principles, will be the means of forcing the Congrefs to treat for a peace, on much more reafonable terms than have yet been mentioned.

Tuefday advice was received exprefs from France, of the Andromaque frigate being arrived at Breft from the Chefapeak.—She failed from thence on the 12th of November, in company with De Graffe's fleet, confifting of thirty-five fail of the line, and three thoufand five hundred troops, which were bound to Martinico; Wafhington and Rochambeau w—— turn to the Jerfeys, havi—— ment under Monf. Le F—— to join Green in South C——

The many idle report—— ftate of the Eaft India C—— Carnatic, which have be—— vailed on a gentleman wh—— a later date than any oth—— from Madras, to commu—— friends; and we have h—— get the following extra—— pended upon as authenti——

Mau——

" I have the pleafure to ——— fituation of our public affairs is much mended fince my laft to you. Sir Eyre Coote took the

" Hyder, with his collected force, marched out of Arcot, and encamped on the plain between Wandewafh and Arnee, fo that we may foon expect to hear of an engagement between the two armies; which, in all likelihood, will decide the great conteft, which has fubfifted near feven months, and laid the whole Carnatic in flames.

" Six French fhips of the line, the Cafolante of 40 guns, the Subtile of 22, and another little veffel of 14, made their appearance in our road on the 27th of laft month. Our apprehenfions at firft were very great, as we had near 200 Paddy veffels laden with provifions lying in the road, an accident to which muft have reduced the fettlement to great diftrefs; but they paffed on quietly without attempting any thing; we had the five Indiamen lately arrived, and feveral country fhips lying in the road.

" There was a degree of ftupidity and indifference in their conduct, which is entirely unaccountable, but it was moft fortunate for us, for they might have rode triumphant on the coaft, deftroying our trade, and intercepting all fupplies of provifions; and if they had put a number of their marines afhore to join Hyder, would have rendered the difpute more unequal; whereas we are now freed from the continual apprehenfion of the French fleet coming, and this muft naturally difpofe Hyder againft them, and may probably have the good effect to make him alter his plan of conqueft; he is too wife not to fee the impracticability of keeping the Carnatic, unlefs ftrongly fupported by an European power. No peace with the Marattas yet, notwithftanding our fuccefles on the other coaft."

Many very fenfible men exprefs great furprife that when Mr. Wafhington made his *feint* towards New York, the Commander in Chief did not offer him battle; or, at leaft that upon his retreat, he did not make a vigorous fally in purfuit of him. Had either of thefe meafures been purfued, or due care been taken to obtain information of the enemy's route, the brave Cornwallis and his army would moft probably have been preferved, and the triumph of rebellion prevented.

Sir Henry Clinton, though with no lefs than 20,000 of the fineft troops in Europe, wrote to the gallant and unfupported Cornwallis, for the loan of 2000 of his little army, to protect him from the threatened attacks of the rebels, confifting of no more than 7000 men.

WEDNESDAY's POST.

---

fall in with them. At ten o'clock yefterday morning faw them: they ftood for us with much

Extracts from the Leyden Gazette, of July 1781.

MADRID, June 26th. The crew of the Dutch frigate la Bruis, complain bitterly of the English for having had the cruelty to fire on them with guns charged with pieces of broken glass and earthen ware; by means of which the wounded have suffered the utmost torture, and their wounds rendered incurable.

PETERSBURGH, July 31. The ratification of the King of Prussia's accession to the armed neutrality was exchanged on the 29th of last month. On this occasion the usual presents have been sent to the Plenipotentiaries who signed the accession. The magnificent presents from our Court, to the two Ministers of State, Count Flackenslen and Baron Herisberg, & also those to the three first Secretaries of the Cabinet, to his Prussian Majesty, will be transmitted to Berlin by a courier, who will be sent off in three days. The Minister from Berlin will send the ratification to his Court by the same conveyance.

PHILADELPHIA, October 3.

We have the pleasure to congratulate the public on the complete re-establishment of American government in the state of Georgia.

Advices from South-Carolina inform that Major General Leslie (who some time since left Virginia in the Carysfort frigate, and arrived in Wilmington, in North-Carolina, from whence he departed in the Blond frigate to take the command of the British forces in South-Carolina) was lost at sea, the frigate having foundered in a storm, and every soul on board perished.

We hear that General Washington began his operations against York, about the 25th ult. and that two French 64's have forced their way up the river a considerable distance above York.

Extract of a letter from Count de Grasse to the Hon. the Chevalier de la Luzerne, Minister Plenipotentiary of France.

Cape Henry, Sept. 13, 1781.

" Nothing gave me greater pleasure than the approach of the armies under General Washington and the Count de Rochambeau. In order to hasten their arrival I had selected out seven vessels that drew the least water to transport them from the mouth of

I could. My putting to sea facilitated the entrance of M. de Barras, and our junction has added much to our strength—I fell in with two of the enemy's frigates, the Iris and the Richmond, of 32 guns each. They had been sent by the English Admiral to cut

---

time closely penned up in York-Town, which, it appears, he has rendered very strong by numerous fortifications; though it was said considerable impression was made on his works by the fire of our heavy cannon, &c. We shall very probably soon have agreeable accounts from that quarter.

Sir Henry Clinton remains quiet in New-York, notwithstanding the imminent danger hanging over the head of his colleague in wickedness Lord Cornwallis; but it is presumed the presence of his YOUNG MASTER will at once dissipate his Fears, and that he, as a " man of spirit," " will be proud to fight in a cause for which the young Gentleman exposes his life."

Extract of a letter from Richmond, dated Sept. 26.

" The following are extracts from letters wrote by Doctors Brown and Johnstone, of the southern army, and handed me by a gentleman at this place.

" At Hutah, near Santee, 55 miles from Charlestown, on the 8th of September, an engagement commenced between Gen. Greene and the main body of the enemy's army, in which the former lost from 250 to 300; the enemy's loss, killed 300, wounded and taken 60, taken, not wounded 340, total 700.

" These letters add, that all the officers in Col. Washington's corps were either killed, wounded or taken, except Capt. Clarke. The Colonel was missing, but returned slightly wounded.

" Monday the 10th a heavy firing was heard, but no account of the event. As Gen. Greene had sent a detachment of fresh troops after the enemy's flying army, there is no doubt of a total defeat.

A list of the officers killed and wounded on our part.

KILLED.

Col. Campbell, Virginia; Maj. Rutherford, N. C. Capts. Dobson, Maryland, Goodman, N. Carolina; Lieuts. Potterfield, do. Goodwin, do. Polk, do. Luff, Dayton, do.

WOUNDED.

Gen. Pickens, S. Carolina; Cols. Henderson, do. Middleton, do. Howard, Maryland, Polk, do. Maj's. Edmonds, Virginia, Erving, Maryland, Martin, S. C. Giles do. Moors, do. Lieuts. Finn, Virginia, Dickson, do. Dudley, do.

October 8.

Extract of a letter from Williamsburg, dated September 29.

I have seen a letter from Brigadier General Jones, of North-Carolina, to the Marquis de la Fayette, which says, that on the 8th of September, Gen. Green had a very severe action with the British, commanded by Col. Stewart, at the Eutaw Springs, 60 miles from Charlestown.—Our troops were hard pushed at first, and lost two field pieces; [...] making a spirited stroke, [...] and took two others [...] followed up the blow, [...] them 6 miles: Col. [...] regiments was pushed [...] came up with them, [...] heard the next morning. [...] the field 250 killed, [...] prisoners were taken, [...] commissioned officers. [...] loss was 250 killed and [...] some valuable officers [...] Washington's cavalry behaved bravely, but are mostly cut to pieces.

HARTFORD, October 16.

Extract of a letter dated head-quarters, Williamsburgh (Virginia) Sep. 24.

" We are at present within six miles of the British army, commanded by Lord Corn [...]

BOSTON, October 18.

A Spanish news-paper of a late date, brought by the vessel arrived at Newbury-Port from Bilboa, contains an account that stock had fallen 17 pr cent. owing to advices lately received, which, though the ministry endeavoured to suppress, had yet obtained credit; that Hyder Ally had taken Madrass, and cut to pieces a body of British troops that had been newly sent to that quarter. The same paper mentions an account, received in Europe by a Danish East-Indiaman, that Commodore Johnstone had arrived with part of his squadron at St. Helena, in a most shattered condition, having had a second engagement, in which the French had taken two ships belonging to the East-India company, and a transport, and taken or sunk a ship of the line.

The Brig Spanish Fame, James Rob, Commander, was lost upon the South Shoal of Hog-Island the 21st September, six Souls perished, two of them of this town, Mr. Chickley and Mr. Prince.

On Sunday evening expir'd after a short illness, in the 14th year of her age, and on Tuesday was interred, Miss Mary Greene, eldest daughter of Mr. Joseph Greene, merchant, of this town. An amiable and benevolent disposition of mind, a grave and serious deportment, and most engaging manners had greatly endeared her to her parents and friends, whose pleasing hopes of future comfort and happiness in her are thus suddenly blasted, and the bereavement peculiarly heavy and afflictive.

" She drops a smile say weeping friends she cries,
What mean the tears that trickle from your eyes,
O! my lov'd Parents could I but reveal
The vast unutterable Bliss I feel,
The glorious vision would your souls inspire,
And warm your bosoms with celestial fire.
Then cease the unavailing flood to pour
The curtain soon will drop your grief be o'er
And we shall meet again to part no more."

the said Thomas Lonnergan was guilty of the murder.—Margaret Murry, a servant in the family, and indicted for aiding abetting this horrid crime, will be tried on Friday next.

"Saturday laft, between 11 and 12 o'clock, an accidental fire broke out in the Cuftom-houfe, which burned for fome time with great violence; but, by the affiftance of the firemen and engines, the fire was happily got under without doing fo much mifchief as it was natural to expect. The Right Hon. the Lord Mayor and the High Sheriffs attended on the firft alarm, and continued there till the fire was extinguifhed; and the different officers and clerks of the Cuftom-houfe removed, on the firft intimation of the fire, all the books and papers to a place of fafety. It was very fortunate that the fire was got under before it reached the fpirits, &c. in the ftores, as the confequences muft have been dreadful."

The Countefs of Donegal, Captain Reed, has arrived in Loughfoil from Charleftown. In her paffage fhe touched at Madeira, where a Portugueze fhip, from Goa for Lifbon, brought intelligence, that the Swallow packet, with Lord Macartney, and feveral Gentlemen, bound to Madras, arrived at Surat, on the Malabar coaft, about the 29th or 30th of May, in a very bad condition, with feveral feet water in her hold, and the lofs of all her guns, which were thrown over-board in a dreadful monfoon or hurricane, in the gulf of Baffora. The paffengers and crew were in tolerable health. After refitting, they proceeded for the Coromandel coaft, which it is fuppofed they made in about three weeks.

We hear from Saltcoats, that, on Friday laft, a fmuggling veffel from Dunkirk, bound for the Trun, ftruck upon a rock, about a mile from that place, and funk: the water was about eight feet above her deck. She mounted 12 guns, and had 32 men on board, who were all faved. Her cargo confifted of above 500 cafks of brandy, and a confiderable quantity of tea. The brandy will turn out a very good prize to the revenue-officers on that coaft.

Extract of a letter from Whitehaven, Nov. 13.

"Three boats, with each fix men on board, which were fifhing near Peeletown when the gale came on, on Tuefday evening, were driven afhore, and by the violence of the breakers were beat to pieces, and all hands perifhed before any affiftance could be given them."

Extract of a letter from Aberdeen, Nov. 19.

"We are informed that the veffel de Gunft van Goede Vrienden, brought in here in April laft, as prize to the Tarter privateer, having been claimed as Pruffian by the mafter, and by the Pruffian ambaffador; The judge admiral, on the 16th inft. ordered her to be reftored to the owners, who are Pruffians, and referves to them to infift afterwards for the damages occafioned by the capture."

ARRIVALS in CLYDE.

Nov. 15. Fanny, Campbell, Jamaica, fugar and rum.
　　　Minerva, Speirs,　do.　　do.
　　　Mary, Hunter,　do.　　do.
　　　Commerce, Symonds, do.　do.
　　　Argyle, Campbell, Dublin, goods.
　　　Greenock, M'Kinlay, do.　do.
　10. St. Andrew, Scott, Jamaica, fugar and rum.

Nov. 17. Phenix, Cuninghame, Dublin, fugar.
　　　Jenny, M'Lean, Highlands, falt and tree.
　　　Arrivals at the Weft End of the Canal.

Thurfday's Exprefs.

This day arrived the Mails from France and Flanders.

From the LONDON GAZETTE, Nov. 17.

Admiralty-Office.

THE following extract of a letter from Admiral Graves, commander of his Majefty's fhips in ——, to Mr. Stephens, were received by Captain Manly, of his Majefty's ——

London, at New York, ——

BE pleafed to acquaint —— the Santa Margaretta —— inftant, with her convoy —— of forty-two fail, for N—— had parted company.

The Carysfort, whi——returned the 8th, and —— good fortune to meet with—— Cape François, on the French King's account, with a confiderable quantity of mafts for large fhips.

The Torbay and Prince William arrived here the 11th, having parted from the Jamaica convoy the 21ft of September.

The Nymphe returned from cruizing off Cape Henry, and brought in five prizes, taken by her and the Amphion.

London, off Sandy Hook, October 19, 1781.

MY laft letter could not fix the time of my failing, the fhips were however moving down as they could be got ready, and on the 17th, fo foon as the tide ferved, I got under fail with the remainder of the fquadron, except the Shrewfbury, Montagu, and Europe, and got down with the help of the afternoon tide to Sandy Hook.

The next morning we embarked all the troops on board the men of war from the tranfports, to the amount of 7149 (officers included;) and this morning the whole fleet failed and got fafe over the Bar, confifting of 25 fail of the line, two fifties, and eight frigates, and the whole are now under fail for the Cheafapeak.

A numerous convoy appears off, which we judge to be the Englifh convoy, as they are making for this place, and the moft advanced fhew Englifh colours.

The fleet above-mentioned proves to be the Centurion and her convoy, which are all arrived (except eight private traders,) and are now ftanding in for the Hook. [*See page 370.*]

PROMOTIONS.—*War-Office, Nov. 17, 1781.*

22d *Regiment of Light Dragoons*, Quarter-Mafter John Anderfon is appointed to be Adjutant, vice Thomas Walker.

15th *Regiment of foot*, Enfign James Gillefpie to be Lieutenant in one of the additional companies, vice Michael Jackfon.

97th *Regiment of foot*, John Ware, gent. to be Enfign, vice Charles Mac Vicar.

101ft *Regiment of foot*, Enfign William Ryan, of Captain A. Campbell's Independent Company, to be Enfign, vice John Quinn.—Enfign William Dane, of Captain Cowan's Independent Company, to be Enfign, vice Robert Robinfon.

Independent Company of foot, Lieutenant James Abercrombie, of 71ft foot, to be Captain.—Enfign William Whatley, of 97th foot, to be Lieutenant.—Enfign Robert Robinfon, of 101ft foot, to be Enfign in Captain Andrew Cowan's Independent Company of foot, vice ——

From the LONDON PAPERS, November 17.

Barcelona, Oct. 17. The officers of a frigate ——

directed againft a poft where it was known that M. de Crillon had placed an hundred of his fineft grenadiers.

The convoy from the Havannah did not arrive the day after the regifter fhips, as was faid in —— only 100 men, of which the enemy had intelligence, gave them every hope of fuccefs; but the befieged lying upon their arms till the French were within piftol-fhot, and then fupported their fire with fuch unabated vigour, that the Frenchmen gave way on all fides, and in their retreat were almoft to a man cut off.

Captain Manly fays, that Sir Henry Clinton and the fleet expected, when he left them, to reach the Chefapeak by the 22d of October; and in that cafe he hoped to relieve Cornwallis by the 26th at fartheft.

We are informed that his Royal Highnefs Prince William Henry, when he delivered his letters to Captain Manly, of the Lively floop, who arrived with the difpatches from America, faid to him, "Here's a letter for my father, another for my mother, and letters for as many of my brothers and fifters as I had time to write to, and pray give my compliments to Sandwich, and tell him, we are juft going to fight the French *in earneft.*"

There is an account from New York, that Gen. Arnold arrived there the 6th of October, and was preparing to execute an expedition up the North River, in the abfence of Wafhington's army. Gen. Robertfon commands at New York during the abfence of the Commander in Chief.

The annals of hiftory do not exhibit a more important period than the prefent. The honour, the intereft, of the nation are in a ftate of temporary fufpenfion. Our hopes, derived from the known courage of our commanders in America, are highly raifed; but it is very much to be feared that the cunning wary Frenchmen will fteal out of the Chefapeak before we fhall be able to prevent them.

Fourteen fhips of the line of battle are preparing, with all poffible expedition, for fome fecret and important expedition, the command of which is to be given to Sir John Lockhart Rofs, or Adm. Kempenfelt. The Edgar and another fhip of the line are alfo fitting out, and, as report fays, are intended for America.

STATE-LOTTERY.

Nov. 16. This day the following numbers were drawn prizes at Guildhall, viz. No. 42,794, as firft drawn, 500l.—Nos. 28,128, 2,005, and ——

35,537, prizes of 50l.
Nov. 17. No. 29,817, as firft drawn, 500l.—No. 756, a prize of 2,000l.—No. 46,905, a ——

LONDON GAZETTE
December 18, 1781

—

The Articles of Capitulation, as accurately reported in the December 18, 1781, *London Gazette*, confirms Yorktown was an American and French victory.

which left New York the 17th of November.

New York, November 13, 1781.

MY LORD,

IN my laſt Diſpatch I had the Honor to acquaint your Lordſhip with my Fears reſpecting the Fate of the Army in Virginia.

It now gives me the deepeſt Concern to inform you, that they were but too well founded, as your Lordſhip will perceive by Lord Cornwallis's Letter to me of the 20th ult. a Copy of which, and the Papers accompanying it, being incloſed for your Information.

Had it been poſſible for the Fleet to have ſailed from hence at the Time it was firſt imagined they would have been able to do, I have not the leaſt Doubt that Lord Cornwallis would have been relieved by the joint Exertions of the Navy and Army; and I therefore cannot ſufficiently lament that they could not have been made ſooner.

Your Lordſhip will be informed by Lord Cornwallis's Letter to me, (a Copy of which accompanies this Diſpatch) of the Force that was oppoſed to his Lordſhip in Virginia; beſides which, by Rebel Accounts, which I have the Honor to incloſe for your Lordſhip's Information, General Green ſeems ſtill to have an Army acting in that Quarter; and there are, at this Inſtant, above 3000 Continental Troops at Weſt Point and in its Vicinity.

My Diſpatches will be delivered to your Lordſhip, without teſtifying to you the high Opinion I have of his Merit, and my entire Approbation of his Conduct ſince he has been on this Service, acting as one of my Aides de Camp, having always ſhewn the greateſt Attention to me, and highly diſtinguiſhed his Spirit, by attending as a Volunteer upon every Expedition and Excurſion which have taken Place ſince his being here.

Copy of a Letter from Lieutenant-General Earl Cornwallis to Sir Henry Clinton, dated York Town in Virginia, October 20, 1781.

SIR,

I HAVE the Mortification to inform your Excellency, that I have been forced to give up the Poſts of York and Glouceſter, and to ſurrender the Troops under my Command, by Capitulation, on the 19th Inſtant, as Priſoners of War to the Combined Forces of America and France.

I never ſaw this Poſt in a very favorable Light; but when I found I was to be attacked in it, in ſo unprepared a State, by ſo powerful an Army and Artillery, nothing but the Hopes of Relief would have induced me to attempt it's Defence; for I would either have endeavoured to eſcape to New York, by rapid Marches, from the Glouceſter Side, immediately on the Arrival of General Waſhingburgh's Troops at Williamſburgh, or I would, notwithſtanding the Diſparity of Numbers, have attacked them in the open Field, where it might have been juſt poſſible that Fortune would have favored the Gallantry of the Handful of Troops under my Command: But being aſſured by your Excellency's Letters, that every poſſible Means would be tried by the Navy and Army to relieve us, I could not think myſelf at Liberty to venture on either of thoſe deſperate Attempts: Therefore, after remaining Two Days in a ſtrong Poſition in Front of this Place, in Hopes of being attacked, upon obſerving that the Enemy were taking Meaſures which could not fail of turning my Left Flank in a ſhort Time; and receiving, on the Second Evening, your Letter of the 24th of Septem-

ber, informing me, that the Relief would ſail about the 5th of October, I withdrew within the Works on the Night of the 29th of September, hoping, by the Labour and Firmneſs of the Soldiers, to protract the Defence until you could arrive.

Every Thing was to be expected from the Spirit of the Troops, but every Diſadvantage attended their Labour, as the Works were to be continued under the Enemy's Fire, and our Stock of Intrenching Tools, which did not much exceed 400, when we began to work in the latter End of Auguſt, was now much diminiſhed.

The Enemy broke Ground on the Night of the 30th, and conſtructed, on that Night and the Two following Days and Nights, Two Redoubts, which, with ſome Works that had belonged to our outward Poſition, occupied a Gorge between Two Creeks or Ravines, which come from the River on each Side of the Town. On the Night of the 6th of October they made their firſt Parallel, extending from it's Right on the River to a deep Ravine on the Left, nearly oppoſite to the Center of this Place, and embracing our whole Left, at the Diſtance of 600 Yards. Having perfected this Parallel, their Batteries opened on the Evening of the 9th againſt our Left; and other Batteries fired at the ſame Time againſt a Redoubt advanced over the Creek upon our Right, and defended by about 120 Men of the 23d Regiment and Marines, who maintained that Poſt with uncommon Gallantry. The Fire continued inceſſant from heavy Cannon, and from Mortars and Howitzers throwing Shells from

remain Priſoners to the United States, the Navy to the naval Army of His Moſt Chriſtian Majeſty.

Article I. Granted.

Article II. The Artillery, Arms, Accoutrements, Military Cheſt, and public Stores of every Denomination, ſhall be delivered, unimpaired, to the Heads of Departments appointed to receive them.

Article III. At Twelve o'Clock this Day the two Redoubts on the Left Flank of York to be delivered, the one to a Detachment of American Infantry, the other to a Detachment of French Grenadiers. The Garriſon of York will march out to a Place to be appointed, in Front of the Poſts, at Two o'Clock preciſely, with ſhouldered Arms, Colours caſed, and Drums beating a Britiſh or German March; they are then to ground their Arms, and return to their Encampment, where they will remain, until they are diſpatched to the Places of their Deſtination. Two Works on the Glouceſter Side will be delivered at One o'Clock to Detachments of French and American Troops appointed to poſſeſs them; the Garriſon will march out at Three o'Clock in the Afternoon; the Cavalry with their Swords drawn, Trumpets ſounding; and the Infantry in the Manner preſcribed for the Garriſon of York: They are likewiſe to return to their Encampment, until they can be finally marched off.

Article III. Granted.

Article IV. Officers to retain their Side Arms;

the Redoubts that covered them, ſpiking 11 Guns, and killing or wounding about 100 of the French Troops who had the Guard of that Part of the Trenches, and with little Loſs on our Side. This Action, though extremely honorable to the Officers and Soldiers who executed it, proved of little Public Advantage; for the Cannon having been ſpiked in a Hurry, were ſoon rendered fit for Service again, and before Dark the whole Parallel and Batteries appeared to be nearly complete. At this Time we knew that there was no Part of the whole Front attacked, in which we could ſhew a ſingle Gun, and our Shells were nearly expended. I had therefore only to chuſe between preparing to ſurrender next Day, or endeavouring to get off with the greateſt Part of the Troops; and I determined to attempt the latter, reflecting, that though it ſhould prove unſucceſsful in it's immediate Object, it might at leaſt delay the Enemy in the Proſecution of further Enterprizes. Sixteen large Boats were prepared, and upon other Pretexts were ordered to the lungs are entirely exhausted, the tongue blistered and inflamed, the stomach closed up, and the heart ossified!—This subject is supposed to have died through want and vexation, and is a striking instance of ministerial inflexibility!

WEDNESDAY's POST.
No foreign Mails.
From the LONDON PAPERS, November 16.

A Letter from Holland of a very late date, says, that the defamatory libels, &c. against the Duke of Brunswick are entirely the production of the French faction there, who still rule with an uncontrolled sway the councils of Holland. The French antipathy to the Duke of Brunswick springs from the open manner in which he has always spoken of the political duplicity of the French, who in almost every alliance, both ancient and modern, have either betrayed or deserted their allies. This letter adds, that a pamphlet has been distributed throughout the Provinces, composed by Van Berkel and the secretary of the French ambassador, displaying in a very pompous manner the courage and seamanship of the Dutch in their former wars with England, magnifying the present power of France, Spain, and America, and diminishing that of Great Britain, while it encourages the Dutch to persist in their warlike operations only for a little time, and the allies will monopolise the whole of the American trade amongst them, and ruin that of England in every part of the globe.

By the last accounts from America, the French and Americans had broken up all the roads, and thrown up every possible impediment that industry could produce, to prevent Lord Cornwallis from making a sally. It is also known, that a number of officers, and many of the American loyalists, have gone upon the expedition from New York, and the British Admiral has taken three light fast sailing vessels with him, in order to give the earliest intelligence to Government here. The above facts were given us by a Gentleman, whose veracity may be depended upon.

The fleet under the command of Admiral Graves, which sailed for the Chesapeak on the 19th of October, consisted of the following vessels, viz.

	Guns.		Guns.
* London, Ad. Graves, Capt. Graves	98	* Shrewsbury, Robinson	74
Prince George, Rear Ad. Digby, C. Williams	98	Torbay, Gidoin	74
		* Princessa, Knatchbull	74
* Barfleur, Ad. Hood, C. Hood	90	Robust, Crosby —	74
		Ramilies — —	74
Canada, Cornwallis	74	Prudent, Burnett —	64
* Alfred, Bayne —	74	Lion, Fooks —	64
* Invincible, Saxton	74	Prince William, Wilkinson — —	64
* Monarch, Reynolds	74	* Belliqueux, Brine —	64
* Centaur, Inglefield	74	* America, Thompson	64
* Resolution, Manners	74	* Europe, Child —	64
* Bedford, Graves	74	* Intrepid, Molloy —	64
* Royal Oak, Ardesoif	74	* Adamant — —	50
* Montague, Bowen	74	* Centurion — —	50
* Ajax, Turrington	74	* Chatham — —	50
* Alcide, Thompson	74	* Warwick — —	50

19 Frigates, and 8 fire-ships.

Those marked * were with Admiral Graves when he engaged de Grasse.

Admiral Rodney will sail for the West Indies about the end of this month with fifteen sail of the line. Sir Richard Bickerton will sail at the same time, as Commodore, with six sail of the line to the East Indies. The East India ships will also sail under his convoy.

tion of three to one; they are now in possession of the greatest part of the Levant and Mediterranean trade. The trade to the port of Ostend has increased so ... ago above 40 ... that place.

The follow ... pany's ships, ... the next con ... barked the re ... have been ra ... his Britannic ... of the Compan ... Worcester, C ... Henry, Dund ... bot, Taylor ... Alfred, Brow ... Dampier.

Most peopl ... fleet either ha ... it, before the ... although they h ... tish, yet it is scarcely to be supposed they will risk a battle, after having avoided it so skilfully in nine different actions this war, in most of which they had a superiority. They will probably keep to their old plan of going off in a line of battle, and so spin out the war, unless they had a certainty of obtaining a victory.

By letters from Petersburgh, of the 19th of September, we are informed, that the British had this season four-fifths of the trade to Petersburgh. On the 11th of September 460 British vessels had been there. The Dutch had three vessels which came there last season, and had not sailed on the 11th of September; and no other vessel from Holland had arrived at that time, nor could this season; so that the British must be in possession of most of the naval stores, such as hemp, iron, &c. From this account, which may be depended on as authentic, the great advantage resulting from Admiral Parker's engagement with the Dutch fleet may be easily conceived.

The Treasury and Secretary of State's office in Cleveland Row, have been busily employed during the course of the last fortnight, in dispatching their circular billets-doux to such peers and members of the lower House as are conceived to be their particular friends in parliament, in which they strongly request their attendance at the opening of the session, as affairs of the highest importance to the state are expected to be agitated the first week after its commencement.

This morning some dispatches were received from Newfoundland, by which we are informed, that upwards of twenty sail of American privateers were cruizing on that station, four of which are taken by his Majesty's cruizers, and carried into St. John's.

A dreadful contagion now rages in this metropolis. On Wednesday evening last, and yesterday morning, several thousand persons were seized with it, and are in a very dangerous way. It is called the "Lottery Pestilence."

It is imagined there are not less than one hundred thousand persons afflicted with the above malady. Its symptoms are a giddiness of head, a wildness of countenance, a restlessness of body, a high pulse, and a total loss of natural reason.——People in health are advised not to go near the sick, lest the effluvia of the disorder should infect them, for 'tis full of contagious particles.

A countryman a few days since going into a lottery-office, and a profusion of policies being

a fortune may be gained."——" Policies!" cry'd the countryman; "methinks the best Policy for me will be to keep my money in my ...

GLASGOW MERCURY
November 22, 1781 (continued from page 337)

The November 22 *Mercury* also revealed irony. The same day Cornwallis surrendered, Clinton sailed from New York with Admiral Graves and "19 frigates and 8 fire ships." Noted on the listing of Graves's ships was the seventy-four gun vessel *Canada*, with a commander named Cornwallis. This was General Cornwallis's younger brother, Captain Sir William Cornwallis. The relief fleet, and Cornwallis's brother, reached Virginia five days later and too late to change history.

Thursday, Nov. 15. This morning the Lottery began drawing at Guildhall, when No. 27,684 was drawn a blank, but as first drawn is entitled to 500l.—Nos. 41,620, and 6,016, 500l. each.—Nos. 6,037, 17,269, and 35,470, 100l. each.—Nos. 15,328, 41,310, 2,747, 10,579, 34,672, 25,826, 21,003, and 38,330, prizes of 50l. each.

Intelligence from LLOYD'S LIST.
November 13.

The Norfolk, ———, with masts, &c. is lost on the rocks near Norway.

The Albion, Oglen, from Liverpool to Cork, and the Rodney, Bramwell, from Waterford to ditto, are taken and carried into Morlaix.

The Nelly, Owen, from Tortola and Cork to Liverpool, is arrived at Milford, after being taken by a Dunkirk privateer, and ransomed for 5000 guineas.

The John, Urry, from London to America, retaken by the Adventure privateer of Weymouth, is arrived at Portsmouth.

The Bee, ———, from Newfoundland to Oporto, was taken off Oporto bar.

The Charming Kitty, Roche, from Tortola and Cork, is on shore at Liverpool, but is expected to be got off without damage.

The Minerva, Squarey, from London to Quebec, is retaken and carried into Halifax.

The Two Brothers, Hans Crow, from Cadiz to Ostend, is lost near Ilfracombe, and only saved 1 hide, 5 bags red wool, 46 barrels cochineal, and 3 bags of indigo.

Two Danes and a Swede are stranded on the coast of Cornwall.

The Brayton, Harrison, from Liverpool to Quebec, with salt, after being retaken, drove on shore near Louisburgh, on her passage to Halifax, and lost her anchors and cables, and received other damage.

The Felicity, Mourant, from Petersburg to Jersey, is lost in the Baltic near Libau; only a small part of the cargo saved.

The Sarah, Newby (or Gale,) from Jamaica to England, which sailed with the fleet and separated, afterwards sprung a leak and put back to Jamaica, where she was to unload and repair, and would then proceed for England.

The Antigallican, Butler, from Liverpool to Charlestown, is on shore near Holyhead.

Portsmouth, Nov. 11. Arrived from Topsham, the Charlotte, Punshon, after engaging a French privateer, and beating her off: The Charlotte had two killed.

Downs, Nov. 12. Sailed to the northward the Sampson and Artois men of war, and Shark sloop.

November 16.

The following ships of war are now at Spithead, viz. Royal George, Dublin, Monsieur, Britannia, Defence, Juno, Victory, Valiant, Anson, Lynx, Defiance, Yarmouth, Tisiphone, Arrogant, Prothée, Furnace, Stag, Queen, Diligente, Success, Duke, Inflexible, Alarm, Union, Sceptre, Daphne, Courageux, Alexander, Agamemnon, Lightning, Cumberland, Renown, Conqueror, Minerva, Edgar, La Prudente, Harpy.

The Edward, Peoples, from New York to Halifax and Quebec, was taken the 11th of August last by the Grayhound privateer, of Portsmouth in New Hampshire.

The Emulation, Simonds, from Quebec to Newfound-

Mharattas difowned all know..
peace, and behaved with the
elty. Before the 28th of May,
taken by Tippoo Saib. His army
more than one hundred thousand
r furrendering, on condition of
onours of war, he forced the gar-
down their arms. Accounts of
urope were then received. Sir Eyre
at Madras on the 26th of April.
been another drawn action between
d Sir Edward Hughes. General
as before Cuddalore, when he recei-
gence of the news of Peace in Europe.
e intelligence was received by the
with the greatest alarm : for though
of France had effected nothing, the
rement of affairs in the country had
y left our whole poffeffions on the
destruction. The dispatches are
th the mutual acculations of the fe-
mmanders.
ollowing, as a true state of the news
dia, is fent to us by a gentleman who
ent in the General Court when it
d, and pledges himself for the truth
ir Eyre Coote arrived at Madras in
with ten lacks of rupees, from Bengal,
aving been chafed by four French ships:
oft unfortunately, this old hero died
ys after he landed. The grand army
Coast of Coromandel, after Tippo Sa-
quitted the Carnatic, marched to at-
he French troops at Cuddalore : they
rced the outworks, and there was no
of their fuccefs against the place, when
gence arrived at Cuddalore of the peace,
hen all hostilities ceased. There was an
between the two fleets in June, but

fo that the whole .. ..
on the shoulders of Mr. Fox ? and ..
bour is indeed Herculean.

TO BE SOLD,
By PUBLIC VENDUE,
At the AMERICAN Coffee-House,
In State-Street,
On THURSDAY next, 22d Inst.
THE GOOD BRIGANTINE

VICTORY,

Burthen 120 Tons, more or lefs,
European built, and well found as fhe came
from Sea, with all her Appurtenances.
N. B. Said BRIGANTINE now lying at
Governor HANCOCK's Wharf.
The SALE beginning at ONE o'Clock.
The INVENTORY to be feen any time
before the Sale, at JOHN JUTAU's Office in
State Street.

BRIG NEW-YORK PACQUET.

THE brig NEW YORK PACQUET,
WILLIAM MORTON, Mafter, will fail
with all poffible dispatch, for NEW-YORK.
For FREIGHT or PASSAGE, apply to the
Mafter on board, at GRAY's wharf; or at
WILLIAM SHATTUCK's ftore, in State-ftreet.
N. B.—Said BRIG has excellent accommo-
dations for PASSENGERS.
BOSTON, January 16, 1784.

Having defen..
this new world... having taught a leffon ..
ful to thofe who inflict, and to thofe who feel
oppreffion, you retire from the great theatre
of action with the bleffings of your fellow
citizens. But the glory of your virtues will
not terminate with your military command--
it will continue to animate remotest ages.
We feel with you our obligations to the army in general, and will particularly charge
ourfelves with the interest of thofe confidential officers who have attended your perfon to
this affecting moment.
We join with you in commending the interests of our dearest country to the protection
of Almighty God, befeeching him to difpofe
the hearts and minds of its citizens to improve the opportunity afforded them of becoming a happy and respectable nation... And
for You, we address to Him our warmest prayers, that a life fo beloved, may be fostered
with all his care----that your days may be
happy as they have been illuftrious, and that
he will finally give you that reward which
this world cannot give.
Extract from the Minutes,
CHARLES THOMSON, Secretary.
Here we must let fall the fcene---few tragedies ever drew more tears from fo many
beautiful eyes, as were affected by the moving
manner in which his Excellency took his final
leave of Congrefs. After which he immediately fet out for Virginia, accompanied
South river by his Excellency ou..
with the warmeft wifhes of the
repofe, health, and happiness.
may be enjoy them !

DELIVERED WITH ELOQUENCE

Introduction

A s British troops and Loyalists evacuated key port towns, peace negotiations in Paris delivered a treaty containing several favorable terms for America. With American independence officially recognized, all eyes turned to the commander in chief, George Washington, who resigned his commission, retired to his farm home at Mount Vernon, Virginia, and formally concluded the Revolution. His return to civilization was a powerful gesture of character and leadership that helped build the foundation for a new nation.

American Herald (Boston)
January 19, 1784

General George Washington
Resigning His Commission
Architect of the Capitol

PERILS OF PEACE

MAKING PEACE TURNED OUT TO BE ALMOST AS DIFficult as making war. The instructions a supine Congress sent to Europe—that American negotiators were to do nothing without the consent of France—put Benjamin Franklin and his two associates, John Jay and John Adams, in a dangerous bind. France had her own territorial goals, mostly in the West Indies. Spanish politicians were making noises about claiming control of the Mississippi and title to all the territory between the Allegheny Mountains and the great river.

Franklin, who conducted the first round of negotiations alone early in July 1782, had no intention of playing second fiddle to the French, no matter what Congress said. He had declared the year prior that he would never sell a drop of the Mississippi. "A neighbor might as well ask me to sell my street door," he said. Moreover, his relationship with the French foreign minister, the Count de Vergennes, was good. When he told the Count that he was going to try for the best possible bargain with the British, Vergennes made no objection.

The seventy-six-year-old American ambassador's opening gambit was nothing short of breathtaking. He informed the chief British negotiator that there were four necessary articles to the treaty of peace: (1) Recognition of American independence and the withdrawal of all British troops. (2) An agreement on the Mississippi as the western boundary, plus the right to use the river. (3) A return of the Canadian boundary to the Great Lakes. (4) The right of Americans to fish in freedom and safety on the Newfoundland Grand Banks. To

Franklin, who conducted the first round of negotiations alone early in July 1782, had no intention of playing second fiddle to the French, no matter what Congress said. He had declared the year prior that he would never sell a drop of the Mississippi.

these four, Franklin added several "advisable" articles—the chief one being the cession of Canada to the United States. He also urged the British to issue a public apology to the people of the United States to restore genuine peace between the two nations.

When Jay and Adams entered the negotiations, matters grew confused. Both suspected the French to the point of paranoia, and this inspired the English to drag their feet and try one last time to divide the two allies. During this wasted interval, victories on distant fronts toughened the British stand. In mid-September 1782, the garrison of Gibraltar beat off a combined Spanish-French assault. In the West Indies, the British thrashed Admiral de Grasse's fleet and captured the admiral.

The revitalized British brushed aside the idea of apologizing for the war, refused to cede Canada, insisted on the payment of all prewar American debts to British merchants, and demanded compensation for the Loyalists whose homes and property had been seized by the rebels. The Americans conceded Canada and the debts, but reimbursing the Loyalists was unacceptable. Franklin maintained they deserved nothing. They had gambled their estates against the rebels' estates and lost. The negotiations teetered toward stalemate.

Franklin proposed requiring Parliament to compensate the Americans for all the seaports the British Navy had burned and for the hundreds of houses their troops had plundered in the previous six years.

The king's negotiators swallowed hard and agreed to a compromise. Congress would ask the states to make some compensation to Loyalists who did not bear arms in the war. At this point, the bankrupt Congress's influence with the states was close to zero. It was a gesture that meant nothing, and everyone knew it.

With the terms settled, the Americans signed the agreement on November 30, 1782, without consulting the French. This was perilously close to violating the terms of America's treaty with France and unquestionably ignored the instructions from Congress. Jay and Adams exulted over this display of American independence. Ambassador Franklin had the task of soothing the Count de Vergennes's extremely ruffled feathers. He not only managed this feat with finesse, but also persuaded the irked foreign minister to agree to one last loan to keep the penniless American government afloat.

On January 20, 1783, the French and the British agreed on terms. Vergennes, pointedly reminding Franklin of the courtesy the Americans had not offered him, invited the ambassador to sign the document with him. Franklin swallowed the rebuke and signed without a murmur. Only one thing mattered to him: the war was over. Later that day, when he arrived at the home of the Duc de la Rochefoucauld for dinner, he threw his arms around this staunch supporter of America and exclaimed, "My friend, could I have hoped, at my age, to enjoy such happiness?"

INDEPENDENT LEDGER (BOSTON), AUGUST 18, 1783
Todd Andrlik

This engraving of thirteen hands grasping one ring adorns the masthead of the *Independent Ledger* and is accompanied by the slogan "All Hands With One Inflamed Enlightened Heart."

THURSDAY, APRIL 10, 1783,

THE
Pennsylvania Packet
OR, THE
GENERAL ADVERTISER.

VOL. XII.] PUBLISHED EVERY TUESDAY, THURSDAY AND SATURDAY.—Price Six-Pence. [NUMB. 1026.

By the February Packet from Falmouth, the ship Vigilant from London, and other late arrivals at New-York from Europe, we have British Prints to the beginning of February, from which the following are taken—

Authentic Copies
OF THE
PRELIMINARY ARTICLES
OF PEACE,
BETWEEN

His Britannic Majesty, the Most Christian King, His Most Catholic Majesty, and The United States of America.

Signed at Versailles, the 20th of January, 1783.

Translation of the Preliminary Articles of Peace, between His Britannic Majesty and the Most Christian King; signed at Versailles the 20th of January, 1783.

In the Name of the Most Holy TRINITY.

THE KING OF GREAT-BRITAIN and the MOST CHRISTIAN KING, equally animated with a desire of putting an end to the calamities of a destructive war, and of re-establishing union and good understanding between them, as necessary for the good of mankind in general as for that of their respective kingdoms, states and subjects, have named for this purpose, viz. on the part of his Britannic Majesty Mr. Alleyne Fitz-Herbert, Minister Plenipotentiary of his said Majesty the King of Great Britain; and on the part of His Most Christian Majesty, Charles Gravier, Comte de Vergennes, Counsellor in all his councils, Commander of his Orders, Counsellor of State, Minister and Secretary of State, and of the Commands and Finances of his said Majesty, for the department of Foreign Affairs; who, after having duly communicated to each other their full powers in good form, have agreed on the following Preliminary

Art. 7. The King of Great Britain shall restore to France the island of St. Lucia, and shall cede and guarantee to her that of Tobago.

Art. 8. The Most Christian King shall restore to Great Britain the islands of Grenada and the Grenadines, St. Vincent, Dominica, St. Christopher's, Nevis, and Montserrat; and the fortresses of those islands conquered by the arms of Great Britain and by those of France, shall be restored in the same condition in which they were when the conquest of them was made, provided that the term of eighteen months, to be computed from the time of the ratification of the definitive treaty, shall be granted to the respective subjects of the Crowns of Great Britain and France, who may have settled in the said islands, and in other places which shall be restored by the definitive treaty, to sell their estates, recover their debts, and to transport their effects and retire without being restrained, on account of their religion, or any other whatever, except in cases of debt or of criminal prosecutions.

Art. 9. The King of Great Britain shall cede and guarantee in full right to his Most Christian Majesty the river of Senegal and its dependencies, with the forts of St. Louis, Podor, Galam, Arguin and Porteudu. His Britannic Majesty shall restore, likewise, the island of Goree, which shall be given up in the condition in which it was when the British arms took possession of it.

Art. 10. The Most Christian King shall, on his side, guarantee to his Majesty, the King of Great Britain, the possession of Fort James, and of the river Gambia.

Art. 11. In order to prevent all discussions in that part of the world, the two Courts shall agree, either by the definitive treaty, or by a separate act, upon the boundaries to be fixed to their respective [...] and French nations carried it on before the [...]

Art. 12. In regard to the rest of the coast of Africa, the subjects of both powers shall continue to frequent them, according to the custom which prevailed hitherto.

Art. 13. The King of Great Britain shall [...] His Most Christian Majesty all the [...] which belonged to him at the commencement of the present war on the coast of Orixa, and in [...] liberty to surround Chandernagor with [...] draining the waters; and his Britannic Majesty [...] to take such measures as may be in his power for securing to the subjects of France, in that part of India, as also on the coast of Orixa, Coromandel, and Malabar, a safe, free, and independent trade, such as was carried on by the late French East India Company, whether it be carried on by them as individuals or as a company.

Art. 14. Pondicherry, as well as Karical, shall likewise be restored, and guaranteed to France; and

Majesty, or by those of his Most Christian Majesty, and which are not included in the present articles, shall be restored without difficulty, and without requiring compensation.

Art. 20. As it is necessary to assign a fixed epoch for the restitutions and the evacuations to be made by each of the high contracting parties, it is agreed, that the King of Great-Britain shall cause to be evacuated the islands of St. Pierre and Miquelon, three months after the ratification of the definitive treaty, or sooner if it can be done; St. Lucia in the West-Indies, and Gorée in Africa, three months after the ratification of the definitive treaty, or sooner if it can be done. The king of Great Britain shall, in like manner, at the end of three months after the ratification of the definitive treaty, or sooner if it can be done, enter again into possession of the Islands of Grenada, the Grenadines, St. Vincent, Dominica, St. Christopher's, Nevis, and Montserrat.

France shall be put into possession of the towns and comptoirs, which are restored to her in the East-Indies, and of the territories which are procured for her, to serve as dependencies round Pondicherry, and round Karical, six Months after the ratification of the definitive Treaty, or sooner if it can be done.

France shall at the end of the same term of six months, restore the towns and territories which her arms may have taken from the English or their allies in the East-Indies.

In consequence whereof, the necessary orders shall be sent by each of the high contracting parties, with reciprocal passports for the ships which shall carry them, immediately after the ratification of the definitive [...]

Translation of the Preliminary Articles of Peace, between His Britannic Majesty and the Most Catholic King; signed at Versailles the 20th of January, 1783.

In the Name of the Most Holy TRINITY.

THE King of Great Britain and the King of Spain, equally animated with a desire of putting an end to the calamities of a destructive war, and of re-establishing union and good understanding between them, as necessary for the good of mankind in general, as [...] for that of their respective kingdoms, states, and sub- [...]

Art. 22. In order to prevent all causes of complaint and dispute which may arise on account of prizes which may be made at Sea after the signing of these preliminary articles, it is reciprocally agreed, that the vessels and effects which may be taken in the Channel and the North-Seas, after the space of twelve days, to be computed from the ratification of the present preliminary articles, shall be restored on each

PENNSYLVANIA PACKET (PHILADELPHIA)
April 10, 1783

The January 20, 1783, preliminary terms of peace between Great Britain and France, and Great Britain and Spain, were shipped across the Atlantic and published in American newspapers, such as the

April 10, 1783, issue of the *Pennsylvania Packet*, which also reprinted the November 30, 1782, terms with America. The treaty with the United States was approved by the Congress of the Confederation on April 15, 1783, signed in Paris on September 3, and ratified by Congress on January 14, 1784, to officially conclude the American Revolutionary War.

Torres, of Villan..
Yoch; Baron of ..
moia, Enipol, Tr..
Antillon, La Alm..
bovillet; Oreau, ..
the Tenance, and ..
Rodellar, the Caf..
Tiurana, de Villa..
Rico Hombre in ..
of the first Clafs, ..
Fleece, and of tha..
the King's Bed-ch..
neral of his Armie..
Chriftian Majefty, w..
cated to each other their full powers in good form, have agreed on the following Preliminary Articles:

Art. 1. AS foon as the Preliminaries fhall be figned and ratified, fincere friendfhip fhall be eftablifhed between his Britannic Majefty and his Catholic Majefty, their kingdoms, ftates and fubjects, by fea and by land, in all parts of the world Orders fhall be fent to the armies and fquadrons, as well as to the fubjects of the two powers, to ftop all hoftilities, and to live in the moft perfect union, forgetting what has paffed, of which their Sovereigns give them the order and example, and for the execution of this article, fea paffes fhall be given on each fide for the fhips which fhall be difpatched to carry the news of it to the poffeffions of the faid Powers.

Art. 2. His Catholic Majefty fhall keep the ifland of Minorca.

Art. 3. His Britannic Majefty fhall cede to his Catholic Majefty Eaft Florida, and his Catholic Majefty fhall keep Weft Florida, provided that the term of eighteen months, to be computed from the time of the ratification of the Definitive Treaty, fhall be granted to the fubjects of his Britannic Majefty who are fettled as well in the ifland of Minorca as in the two Floridas, to fell their eftates, recover their debts, and to tranfport their effects, as well as their perfons, without being reftrained on account of their religion, or under any other pretence whatfoever, except that of debts and criminal profecutions; and his Britannic Majefty fhall have power to caufe all the effects that may belong to him in Eaft Florida, whether artillery or others, to be carried away.

Art. 4. His Catholic Majefty fhall not for the future, fuffer the fubjects of his Britannic Majefty, or their workmen, to be difturbed or molefted, under any pretence whatfoever, in their occupation of cutting, loading and carrying away logwood, in a diftrict of which the boundaries fhall be fixed, and for this purpofe they may build without hindrance, and occupy without interruption, the houfes and magazines neceffary for them, for their families and for their effects, in a place to be agreed upon, either in the definitive treaty, or within fix months after the exchange of the ratifications; and his faid Catholic Majefty affures to them, by this article, the entire enjoyment of what is above ftipulated; provided that thefe ftipulations fhall not be confidered as derogatory in any refpect from the rights of his fovereignty.

Art. 5. His Catholic Majefty fhall reftore to Great-Britain, the Iflands of Providence and the Bahamas, without exception in the fame condition in which they were, when they were conquered by the arms of the King of Spain.

Art. 6. All the countries and territories which may have been, or may be conquered in any part of the world whatfoever, by the arms of his Britannic Majefty, or by thofe of his Catholic Majefty, and which are not included in our prefent articles, fhall be reftored without difficulty, and without requiring compenfations.

Art. 7. By the definitive Treaty, all thofe which have exifted till now between the two High contracting parties, and which fhall not be derogated from either by the faid Treaty, or by the prefent Preliminary Treaty, fhall be renewed and confirmed; and the two Courts fhall name Commiffioners to enquire into the ftate of the commerce between the two nations, in order to agree upon new arrangements of trade, on the footing of reciprocity and mutual convenience; and

Done at Verfailles, the 20th day January, 1783.
ALLEYNE FITZ-HERBERT, (L. S.)
LE COMTE D'ARANDA, (L. S.)

Articles agreed upon by and between Richard Ofwald, efquire, the Commiffioner of his Britannic Majefty, for treating of Peace with the Commiffioners of the United States of America, in behalf of his faid Majefty, on the one part, and John Adams, Benjamin Franklin, John Jay, and Henry Laurens, four of the Commiffioners of the faid States for treating of Peace with the Commiffioner of his faid Majefty, on their behalf, on the other part; to be inferted in and to conftitute the Treaty of Peace propofed to be concluded between the Crown of Great Britain and the faid United States; but which Treaty is not to be concluded until terms of a Peace fhall be agreed upon between Great Britain and France; and his Britannic Majefty fhall be ready to conclude fuch Treaty accordingly.

WHEREAS reciprocal advantages and mutual convenience are found by experience to form the only permanent foundation of peace and friendfhip between States, it is agreed to form the Articles of the propofed Treaty on fuch principles of liberal equity and reciprocity, as that partial advantages, thofe feeds of difcord, being excluded, fuch a beneficial and fatisfactory intercourfe between the two countries may be eftablifhed as to promife and fecure to both perpetual peace and harmony.

Art. 1. His Britannic Majefty acknowledges the faid United States, viz. New-Hampfhire, Maffachufetts-Bay, Rhode Ifland and Providence Plantations, Connecticut, New-York, New-Jerfey, Pennfylvania, Delaware, Maryland, Virginia, North Carolina, South Carolina, and Georgia, to be Free, Sovereign, and Independent States: that he treats with them as fuch; and for himfelf, his heirs and fucceffors, relinquifhes all claim to the government, proprietary, and territorial rights of the fame, and every part thereof: and that all difputes which might arife in future, on the fubject of the boundaries of the faid United States, may be prevented, it is hereby agreed and declared, that the following are and fhall be their boundaries, viz.

Art. 2. From the north weft angle of Nova Scotia, viz. that angle which is formed by a line drawn due north from the fource of Saint Croix River to the Highlands; along the faid iflands, which divide thofe rivers that empty themfelves into the River Saint Laurence from thofe which fall into the Atlantic Ocean, to the north-wefternmoft head of Connecticut River, thence down along the middle of that river to the forty-fifth degree of north latitude, from thence by a line due weft on faid latitude, until it ftrikes the River Iroquois or Cataraquy; thence along the middle of faid river into Lake Ontario, through the middle of faid lake, until it ftrikes the communication by water between that lake and Lake Erie; thence along the middle of faid communication into Lake Erie, through the middle of faid lake until it arrives at the water communication between that lake and Lake Huron; thence along the middle of faid water communication into the Lake Huron; thence through the middle of faid lake to the water communication between that lake and Lake Superior; thence through Lake Superior, northward of the Ifles, Royal and Phelipeaux, to the Long Lake, thence through the middle of faid Long Lake, and the water communication between it and the Lake of the Woods, to the faid Lake of the W...

States, to provide for the reftitution of all eftates, rights, and properties, which have been confifcated, belonging to real British fubjects, and alfo of the eftates, rights, and properties of perfons refident in diftricts, in the poffeffion of his Majefty's arms, and who have not borne arms againft the faid United States. And that perfons of any other defcription fhall have free liberty to go into any part or parts of any of the Thirteen United States, and therein to remain twelve months unmolefted in their endeavours to obtain the reftitution of fuch of their eftates, rights, and properties, as may have been confifcated; and that Congrefs fhall alfo earneftly recommend to the feveral States a reconfideration and revifion of all acts or laws regarding the premifes, fo as to render the faid laws or acts perfectly confiftent, not only with juftice and equity, but with that fpirit of conciliation, which on the return of the bleffings of peace fhould univerfally prevail. And that Congrefs fhall alfo earneftly recommend to the feveral States, that the eftates, rights, and properties of fuch laft mentioned perfons fhall be reftored to them, they refunding to any perfons who may be now in poffeffion the bona fide price (where any has been given) which fuch perfons may have paid on purchafing any of the faid lands or properties fince the confifcation.

And it is agreed, That all perfons who have any intereft in confifcated lands, either by debts, marriage fettlements, or otherwife, fhall meet with no lawful impediment in the profecution of their juft rights.

Art. 6. That there fhall be no future confifcations made, nor any profecutions commenced againft any perfon or perfons for or by reafon of the part which he or they may have taken in the prefent war; and that no perfon fhall, on that account, fuffer any future lofs or damage, either in his perfon, liberty, or property; and that thofe who may be in confinement on fuch charges, at the time of the ratification of the Treaty in America, fhall be immediately fet at liberty, and the profecutions fo commenced be difcontinued.

Art. 7. There fhall be a firm and perpetual peace between his Britannic Majefty and the faid States, and between the fubjects of the one and the citizens of the other, wherefore all hoftilities both by fea and land fhall then immediately ceafe: all prifoners on both fides fhall be fet at liberty, and his Britannic Majefty fhall, with all convenient fpeed, and without caufing any deftruction, or carrying away any negroes, or other property of the American inhabitants, withdraw all his armies, garrifons, and fleets from the faid United States, and from every port, place, and harbour within the fame; leaving in all fortifications the American artillery that may be therein; and fhall alfo order, and caufe all archives, records, deeds, and papers, belonging to any of the faid States, or their citizens, which in the courfe of the war may have fallen into the hands of his officers, to be forthwith reftored and delivered to the proper States and perfons to whom they belong.

Art. 8. The navigation of the Miffiffippi, from its fource to the ocean, fhall for ever remain free and open to the fubjects of Great-Britain and the citizens of the United States.

Art. 9. In cafe it fhould fo happen, that any place or territory belonging to Great-Britain or to the United States, fhould be conquered by the arms of either from the other, before the arrival of thefe articles in America, it is agreed, that the fame fhall be reftored without difficulty, and without requiring any compenfation.

Done at Paris, the thirtieth ...

LAST BOAT OF BRITISH TROOPS LEAVING NEW YORK CITY, 1783
North Wind Picture Archives

Along with British troops, some 29,200 Loyalist refugees evacuated New York, scattering far and wide.

BRITISH AND LOYALIST EVACUATIONS OF AMERICA

By Dennis M. Conrad

A S CAN BE SEEN FROM THE NEWSPAPER ARTICLES PRINTED here, British evacuation of its remaining outposts in the United States was a complex and protracted operation complicated by poor planning on the part of the British ministry, lack of adequate shipping, and the large number of white and black Loyalists and slaves (estimates range from fifty thousand to one hundred thousand—roughly 2 to 3 percent of the population of the United States) that swelled the ranks of those needing transportation. As a result, evacuation dates that were initially set ended up being pushed back for months, and plans that were made initially, such as to evacuate St. Augustine in 1782, were cancelled.

Nonetheless, despite mutual frustration, the handover was done peacefully. The guarantee given by General Anthony Wayne concerning the evacuation of Savannah, which is published in the *Pennsylvania Packet* (August 3, 1782), included an agreement not to attack the retreating British troops. This arrangement was duplicated when Charleston and New York were evacuated so that the turnover of power was done peacefully and order was maintained so there was no looting or civil disturbance.

In defense of the British, a large number of Loyalists chose to leave the United States, which greatly complicated the evacuation process. This outflow of Loyalists was a product of their concern that they would be punished, either personally or through confiscation of their property, by the victorious state governments. For example, Anthony Wayne, in addition to the guarantee he gave to British merchants in Savannah that is published in the August 3, 1782, *Pennsylvania Packet*, issued a proclamation granting amnesty to all Loyalists, except murderers, if those Loyalists would agree to serve in the Georgia Continental line for two years. The Georgia legislature initially agreed to accept this policy but then quickly reneged on it. The Georgia lawmakers were not, in the words of a Wayne biographer, willing to allow "bygones be bygones, as Wayne wished." The passions created by years of civil war were too great to be smoothed over by "easy proclamation."

As a result of such attitudes, which were to be found in every state, Loyalists felt compelled to flee. Some 6,600 Georgia Loyalists and their slaves sought transportation, an estimated 9,127 people (including 5,333 slaves) had to be transported from Charleston, and some 29,200 refugees left New York. These refugees scattered far and wide. Most went to Canada, particularly New Brunswick and Nova Scotia, but others went to Bermuda, to the British Caribbean Islands, especially Jamaica, to England, to East and West Florida (until the Spanish took possession of those territories shortly after the war), and even to the British colony of Sierra Leone in Africa.

It was this outflow of humanity that slowed and complicated the evacuation process. While the author of the "Evacuation Anecdote" published in the *American Herald* (February 16, 1784) could congratulate America on the conduct of its citizens during the turnover of power and argue that it demonstrated the superiority of the American system, the process could have been much quicker and easier had Americans truly practiced the "Clemency and generosity" that the writer claims for them.

The PENNSYLVANIA PACKET

Philadelphia, August 3.

The ship Nonsuch, captain Wells, is arrived in our river from Nantz, which she left about the middle of June. By her we have European papers as late as the 1st of June, from which the most material articles are copied into this paper.

Yesterday morning the brig Mercury, captain Faris, arrived here from Bilboa, after a passage of 50 days. At the time of her sailing a large fleet of French and Spanish ships lay in the bay of Cadiz with a body of 8000 French and 22000 Spanish troops, commanded by the duke de Crillon. This powerful armament was destined for a fresh attack upon Gibraltar, a new plan having been adopted for carrying on the siege of that fortress, which it was not doubted would finally be compelled to surrender.

Besides the account given in our last, of the evacuation of Savannah, we have the pleasure of assuring our readers, that the garrison had arrived at Charlestown before some persons (who arrived in town yesterday from that place, by way of a flag) left it, which was on the 11th ult. They also say, that St. Augustine was certainly abandoned by the enemy.

In addition to the above article our informant says, that a number of heavy cannon, &c. were embarked on board some vessels in Charlestown harbour, and that every appearance indicated a speedy removal of all the British forces from the quarter.

On Tuesday last a court of oyer and terminer, and general gaol delivery, was opened at Newtown, for the county of Bucks, when John Lowright and Jesse Lowright was brought to trial, but acquitted, notwithstanding direct and positive proof, that he was one of the burglars, strong evidence being adduced on his part, that he was at another place when the offence was committed. Next day Vickars was convicted on the full and satisfactory testimony of two persons of undoubted character, although there was an attempt to support an ALIBI in this café also. The persons, whose houses had been broke open were, in both instances, collectors of the public taxes. It is hoped that the conviction of Vickars will curb the disaffected, and disappoint the base arts by which our enemy carries on the war against us.

The following is said to be a copy of an application from some persons in Savannah, to brigadier general Wayne; and of his answer.

SIR,

AS there is reason to believe it is the intention of the British troops to evacuate the town and garrison of Savannah. We are deputed by different classes of inhabitants to wait upon you, as the commander of the army, and also governor Martin, to know whether such of them as are inclined to remain will be protected in their persons and properties, and for more fully discusing this business, we are entrusted with the honour of requesting a conference.

We have the honour &c.
JNO IRVINE,
ANDREW M'LEAN,
JNO WALLACE,
HENRY KEALL,
LD. CECILL.

General WAYNE.
ANSWER.

Should the garrison eventually effect an evacuation, the persons and properties of such inhabitants, or others as chuse to remain in Savannah will be protected by the military, and resigned inviolate to the hands of the civil authority of this state which must ultimately decide.

Given at Head-Quarters, 17th June, 1782.

and the Ruffian plenipotentiary at the Hague. It was then thought proper, under a plaufible pretext to fend to Paris the honourable Mr. T. Grenville, who is now there, continually receives and difpatches meffengers, relative to that great affair.

The 12th inft. Mr. Laurens left England. He is fuppofed to be now near the place where the negociations are to be decifive. It is faid they are on the following terms:

All our iflands, that of Grenada excepted, fhall be reftituted by France, which fhall again be in poffeffion of St. Lucia, Pondicherry, and all her other fettlements in India.

Minorca to be ceded to Spain, who fhall give us Porto Rico, renounce her pretenfions to Jamaica, in confideration of which fhe fhall be put in full poffeffion of Gibraltar.

Florida to be ceded to the Americans.

We fhall reftitute to the Dutch all their poffeffions taken during the war, and fecure to them the exercife of a free and neutral trade, on the terms of the armed neutrality.

America will be granted her independency, and a general liberty of trade. England on her part will equally divide with her the fifheries of Newfoundland and New-England ; preferve the peaceable poffeffion of Canada to its old limits, and all the lands to the northward of that province. We fhall, in confequence of this give up New-York to the Americans, and whatever we poffefs to the fouthward.

Lord Keppel moved yefterday in the houfe of peers, a vote of thanks to admiral Rodney. It paffed unanimoufly ; but lord Sandwich feized this opportunity for obferving, that the fervices done the country by this fortunate commander, were not due to the new adminiftration, which, far from acknowledging them, did in a manner punifh the author of them by recalling him. He demanded lord Keppel's declaration of the motive for that recall ; but this firft lord of the admiralty refufed complying.

May 29. The king has created fir George B. Rodney, baronet and knight of the Bath, barron of the kingdom of Great-Britain, under the ftile of baron Rodney, of Rodney Stoke, in Somerfetfhire ; and fir F. S. Drake, baronet of Great-Britain ; as alfo captain Edmund Afflick. The king has likewife created fir Samuel Hood, baronet, an Irifh peer, under the title of baron Hood, of Cathrington.

The kings of France and Sardinia have fent troops to Geneva, to reftore public tranquility in that unfortunate republic ; and at the fame time took the moft effectual fteps to perfuade the Halvetic body that it was not their intention to make any attempt on the independence of that city.

General Monckton, governor of Portfmouth, died 23d May. Lord George Lenox is to fucceed him.

All the meafures of the new adminiftration are equally oppofed ; that, for inftance, which puts arms into the hands of the people, has occafioned the following paragraph : " When it was propofed to a certain great perfonage to arm the people, he difcovered the greateft repugnance, and made the moft fenfible reprefentations againft it. The chancellor declared, he confidered that meafure as the moft proper for deftroying the very foundation of government : he obferved, that the lofs of America had been effected by armed affociations ; that with the fame affiftance Ireland had difengaged herfelf from all her connections with England, except thofe which fuited her ; and that from the fame caufes, the fame effects ought to be expected from England. The majority carried it in the council, and the king's acquiefcence was founded but on the hopes of feeing the plan mifcarry."

It is faid lord North has been fomewhat nigardly in arranging the prince of Wales's fettlement ; that young dauphin of England, who is doubtlefs more taken up with his pleafures than politics, is fuppofed to tread in the fteps of his predeceffors ; to have the fame principles, and holding necefffarily, by his fituation, to the whig party. The better to keep him in fuch pretended difpofitions, it is given out that the new miniftry out-bid each other for him.

The marquis of Rockingham, fay they, is for fettling upon him an yearly income of 30,000l. fterling. Lord Shelburne would have him to be allowed 45,000l.

GENEVA, May 10.

By advices from Turin we learn, that a body of 4500 Sardinian forces, to be joined by 6000 French, are on their march to quell the diforders in this city. This has raifed great [...] are leaving this place [...] lar party are preparing [...] have begun to repair [...] &c. The fituation [...]

Philadelp[hia]

The fhip Nonfuch [...] river from Nantz, w[...] June. By her we ha[...] 1ft of June, from wh[...] copied into this pape[...]

Yefterday morning [...] ris, arrived here from [...] At the time of her f[...] Spanifh fhips lay in th[...] French and 22000 S[...] duke de Crillon. Th[...] ed for a frefh attack upo[...] been adopted for carrying on the fiege of that fortrefs, which it was not doubted would finally be compelled to furrender.

Befides the account given in our laft, of the evacuation of Savannah, we have the pleafure of affuring our readers, that the garrifon had arrived at Charleftown before fome perfons (who arrived in town yefterday from that place, by way of a flag) left it, which was on the 11th ult. They alfo fay, that St. Auguftine was certainly abandoned by the enemy.

In addition to the above article our informant fays, that a number of heavy cannon, &c. were embarked on board fome veffels in Charleftown harbour, and that every appearance indicated a fpeedy removal of all the Britifh forces from that quarter.

On Tuefday laft a court of oyer and terminer, and general gaol delivery, was opened at Newtown, for the county of Bucks, when John Lowright and Jeffe Vickars were indicted for burglary. On Wednefday Lowright was brought to trial, but acquitted, notwithftanding direct and pofitive proof, that he was one of the burglars, ftrong evidence being adduced on his part, that he was at another place when the offence was committed. Next day Vickars was convicted on the full and fatisfactory teftimony of two perfons of undoubted character, although there was an attempt to fupport an ALIBI in this cafe alfo. The perfons, whofe houfes had been broke open were, in both inftances, collectors of the public taxes. It is hoped that the conviction of Vickars will curb the difaffected, and difappoint the bafe arts by which our enemy carries on the war againft us.

The following is faid to be a copy of an application from fome perfons in Savannah, to brigadier general Wayne ; and of his anfwer.

SIR,

AS there is reafon to believe it is the intention of the Britifh troops to evacuate the town and garrifon of Savannah. We are deputed by different claffes of the inhabitants to wait upon you, as the commander of the army, and alfo governor Martin, to know whether fuch of them as are inclined to remain will be protected in their perfons and properties, and for more fully difcuffing this bufinefs, we are entrufted with the honour of requefting a conference.

We have the honour &c.
JNO. IRVINE,
ANDREW M'LEAN,
JNO. WALLACE,
HENRY KEALL,
LD. CECILL.

General WAYNE.

ANSWER.

Should the garrifon eventually effect an evacuation, the perfons and properties of fuch inhabitants, or others as chufe to remain in Savannah will be protected by the military, and refigned inviolate to the hands of the civil authority of this ftate which muft ultimately decide.

Given at Head-Quarters, 17th June, 1782.

The plague also rages at Angora, a city much connected in trade with Europe, from whence great quantities of yarn are imported via Smyrna.

oner, who had the *fortitude* to walk knee deep into the water, and then returned, having entirely ungarbed himself, on purpose to avoid the fury of a disappointed rabble; however, a *lucky* brick-bat reached his head as he was getting into a boat, which had an *excellent effect*, its *ruby infusion* being the only sport left for the spectators.

Mangalore, which, according to the late overland express from the East Indies, has been taken by the East India company's forces, under the command of Gen. Matthews and Col. M'Leod, is on the Malabar coast, about 50 leagues to the Southward of Onore, which was taken by storm on the 5th of January last. Mangalore is one of the principal settlements in Heider Ali's country, but not his capital, which is called Seringa Patnam (an in land settlement) from which, however, it is distant only 60 miles. Before the Portuguese established themselves at Goa, and made that settlement so capital, Mangalore was called the capital of the ancient kingdom of Visiapoor, which is more than 300 miles in length. It lies in the same latitude as Madras, at opposite sides of the peninsula of India, so that a line drawn from one to the other would pass the heart of the country, the distance between them being upwards of 400 miles.

The English have had better success against the Algerines than any of the other European powers. In 1655, the great admiral Blake entered their harbours, and destroyed their ships—in 1668 sir Thomas Allen forced them to sue for peace—in 1670 commodore Beach, with five men of war, engaged seven of their's, drove two of them on shore, and burnt the other five, clearing four hundred and thirty

him no information, threw it down with a smile. By this honest simplicity, which would have gained the affection of a generous mind, Father Vincenti was so enraged that he gave the word of command, crying out, "Kill ... foot the word ... could not ... at indigna- ... peared, that ... rm exhibit- ... that exe- ... of a world ... uffered as a ... h fix an in- ... Spaniards, ... has passed ... s, that such ... oblivion, ra- ... on they de- ... able to the ... e to embel- ...

... pothecary who ... America, and who carried his medicinal bags on his shoulders from province to province, has lately made a claim on government for the loss of possession as a Loyalist to the amount of 16, 32zl. The Commissioners, we understand, have allowed only the TWO POUNDS. The investigation of the right of claimants is one of the best schemes ever adopted to get at the bottom of the fact; and it must turn out a saving to the kingdom that will astonish parliament, when they find how very much they have been imposed upon in the distribution of the gratuities, and annual payments, to people calling themselves Loyalists.

AMERICA.

NEW-YORK, January 15.

An EVACUATION ANECDOTE.

With some OCCASIONAL OBSERVATIONS.

A FEW days after the evacuation of New-York, and while the British fleet, with the troops and refugees on board, lay within sight of the city, a British officer was sent on shore to remove some effects, which in the hurry of evacuation had been forgotten. Struck, no doubt, with the recollection of the tyrannical conduct of the British army for such a length of time, and apprehensive for his own safety, he applied to the government of the state for a protection; and tho' he was told, that while he conducted himself peaceably and decently, he would meet with no ill usage; he still urged his request, and to ease his fears, was I believe indulged with one.

time of the evacuation, and the immediate repossession of it by its exiled inhabitants, without experiencing a conflict of affecting passions To see so many hundreds immediately happy, by a safe return to their long forsaken homes, and others made wretched by having new habitations to seek, in a comfortless region, and at a stormy season, were circumstances that by contrasting each other produced in the mind a disquieting compound of joy and pity.

Distress in any shape it can be presented to us, will in spite of resentment find a way to soften it; and the difference between threatening revenge and acting it, is so exceedingly great, that those who threaten the highest generally punish the least.

A fallen enemy appears a different being to what he did before, and in our conquest over him, one half our resentments are conquered with him.

Clemency and generosity are as naturally the companions of a great mind, as revenge and cruelty are of a little one. The former disdains to trample on the vanquished, and the latter makes it his only scene of action. If we look into the characters that have been the most eminent throughout the whole of the contest, we shall find greatness and benevolence are united qualities. For the heart that can be generously warmed with the love and principles of liberty, feels its happiness encreased, by sharing it with the world.

COMMON SENSE.

WORCESTER, February 12.

Silas Deane, Esq; has published at London, October 12th, 1783, "An address to the free and independent citizens of the United States of North America;" in which Mr. Deane exhibits a statement of his public accounts, and endeavours to wipe off the aspersions thrown upon his character by his enemies.

It has been observed, that since the first settlement of this country, no two years have produced so many casual deaths as the last twelve months: And it must wound the feelings of every rational being when he reflects that Unnatural and truly Horrible crime of SUICIDE has been more prevalent, not only in Europe, but in this Country, during the aforementioned period, than it has ever been remembered to be before in that space of time.

By the southern papers we learn, that some gentlemen in Trenton and Philadelphia, who have observed the Comet, suppose, that it is advancing towards the sun, and that soon after its perihelion it will make a most splendid appearance in the morning before day break; but it is rather supposed by those who have lately had an opportunity to observe it, that it has already past its perihelion, and is now on its recess from the sun.

christian slaves. The same year sir Edward Spragge destroyed nine of their ships near the castle of Burgia, in which conflict near 1800 of the Moors were killed and drowned. This last victory reduced those free booters to beg a treaty of pacification, and they have shewn a proper regard to the British flag for a series of years.

The following is a copy of the will made by Lieutenant-Colonel Thomas the Evening previous to the fatal interview with Colonel Cosmo Gordon.

London, Sept. 3, 1783.

" I am now called upon, and, by the rules of what is called honour, forced into a personal interview with Colonel Cosmo Gordon—God only can know the event, and into his hands I commit my Soul, conscious only of having done my duty.

" I therefore declare this to be my last will and testament, and do hereby revoke all former wills, &c. I have made at any time.

" In the first place, I commit my Soul to Almighty God, in hopes of his mercy and pardon for the irreligious step I now (in compliance with the unwarrantable customs of this wicked world) put myself under the necessity of taking.

" I leave 150l. in Bank notes, enclosed, to my dear brother, John Thomas, Esq. I bequeath unto him whatever sums may be due to me from the agent of the 1st. regiment of guards, reserving a sufficient sum to pay my debts, which are inconsiderable ; and I also give and bequeath unto him all my books and household furniture, and every thing else of which I am now possessed. I give and bequeath to Tho. Hobber, my servant, 50l. which I request my brother will pay him. What debts may be now owing, I request my brother will immediately discharge.

FRED. THOMAS.

Wednesday Night, Sept. 3, 1783.

" P. S. I commit this into the hands of my Friend, Captain Hill, of the 1st regiment of guards."

ANECDOTE.

When the Spaniards were invading Peru, after the inhabitants of that country were driven to the greatest extremity, one Friar Vincenti was sent by the Spaniards in order to treat with the vanquished. The behaviour of Ata-Nulps, the last Inca of Peru, in his intercourse with Vincenti, appeared particularly striking. He heard the Spanish Missioner with calm attention, and replied, " That it was absurd on the part of the POPE to grant away a territory which did not belong to him, he would still continue to venerate the Gods of his ancestors ; and if the Christians worshipped a God that died, he adored the Sun that never died." He viewed the Prayerbook, which was put into his hands by the Friar, and after saying, that it conveyed to him no information, threw it down with a smile. By this honest simplicity, which would have gained the affection of a generous mind, Father Vincenti was so enraged that he gave the word of command, crying out, " Kill the dogs who trample under foot the word of God." An incident like this could not fail to excite indignation, and that indignation rose still higher, when it appeared, that articles of high treason were in form exhibited against Atra Nulpa, and, after that execrable farce of a state, the Prince of a world just discovered by the Spaniards suffered as a

Observing afterwards that every thing in this city was civil and tranquil, no mobs—no riots—no disorders, he finished unmolested, the business he was sent upon, and prepared to return on board.

Well ! said he to a gentleman in company, this is a strange scene indeed ! Here, in this city, we have had an army for more than seven years, and yet could not keep the peace of it—scarcely a day or night passed without tumults. Now we are gone every thing is in quietness and safety. These Americans, continued he, are a curious original people, *they know how to govern themselves, but nobody else can govern them.*

Though this remark was produced by the force of immediate observation, and with very little reflection, it has something in it that is strong and striking.

To know how to govern ourselves is the nicest point of human wisdom. It is the foundation of character and greatness either in the individual or the nation collectively. The highest abilities or the best of causes without prudence and temper to manage them, lose, in a little time, their grace and influence, and the experience of the world has shewn us, that power without discretion undermines itself.

The British appear to have been exceedingly disappointed and mortified, at the order and regularity which immediately took place, upon the evacuation. They had predicted nothing but riots, revenge and tumults ; and under this expectation, the last scene they were witness to in America, confounded them like a conquest.

It is melancholy to reflect (for reflection will find its way even to the severest heart) how many thousands their assuming arrogance and delusive proclamations have ruined, and how many more their false alarms have unnecessarily frightened away. Hundreds who might have staid in safety, and many no doubt, remain, who can have no good pretensions to be here.

When an enemy suddenly extends his arms and authority over a country, it is impossible for every one to get out of his way. The incumbrance of children and families, the insurmountable difficulty of procuring conveyance for so many thousands at once, the embarrassment of private circumstances which none but themselves can know, the intricacy and influence of dependent connections, the want of money to move with, and, at last, the not knowing where to go, or how to live, will unavoidably leave numbers within their power whose situation being blended with the voluntary traitor, exposes them alike to indiscriminate suspicion. All are not friends or enemies who at first appear so. Misfortune may have the resemblance of guilt, and guilt assume the stile of misfortune ; and to distinguish between them, requires observation, temper and prudence.

It was impossible to view this city at the time of the evacuation, and the immediate repossession of it by its exiled inhabitants, without experiencing a conflict of affecting passions To see so many hundreds immediately happy, by a safe return to their long forsaken homes, and others made wretched by having new habitations to seek, in a comfortless region, and at a stormy season, were circumstances that by contrasting each other produced in the mind a disquieting compound of joy and pity. Distress in any shape it can be presented to us, will in spite of resentment find a way to

RESIGNATION OF GEORGE WASHINGTON AS COMMANDER IN CHIEF

By Robert J. Allison

KING GEORGE III ASKED AMERICAN-BORN PORTRAIT painter Benjamin West what Washington would do after the war. The United States had no effective government. Would the victorious general use his army to hold onto power? No, West said. Washington would return to his farm. "If he does that," the King said, "he will be the greatest man in the world."

As it became clear the war was ending, it also was clear the United States did not have an effective government. Disgruntled Pennsylvania soldiers demanding their pay drove Congress from Philadelphia. Some of Washington's officers plotted to overthrow the ineffective Congress. Washington denounced their threat against the civil power, warning officers not to betray the cause they had served. Washington wrote to state governors urging their support for a stronger union but insisted that citizens, not soldiers, governed.

Facing down a coup d'état, lobbying for a more effective elected government, Washington as commander had to ensure that the British army left. When news that the treaty was signed reached him in October, he wrote to the British commander, General Guy Carleton, about his plans to evacuate New York City. On November 20, Washington accompanied New York governor George Clinton as he crossed into Harlem. Washington and his men were there to restore legitimate civil power. On November 23, the British were on their ships, and the American flag rose at New York's battery. After an emotional farewell to his officers, Washington began his journey home, stopping in Philadelphia to settle his accounts, then on to Annapolis, where Congress met.

As it became clear the war was ending, it also was clear the United States did not have an effective government.

Washington notified Congress of his arrival on December 20; Congress agreed to receive him at noon on December 23. Congress hosted a banquet for Washington and two hundred guests on December 22, and afterward the Maryland government sponsored a gala ball at the State House. To give every lady "the pleasure of dancing with him," Washington danced every set.

At noon the next day, he returned to the State House. The nineteen members of Congress, representing only seven states, remained seated, with their hats on, as Washington entered. Once he was seated, "respectable citizens of Annapolis," the French consul, Governor William Paca, members of the assembly, and "a beautiful group of elegant ladies" filled the gallery and the House floor (*Massachusetts Spy*, January 29, 1784). President Thomas Mifflin told Washington that "the United States in Congress assembled, were prepared to receive his communications." Washington rose and bowed; the members raised their hats. He read his statement, resigning "with satisfaction" the appointment "accepted with diffidence" (*American Herald*, January 19, 1784).

Washington recommended Congress's "favourable notice" to the officers who had formed his official family and commended the "interests of my dearest country to the protection of Almighty God." Now having "finished the work assigned me," he retired "from the great theatre of action," taking "leave of all the employments of public life" (*American Herald*, January 19, 1781). From his pocket he took the commission the Congress of the United Colonies had issued on June 17, 1775, presenting it to President Mifflin.

Virginia delegate Thomas Jefferson wrote the official reply, which Mifflin read with dignity but little feeling. Washington had "defended the standard of liberty in this new world" and "taught a lesson useful to those who inflict, and those who feel oppression."

"[F]ew tragedies ever drew more tears from so many beautiful eyes," the *American Herald* reported (January 19, 1784). All understood the symbolic significance as Washington surrendered military power back into the hands of the civil government, whose authority came from the American people. No one watching knew what their former King had said; but none who saw this remarkable scene would have disagreed, as Washington rode off in haste to spend Christmas as a civilian at home, that they had had a glimpse of the greatest man in the world.

WASHINGTON'S FAREWELL TO HIS OFFICERS AFTER THE REVOLUTION, FRAUNCES TAVERN, NYC
North Wind Picture Archives

After an emotional farewell to his officers in New York, Washington began his journey home, stopping in Philadelphia to settle his accounts, then on to Annapolis, where Congress met.

The MASSACHUSETTS S P Y

BOSTON, January 22.

Extract of a letter, dated Annapolis, 24th December, 1783.

" General Washington having requested to resign his commission, was admitted to a publick audience on Tuesday last. The gallery was filled with a beautiful group of elegant ladies, and some graced the floor of Congress. On this were likewise the Governor, Council and Legislature of the State, several general officers, the Consul General of France, and the respectable citizens of Annapolis. Congress were seated and covered, as Representatives of the sovereignty of the union, the spectators were uncovered and standing. The General was introduced to a chair by the Secretary, who after a decent interval ordered silence. The President then informed the General, That "the United States in Congress assembled were prepared to receive his communications," on which he rose with great dignity and delivered his address. This was followed by his advancing to the President and resigning his commission.—He resumed his place and received in a standing posture, the answer of Congress, which the President delivered with eloquence. The occasion produced a pleasing solemnity that may more easily be conceived than expressed.—To see on the one hand so great and good a man taking his leave of publick employments to spend the residue of his days in retirement, and his country on the other acknowledging his unprecedented merit, and with the most affectionate embraces, loading him with their blessings, exhibited a scene that drew tears from many of the spectators. He is now with his family, and may his rewards and enjoyments be in future adequate to his important services."

Since or last, Major General Knox arrived in Town from Head Quarters.

MASSACHUSETTS SPY (BOSTON)
January 29, 1784

King George III asked American-born portrait painter Benjamin West what Washington would do after the war. The United States had no effective government. Would the victorious general use his army to hold on to power? No, West said. Washington would return to his farm. "If he does that," the King said, "he will be the greatest man in the world."

...period of existence allotted them, and to die chiefly of old age: And, were any obfervations to be made among favages, perhaps the fame would be found to be true of them.—Death is an evil to which the order of Providence has fubjected every inhabitant of this earth; but to man it has been rendered unfpeakably more an evil than it was defigned to be. The greateft part of that black catalogue of difeafes which ravage human life, is the offspring of the tenderneſs, the luxury, and the corruptions introduced by the vices and falſe refinements of civil fociety. That delicacy which is injured by every breath of air, and that rottenneſs of conftitution which is the effect of intemperance and debauchery, were never intended by the Author of Nature; and it is impoſſible, that they fhould not lay the foundation of numberleſs fufferings, and terminate in premature and miferable deaths.

——Let us then value more the fimplicity and innocence of a life agreeable to Nature, and learn to confider nothing as favageneſs but malevolence, ignorance, and wickedneſs. The order of Nature is wife and kind. In a conformity to it confift health and long life; grace, honour, virtue, and joy. But Nature turned out of its way will always punifh. 'The wicked fhall not live out half their days.' Criminal exceſſes imbitter and cut fhort our prefent exiſtence; and the higheſt authority has taught us to expect, that they will not only kill the body, but the foul; and deprive us of an Everlaſting Exiſtence.

HAMBOURG, (Ruſſia) October 12.

A very extraordinary inftance of fecundity has happened in Lower Auftria, to the wife of one Langenloin. After being married a very long time, without having any children, on the 10th of September laft fhe brought forth four. On the 17th fhe felt freſh pains, and was brought to bed of four more. The eight children, which are all boys, have been baptized, and feem likely to live; nor does the mother appear to be at all incommoded by this double delivery.

L O N D O N.

The following copy of a very extraordinary letter was received by a gentleman in London, from a reſpectable correſpondent in Cambridge, who aſſerts that he has feen the original.

Provence, (France) July 12, 1779.

"SIR,

"NOW Mr. Dodd is beyond the reach of his enemies, you may acquaint them that he is here, in found health, though in melancholy fpirits; depreſſed in mind, from the idea of quitting forever his native country, and being neceſſarily compelled to hide his head from publick converſation, which, in England, was his chief enjoyment. Gifted by nature with the moſt fhining talents of fpeech, it muſt be a great mortification to him, that the courtſhip of popular applauſe is at an end; he muſt fink in obſcurity, after raiſing himſelf to the pinnacle of admiration. He is at the houſe of Mr. De Pee, who being my particular friend and relation, I have had an opportunity of feeing the Doctor. The account he gives of his deliverance, which he gathered partly from the information of thoſe to whom he is indebted for his life, and partly from his own knowledge, is this:

worth the purchaſe.

"After the ceremony of congratulation, on one fide and on the other, was over, the next affair to be conſidered (for before, nothing was conſidered by the Doctor's friends) was, how he fhould be diſpoſed of, when it was propoſed, that he fhould fet off the next day for France. A fubſcription for preſent fupply was entered into, and in the evening the Doctor went to his wife's lodgings, which fhe had quitted the evening before, oppoſite Stationer's-Hall. The next day he was equipped in women's apparel, by which, and the great alteration in his countenance, it was hardly poſſible for his moſt intimate friends to know him, unleſs he difcovered himſelf by his fpeech. It was thought proper to conceal all this from Mrs. Dodd, as it might be too fudden a furpriſe, but bring her by degrees to the knowledge of her huſband's exiſtence. The next day the Doctor attended by his friend Mr. H——, went to Dover, and there met with a fair wind, which carried them to Calais, from whence they came here."

NOVEMBER 15.

Mr. Paine, the excellent author of Common Senſe, is, we are told, preparing a hiſtory of the late War in America. Mr. Paine, obviouſly, with all his talents, cannot mount to the fource and fecret fpring—and there is one, who can thus mount, and that is General Waſhington. What a defideratum muſt it be in the world of letters and political attainment, if the General would, without delay, enter on this great work?—Of his talents in literary compoſition, his circular letter alone is a fufficient proof.

Extract of a letter from an Engliſh gentleman at Paris, to his friend in Briſtol, dated October 22.

"The weather has been very cold and foggy in Paris till Sunday laſt, when to my great furpriſe, I faw an advertiſement that Montgolfier and another gentleman were to go up with the globe that has been fo much talked of, the next day. I went to the place, and was a witneſs, among many thouſands, of their executing their promiſe. Mr. M. and no leſs a perſon than a Marquis, an officer in the King's fervice, went up 350 odd feet, and remained in the air fome time, and afterwards defcended without the leaſt hurt or inconvenience. The place they were in was a kind of gallery, conſtructed below the globe.—The next experiment is to give it a direction at will, and mount higher: In fhort, this globe engroſſes every converſation here."

Of all French commanders, not one has fhown more determined bravery than M. Suffrein. In the engagement where his fhip received fo much damage, that fhe funk going into Trincomale, his courage almoſt drove him into a phrenſy; it being well authenticated, that fome of his officers, thinking it impoſſible to carry the fhip out of the line of battle, begun a murmur about ftriking, on which Sufrein inſtantly feized a lighted match, and making towards the powder room, declared that no enemy fhould capture him, and therefore they had no alternative to chooſe, but either to attempt carrying the fhip into port, or be blown up in her. By this threat he preferved himſelf and crew from being made priſoners, though it proved afterwards impoſſible to fave the fhip.

Though the French claim the honour of the new invention of air-globes, there is little doubt but the Engliſh will be the men to make

An act for appraiſing perſonal eſtate taken by execution.

An act to repeal an act of this State, intitled an act in addition to an act paſſed November 28th, 1781, intitled, an act for preventing the fubjects of his Britannick Majeſty, and all other perſons inimical to the United States of North-America, from proſecuting actions, ferving as jurors, or acting as town officers within this State, paſſed the 21ſt day of June, A. D. 1782.

An act for the more fpeedy recovery of fmall debts, and to fave the coſt uſually attending the recovery in the preſent courſe of the law.

A liſt of the members of the Council and Houſe of Repreſentatives, who conſtituted the Aſſembly of this State, at their late Seſſion in Concord, viz.

COUNCIL.

County of ROCKINGHAM. The Hon. Meſhech Weare, Joſiah Bartlett, John M'Clary, Woodbury Langdon, and Nathaniel Folſom, Eſquires.

County of STRAFFORD. Hon. John Wentworth, and George Froſt, Eſqrs.

County of HILLSBOROUGH. Hon. Timothy Farrar, and Francis Blood, Eſqrs.

County of CHESHIRE. Hon. T. Applin, and Enoch Hale, Eſqrs.

County of GRAFTON. Hon. Moſes Dow, Eſquire.

The Hon. Meſhech Weare, Eſq; was unanimouſly choſen Preſident of faid Council. Ebenezer Thomſon, Eſq; Secretary; and Joſeph Pearſon, Eſq: Deputy Secretary.

HOUSE OF REPRESENTATIVES.

COUNTY of ROCKINGHAM.

Portſmouth, George Atkinſon, George Gains, and John Pickering, Eſqrs.

Exeter, Joſeph Gilman, Eſq; and Mr. Jedediah Jewett.

Londonderry, Daniel Runnells, Eſq; and Mr. Archibald M'Murphey.

Cheſter, William White, Eſq; and Mr. Jabez Hoyt.

Hampton, Chriſtopher Toppan, Eſq;

Hampton-Falls, M. Abner Sandborn.

Brintwood, Capt. Levi Morrel.

Stratham, Mark Wiggin, Eſq;

North-Hampton, Moſes Leavitt, Eſq;

Kenſington, Mr. Moſes Shaw.

Newmarket, Capt. Samuel Gilman.

Epping, Capt. Seth Fogg.

South-Hampton, and Newtown, Mr. Benjamin Clough.

Kingſton, and Eaſt-Kingſton, Capt. John Eaſtman.

Greenland, Mr. Stephen March.

Nottingham, Thomas Bartlett, Eſq;

Hawke, and Sandown, Mr. Thomas Page.

Newington, Ephraim Pickering, Eſq;

Rye, Samuel Jenneſs, Eſq;

Atkinſon, and Plaſtow, Nathaniel Peabody, Eſq;

Hampſtead, John Calf, Eſq;

Raymond, John Dudley, Eſq;

Deerfield, and Northwood, Jeremiah Eaſtman, Eſq;

Salem, Captain John Allen.

Candia, Mr. Ezekiel Knowles.

Epſom, and Chicheſter, Capt. James Gray.

Pelham, James Gibſon, Eſq;

Windham, Mr. Gain Armour.

Pembrook, Samuel Daniel, Eſq;

Concord, Timothy Walker, Eſq;

...y, Mr. William Smiley.

Keene, Mr. Benjamin Hall.

Packerſfield, Mr. William Barker.

Swanzey, and Fitzwilliam, Mr. Sam. Kindall.

Hindſdale, and Cheſterfield, Mr. Sam. King.

Richmond, Mr. Oliver Caprice.

Surry, and Alſtead, Nath. Sartill Prentice, Eſq;

Newport, Benj. Giles, Eſq;

Unity, and Ackworth, Mr. Elijah Frink.

Wincheſter, Mr. Simon Willard.

Granfham, and Plainfield, Mr. Nathan Young.

Charleſtown, John Hubbard, Eſq;

Corniſh, Moſes Chace, Eſq;

Waſhington, and Stoddard, Captain Jacob Copland.

COUNTY of GRAFTON.

Plymouth, Francis Wooſter, Eſq;

New Holderneſs, Samuel Livermore, Eſq;

Haverhill, James Woodward, Eſq;

Wentworth, and Warren, Captain Obadiah Clement.

New Cheſter, and Andover, Mr. Enoch Noyce.

Canaan, and Cardigan, Capt. Caleb Church.

Landaff, Mr. John Young.

Orford, Capt. John Mann.

Northumberland, Joſeph Whipple, Eſq;

Lebanon, and Hanover, Bezaleel Woodward, Eſq;

Lyme, Capt. Ebenezer Green.

The Honourable John Dudley, Eſq; was choſen Speaker, and John Calf, Eſq; Clerk of the Honourable Houſe of Repreſentatives; both of whom have been ftaunch friends to their country, and never deſerted our councils in the worſt of times.

The General Court of this State, after finiſhing their late feſſion at Concord, adjourned to the laſt Tueſday of March next, then to meet at the Court-Houſe in Exeter.

BOSTON, January 22.

Extract of a letter, dated Annapolis, 24th December, 1783.

"General Waſhington having requeſted leave to refign his commiſſion, was admitted to a publick audience on Tueſday laſt. The gallery was filled with a beautiful group of elegant ladies, and fome graced the floor of Congreſs. On this were likewiſe the Governor, Council and Legiſlature of the State, feveral general officers, the Conful General of France, and the reſpectable citizens of Annapolis. Congreſs were feated and covered, as Repreſentatives of the fovereignty of the union, the fpectators were uncovered and ftanding. The General was introduced to a chair by the Secretary, who after a decent interval ordered filence. The Preſident then informed the General, That "the United States in Congreſs aſſembled were prepared to receive his communications," on which he roſe with great dignity and delivered his addreſs. This was followed by his advancing to the Preſident and refigning his commiſſion.—He refumed his place and received in a ftanding poſture, the anſwer of Congreſs, which the Preſident delivered with eloquence. The occaſion produced a pleaſing folemnity that may more eaſily be conceived than expreſſed.—To fee on the one hand fo great and good a man taking his leave of publick employments to fpend the refidue of his days in retirement, and his country on the other acknowledging his unprecedented merit, and with the moſt affectionate embraces, loading him with their bleſſings, exhibited a fcene that drew tears from many of the fpectators. He is now with his family, and may his

Column 1 (partial left margin)

RE, in the ship
stage of 34 days,
to the 24th of

... the next day
reigning Duke,
is rout for Italy.
d that the King
the Carnival at

M. Le Febvre
d his post of Con-
ces to the King
was pleased to
The Count de
g sent to know
quired a pension,
that " he should

t of Lisle, was
ntroller General
w Minister is ex-
ing

MBER 13.

braltar mention,
ngly healthy and
tranquility, new
for their accom-
lerable cheap.
d will not return
utenant-General
Lieutenant-Go-

introduced on
St. James's, was
ability, and con-
ds of an hour.
fifty years in the
acquitted himself
the late reign To
f the Prince of
a letter to King
mending him to
strongest terms.

r necessity, in any
maintaining our
sent——Laws
almost to have
owe our confe-
most every great

asis of our great
ommerce of the
at (which is said
y permitting the
te to trade with
es, or by suffer-
this country any
ll desert the na-
marine of Great

ote his celebrated
f navigation had
speaking of that
s, " I am of opi-
, shipping, profit
hoicest and most
nade in England,
not been owners
trading or trade

or authority can he now shelter himself ?
Truly the Court of Proprietors here inter-
pose, vote thanks to the Governor General

terance, and I could scarce congratulate these
more than conquerors, in the name of every
loyal, every honest heart. Well, my lads,
you fought well ; how welcome you are to
every Englishman ! You have a grateful
country to reward your services, which have
been long, laborious, and faithful ; you'll be
promoted.——Sir, interrupted one of ——a,
you are mistaken ; no man has yet noticed
us but yourself ; we have done our duty, Sir,
the King, God bless him, THANKED us for
it. As to promotion, that is at an end we
were relieved, brought to Portsmo——
disbanded : when we get to Scotla——
wives, our children, and our mothers will
rush upon us with open arms. No indifferent man notices individuals. The glory of
the British arms gradually tarnished in my
eyes : the honour of my country sunk away
in a moment ; and though I bore no share
in that *negligence* which disgraces this æra, I
felt my self *less than a man in being a* BRITON !

Nov. 17. It is reported, in the vicinity
of St. James's, that David Hartley, Esq. will
go before Christmas to America in a public
capacity ; but whether as Ambassador, or
Envoy Extraordinary, is not yet determined.

They write from Paris, that an express is
arrived from Monf. de Suffrein at Trincomale, who had been informed of the peace
by a frigate in June last ; and that he had
sent the same vessel as a flag of truce to all the
English settlements with the grateful news.

The emigrators to America may, in the
back settlements, get land almost *for nothing* !
And there, with nature in all her sublimity
of dimension,

" Each like an ocean, each parterre a down,"

they will have the greatest attitude of things,
and may revel in each natural delight ! it is
a *sporting* country, such as a mere European has
no idea of ! Foxes, wolves, bears, &c. are put
up at every turn ! Then as to *society*, when
they understand them, the *natives* will delight them infinitely ! And when, with the
help of bark, and molasses spirits (which are
always at hand in the *adjoining places*, New-
England and Peru) they shall have weathered
but the *first ten or twelve years*, they will be
thoroughly seasoned to the climate, and ague-
proof at every pore ! A *family* will be established after their own name ! and
do not relapse into the habits and some
of the aborigines of the country) their *great
grand children* may, perhaps, become *great
fortunes* !

LONDON, NOVEMBER 22.

IT is with the truest concern we inform the
public, that the advices received yesterday o-
ver land from India, are of a most melancholy
complexion indeed ! The Mharattas have entered into new engagements with the French,
and have already infringed their recent treaty
with us. Tippoo Saib continues a most formidable enemy. Mangalore has furrendered

not decisive. Colonels Macleod and Hum-
berstone were attacked by the Mharratta fleet
and taken before the Mharatta peace was
... latter unfortunately
... former was releas-
... ay. The Mha-
... d, and Madajee
... re complete fa-
... ccident, from the
... ndence had been
... d the Mharattas,
... ng the countries
... ty. General Ma-
... ore, returned to
... acked by Tippo
... as compelled to
... e attacked Man-
... h very great loss
... , and there was no
... holding out, till rein-
forced. Three hundred Europeans had sailed from Madrass, for the purpose, and a
strong detachment from Bombay. No recent accounts from Bengall——all well there
by the last letters.

To-morrow morning the Duke and Duch-
ess of Cumberland will set off to Brightelm-
stone, where they are to embark for France.

The Crocodile frigate, which sailed in February for the East-Indies, carried out an account of the peace ; and the Eurydice,
which has since failed, carried instructions to
Sir Edward Hughes for such ships as are to
return home.

The Prince of Capers, Monarch of the
Graces, and Emperor of taste——the most
puissant and much renowned Monsieur VES-
TRIS, junior, arrived yesterday, at 3 o'clock
in Great Pultney-street, from France, being
engaged at the Opera-House for the ensuing
season.

The system of East-India Government, proposed on Tuesday last by Mr. Fox, is perhaps one of the completest efforts of human
policy that was ever devised by the ingenuity
of man, and will probably, when the rage of
party acrimony has a little subsided, and the
effects of personal enmity are also past, transmit him to posterity, with the brightest character of ancient political wisdom, and invest
him with the glorious titles to which he has
proved indisputable pretensions, of being the
saviour of his country, and the general friend
of mankind.

Mr. Fox assigned as one reason for fixing
the science of Indian Administration here at
home, that Parliament might have their eye
upon the conduct of the Commissioners, and
that the House of Commons might watch it,
and be ready to check each appearance of
misrule or mistake, and keep the current of
the Company's affairs pure, and equally free
from the foulness of corruption, or being diverted from its proper channel by weak management.

The speech of Mr. Fox on Tuesday did the
highest credit to his abilities, but still more to
his force of mind and resolution. His sentiments declaring his readiness to take every
degree of responsibility upon himself for the
bold and arduous attempt of reforming and
regulating India, did him the highest credit
with all who heard him. There is not a doubt
that this measure is completely calculated to
put the affairs of India in a situation of being
substantially useful to this country : It is
manly, vigorous, and comprehensive, and accompanied with a degree of responsibility both
from the nature of the measure and manner
of opening it, that gave a high opinion of the
boldness of the Minister, and his confidence
in the plan.

It is evident from the conclusion of Mr.
Fox's speech on Tuesday, that there is not
the most distant foundation for the reports
that Opposition have wished to propagate relative to diffension among the Administrati-

AMERICA.

ANNAPOLIS, Dec. 25.

The UNITED STATES in CONGRESS
Assembled, December 23, 1783.

According to order, his Excellency the Commander in Chief was admitted to a public
audience, and being seated, the President
after a pause, informed him, that the
United States in Congress Assembled, were
prepared to receive his communications ; whereupon he rose and addressed
Congress as follows :

MR. PRESIDENT,

THE great events on which my resignation depended, having at length taken
place ; I have now the honour of offering my
sincere congratulations to Congress, and of
presenting myself before them to surrender
into their hands the trust committed to me ;
and to claim the indulgence of retiring from
the service of my country.

Happy in the confirmation of our independence and sovereignty, and pleased with the
opportunity afforded the United States of becoming a respectable nation, I resign with
satisfaction the appointment I accepted with
diffidence ; a diffidence in my abilities to accomplish so arduous a task, which, however,
was superceded by a confidence in the rectitude of our cause, the support of the supreme
power of the union, and the patronage of
heaven.

The successful termination of the war has
verified the most sanguine expectations ; and
my gratitude for the interposition of providence, and the assistance I have received from
my countrymen, increases with every review
of the momentuous contest.

While I repeat my obligations to the army
in general I should do injustice to my own
feelings not to acknowledge, in this place, the
peculiar services, and distinguished merits,
of the gentlemen who have been attached to
my person during the war.

It was impossible the choice of confidential officers to compose my family, should have
been more fortunate.

Permit me, sir, to recommend in particular, those who have continued in the service
to the present moment, as worthy of the favourable notice and patronage of Congress.

I consider it as an indispensible duty to
close this last act of my official life, by commending the interests of our dearest country
to the protection of Almighty God, and those
who have the superintendence of them to his
holy keeping.

Having now finished the work assigned me,
I retire from the great theatre of action ; and
bidding an affectionate farewell to this august body, under whose orders I have so
long acted, I here offer my commission, and take my
leave of all the employments of public life.

He then advanced and delivered to the President his commission, with a copy of his address, and having resumed his place, the president returned him the following answer :

SIR,

THE United States in Congress assembled, receive with emotions too affecting for utterance, the solemn resignation of
the authorities under which you have led
their troops with success through a perilous
and doubtful war.

Called upon by your country to defend its
invaded rights, you accepted the sacred
charge before it had formed alliances, and
whilst it was without funds or a government
to support you.

You have conducted the great military
contest with wisdom and fortitude, invariably
regarding the rights of the civil powers thro'
all disasters and changes. You have, by the

Column 5 (partial right margin)

to bring
s own, and
and sacrifice

Joshua Chil
ade, the
or 18 yea
Palladium, fo
ation to
s one of
at ever
which we
our prese
one half
nt."

been,
on nati
on as the
e of Gre
compared
*a Charta
Maritima.*

An orde
ndencies
he Repu
entary
g before
who arr
e Hague
had bee
baffador
tes into
ordered
diately ;
kept fr

ia Com
their losse
o Decem
some of
Parliame
d, in or
ay be
ame time
Ministry
House o
t is mor
refuses
er of tw
er !
which t
uns, is
rt of Di
astings
is the sta
f Parliame
recomm
astings.

of the aborigines of the country) their *great
grand children* may, perhaps, become *great
fortunes* !

LONDON, NOVEMBER 22.

IT is with the trueſt concern we inform the
public, that the advices received yeſterday o-
ver land from India, are of a moſt melancholy
complexion indeed ! The Mharattas have entered into new engagements with the French,
and have already infringed their recent treaty
with us. Tippoo Saib continues a moſt formidable enemy. Mangalore has ſurrendered
to him, and General Mathews and his whole
army are priſoners, on the moſt ignominious
terms. This event happened on the 9th of
March. The Mharatta fleet had taken the
Ranger, and almoſt all our party are killed or
wounded. Colonel Humberſtone is ſlain, and
Colonel Macleod had received three wounds.
At Geriah the Mharattas diſowned all knowledge of the peace, and behaved with the
greateſt cruelty. Before the 28th of May,
Bidnore was taken by Tippoo Saib. His army
conſiſted of more than one hundred thouſand
men. After ſurrendering, on condition of
receiving honours of war, he forced the garriſon to lay down their arms. Accounts of
peace in Europe were then received. Sir Eyre
Coote died at Madras on the 26th of April.
There had been another drawn action between
Suffrein and Sir Edward Hughes. General
Stewart was before Cuddalore, when he received intelligence of the news ofPeace inEurope.
The above intelligence was received by the
Directors with the greateſt alarm : for though
the arms of France had effected nothing, the
miſmanagement of affairs in the country had
apparently left our whole poſſeſſions on the
brink of deſtruction. The diſpatches are
filled with the mutual accuſations of the ſeveral Commanders.

The following, as a true ſtate of the news
from India, is ſent to us by a gentleman who
was preſent in the General Court when it
was read, and pledges himſelf for the truth
of it : Sir Eyre Coote arrived at Madras in
April, with ten lacks of rupees, from Bengal,
after having been chaſed by fourFrench ſhips:
but, moſt unfortunately, this old hero died
two days after he landed. The grand army
on the Coaſt of Coromandel, after Tippo Saib had quitted the Carnatic, marched to attack the French troops at Cuddalore : they
had forced the outworks, and there was no
doubt of their ſucceſs againſt the place, when
intelligence arrived at Cuddalore of the peace,
and then all hoſtilities ceaſed. There was an
action between the two fleets in June, but

that this meaſure is completely calculated to
put the affairs of India in a ſituation of being
ſubſtantially uſeful to this country : It is
manly, vigorous, and comprehenſive, and accompanied with a degree of reſponſibility both
from the nature of the meaſure and manner
of opening it, that gave a high opinion of the
boldneſs of the Miniſter, and his confidence
in the plan.

It is evident from the concluſion of Mr.
Fox's ſpeech on Tueſday, that there is not
the moſt diſtant foundation for the reports
that Oppoſition have wiſhed to propagate relative to diſſenſion among the Adminiſtration, but, on the contrary, Lord North and
Mr. Fox, are as much agreed upon this great
eſſential meaſure for India, and upon every
other relative to the good of the country, as
ever Miniſters were at any period.

Lord North's illneſs renders him wholly incapable of attending to buſineſs of any kind,
ſo that the whole weight of public affairs lies
on the ſhoulders of Mr. Fox ; and the labour is indeed Herculean.

TO BE SOLD,

By PUBLIC VENDUE,

At the AMERICAN Coffee-Houſe,
In State-Street,

On THURSDAY next, 22d Inſt.
THE GOOD BRIGANTINE

VICTORY,

Burthen 120 Tons, more or leſs,
European built, and well found as ſhe came
from Sea, with all her Appurtenances.

N. B. Said BRIGANTINE now lying at
Governor HANCOCK's Wharf.

The SALE beginning at ONE o'Clock.

The INVENTORY to be ſeen any time
before the Sale, at JOHN JUTAU's Office in
State Street.

BRIG NEW-YORK PACQUET.

THE brig NEW YORK PACQUET,
WILLIAM MORTON, Maſter, will ſail
with all poſſible diſpatch, for NEW-YORK.

FOR FREIGHT or PASSAGE, apply to the
Maſter on board, at GRAY's wharf ; or at
WILLIAM SHATTUCK's ſtore, in State-ſtreet.

N. B.—Said BRIG has excellent accommo-
dations for PASSENGERS.

BOSTON, January 16, 1784.

bled, receive with emotions too affecting for utterance, the ſolemn reſignation of
the authorities under which you have led
their troops with ſucceſs through a periſous
and doubtful war.

Called upon by your country to defend its
invaded rights, you accepted the ſacred
charge before it had formed alliances, and
whilſt it was without funds or a government
to ſupport you.

You have conducted the great military
conteſt with wiſdom and fortitude, invariably
regarding the rights of the civil powers thro'
all diſaſters and changes. You have, by the
love and confidence of your fellow citizens,
enabled them to diſplay their martial genius,
and tranſmit their fame to poſterity.

You have perſevered, till theſe United States
aided by a magnanimous King and nation)
have been enabled, under a juſt providence,
to cloſe the war in freedom, ſafety and
independence ; on which happy event we ſin-
cerely join you in congratulations.

Having defended the ſtandard of liberty in
this new world -- having taught a leſſon uſeful to thoſe who inflict, and to thoſe who feel
oppreſſion, you retire from the great theatre
of action with the bleſſings of your fellow
citizens. But the *glory* of your virtues will
not terminate with your military command--
it will continue to animate remoteſt ages.

We feel with you our obligations to the army in general, and will particularly charge
ourſelves with the intereſt of thoſe confidential officers who have attended your perſon to
this affecting moment.

We join with you in commending the in-
tereſts of our deareſt country to the protection
of Almighty God, beſeeching him to diſpoſe
the hearts and minds of its citizens to improve the opportunity afforded them of becoming a happy and reſpectable nation... And
for *You*, we addreſs to *Him* our warmeſt prayers, that a life ſo beloved, may be foſtered
with all his *care*---that your days may be
happy as they have been *illuſtrious*, and that
he will finally give you that reward which
this world cannot give.

Extract from the Minutes,
CHARLES THOMSON, Secretary.

Here we muſt let fall the ſcene---few tragedies ever drew more tears from ſo many
beautiful eyes, as were affected by the moving
manner in which his Excellency took his final
leave of Congreſs. After which he immediately ſet out for Virginia, accompanied to
South river by his Excellency our Governor,
with the warmeſt wiſhes of the city for his
repoſe, health, and happineſs. Long, long
may he enjoy them !

EPILOGUE

By Todd Andrlik

I N 1783, AFTER A BITTER EIGHT-YEAR WAR AGAINST GREAT BRITAIN, AMERICA WON ITS LIBERTY, USH-ering in a new era of hope and optimism. Celebrations were soon tempered by harsh economic realities and the obstacles of a fledgling nation. The world watched with great anticipation.

Among the first major tasks was to create an enduring constitution that enabled a fully functional nation. Under the Articles of Confederation, the first constitution, the Continental Congress had just enough power to fight a war but not enough to run a country. Soaring war debts, coupled with no power to tax, severely depreciated Continental currency and caused colossal inflation.

In the weeks following May 14, 1787, fifty-five delegates convened in the State Hall in Philadelphia for a Federal Convention, presided over by George Washington, to confront the crisis and rewrite a national constitution. Four months later, on September 17, after great debate and compromise among the states, the Convention closed with the introduction of the United States Constitution.

Within weeks, "We the People" was splashed across the pages of newspapers around the globe, including Canada, where the *Quebec Gazette* began publishing the entire Constitution, with French translation, in its November 8, 1787, issue. Through newspaper printings of the Constitution, people learned the construction and powers of the United States's new executive, legislative, and judicial branches of government.

On June 21, 1788, New Hampshire became the ninth and decisive state to ratify the Constitution. Less than a year later, on April 30, 1789, George Washington was sworn in as the first president of the United States. Washington, a leader who Americans trusted to stay true to a constitutional republic, took the oath shortly after noon from the second-floor balcony of Federal Hall in New York City. According to an eyewitness report in the May 6, 1789, *Massachusetts Centinel*:

> At 9 o'clock, all the churches were opened—and the people, in prodigious numbers, thronged these sacred temples—and, with one voice, put up their prayers to Almighty God for the safety of the President. At 12, the procession moved to the Federal State-House, where in the gallery front Broad-Street, in the presence of an immense concourse, his Excellency took the oath, the book being placed on a velvet cushion. The Chancellor then proclaimed him President—and in a moment the air trembled with the shouts of the citizens, and the roar of artillery. His Excellency, with that greatness of soul—that dignity and calmness, which are his characteristicks—then bowed to his 'fellow citizens'—who again huzzaed.

Following the ceremony, Washington stepped into the Senate chamber and delivered the first inaugural address to a joint session of both Houses of Congress, the text of which was also published in the May 6, 1789, *Massachusetts Centinel*.

Nearing the end of two terms as president, Washington knew it was time to resign from public office. With input from James Madison and Alexander Hamilton, Washington penned his thirty-two-page farewell address, declaring he would not seek reelection for a third term.

The sixty-four-year-old Washington never publicly read his farewell address. Instead it was sent directly to newspapers and first published in Philadelphia, then the capital of the United States, on September 19, 1796, in the *American Daily Advertiser*. The milestone address was widely circulated and reprinted in many newspapers, including *The Herald* (New York) on September 21, 1796.

After the Revolutionary War, Washington voluntarily retired as commander in chief of the Continental Army. Now, after two terms as president, Washington was voluntarily retiring from public life again.

Washington used his last public address to impart his wishes, wisdom, and warnings for the fledgling nation. He stressed "unity of government" and "preserving the Union of the whole," cautioning about evident North and South separatism, which escalated and eventually led to the American Civil War. He warned of the effects of political parties and permanent foreign alliances. As a critical source of strength and security, Washington counseled Americans to "cherish public credit. One method of preserving it is, to use it as sparingly as possible."

By the end of 1796, America's republican spirit stretched throughout the colonies and across the globe. America had proved to the world its ability to find great leaders as well as its strength and resolve—militarily, politically, economically, and socially.

Copy of the Result of the Deliberations of the FEDERAL CONVENTION.
In Convention, September 17, 1787.

SIR,

WE have now the honor to submit to the confideration of the United States in Congrefs affembled, that Conftitution which has appeared to us the moft advifeable.

The friends of our country have long feen and defired, that the power of making war, peace and treaties, that of levying money and regulating commerce, and the correfpondent executive and judicial authorities fhould be fully and effectually vefted in the general government of the Union: but the impropriety of delegating fuch extenfive truft to one body of men is evident—Hence refults the neceffity of a different organization.

It is obviously impracticable in the fœderal government of thefe States, to fecure all rights of independent fovereignty to each, and yet provide for the intereft and fafety of all—Individuals entering into fociety, muft give up a fhare of liberty to preferve the reft. The magnitude of the facrifice, muft depend as well on fituation and circumftance, as on the object to be obtained. It is at all times difficult to draw with precifion the line between thofe rights which muft be furrendered, and thofe which may be referved; and on the prefent occafion this difficulty was encreafed by a difference among the feveral States as to their fituation, extent, habits, and particular interefts.

In all our deliberations on this fubject we kept fteadily in our view, that which appears to us the greateft intereft of every true American, the confolidation of our Union, in which is involved our profperity, felicity, fafety, perhaps our national exiftence. This important confideration, ferioufly and deeply impreffed on our minds, led each State in the Convention to be lefs rigid on points of inferior magnitude, than might have been otherwife expected; and thus the Conftitution, which we now prefent, is the refult of a fpirit of amity, and of that mutual deference and conceffion which the peculiarity of our political fituation rendered indifpenfible.

That it will meet the full and entire approbation of every State is not perhaps to be expected; but each will doubtlefs confider, that had her interefts been alone confulted, the confequences might have been particularly difagreeable or injurious to others; that it is liable to as few exceptions as could reasonably have been expected, we hope and believe; that it may promote the lafting welfare of that country fo dear to us all, and fecure her freedom and happinefs, is our moft ardent wifh.

With great refpect, we have the honor to be,
SIR,
Your Excellency's moft obedient and humble fervants,
GEORGE WASHINGTON, Prefident.

By unanimous Order of the Convention.

HIS EXCELLENCY
The Prefident of Congrefs.

WE the People of the United States, *in order to form a more perfect Union, eftablifh Juftice, infure domeftic Tranquility, provide for the common Defence, promote the general Welfare, and fecure the Bleffings of Liberty to ourfelves and our Pofterity, do ordain and eftablifh this* CONSTITUTION *for the United States of America.*

ARTICLE I.

Sect. 1. ALL legiflative powers herein granted fhall be vefted in a Congrefs of the United States, which fhall confift of a Senate and Houfe of Reprefentatives.

Sect. 2. The Houfe of Reprefentatives fhall be compofed of members chofen every fecond year by the people of the feveral ftates, and the electors in each ftate fhall have the qualifications requifite for electors of the moft numerous branch of the ftate legiflature.

No perfon fhall be a reprefentative who fhall not have attained to th[e] age of twenty-five years, and been feven years a citizen of the U[nited] States, and who fhall not, when elected, be an inhabitant of that ft[ate] which he fhall be chofen.

Reprefentatives and direct taxes fhall be apportioned among the f[everal] ftates which may be included within this Union, according to their [re]fpective numbers, which fhall be determined by adding to the whole [num]ber of free perfons, including thofe bound to fervice for a term of [years,] and excluding Indians not taxed, three-fifths of all other perfons. [The] actual enumeration fhall be made within three years after the firft me[eting] of the Congrefs of the United States, and within every fubfequen[t term] of ten years, in fuch manner as they fhall by law direct. The nu[mber] of reprefentatives fhall not exceed one for every thirty thoufand, bu[t each] ftate fhall have at leaft one reprefentative; and until fuch enume[ration] fhall be made, the ftate of New-Hampfhire fhall be entitled to chufe [three,] Maffachufetts eight, Rhode-Ifland and Providence Plantations one, [Con]necticut five, New-York fix, New-Jerfey four, Pennfylvania eight, [De]laware one, Maryland fix, Virginia ten, North-Carolina five, S[outh-] Carolina five, and Georgia three.

When vacancies happen in the reprefentation from any ftate, the E[x]ecutive authority thereof fhall iffue writs of election to fill fuch vacancies.

[...]enators from each ftate, chofen by the legiflature thereof, for fix years; and each fenator fhall have one vote.

Immediately after they fhall be affembled in confequence of the firft election, they fhall be divided as equally as may be into three claffes. The [...]

Copie du Réfultat des délibérations de la CONVENTION FEDERALE.
En Convention, 17 Septembre, 1787.

MONSIEUR,

NOUS avons actuellement l'honneur de foumettre à la confidération des Etats Unis affemblés en congrès, la conftitution qui nous a paru la plus convenable.

Les amis de notre Païs ont longtems vu et defiré, que le pouvoir de faire la guerre, la paix et les traités, celui de lever l'argent et de régler le commerce, ainfi que les autorités exécutives et judiciaires correfpondantes foient pleinement et effectivement confiés au Gouvernement général de l'Union: mais l'impropriété de déléguer un pouvoir fi étendu à un tel corps eft évidente. De là réfulte la néceffité d'une organifation differente.

Il eft évidemment impraticable dans le Gouvernement fédérale de ces Etats, d'affurer tous les droits d'une fouveraineté indépendante à chacun en pourvoyant en même tems aux intérêts et à la fureté de tous. Lorfque les hommes entrent en fociété il leur faut facrifier une partie de leur liberté pour conferver le refte—la grandeur de ce facrifice doit dépendre autant de la fituation et des circonftances que l'objet qu'on veut obtenir. Il eft toujours difficile de féparer avec précifion les droits qu'on doit abandonner de ceux qu'on peut réferver—mais dans l'occurence préfente cette difficulté fe trouve plus grande par la différence qu'il y a entre les Etats relativement à leur fituation, étendue, coutumes et intérêts particuliers,

Nous avons eu conftamment en vue dans toutes nos délibérations fur cet objet, ce qui nous paroit être le plus grand intérêt de chaque véritable Amériquain, la confolidation de notre Union, d'où dépend notre profpérité, félicité, fureté, et peut-être notre exiftence nationale. Cette importante confidération, férieufement et profondement imprimée dans nos efprits, a induit chaque Etat de la convention à être moins rigide relativement à des points moins importans, qu'on eut pû autrement l'efperer. Ainfi la conftitution que nous préfentons maintenant eft le refultat d'un efprit d'amitié, et de cette deférence et conceffion mutuelles, que la particularité de notre fituation politique a rendu indifpenfable.

On ne doit peut-être pas efperer qu'elle fera entierement approuvée de tous les Etats; mais fans doute chacun d'eux confiderera, que fi on n'eut confulté que fon intérêt particulier, les conféquences auroient été particuliérement défagréables ou préjudiciables à d'autres. Nous efperons et croyons qu'elle eft fujette à auffi peu d'exception qu'on peut raifonnablement l'efperer. Quelle puiffe contribuer au bien-être durable de ce païs, fi cher à nous tous, et affurer fa liberté et fa félicité, eft notre vœu très fincère.

Nous avons l'honneur d'être, avec beaucoup de refpect,
MONSIEUR,
de votre Excellence, les très humbles et obéiffants ferviteurs
GEORGE WASHINGTON, Préfident.

Par ordre unanime de la Convention.

SON EXCELLENCE
Le Préfident du Congrès.

Nous, *les peuples des Etats Unis, afin de former une union plus parfaite, établir la juftice, affurer la tranquilité domeftique, pourvoir à la défenfe commune, promouvoir le bien-être général et affurer les avantages de la liberté à nous et à notre pofterité, ordonnons et établiffons la préfente Conftitution pour les Etats Unis d'Amérique.*

ARTICLE I.

Sec. 1. TOUS pouvoirs légiflatifs par le préfent accordés feront commis à un Congrès des Etats Unis, qui fera compofé d'un Sénat et chambre de Répréfentans.

Sec 2. La Chambre des Répréfentans fera compofée de membres choifis tous les deux ans par les peuples des divers états; et les electeurs de chaque état auront les qualifications requifes pour électeurs de la branche [...]

Lorfqu'il arrivera des vacances dans la Réprésentation de quelque état, l'autorité exécutive d'icelle émanera des *writs* ou ordres d'élection [...]

[...] Le Sénat des Etats Unis fera compofé de deux fénateurs de chaque état, choifis par la légiflature d'icelui, pour fix ans, et chaque fénateur aura une voix.
Immédiatement après qu'ils feront affemblés en conféquence de la pre[...]

QUEBEC GAZETTE
November 8, 1787

Soon after the Constitutional Convention closed on September 17, "We the People" was splashed across the pages of newspapers around the globe, including Canada, where the *Quebec Gazette* began publishing the entire U.S. Constitution, with French translation, in its November 8, 1787, issue.

BOSTON, WEDNESDAY, MAY 6, 1789.
RECEIVED YESTERDAY AT NOON.

PROVIDENCE, MAY 4, 1789.

MR. RUSSELL,

A person leaving this place for Boston in the morning, I enclose a New-York paper containing the President's Speech, &c.—I shall be happy if it should give you the latest intelligence from that quarter. I am, your humble servant, CHARLES BULFINCH.

NEW-YORK, MAY 1.

YESTERDAY the great and illustrious WASHINGTON, the favourite son of liberty, and deliverer of his country, entered upon the execution of the office of First Magistrate of the United States of America; to which important station he had been unanimously called by the united voice of the people. The ceremony which took place on this occasion was truly grand and pleasing, and every heart seemed anxious to testify the joy it felt on so memorable an event. His Excellency was escorted from his house, by a troop of Light Dragoons, and the Legion under the command of Col. Lewis, attended by a Committee of the Senate, and House of Representatives, to Federal Hall, where he was formally received by both Houses of Congress, assembled in the Senate Chamber; after which he was conducted to the gallery in front of the Hall, accompanied by all the Members, when the oath preferibed by the Constitution was administered to him by the Chancellor of this State, who then said:

"*Long live* GEORGE WASHINGTON, President of the United States;" which was answered by an immense concourse of Citizens, assembled on the occasion, by the loudest plaudit and acclamation, that love and veneration ever inspired. His Excellency then made a speech to both Houses, and then proceeded, attended by Congress, to St. Paul's Church, where Divine Service was performed by the Right Rev. SAMUEL PREVOST, after which his Excellency was conducted in form to his own house. In the evening a most magnificent and brilliant display of Fire-Works was exhibited at the Fort, under the direction of Col. BEUMAN. The houses of the French and Spanish Ministers were illuminated in a superb and elegant manner; a number of beautiful transparent paintings were exhibited, which did infinite credit to the parties concerned in the design and execution.

His Excellency's Speech to both Houses of Congress.

FELLOW-CITIZENS OF THE SENATE,

AND OF THE HOUSE OF REPRESENTATIVES,

AMONG the vicissitudes incident to life, no event could have filled me with greater anxieties than that of which the notification was transmitted by your order, and received on the 14th day of the present month.—On the one hand, I was summoned by my country, whose voice I can never hear but with veneration and love, from a retreat which I had chosen with the fondest predilection, and, in my flattering hopes, with an immutable decision as the asylum of my declining years:—A retreat which was rendered every day more necessary as well as more dear to me, by the addition of habit to inclination, and of frequent interruptions in my health to the gradual waste committed on it by time. On the other hand, the magnitude and difficulty of the trust to which the voice of my country called me, being sufficient to awaken in the wisest and most experienced of her citizens, a distrustful scrutiny into his qualifications, could not but overwhelm with despondence, one, who

providential agency. And in the system of revolution just accomplished in the system of their United Government, the tranquil deliberations and voluntary consent of so many distinct communities, from which the event has resulted, cannot be compared with the means by which most governments have been established, without some return of pious gratitude along with an humble anticipation of the future blessings which the past seem to presage. These reflections, arising out of the present crisis, have forced themselves too strongly on my mind to be suppressed. You will join with me I trust in thinking, that there are none under the influence of which, the proceedings of a new and free government can more auspiciously commence.

By the article establishing the Executive Department, it is made the duty of the President " to recommend to your consideration, such measures as he shall judge necessary and expedient." The circumstances under which I now meet you, will acquit me from entering into that subject farther than to refer to the Great Constitutional Charter under which we are assembled; and which, in defining your powers, designates the objects to which your attention is to be given. It will be more consistent with those circumstances, and far more congenial with the feelings which actuate me, to substitute in place of a recommendation of particular measures, the tribute that is due to the talents—the rectitude, and the patriotism which adorn the characters selected to devise and adopt them. In these honourable qualifications, I behold the surest pledges, that as on one side, no local prejudices or attachments—no separate views nor party animosities, will misdirect the comprehensive and equal eye which ought to watch over this great assemblage of communities and interests: so, on another, that the foundations of our national policy will be laid in the pure and immutable principles of private morality; and the pre-eminence of a free government be exemplified by all the attributes which can win the affections of its citizens, and command the respect of the world.

I dwell on this prospect with every satisfaction which an ardent love for my country can inspire: since there is no truth more thoroughly established, than that there exists in the economy and course of nature, an indissoluble union between virtue and happiness—between duty and advantage—between the genuine maxims of an honest and magnanimous policy, and the solid rewards of publick prosperity and felicity. Since we ought to be no less persuaded that the propitious smiles of Heaven can never be expected on a nation that disregards the eternal rules of order and right, which Heaven itself has ordained.— And since the preservation of the sacred fire of liberty, and the destiny of the republican model of government, are justly considered as *deeply* perhaps as *finally* staked, on the experiment intrusted to the hands of the American people.

Besides the ordinary objects submitted to your care, it will remain with your judgment to decide how far an exercise of the occasional power delegated by the Fifth Article of the Constitution is rendered expedient at the present juncture by the nature of objections which have been urged ... the degree of inquietude ... them. Instead of ... ommendations on this ... be guided by no lights ... ortunities, I shall again ... fidence in your discern ... ublick good: For I as ... u carefully avoid every ... ndanger the benefits of ... government, or which ... lessons of experience; ... cteristick rights of free ... publick harmony, will ... ur deliberations on the ... rmer can be more im ... latter be safely and ad ...

observations I have one to add, which will be most properly addressed to the House of Representatives. It concerns my ...

supplication, that since he was ... favour the American people with opportunities for deliberating in perfect tranquility, and dispositions for deciding with unparalleled unanimity on a form of government to the security of their Union, and the advancement of their happiness; so his divine blessing may be equally conspicuous in the enlarged views—the temperate consultations—and the wise measures on which the success of this government must depend.

George Washington.

FROM NEW-YORK.

APRIL 30. We have had this day one of those impressive sights which dignify and adorn human nature. At 9 o'clock, all the churches were opened—and the people, in prodigious numbers, thronged these sacred temples—and, with one voice, put up their prayers to Almighty God for the safety of the President.

At 12 the procession moved to the Federal State-House, where in the gallery fronting Broad-Street, in the presence of an immense concourse, his Excellency took the oath, the book being placed on a velvet cushion. The Chancellor then proclaimed him President—and in a moment the air trembled with the shouts of the citizens, and the roar of artillery. His Excellency, with that greatness of soul—that dignity and calmness, which are his characteristicks—then bowed to his " fellow-citizens"—who again huzzaed.

☞ *In having it in our power—through the goodness of our correspondents—to announce thus early the Speech of our beloved President—the congratulatory addresses of the Pennsylvanians, and the answers thereto—as well as the pathetick and elegant valedictory address of the Alexandrians—with its equally pathetick and elegant answer—we feel a felicity which can only be equalled by that which must animate our readers on perusing what we present this day.*

SHIP NEWS.

Capt. Gaze arrived here yesterday from N. Carolina—The 29th ult. in lat. 39. long. 71 30. spoke the Brig ——, Capt. Killim, from Newbury-Port, bound to Philadelphia—out 20 days—who informed, that he had sprung his foremast and maintopmast—and had continual gales of wind most of his passage.

NAVAL-OFFICE, Entered since our last, from
schooner 2-Friends, Knights, St. Thomas
Schooner Harmony, Phinney, N. Carolina
Sloop Nancy, McElroy, Demarara

CLEARED, for
Brig Lisbon-Packet, Rob. Lisbon
Brig Dædalus, Crocker, Baltimore
Sloop Betsy, Stetson, Virginia
Sloop Phœnix, Loring, Philadelphia
Sloop Friendship, Stetson, Philadelphia

On TUESDAY next, 13th inst.
Will be sold by PUBLICK VENDUE, as she now lays at WOODWARD's wharf,

THE Brigantine HANNAH, with all her appurtenances as she lately came from sea, burthen about 150 tons, more or less, a very fast sailer, and well calculated for the Whaling Fishery, Straights or any other trade, and may be sent to sea, with a very little expense.

For Inventory, condition of Sale, &c. apply to LEWIS HAYT, State-Street. The sale will be on board precisely at half-past VII.

COTTON WOOL.

A Quantity of excellent COTTON, just imported in the Ship FRIENDSHIP, Capt. ROBERTS, from India, to be sold cheap, at

John Codman, jun's Store,
South side of the TOWN-DOCK.

At the same place may be had, A few sets of very handsome Tea China, at 48s. per set. May 6, 1789.

APPLETON PRENTISS

INFORMS his friends and customers, that he has REMOVED from Shop, No. 28, CORNHILL, to No. 21, MARLBOROUGH-STREET; Where may be had,

SATURDAY, SEPTEMBER 17.

The opposition papers, for such there must be under the *best government on earth*, begin to vent their spleen against John Adams, Vice President of the United States, with a view to influence the election of President. The Aurora attacks him, as a friend of ranks and *hereditary distinctions!* This calumny is grown *stale*; but as it is the most effectual weapon to be wielded against that old patriot—*the very man* that *planned* our Independence, long before the battle of Lexington, we expect that those papers will continue to dwell on that point, till the election is decided.

The truth is, Mr. Adams is so great an enemy to *orders and hereditary distinctions*, that he spent years in writing his "Defence of the American Constitutions," on purpose to persuade the Americans so to organize their government as forever to prevent such distinctions and guard against all aristocratical influence.

To accomplish this point, Mr. Adams begins with a fact that cannot be denied, viz. that there in every human society such a thing as a *Natural Aristocracy*, that is, *men of wealth, education*, and *a set of parents who have been any way distinguished*, will pride themselves on these advantages, and claim a kind of superiority over their fellow citizens. On the other hand, the people are naturally inclined to pay to such men *more respect*, than to those who have no such advantages. This is so obvious a thing, that every man feels it—he knows it—he *feels it to be true.*

Now, says Mr. Adams, these men who have such advantages, will always be making use of them to extend their power and influence, and will work themselves into places of trust and profit. The business of the framers of a free Constitution, is to *balance* the different branches, as to check such men, and guard the state from any undue influence of theirs.

In short, the whole tenor of Mr. Adams Defence, is, to inculcate the danger of *aristocracy* and *Slave*; to show from what principles of human nature and society, these scourges of freedom, originally proceed; to illustrate his doctrines by facts and examples drawn from history; and to point at the barriers which ought to be erected in a republican government, to *guard against aristocracy* and *faction*. He is in truth, the most decided foe to aristocracy that this country ever produced. . . .

Mr. Adams is a friend to a strong and Independent Executive Power. On this subject many good men differ. But it remains to be proved, that his ideas on this point go *too far.* . . .

The French have imposed on the city of Frankfort a contribution of 37 millions of florins; about six millions and a half sterling.

Accounts from Genoa state that the French government has demanded of the Genoese government to shut all their ports against all English ships of war and merchantmen. It is added the demand is made of Spain, and that the court seemed disposed to comply.

Genoa is a *neutral* State. We may expect the French, in the career of her conquests, may find it convenient to make the same demand of the United States.]

The abject condition of the states of Italy not only the fiefs of the emperor, but the neutral states, and even the allies of France, under the insolent conduct of Buonaparte, is indeed deplorable. Not only laid under contribution, as usual by laws of war, but robbed of those elegant monuments of the fine arts, which are the pride and boast of the country. This despotic exercise of power will go farther than any thing, perhaps, in exciting resentment in the Italians; as it is taking from them what is peculiarly their *own*; the fruits of their *own genius*; and these elegant attractions which lead men of taste from all the world, visit Italy.

20th August, which after mentioning the affair of Captain Jessop, his cruel treatment by Captain Pigot, &c. which have already been fully detailed in this Gazette, goes on to state—that "all at once the proceedings against Pigot were stopped, and report says, that "*the Root of all evil*" softened all the stripes and healed Jessop's beaten back—800 glittering golden guineas said to be the cure. We hope on his arrival in America, he will be able to shew that he is not that despicable wretch we here take him to be."

It is said, that Lieut. Cudwith was lately killed in a duel by Lieut. Geddes, at West-Point.

In the letter from Favarat, French commissioner, giving an account to the Directory of the surrender of the rebels in Morbihan, published in the Minerva of Tuesday, the last paragraph deserves particular remark.

"These deluded men do not dissemble, that it was the *atrocities of government which armed them against the Republic; and that a wise and paternal government has induced them to return to its bosom.*"

This is precisely conformable to the opinions repeatedly published in this paper, "That the opposition made to the establishment of a republic in France, proceeded very much from the sanguinary measures of the government under the domination of the clubs. The severe despotism of Robespierre, and his jacobin agents, has been the principal cause of the factions, massacres and civil war that have distressed that nation. Since that party has been subdued, and kept under the law; since a division of the legislature has placed that body out of the reach of demagogues and intriguers, *government has assumed a milder aspect*—life and property are respected, and the *rebels return to their allegiance and duty.* Such facts as these are a volume of instruction, not only to the French, but to the Americans, who have been in eminent hazard from *private associations of men of the same sanguinary temper*, as those who deluged France with blood.

A member of one of the clubs lately declared in the presence of witnesses, that "he wished the motion made in the Convention of France two or three years ago, to form a band of two thousand assassins, and dispatch them to massacre the kings of Europe, had prevailed and been carried into effect. He thought it would be an act of *humanity*, to murder all those tyrants."

This is exactly the temper of a violent jacobin or democrat. It is precisely, in politics, what the *history of religious fanatics, Popes, Cardinals, and Priests* has been in religion. The *same* spirit, with a *different* education, would preside with zeal in a court of inquisition and burn heretics at the stake.

It is a remark of Condorcet, in his elegant book, on the "Progress of the Human Mind," that the Monks, under the Papal Hierarchy, were so many armies of the Roman Pontiff, spread over Europe, to aid the cause of his despotism. An excellent remark.

Popular societies or clubs, formed for political purposes, and affiliated to a mother club, answer the same purposes in Government, as the monasteries did in religion. They are the *monks of civil society*; scattered thro a country, and corresponding, they form so many different corps of partizans, ready on a call from their chief, to second all his projects, good or bad. The papal power was augmented principally and a long time supported, by these *cloistered* instruments of superstition and sacerdotal tyranny.

The enormous power of the Jesuits, was originally erected and maintained in the same manner, by *detached corps* of their order, established in different countries, but subject to *one head*, acting in close concert! By these simple means, that society had raised a despotism that became formidable to Europe; government took the alarm, and suppressed them, as it had Popular Societies in France, and for similar reasons.

Resignation of the President.

To the PEOPLE of the UNITED STATES:

FRIENDS AND FELLOW-CITIZENS;

THE period for a new election of a Citizen, to administer the executive government of the United States, being not far distant, and the time actually arrived, when your thoughts must be employed in designating the person, who is to be clothed with that important trust, it appears to me proper, especially as it may conduce to a more distinct expression of the public voice, that I should now apprise you of the resolution I have formed, to decline being considered among the number of those, out of whom a choice is to be made.

I beg you, at the same time, to do me the justice to be assured, that this resolution has not been taken, without a strict regard to all the considerations appertaining to the relation, which binds a dutiful citizen to his country; and that, in withdrawing the tender of service which silence in my situation might imply, I am influenced by no diminution of zeal for your future interest; no deficiency of grateful respect for your past kindness; but am supported by a full conviction that the step is compatible with both.

The acceptance of, and continuance hitherto in the office to which your suffrages have twice called me, have been a uniform sacrifice of inclination to the opinion of duty, and to a deference for what appeared to be your desire. I constantly hoped, that it would have been much earlier in my power, consistently with motives, which I was not at liberty to disregard, to return to that retirement, from whence I had been reluctantly drawn. The strength of my inclination to do this, previous to the last election, had even led to the preparation of an address to declare it to you; but mature reflection on the then perplexed and critical posture of our affairs with foreign nations, and the unanimous advice of persons entitled to my confidence, impelled me to abandon the idea.

I rejoice, that the state of your concerns, external as well as internal, no longer renders the pursuit of inclination incompatible with the sentiment of duty, or propriety; and am persuaded whatever partiality may be retained for my services, that in the present circumstances of our country, you will not disapprove my determination to retire.

The impressions with which I first undertook the arduous trust, were explained on the proper occasion. In the discharge of this trust, I will only say, that I have with good intentions, contributed towards the organization and administration of the government, the best exertions of which a very fallible judgment was capable. Not unconscious in the outset, of the inferiority of my qualifications, experience in my own eyes, perhaps still more in the eyes of others, has strengthened the motives to diffidence of myself; and every day the increasing weight of years admonishes me more and more, that the shade of retirement is as necessary to me as it will be welcome. Satisfied that if any circumstances have given peculiar value to my services, they were temporary, I have the consolation to believe, that while choice and prudence invite me to quit the political scene, patriotism does not forbid it.

In looking forward to the moment, which is intended to terminate the career of my public life, my feelings do not permit me to suspend the deep acknowledgment of that debt of gratitude, which I owe to my beloved country, for the many honors it has conferred upon me; still more for the steadfast confidence with which it has supported me; and for the opportunities I have thence enjoyed of manifesting my inviolable attachment, by services faithful and persevering, though in usefulness unequal to my zeal.

---

and which appear to me all important to the permanency of your felicity as a people. These will be offered to you with the more freedom, as you can only see in them the disinterested warnings of a parting friend, who can possibly have no personal motive to bias his counsel. Nor can I forget, as an encouragement to it, your indulgent reception of my sentiments on a former and not dissimilar occasion.

Interwoven as is the love of liberty with every ligament of your hearts, no recommendation of mine is necessary to fortify or confirm the attachment.

The unity of government which constitutes you one people, is also now dear to you. It is justly so; for it is a main pillar in the edifice of your real independence, the support of your tranquility at home, your peace abroad; of your safety; of your prosperity; of that very liberty which you so highly prize. But as it is easy to foresee, that from different causes and from different quarters, much pains will be taken, many artifices employed, to weaken in your minds the conviction of this truth; as this is the point in your political fortress against which the batteries of internal and external enemies will be most constantly and actively (though often covertly and insidiously) directed, it is of infinite moment, that you should properly estimate the immense value of your national Union, to your collective and individual happiness; that you should cherish a cordial, habitual, and immovable attachment to it; accustoming yourselves to think and speak of it as of the Palladium of your political safety and prosperity; watching for its preservation with jealous anxiety; discountenancing whatever may suggest even a suspicion that it can in any event be abandoned; and indignantly frowning upon the first dawning of every attempt to alienate any portion of our country from the rest, or to enfeeble the sacred ties which now link together the various parts.

For this you have every inducement of sympathy and interest. Citizens by birth or choice, of a common country, that country has a right to concentrate your affections. The name of AMERICAN, which belongs to you, in your national capacity, must always exalt the just pride of Patriotism, more than any appellation derived from local discriminations. With slight shades of difference, you have the same religion, manners, habits and political principles. You have in a common cause fought and triumphed together; the Independence and Liberty you possess are the work of joint councils, and joint efforts, of common dangers, sufferings and successes.

But these considerations, however powerfully they address themselves to your sensibility, are greatly outweighed by those which apply more immediately to your interest. Here every portion of our country finds the most commanding motives for carefully guarding and preserving the union of the whole.

The North, in an unrestrained intercourse with the South, protected by the equal laws of a common government, finds in the productions of the latter, great additional resources of maritime and commercial enterprise and precious materials of manufacturing industry. The South in the same intercourse, benefiting by the agency of the North, sees its agriculture grow and its commerce expand. . . . . The East, in a like intercourse with the West, already finds, and in the progressive improvement of interior communications, by land and water, will more and more find a valuable vent for the commodities which it brings from abroad, or manufactures at home.—The West derives from the East supplies requisite to its growth. . . .

THE HERALD (NEW YORK CITY)
September 21, 1796

Nearing the end of two terms as president, Washington knew it was time to resign from public office. With input from James Madison and Alexander Hamilton, Washington penned his 32-page farewell address, declaring he would not seek reelection for a third term. The sixty-four-year-old Washington never publicly read his farewell address. Instead it was sent directly to newspapers.

We have this day, by great exertion, presented our readers with the President's Address to the People of the United States, on declining . . .

tempting to raise the reputation of France on the ruins of genius in a neighboring country. What would Buonaparte himself were a stranger to visit the French . . .

tive example in our annals, that under circumstances in which the passions, agitated in every direction, were liable to mislead, amidst appearances sometimes dubious.—

outlets for its own productions to the weight, influence, and the future maritime strength of the Atlantic side of the union, directed by an indissoluble community of interest as . . .

REVOLUTIONARY PRESS IMPACT

By Carol Sue Humphrey

NEWSPAPERS WERE ABSOLUTELY ESSENTIAL FOR AMERICANS IN THEIR STRUGGLE FOR INDEPEN-dence. Before the fighting started in 1775, newspapers provided information about the arguments with Great Britain and the various protests related to those arguments. During the years of fighting, the press provided news about the war itself, but the press also encouraged the people to support the war effort. Thus, newspapers became the primary morale boosters throughout the Revolutionary War. Printers such as Benjamin Edes and Isaiah Thomas used many means to lift public confidence in the drive for independence. Essays and news stories emphasized the tyranny of the British and the righteousness of the Americans. Patriot newspa-pers sought to destroy any remaining colonial ties to Great Britain as well as point out American successes and future prospects. Printers filled their productions with material on the justness of the American cause and the success of the Continental Army in battle. Newspapers continually worked to increase public resolve by urging readers to put the war above all other concerns.

Printers personally suffered because of the fighting in the Revolution. Many faced problems because of the activities of the armies. Several printers had to move their offices in the face of the approach of the enemy—Isaiah Thomas moved his printing press from Boston to Worcester fol-lowing the Battle of Lexington and Concord. But other printers moved their operation to better serve the public. For example, Samuel Hall moved around to accommodate the government of Massachusetts. He had founded the *Essex Gazette* in Salem in 1768, and he moved to Cambridge in 1775 to better serve the state convention and the army. He then moved to Boston after the British left in 1776.

The press played an important role during the Revolution by keeping Americans engaged in the war even when the fighting occurred far away. Some writers used the newspapers to stir up people's passions against Britain, but the press served primarily to keep Americans informed about the progress of the fight for independence. Americans did gain some information from per-sonal letters, broadsides, and pamphlets, but none of these media circulated as widely as news-papers. From the moment that the colonials received word of Britain's new taxes in 1764 until news of the peace treaty arrived in 1783, newspapers constituted the primary source of informa-tion about the conflict with the mother country. Without the press, many Americans would have known practically nothing about what was happening and could have lost their interest in the outcome of the war. For example, large-scale fighting ended in New England when the British army withdrew from Boston in March 1776. The public remained interested in what was going on in the war with Great Britain for a number of reasons, but constant discussion of battles in the newspapers constituted the major reason for many people. Newspaper printers included as much information about the fighting as they could get. Knowledge produces involvement, and Patriot printers worked hard to make sure that a loss of interest in the Revolution did not occur among the readers of their newspapers.

Patriot newspaper printers also sought to keep people encouraged about how the Revolution was progressing. Thus, they often put a positive spin on reports they published. Military victories and successes were extolled and expanded while defeats and setbacks were downplayed and minimized. For example, printers lavishly praised George Washington and the Continental Army for the relatively small victory at Trenton, New Jersey, in December 1776 while passing off the loss of a five-thousand-man army at Charleston, South Carolina, in May 1780 as a minor setback that would quickly be overcome. Through the use of such reporting techniques, newspaper printers helped to boost morale and keep people engaged in the war.

Newspapers have been a major source of information for Americans for a long time. This proved true for the first time during the American Revolution. There is little doubt that newspapers played an important role during the war. When people wanted information about how the war was going elsewhere, they turned to their local newspaper. Thus, these weekly news-sheets constituted the primary sources of news about the conflict. Their reports were not always accurate, but printers hoped they would boost morale by helping to maintain interest in, and support for, the war effort. By publishing accounts from throughout the colonies, newspapers helped foster a sense of unity and solidarity of purpose that was essential if Americans were going to win their fight for independence.

Contemporaries on both sides believed that the newspapers played an essential role in the war. For example, in 1776, Loyalist Ambrose Serle reported on the potential impact of the press in a letter to Lord Dartmouth: "Among other Engines, which have raised the present Commotion next to the indecent Harangues of the Preachers, none has had a more extensive or stronger Influence than the Newspapers of the respective Colonies. One is astonished to see with what Avidity they are sought after, and how implicitly they are believed, by the great Bulk of the People… Government may find it expedient, in the Sum of things, to employ this popular Engine." And in a 1782 letter to Richard Price, Benjamin Franklin commented on the role of the newspapers during the Revolution: "The ancient Roman and Greek orators could only speak to the number of citizens capable of being assembled within the reach of their voice. Their *writings* had little effect, because the bulk of the people could not read. Now by the press we can speak to nations; and good books and well written pamphlets have great and general influence. The facility, with which the same truths may be repeatedly enforced by placing them daily in different lights in *newspapers,* which are everywhere read, gives a great chance of establishing them. And we now find, that it is not only right to strike while the iron is hot, but that it may be very practicable to heat it by continually striking."

Most Americans concluded that the efforts of Patriot newspaper printers to keep readers informed about the war helped ensure ultimate success by boosting people's morale and rallying Americans to the cause until victory was achieved. By keeping people informed about the war's progress, newspapers made winning independence possible. Newspapers were essential in the fight to win independence and thus were essential in the creation of the United States.

THE VALUE OF PRIMARY SOURCES

By Michelle A. Larson

IT SHOULD BE NO SURPRISE THAT AMERICAN HISTORY BOOKS GLORIFY THE REVOLUTION. WE BELIEVE so strongly in the ideals of that Revolutionary spirit that we allow our textbooks to ignore the complexities that led to the hotly debated decision to declare our independence and the difficult and protracted war that arose afterward. Our education distills nearly twenty years of history down to a handful of momentous events and famous names but glosses over the process by which the colonies shared information and galvanized the population.

While there are many important events in history to cover, no other period is more critical to understanding ourselves as Americans. It is the birth of everything we believe as a nation. While history books credit Thomas Paine and Thomas Jefferson as the major voices of Revolutionary thought, their contributions came about after years of debate. Hundreds of writers had already contributed to the argument. It was the newspapers that provided the platform for that debate and generated the fervor necessary to ignite and sustain the flame of independence where Paine and Jefferson would eventually flourish.

As a teacher, I can't help but encourage the analysis of these valuable primary source documents. Not only do they provide us with a way to help students understand the deeper issues that affected the time, but they also provide us with a way to develop the skills these students need to critically evaluate modern issues.

One of the biggest reasons to read these newspapers is to understand more deeply the issues that the Revolutionaries faced. Since many of the papers included in this volume originate on both sides of the Atlantic, it is possible to evaluate the wide variety of viewpoints as a class. For example, as Americans were resisting attempts to be taxed without representation, members of Parliament disagreed over how to deal with the "childish" Americans. The *New-Hampshire Gazette* of April 14, 1775, published a speech of Lord Chatham arguing for a more reasoned approach but follows it up with a summary from London of the various dissenting attitudes.

Another valuable purpose is to add a dose of reality to our views of the time. The Patriots were not always the "good guys," and their zeal was rife with irony. Several papers in 1765–66 and 1774–75, for example, gleefully describe mobs converging on Loyalists and compelling them to resign their posts or issue apologies for their point of view—not exactly the hallmark of a society that values free speech. Rousing diatribes against colonists serving as slaves to Britain ran side by side with advertisements offering rewards for escaped slaves and indentured servants.

These newspapers also help us to see historical figures as people. Letters in the November 29, 1774, *Essex Gazette* show that General Gage had no real desire to serve as a commander against

America. Benedict Arnold's letter to the Americans in the *London Chronicle* (November 14, 1780) expresses his disillusionment of the goals of the American resistance, but also belies a certain pettiness. Furthermore, the letters exchanged in regards to his captured British accomplice, Major André, show that Washington respected André despite his decision to have him executed as a spy.

There are also many parallels between the American Revolution and the conflicts occurring in our world today. Discussing these issues together can help students gain a greater understanding of media bias. After all, we teach history from an American perspective, so we talk of "revolutionaries," while the British referred to "rebels" and "rabble-rousers." Militias didn't stand much of a chance at fighting the British soldiers in straight lines on formal battlefields, so they shot at the enemy from hidden vantage points. The British considered this barbaric. Taught in concert with a discussion about the "Arab Spring" or the war on terror, for example, we open up a dialogue in which students may begin to look more closely at all sides of modern conflict as well.

As an English teacher, I can't overlook the value of using these articles to discuss literary analysis and writing skills. The *New-Hampshire Gazette* of February 17, 1775, provides a treasure trove of well-constructed arguments and scathing sarcasm. The *Massachusetts Gazette; and the Boston Post-Boy* of January 2, 1775, published a letter by Massachutensis, which argues against the actions of the Americans in response to the British duties on tea. His letter alone provides enough literary devices, formal arguments, and satirical wit to keep a class digging for weeks.

I am also fascinated with the evolution of the printed language in these papers. At the beginning of the Revolution, the language in American papers referring to the King—and Britain in general—is practically dripping with sweetness. This continues until the eve of war. However, in mid-1775, they are referred to as a "crew of enemies to the English constitution." Early papers made veiled attempts to "protect" the identities of those whom they were criticizing by replacing some or nearly all of a person's name with dashes. But as tensions flared, the dashes slowly disappeared and by beginning of the war had vanished almost completely, leaving readers with no doubt as to the target of criticism. Last, early newspapers show inconsistencies in spelling, punctuation, and capitalization, which become almost completely standardized by the end of the Revolutionary period.

As a high school English teacher, I've had my nose in textbooks practically my entire life, so I can say unequivocally that these newspapers are far more interesting reading than anything I have seen in a textbook. They give a glimpse into the daily life, dreams, and desires of the people who gave birth to this nation. Textbooks sanitize and summarize all the juicy bits out of history. Reading a few primary source documents just might reconstitute it!

CONTRIBUTORS

Todd Andrlik

Todd Andrlik is the primary architect of *Reporting the Revolutionary War*. In addition to providing the initial vision for the project, Andrlik authored several sections of the book, recruited more than three dozen contributors, directed more than sixty essays, produced supplemental video, and conceived many of the project's print and digital components. Among America's leading Revolutionary War newspaper archivists, Andrlik built one of the most significant collections of American Revolution newspapers, containing the earliest printed reports of practically every major event and battle from 1763 through 1783. This once-private archive is now publicly exhibited in *Reporting the Revolutionary War*.

Andrlik is curator and publisher of RagLinen.com, an online museum of historically significant newspapers dating back to the sixteenth century. Collaborating with individuals and institutions, including the Library of Congress, Andrlik helps others build private and public collections of these treasured relics. Beyond the acquisition, research, and digital preservation of early newspapers, Andrlik also takes an active role in their physical conservation. Through a partnership with one of the world's top paper conservators, Andrlik helps save damaged newspapers from loss and restores the artifacts as close as possible to original condition.

His passion for newspaper history stems from a career in media and marketing. Andrlik heads the marketing and media operations for Leopardo Companies, one of the nation's largest construction, design-build, and commercial real estate development firms. Andrlik has written or ghost-written thousands of published articles and, as a social media pioneer, created the *Advertising Age* Power 150, a global ranking of the top marketing and media blogs. It was after Andrlik's success in new media that he made a 180-degree turn and focused his attention on old media.

Andrlik earned a bachelor's degree in public relations from Illinois State University and an MBA from Roosevelt University. He studied international business at Salzburg College, Austria. Andrlik serves on the advisory board of the Printing Office of Edes & Gill, the only colonial-era printing experience along Boston's Freedom Trail. He frequently writes for *American Revolution* magazine and is a member of the American Journalism Historians Association (AJHA), the American Revolution Association (ARA), and the Associates of the Omohundro Institute of Early American History and Culture (OIEAHC).

Michael S. Adelberg

Michael S. Adelberg is author of *The American Revolution in Monmouth County: The Theatre of Spoil and Destruction* (History Press, 2010), *The Razing of Tinton Falls: Voices from the American Revolution* (History Press 2012), scholarly articles published in the *Journal of Military History*, the *Journal of the Early Republic*, and *New Jersey History*, and the novel *A Thinking Man's Bully* (Permanent Press, 2011). His historical research has been recognized by the NJSAA, NJTV, and the *Wilson Quarterly*. To learn more about Adelberg, visit www.michaeladelberg.com. Garry Wheeler Stone, historian at Monmouth Battlefield State Park, is thanked for his contributions to this article.

Robert J. Allison

Robert J. Allison, professor of history at Suffolk University in Boston, also teaches at the Harvard Extension School. He is the author of *The American Revolution: A Concise History* (Oxford University Press, 2011), *Stephen Decatur: American Naval Hero* (University of Massachusetts Press, 2005), as well as several books on Boston and the American Revolution. He is vice president of the Colonial Society of Massachusetts, a trustee of the USS *Constitution* Museum, and a consultant to the Commonwealth Museum in Boston.

Charles B. Baxley

Charles B. Baxley earned a BA and JD from the University of South Carolina. He is a practicing attorney in Lugoff, South Carolina, and is the publisher and editor of the magazine *Southern Campaigns of the American Revolution*. Charles has served as president of the Kershaw County Historical Society, as host of several American Revolution symposia, and a guide of Revolutionary War sites. He is the cofounder of the Southern Campaigns Roundtable, Corps of Discovery tour group, and the Archaeological Reconnaissance and Computerization of Hobkirk's Hill battlefield (ARCHH, Inc.) project. Charles is chair of the Battle of Camden battlefield preservation project advisory council.

J. L. Bell

J. L. Bell maintains the Boston1775.net website, dedicated to history, analysis, and unabashed gossip about the start of the American Revolution in New England. Reflecting his interest in the experiences of young people, his study of Boston's Revolutionary youth appeared in *Children in Colonial America* (New York University Press, 2007). He has also published articles about colonial boys' diaries, town watchmen at the Boston Massacre, the wave of bankruptcies in 1765, and the town's raucous Pope Night celebration and has lectured at numerous historical sites in greater Boston.

Wayne Bodle

Wayne Bodle teaches early American history at Indiana University of Pennsylvania. He is the author of *The Valley Forge Winter: Civilians and Soldiers in War* (Penn State Press, 2002) and of a forthcoming monograph on the Middle Colonies of British North America from first European settlement to 1776. He is also working on a biographical account of the American adventures of Charles Wollstonecraft—the youngest brother of the English feminist writer Mary Wollstonecraft—from his arrival in Philadelphia in 1793 until his death in New Orleans in 1817, and another on the life and career of a reputedly "rogue" British colonial governor in America.

John Buchanan

John Buchanan is a military historian who spent almost thirty years on the staff of the Metropolitan Museum of Art, where he was museum archivist, special assistant to the director, and for over twenty years, chief registrar in charge of worldwide art movements. Since his retirement in 1993, he has published three books on early American history, including *The Road to Guilford Courthouse: The American Revolution in the Carolinas* (Wiley, 1999); a novel, *The Rise of Stefan Gregorovic* (iUniverse, 2010), about rebellion in Communist Eastern Europe; and short stories. For more information, visit www.jackbuchanan.net.

Benjamin L. Carp

Benjamin L. Carp is an associate professor of history at Tufts University, where he teaches the history of early America. He has published two books: *Rebels Rising: Cities and the American Revolution* (New York: Oxford University Press, 2007) and *Defiance of the Patriots: The Boston Tea Party and the Making of America* (New Haven: Yale University Press, 2010). He has a BA from Yale University and a PhD from the University of Virginia, and he previously taught at the University of Edinburgh. He has received the Leverhulme Research Fellowship and the Charlotte W. Newcombe Doctoral Dissertation Fellowship.

Bruce Chadwick

Bruce Chadwick, who lives in New Jersey right next door to the winter encampment of the Continental Army, has written five books on the American Revolution and lectures about the war around the world. Chadwick, a former journalist, has also written extensively about the Civil War. He has appeared as a guest scholar on a number of productions for the History Channel and the National Geographic Channel. The historian has also authored a series of books on the history of baseball. He is a history professor at New Jersey City University and an American studies lecturer at Rutgers.

Dennis M. Conrad

Dennis M. Conrad is a historian with the Naval History and Heritage Command in Washington, D.C., and is one of the editors of the series *Naval Documents of the American Revolution*, Vol. 12, which is forthcoming. He is former editor and project director of *The Papers of General Nathanael Greene*, published by the University of North Carolina Press. He has authored an essay on Greene's generalship style for *General Nathanael Greene and the American Revolution in the South*, forthcoming, University of South Carolina Press, and on the career of John Paul Jones in *Sea Raiders of the American Revolution: The Continental Navy in European Waters*.

Diane K. Depew

Diane K. Depew holds a BS in park administration from Shepherd College and an MA in history from Texas A&M University. With over thirty years of National Park Service experience, she previously worked on the Natchez Trace Parkway, Eisenhower National Historic Site, and Gettysburg National Military Park. She started working for Colonial National Historical Park at Yorktown Battlefield in 1988. With a strong interest in military history and having ancestors who served on both sides of the American Revolutionary War, she continues to research and uncover archival material to better tell the Yorktown story.

Robert M. Dunkerly

A native of Lewisburg, Pennsylvania, Robert M. Dunkerly is a park ranger at Richmond National Battlefield Park in Virginia. He holds a degree in history from St. Vincent College and a master's degree in public history from Middle Tennessee State University. He has authored six books and numerous articles on the American Revolution, including *Old Ninety Six* (History Press, 2006). Dunkerly is active in historic preservation and research, promoting the preservation and interpretation of historic sites. He assisted in the 2005 archaeological investigations at Ninety Six and has given many tours of Revolutionary War sites in the Carolinas.

Matthew P. Dziennik

Matthew P. Dziennik is currently a postdoctoral fellow at the New York Historical Society. He was awarded his PhD from the University of Edinburgh with a thesis on the Gaelic military diaspora in the age of the American Revolution. He has held numerous fellowships in Britain, the United States, and Canada and has articles published or forthcoming in the *Journal of British Studies, Historical Research, and Past & Present*. He is currently working on a social and cultural history of revolutionary political organizations in the middle colonies.

Rita Folse Elliott

Rita Folse Elliott (MA, RPA) is an archaeologist, exhibit designer, and former museum curator. She led crews in the archaeological discovery of the 1779 Savannah Battlefield. She has twenty-five years of archaeological and museum experience in eleven states, the Caribbean, three U.S. territories, and several countries. Elliott has authored over fifty monographs and articles and served as a guest editor and reviewer. She participates on committees for museum and archaeology organizations at the state, regional, and national levels. Elliott received the Governor's Award in the Humanities and serves as the education coordinator/research associate for the LAMAR Institute.

Thomas Fleming

Thomas Fleming is one of the most distinguished and productive historians and novelists of our time. He has written twenty nonfiction books that have won prizes and praise from critics and fellow historians, many with a special focus on the American Revolution. His twenty-three novels, many of them bestsellers, explore the lives of men and women in vivid narratives that range from the raw America of the 1730s to the superpower that confronted World War II and endured Korea and Vietnam. He has written frequently for *American Heritage* and many other magazines and is often a guest on C-Span, the History Channel, and PBS.

Don N. Hagist

Don N. Hagist is an independent researcher and author who specializes in the demographics of the British army during the American Revolution. He has written several books and numerous articles concerning the 1775–83 era, including *A British Soldier's Story: Roger Lamb's Narrative of the American Revolution* (Ballindalloch Press, 2004) and *British Soldiers: American War* (Westholme Publishing, 2012). He is also an engineer for a major electronics company and writes humor for several syndicated and freelance cartoonists.

John W. Hall

John W. Hall is the Ambrose-Hesseltine Assistant Professor of U.S. Military History at the University of Wisconsin at Madison. He holds a BS in history from the U.S. Military Academy at West Point and a PhD in history from the University of North Carolina–Chapel Hill. He specializes in early American military history with particular emphasis on partisan and Native American warfare. He is the author of *Uncommon Defense: Indian Allies in the Black Hawk War* (Harvard University Press, 2009) and numerous essays on early American warfare, including "Washington's Irregulars" in *A Companion to George Washington*, edited by Edward Lengel (Wiley-Blackwell, 2012).

Hugh T. Harrington

Hugh T. Harrington is an independent researcher and author whose books include *Remembering Milledgeville* (History Press, 2005), *More Milledgeville Memories* (History Press, 2006), *Civil War Milledgeville* (History Press, 2005), and biography of 1890s magician *Annie Abbott, "The Little Georgia Magnet"* (Createspace, 2010). His articles have appeared in the *Journal of Military History*, *Georgia Historical Quarterly*, *America's Civil War*, *Southern Campaigns of the American Revolution*, *American Revolution*, *Muzzle Blasts*, and others. He has written extensively on Sherlock Holmes and is a member of the Baker Street Irregulars. He lives in Milledgeville, Georgia.

Carol Sue Humphrey

Carol Sue Humphrey has been interested in the Revolutionary War since childhood. She narrowed her interest to the role of the press during the Revolution while in graduate school at the University of North Carolina. She is the author or editor of five books related to the history of the media in the United States, including *This Popular Engine: New England Newspapers During the American Revolution, 1775–1789* (University of Delaware Press, 1992), *Debating Historical Issues in the Media of the Time: The Revolutionary Era* (Greenwood, 2003), and *The Greenwood Library of American War Reporting: The Revolutionary War* (Greenwood, 2005). She currently teaches history at Oklahoma Baptist University.

Neal Thomas Hurst

For nearly a decade, Neal Thomas Hurst has studied and researched all aspects of eighteenth-century history with a focus on colonial men's clothing. Many of his publications and research examine the unique American hunting shirt. Hurst completed a seven-year apprenticeship at the Colonial Williamsburg Foundation as a tailor. He is currently studying history at the College of William and Mary in Virginia, where his primary interests are in early Virginia history and the events and actions leading up to the Williamsburg gunpowder incident.

Benjamin H. Irvin

Benjamin H. Irvin, associate professor of history at the University of Arizona, is a social and cultural historian of early America and the United States, working primarily in the Revolutionary period. His book, *Clothed in Robes of Sovereignty: The Continental Congress and the People Out of Doors*, published by Oxford University Press in April 2011, examines the material culture and ceremonies of state—including, for example, fast days, funeral processions, diplomatic protocols, and presentment swords—by which Congress promoted republicanism and revolution. Central to his study are the many ways that the American people challenged Congress and its vision of the United States.

Michelle A. Larson

Michelle A. Larson is a Pennsylvania high school English teacher and freelance writer who served as transcriptionist on *Reporting the Revolutionary War*. She has twelve years experience teaching British and American literature from a historical perspective. She holds a BSEd in English from Millersville University and an MEd in technology in the classroom from Wilkes University.

Tabitha Marshall

Tabitha Marshall was awarded a PhD in history (2006) by McMaster University in Hamilton, Ontario, Canada, for work on the health of British soldiers during the American Revolution. Current research interests include the health of sailors, as well as a study of the Royal Canadian Army Medical Corps during World War II. After teaching history at Memorial University of Newfoundland and McMaster University, Tabitha now works as an independent scholar and freelance writer in Hamilton, Ontario.

Bruce E. Mowday

Bruce E. Mowday is an award-winning journalist and author from Chester County, Pennsylvania. He has authored books on local history, the American Revolution, and the Civil War. He has also written books on the notorious Johnston gang and on baseball great Richie Ashburn of the Philadelphia Phillies. He was named a local Literacy Hero in 2008. For more than twenty years, he was a newspaper reporter and editor before founding his own media relations firm, the Mowday Group, Inc. For more information on Bruce, see www.mowday.com.

James L. Nelson

James L. Nelson spent a number of years at sea working aboard traditional sailing ships until he decided it would be easier to write about them than work on them. He has since written sixteen works of fiction and nonfiction, including *Glory in the Name* (Harper Perennial, 2004), which won the American Library Association/William Young Boyd Award for best military fiction, and *George Washington's Secret Navy* (Ragged Mountain Press, 2008), winner of the Naval Order's Samuel Eliot Morison Award. He currently lives on the coast of Maine with his former shipmate, now wife, Lisa and their four children.

Julia Osman

Julia Osman is an assistant professor at Mississippi State University, specializing in French, military, and Atlantic history. She received her PhD from the University of North Carolina at Chapel Hill in May 2010. Her work focuses primarily on the French army and its challenges and changes during the seventeenth and eighteenth centuries, as well as North American influences on French military reform. Her current book project, *The Citizen Army of Old Regime France*, traces the intellectual and cultural prehistory of the French Revolutionary army.

Steven H. Park

Steven H. Park wrote his doctoral dissertation on the *Gaspee* Affair and now teaches U.S. history and maritime studies at the University of Connecticut in Storrs and at UConn's campus-by-the-sea at Avery Point. Steve is a sought-after historical speaker for audiences young and mature alike. He teaches a popular class called "Pirates of the Caribbean" that engages undergraduate students in maritime history. He has published in a variety of scholarly print and electronic formats covering mutiny, seamen's missions, seafaring religion, piracy, and privateering. Please see www.stevenpark.org.

Jim Piecuch

Jim Piecuch earned his BA and MA degrees in history at the University of New Hampshire and his PhD at the College of William and Mary. He is an associate professor of history at Kennesaw State University and has published several articles on colonial and Revolutionary history. He is also the author of six books including: *The Battle of Camden: A Documentary History* (History Press, 2006); *Three Peoples, One King: Loyalists, Indians, and Slaves in the Revolutionary South* (University of South Carolina Press, 2008); *"Cool Deliberate Courage": John Eager Howard in the American Revolution* (Nautical & Aviation Pub, 2009), co-authored with John Beakes; and *"The Blood Be Upon Your Head": Tarleton and the Myth of Buford's Massacre* (Southern Campaigns of the American Revolution, 2010).

Ray Raphael

Ray Raphael, author of fifteen books, turned his attention to the Revolutionary Era in the mid-1990s. His several books in that field include *A People's History of the American Revolution*; *Founding Myths: Stories that Hide Our Patriotic Past* (Harper Perennial, 2002); and a detailed study of the Massachusetts Revolution of 1774, *The First American Revolution: Before Lexington and Concord* (New Press, 2002). A complete list of his books and articles, as well as some key historical documents not published elsewhere, can be found at www.rayraphael.com.

Matthew Reardon

Matthew Reardon earned a BA in history and an MA in education from Sacred Heart University. His primary interest lies with early American Military History, focusing on the American Revolution and the Civil War. He currently serves as the executive director of the New England Civil War Museum in Rockville, Connecticut. His first book, *"A Most Desperate Defence": An Interpretive Guide to the Battle of Groton Heights* is forthcoming. Matt resides in Tolland, Connecticut.

John Reda

John Reda is an assistant professor of history at Illinois State University, specializing in colonial and early national American history. He received his PhD from the University of Illinois at Chicago in 2009. His article, "From Subjects to Citizens: Two Pierres and the French Influence on the Transformation of the Illinois Country," appears in the anthology *French and Indians in the Heart of North America, 1630–1815* (Michigan State University Press, 2013). He is currently working on a book for NIU Press entitled *From Furs to Farms: Land, Race, and Sovereignty in the Mississippi Valley, 1762–1825*.

David Paul Reuwer

David Paul Reuwer is editor of *American Revolution* magazine. He earned a JD from Pepperdine University and a BA from Towson University and is currently a historian and practicing attorney, emphasizing historic preservation law. He was an adjunct professor of historic preservation at the College of Charleston. He was the lead investigator of the initial Eutaw Springs battlefield survey and is the plenipotentiary of the magazine *Southern Campaigns of the American Revolution*. David is also a battlefield tour guide.

J. Dennis Robinson

J. Dennis Robinson writes books about American history for young and old. He works from an office in historic Portsmouth, New Hampshire, near the swirling Piscataqua River, where he is also a popular columnist, lecturer, and editor of the award-winning history website SeacoastNH.com. His work includes AASLH award-winning books on the Strawbery Banke Museum and the historic Wentworth by the Sea Hotel, plus juvenile biographies of Jesse James and Lord Baltimore. His most recent books are *America's Privateer: Lynx and the War of 1812* (Lynx Educational Foundation, 2011) and *Under the Isles of Shoals: Archaeological Discovery at Smuttynose Island* (Portsmouth Marine Society, 2012).

David Lee Russell

David Lee Russell was born in Wilmington, North Carolina. After receiving his BS in aerospace engineering from North Carolina State University, he attended the Naval Aviation Officer's Candidate School in Pensacola. Commissioned as an Ensign-Special Duty Intelligence, he served as a Naval Air Intelligence Officer in the Pacific, Southeast Asia, and the Indian Ocean. After leaving active duty service, David began a long career in information technology. He is the author of *The American Revolution in the Southern Colonies* (McFarland, 2009), *Victory on Sullivan's Island: The British Cape Fear/Charles Town Expedition of 1776* (Infinity Publishing, 2002), *Oglethorpe and Colonial Georgia: A History, 1733–1783* (McFarland, 2006), and *The Duke of Southbourne* (CreateSpace, 2011). David resides in Milton, Georgia.

Barnet Schecter

Barnet Schecter, an independent historian, is the author of *George Washington's America: A Biography Through His Maps* (Walker Publishing, 2010), *The Devil's Own Work: The Civil War Draft Riots and the Fight to Reconstruct America* (Walker Publishing, 2007), and *The Battle for New York: The City at the Heart of the American Revolution* (Walker Publishing, 2002). A contributing editor of the three-volume *Encyclopedia of the American Revolution and Landmarks of the American Revolution*, he is also a contributor to the *Encyclopedia of New York City*. In addition to lecturing and leading tours and military staff rides, he has appeared in a variety of television documentaries.

Eric H. Schnitzer

Eric H. Schnitzer, park ranger/historian at Saratoga National Historical Park, has dedicated his life's study to the organization, personnel, and material culture of the British and American armed forces of the Revolution, especially as it relates to the Northern Campaign of 1777. He has written articles for journals such as *The Hessians* and created illustrations for books such as *Philadelphia 1777* and *Wenches, Wives, and Servant Girls*. He and his wife, Jenna, are members of the re-created British 62nd Regiment and live in an eighteenth-century house in the White Creek Historic District near Bennington Battlefield, New York, where they spend much of their time sewing reproduction eighteenth-century garments.

William P. Tatum III

William P. Tatum III is the director of programs and research at the Historical Society of Newburgh Bay and the Hudson Highlands, previously worked at the David Library of the American Revolution, and is an advanced PhD candidate at Brown University. His work focuses on the eighteenth-century British army in its imperial context, as well as larger issues of social control and civil-military relations. He is the author of several articles on the British army during the era of the American Revolutionary War and is currently completing his dissertation, *For the Good of the King's Service: British Military Justice, Society, and Empire, 1715–1785*.

Daniel J. Tortora

Daniel J. Tortora is assistant professor of history at Colby College, where he teaches Native American and early American history. He is writing a book about the Anglo-Cherokee War of 1759–61 and its influence on the American Revolution. He speaks extensively on the South during the French and Indian War era, on Native American military history, and leads battlefield tours. He is currently working on a project in Winslow, Maine, to expand Fort Halifax Park, a reconstructed 1754 blockhouse and the site of an encampment for Benedict Arnold's Quebec campaign.

ACKNOWLEDGMENTS

THIS BOOK IS THE CULMINATION OF FIVE YEARS OF RESEARCH, CURATING, WRITING, AND EDITING. As such, I am indebted to numerous people for their support and contributions along the way.

My parents, Sharon and Robert, taught me to be ambitious, resourceful, creative, and determined, all of which I needed to successfully complete this project, so I am eternally grateful for their love and life instruction. Likewise, my grandmothers, siblings, nieces, nephews, in-laws, and close friends provided tremendous encouragement throughout the whole process, and I owe many thanks to all of them.

To help kick-start the publishing process, book illustrator Leslie Harrington introduced me to book packager Janice Shay, who served as the matchmaker with Sourcebooks. Janice believed in the project from the start and helped convince Sourcebooks that this was a book for them, so a big thank-you to Leslie for making the introduction and to Janice for getting things off the ground.

Sourcebooks instantly recognized the educational importance of historical newspapers and quickly latched on to the concept. I was fortunate to have a publisher so strongly committed to the project from the get-go and who offered a bottomless pit of forward-thinking ideas to help me bring the eighteenth century to the twenty-first. They made the process of publishing my first book a truly wonderful experience. I owe special thanks to Dominique Raccah, Peter Lynch, Todd Stocke, Kelly Bale, Liz Kelsch, Valerie Pierce, Lindsey Tom, Heather Hall, Melanie Jackson, and the entire Sourcebooks team for all their hard work.

Several people provided helpful consulting and aid to various elements of the project, so my sincerest appreciation goes to Ray Raphael, J. L. Bell, David Reuwer, Carol Humphrey, Bob Allison, Ben Carp, Ben Irvin, Will Tatum, Don Hagist, Ben Edwards, Gary Gregory, Danny Maiello, Ernest Kramer, Benjamin Smith, Jaime Ferguson, Craig Bloomfield, Lou Mongello, Brett Sneed, Gil Perez, Matthew Wilding, Jimi Allen, Adam Kelsey, and Hillary Andrlik. I am also extremely grateful to Joyce and Marlon Herring and their family, who provided me with superb hospitality and creative isolation in coastal North Carolina during the early writing and planning stages.

Many thanks to Michelle Larson, a Pennsylvania high school teacher who transcribed several of the newspapers featured in this book and provided an important educational perspective on the project that lent itself to a valuable essay contribution and several of the reading tips featured at the front of the book. Also, thank you to Andrea Wasilko and Karen Vanderzanden, who assisted in the transcriptions.

I would like to give very special thanks to those in and around the historical newspaper community who taught me so much as well as helped me to build and shape the collection featured in this book, including Tim Hughes, Guy Heilenman, Eric Caren, Steve Goldman, Steve Hanly, Mark Mitchell, Joe Felcone, Bob Ward, Brian Zak, Robert Heron, Sam Best, Rick Brown, Phil Barber, Vince Golden, Richard Robinson, Seth Kaller, Will Steere, John Reznikoff, Jim Arsenault, Bill Reese, Rick Mohovich, Scott Nason, Kathy Novak, Matthew Needle, Clarence Wolf, Bob Oswald, Doreen Mileto, Rodger Friedman, Andrew Robinson, Robert Hamm, William Butts, Charles Signer, Rick Stattler, Steve Alsberg, Ed Lake, and Ed King. Also, many thanks to Georgia Higley, Teri Sierra, and Mark Sweeney at the Library of Congress for their support and encouragement over the years.

To help save dozens of the newspapers from loss, I turned to J. Franklin Mowery for his expert paper conservation. Thanks to his collaboration, we restored many of the extremely fragile and tattered papers close to their original condition (many more to go).

This book was made exponentially better by the important essay contributions of 37 professors, scholars, and experts in the field. They helped put the newspaper accounts in context, provided valuable analysis and perspective, and bridged the eighteenth and twenty-first centuries for readers. Their passion for and lifelong commitments to the subject matter is admirable, and I am forever grateful for their generosity and time spent on the project. A full list of contributors and their bios is available within the book.

Thank you to my brothers from Illumination Lodge No. 5 and all my colleagues at Leopardo Companies for their support, especially Jim Leopardo, Rick Mattioda, and John Ward.

Finally, this book is dedicated to Hillary, Rory, and Lincoln, my wife, daughter, and son. I am the luckiest man on earth to be married to such a patient, creative, and helpful wife. Her enduring support helped me get through many long nights and weekends. Thankfully, we share an addiction to hard work and commitment to innovation in both our full-time jobs as well as our hobbies. More importantly, Hillary's objective opinions, sound counsel, artistic talents, and educational acumen helped steer me on several aspects of this project. She is my Abigail Adams. My daughter, Rory, went off to kindergarten, and my son, Lincoln, was born just as this book was being published. They inspire me every day, and when they get older I look forward to sharing all the exciting discoveries and valuable lessons about our nation's founding that I learned from reading eighteenth-century newspapers.

INDEX